Y0-DRV-652

ADVANCED ACCOUNTING

Walter B. Meigs, Ph.D., C.P.A.
PROFESSOR OF ACCOUNTING
UNIVERSITY OF SOUTHERN CALIFORNIA

Charles E. Johnson, Ph.D., C.P.A.
PROFESSOR OF ACCOUNTING
UNIVERSITY OF OREGON

Thomas F. Keller, Ph.D., C.P.A.
ASSOCIATE PROFESSOR OF ACCOUNTING
DUKE UNIVERSITY

NEW YORK ST. LOUIS SAN FRANCISCO

ADVANCED ACCOUNTING

McGraw-Hill BOOK COMPANY

TORONTO LONDON SYDNEY

ADVANCED **ACCOUNTING**

Library of Congress Catalog Card Number: 65-21574

ISBN 07-041432-7

1314 HDBP 754

PREFACE

This is the third volume of the coordinated accounting series which begins with *Accounting: The Basis for Business Decisions* by Meigs and Johnson. *Advanced Accounting* is designed for the student who has completed both an introductory and an intermediate accounting course. The two preceding volumes in the series present the broad theoretical structure of accounting, along with an analysis of problems that arise in applying basic theoretical concepts to financial accounting. Throughout all three volumes, attention is continuously focused on the use of accounting data as a basis for decisions by management, stockholders, creditors, and other users of financial statements and accounting reports.

Advanced Accounting differs from the two preceding volumes in that it covers a series of separate topics of an advanced nature, such as consolidations, price-level changes, and businesses in financial difficulties. Some of these sections (partnerships and present-value concepts, for example) cover in greater depth and detail subject matter to which the student has been introduced in earlier courses. Other sections (consolidations, businesses in financial difficulties, fiduciary accounting, and governmental accounting) are devoted to a discussion of special areas of particular interest to the student who plans a career as a professional accountant. The material in each section is discussed fully, and new terms are carefully defined. In general, however, the level of discussion rests on the assumption that the student has completed an intermediate course in financial accounting. The arrangement of the book into clearly defined topics enables the instructor to choose the desired coverage for his course and to omit certain sections without running into difficulty because of interrelationships among topics.

Organization of subject matter

Part One consists of four chapters devoted to partnerships. Building on the introduction to this subject usually included in introductory accounting, the student is carried to the level of the CPA examination and of the professional accountant dealing with fairly complex problems of profit sharing, changes in personnel, partnership liquidation, and joint ventures.

Part Two contains chapters on installment sales, consignments, and home office and branch accounting. These three topics are logically related since all represent special problems in accounting for sales transactions. In addition, the final chapter on home office and branch accounting is a convenient approach to the study of consolidated financial statements.

Part Three, Consolidated Financial Statements, is less bulky and less laden with procedural details than in older textbooks. We have tried to simplify the discussion of consolidated financial statements and at the same time make this topic more meaningful to the student and less a matter of pushing figures around in voluminous working papers. Rather than follow a strict balance sheet approach with income statement discussion tacked on as an afterthought, we have introduced at the outset all three financial statements: the balance sheet, income statement, and statement of retained earnings. As a result the student is encouraged from the very beginning to think about the effect of various intercompany transactions and relationships on income as well as on financial position.

Following modern working paper techniques, we have avoided cumbersome trial balance working papers. Instead, we have developed as a framework for the discussion of consolidations separate balance sheet and income statement working papers, including an analysis of consolidated retained earnings on the balance sheet working papers. One of the advantages of this approach is that the student sees clearly the effect on net income of various consolidating adjustments at the time the adjusting and eliminating entries are being developed and entered on the working papers. Once the working paper analyses have been made, the completion of financial statements is a routine process of rearranging the data into statement form. Furthermore, the casting of procedures into simplified working papers helps the student to understand clearly what is going on in the consolidating process and enables him to concentrate his attention on the theory and underlying concepts of consolidations.

The basic theory underlying consolidations and the procedures necessary to develop consolidated data are thoroughly covered in six chapters. A seventh is devoted to the special problems of reporting on foreign operations. This chapter covers the theoretical aspects of translating foreign currency balances and utilizes AICPA research statements. Other problem areas range from ordinary purchase and sale transactions to the consolidation of foreign subsidiaries. The material on the reporting of foreign operations leads logically to the discussion of price-level changes. No major topic has been omitted in this condensed coverage of consolidated financial statements, but experience in using these chapters in the classroom indicates that considerably less time and effort are required to give the accounting student a good working knowledge of consolidations.

Part Four, Price-level Changes, a two-chapter section, deals with the general problem of changing prices and accounting for business activity. In Chapter 15, the problems related to changes in the general level of prices and changes in the length of the measuring rod are studied in detail. Changes in specific prices are considered in Chapter 16, the latter part of which summarizes the differences and similarities of accounting for general price-level changes and specific price changes. This treatment is considerably more extensive than is usually found in advanced accounting textbooks.

In Part Five the topic is present-value concepts. Three chapters are devoted to the applications of present-value concepts to accounting valuation and capital budgeting. The usual discussion of compound interest and annuities in advanced texts often bores and frustrates students, because they do not progress beyond the mechanics of the mathematics and therefore do not see the relevance and importance of these concepts in business planning.

The first chapter in this area (17) reviews the basic concepts of the mathematics of finance for those students who do not have a background in the mechanics of compound interest. Emphasis is on an understanding of the basic formulas and the use of interest tables. Chapter 18 focuses on the applications of economic valuation to financial accounting. The concept of income under conditions of certainty is explored in a simple set of illustrations, and this special case is then related to the problem of income measurement under realistic conditions of uncertainty. Present-value applications to the problems of accounting for long-term debt, lease transactions, and depreciation are then explored. The third chapter (19) is devoted to a discussion of applications in the area of capital budgeting and investment decisions. Here the student learns to use present-value concepts in evaluating a variety of investment and borrowing situations. The troublesome concept of the cost of capital is discussed, and the student is given a useful method of approximating the cost of capital of the firm for analytical purposes. Various methods of evaluating investments are compared, and the student is given a basis for choosing the method most relevant and useful for his purpose.

Part Six, Businesses in Financial Difficulties, and Part Seven, Fiduciary Accounting, are more traditional, but again emphasis is placed on explaining *why* the accountant follows certain standards and procedures. The procedural aspects are fully covered and reasons for variations are explained. Our intent is to relate these procedures to accounting concepts already familiar to the student and to make the topics interesting and understandable rather than to stress a memorizing approach to forms and procedures.

Part Eight, Governmental Accounting, presents the basic concepts of fund accounting, with thorough explanations to show why these concepts are well suited to the needs of certain types of organizations.

Problem and case material

An abundance of question and problem material is provided at the end of each chapter. This material is divided into three groups: questions, short cases for analysis, and problems.

The questions are intended for use by the student as a self-testing and review device to measure his comprehension of key points in each chapter. Many of the questions are also of a provocative nature which engenders lively class discussion.

The short cases for analysis are essentially problems that require analytical reasoning but involve little or no quantitative data. In this category of problem material the student is called upon to analyze business situations, to apply accounting principles, and to propose a course of action. He is not required, however, to prepare lengthy schedules or otherwise to manipulate accounting data on an extensive scale. These short cases have all been class-tested and have proved their worth as a means of encouraging students to take clear-cut positions in the argument of controversial accounting issues. A number of the short cases for analysis have been adapted from CPA examination material.

The problems include a wide variety of long and short problems, ranging in difficulty from simple to complex. Most of the problems in the theory and practice sections of recent CPA examinations which are appropriate to advanced accounting are included, although many have been considerably modified. In addition, numerous problems have been designed especially to demonstrate the concepts presented in the theoretical discussion. Probably no more than a third of the total case and problem material would be used in a given course; consequently, ample opportunity exists to vary problem assignments from year to year.

Acknowledgments

We wish to express our appreciation to Professor Arthur M. Lorig of the University of Washington for his advice on the chapters dealing with governmental accounting. Professor A. N. Mosich of the University of Southern California reviewed the manuscript, tested it extensively in classes, and was of immeasurable assistance in the development and testing of problem material. Professor Martin L. Black, Jr., of Duke University reviewed a considerable portion of the book and used this material in classes in mimeographed form. His counsel was most helpful. Professor Edwin I. Pinto of California State College at San Jose utilized the problems in mimeographed form in his classes in advanced accounting and made thorough analyses of student response. Assistance in the development and testing of problem material was also received from Steven De Graff, Mark Klein, and Bruce Jaffe of the University of Southern California, from Arthur Thomas, Jack Ferguson, and Roger Hayman of the University of Oregon, and from Thomas Baxter, Donald Brooks, and Curtis Livingston of Duke University.

We wish also to express our appreciation for permission from the American Institute of Certified Public Accountants to quote from their copyrighted *Accounting Research Studies* and *Accounting Research Bulletins* and to use numerous problems from the Uniform Certified Public Accountant Examination. Finally, we wish to thank our students whose enthusiasm, curiosity, and good humor made a stimulating experience of our testing of both text and problem material in the classroom.

WALTER B. MEIGS
CHARLES E. JOHNSON
THOMAS F. KELLER

CONTENTS

Preface v

PART ONE *Partnerships*

1. **PARTNERSHIPS: ORGANIZATION AND PROFIT SHARING** 3

Appraisal of the partnership form of organization. Characteristics of the partnership. Ease of formation. Limited life. Mutual agency. Unlimited liability. Co-ownership of partnership property. Participation in profits. Deciding between a partnership and a corporation. Is the partnership a separate entity? Articles of partnership. Achieving and maintaining agreement among partners. Owners' equity accounts for partners. Loans to and from partners. Valuation of investments by partners. The partner's equity versus his share in profits. Dividing net income or loss. Equal division of profit and loss. Division of profit and loss in some other agreed ratio. Division of profit and loss in the ratio of partners' capitals. Ratio of original capitals. Ratio of capitals at end of year. Average capital ratio. Interests on partners' capitals with remaining profit and loss divided in an agreed ratio. Interest on partners' loans. Salaries to partners with remaining profit and loss divided in an agreed ratio. Distinguishing between salaries and drawings. Bonus to managing partner. Salaries to partners combined with interest on capital. Income statement—disclosure of profit-sharing data. Statement of partners' capitals. Adjustment of net income of prior periods. Statements and reports for managerial use.

2. **PARTNERSHIPS: CHANGES IN PERSONNEL** 37

Accounting for changes in partnership personnel. Accounting and managerial issues. Admission of a new partner. Purchase of an interest by payment to one partner. Purchase of interest compared with purchase of stock in corporation. Purchase of an interest by payments to two or more partners. Refusal to admit purchaser to partnership. Acquisition of an interest by investment. Bonus or goodwill allowed to old partners. Bonus to old partners. Recognition of goodwill. Comparison of bonus method and goodwill method. Fairness of asset valuation. Bonus or goodwill allowed to new partner. Bonus to new partner. Goodwill to new partner. Computing goodwill or bonus implied by partnership agreement. Bonus to old partners. Goodwill to old partners. Bonus and goodwill to old partners. Bonus to new partner. Goodwill to new partner. Bonus and goodwill to new partner. Other terms for admission of new partner. Retirement of a partner. Computing the settlement price. Recognition of goodwill or payment of bonus. Settlement with retiring partner for less than book value. Death of a partner. Incorporation of a partnership. Retention of partnership books. Establishment of new books for corporation.

3. PARTNERSHIPS: LIQUIDATION 74

The meaning of liquidation. Distribution of loss or gain. Distribution of cash. Determining the settlement with each partner. Division of gain or loss during liquidation. Equity of each partner sufficient to absorb his share of loss on realization. Equity of one partner not sufficient to absorb his share of loss on realization. Equities of two partners not sufficient to absorb their shares of loss on realization. Partnership insolvent but partners personally solvent. Partnership insolvent and partners personally insolvent.

4. PARTNERSHIPS: LIQUIDATION IN INSTALLMENTS 101

Installment payments to partners. General principles guiding installment payment procedures. Installment liquidation when all partners have adequate capital to absorb losses. Installment payments compared with lump-sum settlement. Installment liquidation when one or more partners have insufficient capital to absorb possible losses. Advance planning of cash distribution during liquidation. Withholding of cash for unpaid liabilities. Withholding of cash for future expenses. Joint ventures. History of joint ventures. Present-day ventures. Accounting for a joint venture. Separate set of books for venture. No separate set of books for venture.

PART TWO *Special Problems in Accounting for Sales Transactions*

5. CONSIGNMENTS 129

The meaning of consignments. Distinguishing between a consignment and a sale. Advantages of the consignment method of distributing goods. The consignment contract. Rights of the consignee. Compensation. Reimbursement for expenses and advances. Extension of credit by consignee. Warranty of consigned goods. Duties of the consignee. Care and protection of consigned merchandise. Identification of consigned goods and consignment receivables. Care and diligence in extension of credit. Reporting sales and making payment. The account sales. Accounting methods of consignee. Balance sheet presentation of Consignment In accounts. Accounting methods of consignor. Should profits on consignments be determined separately? Illustration of accounting methods of consignor. Consignment profits determined separately—perpetual inventory basis. Consignment profits determined separately—periodic inventory basis. Consignment profits not determined separately—perpetual inventory basis. Consignment profits not determined separately—periodic inventory basis. Accounting for partial sale of a consignment. Partial sale of consignment; profits determined separately from regular sales. Partial sale of consignment; profits not determined separately—perpetual inventory basis. Partial sale of consignment; profits not determined separately—periodic inventory basis. Disposition of Consignment Shipments account. Return of unsold goods to consignor. Advances from consignee. Varying concepts of the Consignment Out account.

6. INSTALLMENT SALES 160

Installment sales throughout the economy. Special characteristics of installment sales. Methods for recognition of profits on installment sales. Recognition of gross profit at time of sale. Recognition of gross profit in installments. The installment method of accounting. Single sale of real estate on the installment basis. Alternative approaches to recognition of gross profit. Sales of merchandise by a dealer on the installment plan. Use of annual gross profit rates. Classification of cash collections by year of contract. Determining unrealized gross profit by aging installment contracts receivable. Installment method for income tax purposes only. Periodic inventory basis. Departmental gross profit rates. Trade-ins. Defaults and repossessions. Expenses relating to installment sales. Financial statement presentation. Interest on installment contracts. Installment contracts from the buyer's viewpoint.

7. HOME OFFICE AND BRANCH ACCOUNTING 200

Establishment of branches. Sales agency contrasted with branch. Accounting system for a sales agency. Illustrative entries for operation of a sales agency. Accounting system for a branch. Reciprocal accounts. Expenses incurred by home office and charged to branches. Alternative methods of billing shipments to branch. Separate financial statements for branch and home office. Combined statements for home office and branch. Illustrative entries for operation of a branch. Working papers for combined statements. Illustrative combined statements. Accounting for billings to branch in excess of cost. Working papers when billings to branch are in excess of cost. Treatment of beginning inventory priced above cost. Closing entries. Perpetual inventories. Reconciliation of reciprocal accounts. Transactions between branches. Treatment of start-up expenses in new branches.

PART THREE *Consolidated Financial Statements*

8. CONSOLIDATIONS: INTRODUCTION 241

Terminology of consolidations. Why affiliate? Legal status of consolidated statements. When should consolidated statements be prepared? Degree of control. Integrated area of operations. Unconsolidated subsidiaries. Consolidation at date of acquisition—wholly owned subsidiary. Nature of the consolidated balance sheet. Consolidating working papers. Consolidating P and B Companies—acquisition at book value. Consolidating P and B Companies with E Company—acquisition cost greater than book value. Consolidating P, B, and E Companies with U Company—acquisition cost less than book value. Treatment of excess of cost over book value. Net assets of subsidiary undervalued. Payment for advantages of affiliation. An important distinction. Errors in recording parent's cost. Combination of factors. Treatment of excess of book value over cost. Net assets of subsidiary overvalued. Bargain purchase. Errors in recording parent's cost. Consolidation at acquisition—partially owned subsidiary. Purchase at book value. Purchase at more than book value. Summary of procedures when cost exceeds book value. Purchase at less than book value. Summary of procedures when book value exceeds cost. Consolidated balance sheet at date of acquisition. Minority interest on the consolidated balance sheet.

9. CONSOLIDATION AFTER DATE OF ACQUISITION 274

Cost versus equity method of accounting for investment. Consolidation one year after acquisition. Parent records investment at cost. Consolidating working papers—cost basis. Income statement working papers. Balance sheet working papers. Parent records investment on equity (accrual) basis. Equity method—consolidating net income. Equity method—consolidating the balance sheet. Consolidated financial statements. Consolidation more than one period after acquisition. Illustration. Consolidated working papers—cost basis. Income statement working papers. Balance sheet working papers. Consolidating working papers—equity basis. Income statement working papers. Balance sheet working papers. Evaluation of cost and equity methods. Who should use consolidated financial statements? Nonusers. Users.

10. CONSOLIDATIONS: INTERCOMPANY TRANSACTIONS AND PROFITS IN INVENTORIES 311

Intercompany transactions. Intercompany receivables and payables. Discounting intercompany notes. Intercompany revenues and expenses. Intercompany dividends. Intercompany profits. Intercompany sale of land. Intercompany profits in inventories. Illustration—intercompany profits in ending inventories. Why eliminate all the intercompany profit? Summary of procedures to remove intercompany inventory profits. What is the intercompany profit? Intercompany losses on inventories. Intercompany profits in inventories at date of acquisition. Intercompany profits in beginning inventories. Comments on working papers.

11. CONSOLIDATIONS: INTERCOMPANY TRANSACTIONS IN DEPRECIABLE ASSETS AND LONG-TERM DEBT. PURCHASE VERSUS POOLING OF INTEREST INTERPRETATION OF CONSOLIDATIONS 340

Intercompany profits on sale of depreciable assets. Consolidation at date of sale. Elimination of intercompany gain in subsequent periods. Intercompany bondholdings. Bonds acquired from issuing company. Bonds acquired from outsiders. Consolidating working papers at date bonds were acquired. Consolidating working papers after date of bond acquisition. Summary comments—intercompany bondholdings. Amount of gain or loss. Allocation of gain or loss. Subsequent adjustment of gain or loss. Alternative method of allocating gain or loss on intercompany bonds. Pooling of interest versus purchase concept. Illustration. Evaluation of the pooling concept. Summary.

12. CONSOLIDATIONS: SPECIAL PROBLEMS 380

Subsidiaries having both preferred and common stock. Nature of subsidiary's preferred dividends. Stock dividends by subsidiary. Changes in parent's ownership interest in subsidiary. Serial investment by parent. Additional investment after control is achieved. Revaluation alternative. Control achieved in a series of purchases. Sale of shares by parent. Sale or purchase of shares by subsidiary—effect on parent's interest. Subsidiary transactions in treasury shares.

13. CONSOLIDATIONS: INDIRECT AND MUTUAL HOLDINGS 419

Indirect holdings. The valuation problem. Subsidiary becomes a holding company. Holding company becomes a subsidiary. Growth in subsidiaries since acquisition. Father-son-grandson case. Connecting affiliate case. Mutual holdings. Case 1—No outside interests. Case 2—Connecting affiliates; no outside interest. Case 3—Parent and subsidiary with outside interests. Treasury stock assumption (Case 3). Conventional assumption (Case 3). Case 4—Connecting affiliates with outside interests. Other cases.

14. REPORTING FOREIGN OPERATIONS 455

Principles of accounting for foreign activities. Exchange rates. Domestic company with foreign transactions. Foreign purchases. Foreign sales. Realized or unrealized exchange gain or loss. Inventory on consignment in a foreign country. Domestic company with foreign investments. Translation of balance sheet accounts. The AICPA position. The authors' position. Discussion of differences in positions. Translation of income statement accounts. The AICPA position. The authors' position. Discussion of differences. Recognition of exchange gains and losses. Devaluation and foreign investments. Effect of exchange restrictions. Home office and branch operations. Illustration. Accounting for the foreign subsidiary. Translation of account balances. Parent's investment and subsidiary's equity. Intercompany transactions. Illustration. Consolidated statements for parent and foreign subsidiary.

PART FOUR *Price-level Changes*

15. CHANGING PRICE LEVELS AND FINANCIAL REPORTING 495

Measures of general price changes. Measures of specific price changes. Structural price changes versus general price changes. Changing price levels and the assumption of a stable monetary unit. Conversion of recorded dollar cost. Plant accounts. Inventory accounts. Inflation and monetary accounts. Long-term liabilities. Accounting without the stable monetary assumption. Comparative financial statements.

16. REPLACEMENT COST AND FINANCIAL REPORTING 532

Illustration of accounting for replacement cost. Accepted conventions. Advantages and disadvantages of replacement cost. Inventory. Long-lived tangible assets. Determination of replacement cost. Determination of holding gains and losses. Inventories. Long-lived tangible assets. Illustration of replacement cost techniques. Replacement cost and changing general price levels. Techniques for recognition of changing general price levels.

PART FIVE *Present-value Concepts*

17. REVIEW OF COMPOUND INTEREST FUNDAMENTALS 573

Why is compound interest important? The relative significance of simple and compound interest. Simple interest formulas. Compound interest. Amount of a principal sum at compound interest. Simplifying the formula. Present value of a future amount. Present value of $1. Relation of amounts and present values to n and i. Compound interest and compound discount. Annuities. Kinds of standard annuity situations. Computing amounts of annuities. Amount of an ordinary annuity. Amount of an annuity due. Alternative approach to find amount of annuity due. Amount of an open-end annuity. Computing the present value of annuities. Present value of an ordinary annuity. Present value of an annuity due. Alternative approach to find present value of an annuity due. Present value of a deferred annuity. Comparing values over time. Finding an unknown rate of interest (yield). Estimating i when rents are equal. Estimating i when rents are unequal. The borrowing case.

18. COMPOUND INTEREST APPLICATIONS: VALUATION OF ASSETS AND LIABILITIES 612

Direct valuation under conditions of certainty. Illustration. Equipment. Liability—notes payable. Cash receipts and disbursements. Financial statements. Results under indirect valuation. The accountant's valuation problem. Direct valuation and bond issues. Determining bond prices. Alternative method of computing bond prices. Recording interest revenue and expense. Bonds sold at a discount. Bonds sold at a premium. Effective interest versus straight-line average interest. Callable bonds. Issuing bonds between interest dates. Serial bonds. Long-term leases. Valuation of a leasehold. Leases—periodic payments. Opinion No. 5, Accounting Principles Board. Choosing an appropriate interest rate. Depreciation and the interest factor. Annuity method of depreciation. Sinking-fund method of depreciation. Annuity and sinking-fund methods compared. Summary—present-value depreciation methods.

19. DIRECT VALUATION AND INVESTMENT DECISIONS 652

Methods of analysis. Evaluating investment proposals. Evaluating investments by the yield method. The net present value method. Frequency of flows and compoundings. Comparison of yield and net present value methods. Accept or reject decisions. Mutually exclusive investments. Case 1—Same initial outlay and same period of return. Case 2—Different initial outlays; same period of return. Net present value index. Case 3—Unequal periods of benefits. Equivalent average annual cash flows. Equalizing terminal lives. Summary—net present value versus yield method. Income taxes and investment decisions. The cost of capital. The cost of debt and preferred stock. The cost of common stock capital. Measuring the average cost of capital. Estimating the opportunity (lending) rate. Analyzing investment proposals. Lease or buy decisions. Illustrative case. Solution—present value approach (ignoring income taxes). Income tax factors. Bond refunding decisions. Illustrative case. Different terminal lives of debt. Property replacement decisions. Illustrative replacement case. Summary—replacement decisions.

PART SIX *Businesses in Financial Difficulties*

20. BANKRUPTCY AND THE STATEMENT OF AFFAIRS 689

Insolvency defined. Nonjudicial procedures available to debtors in financial distress. Extension of time for payment. Composition agreements. Control by creditor committee. Voluntary assignment of assets. Judicial procedures available to the insolvent business. Equity receivership. Bankruptcy proceedings. Statement of affairs. Classification of assets. Classification of liabilities and capital. Preparation of statements of affairs illustrated. Deficiency account. Items of special interest. Book value columns. Accrued interest. Liabilities with priority. Capital accounts. Assets requiring outlays prior to realization. Rule of offset. Reserve accounts. Prepaid expenses. Interperiod allocation of income taxes. Interests in affiliated organizations. Amount payable to unsecured creditors. Uses of the statement of affairs by a going concern.

21. RECEIVERSHIP ACCOUNTS 722

Receivership in equity. Receivership accounting. Basic procedures illustrated. Statements prepared by receiver. Illustration. Information available. Journal entries to record transactions of the receivership. Termination of the receivership. Working papers. Financial statements.

22. REALIZATION AND LIQUIDATION STATEMENTS, REORGANIZATION, AND ARRANGEMENTS 756

Realization and liquidation statements. Anatomy of the realization and liquidation statement. Illustration. Bookkeeping and the realization and liquidation statement. Old and new accounts. Accrued interest and other payables. Purchases and sales of product. Depreciation and other asset write-offs. Purchase and sales discounts. Composition agreements with creditors. Illustration of a realization and liquidation statement for an operating receivership. Explanation of special problems. Appraisal of the realization and liquidation statement. Reorganization of bankrupt corporations. Legal procedures. Provisions of a reorganization plan. Approval of the plan. Effect of confirmation and final decree. Accounting problems in reorganization. Illustration. Arrangements. Provisions of arrangement. Acceptance of proposed arrangement. Effect of confirmation. Accounting problems of an arrangement.

PART SEVEN *Fiduciary Accounting*

23. ESTATE ADMINISTRATION 795

Fiduciary. Administration of the estate. Duties of the fiduciary. Inventory of assets. Custody of funds. Payment of debts. Taxes on the estate. Distribution of estate properties. Intermediate and final accounting. Fiduciary's accounts. Memorandum entries. Opening accounts. Assets discovered subsequent to inventory. Realization of assets. Payment of expenses or receipt of income. Payment of debts or collection of claims. Payment of expense or collection of income for a legatee. Operation of a going business. Distribution of estate assets to legatees. Entries after the final accounting. Reports of the fiduciary. Illustration. Trial balance. Charge and discharge statement. Closing entries.

24. TRUST ACCOUNTING 829

Types of trusts. Duties of the trustee. Rights of the beneficiary. Principal and income distinguished. Accruals. Classification of receipts and disbursements. Impairment or improvement of trust assets. Private trusts. Accounting for the private trust. Recording principal and income. Trustee's reports. Illustration of accounting procedures. Charitable trusts and foundations. Accounting problems of charitable trusts. Special-purpose funds. Lapsed appropriations and grants. Financial statements.

PART EIGHT *Governmental Accounting*

25. FUND ACCOUNTING: GOVERNMENTS AND INSTITUTIONS 861

Budgeting. Lapsing and continuing appropriations. Annual financial report and the budget. Cash or accrual basis of accounting. Encumbrances and the basis of accounting. Special problems. Interfund receivables and payables. Use of the term revenue. Illustration of fund accounting. General fund. Budget. Revenue. Encumbrances and expenditures. Closing entries.

26. FUND ACCOUNTING: GOVERNMENTS AND INSTITUTIONS (CONCLUDED) 888

Special revenue funds. Working capital or revolving funds. Special assessment fund. Bond funds. Sinking funds. Trust and agency funds. The general fixed asset accounts. General bonded debt and interest accounts. Utility or other enterprise funds. Financial statements.

Compound Interest Tables 927

Index 937

PARTNERSHIPS

PART ONE

1 PARTNERSHIPS: ORGANIZATION AND PROFIT SHARING

Appraisal of the partnership form of organization

Much of our discussion of partnerships will be based on the Uniform Partnership Act which has been adopted by many of the states. This act defines a partnership as "an association of two or more persons to carry on, as co-owners, a business for profit." Although the word "persons" suggests living individuals, a partnership can also include other partnerships among its members; in some states a corporation can become a partner. The creation of a partnership requires no approval by the state; in fact, a partnership may be formed without a written contract or documents of any type, although a carefully formulated written contract is highly desirable. The courts may even hold that a partnership has been created if two or more persons conduct their business activities in such a manner as to imply that a partnership exists.

Partnerships are traditionally associated with the practice of law, medicine, public accounting, and other professions, and also with small business concerns. In many states the licensed professional man such as the CPA is forbidden to incorporate on the grounds that the creation of a corporate entity might weaken the personal relationship of the practitioner to his client. In recent years, however, a number of states have approved legislation designed to permit the incorporation of professional firms. The American Institute of Certified Public Accountants, which has considered the question of incorporation by CPAs at length, has taken the position that such action would not be in the best interests of the public accounting profession. Probably every accounting student is aware that the partnership form of organization is used by the very large CPA firms which carry on a national or international practice. Some large-scale industrial and commercial enterprises also use the partnership form of organization. Although it is a reasonable generalization that partnerships are primarily associated with small-scale organizations, there is abundant evidence that no particular ceiling exists as to the number of partners or the number of branches which may be utilized under the partnership type of organization.

Characteristics of the partnership

The characteristics of a partnership are usually presented in introductory accounting textbooks, and will therefore be only briefly summarized here.

Ease of formation. In contrast to a corporation, a partnership may be created by oral or written agreement between two or more persons or may be implied by their conduct. This advantage of convenience and minimum expense in the formation of a partnership may in some cases be offset by certain difficulties inherent in such an informal and loosely designed organizational structure.

Limited life. A partnership may be ended by the death, retirement, bankruptcy, or incapacity of a partner. The admission of a new member to the firm also ends the existing partnership. Consequently, partnerships tend to be relatively short-lived and may even be regarded as a somewhat unstable form of organization.

Mutual agency. Each partner has the authority to act for the partnership and to enter into contracts binding upon it. Acts beyond the normal scope of business operations, however, such as the borrowing of funds by a partner, generally do not bind the partnership unless specific authority has been given for such transactions.

Unlimited liability. Each partner in a general partnership is personally responsible for the liabilities of the firm. Creditors who are having difficulty in collecting from the partnership will be likely to turn to those individual members of the firm who are known to have other financial resources. In a *limited partnership* one or more of the partners have no personal liability for debts of the firm. The activities of a limited partner are somewhat restricted, and he must maintain an agreed investment in the firm. Statutes providing for limited partnerships require that the firm identify itself publicly as a limited partnership and that at least one member of the firm be a general partner. The term *general partnership* refers to a firm in which all the partners are personally responsible for debts of the business and all have authority to act for the firm. These are attributes of a general partner.

Co-ownership of partnership property. When an individual contributes assets to a partnership, he retains no claim to those specific properties but merely acquires an equity in all assets of the firm.

Participation in profits. Every member of a partnership has an ownership interest in the profits; in fact, participation in profits and losses is one of the tests of the existence of a partnership. The profits of the partnership may be divided equally or in any other manner on which the partners agree. Since the amount of capital, personal ability and experience, and credit standing which partners contribute to the firm may vary widely, it is not surprising that many alternative methods exist for devising an equitable sharing of profits.

Deciding between a partnership and a corporation

One of the most important considerations in choosing between a partnership and the corporate form of organization is the income tax status of the business and of its owners. A partnership pays no income tax but is required to file an information report showing its revenue and expenses, the amount of its net income, and the division of that income among the partners. The partners in turn are obligated to include their respective shares of the ordinary partnership net income and such items as dividends, capital gains and losses, and charitable contributions on their individual income tax returns, regardless of whether they received more or less than this amount of cash from the partnership during the year.

The corporation is a separate legal entity subject to a corporate income tax. The net income after taxes, when and if distributed to stockholders in the form of dividends, is also subject to individual income taxes.

The individual with very large income is subject to individual income tax rates far higher than the rate imposed on corporations. Consequently, to the individual in a high income tax bracket, the corporate form of organization may be particularly attractive. Incorporation of his business may mean that all or a portion of his business income may be retained by the corporation and therefore not subjected to the high individual tax rates which would apply if such profits were derived from a partnership. The total tax burden for a given business organized as a corporation compared with the tax cost of the same business operating as a partnership will be influenced not only by tax rates on corporations and individuals, but also by such factors as types of securities issued, dividend policies, fringe benefits, and deferred compensation plans.

This brief summary of certain tax aspects of partnerships and corporations is by no means complete. For example, certain corporations with not more than ten stockholders are eligible to avoid being taxed as corporations provided their income or loss is fully assumed by their stockholders. These "tax-option corporations" in effect merely file information returns as do partnerships, and their stockholders report on their individual tax returns their respective shares of the year's profit or loss. Some partnerships have chosen to incorporate but to elect to continue being taxed as a partnership. The owners thereby gain advantages peculiar to the corporate form of organization such as limited liability, ready transferability of shares, continuity of existence, and capacity for attracting large amounts of investment capital.

A partnership may under certain conditions elect to be taxed as a corporation. Tax is then payable on the income of the partnership as an entity and the partners will be treated as corporate shareholders subject to certain technical exceptions. This option seldom offers a tax advantage and is rather rarely encountered.

Income tax rates and regulations are subject to frequent change, and new interpretations of the rules often arise. The tax status of the owners is also likely to change from year to year. For all these reasons, management should regularly review the tax implications of the partnership and corporate forms of organization so that the business entity may adapt most successfully to the tax environment.

The burden of taxation is of course not the only factor in making a sound choice between the partnership and the corporate form of organization. Perhaps the factor which most often tips the scales in favor of incorporation is the opportunity of obtaining greater amounts of capital when ownership can be divided into countless shares of stock, readily transferable and offering the many advantages inherent in the separation of ownership and management.

Is the partnership a separate entity?

In the older literature of accounting, the legal aspects of partnerships were sometimes given more emphasis than the managerial and financial issues. Thus, it was common practice to distinguish a partnership from a corporation by saying that the former was an association of persons and the latter a separate entity. Such a distinction unfortunately stresses the outward form rather than the substance of the business organization. In terms of managerial policy and business objectives, many a partnership is as truly a business entity as if it were incorporated. Such partnerships typically are guided by long-range plans not likely to be affected by the admission or withdrawal of a single member. In these firms the accounting policies logically should carry out the concept of the partnership as an entity apart from its individual owners.

Viewing the partnership as a business entity will often aid in developing accounting records and financial statements that provide the most meaningful picture of operating performance. Among the accounting policies to be stressed is continuity in asset valuation, despite changes in the ratio of profit sharing and changes in personnel. Another helpful step may be recognition in expense accounts of the value of personal services rendered by partners who hold managerial positions.

In theoretical discussions considerable support is found for viewing every business as an entity, apart from its owners, regardless of the form of legal organization. A managing partner under this view plays two roles: one as an executive employee of the entity, and the other as an owner. The value of the personal services rendered by the partner is a cost of managing the business entity. Unless this operating cost is deducted from the revenues earned, the measurement of net income is to some extent invalid.

The inclusion among expenses of payments for personal services rendered by partners is not customary practice at present. Opposed to such treatment is the pragmatic argument that partners' salaries may be set at unrealistic levels unrelated to the value of the services rendered. Other deterrents to treating partners' salaries as expense are the existing income tax rules, and the traditional legal view that the partnership is merely an association of individuals in which the partner is an owner and not an employee.

In practice many accountants are accustomed to viewing partnerships as separate entities with continuity of accounting policies and asset valuations not broken by changes in partnership personnel. The literature of accounting, however, has given little attention to this issue. Much work must yet be done before generally accepted standards are adequate to guide the accountant in determining the impact on accounting policies when a partner retires or a new member is admitted to the firm.

The partnership also has the characteristics of a separate entity in that it may hold title to property in its own name, may enter into contracts in its own name, and in some states may sue or be sued as an entity.

Articles of partnership

Although a partnership may exist on the basis of an oral agreement or be implied by the actions of its members, good business policy demands that the articles of partnership be clearly stated in writing. Among the more important points to be covered by the partnership contract are these:

1. The names of the partners and the name and nature of the partnership

2. The date of forming the partnership and the duration of the contract

3. The capital to be invested by each partner, the procedure for valuing non-cash investments, and the penalties for failure to contribute and maintain the agreed amount of capital

4. The authority to be vested in each partner and the rights and duties of each

5. The accounting period to be used, the nature of accounting records, financial statements, and audits by certified public accountants

6. The plan for sharing profits and losses, including the frequency of such income measurement and the distribution to partners

7. The salaries and drawings allowed to partners and the penalties, if any, for excessive withdrawals

8. Insurance on the lives of partners, with the partnership or surviving partners named as beneficiaries

9. Provision for the arbitration of disputes and the liquidation of the partnership at the end of the specified term of the contract or at the death or withdrawal of a partner. Especially important in avoiding costly disputes is agreement upon procedures for valuation of assets, including goodwill, and the method of settlement with the estate of a deceased partner.

Achieving and maintaining agreement among partners

One advantage of developing an adequate partnership contract with the aid of attorneys and accountants is that the process of reaching agreement on these points will develop a fuller understanding among the partners on many issues which might be highly controversial in nature if not settled until after the business had operated for a considerable span of time. Of course, it is seldom possible to cover specifically in a partnership contract every issue which may later arise. To revise the articles of partnership requires the agreement of all partners.

Disputes arising among partners which cannot be resolved by reference to the partnership agreement may be settled by arbitration or in the courts by reference to partnership law. The partner who is not satisfied with the handling of disputed issues always has the right to withdraw from the firm. The relationship of partners is a voluntary one; no one can be forced against his will to continue as a partner regardless of the agreed term of operations. For example, an individual who discovers that one of his partners is engaging in fraudulent or other illegal activities would probably want to end the partnership at once. If he withdraws before the end of the operating period specified in the articles of partnership, he may be subject to suit for breach of contract, but under the circumstances cited, he probably has an adequate defense against any such suit.

Owners' equity accounts for partners

Accounting for a partnership differs from accounting for a sole proprietorship or a corporation chiefly with respect to the sharing of profits and the maintenance of the owners' equity accounts. Although it would be possible to operate a set of partnership records with only one equity account for each partner, the usual practice is to maintain three types of accounts. These equity accounts consist of

(1) capital accounts, (2) drawing or personal accounts, and (3) accounts for loans to or from partners.

The original investment by each partner in the firm is recorded by debiting the assets contributed, crediting any liabilities being assumed by the firm, and crediting the partner's capital account with the fair market value of the net assets invested. Subsequent to the original investment, the partner's equity may be increased by additional investment of cash or other property, by a share of the partnership net income, through the payment by the partner personally of liabilities owed by the firm, or through collection by the partnership of receivables owned personally by the partner.

These possible sources of increase in a partner's equity are paralleled by similar sources of decrease. The partner's equity in the firm may be decreased by withdrawal of cash or other assets, by sharing losses incurred by the firm, through payment of personal debts of the partner from the partnership bank account, and through collection and retention by a partner personally of accounts receivable belonging to the partnership. Clearly, some of these sources of increase and decrease in the partner's equity account reflect the tendency found both in sole proprietorships and partnerships for the owners to intermingle their personal financial affairs with those of the business.

Another possible source of increase or decrease in partners' equity arises from changes in partnership personnel, as discussed in Chapter 2. When a partner retires or a new partner is admitted to the firm, a bonus may be allowed to one or more partners, thus causing a shift between capital accounts. Under some circumstances, partners' capitals may also be changed through recognition of goodwill or revaluation of assets; such write-ups or write-downs should in general be avoided so that asset valuations in the partnership as in other types of organizations will be stated at cost and supported by objective evidence.

The original investment of assets by a partner is recorded by credit to his capital account. Drawings by a partner in anticipation of profits or drawings which are considered as the equivalent of a salary are recorded by debit to his drawing account. However, a large withdrawal which is viewed as a permanent reduction in the equity of the partner is usually recorded by debiting his capital account.

At the end of the accounting period the net income or net loss shown by the Income Summary account is transferred to the capital accounts of the partners in accordance with the profit-sharing agreement. The debit balances in the drawing accounts of the partners at the end of the year are also closed into their respective capital accounts. Consequently, the drawing accounts show zero balances at the beginning of each new accounting period.

Since the accounting procedures for partners' equity accounts are not subject to state regulation as in the case of capital stock and other equity accounts of a corporation, many deviations from the plan described are possible. Some accountants prefer to show the division of partnership net income by closing the Income Summary account into the partners' drawing accounts, and then as a final entry close the drawing accounts into the capital accounts. This variation is purely a procedural one and has no effect on the end results. As another example of alternative procedures, the partners might decide to share profits on the basis of their original capital investments and might therefore prefer to maintain these balances intact with changes resulting from profits, losses, withdrawals, and subsequent investment carried permanently in personal accounts. It is possible to regard the original investment by partners as the equivalent of the capital stock account of a corporation and to maintain the personal accounts as separate measurements of earnings minus distributions to partners. These variations, however, are seldom encountered; it is a safe generalization to say that in the majority of partnerships the Income Summary account and the drawing accounts are closed at the end of each year to the respective capital accounts of the partners. In any event, the partners will usually prefer that the annual balance sheet distributed to outsiders show each partner's equity as a single amount computed by combining his capital account and drawing account.

Loans to and from partners

Occasionally a partner may withdraw a substantial sum from the partnership with the intention of repaying this amount. Such a transaction may be debited to the Notes Receivable account rather than to his drawing account.

On the other hand, a partner may make an advance to the partnership which is viewed as a loan rather than an increase in his capital account. This type of transaction is recorded by a credit to Loans Payable to Partners and is desirably accompanied by the issuance of a note payable. Amounts due from partners may be reflected as assets on the balance sheet and amounts owing to partners shown as liabilities. The classification of these items as current or long-term would, of course, depend upon the maturity date specified in the loan agreement. However, the inclusion of a substantial receivable from a partner in the current asset category calls for solid evidence that the receivable will be collected within the accounting cycle. As for all transactions not consummated at arm's length, a greater weight of evidence is needed to support the prospects for completion of the transaction according to the agreed terms.

If a substantial unsecured loan has been made by a partnership to one of the partners and repayment appears doubtful, the better financial statement presentation may be to offset the receivable against the partner's capital account. If this is not done, the assets shown on the balance sheet and the owners' equity may be inflated to the point of being misleading. In any event, adequate disclosure calls for separate listing and clear labeling of any assets on the balance sheet which are receivables from members of the firm.

Valuation of investments by partners

The investment in the firm by a partner often includes assets other than cash. It is imperative that the partners agree upon the fair market value of these assets at the time of their investment and that the assets be recorded at their fair market values at this time. Any gain or loss resulting from the sale of such assets during the operation of the partnership or at the time of liquidation will be divided according to the established agreement for sharing profits and losses. Fair treatment of the individual partners, therefore, requires a starting point of fair current values recorded for all assets contributed to the firm. It will then follow that partnership gains or losses upon disposal of noncash assets contributed by the partners will be limited to the difference between the disposal price and the fair market value of the property when contributed by the investing partners.

The partner's equity versus his share in profits

The equity of a partner in the firm should be clearly distinguished from his share of profits and losses. Thus to say that A is a one-third partner is not a clear statement. He may have a one-third claim on the assets of the firm but have a share in profits greater or smaller than this proportion. Such a statement might also be interpreted to mean that A was entitled to one-third of the profits or losses, although his capital account represented much more or much less than one-third of the total ownership equity. To state the matter concisely, the partners may agree upon any type of profit-sharing plan, regardless of the amount of their respective capital accounts. The courts have held, however, that if partners fail to specify a plan for sharing profits, it shall be assumed that they intended to share equally. A corollary rule has been that when a specific agreement exists for the sharing of profits but no mention is made of the division of losses, it shall be assumed that losses are to be divided in the same proportion as provided for the division of profits.

To illustrate one result of a disparity in a partner's equity as contrasted with his share of profits, let us assume that A has contributed $40,000 and B has contributed $60,000 to form the new firm of A and B. However, the partners have agreed to share profits and losses equally. It is apparent that the 40:60 relationship of the capital accounts of A and B will soon change because of their division of profits or losses in a different ratio.

Dividing net income or loss

The many possible arrangements for sharing of net income or loss among partners may be summarized into the following classes:

1. Dividing profit and loss equally
2. Dividing profit and loss in some other agreed ratio
3. Dividing profit and loss in the ratio of partners' capitals, or in the ratio of average capitals during the year
4. Allowing salaries to partners and dividing the remaining profit and loss in an agreed ratio
5. Allowing salaries to partners, allowing interest on capitals, and dividing the remaining profit and loss in an agreed ratio

These variations in profit-sharing plans emphasize that the value of personal services rendered by individual partners may vary widely, as may the amounts of capital contributed by each. The amount and quality of managerial services rendered and the amount of capital supplied are clearly important factors in the success or failure of the business. Therefore it is often logical to provide for salaries to partners and interest on their respective capitals as a preliminary step in dividing the net income of the business. Residual profits may then be divided equally.

Another factor affecting the success of the firm may be that one of the partners has very large personal financial resources, which cause the partnership to have a high credit rating merely because of his membership in it. Similarly, a partner with a name widely known in a professional field or even in industry may contribute importantly to the success of the venture even though he may not actively participate in administration of the business. These two factors may be taken into account in devising the profit-sharing plan by judicious selection of the ratio in which residual profits are divided after allowances for partners' salaries and for interest on capital accounts.

We shall now illustrate how each of the principal methods of dividing net income or loss may be applied. This series of illustrations is based on the partnership of A and B, which is assumed to earn net income of $30,000 during the first year of operation. The partnership agreement provides that each partner may withdraw $500 on the last day of each month in anticipation of profits. These drawings are not a factor in dividing net income; they are recorded by debits to the partners' drawing accounts and are not to be regarded as salaries. All other withdrawals and investments will be entered in the capital accounts.

Partner A's original investment on January 1 was $40,000 and he invested an additional $10,000 on April 1. Partner B's investment on January 1 was $80,000, and he withdrew $5,000 on October 1. These assumed transactions are illustrated in the following capital and drawing accounts for the two partners and by the Income Summary account showing the net income of $30,000 to be divided.

A, Capital

		Jan. 1	*40,000*
		Apr. 1	*10,000*

B, Capital

Oct. 1	*5,000*	*Jan. 1*	*80,000*

A, Drawing

Jan.-Dec., inclusive	*6,000*		

B, Drawing

Jan.-Dec., inclusive	*6,000*		

Income Summary

		Dec. 31	*30,000*

Equal division of profit and loss

Many partnership agreements provide that net income or loss will be divided equally. Also, if the partners have made no specific agreement for sharing profits, the courts have generally held that an intent of equal division will be assumed. The net income of $30,000 will therefore be transferred from the Income Summary account to the partners' capital accounts by the following journal entry:

Income Summary	*30,000*	
A, Capital		*15,000*
B, Capital		*15,000*
To divide the net income equally between A and B.		

The drawing accounts will now be closed to the partners' capital accounts so that each partner's capital account at the end of the year will show the equity resulting from combining the positive factors of beginning capital, subsequent investments, and share of net income with the negative factors of regular monthly drawings and any other withdrawals of capital.

If the business owned by A and B had operated at a loss of, say, $20,000 during the first year, the Income Summary account would of course have had a debit balance of $20,000. This loss would have been transferred to the capital accounts by debiting each capital account for $10,000 and crediting Income Summary for $20,000.

Division of profit and loss in some other agreed ratio

In this illustration we shall assume that A and B agree to share profit and loss in the ratio of three-fifths to A and two-fifths to B. This ratio might be selected to reflect the fact that A had greater experience in the field and personal contacts which were important to the success of the firm. The net income of $30,000 is divided as shown in the following entry:

Income Summary	*30,000*	
A, Capital		*18,000*
B, Capital		*12,000*
To divide net income per agreement:		
A: ⅗ × $30,000 . . . $18,000		
B: ⅖ × $30,000 . . . 12,000		
Total $30,000		

The agreement that A should receive three-fifths of the profit because of his greater experience and personal contacts would cause him to suffer a major share of the loss if the business operated unprofitably. If we assume a loss of $20,000 in the first year, A would be charged with three-fifths, or $12,000, while B would bear only an $8,000 reduction in his equity.

Some partnership agreements provide that profits will be divided in a certain ratio such as three-fifths to A and two-fifths to B, but that losses will be divided equally or in some other ratio. Another variation intended to compensate for unequal contributions by the partners provides that the agreed ratio (three-fifths and two-fifths in our example) shall be applicable to a given amount of earnings, but that additional earnings shall be shared in some other ratio. For example, the agreement might require the first $20,000 of net income be divided three-fifths to A and two-fifths to B, with all income in excess of $20,000 to be divided equally. Net earnings of $30,000 would then be divided as follows:

	A	*B*	*Total*
First $20,000 divided ⅗ and ⅖	*$12,000*	*$ 8,000*	*$20,000*
Additional earnings equally	*5,000*	*5,000*	*10,000*
Totals	*$17,000*	*$13,000*	*$30,000*

A profit-sharing agreement of this type places extreme importance on the *timing* of partnership income. Close decisions are often necessary in determining whether a given expenditure shall be treated as expense immediately or as a deferred item. Similar difficult decisions may be necessary in deciding whether certain revenue items belong in the year just ending or in the following year. In the context of our example of the first $20,000 of net income being divided in a different ratio from any additional income, the timing of partnership income may directly affect its division between the partners.

Division of profit and loss in the ratio of partners' capitals

Division of partnership earnings in proportion to the capital provided by each member of the firm is most likely to be found in the type of business in which substantial investment is the principal ingredient for success. For example, a partnership engaged in purchasing raw land and holding it for higher prices might select this method of dividing profits. To avoid controversy, it is essential that the agreement specify whether the profit-sharing ratio is based on the original capital investments, the capitals at the beginning of each year, the capitals at the end of each year, or the average capitals during each year.

Ratio of original capitals. Continuing our illustration of the partnership of A and B, assume that the agreement calls for division of net income in the ratio of the original capitals. The first year's net income will be divided as shown by the following entry:

Income Summary		30,000	
A, Capital			10,000
B, Capital			20,000
To divide earnings in ratio of original capitals:			
A: 40,000/120,000 × $30,000	*$10,000*		
B: 80,000/120,000 × $30,000	*20,000*		
Totals	*$30,000*		

Ratio of capitals at end of year. As a second case, assume that the earnings were to be divided in the ratio of capitals at the end of the year. The entry would be:

Income Summary		30,000	
A, Capital			12,000
B, Capital			18,000
To divide earnings in ratio of ending capitals:			
A: 50,000/125,000 × $30,000	*$12,000*		
B: 75,000/125,000 × $30,000	*18,000*		
Total	*$30,000*		

Average capital ratio. Dividing income on the basis of (1) original capitals; (2) yearly beginning capitals; or (3) yearly ending capitals may prove inequitable if there are significant changes in capital during the period because of withdrawals or added investments by partners. Using average capitals as a basis is preferable in that it reflects the contributed funds actually available for use by the business during the year.

If the partnership agreement provides for sharing profits in the ratio of average capitals during the year, it should also state the amount of drawings each partner may make without affecting his capital account. In our continuing example of the firm of A and B, the partners are entitled to withdraw $500 monthly and these drawings are recorded by debiting their drawing accounts. Any additional withdrawals and any investments are entered in the partners' capital accounts and therefore influence the computation of the average capital ratio. The partnership agreement should also state whether capital balances are to be computed in terms of dollar-months, dollar-weeks, or dollar-days. A common practice is to provide that withdrawals and investments made during the first half of the month shall be treated as having been made as of the first of that month; withdrawals and investments made during the latter half of each month shall not affect the computation of the capital rates until the first of the following month.

In the computation of capital at quarterly or semiannual intervals, it is of course possible to include the interim earnings since the last annual closing date. However, this plan is rarely used, perhaps because of the tentative nature of interim statements and the possibility of major year-end adjustments after an annual audit.

In our example, the ratio of average capitals for A and B is computed as follows:

	Date	Debits	Credits	Capital balance	Months unchanged	Dollar-months
A	Jan. 1		$40,000	$40,000	3	$ 120,000
	Apr. 1		10,000	50,000	9	450,000
					12	$ 570,000
B	Jan. 1		80,000	80,000	9	$ 720,000
	Oct. 1	$5,000		75,000	3	225,000
					12	$ 945,000
Total dollar-months for A and B						$1,515,000

Division of net income:

To A: 570,000/1,515,000 × $30,000	$11,287
To B: 945,000/1,515,000 × $30,000	18,713
	$30,000

In making these calculations we could have computed the average capital for each partner by dividing his dollar-months by 12. Thus, average capital for A was $570,000 ÷ 12, or $47,500; and average capital for B was $945,000 ÷ 12, or $78,750. The ratio between these average capitals is the same as the ratio of dollar-months used in the preceding schedule.

It is worth repeating again that partners may divide profits in any manner they agree upon. Variations from the methods illustrated are virtually unlimited. For example, the division of profits in the ratio of average capitals could be defined in the agreement to include recognition of *all changes* in a partner's equity, including both the capital and drawing accounts. The function of the accountant is twofold: First, to explain to the partners during the formation of the agreement various methods of profit sharing, the reasoning underlying each method, and the results which will flow from these alternative plans under varying levels of profit or loss; and secondly, to interpret the agreement accurately in working out the annual division of net income.

Interests on partners' capitals with remaining profit and loss divided in an agreed ratio

In the preceding section the plan for dividing the entire net income in the ratio of partners' capitals was based on the assumption that invested capital was the dominant factor in profitable operation of the business. In most lines of business, however, the amount of invested capital is only one of several factors which are significant in achieving profitable operation. Consequently, many partnerships choose to divide only a portion of the profits in the capital ratio, and to divide the remainder equally or in some other agreed ratio.

To allow interest on capitals at an agreed rate of, say, 6% is essentially the same thing as dividing a *limited portion* of the profits in the ratio of partners' capitals.

If the partners agree to allow interest on capital as a first step in dividing profits, they should of course specify the interest rate to be used and also state whether the calculation is to be based on capital accounts at specific dates or on average capitals during the year. As previously indicated, partners must make a specific agreement to allow interest on capitals if that is their desire. No matter how unequal the capital accounts of partners may be, the law will assume that they intended to share profits equally unless some other plan for profit sharing has been agreed upon.

Let us use again our basic illustration of the firm of A and B with net income of $30,000 during the first year and capital accounts as shown on page 11. Assume that the partnership agreement allows interest on partners' average capitals at 6% with any residual profit or loss to be divided equally. The following entries show the distribution of net income at the end of the year.

Income Summary			7,575	
A, Capital				2,850
B, Capital				4,725
To allow interest on average capitals as follows:				
A: $40,000 × 6% for 3 months	*$ 600*			
$50,000 × 6% for 9 months	*2,250*	*$2,850*		
B: $80,000 × 6% for 9 months	*$3,600*			
$75,000 × 6% for 3 months	*1,125*	*4,725*		
Total interest allowed		*$7,575*		
Income Summary			22,425	
A, Capital				11,212
B, Capital				11,213
Total income for the year		*$30,000*		
Less: Amounts allowed as interest		*7,575*		
Remaining income to be divided equally		*$22,425*		

The net effect of allowing interest on partners' capitals as shown by these entries (rounded to the nearest dollar) is to divide $7,575 of the year's net income in the ratio of the capital accounts, with the remaining $22,425 divided equally. A received a total of $14,062 and B received $15,938.

Assume for the moment that the partners had agreed that the profit remaining after allowance of interest on capitals should not be divided equally, but in the ratio of the capital accounts. Such a plan would border on the absurd because it would lead in a roundabout manner to the same dollar result produced by dividing the entire profit in the capital ratio.

As a separate case, assume that the partnership of A and B was unsuccessful in its first year and sustained a net loss of $20,000. If the partnership agreement provides for allowing interest on capitals, this provision must be enforced regardless of whether operations are profitable or unprofitable. The only justification for omitting the allowance of interest on partners' capitals during a loss year would be in the case of a partnership agreement containing a specific clause requiring such omission. Notice in the following illustrative entries that the $20,000 debit balance in the Income Summary account resulting from operating losses is increased by allowance of interest to a debit total of $27,575, which is then divided equally between the partners.

			Debit	Credit
Income Summary			7,575	
A, Capital				2,850
B, Capital				4,725
To allow interest on average capitals as follows:				
A: $40,000 × 6% for 3 months	*$ 600*			
$50,000 × 6% for 9 months	*2,250*	*$2,850*		
B: $80,000 × 6% for 9 months	*$3,600*			
$75,000 × 6% for 3 months	*1,125*	*4,725*		
Total interest allowed		*$7,575*		
A, Capital			13,787	
B, Capital			13,788	
Income Summary				27,575
Operating loss for the year		*$20,000*		
Allowance for interest on partners' capital		*7,575*		
Loss to be divided equally		*$27,575*		

The net result of this profit-sharing agreement is that the $20,000 loss from operations was borne $10,937 by A and $9,063 by B, as shown on the following page.

In some cases, the allowance of interest on partners' capitals may result in a net increase in one partner's capital account even though operations for the year resulted in a loss. To illustrate, assume the same conditions as in the preceding

	A	B	Total
Debit balance in Income Summary account			*$20,000*
Add: Allowance for interest	*$ 2,850*	*$ 4,725*	*7,575*
Adjusted debit balance to be divided			*$27,575*
Distribution to partners of residual loss ...	*(13,787)*	*(13,788)*	*(27,575)*
Total loss assigned to each partner	*$(10,937)*	*$(9,063)*	

examples except that the operating loss for the year was $1,000. The following schedule shows that A's capital will be reduced by $1,437 while B's capital will be increased by $437.

	A	B	Total
Debit balance in Income Summary account			*$1,000*
Add: Allowance for interest on capitals	*$2,850*	*$4,725*	*7,575*
Adjusted debit balance to be divided			*$8,575*
Distribution to partners of residual loss	*(4,287)*	*(4,288)*	*(8,575)*
Total loss assigned to each partner.........	*($1,437)*	*$ 437*	

At first thought the idea of a business loss of $1,000 causing one partner's capital to increase and the other partner's capital to decrease may appear unreasonable, but there is sound logic to support this result. Partner B did contribute substantially more capital to the firm than did A; this capital was used to carry on operations, and the fact that a loss was incurred in the first year is no reason to deny recognition of B's greater capital contribution.

A significant contrast between two of the profit-sharing plans we have discussed (the capital ratio plan versus the interest on partners' capitals plan) is apparent if we consider the case of a business operating at a loss. Under the capital ratio plan, the partner who has invested the most capital will be required to bear a larger share of the loss. This result may be considered unreasonable, because the contribution of capital is presumably not the cause of an operating loss. Under the "interest on capitals" plan of sharing profit and loss, the partner who has invested more capital will receive credit for this factor and thereby be charged with a lesser share of the operating loss or may even possibly be credited with a gain.

Still another variation of the plan for allowing interest on partners' capitals is merely to allow interest to the partner with the larger capital on the excess of his capital over that of the other partner. However, this type of plan will give a different end result if the profit or loss remaining after the allowance for interest is to be distributed in any ratio other than equally among partners.

Interest on partners' loans. We have thus far considered interest allowances on partners' capitals as a technique for sharing partnership profits equitably but as having no effect on determining the net income or loss of the business as an entity.

Interest on partners' capitals is not an expense of the business, but interest on loans from partners to the firm is regarded as interest expense and a factor in determining net income for the period. Similarly, interest earned on loans by the firm to partners represents an element of revenue. This treatment is consistent with the point made earlier in this chapter that loans to and from partners are classified as assets and liabilities on the balance sheet of the partnership. Interest on such loans should be accrued in the usual manner at the close of the accounting period.

Another item of expense arising from dealings between a partnership and one of its partners is commonly encountered when the partnership rents property from a landlord who is a partner in the firm. Rent expense and a liability for rent payable should be recognized in such situations. The landlord, although a partner, is also a creditor of the partnership.

Salaries to partners with remaining profit and loss divided in an agreed ratio

In discussing salaries to partners, a first essential is to distinguish clearly between salaries and drawings.

Let us assume that Partner A has greater experience and ability than Partner B and also devotes more time to the partnership. It seems reasonable that the partners will want to recognize the greater contribution of personal services by A in choosing a plan for division of profits. One approach to this objective would be to adopt an unequal ratio: for example, 70% of net income to A and 30% to B. Use of an arbitrary ratio is usually not a satisfactory solution, however, for the same two reasons mentioned in criticizing the capital ratio as a profit-sharing plan. An arbitrary ratio based on the greater contribution of personal services by A may not reflect the fact that other factors apart from personal services of partners are important in determining the profitability of the business. A second significant point is that if the business sustains a loss, the partner rendering the larger amount of personal services will be charged with the larger portion of that loss.

A simple solution to the problem of recognizing unequal personal services by partners is to provide in the partnership agreement for varying salaries to partners, with the remaining profit or loss divided equally or in some other agreed ratio. Salaries to partners have traditionally been treated in financial statements as a device for sharing net income, and not as an expense of the business. Under this view, partners will not necessarily receive payment of their authorized salaries during the year but will merely use their salary allowances at the end of the year as a preliminary step in dividing the year's net income. (Actual monthly cash drawings by the partners may be unrelated to authorized salaries; they are recorded by debits to drawing accounts as shown on page 11.) Let us apply this reasoning to our continuing illustration of the firm of A and B, and assume that the articles of partnership provide for an annual salary of $10,000 to A and $6,000 to B with any remaining profit or loss to be divided equally. The salaries are not actually paid during the year. The first year's net income of $30,000 would be transferred from the Income Summary account to the partners' capital accounts by the following entries:

Income Summary	*16,000*	
A, Capital		*10,000*
B, Capital		*6,000*
To credit each partner with his authorized salary as a first step in dividing the year's net income.		
Income Summary	*14,000*	
A, Capital		*7,000*
B, Capital		*7,000*
To close Income Summary account by transfer to partners' capital accounts of residual profit.		
Total income for the year . . . $30,000		
Less: Amounts allowed as salaries . . . 16,000		
Remaining income to be divided equally . . . $14,000		

The two preceding entries could of course be combined into one entry which would divide the year's net income $17,000 to A and $13,000 to B. The explanation portion of the entry should show clearly how the distribution of the $30,000 net income was computed.

If the partners should choose to take their authorized salaries in cash on a monthly basis, these payments could be debited to partners' salary accounts which, like the drawing accounts, would be closed at the end of the year to the partners' capital accounts. Consequently, the partners' salaries would not influence the amount of net income as shown in the Income Summary account.

Distinguishing between salaries and drawings. Since the word *salary* has a connotation to many people of weekly or monthly cash payments for personal services, the accountant should be quite specific in suggesting and defining the terminology used in accounting for a partnership. We have used the term *drawings* in only one sense: a withdrawal of assets which reduces the partner's equity but plays no part in the division of net income. We shall limit the word *salaries* in partnership accounting to mean a device for sharing the annual net income. When salaries is used with this meaning, the division of net income is the same regardless of whether salaries have been paid in cash or merely used in a year-end computation.

A partnership agreement which permits partners to make regular withdrawals of specific amounts should clearly state whether such withdrawals are intended to be a factor in the division of profit and loss. Assume, for example, that the agreement merely says that Partner A may make drawings of $300 monthly and Partner B $800. If the intent is not clearly stated to include or exclude these drawings as an element in the division of net income, controversy is probable because one interpretation will favor A and the opposing interpretation will favor B.

Bonus to managing partner. When one partner serves as a manager of the business, he is sometimes entitled by contract to receive a bonus equal to a given percentage of the net income. The partnership agreement should state whether the basis of the bonus is net income before deduction of the bonus or net income minus the bonus. For example, assume that the firm of A and B provides for a bonus to B, the managing partner, of 25% of net income before deduction of the bonus and that the remaining net income is to be divided equally. As in the preceding examples, the net income is assumed to be $30,000; the division will be as follows:

	A	B	Total
Net income			*$30,000*
Bonus to B (25% of net income)		*$ 7,500*	*$ 7,500*
Remainder, divided equally	*$11,250*	*11,250*	*22,500*
Totals	*$11,250*	*$18,750*	*$30,000*

On the other hand, if the partnership agreement provides that the basis of the bonus is net income minus the 25% bonus, the bonus may be computed as follows:

$$\begin{aligned}
\text{Bonus} + \text{net income subject to the bonus} &= \$30{,}000 \\
\text{Let } X &= \text{net income subject to bonus} \\
.25X &= \text{bonus} \\
\text{Then } 1.25X &= \text{net income before bonus of } \$30{,}000 \\
X &= \$30{,}000 \div 1.25 = \$24{,}000 \\
.25X &= \$6{,}000 \text{ bonus to B}
\end{aligned}$$

An alternative computation consists of converting the bonus percentage to a fraction. The bonus can then be computed by adding the numerator to the denominator and applying the resulting fraction to the profits before the bonus. In the preceding example, 25% is converted to ¼, and by adding the numerator to the denominator the ¼ becomes ⅕. One-fifth of $30,000 equals $6,000. The distribution of the net income between the partners will then be as follows:

	A	B	Total
Net income			*$30,000*
Bonus to B (25% of net income less bonus)		*$ 6,000*	*$ 6,000*
Remainder, divided equally	*$12,000*	*12,000*	*24,000*
Totals	*$12,000*	*$18,000*	*$30,000*

The concept of a bonus is not applicable to a negative net income: in other words, if the partnership operates at a loss, the bonus provision becomes nonoperative. The partnership agreement may also specify that extraordinary nonoperating gains and losses may be excluded from the basis for the bonus.

Salaries to partners combined with interest on capital

Many partnerships find it reasonable to divide net income by allowing salaries to partners and also interest on their respective capital accounts. Any remaining profit or loss is divided equally or in some other agreed ratio. Such plans have the merit of recognizing that the value of personal services rendered by different partners may vary greatly, and that differences in amounts of invested capital also warrant recognition in devising an equitable plan for sharing profits.

The procedures for carrying out this type of agreement are the same as illustrated in earlier sections. At year-end the Income Summary account is debited and the capital accounts are credited for both the authorized salaries and the interest on partners' capitals. The remaining balance in the Income Summary account (either debit or credit) is then transferred to the capital accounts in the agreed ratio.

Income statement—disclosure of profit-sharing data. Explanations of the division of net income between partners may be added at the bottom of the income statement. This information is sometimes referred to as the distribution section of the income statement. The following illustration shows a highly condensed income statement with the division of net income based on both salary and interest, and the remaining profit or loss divided equally.

A AND B
Income Statement
for the year ended December 31, 19__

Sales	*$300,000*
Cost of sales	*180,000*
Gross profit on sales	*$120,000*
Operating expenses	*90,000*
Net income	*$ 30,000*

Distribution of net income:

	A	*B*	*Total*
Salaries	*$10,000*	*$16,000*	*$26,000*
Interest on capital	*2,850*	*4,725*	*7,575*
	$12,850	*$20,725*	*$33,575*
Less: Excess of salaries and interest over net income	*1,787*	*1,788*	*3,575*
Division of net income	*$11,063*	*$18,937*	*$30,000*

In the illustrated income statement, notice that interest and salaries allowed to the partners exceed the net income for the year. The resulting debit balance in the Income Summary account of $3,575 was charged equally against A and B as the final step in the distribution of the year's income.

Statement of partners' capitals

Each partner will naturally want a complete explanation of the change in his capital account each year. To meet this need a schedule called a *statement of partners' capital* is prepared as a supplement to the balance sheet. Since this information is intended only for the private use of the partners, it is usually presented as a separate statement rather than being inserted within the owners' equity section of the balance sheet.

The following illustrative statement of partners' capitals is based on the ledger accounts presented on page 11, and also uses the division of net income through salaries and interest on capital illustrated on page 21.

A AND B
Statement of Partners' Capitals
for the year ended December 31, 19__

	A	B	Total
Partners' capitals, Jan. 1, 19__	$40,000	$80,000	$120,000
Additional investment and withdrawal of capital	10,000	(5,000)	5,000
Balance before net income and regular drawings	$50,000	$75,000	$125,000
Net income for the year	11,063	18,937	30,000
Totals	$61,063	$93,937	$155,000
Less: Regular drawings	6,000	6,000	12,000
Partners' capitals, Dec. 31, 19__	$55,063	$87,937	$143,000

Adjustment of net income of prior periods

Any business, whether it be organized as a sole proprietorship, partnership, or corporation, will occasionally discover significant errors made in the measurement of income in prior years. Examples include errors in computing prior years' depreciation, errors in inventory valuation, and omission of accruals of revenue or expense. When such errors come to light, the question arises as to whether the corrections should be treated as part of the determination of net income for the current period or treated as direct charges against partners' capitals. In the case of a corporation, exclusion of the adjustment from determination of the current year's income would call for a direct charge or credit to retained earnings. The arguments for these alternative methods were evaluated in Chapter 3 of *Intermediate Accounting* under the discussion of all-inclusive income and current operating performance income. The same considerations apply for a partnership as for a corporation in determining a policy for adjusting errors in income of prior periods. Adherence to the *all-inclusive income* concept would in the case of a partnership call for inclusion of the correction of prior years' errors in the current year's income statement but with careful labeling of the items to achieve full disclosure. On the other hand, adherence to the *current operating performance* concept would call for correction of prior years' errors by direct charges or credits to the partners' capital accounts.

Let us now assume that the income-sharing ratio has been changed by mutual agreement of the partners, the change becoming effective between the year in which the error occurred and the year of its discovery. For example, assume that in Year 1 the reported net income was $50,000 and the partners shared profits equally, but in Year 2 they revised the ratio to 70% for A and 30% for B. During Year 2, it was discovered that the ending inventory for Year 1 had been overstated by $10,000 because of a clerical error. The correction of the error may be made either in the current year's income statement or in the statement of partners' capitals. Whichever method of correction is used, however, the $10,000 adjustment should be divided $5,000 to each partner, in accordance with the profit and loss ratio which prevailed in the *year in which the error occurred.* If the correction is made through the income statement, the division of net income will need to be made in two steps; the correction portion in the equal ratio of Year 1 and the remaining portion in the 70:30 ratio of Year 2.

Somewhat related to the correction of errors of prior years is the treatment of extraordinary gains and losses. When the income-sharing ratio of a partnership is changed, the partners should consider the differences which exist between the book value of assets and their present fair value. As a somewhat extreme example, assume that the partnership of A and B owns marketable securities acquired for $20,000 which have risen in value to $50,000 at the date when the profit-sharing ratio is revised from 50% for each to 70% for A and 30% for B. If the securities were sold for $50,000 just prior to changing the profit-sharing ratio, the $30,000 gain would cause each partner's capital account to rise by $15,000. If the securities were sold for $50,000 immediately after establishment of the 70:30 profit-sharing ratio, the $30,000 gain would be divided $21,000 to A and only $9,000 to B. For most other types of assets, however, objective evidence of current fair value is not readily available.

A solution sometimes suggested for such partnership problems is to revalue the assets to fair market value when the profit-sharing ratio is changed or when a new partner is added or an old one retires. Under certain circumstances the revaluation of assets may be justified, but in general the continuity of cost valuations in a partnership is desirable, for the same reasons that support the use of the cost principle in a corporation. A secondary objection to revaluation of assets is that with a few exceptions such as marketable securities, objective evidence of current fair value is seldom available. A better solution to the problem of change in the ratio of profit sharing may usually be achieved by making appropriate adjustments between partners' capitals rather than by arbitrarily writing asset values up and down.

When the accountant acts in the role of managerial consultant to a partnership, he should bring to the attention of the partners any significant differences between book value and market value, and make them aware of the implications and uncertainties created by a change in the ratio of profit sharing.

Statements and reports for managerial use

Internal reports for use by management in appraising the performance of individual departments or branches may call for different accounting concepts and classifications from those generally used for the financial statements prepared for outsiders. To develop the most meaningful cost data for internal use, it may be helpful to treat partners' salaries as expense rather than as a device for dividing net income. This approach is particularly appropriate if one branch has a partner as active manager and another branch is managed by a salaried employee. The partners must, of course, include the salaries in their individual income tax returns. In large organizations with a number of partners of whom only one or two are active in the management of the business, partners' salaries may realistically be viewed as operating expenses similar to payments to employees. This approach follows the view that the partnership is an entity and that all costs of management must be deducted from revenues to measure the income of the entity.

The inclusion of partners' salaries among the operating expenses may also aid in comparing the income data of a partnership with similar companies operating as corporations. When interest and salaries paid to partners are treated as expenses, these expense accounts should be closed into the Income Summary account and should be listed among the operating expenses on income statements and departmental reports for internal use. This income statement prepared for managerial use will of course show a lower figure for net income, but the overall amount going to each partner, including both salary and share of reported net income, will be the same as if the salaries were treated as a device for dividing net income.

Federal income tax regulations permit a partnership to deduct as expenses payments made to partners for services or for use of capital, provided that the amounts are reasonable and are not based on the net income of the partnership. Such payments generally are not subject to income tax withholding or payroll taxes.

Questions

1. In the formation of a partnership, partners often contribute to the firm such assets as land, buildings, and machinery as well as cash. Should these noncash assets be recorded by the partnership at appraised value, at cost to the partners, or on some other basis of valuation? Give reasons for your answer.

2. Barnes and Cardwell began a partnership business on January 1, with total capital of $50,000, of which $40,000 was contributed by Barnes and $10,000 by Cardwell. The partners made no agreement as to the division of profits or responsibilities. Assuming that the first year's operations resulted in a profit of $10,000, how should this amount be divided? What division would be made if a net loss of $10,000 was incurred in the first year?

3. Some CPA firms have hundreds of staff members and operate on a national or international basis. Would the corporate form of organization not be more appropriate than the partnership form for such large organizations?

4. Explain the proper presentation in the balance sheet of loans to and from partners, and the treatment of interest on such loans.

5. Explain how partners' salaries should be shown in the income statement, if at all.

6. List at least six items that should be covered in a partnership agreement.

7. Compare the capital stock account of a corporation with the capital accounts maintained in a partnership. Indicate both similarities and differences.

8. In the firm of Drew, Long, and Blue, the partnership agreement provided that Drew as managing partner should receive a bonus equal to 20% of the annual net income and that the remaining profits should be divided 40% each to Drew and Long and 20% to Blue. Net income for the first year amounted to $63,600.

Explain two alternative ways in which the bonus provision could be interpreted. Compute the division of the year's net income under each of these interpretations.

9. List at least five methods by which partnership net income may be divided.

10. The partnership of Adams and Barnes offered to admit Crawford to a one-third interest in the firm upon his investment of $50,000. Does this offer mean that Crawford would be entitled to one-third of the partnership net income?

11. Larsen and Lindgren are negotiating a partnership agreement, with Larsen investing $60,000 and Lindgren $20,000. Larsen suggests that interest be allowed on average capitals at 6% and that any remaining profit or loss be divided in the ratio of average capitals. Lindgren prefers that the entire profit or loss be divided in the ratio of average capitals. Comment on these proposals.

12. The partnership agreement of Raymond and Stone is very brief on the subject of profit sharing. It says: "Profits are to be divided 70% to Raymond and 30% to Stone and each partner is entitled to draw $800 a month." What difficulties do you see in carrying out this agreement? Illustrate possible difficulties under the assumption that the firm earned net income of $40,000 in the first year.

Short cases for analysis

1-1 X, Y, and Z, who share profits equally, earned an operating profit of $30,000 during their first year in business. However, near the end of the year, they learned of two unfavorable developments: (a) the bankruptcy of Jones, maker of a two-year promissory note for $20,000 which had been contributed to the firm by Partner X at face value as his original investment; and (b) the appearance on the market of new competing patented devices which rendered worthless a patent contributed to the firm by Partner Y at a valuation of $10,000 as part of his original investment.

The partnership had retained the promissory note with the expectation of discounting it when cash was needed for operating purposes. Quarterly interest payments had been received regularly prior to the bankruptcy of Jones, but present prospects were for no further collections of either interest or principal.

Partner Z states that the $30,000 profit from operations should be divided $10,000 to each partner, with the $20,000 loss on the note charged against the capital account of Partner X and the $10,000 loss on the patent charged against the capital account of Partner Y. Do you agree? Should the apparent loss on the note and the patent be handled in the same manner? Explain.

1-2 When asked how the organizers of a business might choose between a partnership and a corporation in order to minimize the burden of taxation, an accounting student made the following statement:

"The choice is very simple. Organization as a partnership will result in only one Federal income tax, that is, the tax on individual income. If the business is incorporated, it must pay the corporation income tax and in addition the owners must pay individual income taxes as the income of the corporation is distributed to them.

Consequently, the partnership form of organization always provides a lesser burden of taxation."

Do you agree? Explain.

1-3 In your audit of the ABC partnership, you observe that each partner in the firm of ABC has a capital account of $50,000 and that Partner C also has a loan account of $40,000. The partnership agreement provides for equal capital to be provided by each partner and for profits to be shared equally. Supporting the loan account is a one-year note signed by all three partners, dated October 1 and specifying interest at 6%. The year-end adjusting entries included the following entry for interest on the note:

A, Capital	*300*	
B, Capital	*300*	
C, Capital		*600*
To accrue interest on $40,000 note for three months at 6%.		

Comment on the propriety of this treatment.

1-4 Muir and Miller operated a partnership for several years, sharing profits equally. On January 1 of the current year, they agreed to revise the profit-sharing ratio to 70% for Muir and 30% for Miller because of Miller's desire for semiretirement. On March 1 the partnership received $10,000 in a compromise settlement of a lawsuit initiated two years previously. Since the outcome of the litigation had been considered highly uncertain, no asset in the form of a claim or other receivable had ever been entered in the accounts. Explain the accounting you would recommend for the $10,000 cash receipt.

1-5 Doyle and Williams formed a partnership on January 1, Doyle contributing cash of $50,000 and Williams contributing cash of $20,000 and marketable securities worth $80,000. A portion of the securities were sold in January to provide funds for business operations. No gain or loss was incurred.

The agreement stated that "profits were to be divided in the capital ratio and that each partner was entitled to withdraw $1,000 monthly." Doyle withdrew $1,000 on the last day of each month, but Williams made no withdrawals until July 1, when he withdrew all the securities which had not been sold by the partnership. The securities which Williams took had a market value of $46,000 when contributed to the partnership on January 1 and a market value of $62,000 on July 1 when he withdrew them. He instructed the bookkeeper to record the transaction by reducing his capital account by $46,000, which was done. Net income from operations for the first year amounted to $24,000. Income tax issues may be ignored.

You are asked to determine the proper division of net income for the first year. If the profit-sharing agreement is unsatisfactory in any respect, state the assumptions you would make in order to arrive at an equitable interpretation of the partners' intentions. Also indicate what adjustments, if any, you believe should be made in the accounts.

Problems

1-6 Smith and Terry formed a partnership at the beginning of 1967. Their capital accounts show the following changes during 1967:

	Smith	*Terry*
Original investment, Jan. 7, 1967	*$40,000*	*$60,000*
Investments: May 1	*5,000*	
July 1		*5,000*
Withdrawals: Nov. 1	*10,000*	*25,000*
Capital accounts, Dec. 31, 1967	*35,000*	*40,000*

The net income from operations, before salary or interest allowances, amounts to $25,800. The partnership also reported a capital gain of $7,100 on the sale of assets.

Instructions

a. Determine each partner's share of net income to the nearest dollar, assuming the following alternative profit-sharing arrangements:

(1) The agreement is silent as to division of net income.

(2) Net income from operations is to be shared equally after allowing 6% interest on average capitals (computed to the nearest month) and after allowing $10,000 to Smith and $15,000 to Terry as salaries. Capital gains and losses are shared in the ratio of original investments.

(3) Net income from operations is to be shared on the basis of average capitals, and capital gains and losses are to be divided on the basis of original investments.

(4) Net income from operations is shared in a 45:55 ratio between Smith and Terry after allowing a 25% bonus to Terry based on net income after the bonus. Capital gains and losses are to be divided equally.

(5) Salaries are to be allowed at the rate of $800 per month for Smith and $1,000 per month for Terry. The balance of income computed on the all-inclusive basis is to be distributed on the basis of beginning capitals. If the salary allowances exceed net income, the deficiency is to be charged to the partners equally and the amounts so charged carried forward and treated as salary allowances in succeeding years.

b. As a certified public accountant you have been asked to recommend an "equitable profit distribution plan" for Smith and Terry. You are able to ascertain the following information:

(1) Prior to formation of the partnership, Smith was a salaried junior executive with an engineering firm with a salary of $15,500; Terry was a salesman who had earned an average of $12,000 per year for several years, but his earnings for 1966 amounted to only $7,500.

(2) In borrowing money from banks, the partners paid interest at between 6½ and 7½% during 1967.

(3) Smith is experienced in production and product design while Terry has good contacts with local bankers and businessmen who are potential customers.

(4) Smith and Terry are fraternity brothers, go fishing and play golf together, and, according to Smith, decided to form the partnership "in order to be our own bosses and to be able to take time off from business when we feel like it."

1-7 The retail business operated as a partnership by Lord, James, and Nelson was completely destroyed by fire on December 31, 1967. The only assets remaining were the bank account with a balance of $26,100 and a claim against the insurance company which was settled for $206,000. All accounting records were destroyed in the fire. The company had only a few creditors and all of these have presented their claims, which amounted in total to $12,000 at December 31, 1967.

The present three-man partnership had been formed on January 1, 1966. Prior to that time Lord and James had been partners for several years and had shared profits equally. No written contract of partnership was prepared for the new firm, and a dispute has now arisen as to the terms of the partners' oral agreement for sharing profits. The business had not utilized the services of independent accountants except for some assistance with the information return required for income tax purposes at December 31, 1966.

You are retained by the partnership to determine the profit-sharing plan which was followed for the year 1966 and to apply this same plan to the events of 1967, thus determining the present equity of each partner. The partners agree in writing that the profit-sharing plan used in 1966 was correct and should be applied in an identical manner to the net income or loss for 1967. The information available to you consists of the following: a copy of the information tax return of the partnership for 1966, and a statement of the withdrawals made by the partners during 1967. This latter statement has been agreed to in writing by all three partners and appears as follows:

	Lord	*James*	*Nelson*	*Total*
Merchandise	$ 1,500	$850	$2,300	$ 4,650
Salary	8,000		6,000	14,000
Other cash withdrawals	750			750
Totals	$10,250	$850	$8,300	$19,400

Partner Lord explains to you that the $750 in "other cash withdrawals" resulted from the accidental payment by the firm of a personal debt of his when the invoice was sent to the partnership address.

From the information tax return for the preceding year, you obtain the following information:

	Lord	*James*	*Nelson*	*Total*
Capitals, Dec. 31, 1965	$40,000	$50,000	$92,500	$182,500
Capitals, Dec. 31, 1966	$51,000	$61,000	$85,300	$197,300
Net income for 1966				$ 87,600
Division of net income:				
Salaries	$12,000	$15,000	$ 6,000	$ 33,000
Interest on capitals	2,000	2,500	4,625	9,125
Remainder	6,821	13,643	25,011	45,475
Totals	$20,821	$31,143	$35,636	$ 87,600

Instructions

Prepare a statement of partners' capitals for the year 1967, supported by a schedule showing the computation of net income or loss for 1967 and another schedule showing the division of the net income or loss among the partners in accordance with the profit-sharing plan followed in the preceding year.

1-8 Three senior faculty members in the engineering school of a large university decided to form a partnership, Electronic Associates, to produce on a commercial basis an electronic device perfected by one of them. To aid in financing the business they needed outside capital; a tentative agreement to supply most of the funds needed was obtained from the owner of a large resort hotel near the university.

At this preliminary stage of planning, the four prospective partners request you to meet with them and outline the significant accounting and management principles involved in formulating a good plan for profit sharing in a partnership. They inform you that their only specific knowledge of the subject is that partnership agreements usually specify a profit and loss ratio. However, they have heard of such additional profit- and loss-sharing features as salaries, bonuses, and interest allowances on invested capital. To keep the first meeting with you as a consultant reasonably short, it is agreed that the discussion will not include income taxation. However, it is agreed that you are to cover the following specific issues on profit sharing in partnerships:

a. What is the objective of profit- and loss-sharing arrangements? Why may there be a need for features in addition to the profit and loss ratio? Discuss.

b. Discuss the arguments that a partnership is an entity separate from its owners. Also explain the arguments for recording salary and bonus allowances to partners as charges to operations.

c. What are the arguments against treating partnership salary and bonus allowances as expenses? Discuss.

d. In addition to its other profit- and loss-sharing features, a partnership agreement may state that "interest is to be allowed on invested capital." List the additional provision that should be included in the partnership agreement so that "interest to be allowed on invested capital" can be computed.

AICPA adapted

1-9 The partnership of Lee, May, and Nye was formed on January 1, 1957, with capital contributions as follows: Lee, $20,000; May, $30,000; and Nye, $50,000.

The brief partnership agreement stated that each partner was entitled to $5,000 salary as a distribution of profits but made no other provision for sharing profits or losses.

The original partnership agreement was amended as of January 1, 1962, to provide thereafter for distribution of profits after salaries in the original capital ratios. The firm did not utilize the services of independent public accountants until December 31, 1966, when you were retained to examine the records and to determine the proper capital balances. Your examination revealed the following information:

(1) Profit per books:

1957	$15,000	1962	$14,000
1958	17,000	1963	16,000
1959	18,000	1964	20,000
1960	14,000	1965	18,000
1961	16,000	1966	22,000

(2) Total withdrawals made and charged against capital:
Lee and May—each $3,000 per year for the ten years
Nye—$3,000 per year for the first five years and $4,000 per year since

(3) Assets per books Dec. 31, 1966: $270,000; liabilities: $95,000.

(4) Your review of the records disclosed that some material errors had been made at various times. These errors were as follows:
(*a*) Dec. 31, 1959, inventory was overstated by $15,000.
(*b*) Dec. 31, 1959, depreciation was overstated by $3,000.
(*c*) Dec. 31, 1961, inventory was overstated by $8,000.
(*d*) Dec. 31, 1964, depreciation was understated by $3,000.
(*e*) Dec. 31, 1966, inventory was understated by $20,000.

Instructions

Prepare any adjusting entries needed at December 31, 1966, to reflect properly the capital accounts of the partners. To explain such entries, prepare a four-column analysis of the capital accounts individually and in total per the books from the date of original investment up to and including your adjustments at December 31, 1966. Separate schedules should be prepared to support this analysis showing: (1) the correction and distribution of profits for the first five years, and (2) the correction and distribution of profits for the second five years. Finally, prepare a summary analysis of capital accounts as corrected showing the original investments, division of corrected profits for the first five-year period, division of corrected profits for the second five-year period, total withdrawals, and balances at December 31, 1966.

AICPA adapted

1-10 At the beginning of the current year the balance sheet of AB Company, a partnership, is as follows:

AB PARTNERSHIP
Balance Sheet
as of January 1, current year

Assets	*$100,000*	*Liabilities*	*$ 20,000*
		Partner A, Capital	*50,000*
		Partner B, Capital	*30,000*
	$100,000		*$100,000*

The partnership agreement provides that the two partners are to receive credit for 4% interest on their capital balances as of the beginning of each year, that salaries of $8,000 for Partner A and $6,000 for Partner B are to be allowed, and that residual profit or loss should be shared equally.

At the beginning of the current year the balance sheet of the XY Company is as follows:

XY COMPANY
Balance Sheet
as of January 1, current year

Assets	$100,000	*Liabilities*	$ 20,000
		8% preferred stock ($100 par)	40,000
		Common stock ($100 par)	20,000
		Retained earnings	20,000
	$100,000		$100,000

X and Y are the sole stockholders of the company. X owns 250 preferred shares; Y owns 150 preferred shares. X and Y each own 100 common shares. X, as president of the company, receives a salary of $8,000; Y, as secretary-treasurer, receives a salary of $6,000.

At the end of the current year both AB Company and XY Company call in a public accountant, Q, to prepare financial statements. The income statements for the two companies as prepared by Q are shown below:

Income Statements
Current Year

	AB Company	*XY Company*
Sales revenues	$200,000	$200,000
Operating expenses	$180,000	$180,000
Officers' salaries		14,000
Income taxes		1,800
Total expenses	$180,000	$195,800
Net income	$ 20,000	$ 4,200

The XY Company declared $3,200 in preferred dividends at the end of the year, and a dividend of $1,000 on common shares. The drawing accounts of the two partners of AB Company at the end of the year showed drawings of $11,400 for Partner A and $8,600 for Partner B.

AB Company and XY Company both applied to the local bank for loans shortly after the end of the current year, presenting the income statements shown in the above schedule in support of their applications. The bank granted the loan to AB Company, on the grounds that this was a highly profitable firm, but denied the loan to XY Company.

The officers of XY Company pointed out to the accountant, Q, that the operating results of the two companies were essentially identical. They complained that he must have erred in his presentation of the financial statements. Q defended the financial statements, maintaining that he had followed generally accepted accounting principles to the letter.

Instructions

a. Discuss the similarity or lack of similarity in the financial statements of AB Company and XY Company, giving attention to both the income statements and ending balance sheets.

b. Explain and compare the distribution of income in the two companies. How did the withdrawals by the partners of AB Company compare with their respective shares of profits?

c. Do you agree with Q that the financial statements of the two companies were prepared in accordance with generally accepted accounting principles? What alternatives, if any, might the accountant have employed to achieve greater comparability between the statements of the two companies? Give arguments.

d. What reason other than the apparent difference in profitability may have caused the bank to grant a loan to AB Company and reject the application from XY Company?

1-11 The Milburn Company is a partnership formed in 1960 by Rogers, Smith, and Taylor. The partnership agreement provided that records should be maintained on the accrual basis in accordance with generally accepted principles of accounting and that net income should be divided by the partners according to the following plan:

a. Interest at 5% to be allowed each partner on the balance in his capital account at the beginning of the year.

b. To partners Smith and Taylor, in recognition of their technical skill and experience in the industry, a commission to each of 20% of an amount representing net income determined by the cash method of accounting after deducting the provision for depreciation and the authorized interest on capital. In making this application of the cash basis concept, it is agreed that all merchandise purchased is to be treated as expense.

c. The net income remaining after deducting the interest on capital and the commissions due to Smith and Taylor is to be divided equally among the three partners except that the total portion of income allocated to Rogers is not to be less than 50% of the net income determined by the accrual method of accounting. This last provision was agreed upon in recognition of the greater amount of capital provided by Rogers.

Comparative balance sheets of the partnership at December 31, 1966 and 1967, were as shown on page 33 before division of the net income for 1967.

During the year 1967, accounts receivable of $300 were considered uncollectible and charged off to the allowance for doubtful accounts. Also, the amount of $20 was collected on accounts which had been charged to the allowance for doubtful accounts in prior years. No changes occurred in the partners' capital accounts during 1967.

MILBURN COMPANY
Balance Sheets

Assets	*Dec. 31, 1966*		*Dec. 31, 1967*	
Cash		$ 14,000		$ 22,240
Accounts receivable	$ 10,000		$ 12,000	
Allowance for doubtful accounts	200	9,800	240	11,760
Inventory		52,000		48,000
U.S. government bonds, at cost				16,000
Fixed assets, at cost	$240,000		$240,000	
Accumulated depreciation	85,000	155,000	92,600	147,400
Prepaid expenses		2,000		1,600
Total assets		$232,800		$247,000
Liabilities & Capital				
Accounts payable, trade		$ 14,000		$ 8,000
Accrued wages		6,000		10,000
Accrued taxes		1,000		1,000
Deferred income		11,800		—
Net income, year 1967		—		28,000
Partners' capitals:				
Rogers	$160,000		$160,000	
Smith	25,000		25,000	
Taylor	15,000	200,000	15,000	200,000
Total liabilities & capital		$232,800		$247,000

Instructions

a. Determine the net income for 1967 on the cash basis as defined in the agreement. Prepare a schedule supported by clearly detailed computations showing the adjustments necessary to convert the net income for the year 1967 from an accrual basis to a cash basis and the commissions due Smith and Taylor.

b. Prepare a statement supported by clearly detailed computations showing the division among the partners of the net income for the year 1967.

AICPA adapted

1-12 Three years after the organization of the Midland Company, the partners decided upon an audit by a certified public accountant as a preliminary step toward possible change in the number of partners and the method of dividing profits. You are retained by the partners, Long, Davis, and Brink, in January, 1968, to review the records for the entire three years of the firm's existence.

From study of the partnership agreement and amendments thereto, you learn that the profit-sharing plans used to date have been as follows:

	Salaries	Interest on capitals, %	Residual shares, %
For the years 1965 and 1966:			
Long	*$10,000*	*6*	*20*
Davis	*12,000*	*6*	*30*
Brink	*15,000*	*6*	*50*
For the year 1967:			
Long	*$12,000*	*6*	*30*
Davis	*14,400*	*6*	*35*
Brink	*18,000*	*6*	*35*

Drawings by partners were authorized in the agreement in the amount of $1,000 to each partner monthly.

The original agreement for allowing 6% interest on partners' capitals provided that: "The capital amount to be used as a basis for computation of the interest credit shall be the average of each partner's capital at the beginning and close of each calendar year. The capital of a partner at the close of the year shall include *his share of the current year's profits computed without consideration of the interest credit* for such current year. Drawings during the year shall be considered in computing the year-end capital of each partner."

On January 1, 1966, the partnership agreement was amended as to the base to be used in 1966 and subsequent years in computing interest on capitals. The amendment stated that: "Effective January 1, 1966, interest on partners' capitals shall be allowed at 6% per annum based on the capital balance of the partner at the beginning of each year. If drawings during the year are in excess of the authorized amount of $1,000 monthly, the excess shall be deducted from the base used for computation of interest."

On January 1, 1967, the profit-sharing plan was changed again, as shown in the preceding schedule, by increasing salaries and by adjusting the shares in residual profit or loss to reflect changes which had occurred in the personal relationships of individual partners to major customers of the firm.

The net income as shown by the Midland Company's financial statements for the three years covered by your investigation was as follows: 1965, $45,000; 1966, $75,000; and 1967, $140,000. Transactions involving capital contributions, drawings, and loans from partners had occurred as follows:

	Long	Davis	Brink
Original investment, Jan. 1, 1965	*$50,000*	*$100,000*	*$100,000*
Drawings per month (1965, 1966, and 1967)	*1,000*	*1,000*	*1,000*
Loan from partner at 6% on Jan. 1, 1967, due June 15, 1968		*25,000*	

During your examination you discover that the inventory taken at December 31, 1965, had been overstated $10,000 because of a computational error, and that a similar error at December 31, 1966, had caused inventory at that date to be understated by $15,000. No other material errors were found. Interest had been paid quarterly on the loan from Davis.

Instructions

a. Determine corrected net income for the years 1965, 1966, and 1967 and the proper sharing of that income under the partnership agreement and amendments thereto.

b. Prepare a statement of partners' capitals covering the three years. Show separately the income, drawings, and ending capital balance for each year.

1-13 The partnership agreement of Foote, Cane, and Welding provided for the division of net income as follows: interest at 6% on capital balances as of the beginning of each fiscal year; salaries to partners, Foote $12,000, Cane $15,000, and Welding $20,000; remaining profit or loss, Foote 20%, Cane 30%, and Welding 50%.

During the first several months of the fiscal year ended June 30, 1967, Foote and Cane each withdrew $1,000 a month and Welding withdrew $1,500 a month.

FOOTE, CANE, AND WELDING
Adjusted Trial Balance
June 30, 1967

Cash	$ 37,650	
Notes receivable	12,000	
Accrued interest on notes receivable	180	
Accounts receivable	160,878	
Allowance for bad debts		$ 1,250
Inventory, June 30, 1966	408,090	
Furniture and fixtures	207,000	
Accumulated depreciation		31,900
Accounts payable		33,770
Accrued interest and taxes payable		2,750
Cane, loan payable		40,000
Foote, capital, June 30, 1966		70,000
Foote, drawings	870	
Cane, capital, June 30, 1966		180,000
Cane, drawings	1,292	
Welding, capital, June 30, 1966		200,000
Sales		1,760,000
Purchases	1,245,000	
Transportation—in	12,840	
Selling expenses	116,000	
General and administrative expenses	93,700	
Interest earned		430
Interest on partners' loans	600	
Foote, salary	9,000	
Cane, salary	6,000	
Welding, salary	9,000	
	$2,320,100	$2,320,100

Foote and Cane also withdrew miscellaneous amounts of cash and merchandise from time to time. On December 15 in a partners' meeting, the possibility of a shortage of working capital was discussed. After this Cane and Welding made no further withdrawals for the rest of the fiscal year, but Foote withdrew $500 on the first of each month. The bookkeeper recorded all regular monthly withdrawals in partners' salary accounts. Other withdrawals of varying amounts of cash and merchandise were recorded by charges to the partners' drawing accounts.

At June 30, 1967, the end of the fiscal year, the adjusted trial balance of the partnership was as shown on page 35.

Inventory at June 30, 1967, was $186,800.

Instructions

a. Comment on the bookkeeper's treatment of partners' salaries and drawings during the year. Does the separation of salaries and drawings have any effect on the division of net income in this case?

b. Prepare an income statement, statement of partners' capital, and balance sheet.

c. Prepare entries to close the books at June 30.

2 PARTNERSHIPS: CHANGES IN PERSONNEL

Accounting for changes in partnership personnel

Most changes in partnership personnel are accomplished without interrupting the regular operation of the business. For example, when a large and well-established partnership promotes one of its employees to partnership status, there is usually no significant change in the financial condition, the accounting policies, or the operating routines of the business. From a legal viewpoint, however, a partnership is dissolved by the retirement or death of a partner or by the admission of a new partner to the firm.

Dissolution of a partnership may also result from such causes as the bankruptcy of the firm or of any single partner, the expiration of a time period stated in the partnership agreement, or the mutual agreement of the partners to end their association.[1]

Before trying to summarize accounting principles applicable to dissolution of a partnership, we must consider the tremendous range of business events to which the term *dissolution* may be applied. These events include, on the one hand, a minor change of ownership interest not affecting operation of the business; on the other hand, a joint decision of all members of a firm to end entirely their business relationships. In the one type of event the going-concern concept, which is so fundamental to accounting policies, is left undisturbed; in the more serious example of dissolution, the going-concern concept must be abandoned as a basis for accounting interpretations and decisions. Consequently, it is difficult to formu-

[1] The dissolution of a partnership is defined by the Uniform Partnership Act as "the change in the relation of the partners caused by any partner ceasing to be associated in the carrying on as distinguished from the winding up of the business."

late a single set of accounting rules to be applied universally to all changes in partnership personnel.

The professional accountant is concerned with the substance of a transaction rather than with its outward form. Therefore, he must evaluate carefully all the circumstances of the individual case in determining how a change in partnership personnel can most effectively be reflected in the accounting records and in the financial statements. Our approach in this chapter will be to consider one by one the principal kinds of changes in partnership personnel, and to illustrate one or more acceptable accounting treatments for each type of change.

Accounting and managerial issues

Although a partnership association is ended in a legal sense when a partner withdraws or a new partner is added, the business as a going concern often continues with little outward evidence of change. In current accounting practice, a partner's interest is often viewed as a share in a continuing business which may be transferred, much as shares of stock are transferred between stockholders, without disturbing the continuity of the enterprise. For example, in a successful firm of certified public accountants, if a partner wishes to retire or a new partner enters the firm, the agreement for the change in ownership is usually carefully planned to avoid disturbing client relationships. A smooth transition through a period of change in partnership personnel is greatly facilitated if the retiring partner reduces his participation in operations gradually over a period of time and uses his influence during this period to encourage full acceptance by clients of any new partners involved in the realignment of the firm.

In a very large CPA firm with a hundred or more partners scattered throughout the country, the decision to promote an employee to the rank of partner may often be made by a governing group similar to a board of directors rather than by the direct and unanimous action of all partners.

Changes in partnership personnel in any line of business raise a number of complex accounting and managerial issues upon which the professional accountant can serve as consultant. Among these issues are the determination of the amount to be paid to a retiring partner, the setting of terms for admission of a new partner, the possible revaluation of assets, the recognition of goodwill, and the development of a new basis for division of income.

Of particular importance is the establishment of a new plan for sharing profits. Since a change in partnership personnel changes the relationship of partners, it wipes out the former profit-sharing agreement. Unless a new plan for division of profits is clearly stated, there may be some legal basis for assuming that equal profit sharing is intended in the new firm even though the capital and services contributed by individual partners vary greatly. A change in partnership personnel also raises a question as to the sharing of unrealized profits among old partners and a new partner.

Admission of a new partner

When a new partner is admitted to a small firm of perhaps two or three partners, it is particularly appropriate to consider the fairness and adequacy of past accounting policies and the need for correction of errors in prior years' accounting data. The terms of admission of a new partner are often influenced by the level and trend of past profits, since these profits are indicative of future earnings. Sometimes specific accounting policies, such as the "completed contract" method of recognizing profits on long-term construction contracts, may cause the records to convey a misleading impression of operating results in the periods preceding the admission of a new partner.

Adjustments of the records may be necessary to provide an equitable statement of partners' capitals and other elements of financial condition before the change in membership of the firm is carried out. Book values and fair market value of assets are often far apart.

As an alternative to revaluing the assets, it may be preferable to evaluate the dollar significance of any discrepancies between the accounts and current economic values and to make appropriate adjustment in the terms set for admission of the new partner. In other words, the amount invested or price paid by the incoming partner can be set at a level which reflects the current values of the business even though the carrying value of assets remains unchanged on the books. Consideration must be given to the fact that if assets have appreciated in value but such appreciation is ignored, the subsequent sale of the assets after admission of a new partner will cause him to share in profits which existed prior to his joining the firm.

The admission of a new partner to a firm may occur in either of two ways: (1) through the *purchase* of all or part of the interest of one or more of the existing partners, or (2) through the *investment* of assets in the firm by the new partner, thus increasing the resources of the partnership.

Purchase of an interest by payment to one partner

If the incoming partner purchases his interest from one of the original partners, the transaction is recorded by opening a capital account for the new partner and decreasing the capital account of the selling partner by the same amount. No funds are received by the partnership; the transfer of assets is between the two individuals.

As a very simple illustration of this situation, assume that L and M are partners sharing profits equally and each having a capital of $60,000. Partner L (with the consent of M) sells half of his interest to N. The entry to record this change in ownership is:

L, Capital	*30,000*	
N, Capital		*30,000*
To record the transfer of one-half of L's capital to the incoming partner, N.		

The price paid by N in buying half of L's interest may have been the book value of $30,000 or it may have been more or less than book value. Possibly no price was established; L may have made a gift to N of one-half of his interest in the partnership, or perhaps N won it in a poker game. Regardless of the terms of the transaction between L and N, the entry illustrated above is all that is required on the partnership's books. No change has occurred in the assets, the liabilities, or the total of the owners' equity.

To explore further some of the implications involved in the purchase of an interest by an incoming partner, assume that N paid $40,000 to L for one-half of his $60,000 equity in the business. Some accountants have suggested that the willingness of the new partner to pay $10,000 in excess of book value for a one-fourth interest in capital indicates that the total capital of the partnership should be valued at $40,000 more than presently shown by the books. From this assumption they reason that the assets of the old firm should be written up by $40,000, or goodwill of $40,000 should be recorded as an asset with offsetting credits of $20,000 each to the capital accounts of the old partners, L and M. Most accountants, however, take the position that the payment by N to L is a personal transaction between them and that the partnership, which has neither received nor paid any funds, should make no entry except to transfer one-half of L's capital to N, the new partner.

What are the arguments for these two opposing views of the purchase of an interest by a new partner? Those who advocate a write-up of assets stress the legal concept of dissolution of the old firm and formation of a new partnership. This change in identity of owners, it is argued, justifies departure from the going-concern principle and the revaluation of assets at fair market value in order to achieve an accurate measurement of the capital contributed by each member to the new partnership.

The opposing argument, that the purchase of an interest by an incoming partner requires only a transfer from the capital account of the selling partner to the capital account of the new partner, is based on several points. First, the partnership as an entity did not participate in negotiating the price paid by N to L for one-half of his interest in the firm. Many factors other than the valuation of assets may have been involved in the negotiations between the two individuals concerned. Perhaps N paid more than book value because he was allowed very generous credit terms in paying the agreed price. Perhaps he gave noncash assets in payment which were themselves overvalued. Perhaps he received more than a one-fourth share in profits as part of his purchase agreement. (As emphasized in Chapter 1, partners do not necessarily share profits in proportion to their capital accounts.) Perhaps the new partner was very anxious to join the firm of L and M because of his confidence in their personal abilities or because he anticipated great growth in the particular industry or community. Perhaps N accepted the interest in the partnership as the only convenient means of collecting a past-due $40,000 debt owed to him by L. It is even possible that the price paid by N to L was not accurately reported to the partnership since it was a personal transaction with details known only to the buyer and seller. In some cases the buyer and seller of an interest may be members of the same family, and noneconomic factors may influence the sales price.

Because of these and other similar reasons, we may conclude that the purchase price of an interest transferred from one of the old partners to a new partner is not highly dependable or verifiable evidence to support extensive changes in the carrying value of the partnership's assets. This conclusion is just as applicable when the new partner pays less than book value for his interest as when he reports having paid a price in excess of book value.

Purchase of interest compared with purchase of stock in corporation

Is the purchase of an interest in a partnership basically different from the purchase of stock by a new investor from one of the original stockholders in a corporation? In neither case is the business entity a party to the transaction. The one transaction may have no greater impact on management control than the other. The incoming partner might be a silent partner with no voice in management or a limited partner whose authority is limited by statute.

On the other hand, the purchaser of stock in a corporation from an original stockholder might acquire a controlling interest. The price paid for the stock would not justify adjusting the book value of the corporation's assets. Is there any greater reason for writing up or down the assets owned by a partnership on the basis of the price reportedly paid by one individual in acquiring an interest from one of the original partners? Practicing accountants appear to be increasingly inclined to view the partnership as a business entity and to stress the continuity of the entity despite shifts in ownership.

Purchase of an interest by payments to two or more partners

As a second illustration of change in partnership personnel by purchase of an interest, assume that the partnership of R, S, and T has the following capital accounts and income-sharing ratio:

	Capital accounts	*Income-sharing ratio, %*
R	*$ 80,000*	*60*
S	*50,000*	*30*
T	*30,000*	*10*
	$160,000	*100*

The incoming partner, U, purchases for $32,000 a one-fifth interest in both partnership capital and earnings, with each of the old partners transferring one-fifth of his equity to U. The admission of U as a partner is recorded by the following entry:

R, Capital	*16,000*	
S, Capital	*10,000*	
T, Capital	*6,000*	
U, Capital		*32,000*
To record the transfer to U of a one-fifth interest in the business.		

In this example the partnership again neither received nor paid funds. Cash (or other property) was paid by U to R, S, and T personally in the amounts by which their capitals were reduced. The price paid for purchase of an interest by U was equal to book value.

The income-sharing ratio for the new firm should be clearly stated in the new partnership agreement. If the three original partners are to maintain the same relationship previously existing among them, the new ratios will be R 48%, S 24%, T 8%, and U 20%. In other words, the ratio for each of the old partners was reduced by one-fifth.

Next, as an independent case, let us consider the purchase of a one-fifth interest by U at a price $18,000 above book value; that is, he agrees to pay $50,000 for a one-fifth interest in the total capital of $160,000. Again assume that R, S, and T all agree to transfer one-fifth of their respective capitals to the new partner. Assume also that they agree that the payment in excess of book value ($18,000) shall be divided among them in the ratio in which they have previously shared profits; that is, R 60%, S 30%, and T 10%. The changes in partners' capitals are shown by the following schedule:

	R	*S*	*T*	*U*	*Total*
Capitals before sale	*$80,000*	*$50,000*	*$30,000*		*$160,000*
Capitals transferred to U	*16,000*	*10,000*	*6,000*	*$32,000*	
Totals	*$64,000*	*$40,000*	*$24,000*	*$32,000*	*$160,000*

The cash payments by the new partner to R, S, and T personally will be divided as follows, since we have assumed that all the transfers were negotiated on a uniform basis and gains were divided in the established profit-sharing ratio.

	R	*S*	*T*	*Total*
Payment for ⅕ capital accounts	*$16,000*	*$10,000*	*$6,000*	*$32,000*
Payment in excess of book value	*10,800*	*5,400*	*1,800*	*18,000*
Total payments	*$26,800*	*$15,400*	*$7,800*	*$50,000*

Note that in this example the three old partners have acted as a unit in agreeing that each should transfer one-fifth of his capital to U and that the excess of the selling price above book value should be divided in the established ratio for sharing profits. By these rigorous assumptions, we have in effect made the buyer negotiate with the partnership rather than with the old partners as individuals. Otherwise the buyer might have negotiated different prices with the individual partners, depending on their eagerness to sell and their bargaining abilities. In fact, the transaction as we have defined it is almost the same as if the new partner had made his $50,000 payment to the firm and the partners had immediately withdrawn cash corresponding to their sale of capital plus the gain on such sale.

Under these circumstances, accounting literature has sometimes suggested adjusting the assets of the firm to an amount indicated by the price paid by U. For example, goodwill of $18,000 might be entered in the accounts with offsetting credits to the capital accounts of R, S, and T in the profit-sharing ratio. A second alternative might be to recognize $90,000 of goodwill, on the grounds that payment of $50,000 for a one-fifth interest is evidence that the total owners' equity is properly stated at $250,000 rather than the recorded amount of $160,000. A third alternative is that certain tangible assets might be written up if their undervaluation appeared to explain the premium paid by U for his interest.

As a practical matter, most business concerns are not interested in placing large amounts of goodwill on their balance sheets. To do so is certain to create a skeptical reaction from bankers, creditors, and other users of the statements. A CPA engaged to audit a firm which had written up assets in this manner would probably feel compelled to issue an adverse opinion.

The purchase of an interest by a new partner may occur under an almost endless variety of conditions. He may buy an interest from one partner or from several. If he buys his interest from more than one partner, the terms of payment agreed upon may be consistent or inconsistent among the selling partners. In one case the purchase may be for cash and in another it may involve long-term credit. The share of profits acquired by the incoming partner may or may not correspond to the percentage of total capital which he acquires. The relative size of the interest purchased by the incoming partner may vary so greatly as to change the basic meaning of the transaction. A purchase of an 80% interest in capital at a price above or below book value suggests a significant break in the continuity of the business; it might be viewed as a more valid reason for recognizing goodwill or adjusting asset valuations than would the purchase of a 10% interest.

As a general rule we may conclude that when an incoming partner purchases an interest from one or more of the original partners, the only accounting entry required is a transfer between capital accounts. In a few exceptional cases, however, the evidence may justify some adjustment of asset values or recognition of goodwill. Such adjustments are seldom encountered in practice; a CPA confronted with adjustments of this nature would as a minimum insist upon their full disclosure before giving his approval to the financial statements. Adjustments of this character, if made at all, should be substantiated by objective evidence capable of verification.

Refusal to admit purchaser to partnership

Usually when a partner sells all or part of his interest, the transaction is arranged with the consent of all members of the firm. Their consent indicates the formation of a new partnership. On the other hand, if the partners do not consent to the admission of the purchaser, he does not become a partner. Under the common law, the partner who sells an interest without the consent of his partners thereby dissolves the partnership and may be liable to his partners for any loss thus imposed upon them. The purchaser of the interest, although he does not become a partner, is entitled to receive an appropriate settlement after the assets have been sold and the liabilities paid.

Under the Uniform Partnership Act, the treatment is somewhat different. The sale of an interest without mutual consent of all partners does not dissolve the firm; the purchaser does not become a partner but he does acquire a right to the profits and to assets in event of dissolution in accordance with his contract with the selling partner. Since he does not become a partner, he cannot exercise any influence on the conduct of the business. Under both the common law and the Uniform Partnership Act, the principle is maintained that the relationship between partners is a voluntary one. One person cannot be forced to accept another as a partner.

Acquisition of an interest by investment

An incoming partner may gain admission to the firm by making payment directly to the partnership. The assets which he contributes are recorded on the firm's books, and consequently the total assets of the firm and its total capital are increased. If the new partner contributes assets other than cash, it is necessary to determine their fair market value as a basis for measuring the amount of his investment. If such noncash assets are later sold by the partnership, any difference between the selling price and the recorded book value will be a gain or loss of the partnership to be divided in the agreed ratio for division of net income.

As an example, assume that X and Y are partners operating an automobile rental business. They share profits equally and each has a capital account of $60,000. Assume also that the carrying value of the partnership assets is approximately the same as current fair market value. Adjacent to the business is a tract of land owned by Z which could be used for expansion of operations. X and Y agree to admit Z to the partnership upon his investment of the land; profits and losses of the new firm are to be shared equally. Cost of the land to Z a few years ago was $60,000, but a current appraisal indicates it is now worth $80,000.

The admission of Z to the partnership is recorded by the following entry:

Land	*80,000*	
Z, Capital		*80,000*
To record admission of Z as a partner with a one-third share in profits and losses.		

The new partner has a capital account $20,000 larger than the capitals of his partners. In other words he owns a 40% (80,000/200,000) interest in the firm. The fact that the three partners share profits equally does not require that their capital accounts be equal.

Assume for the moment that the land contributed by Z had been recorded at $60,000 in order to make his capital account equal to the capitals of X and Y (or because the cost of the land to him had been $60,000). Assume further that the partnership shortly thereafter sold the land for $80,000 cash. The $20,000 excess of selling price over book value would be a partnership gain divided equally among the three partners. Such inequities will be avoided if the assets invested by the incoming partner are recorded at fair market value at the time of forming the new firm.

Bonus or goodwill allowed to old partners

In a profitable, well-established firm, the partners may insist that a portion of the investment by a new member be allowed to them as a bonus or that goodwill be recognized and credited to the original partners. The incoming partner may reasonably agree to such terms because of the benefits to be gained by becoming a member of a firm of proved earning power.

Bonus to old partners. Assume that A and B are partners who share profits equally and have capitals of $45,000 each. Asset valuations are assumed to approximate fair market value. The partners agree to admit C to a one-third interest in assets and a one-third share in profits upon investment of $60,000 in the firm. The total assets of the new firm will therefore amount to $150,000. The following entry to record the investment by C will give him the agreed one-third interest and will divide the $10,000 bonus equally between A and B in accordance with their prior agreement to share profits equally.

Cash	*60,000*	
A, Capital		*5,000*
B, Capital		*5,000*
C, Capital		*50,000*
To record investment by C for a one-third interest with bonus divided equally between old partners.		

Recognition of goodwill. In the preceding illustration, C invested $60,000 but received a capital account of only $50,000, representing a one-third interest in the firm. He might prefer that his capital account show the full amount of his investment. This could be done while still allotting him a one-third interest if goodwill is placed on the books with the offsetting credit divided equally between the two original partners. If C is to be given a one-third interest represented by a capital account of $60,000, the total indicated capital is $180,000, and the capitals of A and B together must total $120,000. Since their present combined capitals amount to $90,000, a write-up of $30,000 may be made. The following two entries will record the admission of C under these conditions:

Goodwill	*30,000*	
A, Capital		*15,000*
B, Capital		*15,000*
Cash	*60,000*	
C, Capital		*60,000*

Comparison of bonus method and goodwill method. When the incoming partner invests an amount greater than the book value of the interest he acquires, the transaction is usually handled by allowing a bonus to the old partners. The bonus method has the advantage of adhering to the cost principle of asset valuation and is in accord with the concept of a partnership as a continuing business entity. However, an alternative method which has received considerable attention in accounting literature consists of recognizing and recording in the accounts the amount of goodwill *implied* by the purchase price. Use of this method signifies the substitution of estimated fair value of an asset rather than valuation on a cost basis. The goodwill of $30,000 shown in the preceding example was not purchased. Its existence is merely implied by the price the incoming partner paid for a one-third interest in the firm. As previously pointed out, the price paid by the incoming partner may have been influenced by many factors, some of which may be personal rather than economic in nature. To attribute the excess of the purchase price over book value to goodwill is an assumption which is usually difficult to support with objective evidence.

Apart from the questionable theoretical basis for such recognition of goodwill, there are other practical difficulties. The presence of goodwill created in this manner is likely to evoke criticism of the company's financial statements, and such criticism may lead the partnership to amortize or to write off the goodwill. Also, if the business should be liquidated, the goodwill will probably have to be written off as a loss. Will the recording of goodwill and its subsequent write-off injure one partner and benefit another? The net results to the individual partners will be the same under the bonus and goodwill methods only if two specific conditions are met. First, the incoming partner's share of profits must be equal to his percentage equity in assets at the time of his admission, and second, the original partners must continue to share income between themselves in the same ratio as in the original partnership. Both these conditions were met in our example; that is, the new partner, C, received a one-third interest in the assets and a one-third share of profits. Secondly, the original partners shared profit and loss equally both before and after the admission of C.

Under these circumstances if the firm of A, B, and C decides to write off the goodwill, the capital account of each partner will be decreased to the same amount it would have been if the bonus method had been used in admitting C to partnership.

	A	*B*	*C*	*Total*
Capitals if bonus method is used	*$50,000*	*$50,000*	*$50,000*	*$150,000*
Capitals when goodwill method is used	*$60,000*	*$60,000*	*$60,000*	*$180,000*
Write-off of goodwill (⅓ each)	*10,000*	*10,000*	*10,000*	*30,000*
Capitals (same as under bonus method)	*$50,000*	*$50,000*	*$50,000*	*$150,000*

Assume, however, that the three partners agreed on a profit and loss ratio of A 40%, B 40%, and C 20%; the goodwill method would then benefit C and injure A and B as compared with the bonus method. The first of the two necessary conditions for equivalent results from the bonus method and goodwill method is no longer met. The incoming partner's share of profit and loss is not equal to his share in assets. C is now assumed to have a 20%, or one-fifth, share in profit and loss, although as in the preceding example he has a one-third interest in assets.

	A	*B*	*C*	*Total*
Capitals if bonus method is used	*$50,000*	*$50,000*	*$50,000*	*$150,000*
Capitals if goodwill method is used	*$60,000*	*$60,000*	*$60,000*	*$180,000*
Write-off of goodwill (40%, 40%, 20%)	*12,000*	*12,000*	*6,000*	*30,000*
Capitals after write-off of goodwill	*$48,000*	*$48,000*	*$54,000*	*$150,000*

The use of the goodwill method in admitting C and the subsequent write-off of the goodwill caused a $4,000 shift of capital from A and B to C.

A similar result will emerge if we choose an example in which the incoming partner's share of profit and loss is equal to his interest in assets but the two original partners do not continue to share profits between themselves in the same ratio as in the original partnership. To illustrate, assume that in the new firm profit and loss is divided one-half to A, one-sixth to B, and one-third to C.

	A	B	C	Total
Capitals if bonus method is used	$50,000	$50,000	$50,000	$150,000
Capitals if goodwill method is used	$60,000	$60,000	$60,000	$180,000
Write-off of goodwill (½, ⅙, ⅓)	15,000	5,000	10,000	30,000
Capitals after write-off of goodwill	$45,000	$55,000	$50,000	$150,000

Under these assumptions the final results of using the goodwill method rather than the bonus method were a $5,000 decrease in A's capital and a corresponding increase for B. This shift resulted because A and B were credited in one ratio when goodwill was recorded and charged in a different ratio when goodwill was eliminated.

These illustrations, viewed as a group, show that the end result of recording goodwill and later writing it off is likely to affect partners differently than the bonus method. A generalized statement that one method will always give more equitable results than the other cannot be supported.

The advocates of the goodwill method argue that if the old partnership truly possesses goodwill which can be measured by objective evidence, recognition of the asset is desirable to present a full picture of the business. If the goodwill is later dissipated, thus necessitating its removal from the accounts, the loss should be divided among the partners in the ratio prevailing at the time of the loss. This line of reasoning raises the familiar theoretical issue as to whether goodwill normally is subject to amortization or has an unlimited term of existence. If the partners at the time of choosing between the bonus method and goodwill method will consider the ultimate results which will flow from the writing off of goodwill in the future, they will be able to make a more intelligent decision on the advisability of recording it. As a matter of current practice, the goodwill method is rarely used.

Fairness of asset valuation. In the preceding examples of bonus or goodwill allowed to the original partners, it was assumed that the carrying values of assets on the books of the old partnership approximated fair market value. If such assets as land and buildings have been owned by the partnership for many years, it is probable that book value and fair market value are quite far apart. Inventory priced on the lifo basis may also differ substantially from its current replacement cost.

To bring this problem into focus, let us assume that the assets of the partnership of A and B carried at $90,000 were estimated to have a fair market value of $120,000 at the time of admitting C as a partner. Our previous example called for C to receive a one-third interest upon investment of $60,000. Why not write up the assets from $90,000 to $120,000, with a corresponding increase in the capitals of the original partners? Neither a bonus nor the recognition of goodwill would then be necessary to record the admission of C to a one-third interest upon investment of $60,000 because his investment would now be at book value.

Such restatement of asset values would not be acceptable practice in a corporation merely because the corporation's stock had risen in price. If we assume the existence of certain conditions in a partnership, then adherence to cost as a basis for asset valuation is as appropriate a policy as for a corporation. These specific conditions are that the ratio for sharing profit and loss should correspond to the share of equity held by each partner, and that the profit and loss ratio continue unchanged. When these conditions do not exist, a restatement of assets from cost to market value may be the most convenient method of achieving equity among the partners.

One objection to substitution of estimated market values for assets in any type of organization is that such estimates are subject to a wide range of opinion. They are less objective in nature than are cost data. Furthermore, the function of independent verification by a certified public accountant becomes almost meaningless if financial statements are presented in terms of estimated current values. Public confidence in financial statements would probably be lessened by a significant degree if accounting practice condoned the substitution of appraisal amounts for the cost basis of valuation.

In certain circumstances the use of appraised values for assets rather than cost may be justified regardless of the form of business organizations. For example, if the assets consist solely of marketable securities, a strong argument can be made for their valuation at current market price which is readily determinable and quite easily verified. Or, if assets consist of low-cost desert land which has suddenly been converted into an oil field, adherence to cost valuations might produce meaningless financial statements. Such exceptional cases, however, are not sufficient basis for establishing generally useful accounting policies.

Bonus or goodwill allowed to new partner

An existing partnership may be very anxious to bring a new member into the firm, because the business is desperately in need of cash or because the prospective new member has unusual ability or extraordinary business contacts. To ensure the admission of the new partner, the present firm may offer him a capital account larger than the amount he invests.

Bonus to new partner. Assume that F and G, who have capitals of $35,000 each and share profit and loss equally, offer to admit H to a one-third interest in assets and a one-third share of income upon his investment of $20,000. Their offer is based on a desperate need for more cash and upon the conviction that H's personal abilities and business contacts will be of great value to the business. The investment of $20,000 cash in the firm by the new partner, when added to the existing net assets of $70,000, gives a total capital of $90,000 of which H is entitled to one-third, or $30,000. The excess of H's capital account over his investment represents a $10,000 bonus allowed him by the old partners. Since F and G share profit and loss equally, the $10,000 bonus will be deducted from their capital accounts in equal amounts, as shown by the following entry to record admission of the new partner.

Cash	*20,000*	
F, Capital	*5,000*	
G, Capital	*5,000*	
H, Capital		*30,000*

In outlining this method of accounting for the admission of H, we have assumed that the assets of the old partnership were properly valued. On the contrary, if the admission of the new partner to a one-third interest upon investment of $20,000 was based upon recognition that the assets owned by the old partnership were worth only $60,000, consideration should be given to writing down certain assets. Such write-downs would be proper if accounts receivable, for example, included uncollectible or doubtful accounts, or if inventory were obsolete. On the other hand, the write-down of plant and equipment would not be justified merely because its estimated market value was below book value. Accounting principles applicable to fixed assets in a going concern do not purport to maintain book values in line with current replacement cost or with estimated sales value. It is clear, however, that under certain conditions the admission of a new partner for an investment less than book value may indicate that unrecorded losses have occurred and that downward adjustment of assets is warranted.

Goodwill to new partner. Assume that the incoming partner is the owner of a successful business which he contributes to the partnership rather than making his investment in cash. Using the same data as in the preceding example, assume that F and G with capitals of $35,000 each admit H to a one-third interest in assets and in profits. The tangible assets comprising the business owned by H are worth $20,000 but, because of its superior earnings record, a fair value for his business as an entity is agreed to be $35,000. The admission of H as a partner is then recorded as follows:

Various Tangible Assets	*20,000*	
Goodwill	*15,000*	
H, Capital		*35,000*

The point to be stressed here is that goodwill is recognized as part of the investment of a new partner only when he contributes a going business of superior earning power. If H is admitted by reason of a cash investment and credited with a capital larger than the cash invested, the proper accounting for the transaction is to subtract this differential from the capitals of the old partners or to write down any overvalued asset accounts. Goodwill should be recognized in the accounts only when substantiated by objective evidence; it should never be recorded to avoid recognition of a loss or merely as a convenient balancing device.

Computing goodwill or bonus implied by partnership agreement

Agreements for admission of a new partner sometimes fail to mention whether a bonus or recognition of goodwill is involved. However, the amount of bonus or goodwill *implied* by the agreement can be determined if the total capital of the new firm and the new partner's fractional share in the capital are specified in the agreement.

For example, assume that J and K have capitals of $50,000 and $25,000, respectively, and share profit and loss equally. It is agreed that L is to be admitted as a partner by making an investment of cash or other assets in the firm as indicated by the following independent cases.

Bonus to old partners. The incoming partner, L, invests $29,000 cash for a one-fourth interest in total capital of $104,000. To meet these conditions, it is necessary to establish a $26,000 capital account for L; therefore, the $3,000 excess of his investment over his capital credit represents a bonus to be divided equally between the old partners.

Cash	*29,000*	
J, Capital		*1,500*
K, Capital		*1,500*
L, Capital		*26,000*
To record admission of L to a one-fourth interest in total capital of $104,000.		

Goodwill to old partners. The incoming partner invests $30,000 cash for a one-fourth interest and it is agreed that his capital balance shall be $30,000. The total capital must necessarily be four times $30,000 or $120,000, in order that L's capital be one-fourth of the total. The recorded capital of J and K plus the $30,000 invested by L totals $105,000; therefore goodwill of $15,000 may be recorded and credited to the old partners. The objections to such writing up of asset values based on a change in partnership personnel have been covered earlier in this chapter.

Cash	*30,000*	
Goodwill	*15,000*	
J, Capital		*7,500*
K, Capital		*7,500*
L, Capital		*30,000*
To record admission of L with a capital of $30,000, representing a one-fourth interest.		

Bonus and goodwill to old partners. The agreement requires that the incoming partner, L, invest $30,000 for a one-fourth interest in total capital of $112,000. The combined capitals of J and K plus the investment of L equal a total of $105,000. To bring this amount up to the required total capital of $112,000 will require recognition of $7,000 in goodwill to be credited equally to the two original partners. Also, the $30,000 investment by L is $2,000 greater than the one-fourth interest in total capital ($\frac{1}{4} \times \$112,000 = \$28,000$) which he has agreed to accept. This $2,000 excess of L's investment over his agreed capital represents a bonus to be credited equally to J and K.

Cash	*30,000*	
Goodwill	*7,000*	
J, Capital		*4,500*
K, Capital		*4,500*
L, Capital		*28,000*
To record investment by L of $30,009 for a one-fourth interest in total capital of $112,000.		

Bonus to new partner. The incoming partner invests cash of $21,000 for a one-fourth interest in total capital of $96,000. The combined capitals of J and K plus L's investment total $96,000, so no increment through the recognition of goodwill is permissible. Since L must be assigned a capital account equal to one-fourth of $96,000, or $24,000, and he invested only $21,000, he is allowed a bonus of $3,000, which must be deducted from the two original partners in equal amounts.

Cash	*21,000*	
J, Capital	*1,500*	
K, Capital	*1,500*	
L, Capital		*24,000*
To record admission of L to a one-fourth interest in capital of $96,000.		

Goodwill to new partner. The incoming partner invests various tangible assets comprising a business he has been operating profitably. These assets are valued at $20,000 and it is agreed L shall have a one-fourth interest in a total capital of $100,000. The recorded capitals of J and K plus the $20,000 of tangible assets invested by L total $95,000; therefore goodwill of $5,000 may be recognized and credited to the new partner. This will give him an interest of $25,000, or one-fourth of the agreed total capital of $100,000.

Various Tangible Assets	*20,000*	
Goodwill	*5,000*	
L, Capital		*25,000*
To record admission of L to a one-fourth interest in total capital of $100,000 by contribution of a going business.		

Bonus and goodwill to new partner. This example is the same as the preceding one except that the agreement calls for the new partner to receive a one-third interest in total capital of $100,000. In other words, the incoming partner invests various tangible assets comprising a business he has been operating profitably. These assets are valued at $20,000 and it is agreed that he shall have a one-third interest in total capital of $100,000. The recorded capitals of J and K plus the $20,000 of tangible assets invested by L total $95,000; therefore goodwill of $5,000 is recognized and credited to the new partner. To bring L's capital account up to the required one-third of $100,000 total capital, he must also be credited with a bonus of $8,333, which is deducted in equal amounts from the capitals of the two original partners.

Various Tangible Assets	*20,000*	
Goodwill	*5,000*	
J, Capital	*4,167*	
K, Capital	*4,166*	
L, Capital		*33,333*
To record admission of L to a one-third interest in total capital of $100,000.		

Other terms for admission of new partner

An agreement for the admission of a new partner may not indicate any agreed amount of total capital for the new firm. For example, assume that J and K have capitals of $50,000 and $25,000 and share profits equally. They agree to admit L to a one-fourth interest upon investment of $33,000. Since there is no agreement on the amount of L's capital account or the total capital of the firm, two alternative ways of recording L's admission are mechanically possible. The capitals of J and K plus the investment of L equal a total of $108,000. The required one-fourth interest for L may be achieved by crediting him with only $27,000 and dividing the remaining $6,000 of the investment as a bonus between the two original partners. This method is the preferable approach.

Cash	*33,000*	
J, Capital		*3,000*
K, Capital		*3,000*
L, Capital		*27,000*
To record admission of L to a one-fourth interest.		

An alternative method (subject to the objections previously discussed) is to record the implied goodwill. The admission of L to the firm could be recorded by crediting him with the full $33,000 he invested and increasing the capitals of the original partners by recording goodwill of sufficient amount to give them the required three-fourths of total capital. If L is to have a capital of $33,000 representing a one-fourth interest, then J and K together must have a capital of three times $33,000, or $99,000. This will require recognition of $24,000 in goodwill to be divided equally between J and K as shown by the following entry:

Cash	*33,000*	
Goodwill	*24,000*	
J, Capital		*12,000*
K, Capital		*12,000*
L, Capital		*33,000*
To record admission of L to a one-fourth interest.		

In choosing between these alternative methods, the partners should consider the consequences of a later write-off of goodwill, as discussed on pages 46 and 47, and also the current trend toward viewing the partnership as a continuing business entity with asset valuations undisturbed by changes in partnership personnel.

Retirement of a partner

When a partner retires, he usually receives a settlement representing the amount of his equity paid from partnership assets. It is also possible that he might arrange for the sale of his equity to one or more of the continuing partners as individuals, or that he might sell his interest in the firm to an outsider. Since we have already considered the accounting principles applicable to the purchase of an interest by an incoming or continuing partner, it is unnecessary to review such transactions again from the viewpoint of the selling partner. Emphasis has previously been placed on the preferred accounting treatment: that is, to transfer the capital balance of the selling partner to the capital account of the partner acquiring the interest without regard to the amount of the payment between the individuals involved.

At this point our discussion of the retirement of a partner is therefore limited to the situation in which the partner receives settlement from the assets of the partnership.

Another assumption underlying this discussion is that the partner has a right to withdraw under the terms of the partnership agreement. A partner always has the *power* to withdraw, as distinguished from the *right* to withdraw. If a partner withdraws in violation of the terms agreed upon in the partnership contract and without the consent of his partners, he may be liable for damages caused his partners by his violation of the contract. The liability for damages could be offset against the amount he is entitled to receive in settlement for his equity. Such cases are infrequent and stress legal rather than accounting issues; they are not considered in the following discussion.

Computing the settlement price

What is a fair measurement of the equity of a retiring partner? A first indication is the amount of his capital account, but this amount may require various adjustments before it represents an equitable settlement. These adjustments may include (1) correction of errors in accounting data, (2) recognition of differences in book values of assets and current market values, and (3) recognition of goodwill. In approaching these adjustments, the accountant will first refer to the partnership agreement, which may contain specific instructioins for computing the amount to be paid a retiring partner. These instructions, for example, might provide for the appraisal of assets, might call for an audit by independent public accountants, and might prescribe a formula to be used in determining a figure for goodwill. If the business has not maintained good accounting records or has not been regularly audited, it is possible that the capital accounts are grossly misstated because of improper depreciation charges, failure to provide for bad debts, and other deficiencies in accounting.

If the articles of partnership do not contain provisions for computing the equity of a retiring partner, the accountant may be able to obtain joint authorization from the partners to follow a specific approach to determining an equitable settlement amount.

In most cases the equity of the retiring partner is computed on the basis of current fair market values for all assets. The gain or loss indicated by the difference between the book value of assets and their appraised value is divided in the profit and loss ratio. This calculation of the fair market value of a partner's equity may be made on a work sheet without any entries being made in the accounts to change assets values or capital accounts. The computation of an estimated current value for the partner's equity is a necessary step in reaching a settlement; an independent decision should be made as to whether the appraised values and changes in capitals should be introduced into the accounting records.

If the retirement of the partner is viewed as ending the life of one business entity and the association of the continuing partners is viewed as the beginning of a new entity, then accounting entries may be made for the revaluation of the assets. Under this approach, asset values would be written up or down to the appraised amounts and the net gain or loss would be entered in the partners' capital accounts in the profit and loss ratio.

After the equity of the retiring partner has been computed in terms of current valuations for assets, the partners may agree to settle by payment of this amount or they may agree upon a higher or lower amount.

Recognition of goodwill or payment of bonus

The partnership agreement may provide for recognition of goodwill at the time of a partner's retirement and may specify the methods of computing it. Usually the amount of the computed goodwill will be attributable to the partners in the profit and loss ratio. For example, assume that C is to retire from the firm of A, B, and C. Each partner has a capital of $60,000 and profits and losses are shared equally. The partnership agreement states that a retiring partner is entitled to receive the balance shown by his capital account plus goodwill. At the time of C's retirement, goodwill in the amount of $30,000 is computed in accordance with the formula prescribed by the partnership contract or presently agreed to by the partners. The purpose of this computation is to determine an equitable price for C's interest in the firm. It is not necessary that the goodwill be entered on the books; the essential point is that the total payment to C be properly computed. If the computed goodwill is recorded in the accounts, the entry will be:

Goodwill	*30,000*	
A, Capital		*10,000*
B, Capital		*10,000*
C, Capital		*10,000*
To record as an asset the amount of goodwill computed as specified by the partnership contract in event of a partner's retirement.		

Serious objections exist to recording goodwill as shown in this illustration. Since only $10,000 of the goodwill is included in the payment for C's equity, the remaining $20,000 of goodwill has not been purchased by the continuing partnership.

Its inclusion in the balance sheet of the partnership is not supported by the cost principle nor by any objective verifiable evidence. The fact that the partners "voted" for $30,000 of goodwill does not meet our need for objective evidence of asset value.

A second alternative in accounting for C's retirement is to enter in the accounts only $10,000 of goodwill, since this amount was "paid for" by the continuing partnership in acquiring C's interest. The entry would be:

Goodwill	*10,000*	
C, Capital		*10,000*
To record as an asset the amount of goodwill included in payment for the equity of the retiring partner.		

This method is perhaps more justifiable than that in the previous illustration, but evidence is still lacking that a valid intangible asset exists. Since the computation of goodwill was made in accordance with an agreement created at the inception of the partnership, the amount is not related to the actual earnings record of the firm. It is conceivable that a partnership might choose to recognize goodwill in this manner even though the business was incurring operating losses.

A further objection to both methods of recording goodwill is the possibility of inequitable results between the continuing partners if the goodwill is later written off when the partners are no longer sharing profit and loss in the same ratio. The possible inequities were discussed in some detail earlier in this chapter.

In the opinion of the authors, a more satisfactory method of accounting for the retirement of partner C is to treat the computed amount of goodwill as a $10,000 bonus. Since the settlement with C is for the amount of his capital account ($60,000) plus estimated goodwill of $10,000, the following entries could be made to record C's retirement:

C, Capital	*60,000*	
A, Capital	*5,000*	
B, Capital	*5,000*	
Liability to C		*70,000*
To record the obligation to retiring partner C computed per agreement as his capital balance plus bonus for estimated goodwill.		

The bonus method illustrated here is appropriate whenever the settlement with the retiring partner exceeds the book value of his capital. The agreement for settlement may or may not use the term goodwill; the essence of the matter is determining the amount to be paid to the retiring partner.

The bonus method is consistent with the current trend toward viewing a partnership as a continuing business entity, with asset valuations and accounting policies remaining undisturbed by the retirement of a partner. Of course, if the retirement of a partner causes the termination of the business, the going-concern concept no longer applies.

Settlement with retiring partner for less than book value

A partner may be so anxious to escape from an unsatisfactory business situation that he surrenders his equity for less than book value. In other cases, willingness by the retiring partner to accept a settlement below book value may reflect personal problems entirely apart from the business. Another possible explanation is that the retiring partner considers the assets overvalued, or that he anticipates declining profits or even operating losses in future years.

In brief, there are many subjective and unmeasurable factors which may induce a partner to accept less than book value in settlement for his equity in the business. Since a settlement below book value is seldom supported by objective evidence of overvaluation of assets, the preferred accounting treatment is to leave asset valuations undisturbed. The difference between the retiring partner's capital account and the amount he accepts in settlement should be credited to the continuing partners in the profit and loss ratio.

For example, assume that in the firm of A, B, and C with capitals of $60,000 each, partner B retires upon payment of $50,000. Assuming that profit and loss is shared equally, the entry is:

B, Capital	*60,000*	
Liability to B		*50,000*
A, Capital		*5,000*
C, Capital		*5,000*
To record surrender by B of his equity for an amount below book value.		

The final settlement with a retiring partner is often deferred for some time after his withdrawal to permit the accumulation of cash, the obtaining of bank loans, or other steps needed to complete the transaction. Since he is not a partner during this interim period, his capital account should be closed and replaced with a liability account with a descriptive title. The retirement of a partner does not terminate his personal responsibility for partnership debts existing at the date of his retirement unless the creditors agree to release him.

Death of a partner

The partnership agreement often provides that partners shall purchase life insurance policies on each others' lives so that funds will be available for settlement with the estate of a deceased partner. A buy and sell agreement may be formed by the partners with a trustee appointed to carry out the plan. Under a buy and sell agreement, the partners commit their estates to sell their interests in the business and the surviving partners to buy such interests. Another form of such an agreement gives the surviving partners an option to buy or "first refusal" rather than imposing an obligation to buy. The agreement should include provision for determining the transfer price of an interest, and the insurance policies should be of sufficient amount to permit the payment for the interest each partner may be required to purchase. Each partner pays the premiums on the lives of his partners and has title to their policies.

Upon the death of a partner, the trustee named in the buy and sell agreement will receive payment from the insurance company, make payment to the estate of the deceased partner, and transfer the deceased partner's equity to the surviving partners. A plan of this type avoids the possibility of forced liquidation of the business or of financial crisis to the surviving partners. It also assures the estate of the deceased partner of prompt settlement.

Since a partnership is dissolved by the death of a partner, it is ordinarily necessary to close the books and determine the net income or loss to be divided among the partners for the fractional period since the last regular closing date. The closing process may necessitate a physical inventory and an independent audit, depending upon the size and nature of the business and any specific prior agreement.

Some partnership agreements provide that the equity of a deceased partner need not be determined until the end of the regular fiscal period. These arrangements usually include agreement for prorating to the estate of the deceased partner a portion of the year's earnings corresponding to the portion of the year elapsed at the date of death.

If the partnership agreement provides for the liquidation of the business upon the death of a partner, the surviving partners are obligated to wind up the enterprise by selling the assets, paying creditors, and making distributions to partners and to the estate of the deceased partner. Gains and losses from the disposal of assets are divided in the established ratio for sharing profit and loss, including the share going to the account of the deceased partner.

Incorporation of a partnership

Most successful partnerships give consideration at times to the possible advantages to be gained by incorporating. Among the advantages are limited liability, ease of attracting outside capital without loss of control, and possible tax savings.

A new corporation formed to take over the assets and liabilities of a partnership will usually sell stock to outsiders for cash either at the time of incorporation or at a later date. To assure that the former partners receive an equitable portion of the total capital stock, the assets of the partnership will need to be adjusted to fair market value before being transferred to the corporation. Any goodwill developed by the partnership should be recognized as part of the assets transferred.

For tax purposes, no gain or loss is recognized on the transfer of assets if the former partners hold control of the corporation. Control is defined as ownership of 80% or more of the voting stock and 80% or more of other classes of stock. An important part of this tax rule is that the basis of the property transferred remains unchanged, so that for tax purposes the depreciation program continues on the basis of the original cost of the assets to the partnership. Assume that the incorporation of a partnership is to follow the theoretical concept of a change in business entities despite continuity of individual ownership and that the assets are revalued to reflect current market prices. From this point on, the depreciation recorded in the accounts and shown in financial statements of the corporation will differ from the amount of depreciation which can be deducted on the corporate income tax return.

The accounting records of a partnership may be modified and continued in use when the firm changes to the corporate form. As an alternative, the partnership books may be closed and a new set of accounting records established for the corporation. Since the procedures to be followed under both of these alternatives are illustrated in detail in *Intermediate Accounting,* they will be only briefly summarized here.

Retention of partnership books. If the accounting records used by the partnership are to be continued in use by the corporation, a first step consists of entries needed to adjust assets and liabilities to reflect current fair value. The gain or loss from this revaluation may be entered first in a Revaluation and Summary Account, which is then closed to the partners' capital accounts in the profit and loss ratio. If adjustments are few, they may conveniently be charged or credited directly to the capital accounts. To complete the changeover, the partners' capital accounts are closed, with offsetting credits to the capital stock and paid-in capital accounts. The accounting records are then ready for recording transactions by the corporation.

Establishment of new books for corporation. If new accounting records are to be opened for the corporation, entries should first be made in the partnership books for revaluation of assets, liabilities, and partners' capitals. The next step is to transfer the assets and liabilities to the corporation, setting up a special receivable for the net amount due. This receivable is collected through receipt by the partnership of capital stock. The final entry to close the partnership books is based on distribution of the shares of stock to the partners by debiting their capital accounts and crediting the asset account representing capital stock held by the partnership.

The entries on the corporation books consist of recording the assets and liabilities acquired from the partnership at the adjusted valuations, with an offsetting liability for the net amount owed to the partnership. This liability is discharged by delivery of shares of stock to the partnership, accompanied by credits to the capital stock and paid-in capital accounts.

The results produced by the opening of a new set of books are the same as if the partnership books were retained for use by the corporation. Under either method the corporation must decide whether to transfer the accumulated depreciation accounts or to record the net value of the depreciable assets as the cost to the corporation.

Questions

1. Should the valuation of assets as shown by the accounting records of a partnership be changed to correspond to current fair market value whenever a partner withdraws or a new partner is admitted to the firm? Explain fully and give specific examples.

2. John Bell and Ray Jones are partners sharing profits equally; each has a capital account of $100,000. Jones (with the consent of Bell) sells one-fifth of his interest to his son, Arthur, for a price of $25,000, with payment to be made in five annual installments without any interest charge. Give the entry to record the change in ownership, and explain why you would or would not recommend a change in the valuation of assets on the partnership books.

3. Rogers purchases for $50,000 cash a one-fourth interest in the net assets and earnings of the Web Company. The Web Company had been a partnership of three men, White, Edwards, and Barnes, each having a one-third interest in capital and in profits. Total capital before admission of Rogers was $120,000; there was no recorded goodwill. The agreements do not specify the dollar amount of capital to be credited to Rogers or the total capital of the firm. The cash payments are made by Rogers not to the firm but to each of the three old partners individually in equal amounts. Suggest four alternative ways in which the admission of Rogers might be recorded, and state a reason in support of each.

4. L and M are partners with capital accounts of $70,000 each who share profits equally. The partners agree to admit N to a one-third interest in assets and a one-third share in profits upon investment by him in the firm of $100,000. Assume that the assets are fairly valued and that his admission is recorded by allowing a bonus to the old partners. Give the entry or entries to record the admission of N to the firm.

5. When a new partner is admitted to an established firm, he is often required to invest an amount larger than the book value of the interest he acquires. In what two ways can such a transaction be recorded? What is the principal argument for each method?

6. Assume that A and B are partners in a successful business, sharing profits in a 60:40 ratio. Their capital accounts are A, $60,000 and B, $40,000. They agree to admit C to a 30% interest in assets and a 20% interest in profits upon his investment of $50,000. The new profit-sharing ratio is to be 48:32:20 for A, B, and C, respectively. The partners are discussing whether to record the admission of C by a bonus to A and B or by recording goodwill. What would be the amount of the bonus to A and B, respectively? What would be the total goodwill implied by C's investment? Would the goodwill method be more advantageous to C if we assume the goodwill were written off the books two years later? What would be the dollar amount of the advantage or disadvantage to C from use of the goodwill method?

7. Assume that an incoming partner invests an amount greater than the book value of the interest he receives. Under what specific circumstances will the recording of the implied goodwill and its write-off in a subsequent year have the same net results for the individual partners as would the use of the bonus method?

8. Bennett, Cross, and Davis have operated a partnership business for many years and have shared profits equally. The partners now agree that Gray, a key employee of the firm who is an able manager but has limited financial resources, should become a partner with a one-sixth interest in capital. It is further agreed that the four partners will share profits equally in the future. Bennett suggests that the assets on the books of the old partnership should be restated at current market value at the time of admitting Gray, but Cross and Davis advocate that the accounts be left undisturbed in order to have a consistent accounting record. What is the argument for restating assets at the time of Gray's admission? What alternative, if any, would you suggest for such restatement of asset values?

9. The partnership of James, Wylie, and Martin has operated successfully for many years but Martin has now reached retirement age. In discussing the settlement to be made with Martin, the point was made that the inventories of the firm had consistently been valued on a lifo basis for many years. Martin suggested that the current replacement value of the inventory be determined and the excess of this sum over the book value be regarded as a gain in which he would share. James objected to this suggestion on the grounds that any method of inventory valuation would give reasonably accurate results provided it were followed consistently and that a departure from the long-established method used by the partnership would produce an erroneous picture of the profits realized over the life of the firm. Evaluate these arguments.

10. Land and Marlin are partners who share profits equally. They offer to admit Naylor to a one-third interest in assets and in profits upon his investment of $50,000 cash. The total capital of the partnership prior to the admission of Naylor was $110,000. Naylor makes a counteroffer of $40,000, explaining that his investigation of the business indicates that many receivables are past due and that a significant amount of obsolescence exists in the inventory. Land and Marlin deny both these points. They contend that inventory is valued in a normal and reasonable manner and that the receivables are fully collectible. However, after prolonged negotiation, the admission price of $40,000 proposed by Naylor is agreed upon. Explain two ways in which the admission of Naylor *could* be recorded and indicate which method is more justifiable. Comment on the possibility of recording goodwill.

Short cases for analysis

2-1 Blake and Carter have been in business for many years and have shared profits equally. They own and operate a resort hotel which includes a golf course and other recreational facilities. Blake has maintained a larger capital investment than Carter, but Carter has devoted much more time to the management of the business.

The business is located in one of the fastest-growing areas in the country and has been expanding rapidly. To help meet the problems of this expansion, the partners decide to admit Davis as a partner with a one-third interest in the firm and a one-third share in profits. Davis is known as an excellent administrator and has ample cash to invest for his share in the firm. You are retained by the partnership to give advice upon any accounting issues created by the admission of Davis as a partner. List the factors that you believe deserve consideration and prepare a brief set of recommendations to guide the partners in dealing with these issues.

2-2 Austin and Bradford are partners who share profits equally and have equal capital accounts. The net assets of the firm are carried on the books at $40,000. Crane is admitted to the partnership with a one-third interest in profits and net assets. To acquire his interest, Crane pays $18,000 cash into the partnership.

Instructions

Prepare journal entries to show three possible methods of recording on the partnership books the admission of Crane. State the conditions under which each method would be appropriate.

AICPA adapted

2-3 The partnership of Welborn, Dickson, and Graf has maintained its accounting records in accordance with the policy of stating assets at cost less accumulated depreciation or valuation allowances. At December 31, 1967, Welborn, who has a 40% interest in profits and assets, is to withdraw from the firm. The partnership holds a building under a lease having 30 years of remaining life. Because of increased rental rates since the time when the partnership leased the building from the owner, the lease now has substantial value, although the partnership has paid nothing for it except current rentals. An offer of $450,000 has been received for the lease from a large national corporation. The partnership agreement contains no provision as to method of valuing assets in the event of liquidation of the business or withdrawal of a partner.

Instructions

State with reasons:

a. Your opinion as to how the lease should be treated to produce equitable results in computing the amount to be paid to Welborn, the withdrawing partner.

b. Whether you think the accounting records of the partnership have been properly maintained with regard to this lease.

c. How any settlement with Welborn in excess of the balance in his capital account should be recorded in the accounts.

AICPA adapted

Problems

2-4 Allen, Bates, and Crest are partners sharing profits in a 3:2:1 ratio. The business has been successful, as indicated by the following data concerning the partners' capital accounts:

	Original investments	*Retained earnings*	*Present balances*
Allen, capital	$30,000	$42,000	$ 72,000
Bates, capital	22,400	28,000	50,400
Crest, capital	11,500	12,500	24,000
	$63,900	$82,500	$146,400

At this time Crest becomes ill and retires from the partnership, receiving $30,000 in full payment for his equity. Allen and Bates decide to continue in partnership and to share profits equally. However, as a condition of this change in profit sharing, Bates agrees to invest an additional $10,000 cash in the firm. The investment is made but the partners have difficulty in agreeing on the method to be used in recording Crest's withdrawal from the firm. Allen wants to record the entire goodwill of the partnership as implied by the amount paid for Crest's interest. Bates argues that the amount of goodwill to be recorded should not be greater than the amount paid for Crest's share of the partnership goodwill. The accountant for the firm points out that the profit-sharing ratio is being changed and suggests that this is a reason for recognizing the goodwill of the business prior to Crest's withdrawal. Crest suggests that the entire controversy over goodwill can be avoided by treating the amount paid to him in excess of his capital account as a bonus from Allen and Bates.

Instructions

a. Give the entries on the books of the partnership required by the recommendation of each of the three partners (three independent sets of entries).

b. Assume that the business is sold for $162,400 in cash shortly after the withdrawal of Crest, with the buyer assuming the liabilities. Prepare orderly schedules showing how the cash would be divided between Allen and Bates under each of the three alternative methods for handling the withdrawal of Crest as previously described.

c. For this portion of the problem, assume the same data as to original investments and retained earnings by Allen, Bates, and Crest. However, rather than having Crest withdraw from the partnership, assume that the three partners agree to admit Davis as a fourth partner for an investment of $40,000 cash in the firm. Davis is given a 25% interest in the partnership net assets and a 25% share in profits. Allen, Bates, and Crest will share the remaining 75% of partnership profits in the same original ratio existing among them prior to admission of Davis to the firm. Allen, Bates, and Crest each withdraw $10,000 cash from the business. Prepare the journal entries needed to record the withdrawals of cash and the admission of Davis into the partnership using (1) the goodwill method and (2) the bonus method.

d. Assume the same facts presented in (c) above, and further that the business is sold for $162,400 shortly after the admission of Davis to the firm. The buyer assumes the liabilities. Prepare a schedule showing how the cash would be distributed among the four partners if the admission of Davis had been recorded by using (1) the goodwill method and (2) the bonus method.

2-5 The partnership of Jackson and Klein has maintained accounting records on the accrual basis except for the method of handling credit losses. Bad debts have been recognized by a direct charge-off to expense at the time individual accounts receivable were determined to be uncollectible.

The partners are anticipating the admission of a third member, Lewis, to the firm and they retain you as an accountant to review the records before this action is taken. You suggest that the firm change retroactively to the allowance method of accounting for bad debts so that the planning for admission of Lewis to partnership can be based upon a full accrual system. The following information is available:

Accounts receivable	*Accounts written off*			*Additional estimated losses*
	1964	*1965*	*1966*	
1963	*$1,200*	*$ 200*		
1964	*1,500*	*1,300*	*$ 600*	*$ 150*
1965		*1,800*	*1,400*	*1,250*
1966			*2,200*	*3,750*
	$2,700	*$3,300*	*$4,200*	*$5,150*

The partners shared profits equally until 1966. In 1966 the profit-sharing plan was changed as follows: salaries of $8,000 and $6,000 to be allowed Jackson and Klein, respectively, any balance to be divided 60% to Jackson and 40% to Klein. Net income of the partnership for 1966 according to the records was $28,000.

Instructions

a. Prepare a compound entry giving effect to the change in accounting method for uncollectible accounts. Support your entry with a carefully prepared schedule showing changes in net income for each year.

b. Assume that after you prepared the entry in (a) above, Jackson's capital is reported at $48,000 and Klein's capital is reported at $22,000. If Lewis invests $25,000 for a 20% interest in total assets of the partnership and a 25% share in income, illustrate by journal entries two methods that may be used to record his admission into the partnership. Any increment in capital of old partners is to be divided 60% and 40%. Which method would be more advantageous to Lewis if the goodwill is later substantiated through a profitable sale of the business? Which method would be more advantageous to Lewis if we assume that the goodwill is written off by the partnership in the year following his admission to the firm?

2-6 The partnership of Bryson and Jones has assets of $800,000. Bryson's capital account is $300,000 and he has a 70% share in profits. Jones's capital account is $200,000 and his share in profits is 30%.

Negotiations have been conducted with Smith for some time concerning his admission to the firm. Agreement has been reached that Smith shall be admitted and that he shall have a one-fourth interest in capital and in profits. The three men are presently considering whether Smith should invest directly in the firm or should purchase his interest from Bryson. An independent appraisal of the firm's properties is obtained which indicates that current market value is approximately the same as the book value of the assets.

Instructions

a. Assuming that Smith buys his one-fourth interest from Bryson, what price should he pay?

b. Assuming that Smith acquires his one-fourth interest by investing in the partnership, what price should he pay? Would this be more or less advantageous to Smith than the purchase described in (a)?

c. Assume that Smith, in addition to his business activities, is also a candidate for political office and that Bryson is a very influential and prominent figure in the community. Smith made the following proposal to Bryson: "If you would play an active role in my political campaign by giving several speeches and interviews in my behalf I believe this would assure my election. I do not feel it appropriate to offer pay for such services, but I recognize the time required would restrict your other activities. Therefore, I propose that in buying a one-fourth interest in the Bryson-Jones partnership I shall pay you $10,000 in addition to the book value price we have previously discussed."

If this plan is carried out and Smith purchases his interest directly from Bryson, how should his admission be recorded on the partnership books? Give the journal entry and your reasons.

d. Assume that Bryson, after considering the offer made by Smith in (c) above, decides that such a transaction might offend his partner, Jones. He therefore counters with the suggestion that Smith invest directly in the partnership, making a payment $10,000 above that indicated by the carrying value of the partnership assets. If this proposal is carried out, how would Smith's admission be recorded by the partnership? Explain fully.

2-7 The partnership of Mark, Neal, and Patrick was formed January 1, 1966, with Mark and Neal furnishing most of the required capital and Patrick serving as general manager. Beginning capital balances were Mark $70,000, Neal $60,000, and Patrick $10,000. The partners agreed that a division of profits in the ratio of 40% to Mark, 35% to Neal, and 25% to Patrick would be equitable in view of the differences in amounts of capital and personal services contributed by each man to the firm.

On January 1, 1967, Patrick received a substantial inheritance and used a portion of these funds to increase his capital in the partnership by $60,000. Because of the improvement in his personal financial affairs and a desire to take a world cruise, Patrick asked to be relieved as general manager; he was replaced by Neal. In view of these changes, the profit-sharing ratio was revised on January 1, 1967, as follows: Mark 30%; Neal 50%; and Patrick 20%.

The net income of the partnership was reported as $44,000 for 1966 and as $72,000 for 1967. Each partner withdrew $800 monthly during 1966 and $1,000 monthly during 1967. In January, 1968, Patrick decided he would like to free himself from all business obligations and offered to sell his interest in the firm to Mark and Neal at book value as of December 31, 1967 (subject to any adjustments indicated by an independent audit) plus $15,000 for his share of estimated goodwill accumulated by the firm.

Mark and Neal accepted this offer and a CPA firm was engaged to perform the audit. The books had been closed at December 31, 1967, prior to the beginning of the audit work, but the partners agreed that the audit fee of $1,500 should be treated as an expense of the year 1967. The partnership had not been audited previously and the examination disclosed that the following errors had occurred during the two years of operation.

(1) Expenditures of $6,000 for equipment on October 1, 1966, had been recorded as Repair and Maintenance Expense. Estimated life of the equipment was

10 years. The depreciation policy applied by the firm to other similar equipment was the double-declining-balance method.

(2) The inventory taken at December 31, 1966, had been understated in the amount of $7,200 because of a clerical error on the inventory summary sheet. A similar error in the inventory taken at December 31, 1967, caused an overstatement of $1,000.

(3) Expenses in the amount of $1,500 had been incurred but were unrecorded at December 31, 1966. At December 31, 1967, similar unrecorded expenses of $4,200 were disclosed by the auditors.

Instructions

Disregard income taxes.

a. Prepare a separate journal entry to correct the errors in each of the above-numbered paragraphs and an entry to reflect the audit fee as if it were a 1967 expense.

b. Compute the corrected annual net income for 1966 and 1967.

c. Compute the amount Patrick should receive for the sale of his interest to Mark and Neal. Draft the journal entry to record the settlement with Patrick, assuming that a note for $40,000 is issued and the remainder is paid in cash.

2-8 The partnership of A and B is distributor for a nationally advertised line of farm implements in a small town. The partnership also operates a small lumberyard. B is retired and has agreed to sell his interest in the partnership to A at book value as of March 31, 1967. B is willing to accept A's 5% notes payable in four annual installments of $3,000 each, beginning October 1, 1967, and all the notes receivable held by the partnership in part payment for his interest, the remainder of the purchase price to be paid during April, 1967, from cash of the dissolved partnership.

The trial balance of the partnership as of March 31, 1967, and additional information follow:

Cash	*$ 7,100*	
Accounts receivable	*12,050*	
Merchandise account	*22,500*	
Property	*7,250*	
Expense	*6,550*	
Accounts payable		*$17,600*
A, capital		*20,550*
B, capital		*17,300*
	$55,450	*$55,450*

Additional information

(1) A is the active manager of the business and draws a salary of $500 per month. The remaining profits or losses are distributed equally between the partners. The partnership normally closes its books on a calendar-year basis.

(2) The cash account is properly stated.

(3) The aggregate of the detail accounts receivable is $14,900 and includes $5,650 in notes receivable. Prior years' tax returns indicate that certain accounts

have been written off but no record has been kept of the detail of such write-offs. The partners agree that all the notes receivable are collectible but that $1,050 of the accounts are uncollectible.

(4) The latest physical inventory was taken on December 31, 1966, and consisted of the following: implements, $10,300; implement parts, $7,800; lumber, $4,400; and a used truck, $1,200. The truck is used in the business and was priced at estimated resale value. The cost of the truck is not known, but the partners estimate that it had a useful life of three years at December 31, 1966. The inventory was charged to the merchandise account on January 1, 1967. Other transactions recorded in the merchandise account to March 31, 1967, consist of purchases of $38,400 and sales of $39,600. Purchases have been set up in accounts payable.

(5) Property consists of land, $250; buildings, $2,000; and equipment, $5,000. The detail records indicate that these amounts represent cost.

(6) Expenses for the three months include A's salary. Other salaries and wages for the same period aggregated $3,500.

(7) Accounts payable to vendors other than the implement manufacturer have been accrued on the basis of statements received. No vendors have been omitted in this accrual. The account payable to the implement manufacturer as shown by the books does not agree with that vendor's statement as of March 31, 1967. You are able to determine that the difference is due to improper handling of the 2% cash discount allowed on $30,000 of invoices paid during the first three months of 1966. These invoices were accrued gross, but only the net amount paid has been charged against the accounts payable control account.

(8) Your review of tax returns for the most recent three years reveals that the invoice cost of merchandise sold has averaged 75% of sales. You also note that $2,000 of accumulated depreciation appears on the balance sheet in the 1966 tax return. Depreciation has been provided in the return on the basis of a 20-year life for the buildings and a 10-year life for machinery and equipment.

Instructions

a. Prepare an eight-column work sheet for A and B Company at March 31, 1967 (trial balance, adjustments, income statement, and balance sheet columns).

b. Prepare balance sheets for the partnership as of March 31, 1967, and for the new proprietorship as of April 1, 1967. (The notes payable issued to B in partial settlement of his interest should be included among the liabilities of the new proprietorship.)

AICPA adapted

2-9 The law firm of Day, East, and Fox came into being on January 1, 1967, when the three attorneys decided to consolidate their individual law practices. The partners reached agreement on the following matters:

a. Each partner would contribute to the firm the assets and liabilities of his individual practice and would be credited with a capital contribution equal to the net assets taken over by the partnership. The receivables contributed by each partner were personally guaranteed by him to be collectible. The assets and liabilities acquired by the partnership in this manner were as follows:

	Day	East	Fox
Cash	$10,000	$10,000	$10,000
Accounts receivable	28,000	12,000	32,000
Law library and furniture	8,600	5,000	12,400
Accumulated depreciation	(4,800)	(3,000)	(9,400)
Total assets	$41,800	$24,000	$45,000
Less: Accounts payable	600	2,800	1,400
Net assets (capital contributed)	$41,200	$21,200	$43,600

b. The partnership decided to occupy Fox's office space until his lease expired on June 30, 1967. The monthly rental was $1,200 but the partners agreed that this was an excessive rate for the space provided and that $900 monthly would be reasonable. They therefore agreed that the excess rent would be charged to Fox at the end of the year. When the lease expired on June 30, 1967, the partners moved to a new office with a monthly rental of $1,000.

c. The profit-sharing agreement did not provide for salaries to the partners but specified that individual partners should receive 20% of the gross fees billed to their respective clients during the first year of the partnership. The balance of the fees after deduction of operating expenses was to be credited to the partners' capital accounts in the following proportions: Day, 40%; East, 35%; Fox, 25%.

A new partner, Gray, was admitted to the partnership on April 1, 1967; he was to receive 20% of the fees from new business obtained after April 1 after deducting expenses applicable to that new business. Expenses were to be apportioned to the new business in the same ratio that total expenses, other than bad debt losses, bore to total gross fees.

The following information pertains to the partnership's activities in 1967:

(1) Fees were billed as follows:

Day's clients	$ 44,000
East's clients	24,000
Fox's clients	22,000
New business:	
Prior to April 1	6,000
After April 1	24,000
Total	$120,000

(2) Total expenses, excluding depreciation and bad debt expenses, were $38,700 including the total amount paid for rent. Depreciation was to be computed at the rate of 10%. Depreciable assets purchased during 1967, on which one-half year's depreciation was to be taken, totaled $10,000.

(3) Cash charges to the partners' accounts during the year were:

Day	$10,400
East	8,800
Fox	11,600
Gray	5,000
Total	$35,800

(4) Accounts receivable acquired from Day in the amount of $2,400 and from East in the amount of $900 proved to be uncollectible. Also, a new client billed in March for $3,200 had been adjudged bankrupt and a settlement of 50 cents on the dollar was made.

Instructions

Prepare a statement of the partners' capital accounts for the year ended December 31, 1967. All supporting computations should be carefully organized and presented in good form. Depreciation should be based on the original cost of assets to individual partners. Income taxes are to be disregarded.

AICPA adapted

2-10 Ryan, Smith, and Thomas were partners in a service business until February 15, 1967, at which time Smith withdrew. Ryan and Thomas continued the business until July 1, 1967, when they admitted Doe as a partner. They have continued to operate the same business.

Comparative balance sheets and additional information follow:

	Balance Dec. 31, 1966	*Balance Dec. 31, 1967*	*Increase or (decrease)*
Cash	$ 3,675	$13,239	$ 9,564
Trade accounts receivable	3,241	5,526	2,285
Sundry receivables	420	100	(320)
Cash value of life insurance	8,280	5,020	(3,260)
Supplies and prepaid expenses	983	1,232	249
Notes receivable—trade	2,050	3,140	1,090
Goodwill	5,000	1,311	(3,689)
Land	3,000	3,000	-0-
Building and equipment	32,338	38,738	6,400
Allowance for depreciation	(14,211)	(13,374)	837
	$44,776	$57,932	$13,156
Trade accounts payable	$ 2,680	$ 950	$ (1,730)
Notes payable—Smith	-0-	10,000	10,000
Bank loan	-0-	1,000	1,000
Installment equipment notes	-0-	7,600	7,600
Accrued expenses	1,406	1,972	566
Ryan, capital	12,372	12,370	(2)
Smith, capital	15,946	-0-	(15,946)
Thomas, capital	12,372	11,170	(1,202)
Doe, capital	-0-	12,870	12,870
	$44,776	$57,932	$13,156

Additional information

(1) Until February 15, 1967, Ryan, Smith, and Thomas divided profit and loss equally. On February 15, 1967, Smith withdrew from the partnership under an agreement that he was to accept $4,000 in cash and a partnership note for $10,000 in full settlement of his interest. The note is payable in installments of $2,000 each six months starting March 1, 1968. At the time of his withdrawal his drawings for the year to date had exceeded his $570 share of net profits by $420.

In connection with Smith's withdrawal, the entire Goodwill account was written off against capital and the insurance policy on Smith's life was canceled at its cash surrender value of $5,360.

(2) Ryan and Thomas continued as equal partners from February 15 until Doe was admitted to the firm on July 1, 1967, during which period profits amounted to $8,212. On July 1, 1967, Doe paid in $12,000 cash, for which he received a one-third interest in the assets and in profits and losses. The net assets at June 30, 1967, amounted to $26,622.

(3) Ryan withdrew $7,200 and Thomas $8,400 during the entire year. Doe withdrew $4,700 after he became a partner. Except for the transactions described, the only other entries in the partners' capital accounts were for division of profit and loss.

(4) During the last half of the year some equipment was sold for $1,000 cash. The original cost of this equipment was $3,700 and accumulated depreciation was $2,940. New equipment costing $10,100 was purchased. Installment notes of $8,000 due $200 per month were given in part payment.

(5) In December, $947 of accounts receivable were written off as uncollectible and obsolete supplies amounting to $369 were written off to expense. The notes receivable are due within one year and are believed to be collectible.

Instructions

You are to prepare a statement showing source and application of funds for the business for the year from January 1, 1967, to December 31, 1967. Also prepare a schedule in good form showing changes in working capital. Preparation of a work sheet is not required, but your principal computations should be presented in good form.

AICPA adapted

2-11 In conjunction with your regular year-end audit of Encino Motors, a partnership, you pointed out certain tax, financial, and legal advantages in operating the business as a corporation. Although the partnership has been extremely profitable, the partners have been finding it difficult to accumulate a sufficient equity in the business to enable them to borrow the large amounts of capital required. The partners have also been handicapped by the relative inflexibility of their personal wealth, most of which consists of their equity in the partnership.

The partners gave your recommendation serious consideration and after consulting with their attorneys decided to incorporate by issuing 100,000 shares of

$1 par value stock to be distributed to the partners in proportion to their capitals. The incorporation of Encino Motors, Inc., became effective July 1, 1968. An adjusted trial balance as of June 30, 1968, is presented below. General and administrative expenses include $2,000 of legal and other costs relating to incorporation; all other accounts are satisfactorily stated. The partners share profits as follows: Stanton, 40%; Thompson, 30%; Udall, 30%.

ENCINO MOTORS
Adjusted Trial Balance
June 30, 1968

Cash	*$ 65,400*	
Accounts receivable	*240,000*	
Less: Estimated uncollectibles		*$ 4,750*
Inventories (including supplies)	*310,100*	
Equipment	*120,000*	
Less: Accumulated depreciation—equipment		*32,000*
Building	*122,000*	
Less: Accumulated depreciation—buildings		*27,500*
Land	*40,500*	
Deferred moving costs	*2,500*	
Accounts payable		*175,600*
Accrued liabilities		*7,650*
Notes payable		*255,000*
Stanton, capital		*112,000*
Stanton, drawing	*8,200*	
Thompson, capital		*75,380*
Thompson, drawing	*11,500*	
Udall, capital		*89,920*
Udall, drawing	*7,600*	
Sales		*810,900*
Cost of sales	*534,700*	
Selling expense control	*85,200*	
General expense control	*43,000*	
	$1,590,700	*$1,590,700*

Instructions

a. Assuming that the partnership books are retained for use by the corporation, prepare all entries required to convert the partnership into a corporation. Show how the shares are divided among the partners.

b. Assuming that a new set of books is opened for the corporation, prepare all entries required on the books of the partnership after the income summary and drawing accounts have been closed.

c. Prepare all entries required on the books of the corporation, assuming that the valuation accounts for depreciable assets are carried forward to the corporation's books.

2-12 Ames, Bay, Call, and Day are partners in a firm which has been engaged in jobbing refrigerators and other household appliances.

The firm started operating on January 1, 1966. At that time Ames and Bay contributed $20,000 and $30,000, respectively, as capital for the business. On July 1, 1966, Call was admitted to the firm, paying in $25,000, and January 1, 1967, Day was admitted and paid in $12,000. No interest was to be allowed on the partners' investments. All partners devoted their entire effort to the business during the time they were partners and were to be compensated at the following annual rates: $8,000 each for Ames and Bay, $7,500 for Call, and $6,000 for Day. Because of the need for increased working capital, salary withdrawals were limited to $300 per month for each partner. The partnership agreement, as finally drawn up, provided for a split of the net profit and loss after salary allowances among the partners involved for each six months in the following ratios: Ames—3, Bay—3, Call—2, Day—2.

Formal books of account were not maintained but a running analysis of cash revealed the following facts:

	Six months ended			
	June 30, 1966	*Dec. 31, 1966*	*June 30, 1967*	*Dec. 31, 1967*
Collections on sales made in the six-month period ended:				
June 30, 1966	*$36,600*	*$ 6,200*	*$ 4,100*	*$ 2,500*
Dec. 31, 1966		*124,200*	*34,500*	*8,200*
June 30, 1967			*192,500*	*53,900*
Dec. 31, 1967				*347,300*
Payments on purchases	*65,871*	*152,382*	*185,699*	*338,546*
Rent and other fixed costs	*5,698*	*6,550*	*10,891*	*12,141*
Other expenses	*2,620*	*14,120*	*22,620*	*23,341*
Withdrawals	*3,600*	*5,400*	*7,200*	*7,200*

Unpaid customers' accounts considered collectible at December 31, 1967, by period of origin, were:

Sales made during six months ended	*Amount*
June 30, 1966	*$ 1,600*
Dec. 31, 1966	*3,100*
June 30, 1967	*8,600*
Dec. 31, 1967	*26,700*

A physical inventory on December 31, 1967, showed that the merchandise inventory on hand at cost, including that covered by unpaid invoices of $14,285, amounted to $83,084.

The partners have agreed:

(1) That "rents and other fixed costs" are to be divided equally over the four six-month periods.

(2) That the cost of merchandise sold during these periods may be assumed to have been 70, 75, 80, and 80%, respectively, of sales.

(3) That any merchandise "loss" resulting from the application of the above amounts and percentages may be regarded as a proper addition to "other expenses."

(4) That "other expenses" are to be spread over the four periods in proportion to sales.

Instructions

a. Prepare a summary operating statement for each six-month period of the firm's existence.

b. Prepare an analysis of changes in partners' capital accounts for each six-month period.

c. Prepare a balance sheet at December 31, 1967.

AICPA adapted

2-13 The partnerships of Kay & Lee and Mann & Neal started in business on July 1, 1964; each partnership owns one retail appliance store. It was agreed as of June 30, 1967, to combine the partnerships to form a new partnership to be known as Four Square Company.

The June 30, 1967, post-closing trial balances of the partnerships were as follows:

	Kay & Lee Trial balance June 30, 1967		*Mann & Neal Trial balance June 30, 1967*	
Cash	*$ 20,000*		*$ 15,000*	
Accounts receivable	*100,000*		*150,000*	
Allowance for doubtful accounts		*$ 2,000*		*$ 6,000*
Merchandise inventory	*175,000*		*119,000*	
Land	*25,000*		*35,000*	
Buildings and equipment	*80,000*		*125,000*	
Allowance for depreciation		*24,000*		*61,000*
Prepaid expenses	*5,000*		*7,000*	
Accounts payable		*40,000*		*60,000*
Notes payable		*70,000*		*75,000*
Accrued expenses		*30,000*		*45,000*
Kay, capital		*95,000*		
Lee, capital		*144,000*		
Mann, capital				*65,000*
Neal, capital				*139,000*
	$405,000	*$405,000*	*$451,000*	*$451,000*

The following additional information is available:

(1) The profit- and loss-sharing ratios for the former partnerships were 40% to Kay and 60% to Lee, and 30% to Mann and 70% to Neal. The profit- and loss-

sharing ratio for the new partnership will be Kay, 20%; Lee, 30%; Mann, 15%; and Neal, 35%.

(2) The opening capital ratios for the new partnership are to be the same as the profit- and loss-sharing ratios for the new partnership. The capital to be assigned to Kay & Lee will total $225,000. Any cash settlements among the partners arising from capital account adjustments will be a private matter and will not be recorded on the partnership books.

(3) The partners agreed that the allowance for bad debts for the new partnership is to be 3% of the accounts receivable balances.

(4) The opening inventory of the new partnership is to be valued by the fifo method. The inventory of Kay & Lee was valued by the fifo method and the Mann & Neal inventory was valued by the lifo method. The lifo inventory represents 85% of its fifo value.

(5) Depreciation is to be computed by the double-declining-balance method with a 10-year life for the depreciable assets. Depreciation for three years is to be accumulated in the opening balance of the Allowance for Depreciation account. Kay & Lee computed depreciation by the straight-line method, and Mann & Neal used the double-declining-balance method. All assets were obtained on July 1, 1964.

(6) After the books were closed, an unrecorded merchandise purchase of $4,000 by Mann & Neal was discovered. The merchandise had been sold by June 30, 1967.

(7) The accounts of Kay & Lee include a vacation pay accrual. It was agreed that Mann & Neal should make a similar accrual for their ten employees, who will receive a two-week vacation at $100 per employee per week.

Instructions

a. Prepare an eight-column work sheet to determine the opening balances of a new partnership after giving effect to the above information. Also prepare formal journal entries with explanations for each adjustment or combining entry. Supporting computations, including the computation of goodwill, should be in good form. The following column headings are suggested for the work sheet: Kay & Lee, Trial Balance, June 30, 1967; Mann & Neal, Trial Balance, June 30, 1967; Adjusting & Combining Entries; and Four Square Company, Beginning Balances.

b. Prepare a schedule computing the cash to be exchanged between Kay & Lee, and between Mann & Neal in settlement of the affairs of each original partnership.

3 PARTNERSHIPS: LIQUIDATION

The meaning of liquidation

The liquidation of a partnership means winding up the business, usually by selling the assets, paying the liabilities, and distributing the remaining cash to the partners. In some cases, the business may be sold as a unit, possibly with the purchaser agreeing to assume the liabilities; in other cases, particularly for unsuccessful firms, the assets are sold on a piecemeal basis and most or all of the cash received must be used to pay creditors. A business which has ended normal operations and is in the process of converting its assets into cash and making settlements with its creditors is said to be *in liquidation* or in the process of being liquidated. This process of liquidation may be completed quickly or it may require several months or years, depending upon the amount and kinds of assets to be disposed of and the ability to pay creditors in full.

The term *liquidation* is also used in a narrower sense to mean the payment of liabilities; in this chapter, however, we shall use it only in the broader sense of breaking up and discontinuing the business of a partnership. Another term commonly used by a business in process of liquidation is *realization,* which means the conversion of assets into cash.

When the decision is made that a partnership is to be liquidated, the books should be adjusted and closed, and the net income or loss for the final period of operations entered in the capital accounts of the partners.

The liquidation process usually begins with the sale of assets. The gains or losses from conversion of assets should be divided among the partners in the profit and loss ratio and entered in their capital accounts. The amounts shown as their respective equities at this point are the basis for settlement. However, before any payment to partners, all outside creditors must be paid in full. If the cash obtained through conversion of assets is insufficient to pay liabilities in full, any unpaid creditor may act to enforce collection from the personal resources of any partner, regardless of whether that partner has a debit or credit balance in his capital account. As pointed out in the preceding chapter, the partnership is viewed as an entity for many purposes such as changes in partnership personnel, but it cannot use the shield of a separate entity to protect partners personally against the claims of partnership creditors.

Partnerships are of course not the only form of business subject to liquidation. Corporations, sole proprietorships, and estates are examples of other economic units which may undergo the process of liquidation.

Distribution of loss or gain

The underlying theme in accounting for the liquidation of a partnership may be briefly stated: *Distribute the loss or gain from the sale of assets before distributing the cash.* As assets are sold, the loss or gain realized is apportioned among the partners' capital accounts in the established ratio for sharing profit or loss. The amount of cash, if any, which a partner is entitled to receive in liquidation cannot be determined until his capital account has been increased or decreased by his share of the gain or loss from disposal of the assets. Strictly interpreted, this reasoning might indicate that no cash can safely be distributed to a partner until after all the assets have been sold since the total gain or loss will not be known until the conversion of all assets has been completed. In this chapter we shall be concerned only with liquidations in which the realization of assets is completed before any payments are made to partners. In Chapter 4 we shall consider liquidation in installments; that is, payments to partners after some of the assets have been sold and the liabilities paid but with final gain or loss from sale of the remaining assets not yet known. The installment payments to partners are computed by a method which provides a safeguard against overpayment. Liquidation in installments may clearly be demanded when the realization of assets requires a long period of time.

An important service by the accountant to a partnership in liquidation is to determine proper distribution of cash or other assets to individual partners after the liabilities have been paid. The partners may of course choose to receive certain assets, such as automobiles or furniture, in kind rather than to convert such property into cash. Regardless of whether cash or other assets are being distributed to partners, it is imperative to follow the basic rule that no distribution of assets be made until after all losses and gains have been allocated to the capital accounts. Failure to follow the basic rule may result in overpayment of a partner. If the partner is unable to return the excess payment, the person who authorized the improper distribution may become personally liable for the loss forced on the other partners by his error.

Distribution of cash

Traditionally, accounting textbooks have listed the proper order for distribution of cash as (1) payment of creditors in full, (2) payment of partners' loan accounts, and (3) payment of partners' capital accounts. The indicated priority of partners' loans over partners' capitals appears to be a legal fiction. Although the Uniform Partnership Act states that partners' loans rank ahead of partners' capitals in order of payment, this rule is nullified for all practical purposes by an established legal doctrine called the *right of offset*. If a partner has a debit balance in his capital account (or even a potential debit balance depending on possible future losses), any credit balance in his loan account must be offset against the deficiency or potential deficiency in his capital account. Because of the right of offset, the total amount of cash received by a partner during the liquidation process will always be the same as if his loan to the partnership had been recorded as an additional investment in his capital account. Furthermore, the existence of a partner's loan account will not advance the time of any payment during the liquidation. Consequently, in setting up a work sheet or statement of liquidation, the accountant may prefer to reduce the number of columns and simplify the statement by combining the amount of a partner's loan with the amount shown in his capital account. The statement of liquidation will then include only one column for each partner; the top figure in the column will be the total interest of the partner at the beginning of the liquidation. A slight variation of this procedure is to use one column for each partner, but to list therein first the amount of the capital account, secondly, the amount of the loan account, and thirdly the total interest of the partner. The distribution of cash will not be changed by combining these two elements of a partner's total interest in the firm.

Combining the capital and loan accounts of a partner on the statement of liquidation does not imply merging these accounts in the ledger. Separate ledger accounts for a partner's capital and for his loan to the firm should be maintained to provide a clear permanent record of the terms under which funds were provided by the partners. Separate accounts are especially useful if interest is payable on loan balances.

Determining the settlement with each partner

The amount which each partner receives from the liquidation of a partnership will be equal to (1) the capital he invested in the business, whether recorded in a capital account or in a loan account; (2) his share of operating net income or loss minus his drawings; and (3) his share of gain or loss from the sale of assets in liquidation.

In other words, each partner will receive in the settlement the amount of his equity in the business. The amount of a partner's equity is increased by the positive factors of investing capital and sharing in profits; it is decreased by the negative factors of drawings and sharing in losses. If the negative factors are the greater, the partner will have a capital deficiency (a debit balance in his capital account), and he must pay in to the partnership the amount of such deficiency. Failure to make good a capital deficiency by payment to the firm would mean that the partner had not lived up to the partnership agreement for sharing profit and loss. This would cause his fellow partners to bear more than their contractual share of losses, or, stated conversely, to receive less in settlement than their equities in the business.

Division of gain or loss during liquidation

The profit or loss ratio used during the operation of the partnership is also applicable to the gains and losses during liquidation unless the partners have made a specific agreement to the contrary. A partnership is not dissolved because of the decision to cease operations; the agreement for division of profit or loss therefore continues in force.

Accountants are agreed that the net income or net loss of a business cannot be measured with complete accuracy except over the entire life span of the enterprise. Annual or quarterly determinations of net income are merely approximations because of the estimates they necessarily involve on such matters as the useful life of plant and equipment and the collectibility of receivables. Errors in these estimates affect the periodic net income divided among the partners, but when the business is liquidated the gains or losses from conversion of assets will tend to correct or counterbalance prior errors in determination of net income. For example, if insufficient provision for bad debts was made during the period of operations, the net income was thereby overstated. However, the receivables are overvalued and a loss will be incurred on them during the liquidation process. Consequently, the profit or loss resulting from the liquidation of a partnership should logically be divided among the partners in the same ratio used in dividing net income during the operating period of the partnership's existence.

When the gain or loss from liquidation is divided among the partners in accordance with the profit and loss ratio, the final balances in the partners' capital and loan accounts will be equal to the cash available for distribution to them. Payments are then made in the amounts of their respective interests in the business.

Equity of each partner sufficient to absorb his share of loss on realization

Assume that A and B, who share profit and loss equally, decide to liquidate their partnership. A condensed balance sheet prepared just prior to liquidation is as follows:

A AND B
Balance Sheet
June 30, 19__

Assets		*Liabilities & Partners' Equities*	
Cash	$10,000	Liabilities	$20,000
Other assets	75,000	B, loan	20,000
		A, capital	40,000
		B, capital	5,000
	$85,000		$85,000

As a first step in the liquidation, the noncash assets with a book value of $75,000 are sold for cash of $35,000, thus creating a loss of $40,000 to be shared equally by A and B. Since B's capital account is only $5,000, it will be necessary to exercise the right of offset by transferring $15,000 from his loan account to his capital account. The following liquidation statement shows the division of the loss between the partners, the payment of creditors, and the distribution of the remaining cash to the partners. The heading of the statement will usually show a period of time, although in rare cases the sale of the assets and distribution of cash might be completed on a single day.

A AND B
Statement of Partnership Liquidation
July, 19__

	Assets		Liabilities	B, loan	Partners' capitals	
	Cash	Noncash			A	B
Profit and loss ratio					50%	50%
Balances before liquidation	$10,000	$75,000	$20,000	$20,000	$40,000	$ 5,000
Sale of assets at a loss	35,000	(75,000)			(20,000)	(20,000)
Balances	$45,000		$20,000	$20,000	$20,000	$(15,000)
Payment to creditors	(20,000)		(20,000)			
Balances	$25,000			$20,000	$20,000	$(15,000)
Offset capital deficit of B against loan account				(15,000)		15,000
Balances	$25,000			$ 5,000	$20,000	
Payment to partners	(25,000)			(5,000)	(20,000)	

To demonstrate that the statutory priority of a partner's loan account has no significance in determining either the amount of cash a partner receives in liquidation or the timing of his payment, let us now present a second illustration of the liquidation of the firm of A and B. All data are exactly the same as before, but as a matter of convenience in preparing the schedule we shall add together B's loan account of $20,000 and his capital account of $5,000 at the top of the statement, thus showing a single equity figure of $25,000 for B.

A AND B
Statement of Partnership Liquidation
July, 19__

	Assets		Liabilities	Partners' capitals	
	Cash	Noncash		A	B
Profit and loss ratio				50%	50%
Balances before liquidation	$10,000	$75,000	$20,000	$40,000	$25,000
Sale of assets at a loss	35,000	(75,000)		(20,000)	(20,000)
Balances	$45,000		$20,000	$20,000	$ 5,000
Payment to creditors	(20,000)		(20,000)		
Balances	$25,000			$20,000	$ 5,000
Payment to partners	(25,000)			(20,000)	(5,000)

Note that in both the preceding illustrations, A received a settlement of $20,000 and B a settlement of $5,000. Neither received payment until after creditors had been paid in full. Since at this point the only asset was cash of $25,000, it is reasonable to assume that checks to A and B for $20,000 and $5,000, respectively, were written and delivered to the partners at the same time. Which check was written first is clearly of no practical importance. Some accountants, however, in preparing the schedule would show the payment to B occurring just prior to the payment to A because B's equity was in the form of a loan account. Such a priority is an empty gesture since under no circumstances will a partner receive any more cash or be paid any sooner during the liquidation process if his investment is partially in the form of a loan account.

In succeeding illustrations, therefore, we shall not show a partner's loan account in a separate column of the statement of liquidation. Whenever a partner's loan account is encountered, it may be combined with the partner's capital account in scheduling the steps of the liquidation process.

Equity of one partner not sufficient to absorb his share of loss on realization

In this case, the loss on realization of assets when distributed in the profit and loss ratio creates a debit balance in the capital account of one of the partners. It may be assumed that the partner with a debit balance has no loan account, or that the total of his capital account and loan account combined is less than his share of the loss on realization. To fulfill his agreement to share a given percentage of partnership profit and loss, the partner must pay in to the firm sufficient cash to eliminate his capital deficiency. If he is unable to do so, his debit balance must be absorbed by the other partners as an additional loss to be shared in the same proportion as they have previously shared profit and loss among themselves. Assume the following balance sheet for D, E, and F just prior to liquidation.

D, E, AND F
Balance Sheet
June 30, 19__

Assets		*Liabilities & Partners' Capitals*	
Cash	$ 20,000	Liabilities	$ 30,000
Other assets	80,000	D, capital	40,000
		E, capital	21,000
		F, capital	9,000
	$100,000		$100,000

The division of profit and loss is D 20%, E 40%, and F 40%. The other assets carried at $80,000 on the balance sheet are sold for $50,000 cash, resulting in a loss of $30,000 to be divided among the partners. Partner F is charged with 40% of this loss, or $12,000, which creates a debit balance of $3,000 in his capital account. In the following statement of liquidation, it is assumed that F pays in $3,000. If he had not done so, an additional loss of $3,000 would have been divided between D and E.

D, E, AND F
Statement of Partnership Liquidation
July, 19__

	Assets		Liabilities	Partners' capitals		
	Cash	Noncash		D	E	F
Profit and loss ratio				20%	40%	40%
Balances before liquidation	$20,000	$80,000	$30,000	$40,000	$21,000	$ 9,000
Sale of assets at a loss	50,000	(80,000)		(6,000)	(12,000)	(12,000)
Balances	$70,000		$30,000	$34,000	$ 9,000	$(3,000)
Payment to creditors	(30,000)		(30,000)			
Balances	$40,000			$34,000	$ 9,000	$(3,000)
Cash paid in by F	3,000					3,000
Balances	$43,000			$34,000	$ 9,000	
Payments to partners	(43,000)			(34,000)	(9,000)	

Next let us change one condition of the preceding illustration by assuming that Partner F was not immediately able to pay in his $3,000 debt to the partnership indicated by the debit balance in his capital account. If the cash on hand after payment of creditors is to be distributed to D and E without waiting to determine the collectibility of the $3,000 claim against F, the statement of liquidation will appear as follows:

D, E, AND F
Statement of Partnership Liquidation
July, 19__

	Assets		Liabilities	Partners' capitals		
	Cash	Noncash		D	E	F
Profit and loss ratio				20%	40%	40%
Balances before liquidation	$20,000	$80,000	$30,000	$40,000	$21,000	$ 9,000
Sale of assets at a loss	50,000	(80,000)		(6,000)	(12,000)	(12,000)
Balances	$70,000		$30,000	$34,000	$ 9,000	$(3,000)
Payment to creditors	(30,000)		(30,000)			
Balances	$40,000			$34,000	$ 9,000	$(3,000)
Payment to partners	(40,000)			(33,000)	(7,000)	
Balances				$ 1,000	$ 2,000	$(3,000)

The cash payments of $33,000 to D and $7,000 to E leave each partner with a sufficient credit balance to absorb his share of the additional loss if F fails to make good the $3,000 debit balance in his capital account. The profit and loss shares were 20% for D and 40% for E; consequently, the possible additional loss of $3,000 would be charged to them in the proportion of ($20/60 \times \$3,000$) or

$1,000 to D, and (40/60 × $3,000) or $2,000 to E. The payment of the $40,000 cash available to partners is therefore divided between them in a manner that pays D down to a balance of $1,000 in his capital account and pays E down to a balance of $2,000.

If F later pays in the $3,000 he owes to the partnership, this amount will be divided by paying $1,000 to D and $2,000 to E. The preceding statement of liquidation could be completed as follows:

	Cash	D	E	F
Balances (as above)		*$1,000*	*$2,000*	*$(3,000)*
Cash paid in by F	*$3,000*			*3,000*
Payments to partners	*(3,000)*	*(1,000)*	*(2,000)*	

On the other hand, if the $3,000 due from F is determined to be uncollectible, the statement of liquidation would be completed by showing the write-off of F's debit balance as an additional loss borne by D and E as follows:

	D	E	F
Balances as above	*$1,000*	*$2,000*	*$(3,000)*
Additional loss from noncollection of debit balance from F	*(1,000)*	*(2,000)*	*3,000*

Equities of two partners not sufficient to absorb their shares of loss on realization

We have already observed that inability of a partner to make good a debit balance in his capital account causes an additional loss to the other partners. A partner may have sufficient capital or combination of capital and loan accounts to absorb his direct share of loss on the realization of assets, but not a sufficient equity to absorb his share of the additional actual or potential loss caused by inability to collect the debit balance in another partner's capital account. In brief, one capital deficiency if not collectible may cause a second capital deficiency, which may or may not be collectible.

Assume that J, K, L, and M are partners sharing profit and loss in the ratio of 10%, 20%, 30%, and 40%. Their capital accounts are as shown in the statement of liquidation on page 82. The assets are converted into cash at a loss of $80,000, and creditors are paid in full. Cash of $20,000 is available for distribution to the partners. In making this distribution, the guiding principle is to pay each partner an amount equal to the excess of his capital account over any possible charges against him. In other words, pay a partner's capital account down to the level necessary to absorb any additional losses which may be charged against him because of the uncollectibility of debit balances owed by other partners.

J, K, L, AND M
Statement of Partnership Liquidation
July, 19__

	Assets		Liabilities	Partners' capitals			
	Cash	Noncash		J	K	L	M
Profit and loss ratio				10%	20%	30%	40%
Balances before liquidation	$ 20,000	$200,000	$120,000	$30,000	$32,000	$30,000	$ 8,000
Sale of assets at a loss	120,000	(200,000)		(8,000)	(16,000)	(24,000)	(32,000)
Balances	$140,000		$120,000	$22,000	$16,000	$ 6,000	$(24,000)
Payment to creditors	(120,000)		(120,000)				
Balances	$ 20,000			$22,000	$16,000	$ 6,000	$(24,000)
Payment to partners (Schedule A)	(20,000)			(16,000)	(4,000)		
Balances				$ 6,000	$12,000	$ 6,000	$(24,000)

J, K, L, AND M
Schedule A
Computation of cash payments to partners

	Partners' capitals			
	J	K	L	M
Profit and loss ratio	10%	20%	30%	40%
Capital balance before distributing cash to partners	$22,000	$16,000	$ 6,000	$(24,000)
Additional loss to J, K, and L if M's debit balance is uncollectible (ratio of 10:20:30)	(4,000)	(8,000)	(12,000)	24,000
Balances	$18,000	$ 8,000	$ (6,000)	
Additional loss to J and K if L's debit balance is uncollectible (ratio of 10:20)	(2,000)	(4,000)	6,000	
Amounts which may safely be paid to partners	$16,000	$ 4,000		

The preceding statement of liquidation and its supporting schedule show that the $20,000 of cash in hand can safely be distributed $16,000 to J and $4,000 to K. If the debit balance in M's capital account proves uncollectible, the additional loss to be divided among the other three partners will cause L's capital account to change from a $6,000 credit balance to a $6,000 debit balance. He is therefore not eligible to receive a cash payment. If this debit balance in L's account proves uncollectible, the balances remaining in the capital accounts of J and K after the cash payment indicated above will be exactly the amounts needed to absorb the additional loss shifted from L's account.

Partnership insolvent but partners personally solvent

If a partnership is insolvent, at least one and perhaps all of the partners will have debit balances in their capital accounts. In any event the total amount of the debit balances will exceed the total of the credit balances. If the partner or partners with a capital deficiency pay in the required amount, the partnership will have funds to pay its liabilities in full. However, the creditors may demand payment from any partner individually, regardless of whether his capital account shows a debit or credit balance. In terms of relationships with creditors, the partnership is not a separate entity. A partner who personally makes payment to partnership creditors of course receives a credit to his capital account. As an illustration of an insolvent partnership with partners personally solvent, assume that N, O, and P, who share profit and loss equally, present the following condensed balance sheet just prior to liquidation of the business.

The other assets shown in the balance sheet at a book value of $85,000 are sold for $40,000 cash, which causes a loss of $45,000 to be divided equally among the partners. The total cash of $55,000 is paid to the creditors, which leaves

N, O, AND P
Balance Sheet
June 30, 19__

Assets		*Liabilities & Partners' Capitals*	
Cash	$ 15,000	*Liabilities*	$ 65,000
Other assets	85,000	*N, capital*	18,000
		O, capital	10,000
		P, capital	7,000
	$100,000		$100,000

unpaid liabilities of $10,000. Partner N has a credit balance of $3,000 after absorbing his one-third share of the loss on realization. Partners O and P owe the partnership $5,000 and $8,000, respectively. If O and P pay in the amounts of their debit balances, the partnership will use $10,000 of this new cash to pay the remaining liabilities and will distribute $3,000 to N in settlement of his equity. These events are portrayed in the following statement of liquidation.

N, O, AND P
Statement of Partnership Liquidation
July, 19__

	Assets		*Liabilities*	*Partners' capitals*		
	Cash	*Noncash*		*N*	*O*	*P*
Profit and loss ratio				⅓	⅓	⅓
Balance before liquidation	$15,000	$85,000	$65,000	$18,000	$10,000	$ 7,000
Sale of assets at a loss	40,000	(85,000)		(15,000)	(15,000)	(15,000)
Balances	$55,000		$65,000	$ 3,000	$ (5,000)	$ (8,000)
Partial payment to creditors	(55,000)		(55,000)			
Balances			$10,000	$ 3,000	$ (5,000)	$ (8,000)
Cash paid in by O and P	$13,000				5,000	8,000
Balances	$13,000		$10,000	$ 3,000		
Final payment to creditors	(10,000)		(10,000)			
Balances	$ 3,000			$ 3,000		
Payment to N	(3,000)			(3,000)		

Assume that there was some delay in collecting the debit balances from O and P and during this period the creditors demanded and received payment of their $10,000 in claims from Partner N. This payment by N would cause his equity to rise from $3,000 to $13,000. When O and P paid in their debit balance totaling $13,000, this amount of cash would then go to N in settlement of the credit balance in his capital account.

Another alternative is that creditors might collect the final $10,000 due them directly from O or P. Payments by these partners to creditors would increase their equities and eliminate or reduce their indebtedness to the firm. So long as we assume that the partners with debit balances make good their capital deficiencies either by payment to the partnership or directly to partnership creditors, the results are the same. Creditors will be paid in full and partners will share losses as provided in the partnership agreement.

Partnership insolvent and partners personally insolvent

In the preceding illustration of an insolvent partnership, we assumed that the partners were personally solvent and therefore able to make good their capital deficiencies. Now we are ready to consider an insolvent partnership in which one or more of the partners are personally insolvent. This situation raises a question as to the relative rights of two groups of creditors: (1) those persons who extended credit to the partnership, and (2) those persons who extended credit to the partners as individuals. The relative rights of these two groups of creditors are governed by the legal rules of *marshaling of assets*. These legal rules provide that assets of the partnership are first available to creditors of the partnership, and that assets owned individually by a partner are first available to his personal creditors. After the debts of the partnership have been paid in full, if any assets remain in the firm, the creditors of an individual partner have a claim against the firm assets to the extent of the partner's credit balance.

After the personal creditors of a partner have been paid in full from his personal assets, any remaining assets are available to creditors of the partnership regardless of whether the partner's capital account shows a credit or debit balance. Such claims by creditors of the partnership are of course permitted only when these creditors are unable to obtain payment from the partnership.

To illustrate the relative rights of creditors of an insolvent partnership and personal creditors of an insolvent partner, assume that R, S, and T, who share profit and loss equally, have the following balance sheet just prior to liquidation:

R, S, AND T
Balance Sheet
June 30, 19__

Assets		Liabilities & Partners' Capitals	
Cash	$ 10,000	Liabilities	$ 60,000
Other assets	100,000	R, capital	5,000
		S, capital	15,000
		T, capital	30,000
	$110,000		$110,000

Assume also that the partners as individuals have the following assets and liabilities apart from their equities in the partnership:

	Assets	Liabilities
R	$100,000	$25,000
S	50,000	50,000
T	5,000	60,000

The conversion of partnership assets into cash results in a loss of $60,000, as shown in the following statement of liquidation.

R, S, AND T
Statement of Partnership Liquidation
July, 19__

	Assets		Liabilities	Partners' capitals		
	Cash	Noncash		R	S	T
Profit and loss ratio				⅓	⅓	⅓
Balances before liquidation	$10,000	$100,000	$60,000	$ 5,000	$15,000	$30,000
Sale of assets at a loss	40,000	(100,000)		(20,000)	(20,000)	(20,000)
Balances	$50,000		$60,000	$(15,000)	$ (5,000)	$10,000
Payment to creditors	(50,000)		(50,000)			
Balances			$10,000	$(15,000)	$ (5,000)	$10,000

The creditors of the partnership have received all the firm's assets and still have unpaid claims of $10,000. They cannot collect from S or T personally because the personal resources of these two partners are insufficient or just sufficient to meet their personal liabilities. However, the partnership creditors can collect the $10,000 in full from R who is personally solvent. By chance, R has a debit balance in his capital account, but this is of no concern to the creditors. They could collect in full from any partner who had sufficient personal resources regardless of whether his capital account showed a debit or credit balance. The liquidation statement shown above is now continued to show the payment by R personally of the final $10,000 due to partnership creditors. Since our assumptions about R's personal finances showed that he had $100,000 of assets and only $25,000 in liabilities, he is also able to pay into the firm the additional $5,000 needed to make good his capital deficiency. This $5,000 of cash is promptly paid to partner T, the only partner with a credit balance.

	Cash	Liabilities	Partners' capitals		
			R	S	T
Balances		$10,000	$(15,000)	$(5,000)	$10,000
Payment by R to partnership creditors		(10,000)	10,000		
Balances			$ (5,000)	$(5,000)	$10,000
Additional investment by R	$5,000		5,000		
Balances	$5,000			$(5,000)	$10,000
Payment to T	(5,000)				(5,000)
Balances				$(5,000)	$ 5,000

The continued statement of partnership liquidation now shows that S owes $5,000 to the firm; however, his personal assets of $50,000 are exactly equal to his personal liabilities of $50,000. Under the Uniform Partnership Act, all the personal assets of S will go to his personal creditors, therefore the $5,000 debit balance in his capital account represents an additional loss to be shared equally between R and T. To conclude the liquidation, R, who is personally solvent, will be required to contribute $2,500 to the partnership and the amount will go to T or to his personal creditors since T is hopelessly insolvent. These payments are shown below in concluding the statement of liquidation.

	Cash	Partners' capitals		
		R	*S*	*T*
Balances carried forward			*$(5,000)*	*$5,000*
Write-off debit balance from S as uncollectible		*$(2,500)*	*5,000*	*(2,500)*
Balances		*$(2,500)*		*$2,500*
Cash paid in by R	*$2,500*	*2,500*		
Balances	*$2,500*			*$2,500*
Payment to T	*(2,500)*			*(2,500)*

The final results of the liquidation show that the partnership creditors received payment in full because of the personal financial strength of partner R. Since R was personally solvent, his personal creditors could also collect in full. The personal creditors of S were paid in full, thereby exhausting his personal assets; he failed to make good the $5,000 debit balance in his capital account, thus shifting an additional loss to his partners. The personal creditors of T received all his personal assets and also $7,500 from the partnership, representing T's equity in the firm. However, T's personal creditors were able to collect a total of only $12,500 on their claims of $60,000.

Under the common law, the final stages of the dissolution would be handled somewhat differently. Partner S had a $5,000 debit balance in his capital account. This capital deficiency of $5,000 by S would have ranked equally with his indebtedness to personal creditors. He would then have owed total debts of $55,000, compared with personal assets of $50,000. A pro rata settlement by S would have made 50/55 of $5,000, or $4,545, available to the partnership and would have forced a loss of this amount on his personal creditors. This contribution to the partnership by S would have reduced the additional loss thrown on his partners by $2,272.50 each. Consequently, the personal creditors of T, under the common law rules, would have received $2,272.50 more than if the settlement were made under the Uniform Partnership Act.

Questions

1. Adams and Barnes have capital accounts of $60,000 and $80,000, respectively. In addition, Adams has made a non-interest-bearing loan of $20,000 to the firm. Adams and Barnes now decide to liquidate their partnership. What priority or advantage, if any, will Adams enjoy in the liquidation with respect to his loan account?

2. State briefly the procedure to be followed in a partnership liquidation when a debit balance arises in the capital account of one of the partners.

3. In the liquidation of the partnership of Baynes, Cross, and David, the sale of the assets resulted in a loss which produced the following balances in the capital accounts: Baynes, $25,000 credit; Cross, $12,500 credit; and David, $5,000 debit. The partners shared profits and losses in a 5:3:2 ratio. All liabilities have been paid and $32,500 of cash is available for distribution to partners. However, it is not possible to determine at present whether David, who is ill, will be able to make good his $5,000 capital deficiency. Can the cash on hand be distributed without waiting to determine the collectibility of the amount due from David? Explain.

4. After disposing of all assets and distributing all cash to creditors, the partnership of A, B, and C still had accounts payable of $12,000. The capital account of partner A showed a credit balance of $16,000 and that of B a credit balance of $2,000. Creditors of the firm demanded payment from A personally, but he replied that the three partners shared profits and losses equally and had begun operations with equal capital investments. A, therefore, offered to pay the creditors one-third of their claims and no more. What is your opinion of the position taken by A? What is the balance in C's capital account? What entry, if any, should be made on the partnership books for a payment by A personally to the partnership creditors?

5. In the partnership of Jones, Kendall, and Littrell, Jones serves as general manager. The partnership agreement provides that Jones is entitled to an annual salary of $12,000, payable in 12 equal monthly installments, and that remaining profits or losses shall be divided equally. On June 30, the firm suspended operations and began liquidation. Because of a shortage of working capital, Jones had not drawn his salary for the last two months of operation. How should his claim for $2,000 of "unpaid wages" be handled in the liquidation of the partnership?

6. Liquidation of the firm of A and B left partner B with a debit balance of $13,000 in his capital account and a credit balance of $15,000 in his loan account. A has a credit balance of $6,000 in his capital account. All assets have been realized and all liabilities have been paid, but the partnership is contingently liable on a $5,000 note receivable discounted at the bank. The note has one month to run before maturity. How much cash does the partnership have? When and how should the distribution of cash be made to the partners?

7. Grant and Hall are partners who share profits and losses in a 60:40 ratio. They have decided to liquidate their partnership. A portion of the assets have been sold but other assets with a book value of $32,000 must still be disposed of. All liabilities have been paid, and cash of $20,000 is available for distribution to partners. The capital accounts show balances of $30,000 for Grant and $22,000 for Hall. How should the cash be divided? Explain the basis used.

8. A and B are partners and have agreed to share profits and losses equally. State your reasons in support of one of the following methods of dividing losses incurred in liquidation of the partnership.
   a. Profit and loss ratio
   b. Ratio of capital balances

Short cases for analysis

3-1 Wayne and Flint formed a partnership and agreed to share profits and losses equally. Although they began business with equal capitals, Wayne made more frequent withdrawals than Flint, with the result that his capital account became the smaller of the two. The partners have now decided to liquidate their business at June 30; on that date the books were closed and financial statements prepared. The balance sheet showed a capital account for Wayne of $40,000 and Flint's capital as $60,000. In addition the balance sheet showed that Flint had made a $10,000 loan to the partnership.

The liquidation of the partnership was managed by Wayne because Flint was hospitalized by an auto accident on July 1, the day after regular operations were suspended. The procedures followed by Wayne were as follows: First, to sell all the assets at the best prices obtainable; second, to pay the creditors in full; third, to pay Flint's loan account; and fourth to divide all remaining cash between Flint and himself in the 40:60 ratio represented by their capital accounts.

When Flint was released from the hospital on July 5, Wayne met him and informed him that through good luck and hard work, he had been able to find buyers for the assets and complete the liquidation during the five days of Flint's hospitalization. As the first step in the liquidation, Wayne delivered two cashier's checks to Flint at the moment of his release from the hospital. One check was for $10,000 in payment of the loan account; the other was in settlement of Flint's capital account.

Instructions

a. Do you approve the procedures followed in the liquidation? Explain fully.

b. Assume that the liquidation procedures followed resulted in the payment of $24,000 to Flint in addition to the payment of his loan account in full. What was the amount of gain or loss on the liquidation? If you believe that other methods should have been followed in the liquidation, explain how much more or less Flint would have received under the procedure you recommend.

3-2 In reply to a question as to how settlement with partners should be made during liquidation of a partnership, Student A made the following statement:

"Accounting records are usually based on cost and reflect the 'going-concern' concept. When a business is broken up, it is often necessary to sell the assets for a fraction of their book value. Consequently, a partner usually receives in liquidation a settlement far below the amount of his equity in the business."

Student B offered the following comment:

"I agree fully with what A has said, but he might have gone further and added that no payment should ever be made to any partner until all the assets of the partnership have been sold and all creditors have been paid in full. Until these steps have been completed, the residual amount available for distribution to partners is unknown, and therefore any earlier payment to a partner might have to be returned. If he were unable to return such amount, the person who authorized the payment might be held personally responsible."

Student C made the following statement:

"In the liquidation of a partnership, each partner receives the amount of his equity in the business; no more and no less. As to timing of payments, it is often helpful to a partner to receive a partial payment before the assets are sold and creditors are paid. If proper precautions are taken, such early partial payments are quite satisfactory."

Instructions

Evaluate the statements made by each student.

3-3 The partnership of Bell, Cave, and Dart is insolvent and in process of liquidation under the Uniform Partnership Act. After conversion of the assets into cash and distribution of the loss equally among the three partners, their positions are as follows:

	Equity in partnership	*Personal financial condition other than equity in partnership*	
		Assets	*Liabilities*
Bell	$20,000	$110,000	$45,000
Cave	(21,000)	20,000	40,000
Dart	(55,000)	55,000	35,000

Explain the prospects for collection by (a) the creditors of the partnership, (b) the personal creditors of each partner, and (c) Partner Bell from his copartners. Starting from the assumption that Bell has a $20,000 equity in the firm, what is the amount of loss he should sustain?

Problems

3-4 The balance sheet of the Utility Equipment Co., a partnership owned by X, Y, and Z, appeared as follows immediately prior to liquidation:

UTILITY EQUIPMENT CO.
Balance Sheet
December 31, 1967

Cash	$ 20,000	*Liabilities*	$ 50,000
Receivable from X	10,000	*Y, loan*	5,000
Other assets	170,000	*X, capital*	50,000
		Y, capital	45,000
		Z, capital	50,000
	$200,000		$200,000

At the time the partnership was organized in 1963, the partners agreed to share profits equally except that X was entitled to a bonus equal to 10% of the profits in excess of $20,000 for any year. Beginning in 1967 the profit-sharing agreement was changed to the following plan:

	Salary	*Profits*
X	*$10,000*	*40%*
Y	*8,000*	*30%*
Z	*6,000*	*30%*

The earnings reported of the partnership follows:

Year	*Net income*
1963	*$ 9,000*
1964	*18,300*
1965	*(4,200) loss*
1966	*19,700*
1967	*(23,000) loss*

In order to mitigate the reported loss in 1965, the inventory was purposely inflated by Y, who was in charge of taking inventory. The amount of this overstatement was $4,800. An audit of 1967 activities discloses the following:

(1) Inventory as of January 1, 1967, was understated by $1,500.

(2) The partnership books report a purchase of lumber and paint used to remodel Z's beach home. The invoice for $1,200 was recorded as a purchase of merchandise and the invoice was paid on June 10, 1967.

(3) On April 10, 1967, X instructed the bookkeeper to write a check covering the second installment of property taxes on X's residence. The check for $500 was charged to Property Taxes.

(4) The partnership agreement states that interest at 6% is to be charged partners on loans from the partnership or credited at the same rate for funds loaned by individual partners to the partnership. Both loans were made on June 30, 1967.

The net loss of $23,000 for 1967 was correctly distributed among the partners.

Instructions

a. Prepare any correcting entries required on December 31, 1967, prior to liquidating the partnership.

b. Prepare a statement of partnership liquidation, assuming that other assets are sold for $120,000 and that all partners are personally solvent.

c. Prepare a statement of partnership liquidation, assuming that other assets are sold for $65,000 and that all partners are personally insolvent.

d. Prepare all entries required to wind up the partnership liquidation if other assets are sold for $65,000 and partners are personally insolvent as in (c) above.

3-5 Hall, Irvin, and Jones decide to form a partnership early in 1967. Their capital contributions and profit-sharing ratio are listed below:

Hall: $15,000—50%
Irvin: $10,000—30%, with a guarantee of $6,000 per year or a proportionate amount for a period less than a year.
Jones: $8,000—20%

During the first six months of 1967, the partners were not particularly concerned over the poor volume of business and the loss of $14,000 reported by their bookkeeper since they had been told that it would take at least six months to establish their business and to achieve profitable operations. Business during the second half of the year did not improve and the partners decided to go out of business before additional losses were incurred. The decision to liquidate was hastened when two large customers filed bankruptcy proceedings.

The sale of assets was completed during October and all available cash was paid to creditors. Suppliers' invoices of $1,800 remained unpaid at this time. The personal financial status of each partner on October 31, 1967, was as follows:

	Personal assets	*Personal creditors*
Hall	*$10,000*	*$ 8,500*
Irvin	*20,000*	*5,000*
Jones	*25,000*	*14,000*

The partners had made no cash withdrawals during 1967; however, in August Jones had withdrawn merchandise with a cost of $400 and Irvin had taken title to some surplus equipment at an agreed consideration of $250.

The partners have agreed to end the partnership immediately and to arrive at a settlement among themselves in accordance with the provisions of the Uniform Partnership Act.

Instructions

Prepare a four-column statement of partners' capitals (including liquidation) as of October 31, 1967. You need not show the changes in liabilities, cash, or noncash assets, merely the changes in the total capital and individual capitals of the three partners.

3-6 The partnership of Giant Stores was formed on January 2, 1966, by equal contributions from George Allen and Henry Ball. Allen, who was in the toy business, contributed $10,000 of inventory for his 50% interest and Ball, who was a distributor of appliances, contributed inventory valued at $8,000 plus $2,000 in cash for his 50% interest. The partners agreed to share profits and losses equally.

The operation of Giant Stores did not prove profitable, and after the Christmas shopping season of 1966, Allen and Ball agreed to dissolve the partnership. They retained you at this time to assist in the termination of the business. Your investigation reveals the following information:

(1) The part-time bookkeeper employed by Giant Stores was also bookkeeper for Ball's appliance business. The condition of the records indicated a lack of competence on his part. He had discarded all cash register tapes and invoices for expenses and purchases.

(2) The partners assure you in writing that the only liabilities are to the two firms which they own as sole proprietorships. The amounts are $9,740 owing to Allen Toy Company and $5,260 owing to Ball Appliance Company.

(3) Through an analysis of bank statements and paid checks you are able to construct the following summary of cash transactions:

Opening cash balance		*$ 2,000*
Receipts:		
Sales	*$70,000*	
Inventory liquidation	*7,000*	*77,000*
		$79,000
Disbursements:		
Purchases	*$36,000*	
Operating expenses	*26,000*	
Leasehold improvements (five-year lease)	*6,000*	
Liquidating expenses	*4,000*	*72,000*
Balance, Dec. 31, 1966		*$ 7,000*

(4) Payments of $3,500 were made to each of the partners on December 31, 1966, in partial settlement of the firm's liabilities.

(5) You are informed by the partners that the dollar amounts of regular sales during the year were divided approximately equally between toys and appliances and that the dollar amounts of liquidating sales of toys and appliances were also approximately equal. The markup was uniformly 40% of cost on toys and 25% of cost on appliances. All sales were for cash. The ending inventory of shopworn merchandise was liquidated on December 31, 1966, for 50% of the retail sales price. The partners believe that some appliances may have been returned to Ball Appliance Company, but the bookkeeper failed to record any such returns on the books of either organization.

Instructions

a. Prepare a schedule showing the computation of unrecorded returns of merchandise by Giant Stores. Assume that no theft of merchandise has occurred.

b. Prepare an income statement for Giant Stores for the period from January 2 to December 31, 1966.

c. Prepare a statement of partners' capital accounts.

AICPA adapted

3-7 The partnership of X, Y, and Z is unable to meet the demands of its creditors; furthermore, two of the partners are personally insolvent. The partners share profits and losses in the ratio of 4, 3, and 2, respectively. The balance sheet of the firm is as follows:

X, Y, AND Z PARTNERSHIP
Balance Sheet

Assets		*Liabilities & Capital*	
Cash	*$ 500*	*Accounts payable*	*$37,000*
Other assets	*60,500*	*Partners' capitals:*	
		X, capital	*10,000*
		Y, capital	*6,000*
		Z, capital	*8,000*
	$61,000		*$61,000*

The financial position of the partners as individuals is shown in the following tabulation:

Partner	*Cash and cash value of personal assets*	*Liabilities*
X	$31,000	$20,000
Y	9,450	11,900
Z	4,000	5,000

Instructions

a. Assuming that the "other assets" are sold for $33,500 cash, prepare a statement of partnership liquidation showing the payment to partnership creditors and the amount, if any, to be distributed to partners. Also prepare a separate schedule showing the distribution to personal creditors of the three partners of their personal assets.

b. Compute the minimum amount which must be realized from the sale of the partnership assets other than cash so that the personal creditors of Y would receive full settlement of their claims.

AICPA adapted

3-8 Mason and Parks were attorneys and automobile fanciers who became acquainted because of their interest in imported automobiles. They decided to become partners in a law firm and persuaded a third attorney, Naylor, to join with them. The partnership maintained only meager accounting records, but a secretary in the firm did maintain a careful daily record of cash receipts, which were almost entirely in the form of checks received through the mail. The only other systematically maintained record was the checkbook used for all disbursements by the partnership. Some miscellaneous work papers were on file relating to income tax returns of prior years but these were not very informative.

Early in 1967 the partners quarreled over the use of partnership funds to buy expensive automobiles; this quarrel led to a decision to dissolve the firm as of June 30, 1967. You were retained to assemble the financial data needed for an equitable distribution of assets. You learn that the partnership was formed four years ago with equal capital investments and an agreement to share profits equally. By inspection of the income tax return for the calendar year 1966, you determine that the amounts of fixed assets and accumulated depreciation were as follows at December 31, 1966:

	Fixed assets	*Accumulated depreciation, Dec. 31, 1966*
Office equipment	$ 7,500	$ 2,250
Library	4,500	900
Automobiles:		
Bentley—assigned to Mason	10,000	3,000
Buick—assigned to Naylor	5,000	1,000
Rolls-Royce—assigned to Parks	15,000	3,000
	$42,000	$10,150

By reference to the cash records, you find that cash receipts for the first six months of 1967 amounted to $300,000. The cash disbursements could be summarized as follows:

Automobile and miscellaneous expense	*$ 5,000*
Entertainment expense	*20,000*
Wages and salaries expense	*10,510*
Rent expense	*7,000*
Drawings: Mason	*45,000*
Drawings: Naylor	*50,000*
Drawings: Parks	*60,000*
	$197,510

The automobiles were depreciated on a straight-line basis over a five-year life and depreciation was treated as a charge against partnership revenues. A 10-year life was used for depreciation of office equipment and books. As one step in the dissolution, the partners agree that the automobiles which were purchased from partnership funds should be retained by the partners to whom assigned. They also agree upon equal distribution of the office equipment among them in kind. The entire library will be distributed to Mason.

Cash on hand and in bank at June 30, 1967, amounted to $149,990. The capital accounts of the partners were equal as of December 31, 1966.

Instructions

Prepare a schedule showing the changes in partners' capital accounts from January 1, 1967, to June 30, 1967, and the final distribution of cash and other assets to partners. To support this schedule, prepare an income statement for the six months ended June 30, 1967.

AICPA adapted

3-9 Randall and Mason have operated the Pacific Marina as a partnership for several years and have shared profits equally. For the last year Mason has been suggesting that he had reached retirement age. On April 1, 1967, the partners agreed that Randall should buy Mason's interest and dissolve the partnership.

Since the accountant employed by Pacific Marina is capable of handling only routine matters, you are retained to act as a consultant to him. The books were last closed on December 31, 1966, and you find the following trial balance has been prepared at March 31, 1967.

	Debit	*Credit*
Cash	*$ 630*	
Petty cash	*100*	
Prepaid insurance	*1,360*	
Land	*32,500*	
Building	*75,000*	
Allowance for depreciation: Building		*$ 15,000*
Equipment	*30,000*	
Allowance for depreciation: Equipment		*10,800*
Mortgage payable: ABC Life Insurance Company		*53,000*

Randall, capital		28,265
Mason, capital		28,265
Rental revenue		17,249
Wages	3,545	
Advertising and supplies	2,755	
Repairs and utilities	2,234	
Office expense	114	
Taxes	166	
Depreciation	3,770	
Interest	405	
	$152,579	$152,579

Upon a careful inspection of details of the settlement between Randall and Mason, you learned that no adjustment for supplies, taxes, interest, and insurance had been recorded on March 31, 1967.

The following transactions occurred on April 1, 1967, in the settlement:

(1) The partnership bank account was closed by drawing equal checks payable to each partner.

(2) Randall paid Mason $235 to be applied as follows:

One-half of petty cash	$ 50
One-half of supplies inventory	185
	$235

(3) It was necessary for Randall to borrow additional funds on the business property. Complete refinancing was worked out with the Second National Bank as set forth in the following disbursement statement prepared by the bank:

Amount of loan from the Second National Bank				$84,000
Amount of check from Mr. Randall				500
Total				$84,500
Less: Payoff of mortgage due ABC Life Insurance Company			$56,150	
Amount due Mason		$28,950		
Add: One-half unexpired fire insurance premium due Mason, prorated Apr. 1, 1967, to Apr. 1, 1968; original premium was $3,180		500		
		$29,450		
Less: One-half penalty due ABC Insurance Company	$1,325			
One-half interest due ABC Insurance Company from Feb. 6, 1967, to Apr. 1, 1967	250			
One-half real estate taxes from Jan. 1, 1967, to Apr. 1, 1967	150			
Total		1,725		
Amount due to Mason			27,725	83,875
Total				$ 625
Less: Financing costs				625

(4) In addition, Mason accepted a $30,000 second mortgage payable in equal monthly installments.

(5) An appraisal of the Marina property indicated the following values, which the partners agreed to accept as a basis for settlement. These values are to be entered in the books.

Land	*$ 45,500*
Buildings	*78,000*
Equipment	*18,200*
Total	*$141,700*

Instructions

a. Prepare necessary adjusting entries (with explanations) and entries for dissolution of the partnership.

b. Prepare a work sheet with columns to show the following information:

(1) Adjustments necessary to bring accounts into agreement with data as presented, showing facts of dissolution agreement

(2) Income statement of the partnership for the period January 1, 1967, to March 31, 1967

(3) Balance sheet as of March 31, 1967

(4) Adjustments for dissolution

(5) Opening balances for Randall's books

AICPA adapted

3-10 Day, East, Fry, and Garth were partners for 15 years. Following Day's death early in 1967, the remaining partners decided to sell the business to an eastern syndicate for $1 million. The latest balance sheet for the partnership, prepared on January 31, 1967, contains the following information:

Day, capital	*$115,000*
East, capital	*88,000*
Fry, capital	*79,500*
Garth, capital	*44,400*
Fry, loan	*10,000*
Receivable from Garth	*12,500*

You have been engaged to audit the capital accounts in order to determine the proper partnership equities. The partners provide you with a copy of the partnership agreement dated January 12, 1952, which covers among other matters the following points:

(1) Profits and losses to be shared among Day, East, Fry, and Garth in a 3:2:2:1 ratio.

(2) Books of account to be maintained on the accrual basis.

(3) Each partner's life to be insured for the benefit of his copartners, the premium payments and policy settlements to be divided among the three beneficiaries in the profit and loss ratio.

(4) Each partner to be insured under a major medical policy, the partnership to pay all premiums and to charge each partner's drawing for the premium cost. Should any partner fail to qualify for such policy, he shall be entitled to withdraw an amount equal to the average premiums paid by the insured partners.

Upon careful investigation of records you discover the following:

(1) Uncollectible accounts have been written off by a charge to bad debt expense, no allowance for bad accounts having been provided. Certain accrued and deferred items were not recognized on the financial records. It is now determined that an estimate of bad debts, accruals, and deferrals should have been recognized as follows:

	Fiscal year ended Jan. 31	
	1966	*1967*
Estimated uncollectible accounts at year-end determined by aging of accounts	*$2,500*	*$3,500*
Prepaid expenses	*1,000*	*1,100*
Accrued expenses	*3,200*	*1,800*
Unearned revenues	*–0–*	*600*
Accrued revenues	*1,200*	*–0–*

(2) All premiums paid on life policies were charged to Insurance Expense. The aggregates of these premiums on the life of each partner are:

On Day's life ($150,000 face value)	*$18,100*
On East's life ($200,000 face value)	*24,000*
On Fry's life ($160,000 face value)	*21,000*
On Garth's life ($150,000 face value)	*17,500*
	$80,600

(3) The life policies had no cash surrender value. The face of the policy on Day's life, $150,000, was collected on February 26, 1967, and this amount was immediately distributed to the appropriate partners. No entries have been made to record the receipt or payment of life insurance proceeds.

(4) The amounts paid on partners' health policies have also been erroneously charged to Insurance Expense. The aggregate of such payments since 1952 amounts to $15,600 for equal insurance on Day, Fry, and Garth. East did not qualify for a health policy and was paid a total of $5,200 by the partnership. Payments to East were also recorded as insurance expense.

The partnership was sold on March 1, 1967, the purchasers assuming all liabilities to outside creditors. Each of the insured partners continues to carry the health policy but the life insurance policies, which have an anniversary date on March 1, are terminated. Profits for the month of February amounted to $15,000. Day's estate is entitled to participate in these profits. There were no drawings other than the distribution of the life insurance proceeds.

Instructions

a. Prepare all entries necessary to develop the correct balances in the partners' capital accounts as of March 1, 1967, and to record the sale of the assets.

b. Determine how the $1 million should be distributed among Day's estate, East, Fry, and Garth. Present this information in the form of a statement of partners' capitals beginning with the unadjusted balances at January 31, 1967. Include in the statement each correction or adjustment needed to develop the proceeds to be distributed in liquidation.

3-11 The ABC partnership, doing business as Exotic Flowers, has never been audited. In January of 1967, the partners were forced to liquidate their wholesale evergreens and flowers business in downtown Los Angeles to make room for a new building. The partners have been leasing the building since 1955, and A has been in this business since 1935. Early in 1955 he admitted B and C to partnership in order to expand sales. A's balance sheet, prepared by his bookkeeper at the end of 1955, appears below:

Cash	$18,000	*Accounts payable*	$ 7,000
Customers	10,000	*A, capital*	24,000
Furniture and equipment	4,500		
Less: Depreciation	(1,500)		
	$31,000		$31,000

B and C did not invest any capital in the business; the partnership agreement included the following rather unusual provisions:

"Profits shall be shared equally and the 'dividends' withdrawn by B and C shall be reduced by at least $3,000 each December until the aggregate 'dividends' withdrawn by A amount to $15,000 in excess of the individual amounts withdrawn by B and C. Withdrawals by A in excess of those drawn by B and C are to be treated as capital withdrawals to the extent of the first $24,000 of such withdrawals and $6,000 as payment for goodwill. Goodwill of $6,000 is to be recorded on the books prior to the formation of the partnership."

Immediately prior to liquidation in January, 1967, B prepared the following balance sheet for the firm:

Cash	$21,000	*Accounts payable*	$15,000
Accounts receivable	23,000	*Partners' capitals*	45,000
Goodwill	6,000		
Furniture and equipment	18,000		
Less: Accumulated depreciation	(8,000)		
	$60,000		$60,000

All profits and drawings were recorded in a single account entitled Partners' Capitals. Aggregate profits for the partnership have amounted to $435,000. A has withdrawn $160,000 since formation of the partnership and each of the other partners has withdrawn $130,000.

The partners have not been getting along well in recent years and do not wish to continue their business association. Accordingly they carry out the following liquidation program:

(1) A is to be allowed to open a new location using the firm name of Exotic Flowers. The partners agree that a value of $4,500 should be placed on the trade name.

(2) Accounts receivable are sold for $20,300 and A agrees to take over the furniture and equipment for $10,900, with the understanding that he will invest additional cash in the partnership in order to make good his capital deficiency.

(3) All creditors are paid in full except for one disputed invoice recorded on the books at $1,300. The account was settled for $1,000.

Instructions

a. Prepare a statement of liquidation for the partnership.

b. Prepare entries to record the liquidation on the books of the partnership. Open a separate capital account for each partner. Use a Loss on Liquidation account to accumulate the losses and gains from the series of events comprising the liquidation. This account should be closed prior to the distribution of cash to partners.

4 PARTNERSHIPS: LIQUIDATION IN INSTALLMENTS

Installment payments to partners

In the illustrations of partnership liquidation in the preceding chapter, all the firm's assets were sold and the total loss on realization was divided among the partners before any payments were made to them. The liquidation of some businesses, however, may extend over several months; in these extended liquidations the partners will usually want to receive cash as it becomes available rather than waiting until the last asset has been converted into cash. Installment payments to partners are quite proper so long as the necessary safeguards are employed to ensure that all creditors are paid in full and that no partner is paid more than the amount to which he is ultimately entitled after all losses on realization have become known.

Liquidation in installments may be regarded as a process of selling some of the assets, paying creditors, paying the remaining available cash to partners, selling more of the assets, and making further payments to partners. The liquidation continues until all assets have been sold and all cash distributed.

The circumstances of installment liquidation are likely to vary from one case to the next; consequently, our approach is to emphasize the general principles guiding liquidation in installments rather than to provide illustrative models of all possible liquidation situations. Among the variables which cause partnership liquidations to differ are the sufficiency of each partner's capital to absorb his share of the possible losses remaining after each installment, the shifting of losses from one partner to another because of inability to collect a debit balance, the offsetting of loan accounts against capital deficiencies, and the possible need for setting aside cash to meet future expenses or unpaid liabilities.

General principles guiding installment payment procedures

The critical element in installment liquidations is that the liquidator authorizes cash payments to partners before he knows what losses may be incurred and charged against the partners. If a payment is made to a partner and later losses cause a debit balance to develop in his capital account, the liquidator will have to ask for the return of the payment. If he cannot recover the payment, he may be personally liable to the other partners for the loss caused them by his unwise distribution of cash. Because of this danger, the only safe policy for determining installment cash payments to partners may be summarized into the following rules.

Assume a total loss on all remaining assets. Assume also that any partner with a capital deficiency or a potential capital deficiency will be unable to pay anything to the firm. In other words, distribute each installment of cash as if no more cash would be forthcoming either from sale of assets or from collection of debts from partners. Under these assumptions the liquidator will authorize a payment to a partner only if he has a credit balance in his capital account (or in his capital and loan account combined) in excess of the amount required to absorb his share of the maximum possible loss which may be incurred. In this statement, a partner's "share of the maximum possible loss" will include any loss that may be shifted to him because of the inability of his partners to make good any debit balance which may arise in their capital accounts.

When installment payments are made according to these rules, the effect will be to bring the equities of the partners into the profit and loss ratio as quickly as possible. When installment payments have proceeded to the point that the partners' capitals correspond to the profit and loss ratio, all subsequent payments can be divided in that ratio, because each partner's capital will be sufficient to absorb his share of the maximum possible remaining loss.

Installment liquidation when all partners have adequate capital to absorb losses

In the first illustration of liquidation in installments, we shall assume that each partner has sufficient capital (or capital and loan accounts combined) to absorb his share of all possible losses, and that the first installment paid to the partners brings their capitals into the profit and loss ratio. A, B, and C, who share profits and losses equally, present the following partnership balance sheet just prior to liquidation.

A, B, AND C
Balance Sheet
June 30, 19__

Assets		*Liabilities & Partners' Capitals*	
Cash	$ 5,000	*Liabilities*	$ 40,000
Other assets	155,000	*A, capital*	30,000
		B, capital	40,000
		C, capital	50,000
	$160,000		$160,000

During July, assets carried on the books at $80,000 are sold for $65,000. The liabilities are paid in full, which leaves cash of $30,000 available for distribution to the partners. The July transactions and the resulting account balances are shown in the following tabulation.

	Assets		*Liabilities*	*Partners' capitals*		
	Cash	*Noncash*		*A*	*B*	*C*
Balances before liquidation . . .	*$ 5,000*	*$155,000*	*$40,000*	*$30,000*	*$40,000*	*$50,000*
Sale of assets at a loss	*65,000*	*(80,000)*		*(5,000)*	*(5,000)*	*(5,000)*
Balances	*$70,000*	*$ 75,000*	*$40,000*	*$25,000*	*$35,000*	*$45,000*
Payment of creditors	*(40,000)*		*(40,000)*			
Balances	*$30,000*	*$ 75,000*		*$25,000*	*$35,000*	*$45,000*

How should the $30,000 of cash on hand be divided among the three partners? The guidelines to this decision, as previously explained, are to assume that the remaining noncash assets will prove worthless and that the $30,000 of cash now available will be all that the partners will receive. The possible loss is therefore $75,000; equal division of this loss among the three partners would reduce each partner's capital by $25,000. A's interest would be reduced to zero, B's interest to $10,000, and C's interest to $20,000. The only safe plan for distribution of this first installment of $30,000 is to give $10,000 to B and $20,000 to C. Partner A receives nothing because his capital is just sufficient to absorb his share of the possible remaining loss. These computations of installment payments to the partners are shown in the following schedule prepared to support and explain the statement of liquidation.

Schedule A

A, B, AND C
Computation of Installment Payments to Partners
July 31, 19__

	Partners' capitals		
	A	*B*	*C*
Capitals before first installment payments	*$25,000*	*$35,000*	*$45,000*
Possible remaining loss ($75,000 noncash assets)	*(25,000)*	*(25,000)*	*(25,000)*
Amounts safely payable to partners		*$10,000*	*$20,000*

Distribution of the $30,000 first installment to B and C in the amounts of $10,000 and $20,000, respectively, will leave each of the three partners with a capital account of $25,000. Regardless of whether the remaining assets prove to be worthless or worth their full book value or any other amount, this initial distribution is a safe one. The capital accounts are now in the profit and loss ratio; therefore, any further installment payments can be made in that ratio, that is, one-third to each partner.

Let us assume that during August assets with a book value of $42,000 were sold for $24,000 cash and that during September the remaining assets with a book value of $33,000 were sold for $12,000 cash. As cash was received by the firm, it was promptly distributed to the partners. The following statement of liquidation gives a complete picture of the liquidation of the firm of A, B, and C.

A, B, AND C
Statement of Partnership Liquidation
July 1 to September 30, 19__

	Assets		Liabilities	Partners' capitals		
	Cash	Noncash		A	B	C
July installment:						
Balances before liquidation	$ 5,000	$155,000	$40,000	$30,000	$40,000	$50,000
Sale of assets at a loss	65,000	(80,000)		(5,000)	(5,000)	(5,000)
Balances	$70,000	$ 75,000	$40,000	$25,000	$35,000	$45,000
Payment of creditors	(40,000)		(40,000)			
Balances before paying partners	$30,000	$ 75,000		$25,000	$35,000	$45,000
Payment to partners (Schedule A)	(30,000)				(10,000)	(20,000)
Balances		$ 75,000		$25,000	$25,000	$25,000
August installment:						
Sale of assets at a loss	$24,000	(42,000)		(6,000)	(6,000)	(6,000)
Balances before paying partners	$24,000	$ 33,000		$19,000	$19,000	$19,000
Payment to partners	(24,000)			(8,000)	(8,000)	(8,000)
Balances		$ 33,000		$11,000	$11,000	$11,000
September installment:						
Sale of assets at a loss	$12,000	(33,000)		(7,000)	(7,000)	(7,000)
Balances before paying partners	$12,000			$ 4,000	$ 4,000	$ 4,000
Payment to partners	(12,000)			(4,000)	(4,000)	(4,000)

In journalizing the transactions comprising the liquidation of a partnership, no entries are made for the possible losses computed for future sales of assets. In accordance with standard accounting practice, entries are made in the accounts only for actual sales and actual changes in partners' capital accounts. The journal entries for the preceding illustrated liquidation of the A, B, and C partnership are as follows:

Account	Debit	Credit
Cash	65,000	
A, Capital	5,000	
B, Capital	5,000	
C, Capital	5,000	
Other Assets		80,000
To record sale of assets at a loss during July, and division of loss among partners.		
Liabilities	40,000	
Cash		40,000
Paid creditors in full.		
B, Capital	10,000	
C, Capital	20,000	
Cash		30,000
Paid first installment to partners in manner that leaves each partner with sufficient capital to absorb his share of possible remaining losses.		
Cash	24,000	
A, Capital	6,000	
B, Capital	6,000	
C, Capital	6,000	
Other Assets		42,000
To record sale of assets at a loss during August, and division of loss among partners.		
A, Capital	8,000	
B, Capital	8,000	
C, Capital	8,000	
Cash		24,000
Paid second installment to partners, corresponding to profit and loss ratio.		
Cash	12,000	
A, Capital	7,000	
B, Capital	7,000	
C, Capital	7,000	
Other Assets		33,000
To record sale of remaining assets at a loss during September, and division of loss among partners.		
A, Capital	4,000	
B, Capital	4,000	
C, Capital	4,000	
Cash		12,000
Paid final installment to partners, corresponding to profit and loss ratio.		

Installment payments compared with lump-sum settlement

The installment payments shown in the preceding illustration of the ABC partnership liquidation produced exactly the same final results as if the liquidator had made no payments to partners until all assets had been sold. The entire liquidation consisted of selling assets with a book value of $155,000 for cash of $101,000, which provided a total loss of $54,000. This loss divided equally among the partners reduced the capital account of each by $18,000. The remaining capital accounts were $12,000, $22,000, and $32,000, respectively, for A, B, and C. Each partner received cash equal to the amount in his capital account, as shown by the following summary schedule.

		Partners' capitals		
	Total	*A*	*B*	*C*
Balances before liquidation	*$120,000*	*$30,000*	*$40,000*	*$50,000*
Loss on sale of assets	*(54,000)*	*(18,000)*	*(18,000)*	*(18,000)*
Balances	*$ 66,000*	*$12,000*	*$22,000*	*$32,000*
Installment payments to partners:				
July payment	*$ 30,000*		*$10,000*	*$20,000*
August payment	*24,000*	*$ 8,000*	*8,000*	*8,000*
September payment	*12,000*	*4,000*	*4,000*	*4,000*
Total payments (equal to capitals)	*$ 66,000*	*$12,000*	*$22,000*	*$32,000*

Assume for the moment that Partner A's interest in the business at the beginning of the liquidation process had consisted of a loan account of $15,000 and a capital account of $15,000 rather than a capital account of $30,000 as in our illustration. Partner A might have objected to the first installment payment, which gave him nothing but gave $10,000 cash to B and $20,000 to C. His protest would presumably have been based on the statutory priority in the Uniform Partnership Act which indicates that partners' loans should be paid before payment of capital accounts. In the face of such a protest by A, the only alternative open to the liquidator would be to make no payments to the partners until all the assets had been sold and the total loss determined. Any installment payment plan other than the one illustrated would create the risk of forcing one partner to bear more than his contractual share of losses.

Installment liquidation when one or more partners have insufficient capital to absorb possible losses

This case illustrates installment liquidation when two members of a four-man partnership have insufficient capital to bear their shares of the total possible loss. The following balance sheet was prepared just prior to liquidation.

J, K, L, AND M
Balance Sheet
June 30, 19__

Assets		*Liabilities & Partners' Capitals*	
Cash	$ 6,000	*Liabilities*	$ 50,000
Other assets	174,000	*J, loan*	10,000
		J, capital	27,000
		K, capital	50,000
		L, capital	21,000
		M, capital	22,000
	$180,000		$180,000

The profit- and loss-sharing ratio is 20% to J; 40% to K; 10% to L; and 30% to M. The disposal of assets, extended over a four-month period, is as follows:

	Book value of assets sold	*Loss*	*Cash received*
First month	$ 84,000	$30,000	$ 54,000
Second month	70,000	20,000	50,000
Third month	16,000	4,000	12,000
Fourth month	4,000	3,000	1,000
	$174,000	$57,000	$117,000

Note that in the liquidation statement on page 108, the loan account and capital account of Partner J have been combined into a single amount representing his equity at the beginning of liquidation. This step simplifies the liquidation statement and does not affect the distribution of cash among the partners.

The creditors were paid in full during the first month of the liquidation. Payments were made to partners at the end of each month to the extent of cash available. The distribution of cash among partners was made on the assumption that any remaining noncash assets would prove worthless and that any partner with a capital deficiency would be unable to pay in such indebtedness to the firm. After the payment of cash to the partners at the end of the second month, the amounts remaining in the capital accounts corresponded to the profit and loss ratio. The cash distributions in the following months could therefore be made in the profit and loss ratio because each partner's capital was equal to his share of the maximum possible loss.

J, K, L, AND M
Statement of Partnership Liquidation
July 1 to October 31, 19__

	Assets		Liabilities	Partners' capitals			
	Cash	Noncash		J	K	L	M
Profit and loss ratio				20%	40%	10%	30%
Balances before liquidation	$ 6,000	$174,000	$50,000	$37,000	$50,000	$21,000	$22,000
First installment:							
Sale of assets at a loss	54,000	(84,000)		(6,000)	(12,000)	(3,000)	(9,000)
Balances	$60,000	$ 90,000	$50,000	$31,000	$38,000	$18,000	$13,000
Payment of creditors	(50,000)		(50,000)				
Balances before paying partners	$10,000	$ 90,000		$31,000	$38,000	$18,000	$13,000
Payment to partners (Schedule A)	(10,000)			(5,000)		(5,000)	
Balances		$ 90,000		$26,000	$38,000	$13,000	$13,000
Second installment:							
Sale of assets at a loss	$50,000	(70,000)		(4,000)	(8,000)	(2,000)	(6,000)
Balances	$50,000	$ 20,000		$22,000	$30,000	$11,000	$ 7,000
Payment to partners (Schedule A)	(50,000)			(18,000)	(22,000)	(9,000)	(1,000)
Balances		$ 20,000		$ 4,000	$ 8,000	$ 2,000	$ 6,000
Third installment:							
Sale of assets at a loss	$12,000	(16,000)		(800)	(1,600)	(400)	(1,200)
Balances	$12,000	$ 4,000		$ 3,200	$ 6,400	$ 1,600	$ 4,800
Payment to partners	(12,000)			(2,400)	(4,800)	(1,200)	(3,600)
Balances		$ 4,000		$ 800	$ 1,600	$ 400	$ 1,200
Fourth installment:							
Sale of assets at a loss	$ 1,000	(4,000)		(600)	(1,200)	(300)	(900)
Balances	$ 1,000			$ 200	$ 400	$ 100	$ 300
Payment to partners	(1,000)			(200)	(400)	(100)	(300)

Advance planning of cash distribution during liquidation

The preceding illustrations of partnership liquidation in installments have included a month-by-month division among partners of the losses on disposal of assets. The statements of partnership liquidation and the supporting schedules also show the amounts of cash which could safely be distributed to each partner each month after calculating the impact on partners' capitals of the maximum possible remaining loss. Although the method demonstrated is entirely sound, it does not show at the beginning of the liquidation how the cash which becomes available will be divided among the partners.

The partners may want a complete cash distribution program prepared in advance to show how the cash which is realized during the liquidation will be divided. If such a plan of cash distribution is prepared, any amounts of cash received from disposal of partnership assets can be distributed to the partners as

Schedule A

J, K, L, AND M
Computation of Installment Payments to Partners
July and August, 19__

	Partners' capitals			
	J	K	L	M
Profit and loss ratio	20%	40%	10%	30%
First month:				
Capitals (including loan) before first installment payment	$31,000	$38,000	$18,000	$13,000
Possible remaining loss ($90,000 noncash assets)	(18,000)	(36,000)	(9,000)	(27,000)
Balances	$13,000	$ 2,000	$ 9,000	$(14,000)
Additional possible loss from capital deficiency of M (in ratio of 2/7 to J, 4/7 to K, and 1/7 to L)	(4,000)	(8,000)	(2,000)	14,000
Balances	$ 9,000	($6,000)	$ 7,000	
Additional possible loss from capital deficiency of K (2/3 to J and 1/3 to L)	(4,000)	6,000	(2,000)	
Safe payments to partners	$ 5,000		$ 5,000	
Second month:				
Balances before payment to partners . . .	$22,000	$30,000	$11,000	$ 7,000
Possible remaining loss ($20,000 noncash assets)	(4,000)	(8,000)	(2,000)	(6,000)
Possible balances and safe payments to partners	$18,000	$22,000	$ 9,000	$ 1,000

specified in this plan. The preparation in advance of a cash distribution plan is therefore an alternative method to the procedure previously described for computing installment payments to partners.

Assume that R, S, and T, who share profits and losses 40%, 30%, and 30%, decide to liquidate their business and want a complete cash distribution plan prepared in advance. The balance sheet just prior to liquidation is as follows:

R, S, AND T
Balance Sheet
June 30, 19__

Assets		Liabilities & Partners' Capitals	
Cash	$ 8,000	Liabilities	$ 61,000
Other assets	192,000	R, capital	40,000
		S, capital	45,000
		T, capital	54,000
	$200,000		$200,000

As a first step, we shall compute the amount of the loss which would eliminate the capital account of each partner and therefore make him ineligible to receive any cash. The computation consists of dividing the capital account by the partner's percentage of profit and loss as follows:

Partner	Capital	Profit & loss percentage	Amount of loss
R..................	$40,000	40%	$100,000
S..................	45,000	30%	150,000
T..................	54,000	30%	180,000

This computation shows that a loss on disposal of assets in the amount of $100,000 would wipe out R's capital account, thus postponing his right to receive cash. A loss of $150,000 would eliminate S's capital, and a loss of $180,000 would eliminate the capital of Partner T.

The following schedule is prepared to determine the balance which would be left in each partner's capital account if losses were incurred in amounts sufficient to eliminate first the equity of Partner R and secondly the equity of Partner S.

	Total	Partners' capitals		
		R	S	T
Profit and loss ratio.................	*100%*	*40%*	*30%*	*30%*
Balances before liquidation...........	*$139,000*	*$40,000*	*$45,000*	*$54,000*
Loss which would eliminate R, who is least able to absorb losses..........	*(100,000)*	*(40,000)*	*(30,000)*	*(30,000)*
Balances..........................	*$ 39,000*		*$15,000*	*$24,000*
Loss which would eliminate S (losses divided equally between remaining partners)........................	*(30,000)*		*(15,000)*	*(15,000)*
Balances..........................	*$ 9,000*			*$ 9,000*

By using the priorities suggested by the preceding table, we can now prepare a schedule of planned payments for the distribution of whatever amount of cash is available during the liquidation.

Planned Payments of Cash during Liquidation

	Cash	Liabilities	Partners' capitals		
			R	S	T
First..........................	*$ 61,000*	*$61,000*			
Next..........................	*9,000*				*$9,000*
Next..........................	*30,000*			*50%*	*50%*
All cash in excess of.............	*$100,000*		*40%*	*30%*	*30%*

Assume that the cash of $8,000 shown by the partnership balance sheet at June 30 just prior to liquidation is paid to creditors on July 1. Also assume that the realization of assets is as follows during July, August, and September.

Month	Book value of assets sold	Loss on sale	Cash received
July	$ 62,000	$12,000	$ 50,000
August	66,000	30,000	36,000
September	64,000	43,000	21,000
	$192,000	$85,000	$107,000

To determine how the cash made available through the realization of assets should be used to pay creditors and partners, we apply the schedule of planned payments to the cash available as shown by the following schedule.

Distribution of Cash to Creditors and Partners

Month	Cash	Liabilities	Partners' capitals		
			R	S	T
July	$ 50,000	$50,000			
August	36,000	3,000			$ 9,000
				$12,000	12,000
September	21,000			3,000	3,000
			$6,000	4,500	4,500
	$107,000	$53,000	$6,000	$19,500	$28,500

The statement of partnership liquidation is exactly the same as if the method presented earlier in this chapter had been followed. In other words, the preparation in advance of a planned program of cash payments for the entire period of liquidation will provide for the same distribution of cash as if the payments were computed each month on the basis of each partner's ability to absorb his contractual share of the possible remaining losses. The statement of partnership liquidation follows on page 112.

Withholding of cash for unpaid liabilities

As previously emphasized, creditors are entitled to payment in full before anything is paid to partners. In some cases, however, the liquidator may find it more convenient merely to set aside in a separate fund the cash required to pay certain liabilities, and to distribute the remaining cash to the partners. The withholding of cash for payment of recorded liabilities is appropriate when for any reason it is not practicable to pay an obligation before distributing cash to partners. An

R, S, AND T
Statement of Partnership Liquidation
July 1 to September 30, 19__

	Assets		Liabilities	Partners' capitals		
	Cash	Noncash		R	S	T
Profit and loss ratio				40%	30%	30%
Balances before liquidation	$ 8,000	$192,000	$61,000	$40,000	$45,000	$54,000
July installment:						
Sale of assets at a loss	50,000	(62,000)		(4,800)	(3,600)	(3,600)
Balances	$58,000	$130,000	$61,000	$35,200	$41,400	$50,400
Payment of creditors	(58,000)		(58,000)			
Balances		$130,000	$ 3,000	$35,200	$41,400	$50,400
August installment:						
Sale of assets at a loss	$36,000	(66,000)		(12,000)	(9,000)	(9,000)
Balances	$36,000	$ 64,000	$ 3,000	$23,200	$32,400	$41,400
Payment of creditors	(3,000)		(3,000)			
Balances before paying partners	$33,000	$ 64,000		$23,200	$32,400	$41,400
Payment to partners	(33,000)				(12,000)	(21,000)
Balances		$ 64,000		$23,200	$20,400	$20,400
September installment:						
Sale of assets at a loss	$21,000	(64,000)		(17,200)	(12,900)	(12,900)
Balances	$21,000			$ 6,000	$ 7,500	$ 7,500
Payment to partners	(21,000)			(6,000)	(7,500)	(7,500)

amount of cash equal to recorded unpaid liabilities which is set aside in a fund is not a factor in computing possible future losses. The possible future loss is measured by the amount of noncash assets.

Withholding of cash for future expenses

Any expenses incurred during the realization of assets may be deducted in determining the net cash available for distribution. Expenses of liquidation are thereby treated as part of the loss on realization of assets. However, in some cases, the liquidator may wish to withhold cash in anticipation of future expenses. The amount of cash withheld or set aside for future expenses or for payment of liabilities not recorded in the accounts should be combined with the noncash assets in computing the maximum possible loss in the remainder of the liquidation.

If noncash assets such as an automobile or patent are distributed to a partner, the agreed fair value of such property should be treated as the equivalent of a cash payment. Such a cash-equivalent distribution may be in excess of the scheduled amount of cash to which the partner is currently entitled, and therefore may alter the subsequent distribution of cash. To safeguard himself, the liquidator may also choose to require a bond from the partner receiving the premature distribution or may arrange for such noncash assets to be placed in trust temporarily.

Joint ventures

History of joint ventures

A joint venture differs from a partnership in that it is limited to carrying out a single project, such as the sale of a given lot of merchandise or construction of a given building. Historically, joint ventures were used to finance the sale or exchange of a cargo of merchandise in a foreign country. In an era when marine transportation and foreign trade involved many hazards, individuals would band together to undertake a venture of this type. The capital required was usually larger than one person could provide, and the risks were too great to be borne singlehanded. Because of the risks involved and the relatively short duration of the project, no income was recognized until the venture had been completed. At the end of the voyage, the gain or loss was divided among the participants and their association was ended. A joint venture may therefore be regarded as a type of partnership which comes to an end with the attainment of a specific objective.

In its traditional form, the accounting for a venture did not follow the accrual concept. The present-day common assumption of continuity for most business entities was not appropriate; instead of the determination of income at regular intervals, the measurement and reporting of income awaited the completion of the venture. Even today, for many joint ventures the final events in the completing of the venture are often of such critical importance as to preclude any earlier recognition of gain or loss.

Present-day ventures

In today's business community, joint ventures are less common but are still employed for many projects such as (1) the purchase, development, and sale of a specific tract of real estate; (2) the sale of agricultural products; (3) exploration for oil and gas; or (4) the construction of a bridge, building, or dam. Large corporations sometimes form teams to handle highly technical, large-scale government contracts. Since these associations are formed to carry out a specific project, they may be called joint ventures.

The term *joint venture* is also used at present by many large American corporations to describe overseas operations by a company whose ownership is divided evenly between the American corporation and a foreign company. For example, in a recent annual report, Gulf Oil Corporation states that:

"In Sardinia, a new company called S.I.R.G., jointly owned by Societa Italiana Resine and Gulf, was created. This joint-venture company is building a plant in Sardinia to produce phenol and acetone from cumene made at Philadelphia."

Many such examples of jointly owned companies are found in the petrochemical industry. Since these companies are organized as corporations and may be intended for permanent operation, their accounting problems largely fall within the area of parent and subsidiary corporate relations, as presented in Chapters 8 through 14. Our use of the term joint venture in this chapter is in the traditional meaning of a partnership limited to carrying out a single project.

The term *single venture* may be used to describe a project undertaken by one individual or one company which is apart from normal operations of the business and tends to be of limited duration.

The accounting for a single venture may consist of establishing a general ledger account in the name of the venture, debiting it with all costs incurred, and crediting it with all revenues received. At the conclusion of the venture, a debit balance in the account indicates a loss; a credit balance represents a gain from the venture. The venture account is closed by transferring its balance (gain or loss) to the Income Summary account.

Accounting for a joint venture

The key issue in accounting for a joint venture is whether to establish an independent separate set of books for the venture. If a separate set of books is not established, two alternative methods are commonly used. One of these two methods calls for each participant to record all transactions of the venture in his own accounting records. He will open a Joint Venture account and also a receivable or payable with each other participant. The other commonly used procedure calls for each participant to record in his own books only those transactions in which he participates directly.

Separate set of books for venture. The complexity of modern business, the emphasis upon good organization and strong internal control, the importance of income taxes, the extent of government regulation, and the need for preparation and retention of adequate records are strong arguments for establishing a complete independent set of records for every joint venture of large size and long duration. This approach views the joint venture as a separate entity. Each participant is credited for the amount of cash or for the fair value of noncash assets which he contributes. The fiscal year of the joint venture may or may not coincide with the fiscal years of the participants, but the use of accrual accounting and periodic financial statements for the venture permit regular reporting of the share of profit or loss allocable to each participant.

The accounting records of such a joint venture will include all usual accounts for assets, liabilities, owners' equity, revenue, and expense. The entire accounting process will conform to generally accepted accounting practices customarily followed in a partnership or corporate organization, from the recording of transactions to the preparation of financial statements.

Each participant in the venture will open an account in his general ledger entitled Joint Venture. This account is debited for capital contributed to the venture, for any services billed to the venture, and for the proper share of venture profits realized. The Joint Venture account is credited for any amounts received from the venture and for a proper share of any losses reported. The account will normally have a debit balance, representing the net investment in the venture. A participant does not make any accounting entry in his records for transactions between the venture and the other participants. The account Joint Venture or Investment in Joint Venture will appear in the balance sheet as an asset, either current or noncurrent, depending upon the expected completion date for the venture.

No separate set of books for venture. If an independent set of records is not maintained by the venture as an entity, there are, as previously explained, two common alternative methods available. Each participant may record in his own records all transactions entered into by the venture, or each participant may record only those transactions to which he is a party. Let us assume the first method is in use. Thus, if Participant A contributes merchandise to the venture, he debits Joint Venture and credits Inventory. Each of the other participants makes an entry debiting Joint Venture and crediting Participant A. When sales are made, the participant handling the transaction debits Cash or Accounts Receivable and credits Joint Venture. The other participants debit the participant who executed the sale and credit Joint Venture. In brief, each participant maintains in his own books a complete record of all transactions by the joint venture and of the equities of the other participants.

Upon completion of the venture, the net gain or loss is shown by the balance in the Joint Venture account. Assuming that a profit has been realized, the entry to divide the profit and to close the Joint Venture account will be to debit Joint Venture for the balance, credit each other participant for his share of the profit, and credit Income Summary for the participant's own share. Each participant will then have an account with each of the other participants; the final step is to make payment or collection of these accounts.

If a venture has not been completed at the date one of the participants prepares a balance sheet, only the equity of that participant should be presented as an asset. Since the ledger account Joint Venture shows the total investment by all participants, the balance of this account should be listed in the balance sheet and deductions made for the equities of the other participants.

The operation of a joint venture without a separate set of records is appropriate when the venture is expected to be of short duration and not to require complex involved transactions. If prompt communication among participants is not practicable, convenience may dictate that each participant record only transactions of the venture for which he is personally responsible.

Questions

1. State briefly the basic rule or principle to be observed in distributing cash to partners when the liquidation of a partnership business extends over several months.

2. After sale of a portion of the assets of the ABC partnership, which is being liquidated, the capital accounts are A $35,000, B $40,000, and C $43,000. Cash of $42,000 is on hand, and other assets amount to $78,000 in book value. Creditors' claims total $2,000. A, B, and C share profits equally. What cash payments can be made to the partners at this time? Explain.

3. During the installment liquidation of a partnership, it is necessary to determine the possible future loss from sale of the remaining assets. What entries, if any, should be made to reflect in the partners' capital accounts their respective shares of the maximum possible loss which may be incurred during the remaining stages of dissolution?

4. The XYZ partnership is liquidated over a period of several months with several distributions of cash to the partners. Will the total amount of cash received by each partner under these circumstances be more, less, or the same amount as if the liquidator had retained all cash until all assets had been sold and had then made a single payment to the partners?

5. Under what circumstances, if any, is it sound practice for a partnership undergoing installment liquidation to distribute cash to partners in the profit and loss ratio?

6. Jones, Klein, and Lund, who share profits equally, have capital balances of $30,000, $25,000, and $21,000, respectively, when the firm begins the process of liquidation. Among the assets is a note receivable from Klein in the amount of $7,000. All liabilities have been paid. The first assets sold during the liquidation are some marketable securities carried on the books at $15,000; cash of $18,000 is received from their sale. How should this $18,000 of cash be divided among the partners?

7. When the partnership of R, S, and T began the process of liquidation, the capital accounts were R $38,000, S $35,000, and T $32,000. When the liquidation was complete, R had received less cash than either of his partners. Name several factors which might explain why the partner with the largest capital account might receive the smallest amount of cash in liquidation.

8. Landon and Hayes, partners who shared profits equally, were both incapacitated in an airplane accident and a liquidator was appointed to wind up their business. The books showed cash, $30,000; noncash assets, $100,000; liabilities, $20,000; Landon, capital, $61,000; and Hayes, capital, $49,000. Because of the highly specialized nature of the noncash assets, the liquidator anticipated that considerable time would be required to dispose of them. He estimated that the expenses of liquidating the business, including advertising, rent, travel, and his fee might approximate $7,000. How much cash can safely be distributed to each partner at this point? Explain.

9. How does a joint venture differ from a partnership? Distinguish between a joint venture and a single venture.

10. When the concept of the joint venture is viewed from the historical viewpoint, how has the process of income determination differed from that of a partnership or corporation? Does this difference prevail in present practice?

Short cases for analysis

4-1 On April 1, in beginning the liquidation of the LMN partnership, the liquidator found that an 8% note payable for $100,000 issued by the firm had six months remaining until maturity on September 30. Interest had been paid to the current date. Terms of the note provided that interest at 8% to the due date must be paid in full even though the note was paid prior to maturity. The liquidator had paid all other liabilities and had on hand cash of $150,000. The remaining noncash assets had a book value of $200,000, and the liquidator believed that six months would be required to dispose of them. He estimated that the sale of assets over this period would produce cash at least 25% in excess of book values.

Partner L made the following statement to the liquidator: "I realize you can't pay the partners until creditors have been paid in full, but I need cash for another business I'm starting. So I'd like for you to pay off the note and interest immediately and distribute the remaining available cash to the partners." Partner M objected to this proposal for immediate cash payments on the ground that it would entail a loss of $4,000. He argued that if such action were taken, the interest cost of $4,000 be charged entirely against L's capital account. Partner N said that he had no particular concern about the matter but as a convenience to his partners he would assume the note liability personally, if $102,000 in cash were turned over to him immediately. To insure the noteholder against loss, he would deposit collateral of $104,000 in government bonds. The noteholder expressed his willingness to accept this arrangement. Partner N specified that the proposed payment of $102,000 to him would be in his new role as a creditor and that it would not affect his right to share in any cash distributions to the three partners.

Instructions

Evaluate the proposal by each partner. State with reasons the action you would recommend be taken by the liquidator. Would your answer differ if the assumptions were changed to indicate a probable loss on the sale of the remaining noncash assets?

Problems

4-2 Arnold, Barr, and Casey, who share profits equally, present the following balance sheet on September 30 just prior to liquidation of the partnership.

ARNOLD, BARR, AND CASEY
Balance Sheet
September 30, 1967

Assets		*Liabilities & Partners' Capitals*	
Cash	*$ 10,000*	*Liabilities*	*$ 70,000*
Other assets	*280,000*	*Arnold, capital*	*60,000*
		Barr, capital	*70,000*
		Casey, capital	*90,000*
	$290,000		*$290,000*

During October, assets with a book value of $100,000 were sold for $70,000 cash. During November, assets with a book value of $138,000 were sold for $102,000 cash, and in December the remaining assets with a book value of $42,000 were sold for $15,000 cash. The cash which became available each month was promptly distributed.

Instructions

a. Prepare a statement of partnership liquidation covering the entire period of liquidation, and a supporting schedule showing the computation of installment payments to partners.

b. At what point in the liquidation did the partners' capital accounts have balances corresponding to the profit and loss ratio? Of what significance is this relationship with respect to subsequent cash distributions to partners?

4-3 A, B, C, and D decide to form a joint venture and to try their luck at the races. They agree to share profits and losses equally and to allow each member to place bets at his discretion. Each is to place bets from personal resources and is to cash in any win, place, or show tickets. The only other provisions of the agreement are:

(1) Limit of $10 on each bet.

(2) No more than two selections on each race.

(3) D, being from Florida, does not wish to participate on bets placed on any California-bred horses.

The bets and winnings of each man are summarized below:

	A	B	C	D
Bets placed, including $6 bet by A on a California horse, Miami Moon, on which A collected $360	$ 80	$ 66	$100	$40
Tickets cashed	400	116	35	5

Instructions

Prepare an orderly schedule showing how settlement should be made between the four sportsmen.

4-4 The Oceanside Realty Company is a partnership in the process of liquidation. At April 30 the liabilities, the equities of partners, and the profit-sharing ratios were as follows:

Current liabilities	$17,500
Real estate loans payable	90,000
Peters, loan	10,000
Peters, capital (40%)	32,000
Queen, capital (30%)	20,400
Robb, capital (20%)	2,000
Sanders, capital (10%)	15,000

As the liquidation proceeded, cash became available for payment of liabilities and distribution to partners according to the following schedule:

May	$ 80,000
June	40,000
July	50,500
August	30,000
	$200,500

The partners wish to distribute cash in such a way as to avoid any possibility of a partner having subsequently to return any cash received in the process of liquidation.

Instructions

a. You are retained by the firm at April 30 to prepare in advance a plan of distribution showing how cash which becomes available during the liquidation should be divided among the partners. In separate schedules, show (1) the amount of loss which can be absorbed by each partner; (2) the balance left in each partner's account if losses were incurred in amounts sufficient to eliminate the equity of each partner in turn; and (3) planned payments of cash during liquidation based on the priorities suggested by the preceding schedule.

b. Subsequently you were asked by the partnership to prepare a schedule showing by months the proper distribution of cash which actually became available in May, June, July, and August. This schedule should utilize the data previously developed in the schedule of planned payments.

4-5 F, G, and H started a partnership in 1960 and shared profits in a 3:2:1 ratio. On December 31, 1966, their equities in the partnership were as follows: F, $140,500; G, $112,000; and H, $47,500.

On January 1, 1967, H sold his interest to I for $35,000. The accountant transferred the balance in H's capital account to I's capital account. At the same time the partners decided to admit J into the partnership. J is an experienced business consultant and he has convinced the partners that he can help them solve their production and distribution problems by installing a computer-oriented quality control system and by completing an extensive consumer survey within the firm's sales territory. J is to be allowed a 10% interest in the net assets of the firm by investing assets as follows:

Patent on quality control system—agreed value	*$10,000*
Cash	*4,000*
Face value of note (payable to J)	*10,000*
Total	*$24,000*

J is to share in profits only after the other three partners receive interest at the rate of 6% on the beginning balances of their capital accounts as adjusted at January 1, 1967, after admission of J. The remaining profits or losses are to be divided as follows: F, 45%; G, 25%; I, 15%; and J, 15%.

J's admission is to be recorded by the bonus method. Any bonus to or from J is to be divided between F, G, and I in a 3:2:1 ratio, respectively.

J approached with vigor the challenge of reversing the unfavorable trend in sales and operating losses. Substantial loans were obtained and the proceeds "invested" in additional research on the quality control system and on the consumer survey. The results were not encouraging. Evidence mounted that placing the quality control ideas into operation would require additional financing which was not available to the firm. The consumer survey yielded conflicting and inconclusive results. Sales continued to deteriorate and F was disturbed when a friend at the country club commented: "J tried to sell his patent to us but I wouldn't give him a dime for it. We terminated his consulting services with us after we discovered that he was creating more problems for us than he was solving."

Late in August, 1967, F called his partners together and confronted J with several questions. J admitted that he, too, was discouraged with his efforts and suggested that the patent be written off against his capital account. The other partners agreed and also decided to liquidate and to form a new partnership to engage in the development of land in Arizona. The accountant for the present firm prepared a balance sheet as of August 31, 1967, as follows:

F, G, I, AND J
Balance Sheet
August 31, 1967

Assets		*Liabilities & Partners' Capitals*	
Cash	$ 11,200	*Notes payable*	$ 65,000
Accounts receivable	120,500	*Accounts payable*	77,136
Allowance for bad debts	(6,500)	*Total liabilities*	$142,136
Merchandise	135,000	*F, capital*	136,300
Machinery	220,000	*G, capital*	109,200
Accumulated depreciation	(120,000)	*I, capital*	46,100
Patents	10,000	*J, capital*	32,400
Other assets	15,000	*Loss Jan. 1–Aug. 31, 1967*	(80,936)
	$385,200		$385,200

The liquidation is summarized as follows:

	Cash received	*Liabilities paid*	*Cash to partners*	*Cash retained*
September (all assets sold except machinery)	$170,000	$132,000	$37,044	$12,156
October (machinery sold)	90,000	10,136	92,020*	–0–

* *Plus any amounts received from deficient partners.*

Interest is not to be allowed to partners after August 31, 1967. All notes are paid in September. All partners are personally solvent and are able to make good any deficiency resulting from the liquidation.

Instructions

a. Prepare a statement of partners' capital accounts for the period from January 1 to October 31, 1967.

b. Prepare all entries on the books of the partnership to record the liquidation, including the closing of the Income Summary account to the capital accounts. Losses on sales of assets should be charged directly to partners' capitals.

4-6 The partnership of Dane, Frost, and Garth has called upon you to assist in winding up the affairs of the partnership.

You are able to gather the following information:

(1) The trial balance of the partnership at June 30, 1967, is as follows:

Cash	*$ 6,000*	
Accounts receivable	*22,000*	
Inventory	*14,000*	
Plant and equipment (net)	*99,000*	
Dane, loan	*12,000*	
Garth, loan	*7,500*	
Accounts payable		*$ 17,000*
Dane, capital		*67,000*
Frost, capital		*45,000*
Garth, capital		*31,500*
	$160,500	*$160,500*

(2) The partners share profits and losses as follows: Dane, 50%; Frost, 30%; and Garth, 20%.

(3) The partners are considering an offer of $100,000 for the accounts receivable, inventory, and plant and equipment as of June 30. The $100,000 would be paid to the partners in installments, the number and amounts of which are to be negotiated.

Instructions

a. Prepare a cash distribution schedule as of June 30, 1967, showing how the $100,000 would be distributed as it becomes available.

b. Assume the same facts as in (a), except that the partners have decided to liquidate their partnership instead of accepting the offer of $100,000. Cash is distributed to the partners at the end of each month.

A summary of the liquidation transactions follows:

July:

$16,500—collected on accounts receivable, balance is uncollectible.
$10,000—received for the entire inventory.
$ 1,000—liquidation expenses paid.
$ 8,000—cash retained in the business at end of the month.

August:

$ 1,500—liquidation expenses paid.
As part payment of his capital, Garth accepted a piece of special equipment that he had developed which had a book value of $4,000. The partners agreed that a value of $10,000 should be placed on the machine for liquidation purposes.
$ 2,500—cash retained in the business at end of the month.

September:

$75,000—received on sale of remaining plant and equipment.
$ 1,000—liquidation expenses paid.
No cash retained in the business.

Prepare a schedule of cash payments as of September 30, 1967, showing how the cash was actually distributed.

AICPA adapted

4-7 Allen and Barr form a joint venture for the purchase of some specialized construction equipment at an auction. They believe very large profits are possible, but since only a few companies have need for such equipment the success of the venture depends upon locating interested buyers. The two participants agree to share profits equally although their individual contributions of cash to purchase the used equipment were $5,500 by Allen and $4,500 by Barr. The lower contribution by Barr was considered reasonable because of his prior experience in buying and selling equipment of this type. Each participant took approximately one-half the equipment and placed it on display, each lot in a different city.

No separate set of books was established for the venture. At the time of the purchase, entries were made by the two participants in their respective sets of books as follows:

Allen's Books

Joint Venture with Barr	*10,000*	
Cash		*5,500*
Barr, Venture Capital		*4,500*
To record own investment in venture and also that of coparticipant.		

Barr's Books

Joint Venture with Allen	*10,000*	
Cash		*4,500*
Allen, Venture Capital		*5,500*
To record own investment in venture and also that of coparticipant.		

Although this initial transaction reflected in each participant's books the investment by the other, the later entries for expenses and sales were made by each participant only for his own transactions. Neither had knowledge of the expenses incurred and sales arranged by the other. At the time of a sale, the participant executing the transaction debited Cash and credited the Joint Venture account; expenses were recorded by debiting the Joint Venture account and crediting Cash.

After a few months Allen and Barr decided to make an accounting and to terminate the venture. The unsold equipment was valued at prices satisfactory to both and taken over by the partner having possession. Pertinent information relating to venture activities was as follows:

	Allen	*Barr*
Joint venture account balance	*$8,000 cr*	*$9,200 cr*
Value of inventory held	*300*	*1,100*
Expenses charged to venture account	*400*	*900*

Instructions

a. Prepare an income statement for the joint venture. Attach a supporting schedule showing the computation of sales.

b. Prepare a schedule showing the amount of cash to be paid by one participant to the other in final settlement of the venture.

c. Prepare entries for each participant's books to record (1) the venture transactions completed by his coparticipant; (2) the division of profit; and (3) the cash settlement between participants. (In making these entries, you should bear in mind that each participant has made the entry previously shown for the initial investment of $10,000, but that each participant thereafter recorded only his own transactions. Information is now available for each to record the transactions of the other participant. You may find it helpful to set up T accounts for the joint venture and for capital accounts.)

4-8 A joint venture of quite limited duration was formed by X, Y, and Z when they agreed to sell hot dogs on July 3 and 4. X agreed to construct a stand on the front lawn of Z and charge the cost to operations. Z agreed to the use of his front lawn but asked $25 for the cost of sod replacement and cleaning up his lawn after July 4. X, Y, and Z decided that profits, if any, would be distributed first by the $25 payment to Z and then by a 40% commission on individual sales. The balance would be distributed 75% to X and 25% to Y. They agreed that a cash box would only complicate matters and that all purchase and sales transactions would be out-of-pocket and the responsibility of the individual. Sales to X, Y, and Z were to be at cost, except that the ending inventory might be purchased at 50% of cost. All other sales were to be made at 100% markup on cost.

The activity of the venture was as follows:

July 2 X constructed the stand on the front lawn of Z at a cost of $100.

July 3 X paid $1,000 for supplies. Z paid $50 for a permit to operate the concession.

July 4 X purchased additional supplies for $1,500, using $500 given to him by Y and $1,000 of his own money. Sales for the day were as follows: X, $1,700; Y, $2,600; and Z, $600.

July 5 Z paid $90 for fire extinguishers; these were distributed equally among X, Y, and Z for their personal use at home. Z agreed to pay $50 for the stand. The balance of the inventory was taken by X.

Instructions

Prepare a work-sheet analysis of the transactions which will give X, Y, and Z the following information:

a. Net profit or loss from the operation

b. Distribution of profit or loss to X, Y, and Z

c. The final cash settlement

The following headings are suggested for the work sheet:
- Explanation of transaction
- Inventory reconciliation at cost
- Expenses
- Sales
- X (Debit and credit columns)
- Y (Debit and credit columns)
- Z (Debit and credit columns)

AICPA adapted

4-9 You have been engaged to prepare a cash forecast for James Norton, a very successful young real estate and lumber investor. You are able to project the cash receipts and disbursements for 1968 without much difficulty except for possible receipts from a joint venture with Abner Olmstead and Elwood Parker.

During December 1967, Norton, Olmstead, and Parker agreed to acquire a subordinated mortgage note on a large building. On December 31, 1967, they paid $100,000 for the note, which bears interest at the rate of 8% a year payable quarterly, the next payment being due on March 31, 1968. The unpaid balance of the note at December 31, 1967, is $120,000, and principal payments are due at the rate of $2,000 each quarter. Because of the speculative nature of the note, the three men agree not to recognize any of the discount as income until the full amount of their investment has been recovered. Each member of the venture invests cash as follows:

Norton	*$55,500*
Olmstead	*32,000*
Parker	*12,500*

Because Norton and Parker arranged the purchase of the note, they agree that Olmstead's share of profits should be less than warranted by his cash investment. As a result, a profit-sharing ratio of 4:2:1 for Norton, Olmstead, and Parker is deemed satisfactory.

The projected cash receipts and payments for the joint venture are as follows:

	Receipts		*Payments of collection expenses*
	On principal	*On interest*	
Mar. 31, 1968	*$2,000*	*$2,400*	*$60*
June 30, 1968	*2,000*	*2,360*	*70*
Sept. 30, 1968	*2,000*	*2,320*	*30*
Dec. 31, 1968	*2,000*	*2,280*	*45*

You present the foregoing facts to your former professor of accounting at the local university and, without hesitation, he states, "Give the first $4,250 of cash available for distribution to Olmstead, then pay the next $8,250 to Norton and

Olmstead in a 2:1 ratio, and any additional cash can be paid to the three men in the profit-sharing ratio."

Instructions

a. Illustrate how the professor determined the cash to be distributed to the three men.

b. Estimate Norton's cash receipts from the venture for each quarter of 1968.

4-10 Partners P, Q, and R share profits and losses in a ratio of 5:3:2. At the end of a very unprofitable year, they decide to liquidate the firm. The partners' capital accounts at this date were as follows: P, Capital, $22,000; Q, Capital, $27,000; R, Capital, $14,000. The liabilities shown on the balance sheet amounted to $28,000, including a loan of $8,000 from Partner P. The cash balance was only $3,280.

The partners plan to sell the noncash assets on a piecemeal basis and to distribute cash as rapidly as it becomes available. So far as is known, all three partners are solvent.

Instructions

Answer each of the following questions and show how you reached your conclusions. (Each question is independent of the others.)

a. If Q received $5,000 on the first distribution of cash, how much did P and R receive at this time?

b. If P receives a total of $25,000 as a result of the liquidation, what was the total amount realized on the sale of the noncash assets?

c. If R receives $3,000 on the first distribution of cash, how much did P receive at this time?

4-11 The partners of Able, Bright, Cool, and Dahl have decided to dissolve their partnership. They plan to sell the assets gradually in order to minimize losses. They share profits and losses as follows: Able, 40%; Bright, 35%; Cool, 15%; and Dahl, 10%. Presented below is the partnership's trial balance as of October 1, 1967, the date on which liquidation begins.

	Debit	*Credit*
Cash	*$ 200*	
Receivables	*25,900*	
Inventory, Oct. 1, 1967	*42,600*	
Equipment (net)	*19,800*	
Accounts payable		*$ 3,000*
Able, loan		*6,000*
Bright, loan		*10,000*
Able, capital		*20,000*
Bright, capital		*21,500*
Cool, capital		*18,000*
Dahl, capital		*10,000*
	$88,500	*$88,500*

Instructions

a. Prepare a statement as of October 1, 1967, showing how cash will be distributed among partners by installments as it becomes available.

b. On October 31, 1967, cash of $12,700 became available to creditors and partners. How should it be distributed?

c. If instead of being dissolved, the partnership continued operations and earned a profit of $23,625, how should that profit be distributed if, in addition to the aforementioned profit-sharing arrangement, it was provided that Dahl receive a bonus of 5% of the net income from operations after treating such bonus as an expense?

AICPA adapted

SPECIAL PROBLEMS IN ACCOUNTING FOR SALES TRANSACTIONS

PART TWO

5 CONSIGNMENTS

The meaning of consignments

The term *consignment* means a transfer of merchandise from the owner to another person who acts as the sales agent of the owner. Title to the goods remains with the owner, who is called the *consignor;* the sales agent who has possession of the goods is called the *consignee.*

From a legal viewpoint a consignment represents a bailment. The relationship between the consignor and consignee is that of principal and agent, and the law of agency controls the determination of the obligations and rights of the two parties to the consignment contract.

The consignee is responsible to the consignor for the goods placed in his custody until they are sold or returned. Since the consignee does not acquire title to the goods, he does not include them in his inventory and records no account payable or other liability. His only obligation is to give reasonable care to the consigned goods and to account for them to the consignor. When the goods are sold by the consignee, the resulting account receivable is the property of the consignor. At this point the consignor recognizes the passage of title to the goods to the purchaser and also recognizes any gain on the sale.

The shipment of goods on consignment may be referred to by the consignor as a *consignment out,* and by the consignee as a *consignment in.*

Distinguishing between a consignment and a sale

Although both a sale and a consignment involve the shipment of merchandise, a clear distinction between the two is necessary for the proper determination of income. Since the title does not pass when goods are shipped on consignment, the consignor continues to carry the consigned merchandise on his books as part of his inventory. No profit can be recognized at the time of the consignment shipment because there is no change in ownership of goods. If the consignee's business should fail, the consignor would not be in the position of a creditor hoping to recover a part of his claim; instead he would have the right to take possession of the consigned merchandise to which he has title.

Advantages of the consignment method of distributing goods

Why should a producer or wholesaler of merchandise prefer to consign goods rather than to make outright sales? One possible reason, especially with new products, is that he may be able to persuade dealers to stock the items on consignment whereas they would not be willing to purchase the goods outright. Secondly, the consignor avoids the risk inherent in selling goods on credit to dealers of questionable financial strength. Still another favorable factor is that the consignor can control the selling price to the consumer, which he might not be able to do if he made outright sales to dealers.

From the viewpoint of a consignee, the acquisition of a stock of merchandise on consignment rather than by purchase has the obvious advantage of requiring less capital investment in his business. He also avoids the risk of loss if he is unable to sell all the goods, and he avoids the risks of style obsolescence and physical deterioration of inventory.

The consignment contract

When goods are shipped on consignment, a written contract is needed to provide specific rules on such points as credit terms to be granted to customers by the consignee, expenses of the consignee to be reimbursed by the consignor, commissions allowable to the consignee, frequency of reporting and payment by the consignee, and handling and care of the consigned goods.

Rights of the consignee

The rights of the consignee usually include the following:

Compensation. The consignee is entitled to receive compensation, usually computed as a percentage of the price of the consigned goods he sells. In some cases his compensation may be the excess of the sale price over a specified amount.

Reimbursement for expenses and advances. The consignee usually incurs some expenses such as freight, cartage, and insurance which he is entitled to charge to the consignor. These expenses, plus any advances which the consignee may have made to the consignor, constitute a lien against the consigned goods. The consignee will ordinarily recover these amounts by deducting them from the proceeds of sale of consigned merchandise. The lien on the goods is discharged as the consigned merchandise is sold, but the consignee then acquires a lien against the receivables or other proceeds of the sale.

Extension of credit by consignee. The consignee has the right to sell consigned goods on credit if it is the custom of the trade and the consignor has not forbidden him to do so. In granting credit, as in caring for the consigned goods, the consignee is obliged to act prudently and to protect the interests of the consignor. Since the receivables from sale of consigned goods are the property of the consignor, he bears any credit losses, providing the consignee has exercised due care in granting credit and making collections. However, by special agreement, the consignee may guarantee the collection of receivables; under this type of consignment contract, he is said to be a "del credere agent."

Warranty of consigned goods. In selling consigned goods, the consignee is entitled to make the usual warranties as to the merchandise, and the consignor becomes obligated by such warranties. On the other hand, the consignor would not be bound by any extraordinary warranties which the consignee might choose to make.

Duties of the consignee

The duties of the consignee include the following:

Care and protection of consigned merchandise. The consignee must give care and protection reasonable in relation to the nature of the consigned goods. He must also follow any special instructions by the consignor as to care of the goods. If the consignee acts prudently in providing appropriate care and protection, he is not liable for any damage to the goods which may occur.

Identification of consigned goods and consignment receivables. The consignee must keep the consigned merchandise separate from his own goods, or if this is not practicable, he must, by maintenance of records or other means, be able to identify the consigned goods. Similarly, the consignee must maintain records which serve to keep the consignment receivables separate from his own accounts receivable. Although he is not usually obligated to maintain a separate bank account for cash from consignment sales, a strict legal view of the relationship between consignor and consignee requires separate identification of all property belonging to the consignor.

Care and diligence in extension of credit. As previously noted in discussing the extension of credit by the consignee, he is obligated when selling consigned goods on account to use care in selecting credit risks and to be diligent in collecting receivables.

Reporting sales and making payment. The consignee must render regular reports and make payments in accordance with the terms of each consignment. The report rendered by the consignee is called an *account sales;* it shows the goods received, goods sold, expenses incurred, advances made, and amounts owed or remitted. Payments may be scheduled as agreed portions of the shipment are sold or may not be required until the entire consignment has been disposed of.

The account sales

Assume that Lane Company ships on consignment to Ralph Brothers 10 television sets to be sold at $400 each. The consignee is to be reimbursed for any transportation expense and is to receive a commission of 20% of the authorized selling price. After selling all the consigned goods, Ralph Brothers sends the consignor an account sales similar to the one shown, accompanied by a check for the amount due.

Ralph Brothers
Rockport, Missouri

ACCOUNT SALES

________________, 19___
(date)

Sales for account and risk of:

Lane Company

Pittsburgh, Pennsylvania

Sales:		
10 TV sets @ $400		*$4,000*
Charges:		
Transportation-in	*$135*	
Commission (20% of $4,000)	*800*	*935*
Balance—(check enclosed)		*$3,065*
Consigned merchandise on hand	*None*	

Accounting methods of consignee

The receipt of the consignment shipment of 10 television sets by Ralph Brothers could be recorded in any of several ways. The objective is to create a memorandum record of the consigned goods; no purchase has been made and no account payable exists. The receipt of the consignment could be recorded by a memorandum notation in the journal, or by an entry in a separate ledger of consignment shipments, or by a memorandum entry in a general ledger account entitled Consignment In—Lane Company. In this illustration, the latter method is used and the ledger account would appear as follows:

Consignment In—Lane Company	
10 TV sets	

The entries by Ralph Brothers to record the incurring of transportation charges on the shipment and subsequently the sale of the merchandise would be as follows:

Consignment In—Lane Company	*135*	
Cash		*135*
Inbound transportation charges.		
Cash	*4,000*	
Consignment In—Lane Company		*4,000*
Sold 10 TV sets at $400 each.		

The entry to record the 20% commission earned by the consignee consists of a debit to the Consignment In account and a credit to a separate revenue account, as follows:

Consignment In—Lane Company	*800*	
Commissions on Consignment Sales		*800*
Commission of 20% earned on units sold.		

The payment by the consignee of the full amount owed will be recorded by a debit to the Consignment In account and will result in closing that account. The entry is:

Consignment In—Lane Company	*3,065*	
Cash		*3,065*
Payment in full to consignor.		

After the posting of this entry, the ledger account for the consignment will appear as follows in the consignee's records:

Consignment In—Lane Company

10 TV sets:		*Sales—10 sets*	*4,000*
Transportation-in	*135*		
Commissions earned	*800*		
Payment to consignor	*3,065*		
	4,000		*4,000*

Several variations from the basic pattern of entries illustrated might be mentioned. If the policy of Ralph Brothers is to charge inbound freight on both consignment shipments and purchases of merchandise to a Freight In account, the portion applicable to the Lane Company consignment should later be reclassified by debiting Consignment In—Lane Company and crediting Freight In. If an advance is made by the consignee to the consignor, it is recorded as a debit to the Consignment In account, and the final payment is reduced by the amount of the advance. If goods are received on consignment from several suppliers, a controlling account entitled Consignments In may be established in the general ledger, and a supporting account for each consignment set up in a separate consignment ledger.

If the consignee, Ralph Brothers, does not wish to determine profits from consignment sales separately from regular sales, the sale of the consigned goods may be credited to the regular Sales account. Concurrently, an entry should be made debiting Cost of Sales (or Purchases) and crediting Consignment In—Lane Company, for the amount payable to the consignor for each unit sold (sales price minus agreed commission). Expenses chargeable to the consignor would be recorded by debiting this same account with the consignor and crediting cash or expense accounts. No entry would be made for commissions earned since the profit element would be represented by the difference between the amount credited to Sales and the amount debited to Cost of Sales (or Purchases). The Consignment In account would be closed by debiting it with the payment made to Lane Company in settlement for the consigned goods. This method is usually less desirable, since information on the profits earned on consignment sales as compared with other sales is usually needed by the consignee as a basis for sound operating decisions.

Balance sheet presentation of Consignment In accounts

Since a separate Consignment In account is desirable for each shipment of merchandise received on consignment, most companies will use a general ledger controlling account representing all consignments in, supported by a subsidiary ledger of individual Consignment In accounts.

At the end of the accounting period when financial statements are prepared, some Consignment In accounts may have debit balances and others credit balances. A debit balance will exist in a Consignment In account if the total of expenses, commissions, and advances is larger than the proceeds of sales of that particular lot of consigned goods. A credit balance will exist if the proceeds of sales are in excess of the expenses, commissions, and advances. The total of the Consignment In accounts with debit balances should be shown as an asset on the balance sheet; the total of the Consignment In accounts with credit balances should be classified as a liability. Any commissions earned but not recorded should of course be entered in the accounts before financial statements are prepared.

The balance of the controlling account represents the difference between the Consignment In accounts with debit balances and those with credit balances. This net figure should not be used on the balance sheet, because it is merely the result of offsetting asset and liability accounts.

Accounting methods of consignor

When the consignor ships merchandise to consignees, it is essential that he have a record of the location of this portion of his inventory. Therefore, he may establish in the general ledger a Consignment Out account for every consignment shipment. If consignment shipments are very numerous, the consignor may prefer to use a control account in the general ledger supported by individual consignment accounts in a subsidiary consignment ledger. Note that a separate account is maintained for each consignment shipment rather than with each consignee. Each consignment of goods is accounted for separately; therefore, successive consignments to a given consignee require separate accounts. The Consignment Out accounts should not be intermingled with accounts receivable, because they represent a special category of inventory rather than receivables.

Should profits on consignments be determined separately?

First, let us distinguish between a separate determination of *net income* on consignment sales and a separate determination of *gross profits* on consignment sales. Another possibility to consider is merely a separate determination of consignment revenues apart from other sales revenues.

Naturally, it would be interesting and useful to have very detailed information on the relative profitability of selling through consignees as compared with selling through other channels of distribution. However, our inclination to develop such information must be influenced by several practical considerations. First, the determination of a separate net income from consignment sales is seldom feasible because this would require allocations of many administrative and general overhead costs on a rather arbitrary basis. The work required would be extensive and the resulting data would be no better than the arbitrary decisions underlying it. In general, therefore, the determination of net income from consignment sales cannot be justified.

The determination of gross profits from consignment sales as distinguished from gross profits on other sales is much simpler, since it is based on the identification of direct costs associated with the consignments. However, the compilation of these direct costs can be an expensive process, especially if the gross profit is computed by individual consignments or consignees. Management should weigh the cost of this extra work against the need for information on consignment profits. In general, a separate determination of profits on consignments becomes more desirable if consignment transactions are substantial in relation to other sales.

A separation of consignment sales from other sales is usually a minimum step to develop information needed by management if consignment sales are an important part of total sales volume. On the other hand, no separation of consignment sales from other sales may be justified if only an occasional sale is made on a consignment basis.

Illustration of accounting methods of consignor

The choice of accounting methods by the consignor depends upon whether (1) consignment profits are to be determined separately from profits on regular sales or (2) sales on consignment are to be merged with regular sales without any effort to measure profits separately for the two types of transactions.

The entries required under these alternative methods of accounting for consignment shipments will now be illustrated; first under the assumption that profits on consignment sales are to be determined separately and secondly on the assumption that consignment sales are to be merged with regular sales without a separate determination of profits. The assumed transactions for these illustrations have already been described from the consignee's viewpoint but are now restated to include the cost data available to the consignor.

Lane Company shipped on consignment to Ralph Brothers 10 television sets which cost $250 each. Authorized selling price was $400 each. The cost of packing the merchandise for shipment was estimated to be $30; all expenses of the company's packing department are charged to the Packing Expense account. Transportation charges of $135 by an independent truck line to deliver the shipment to Ralph Brothers were paid by the consignee. All 10 sets were sold by the consignee at the authorized price of $400 each. After deducting the agreed commission of 20% and the transportation charges of $135, Ralph Brothers sent a check for $3,065 and the account sales illustrated on page 132 to Lane Company.

Consignment profits determined separately—perpetual inventory basis. Under the assumption of a separate accounting for consignment profits and a perpetual inventory system, the following series of entries will be made by the consignor.

For shipment on consignment:

Consignment Out—Ralph Brothers	*2,500*	
Inventory		*2,500*
To transfer the cost of consigned goods to a separate inventory account.		

This entry is based on the assumption that a perpetual inventory system is maintained. If the company uses the periodic inventory system, the credit side of the entry would be to the Purchases account or to the Consignment Shipments account.

The credit portion of this entry is a factor in determining the cost of sales for merchandise disposed of through direct sales rather than by consignment. The credit to the perpetual inventory account, Inventory, reflects the reduction in the stock of goods remaining on hand.

Packing expense:

Consignment Out—Ralph Brothers	*30*	
Packing Expense		*30*
To transfer packing expenses applicable to the consignment shipment to the Consignment Out account.		

Sales reported and payment received:

Cash	*3,065*	
Consignment Out—Ralph Brothers	*135*	
Commissions Expense—Consignment Sales	*800*	
Consignment Sales		*4,000*
Received account sales reporting sale of 10 TV sets at $400 each, less 20% commission and freight paid by consignee.		

If the consigned merchandise is sold on credit by the consignee, he may send the consignor an account sales but no check. In this case the debit will be to an account receivable rather than to cash.

Recording cost of consignment sales:

Cost of Consignment Sales	*2,665*	
Consignment Out—Ralph Brothers		*2,665*
To close the Consignment Out account and recognize cost of goods sold on consignment.		

After this series of entries affecting the Consignment Out account has been posted, the account will have been closed out, as shown by the following illustration.

Consignment Out—Ralph Brothers

10 TV sets at cost	*2,500*	*Cost of 10 TV sets sold*	*2,665*
Packing costs	*30*		
Freight	*135*		
	2,665		*2,665*

Consignment profits determined separately—periodic inventory basis. The same transactions previously illustrated are now presented again under the assumption that Lane Company relies on a periodic physical inventory and does not maintain perpetual inventory records.

For shipment on consignment:

Consignment Out—Ralph Brothers	*2,500*	
Consignment Shipments (or Purchases)		*2,500*
To record the cost of consigned goods.		

The credit side of this entry is a factor in determining the cost of sales of merchandise being disposed of through direct sales rather than on consignment. The determination of cost of goods available for direct sales transactions can be made on the income statement by deducting the Consignment Shipments account from the total of the beginning inventory and purchases. If the credit is made directly to the Purchases account rather than to Consignment Shipments, the Purchases account is thereby reduced to the amount to be used in computing cost of sales for direct sales transactions.

Packing expense:

Consignment Out—Ralph Brothers	*30*	
Packing Expense		*30*
To transfer packing expenses applicable to the consignment shipment to the Consignment Out account.		

Sales reported and payment received:

Cash	*3,065*	
Consignment Out—Ralph Brothers	*135*	
Commissions Expense—Consignment Sales	*800*	
Consignment Sales		*4,000*
Received account sales reporting sale of 10 TV sets at $400 each, less 20% commission and freight paid by consignee.		

Recording cost of consignment sales:

Cost of Consignment Sales	*2,665*	
Consignment Out—Ralph Brothers		*2,665*
To close the Consignment Out account and recognize cost of goods sold on consignment.		

Closing Consignment Shipments account:

Consignment Shipments	*2,500*	
Income Summary		*2,500*
To close the Consignment Shipments account.		

Consignment profits not determined separately—perpetual inventory basis. The following series of entries shows the same transactions of Lane Company, but under the assumption of a perpetual inventory and no separation of sales on consignment from regular sales.

For shipment on consignment:

Consignment Out—Ralph Brothers	*2,500*	
Inventory		*2,500*
To transfer the cost of consigned goods to a separate inventory account.		

Packing expense: No entry. Packing expenses are regularly charged to the Packing Expense account; there is no reason to reclassify the $30 of packing expense applicable to the Ralph Brothers consignment since profits on consignments are not to be separately determined.

Sales reported and payment received:

Cash	*3,065*	
Freight Expense	*135*	
Commissions Expense	*800*	
Sales		*4,000*
Received account sales reporting sale of 10 TV sets at $400 each, less 20% commission and freight paid by consignee.		

Note that the account credited is not Consignment Sales but Sales, since there is no intent to separate direct sales from consignment sales. Similarly, commissions paid to consignees are merged with other commissions expense, and freight applicable to the consignment shipment is merged with other freight expense.

Recording cost of sales:

Cost of Sales	*2,500*	
Consignment Out—Ralph Brothers		*2,500*
To close the Consignment Out account.		

The preceding entry shows a debit to Cost of Sales rather than to Cost of Consignment Sales since there is no need for a separation of the cost of goods sold directly and sold on consignment.

Consignment profits not determined separately—periodic inventory basis. This final series of entries for the Lane Company is based on the assumptions of the periodic inventory basis and no separation of consignment sales from regular sales.

For shipment on consignment:

Consignment Out—Ralph Brothers	*2,500*	
Consignment Shipments		*2,500*
To create a memorandum record of cost of goods on consignment.		

Packing expense: No entry.

Sales reported and payment received:

Cash	*3,065*	
Freight Expense	*135*	
Commissions Expense	*800*	
Sales		*4,000*
Received account sales reporting sale of 10 TV sets at $400 each, less 20% commission and freight paid by consignee.		

Closing Consignment Shipments account:

Consignment Shipments	*2,500*	
Consignment Out—Ralph Brothers		*2,500*
To close the memorandum record showing goods on consignment.		

Freight charges applicable to consigned goods are included in the valuation of inventory out on consignment when a balance sheet is prepared. For this reason it may be convenient to maintain a memorandum record of freight charges on each separate consignment shipment even though the company does not intend to determine profits on consignment sales separately from regular sales. The alternative is to analyze the freight expense account for outbound shipments and to make an appropriate allocation to the ending inventory of unsold goods on consignment.

Accounting for partial sale of a consignment

In the preceding examples, we have assumed that the consignor received an account sales showing that the entire consignment had been sold by the consignee. The account sales was accompanied by remittance in full, and the consignor's accounting entries were designed to record the profit from the completed consignment.

Let us now change our conditions by assuming that only four of the ten TV sets consigned by Lane Company to Ralph Brothers had been sold by the end of the accounting period. In order to prepare financial statements, the consignor must determine the amount of profit realized on the four consigned units sold and also determine the inventory value of the six unsold units.

Assume that an account sales is received by the consignor reporting the following information at year-end:

Sales: 4 TV sets at $400		*$1,600*
Less: Transportation-in	*$135*	
Commission (20% of $1,600)	*320*	*455*
Balance (check enclosed)		*$1,145*
Consigned merchandise on hand	*6 TV sets*	

Partial sale of consignment; profits determined separately from regular sales. If the consignor, Lane Company, measures profits on consignment sales separately from profits on regular sales, the account Consignment Out—Ralph Brothers will appear as follows before the data that are reported by the account sales are recorded.

Consignment Out—Ralph Brothers

10 TV sets at cost	*2,500*		
Packing expenses	*30*		

The entries by the consignor to record partial sale of the consignment are as follows:

Cash	*1,145*	
Consignment Out—Ralph Brothers	*135*	
Commissions Expense—Consignment Sales	*320*	
Consignment Sales		*1,600*
Received account sales reporting freight paid by consignee and sale of four of ten units consigned.		

Cost of Consignment Sales	*1,066*	
Consignment Out—Ralph Brothers		*1,066*
To record cost of goods sold on consignment and to adjust the Consignment Out account to year-end inventory value, as follows:		

10 TV sets at cost	*$2,500*
Packing costs	*30*
Freight	*135*
Total	*$2,665*
Allocable to 6 unsold units (60%)	*1,599*
Allocable to 4 units sold (40%)	*$1,066*

After the two preceding entries have been posted, the account Consignment Out—Ralph Brothers will show a debit balance of $1,599, which should appear in the current asset section of the balance sheet as Inventory on Consignment. The ledger account will appear as follows:

Consignment Out—Ralph Brothers

10 TV sets at cost	*2,500*	*Cost of 4 TV sets sold*	*1,066*
Packing costs	*30*		
Freight	*135*	*Balance down—6 sets unsold*	*1,599*
	2,665		*2,665*
Balance, 6 TV sets	*1,599*		

Under the periodic inventory system, an additional entry will be necessary to close the Consignment Shipments account to the Income Summary. This entry (as illustrated on page 138) is the same regardless of whether all, part, or none of the shipment has been sold by the closing date.

In the preceding illustration of partial sale of a consignment, we have employed the familiar accounting principle of carrying forward as part of inventory value a pro rata portion of those costs incurred to place the goods in a location and condition necessary for their sale. The selling commission allowed to the consignee on the units sold is of course deducted from revenues in the current period in order to achieve a logical matching of costs and revenues.

The income statement data we have developed may be summarized as follows:

Consignment sales	*$1,600*
Less: Cost of consignment sales	*1,066*
Gross profit on consignment sales	*$ 534*
Less: Commissions expense—consignment sales	*320*
Profit on consignment sales	*$ 214*

This information may be inserted in full or in part in the income statement. Whether to use a single net figure representing the profit from consignments or to include all the above data usually depends upon the relative importance of consignment sales to regular sales.

Partial sale of consignment; profits not determined separately—perpetual inventory basis. Under these assumptions the sequence of entries to be made by the consignor, Lane Company, is as follows:

For shipment on consignment:

Consignment Out—Ralph Brothers	*2,500*	
Inventory		*2,500*
To transfer the cost of consigned goods to a separate inventory account.		

Packing expense: No entry. All packing expenses are treated alike.

Partial sale reported and payment received:

Cash	*1,145*	
Freight Expense	*135*	
Commissions Expense	*320*	
Sales		*1,600*
Received account sales reporting sale of four TV sets at $400 each, less 20% commission and freight on entire consignment paid by consignee.		

Recording cost of sales:

Cost of Sales	*1,000*	
Consignment Out—Ralph Brothers		*1,000*
To record cost of units sold (40% × $2,500).		

Adjusting entry to defer consignment expense:

Deferred Packing and Freight Expense	*99*	
Packing Expense		*18*
Freight Expense		*81*
To defer expenses applicable to six units unsold at year-end ($30 packing expense + $135 freight) × 60%.		

Partial sale of consignment; profits not determined separately—periodic inventory basis. The entries to be made by Lane Company, the consignor, under these assumptions are as follows:

For shipment on consignment:

Consignment Out—Ralph Brothers	*2,500*	
Consignment Shipments		*2,500*
To create a memorandum record of cost of goods on consignment.		

Packing expense: No entry.

Partial sale reported and payment received:

Cash	*1,145*	
Freight Expense	*135*	
Commissions Expense	*320*	
Sales		*1,600*
Received account sales reporting sale of four TV sets at $400 each, less 20% commission and freight on entire consignment paid by consignee.		

Adjusting the memorandum record of consignment shipments:

Consignment Shipments	*1,000*	
Consignment Out—Ralph Brothers		*1,000*
To adjust the memorandum record showing goods on consignment.		

Adjusting entry to defer consignment expenses:

Deferred Packing and Freight Expense	*99*	
Packing Expense		*18*
Freight Expense		*81*
To defer expenses applicable to six units remaining unsold at year-end ($30 packing expense + $135 freight) × 60%.		

Disposition of Consignment Shipments account

In comparing the several alternative accounting methods which have been illustrated for use by the consignor, the disposition of the Consignment Shipments account deserves some attention. This account is used only with the periodic inventory method; it is credited with the cost of goods that have been shipped on consignment.

The method of closing the Consignment Shipments account depends upon whether the system is designed for a separate determination of profits on consignment sales, or for profits on consignments to be merged with profits on ordinary sales. If profits on consignment sales are to be determined separately, the Consignment Shipments account is closed to the Income Summary account. If the system is not designed to determine profits on consignments separately, then Consignment Shipments is merely a memorandum account which is closed against the Consignment Out account. The closing entry is simply a reversal of the memorandum entry made at the time of shipping goods to the consignee. Under these circumstances the function of the two accounts, Consignment Out and Consignment Shipments, is limited to providing a memorandum record of goods in the hands of consignees.

Return of unsold goods to consignor

We have stressed that the costs of packing and shipping goods to a consignee, whether paid directly by the consignor or by the consignee, are properly included in the inventory value assigned to merchandise on consignment. However, if the consignee for any reason returns goods to the consignor the packing and freight costs incurred on the original outbound shipment should immediately be written off as expense of the current period. The "place utility" originally created by these expenditures was lost when the goods were returned. Any charges borne by the consignor on the return shipment should also be treated as expense, along with any repair expenditures necessary to place the merchandise in salable condition.

Finally, a clear distinction should be made between freight costs on consignment shipments and outbound freight on regular sales. The latter is a current expense because the revenue from sale of the merchandise is recognized in the current period. The transportation cost of shipping goods to a consignee creates an increment in value of the merchandise, which is still the property of the consignor. This increment, along with the cost of acquiring or producing the goods, is to be offset against revenue in the accounting period in which the consigned goods are sold.

Advances from consignees

Although cash advances from a consignee are sometimes credited to the Consignment Out account, a better practice is to credit a liability account, Advances from Consignees. The Consignment Out account will then continue to show the asset value of goods on consignment rather than being shown net of a liability to the consignee.

Varying concepts of the Consignment Out account

When the student of accounting encounters a ledger account such as Consignment Out for the first time, he may gain a clear understanding of its function more quickly by considering where it belongs in the basic five types of accounts: assets, liabilities, owners' equity, revenue, and expense. Classification of the Consignment Out account within this structure will depend upon the methods employed by a particular company in accounting for consignments. If the company uses a system of determining profits on consignment sales separately from regular sales and also maintains a perpetual inventory system, then clearly the Consignment Out account belongs in the asset category. The account is debited with the cost of merchandise shipped to a consignee; when the consignee reports sale of all or a portion of the goods, the cost is transferred from Consignment Out to Cost of Consignment Sales. To be even more specific, Consignment Out is a current asset, one of the inventory group to be listed on the balance sheet as Inventory on Consignment, or perhaps merged with other inventories if the amount is not material. The costs of packing and transporting the consignment shipment to the consignee constitute an element of inventory cost. These costs may be charged to the Consignment Out account or carried in separate accounts, but under either method the costs of packing and shipping goods on consignment are to be deducted from revenue in the accounting period in which the consigned goods are sold. Consequently, the packing and shipping costs applicable to unsold goods on consignment at the balance sheet date should be treated as an asset—a part of the inventory valuation or a separate item of deferred expense.

Suppose that a company determines profits on consignments separately from regular sales but uses the periodic inventory system. Reference to the accounting entries presented earlier in this chapter for this set of conditions will show that actually the Consignment Out account functions as a perpetual inventory account even though the company does not maintain perpetual inventory records for its inventories other than those on consignment. The Consignment Out account is debited with the cost of goods shipped on consignment, with an offsetting credit to Shipments on Consignment. When the consigned goods are sold, the cost is transferred from Consignment Out to Cost of Consignment Sales. We may, therefore, conclude that the Consignment Out account belongs in the asset category just as in the preceding example.

The third alternative we have considered is that of the company which does not separate consignment sales from regular sales but does maintain perpetual inventory records. Again we must classify the Consignment Out account as an asset. It is debited with the cost of goods shipped to the consignee and credited with cost of goods sold by the consignee. This credit is offset by a debit to Cost of Sales. The Consignment Out account therefore continuously represents the cost of inventory in the hands of a consignee.

The last of the four alternative methods of accounting for consignments illustrated in this chapter was that of the company which did not separate consignment sales from regular sales and which relied upon a periodic inventory system. Under this system Consignment Out was debited and Consignment Shipments credited with the cost of goods shipped to a consignee. The two accounts were described as memoranda accounts, that is, related accounts with equal but opposing balances which provide valuable supplementary information but cancel each other out when financial statements are prepared. When the consignee reports the sale of consigned goods under this system, the consignor reverses the entry for shipment. If only a part of the consignment is sold, the reversing entry is for a proportionate amount of the original entry for shipment. Memoranda accounts are a special category outside our basic fivefold classification, because that classification is limited to the five types of accounts which comprise the financial statements. However, we should note that the Consignment Out account under this system, as in all the others, gives us a continuous record of the cost of goods held by a consignee. It affords the same control function as in the other examples, although it is continually offset by the Consignment Shipments account and therefore is eliminated in the process of preparing financial statements.

Still another concept of the Consignment Out account not illustrated previously in this chapter but used by some companies will now be summarized briefly. The Consignment Out account may be debited with the cost of merchandise shipped to the consignee and credited with the sales proceeds remitted by the consignee. This will normally result in a credit balance in Consignment Out when the entire shipment has been sold. This credit balance represents the profit earned by the consignor. The account is now closed by debiting Consignment Out and crediting a revenue account such as Profit on Consignment Sales. No separate account is used for Consignment Sales, and the income statement does not show the amount of sales made through use of consignees. Under this system the Consignment Out account does not fit into any of the five basic classes of accounts. It is a mixture of asset elements and revenues and must be closed or reduced to its asset element (cost of unsold consigned goods) before financial statements are prepared.

The methods we have illustrated in accounting for consignments are widely used, but many variations from these methods are quite acceptable. Our real concern lies in recognizing the issues which arise in accounting for consignment shipments under various assumptions as to inventory records and profit measurement. The most appropriate pattern of entries can only be determined in the light of conditions prevailing in a particular business. The choice of method is likely to be influenced by the nature and price of the commodities shipped on consignment, by the volume of transactions, by the degree of management's interest in internal control, and by the extent to which management utilizes accounting information as a basis for operating decisions.

Questions

1. How does a consignment of merchandise differ from a sale?

2. Avery Corporation sells goods outright for cash and on 30-day credit; it also makes sales through consignees. Explain how the two methods of marketing differ with respect to the time when income is recognized. What relationship, if any, exists between the recognition of profit and the receipt of payment by Avery Corporation?

3. Give reasons why the use of consignments may be advantageous from the viewpoint of both the consignor and the consignee.

4. On December 31, Mavis Company received a report from one of its consignees that 40 motors out of a consignment of 100 had been sold. No check was enclosed but the report indicated that payment would be made later. Mavis Company keeps its records on a calendar-year basis and maintains perpetual inventory records. It determines profits on consignment sales separately from profits on regular sales. What accounting action, if any, should be taken by Mavis Company at December 31 with respect to the consignee's report?

5. A Denver manufacturer of outboard motors accumulates production costs on job cost sheets. On March 20, Lot No. K-37, consisting of 100 identical motors, was completed at a cost of $14,000. Of the motors 25 were immediately shipped on consignment to a dealer in Florida and another 25 were sent to a consignee in California. The remaining 50 motors were still in the manufacturer's stockroom at March 31, the end of the fiscal year. Neither of the consignees submitted an account sales for March. Explain the quantity and valuation of motors in the manufacturer's balance sheet at March 31.

6. Give the entries to be made on the books of both the consignor and the consignee for each of the following transactions, assuming that both companies maintain perpetual inventories and measure profit on consignments separately from profits on other sales. Assume that the consignor receives no report from the consignee until all goods have been sold and receivables collected.
   a. Shipment of merchandise from consignor to consignee
   b. Payment of packing costs by consignor
   c. Payment of transportation charges by consignee upon arrival of consigned goods
   d. Advance by consignee to consignor
   e. Payment of advertising expenses by consignee applicable to consigned goods but not reimbursable by consignor
   f. Sale of consigned merchandise on account
   g. Collection of receivables by consignee
   h. Submission of account sales and check by consignee after deducting his commission and all reimbursable items

7. Morley Hardware received on consignment a shipment of 10 video tape recorders to be sold at a retail price of $900 each with a 20% commission specified in the consignment agreement. The transportation charges of $90 had been prepaid by the consignor. After one month of displaying the merchandise without making a sale, Morley decided the equipment was too costly to appeal to his clientele, so he shipped the entire lot back to the consignor on a collect basis. The return freight charges of $90 were paid by the consignor to the freight line at time of delivery. Assume that the consignor maintains perpetual inventory records and determines profits on consignment sales separately. The original cost of the recorders to the consignor was $600 each. What entries should be made by the consignor and by the consignee for this return of an unsold consignment?

8. Identify each of the following accounts by indicating whether it belongs in the ledger of the consignor or the consignee; whether it normally has a debit or credit balance; and how the account would be classified in the financial statements.
   a. Cost of Consignment Sales
   b. Consignment Out
   c. Consignment Sales
   d. Consignment In
   e. Consignment Shipments

9. During your first audit of the Douglas Corporation you find that an occasional shipment of goods is made on a consignment basis but that such transactions represent an extremely small portion of the total volume of sales. In reviewing these consignment transactions you note that freight charges are treated as expense at the time of shipment and that no adjustment has been made at year-end to defer the portion of the freight charge applicable to unsold units in the hands of consignees. In theoretical terms what is the issue involved? As auditor of the Douglas Corporation, what position would you take?

10. What difference, if any, do you see between outbound freight expense on regular sales and outbound freight expense on consignment shipments?

11. Bronson Company received a shipment of merchandise on consignment shortly before the end of its fiscal year and made a memorandum record of the goods. A portion of the consigned goods were sold before the end of the period and credited to the Consignment In account, but no account sales was submitted since it was expected that the remainder of the goods would be sold within a few weeks and a complete report could then be filed with the consignor and settlement made. Will the failure to submit an account sales to the consignor prevent a proper presentation of year-end financial statements by Bronson Company? What adjusting entries, if any, do you consider appropriate in the light of the above information?

12. Jameson Company makes a number of shipments on consignment, although most of its output is sold outright on 30-day credit. Consignment shipments are recorded on sales invoices which are posted as debits to Accounts Receivable and credits to Sales. The Jameson Company has never before been audited by independent public accountants, but at the suggestion of the company's bank you are retained to make an audit for the current year.

Would you as an independent auditor take exception to the company's method of accounting for consignments? Explain. What adjustments, if any, would be needed at year-end?

Short cases for analysis

5-1 The public accounting firm of Stuart and Burt, certified public accountants, is attempting to develop the management advisory services area of its practice. One of the firm's tax clients, Zero Corporation, affords an opportunity for work along this line. Zero Corporation, a manufacturer of machinery, has in the past sold its products through wholesalers and also directly to some large retail outlets.

During a telephone conversation on tax matters between the president of Zero Corporation and Mr. Stuart, the president posed the following question: "We are considering making sales of our products on a consignment basis as well as through our present outlets; would it be feasible to establish accounting methods that would show separately the net income we earned on the consignment transactions? I don't have time to discuss it now, but write me a memo and let me have your reactions."

Instructions

Write the memo requested, making any assumptions you deem necessary, and summarizing the issues involved and the alternatives available.

5-2 A professor of accounting posed the following question to a group of students: "Assume that two established wholesaling companies, East Corporation and West Corporation, decide to try sales on consignment as an additional method of marketing. They want to determine profits on consignments separately from profits on other sales. The two companies are identical in all but one respect: East Corporation maintains a perpetual inventory, and West Corporation relies on periodic inventories. What effects, if any, will this factor have upon the choice of appropriate methods of accounting for consignment sales and the internal control achieved?"

Student A replied as follows: "The existence of a perpetual inventory record will greatly influence the methods of accounting for consignments. As goods are shipped to consignees by East Corporation, the accounts will show a transfer at cost from one inventory account to another. However, West Corporation, which does not have perpetual inventories, will not be able to maintain this type of control over its goods on consignment. It will have to use a Consignment Shipments account and will have no clear continuous picture of the value of goods held by consignees.

Student B took a different position: "I disagree completely with A. The control over goods shipped on consignment can be just as strong for one company as the other. A doesn't seem to understand the use of a Consignment Shipments account."

Student C offered the following comment: "I think the principal difference in accounting for consignments by East and West is that West would not know until the year-end physical inventory whether its consignment business was profitable, but East could determine the profit or loss on each consignment."

Instructions

Evaluate the views expressed by each student and add any significant points that you feel may have been overlooked by them.

5-3 Manning Company made the four journal entries shown below to record various transactions relating to a consignment of merchandise received from a manufacturer.

1967			
Mar. 27	*Consignment In*	*24*	
	Cash		*24*
Apr. 25	*Cash*	*800*	
	Consignment In		*800*
Apr. 25	*Consignment In*	*200*	
	Commissions Earned		*200*
May 5	*Consignment In*	*576*	
	Cash		*576*

Instructions

a. Describe fully each of the transactions which were recorded by journal entries.

b. Prepare journal entries to record the consignment transactions on the books of the consignor. Assume that the consigned goods cost $400 and that the consignor maintains perpetual inventory records.

c. State how the facts should be presented on the balance sheets of both the consignee and the consignor as of April 30, 1967. Explain your reasons for such presentation.

AICPA adapted

Problems

5-4 Hall Company makes only a small part of its sales through consignees and does not make a separate determination of profits on consignment sales. The company relies on a periodic inventory. During June the company shipped ten machines to a consignee, under an agreement that he should receive a 25% commission on a retail sales price of $4,000 for each machine. Packing expenses of $300 and transportation charges of $1,200 were paid by the consignor. The machines had been purchased by Hall Company for $2,000 each.

At June 30, Hall Company received a check for $11,500 from the consignee along with an account sales reporting that eight machines had been sold, that $12,000 in accounts receivable was outstanding, that $500 in reimbursable repair expenses had been incurred on one of the machines sold, and that two machines remained unsold.

Instructions

a. Assuming that Hall Company had made appropriate accounting entries up to this point, give the entries to be made upon receipt of the account sales and any adjustments required by the June 30 closing of the books.

b. What items, if any, should appear in Hall Company's balance sheet at June 30 relating to the consignment? Explain.

5-5 The Larsen Corporation sells a limited number of its products through agents on a consignment basis. In the spring of 1968, the company arranged to sell outboard motors through a consignee, the Marine Supply Co. in Newport Beach, California. The motors were to be sold by the consignee at a fixed price of $300 each, and the consignee allowed a 15% commission on gross sales price. The consignee agreed to guarantee the accounts receivable and to remit all collections less the commission on accounts collected. The consignee was also allowed to deduct certain agreed reimbursable costs; these costs were chargeable to the consignor as incurred. Both companies maintain perpetual inventory records.

Transactions relating to the consignment during the first six months of 1968 were as follows:

Consignor's transactions:

Apr. 10	*Sent 30 motors to Marine Supply Co., cost of each motor $180. Total packing costs paid for shipment $120.*
June 30	*Received account sales from Marine Supply Co. and check for $4,255.*

Consignee's transactions:

Apr. 15	*Received 30 motors and paid freight charges, $150.*
May 1–June 23	*Sold 20 motors and collected $5,200.*
June 2	*Paid $15 for minor repairs on two motors sold.*
June 30	*Sent account sales to Larsen Corporation with a check for $4,255 enclosed.*

Instructions

a. Prepare all entries on the books of the Larsen Corporation and on the books of the Marine Supply Co., assuming that both companies wish to report profits on consignment sales separately. Closing entries are not required.

b. Prepare all entries on the books of the Larsen Corporation and on the books of the Marine Supply Co., assuming consignment sales are combined with regular sales. Closing entries are not required.

c. Would the balance of the Consignment In account maintained by Marine Supply Co. be of the same amount at June 30 under the differing assumptions in (a) and (b) above? What is the balance of that account and how should it be shown in the financial statements of Marine Supply Co. at June 30?

5-6 Henry Hill sells pianos for Keys, Inc., on a consignment basis. His ledger shows the following account summarizing consignment activities for the month of May:

Consignment In—Keys, Inc.

Memo: Received 10 pianos		*Sale of 6 pianos*	*4,818*
Paid freight and insurance	*120*		
Delivery to customers of 6 pianos	*80*		
Commissions earned	*723*		
Storage fees on 4 unsold pianos (as agreed)	*20*		
Remittance	*2,100*		

The cost of the pianos to Keys, Inc., was $480 each. The accounting policies of Keys, Inc., provide for a separate determination of profits on consigned goods as distinguished from profits on direct sales. The company maintains perpetual inventory records and also maintains a separate Consignment Out account for each consignee. All costs applicable to a consignment of pianos are charged to the Consignment Out account. When sales are reported by a consignee, the gross sales price is credited to Consignment Sales. The Consignment Out account is then relieved of the cost of the units sold by transferring this amount to Cost of Consignment Sales.

Instructions

a. Give all entries required on the books of the consignor, Keys, Inc., during May.

b. Construct the Consignment Out ledger account applicable to the transactions with Henry Hill showing all entries during May.

c. How should the month-end balances in the Consignment Out and Consignment In accounts appear on the financial statements of the consignor and the consignee at May 31?

5-7 You are examining the December 31, 1967, financial statements of the Davis Sales Company, a new client. The company was established on January 1, 1966, and is a distributor of air-conditioning units. The company's income statements for 1966 and 1967 were presented to you as follows:

DAVIS SALES COMPANY
Statements of Income and Expense
for the years ended December 31, 1967 and 1966

	1967	1966
Sales	$1,287,500	$1,075,000
Cost of sales	669,500	559,000
Gross profit	$ 618,000	$ 516,000
Selling and administration expense	403,500	330,000
Net income before income taxes	$ 214,500	$ 186,000
Provision for income taxes, at 50%	107,250	93,000
Net income	$ 107,250	$ 93,000

Your examination disclosed the following:

(1) Some sales were made on open account; other sales were made through dealers to whom units were shipped on a consignment basis. Both sales methods were in effect in 1966 and 1967. In both years, however, the company treated all shipments as outright sales.

(2) The sales price and cost of the units were the same in 1966 and 1967. Each unit had a cost of $130 and was uniformly invoiced at $250 to open-account customers and to consignees.

(3) During 1967 the amount of cash received from consignees in payment for units sold by them was $706,500. Consignees remit for the units as soon as they are sold. Confirmations received from consignees showed that they had a total of 23 unsold units on hand at December 31, 1967. Consignees were unable to confirm the unsold units on hand at December 31, 1966.

(4) The cost of sales for 1967 was determined by the client as follows:

		Units	
Inventory on hand in warehouses, Dec. 31, 1966		1,510	
Purchases		4,454	
Available for sale		5,964	
Inventory on hand in warehouse, Dec. 31, 1967		814	
Shipments to: Open-account customers	3,008		
Consignee customers	2,142	5,150	@ $130 = $669,500

Instructions

a. Compute the total amount of the Davis Sales Company's inventory at December 31, 1967, and December 31, 1966.

b. Prepare the auditor's work-sheet journal entries to correct the financial statements for the year ended December 31, 1966.

c. Prepare the formal adjusting journal entries to correct the accounts at December 31, 1967. (The books have not been closed. Do not prepare the closing journal entries.)

AICPA adapted

5-8 Evans and Farmer operate a retail business with profits shared in a 3:2 ratio. Financial statements at the end of 1968 were prepared by their bookkeeper as follows:

EVANS AND FARMER
Balance Sheet
December 31, 1968

Cash	$ 6,230	*Accounts payable*		$ 14,210
Accounts receivable	24,000	*Accrued liabilities*		2,100
Less: Allowance for bad debts	(600)	*Purchase-money mortgage payable, 6½%*		15,000
Merchandise	31,300	*Total liabilities*		$ 31,310
Plant and equipment	62,000			
Less: Accumulated depreciation	(21,600)	*Evans, capital*	$47,300	
		Farmer, capital	30,510	77,810
Other assets (noncurrent)	7,790			
Total assets	$109,120	*Total liabilities & capital*		$109,120

EVANS AND FARMER
Income Statement
for year ended December 31, 1968

Sales		$160,800
Less cost of sales		120,600
Gross profit		$ 40,200
Operating expenses:		
Selling	$6,200	
General	8,660	14,860
Operating income		$ 25,340
Interest expense on mortgage		1,120
Net income		$ 24,220

EVANS AND FARMER
Statement of Fund Flows
for year ended December 31, 1968

Funds were provided:		
Operations—net income	$24,220	
Add: Depreciation	4,500	$28,720
Funds were applied:		
Partners' drawings (equally)	$17,500	
Reclassification of portion of purchase money mortgage from noncurrent to current	3,000	20,500
Increase in working capital		$ 8,220

On January 3, 1969, the partners present the foregoing financial statements to a local bank in an effort to borrow $40,000. The money would be used to open a branch store in the south part of the city where the partnership has been distributing its products through a consignee.

The banker is inclined to grant the loan but he wants the financial statements revised because of the following information which comes to his attention:

(1) The partners determined the inventory on December 31, 1968, by starting with the inventory on December 31, 1967 (excluding goods in hands of consignees) of $26,000, adding purchases for the year, and deducting 75% of sales. No physical inventory was taken on December 31, 1968.

(2) Shipments to the consignees are not recorded on the books, and receivables from consignees are not included in the general ledger or on the financial statements. However, a complete memorandum record is maintained with each consignee and includes the following information:

	Dec. 31, 1967	*Dec. 31, 1968*
Receivable from consignees—on account of sales completed		*$1,200*
Cost of merchandise in hands of consignees (including deferrable costs)	*$4,200*	*7,150*
Sales value of merchandise in hands of consignees	*5,400*	*9,050*

When remittances are received from consignees, it is the company's practice to debit Cash and credit Sales. Selling expenses not recorded as a result of this procedure amount to $380.

(3) An inventory of sales supplies amounting to $650 and accrued general expenses of $240 were overlooked in preparing the financial statements on December 31, 1968.

The purchase-money mortgage matures at the rate of $1,500 every six months. The partners are able to determine that the inventory actually on hand December 31, 1968, amounted to $36,180, excluding goods in hands of consignees. Other assets include delivery equipment not used in business on which depreciation of $250 was recorded and credited to the Accumulated Depreciation account. The equipment is up for sale at a figure substantially in excess of book value.

Instructions

a. Prepare working papers to restate the accounts as of December 31, 1968. Include revenue and expense accounts, and show the beginning balances of the partners' capital accounts in the trial balance. The following pairs of columns are suggested: Trial balance, Dec. 31, 1968; Corrections; Income statement; and Balance sheet. Add a legend showing brief explanations for each correcting entry and a supporting schedule showing the computation of purchases for 1968.

b. Prepare a revised income statement and a classified balance sheet.

c. Prepare a summary entry to correct the books of the partnership, assuming that closing entries for 1968 have been posted.

d. Prepare a revised statement of working capital flows. Indicate the corrected amount of working capital as of December 31, 1967.

5-9 The Sunset Mfg. Co. is engaged in production of custom-made deep freezers and sells a part of its output through consignees. Seventy-five freezers were sent to various consignees late in 1968, including 30 units to Forrester Appliances. Account sales received by the Sunset Mfg. Co. from Forrester Appliances at the end of November and at the end of December follow:

FORRESTER APPLIANCES
Tucson, Arizona
Account Sales

November 30, 1968

Sales for account and risk of:

Sunset Mfg. Co.
Denver, Colorado

Sales—12 freezers @ $495		*$5,940*
Charges: Transportation expenses	*$ 240*	
Delivery of 12 units sold	*60*	
Commission (20% of $5,940)	*1,188*	*1,488*
Balance		*$4,452*
Check enclosed		*3,052*
Balance due, Nov. 30, 1968 (accounts not collected)		*$1,400*

Consigned merchandise on hand, 18 freezers.

FORRESTER APPLIANCES
Tucson, Arizona
Account Sales

December 31, 1968

Sales for account and risk of:

Sunset Mfg. Co.
Denver, Colorado

Balance due, Nov. 30, 1968		*$1,400*
Sales—10 freezers @ $495	*$4,950*	
6 freezers @ $465	*2,790*	*7,740*
		$9,140
Charges: Delivery of 16 units sold	*$ 88*	
Replacement of parts on last 4 units (including 2 unsold units)	*24*	
Commission (20% of $7,740)	*1,548*	*1,660*
Balance		*$7,480*
Cash enclosed		*5,080*
Balance due, Dec. 31, 1968 (accounts not collected)		*$2,400*

Consigned merchandise on hand, 2 freezers.

The 30 sets consigned to Forrester Appliances were produced on job order 37 for 60 freezers. The cost sheet for job order 37 shows the following information:

Direct materials	*$5,100*	
Direct labor	*4,400*	
Factory overhead, 125% of labor	*5,500*	*$15,000*

Costs applicable to job order 37 have been transferred from work in process to the finished goods inventory account. No other costs were incurred by the Sunset Mfg. Co. Late in December the consignee was instructed to reduce the price on the freezers to $465 per unit. The consignee remits cash to the consignor as soon as collections are made from customers. At the end of each month the Sunset Mfg. Co. wished to have an allowance for bad accounts equal to 5% of accounts receivable from consignees.

The Sunset Mfg. Co. uses a perpetual inventory system. Among the ledger accounts used for consignment transactions are Consignment Sales, Cost of Consignment Sales, Accounts Receivable from Consignees, Consignment Out—Forrester Appliances, Transportation Expense—Consignment Sales, Delivery Expense—Consignment Sales, Commissions Expense—Consignment Sales, Bad Debt Expense—Consignment Sales, Allowance for Bad Debts—Consignment Receivables, and Miscellaneous Expense—Consignment Sales.

Delivery expense is defined as charges for delivery by consignee to customers of units sold; such charges are reimbursable from the consignor. Transportation Expenses—Consignment Sales is charged with the portion of costs of moving goods from consignor to consignee which is applicable to units sold. Transportation costs applicable to unsold units are recorded in the Consignment Out account, but as these units are reported to be sold the transportation cost is shifted from the Consignment Out account to the expense account. Consequently, the Cost of Consignment Sales accounts shows only manufactured cost of units sold.

Forrester Appliances combines consignment sales with regular sales and relies on a periodic inventory rather than maintaining perpetual inventory records. When consigned goods are sold, the full sales price is credited to the regular Sales account. To distinguish consignment receivables from other accounts receivable, the company uses the account title of Consignment Accounts Receivable.

Instructions

a. Give all entries required on the books of the Sunset Mfg. Co. for 1968 relating to the Forrester Appliances consignment.

b. Give all entries required on the books of Forrester Appliances for 1968 relating to the consignment from the Sunset Mfg. Co.

c. Give the balances that should be reported in the following accounts on December 31, 1968, and state the classification of each account.

For consignor:

Consignment Out

Accounts Receivable from Consignees

For consignee:

Consignment In

5-10 The Barnard Company decided at the beginning of 1968 to try selling its products on consignment in addition to its established policy of selling on 30-day credit to retail stores. The consignment contracts stipulated that receivables from sale of consigned goods were guaranteed by the consignees. The following entries show in summary form the accounts used and procedures followed by the Barnard Company in accounting for its transactions with consignees.

Jan. 2–June 30, 1968

Transportation Expense	425	
Accounts Receivable	21,500	
Cost of Sales	13,400	
Sales		21,500
Inventory		13,400
Cash		425

Shipped following merchandise on consignment:

Product	*Quantity*	*Total cost*	*Sales price*	*Transportation*	*Consignee*
A	100	$2,000	$ 3,000	$ 40	Axel
B	80	2,400	4,000	120	Barnes
C	50	3,000	5,500	65	Cox
D	200	6,000	9,000	200	Davis
		$13,400	$21,500	$425	

Jan. 2–Dec. 28, 1968

Cash	11,362	
Accounts Receivable		11,362

To record remittances from consignees as follows:

Consignee	*Units sold*	*Total sales*	*Commissions*	*Installation expenses applicable to units sold*	*Net*	*Cash enclosed*
Axel	40	$ 1,200	$ 120	$ 18	$ 1,062	$ 1,062
Barnes	50	2,500	375	35	2,090	1,000
Cox	40	4,400	660	78	3,662	3,400
Davis	180	8,100	1,620	104	6,376	5,900
		$16,200	$2,775	$235	$13,190	$11,362

On December 31, the Barnard Company received a letter from a consignee confirming the following additional sales to December 31, 1968:

Consignee	*Units sold*	*Total sales*	*Commissions*	*Installation expenses*	*Net*	*Cash enclosed*
Axel	20	$600	$60	$10	$530	-0-

Instructions

Prepare required correcting and adjusting entries for the Barnard Company as of December 31, 1968, assuming that consignment and regular sales data are combined in the accounts. A separate receivable account showing unremitted proceeds from consignees should be used. Include in the explanation of each correcting or adjusting entry a schedule or other detailed explanation of the underlying data.

5-11 The General Products Co. is engaged in the production of a broad line of products at eight different factory locations. Management is currently studying two problems: The first is the possibility of opening Plant 9 for the production of a new line of lawn mowers operated by remote control on a solar cell. The mowers would be sold through consignees for a commission of 10% of sales price. The projected costs for 20,000 mowers have been prepared by company engineers and cost accountants as follows:

Type of cost	*Total costs*	*Variable portion of total costs, %*
Direct materials	*$ 525,000*	*100*
Direct labor	*375,000*	*80*
Factory overhead	*300,000*	*65*
General and administrative (excluding commissions)	*120,000*	*50*
	$1,320,000	

The company wants to know whether or not the mowers could be sold at a price to yield a 15% net income before taxes on sales of 20,000 units and what the approximate break-even point would be at the projected price.

The other problem confronting management concerns Plant 5, which produces golf carts and has been operating in excess of its normal monthly capacity of 50,000 labor-hours. All output of Plant 5 is sold through four consignees. Management has requested its accounting staff to prepare a breakdown of the sales, costs, and profits from each of the four consignees. The company has been operating 60,000 labor-hours per month but it does not wish to do so in the future. Consequently, it is now necessary to allocate output among the four consignees. The consignees are allowed to set the price on the carts at any figure above $40 per cart. Commission to consignees is determined as follows:

On price of $40 per cart	*$5*
On price in excess of $40 per cart	*40% of excess*

The breakdown of monthly sales and cost data, as experienced during the last year, is shown in the following table:

	Consignees				
	A	*B*	*C*	*D*	*Total*
Carts shipped and sold	*10,000*	*4,000*	*4,000*	*2,000*	*20,000*
Average sales price	*$42*	*$48*	*$47*	*$50*	*$45*
Cost of shipping (per cart)	*$1.50*	*$1.20*	*$2.00*	*$1.00*	*$1.49*
Consignees' reimbursable costs (per cart)	*$0.70*	*$1.00*	*$1.50*	*$2.50*	*$1.10*
Commissions (per cart)	*$5.80*	*$8.20*	*$7.80*	*$9.00*	*$7.00*

The manufacturing cost per cart at normal capacity is $15 of variable costs and $7 of fixed costs. Other selling and administrative costs for Plant 5 amount to $10,000 and their behavior pattern is relatively fixed.

Instructions

a. Determine the selling price that should be charged on the lawn mowers to be produced by Plant 9 in order for General Products Co. to realize a pretax profit of 15% on sales volume of 20,000 units.

b. How many units must be sold in order for Plant 9 to break even, based on the selling price determined in (a)?

c. Determine the marginal income earned by Plant 5 on carts sold by each consignee. Compute both the marginal income per cart and the total marginal income from each consignee. ("Marginal income" as used in this problem means average sale price minus commissions, reimbursable selling costs incurred by consignees, shipping costs, and a variable portion of production cost.)

d. Since the monthly production of Plant 5 should be reduced by approximately 3,333 carts in order to reduce the monthly labor-hours worked from 60,000 to 50,000 hours, how would you recommend that the 16,667 carts to be produced each month be allocated to the consignees? Your answer need not specify quantities but should indicate which consignees constitute most profitable outlets. What other actions would you recommend for consideration by management to increase the profitability of Plant 5?

6 INSTALLMENT SALES

Installment sales throughout the economy

"Fly Now, Pay Later" is the term used by the airlines to describe the installment sales plan now available to air travelers. Under this plan the airline passenger may make a down payment of as little as 10% and pay the remaining cost of his ticket over a period as long as two years. Although the concept of the installment sale was first developed in the field of real estate and for high-priced durable goods such as automobiles, it has now spread through nearly every sector of the economy, embracing personal services as well as real estate and personal property. Almost all single-family residences are sold on the installment plan, with monthly payments extending as long as 25 to 30 years. Installment sales also are very widely used by dealers in home furnishings and appliances and in farm equipment. For these products the installment payments are usually due monthly for periods of from 6 to 36 months.

The current annual report of Sears, Roebuck and Co. indicates that its approximately two billion dollars of receivables are principally customer installment accounts. The company has more than thirteen million individual installment accounts. These receivables constitute the largest single asset on the balance sheet and represent more than half the company's total assets.

For many types of business, the technique of installment sales has been a key factor in achieving large-scale operation. The automobile industry, for example, could hardly have developed to anything like its present size without the use of installment sales. The huge volume of output achieved by the auto industry has in turn made possible economies in tooling, production, and distribution which could not have been achieved on a small scale of operation. Credit losses are often increased when a business adopts an installment sales plan but this disadvantage may be more than offset by the expanded sales volume.

To the accountant, installment sales pose some puzzling problems. The most basic of these issues is the proper matching of costs and revenues. Should the gross profit inherent in an installment sale be treated as revenue in the period the sale occurs, or should it be spread over the life of the installment contract? What should be done with collection expenses and other expenses which occur in periods subsequent to the sale? How should defaults and repossessions be handled?

Certain methods of accounting for installment sales are acceptable for income tax purposes and offer significant tax advantages. The practicing accountant is therefore under pressure in designing an accounting system to follow the tax-approved methods regardless of whether some other approach might produce a better matching of costs and revenues or might be more defensible from a theoretical standpoint.

Regardless of the accounting dilemmas raised by installment sales, we can realistically assume that installment contracts will continue to be a major element in the economy. The accountant, therefore, must examine the issues and develop the most effective techniques possible for measuring, controlling, and reporting installment sales. At the same time the accounting profession bears the responsibility of developing a broad structure of accounting theory which will encompass logical and improved methods of accounting for installment sales as well as regular credit sales. As we progress through this chapter, it will be apparent that installment sales are one of the many thorny problems confronting the accounting profession as it searches for a consistent set of universally useful accounting principles.

Special characteristics of installment sales

An installment sale is a sale of real or personal property or services which provides for a series of payments over a period of months or years. A down payment is usually but not always required. Since the seller must wait a considerable period of time to collect the full sales price, it is customary to provide for interest on the unpaid balance, or to include a "load factor" in the sales price.

The risk to the seller of noncollection is greatly increased by use of the installment plan. The customers generally are in weaker financial condition than those who buy on open account; furthermore, the credit rating of the customer and his ability to pay may change significantly during the long time period covered by an installment contract.

To protect himself against this greater risk of noncollection, the seller of real or personal property usually selects a form of contract which enables him to repossess the property if the buyer fails to make all the agreed payments. Among the more common contractual arrangements to permit recovery of goods are the following:

1. Conditional sales contract. Title to the goods does not pass at time of delivery but is retained by the seller until the final payment under the contract has been received. Strictly speaking, such a transaction is not a sale but a contract to sell. For accounting purposes, however, it is customary to treat a conditional sales contract as a sale.

2. Trust deed. At date of delivery of the goods, title is conveyed to a trustee. When the final payment is received by the seller, the trustee gives title to the buyer. In the event of nonpayment, title reverts to the seller.

3. Mortgage. Title to the property passes to the purchaser immediately, but it is subject to a mortgage or lien on the property for the unpaid portion of the sales price.

4. Lease-option plan. Title is retained by the seller, with the purchaser having possession of the property under a lease-option agreement. After lease payments approximately equal to the purchase price have been made, the customer has the option of acquiring title by making a final payment.

The value and effectiveness of the seller's right to repossess goods varies greatly by type of industry. As previously indicated, installment sales are often made by service enterprises such as the airlines; for the service-type business, repossession is obviously not available as a safeguard against credit losses. In reality, for many types of personal property as well, the seller's right to repossess the goods may be more of a threat than a real assurance against loss. The merchandise may have been damaged or may have depreciated to a point that it is worth less than the balance due on the installment contract. A basic rule in attempting to minimize losses from nonpayment of installment contracts is to require a sufficient down payment to cover the loss of value when property moves out of the "new merchandise" category. A corollary rule is that the payment schedule should not be outstripped by the projected decline in value of the article sold. In other words, the payments required up to any given date in the contract should be at least as much as the loss in market value of the goods. For example, if a customer buying an automobile on the installment plan finds after a year or so that his car is currently worth less than the balance still owed on the contract, his motivation to continue the payments may be considerably reduced.

Often competitive pressures within an industry will not permit a business to adhere to these standards. Furthermore, repossession may be a difficult and expensive process, especially if the customer is noncooperative or perhaps has disappeared. The sales value of repossessed merchandise is sometimes difficult to determine. Reconditioning and repair may be necessary to make the goods salable and even after such expenditures, sale of repossessed merchandise may be more difficult than for similar new goods. For these reasons, credit losses are likely to be significantly higher on installment sales than on regular credit sales.

A related problem is the increased collection expense when payments are spread over an extended period. Accounting costs also are multiplied by the use of installment sales, and large amounts of working capital are tied up in receivables. In recognition of these problems, many businessmen have concluded that the handling of installment receivables is a separate business and they therefore sell their installment contracts receivable to finance companies which specialize in credit and collection activities. Some of the airlines, for example, inform customers who buy tickets on the installment plan that the credit will be handled by a separate finance company. In the automobile industry, subsidiary corporations have been formed by some manufacturers to finance customers' installment contracts.

Methods for recognition of profits on installment sales

The determination of net income on installment sales is complicated by the fact that the amounts of revenue and related expenses are seldom known quantities in the period when the sale is made. Substantial expenses (as for collection, accounting, repairs, and repossession) are likely to be incurred in subsequent periods. In some specific businesses, the risk of noncollection may even be so great as to raise doubts as to the recognition of any profit at the inception of the contract.

The first objective in developing accounting policies for installment sales should be a reasonable matching of revenues and expenses. In recognition of the diverse business conditions under which installment sales are made, however, accountants have sanctioned alternative approaches to the problem.

Two general plans of accounting for installment sales are widely used: (1) the gross profit (excess of sales price over cost of goods sold) is recognized at the time of the sale, and (2) the gross profit is recognized in installments over the life of the contract on the basis of cash collections.

Recognition of gross profit at time of sale. To recognize the entire gross profit at the time of making an installment sale is to say in effect that installment sales should be treated like regular sales on credit.[1] The goods have been delivered to the customer and an enforceable receivable of definite amount has been acquired. The excess of the receivable contract over the cost of goods delivered is realized profit in the traditional meaning of the term. The accounting entry consists of a debit to Installment Contracts Receivable and a credit to Installment Sales. If perpetual inventories are maintained, a companion entry is needed to transfer the cost of the goods from Inventory to Cost of Installment Sales. No recognition is given to the seller's retention of title to the goods, since the normal expectation is completion of the contract through collection of the receivable. Implicit in this recognition of gross profit at the time of sale is the assumption that all expenses relating to the sale will be recognized in the same period so that the determination of net income will be a valid process.

The expenses associated with the sale include collection expenses, repossession expenses, and bad debts. Recognition of these expenses in the period of sale requires an estimate of the customer's performance over the entire life of the installment contract. Such an estimate may be considerably more difficult to make than the normal provision made for bad debts from regular sales, which involves credit extension for only 30 or 60 days. However, with careful study of experience in the industry and in the particular business, reasonably satisfactory estimates can probably be made. The accounting entries would consist of year-end debits

[1] "There is no sound accounting reason for the use of the installment method for financial statement purposes in the case of closed transactions in which collection is dependent upon lapse of time and the probabilities of realization are properly evaluated. In the opinion of the Committee, such income has accrued and should be recognized in the financial statements even though deferred for tax purposes." *Accounting and Reporting Standards for Corporate Financial Statements,* issued in 1957 by the Committee on Concepts and Standards Underlying Corporate Financial Statements, American Accounting Association.

to expense accounts and credits to valuation accounts such as Allowance for Bad Debts and Allowance for Collection and Repossession Expenses. These valuation accounts would be debited in later periods as expenses applicable to the installment contracts became known.

This method of accounting for installment sales is widely used by retail stores which make only a portion of their sales on the installment plan and which often sell these installment contracts to finance companies. The method is clearly within the framework of generally accepted accounting principles. As followed in most companies, however, the procedures described are subject to one important modification: no provision is made for collection and repossession expenses. Such an estimated expense is not a permissible deduction for the determination of taxable income. Some companies, however, prefer to make provision for these later expenses in order to develop more accurate accounting data for managerial use; they must then carry out appropriate adjustments in computing taxable income.

Recognition of gross profit in installments. The alternative approach to income determination for installment sales is to recognize gross profit in installments over the life of the contract on the basis of cash collections. Emphasis is shifted from the acquisition of a receivable to the collection of that receivable as the basis for realization of profit; in other words, a modified cash basis of accounting is substituted for the accrual basis.

The installment method of accounting

The term *installment method of accounting* means that each collection on the contract is regarded as including both a return of cost and a realization of gross profit in the ratio in which these two elements were included in the total sales price.

For example, assume that a farm equipment dealer sells for $1,000 a machine which cost him $600. The $400 excess of the sales price over cost is regarded as *deferred gross profit.* Since cost and gross profit constituted 60% and 40%, respectively, of the sales price, this 60:40 ratio is used to divide each collection under the contract between the recovery of cost and realization of gross profit. If $100 is received as a down payment, then $40 of the deferred gross profit has become realized and is taken into income of the current period. At the end of each accounting period, the Deferred Gross Profit account will equal 40% of the installment receivable remaining uncollected. The revenue account, Realized Gross Profit on Installment Sales, will show for each period an amount equal to 40% of the collections during that period. In this illustration the question of interest charges is purposely omitted; it is considered later in the chapter.

The method described is acceptable under income tax regulations. In fact, the opportunity to postpone the recognition of income for tax purposes is undoubtedly responsible for the current popularity of the installment method of accounting. The tax advantages are readily apparent; the theoretical support for the method is much less impressive. The installment method of accounting, however, is considered within the scope of generally accepted accounting principles.

Accounting Research Study No. 3, "A Tentative Set of Broad Accounting Principles for Business Enterprises," emphasizes that revenues should be identified with the accounting period in which the major economic activities necessary to the creation and disposition of goods and services are performed. The study then criticizes the installment method of accounting in the following statement:

> Collectibility of receivables is not necessarily less predictable because collections are scheduled in installments. The postponement of recognition of revenues until they can be measured by actual cash receipt is not in accordance with the concept of an accrual accounting. Any uncertainty as to collectibility should be expressed by a separately calculated and separately disclosed estimate of uncollectibles rather than by a postponement of the recognition of revenue.[2]

Single sale of real estate on the installment basis

The holder of real estate which has appreciated greatly in value is often willing to sell only on the installment basis so that he can spread the profit over several years for tax purposes. Federal tax regulations presently permit the use of the installment method for the sale of real estate if the payment received during the year of the sale does not exceed 30% of the sales price.

Let us assume that on November 1, 1966, John Stone sells for $105,000 a tract of land acquired some years ago for $40,000. Commission and other expenses pertaining to the sale amount to $5,000. Since Stone is not in the real estate business, he treats these expenses as a deduction in determining the gross profit on the sale rather than charging them to business expense accounts. (This handling of expenses incident to the sale is the same as that used by an individual investor who sells investment securities and deducts the broker's commission in computing the gross profit on the sale.) The net amount receivable from the sale is therefore $100,000, of which 40% represents the return of cost and 60% represents deferred gross profit. All collections under the sale, including the down payment, will be regarded as consisting of 40% return of cost and 60% realization of gross profit. Stone maintains his accounting records on a calendar-year basis.

The sales agreement signed by Stone called for a down payment of $25,000 and a note secured by a trust deed payable $5,000 every six months, plus 6% interest on the unpaid balance. The entries on page 166 show the sales transaction, the interest accrual at year-end, the collections on the note during the next year, and the realization of a portion of the deferred gross profit. Since this transaction is an isolated sale by a nondealer, there is no need to use an Installment Sales account; the Deferred Gross Profit account can be set up immediately rather than waiting until the end of the year to determine the average profit rate.

Entries for the remaining life of the note would follow the same pattern illustrated for the years 1966 and 1967, assuming that the debtor makes all payments

[2] *Accounting Research Study No. 3,* by Robert T. Sprouse and Maurice Moonitz, published by the Director of Accounting Research of the AICPA, has not been approved by the Accounting Principles Board. The position of the board is expressed in part by its statement that ". . . while these studies are a valuable contribution to accounting thinking, they are too radically different from present generally accepted accounting principles for acceptance at this time."

Nov. 1, 1966		
Cash	*25,000*	
Note Receivable	*75,000*	
Land		*40,000*
Deferred Gross Profit on Installment Sale		*60,000*
Sold real estate on installment plan, receiving note secured by trust deed payable $5,000 every six months plus 6% interest. Broker's commission of $5,000 withheld and deducted in computing gross profit.		
Dec. 31, 1966		
Deferred Gross Profit on Installment Sale	*15,000*	
Realized Gross Profit on Installment Sale		*15,000*
Realized profit computed at 60% of cash collected during the period.		
Accrued Interest on Note Receivable	*750*	
Interest Earned		*750*
To accrue interest for two months on $75,000 note receivable at 6%.		
May 1, 1967		
Cash	*7,250*	
Accrued Interest on Note Receivable		*750*
Interest Earned		*1,500*
Note Receivable		*5,000*
Collected semiannual installment on note receivable plus interest on unpaid balance.		
Nov. 1, 1967		
Cash	*7,100*	
Interest Earned		*2,100*
Note Receivable		*5,000*
Collected semiannual installment on note receivable plus interest on unpaid balance.		
Dec. 31, 1967		
Deferred Gross Profit on Installment Sale	*6,000*	
Realized Gross Profit on Installment Sale		*6,000*
Realized profit computed at 60% of amount collected on principal of note during the year.		
Accrued Interest on Note Receivable	*650*	
Interest Earned		*650*
To accrue interest for two months on $65,000 unpaid balance of note receivable at 6%.		

as required by the note. The use of the installment method has caused the total profit of $60,000 to be spread over a span of years, as shown by the following ledger account.

Deferred Gross Profit on Installment Sale

Dec. 31, 1966	*Profit realized*	*15,000*	*Nov. 1, 1966*	*60,000*
Dec. 31, 1967	*Profit realized*	*6,000*		
Dec. 31, 1968	*Profit realized*	*6,000*		
Dec. 31, 1969	*Profit realized*	*6,000*		
Dec. 31, 1970	*Profit realized*	*6,000*		
Dec. 31, 1971	*Profit realized*	*6,000*		
Dec. 31, 1972	*Profit realized*	*6,000*		
Dec. 31, 1973	*Profit realized*	*6,000*		
Dec. 31, 1974	*Profit realized*	*3,000*		
		60,000		*60,000*

This example brings out forcibly the contrast between the timing of profits on ordinary sales and on sales accounted for by the installment method. If the land sold by Mr. Stone had been recorded as an ordinary sale, a profit of $60,000 would have been reported in the year of sale. Use of the installment method led to the recognition of only $15,000 profit in the year of sale, followed by a profit of $6,000 in each of the next seven years and a profit of $3,000 in the ninth year.

To round out this example, let us assume that a severe business depression developed shortly after the sale, and real estate prices dropped sharply. The buyer was unable to make the semiannual payment due on November 1, 1967, and no further collection from him appeared possible. The seller repossessed the land, having received only the down payment of $25,000 and the first semiannual payment of $5,000 plus interest of $2,250, accrued to May 1, 1967.

In view of the default by the buyer, the seller should write off both the note receivable and the deferred gross profit applicable to the uncollected installments. The unpaid balance of the note at date of default was $70,000; accrued interest was $2,100. The accrued interest should preferably be recorded as earned if the property repossessed is worth as much as the defaulted note plus the accrued interest. In our example, we shall assume that the land when repossessed was appraised at a fair value of only $60,000, that is, less than the unpaid balance of the note; consequently, the accumulated but uncollectible interest is not entered in the accounts. The journal entry to record the repossession would be:

Land	*60,000*	
Deferred Gross Profit on Installment Sale	*42,000*	
Note Receivable		*70,000*
Gain on Repossession		*32,000*
To record default on note receivable, cancellation of deferred gross profit, and repossession of land sold on installment plan.		

The $32,000 gain on repossession represents the excess of the present appraised value of the land ($60,000) over the cost element ($28,000) contained in the defaulted contract. The data may be tabulated as follows:

Cash collected:		
Down payment, Nov. 1, 1966	*$25,000*	
First installment, May 1, 1967	*5,000*	*$30,000*
Property repossessed at fair value		*60,000*
Total received		*$90,000*
Cost of property sold		*40,000*
Total profit		*$50,000*
Portion realized through collection of installments (60% × $30,000)		*18,000*
Gain on repossession		*$32,000*

Note that the fair value of $60,000 at which the repossessed property is now shown on Stone's books is in excess of the cost basis of $40,000 at which the same land was carried by Stone prior to its sale under the installment plan.

Would accounting theory sanction placing the repossessed property on the books at the original cost basis of $40,000 rather than the $60,000 appraised value at date of repossession? It might be argued that the buyer's default on the installment contract and the repossession of the land by the seller were in effect a nullification of the sale, and the original cost basis was still applicable. The argument for reinstatement of the land at its original cost might be strengthened by the fact that title never passed to the purchaser and that most of the alleged "profit on the sale" was deferred pending collections that never came about. Such arguments are really an attack on the validity of the installment method of determining income. If one disposes of property in an ordinary sale and later reacquires it, either by outright purchase or by bid in a foreclosure proceeding, there is no question that a gain or loss was realized on the sale and a new cost basis established when the land was reacquired. The principal reasons for doubting the authenticity of a new cost basis for land repossessed after default by an installment buyer is that the installment method denies the realization of a profit or loss upon execution of the sale; instead, the realization of profit is based upon subsequent collections. In the opinion of the authors, the theoretical support for the installment method is somewhat questionable and contains elements of contradiction.

Since accountants generally emphasize the economic and managerial substance of a transaction rather than its outward legal form, an installment sale should be viewed as a genuine sale. Under this view a seller who later repossesses the property acquires a new cost basis. The only theoretical flaw appears to lie in the basic assumption of the installment method: the assumption that profit is not realized at the date of sale.

Alternative approaches to recognition of gross profit

Accountants have given limited consideration to two other versions of recognizing gross profit by installments. One of these methods is to treat the first collections as a return of cost and the later collections as realization of gross profit. Perhaps the most appropriate circumstances for using this highly conservative method are in the sale of services or products of a nature not permitting repossession, and when the customers' notes have no fair market value.

A second method deserving of brief mention calls for recognizing the first collections as gross profit realized and the later collections as return of cost. The weakness of this method lies in the probability of showing large losses when customers default, and a tendency toward overstatement of income. Neither of these two methods is acceptable for tax purposes and neither is used to any significant extent. As a practical matter, the recognition of profits on an installment basis is limited almost entirely to the method in which gross profit is recognized in proportion to collections received.

Sales of merchandise by a dealer on the installment plan

In the preceding example we dealt with a casual sale of real property on the installment plan by a nondealer. Now we shall consider a large volume of installment sales of merchandise by a retailer.

A first requirement is to keep separate all sales made on the installment basis as distinguished from ordinary sales. The records of installment receivables are usually maintained by contract rather than by customer; if several articles are sold on the installment plan to one customer, it is convenient to account for each contract separately. However, it is not necessary to compute the rate of gross profit on each individual installment sale, or to apply a different rate to collections on each individual contract. The average rate of gross profit on all installment sales during a given year is computed and applied to all collections received on installment receivables originating in that year.

To illustrate the procedures of accounting for merchandise sales on the installment plan, assume that the Gridley Company is organized on January 1, 1967, and shows the following initial balance sheet:

Assets		*Stockholders' Equity*	
Cash	*$800,000*	*Capital stock*	*$800,000*

The policies of the new company include the leasing of fixed assets, the maintenance of perpetual inventories, and the sale of merchandise both by ordinary sales and by sales on the installment plan. On an installment sale the customer's account is debited for the full amount of the sale price and then credited with the down payment, if any. The installment contract receivable thus provides a complete record of the transaction. Assume that the first year of operations produced the following data:

Purchases of merchandise	*$1,000,000*
Payments to suppliers	*900,000*
Installment sales	*600,000*
Cost of installment sales	*360,000*

(continued)

Gross profit on installment sales	*240,000*
Rate of gross profit on installment sales	*40%*
Cash collected during 1967 on installment sales	*420,000*
Gross profit realized (40% × $420,000)	*168,000*
Sales other than installment sales	*200,000*
Cost of sales other than installment sales	*150,000*
Cash collected on sales other than installment sales	*170,000*
Selling expenses	*60,000*
General expenses	*40,000*
Income taxes	*59,000*

The following entries summarize the operations during 1967 up to the year-end entries for adjusting and closing the books.

Inventory	*1,000,000*	
Accounts Payable		*1,000,000*
To record purchases during 1967.		
Installment Contracts Receivable	*600,000*	
Installment Sales		*600,000*
To record installment sales during 1967.		
Cost of Installment Sales	*360,000*	
Inventory		*360,000*
To transfer cost of goods sold out of inventory.		
Cash	*420,000*	
Installment Contracts Receivable		*420,000*
To record collections on installment sales during 1967.		
Cash	*170,000*	
Accounts Receivable	*30,000*	
Sales (other than installment sales)		*200,000*
To record regular sales and collections thereon during 1967.		
Cost of Sales	*150,000*	
Inventory		*150,000*
To record cost of goods sold applicable to sales other than installment sales.		
Accounts Payable	*900,000*	
Selling Expenses	*60,000*	
General Expenses	*40,000*	
Cash		*1,000,000*
To record payments to suppliers and payment of operating expenses.		

The adjusting and closing entries made at December 31, 1967, include those which set up the deferred gross profit on installment sales and recognize the gross profit realized on the basis of cash collections.

Installment Sales	*600,000*	
Cost of Installment Sales		*360,000*
Deferred Gross Profit on Installment Sales		*240,000*
To set up deferred gross profit and to close the accounts for Installment Sales and for Cost of Installment Sales.		
Deferred Gross Profit on Installment Sales	*168,000*	
Realized Gross Profit on Installment Sales		*168,000*
To recognize realized profit equal to 40% of collections on installment contracts during 1967 ($420,000 × .40 = $168,000).		
Realized Gross Profit on Installment Sales	*168,000*	
Income Summary		*168,000*
To close the revenue account relating to installment sales.		

The remaining adjusting and closing entries are of a routine nature designed to accrue income tax and to close the remaining operating accounts as follows:

Income Taxes Expense	*59,000*	
Income Taxes Payable		*59,000*
To accrue income taxes at 50% of net income.		
Sales (other than installment sales)	*200,000*	
Income Summary	*109,000*	
Cost of Sales		*150,000*
Selling Expenses		*60,000*
General Expenses		*40,000*
Income Tax Expense		*59,000*
To close remaining nominal accounts.		
Income Summary	*59,000*	
Retained Earnings		*59,000*
To close Income Summary account.		

The ledger accounts for Deferred Gross Profit on Installment Sales and for Realized Gross Profit on Installment Sales will appear as shown on page 172 after the preceding entries have been posted.

The account for Realized Gross Profit on Installment Sales is closed into the Income Summary in the same manner as any other revenue account. The account for Deferred Gross Profit on Installment Sales, with a credit balance of $72,000, appears on the balance sheet shown on page 172 as a deferred credit at the end of the liability section. This $72,000 balance will become realized gross profit in sub-

Deferred Gross Profit on Installment Sales—1967			
Realized in 1967	*168,000*	*Total gross profit*	*240,000*

Realized Gross Profit on Installment Sales			
Closed to Income Summary	*168,000*	*Realized in 1967*	*168,000*

sequent years as the remaining 1967 installment contracts receivable are collected. More detailed consideration is given to the nature of this account at a later point in the chapter, and alternative balance sheet classifications are discussed.

GRIDLEY COMPANY
Balance Sheet
December 31, 1967

Assets		
Current assets:		
Cash		*$ 390,000*
Accounts receivable		*30,000*
Installment contracts receivable, due in 1968		*180,000*
Inventory		*190,000*
Total assets		*$1,090,000*
Liabilities & Stockholders' Equity		
Current liabilities:		
Accounts payable	*$100,000*	
Income taxes payable	*59,000*	
Total current liabilities		*$ 159,000*
Deferred gross profit on installment sales		*72,000*
Total liabilities		*$ 231,000*
Stockholders' equity:		
Capital stock	*$800,000*	
Retained earnings	*59,000*	*859,000*
Total liabilities & stockholders' equity		*$1,090,000*

Use of annual gross profit rates. During the first year of operations of the Gridley Company, the rate of gross profit on installment sales was 40% and this rate was applied to collections to determine the gross profit realized. The rate of gross profit will probably vary from year to year, but the gross profit percentage of a given year should be applied consistently to all collections made on contracts originating in that year. To illustrate this point, let us assume that the gross profit rates on installment sales by the Gridley Company during the first three years of operation were 40%, 45%, and 50%, respectively. The following schedule shows how the three gross profit rates would be used in computing gross profit realized.

	1967	1968	1969
Installment sales	*$600,000*	*$700,000*	*$900,000*
Cost of installment sales	*360,000*	*385,000*	*450,000*
Gross profit on installment sales	*$240,000*	*$315,000*	*$450,000*
Rate of gross profit	*40%*	*45%*	*50%*
Collections:			
On 1967 contracts	*$420,000*	*$120,000*	*$ 60,000*
On 1968 contracts		*500,000*	*130,000*
On 1969 contracts			*600,000*
Gross profit realized:			
Collections on 1967 contracts × 40%	*$168,000*	*$ 48,000*	*$ 24,000*
Collections on 1968 contracts × 45%		*225,000*	*58,500*
Collections on 1969 contracts × 50%			*300,000*

This schedule indicates that cash collected in 1968 was derived partially from 1967 contracts and partially from 1968 contracts. Two gross profit rates therefore had to be applied. In 1969, cash collections included amounts applicable to 1967 contracts, to 1968 contracts, and to 1969 contracts. Consequently, three gross profit rates were applied to determine the gross profit realized in 1969.

Classification of cash collections by year of contract. The sales journal may be designed with extra columns to record and accumulate separately installment sales, as distinguished from regular credit sales and cash sales. Similarly, the cash receipts journal may be expanded by using separate columns to record and accumulate collections on installment receivables, as distinguished from collections on regular accounts receivable. To go one step further in classification of cash received, we can add special columns in the cash receipts journal for collections on installment receivables of the present year and installment receivables of each prior year.

In our example of the Gridley Company, the special columns in the cash receipts journal could be entitled Installment Contract Receivables—1967, Installment Contract Receivables—1968, and Installment Contract Receivables—1969.

In addition to special columns in the journals, we shall use some additional ledger accounts to maintain a continuing record of installment receivables by year of origin. A separate controlling account and subsidiary ledger may be established for the installment contracts receivable originating each year. Also, a separate deferred gross profit account will be set up for the installment sales of each year. The three controlling accounts for installment receivables and the three related accounts for deferred gross profit are now illustrated for the data previously presented for the Gridley Company.

Installment Contracts Receivable—1967

Installment sales in 1967	*600,000*	*Collected during 1967*	*420,000*
		Collected during 1968	*120,000*
		Collected during 1969	*60,000*

Installment Contracts Receivable—1968

Installment sales in 1968	*700,000*	*Collected during 1968*	*500,000*
		Collected during 1969	*130,000*

Installment Contracts Receivable—1969

Installment sales in 1969	*900,000*	*Collected during 1969*	*600,000*

Deferred Gross Profit on Installment Sales—1967

Portion realized in 1967	*168,000*	*Total gross profit*	*240,000*
Portion realized in 1968	*48,000*		
Portion realized in 1969	*24,000*		

Deferred Gross Profit on Installment Sales—1968

Portion realized in 1968	*225,000*	*Total gross profit*	*315,000*
Portion realized in 1969	*58,500*		

Deferred Gross Profit on Installment Sales—1969

Portion realized in 1969	*300,000*	*Total gross profit*	*450,000*

Only one account is needed for Realized Gross Profit on Installment Sales. This revenue account, which is closed to the Income Summary at the end of each year, would contain during 1969 the profits realized in that year on three separate groups of contracts originating in the years 1967, 1968, and 1969, respectively. Entries in this ledger account are shown in the following illustration for the three-year period from 1967 through 1969.

Realized Gross Profit on Installment Sales

		Debits	*Credits*	*Balance*
1967:	*Realized from collections on 1967 sales*		*168,000*	*168,000*
	Closed to Income Summary	*168,000*		*-0-*
1968:	*Realized from collections on 1967 sales*		*48,000*	*48,000*
	Realized from collections on 1968 sales		*225,000*	*273,000*
	Closed to Income Summary	*273,000*		*-0-*
1969:	*Realized from collections on 1967 sales*		*24,000*	*24,000*
	Realized from collections on 1968 sales		*58,500*	*82,500*
	Realized from collections on 1969 sales		*300,000*	*382,500*
	Closed to Income Summary	*382,500*		*-0-*

An income statement for 1969 for the Gridley Company is now presented, based on the information previously illustrated plus some additional assumed data.

GRIDLEY COMPANY
Income Statement
for the year ended December 31, 1969

		Installment sales	Other sales	Totals
Sales		$900,000	$300,000	$1,200,000
Cost of sales		450,000	225,000	675,000
Gross profit		$450,000	$ 75,000	$ 525,000
Less: Deferred gross profit on installment sales made in 1969		150,000		150,000
Realized gross profit on 1969 sales		$300,000	$ 75,000	$ 375,000
Add: Realized gross profit based on prior years' installment sales (see Note A):				
Installment contracts, 1967				24,000
Installment contracts, 1968				58,500
Total realized gross profit				$457,500
Operating expenses:				
Selling expenses			$90,000	
General expenses			60,000	150,000
Net income before income taxes				$307,500
Income taxes				153,750
Net income				$153,750

Note A

Analysis of Realized Gross Profits on Installment Sales
for the year ended December 31, 1969

	1967	1968	1969
Installment sales	$600,000	$700,000	$900,000
Cost of installment sales	360,000	385,000	450,000
Gross profit	$240,000	$315,000	$450,000
Rate of gross profit	40%	45%	50%
Cash collections during 1969	$ 60,000	$130,000	$600,000
Gross profit realized	$ 24,000	$ 58,500	$300,000

Determining unrealized gross profit by aging installment contracts receivable

The method previously illustrated for determining gross profit realized each year required (1) a separate control account for the receivables of each year, (2) a separate subsidiary ledger corresponding to each control account, (3) a deferred gross profit account for sales of each year, and (4) special columns in the cash receipts journal to classify collections by the years to which they applied.

We are now ready to consider an alternative method which requires only one controlling account for all installment receivables and one subsidiary ledger. Also, a single account is used for the deferred gross profit arising in the several years, and the special classification columns in the cash receipts journal are eliminated. To achieve the same end results with this smaller number of accounts, we must at the end of each year analyze the installment receivables and classify them by year of origin. The gross profit rate for each year is then applied to the remaining receivables from that year to determine the deferred gross profit.

Let us apply this method to the data previously presented for the Gridley Company. The single controlling account would contain the following entries.

Installment Contracts Receivable

	Debits	*Credits*	*Balance*
1967 sales	*600,000*		
Collections		*420,000*	
Balance at year-end			*180,000*
1968 sales	*700,000*		
Collections on current and prior years' sales		*620,000*	
Balance at year-end			*260,000*
1969 sales	*900,000*		
Collections on current and prior years' sales		*790,000*	
Balance at year-end			*370,000*

To determine the age of the receivables comprising the balance shown in the controlling account, an analysis of the subsidiary ledger would be made at the end of each year. For the Gridley Company, this analysis would reveal the following aging schedule, based on the data presented on page 173.

Aging Schedule for Installment Contracts Receivable as of December 31

Date of analysis	*1967*	*1968*	*1969*
Receivables originating in 1967	*$180,000*		
Receivables originating in 1967		*$ 60,000*	
Receivables originating in 1968		*200,000*	
Receivables originating in 1968			*$ 70,000*
Receivables originating in 1969			*300,000*
	$180,000	*$260,000*	*$370,000*

From this schedule the amount of deferred gross profit which should appear on the balance sheet at the end of each year is computed as follows:

Computation of Deferred Gross Profit
at December 31, 1967, 1968, and 1969

	Deferred gross profit
At Dec. 31, 1967:	
Gross profit rate of 40% × 1967 receivables of $180,000	*$ 72,000*
At Dec. 31, 1968:	
1967 gross profit rate of 40% × 1967 receivables of $60,000	*$ 24,000*
1968 gross profit rate of 45% × 1968 receivables of $200,000	*90,000*
	$114,000
At Dec. 31, 1969:	
1968 gross profit rate of 45% × 1968 receivables of $70,000	*$ 31,500*
1969 gross profit rate of 50% × 1969 receivables of $300,000	*150,000*
	$181,500

Since these computations show the amount of deferred gross profit to appear in the balance sheets for each of the three years, we can readily compute the amount of realized gross profit which should appear in each of the annual income statements, as follows:

	1967	*1968*	*1969*
Deferred gross profit at beginning of year		*$ 72,000*	*$114,000*
Gross profit on current year's sales	*$240,000*	*315,000*	*450,000*
Total	*$240,000*	*$387,000*	*$564,000*
Less: Deferred gross profit at year-end (amounts computed in preceding schedule)	*72,000*	*114,000*	*181,500*
Gross profit realized during year	*$168,000*	*$273,000*	*$382,500*

Installment method for income tax purposes only

Both the methods illustrated for the Gridley Company produce the same end results in the financial statements; however, the second method illustrated requires less daily record keeping. It is also well suited to the needs of a company that wishes to use the installment method of recognizing profit in computing taxable income *but prefers regular accrual accounting for all other accounting purposes.*

The popularity of the installment method for tax purposes is readily explained by its capacity for postponing the recognition of taxable income and the payment of income taxes. For example, assume that the Gridley Company in the preceding illustration recognized profits on installment sales at the date of sale just as with its sales on open account. In other words, the company used the accrual method rather than the installment method in its accounting records and financial statements. However, the company did wish to make a work sheet adjustment at year-end to determine taxable income under the installment method of accounting.

The net income before taxes for 1967 (using the data on pages 169 and 170) would be $190,000, as indicated by the following condensed income statement:

Sales		*$800,000*
Cost of sales		*510,000*
Gross profit on sales		*$290,000*
Operating expenses:		
Selling expenses	*$60,000*	
General expenses	*40,000*	*100,000*
Net income before income taxes		*$190,000*

To take advantage of the installment method for income tax purposes, the net income would be adjusted as follows:

Net income per books	*$190,000*
Deduct deferred gross profit on installment sales at Dec. 31, 1967	*72,000*
Net income after adjustment to installment basis	*$118,000*

Since this was the first year of operation for the Gridley Company, there was no adjustment for deferred gross profit at the beginning of the year. In 1968 and subsequent years, the adjustment to compute taxable income would require adding the deferred gross profit at the beginning of the year to the book net income and deducting the deferred gross profit at the end of the year. In other words, if deferred gross profit is greater at the end of the year than at the beginning, the increment is subtracted from net income per the books to arrive at taxable net income. This is a work sheet adjustment only and is not entered in the accounting records, which are maintained in accordance with accrual accounting.

The use of the installment method for tax purposes concurrently with the accrual method for financial reporting will usually cause income tax to be paid on a lesser amount than the net income shown in the financial statements. The tax on the profit to be recognized later for tax purposes on the basis of collection of receivables should be computed and presented in the balance sheet as a liability with a title such as deferred income taxes. The Note to Financial Statements appearing in the annual report of Sears, Roebuck and Co. is a succinct explanation of this point.

> For income tax purposes, the Company uses the installment method of reporting its income. Under this method, the tax on profits from installment sales is payable when the profit is realized by collection from customers or through the sale of accounts. However, the Company prepares its consolidated financial statements on the accrual basis wherein the profit on installment sales

is included in income at the time of sale, and the provision for Federal income taxes is charged against income concurrently. The Company computed the provision for deferred Federal income taxes on profits from installment sales at the rate that will be in effect at the time collections on account are made, and at which time the taxes, reported under the installment method, are payable.

In this particular example, the deferred income taxes represented a liability of over 300 million dollars. For a thorough discussion of this problem of income tax allocation, the reader should refer to Chapter 25 of *Intermediate Accounting* in this series.

Periodic inventory basis

The illustrations thus far of installment sales have rested on the assumption that perpetual inventories were maintained. This is in general a reasonable assumption, because many of the types of goods sold on the installment plan are relatively high-cost items which can best be controlled by the perpetual inventory method.

The rate of gross profit on installment sales usually differs from that on regular sales because of the "load" added to the normal selling price. Consequently, it is essential to determine separately the cost of the goods sold on the installment plan. If a company using the periodic inventory system charges a single Purchases account with the cost of merchandise which will be sold both on the installment plan and on open account, some method must be designed to determine the cost of installment sales. The annual year-end physical inventory, when deducted from the total of beginning inventory and purchases, indicates the cost of *all* goods sold but not the cost of installment sales. A memorandum record of goods sold under installment contracts may be maintained to permit the calculation of cost of installment sales during the year.

The periodic inventory basis thus requires some supplementary records if the business sells goods both on regular credit terms and on the installment plan and the gross profit rates differ as between the two types of sales. If the gross profit rates were identical, the multiplication of this rate by the installment sales for the year would of course produce the amount of deferred gross profit.

In most cases the use of the periodic inventory basis will necessitate some special record keeping to determine the cost of goods sold on the installment plan, and to remove this accumulated cost from the Purchases account at the end of the year. This transfer of cost is made by debiting Cost of Installment Sales and crediting Purchases, but the detailed work in developing this cost figure may approximate the record keeping required to maintain a perpetual inventory system.

Departmental gross profit rates

Many a business enterprise is organized into several departments, each making sales on the installment basis at a different rate of gross profit. Can we safely average these departmental profit rates and apply the average gross profit rate to all cash collections applicable to the installment contracts of a given year? Or must we classify cash collections by departments, and apply different departmental rates to collections in computing realized gross profit?

The choice between these two approaches depends upon whether the several departments make collections on their sales at the same rate per period. For example, if all departments collect 50% of annual sales in the year of sale, 30% in the next year, and the remaining 20% in the following year, an average rate of gross profit for the entire business may be applied to total collections in determining realized gross profit. The results will be the same as if collections were classified by departments and departmental gross profit rates applied.

On the other hand, if the rate of collection per period differs among departments, the use of an average gross profit rate will not lead to the same figures for realized gross profit as will the use of separate departmental gross profit rates. The accountant must consider the extent of variations in departmental gross profit rates and rates of collection in the individual business to determine whether the additional work of classification and analysis on a departmental basis is justified by the greater degree of accuracy in measuring realized gross profit.

Trade-ins

The automobile business is a familiar example of the use of trade-ins; that is, the acceptance by the dealer of a used automobile as partial payment for a new car. An accounting problem is raised only if the dealer grants an *overallowance* on the used car taken in trade. An overallowance is the excess of the trade-in valuation over the inventory value of the used merchandise in terms of the dealer's ability to resell it at a price covering his expenses and a normal profit. A rough approximation of inventory value or "fair value" of the used automobile to the dealer may be the currently quoted wholesale price for used cars of the particular make and model.

An overallowance on trade-ins is significant to the accountant because it actually represents a reduction in the stated sales price of the new merchandise. The stated sales price must be reduced by the amount of the overallowance to arrive at a valid amount for the net sales price. This net sales price as compared with cost indicates the rate of gross profit.

As an illustration, assume that an article with a cost of $2,400 is sold for $3,300. Used merchandise is accepted as a trade-in at a valuation of $1,100, but the dealer expects to spend $50 in reconditioning the used merchandise before reselling it for $1,000. Assume that the customary gross profit rate on used merchandise of this type is 15%, which will cover the selling expenses, various elements of overhead, and also provide a reasonable rate of net profit.

The inventory value of the trade-in and the amount of the overallowance may be computed as follows:

Trade-in allowance			*$1,100*
Deduct inventory value of trade-in:			
Estimated sales value of trade-in		*$1,000*	
Less: Reconditioning cost	*$ 50*		
Profit margin (15% × $1,000)	*150*	*200*	
Inventory value of trade-in			*800*
Overallowance			*$ 300*

The journal entry to record the sale under these conditions could be made as follows:

Inventory of Used Merchandise	*800*	
Overallowance on Trade-ins	*300*	
Installment Contracts Receivable	*2,200*	
Installment Sales		*3,300*

The net sales price is equal to $3,300 minus the overallowance of $300, or $3,000. Cost was assumed to be $2,400; therefore the deferred gross profit on this installment sale amounts to $600. The gross profit rate is 600/3,000, or 20%. This rate will be applied in determining the realization of deferred gross profit on the basis of collections. The value of merchandise taken in trade, $800, is viewed as a collection for this purpose.

An alternative method of recording the preceding trade-in transaction consists of omitting the account for Overallowance on Trade-ins and reducing the credit to Installment Sales to the net sales price of $3,000. However, the account for Overallowance on Trade-ins may serve a useful internal purpose by providing management with current information on the amount and trend of overallowances being granted to customers. In the preparation of annual financial statements for distribution outside the company, management may prefer to eliminate the overallowance account against the sales account to establish a more meaningful amount for net sales, and to achieve greater uniformity with financial reporting practices of other companies and other industries.

Defaults and repossessions

A default and a repossession of real estate sold on the installment plan by a nondealer were illustrated on pages 167 to 168. We now need to consider defaults and repossessions from the viewpoint of a business selling merchandise or services and using the installment method of accounting.

If a customer defaults on an installment contract payable for services and no further collection can be made, we have an example of default without the possibility of repossession. A similar situation exists for certain types of merchandise which have no significant resale value. The accounting entry required in such cases is to write off the uncollectible installment contract receivable, cancel the deferred gross profit related to the receivable, and debit Loss on Defaulted Contracts for the difference between the two. In other words, the loss is equal to the element of unrecovered cost contained in the installment contract receivable.

For many lines of business, however, a default by a customer leads to repossession of merchandise. The loss is reduced by the value of the property repossessed and it is possible, though not likely, for the repossession to result in a gain. The recognition of gain or loss at the time of repossession is in accordance with present Federal income tax regulations.

The principal difficulty in accounting for defaults followed by repossession is in estimating the fair value of the merchandise at the time of repossession. In setting a fair value, the objective is to choose an amount that will allow for any necessary reconditioning costs and provide a normal gross profit on resale. As reconditioning costs are incurred, they should be added to the inventory value, provided this does not become unreasonable in relation to the expected selling price.

The difficulties of estimating the value of certain types of repossessed merchandise have led some finance companies and other businesses to adopt a policy of not recording the repossessed article as an asset. This approach calls for treating the excess of the installment receivable over the deferred gross profit as a loss at date of repossession. When the repossessed merchandise is sold, the entire proceeds are classified as revenue. The principal objection to this approach is that some repossessed goods may be on hand but not recorded as inventory at the end of the accounting period. Unless an appropriate value is assigned to such goods, the financial statements will show an understated net income, and an understatement of assets and owners' equity. The estimating of a fair value for the year-end inventory of repossessed merchandise may, however, be a less burdensome task than establishing a value for all repossessed goods at the time of repossession.

Another method of avoiding the need for estimating the fair value of repossessed merchandise is to bring the repossessed goods on the books at the amount of unrecovered cost contained in the defaulted installment receivable. The recognition of gain or loss is thereby postponed until the date of resale. If resale does not occur until the next accounting period, this method is deficient in that the inventory of repossessed goods would be reflected in the financial statements at an arbitrary valuation.

To illustrate a common type of default and repossession transaction, assume that a retail appliance dealer during 1967 showed a gross profit rate of 30%. An article sold in that year for $1,000 had cost $700. Payments by the customer during 1967 amounted to $200. In 1968, after making additional payments totaling $250, the customer defaulted and the article was repossessed. The estimated value of the article when repossessed was $160, after making allowance for reconditioning and a normal profit on resale.

The loss on the repossession may be computed as follows:

Installment contract receivable written off:		
Face amount ($1,000 – $450)	*$550*	
Less: Deferred gross profit (30%)	*165*	*$385*
Fair value of property repossessed		*160*
Loss on repossession		*$225*

The journal entry to record the default and repossession is as follows:

Inventory of Repossessed Merchandise	*160*	
Deferred Gross Profit on Installment Sales—1967	*165*	
Loss on Repossessions	*225*	
Installment Contracts Receivable		*550*
To write off defaulted installment contract and cancel related gross profit.		

This entry accomplishes four things: (1) to write off the defaulted installment receivable; (2) to cancel the deferred gross profit (30% × $550) applicable to the defaulted contract; (3) to record as an asset the fair value of the repossessed merchandise; and (4) to recognize the loss on the repossession. Note that the loss of $225 is computed by deducting the value of the repossessed goods, $160, from the $385 cost element of the receivable. In other words, the cancellation of the $165 of deferred gross profit serves to reduce the receivable from its face amount of $550 to a cost basis of $385. It should be emphasized that a loss cannot be recognized with respect to the deferred gross profit element contained in the installment contract receivable.

The illustrated entry was based on the assumption of perpetual inventories. If the company relies on the periodic inventory system, the repossessed goods would be debited to an account entitled Merchandise Repossessed which would be treated in the same way as the Purchases account in determining the cost of goods sold.

A default by a customer and the repossession of the merchandise may occur in the year in which the original sale was made, before the gross profit rate for the year is known. Under these circumstances an estimated gross profit percentage may be used in recording the default and repossession. After the gross profit rate has been determined at the end of the year, a correcting entry may be made to adjust the gain or loss on the repossession. Losses on defaults and repossessions may be shown on the income statement as a deduction from the realized gross profit, and the resulting balance labeled as Total Realized Gross Profit after Deduction of Losses on Defaulted Contracts.

Expenses relating to installment sales

Since the installment method of accounting defers gross profit from the period of sale to the period of collecting the installment receivables, why should we not defer operating expenses as well? An objective approach to the determination of income suggests that deferral of expenses would produce a better matching of revenues and related expenses. As a practical matter, two important objections exist with respect to deferral of expenses. First, the income tax rules permit expenses to be deducted in the period incurred, and the companies that adopt the installment method of accounting are usually influenced by a desire to postpone the recognition of taxable income. To defer expenses would tend to reduce the tax advantage of the installment method. Secondly, a determination of the amount of expense to be deferred on grounds of its relationship to installment sales would be difficult to make and would involve additional accounting work.

Some accountants have defended the deferral of gross profit without the deferral of related expenses by the argument that the realization of gross profit was contingent on future collections whereas the expenses were definitely incurred. This viewpoint is subject to criticism, however, because it ignores the problem of matching revenues with related expenses.

As previously stated, most companies using the installment method of accounting deduct operating expenses in the period incurred; however, bad debts expense is not provided for in the usual manner. The provision for bad debts as customarily set up under accrual accounting is not permissible under the installment method of accounting. Inability to collect installment receivables results in a loss or gain on defaults and repossessions.

Under the accrual method of accounting, the gross profit on a credit sale is immediately taken into income; consequently, it is logical to provide for credit losses by debiting bad debt expense and crediting an allowance for bad debts. Proper income determination under the accrual method requires a charge against the recorded revenue to provide for the expenses associated with that revenue.

Under the installment method of accounting, however, recognition of revenue is deferred until support in the form of cash collections is received. In fact, the entire amount of the account Deferred Gross Profit on Installment Sales could be regarded as an allowance to cover noncollection of receivables.

Financial statement presentation

Installment receivables are classified as current assets although the collection schedule often extends more than a year beyond the balance sheet date. The definition of current assets in the AICPA publication, *Accounting Research and Terminology Bulletins, Final Edition,* specifically includes "installment or deferred accounts and notes receivable if they conform generally to normal trade practices and terms within the industry." This classification is implicit in the concept that current assets include all resources "expected to be realized in cash or sold or consumed during the normal operating cycle of the business."

The listing of installment receivables in the current asset section may be made most informative by showing separately the amounts maturing each year or by disclosing this information in notes accompanying the financial statements.

Where to place Deferred Gross Profit on Installment Sales on the balance sheet is a question that has long troubled accountants. The most common practice is to classify it as a deferred credit to income at the end of the liability section. Critics of this treatment point out that no obligation to an outsider exists, and therefore the liability classification is improper.

The existence of a deferred gross profit account is based on the argument that the profit element of an installment sale has not yet been realized. Acceptance of this view suggests that the related installment receivable will be overstated unless the deferred gross profit account is shown as a deduction from installment contracts receivable. This classification as an asset valuation account seems theoretically preferable, but the effect is to show installment receivables at a value equal to the unrecovered cost of the merchandise sold. Many businessmen and other users of the financial statements believe this method causes a misleading understatement of assets. In many cases the installment receivables could probably be sold for substantially more than their face amount reduced by the deferred gross profit.

Efforts to find an acceptable compromise to these conflicting views have brought forth the suggestion that deferred gross profit be subdivided into three portions: (1) an allowance for collection expenses and bad debt losses which would be deducted from receivables; (2) a liability representing future income taxes applicable to the profits not yet reported as realized; and (3) a residual profit element. This third element would be classified by some as a separate item in the owners' equity section and by others in an undefined no-man's-land between liabilities and stockholders' equity. Such a detailed classification of deferred gross profit on the balance sheet is rarely, if ever, encountered in actual practice.

The lack of agreement on proper balance sheet classification of deferred gross profit is evidence of the inherent contradiction between the installment method of accounting and the basic assumptions of accrual accounting. Since the chief reason for the existence of the installment method in most companies is the income tax advantage it affords, the most satisfactory solution may be to recognize profits on installment sales on an accrual basis for general accounting purposes and to defer recognition of profits for tax purposes.

At the present time, however, most practicing accountants would no doubt regard as acceptable the classification of deferred gross profit as a deferred credit to income within the liability section of the balance sheet. Classification as an asset valuation account to be deducted from installment receivables would also be considered within the scope of generally accepted accounting principles, although this classification is seldom encountered.

Interest on installment contracts

Installment contracts usually provide for an interest charge payable concurrently with each installment payment on the principal. Only that portion of the payment which is applied to reduce the principal of the contract is considered in measuring the realization of profit under the installment method of accounting.

The arrangement for payment of interest generally follows one of the following plans:

1. Interest is computed throughout the contract on the basis of the original amount of the sale minus any down payment.

2. Interest is computed each month on the uncollected balance of the principal.

3. Equal periodic payments are made, with each payment including interest on the uncollected balance of the principal.

4. Interest is computed on each individual installment from the beginning date of the contract to the date of paying the installment.

To illustrate these four alternative arrangements for interest payments, assume that a retailer on March 31 sells merchandise for $650. Terms of the installment sale call for a down payment of $50, with the balance of $600 to be paid in six monthly payments with interest at 6% a year, or ½ of 1% a month.

1. Interest computed throughout contract on basis of original amount of sale minus down payment. This method causes the effective rate of interest to be almost double the stated 6% rate, and almost twice as much as that for any of the three other plans illustrated. It might be described as an interest plan for the "unthinking customer" or for the customer who cannot qualify for credit elsewhere. A schedule showing the down payment and the six monthly payments follows:

Date	Amounts collected			Uncollected balance of principal
	Total	Interest on original balance	Principal	
Mar. 31				$650.00
Mar. 31 (down payment)	$ 50.00	-0-	$ 50.00	600.00
Apr. 30	103.00	$ 3.00	100.00	500.00
May 31	103.00	3.00	100.00	400.00
June 30	103.00	3.00	100.00	300.00
July 31	103.00	3.00	100.00	200.00
Aug. 31	103.00	3.00	100.00	100.00
Sept. 30	103.00	3.00	100.00	-0-
	$668.00	$18.00	$650.00	

The average amount owed during the six months of the contract was $350 [($600 + $100) ÷ 2]. Interest on $350 for six months at 6% per year is $10.50. Although the contract speaks of a 6% interest rate, the total interest charge of $18 represents an effective rate of more than 10% on the average amount of the debt.

In the accounting records of the seller, the entry to record collection of each of the six monthly payments would be:

Cash	*103*	
Installment Contracts Receivable		*100*
Interest Earned		*3*

2. ***Interest computed each month on uncollected balance of principal.*** Under this plan the effective interest rate is the same as the stated rate of 6%. Since the uncollected principal is smaller each month, the interest payments decline throughout the life of the contract. A schedule showing the down payment and the six monthly payments by the customer follows:

Date	*Amounts collected*			*Uncollected balance of principal*
	Total	*Interest on unpaid balance*	*Principal*	
Mar. 31				*$650.00*
Mar. 31 (down payment)	*$ 50.00*	*-0-*	*$ 50.00*	*600.00*
Apr. 30	*103.00*	*$ 3.00*	*100.00*	*500.00*
May 31	*102.50*	*2.50*	*100.00*	*400.00*
June 30	*102.00*	*2.00*	*100.00*	*300.00*
July 31	*101.50*	*1.50*	*100.00*	*200.00*
Aug. 31	*101.00*	*1.00*	*100.00*	*100.00*
Sept. 30	*100.50*	*0.50*	*100.00*	*-0-*
	$660.50	*$10.50*	*$650.00*	

Note that the $10.50 of total interest payments under this plan is equal to 6% of the average indebtedness of $350 for the six-month period of the contract ($350 × .06 × ½).

The accounting entries to be made by the seller at the time of the sale and upon collection of the first monthly installment will be as follows:

Installment Contracts Receivable	*650*	
Installment Sales		*650*
To record installment sale with terms of $50 down, six monthly payments of $100 plus interest at 6% on uncollected principal.		

Cash	*50*	
Installment Contracts Receivable		*50*
Collected down payment.		
Cash	*103*	
Installment Contracts Receivable		*100*
Interest Earned		*3*
Collected first monthly installment.		

Each of the remaining five installments will be recorded in the same way although the interest payment will be less each month.

3. Equal periodic payments with each payment including interest on uncollected balance of principal. This method is popular because of the convenience to the customer of making monthly payments of uniform amount. The uniformity of monthly payments may also be an advantageous factor to the dealer in designing an efficient system for processing collections. Since the uncollected principal is smaller after each payment, the portion of the monthly payment constituting interest declines each month and the portion applicable to principal increases.

The calculation of the amount of the uniform periodic payment required to cover interest charges and to extinguish the principal of an installment contract calls for an understanding of annuities as illustrated in Chapter 17. In our present example, six equal monthly payments of $101.76 will pay the installment contract of $600 with interest of ½ of 1% per month, as shown by the following schedule. The final payment to liquidate the principal and cover interest for the last month is 2 cents less than the other payments.

Date	*Amounts collected*			*Uncollected balance of principal*
	Total	*Interest*	*Principal*	
Mar. 31				*$650.00*
Mar. 31 (down payment)	*$ 50.00*	*-0-*	*$ 50.00*	*600.00*
Apr. 30	*101.76*	*$ 3.00*	*98.76*	*501.24*
May 31	*101.76*	*2.51*	*99.25*	*401.99*
June 30	*101.76*	*2.01*	*99.75*	*302.24*
July 31	*101.76*	*1.51*	*100.25*	*201.99*
Aug. 31	*101.76*	*1.01*	*100.75*	*101.24*
Sept. 30	*101.74*	*0.50*	*101.24*	*-0-*
	$660.54	*$10.54*	*$650.00*	

The seller will record the collection of the first monthly payment by the following entry:

Cash	*101.76*	
Installment Contracts Receivable		*98.76*
Interest Earned		*3.00*

4. Interest computed on individual installment. The interest payable on each installment runs from the beginning of the contract; consequently, the later installments are larger because of the longer period covered in the interest computation.

However, interest earned should be recognized as income in the period it accrues, regardless of the payment date. The monthly financial statements should, therefore, include interest accrued on the uncollected principal of all installment contracts. Thus in the first month of our example, the customer pays $100 on principal plus interest for one month, or $0.50. However, the interest earned by the dealer in that first month is $3.00, representing interest at 6% per annum on the entire balance of $600. The following schedule shows the interest accruing each month as well as the payments applicable to interest and to principal.

Date	Interest		Amounts collected			Uncollected balance of principal
	Accrued	Uncollected	Total	Interest	Principal	
Mar. 31.....						$650.00
Mar. 31.....	-0-	-0-	$ 50.00	-0-	$ 50.00	600.00
Apr. 30.....	$ 3.00	$2.50	100.50	$ 0.50	100.00	500.00
May 31.....	2.50	4.00	101.00	1.00	100.00	400.00
June 30.....	2.00	4.50	101.50	1.50	100.00	300.00
July 31.....	1.50	4.00	102.00	2.00	100.00	200.00
Aug. 31.....	1.00	2.50	102.50	2.50	100.00	100.00
Sept. 30.....	0.50	-0-	103.00	3.00	100.00	-0-
	$10.50		$660.50	$10.50	$650.00	

The seller will make an entry each month to record the interest accrued as well as an entry for receipt of the monthly installment payment. The following entries at April 30 are illustrative.

Accrued Interest on Installment Contracts Receivable....	*3.00*	
Interest Earned..........................		*3.00*
To accrue interest earned on $600 balance of contract for month of April.		
Cash..	*100.50*	
Installment Contracts Receivable.............		*100.00*
Accrued Interest on Installment Contracts Receivable..........................		*.50*

In the early months of the contract, interest is accrued in excess of that collected, but in the later months the situation is reversed. Over the life of the contract, interest collected exactly offsets interest accrued.

Installment contracts from the buyer's viewpoint

Many business concerns buy fixed assets under installment contracts. Although legal title is usually not acquired until final payment is made, equitable title is acquired immediately. The asset should be recorded at once, net of financing charges, and the depreciation program should be begun. Since the asset is being used in operations, a depreciation charge must be recognized to secure a reasonable relationship between costs of owning the asset and revenues realized through its use.

The financing charges should be treated as expense in proportion to the amounts and timing of the installment contracts. Thus the financing charge is treated as a deferred item subject to amortization over the life of the installment contract. Straight-line amortization is often used because of its simplicity, but this approach has little theoretical justification. The amortization charges should logically be greater in the early stages of the contract and should decline with each payment. For example, on a 24-month contract the amortization under the "payments outstanding method" would be 24/300 of the total financing charge for the first month, 23/300 the second month, and only 1/300 in the final month. The deferred interest and finance charge should appear in the balance sheet of the debtor as a deduction from the face value of the note, not as a deferred charge type of asset.

To include the interest charges arising from purchase of assets on the installment plan as part of the cost of the asset is not satisfactory, because this would spread the interest charge over the life of the asset rather than over the period of credit extension. As an alternative to acquiring fixed assets under installment contracts, a company may choose to obtain cash through a bank loan and purchase the assets for cash. In either case, the interest charges should be treated as expense of the periods during which the liability exists.

Questions

1. What do you consider to be the most important characteristics that distinguish an installment sale from an ordinary charge sale on 30-day credit?

2. The Madden Company is entering the appliance business and plans to make most of its sales on the installment plan. Outline two general plans of accounting for installment sales from which the company might choose. Do not suggest plans which are unacceptable from the standpoint of either general accounting practice or income tax regulations.

3. In a discussion of the theoretical support for the installment method, one student made the following statement: "If a business is going to sell personal property over a period as long as 36 months, no one can predict how difficult or costly collections may be. To recognize the gross profit as earned at the time of sale would violate well-established accounting principles such as conservatism and the 'completed transaction' concept." What opposing arguments can you offer?

4. On December 1, Jones agreed to sell for $150,000 a tract of land acquired by him several years ago at a cost of $60,000. The buyer offered to pay $50,000 down and the balance in 20 semiannual installments plus 6% interest on the unpaid balance. Jones agreed to these terms except that he insisted that the down payment be only $44,000 and the semiannual payments increased accordingly. The buyer quickly agreed and the deal was completed. Why did Jones insist on reducing the down payment? Assume that Jones (who is not a dealer in real estate) computes his income on a calendar-year basis and chooses to use the special installment method of accounting. How much income did he realize in the year of sale on this transaction?

5. Graham, a physician, invested in vacant land at a cost of $20,000; several years later he sold it to Hall on the installment plan at a total price of $80,000. Graham received $10,000 as a down payment and six semiannual payments of $2,000 each plus interest. Hall then defaulted on the contract and Graham repossessed the property. At the time of repossession, an independent appraiser estimated the land to have a current fair value of $60,000. At what valuation should the land be entered on Graham's books? Give reasons. Also, draft the journal entry to record the default and repossession.

6. Zenith Company changes its policy from selling on open account to selling on the installment plan and concurrently adopts the special installment method of accounting. In the past Zenith has maintained an allowance for bad debts by an annual provision equal to 2% of credit sales. What change, if any, do you think should be made with respect to provision for bad debts under the new accounting policy?

7. In your audit of the Midway Auto Company, you find in the ledger an account entitled Overallowance on Trade-ins. How should this account be treated in the preparation of financial statements for publication and general distribution?

8. You observe the following journal entry on the books of a company using the special installment method of accounting:

Inventory of Repossessed Merchandise	*225*	
Deferred Gross Profit on Installment Sales—1967	*301*	
Loss on Repossessions	*334*	
Installment Contracts Receivable		*860*

What was the rate of gross profit on the original sale? What was probably the source of the $225 debit?

9. The Courtesy Finance Company finds that estimating the fair value of the merchandise it repossesses under defaulted contracts is a time-consuming and somewhat uncertain process. The company's policy is to sell this used merchandise for cash as quickly as possible even though successive reductions in price are necessary to make sales. What method can you suggest of accounting for defaults and repossessions that would avoid the need for an appraisal in each case?

10. Discuss briefly the location or classification of deferred gross profit in the financial statements, touching on both current practice and theoretical considerations in your answer.

Short cases for analysis

6-1 The Atlantic Company sells furniture on the installment plan. For its Federal income tax returns, it reports its profit from sales on the installment basis. For its financial reports, it considers the entire profit to be earned in the year of sale.

Instructions

a. Discuss the relative merits of the two methods of reporting income.

b. Explain the installment basis as used for income tax purposes.

c. Discuss the effects of the concurrent use of these two bases by the Atlantic Company on the significance of its reported annual income. What recommendation would you make to the company to produce an income statement in accordance with generally accepted accounting principles?

AICPA adapted

6-2 The generally accepted rule in accounting is that revenue is recognized when the sale is made.

Instructions

a. Why has the sale been chosen as the point at which to recognize the revenue resulting from the entire producing and selling process?

b. What is the justification for the following deviations from recognizing revenue at the time of sale?

(1) Installment sales method of recognizing revenue
(2) Recognition of revenue during production in gold mining
(3) The percentage-of-completion basis in long-term construction contracts

AICPA adapted

6-3 Zenith Trucking Corporation purchased two new trailers on September 30, 1967. The purchase contract specified a total price of $15,752 and a down payment of $5,000. The balance was covered by a non-interest-bearing installment note to be paid in 24 monthly installments of $448. The first payment was due on October 31, 1967. Included in the total price was an interest and finance charge of $1,152.

The purchase was recorded by the following entry:

Trailers	*14,600*	
Deferred Interest and Finance Charge	*1,152*	
Cash		*5,000*
Installment Note Payable		*10,752*

Instructions

a. In journal entry form, record the October 31, 1967, payment and adjustment of the Deferred Interest and Finance Charge account. Use the straight-line method of amortization.

b. Give arguments for and against the straight-line method of amortizing the deferred interest.

c. The corporation wishes to show the deferred interest as a deduction from the installment note payable on its balance sheet. Give arguments for and against this treatment, even though you may be convinced personally that only one side of the issue is well supported.

AICPA adapted

6-4 On January 2, 1966, the Rogers Company purchased display equipment for its store under the following terms: $2,000 to be paid upon installation, plus five annual payments of $1,000, the first payment to be made on December 31, 1966. Title to the display equipment was retained by the seller until the final payment was made. It is estimated that the display equipment will be used for ten years, with no residual value.

This same display equipment was available at a cash price of $6,600.

Instructions

Make all accounting entries relating to the display equipment as of January 2 and December 31, 1966, and as of December 31, 1967. For each entry, give your supporting reasons. Do not consider income tax aspects of the transaction.

AICPA adapted

6-5 The Freeway Music Company, which maintains its accounts on a calendar-year basis, sold a stereo set to Kearns on October 1, 1967. Cost of the set was $800 and the sales price was $1,200. A down payment of $300 was received along with a contract calling for the payment of $50 on the first of each month for the next 18 months.

Kearns paid the monthly installments promptly on November 1 and December 1, 1967. He also made five payments in 1968 but then defaulted on the contract. Freeway Music Company repossessed the set on November 1, 1968.

Instructions

a. State three different amounts which *might* be reported as realized income from this transaction for the year 1967, and indicate the circumstances under which each of the three amounts might be acceptable.

b. Without regard to income tax advantages or disadvantages, which of the three amounts do you believe has the strongest support from a theoretical standpoint? Which has the weakest support? Explain.

c. If the stereo set repossessed on November 1, 1968, has a wholesale value of $100 and a retail value of $150, prepare a journal entry to record the repossession under the installment method of accounting. Explain fully the reasoning applicable to your entry.

Problems

6-6 The Grayson Company started business on January 1, 1966. Separate accounts were set up for installment and cash sales, but no perpetual inventory record was maintained. On the installment sales a down payment of one-third was required, with the balance payable in 18 equal monthly installments. At the end of each year the company adjusted its books to the "installment basis" by use of a Deferred Gross Profit account. When contracts were defaulted, the unpaid balances were charged to a Bad Debt Expense account, and sales of repossessed merchandise were credited to the account. The expense account was adjusted at the year-end to reflect the actual loss.

Information about the transactions of the Grayson Company follows:

	1966	*1967*
Sales:		
New merchandise for cash	*$ 21,348*	*$ 29,180*
New merchandise on installment (including the one-third cash down payment)	*188,652*	*265,320*
Repossessed merchandise	*600*	*700*
Purchases	*154,000*	*173,585*
Physical inventories at Dec. 31:		
New merchandise at cost	*36,400*	*48,010*
Repossessions at realizable value	*150*	*160*
Unpaid balances of installment contracts defaulted:		
1966 sales	*2,865*	*3,725*
1967 sales		*3,010*
Cash collections on installment contracts, exclusive of down payments:		
1966 sales	*42,943*	*61,385*
1967 sales		*55,960*

Instructions

a. Compute the gross profit percentages (for new merchandise) for the years 1966 and 1967.

b. In T-account form, reproduce the ledger accounts for installment contracts receivable. Sales may be recorded net of down payments and collections exclusive of down payments.

c. Calculate the net loss on defaulted accounts for the year 1966.

d. Prepare a schedule showing the realized gross profit for the year 1967 that would be reported in the income statement.

AICPA adapted

6-7 The Portola Company uses the installment sales basis of determining net income, recognizing gross profit earned in proportion to cash collections on sales. Installment sales are recorded by debiting Installment Contracts Receivable and crediting Installment Sales. At the same time an entry is made to record the cost of goods sold by debiting Cost of Installment Sales and crediting Inventory.

The balances in the controlling accounts for Installment Contracts Receivable were as follows at the beginning and end of 1967:

	Jan. 1, 1967	*Dec. 31, 1967*
Installment contracts receivable—1965	$ 30,000	-0-
Installment contracts receivable—1966	200,000	$ 80,000
Installment contracts receivable—1967	-0-	300,000
	$230,000	$380,000

The sales and cost of sales of the Portola Company for a three-year period were as follows:

	1965	*1966*	*1967*
Installment sales	$500,000	$480,000	$600,000
Cost of installment sales	400,000	360,000	468,000

Late in 1967 the company repossessed merchandise that had been sold for $10,000 in 1966. Collections on these defaulted installment contracts had been $7,000 and the company estimated the value of the repossessed merchandise at $2,400. The entries in the accounts to record the repossessions had consisted of crediting Installment Contracts Receivable and debiting Repossessed Merchandise for $3,000. None of the repossessed merchandise had been sold as of December 31, 1967.

Instructions

a. Prepare all necessary adjusting entries at December 31, 1967, to reflect income on the Portola Company's books on the installment method of accounting. Show all supporting computations in schedules or other explanatory form.

b. As controller of the Portola Company, you are asked to summarize briefly for the board of directors the effect on profits and income taxes during the three-year period ended December 31, 1967, of using the installment method of accounting as opposed to the regular sales method of recognizing profit. To facilitate compilation of specific dollar data, you are asked to assume that the choice of accounting method had no effect on operating expenses except that under the regular sales method of accounting a bad debt provision equal to ½ of 1% of sales would be made each year. You are also to assume an income tax rate of 50% during the three years.

6-8 The McGee Company was formed on July 31, 1965, and sells household appliances at retail on installment-payment contracts.

The following information was taken from the accounts of the McGee Company at year-end:

	July 31	
	1967	*1966*
Installment contracts receivable:		
1966 contracts	*$ 4,000*	*$ 63,000*
1967 contracts	*80,000*	
Sales	*250,000*	*150,000*
Merchandise inventory, new, at cost	*42,250*	*32,250*
Purchases	*155,000*	
Selling and administrative expenses	*70,000*	
Loss on defaulted contracts	*8,550*	*500*
Allowance for defaulted contracts	*4,500*	*4,500*

The CPA's audit at July 31, 1967, disclosed the following:

(1) When a contract is in default, the merchandise is repossessed and the contract written off to Loss on Defaulted Contracts. Information regarding repossessed merchandise is kept on a memo basis and is not recorded on the books. Any income derived from the sale of this merchandise is credited to Loss on Defaulted Contracts. No repossessed merchandise was sold in 1966 or 1967 for more than the unpaid balance of the original contract. An analysis of the Loss on Defaulted Contracts account for the year ended July 31, 1967, follows:

Contracts written off during 1967:		
1966 contracts		*$ 7,500*
1967 contracts		*3,000*
		$10,500
Less: Sale of repossessed merchandise during 1967:		
1966 contracts	*$1,600*	
1967 contracts	*350*	*1,950*
Balance		*$ 8,550*

The market value of the repossessed merchandise inventory on hand at July 31, 1967, was $400, all of which was repossessed from 1966 contracts. There was no merchandise repossessed during the year ended July 31, 1966.

The $4,000 balance of 1966 installment contracts receivable is considered collectible.

(2) The gross profit ratio for 1966 was 40%.

(3) The company's financial statements are prepared on the accrual basis, and the installment method of reporting income is used for income tax purposes. The company is on the charge-off method for losses on defaulted contracts for income tax purposes.

Instructions

a. Prepare a schedule to compute the adjustment to the balance of Allowance for Defaulted Contracts account that the CPA would suggest at July 31, 1967. The rate of bad debt losses for 1967 is expected to be the same as the experience rate for 1966 based on sales. (Compute the rate of bad debt losses to sales based on 1966 contracts, utilizing in this computation all data accumulated throughout 1966 and 1967 applicable to the 1966 contracts.)

b. Prepare a schedule computing taxable income on the installment sales method for the year ended July 31, 1967. The following supporting schedules should be in good form:

(1) Computation of realized gross margin on 1966 sales.

(2) Computation of losses on defaults on 1966 contracts and 1967 contracts.

AICPA adapted

6-9 On January 1, 1966, the Colorama Television Store began making installment sales with the objective of securing a higher volume of operation by offering liberal credit terms. To hold down operating costs, the company decided against maintaining a perpetual inventory system. Although installment sales were emphasized, the company also sold many sets for cash. Separate ledger accounts were used for cash sales and for installment sales.

The price of television sets to installment customers was set at 106% of the cash sale price. This 6% increment included all interest charged to the customer. Installment customers were required to sign a contract for an amount equal to 106% of the cash price; this contract provided for a down payment of one-quarter of the installment price, with the balance payable in 15 equal monthly installments. As each monthly payment by an installment customer was received, the Colorama Television Store treated as interest earned an amount equal to 1% of the *unpaid* cash sale price equivalent. For example, a television set with a cash sales price of $1,000 would be sold under an installment contract of $1,060, with a 25% down payment of $265 and 15 equal monthly installments of $53. Upon receipt of the first monthly installment, the store would record as interest earned the amount of $7.35, representing 1% of the unpaid cash sales price equivalent at that date.

Installments receivable and installment sales were recorded at the contract price. When contracts were defaulted, the unpaid balances were charged to Bad Debt Expense. Sales of repossessed merchandise were credited to Bad Debt Expense.

Sales:	
Cash sales	*$126,000*
Installment sales	*265,000*
Repossessed sales	*230*
Inventory, Jan. 1, 1966:	
Merchandise inventory	*58,060*
Purchases, 1966:	
New merchandise	*209,300*
Inventories, physical, Dec. 31, 1966:	
New merchandise	*33,300*
Repossessed inventory	*180*
Cash collections on installment contracts, 1966:	
Down payments	*66,250*
Subsequent installments (average six monthly installments on all contracts except on defaulted contracts)	*79,341*

Five contracts totaling $1,060 were defaulted, in each case after three monthly installments were paid.

Interest should be recognized in the period earned.

Instructions

Compute or prepare the following:

a. The gross profit percentage for 1966. (Compute total sales at cash sales price equivalent.)

b. A schedule showing for each of the first six monthly payments: the cash sale price equivalent, the contract balance, the amount of interest earned, and the cash collected on a $1,060 installment sale contract.

c. The net gain or loss on defaulted contracts during 1966.

d. The realized gross profit for 1966.

AICPA adapted

6-10 The Whitewall Appliance Company, your client, has followed the policy of selling its merchandise at retail for cash only. During the past year it expanded its line of appliances to include higher-priced items and provided an 18-month installment payment plan for its customers.

Under Whitewall's installment payment plan the customer's contract includes a financing charge of 10% of the sales price of the merchandise. Whitewall has decided to retain the installment contracts receivable and not discount them with a finance company. Whitewall intends to obtain the necessary additional working capital by short-term bank loans.

You learn that Whitewall has decided to report the unearned portion of the 10% finance charges as a current liability in the balance sheet with full disclosure in a footnote, an acceptable treatment. You know that the unearned portion of the finance charges might be reported by alternative accounting procedures.

Instructions

a. What arguments do you expect from Whitewall to support its decision to report the unearned portion of the 10% finance charges as a current liability?

b. What reasons could you offer Whitewall for reporting the unearned portion of the finance charges as deferred income in a section of the balance sheet between liabilities and stockholders' equity?

c. The unearned portion of the finance charges may be reported as a deduction from the total contracts receivable on the asset side of the balance sheet. What reasons would you offer for this procedure?

d. Discuss the validity of the arguments for the three methods. Which method do you recommend?

e. Whitewall has not given any consideration to the accounting method to be used for recognizing revenue on the installment sales. Give the methods of recognizing revenue (you may write in terms of gross profit) from installment sales and discuss the acceptability of each method.

AICPA adapted

6-11 The Installment Jewelry Company has been in business for five years but has never had an audit made of its financial statements. Although nearly all the sales are on the installment plan, the company does not use the special installment method of accounting. Engaged to make an audit for 1967, you find that the company's balance sheet carries no allowance for bad accounts, bad accounts having been expensed as written off and recoveries credited to income as collected. The company's policy is to write off at December 31 of each year those accounts on which no collections have been received for three months. The installment contracts generally are for two years.

Upon your recommendation, the company agrees to revise its accounts for 1967 to give effect to bad account treatment on the reserve basis. The allowance is to be based on a percentage of sales which is derived from the experience of prior years. The year 1967 is to be charged with an amount of bad debt expense sufficient to change to the reserve method and establish the proper balance in the valuation allowance. The portion of this charge relating to receivables originating in prior years is not regarded as sufficiently material to warrant a direct charge to retained earnings.

Statistics for the past five years are as follows:

Year	*Charge sales*	*Accounts written off and year of sale*			*Recoveries and year of sale*
1963	*$100,000*	*(1963)* *$ 550*			
1964	*250,000*	*(1963)* *1,500*	*(1964)* *$1,000*		*(1963)* *$100*
1965	*300,000*	*(1963)* *500*	*(1964)* *4,000*	*(1965)* *$1,300*	*(1964)* *400*
1966	*325,000*	*(1964)* *1,200*	*(1965)* *4,500*	*(1966)* *1,500*	*(1965)* *500*
1967	*275,000*	*(1965)* *2,700*	*(1966)* *5,000*	*(1967)* *1,400*	*(1966)* *600*

Accounts receivable at December 31, 1967, were as follows:

1966 sales	*$ 15,000*
1967 sales	*135,000*
	$150,000

Instructions

Prepare the adjusting journal entry or entries with appropriate explanations to set up the Allowance for Bad Accounts. Support each item with organized computations; income tax implications should be ignored. In computing the percentage of bad debts to sales, you should rely upon the experience of the years 1963 through 1965, for which complete data are now available. Treat the transactions of this three-year period as a single group; percentage relationships need not be computed for individual years. Since the receivables at December 31, 1967, include accounts which originated in 1966 as well as those from 1967 sales, the allowance should be computed by applying a percentage of sales to the sales of both years and deducting from the resulting amount the net write-off during both years.

AICPA adapted

6-12 The Madison Company commenced business operations on January 1, 1967. All sales are made on installment contracts and inventory records are on a periodic basis. Contract receivables are kept separate by years. At the end of each year adjustments for unrealized and realized gross profits are made through a Deferred Gross Profit on Installment Sales account. Defaulted contracts are recorded by debiting the Loss on Defaults account and crediting the appropriate contracts receivable account for the amount unpaid at the time of default. All repossessed merchandise and trade-ins should be recorded at realizable values. Presented below is information taken from the accounts of the Madison Company.

	1967	*1968*
Contracts receivable (unpaid balances):		
1967 accounts	*$ 62,425*	*$ 3,175*
1968 accounts		*101,375*
Installment sales	*138,675*	*220,925*
Purchases	*160,000*	*154,600*
New merchandise inventory, Dec. 31, at cost	*60,154*	*73,042*
Loss on defaults		*5,000*

Additional information

In the process of your audit you find that the following items were not included in the inventory taken on December 31, 1968:

(1) Merchandise received as a trade-in on December 15, 1968, for which an allowance was given. The realizable value of the merchandise is $500, which was the allowance for the trade-in. No entry was made to record this merchandise on the books at the time it was received.

(2) Repossessed merchandise, originally sold in 1967, representing the only default and repossession by the company to date, had a realizable value of $2,000 at the time of repossession and at December 31, 1968. No entry has been made to record this repossessed merchandise.

Instructions

a. Prepare the adjusting entry to record the trade-in merchandise.

b. Compute the gross profit percentages for 1967 and 1968.

c. Reconstruct the Deferred Gross Profit on Installment Sales account by years through December 31, 1968, showing in good form all computations for the amounts included in the account. Only one ledger account for Deferred Gross Profit on Installment Sales should be used, but entries for 1967 and 1968 should be shown separately and clearly labeled.

d. Prepare the entry necessary to adjust the Loss on Defaults account. Do not reverse the original entry writing off the defaulted receivable since this is an established company practice. Merely make the adjusting entry necessary to produce correct year-end amounts for the financial statements.

AICPA adapted

7 HOME OFFICE AND BRANCH ACCOUNTING

Establishment of branches

As a business grows it often establishes branches in order to market its products over a larger territory. The term *branch* has traditionally been used to describe a company unit located at some distance from the home office which carries a stock of merchandise, makes sales for cash and on credit in its local area, approves customers' credit, and makes collection of its own receivables.

The merchandise handled by a branch may be obtained solely from the home office or a portion may be purchased from outside suppliers. The cash receipts of the branch are often deposited in a bank account belonging to the home office; the expenses are then paid from an imprest fund provided by the home office. As the fund is depleted, the branch submits a list of disbursements supported by vouchers and receives a check from the home office to replenish the fund.

The use of a working fund gives the home office strong control over the cash receipts and disbursements of the branch. However, in larger, more autonomous branches it is common practice for the branch to maintain its own bank accounts, that is, to deposit its cash receipts and issue its own checks to cover expenses without intervention by the home office. In summary, we may say that the extent of independence and responsibility given to a branch will vary greatly in different companies and even among different branches within the same company.

Sales agency contrasted with branch

The term *sales agency* is sometimes applied to a company unit which performs only a small portion of the functions traditionally associated with a branch. For example, a sales agency usually carries samples of company products but does not have a stock of merchandise. Orders are taken from customers and transmitted to the home office, which passes on the customers' credit standing and ships the merchandise directly to them. The accounts receivable are maintained at the home office, which also performs the collection function. A working fund on the imprest basis is maintained at the sales agency to permit payment of its expenses.

Accounting system for a sales agency

A sales agency which does not carry stocks of merchandise, maintain receivables, or make collections has no need for a complete set of accounting records. All that is needed is a record of sales to customers and a listing of cash disbursements supported by vouchers.

If the home office wants to measure the profitability of each sales agency separately, it will establish in the general ledger special revenue and expense accounts in the name of the agency, for example, Sales: Lakeview Agency; Rent Expense: Lakeview Agency. The cost of goods sold by each agency must also be determined. If perpetual inventories are maintained, shipments to the Lakeview Agency would be charged to Cost of Sales: Lakeview Agency.

If a periodic inventory system is in use, a shipment of goods sold by an agency may be recorded by debiting Cost of Sales: Lakeview Agency and crediting Shipments of Merchandise: Agencies. This entry will be necessary only at the end of the accounting period if a memorandum record is maintained during the period listing the cost of goods shipped to fill sales orders received from agencies. At the end of the period the account Shipments of Merchandise: Agencies will be offset against the total of beginning inventory and purchases to determine the cost of goods available for sale by the home office in its own operations.

Office furniture or other assets located at a sales agency may be carried in a separate account in the general ledger of the home office, or control over such assets may be achieved by use of an equipment ledger with a card for each item showing location as well as cost and other data.

Illustrative entries for operation of a sales agency. The accounting entries made by the home office in connection with operation of a sales agency are now illustrated, based on the assumption of a periodic inventory system.

Inventory of Samples: Lakeview Agency	*1,500*	
Shipments of Merchandise: Lakeview Agency		*1,500*
Shipped merchandise to agency for use as samples.		
Working Fund: Lakeview Agency	*1,000*	
Cash		*1,000*
To establish agency working fund on imprest basis.		
Accounts Receivable	*50,000*	
Sales: Lakeview Agency		*50,000*
To record filling of sales orders received through Lakeview Agency.		

(continued)

Various Expense Accounts: Lakeview Agency	*10,000*	
Cash		*10,000*
To replenish working fund. (This entry represents several checks sent to the agency during the period.)		
Cost of Sales: Lakeview Agency	*35,000*	
Shipments of Merchandise: Lakeview Agency		*35,000*
To summarize memorandum record of cost of goods shipped during period to fill orders received through agency.		
Sales: Lakeview Agency	*50,000*	
Cost of Sales: Lakeview Agency		*35,000*
Various Expense Accounts: Lakeview Agency		*10,000*
Income Summary: Lakeview Agency		*5,000*
To close revenue and expense accounts into a separate Income Summary account for sales agency.		
Income Summary: Lakeview Agency	*5,000*	
Income Summary		*5,000*
To close the agency Income Summary account to the general Income Summary account.		

Accounting system for a branch

The extent of the accounting activity at a branch depends upon company policy. The policies of one company may provide for a complete accounting structure at each branch; the policies of another company may call for concentration of all accounting records in the home office. In some of the drug and grocery chain stores, for example, the branches submit daily reports and documents to the home office, which records all transactions by branches in journals and ledgers kept in one central location. The home office may not even conduct operations on its own but merely serve as an accounting and control headquarters.

In many fields of business, however, the branch maintains a complete, self-balancing set of records with journals, ledgers, and a chart of accounts similar to those of an independent business. Financial statements are prepared at regular intervals by the branch and forwarded to the home office. The number and type of accounts, the internal control practices, the form and content of financial statements, and the accounting policies generally are prescribed by the home office. Internal auditors may perform examinations to determine whether branch personnel apply these policies and procedures in a uniform and consistent manner.

In the remainder of this chapter we shall be concerned with a branch operation that includes a complete set of accounting records. The range of transactions to be accounted for by the branch should ordinarily include all controllable expenses and revenues for which the branch manager is held responsible. If his responsibility includes all assets and all expenditures, then the accounts should reflect this responsibility. More commonly, expenses such as depreciation of plant and equipment are regarded as not subject to control by the branch manager, and both the fixed asset and related depreciation accounts are maintained by the home office.

Reciprocal accounts

The ledger maintained by the branch will include an account entitled Home Office which will be credited for all merchandise, cash, or other resources provided by the home office. It will be debited for all cash, merchandise, or other resources sent by the branch to the home office or to other branches. The Home Office account is a proprietorship account which shows the investment made in the branch. It replaces the capital stock and retained earnings accounts or the capital accounts used by an independent business. At the end of the accounting period when the branch closes its books, the Income Summary account is closed into the Home Office account. A net income increases the credit balance of the Home Office account; a net loss decreases this balance.

On the home office books a reciprocal account with a title such as Investment in Branch or Springfield Branch is maintained. This account is debited for the cash, merchandise, and services provided to the branch, and for net income earned by the branch. It is credited for the cash or other assets received from the branch, and for any net loss incurred by the branch.

A separate account is maintained by the home office for each branch. If there is only one branch, the account title is likely to be Investment in Branch. If there are numerous branches, each account title will include a name or number to identify the individual branch. Traditionally, the account titles for the reciprocal accounts were Branch Current and Home Office Current but the word *current* appears to have been dropped from use in reciprocal accounts in recent years.

Expenses incurred by home office and charged to branches

Some companies follow a policy of notifying branches of expenses incurred by the home office in their behalf. As previously mentioned, fixed assets located at branches are commonly carried on the home office books. This practice facilitates the use of standard depreciation procedures throughout the company. If the fixed asset is purchased by the home office for the branch, the entry for the acquisition is the usual one of debiting an asset account and crediting Cash or Accounts Payable. If the branch makes the purchase of a fixed asset, it will debit the Home Office account and credit Cash or Accounts Payable. The home office will then make an entry debiting a fixed asset account such as Plant and Equipment: Springfield Branch and crediting the reciprocal account Springfield Branch.

The home office also usually purchases insurance, pays taxes, and places some advertising which benefits all branches. Clearly such expenses as depreciation, taxes, insurance, and advertising must be considered in determining the profitability of a branch. A policy decision must be made as to whether these expense data are to be retained at the home office or are to be reported to the branches so that the operating statement prepared by each branch will give a complete picture.

If the home office does not make sales itself but functions only as a control agency, most or all of its expenses may be allocated to the branches. In order to facilitate comparison of the operating results achieved by the various branches, the home office may charge each branch interest on the total resources used by it. Such interest expense recorded by the branches would of course be offset by interest income to the home office and would not appear in the combined financial statements of the company as a whole.

In some companies the expenses incurred by the home office relating to branch operations are not transmitted to the branches but are used in the home office in modifying and analyzing the financial reports prepared by the branches.

Alternative methods of billing shipments to branch

Three alternative methods are available to the home office in pricing merchandise shipped to a branch. The merchandise shipped may be billed (1) at cost, (2) at cost plus an arbitrary percentage, or (3) at retail sales price. Of course the shipment of merchandise to a branch does not constitute a sale because ownership of the goods does not change.

Billing at cost is the simplest procedure and the most widely used one. It avoids the complication of unrealized profit in inventories and permits the financial statements of the branch to give a meaningful picture of operations. However, billing goods to branches at cost attributes all profits of the organization to the branches, even though some of the goods may be manufactured by the home office. Under these circumstances cost may not be the most realistic basis for pricing shipments to branches.

Billing shipments to the branch at an arbitrary percentage above cost (such as 110% of cost) may be intended to allocate a reasonable profit to home office operations or may be used merely to prevent branch personnel from knowing the profits earned by the branch. This latter reason is a dubious one because a competent branch manager will necessarily be well aware of the cost of merchandise in his own store and also the costs of competing lines. Moreover, the internal process of arbitrarily writing up the value of merchandise shipped to branches is necessarily known by some employees; such information is likely to flow through the organization faster than the goods to which it relates.

When goods are billed to the branch at a price in excess of cost, the profits reported by the branch will necessarily be reduced and the ending inventory will be overstated. Adjustments must be made by the home office to compensate for the excess of inventory valuation above cost before completing the accounting work each period.

Billing shipments to a branch at retail sales price may be based on a desire to conceal profit information from branch personnel and also to strengthen internal control over inventories. The merchandise accounts of the branch show the merchandise received at retail sales price and show units sold at the same prices. Consequently, the accounts will show the ending inventory which *should* be on hand priced at retail sales price. The home office record of shipments to a branch, when considered along with sales reported by the branch, provides a perpetual inventory stated at sales price. If the physical inventory taken periodically at the branch does not agree with the book figure, some type of error or theft is indicated and can be promptly investigated.

Separate financial statements for branch and home office

A separate income statement and balance sheet will be prepared by the branch so that management can review the operating results and financial position of the branch. The income statement has no unusual features if merchandise is billed to the branch at cost. However, if merchandise is billed to the branch at retail sales price, the income statement will necessarily show a net loss equal to the amount of operating expenses. The only unusual aspect of the balance sheet for a branch is the use of the Home Office account in lieu of the capital accounts used by an independent business. The separate financial statements prepared by a branch may be revised in the home office to include expenses incurred by the home office but allocable to the branch, and also to show branch operations after elimination of any interoffice profit.

Separate financial statements are also usually prepared for the home office so that management will be able to appraise the results of its operations and its financial condition. It is important to emphasize, however, that separate statements of the home office and of the branch are for internal use only. They do not meet the needs of investors, bankers, or other outsiders.

Combined statements for home office and branch

A balance sheet for distribution to bankers, creditors, stockholders, and government agencies must show the financial position of the business as one unit. A convenient starting point in creating such a combined statement consists of the adjusted trial balances of the home office and of the branch. A working paper for the combination of these trial balances is illustrated on page 208.

The assets and liabilities of the branch are substituted for the Investment in Branch account shown on the home office trial balance. Like accounts are combined to produce one amount for the total cash of the business, one amount for accounts receivables, and similarly for other assets and liabilities.

In the preparation of a combined balance sheet, reciprocal accounts are eliminated because they lose all significance when one views the complete enterprise as one entity. The Home Office account is offset against the Investment in Branch account; also any receivables and payables between branches or between the home office and a branch are eliminated.

The operating results of the entire business are shown by an income statement in which the revenues and expenses of the branch are combined with corresponding accounts for the home office. Interoffice profits must be eliminated. The stockholders, creditors, and other outsiders interested in the company naturally want to see an income statement which reveals the earnings for the business as a whole.

In the preparation of a combined income statement, the two accounts showing transfer of merchandise between home office and branch must be eliminated. The account on the branch books called Shipments from Home Office is eliminated by offsetting it against Shipments to Branch on the home office books.

Illustrative entries for operation of a branch

Assume that Ryan Company bills merchandise to Branch X at cost, and that the branch maintains complete accounting records and prepares monthly financial statements. Both the home office and the branch use the periodic inventory system. Fixed assets used at the branch are carried on the home office books. Certain expenses, such as advertising and insurance, are incurred by the home office in behalf of the branch and are billed to the branch so that its records will give a realistic picture of operating results. During the first year of operation of the branch, the transactions may be summarized as follows:

(1) Cash of $1,000 sent to branch
(2) Merchandise with a cost of $60,000 shipped to branch
(3) Equipment purchased by branch for $500, to be carried on home office books (Other fixed assets for branch purchased by home office)
(4) Sales by branch on credit, $80,000
(5) Collections of accounts receivable, $62,000
(6) Payment of expenses by branch, $20,000
(7) Cash remittance to home office, $37,500
(8) Expenses incurred by home office charged to branch, $3,000

These transactions are recorded by the home office and by the branch with the following journal entries.

	Home Office Books			*Branch Books*		
(1)	*Branch X*	1,000		*Cash*	1,000	
	Cash		1,000	*Home Office*		1,000
(2)	*Branch X*	60,000		*Shipments from Home Office*	60,000	
	Shipments to Branch X		60,000	*Home Office*		60,000
(3)	*Equipment: Branch X*	500		*Home Office*	500	
	Branch X		500	*Cash*		500
(4)				*Accounts Receivable*	80,000	
				Sales		80,000
(5)				*Cash*	62,000	
				Accounts Receivable		62,000
(6)				*Expenses*	20,000	
				Cash		20,000
(7)	*Cash*	37,500		*Home Office*	37,500	
	Branch X		37,500	*Cash*		37,500
(8)	*Branch X*	3,000		*Expenses*	3,000	
	Expenses		3,000	*Home Office*		3,000

Branch X

	Debit	*Credit*	*Balance*
Cash sent to branch	1,000		1,000
Merchandise billed to branch at cost	60,000		61,000
Equipment purchased by branch, recorded as asset on home office books		500	60,500
Cash received from branch		37,500	23,000
Expenses billed to branch	3,000		26,000

On the home office books, the ledger account entitled Branch X has a debit balance of $26,000 before the books are closed and the branch net income is debited to the account.

On the branch books, the ledger account entitled Home Office has a credit balance of $26,000 before the books are closed and the net income of $12,000 is credited to the account.

Home Office

	Debit	Credit	Balance
Cash received from home office		1,000	1,000
Merchandise received from home office		60,000	61,000
Equipment purchased	500		60,500
Cash sent to home office	37,500		23,000
Expenses billed by home office		3,000	26,000

Assume that the inventory at the end of the period amounts to $15,000 for the branch. The adjusting and closing entries relating to the branch are as follows:

Home Office Books			*Branch Books*		
			Inventory	15,000	
			Sales	80,000	
			Shipments from Home Office		60,000
			Expenses		23,000
			Income Summary		12,000
Branch X	12,000		*Income Summary*	12,000	
Income Summary: Branch X		12,000	*Home Office*		12,000
Income Summary: Branch X	12,000				
Income Summary		12,000			

On the home office books, the Shipments to Branch account will be closed to the Income Summary along with the closing of the other nominal accounts.

Working papers for combined statements

Working papers for combined statements have three distinctive purposes: (1) to combine accounts with like assets and like liabilities, (2) to eliminate interoffice profits, and (3) to eliminate reciprocal accounts. The following working papers for the Ryan Company are based on the branch transactions illustrated on pages 206–207 and additional assumed data for the home office trial balance. All the routine year-end adjusting entries are assumed to have been made and the working

RYAN COMPANY

Working Papers for Combined Statements of Home Office and Branch X
for the year ended December 31, 1967

(First year: Billings at cost)

	Adjusted trial balances				Eliminations		Combined	
	Home Office		Branch					
	Dr	Cr	Dr	Cr	Dr	Cr	Dr	Cr
Income statement:								
Sales		400,000		80,000				480,000
Inventory, Dec. 31, 1966	40,000						40,000	
Purchases	300,000						300,000	
Shipments to Branch X		60,000			(a) 60,000			
Shipments from Home Office			60,000			(a) 60,000		
Inventory, Dec. 31, 1967		45,000		15,000				60,000
Expenses	90,000		23,000				113,000	
Subtotals	430,000	505,000	83,000	95,000				
Net income (down)	75,000		12,000				87,000	
Totals	505,000	505,000	95,000	95,000			540,000	540,000
Statement of retained earnings:								
Retained earnings, Dec. 31, 1966		70,000						70,000
Net income (as above)		75,000		12,000				87,000
Dividends	40,000						40,000	
Retained earnings, Dec. 31, 1967 (down)							117,000	
Totals							157,000	157,000
Balance sheet:								
Cash	24,000		5,000				29,000	
Accounts receivable	40,000		18,000				58,000	
Inventory, Dec. 31, 1967	45,000		15,000				60,000	
Branch X	26,000					(b) 26,000		
Plant and equipment	150,000						150,000	
Accumulated depreciation: plant & equipment		10,000						10,000
Accounts payable		20,000						20,000
Home office				26,000	(b) 26,000			
Capital stock		150,000						150,000
Retained earnings (as above)								117,000
Totals	325,000	325,000	38,000	38,000	86,000	86,000	297,000	297,000

(a) To eliminate reciprocal accounts for merchandise shipments.
(b) To eliminate reciprocal accounts for branch X and home office.

papers are begun with the adjusted trial balances of the home office and the branch.

Note that the $26,000 debit amount in the Branch X account and the $26,000 credit amount in the Home Office account are the balances before the books are closed, that is, before the $12,000 net income of the branch is entered in these two reciprocal accounts. In the Eliminations columns, entry (a) offsets the Shipments to Branch X account against the Shipments from Home Office account. Entry (b) offsets the Branch X account against the Home Office account. These elimination entries appear in the working papers only. They are not recorded in the accounts of either the home office or branch, because their only purpose is to aid in the preparation of combined statements.

Illustrative combined statements

These working papers provide the information for the financial statements of Ryan Company given below.

RYAN COMPANY
Income Statement
for the year ended December 31, 1967

Sales		$480,000
Cost of sales:		
Inventory, Dec. 31, 1966	$ 40,000	
Purchases	300,000	
Cost of goods available for sale	$340,000	
Inventory, Dec. 31, 1967	60,000	280,000
Gross profit on sales		$200,000
Expenses		113,000
Net income		$ 87,000

RYAN COMPANY
Statement of Retained Earnings
for the year ended December 31, 1967

Retained earnings, Dec. 31, 1966	$ 70,000
Net income for the year	87,000
Total	$157,000
Less: Dividends declared	40,000
Retained earnings, Dec. 31, 1967	$117,000

RYAN COMPANY
Balance Sheet
December 31, 1967

Assets

Cash		$ 29,000
Accounts receivable		58,000
Inventory		60,000
Plant and equipment	$150,000	
Less: Accumulated depreciation	10,000	140,000
Total assets		$287,000

Liabilities & Stockholders' Equity

Liabilities:		
Accounts payable		$ 20,000
Stockholders' equity:		
Capital stock	$150,000	
Retained earnings	117,000	267,000
Total liabilities & stockholders' equity		$287,000

Accounting for billings to branch in excess of cost

As explained earlier, some companies prefer to bill merchandise to branches at cost plus an arbitrary percentage, or at retail sales price. Since both these methods involve similar modifications of accounting procedures, a single example will illustrate the key points involved. We shall now repeat the Ryan Company illustration with one changed assumption: the home office bills merchandise to the branch at 50% above cost.

Under this assumption the entries for the first year's transactions by the home office and the branch will be the same as those previously presented on page 206 except for the entries showing shipment of merchandise from the home office to the branch. These shipments will be recorded as follows:

Home Office Books			Branch Books		
(2) Branch X	90,000		Shipments from Home Office	90,000	
Shipments to Branch X		60,000	Home Office		90,000
Allowance for Overvaluation of Inventory: Branch X		30,000			

On the home office books the ledger account entitled Branch X now has a debit balance of $56,000 before the books are closed and the net income or loss of the branch is entered in the account. This amount is $30,000 higher than the $26,000 balance in our prior illustration; the increase represents the increase in invoiced prices of the merchandise shipped to the branch.

Branch X

	Debit	Credit	Balance
Cash sent to branch	*1,000*		*1,000*
Merchandise billed to branch at 50% above cost	*90,000*		*91,000*
Equipment purchased by branch, recorded as asset on home office books		*500*	*90,500*
Cash received from branch		*37,500*	*53,000*
Expenses billed to branch	*3,000*		*56,000*

On the branch books the ledger account entitled Home Office now has a credit balance of $56,000 before the books are closed and the net income or loss is entered in the account.

Home Office

	Debit	Credit	Balance
Cash received from home office		*1,000*	*1,000*
Merchandise received from home office		*90,000*	*91,000*
Equipment purchased	*500*		*90,500*
Cash sent to home office	*37,500*		*53,000*
Expenses billed by home office		*3,000*	*56,000*

The branch recorded the merchandise received from the home office at the invoiced amount of $90,000. The $90,000 debit balance in the account Shipments from Home Office is reciprocal to two accounts on the home office books. These two accounts are Shipments to Branch X with a credit balance of $60,000 and Allowance for Overvaluation of Inventory: Branch X with a credit balance of $30,000.

The use of two reciprocal accounts rather than one enables the home office to maintain a record of the *cost* of goods shipped to the branch, as well as the amount of "write-up" on shipments. The home office will deduct the Shipments to Branch X account, which is stated at cost, from the total of the beginning inventory and purchases to determine the cost of goods available for sale by the home office.

At the end of the period the branch will report its inventory (based on invoice prices) at $22,500. The cost of this inventory is $15,000 ($22,500 ÷ 1.50). On the home office books, the required balance in the account entitled Allowance for Overvaluation of Inventory: Branch X is therefore only $7,500 and the account should be reduced from its present balance of $30,000 to $7,500. The reason for this reduction is that the 50% write-up of merchandise over cost has become realized profit with respect to the goods sold by the branch. Consequently, at the end of the year the home office should reduce its allowance for overvaluation of the branch inventory to the $7,500 excess valuation contained in the ending inventory. This adjustment of $22,500 in the allowance account is transferred as a credit to Income Summary: Branch X, because it represents additional profit on branch operations over that reported by the branch. (An alternative interpretation is to regard the $22,500 portion of the year's income as realized profit attributable to the operations of the home office.)

Of course the actual profit earned through operation of the branch will be the same amount of $12,000 as shown in our prior illustration when merchandise was billed to the branch at cost. Under the present assumptions, however, the branch will *report* a net loss of $10,500. This amount will be picked up by the home office and adjusted to a net income of $12,000, as shown by the following year-end entries relating to branch operations.

Home Office Books

Income Summary: Branch X	*10,500*	
Branch X		*10,500*
To record operating loss reported by branch.		
Allowance for Overvaluation of Inventory: Branch X	*22,500*	
Income Summary: Branch X		*22,500*
To reduce allowance to amount by which ending inventory is in excess of cost.		
Income Summary: Branch X	*12,000*	
Income Summary		*12,000*
To close branch net income to Income Summary.		

After these entries have been recorded, the ledger accounts on the home office books used to portray branch operations will be as follows:

Branch X

	Debit	*Credit*	*Balance*
Cash sent to branch	*1,000*		*1,000*
Merchandise billed to branch at 50% above cost	*90,000*		*91,000*
Equipment purchased by branch, recorded as asset on home office books		*500*	*90,500*
Cash received from branch		*37,500*	*53,000*
Expenses billed to branch	*3,000*		*56,000*
Operating loss reported by branch		*10,500*	*45,500*

Allowance for Overvaluation of Inventory: Branch X

	Debit	Credit	Balance
Write-up of merchandise shipped to branch by 50% of cost		30,000	30,000
Realization of 50% write-up on goods sold by branch	22,500		7,500

Income Summary: Branch X

	Debit	Credit	Balance
Operating loss reported by branch	10,500		10,500
Realization of 50% write-up on goods sold by branch		22,500	12,000 (cr)
Net income of branch closed to Income Summary account	12,000		-0-

A separate balance sheet prepared for the home office alone would show the $7,500 credit balance in allowance for Overvaluation of Inventory: Branch X as a deduction from the $45,500 debit balance in the asset account Branch X. As an alternative the net amount of $38,000 could be shown.

The closing entries by the branch at year-end are as follows:

Branch Books

Inventory	22,500	
Sales	80,000	
Income Summary	10,500	
Shipments from Home Office		90,000
Expenses		23,000
To record the ending inventory and to close the nominal accounts.		
Home Office	10,500	
Income Summary		10,500
To close the operating loss in the Income Summary account to the Home Office account.		

After these closing entries have been posted by the branch, the proprietorship account, Home Office, will show a credit balance of $45,500.

Home Office

	Debit	*Credit*	*Balance*
Cash received from home office		*1,000*	*1,000*
Merchandise received from home office		*90,000*	*91,000*
Equipment purchased	*500*		*90,500*
Cash sent to home office	*37,500*		*53,000*
Expenses billed by home office		*3,000*	*56,000*
Operating loss for the year	*10,500*		*45,500*

Working papers when billings to branch are in excess of cost

The working papers to develop combined statements when billings to the branch are in excess of cost are presented on page 215. They differ from the previously illustrated working papers by the inclusion of entries to adjust the ending inventory of the branch to a cost basis. Also the net loss reported by the branch is adjusted by the $22,500 of merchandise "write-up" which has become realized profit through the sale of the goods by the branch. Bear in mind that the entries in the Adjustments and Eliminations columns appear only on the working papers. They represent a mechanical step to aid in the preparation of combined statements and are not placed in the accounting records of the home office or the branch.

Note that the amounts in the "Combined" columns of these working papers are exactly the same as in the working papers prepared when the shipments to the branch were billed at cost. Consequently, the financial statements would be identical with those presented on pages 209–210.

Treatment of beginning inventory priced above cost

The working papers on page 215 show how the ending inventory and the related allowance for overvaluation of inventory were handled at the end of the first year of operations. However, since this was the first year of operation for the branch, no beginning inventory was involved.

We shall now continue the illustration of the Ryan Company into a second year of operations in order to demonstrate the handling of a beginning inventory carried by the branch at a value in excess of cost. The beginning inventory for 1968 was carried by the branch at $22,500, or 150% of the cost of $15,000. Assume that during the second year the home office shipped to the branch goods which cost $80,000 and were billed at $120,000. The branch inventory at the end of 1968 amounted to $30,000 at billed prices, representing cost of $20,000 plus a 50% write-up by the home office at time of shipment to the branch.

RYAN COMPANY

Working Papers for Combined Statements of Home Office and Branch X
for the year ended December 31, 1967

(First year: Billings above cost)

	Adjusted trial balances				Adjustments and eliminations		Combined	
	Home Office		Branch					
	Dr	Cr	Dr	Cr	Dr	Cr	Dr	Cr
Income statement:								
Sales		400,000		80,000				480,000
Inventory, Dec. 31, 1966	40,000						40,000	
Purchases	300,000						300,000	
Shipments to Branch X		60,000			(a) 60,000			
Shipments from Home Office			90,000			(a) 90,000		
Inventory, Dec. 31, 1967		45,000		22,500	(b) 7,500			60,000
Expenses	90,000		23,000				113,000	
Subtotals	430,000	505,000	113,000	102,500			453,000	540,000
Net income (down)	75,000			10,500	(c) 22,500		87,000	
Totals	505,000	505,000	113,000	113,000			540,000	540,000
Statement of retained earnings:								
Retained earnings, Dec. 31, 1966		70,000						70,000
Net income (as above)		75,000	10,500			(c) 22,500		87,000
Dividends	40,000						40,000	
Retained earnings, Dec. 31, 1967 (down)							117,000	
Totals							157,000	157,000
Balance sheet:								
Cash	24,000		5,000				29,000	
Accounts receivable	40,000		18,000				58,000	
Inventory, Dec. 31, 1967	45,000		22,500			(b) 7,500	60,000	
Allowance for overvaluation of inventory: Branch X		30,000			(a) 30,000			
Branch X	56,000					(d) 56,000		
Plant and equipment	150,000						150,000	
Accumulated depreciation: plant & equipment		10,000						10,000
Accounts payable		20,000						20,000
Home office				56,000	(d) 56,000			
Capital stock		150,000						150,000
Retained earnings (as above)								117,000
Totals	355,000	355,000	56,000	56,000	176,000	176,000	297,000	297,000

(a) To eliminate reciprocal accounts for merchandise shipments.
(b) To reduce ending inventory of branch to a cost basis.
(c) To increase reported net income of branch by the portion of merchandise write-up which has become realized profit.
(d) To eliminate reciprocal accounts for branch X and home office.

The flow of merchandise at the branch during the second year may be summarized as follows:

	Cost	Billed price
Beginning inventory	$15,000	$ 22,500
Shipments from home office	80,000	120,000
Available for sale	$95,000	$142,500
Ending inventory	20,000	30,000
Goods sold	$75,000	$112,500

The 1968 activities of the branch as shown by the home office books are reflected in the following ledger accounts.

Branch X

	Debit	Credit	Balance
Balance, Dec. 31, 1967			45,500 (dr)
Merchandise billed to branch at 50% above cost	120,000		165,500
Cash received from branch		113,000	52,500
Expenses billed to branch	4,500		57,000
Operating profit reported by branch	10,000		67,000

Allowance for Overvaluation of Inventory: Branch X

	Debit	Credit	Balance
Balance, Dec. 31, 1967 (see page 213)			7,500 (cr)
Write-up of merchandise shipped to branch during 1968 (50% of cost)		40,000	47,500
Realization of 50% write-up on merchandise sold by branch during 1968	37,500		10,000

Income Summary: Branch X

	Debit	Credit	Balance
Operating income reported by branch		10,000	10,000 (cr)
Realization of 50% write-up of merchandise sold by branch during 1968		37,500	47,500
To close branch net income to Income Summary	47,500		-0-

On the home office books, at the end of the second year the balance required in the account Allowance for Overvaluation of Inventory: Branch X is $10,000, that is, the billed price of $30,000 less cost of $20,000 for goods in the ending inventory. The account should therefore be reduced from its present balance of $47,500 to $10,000. This reduction of $37,500 represents the 50% write-up of merchandise in excess of cost which has become realized profit on goods sold by the branch during 1968 and is credited to Income Summary: Branch X.

On the branch books the account with the home office showed the following activity for the year 1968.

Home Office

	Debit	*Credit*	*Balance*
Balance, Dec. 31, 1967			*45,500 (cr)*
Merchandise received from home office		*120,000*	*165,500*
Cash remitted to home office	*113,000*		*52,500*
Expenses billed by home office		*4,500*	*57,000*
Net income for the year		*10,000*	*67,000*

The working papers for the second year (page 218) are very similar to those of the first year (page 215), except for one additional entry in the pair of columns for Adjustments and Eliminations. Entry (b) reduces the beginning inventory of the branch by the $7,500 of unrealized profit contained therein, with an offsetting debit to the Allowance for Overvaluation of Inventory: Branch X. All the other adjustment and elimination entries follow the pattern previously shown in the working papers for the first year.

Closing entries. On the branch books, the closing entries at the end of the second year are as follows:

Inventory, Dec. 31, 1968	*30,000*	
Sales	*150,000*	
Inventory, Dec. 31, 1967		*22,500*
Shipments from Home Office		*120,000*
Expenses		*27,500*
Income Summary		*10,000*
To record the ending inventory and to close the beginning inventory and the nominal accounts.		
Income Summary	*10,000*	
Home Office		*10,000*
To close the operating profit in the Income Summary account to the Home Office account.		

RYAN COMPANY
Working Papers for Combined Statements of Home Office and Branch X
for the year ended December 31, 1968

(Second year: Billings above cost)

	Adjusted trial balances				Adjustments and eliminations		Combined	
	Home Office		Branch					
	Dr	Cr	Dr	Cr	Dr	Cr	Dr	Cr
Income statement:								
Sales		500,000		150,000				650,000
Inventory, Dec. 31, 1967	45,000		22,500			(b) 7,500	60,000	
Purchases	400,000						400,000	
Shipments to Branch X		80,000			(a) 80,000			
Shipments from Home Office			120,000			(a) 120,000		
Inventory, Dec. 31, 1968		70,000		30,000	(c) 10,000			90,000
Expenses	120,000		27,500				147,500	
Subtotals	565,000	650,000	170,000	180,000			607,500	740,000
Net income (down)	85,000		10,000		(d) 37,500		132,500	
Totals	650,000	650,000	180,000	180,000			740,000	740,000
Statement of retained earnings:								
Retained earnings, Dec. 31, 1967		117,000						117,000
Net income (as above)		85,000		10,000		(d) 37,500		132,500
Dividends	60,000						60,000	
Retained earnings, Dec. 31, 1968 (down)							189,500	
Totals							249,500	249,500
Balance sheet:								
Cash	30,000		9,000				39,000	
Accounts receivable	64,000		28,000				92,000	
Inventory, Dec. 31, 1968	70,000		30,000			(c) 10,000	90,000	
Allowance for overvaluation of inventory: Branch X		47,500			(a) 40,000 (b) 7,500			
Branch X	57,000					(e) 57,000		
Plant and equipment	158,000						158,000	
Accumulated depreciation: plant & equipment		15,000						15,000
Accounts payable		24,500						24,500
Home office				57,000	(e) 57,000			
Capital stock		150,000						150,000
Retained earnings (as above)								189,500
Totals	439,000	439,000	67,000	67,000	232,000	232,000	379,000	379,000

(a) To eliminate reciprocal accounts for merchandise shipments.
(b) To reduce beginning inventory of branch to a cost basis.
(c) To reduce ending inventory of branch to a cost basis.
(d) To increase reported net income of branch by portion of merchandise write-up which has become realized profit.
(e) To eliminate reciprocal accounts for branch X and home office.

On the home office books, the closing entries at the end of the second year will be:

Branch X	*10,000*	
Income Summary: Branch X		*10,000*
To record the operating profit reported by the branch.		
Allowance for Overvaluation of Inventory: Branch X	*37,500*	
Income Summary: Branch X		*37,500*
To recognize as realized income the write-up of merchandise applicable to goods sold by the branch during the year.		
Income Summary: Branch X	*47,500*	
Income Summary		*47,500*
To close separate Income Summary account applicable to branch operations.		
Inventory, Dec. 31, 1968	*70,000*	
Sales	*500,000*	
Shipments to Branch X	*80,000*	
Inventory, Dec. 31, 1968		*45,000*
Purchases		*400,000*
Expenses		*120,000*
Income Summary		*85,000*
To record new inventory and to close old inventory and nominal accounts.		
Income Summary	*132,500*	
Retained Earnings		*132,500*
To close Income Summary account.		
Retained Earnings	*60,000*	
Dividends		*60,000*
To close Dividends account.		

Perpetual inventories

If the home office and branch maintain perpetual inventory records, the ledger accounts, Shipments to Branch X and Shipments from Home Office, shown in the preceding illustrations will be unnecessary. The home office will credit its perpetual inventory account for the cost of goods shipped to the branch. Any excess of billed price over cost will be credited to Allowance for Overvaluation of Inventory: Branch X. Upon receipt of the merchandise, the branch will debit Inventory of Merchandise and credit Home Office at the billed price. At the end of the period the home office will reduce its Allowance for Overvaluation of Inventory: Branch X to the amount of overvaluation existing in the ending inventory. The offsetting credit will be to Income Summary: Branch X.

Reconciliation of reciprocal accounts

The year-end balance of the branch account on the home office books may not agree with the home office account on the branch books because certain transactions may have been recorded by one office but not by the other. The situation is comparable to that of reconciling the ledger account for Cash in Bank with the balance shown by the bank statement. The lack of agreement between the reciprocal accounts causes no difficulty during the accounting period, but at the balance sheet date the interoffice accounts must be brought into agreement before combined statements are prepared.

As an illustration of the procedure for reconciling reciprocal accounts at the year-end, assume that the branch and home office accounts contain the following data:

On the home office ledger:

Branch A

Nov. 30	*Balance*	*45,000*	*Dec. 10*	*Cash received from branch*	*20,000*
Dec. 29	*Merchandise shipped to branch*	*10,000*	*Dec. 27*	*Collection of branch account receivable*	*1,000*

On the Branch A ledger:

Home Office

Dec. 7	*Cash sent to home office*	*20,000*	*Nov. 30*	*Balance*	*45,000*
Dec. 28	*Purchased office equipment*	*3,000*	*Dec. 30*	*Collection of home office account receivable*	*2,000*

Comparison of these accounts shows the existence of four reconciling items, which may be described as follows:

1. A debit of $10,000 in the Branch A account without a related credit in the Home Office account.

On December 29 the home office shipped merchandise to the branch in the amount of $10,000. The home office will normally debit its account with the branch on the date of shipping merchandise, but the branch will not credit its account with the home office until the merchandise is received, perhaps several days later. The required adjustment at year-end for this type of reconciling item will be an entry on the branch books as follows:

Shipments from Home Office—In Transit	*10,000*	
Home Office		*10,000*

In preparing the income statement for the branch, the $10,000 balance in the account Shipments from Home Office—In Transit will be combined with the account Shipments from Home Office. The total will be equal to the amount shown on the home office books for Shipments to Branch; therefore these two reciprocal accounts can be eliminated for the purpose of preparing a combined income statement.

In determining its year-end inventory of merchandise, the branch must also add to the inventory on hand the $10,000 of merchandise in transit. This lot of merchandise will therefore appear on the branch balance sheet and also as part of the total inventory in the combined financial statements.

2. A credit of $1,000 in the Branch A account without a related debit in the Home Office account.

On December 27 an account receivable belonging to the branch was collected directly from the customer by the home office. The collection was recorded by the home office by debiting Cash and crediting Branch A. No entry has been made by the branch; therefore, the following entry is needed at the year-end on the branch books:

Home Office	*1,000*	
Accounts Receivable		*1,000*

3. A debit of $3,000 in the Home Office account without a related credit in the Branch A account.

On December 28 the branch purchased some office equipment at a cost of $3,000. Since the fixed assets in use at the branch are carried on the home office books, the entry made by the branch was to debit Home Office and credit Cash. No entry has yet been made by the home office; therefore, the following entry will be made at December 31 on the home office books:

Office Equipment	*3,000*	
Branch A		*3,000*

4. A credit of $2,000 in the Home Office account without a related debit in the Branch A account.

On December 30 an account receivable belonging to the home office was collected directly from the customer by the branch. The collection was recorded by the branch by debiting Cash and crediting Home Office. No entry has been made by the home office; therefore, the following entry is needed at the year-end on the home office books.

Branch A	*2,000*	
Accounts Receivable		*2,000*

The effect of these four year-end entries is to bring the reciprocal accounts into agreement, as shown by the following schedule:

	Branch A account (In home office ledger)	*Home Office account (In branch ledger)*
Balances prior to adjustment	*$34,000 (dr)*	*$24,000 (cr)*
Increases by adjusting entries:		
(1) Merchandise shipped to branch		*10,000*
(4) Receivable owned by home office, collected by branch	*2,000*	
	$36,000 (dr)	*$34,000 (cr)*
Decreases by adjusting entries:		
(2) Receivable owned by branch, collected by home office		*1,000*
(3) Office equipment purchased by branch	*3,000*	
Adjusted balances	*$33,000 (dr)*	*$33,000 (cr)*

Transactions between branches

Efficient operations may on occasion require that merchandise or equipment be transferred from one branch to another. A branch should not carry an account with another branch but should clear the transfer through its account with the home office. For example, if Branch A ships merchandise to Branch B, Branch A will debit Home Office and credit Shipments from Home Office. Upon receipt of the goods, Branch B will debit Shipments from Home Office and credit Home Office. The home office will record the transfer between branches by crediting its account Branch A and debiting Branch B.

The transfer of merchandise from one branch to another does not justify increasing the inventory value by the additional freight charges incurred because of the indirect routing. The amount of freight charges properly included in merchandise inventory at a branch is limited to the transportation cost of shipping the goods directly from the home office to their present location. Excess freight charges should be treated as expense of the current period on the books of the home office.

To illustrate the accounting for excess freight charges on interbranch transfers of merchandise, assume the following data. The home office shipped goods costing $6,000 to Branch D and paid freight charges of $400. Shortly afterward, the home office instructed Branch D to transfer these goods to Branch E. Freight charges of $300 were paid by Branch D to carry out this order. If the merchandise had been shipped directly from the home office to Branch E, the freight cost would have been $500. The entries to be made on the three sets of books are as follows:

Home office books:

Branch D	*6,400*	
Shipments to Branch D		*6,000*
Cash		*400*
To record shipment of merchandise and payment of freight thereon.		
Branch E	*6,500*	
Shipments to Branch D	*6,000*	
Excess Freight Expense—Interbranch Transfers	*200*	
Shipments to Branch E		*6,000*
Branch D		*6,700*
To record transfer of goods from Branch D to Branch E. Interbranch freight of $300 paid by Branch D caused total freight charges on these goods to exceed direct shipment costs by $200.		

Branch D books:

Shipments from Home Office	*6,000*	
Freight In	*400*	
Home Office		*6,400*
Received merchandise from home office with freight paid in advance.		
Home Office	*6,700*	
Shipments from Home Office		*6,000*
Freight In		*400*
Cash		*300*
Transferred goods to Branch E at instruction of home office. Paid freight of $300 to ship goods.		

Branch E books:

Shipments from Home Office	*6,000*	
Freight In	*500*	
Home Office		*6,500*
Received merchandise from Branch D transferred by order of home office; recorded normal freight cost billed by home office.		

The practice of treating excess freight charges on merchandise transferred from one branch to another as an expense of the current period is a specific example of the accounting principle that losses should be given prompt recognition rather than being concealed by inflating asset values. The excess freight charges from cross-shipment of goods between branches are in most cases the result of imperfect planning of original shipments. The expense arising from such errors does not add to the utility of the merchandise and should not be counted as an element of inventory cost.

In treating excess cost of interbranch transfers as an expense attributable to the home office, we have assumed that the home office makes the decisions directing all shipments. If the branch offices are given authority to order shipments, then the loss from errors in such orders should be borne by the branches.

Treatment of start-up expenses in new branches

The establishment of a new branch often requires the incurring of considerable expense before a significant flow of revenue has been generated. Operating losses in the first few months are very likely. Some companies have made a practice of capitalizing these "start-up" losses on the grounds that such unprofitable operation is a necessary prelude to successful operation at a new location. However, most companies write off start-up charges in a new branch in the period incurred.

The decision should be based on the particular circumstances and on the familiar concept that net income is measured by matching costs and expenses against related revenues. If a given expense can clearly be shown to benefit future periods, it should be assigned to those periods. However, if conservatism is accepted as an accounting principle, the burden of proof should be borne by the advocate for deferral of start-up expenses. Seldom is there any positive assurance that a new branch will achieve a profitable level of operations in later years. If material start-up losses are capitalized, disclosure of this action should be made in the financial statements.

Questions

1. Explain briefly the usual distinctions between a "sales agency" and a "branch."

2. The Northridge Company has several sales agencies and wishes to determine the profitability of each. Describe briefly the principal accounting procedures that you would recommend be performed by the home office and by the individual sales agencies to achieve this goal.

3. Some branches maintain complete accounting records and prepare financial statements in much the same way as an autonomous business. Other branches perform only limited accounting functions, with most accounting activity concentrated in the home office. Assuming that a branch has a fairly complete set of accounting records, what criterion or principle would you suggest be used in deciding whether various types of expense applicable to the branch should be accounted for in the home office or in the branch?

4. Explain the use of "reciprocal accounts" in the area of home office and branch accounting.

5. The branch and home office reciprocal accounts of the Dawson Company are out of balance at the year-end by a substantial amount. What factors might have caused this lack of agreement?

6. Bonanza Company operates a number of branches but centralizes its accounting activities in the home office and maintains rigorous control of branch operations. The home office finds that Branch D has ample stock of a certain type of merchandise but that Branch E is almost out of this item. The home office therefore instructs Branch D to ship merchandise with a cost of $5,000 to Branch E. What entry should Branch D make, and what principle should guide the treatment of freight charges?

7. The president of Linnfield Company informs you that a branch store is being opened and requests your advice in the following words: "I have been told that we can bill goods to the branch at cost, at selling price, or anywhere in between. Do you as an independent public accountant really have that much latitude in your definition of generally accepted accounting principles?"

8. The policies of the Harmon Company provide that fixed assets in use by its branches shall be carried on the books of the home office. The purchase of new assets may be carried out either by the home office, or by a branch with the approval of the home office. Branch X, with the approval of the home office, purchases new office equipment at a cost of $8,000. Give the entries to be made by the branch and by the home office for acquisition of this equipment.

9. The Bell Company, which uses the periodic inventory method, established the Bodega Bay Branch on January 1. During the first year of operation, Bell Company shipped to the branch merchandise which cost $100,000. Billings were made at prices 20% in excess of cost. Freight charges amounted to $3,500 and were paid by the home office. Sales by the branch were $150,000 and operating expenses $32,000, all on a cash basis. At the end of the year the branch took a physical inventory which showed goods on hand of $24,000 at billed prices. Give entries to record on both the home office and branch books the shipment of goods, payment of freight, setting up of year-end inventory, and other related entries at year-end.

10. The Layton Company operates ten branches in addition to its main store, and bills merchandise to the branches at 10% above cost. The fixed assets for the entire company are carried on the home office books. The home office also conducts a regular advertising program which benefits all the branches. Each branch maintains its own accounting records and prepares financial statements. In the home office, the accounting department prepares (a) financial statements for the main store; (b) revised financial statements for each branch; and (c) combined financial statements for the company as a whole.

Explain briefly the purpose of the financial statements prepared by the branches, the home office statements, the revised statements for the branches, and the combined statements.

Short cases for analysis

7-1 You are engaged in the audit of the Ryan Corporation, which opened its first branch office in 1967. During the audit the Ryan president raises the question of the accounting treatment of the branch office operating loss for its first year, which is material in amount.

The president proposes to capitalize the operating loss as a "starting-up" expense to be amortized over a five-year period. He states that branch offices of other firms engaged in the same field generally suffer a first-year operating loss which is invariably capitalized, and you are aware of this practice. He argues, therefore, that the loss should be capitalized so that the accounting will be "conservative"; further, he argues that the accounting must be "consistent" with established industry practice.

Instructions

a. Discuss the president's use of the words "conservative" and "consistent" from the standpoint of accounting terminology. Discuss the accounting treatment you would recommend.

b. What disclosure, if any, would be required in the financial statements?

AICPA adapted

7-2 The Mammoth Company operates a number of branches as well as a main store. Each branch carries in stock a complete line of merchandise which is obtained almost entirely from the home office. The branches also handle their own billing, approve customer credit, and make collections. Each branch has its own bank account and each maintains complete accounting records. All fixed assets at the branches, consisting chiefly of furniture and office equipment, are carried on the home office books and depreciated by the straight-line method at 10% a year.

On July 1, 1967, the Raytown branch purchased some office equipment on the orders of the newly appointed branch manager. The equipment had a list price of $2,400 but was acquired on the installment payment plan with no down payment and 24 monthly payments of $110 beginning August 1, 1967. No entry was made for this transaction by the branch until August 1, when the first monthly payment was recorded by debiting Miscellaneous Expense. The same entry was made for the next four monthly payments made during 1967. On December 2 the branch manager became aware during a meeting at the home office that fixed assets could be purchased by the branches only with prior approval by the home office. Regardless of whether the home office or the branches purchased fixed assets, such assets were to be carried on the home office books. In an effort to avoid criticism, the Raytown branch manager immediately disposed of the equipment acquired July 1 by sale for $1,500 cash to an independent store in a nearby town. The manager then paid off the balance due on the installment contract using his own funds (a personal check) and the $1,500 check he had received from sale of the equipment. In consideration of the advance payment of the remaining installments on December 3, the equipment dealer agreed to a $100 reduction in the total of the contract. No entry was made for the disposal of the equipment or the settlement of the liability.

Assume that you are a CPA engaged to perform a year-end audit of the Mammoth Company. During your visit to the Raytown branch you analyze the Miscellaneous Expense account and investigate the five monthly charges of $110. This investigation discloses the acquisition and subsequent disposal of the office equipment. After some hesitation the branch manager gives you a full account of the events.

Instructions

a. Would you, as an independent auditor, take any action on this matter? Indicate the major issues involved rather than the accounting details. Give reasons for your answers.

b. Draft the entries which should have been made for the entire series of events on the books of the branch. Assume that the company accepts responsibility for the branch manager's actions.

c. Draft the entries which should have been made on the home office books for the entire series of events, assuming that the home office was currently informed of each event and accepts responsibility for all actions by the branch manager.

d. As an independent situation from (b) and (c), draft the entries which could best be made at the time of your audit to correct the accounts with a minimum of work. One compound entry on each set of books is suggested. Assume the net interest cost belongs on branch books. Also assume that the company wishes to show on the branch books a liability to the manager for personal funds contributed and will consider later any disciplinary action to be taken. The books have not been closed.

Problems

7-3 On January 1, 1967, Judson Company opened its first branch with instructions to the branch manager that he should, among other duties, perform the functions of granting credit, billing customers, accounting for receivables, and making col-

JUDSON COMPANY
Trial Balances
December 31, 1967

	Home Office		Valley Branch	
	Debit	Credit	Debit	Credit
Cash	$ 41,600		$ 8,600	
Notes receivable	7,000			
Accounts receivable (net)	120,400		20,200	
Inventory, Dec. 31, 1966	90,500			
Furniture & equipment (net)	48,100			
Accounts payable		$ 41,000		
Capital stock		150,000		
Retained earnings		25,000		
Sales		400,000		$ 95,100
Purchases	286,300			
Expenses	69,500		18,900	
Shipments to branch		110,000		
Shipments from home office			110,000	
Valley branch	62,600			
Home office				62,600
	$726,000	$726,000	$157,700	$157,700

lections. The branch paid its operating expenses by checks drawn on its bank account. The branch obtained merchandise solely from the home office; billings for these shipments were on the basis of cost to the home office. The trial balances for the home office and for the branch after one year were as shown on page 227.

The physical inventories taken on December 31, 1967, amounted to $95,800 for the home office and $24,200 for the branch.

Instructions

a. On the branch books, prepare the closing entries needed at December 31, 1967.

b. On the home office books, prepare the adjusting entries pertaining to Valley Branch and also all closing entries for the home office.

c. Prepare an eight-column working paper for combined statements of home office and branch.

7-4 The Handley Company operates a branch at Sun City to which it bills merchandise at prices 30% above Handley's cost. The branch obtains goods only from the home office and sells the merchandise at prices averaging 15% above the prices billed by the home office. Both the home office and the branch maintain perpetual inventory records and both close their books on December 31.

On February 18, 1967, a fire at the branch destroyed a part of the inventory. Immediately after the fire, a physical inventory taken of the stock of merchandise on hand and not damaged showed it to have a selling price of $1,495. On January 1, 1967, the inventory of the branch at billed price had been $3,900. Shipments from the home office during the period January 1 to February 18 were billed to the Sun City branch in the amount of $14,300. The branch records show that sales during this period were $10,368, less sales returns of $202.

Instructions

Give the journal entries necessary to record the loss from the fire on (a) the branch books, and (b) the home office books. Show how all amounts were determined.

7-5 The Morgan Music Company, a sole proprietorship owned by John Morgan, operates two retail music stores, one located in Seattle and the other in Tacoma. Each store maintains a complete and independent set of accounting records including a capital account. Neither store is regarded as a "home office" and no such account is in use. However, since both stores are owned and controlled by John Morgan, they engage in intercompany transactions whenever such actions are beneficial. Intercompany transfers or transactions are recorded by the Seattle store in an account entitled "Intercompany Account—Tacoma"; the Tacoma store maintains a similar account entitled "Intercompany Account—Seattle."

Purchases of major items of inventory such as organs or pianos are charged to Organ Purchases or Piano Purchases. Perpetual inventories are not maintained. Purchases are usually made under a financial arrangement with a local bank advancing 90% of the invoice price and the company paying 10%. If the bank note remains unpaid at the end of 90 days, the company is required to pay an additional 10% of the invoice price as a payment on the note.

In August, 1967, the Seattle store purchased an organ for which the seller's draft in the amount of $6,300 was sent to The First National Bank of Seattle, which refused to finance the purchase of the instrument. Because of the refusal by the bank, the Seattle store made no entry to record the purchase. Instead arrangements were made through the Tacoma store with The Citizens Bank of Tacoma to provide the financing. The bank lent Tacoma 90% of the invoice price, or $5,670, which Tacoma deposited and credited to Notes Payable. The Seattle store drew a check payable to the Tacoma store for $630, or 10% of the invoice price, charging Tacoma intercompany account on its books. Tacoma took up the deposit crediting the intercompany account carried with Seattle.

Tacoma, using the 10% received from Seattle and the 90% advanced by the bank, drew a check payable to The First National Bank of Seattle in full payment of the draft, charging Notes Payable.

In November, Seattle made the second payment of $630 directly to the Tacoma bank, charging Tacoma intercompany account, and also notified the Tacoma bookkeeper that the payment had been made. Tacoma took up the transaction, charging Organ Purchases and crediting Seattle. In December Seattle paid off the balance on the note charging Organ Purchases. Interest charges may be disregarded.

Instructions

a. What amount has been recorded in the Organ Purchases account of the Seattle store with respect to the purchase of the organ?

b. Give the adjusting entries, with detailed explanations, to be recorded on each set of books to correct the account balances.

AICPA adapted

7-6 The Sunshine Company is a merchandising business which makes sales at its home office location and also through a branch located a few hundred miles away. The home office bills goods to the branch at 125% of cost, and is the only supplier of merchandise to the branch. The shipment of merchandise to the branch is recorded by credit to the Sales account for the invoice price.

The company engages you to conduct an audit for the year ended December 31, 1966. This is the first time the company has utilized the services of independent accountants. You are provided with the following trial balance:

Debits	*Home Office*	*Branch*
Cash	*$ 15,000*	*$ 2,000*
Accounts receivable	*20,000*	*17,000*
Inventory—Dec. 31, 1966	*30,000*	*8,000*
Fixed assets—net	*150,000*	
Branch office current account	*44,000*	
Cost of sales	*220,000*	*93,000*
Expense	*70,000*	*41,000*
Total	*$549,000*	*$161,000*

Credits	*Home Office*	*Branch*
Accounts payable	*$ 23,000*	
Mortgage payable	*50,000*	
Capital stock	*100,000*	
Retained earnings, Jan. 1, 1966	*26,000*	
Sales	*350,000*	*$150,000*
Accrued expenses		*2,000*
Home office current account		*9,000*
Total	*$549,000*	*$161,000*

Additional information disclosed by your examination includes the following items:

(1) On January 1, 1966, inventory of the home office was $25,000. Inventory at this date was shown by the branch books at $6,000. During 1966 the branch was billed for $105,000 for shipments from the home office.

(2) At December 31, 1966, the home office billed the branch for $12,000, representing the branch's share of expenses paid at the home office. This billing has not been recorded by the branch.

(3) All cash collections made by the branch are deposited in a local bank to the account of the home office. Deposits of this nature included the following:

Amount	*Date deposited by branch*	*Date recorded by home office*
$5,000	*Dec. 28, 1966*	*Dec. 31, 1966*
3,000	*Dec. 30, 1966*	*Jan. 2, 1967*
7,000	*Dec. 31, 1966*	*Jan. 3, 1967*
2,000	*Jan. 2, 1967*	*Jan. 5, 1967*

(4) Expenses incurred locally by the branch are paid from an imprest bank account which is reimbursed periodically by the home office. Just prior to the end of the year, the home office forwarded a reimbursement check in the amount of $3,000 which was not received by the branch office until January, 1967.

Instructions

a. You are to prepare a columnar work sheet for the company and its branch with columns for "Trial balance," "Adjustments and eliminations," "Branch income statement," "Home office income statement," and "Balance sheet." Complete the work sheet and key and explain all adjustments and eliminations. (The income statements should be on a cost basis.)

b. Prepare a reconciliation of branch office and home office current accounts showing the *corrected* book balances, ignoring income tax considerations.

AICPA adapted

7-7 You are engaged to make an audit of the Drexal Company, which carries on merchandising operations at both a home office and a branch location. The trial balances of the home office and of the branch are as follows:

THE DREXAL COMPANY
Trial Balance
for the year ended December 31, 1966

Debits	*Home*	*Branch*
Cash	*$ 17,000*	*$ 200*
Inventory—home	*23,000*	
Inventory—branch		*11,550*
Sundry assets	*200,000*	*48,450*
Branch current account	*60,000*	
Purchases	*190,000*	
Purchases from home		*105,000*
Freight in from home		*5,500*
Sundry expenses	*42,000*	*24,300*
	$532,000	*$195,000*
Credits		
Sundry liabilities	*$ 35,000*	*$ 3,500*
Home current account		*51,500*
Sales	*155,000*	*140,000*
Sales to branch	*110,000*	
Allowance for markup in branch inventory	*1,000*	
Capital stock	*200,000*	
Retained earnings	*31,000*	
	$532,000	*$195,000*

The audit at December 31, 1966, disclosed the following:

(1) The branch office deposits all cash receipts in a local bank for the account of the home office. The audit work sheet for the cash cutoff revealed:

Amount	*Date deposited by branch*	*Date recorded by home office*
$1,050	*Dec. 27, 1966*	*Dec. 31, 1966*
1,100	*Dec. 30, 1966*	*Jan. 2, 1967*
600	*Dec. 31, 1966*	*Jan. 3, 1967*
300	*Jan. 2, 1967*	*Jan. 6, 1967*

(2) The branch office pays expenses incurred locally from an imprest bank account that is maintained with a balance of $2,000. Checks are drawn once a week on this imprest account and the home office is notified of the amount needed to replenish the account. At December 31, an $1,800 reimbursement check was mailed to the branch office.

(3) The branch office receives all its goods from the home office. The home office bills the goods at cost plus a markup of 10% of cost. At December 31 a shipment with a billing value of $5,000 was in transit to the branch. Freight costs are typically 5% of billed values. Freight costs are considered to be inventoriable costs.

(4) The trial balance opening inventories are shown at their respective costs to the home office and to the branch office. The inventories at December 31, excluding the shipment in transit, are

Home office, at cost	*$30,000*
Branch office, at billing value	*10,400*

Instructions

Prepare a columnar work sheet for the Drexal Company and its branch with columns for "Trial balance," "Adjustments and eliminations," "Home income statement," "Branch income statement," and "Combined balance sheet." The branch income statement should be prepared on the basis of home office cost. Disregard income taxes. (Formal journal entries are not required. Supporting computations must be in good form.) Number your work-sheet adjusting and eliminating entries.

AICPA adapted

7-8 The following reciprocal accounts are found in the records of the home office and branch of the Palos Verdes Trading Company:

Branch Account

Feb. 1	*Balance*	*92,408*	*Mar. 31*	*Cash received*	*5,000*
Feb. 6	*Shipment of merchandise*	*7,840*	*Apr. 2*	*Merchandise returned*	*450*
Feb. 17	*Note collected by branch*	*2,500*	*Apr. 29*	*Corrected loss on sale of branch equipment from $780 to $250*	*530*
Apr. 26	*Loss on sale of branch equipment*	*780*			
Apr. 28	*Expenses chargeable to branch*	*4,200*			

Home Office Account

Mar. 30	*Deposited cash in bank account of home office*	*5,000*	*Feb. 1*	*Balance*	*92,408*
Mar. 31	*Returned merchandise*	*450*	*Feb. 8*	*Merchandise, 160 cases @ $49*	*7,480*
Mar. 31	*Paid a repair bill for the home office*	*375*	*Feb. 14*	*Received shipment directly from supplier, invoice to be paid by home office*	*2,750*
Mar. 31	*Returned surplus merchandise*	*1,100*	*Feb. 15*	*Note collected for home office*	*2,500*
			Apr. 30	*Profit for quarter (tentative)*	*9,210*

You have been called in by the company to assist them with some accounting work preliminary to the preparation of financial statements for the quarter ended

April 30. Your first task is to prepare a reconciliation of the reciprocal accounts. Additional information available to you is as follows:

(1) Branch equipment is carried on the books of the home office; the home office notifies the branch periodically as to the amount of depreciation applicable to equipment used by the branch. Gains or losses on disposal of branch equipment are reported to the branch and included on the branch income statement.

(2) Despite the error on February 8 in recording the shipment from the home office, the sale of goods has been properly charged to cost of sales at $49 per case.

(3) The branch frequently makes collection on home office accounts and the home office also collects receivables belonging to the branch. On April 30, the branch collected a receivable of $350 belonging to the home office but the branch employee who recorded the collection mistakenly treated the receivable as belonging to the branch.

(4) The branch recorded the tentative profit of $9,210 by a debit to Income Summary and a credit to Home Office, although the revenue and expense accounts had not been closed.

Instructions

a. Reconcile the interbranch accounts to the correct total as of April 30. Use a four-column schedule (debit and credit columns for the Branch account on the Home Office books and debit and credit columns for the Home Office account on the Branch books). Start with the unadjusted balances at April 30 and work to corrected balances, inserting full explanations of all adjusting or correcting items.

b. Prepare individual entries on the books of the branch to bring the books up to date, assuming that corrections can still be made to revenue and expense accounts.

c. Prepare required entries on the books of the home office.

7-9 Seaman Tire Company operates many stores in and near the city of York. The account with the Tenth & Todd branch shows the following charges and credits during 1968:

Charges:	
Balance, Jan. 1	*$ 65,760*
Shipments of merchandise at 25% above cost	*45,600*
Payment of branch expenses (including replenishment of imprest fund several times during year)	*16,299*
Increase in imprest fund from $500 to $750	*250*
Allocation of depreciation	*1,260*
Net income reported by branch for year ended Dec. 31, 1968	*8,376*
Total charges	*$137,545*
Credits:	
Bank deposits to account of home office	*$ 72,112*
Correction of a transposition error in branch inventory as of Dec. 31, 1967. Inventory was erroneously reported at billed price of $12,100 when correct billed price was $11,200	*900*
Balance, Dec. 31, 1968	*64,533*
Total credits	*$137,545*

All cash received by the branch is deposited in a checking account for the Seaman Tire Company on which only the home office can draw checks. Payments for major expenses of the branch are made by the home office but are billed to the branch so that the branch can maintain fairly complete records of expenses and can prepare income statements. The branch maintains an imprest fund which is used for payment of a variety of minor expenditures and is also used as a change fund.

The income statement prepared by the branch for the year 1968 did not include any depreciation expense. Depreciable assets in use at the branch are carried on the home office books and depreciation is computed by the home office. The income statement as prepared by the branch reflected merchandise costs on the basis of billed prices; it also included $125 of expense vouchers in the imprest fund.

The physical inventory taken at the branch by home-office personnel on December 31, 1968, amounted to $9,800 at prices billed by the home office. The accountant at the home office responsible for control of inventories wanted to "confirm" the physical inventory through use of the retail inventory method. He was pleased when his computation showed the estimated billed price of the ending inventory to be $9,975. This discrepancy was considered minor because billed price was not uniform on all lines of tires.

The correction to the inventory of December 31, 1967, was recorded on the home office books as follows:

Allowance for Overvaluation of Inventory: Tenth & Todd Branch	*180*	
James Seaman, Capital	*720*	
Tenth & Todd Branch		*900*

The net income, as reported by the branch, was equal to 12% of sales. Shipments amounting to $2,000 were in transit to the branch at year-end. These goods were neither recorded by the branch nor included in the ending inventory.

Instructions

a. Put yourself in the role of an accountant for the home office and prepare a revised income statement for the Tenth & Todd branch. (Show all data in the cost of goods section at "home-office cost" rather than at billed prices, including the merchandise in transit from the home office at year-end. The income statement should be free from all effects of the practice of billing the branch at more than cost.)

b. Prepare entries on the books of the home office (1) to correct the branch net income for failure to record depreciation, and (2) to adjust the inventory overvaluation account as of December 31, 1968.

7-10 Redmond Furniture Company operates a main store and three branch stores. The records are centralized at the main store and little effort is made to measure the net income of each store. Sales records, however, are maintained with care by each store manager.

A bonus equal to 3% of sales is paid to the manager of each store. Each store manager has authority to reduce the selling price from a suggested list prepared by the general manager but not below a "rock bottom" price which is set on each furniture item. Records of shipments to the branches are maintained in memorandum form by the home office; vouchers for all expenses incurred by the branches are mailed to the main store for payment.

After several years of doing business in this manner, the owners ask you early in 1968 to assist them in improving their net income by establishing complete profit centers at each store and designing a better incentive plan for store managers. They would also like for you to evaluate their pricing policy, although they feel this is the least worrisome aspect of their business.

You approach your assignment energetically and after several days of hard work you assemble the following facts relating to 1967 operations:

	Company total	*Main store*	*Branch 1*	*Branch 2*	*Branch 3*
Sales	*$450,000*	*$250,000*	*$80,000*	*$70,000*	*$50,000*
Cost of sales	*322,500*	*175,000*	*55,000*	*52,500*	*40,000*
Gross profit	*$127,500*	*$ 75,000*	*$25,000*	*$17,500*	*$10,000*
Operating expenses:					
Direct—fixed	*$ 34,000*	*$ 20,000*	*$ 6,000*	*$ 4,000*	*$ 4,000*
variable	*55,000*	*33,000*	*10,000*	*7,000*	*5,000*
*Indirect—fixed**	*7,000*	*2,000*	*2,000*	*1,500*	*1,500*
*variable**	*4,500*	*1,500*	*1,500*	*750*	*750*
Total operating expenses	*$100,500*	*$ 56,500*	*$19,500*	*$13,250*	*$11,250*
Net income or loss	*$ 27,000*	*$ 18,500*	*$ 5,500*	*$ 4,250*	*$ (1,250)*
Inventory (average for 1968)	*$ 55,000*	*$ 25,000*	*$11,000*	*$15,000*	*$ 4,000*
Receivables (average for 1968)	*44,875*	*15,625*	*8,000*	*8,750*	*12,500*

Industry standards (local area):

Sales to inventory (at cost)†	*5%*
Net income as percentage of sales	*8%*
Collection period (average)	*45 days*
Gross profit on sales	*34%*

* *Allocated by manager of main store.*
† *Equivalent to an inventory turnover of 3.3 times.*

The sales volume does not fluctuate materially during the year. Terms of sale are 2/10, n/30.

Instructions

a. Determine the following for the company as a whole and for each store:

(1) Gross profit percentage
(2) Percentage of operating expenses to sales
(3) Net income as percentage of sales
(4) Inventory annual turnover rate
(5) Accounts receivable turnover rate

b. How do the measurements in (a) compare with the industry standards? Do you see any significant variations among the four stores?

c. Do you think that the indirect expenses were equitably allocated? Explain briefly.

d. Would you recommend a change in the incentive plan for store managers? Why?

e. What is your evaluation of the pricing policy of the Redmond Furniture Company? Explain briefly.

7-11 Comparative balance sheets for the Home Office of Hoover Sales Company follow.

	Dec. 31, 1966	*Dec. 31, 1967*
Cash	$ 25,600	$ 38,000
Accounts receivable	80,000	85,000
Less: Allowance for bad debts	(2,400)	(3,000)
Merchandise	112,000	100,000
Plant and equipment (net)	180,000	200,000
Branch office		120,000
Investment in Slauson Corp. (100%)	80,000	
	$475,200	$540,000
Accounts payable	$ 95,300	$ 88,000
Accrued expenses	2,700	3,500
Capital stock, $5 par value	200,000	200,000
Retained earnings	177,200	248,500
	$475,200	$540,000

The home office purchased equipment for $50,000 during the year and equipment having a book value of $10,000 was sold at a loss of $3,000. The loss was charged to Retained Earnings. Dividends of $12,000 were paid during the year and earnings amounted to $86,300, including $40,000 earned by the branch. The branch remitted $10,000 to the home office during the year. The remittance was credited in error to Accounts Receivable.

Comparative balance sheets for the branch are shown below:

	Dec. 31, 1966	*Dec. 31, 1967*
Cash	$ 15,000	$ 28,000
Accounts receivable (net)	20,000	25,000
Merchandise	65,000	70,500
Prepaid expenses	2,000	1,500
	$102,000	$125,000
Accounts payable	$ 22,000	$ 15,000
Capital stock, $1 stated value	10,000	
Retained earnings	70,000	
Home office		110,000
	$102,000	$125,000

The branch was operated as a wholly owned subsidiary corporation until January 1, 1967, at which time the corporate form was abandoned.

Instructions

a. Prepare a combined balance sheet for Hoover Sales Company on January 1 and December 31, 1967.

b. Prepare a statement of working capital flow for Hoover Sales Company for 1967, assuming that the Slauson Corporation accounts were consolidated with the accounts of Hoover Sales Company as of January 1, 1967.

c. Prepare a statement of cash flow for Hoover Sales Company for 1967.

CONSOLIDATED FINANCIAL STATEMENTS

PART THREE

8 CONSOLIDATIONS: INTRODUCTION

In the eyes of the law, corporations are separate legal entities. For many purposes the legal entity is also a suitable accounting entity. Financial statements of individual corporations are prepared under the assumption that the corporate legal entity is the accounting unit. When one corporation owns a substantial portion of the outstanding shares of another or where a group of corporations are operated under common control exercised by stock ownership, however, the assumption that the accounting and legal entities coincide becomes less useful. Managers and outsiders who have an interest in the consolidated group need reports of the financial position and operating results of the affiliated companies as a unified *economic entity*. Consolidated financial statements were devised by accountants to meet this need. The consolidating process is designed to lift the legal curtain of corporate separateness and reveal, within the accounting framework, the financial and operating history of the affiliated companies viewed as an economic unit operating under unified management and control.

Terminology of consolidations

A corporation that controls the activities of another corporation through stock ownership is called a *parent* company. What constitutes control is discussed later in this chapter. The company or companies controlled by a parent are called *subsidiaries*. Both parents and subsidiaries are sometimes referred to as *affiliated* companies. A parent company formed for the sole purpose of holding the stock of other corporations and supervising their activities is designated a *holding* company. The stock interest held by a parent company in a subsidiary is called the *controlling interest* (or majority interest); the remainder of the stock owned outside the consolidated group is referred to as the *minority interest.* A *wholly owned* subsidiary is a company all of whose stock is held within the consolidated group.

Why affiliate?

Corporate affiliations based on stock ownership are a common phenomenon in most industrial economies. The majority of companies whose stocks are listed on the New York Stock Exchange have one or more subsidiaries and publish financial reports on a consolidated basis. Operating through 25 or more active subsidiaries is not at all unusual among larger companies. What benefits do the owners and managers of these companies see in corporate affiliation?

Most subsidiary companies were once independent corporations and were acquired by a parent company bent on expansion. There are obvious advantages in growing and diversifying by acquiring an existing business. Purchase of a controlling stock interest is easier to arrange and often requires less capital investment than other means of acquiring assets. Exchanging a parent's shares for the stock of a subsidiary is a common means of acquiring a controlling interest. Organizing divisions as legal subsidiaries is often a convenient way to establish decentralized responsibility. The limited liability feature of the corporate form of organization makes it possible to enter a speculative venture through a subsidiary with minimum risk to the parent. An unprofitable subsidiary may be easily separated by selling its shares. Savings in income and other taxes are sometimes possible by operating through subsidiaries.

This is not a complete list of the possible advantages of affiliation, but it helps to explain why corporate combinations are so prevalent and why the process of consolidating the financial data of two or more corporations is an important area of financial accounting.

Legal status of consolidated statements

In general the courts tend to uphold the legal insulation between companies in an affiliated group. The parent corporation is not liable for the acts or obligations of its subsidiary. Only in unusual circumstances, where the corporate form is used as a device to defeat public policy or to perpetrate a fraud, will the courts ignore the legal boundaries of the corporate entity.

For some purposes, however, consolidated statements have attained a substantial legal status. Consolidated income statements are permitted but not required for income tax purposes. Both the Securities and Exchange Commission and the Federal Trade Commission have the power to call for consolidated financial statements whenever such information has regulatory significance. The New York Stock Exchange requires periodic submission to stockholders of a consolidated balance sheet, income statement, and statement of retained earnings except in unusual circumstances. These requirements and the general widespread acceptance of consolidated statements by financial analysts testify to the usefulness of accounting information developed from the viewpoint of the economic rather than the legal entity.

When should consolidated statements be prepared?

In general consolidated financial statements are likely to be useful whenever we find two or more separate corporations operating under centralized control exercised through stock ownership.[1]

Degree of control. The question of control is one of economic fact as well as legal right. The ownership of more than 50% of the voting stock of a subsidiary corporation constitutes legal control. Substantially less than 51% ownership is often sufficient to provide effective operational control because the stock ownership of major corporations is often widely dispersed among small stockholders who do not exercise their voting rights. On the other hand, some accountants hold that ownership of 67 to 75% of the outstanding shares of a company is necessary for absolute control since major corporate actions may require the approval of two-thirds or three-fourths of the stockholders or members of the board of directors.

The exact degree of control necessary to warrant the preparation of consolidated financial statements is thus a matter of judgment. Whenever a parent owns directly or indirectly more than 50% of the voting shares of one or more subsidiaries, consolidated financial statements should be prepared unless there are persuasive reasons why such statements are inappropriate. It is conceivable that consolidation may provide useful information even when in fact control is exercised through other means than a majority stockholding. The case for consolidation becomes stronger the larger the percentage of stock ownership, and the reasons for not furnishing consolidated financial statements must be correspondingly more cogent.

Control of a subsidiary may be indirect. For example, if A Company owns 80% of the stock of B Company, which in turn owns 80% of the stock of C Company, there is no question that A controls C Company although it does not directly own a single share in C.

Integrated area of operations. If an automobile company owns a controlling interest in a steel manufacturer, a glass factory, and an installment finance company, this group of firms constitutes an integrated area of operations in manufacturing and selling automobiles. But the term *integrated area of operations* may be broadened to include the performance of any business function which the parent company could conduct through a division or branch instead of a separate controlled subsidiary. Some large companies are engaged in widely diversified activities, in some cases through separate divisions and in some cases through subsidiary corporations. Such companies, which often defy classification within

[1] In his recent inventory of accepted principles of accounting, Paul Grady lists as one of the objectives of accounting that, "Reporting to investors should be performed on an entity basis." As a corollary of this proposition he deduces the following principle: "Where there is a parent company and one or more subsidiaries, there is a presumption that consolidated statements are more meaningful than separate statements." Grady does not discuss the basis for this presumption. Perhaps he finds obvious the proposition that readers of financial statements will find it useful to have information about the entire collection of resources under the control of the business entity in which they have an interest, and the results obtained from using these resources. AICPA, *Inventory of Generally Accepted Accounting Principles for Business Enterprises,* Accounting Research Study No. 7 (New York: 1965), pp. 67, 318.

any industry group, have been described as being in the business of making money. The fact that highly dissimilar kinds of business activity can be carried on successfully under unified management and control suggests that the term *economic entity* should be broadly interpreted. Consolidated financial statements are appropriate whenever it is useful to have an accounting picture of the entire area of operations represented within an economic entity composed of affiliated corporations.

There are some cases where affiliated companies are engaged in activities so disparate in nature as to make consolidated statements of doubtful worth. If, for example, a manufacturing company owns a controlling interest in a bank, or a retail firm owns a controlling interest in an insurance company, the combination of their accounts is not likely to yield meaningful information. Furthermore, the existence of separate corporations in these cases is not accidental; legally, banks and insurance companies cannot be operated as branches or divisions of industrial companies.

Unconsolidated subsidiaries. Exclusion of subsidiaries from consolidation does not mean that they are ignored in published financial statements. The investment in such subsidiaries will appear as an asset on the statement of the parent and its consolidated subsidiaries. In addition, there should be a disclosure of the identity of all nonconsolidated subsidiaries, the extent of the parent's interest, the reason for nonconsolidation, the parent's share of the subsidiaries retained earnings since acquisition, and current year's earnings. Where the investment in a nonconsolidated subsidiary is significant in relation to the total assets of the parent, the separate financial statements of the unconsolidated subsidiary should be included along with the published consolidated statements.

Corporate joint ventures, an arrangement whereby two or more corporations pool their resources to set up a new corporation whose ownership they share, usually result in unconsolidated subsidiaries. Typically the joint venture corporation undertakes some activity which the management of the owner-corporations believe their companies cannot do as well alone. Steel companies have established jointly owned corporations to share the large investment necessary to mine newly discovered ore reserves in remote parts of the world. Oil companies share the risk and cost of searching for and developing foreign oil fields through corporate joint ventures. In recent years a number of newspapers in large cities have formed joint venture corporations to operate common printing facilities and thus share the cost of expensive high-speed presses. It is usually not feasible to consolidate the financial statements of joint venture corporations with the statements of the parent companies because control is shared; neither parent controls the corporate joint venture. Each parent company carries its investment in the joint venture corporation as an asset on its balance sheet.

Consolidation at date of acquisition—wholly owned subsidiary

A balance sheet is the only consolidated financial statement that can be prepared as of the date on which a parent acquires a controlling interest in a subsidiary since the consolidated entity has no operating history.[2] A number of important

[2] Consolidated income statements for the year prior to acquisition or the year in which acquisition took place are sometimes prepared for comparative purposes, to provide some basis for judging performance of the economic entity during the first year after acquisition.

consolidating problems arise in connection with the beginning position statement of the affiliated companies. As a basis for discussing the preparation of a consolidated balance sheet at date of acquisition, we shall use the following statement of a parent and three subsidiary companies. It is assumed that the statements were prepared immediately after P Company had acquired 100% of the capital stock of B Company, E Company, and U Company.

P, B, E, AND U COMPANIES
Balance Sheets
at date of acquisition—January 1, current year

	P Company	B Company	E Company	U Company
Investment in B Company	$ 50,000			
Investment in E Company	75,000			
Investment in U Company	35,000			
Other assets	200,000	$70,000	$90,000	$75,000
Total assets	$360,000	$70,000	$90,000	$75,000
Less: Liabilities	60,000	20,000	40,000	25,000
Net assets	$300,000	$50,000	$50,000	$50,000
Owners' equity:				
Capital stock	$200,000	$25,000	$20,000	$70,000
Retained earnings (deficit)	100,000	25,000	30,000	(20,000)
Total owners' equity	$300,000	$50,000	$50,000	$50,000

A parent company may acquire the capital stock of a subsidiary by purchase for cash or other assets, or through an exchange of its own securities (stocks or bonds) for subsidiary shares. On the parent's books, the investment is recorded initially at cost. When assets other than cash are given up, the fair value of these assets at the date of acquisition is a reasonable measure of cost. When the parent issues stocks or bonds in exchange for subsidiary shares, the opportunity cost of the parent's securities (that is, the price at which they could have been sold in the market) may be used as a measure of the purchase price.[3]

The cost of the parent's ownership interest in the subsidiary's net assets at date of acquisition is indirect evidence of the fair market value of the assets and liabilities of the subsidiary at that time. Assuming that the parties deal at arm's length, the price paid for the subsidiary's shares is an objective piece of financial information and may well become the basis for revaluing the net assets of the subsidiary to establish a new basis of accountability.

There are three possible relationships between the price paid (value given up) by the parent and the book value of a subsidiary's net assets:

[3] An alternative consolidating assumption known as the "pooling of interest" concept is discussed in chap. 11.

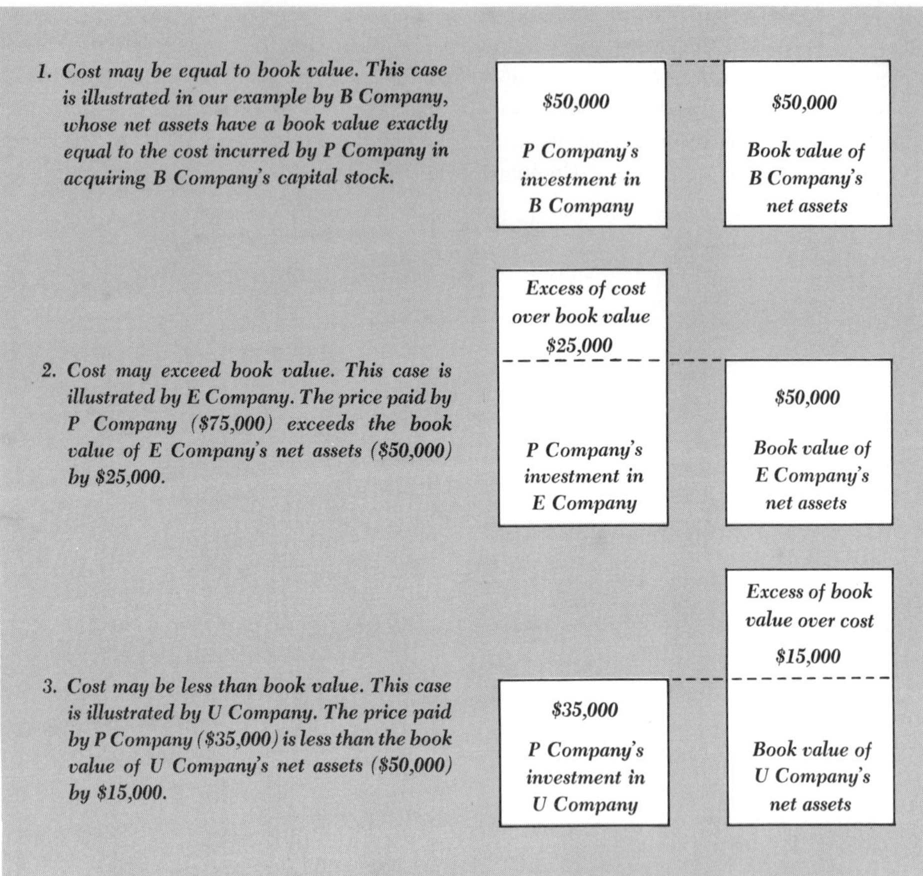

Nature of the consolidated balance sheet. The objective in preparing a consolidated balance sheet for P, B, E, and U Companies is to combine the assets, liabilities, and ownership equity accounts of all four companies into a position statement for the economic entity as a whole. If we were to do this by simply summing these elements as they appear on the individual statements of the affiliated companies, however, we would be double counting both assets and ownership equity. It would be improper to add together P's investment accounts and the assets of the subsidiary companies, because P's investments represent an ownership interest in the underlying net assets of the subsidiaries. Similarly it would be improper to combine the ownership equity accounts of the four affiliated companies. From the viewpoint of the consolidated entity, only the common stock of the parent company represents an ownership interest in the collective resources of the economic entity. The shares of the three subsidiaries are all held within the family, since all these shares are owned by P Company.

In essence the consolidating procedure at date of acquisition is to eliminate this potential double counting by offsetting the investment accounts of P Company against the ownership equity accounts of the three subsidiaries. If we can arrange this offset so that we eliminate an equal dollar amount of assets and ownership equity, we can add together the remaining assets, liabilities, and equity accounts and maintain the integrity of the accounting equation (assets − liabilities = ownership equity) for the consolidated entity. The effect of this consolidating procedure is to substitute on the consolidated balance sheet the underlying net assets of the subsidiary companies for P Company's investment accounts. This is a logical substitution since P Company's investments represent an ownership interest in the net assets of the affiliated subsidiaries.

Consolidating working papers. To assure that the integrity of the basic accounting equation ($A - L = OE$) is maintained in the process of consolidation, it is convenient to make the necessary adjustments and offsets of amounts on the parent's and subsidiaries' statements on consolidating working papers. The accounts are consolidated through a series of working-paper journal entries which cut across company boundaries to eliminate or adjust simultaneously the accounts of two or more companies in the affiliated group. The basic consolidating procedure at date of acquisition is to eliminate the investment accounts on the parent company's balance sheet against the owners' equity accounts on the statements of the subsidiary companies. When the remaining assets and liabilities of the three companies are combined, the result is to replace the parent's investments with the specific assets and liabilities of the subsidiary companies.

Intercompany eliminations and adjustments are made on the consolidating working papers in the form of journal entries, in which the familiar equality of debits and credits operates as a control feature to assure the accountant that the integrity of the accounting equation is maintained. It is important to note that the individual statements of the affiliated companies are *not* altered by these entries. Consolidating journal entries appear only on the consolidating working papers; they are not recorded on the books of the parent and subsidiary companies.

To illustrate the consolidating process, the balance sheet of P Company will be consolidated with the balance sheets of each of the three subsidiary companies. It would be possible to consolidate all four companies on one set of working papers. To demonstrate clearly the points involved, however, we shall make the consolidation in three separate steps: consolidating first P and B Companies, then consolidating P and B Companies with E Company, and finally consolidating P, B, and E Companies with U Company.

Consolidating P and B Companies—acquisition at book value. Since P Company's investment in B Company was made at a cost *equal* to the book value of B's underlying net assets, no problems arise in making the elimination of P Company's investment against the ownership equity of B Company on the working papers (on page 248).

Note that the figures in the right-hand column of the working papers represent only a partially consolidated balance sheet of the four companies in the affiliated group. Since Companies E and U have not been consolidated, P Company's interests in these companies are shown as investments on the consolidated balance sheet of P and B Companies. The effect of the eliminating entry (a) is to substitute the \$50,000 of net assets of B Company (assets of \$70,000 minus liabilities of \$20,000) for the investment account on P Company's books and to eliminate the ownership equity accounts of B Company.

P AND B COMPANIES
Working Papers—Consolidated Balance Sheet
at date of acquisition—January 1, current year

	P Company	B Company	Eliminating entry Dr	Eliminating entry Cr	Consolidated balance sheet
Assets:					
Investment in B—100%	50,000			(a) 50,000	
Investment in E—100%	75,000				75,000
Investment in U—100%	35,000				35,000
Other assets	200,000	70,000			270,000
Totals	360,000	70,000			380,000
Liabilities & Equity:					
Liabilities	60,000	20,000			80,000
Capital stock—P	200,000				200,000
Retained earnings—P	100,000				100,000
Capital stock—B		25,000	(a) 25,000		
Retained earnings—B		25,000	(a) 25,000		
Totals	360,000	70,000			380,000

Consolidating P and B Companies with E Company—acquisition cost greater than book value. P Company's investment in E Company was made at a cost that is $25,000 greater than the book value of E's net assets. As a result we can no longer make a simple elimination of P's investment against the ownership equity of E Company, since the $75,000 investment account is larger than the $50,000 ownership equity of E Company. We shall consider the nature of this excess in detail in a later section of this chapter. For the moment we shall solve the problem by assuming that the price paid by P is evidence of unrecorded goodwill of E Company in the amount of $25,000.

In the papers at the top of page 249, entry (a) reflects the upward revaluation of net assets of E Company, based on the evidence that P Company paid $75,000 for a 100% interest in E Company. Once this adjustment of E's assets has been made, the investment account on P's books eliminates against the revised owners' equity of E Company, entry (b). Note that the appraisal capital account is eliminated in the consolidating process, and the asset Goodwill emerges on the consolidated balance sheet. Since U Company is not consolidated, the $35,000 investment in U is simply carried forward onto the consolidated balance sheet, representing the dollar investment in an unconsolidated subsidiary.

Consolidating P, B, and E Companies with U Company—acquisition cost less than book value. The cost of P Company's investment in the stock of U Company is *less than* the book value of U Company's net assets. We shall assume that P's purchase price of $35,000 is valid evidence of the fair value of U Company's net assets, and that the $15,000 difference between book value and investment represents an overvaluation of certain specific assets carried on U Company's books. The consolidating working papers are shown at the bottom of page 249.

P, B, AND E COMPANIES
Working Papers—Consolidated Balance Sheet
at date of acquisition—January 1, current year

	P and B Companies	E Company	Eliminations Dr	Eliminations Cr	Consolidated balance sheet
Assets:					
Investment in E	75,000			(b) 75,000	
Investment in U	35,000				35,000
Other assets	270,000	90,000			360,000
Goodwill			(a) 25,000		25,000
Totals	380,000	90,000			420,000
Liabilities & Equity:					
Liabilities	80,000	40,000			120,000
Capital stock—P	200,000				200,000
Retained earnings—P	100,000				100,000
Capital stock—E		20,000	(b) 20,000		
Retained earnings—E		30,000	(b) 30,000		
Appraisal capital			(b) 25,000	(a) 25,000	
Totals	380,000	90,000			420,000

(a) To record E Company's goodwill, based on the evidence of the price paid by P Company for its 100% investment in E Company.
(b) To eliminate P Company's investment account and E Company's ownership equity accounts.

P, B, E, AND U COMPANIES
Working Papers—Consolidated Balance Sheet
at date of acquisition—January 1, current year

	P, B, and E Companies	U Company	Eliminations Dr	Eliminations Cr	Consolidated balance sheet
Assets:					
Investment in U—100%	35,000			(b) 35,000	
Other assets	360,000	75,000		(a) 15,000	420,000
Goodwill	25,000				25,000
Totals	420,000	75,000			445,000
Liabilities & Equity:					
Liabilities	120,000	25,000			145,000
Capital stock—P	200,000				200,000
Retained earnings—P	100,000				100,000
Capital stock—U		70,000	(b) 70,000		
Deficit—U		(20,000)	(a) 15,000	(b) 35,000	
Totals	420,000	75,000			445,000

(a) To write down U Company's overvalued assets.
(b) To eliminate investment account.

The write-down of U Company's assets to reflect the overvaluation indicated by P's purchase price is made in entry (a). This adjustment makes it possible to eliminate P's investment against the owners' equity accounts of U Company. Note that the eliminating entry (b) cancels out the increase in U Company's deficit resulting from the downward revaluation of U's assets. The net effect is to bring U Company's net assets onto the consolidated balance sheet at a valuation of $35,000, rather than the $50,000 book value appearing on U Company's books [$75,000 (assets) − $15,000 (write-down) = $60,000 − $25,000 (liabilities) = $35,000].

Treatment of excess of cost over book value

When a parent company pays more for its interest in a subsidiary than the book value of the underlying net assets, the reason for the difference should be carefully considered in determining the disposition of this excess in consolidating the two companies. What are the possible reasons for an excess of cost over book value?

Net assets of subsidiary undervalued. The parent company may pay a price greater than the underlying book value of the net assets of the subsidiary because it believes the subsidiary's assets are undervalued or its liabilities are overstated. Such an undervaluation of net assets might stem from a number of sources:

1. There may be errors on the subsidiary's books or the subsidiary may have followed unduly conservative accounting practices in the past. For example, excessive depreciation may have been taken on depreciable assets, or estimated liabilities may be overstated. Errors should be corrected on the books of the subsidiary prior to consolidation. Adjustments of subsidiary asset or liability valuations not made on the subsidiary's books may be made as a part of the consolidating process.

2. Legitimate accounting valuations may be less than fair market value at the date of acquisition. It is possible that the assets of the subsidiary are valued on an acceptable cost basis but because of inflation or specific price changes the current fair value of certain assets is in excess of their book value. Subsidiary inventories may be carried at lifo, for example, but economic decisions to buy and sell are not predicated on such meaningless figures. Land owned by the subsidiary may have appreciated in value above its cost. Because the current worth of the subsidiary's assets was probably carefully assessed in negotiating the purchase of its stock, the accountant may view the purchase price as objective evidence of the current worth of undervalued subsidiary assets. On this basis the parent company might authorize the revaluation of these assets on the subsidiary's books, with a balancing credit to an appraisal capital account. Alternatively, the parent may prefer to recognize the increased asset value only on the consolidating working papers.

3. Unrecorded goodwill or other intangibles may account for the excess of purchase price over underlying book value. The price paid by the parent may simply reflect the fact that because of superior earning power the subsidiary is worth more than the sum of the valuations assigned to its individual assets. This situation implies that the subsidiary has unrecorded goodwill or other intangible assets, and the parent may authorize the subsidiary to record such intangibles on an appraisal basis. Alternatively, goodwill of the subsidiary may be recognized only on the consolidated working papers. In either case the price paid by the parent for its interest provides objective evidence of the exchange value of goodwill or other intangibles.

If the subsidiary company revalues its assets upward on the basis of the parent's purchase price as evidence of undervaluation, the effect is to restate the net assets of the subsidiary and remove the difference between underlying book value (as revised) and the parent's investment. Depreciation and amortization will then be recorded by the subsidiary in future periods on the basis of restated values, and no further consolidating adjustments are necessary. If the upward revaluation is made only on consolidating working papers, adjustments for amortization in subsequent accounting periods will have to be made as a part of the consolidating process. The detailed procedures for making such adjustments are discussed in a later chapter.

Payment for advantages of affiliation. In negotiating the purchase price of subsidiary shares, the parent company may have been willing to pay for advantages that were expected to accrue to the controlling interest as a result of the affiliation. The excess of cost over subsidiary book value in these circumstances may be attributed to an intangible asset of the consolidated group representing increased earnings expected to stem from the association. This intangible asset should be identified as specifically as possible, but if its exact nature is uncertain it may be labeled *consolidated goodwill* or *excess of cost over book value of investment in subsidiaries.*

An important distinction. Consolidated goodwill should be carefully distinguished from the case of unrecorded goodwill of the subsidiary company. Goodwill of the subsidiary company is evidenced by past and potential superior earning power inherent in the subsidiary's economic position at the time of acquisition. Recording subsidiary goodwill as a part of the consolidation process is in effect revaluing the net assets of the subsidiary upward. Consolidated goodwill, on the other hand, simply reflects some economic advantage which the parent sees in the future operation of the consolidated group under centralized control, and for which it is willing to pay over and above the value of the subsidiary's net assets. For example, the parent might anticipate buying more of its raw material requirements from the subsidiary and the resulting increase in the subsidiary's volume may produce cost savings that will be reflected in the future earnings of both companies. Consolidated intangibles are recorded only on the consolidated balance sheet. Since the economic advantages of centralized control may be eroded by competitive forces, consideration should be given to amortizing the amount of consolidated goodwill over some reasonable period of time subsequent to the date of acquisition.

When subsidiaries are wholly owned (as in the cases we have just discussed) the total assets on the consolidated balance sheet will be the same whether we interpret the excess of the parent's investment over the underlying book value of its interest in the subsidiary as the cost of an intangible advantage of affiliation, or as evidence of an understatement of the assets of the subsidiary. This is true because the price paid by the parent company represents the purchase of a 100% interest in the subsidiary's net assets.

When control is achieved by the purchase of *less than a 100% interest,* however, the interpretation of the excess of the parent's investment over the book value of its underlying interest *will* affect the amount of total assets appearing on the consolidated balance sheet. It is important to understand why this is so. When a parent acquires less than a 100% interest in a subsidiary and the price paid for its investment is considered evidence of an undervaluation of the assets of the subsidiary, the implied undervaluation is *greater* than the difference between cost and book value because we are inferring something about the total net assets of the subsidiary from a price paid to buy an interest in only a portion of those net assets. On the other hand, if we do not make this inference and simply treat the excess of the cost of the parent's investment over underlying book value as an intangible asset *of the parent,* then we are accounting only for the difference between cost and book value that relates to the parent's less than 100% interest in the subsidiary. To illustrate this point, suppose that P Company pays $80,000 for 80% of the outstanding common stock of S Company at a time when the book value of S Company's total net assets is $90,000. The book value of P's interest in S is $72,000 (80% of $90,000) and the cost of its investment ($80,000) exceeds book value by $8,000. If we assume P Company paid $8,000 for the advantages inherent in achieving centralized control, an intangible asset in the amount of $8,000 will be carried over to the consolidated statement from P Company's books. If, on the other hand, we use the price paid by P Company for its investment as evidence of an understatement of assets on S Company's books, the fact that P Company paid $8,000 more than book value for its 80% interest implies that the total net assets of S Company are undervalued by $10,000. This interpretation will lead us to revalue the assets of S Company upward by $10,000 (or to establish $10,000 of unrecorded goodwill for S Company) and this increase in S Company's total net assets will be carried over into the consolidated balance sheet. Thus consolidated net assets will differ by $2,000 ($10,000 – $8,000) depending on our interpretation of the difference between cost and book value in this case. The consolidating procedures when subsidiaries are less than wholly owned are discussed in a later section of this chapter beginning on page 255.

The important point to note at this time is simply that differences in the interpretation of the excess of cost over book value will produce differences in consolidated results.

Errors in recording parent's cost. In some cases what appears to be an excess of cost over the book value of the subsidiary may be nothing more than an error in recording the parent's cost. To illustrate, assume that P Company owns marketable securities carried at $212,000 on its books. At a time when these securities are worth $200,000, P Company exchanges them for a 100% interest in S Company, whose book value at the date of acquisition is $200,000. If P Company should record its investment at $212,000, the carrying value of the securities it gave up, there would be an apparent $12,000 excess of cost over book value of the net assets of S Company. It is clear, however, that the parent company in this case has simply failed to recognize a $12,000 loss on marketable securities and has overstated its cost by this amount. The appropriate consolidating adjustment in this case would be to decrease P's investment account and charge the loss against the parent's retained earnings, thus removing the apparent excess of cost over book value.

Combination of factors. In any given situation the total difference between the parent's investment and the book value of the subsidiary's net assets may be attributed to a combination of the three factors just discussed. For example, some of the subsidiary's tangible assets may be undervalued, unrecorded subsidiary goodwill may be present, and some portion of the purchase price may represent an amount paid for the advantages of affiliation. The accountant should not follow rule-of-thumb solutions to avoid the necessity of analyzing the reasons for the excess of cost over book value.

To illustrate, let us use the data from the case of P Company and E Company from our previous example (see page 249). P Company paid $75,000 for its investment in E Company, which had a book value of $50,000. Suppose it had been determined that this $25,000 excess was attributable as follows: $10,000 to undervaluation of land on E's books, $14,000 to consolidated goodwill (advantages of affiliation), and $1,000 to an error in recording the price paid by P Company. The consolidating adjustment and eliminating entries, on the basis of these assumptions, would be:

Entry (a) (adjustment)

Consolidated Goodwill	*14,000*	
Land (E Company)	*10,000*	
Retained Earnings (P Company)	*1,000*	
Investment in E Company		*15,000*
Unrealized Appraisal Capital (E Company)		*10,000*

Entry (b) (elimination)

Capital Stock (Company E)	*20,000*	
Retained Earnings (Company E)	*30,000*	
Unrealized Appraisal Capital (E)	*10,000*	
Investment in E Company		*60,000*

Treatment of excess of book value over cost

When a parent company pays for its interest in a subsidiary an amount less than the book value of the underlying net assets, the disposition of the excess of book value over cost in the process of consolidating the companies depends on the reason for its existence. There are a number of possible explanations:

Net assets of subsidiary overvalued. If the price paid by the parent company reflects a careful evaluation of the subsidiary's net assets, an excess of book value over cost should be interpreted as evidence of an overvaluation of the net assets of the subsidiary. This overvaluation may result from erroneous accounting practices in past periods (for example, recording inadequate amounts of depreciation), from an unrecorded decline in the value of assets below original cost, or from a failure to record certain liabilities. Alternatively, the net assets of the subsidiary as a whole may simply be worth less than the sum of their individual valuations. This case of a general overvaluation of the subsidiary is the inverse of the goodwill case previously discussed. Goodwill may be either negative or positive. *Negative goodwill* is a general valuation account reflecting the fact that the subsidiary's earning power is abnormally low and the present value of its future expected earnings is thus less than the algebraic sum of reasonable valuations assigned to specific assets and liabilities. Negative goodwill should be reported on the consolidated balance sheet as a general valuation account deducted from total assets under a heading such as Allowance for Overvaluation of Assets.

When the price paid by the parent for its investment is considered evidence of an overvaluation of subsidiary assets, either individually or collectively, the appropriate adjustment writing down both assets and stockholders' equity may be made in the accounts of the subsidiary prior to consolidation. When this is done, the consolidating elimination is simply an offsetting of the parent's investment against the revised owners' equity accounts of the subsidiary. Alternatively, the downward revaluation of the subsidiary's assets may be confined to the consolidating working papers, in which case it may be necessary to make adjustments in subsequent periods to maintain a consistent accounting basis for the subsidiary's expense charges. The details of this procedure are discussed in a later chapter.

Bargain purchase. It is sometimes contended that an excess of subsidiary book value over cost to the parent is evidence that the parent acquired its interest at a bargain price. If this assumption were accepted, the logical consolidating procedure would be to write up the parent's investment account to full value (presumably the book value of the underlying interest in the subsidiary) and record an offsetting increase in the parent's ownership equity under a title such as Increased Capital from Consolidation.

The bargain-purchase assumption, however, is not generally accepted. Bargain purchases are conceivable but their existence is difficult to substantiate objectively, and for this reason there is an accounting presumption against the recognition of gains on purchases. In the parallel case of cost in excess of book value, note that the asset consolidated goodwill is evidenced by a market price paid by the parent for its interest at date of acquisition. This price is an objective and current bit of economic evidence. In the bargain-purchase case, however, we are asked to ignore a price established in an arm's-length market transaction and to substitute the book values in the records of S Company or some other evidence that the interest acquired is worth more than the consideration given for it.

The bargain-purchase assumption has been rejected by the AICPA's Committee on Accounting Procedures; it states, "Where the cost to the parent is less than its equity in the net assets of the purchased subsidiary, as shown by the books of the subsidiary at date of acquisition, the amount at which such net assets are carried in the consolidated statements should not exceed the parent's cost."[4]

Errors in recording parent's cost. An apparent excess of book value over cost may be attributable to an error in recording the parent company's cost. For example, suppose a parent company gave 10,000 shares of its $50 par value common stock in exchange for its interest in a subsidiary and recorded the investment at $500,000. If the parent's stock was selling on a recognized market at $60 per share, there is evidence that the cost of the investment is understated by $10 a share, or $100,000. The entry to correct this record should be made on P's books, adding $100,000 to the Investment account and crediting Additional Paid-in

[4] AICPA, *Accounting Research Bulletins, Final Edition,* Bulletin No. 51 (New York: August, 1959), p. 44.

Capital for the same amount. This entry might remove all or part of the difference between the investment account and the book value of the subsidiary net assets, or it might actually establish an excess of cost over book value.

Consolidation at acquisition—partially owned subsidiary

When a parent company owns less than 100% of the capital stock of a subsidiary, the control over the net assets of the subsidiary is based on less than complete ownership. Assuming control does exist, the consolidated balance sheet should show *all* the subsidiary's assets and liabilities as a part of the affiliated economic position, but the ownership equity in the entire collection of consolidated net assets will be broader than that of the parent company's controlling interest. An element of consolidated owners' equity called *minority interest* is introduced, representing the equity interest of the shares of stock in the subsidiary held outside the consolidated group.

To illustrate the consolidating process when the parent acquires less than a 100% interest in a subsidiary, assume that P Company acquires a 90% interest in S Company, whose book value at date of acquisition is $60,000, measured in either of two ways:

Book Value of S Company at Date of Acquisition

Total assets	*$95,000*	*Capital stock*	*$20,000*
Less: Total liabilities	*35,000*	*Retained earnings*	*40,000*
Net assets	*$60,000*	*Stockholders' equity*	*$60,000*

A 90% interest in S Company has a book value of $54,000 (90% of $60,000). We shall consider the problem of consolidating P and S Companies under three different assumptions: purchase at book value, purchase at more than book value, and purchase at less than book value.

Purchase at book value. Assuming that P pays book value, $54,000, for its 90% investment in S, the working papers on page 256 illustrate the consolidation of the two companies at date of acquisition.

Since P's investment is carried at 90% of S Company's book value, the elimination of the investment account against S Company's total ownership equity of $60,000 leaves a 10% equity ($6,000) representing the residual interest of the minority stockholders of S Company. In the eliminating entry (a), all the capital stock and retained earnings of S Company are eliminated and the 10% minority interest in S is established as a separate item and extended into the consolidated balance sheet columns. If the details of the minority interest are to be presented on published consolidated statements, it is a simple matter to determine that the $6,000 minority interest consists of $2,000 stated capital and $4,000 interest in retained earnings. It is doubtful whether a more detailed presentation of minority interest than the total dollar amount is useful. Minority stockholders must look to the individual financial statements of S Company to obtain any meaningful picture of their equity interest; from a consolidated viewpoint they are simply an outside residual interest.

P AND S COMPANIES
Working Papers—Consolidated Balance Sheet
as of January 1, current year
(Assumption: Acquisition at book value)

	P Company	S Company	Eliminations Dr	Eliminations Cr	Consolidated balance sheet
Assets:					
Investments in S (90%)	54,000			(a) 54,000	
Other assets	300,000	95,000			395,000
Totals	354,000	95,000			395,000
Liabilities & Equity:					
Liabilities	60,000	35,000			95,000
Capital stock—P	200,000				200,000
Retained earnings—P	94,000				94,000
Capital stock—S		20,000	(a) 20,000		
Retained earnings—S		40,000	(a) 40,000		
Minority interest—S				(a) 6,000	6,000
Totals	354,000	95,000			395,000

The following diagram illustrates the nature of the consolidating process when a minority interest is present:

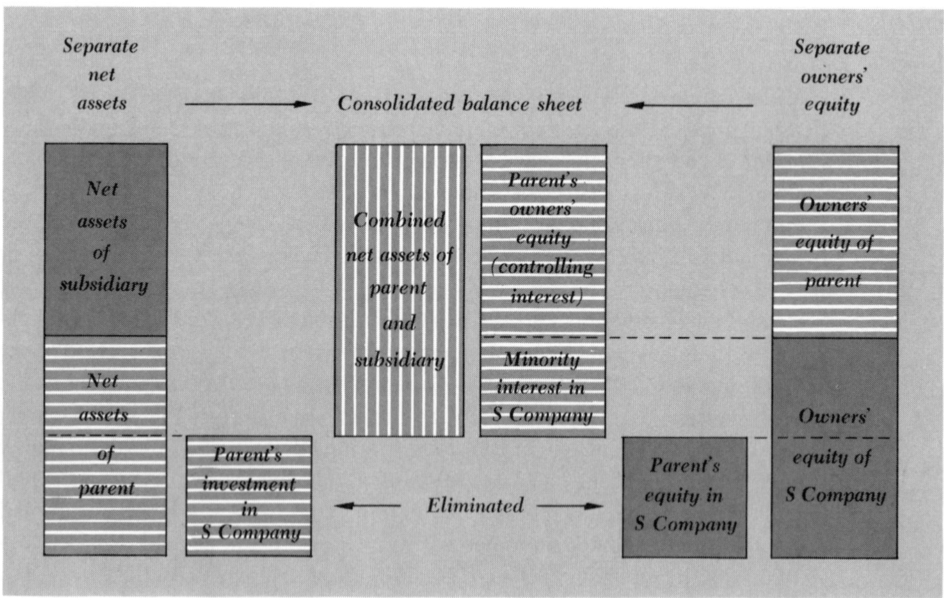

Purchase at more than book value. Assume now that P Company paid $81,000 for its 90% interest in the capital stock of S Company. The following schedule shows the amount by which P's cost is in excess of the book value of its underlying interest in S Company's net assets and the implications of this difference on the minority interest in S Company:

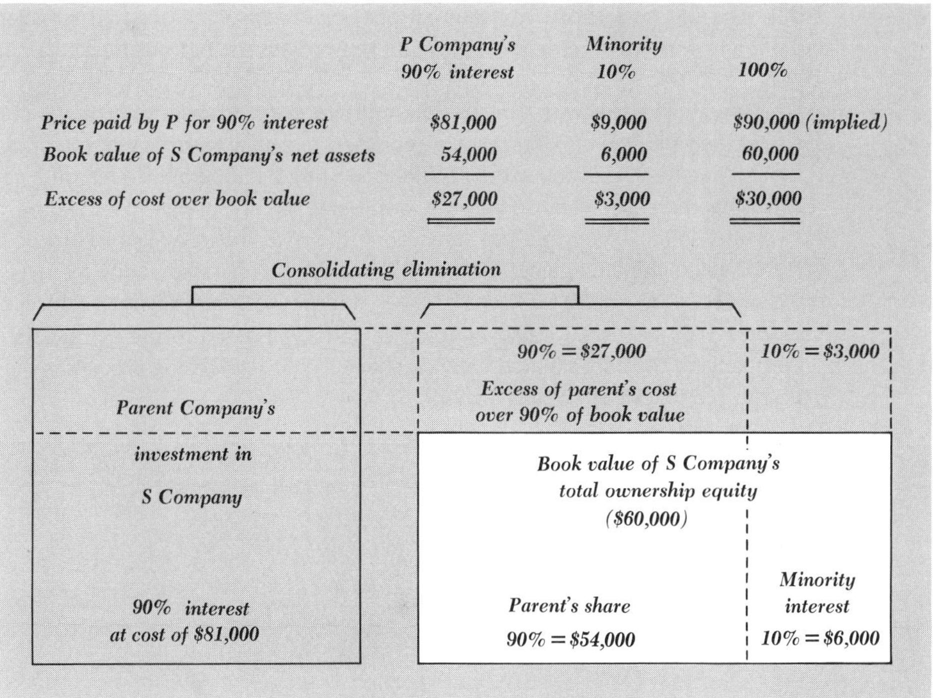

	P Company's 90% interest	*Minority 10%*	*100%*
Price paid by P for 90% interest	*$81,000*	*$9,000*	*$90,000 (implied)*
Book value of S Company's net assets	*54,000*	*6,000*	*60,000*
Excess of cost over book value	*$27,000*	*$3,000*	*$30,000*

The problem we face in consolidating P and S Companies at date of acquisition is now clear. P Company's investment of $81,000 must be eliminated against $54,000 of S Company's ownership equity, representing a 90% interest in the book value of the net assets of S Company. The appropriate solution to this problem, as we have previously noted, depends on the reason for the $27,000 difference between cost and book value. We shall illustrate the consolidating process under two different assumptions as to the reason for this difference.

*1. **Net assets of S Company undervalued.*** One assumption, as indicated in our previous discussion, is that the $81,000 price paid by P Company for its 90% interest represents evidence of an undervaluation of the net assets of S Company. If this is the case, we should first revalue upward the net assets of S Company, either by increasing the valuation of specific assets or by recognizing unrecorded goodwill of S Company.

But we now face an additional question not raisèd in the wholly owned subsidiary cases previously discussed. Do we revalue only P Company's 90% interest in S Company's net assets, or do we revalue the entire net assets of S Company, including the minority interest? There is only one logical answer to this question. If the price paid for P's 90% interest is valid evidence of the worth of S Company's net assets, it is as good evidence of the current value of *all* the assets as of 90%, since there is no specific collection of net assets associated with a 90% interest.[5] Since the entire net assets of S Company are reported on the consolidated balance

[5] As one writer points out: "The parent paid the price it did because, presumably, the subsidiary is worth more than book value, and the amount of the excess does not vary with an alteration in the size of the parent's interest." Maurice Moonitz, *The Entity Theory of Consolidated Statement,* The American Accounting Association (Madison: 1944), p. 66.

sheet, it would be a rather nonsensical position to claim that we had sufficient evidence to warrant revaluation of 90% of the net assets, but not the remaining 10%.

This reasoning suggests that the appropriate consolidating adjustment is to increase the valuation of S Company's net assets (we shall assume that the undervaluation can be associated with specific assets) by $30,000 and to record a corresponding increase in S Company's ownership equity under the heading of Appraisal Capital. When this has been done the investment account balance of $81,000 will eliminate against 90% of S Company's ownership equity as revised [90% of ($60,000 + $30,000) = $81,000] and the 10% minority interest will be valued at 10% of the $90,000 adjusted valuation assigned to the net assets of S Company on the consolidated balance sheet. The consolidating process is illustrated in the following working papers:

P AND S COMPANIES
Working Papers—Consolidated Balance Sheet
as of January 1, current year
(P buys 90% interest in S for more than book value.
Assumption: Assets of S Company are undervalued.)

	P Company	S Company	Eliminations		Consolidated balance sheet
			Dr	Cr	
Assets:					
Investment in S—90%	81,000			(b) 81,000	
Other assets	273,000	95,000	(a) 30,000		398,000
Totals	354,000	95,000			398,000
Liabilities & Equity:					
Liabilities	60,000	35,000			95,000
Capital stock—P	200,000				200,000
Retained earnings—P	94,000				94,000
Capital stock—S		20,000	(b) 20,000		
Retained earnings—S		40,000	(b) 40,000		
Appraisal capital—S			(b) 30,000	(a) 30,000	
Minority interest in S				(b) 9,000	9,000
Totals	354,000	95,000			398,000

(a) To revalue assets of S Company on the basis of price paid by P Company for its 90% interest.
(b) To eliminate P's investment against S Company's owners' equity accounts and record the 10% minority interest in S's net assets as adjusted.

2. *Goodwill from consolidation.* Another possible explanation of the $27,000 excess of cost over book value is that P Company was willing to pay this amount to obtain certain intangible advantages expected to result from the affiliation. The directors of P Company may believe that S Company's net assets are fairly valued on the books, but they see certain intangible advantages from affiliation that are worth at least $27,000. Thus the evidence in this case does not point to an upward revaluation of S Company's net assets, but to the recognition of an intangible asset of the parent company arising out of the consolidation. This is the case of consolidated goodwill, previously discussed, and the appropriate consolidating adjustment is to transfer $27,000 out of P Company's investment account to a separate asset account labeled Consolidated Goodwill or Excess of Cost over Book Value of Interest in Subsidiary. This asset will appear on the consolidated balance sheet and the remaining balance in the investment account will eliminate against 90% of the subsidiary's ownerships equity accounts, as illustrated in the following working papers:

P AND S COMPANIES
Working Papers—Consolidated Balance Sheet
as of January 1, current year
(P Company purchases 90% interest in S at more than book value.
Assumption: Excess represents advantages of consolidation.)

	P Company	S Company	Eliminations Dr	Eliminations Cr	Consolidated balance sheet
Assets:					
Investment in S—90%	81,000			(a) 27,000 (b) 54,000	
Other assets	273,000	95,000			368,000
Excess of cost over book value of interest in subsidiary			(a) 27,000		27,000
Totals	354,000	95,000			395,000
Liabilities & Equity:					
Liabilities	60,000	35,000			95,000
Capital stock—P	200,000				200,000
Retained earnings—P	94,000				94,000
Capital stock—S		20,000	(b) 20,000		
Retained earnings—S		40,000	(b) 40,000		
Minority interest in S				(b) 6,000	6,000
Totals	354,000	95,000			395,000

(a) *To reclassify cost in excess of book value to show amount paid by P Company for intangible advantages of affiliation.*
(b) *To eliminate P's investment against S Company's owners' equity and recognize minority interest in S Company.*

Note that since there is no revaluation of S Company's net assets in this case, the minority interest in S Company is 10% of the book value of the net assets as reported on S Company's individual balance sheet [10% ($95,000 − $35,000) = $6,000]. A comparison between the working papers on page 258 and those above will show that the major difference in the results under these two assumptions is a $3,000 reduction in the total amount of consolidated assets and in the minority interest.

We might pose a number of other possible assumptions: an error in recording the $81,000 cost on P Company's books, or a combination of factors involving some revaluation of S Company's assets and some payment for the advantages of affiliation. The basic accounting issue has been isolated in these two examples, however, and any variations will affect only the procedural details.

Summary of procedures when cost exceeds book value. We can summarize the major alternatives when cost exceeds book value as follows:

Assumption	*Consolidating procedure*
1. Net assets of subsidiary are undervalued, either collectively or in terms of specific assets or liabilities.	1. Determine 100% of the undervaluation as indicated by the price paid by the parent for its interest, and restate the net assets and owners' equity of the subsidiary accordingly.
2. Parent paid for goodwill or other intangibles arising from the affiliation of the two companies.	2. Remove from the parent's investment account the amount paid for intangible benefits and reclassify it as a special intangible asset arising out of the consolidation.
3. The parent sustained a loss on purchase, or has made an error in recording the cost of the investment.	3. Restate the investment account on P Company's statement to the proper figure, with an appropriate offsetting reduction of P's ownership equity.

Purchase at less than book value. Assume now that P Company paid only $35,100 for its 90% interest in S Company. P Company's cost in this situation is less than the $54,000 book value of the underlying net assets of S Company. The implications of this excess of book value over cost on the appropriate total valuation of S Company and the minority interest are indicated in the following schedule and diagram:

	P Company's 90% interest	*Minority 10% interest*	*100%*
Book value of S Company's net assets	*$54,000*	*$6,000*	*$60,000*
Price paid by P Company for 90% interest	*35,100*	*3,900*	*39,000 (implied)*
Excess of book value over cost	*$18,900*	*$2,100*	*$21,000 (implied)*

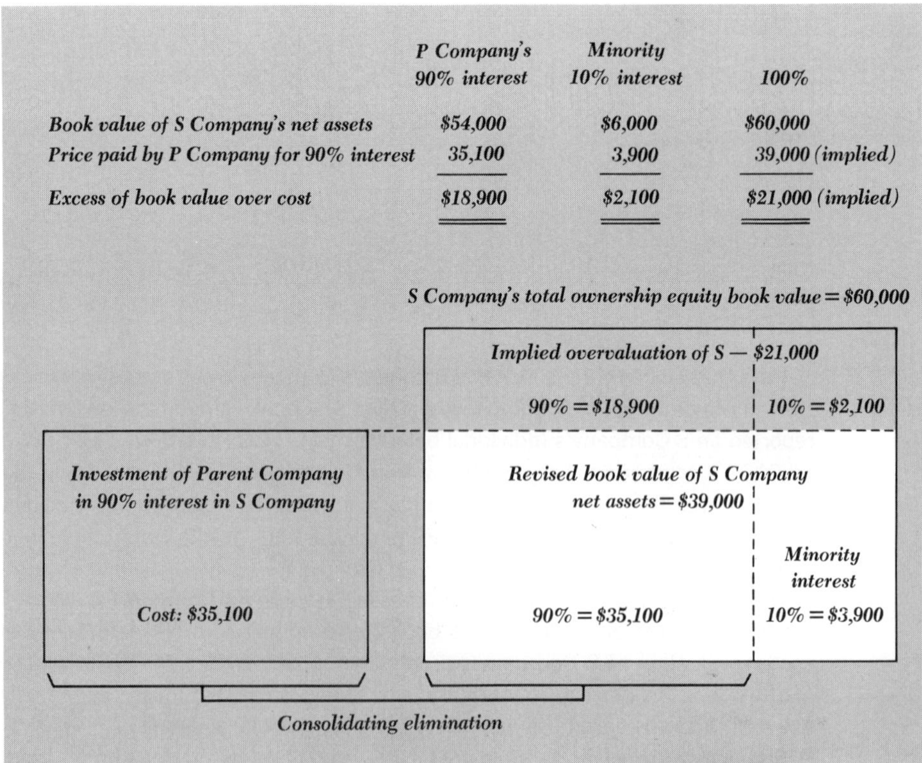

1. S Company's net assets overvalued. If we assume that the price paid by P Company for its 90% interest may be used as evidence of the value of the net assets of S Company, the appropriate consolidating procedure is to write down S Company's net assets by $21,000. If 90% of S Company is worth $35,100, this implies that the entire net assets of S Company have a current fair value of $39,000 ($35,100 ÷ .90). If we cannot identify specific assets of S Company that are overstated, we can accomplish the revaluation by establishing a general allowance for overvaluation (or negative goodwill) account to indicate the reduction in the total valuation assigned to S Company's assets. The revaluation of S Company's net assets from $60,000 to $39,000 and the consolidation of the two companies are illustrated in the following working papers:

P AND S COMPANIES
Working Papers—Consolidated Balance Sheet
at date of acquisition—January 1, current year
(P purchases 90% of S Company at a cost less than book value.
Assumption: Net assets of S Company are overvalued.)

	P Company	S Company	Adjustments and eliminations		Consolidated balance sheet
			Dr	Cr	
Assets:					
Investment in S—90%	35,100			(b) 35,100	
Other assets	318,900	95,000			413,900
Allowance for overvaluation of assets				(a) 21,000	(21,000)
Totals	354,000	95,000			392,900
Liabilities & Equity:					
Liabilities	60,000	35,000			95,000
Capital stock—P	200,000				200,000
Retained earnings—P	94,000				94,000
Capital stock—S		20,000	(b) 20,000		
Retained earnings—S		40,000	(a) 21,000 (b) 19,000		
Minority interest in S				(b) 3,900	3,900
Totals	354,000	95,000			392,900

(a) *To adjust for overvaluation of net assets of S Company as indicated by the price paid by P for a 90% interest.*
(b) *To eliminate P's investment in S and to recognize minority interest in S at 10% of new book value [10% ($60,000 − $21,000) = 3,900].*

2. Bargain-purchase assumption. The alternative to restating S Company's net assets at a valuation consistent with the price paid by P Company for its interest is to assume that P Company has made a bargain purchase and acquired an interest worth $54,000 for only $35,100. If this assumption were accepted, the consolidating adjustment would be to add $18,900 to the investment of P Company and record a gain on acquisition of this same amount as an addition to P Company's ownership equity accounts. The investment account would thereby be restated at $54,000 ($35,100 + $18,900) and this amount would eliminate against 90% of the ownership equity of S Company. As previously noted, the assumption of a gain on purchase is difficult to justify and is not currently a generally accepted accounting procedure.

Summary of procedures when book value exceeds cost. The major alternative consolidating procedures when the book value of an interest in a subsidiary exceeds the parent's cost are summarized below:

Assumption	*Consolidating procedure*
1. Net assets of the subsidiary are overvalued, either collectively or in terms of specific assets and liabilities.	*1.* Determine 100% of the overvaluation as indicated by the price paid by the parent for its interest and write down the net assets and owner's equity of the subsidiary by this amount.
2. An error was made on the parent's books in recording the cost of its investment.	*2.* Increase the parent's investment account by the amount of the error, and make the appropriate offsetting adjustment of any affected asset, liability, or owners' equity accounts of the parent company.
3. The parent company has purchased its interest at a bargain price.	*3.* Consolidation on the basis of this assumption is not generally accepted. Such an assumption would call for an increase in the parent's investment account and recognition of a gain on purchase as an increase in the parent's owners' equity.

Consolidated balance sheet at date of acquisition

The illustrations in this chapter have been highly condensed in order to focus attention on the basic consolidating principles. All assets not germane to the discussion have been lumped together and liabilities have been treated as a single figure. In this process we have not omitted anything of significance from the discussion, since any individual assets and liabilities not affected by consolidating adjustments or eliminations are simply combined in the consolidated balance sheet. For example, the cash account of the parent is combined with the cash account of the subsidiary; similarly other like assets and like liabilities of the parent and subsidiary are combined.

This point is illustrated by the consolidated balance sheet for P Company and S Company shown on the next page. The details of the combined assets and liabilities have been assumed; the figures would be obtained by simply adding the specific asset and liability accounts appearing on the separate statements of P Company and S Company. The total assets of $392,900 and the total liabilities of $95,000 agree with the data in the working papers on page 261, since the statement is based on that illustration.

P AND S COMPANIES
Consolidated Balance Sheet
at date of acquisition—January 1, current year
(Based on working papers appearing on page 261 of text)

Assets

Current assets:				
Cash				$ 15,000
Accounts receivable (net of $2,300 allowance for uncollectibles)				20,700
Inventories (at fifo cost)				44,300
Short-term prepayments				8,400
Total current assets				$ 88,400
Plant and equipment:				
	Cost	*Accumulated depreciation*	*Book value*	
Land	$ 30,000	-0-	$ 30,000	
Buildings	500,000	$260,000	240,000	
Equipment	80,000	24,500	55,500	
	$610,000	$284,500		325,500
Allowance for overvaluation of subsidiary net assets				(21,000)
Total assets				$392,900

Liabilities & Stockholders' Equity

Current liabilities:		
Notes payable		$ 10,000
Accounts payable		42,400
Accrued liabilities		17,600
Total current liabilities		$ 70,000
Equipment mortgage, due in five years		25,000
Total liabilities		$ 95,000
Stockholders' equity:		
Common stock, $50 par value, authorized 10,000 shares, issued and outstanding 4,000 shares	$200,000	
Retained earnings	94,000	294,000
Minority interest in S Company		3,900
Total liabilities & stockholders' equity		$392,900

Minority interest on the consolidated balance sheet. In practice the minority interest in subsidiary companies is often reported as a liability on the consolidated balance sheet, or in the limbo between the liability and owners' equity section of the statement. In theory the minority interest is clearly a part of the ownership equity on the consolidated balance sheet. The minority interest is certainly not an unliquidated obligation in any sense, and classifying it in the no-man's-land between liabilities and capital simply avoids the issue. Since the consolidated assets and liabilities are those of the affiliated group as a whole, the treatment of minority interest as a specially designated element of the ownership equity is in conformity with the basic assumptions of the consolidating process.

Minority shareholders must look to the separate statements of the subsidiary for information about their investment. The reader of consolidated statements, therefore, is not likely to be interested in the composition of the minority interest. Thus the minority interest may be reported as a single amount, combining the minority shareholders' interest in retained earnings and invested capital. An exception may be made if the subsidiary has a deficit which impairs stated capital. This situation should be disclosed; a separation of the minority interest into stated capital and deficit components may be a convenient means of disclosure.

Questions

1. Explain the significance of unified control and an integrated area of operations as criteria for determining whether two or more business units constitute an economic entity for which consolidated statements would be useful.

2. A parent company owns 46% of the outstanding common stock of a subsidiary and excludes the subsidiary from consolidation. Where will the parent's equity in this subsidiary be reported on a consolidated balance sheet?

3. A parent company pays more than book value for a common stock interest in a subsidiary company. What are two possible explanations of the parent's willingness to pay more than book value for its interest? What balance sheet treatment of the excess of cost over book value is appropriate under each of the two interpretations if the parent buys 100% of the common stock? If the parent buys 90% of the common stock?

4. A parent company buys a substantial common stock interest in a subsidiary, paying less than the book value of its interest. What are two possible explanations for the excess of book value over the cost of the parent's investment? How should this excess be reported on a consolidated balance sheet?

5. P Company acquired a controlling interest in Q Company for more than book value. The excess of the cost of P's investment over the book value of its interest is attributed to unrecorded goodwill of Q Company. The book value of Q's net assets at date of acquisition was $500,000. If the proper amount of goodwill on a consolidated balance sheet prepared at date of acquisition is $45,000, what price did P Company pay for its interest in Q Company if it owns (a) 100% of the common stock, (b) 90% of the common stock, (c) 80% of the common stock?

6. On January 1, Year 1, P Company reported $700,000 of net assets and S Company reported $300,000 of net assets. On this date, P Company acquired an 80% interest in S Company for $280,000. In a consolidated balance sheet prepared at date of acquisition, one accountant believes the net assets of the consolidated entity should be reported as $760,000; another accountant believes the net assets should be $770,000. Explain the basis for this difference in the interpretation of the data.

7. P Company acquired a controlling interest in F Company for $120,000. The book value of P's equity interest at date of acquisition was $90,000. If we assume that F Company's net assets are undervalued at the date of acquisition, what is the amount of the undervaluation if P acquired (a) a 100% interest, (b) a 70% interest, (c) a 60% interest?

8. P Company acquired a 75% interest in R Company for $600,000. The book value of R Company's net assets at date of acquisition was $860,000. It is agreed by the board of directors that certain plant assets on R's books are misstated at the date of acquisition. What is the amount of the overstatement or understatement of R's plant? What adjusting entry would be appropriate to revise the net assets of R Company prior to consolidation?

9. Explain the nature of minority interest and its proper presentation on a consolidated balance sheet.

10. P Company acquired a controlling interest in X Company at a cost in excess of the book value of the stock acquired. In the process of preparing consolidated statements, the assets of X Company were revalued on the basis of the price paid by P for its equity interest, with an offsetting credit to an appraisal capital account. Will the appraisal capital account appear on the consolidated balance sheet? Explain why or why not.

Short cases for analysis

8-1 In each of the three cases described below, the question is whether there is sufficient control over the economic entity by one of the affiliated companies to warrant the preparation of consolidated financial statements.

Case 1. Arne owns 55% of the common stock of Mohr Corporation and 70% of the common stock of Senner Corporation. Mohr Corporation holds the remaining 30% of the stock of Senner Corporation. Arne is chairman of the board of both Mohr and Senner Corporations. The remaining 45% of the shares of Mohr common stock are held by 10,000 stockholders, and the stock is sold over the counter nationally. Arne suggests that consolidated financial statements might be prepared for submission to the stockholders of Mohr Corporation, but the controller objects that this would be improper since Mohr Company owns only 30% of the shares of Senner.

Case 2. Weatherhead Company has the following capitalization:

Class A common, 200,000 shares outstanding, nonvoting, no par, stated value $100 per share	*$20,000,000*
Class B common, 100,000 shares outstanding, voting, no par, stated value $10 per share	*1,000,000*

Crockett Company owns 51% of the Class B common stock of the Weatherhead Company. The Class A common, which is widely held, is nonvoting but is entitled to receive dividends per share equal to 10 times any per-share dividends declared on Class B common. To the suggestion that consolidated financial statements might be prepared, the president of Crockett Company replies, "Consolidated statements would be inappropriate since we have a minority interest in the ownership equity of Weatherhead Company."

Case 3. Patton Company owns 50% of the common stock of Simpson Company. Patton Company also holds a contract with the remaining shareholders of Simpson Company which entitles the directors of Patton Company to elect a majority of the board of directors of the Simpson Company. This contract runs for 30 years and is renewable for two additional 30-year periods if approved by the owners of one-third of the 50% of Simpson Company shares held by outsiders. One of the directors of Patton Company makes a case for the preparation of consolidated financial statements on the grounds that "We exercise effective control over Simpson, and it would be useful to have a picture of the financial resources of the combined companies."

Instructions

Discuss the possible usefulness of consolidated financial statements in each of the above cases, and state whether, in your opinion, consolidated statements would be appropriate, giving reasons for your conclusion.

8-2 The working capital position as shown on separate statements of Haupt and Allide Companies and on a consolidated balance sheet at the end of the current year is as follows:

	Haupt Company	*Allide Company*	*Consolidated*
Cash	*$ 200,000*	*$ 60,000*	*$ 260,000*
Receivables	*350,000*	*310,000*	*660,000*
Inventories	*450,000*	*430,000*	*880,000*
Total current assets	*$1,000,000*	*$ 800,000*	*$1,800,000*
Notes payable	*$ 100,000*	*$ 900,000*	*$1,000,000*
Accounts payable	*220,000*	*600,000*	*820,000*
Accrued liabilities	*80,000*	*100,000*	*180,000*
Total current liabilities	*$ 400,000*	*$1,600,000*	*$2,000,000*
Working capital	*$ 600,000*	*$ (800,000)*	*$ (200,000)*

The net assets of Allide Company have a book value at the end of the current year of $750,000. Haupt Company owns 70% of the common stock of Allide, which is carried on Haupt's balance sheet at a figure approximating the underlying book value of $525,000.

Haupt and Allide Companies have issued consolidated financial statements in the past, but at the end of the current year one of the directors of Haupt urges that this policy be discontinued in view of the precarious working capital position of Allide. "Why should we hide our sound working capital position in consolidated statements?" he asks at a meeting of the board. "We have a good current ratio and despite the bind Allide is in, our investment is well protected by the value of their plant and equipment. Consolidated statements are distorting our financial picture."

Instructions

Discuss the question raised by the member of the board. Are consolidated financial statements misleading under these circumstances? As a stockholder or creditor of Haupt, would you find Haupt Company's unconsolidated statement, showing its investment in Allide as an asset, more useful? Explain your position on these questions.

8-3 The management of Mills Company is considering the acquisition of 80% of the common stock of Nesco Company. At the date of acquisition Nesco Company has the following assets:

Cash	*$ 62,000*
Receivables	*56,000*
Inventories	*80,000*
Marketable securities	*2,000*
Plant and equipment (net)	*500,000*
Total assets	*$700,000*

An appraisal of the Nesco plant at date of acquisition indicates a current fair value of $490,000, and this is regarded by the management of Mills to be sufficiently close that they will accept book value figures. Nesco inventories are carried at lifo; current replacement cost is $100,000. Cash and receivables are fairly stated. The marketable securities are 2,000 shares of JK Company, valued at $1 per share. These shares were purchased at the inception of JK Company, whose stock sold over the counter for several subsequent years at prices ranging from $1 to $10 per share. Five years ago JK Company stock was listed on the Pacific Coast Stock Exchange, and at the current date its 400,000 outstanding shares are quoted at $32 per share.

An evaluation of Nesco Company, in a report prepared by Mills's controller, recommending acquisition of the shares, is shown below:

Book value of Nesco's total assets at current date		*$700,000*
Less: Total liabilities		*200,000*
Book value of net assets		*$500,000*
Add: Increased valuation of inventory	*$20,000*	
Less: 50% income taxes on increase	*10,000*	*10,000*
Increased valuation of marketable securities	*$62,000*	
Less: 25% capital gains tax on increase	*15,500*	*46,500*
Revised book value of Nesco's net assets		*$556,500*
Recommended offer for 80% of Nesco's common (80% of $556,500)		*$445,200*

After some negotiation, Mills Company paid $450,000 in cash for 80% of the stock of Nesco Company. In preparing a consolidated balance sheet at the date of acquisition, the controller of Mills Company faces the problem of a proper valuation of Nesco's assets and the treatment of the difference between the cost of the 80% interest and the underlying book value. The controller believes that since

Mills Company carries its inventory on a fifo basis, Nesco's inventory should be restated to a fifo basis for consolidated statements, but he is uncertain whether to make the write-up net of the income tax factor. The assistant controller argues that income taxes should be deducted from any write-up of both inventories and marketable securities. "I think we should state marketable securities at $48,500," he contends. "Then if the securities are sold for $64,000, Nesco would report a taxable gain of $62,000 which would be subject to tax of $15,500, and we would break even on the basis of revised book values."

Instructions

a. Prepare a statement recommending an appropriate valuation of Nesco's assets on consolidated statements, explaining the basis for your position.

b. Present journal entries to revise the statements of Nesco at date of acquisition, and the eliminating entry that would appear on the consolidated working papers to eliminate Mills Company's investment in Nesco at that date.

Problems

8-4 Condensed balance sheets for P, H, K, and L Companies as of December 31 of the current year are given below:

	P Company	*H Company*	*K Company*	*L Company*
Assets	*$800,000*	*$250,000*	*$400,000*	*$200,000*
Liabilities	*$100,000*	*$ 50,000*	*$150,000*	*$ 25,000*
Capital stock ($100 par)	*400,000*	*300,000*	*200,000*	*100,000*
Retained earnings (deficit)	*300,000*	*(100,000)*	*50,000*	*75,000*
Total liabilities & equities	*$800,000*	*$250,000*	*$400,000*	*$200,000*

As of this date P Company acquired all the capital stock of the other three companies. For the stock of H Company, P Company paid $160,000 in cash. P Company paid $200,000 in cash and issued five-year interest-bearing notes for $100,000 to the stockholders of K Company. P Company issued 1,000 shares of its capital stock in exchange for the 1,000 outstanding shares of L Company common stock.

Instructions

a. Prepare journal entries to record on P Company's books the acquisition of the shares of H, K, and L Companies.

b. Prepare a consolidated balance sheet for the four companies as of the date of affiliation. You may use working papers or may prepare the statement directly and show in supporting schedules how balances were derived.

8-5 W Company acquired control of X Company on July 1 of the current year. Immediately after the acquisition the financial position of the two companies was as follows:

Assets	*Company W*	*Company X*
Cash	*$ 32,000*	*$ 25,000*
Accounts receivable	*48,000*	*30,000*
Inventories	*65,000*	*18,000*
Plant and equipment (net)	*350,000*	*187,000*
Investment in stock of X Company (90%)	*217,000*	
	$712,000	*$260,000*
Liabilities & Owners' Equity		
Liabilities	*$116,000*	*$ 50,000*
Capital stock ($10 par value)	*300,000*	*80,000*
Additional paid-in capital	*90,000*	*40,000*
Retained earnings	*206,000*	*90,000*
	$712,000	*$260,000*

W Company authorized an audit of the accounting records of X Company as of July 1. The audit disclosed that X Company's inventories were carried on a lifo basis; in order to restate them on a fifo basis, comparable with W Company, the book value should be increased by $12,000. Uncollectible receivables of $7,500 should be written off on X Company's books, as no allowance for bad debts has been provided. The current sound depreciated value of X Company's plant and equipment as of July 1 is $220,000. The auditor discovered that $20,000 of customers' advances were carried by X Company as an appropriation of retained earnings. After these adjustments, any excess of cost over the book value of the investment in X Company is to be considered an amount paid to achieve control.

Instructions

a. Prepare the necessary journal entries to adjust the records of X Company prior to consolidation.

b. Prepare consolidated working papers for the parent and subsidiary companies, after the books of the subsidiary are adjusted.

c. Prepare a consolidated balance sheet.

8-6 The balance sheets of Par and Sub Companies at the close of the current year are as follows:

	Par Company	*Sub Company*
Cash	*$150,000*	*$ 25,000*
Other assets	*650,000*	*125,000*
	$800,000	*$150,000*
Liabilities	*$100,000*	*$ 20,000*
Capital stock ($50 par value)	*350,000*	*100,000*
Additional paid-in capital	*200,000*	*10,000*
Retained earnings	*150,000*	*20,000*
	$800,000	*$150,000*

Instructions

Prepare a consolidated balance sheet for Par and Sub Companies, under each of the independent assumptions listed below:

a. Par Company acquires all the stock of Sub Company by buying the stock from stockholders for $60 per share.

b. Par Company acquires 80% of the stock of Sub Company, paying $112,000 in cash for 1,600 shares.

c. Par Company acquires 80% of the stock of Sub Company by issuing additional shares of its own common stock in exchange for Sub Company shares, on the basis of one share of Par Company stock for each two shares of Sub Company stock. The market value of Par Company stock at this time is $160 and of Sub Company stock is $80.

Note: In each of the above cases, assume that any difference between the cost and book value of Par Company's investment may be attributed to an overvaluation or undervaluation of "other assets" on the books of Sub Company.

8-7 The position statements of Companies P, Q, and R, immediately after the acquisition of control in Q and R by P Company were as follows:

	P Company	*Q Company*	*R Company*
Current assets	$ 635,000	$ 20,000	$200,000
Plant and equipment	1,988,000	900,000	798,000
Investment in Q (70%)	427,000		
Investment in R (80%)	800,000		
Total assets	$3,850,000	$920,000	$998,000
Liabilities	$ 450,000	$220,000	$ 98,000
Capital stock ($100 par value)	2,000,000	600,000	400,000
Additional paid-in capital	600,000	300,000	200,000
Retained earnings (deficit)	800,000	(200,000)	300,000
Total liabilities & owners' equity	$3,850,000	$920,000	$998,000

Under some conditions, an appropriate eliminating entry to consolidate the balance sheets of P Company and Q Company on this date would be:

Capital Stock—Q Company	600,000	
Additional Paid-in Capital—Q Company	300,000	
Investment in Q Company		427,000
Retained Earnings—Q Company		200,000
Minority Interest in Q Company		210,000
Excess of Book Value over Cost of Investment in Q Company		63,000

Instructions

a. Prepare a similar combined journal entry to eliminate the investment of P Company in Q Company under each of the following assumptions:

(1) That the plant and equipment of Q Company are overvalued by an amount indicated by the price paid by P Company for a 70% interest in Q Company.

(2) That P Company gave 4,270 shares of its common stock in exchange for 4,200 shares of Q Company stock, which had a market value of $490,000 at the time of exchange.

b. Prepare combined journal entries to eliminate the investment of P Company in R Company under each of the following assumptions:

(1) That R Company has unrecorded goodwill in an amount evidenced by the price paid by P Company for its 80% interest.

(2) That R Company's plant and equipment is undervalued by $100,000.

(3) That R Company has patents which have a current fair market value of $60,000 but which have been fully amortized on R Company's books. P Company took these patents into account in setting its purchase price and also paid an additional amount for some intangible benefits which the officers believe will result from acquiring control of R Company.

c. What is the nature of the $63,000 credit balance in the account, Excess of Book Value Over Cost of Investment in Q Company, shown in the illustrative journal entry?

8-8 Below is given condensed balance sheet information for two companies at the end of the current year, just prior to the purchase of the stock of Crite Company by Hurt Company:

	Hurt Company	*Crite Company*
Current assets	*$ 97,000*	*$ 40,000*
Other assets	*115,000*	*67,000*
Total assets	*$212,000*	*$107,000*
Liabilities	*$ 40,000*	*$ 35,000*
Capital stock, $100 par value	*100,000*	*50,000*
Retained earnings	*72,000*	*22,000*
Total liabilities & owners' equity	*$212,000*	*$107,000*

On the date of the above balance sheets, assume that Hurt Company acquired stock of Crite Company for cash under the following six sets of circumstances:

A. Hurt Company acquired all the stock of Crite Company at the following prices:
   (1) At $144 per share.
   (2) At $166 per share. Current assets of Crite Company are overstated by $4,000; Crite Company has unrecorded goodwill.
   (3) At $128 per share. Other assets of Crite Company are overvalued.

B. Hurt Company acquired 400 shares of the stock of Crite Company at the following prices:
   (1) At $144 per share.
   (2) At $112 per share. Other assets of Crite Company are overvalued.
   (3) At $174 per share. Other assets of Crite Company are undervalued by $10,000, and Hurt Company anticipates certain benefits from the affiliation.

Instructions

Set up a six-column schedule, with columns headed A-1, A-2, A-3, B-1, B-2, B-3, and prepare consolidated balance sheets for Hurt and Crite Companies under each of the above stated conditions, entering the appropriate balances in each of the columns. Show supporting computations in footnotes.

8-9 The condensed balance sheets of Port, Arkin, and Bule Companies at the date of the acquisition by Port Company of a controlling interest in Arkin and Bule Companies is shown below:

	Port Company	*Arkin Company*	*Bule Company*
Current assets	*$ 20,000*	*$36,000*	*$ 50,000*
Investment in Arkin Company (90%)	*72,000*		
Investment in Bule Company (80%)	*36,000*		
Other assets	*154,000*	*44,000*	*40,000*
Total assets	*$282,000*	*$80,000*	*$ 90,000*
Liabilities	*$ 32,000*	*$10,000*	*$ 30,000*
Capital stock ($10 par value)	*200,000*	*50,000*	*100,000*
Retained earnings (deficit)	*50,000*	*20,000*	*(40,000)*
Total liabilities & owners' equity	*$282,000*	*$80,000*	*$ 90,000*

In negotiating the purchase of the two companies, the management of Port Company made a thorough investigation of the financial condition of Arkin Company and Bule Company. The price paid for the stock of the respective companies reflects agreement as to the current fair market value of the net assets of the respective companies, and unrecorded goodwill (either positive or negative) is to be reflected in the consolidated balance sheet.

Instructions

a. Prepare consolidating working papers for the consolidated balance sheet of the three companies at the date of acquisition.

b. Describe an alternative treatment of the differences between the cost of the stock and the book value, and compute the amount of the minority interest that would appear on the consolidated balance sheet if the alternative method had been used.

8-10 Condensed balance sheet information for the Proxy, Stan, and Truax Companies at the beginning of Year 1 is as follows:

	Proxy Company	Stan Company	Truax Company
Other assets (details omitted)	$349,000	$210,000	$230,000
Investment in Stan Company (80%)	158,800		
Investment in Truax Company (90%)	142,200		
Total assets	$650,000	$210,000	$230,000
Liabilities	$150,000	$ 20,000	$ 60,000
Capital stock—$100 par value	300,000	150,000	200,000
Retained earnings or (deficit)	200,000	40,000	(30,000)
Total liabilities & owners' equity	$650,000	$210,000	$230,000

Proxy Company acquired 80% of the stock of Stan Company at the beginning of Year 1 by paying $38,800 in cash and issuing $120,000 in 5% notes in exchange for 1,200 shares of Stan's common stock. An audit of Stan Company indicates that Stan Company's net assets are fairly valued except that unrecorded liabilities of $6,500 do not appear on the above balance sheet at the beginning of Year 1, and other assets are considered to be worth $220,000.

Proxy Company acquired 90% of the stock of Truax Company at the beginning of Year 1 by paying $42,200 in cash and issuing 1,000 shares of additional common stock in exchange for the 1,800 shares of Truax common. Proxy Company recorded the issue of its common stock at par value. The net assets of Truax Company are assumed to be fairly valued on the above balance sheet except that the Allowance for Bad Debts should be increased by $1,800.

Instructions

On the basis of the above information, prepare working papers for a consolidated balance sheet at the date of acquisition. Explain in supporting footnotes the assumptions you have followed in dealing with differences between the cost and book value of Proxy's investment in subsidiaries.

9 CONSOLIDATION AFTER DATE OF ACQUISITION

At the time of acquisition, a parent company normally records its investment in the capital stock of a subsidiary at cost, which may differ from the book value of the underlying net assets. Subsequent to acquisition the subsidiary company earns income, suffers losses, or perhaps pays dividends. These activities change the book value of the subsidiary's net assets so that any original difference between the cost and book value of the parent's equity is affected. Thus in preparing consolidated statements, we must distinguish the initial gap between cost and book value *at date of acquisition* from the *subsequent growth* (or decline) in the subsidiary's net assets as a result of operations.

From a consolidated viewpoint, the growth in the net assets of both the parent and subsidiary as a result of operations is properly included in consolidated income. Just as the combined assets and liabilities of the parent and subsidiary are reported on a consolidated balance sheet, the combined revenues and expenses should be reported on the consolidated income statement. Eliminations to avoid duplication are necessary, and some consolidating adjustments may be required to reflect properly transactions between the parent and subsidiary company from the viewpoint of the consolidated entity. These eliminations and adjustments will be discussed in later sections of this chapter.

Cost versus equity method of accounting for investment

The procedures necessary to arrive at consolidated statements after date of acquisition will differ depending on whether the parent company uses a cost or an equity basis in accounting for its investment in the subsidiary. Under the *cost method,* the parent continues to carry its investment in a subsidiary at cost, records any dividends received as dividend revenue, and does not adjust the investment account to reflect the growth in the subsidiary's net assets resulting from retained earnings. Under the *equity method* (sometimes called the *accrual* method), the parent adds periodically to the investment account its share of the subsidiary's earnings (or deducts its share of any losses) and records the receipt of any dividends as a realization of some portion of the growth in the investment account, that is, as a reduction of the investment account balance. The following illustrations will demonstrate the appropriate consolidating procedures under each of the two methods of accounting for the investment in subsidiary on the parent's books.

Consolidation one year after acquisition

Assume that P Company acquired an 80% interest in S Company on January 1st, Year 1, at a cost of $48,000. At this date the book value of S Company's net assets was $75,000, but the directors of P Company estimated that patents carried by S Company at $30,000 were overvalued by $15,000. S Company had been amortizing these patents on a straight-line basis over a period which ended 5 years after the date of acquisition. During Year 1, S Company earned net income of $7,000 (after patent amortization of one-fifth of $30,000, or $6,000) and paid dividends at the end of Year 1 of $3,000.

Parent records investment at cost

Under the cost method the entries that would be made on P Company's books to record the transactions relating to the investment would be as follows:

Year 1			
Jan. 1	*Investment in S Company*	*48,000*	
	Cash		*48,000*
	To record purchase of 80% of S Company's outstanding capital stock at the beginning of Year 1.		
Dec. 31	*Cash*	*2,400*	
	Dividend Revenue		*2,400*
	To record receipt of dividends on S Company stock.		

Condensed income statements for Year 1 and balance sheets at the end of Year 1 for P and S Companies are shown at the top of page 276.

Consolidating working papers—cost basis

In preparing consolidated financial statements for P and S Companies one year after acquisition, working papers are a convenient device for scheduling the necessary consolidating adjustments and eliminations. Our objective is to arrive at data for a consolidated income statement, a consolidated balance sheet, and a

P AND S COMPANIES
Income Statements
Year 1

	P Company	S Company
Operating revenues (details not shown)	$ 96,000	$ 56,000
Dividend revenue	2,400	
Total revenues	$ 98,400	$ 56,000
Operating expenses (details not shown)	$ 68,400	$ 40,000
Patent amortization		6,000
Income taxes	9,000	3,000
Total expenses	$ 77,400	$ 49,000
Net income	$ 21,000	$ 7,000

P AND S COMPANIES
Balance Sheets
end of Year 1

	P Company	S Company
Assets:		
Various assets (details not shown)	$ 71,800	$70,000
Investment in S Company	48,000	
Patents		24,000
Total assets	$119,800	$94,000
Liabilities & Stockholders' Equity:		
Various liabilities (details not shown)	$ 22,000	$15,000
Capital stock	60,000	50,000
Retained earnings—Jan. 1	25,800	25,000
Net income	21,000	7,000
Dividends paid	(9,000)	(3,000)
Total liability & stockholders' equity	$119,800	$94,000

consolidated statement of retained earnings. We might accomplish this by starting with the ending trial balances of P and S Companies and developing in a single comprehensive working paper all three statements. It is often more convenient for analytical purposes, however, to prepare one working paper for the consolidated income statement, and a separate working paper for the consolidated balance sheet and statement of retained earnings. The reasons for this will become apparent as we proceed with the illustration.

Income statement working papers. The working paper for the consolidated income statement appears on page 278. A number of features of this working paper are worth noting. In order to avoid the necessity of having separate debit and credit columns, the various elements of net income are classified on the working paper in terms of their normal balance—credits first and debits below. This is a handy procedural device which reduces the number of columns required.

Note also that the income statement working paper is prepared in *balancing form;* that is, total debits are equal to total credits. This procedure is useful for a number of reasons which will be demonstrated in our discussion, but at the outset it requires that the student shift mental gears and think of the *net income* figure on the balancing income statement as a debit balance. Ordinary income statements do not balance; the net income figure is a residual credit balance which summarizes the effect of changes in net assets as a result of operations and is the link between the income statement and the balance sheet. The relationship between the trial balance, balance sheet, and income statement is reviewed in the following simplified schedule:

	Trial balance		*Balance sheet*		*Income statement*	
	Dr	*Cr*	*Dr*	*Cr*	*Dr*	*Cr*
Assets	1,000		1,000			
Liabilities		400		400		
Owners' equity—beginning		500		500		
Revenues		2,000				2,000
Expenses	1,900				1,900	
Net income				100	100	
Balancing totals	2,900	2,900	1,000	1,000	2,000	2,000

Now suppose we wish to deal procedurally with the income statement as a self-balancing statement. The net income figure of $100 appears as a balancing figure on the *debit* side, and must therefore be thought of *in the income statement* as a figure having a debit balance. To illustrate, assume that there is an error in the above figures: assets are overstated by $50 and revenues by $50. If we are analyzing data in working papers, each of these three kinds of financial summaries may be treated as a separate self-balancing statement; the working paper adjusting entry to correct this error would be as follows:

Item debited or credited	*Trial balance*		*Balance sheet*		*Income statement*	
	Dr	*Cr*	*Dr*	*Cr*	*Dr*	*Cr*
Revenues (debited)	50				50	
Net income (debited)			50			
Assets (credited)		50		50		
Net income (credited)						50

The effect of this simple adjustment is to *reduce* net income. On the self-balancing income statement, however, net income must be thought of as a debit balance and therefore a *credit* of $50 is necessary to reflect a *reduction* in the net income figure. Conversely if we were to make an income statement entry increasing revenues and net income, the *increase* in net income would be reflected in the income statement entry as a *debit*.[1]

The self-balancing idea is particularly useful in developing consolidating working papers because it enables the accountant to treat the net income figure of each company in the affiliation as a separate identifiable amount and to analyze the effect of any given adjusting or eliminating entry on the net income of the particular company involved.

P AND S COMPANIES
Consolidated Income Statements
Year 1

	P Company	S Company	Adjustments and eliminations		Consolidated income statement
			Dr	Cr	
Credits:					
Dividend revenues	2,400		(a) 2,400		
Other revenues	96,000	56,000			152,000
Totals	98,400	56,000			152,000
Debits:					
Patent amortization		6,000		(b) 3,000	3,000
All other expenses	68,400	40,000			108,400
Income taxes	9,000	3,000			12,000
Net income—P	21,000		(c) 8,000	(a) 2,400	26,600
Net income—S		7,000	(b) 3,000	(c) 10,000	
Minority interest in S income			(c) 2,000		2,000
Totals	98,400	56,000			152,000

(a) *To eliminate dividend revenues from the income of P Company. From a consolidated viewpoint this is a duplication, since these dividends were earned by S Company.*

(b) *To eliminate overstatement of patent amortization expense from income of S Company. Patents are overvalued from consolidated viewpoint.*

(c) *To close S Company's adjusted net income of $10,000, distributing parent company's share (80%) and share of minority interest (20%). As a result of this entry, the amount ($26,600) extended into the consolidated columns opposite the title, Net income—P, becomes the controlling interest in consolidated net income.*

We can now demonstrate the advantages of this procedure by considering the three eliminating entries on the working paper for the consolidated income statements of P and S Companies shown above. In entry (a) dividend revenues of P Company are eliminated from the revenue figure (by debiting revenues) and

[1] When the accountant records transactions and adjustments in the formal accounting records, his journal entries are made on a "trial balance" basis since he is dealing with the set of account balances summarized by the trial balance. In working paper analysis, however, he may find it convenient to deal with financial statements in self-balancing form even though, as shown on page 277, two working paper entries are required to schedule the effect of an adjustment that if recorded on the books would be more simply entered as a single entry. This is particularly true in consolidating working papers since most of the so-called adjusting and eliminating entries reflected in consolidated data are never made in a formal ledger of accounts.

from P's net income figure (by crediting net income) because these dividends are based on S Company's earnings which, from a consolidated viewpoint, will be included in the final consolidated net income figure. To allow the dividends received by P to be included in P's income and also reflected in S's income would result in double counting. Because we are dealing with a self-balancing income statement, we can incorporate in the entry its effect on the net income of P Company. If we had scheduled the income statements in the normal residual form, there would be no convenient way of showing which company's income was reduced by this eliminating entry.

In entry (b) the excess patent amortization cost is eliminated as an element of S Company's income; patents belonging to S Company are overvalued from a consolidated viewpoint. This entry corrects the expense account; the correction of S Company's assets will be taken care of on the balance sheet working papers illustrated later in this section.

The purpose of entry (c) is to distribute S Company's adjusted net income ($10,000) between the controlling and minority interests. The parent company's 80% share, or $8,000, is combined with P Company's adjusted net income of $18,600 ($21,000 – $2,400) to arrive at consolidated net income of $26,600. At the same time we isolate the 20% minority interest ($2,000) in S's adjusted income.

Note that S Company reported $7,000 net income on its books, but for consolidated purposes its net income is $10,000 because we have eliminated $3,000 of patent amortization expense as a result of the $15,000 overvaluation of patents on S's books. The effect for consolidation purposes is the same as if S Company had written down its patents by $15,000 on its own books as of the beginning of Year 1 and as a result had amortized only $3,000 rather than $6,000 of patent cost during the year. One may well argue that the patent valuation established from a consolidated viewpoint is valid and that S Company should, in fact, make this adjustment on its records. On the other hand, if S Company continues to record the patents at $30,000 and amortize them at the rate of $6,000 per year because, for example, it wishes to maintain its accounting records on a tax basis and would have difficulty in establishing the validity of an immediate $15,000 write-down for tax purposes, there is no reason why this consideration should be allowed to distort the consolidated financial statements.

The objection may be raised that minority stockholders may find their interest valued at a different amount on the individual financial statements of S Company than on consolidated financial statements. In our current example this will certainly be the case if the patent adjustment is made only on consolidated working papers. But we should remember that consolidated financial statements are prepared not to inform minority stockholders, but to inform the controlling interest (see discussion in Chapter 8). Minority stockholders should look to the statements of S Company as their primary source of financial information. The minority viewpoint should not be allowed to control accounting issues that arise in developing consolidated statements.

Balance sheet working papers. The working papers used in preparing a consolidated balance sheet for P and S Companies appear on page 280. The four adjusting and eliminating entries, (a) through (d), are explained at the bottom of the working papers. Note that entries (a), (b), and (c) are the balance sheet counterparts of the three entries already made on the income statement working papers on page 278.

In setting up balance sheet working papers it is desirable to schedule the stockholders' equity elements of each company on separate lines, since there will usually be a number of eliminating and adjusting entries affecting these accounts and it is important to maintain a clear distinction between the equity accounts of the parent and subsidiary company.

Another significant feature of these working papers is that all elements of the change in retained earnings during Year 1, for both P and S Companies, are listed

P AND S COMPANIES
Consolidated Balance Sheet
end of Year 1

	P Company	*S Company*	*Adjustments and eliminations*		*Consolidated balance sheet*
			Dr	*Cr*	
Assets:					
Investment in S—80%	48,000			(d) 48,000	
Other assets	71,800	70,000			141,800
Patents		24,000	(b) 3,000	(b) 15,000	12,000
Totals	119,800	94,000			153,800
Liabilities & Equity:					
Liabilities	22,000	15,000			37,000
Capital stock—P	60,000				60,000
Beginning retained earnings—P	25,800				25,800
Net income—P	21,000		(a) 2,400	(c) 8,000	26,600
Dividends—P	(9,000)				(9,000)
Capital stock—S		50,000	(d) 50,000		
Beginning retained earnings—S		25,000	(b) 15,000 (d) 10,000		
Net income—S		7,000	(c) 10,000	(b) 3,000	
Dividends—S		(3,000)		(a) 3,000	
Minority interest in S			(a) 600	(c) 2,000 (d) 12,000	13,400
Totals	119,800	94,000			153,800

(a) To eliminate dividends paid by S Company and P Company and record minority interest in S Company dividends.

(b) To write down patents by $15,000 as of the beginning of the year, and adjust Year 1 amortization downward by $3,000, thus increasing S Company income by $3,000.

(c) To close S Company's adjusted net income, distributing 80% to parent and 20% to minority interest.

(d) To eliminate the owners' equity of S Company as of the beginning of the year (date of acquisition) against P's investment account (80% of $60,000 = $48,000), and record minority interest as of the beginning of the year (20% of $60,000 = $12,000).

Book value of S Company net assets at beginning of year	$75,000
Less: Overvaluation of patents as of beginning of year (entry b)	15,000
Adjusted book value of S Company net assets at beginning of year	$60,000

separately. Note, for example, that the separate balances of beginning retained earnings, net income, and dividends for each company are set out on the working papers, rather than simply a single figure representing the ending retained earnings balance. There are several advantages in this technique: (1) We can eliminate the parent's investment account against the ownership equity balances *as of the beginning of the year* so that our eliminating entries are not complicated by this year's income statement adjustments, as shown by entry (d); (2) the entries on the balance sheet papers which are a counterpart of entries on the self-balancing income statement, entries (a), (b), and (c), can be readily distinguished, and the consolidated net income figure ($26,600) which is the link between the two sets of working papers can be readily verified; (3) all the amounts needed to prepare a statement of consolidated retained earnings for the year are developed in separately labeled items on the balance sheet working papers without the necessity of adding columns to the working papers.

A statement of consolidated (controlling interest) retained earnings for Year 1, for example, may be prepared simply by taking figures from the working papers as follows:

P AND S COMPANIES
Statement of Consolidated Retained Earnings
Year 1

Beginning balance of retained earnings	*$25,800*
Add: Consolidated net income	*26,600*
Less: Dividends	*(9,000)*
Ending balance of retained earnings	*$43,400*

Note that dividends from a consolidated viewpoint are limited to the $9,000 of parent company dividends. Any dividends paid by the subsidiary company either are a reduction of the minority interest [see, for example, the $600 debit to minority interest in entry (a)] or reflect a transfer of assets within the consolidated group based on earnings which are already included in the consolidated net income figure [see the $2,400 elimination from P's income in entry (a) on both the income statement and balance sheet working papers].

The total minority interest as of the end of Year 1 ($13,400) is accumulated as a separate item on the working papers. For consolidated statement purposes only the total ending balance has much significance, but if we wish we can explain its composition as the minority 20% share in the beginning stockholders' equity of S (20% of $60,000 = $12,000) plus the minority share in S's net income ($2,000), less the minority share in S's dividends ($600).

Parent records investment on equity (accrual) basis

If P Company, in the previous example, had used the equity (or accrual) method of accounting for its investment in S Company, the following entries would have been made on P's books during Year 1:

Year 1			
Jan. 1	*Investment in S Company*	*48,000*	
	Cash		*48,000*
	To record purchase of 80% of S Company's capital stock.		
Dec. 31	*Investment in S Company*	*5,600*	
	Investment Income—Earnings of Subsidiary		*5,600*
	To record the accrual of 80% of earnings reported by S Company for Year 1 (80% of $7,000).		
Dec. 31	*Cash*	*2,400*	
	Investment in S Company		*2,400*
	To record receipt of dividend from S Company (80% of $3,000).		

The individual financial statements for S Company at the end of Year 1 would be exactly the same as those illustrated on page 276. P Company would report net income of $24,200 for Year 1 instead of $21,000, as a result of the inclusion of $3,200 of accrued but undistributed earnings of S Company in its investment income account. On P's balance sheet the investment account would be carried at $51,200 rather than $48,000, and thus both total assets and stockholders' equity would be increased by $3,200 ($5,600 − $2,400).

The use of the equity method by P Company will have some effect on the details of the consolidating process and on the entries made in the consolidating working papers, but the resulting consolidated financial statements *will be exactly the same.* This is an important point; the choice between the cost or equity methods of accounting for investments will affect P's individual financial statements, but it will have no effect on the consolidated financial statements. Since P's share of S Company's earnings is included in the consolidated income statement and since any growth in S Company's net assets as a result of operations is incorporated in the consolidated balance sheet, the particular method used by the parent company in accounting for its investment in a subsidiary cannot change the consolidated results.

Equity method—consolidating net income. The working papers to consolidate the income statements of P and S Companies are shown on page 283. A comparison of this schedule with that on page 278 will show that the elements of consolidated net income are exactly the same after consolidated entries have been made. Some comment on the three eliminating entries is in order.

The purpose of entry (a) is to correct the patent amortization on S Company's books; this entry is not changed from the cost method illustration. Entry (b) eliminates the share of S's reported earnings that has been accrued by P Company on its books (80% of $7,000 = $5,600), to avoid double counting. In entry (c) the *adjusted* net income of S Company ($10,000) is allocated between the parent (80%) and minority (20%) interest. In effect we put back the $5,600 eliminated in entry (b) and also 80% of the $3,000 addition to S's net income as a result of the correction in entry (a). It would of course be possible to achieve the same results by combining entry (b) and (c) into the following entry:

Investment Income—Earnings of S Company	*5,600*	
Net Income—P Company	*2,400*	
Minority Interest in S Company Income	*2,000*	
Net Income—S Company		*10,000*

When the combined figures are extended into the consolidated income statement column, the figure opposite "Net income—P" ($26,600) will represent consolidated net income since it includes P's individual income plus P's share of the adjusted net income of the subsidiary.

P AND S COMPANIES
Consolidated Income Statement Working Papers
Year 1
(Assuming P Company records investment in S on the equity basis)

	P Company	*S Company*	*Adjustments and eliminations*		*Consolidated income statement*
			Dr	*Cr*	
Credits:					
Other revenues	*96,000*	*56,000*			*152,000*
Investment income—earnings of S Company	*5,600*		*(b) 5,600*		
Totals	*101,600*	*56,000*			*152,000*
Debits:					
Patent amortization		*6,000*		*(a) 3,000*	*3,000*
Other expenses	*68,400*	*40,000*			*108,400*
Income taxes	*9,000*	*3,000*			*12,000*
Net income—P	*24,200*		*(c) 8,000*	*(b) 5,600*	*26,600*
Net income—S		*7,000*	*(a) 3,000*	*(c) 10,000*	
Minority interest in S net income			*(c) 2,000*		*2,000*
Totals	*101,600*	*56,000*			*152,000*

(a) To correct S Company's patent amortization. Patent overvalued on balance sheet; amortization of revised valuation should be $3,000.
(b) To eliminate 80% of S Company's income already recorded by P Company, to avoid double counting.
(c) To allocate S Company's adjusted net income ($10,000) between the parent (80%) and minority (20%) interests.

Equity method—consolidating the balance sheet. The working papers used to develop consolidated balance sheet data for P and S Companies appear on page 284. The following comments apply to the adjusting and eliminating entries on these working papers:

S Company's patents were overvalued by $15,000 at the beginning of Year 1, the date of acquisition. By the end of Year 1, $3,000 of this overvaluation had been written off to expense. Therefore as of the end of Year 1, the asset account, Patents, is overstated by only $12,000. In entry (a) the asset is written down by $12,000, the retained earnings at the beginning of the year is reduced by $15,000 (the overvaluation at that date), and $3,000 is added to S's net income to adjust for the overstatement of patent amortization expense during Year 1. Since S Company's income is increased by $3,000 in entry (a), it is necessary to add 80% of this increase ($2,400) to P's investment account and P's net income in order to

P AND S COMPANIES
Consolidated Balance Sheet
December 31, Year 1
(Assuming P records investment in subsidiary on the equity basis)

	P Company	S Company	Adjustments and eliminations		Consolidated balance sheet
			Dr	Cr	
Assets:					
Investment in S—80%	51,200		(b) 2,400	(c) 53,600	
Other assets	71,800	70,000			141,800
Patents		24,000		(a) 12,000	12,000
Totals	123,000	94,000			153,800
Liabilities & Equity:					
Liabilities	22,000	15,000			37,000
Capital stock—P	60,000				60,000
Beginning retained earnings—P	25,800				25,800
Net income—P	24,200			(b) 2,400	26,600
Dividends—P	(9,000)				(9,000)
Capital stock—S		50,000	(c) 50,000		
Beginning retained earnings—S		25,000	(a) 15,000 (c) 10,000		
Net income—S		7,000	(c) 10,000	(a) 3,000	
Dividends—S		(3,000)		(c) 3,000	
Minority interest in S				(c) 13,400	13,400
Totals	123,000	94,000			153,800

(a) *To write down S's patents as of the end of Year 1, and S's beginning retained earnings. The difference of $3,000 represents the excess of patent amortization on S's books ($6,000) over the appropriate amortization on the basis of the revised valuation for patents ($3,000) and is a correction of S's net income.*
(b) *To correct P's investment and net income accounts for 80% of the $3,000 addition made to S's net income in entry (a). P's investment will now reflect the change in S's stockholders' equity during Year 1, as adjusted.*
(c) *To eliminate S's stockholders' equity as of the end of Year 1, as follows:*

Capital stock	$50,000		
Retained earnings, beginning of Year 1	10,000	*P's share (80%)*	$53,600
Net income (as adjusted)	10,000	*Minority interest 20%*	13,400
Less: Dividends	(3,000)		
	$67,000		$67,000

bring P Company's investment records up to date with respect to P's share of the growth in S Company's net assets as a result of operations during Year 1. This is done in entry (b), which in effect puts P Company's statements on an adjusted equity basis consistent with the new valuation assigned to S Company's net assets.

It is now possible to eliminate P's investment account (stated on an adjusted equity basis) against the owners' equity accounts of S Company *as of the end of Year 1*. When P Company recorded its investment on a cost basis, it was convenient to make the elimination of the investment on the working papers as of the beginning of the year. However when P Company accounts for its investment on an equity basis, thus including in the investment account its share of S Company's profits and dividends for the current year, it is easier to make the elimination as of the end of the year in order to avoid having to restate P's investment account to a beginning of the year balance. The following schedule demonstrates the relationship between P's investment account and the book value of S's net assets:

		Total for S Company	*P Company's 80% interest*	*Minority 20% interest*
Capital stock		*$50,000*	*$40,000*	*$10,000*
Retained earnings at date P acquired its investment		*25,000*	*20,000*	*5,000*
Less: Write-down of patents		*(15,000)*	*(12,000)*	*(3,000)*
Owners' equity at date of acquisition (beginning of Year 1)		*$60,000*	*$48,000**	*$12,000*
Add: Net income	*$7,000*			
Less: Dividends	*(3,000)*	*4,000*	*3,200*	*800*
Owners' equity at end of Year 1		*$64,000*	*$51,200†*	*$12,800*
Adjustment increasing S's net income for Year 1		*3,000*	*2,400‡*	*600*
Owners' equity (adjusted) at date of consolidation		*$67,000*	*$53,600*	*$13,400*

* *Price paid by P for its 80% interest in S Company.*
† *Balance in Investment account on P's books at the end of Year 1.*
‡ *Working paper entry (b) increasing P's investment account by its share (80%) of the $3,000 addition to S Company's net income as a result of the reduction in patent amortization expense.*

The above schedule shows that the $13,400 minority interest that will appear on the consolidated balance sheet is equal to 20% of the stockholders' equity of S Company after all consolidating adjustments have been made.

Consolidated financial statements

The three major consolidated financial statements—the balance sheet, income statement, and statement of retained earnings—may now be prepared from the two sets of consolidating working papers just illustrated. These statements (in condensed form) are shown on the following page. Remember that these statements will be exactly the same whether P Company has accounted for its investment in S Company on the cost or on the equity method.

P AND S COMPANIES
Consolidated Balance Sheet
as of December 31, Year 1

Assets		
Various combined assets of parent and subsidiary (details omitted)		$141,800
Patents (net of amortization)		12,000
Total assets		$153,800
Liabilities & Stockholders' Equity		
Combined liabilities of parent and subsidiary (details omitted)		$ 37,000
Stockholders' equity:		
Capital stock, $100 par value, 6,000 shares issued and outstanding	$60,000	
Retained earnings (see statement)	43,400	103,400
Minority interest in S Company		13,400
Total liabilities & stockholders' equity		$153,800

P AND S COMPANIES
Consolidated Income Statement
Year 1

Combined revenues (details omitted)		$152,000
Operating expenses:		
Combined expenses of parent and subsidiary (details omitted)	$108,400	
Patent amortization	3,000	111,400
Net income before income taxes		$ 40,600
Less: Provision for income taxes		12,000
Net income after taxes (consolidated entity)		$ 28,600
Less: Minority interest in net income		2,000
Net income added to retained earnings (controlling interest)		$ 26,600

P AND S COMPANIES
Statement of Consolidated Retained Earnings
Year 1

Retained earnings, Jan. 1, Year 1	$ 25,800
Add: Consolidated net income	26,600
	$ 52,400
Less: Dividends declared or paid	9,000
Retained earnings, Dec. 31, Year 1	$ 43,400

In these statements, and in the working papers on which they are based, we have shown only the amount of detail necessary to make the consolidating process clear. It has not been necessary to consider the details of the asset and liability accounts of the two companies. In later chapters as additional features are introduced we shall expand the list of balance sheet and income statement accounts to show in greater detail the composition of assets, liabilities, revenues, and expenses.

One point in connection with the consolidated income statement on page 286 requires comment. The net income transferred to consolidated retained earnings is $26,600. Net income from the viewpoint of the consolidated entity, however, is $28,600, since this is the increase during the period in the total ownership equity interest in consolidated net assets. In theory we should report consolidated net income of $28,600 and then show that this income is allocated between the controlling ($26,600) and minority ($2,000) interests. If we are interested in the rate of income per dollar of sales or in the rate of return on the total assets or net assets of the consolidated entity, the $28,600 income figure is clearly the appropriate amount to use. In published consolidated statements the minority interest in income is usually deducted on the income statement to arrive at a final figure, labeled "consolidated net income," which in reality is simply the controlling interest in consolidated income. The net income attributed to the minority interest is thus excluded in arriving at the net income applicable to the controlling interest in the consolidated entity. Since the minority interest in consolidated net assets is shown as a single figure on the balance sheet and since the statement of consolidated retained earnings is normally limited to the controlling interest in retained earnings of the consolidated entity, the procedure labeling the controlling interest in net income as consolidated net income may be justified as a means of showing clearly the link between the income statement and the statement of changes in retained earnings. The accountant should be aware of the theoretical inconsistency involved, however, particularly when the minority interest in net income is a significantly large amount.

Consolidation more than one period after acquisition

The procedures and reasoning involved in preparing consolidated statements two or more periods after acquisition are simply an extension of the case illustrated above for the first year after acquisition. In order to lay the foundation for the discussion in the next chapter, however, a consideration at this point of the consolidating procedures in a very simple case is worthwhile. Once more we shall condense the details of assets and liabilities in order to focus attention only on the elements of the financial statements that are pertinent to the consolidating process at this stage of our discussion.

Illustration

The data on which the illustration is based are shown on page 288. We shall assume that P Company acquired its interest in S Company at the beginning of Year 1, and that the problem is to prepare consolidated financial statements as of the end of Year 4. Since we are interested in noting how the procedures vary depending on whether P Company has used the cost or the equity method of recording its investment, Year 4 financial statements for P Company under both assumptions are given. Balance sheet information at date of acquisition (beginning of Year 1) is given for S Company as well as the data for Year 4 in order to show clearly the subsidiary's position at the time P Company's investment was originally made.

P AND S COMPANIES—DATA FOR ILLUSTRATION

	P Company—Year 4		*S Company*	
	Cost basis	*Equity basis*	*At acquisition*	*Year 4*
Balance sheet data (end of Year 4):				
Assets:				
Investment in S—70%	$ 39,200	$ 54,950		
Other assets	117,800	117,800	$64,000	$94,500
Total	$157,000	$172,750	$64,000	$94,500
Liabilities & Equity:				
Liabilities	$ 27,000	$ 27,000	$14,000	$22,000
Capital stock	75,000	75,000	30,000	30,000
Additional paid-in capital	25,000	25,000	12,000	12,000
Retained earnings:				
Beginning of Year 1			8,000	
Beginning of Year 4	26,000	37,900		25,000
Income—Year 4	15,000	18,850		9,000
Dividends—Year 4	(11,000)	(11,000)		(3,500)
Total	$157,000	$172,750	$64,000	$94,500
Income statement data (Year 4):				
Revenues	$150,000	$150,000		$80,000
Income from subsidiary:				
Dividends	2,450			
Share of earnings		6,300		
Total revenues	$152,450	$156,300		$80,000
Operating expenses	$130,950	$130,950		$67,000
Income taxes	6,500	6,500		4,000
Total expenses	$137,450	$137,450		$71,000
Net income	$ 15,000	$ 18,850		$ 9,000

Let us look first at some pertinent data relating to our consolidating problem that can be gleaned from an analysis of the statements of P Company and S Company:

		P's investment		70% of book value of S Company's owners' equity	Excess of P's cost over book value
		Equity basis	Cost basis		
At date of acquisition (beginning of Year 1)		$39,200	$39,200	$35,000	$4,200
70% of growth in S Company from beginning of Year 1 to beginning of Year 4:					
Net assets of S, beginning of Year 4.....	$67,000				
Net assets of S, beginning of Year 1.....	50,000				
Increase	$17,000	11,900		11,900	
Growth in S Company during Year 4 (income minus dividends)	$ 5,500	3,850		3,850	
Balances at end of Year 4		$54,950	$39,200	$50,750	$4,200

S Company's Net Assets Represented by

Capital stock....................................	$30,000
Additional paid-in capital..........................	12,000
Retained earnings—beginning of Year 4...............	25,000
Year 4 net income..................................	9,000
Dividends (Year 4).................................	(3,500)
Total ownership equity of S Company...............	$72,500
P Company's share—70%........................	$50,750

This analysis shows that there is a $4,200 discrepancy between the amount P Company paid for its 70% interest in S ($39,200) and 70% of the book value of S's net assets at date of acquisition ($35,000). If P Company follows the equity method of accounting for its investment, the balance of the investment account on P's books and the book value of S's net assets move in tandem, and the difference between the investment balance at the end of Year 4 ($54,950) and 70% of S Company's stockholders' equity ($50,750) is still $4,200. If P Company follows the cost method, however, we must compare investment cost and book value *at date of acquisition* to isolate the $4,200 excess of cost over book value.

We shall assume that this $4,200 excess is accounted for by the existence of unrecorded goodwill in S Company of $6,000 at the beginning of Year 1. In other words, the evidence that 70% of S Company is worth $4,200 more than book value implies that 100% of S Company is worth $6,000 ($4,200/.70) more than the book value of S's net assets. We shall also assume that on consolidated statements it is reasonable to amortize the $6,000 of S Company's unrecorded goodwill on a straight-line basis over a 10-year period after date of acquisition. This means that $1,800 ($600 × 3) of goodwill has been amortized up to the beginning of Year 4, and $600 should be amortized during the current year on consolidated working papers.

Consolidated working papers—cost basis

The procedures illustrated in the consolidating working papers shown below are similar to those in the illustration at the beginning of this chapter. In practice we would have the consolidated statements for Years 1, 2, and 3 for reference in preparing statements for Year 4. For purposes of this discussion, however, we shall have to consider the events of the entire four-year period and in some cases reconstruct consolidated information as of the beginning of Year 4.

Income statement working papers. The working papers to consolidate the Year 4 income statements of P and S Companies are shown below. Three elimination entries are required. Entry (a) is necessary to eliminate the duplication of income represented by dividends received by P from S during Year 4. Entry (b) reflects the amortization of one-tenth of the $6,000 of S Company goodwill established from the consolidated viewpoint on the basis of the price paid by P Company for its investment in S. S Company's income is reduced and $600 of goodwill amortization appears as an expense on the consolidated income statement.

P AND S COMPANIES
Consolidated Income Statement
Year 4
(Assuming P carries investment in subsidiary on the cost basis)

	P Company	*S Company*	*Adjustments and eliminations*		*Consolidated income statement*
			Dr	*Cr*	
Credits:					
Revenues	150,000	80,000			230,000
Dividend revenues	2,450		(a) 2,450		
Totals	152,450	80,000			230,000
Debits:					
Operating expenses	130,950	67,000			197,950
Goodwill amortization			(b) 600		600
Income taxes	6,500	4,000			10,500
Net income—P	15,000		(c) 5,880	(a) 2,450	18,430
Net income—S		9,000		(b) 600 (c) 8,400	
Minority interest in S Company's income			(c) 2,520		2,520
Totals	152,450	80,000			230,000

(a) *To eliminate P's share of dividends declared by S Company.*
(b) *To record Year 4's amortization of $6,000 S Company's goodwill recognized in consolidation.*
(c) *To close S Company's net income (as adjusted), allocating 70% to parent and 30% to minority interest.*

The adjusted income of S Company ($9,000 − $600 = $8,400) is allocated between the controlling and minority interests in entry (c). The controlling interest in consolidated net income is thus $18,430, which may be analyzed as follows:

P Company's reported net income	*$15,000*
Less: Intercompany dividends	*(2,450)*
P's income other than dividends from S	*$12,550*
Add: P's share (70%) of S's adjusted net income (70% of $8,400)	*5,880*
Controlling interest in consolidated net income	*$18,430*

Balance sheet working papers. The working papers to consolidate the balance sheets of P and S Companies appear on page 292. The following explanatory comments relate to items on the working papers:

Entry (a). The purpose of this entry is to recognize S Company's unrecorded goodwill as of the date of acquisition. The computation of the $6,000 goodwill figure was discussed on pages 289 and 290.

Entry (b). This entry is to record the amortization of the $6,000 goodwill of S Company for the four years since acquisition. Goodwill is to be amortized at the rate of $600 per year for 10 years. Amortization for the first three years ($600 × 3 = $1,800) is charged against S Company's beginning retained earnings, since the three-year write-off for consolidated purposes will have reduced retained earnings attributable to S Company by this amount. Amortization of $600 for Year 4 is charged against net income, as a counterpart of entry (a) appearing on the consolidated income statement working papers. Goodwill is reduced by the total four-year amortization of $2,400.

Entry (c). When the parent company carries its investment at cost, it is convenient to determine the subsidiary's ownership equity *as of the beginning* of the year under consideration, adjust the investment account to the accrual basis as of this date, and make the elimination of P's investment against S's ownership equity as of the beginning of the current year. By following this procedure we can readily and clearly develop on our working papers the amount of the beginning consolidated retained earnings, and the consolidated net income, each of which is needed for the retained earnings statement.

We have already recorded S Company's goodwill, thus bringing the book value of S Company into agreement with the investment account as of date of acquisition. The only remaining difference between P's investment account balance and 70% of S Company's net assets (or stockholders' equity) is the growth in retained earnings since acquisition. This growth may be computed as follows:

S Company's retained earnings (per books) at the beginning of Year 4	*$25,000*	
Adjustment (b) recording goodwill amortization	*(1,800)*	*$23,200*
S Company's retained earnings (per books) at the date of acquisition (beginning of Year 1)		*8,000*
Growth in S Company's retained earnings from Year 1 to the beginning of Year 4		*$15,200*
P Company's share of this growth (70% of $15,200)		*$10,640*

In determining the change in S Company's retained earnings from date of acquisition to the beginning of the current year, it is necessary to include any adjustments of S Company's earnings during this period that are made in the consolidating process. S Company's cumulative reported net income less dividends will automatically be included in its retained earnings balance at the beginning

P AND S COMPANIES
Consolidated Balance Sheet
end of Year 4
(Assuming parent maintains investment account on the cost basis)

	P Company	S Company	Eliminations and adjustments Dr	Eliminations and adjustments Cr	Consolidated balance sheet
Assets:					
Investment in S—70%	39,200		(c) 10,640	(d) 49,840	
Goodwill—S			(a) 6,000	(b) 2,400	3,600
Other assets	117,800	94,500			212,300
Totals	157,000	94,500			215,900
Liabilities & Equity:					
Liabilities	27,000	22,000			49,000
Capital stock—P	75,000				75,000
Additional paid-in capital—P	25,000				25,000
Retained earnings—P	26,000			(c) 10,640	36,640
Net income—P	15,000		(f) 2,450	(e) 5,880	18,430
Dividends—P	(11,000)				(11,000)
Capital stock—S		30,000	(d) 30,000		
Additional paid-in capital—S		12,000	(d) 12,000		
Beginning retained earnings—S		25,000	(b) 1,800 (d) 23,200		
Appraisal capital—S			(d) 6,000	(a) 6,000	
Net income—S		9,000	(b) 600 (e) 8,400		
Dividends—S		(3,500)		(f) 3,500	
Minority interest—S			(f) 1,050	(d) 21,360 (e) 2,520	22,830
Totals	157,000	94,500			215,900

(a) To record S Company's goodwill as evidenced by price paid by P Company for 70% interest.
(b) Amortization of goodwill for four years at rate of 10% per year.
(c) To record P's share of the growth in S Company's retained earnings, as adjusted by (b), from Year 0 to beginning of Year 4.
(d) To eliminate P's investment against S Company's ownership equity as of the beginning of Year 4.
(e) To close S Company's net income (as adjusted), allocating 70% to P and 30% to minority interest.
(f) To close S Company's dividends, allocating 70% to P and 30% to minority interest.

of the current year, but any adjustments (such as goodwill amortization in this example) that are made in the consolidating process and appear only on the periodic consolidating working papers must be taken into account in deriving the changes that have taken place since acquisition.

Note that the growth in S Company's net assets resulting from the valuation of goodwill *does not* constitute growth *since date of acquisition.* This is a consolidating adjustment to revalue S's net assets to an amount consistent with the cost of P's investment in S Company stock. Thus any revaluation of a subsidiary's net assets made at the date of acquisition should be ignored in determining changes that have taken place since acquisition.

Entry (d). The effect of entries (a) and (c) is to restate the balance in P's investment account to an amount that is 70% of the adjusted ownership equity of S Company as of the beginning of Year 4. Entry (d) then serves to eliminate 100% of S's ownership equity accounts against P's investment account (70%) and to establish the residual 30% as the minority interest in S Company. The following schedule shows the effect:

	S Company's ownership equity	*Allocation between controlling and minority interests*	
Accounts:			
Capital stock	*$30,000*		
Additional paid-in capital	*12,000*	*P Company's share, 70% of $71,200*	*$49,840*
Retained earnings at beginning of Year 4 (adjusted)	*23,200*	*Minority interest, 30% of $71,200*	*21,360*
Appraisal capital	*6,000*		
Owners' equity at beginning of Year 4	*$71,200*		*$71,200*

Entries (e) and (f). The remaining two eliminating entries are counterparts of entries appearing on the income statement working papers. Their purpose is to allocate S Company's net income and dividends among controlling and minority interests. When this has been done the figure opposite the caption "Net income—P" becomes the controlling interest in consolidated net income ($18,430), which agrees with the amount shown on the consolidated income statement. The ending minority interest of $22,830 is derived from the interest at the beginning of Year 4 ($21,360) plus the minority share of S's income ($2,520), less the minority share of S's dividends ($1,050).

The preparation of consolidated financial statements from these working papers is straightforward and therefore need not be illustrated. The statement of consolidated retained earnings for Year 4 would be as shown at the top of the next page:

P AND S COMPANIES
Consolidated Retained Earnings
Year 4

Retained earnings—Jan. 1, Year 4	*$36,640*
Add: Consolidated net income (controlling interest)	*18,430*
	$55,070
Less: Dividends	*11,000*
Retained earnings, Dec. 31, Year 4	*$44,070*

Consolidating working papers—equity basis

As previously noted, the consolidated financial statements will be the same whether P Company uses the cost or the equity basis. Some modifications in working paper procedures are necessary if the equity method has been used, since in this case P Company will have accrued (both in its asset and income accounts) 70% of S Company's reported net income during the four-year period since the date of acquisition. The consolidating working papers for P and S Company,

P AND S COMPANIES—Working Papers
Consolidated Income Statement
Year 4
(Assuming P carries investment in subsidiary on an equity basis)

	P Company	S Company	Adjustments and eliminations		Consolidated income statement*
			Dr	Cr	
Credits:					
Revenues	150,000	80,000			230,000
Share of subsidiary earnings	6,300		(a) 6,300		
Totals	156,300	80,000			230,000
Debits:					
Operating expenses	130,950	67,000			197,950
Goodwill amortization			(b) 600		600
Income taxes	6,500	4,000			10,500
Net income—P	18,850		(c) 5,880	(a) 6,300	18,430
Net income—S		9,000		(b) 600 (c) 8,400	
Minority interest in S Company net income			(c) 2,520		2,520
Totals	156,300	80,000			230,000

(a) *To eliminate P's share of S Company's earnings from P's net income to avoid duplication.*
(b) *To record amortization of S Company goodwill recorded as a consolidating adjustment.*
(c) *To allocate S Company net income (as adjusted) to parent company (70%) and minority interest (30%).*

* *Note that the figures in this column are identical to those appearing in the illustration of the cost method on page 290.*

P AND S COMPANIES
Consolidated Balance Sheet
as of end of Year 4
(Assuming parent has maintained its investment account on the equity basis)

	P Company	S Company	Adjustments and eliminations Dr	Cr	Consolidated balance sheet*
Assets:					
Investment in S—70%	54,950			(c) 1,680 (d) 53,270	
Other assets	117,800	94,500			212,300
Goodwill—S			(a) 6,000	(b) 2,400	3,600
Totals	172,750	94,500			215,900
Liabilities & Equity:					
Liabilities	27,000	22,000			49,000
Capital stock—P	75,000				75,000
Additional paid-in capital—P	25,000				25,000
Beginning retained earnings—P	37,900		(c) 1,260		36,640
Net income—P	18,850		(c) 420		18,430
Dividends—P	(11,000)				(11,000)
Capital stock—S		30,000	(d) 30,000		
Additional paid-in capital—S		12,000	(d) 12,000		
Beginning retained earnings—S		25,000	(b) 1,800 (d) 23,200		
Appraisal capital			(d) 6,000	(a) 6,000	
Net income—S		9,000	(b) 600 (d) 8,400		
Dividends—S		(3,500)		(d) 3,500	
Minority interest—S				(d) 22,830	22,830
Totals	172,750	94,500			215,900

(a) To record S Company's goodwill at time of acquisition as evidenced by price paid by P Company for a 70% investment.
(b) Amortization of goodwill at 10% per year for four years (Year 0 to Year 4).
(c) To adjust P's investment and income for P's share (70%) of the amortization of S Company goodwill.
(d) To eliminate P's investment account against the ownership equity of S Company as of the end of Year 4. (See explanation on page 296.)
** Note that the figures in this column are identical to those in the illustration of the cost method on page 292.*

assuming that P Company has maintained its investment account on an equity basis are illustrated on page 294 and above.

Income statement working papers (page 294). Since P Company has picked up as an element of its income $6,300, or 70% of the $9,000 income reported by S Company, we need only consider the effect of any consolidating adjustment to S's income. In this illustration there is a consolidating adjustment to write off $600 of S Company's goodwill, which reduces S's income from $9,000 to $8,400, as shown in entry (b). On the working papers in entry (a), we have first eliminated the income already picked up by P Company and then in entry (c) allocated the adjusted income of S Company between the majority (70% of $8,400 = $5,880) and the minority (30% of $8,400 = $2,520) interests. Other possible working paper entries are equally satisfactory so long as they accomplish the same results.

Balance sheet working papers (page 295). Entries (a) and (b) on the balance sheet working papers are identical to those illustrated for the cost method. The purpose of entry (c) is to correct P Company's records to reflect the amortization of S Company goodwill at the rate of $600 per year for four years. From a consolidated viewpoint, this amortization reduces S Company's reported income during the four-year period by $2,400, and P Company's share of this reduction is 70%, or $1,680. Of this amount three-fourths, or $1,260, is applicable to P's beginning retained earnings and one-fourth, or $420, is applicable to Year 4 income.

Entry (d) reflects another difference in the consolidating working papers when P uses the equity method. This entry is designed to eliminate P's investment account against S's ownership equity and establish the amount of minority interest in S *as of the end of Year 4* rather than as of the beginning of the year as was done in the illustration of the cost method. The end-of-the-year approach is appropriate in this case because P's investment account, beginning retained earnings, and reported net income already include the controlling interest in S Company's reported growth through earnings since date of acquisition. The necessary adjustment of this growth to reflect the amortization of goodwill from a consolidated viewpoint was made in entry (c). Therefore, if we eliminate the investment and ownership equity accounts as of the end of the year, we shall not affect the computation of consolidated net income and consolidated beginning retained earnings. Thus the factors which made it desirable to eliminate the investment account as of the beginning of the year in the cost-method illustration are not present in the equity-method situation. The basis for eliminating entry (d) on the working papers on page 295 is demonstrated below:

		Owners' equity of S Company	*Allocation between controlling and minority interests*	
Accounts:				
Capital stock		*$30,000*		
Additional paid-in capital		*12,000*		
Beginning retained earnings:			*P Company's*	
Per S Company books	*$25,000*		*share, 70%*	
Adjustment (goodwill amortization)	*1,800*	*23,200*	*of $76,100*	*$53,270*
Net income:			*Minority*	
As reported by S Company	*$ 9,000*		*interest, 30%*	
Goodwill amortization adjustment	*600*	*8,400*	*of $76,100*	*22,830*
Appraisal capital		*6,000*		
Dividends		*(3,500)*		
S Company's ownership equity (as adjusted) at the end of Year 4		*$76,100*		*$76,100*

Evaluation of cost and equity methods

We have noted that a parent company may carry its investment in a subsidiary company on either the cost or equity method. With respect to the consolidating process we have demonstrated (1) that some procedural differences are involved in consolidating financial data depending on whether the parent company uses the cost or equity method; (2) that the parent's choice between the cost and equity methods of recording its investment in consolidated subsidiaries has no affect on the resulting consolidated financial statements.

The choice between the cost or equity methods will, however, affect the *parent company* statements one or more periods after date of acquisition. More important, if a parent company has an investment in unconsolidated subsidiaries, this investment will appear on consolidated statements as an asset valued on either a cost or an equity basis and the choice of method will in this situation affect consolidated statements. An evaluation of the cost and equity methods therefore must be made from the viewpoint of the parent's statements standing alone, or in the light of the resulting effect on consolidated statements when unconsolidated subsidiaries are present.

In published financial statements, the investment in unconsolidated subsidiaries is usually shown at cost, and the equity of the parent in the net assets and current earnings of the subsidiary is disclosed in supplementary statements or notes to the financial statements.[2]

The objections to the use of the equity method and answering arguments are summarized below:

Objection: The equity method represents a departure from the accountant's concept of realization. Income of a subsidiary is not realized by the parent until there has been a transfer of liquid assets (that is, dividends declared or paid).

Answer: An exchange of liquid assets is not the only acceptable evidence of realization. The change in the net assets of a subsidiary as a result of operations is based on evidence equally as good as that used to establish the realized growth of net assets which produces the income of the parent. Since the parent has a controlling interest in the subsidiary, there is no question of ultimate control over the increase in net assets; therefore, recognition on the parent's books of its share of any undistributed income of the subsidiary is warranted.

Objection: Recognizing the earnings of a subsidiary as a part of the earnings of the parent is based on an economic view which is the reason for the preparation of consolidated statements. Separate statements prepared from a legal entity viewpoint should not reflect an economic entity viewpoint.

Answer: In statements prepared from the legal entity viewpoint, the issue of proper asset valuation is still present. The original cost of an investment in an unconsolidated subsidiary becomes an outdated historical figure as time passes and the subsidiary grows through the retention of earnings. Since the accountant has objective evidence (in the sub-

[2] AICPA, *Survey of Consolidated Financial Statement Practices* (New York: 1956), p. 16.

sidiaries' financial statements) of the amount of this growth, he should use this information to update the valuation of the investment.

Objection: The valuation of an investment in a subsidiary when it is accounted for on an equity basis is a hodgepodge—neither original cost nor current value. Any difference between cost and the book value of the subsidiary's net assets at date of acquisition remains, and the equity basis valuation of cost plus or minus changes in the underlying book value of subsidiary net assets defies interpretation.

Answer: The price paid by the parent for its investment is more likely to reflect current value at that time than the book value of the parent's equity in the subsidiary. Thus the equity method begins with a valid basis of valuation and this valuation is then adjusted for changes which can be objectively measured on the basis of the same accounting concepts as used by the parent.

As with many difficult issues, there is merit in the arguments on both sides. On balance, however, the case for the use of the equity method in reporting an investment in unconsolidated subsidiaries is a convincing one. On this subject one authority writes:

> The fundamental point at issue is the problem of the proper timing and amount of income accruing to a parent from its investment in affiliates. The contention here is that income accrues when the investment increases in value; the investment increases in value when the equities they represent grow; the equities of which they are a reflection grow when *bona fide* increases in subsidiaries' proprietary equities occur.[3]

The Committee on Accounting Procedure of the AICPA takes the position that the equity method is preferable in reporting unconsolidated subsidiaries on financial statements. They accept, however, the alternative cost method provided there is a full disclosure of the equity in the net assets of unconsolidated subsidiaries, dividends received during the current period, and the equity of the controlling interest in the current year's earnings.[4]

Who should use consolidated financial statements?

We have now examined the consolidating process in sufficient detail to consider the groups or interests to whom consolidated financial statements will prove useful. We have previously noted that consolidated statements are auxiliary to the legal statements of the individual companies in an affiliated group. We may conclude, therefore, that parties looking to their *legal* rights will not find them revealed in consolidated financial statements. This general principle provides the means for classifying the appropriate users and nonusers of consolidated data in the following way:

[3] Maurice Moonitz, *The Entity Theory of Consolidated Statements,* The American Accounting Association (Madison: 1944), p. 59.
[4] AICPA, *Accounting Research and Terminology Bulletins, Final Edition,* Research Bulletin No. 51 (New York: 1961), pp. 46–47.

Groups primarily concerned with consolidated statements	*Groups that will probably not find consolidated statements useful*
Management of the parent company	Creditors of subsidiary companies
Stockholders of the parent company	Minority stockholders of subsidiary companies
	Creditors of the parent company

Nonusers. Minority stockholders have no interest in consolidated statements because their equity interests do not run beyond the legal boundaries of the subsidiary company whose stock they own. It is assumed that creditors in general will not find consolidated statements of primary usefulness because they must look to the net assets and operating results of the company which assumes legal responsibility for the debt. Creditors of a subsidiary obviously have no claim against net assets of the parent company, unless there is an intercompany guarantee of the debts of the subsidiary by the parent. Long-term creditors of the parent company may have some interest in consolidated statements since the success of the consolidated group as a whole may ultimately affect the long-range debt-paying ability of the dominant company. If creditors of the parent should be forced to exercise their legal rights in a time of financial difficulty, however, their claim cannot be exercised against the underlying net assets of the subsidiary companies in the affiliation. Therefore the parent's *individual* statements are of primary interest to its creditors.

Users. For management and stockholders of the dominant company, consolidated statements overshadow in importance the individual statements of the dominant company. This conclusion is supported by the fact that the vast majority of published annual reports contain only consolidated financial statements. Management's interest stems from its responsibility to direct the day-to-day operations of the consolidated economic entity. Stockholders of the dominant company see in consolidated statements an overview of the entire scope of their investment. Obviously consolidated statements are not primary in such narrow issues as the maximum legal dividends that may be declared by the parent company, but for most going concerns the declaration of dividends depends more on economic results and discretion of the board of directors than on bare legal rights. Over the long run it is likely that the value of the stock in the dominant company and the dividend policy of its directors will be governed by the economic progress of the affiliated group, and the clearest picture of the resources controlled by the dominant group and the earnings performance attained through their use is contained in the consolidated financial statements.

Questions

1. A parent company owns 80% of the common stock of a subsidiary and carries its investment at cost. Six years after date of acquisition, the book value of this 80% interest is $500,000 larger than original cost. Explain the possible sources of this difference.

2. Explain the difference between the cost and accrual (or equity) method of accounting for an investment in a subsidiary.

3. P Company owns 70% of the common stock of a subsidiary, purchased at a cost of $700,000. Subsequent to the date of acquisition, the subsidiary earned $300,000 and paid $180,000 in dividends. What will be the differences in the balances of the asset, liability, and ownership equity accounts on the parent company's books if the parent accounts for this investment on the accrual (equity) basis rather than the cost basis?

4. On a balancing consolidated net income working paper, the following entry appears in the adjusting and eliminating columns:

Net Income—Parent	*75,000*	
Minority Interest—Subsidiary	*25,000*	
Net Income—Subsidiary		*100,000*

Explain the nature and purpose of the entry and the reason for each of the debit and credit items.

5. It is possible that the minority interest appearing on a consolidated balance sheet may be larger or smaller than the minority interest in the net assets of the subsidiary as shown at book value on the individual balance sheet of the subsidiary company. Explain why this is true, and give an example which illustrates such a situation.

6. In working papers for a consolidated balance sheet, it is usually desirable to eliminate the parent's investment account against the appropriate ownership equity accounts of the subsidiary as of the *beginning* of the current accounting period. Explain the advantages of this procedure.

7. A parent company owns an 80% interest in a subsidiary. Subsequent to the date of acquisition, the subsidiary reported earnings of $250,000 and dividends on common stock of $400,000. What would be the difference in the parent's investment account if the parent accounted for its investment on an accrual (equity) basis rather than the cost basis?

8. The following entry appears in the adjusting and eliminating columns of a balancing consolidated net income working paper:

Dividend Revenues from Subsidiary.........	*20,000*	
Net Income—Parent		*20,000*

Explain the nature and purpose of this entry. What is the counterpart of this entry on the balance sheet working papers?

9. If a parent company uses the accrual (equity) method of accounting for its investment in a subsidiary, rather than the cost method, what effect will this have on the consolidated financial statements? Why?

10. Net income, from the viewpoint of a consolidated entity, is usually larger than the figure that is labeled ''consolidated net income'' and transferred to consolidated retained earnings. Explain the nature of this difference and the reason for it. Which net income figure would be more relevant in computing return on investment for the consolidated entity? Why?

11. Of the various groups having an interest in financial statements: management, stockholders, creditors, and the public, which will find consolidated financial statements most useful? Explain.

Short cases for analysis

9-1 The ownership equity of a parent company and its 90% owned subsidiary at the beginning of Year 1 is shown below:

	Parent Co.	*Subsidiary Co.*
Capital stock, $100 par value	*$ 600,000*	*$400,000*
Additional paid-in capital	*700,000*	*180,000*
Retained earnings	*40,000*	*120,000*
Total ownership equity	*$1,340,000*	*$700,000*

Parent Company acquired 90% of the stock of Subsidiary Company at the beginning of Year 1 for $650,000. During the next two years the subsidiary's earnings and dividends were as follows:

	Year 1	*Year 2*
Net income (loss)	*70,000*	*(90,000)*
Dividends	*40,000*	*40,000*

The parent company's accountant recorded dividend revenues of $36,000 (90% of $40,000) in each of the two years, and on consolidated balance sheets reported $20,000 as the excess of the cost of the parent's investment in its subsidiary over book value. In connection with the Year 2 audit, the auditor of the parent company objected to this treatment. He argued that the subsidiary Year 2 loss of $90,000 plus the $80,000 of dividends paid in Years 1 and 2 had impaired the investment of the parent by $90,000, or 90% of the reduction in the subsidiary's retained earnings since date of acquisition. The parent accountant replied: "We have received $36,000 in dividend revenues in each year and have used these funds to pay dividends on our own shares. If we write down our investment in the subsidiary by $90,000, we shall show dividends in excess of net income for Year 2. Why should we be penalized for the losses of our subsidiary?"

Instructions

a. Prepare a schedule showing the accounting for the parent's investment in its subsidiary if the equity method had been followed.

b. Discuss the controversy between the auditor and the parent company's accountant, and state your views.

9-2 Cable Company acquired a controlling interest in Bar Company at the beginning of Year 1, by exchanging shares of Cable Company's common stock, having a par value of $40,000, for shares of Bar Company common stock. The book value of Bar Company's net assets at the end of Year 3 is $50,000.

An appropriate eliminating entry to effect a consolidation of the statements of Cable and Bar Companies at the *end* of Year 3 is as follows:

Capital Stock—Bar Company	*30,000*	
Retained Earnings—Bar Company	*20,000*	
Discount on Capital Stock—Cable Company	*2,200*	
Investment in Bar Company		*47,200*
Minority Interest in Bar Company		*5,000*

Instructions

Answer each of the following questions, explaining the reasoning by which you arrived at your conclusion:

a. Does Cable Company use the equity or cost method of accounting for its investment in Bar Company?

b. What percentage of Bar's total outstanding shares does Cable Company hold at the end of Year 3?

c. What was the book value of Bar Company's net assets at the date Cable Company acquired its interest in Bar's common shares?

9-3 Condensed separate and consolidated financial statements for Carr and Foundry Companies at the end of Year 5 are shown below:

	Carr Company	*Foundry Company*	*Consolidated*
Current assets	*$180,000*	*$ 80,000*	*$ 260,000*
Investment in Foundry (cost)	*320,000*		
Other assets	*200,000*	*720,000*	*920,000*
Total assets	*$700,000*	*$800,000*	*$1,180,000*
Liabilities	*$250,000*	*$100,000*	*$ 350,000*
Capital stock ($100 par value)	*600,000*	*300,000*	*600,000*
Retained earnings (deficit)	*(150,000)*	*400,000*	
Consolidated retained earnings			*90,000*
Minority interest in Foundry			*140,000*
Total liabilities & equities	*$700,000*	*$800,000*	*$1,180,000*

During Year 5 the Carr Company suffered a loss of $30,000, while Foundry Company reported net income of $70,000. On the basis of consolidated retained earnings and net income, the Carr Company board of directors declared a dividend of $4 per share on the 6,000 shares of Carr Company stock outstanding. Foundry Company did not declare a dividend during Year 5 because of a tight working capital position.

Instructions

a. Discuss the propriety of the dividend action of the Carr Company board of directors.

b. On the basis of an analysis of the above information, determine the following, explaining your reasoning in each case:

(1) The percentage of Foundry stock owned by Carr Company
(2) The consolidated net income for Year 5
(3) The retained earnings of Foundry at the date of Carr's stock acquisition

Problems

9-4 Condensed financial information of Acme and Best Companies is shown below:

Balance Sheet Data
end of Year 2

	Acme Company	*Best Company*
Current assets	$ 86,394	$ 36,470
Investment in Best—70% (equity)	130,846	
Other assets	320,000	190,000
Total assets	$537,240	$226,470
Liabilities	$ 61,480	$ 36,190
Capital stock, $50 par value	300,000	150,000
Retained earnings	175,760	40,280
Total liabilities & equities	$537,240	$226,470

Analysis of Retained Earnings
Years 1 and 2

Balance at beginning of Year 1	$115,460	$ 10,500
Year 1: Net income	53,930	32,420
Dividends	(25,000)	(15,000)
	$144,390	$ 27,920
Year 2: Net income	61,370	27,360
Dividends	(30,000)	(15,000)
Balance at end of Year 2	$175,760	$ 40,280

Income Statement Data
Year 2

Sales revenues	$426,400	$319,180
Share of earnings of subsidiary	19,152	
Total revenues	$445,552	$319,180
Cost of goods sold	$247,210	$183,400
Operating expenses	86,972	88,420
Income taxes	50,000	20,000
Total expenses	$384,182	$291,820
Net income	$ 61,370	$ 27,360

Acme purchased a 70% interest in Best Company at the beginning of Year 1 at a price $2,350 below the book value of its interest in Best Company's net assets at date of acquisition. Acme Company accounts for its investment on an equity basis.

Instructions

a. Prepare consolidating working papers for a consolidated balance sheet as of the end of Year 2, and a consolidated income statement for Year 2.

b. Prepare a statement of consolidated retained earnings for Year 2.

c. Compute the price paid by Acme for its interest in Best Company.

9-5 Condensed financial information for Prince Company and Thom Company is given below:

Balance Sheet Data
end of Year 2

	Prince Company	*Thom Company*
Current assets	*$140,000*	*$110,000*
Investment in Thom Company—80%	*200,000*	
Other assets	*460,000*	*148,000*
Total assets	*$800,000*	*$258,000*
Liabilities	*$148,000*	*$ 18,000*
Capital stock, $25 par value	*400,000*	*200,000*
Retained earnings	*252,000*	*40,000*
Total liabilities & equities	*$800,000*	*$258,000*

Statement of Retained Earnings
from beginning of Year 1 to end of Year 2

	Prince Company	*Thom Company*
Balance, beginning of Year 1	*$204,000*	*$ 25,000*
Year 1: Net income	*46,000*	*22,000*
Dividends	*(25,000)*	*(15,000)*
Year 2: Net income	*52,000*	*26,000*
Dividends	*(25,000)*	*(18,000)*
Balance, end of Year 2	*$252,000*	*$ 40,000*

Income Statement Data
Year 2

	Prince Company	*Thom Company*
Sales revenues	*$600,000*	*$210,000*
Dividend revenues	*14,400*	
Total revenues	*$614,400*	*$210,000*
Cost of goods sold	*$302,300*	*$134,000*
Operating expenses	*212,100*	*32,000*
Income taxes	*48,000*	*18,000*
Total expenses	*$562,400*	*$184,000*
Net income	*$ 52,000*	*$ 26,000*

Prince Company purchased an 80% interest in Thom Company for $200,000 at the beginning of Year 1. In negotiating this purchase, the management of Prince Company agreed that the book value of Thom's assets approximated their fair market value at date of acquisition. Prince Company was willing to pay something more than book value in order to gain control of Thom. The board of directors of

Prince directed that the investment in Thom be carried at cost in Prince's balance sheet but authorized the amortization of the excess of cost over book value on consolidated statements over a period of five years after date of acquisition by a charge against income.

Instructions

a. Prepare consolidating working papers for a consolidated balance sheet at the end of Year 2, and a consolidated income statement for Year 2.

b. Prepare a statement of consolidated retained earnings for Year 2.

9-6 Able Company acquired an 80% interest in Baker Company at the beginning of Year 1 for $128,800. The stock was purchased from the president and founder of the Baker Company. In negotiating the purchase price, it was agreed that a market value per share in excess of book value was justified because of the strong foothold in the market established by a newly launched product, Bakerbee Instant Soups. Competitive brands are now coming onto the market, however, and the management of Able Company believes that the initial advantage gained by Baker's new product will be dissipated in the next five years.

Condensed financial data for the two companies at the end of Year 1 are shown below:

Balance Sheet Data
as of December 31, Year 1

	Able Company	*Baker Company*
Investment in Baker Company stock—80%	*$128,800*	
Dividend receivable from Baker Company	*2,400*	
Other assets	*374,800*	*$200,000*
Total assets	*$506,000*	*$200,000*
Liabilities	*$ 96,500*	*$ 41,000*
Dividends payable	*7,500*	*3,000*
Capital stock	*300,000*	*100,000*
Retained earnings, Jan. 1	*84,000*	*40,000*
Net income, Year 1	*33,000*	*22,000*
Dividends declared	*(15,000)*	*(6,000)*
Total liabilities & equities	*$506,000*	*$200,000*

Income Statement Data
Year 1

	Able Company	*Baker Company*
Sales revenues	*$495,200*	*$181,000*
Dividend revenues	*4,800*	
Total revenues	*$500,000*	*$181,000*
Cost of goods sold	*$313,400*	*$121,600*
Operating expenses	*135,200*	*30,200*
Income taxes	*18,400*	*7,200*
Total expenses	*$467,000*	*$159,000*
Net income	*$ 33,000*	*$ 22,000*

The controller of Able Company has written the following memo to his assistant: "In preparing consolidated statements for Year 1, we shall establish an intangible asset 'Product Research' to explain the full difference between the fair market value and book value of Baker's net assets at date of acquisition. Amortize this intangible on the consolidated statements on a sum of the years' digits basis over a five-year period."

Instructions

a. As the assistant, prepare working papers for a consolidated balance sheet and consolidated income statement at the end of Year 1.

b. Prepare a statement of changes in consolidated retained earnings and of minority interest during the year.

c. What is the Year 1 net income of the entire consolidated entity? Explain the difference between this figure and the figure commonly referred to as "consolidated net income."

9-7 Elsy Company acquired 75% of the common stock of Fargo at the beginning of Year 1 for $360,000, a price below the book value of the underlying net assets. Part of Fargo's plant is obsolete and is carried at a figure which the directors of Elsy believe is in excess of current fair market value. Because substantial plant expenditures will be necessary in the near future, the directors of Fargo Company authorized, near the end of Year 1, the creation of a Reserve for Plant Expansion by a charge during each of the next three years against retained earnings equal to the net income of each year. Elsy carries its investment on an equity basis.

Financial data for the two companies at the end of Year 1 are summarized below:

	Elsy Company	*Fargo Company*
Current assets	$ 85,000	$ 130,000
Investment in Fargo	397,500	
Other assets	125,000	630,000
Cost of goods sold	396,000	305,000
Operating expenses	169,500	65,000
Income taxes		40,000
Dividends	4,000	
Total assets	$1,177,000	$1,170,000
Liabilities	$ 82,500	$ 150,000
Capital stock—$100 par	400,000	250,000
Additional paid-in capital	50,000	175,000
Retained earnings	107,000	85,000
Sales revenues	500,000	460,000
Earnings of subsidiary	37,500	
Reserve for plant expansion		50,000
Total liabilities & equities	$1,177,000	$1,170,000

Instructions

a. Prepare separate consolidating income statement and balance sheet working papers for Elsy and Fargo Companies for Year 1. The write-down of obsolete plant of Fargo Company is to be treated as a special charge against Fargo's retained earnings at the beginning of Year 1. However, during Year 1 Fargo Company charged against operations as expense $12,000 of the overvaluation of obsolete plant as of the beginning of Year 1.

b. Prepare a statement of consolidated retained earnings for Year 1.

c. What was Elsy Company's net income during Year 1?

d. Why does a Reserve for Plant Expansion not appear on the consolidated balance sheet? What purpose is served by creating such a reserve?

9-8 The data shown below were extracted from the financial statements of the Dorn and Esty Companies as of the end of Year 6:

	Dorn Company	*Esty Company*
Current assets	*$ 50,000*	*$123,000*
Investment in Esty—90% (equity basis)	*297,000*	
Other assets	*243,000*	*210,000*
Total assets	*$590,000*	*$333,000*
Current liabilities	*$ 85,000*	*$ 28,000*
Capital stock	*250,000*	*50,000*
Additional paid-in capital	*75,000*	*50,000*
Retained earnings—Jan. 1, Year 6	*150,000*	*190,000*
Net income—Year 6	*45,000*	*25,000*
Dividends	*(15,000)*	*(10,000)*
Total liabilities & equities	*$590,000*	*$333,000*

Dorn Company acquired a 90% interest in Esty Company on January 1, Year 1, for $220,500. At the date of acquisition, Esty Company's net assets had a book value of $200,000, but the price paid by Dorn Company included a payment for unrecorded goodwill of Esty Company, based on prospective superior earning power, and reflected an estimate that land owned by Esty Company (included in other assets) was undervalued by $10,000. Esty Company's unrecorded goodwill has been amortized on consolidated financial statements for Years 1 to 5 at the rate of 10% per year.

Dorn Company carries its investment in Esty Company on an equity basis but has recorded no changes in the investment account during Year 6 other than the receipt of $4,500 in dividends in June of Year 6. Esty Company declared a second $5,000 dividend on December 31, Year 6, but no record of this dividend has been made as of the end of Year 6 by Dorn Company.

Instructions

a. Prepare working papers for a consolidated balance sheet as of the end of Year 6 and a statement of consolidated retained earnings for Year 6.

b. In the consolidated balance sheet at the end of Year 5, current assets were $160,000 and other assets (including goodwill) were $421,000. There were no changes during Year 6 in the amount of paid-in capital. On the basis of this information and the data developed in your working papers in (a), prepare a comparative consolidated balance sheet for Esty and Dorn Companies showing the consolidated position at the end of both Years 5 and 6. Show how you derive all necessary Year 5 balances.

9-9 In each of the following described situations, determine the amounts asked for, showing all computations:

Case A. P Company acquired an interest in S Company on January 1, Year 1, for $188,600 and carries its investment at cost. In the consolidated balance sheet at the end of Year 5 appeared a $5,100 asset titled "Excess of investment in subsidiary over book value, less amortization since date of acquisition." A footnote explained that the original excess had been amortized in consolidated statements at the rate of 12½% per year. The amortization was not recorded on P's books. The book value of S Company's net assets was $200,000 at the beginning of Year 1 and $242,000 at the end of Year 5. P Company's retained earnings at the end of Year 5 was $232,000.

Instructions

a. Determine the percentage of S's common stock owned by P Company.

b. Compute the amount of consolidated retained earnings (controlling interest) as of the end of Year 5.

Case B. Q Company purchased an 80% interest in R Company at the beginning of Year 1 for a price which was $20,000 less than the book value of Q's interest in R's net assets at the time. At the end of Year 3, Q Company carries its investment on an equity basis at $572,800. In consolidated financial statements, the net assets of R Company were written down to a valuation consistent with the price paid by Q Company for its interest. The minority interest in R Company on consolidated statements prepared immediately after acquisition was $125,000. R Company paid annual dividends of $15,000 in Year 1, Year 2, and Year 3.

Instructions

a. Compute the book value of R Company's net assets at the end of Year 3.

b. Compute the amount of R Company's earnings during Years 1 to 3.

Case C. L Company purchased a 70% interest in M Company for $168,000 at the beginning of Year 1, and an 80% interest in N Company for $728,000 at the beginning of Year 3. At the dates of acquisition, M Company had capital stock of $100,000; N Company had capital stock of $500,000. On consolidated financial statements, the difference between purchase price and book value of L Company's interest was attributed to unrecorded goodwill of the respective subsidiary companies, and such goodwill was amortized on a straight-line basis over a 10-year period. L Company carries its investment in M Company at cost, and its investment in N Company on an equity basis. The retained earnings of the three companies for Years 1 through 4 is summarized on the following page:

	L Company	M Company	N Company
Retained earnings, beginning of Year 1	*$173,000*	*$110,000*	*$320,000*
Add: Net income or (loss)			
Year 1	*52,000*	*40,000*	*28,000*
Year 2	*68,000*	*50,000*	*12,000*
Year 3	*67,000*	*60,000*	*(20,000)*
Year 4	*63,000*	*70,000*	*(10,000)*
Less: Dividends			
Year 1	*(30,000)*	*(20,000)*	*(10,000)*
Year 2	*(30,000)*	*(20,000)*	*(10,000)*
Year 3	*(30,000)*	*(25,000)*	*(10,000)*
Year 4	*(30,000)*	*(45,000)*	*(10,000)*
Retained earnings, end of Year 4	*$303,000*	*$220,000*	*$290,000*

Instructions

a. Compute the consolidated net income for Year 4.

b. Compute the consolidated retained earnings (controlling interest) at the end of Year 4.

c. Compute the total minority interest as of the end of Year 4.

9-10 The following are the balance sheets of Parco, Inc., and Subco, Inc., as of December 31, Year 1.

	Parco, Inc.	*Subco, Inc.*
Cash	*$ 432,576*	*$ 32,569*
Accounts receivable	*825,620*	*225,627*
Inventories	*1,628,429*	*625,375*
Prepaid expenses	*36,475*	*5,648*
Total	*$2,923,100*	*$889,219*
Accounts payable	*$ 325,647*	*$437,989*
Federal income tax payable	*250,000*	*15,000*
Capital stock	*300,000*	*50,000*
Retained earnings	*2,047,453*	*386,230*
Total	*$2,923,100*	*$889,219*

As of December 31, Year 1, Parco, Inc., acquired from the stockholders all the shares of stock of Subco, Inc., in exchange for $550,000 of Parco's 4% 10-year debentures. The excess cost of acquisition (excess of the purchase price over the net assets of Subco) is to be amortized on Parco's books by charges to income over a 10-year period.

In Years 2 and 3, operations of Subco, Inc., resulted in losses of $52,376 and $15,226, respectively, and operations of Parco, Inc., resulted in profits of $387,465 and $420,009, respectively. Parco provided a reserve on its books by charges to income for the losses of its subsidiary. The profits shown above for

Parco are before provision for amortization of the excess cost of acquisition and for the losses of its subsidiary, Subco. Dividends of $150,000 were paid by Parco in each of Years 2 and 3.

The remaining assets and liabilities of Parco and Subco at December 31, Year 2 and Year 3, were as shown below:

Assets and Liabilities of Parco and Subco

	Parco		*Subco*	
	Year 2	*Year 3*	*Year 2*	*Year 3*
Assets				
Cash	$ 426,879	$ 490,327	$ 30,194	$ 31,187
Accounts receivable	897,426	940,227	200,525	203,287
Inventories	1,826,162	1,952,173	600,476	535,711
Advances to Subco, Inc.	165,000	180,000		
Prepaid expenses	32,879	34,327	5,347	4,621
Liabilities				
Accounts payable	357,428	298,627	287,688	226,178
Federal income taxes payable . . .	406,000	443,500		
Advances from Parco, Inc.			165,000	180,000

Instructions

Prepare working papers for a consolidated balance sheet as of the end of Year 3. Key and explain all adjustments and eliminations made either as part of the working papers or prior to entering balance sheet data on the working papers. Show beginning retained earnings, net income (or loss), and dividends for both companies on the balance sheet working papers so that the changes in consolidated retained earnings during Year 3 will appear as distinct items on the working papers.

AICPA adapted

10 CONSOLIDATIONS: INTERCOMPANY TRANSACTIONS AND PROFITS IN INVENTORIES

Transactions between affiliated companies are usually recorded by each company in the same manner as if the transaction were with a company outside the affiliated group. When the financial statements of the affiliated companies are consolidated, however, the accountant adopts an economic rather than legal entity viewpoint, and this shift in viewpoint may require that the record of intercompany transactions be modified. From a consolidated viewpoint only transactions between affiliated companies and outsiders represent external evidence of exchanges at market values.

Internal transactions within the group of affiliated entities distort consolidated statements in two major respects: (1) Some intercompany transactions result in a double counting of assets and liabilities or revenues and expenses from a consolidated viewpoint. For example, if one affiliated company owes money to another there is no net asset nor liability from a consolidated viewpoint. (2) Prices established in intercompany transactions may not be objectively determined and therefore the profit recognized by one affiliate on a sale to another is not realized in the sense that there has been an exchange at a price established in arm's-length bargaining. If consolidated statements are to be consistent with the statements of nonaffiliated companies, the evidence used to establish gains and losses should be comparable. Since profits or losses are not usually recognized on transfers between the divisions of a single company, a comparable accounting treatment should be accorded transfers between affiliated companies that are welded into an economic entity by stock ownership.

In this chapter and the next we shall consider the problem of eliminating duplication resulting from intercompany transactions, and second the problem of eliminating intercompany profits established in transactions between affiliated companies.

Intercompany transactions

Intercompany transactions between affiliated companies result in duplication from a consolidated viewpoint whenever an asset on the books of one affiliated company is represented by a debt on the books of another, and whenever an element of the revenue of one affiliate is an expense or income distribution of another. The typical situations are discussed below.

Intercompany receivables and payables

On individual financial statements a receivable from an affiliated company is an asset of the creditor and a liability of the debtor company. From a consolidated viewpoint the intercompany obligation simply reflects a potential transfer of cash from one segment of the entity to another, and neither an asset nor a liability exists. Failure to pay such debts cannot alter the net assets of the consolidated group since neither payment nor nonpayment will change the total cash balances of the affiliated group as an economic entity. Therefore these reciprocal receivable and debt accounts should be eliminated in the process of consolidation.

The partial consolidating working papers for P Company and its 80% owned affiliate, S Company, shown on page 313, illustrate the procedure to be followed in eliminating intercompany receivables and payables. Four different kinds of intercompany debt are included in the illustration: trade receivables, advances, accrued interest, and dividends declared. In two cases (interest and dividends) there is a residual debt owed to parties outside the affiliated entity which will appear on the consolidated balance sheet.

Discounting intercompany notes

If one company in an affiliated group discounts a customer's note at the bank this transaction is reported on consolidated statements in the normal fashion; that is, the contingent liability on the discounted note is disclosed through the use of a Notes Receivable Discounted account or in a footnote to the consolidated balance sheet. When one affiliate holds the note of another company in the affiliation and discounts this note at the bank, however, the consolidated entity has an actual, not a contingent, liability. To illustrate, assume that S Company gives P Company a note for $10,000 in payment for intercompany purchases, and P Company discounts S's note at the bank. From a consolidated viewpoint the affiliated entity owes the bank $10,000. The eliminating procedure to show this obligation properly on the consolidated balance sheet is illustrated in the partial consolidating working papers on page 314 in entries (a) and (b). Since P Company has discounted S Company's note, the net effect is that S Company owes the bank $10,000. Entry (a) eliminates the note receivable on P's books against the note payable on S's books. Entry (b) transfers $10,000 from the Notes Receivable Dis-

P AND S COMPANIES
Partial Consolidating Working Papers—Eliminating Intercompany Debt

	P Company	S Company	Eliminations Dr	Eliminations Cr	Consolidated balance sheet
Assets:					
Accounts receivable from P Company		8,750		(a) 8,750	
Advances to S Company	20,000			(b) 20,000	
Dividends receivable from S Company	6,000			(d) 6,000	
Interest receivable from S Company	800			(c) 800	
Total assets	xx,xxx	xx,xxx			xx,xxx
Liabilities:					
Accounts payable to S Company	8,750		(a) 8,750		
Advances from P Company		20,000	(b) 20,000		
Dividends payable		7,500	(d) 6,000		1,500
Interest payable		980	(c) 800		180
Total liabilities & equities	xx,xxx	xx,xxx			xx,xxx

(a) This is an example of a simple intercompany receivable on S Company's records and payable on P's records. There is no asset or liability from a consolidated viewpoint.

(b) P Company has advanced $20,000 to S under an agreement that the debt is due on call and will bear interest at 4%. This entry eliminates the principal of the debt.

(c) This entry eliminates the 4% accrued interest on the intercompany advance from P to S. Presumably S Company has other accrued interest payable of $180 which is extended into the consolidated balance sheet columns, since this is a liability of the consolidated group.

(d) Apparently S Company has declared dividends on its shares totaling $7,500. Since P Company owns 80% of the shares of S Company, it is entitled to 80%, or $6,000 of this dividend. This entry eliminates the intercompany portion; dividends owed to the outside minority interest are extended into the consolidated column since this is a legitimate liability of the consolidated entity to one group of stockholders.

counted account on P's books to a Notes Payable item on the consolidated statement, to reflect as a debt of the consolidated entity the $10,000 obligation of S Company to the bank.

A variation of this situation occurs when one affiliate discounts its customers' notes with another affiliate. This case is illustrated on page 314 by eliminating entry (c). Among the assets of P Company are $33,000 of customers' notes receivable. P Company has discounted $18,000 of these notes with Company S. On S Company's books the $18,000 of discounted notes shows up as notes receivable, since S Company has presumably paid P Company for these notes and will ultimately collect from P's customers. On P Company's books the $18,000 of notes discounted with S Company is included in the Notes Receivable—Customers account, and also as a contra-asset in the Notes Receivable Discounted (customers) account.

P AND S COMPANIES
Partial Consolidating Working Papers—Eliminating Discounted Notes

	P Company	S Company	Eliminations		Consolidated balance sheet
			Dr	Cr	
Assets:					
Notes receivable from S Company	10,000			(a) 10,000	
Notes receivable discounted (S note)	(10,000)		(b) 10,000		
Notes receivable, customers	33,000	18,000		(c) 18,000	33,000
Notes receivable discounted (customers)	(18,000)		(c) 18,000		
Total assets	xx,xxx	xx,xxx			xx,xxx
Liabilities:					
Notes payable to P Company		10,000	(a) 10,000		
Notes payable, other	25,000			(b) 10,000	35,000
Total liabilities & equities	xx,xxx	xx,xxx			xx,xxx

(a) To eliminate note payable owed by S Company to P Company.
(b) To eliminate notes receivable discounted on P Company's books and establish the actual liability to the bank represented by S Company's note.
(c) To eliminate $18,000 of notes receivable (customers) on S Company's books against the notes receivable discounted account on P Company's books. These notes are owed to the consolidated entity by customers of P Company, and prior to this elimination are duplicated on P and S Companies' books.

From a consolidated viewpoint there is an asset, Notes Receivable, representing the $18,000 owed to the consolidated entity by customers of P Company. Eliminating entry (c) eliminates the double counting of these customers' notes as assets on the books of P and S Companies. The $33,000 of customers' notes receivable extended into the consolidated balance sheet column includes $18,000 of customers' notes which P Company has discounted with S Company, and the remaining $15,000 of customers' notes on P's books. Both these amounts are legitimate assets from a consolidated viewpoint.

Intercompany revenues and expenses

When intercompany transactions result in revenues for one affiliate and an equal amount of expense for another, no net income accrues to the consolidated entity. Examples of this situation are: interest paid by one affiliate to another, rent paid by one affiliate to another for the use of property, sales of goods or services by one affiliate to another. We shall defer discussion of the intercompany sale of goods to a later section of this chapter since proper inventory valuation is a complicating issue.

The elimination of intercompany transactions involving interest and rent is illustrated on the partial consolidating working papers on page 315. In this example P Company has paid $1,000 of interest to S Company; and S Company has paid

$3,400 of rent to P Company. The entries to record these transactions on the individual records of the two companies are shown below:

Entries on P Company's books			*Entries on S Company's books*		
Rent Receivable	*3,400*		*Rent Expense*	*3,400*	
Rent Revenues		*3,400*	*Rent Payable* . . .		*3,400*
Interest Expense	*1,000*		*Interest Receivable*	*1,000*	
Interest Payable		*1,000*	*Interest Revenue*		*1,000*

Neither of these two transactions produces any change in the net assets, revenues, or expenses of the consolidated entity. Payment of the rent and interest will shift cash from one affiliate to the other, but this transfer will not change the resources of the consolidated group. The consolidated entity owns certain property (appearing on P's books) which is used by S Company to produce income, and incurs certain costs such as depreciation, property taxes, insurance, etc., recorded as expenses on P Company's books. When the intercompany revenues and expenses have been eliminated the net income from a consolidated viewpoint will thereby be limited to the excess of revenues earned from the property (by S) over the costs of owning and maintaining it (incurred by P). The intercompany receivables and payables will be completely eliminated on the balance sheet working papers. None of these eliminations will have any net effect on consolidated net assets nor on consolidated net income; their effect is simply to remove double-counted items from consolidated data.

P AND S COMPANIES

Partial Consolidating Working Papers—Eliminating Intercompany Revenues and Expenses

	P Company	*S Company*	*Eliminations*		*Consolidated income statement*
			Dr	*Cr*	
Revenues (credits):					
Rental revenues	*3,400*		*(b) 3,400*		
Interest revenue		*1,900*	*(a) 1,000*		*900*
Total revenue	*xx,xxx*	*xx,xxx*			*xx,xxx*
Expenses (debits):					
Rental expense		*3,400*		*(b) 3,400*	
Interest expense	*1,600*			*(a) 1,000*	*600*
Depreciation, taxes, insurance on rented property	*2,800*				*2,800*
Total expenses	*xx,xxx*	*xx,xxx*			*xx,xxx*

(a) To eliminate intercompany interest revenues and expenses on debt owed by P Company to S Company.

(b) To eliminate intercompany rental revenues and expenses. Property of P Company is rented by S Company.

Intercompany dividends

If P Company owns 75% of the common stock of S Company and S Company declares and pays a $10,000 dividend during the current period, the appropriate elimination entries on consolidated working papers are as follows (assuming P carries its investment on a cost basis):

On income statement working papers			*On balance sheet working papers*		
Dividend Revenues (P Company)	7,500		*Net Income (P Company)*	7,500	
Net Income (P Company)		7,500	*Minority Interest in S Company*	2,500	
			Dividends or Retained Earnings (S Company)		10,000

It is easy to see why these entries work mechanically; understanding the effect of this procedure requires a bit of thought. The net effect of this pair of working paper entries is to restore the $10,000 dividend to the retained earnings of S Company, and to reduce (through net income) the ownership equity of P Company by $7,500 and the ownership equity assigned to the minority interest in S Company by $2,500. Why are these results appropriate?

When one affiliate pays a dividend to another, the result is to shift net assets from the paying firm to the receiving firm, increasing the ownership equity of the receiving entity and decreasing the ownership equity of the paying entity. From the viewpoint of the consolidated entity, however, no income is earned from such an intercompany asset transfer. There *will* be some reduction in consolidated net assets if a portion of the dividend is distributed outside the entity to the minority stockholders of the paying affiliate. In the example above, when the net assets of S Company increased during the period as a result of earnings, 75% of this increase belonged to P Company and 25% to the outside stockholders of S. In the consolidating process the net income of S Company will be allocated between controlling and minority interests in exactly this proportion. The $2,500 reduction in the minority interest caused by S's dividend distribution is charged against the minority interest in the balance sheet entry shown above. Insofar as the $7,500 dividend to P Company is concerned, there was a transfer of assets in this amount from S to P, but this transfer did not alter the ownership interest in consolidated net assets in any way. This $7,500 belonged to the controlling interest when the assets were in S Company; it still belongs to the controlling interest after the assets are shifted to P Company. When P Company's share of S's net income is allocated to the controlling interest in the process of consolidation, the allocation will include P's ownership interest in the $7,500 of net assets represented by the dividend. If we allowed the $7,500 dividend to be included in P's income and *also* represented in P's share of the net income of S, we should have accounted for more ownership interest than there are net assets in the consolidated entity. Thus the effect of the entries eliminating intercompany dividends is to remove this double counting and to assign to the minority interest the actual decrease in consolidated net assets resulting from the distribution to them.

Intercompany profits

When intercompany transactions shift resources from one affiliated company to another, with no change in the valuation of the assets transferred, the proper consolidating procedure is to remove any double counting of revenues and expenses that results from combining the financial data of the individual affiliated companies.

A different and more complex problem arises when resources are shifted between affiliates at a transfer price above or below their book value on the records of the transferor company. A typical situation might be described as follows: P Company owns an 80% interest in S Company. During the current year P Company sells an asset, carried on P's books at a cost of $100, to S Company at a price of $150. The asset in question is valued at $150 on S Company's balance sheet at year-end, and P Company includes the $50 markup in its profit for the year. In consolidating the financial data of these two companies, the accountant adopts the view that this $50 increase in asset value has not been realized by the economic entity since the transfer price was established within the entity rather than in an arm's-length transaction between the consolidated entity and outsiders. Consolidated financial statements are prepared on the assumption that an economic entity exists, and transfer prices established in transactions which shift resources *within* a given accounting entity are not normally considered valid external evidence to support a revaluation of the assets involved. The appropriate consolidating procedure is to write down the asset held by S Company by $50, and remove the $50 profit from the records of P Company.

Carrying the above illustration one step further, assume that during the second period S Company sold the asset in question for $175 to a company outside the affiliation. From a consolidated viewpoint the result of this transaction is not only to establish a realized profit of $25 for S Company, but to validate the $50 markup of P Company in the original intercompany transfer. The consolidated entity now has a realized profit of $75 (ignoring incidental expenses) of which $50 accrues to P Company and $25 to S Company. The appropriate consolidating procedures will be discussed below; for the moment we are interested only in demonstrating that the basic intercompany profit issue is to decide *when* profits (increases in asset values) are realized by the consolidated entity. The standard accounting test of profit realization for *legal* entities requires objective external evidence of increases in value.[1] In preparing consolidated statements we should apply this basic test consistently in dealing with the *economic* entity represented by the affiliated companies as a whole.

[1] For a more detailed discussion of the realization concept, see *Intermediate Accounting* in this series, pp. 91–94.

Intercompany sale of land

The simplest intercompany profit situation involves the transfer of an asset, such as land, which is not included in periodic inventory and not subject to depreciation. Suppose that P Company owns a building site carried on its books at cost, $70,000. P Company sells this land to S Company, a 90% owned affiliate, for $150,000. S Company records the land at its cost, $150,000; and P Company records an $80,000 gain on the transaction as a special credit to retained earnings.

In consolidating working papers for the year in which this intercompany transaction occurred, the following eliminations would be required:

P AND S COMPANIES
Partial Consolidating Working Papers—Balance Sheet
Eliminating Intercompany Profit on Sale of Land

	P Company	S Company	Eliminations Dr	Eliminations Cr	Consolidated balance sheet
Assets:					
Land		*150,000*		*(a) 80,000*	*70,000*
Total assets	*xx,xxx*	*xx,xxx*			*xx,xxx*
Owners' Equity:					
Beginning retained earnings—P Company	*740,000*				*740,000*
Gain on sale of land—P Company	*80,000*		*(a) 80,000*		
Total liabilities & owners' equity	*xx,xxx*	*xx,xxx*			*xx,xxx*

Eliminating the $80,000 gain on sale of land from the ownership equity of P Company and from S Company's land account restates the land to a cost basis from the consolidated viewpoint. The same elimination should be made in each subsequent year's consolidating working papers, except that the debit would be to P Company's *beginning* retained earnings since the gain on sale of land would be included in the beginning retained earnings in all years after that in which the sale occurred.

If at some future date S Company should sell this land for more than $70,000, an increased value would then be established for the consolidated entity. If, for example, S Company sold the land for $175,000, the total gain of $105,000 ($175,000 – $70,000) would be allocated $25,000 to S and $80,000 to P on consolidated statements. If S sold the land for $100,000, the net consolidated gain of $30,000 would be allocated as a $50,000 loss to S and an $80,000 gain to P. After the disposal of the land by S, no further consolidating eliminations would be necessary.

Intercompany profits in inventories

When one affiliated company buys merchandise from another at a price above cost and in the same accounting period sells this merchandise to outsiders, the profit of both affiliated companies is fully realized from a consolidated viewpoint since the total increase in the value of net assets resulting from these transactions is substantiated by cash or accounts receivable on the books of the affiliate completing the sale to outsiders. For example, if affiliate A sells merchandise costing $8,000 to affiliate B for $10,000 and B sells all these goods to outsiders for $14,000, the entire gain of $6,000 is realized by the consolidated entity. The only consolidating eliminations required in this case would be to offset $10,000 of A's sales against $10,000 of B's cost of goods sold to remove double counting. The net effect of this elimination would be to leave $14,000 of sales revenues (B Company's) and $8,000 of cost of goods sold (A Company's) in the consolidated income statement. The total gross profit of $6,000 would thus be included in consolidated income and would still be allocated $2,000 to A and $4,000 to B, since the net income figures of the individual affiliates are not affected by a simple offset of revenues and expenses on consolidating working papers.

Now, however, assume that affiliate A sells merchandise to affiliate B during the period (under the same conditions described in the preceding paragraph) and at the end of the period affiliate B has half the merchandise still on hand. We must still eliminate the $10,000 of double counting from A's sales and B's merchandise purchases since the intercompany transfer of goods added neither to revenues or expenses from a consolidated viewpoint. *In addition* we face the problem of removing the intercompany markup from the valuation of the inventory of unsold goods on the books of the buyer and from the gross profit of the selling company. In our example the ending inventory was marked up from $4,000 (½ of A's $8,000 cost) to $5,000 (½ of the $10,000 price to B) in the process of intercompany transfer, and this $1,000 gain now appears in A Company's gross profit. In consolidating we would write down the inventory of the buying affiliate (B Company) from $5,000 to $4,000 and remove $1,000 from the net income of the selling affiliate (A Company) thereby valuing the inventory on a cost basis to the consolidated entity.

The reasoning employed above applies generally in dealing with intercompany profits *without regard to the identity of the buying and selling affiliate.* The principle is the same whether a parent sells to a subsidiary, a subsidiary sells to a parent, or one subsidiary sells to another. Our objective is to value consolidated inventories and recognize income to the consolidated entity on the same basis followed in accounting for the position and operating results of a single legal entity. This can be accomplished by removing any intercompany markup from the inventories of the affiliate that holds them at statement date and removing this same markup from the profit of the affiliate(s) that sold the goods within the consolidated group. Note that we are concerned not with the markup on *all* goods transferred intercompany during the period but only with the markup on goods *remaining* in the consolidated inventory at the end of the period.

Illustration—intercompany profits in ending inventories. The following example will illustrate the working paper procedures to eliminate intercompany profits in ending inventories. Assume that P Company acquired an 80% interest in S Company at exactly book value at the beginning of Year 1. During Year 1 $30,000 of S Company's sales were to P Company, at an average markup of 25%; that is, S Company's cost was 75% of $30,000, or $22,500. P Company's inventory at the end of Year 1 includes $16,000 of merchandise purchased from S, priced to include a $4,000 intercompany markup above their cost of $12,000 to S Company. P Company also rents a warehouse from S Company, paying a total rental of $4,700 during Year 1. At the end of Year 1, P Company owes S Company $3,300 on open account.

The working papers to consolidate the income statements of P and S Companies appear as follows:

P AND S COMPANIES
Working Papers—Consolidated Income Statement
Year 1

	P Company	*S Company*	*Adjustments and eliminations*		*Consolidated income statement*
			Dr	*Cr*	
Credits:					
Sales revenues	124,000	90,000	(a) 30,000		184,000
Rental revenues		4,700	(b) 4,700		
Ending inventory	24,000	14,600	(c) 4,000		34,600
Totals	148,000	109,300			218,600
Debits:					
Beginning inventory	19,800	9,300			29,100
Purchases	67,700	52,000		(a) 30,000	89,700
Rental expense	4,700			(b) 4,700	
Other expense	26,300	32,000			58,300
Net income—P Company	29,500		(d) 9,600		39,100
Net income—S Company		16,000		(c) 4,000 (d) 12,000	
Minority interest in net income of S Company			(d) 2,400		2,400
Totals	148,000	109,300			218,600

(a) To eliminate intercompany sales by S Company to P Company.
(b) To eliminate intercompany rental paid by P Company to S Company.
(c) To eliminate intercompany markup of $4,000 on goods in the ending inventory of P which were purchased from S Company.
(d) To allocate the adjusted net income of S Company ($12,000) between the controlling (80%) and minority (20%) interests.

Note that the elimination of intercompany sales of $30,000 as shown in entry (a) and intercompany rentals of $4,700 in entry (b) do not affect the consolidated net income. These eliminations simply remove an offsetting overstatement of revenues and expenses from a consolidated viewpoint.

The elimination of the $4,000 intercompany markup in P Company's ending inventory in entry (c), however, *does* affect consolidated net income. The debit to the ending inventory of P removes the $4,000 overstatement of inventory, in effect increasing consolidated cost of goods sold, since the ending inventory is deducted in computing cost of goods sold. The credit to S Company's net income in entry (c) removes from the net income of S the $4,000 gross profit on these goods recognized by S Company at the time of their sale to P Company. The reduction of S Company's net income is allocated between the controlling and minority interests in S; in effect 20% of $4,000 is charged against the minority interest and 80% of $4,000 is charged against the controlling interest. This result is demonstrated in the following schedule:

	Total	*Controlling interest—80%*	*Minority interest—20%*
Net income reported by S Company	*$16,000*	*$12,800*	*$3,200*
Distribution of S Company's income on working papers in entry (d)...	*12,000*	*9,600*	*2,400*
Difference: Intercompany profit eliminated in consolidating......	*$ 4,000*	*$ 3,200*	*$ 800*

Working papers to consolidate the balance sheets of P and S Companies are illustrated on page 322.

Since P Company acquired its 80% interest in S Company at the beginning of Year 1 at book value, the elimination of P's investment against the ownership equity accounts of S Company *as of the beginning of the year* is straightforward. In entry (c) on the balance sheet working papers, 80% of $65,000, or $52,000, is eliminated from P's investment account and the remaining 20%, or $13,000, is established as the minority interest in S at the beginning of Year 1.

The purpose of entry (b) on the balance sheet working papers is to eliminate the intercompany debt owed by P Company to S Company.

Entry (a) on the balance sheet working papers is the counterpart to entry (c) on the income statement working papers; it eliminates $4,000 from the ending inventory of P Company on the balance sheet, and from S Company's net income which appears among the ownership equity accounts.

Entry (d) allocates S Company's net income between the minority and controlling interests, adding 80%, or $9,600, to P's net income to produce the $39,100 consolidated income figure which is extended into the balance sheet columns. The ending minority interest balance of $15,400, composed of the minority interest at the beginning of Year 1 plus 20% of S's net income, is similarly extended into the consolidated balance sheet column.

Why eliminate all the intercompany profit?

One may well ask at this point: Why eliminate 100% of the intercompany profit? Referring to our previous example, has not a sale between S and P Company been effected and, insofar as the minority stockholders of S Company are concerned, 20% of any gain actually realized? Why not treat the $800 minority share of intercompany profit (20% of $4,000) as realized income, and eliminate only the $3,200 share of the controlling interest?

To answer these questions we should recall one of the basic assumptions underlying the consolidating process. Consolidated statements are prepared for an economic entity consisting of a collection of net assets owned by two major stock-

P AND S COMPANIES
Working Papers—Consolidated Balance Sheet
as of the end of Year 1

	P Company	S Company	Adjustments and eliminations Dr	Adjustments and eliminations Cr	Consolidated balance sheet
Assets:					
Investment in S Company—80%	52,000			(c) 52,000	
Cash	14,800	16,400			31,200
Accounts receivable	19,200	27,000		(b) 3,300	42,900
Inventories	24,000	14,600		(a) 4,000	34,600
Other assets	90,000	40,000			130,000
Totals	200,000	98,000			238,700
Liabilities & Equity:					
Liabilities	59,000	17,000	(b) 3,300		72,700
Capital stock—P	80,000				80,000
Beginning retained earnings—P	31,500				31,500 } °
Net income—P	29,500			(d) 9,600	39,100 }
Capital stock—S		50,000	(c) 50,000		
Beginning retained earnings—S		15,000	(c) 15,000		
Net income—S		16,000	(a) 4,000 (d) 12,000		
Minority interest in S				(c) 13,000 (d) 2,400	15,400
Totals	200,000	98,000			238,700

(a) To eliminate intercompany profit from the portion of P's ending inventory which was acquired from S.
(b) To eliminate intercompany payable owed by P to S.
(c) To eliminate P's investment against S's owners' equity as of the beginning of the year, and record minority interest at that date.
(d) To allocate the adjusted net income of S Company between the controlling (80%) and minority (20%) interests.
° Consolidated retained earnings at the end of Year 1 = $70,600 ($31,500 + $39,100).

holder groups: the stockholders of the parent and the minority stockholders of the subsidiary. Since the total net assets are under a single unified control, it is reasonable to assume that members of the affiliated group of companies cannot deal with each other on a truly arm's-length basis. The transfer prices at which goods and services exchange among affiliates are controlled by the management of the parent company, subject only to the test that minority stockholders must be treated equitably. This reasoning is the basis for the accountant's position that the entire amount of any increase in the recorded valuation of assets resulting from intercompany transfers among affiliates is not realized profit and should be eliminated in the process of consolidation. The result is to state assets in general at cost to the selling company, the same basis as would be used if the legal boundaries between affiliated companies did not exist.

There are those who argue that only the controlling share (in our example, 80%) of intercompany profits should be eliminated on the grounds that, from the viewpoint of the 20% minority interest in S, the sale to P Company is a closed transaction and any gain or loss to S Company is fully established. This contention is true, but it is not really pertinent to the issue.

Consolidated statements are not prepared for the benefit of minority stockholders in subsidiaries. The minority interest is a limited one; it extends only to the net assets of the subsidiary. Minority stockholders, therefore, should look to statements of the subsidiary company in which they have an interest as the source of information about the status of their investment, not to consolidated statements.

From a consolidated viewpoint, as in the case of any other accounting entity, the accountant's problem is to assign a valuation to the independent variables—the assets and liabilities under common control. Once this is done on a basis consistent with the valuation assumptions of accounting, the only remaining problem is to allocate the total interest between the controlling and minority interests. It would be entirely improper to reason backward and, by applying some assumption about the nature of the minority equity interest, value some portion of the consolidated net assets on one basis and another portion (perhaps identical assets) on another basis.

At one time the position that only the controlling share of intercompany profits should be eliminated was the dominant view among accountants. The case for 100% elimination of intercompany profits was made in 1944 by Maurice Moonitz as an element of his entity theory of consolidated statements.[2] Since that time the weight of authority has gradually shifted until it is now solidly behind the entity theory and 100% elimination.[3]

Summary of procedures to remove intercompany inventory profits. The general rule for eliminating intercompany profits in inventories may be stated simply: Eliminate 100% of any intercompany profit from the inventory of the company holding an inventory of goods acquired in intercompany transactions, and eliminate the same amount from the net income of the affiliate that sold the goods and recognized profit on the transaction. The following examples illustrate the application of this rule:

Case 1: Parent sells to subsidiary. Eliminate intercompany profit from subsidiary's inventory and from parent's net income.

Case 2: Subsidiary sells to parent. Eliminate intercompany profits from parent's inventory and from subsidiary's net income.

Case 3: Subsidiary sells to another subsidiary. Eliminate intercompany profit from inventory of buying subsidiary and from income of selling subsidiary.

Case 4: Merchandise is sold by one affiliate to a second, by the second to a third, by the third to a fourth, etc. Eliminate the entire amount of intercompany profit from the inventory of the affiliate holding the inventory at statement date, and

[2] Maurice Moonitz, *The Entity Theory of Consolidated Statements,* Monograph No. 4, The American Accounting Association (Madison: 1944), pp. 78–84.

[3] Committees of both the AICPA, in "Consolidated Financial Statements," Accounting Research Bulletin No. 51 (New York: 1959), p. 45, and The American Accounting Association, "Accounting and Reporting Standards for Corporate Financial Statements," *Supplementary Statement No. 7* (Iowa City: 1957), pp. 44–45, are on record in support of the full-elimination position.

eliminate the proportional profit earned by each of the selling subsidiaries from their net income. For example, assume that S-1 sells goods to S-2 at a $2,000 markup, and S-2 sells these goods to S-3 at a $3,000 markup, and S-3 sells to the parent at a $1,500 markup. The entire markup of $6,500 would be eliminated from the parent's inventory and $2,000 would be eliminated from S-1's income, $3,000 from S-2's income, $1,500 from S-3's income.

What is the intercompany profit? The appropriate amount of intercompany markup to be eliminated from inventories is the gross margin of the selling company reduced by any inventoriable costs incurred in moving goods from one affiliate to another.

If only the net profit of the selling affiliate were eliminated, the result would be to capitalize in the consolidated inventory the average selling and administrative expenses of the selling affiliate. To illustrate, assume that S Company sells its entire output to P Company. S Company's income percentages are:

	Average percentage	*Merchandise in P's inventory*
Sales revenue	*100*	*$10,000*
Cost of goods sold	*60*	*6,000*
Gross margin	*40*	*$ 4,000*
Selling expenses	*15*	
Administrative expenses	*11*	*3,200*
Income taxes	*6*	
Net income	*8*	*$ 800*

If the entire $4,000 gross margin is eliminated from the goods in P's inventory, the inventory will be valued at $6,000 on consolidated statements. If only the net markup of $800 (8% of $10,000) were eliminated, the goods would be valued at $9,200 on the balance sheet, in effect adding S's average selling, administrative, and tax expenses to the cost of inventory items. Capitalizing these expenses would be improper accounting for a single firm; it is similarly objectionable from a consolidated viewpoint. If packing, shipping, and transportation costs in moving goods from S Company to P Company amounted to 3% of S's selling price, however, it would be appropriate to eliminate only 37% as markup, thus pricing the goods in inventory at $6,300 and capitalizing the $300 of legitimate inventoriable costs incurred by the consolidated entity in preparing the goods for ultimate sale.

Intercompany losses on inventories. Losses on intercompany sales are no more realized in an accounting sense than intercompany profits. Intercompany losses should be added to the inventory valuation of the buying affiliate and also added back to the net income of the selling affiliate until the loss is established by sale to outsiders.

Since the lower of cost or market is an acceptable accounting basis for inventory valuation, a loss incurred by a selling affiliate because of a decline in "market value" of goods transferred intercompany need not be eliminated, if the result is to state consolidated inventories on a lower of cost or market basis. The appropriate consolidating procedure would be first to eliminate the amount of intercompany loss, and then to establish an appropriate lower of cost or market valuation from the consolidated viewpoint.

Intercompany profits in inventories at date of acquisition. A special problem arises when companies that have been doing business with each other become members of a consolidated group. For example, suppose A Company sells merchandise to B Company, and B holds $50,000 of such merchandise at the end of Year 1 when A Company acquires a controlling interest in B. Should A's profit on these goods be eliminated in preparing a consolidated balance sheet at date of acquisition and an income statement for Year 1?

One view of this situation is that A Company in effect has reacquired goods which it had previously sold, and therefore these goods should be valued at cost until there is evidence of realization through sale outside the affiliation. This view points to an elimination of these intercompany profits.

Another view is that the sale from A to B prior to affiliation was an arm's-length transaction, at a price not controlled by A Company at that time. Therefore the increase in valuation has been established by an objective, external transaction and the related profits are fully realized. Under this view no elimination is necessary.

There is no easy answer to this question. The goods in question are held within the consolidated entity, and presumably should be valued on a basis consistent with that applied to other goods so held. On the other hand the evidence of increased value is of the same quality as would be accepted as a test of realization for a single entity. On balance the authors favor the view that elimination of intercompany profits at date of acquisition is not necessary. One special difficulty in attempting to eliminate such profits is that B's inventory is an element of the book value of B's net assets at date of acquisition. If the inventory value is written down to A's cost, this changes the book value of the shares of B's capital stock owned by A and affects any difference that exists between the price paid by A for its interest, and the underlying book value of B's net assets.

Intercompany profits in beginning inventories. Thus far we have considered only intercompany profits in *ending* inventories. But the ending inventory of one period is the beginning inventory of the next (for both legal and consolidated entities) and the elimination of intercompany profits at the end of Year 1 inevitably affects consolidated net income reported for Year 2, as well as the balance of consolidated retained earnings at the start of Year 2.

Adding this new element to our problem introduces no new concepts, since we must simply carry forward the consolidated results at the end of one year to the consolidating process of the next year. Some new procedural complexities are involved, however, and it may be helpful to illustrate working paper procedures by continuing our previous example of P Company and its 80% owned subsidiary S Company, through Year 2 (see pages 326 and 327 for the basic data).

At the end of Year 1 there was a $4,000 intercompany profit in the ending inventory of P Company resulting from the purchase by P of goods from S at an average markup of 25%. We shall now assume that at the end of Year 2, P Company also held goods which had been acquired from S at a cost of $8,800. S Company's 25% markup on these goods was $2,200, and thus the cost of these goods to S Company was $6,600. The consolidating working papers for the Year 2 income statement and the balance sheet at the end of Year 2 are illustrated on pages 326 and 327.

Comments on working papers: In the following income statement working paper, ending inventories are shown among the credits, since they are deducted to arrive at cost of goods sold. In entry (b) the debit of $2,200 to ending inventories reduces the consolidated ending inventory figure (increasing consolidated cost of goods sold) and the credit to the net income of S Company eliminates the intercompany profit on these goods.

P AND S COMPANIES
Working Papers—Consolidated Income Statement
Year 2

	P Company	S Company	Adjustments and eliminations Dr	Adjustments and eliminations Cr	Consolidated income statement
Credits:					
Sales revenues	133,900	94,700	(a) 40,000		188,600
Rental revenues		4,700	(d) 4,700		
Ending inventories	17,800	16,000	(b) 2,200		31,600
Totals	151,700	115,400			220,200
Debits:					
Beginning inventories	24,000	14,600		(c) 4,000	34,600
Purchases	68,000	51,000		(a) 40,000	79,000
Rental expense	4,700			(d) 4,700	
Other expense	25,000	34,000			59,000
Net income—P	30,000		(e) 14,080		44,080
Net income—S		15,800	(c) 4,000	(b) 2,200 (e) 17,600	
Minority interest in net income of S			(e) 3,520		3,520
Totals	151,700	115,400			220,200

(a) *To eliminate intercompany sales from S to P Company.*
(b) *To eliminate intercompany profit in P's inventory at end of Year 2.*
(c) *To eliminate intercompany profits in P's inventory at beginning of Year 2 (same as at end of Year 1).*
(d) *To eliminate intercompany rental paid by P to S Company.*
(e) *To allocate adjusted profit of S Company ($17,600) between controlling (80%) and minority (20%) interest.*

Beginning inventories appear as a debit balance on the income statement. Refer to the Year 1 working papers (see page 320) and note that the consolidated inventory at the end of Year 1 was $34,600 after eliminating $4,000 of intercompany profit recognized by S Company. The consolidated inventory at the *beginning* of Year 2 must be the same as the inventory at the *end* of Year 1. Therefore we should reduce (credit) P's beginning inventory for $4,000 and add (debit) this amount to the net income of S for Year 2. This is done in eliminating entry (c). The result squares with our accounting reasoning: reducing a beginning inventory figure makes cost of goods sold smaller and net income larger. The remainder of the eliminations on the income statement working papers are self-explanatory.

On the balance sheet working papers (page 327) eliminating entry (a) removes $2,200 from the *ending* inventory and reduces S's income by an equal amount.

P AND S COMPANIES
Working Papers—Consolidated Balance Sheet
as of the end of Year 2

	P Company	S Company	Adjustments and eliminations		Consolidated balance sheet
			Dr	Cr	
Assets:					
Investment in					
S Company—80%	52,000		(d) 9,600	(e) 61,600	
Cash	16,200	12,800			29,000
Accounts receivable	22,000	23,000		(c) 5,000	40,000
Inventories	17,800	16,000		(a) 2,200	31,600
Other assets	103,000	60,000			163,000
Totals	211,000	111,800			263,600
Liabilities & Equity:					
Liabilities	40,000	15,000	(c) 5,000		50,000
Capital stock—P	80,000				80,000
Beginning retained earnings—P	61,000			(d) 9,600	70,600
Net income—P	30,000			(f) 14,080	44,080
Capital stock—S		50,000	(e) 50,000		
Beginning retained earnings—S		31,000	(b) 4,000 (e) 27,000		
Net income—S		15,800	(a) 2,200 (f) 17,600	(b) 4,000	
Minority interest in S				(e) 15,400 (f) 3,520	18,920
Totals	211,000	111,800			263,600

(a) To eliminate intercompany profit in ending inventory of P.
(b) To eliminate intercompany profit in beginning inventory of P from the beginning retained earnings of S and add to S Company's Year 2 income.
(c) To eliminate intercompany debt owed S Company by P Company.
(d) To add to P's investment account P's share of the growth in S Company (as adjusted) during Year 1 (80% of $12,000).
(e) To eliminate P's investment account against the ownership equity of S Company as of the beginning of Year 2.
(f) To allocate adjusted net income of S for Year 2 between minority and controlling interests.

The *beginning* inventory does not appear on the balance sheet. At the end of Year 1, however, S's net income was reduced by the elimination of $4,000 intercompany profit from Year 1 inventory. Therefore when S's Year 1 reported income of $16,000 was closed to retained earnings, the retained earnings balance at the end of Year 1 was overstated by $4,000 from a consolidated viewpoint. Balance sheet eliminating entry (b) readjusts S's beginning retained earnings by removing $4,000, and adds this $4,000 to S's Year 2 net income. The result is sensible: In Year 1 we eliminated the $4,000 profit recognized by S on sales to P because the goods remained in P's inventory; during Year 2, P Company presumably sold these goods outside the affiliation, thus establishing the original intercompany markup of S Company as fully realized profit in Year 2 from a consolidated viewpoint.

It is convenient on the balance sheet working papers to eliminate P's investment account as of the *beginning* of Year 2 rather than at the end, since P's share of S's Year 2 income may then be treated as a separate allocation in arriving at Year 2 consolidated income. Since P carries its investment in S at cost, it will first be necessary to restate the investment to an accrual basis as of the beginning of Year 2. In entry (d) P Company's share of the growth in S Company during Year 1 (80% of $12,000) is added to P's investment and beginning retained earnings. As a result the consolidated figure opposite the heading "Beginning retained earnings—P" becomes the beginning consolidated retained earnings of $70,600 which agrees with the consolidated retained earnings at the end of Year 1 (see page 322). The investment balance of $61,600 may now be eliminated in entry (e) against the $77,000 beginning owners' equity of S (capital stock and beginning retained earnings) and the beginning minority interest of $15,400 established.

The final balance sheet entry (f) allocates the adjusted Year 2 income of S ($17,600) between the controlling ($14,080) and minority ($3,520) interests.

This working paper procedure accomplishes two important results: (1) The consolidated net income figure ($44,080) and minority interest in S's income ($3,520) provide a link with the income statement working papers as a test of consistency and accuracy; (2) the beginning consolidated retained earnings balance, necessary to prepare a statement of consolidated retained earnings, appears on the balance sheet working papers. The figures in the statement below were taken directly from the consolidating working papers:

P AND S COMPANIES
Statement of Consolidated Retained Earnings and Change in Minority Interest during Year 2

	Consolidated retained earnings	*Minority interest*
Balance, beginning of Year 2	*$ 70,600*	*$15,400*
Add: Net income	*44,080*	*3,520*
Balance at end of Year 2	*$114,680*	*$18,920*

Questions

1. Describe an intercompany transaction that will result in an overstatement of consolidated assets, liabilities, revenues, and expenses unless appropriate eliminations are made.

2. Describe the nature of the liability or asset that exists from a consolidated viewpoint:
   a. When one affiliated company discounts at a bank a note of another company in the affiliated group
   b. When one affiliated company discounts its customers' notes with another company in the affiliated group

3. P Company owns a controlling interest in S Company. During the year P Company rented equipment from S Company, paying $12,000 in rent. Explain why the elimination of this $12,000 of intercompany rent does not affect the consolidated net income.

4. A parent company receives $10,000 in cash dividends on common stock from its subsidiary during a given year. Explain the adjustments and eliminations relating to dividends that are necessary to consolidate the accounts of the parent and subsidiary. Where will these dividends appear on consolidated financial statements?

5. A subsidiary sells to a parent company parts which are incorporated in a finished product and in turn sold by the parent to customers. From a consolidated viewpoint, when is the subsidiary's profit on the manufacture of these parts realized? Explain.

6. A Company owns 80% of the common stock of B Company, and purchases paints and glues from B Company at B's cost plus 50%. At the close of the current year there is in A's inventory a stock of paints and glues purchased from B Company for $225,000. The assistant controller argues that in consolidating the accounts of the two companies 80% of the $75,000 intercompany markup in A's inventory should be eliminated because, from the viewpoint of the minority shareholders of B, 20% of the profit has been realized. Explain why you agree or disagree with this position.

7. X Company owns 70% of the common stock of Y Company. During the current year X Company sold goods for $1 million to Y Company on which X recorded a gross profit of 20%. At the end of the period $300,000 of goods purchased from X are in Y's inventory. Explain why the intercompany profit elimination in consolidating the accounts of these companies should be $60,000 rather than $200,000.

8. K Company is a subsidiary of J Company. K sells goods to J Company at an average markup of 25% of selling price. J Company's beginning inventory includes $100,000 of goods purchased from K, and J's ending inventory includes $150,000 of goods purchased from K. In consolidating the accounts of these companies, what amount of intercompany profit will be eliminated from K Company's beginning retained earnings and from K Company's net income for the current year? Explain why the elimination of intercompany profit from K's beginning retained earnings is necessary.

9. In consolidating the accounts of a parent and subsidiary only the *net* profit realized by the subsidiary on sales to the parent is removed from the parent's ending inventory. What effect would this procedure have on the valuation of inventories from a consolidated viewpoint?

10. Q Company has purchased goods from R Company for many years. On January 1 of the current year, Q Company bought a controlling interest in R Company. Included in Q's January 1 inventory were goods purchased from R for $180,000 on which R Company had recorded a $36,000 gross profit. The controller of Q Company decided not to eliminate this intercompany profit in consolidating the accounts of the two companies as of January 1. What arguments may be presented in support of the controller's position?

Short cases for analysis

10-1 P Company owns an 80% interest in the common stock of Q Company. During the current year P Company leased property from Q Company, paying rent of $48,000 to Q Company. Rent expense on P's books became a part of its cost of goods manufactured for the year, and thus became an element in the cost of its ending work in process and finished goods inventories. An analysis of these inventory accounts indicates that $480 of the work in process inventory and $960 of the finished goods inventory cost are attributable to the intercompany rent.

At the end of the year, in preparing consolidating working papers, the controller of P Company has eliminated the intercompany rental revenue and rental expense on consolidating working papers. His assistant has raised the question whether anything should be done about the rental element that has been capitalized in inventories. The assistant argues that, since the intercompany lease rents have been eliminated, it is also necessary to eliminate the $1,440 rental element in inventories. The controller is not particularly concerned, in view of the relative immateriality of the amounts involved, but has difficulty in explaining to his assistant why the elimination should not be made on theoretical grounds.

Instructions

Write a brief statement (ignoring the issue of materiality) explaining why the indicated elimination from the ending inventories of P Company and the net income of Q Company should or should not be made.

10-2 John Penn has just accepted a position as assistant controller of the Carol Company, and has been given the assignment of preparing consolidated financial statements at the end of the current year for Carol and Durn Companies. Carol Company purchased 72% of the common stock of Durn Company three months prior to the end of the current year.

Carol Company had purchased parts from Durn for a number of years, and during the current year, prior to date of acquisition, Durn had sold $985,000 of parts to Carol. At the date of acquisition, Carol had $113,000 of parts purchased from Durn in its inventory. In the three-month period since acquisition, Carol Company purchased an additional $450,000 of parts from Durn, and held $240,000 of Durn parts in its year-end inventory. Durn Company reports an average gross profit of 32% for the year and a net profit of 11% after selling, administrative, and income tax expenses.

John Penn is uncertain about a number of points in preparing consolidated statements. Should the statements of Carol and Durn Companies be consolidated in view of the short period of affiliated operations? Should he eliminate intercompany profits from the inventory at date of acquisition? If so, should he eliminate 32% of Carol's cost on parts purchased from Durn, or should he eliminate 11%, or some percentage in between these two figures?

Prior to Carol's acquisition of a controlling interest in Durn Company, Durn had sold land to Carol Company as a site for a factory. An examination of Durn's records shows that the land, which was sold to Carol for $185,000, had originally cost Durn $200,000. After date of acquisition, Carol Company sold the land back to Durn for $200,000, recording a $15,000 profit on the transaction. Penn is uncertain as to the proper valuation of this land on the consolidated statements, and the proper consolidating treatment of the gain and loss.

Instructions

Write a statement advising Penn on the following points, and explaining your position:

a. Should consolidated financial statements be prepared at the end of the current year? If so, how should the revenues and expenses before and after acquisition be handled? If not, how should Carol Company report its investment in Durn Company on its individual financial statement?

b. If consolidated statements are prepared, how should the intercompany sales of parts and the intercompany profits on inventories at date of acquisition and at the end of the current year be handled?

c. If consolidated statements are prepared, at what valuation should the plant site appear on the consolidated balance sheet, and what disposition should be made of Durn's loss and Carol's gain on the two sale transactions?

10-3 Plato Company owns 90% of the capital stock of Rush Company and 80% of the stock of Tabor Company. On April 1 of the current year, Rush Company sold merchandise (which cost Rush Company $37,625) to Tabor Company and received five non-interest-bearing notes of $10,000 each, due respectively on May 1, June 1, July 1, August 1, and September 1 of the current year. Rush Company immediately (on April 1) discounted the notes due on May 1 and June 1, respectively, with its bank and was credited with the proceeds of $19,925. The other three notes Rush Company plans to hold to maturity.

Instructions

a. Present all the entries that Rush Company should have made relating to the above transactions up to April 30, which is the close of its fiscal year. The bank's rate of discount is ¼% per month. Assume that Rush Company records its sale to Tabor at present value, using the bank discount rate to determine the value of the notes at the date of sale.

b. In consolidating the three companies at April 30 of the current year, how should the transactions involving the above notes be handled? You may assume that one-fourth of the merchandise remains in Tabor's inventory at that time. Explain all consolidating adjustments and eliminations necessary on April 30 that relate to the intercompany sale transaction between Rush and Tabor Companies.

AICPA adapted

Problems

10-4 Income statement information for two affiliated companies, Knoff and Lusk Companies, for the current year is presented at the top of the next page:

	Knoff Company	Lusk Company
Sales revenues	$732,000	$840,000
Dividend revenues	43,800	-0-
Rental revenues	33,000	-0-
Total revenues	$808,800	$840,000
Cost of goods sold:		
Beginning inventory	$ 60,000	$123,000
Purchases	611,300	471,200
Less: Ending inventory	(310,000)	(65,000)
Cost of goods sold	$361,300	$529,200
Operating expenses	261,100	151,500
Income tax provision	90,000	75,000
Total expenses	$712,400	$775,700
Net income	$ 96,400	$ 84,300
Dividends paid or declared	70,000	50,000
Net income transferred to retained earnings	$ 26,400	$ 34,300

Knoff Company owns 78% of the stock of Lusk Company. During the current year 60% of Lusk Company's sales were made to Knoff Company at the same average prices charged to outside customers. An analysis of Knoff's inventories shows that 90% of its beginning inventory and 70% of its ending inventory consisted of goods purchased from Lusk. Knoff rents a store building to Lusk for $15,000 per year.

Instructions

a. Prepare working papers for a consolidated income statement.

b. Comment on the relation between the provision for income taxes and the net income figure on the consolidated income statement.

10-5 Bowles Company purchased a 75% interest in Curry Company several years ago in order to obtain retail outlets for its major products. Since that time Bowles has sold to Curry Company a substantial portion of its merchandise requirements. At the beginning of the current year Curry Company's inventory of $690,000 was composed 80% of goods purchased from Bowles at markups averaging 30% of Bowles Company's selling price. Sales from Bowles to Curry during the current year were $5,600,000. The estimated intercompany profit in Curry's ending inventory was $194,000.

Bowles Company owns buildings and land used in Curry Company's retail operations and leased to Curry Company. Lease rentals paid by Curry Company to Bowles Company during the current year amounted to $743,000. At the end of the current year, Bowles sold to Curry for $250,000 land to be used in the development of a shopping center which had cost Bowles $203,500. The gain was included in Bowles Company's net income for the current year. Curry paid $50,000 in cash and gave Bowles Company a $200,000 note for the balance. Bowles also holds a $750,000, one-year, 6% note of Curry Company on which it has accrued interest revenues of $22,500 during the current year.

During the current year Bowles Company reported net income of $486,300, and Curry Company reported net income of $384,760.

Instructions

a. Prepare in journal entry form the necessary adjusting and eliminating entries to eliminate intercompany debts, revenues and expenses, and profits for the current year on balance sheet and income statement working papers. Be sure to designate which company's account is affected in the account titles used in your journal entries.

b. Compute the consolidated net income of the two companies for the current year.

10-6 The balance sheets at the end of the current year, and the income statements for the current year, for the Caplan and Hayman Companies are given below:

Balance Sheet Data

	Caplan Company	*Hayman Company*
Cash	$ 13,000	$ 47,000
Receivables	31,000	106,000
Inventories	80,000	62,000
Investment in Hayman Company	201,240	
Other assets	114,760	157,000
Total assets	$440,000	$372,000
Current liabilities	$160,000	$ 58,000
Notes receivable discounted		25,000
Capital stock	200,000	150,000
Beginning retained earnings	64,000	126,000
Net income	41,000	63,000
Dividends	(25,000)	(50,000)
Total liabilities & capital	$440,000	$372,000

Income Statement Data

Sales revenues	$340,000	$820,000
Dividend revenues	45,000	
Interest revenues		1,250
Gain on sale of land	13,000	
Total revenues	$398,000	$821,250
Beginning inventory	$ 44,000	$110,000
Purchases	237,000	583,400
Ending inventory	(80,000)	(62,000)
Cost of goods sold	$201,000	$631,400
Operating expenses	135,600	84,050
Interest expense	6,500	
Income taxes	13,900	42,800
Total expenses	$357,000	$758,250
Net income	$ 41,000	$ 63,000

Caplan Company owns 90% of the stock of Hayman Company, purchased for $225,000 six years ago when Hayman's retained earnings were $56,000. Since that date the Caplan Company has amortized 60% of the excess of the cost of the investment over the book value of the underlying net assets of Hayman. The management of Caplan regarded this excess payment as the cost of the intangible benefits associated with affiliation, and authorized amortization over a period of 10 years. Amortization for the current year has been charged to Caplan Company's operating expenses.

Caplan Company owes Hayman Company $50,000 on two $25,000, three-year, 5% notes. Hayman Company has discounted one of these notes at a bank. During the current year Caplan Company sold to Hayman land at a price $13,000 in excess of Caplan's cost.

Caplan Company buys all its merchandise from Hayman and has done so for several years. The average gross profit realized by Hayman on these sales is approximately the same as on sales to outsiders and has remained stable for the last two years.

Instructions

a. Prepare working papers for a consolidated balance sheet and income statement for these two companies for the current year.

b. Prepare a statement of consolidated retained earnings for the current year.

c. Comment on any significant differences between the financial position and operating results of the individual companies, and the results shown on consolidated statements.

10-7 The income statements of the Evers Company and the Felkel Company for the current year are shown below:

	Evers Company	*Felkel Company*
Sales revenues	$450,000	$600,000
Dividend revenues	32,000	
Rent revenues	33,600	
Interest revenues		18,000
Total revenues	$515,600	$618,000
Cost of goods sold	$288,000	$353,000
Operating expenses	104,000	146,000
Interest expense	30,000	
Income taxes	31,700	43,500
Total expenses	$453,700	$542,500
Net income	$ 61,900	$ 75,500
Beginning retained earnings	632,000	348,000
Dividends	(30,000)	(40,000)
Ending retained earnings	$663,900	$383,500

Evers Company owns 80% of the outstanding common stock of Felkel Company, purchased at the time the latter company was organized.

Evers Company sells parts to Felkel Company at a price which is 25% above cost. Total sales from Evers to Felkel during the year were $85,000. Included in Felkel's inventories were parts purchased from Evers amounting to $21,250 in beginning inventories and $28,750 in the ending inventory.

Felkel Company sells back to Evers Company certain finished goods, at a price which gives Felkel an average gross profit of 30% on these intercompany sales. Total sales from Felkel to Evers during the year were $177,000. Included in the inventories of Evers Company were parts acquired from Felkel amounting to $11,000 in beginning inventories and $3,000 in ending inventories.

Felkel Company rents an office building from Evers Company, paying $2,800 per month in rent. Evers Company has borrowed $600,000 through a series of 5% notes, of which Felkel Company holds $360,000 as notes receivable.

Instructions

a. Prepare working papers for the consolidated income statement for these companies.

b. Prepare a statement of consolidated retained earnings for the current year.

c. What change would there be in consolidated net income if both Evers Company and Felkel Company had engaged in the same transactions but all purchases, sales, lending, and borrowings had been with firms outside the affiliated entity? Explain the source of the amount of any difference.

10-8 The balance sheets of P, S, and T Companies as of December 31, Year 2, are shown below. P Company carries its investment accounts on a cost basis.

P, S, AND T COMPANIES
Balance Sheets
December 31, Year 2

	P Company	*S Company*	*T Company*
Cash	*$ 20,000*	*$ 12,000*	*$ 17,000*
Accounts receivable	*40,000*	*25,000*	*110,000*
Notes receivable	*20,000*	*35,000*	
Notes receivable discounted	*(20,000)*	*(30,000)*	
Inventories	*80,000*	*25,000*	*30,000*
Investment in S—90%	*130,000*		
Investment in T—80%	*200,000*		
Other assets	*94,000*	*103,000*	*128,000*
Total assets	*$564,000*	*$170,000*	*$285,000*
Notes payable	*$ 15,000*		
Other liabilities	*35,000*	*$ 30,000*	*$ 15,000*
Capital stock, $100 par value	*500,000*	*100,000*	*200,000*
Retained earnings	*14,000*	*40,000*	*70,000*
Total liabilities & equities	*$564,000*	*$170,000*	*$285,000*

P Company bought a 90% interest in S Company on January 1, Year 1, at a time when the retained earnings of S Company were $60,000. P Company acquired its interest in an exchange of stock, giving 1,300 shares of its own $100 par value capital stock in exchange for 90% of the stock of S Company.

P Company bought an 80% interest in T on January 1, Year 2, for $200,000 in cash. You may assume that nondepreciable "other assets" of T Company were misvalued at the time.

P Company is liable to S Company on three notes for $5,000 each at the end of Year 2. In addition, P Company discounted $20,000 of its customers' notes receivable with S Company during Year 2. S Company has discounted two of the notes of P Company and has rediscounted all the customers' notes with a finance company.

Included in the ending inventory of P Company is merchandise valued at $30,000 which was purchased from T Company. T Company has an average markup on its sales of 40% of selling price. There were no intercompany sales prior to Year 2.

The $15,000 liability on the books of T Company represents a dividend declared by T on December 30, Year 2. P Company has not recognized this event on its books as of that date.

The retained earnings of the three companies during Year 2 changed as follows:

	P Company	*S Company*	*T Company*
Balance on Jan. 1, Year 2	*$30,000*	*$48,000*	*$20,000*
Net income (loss)	*(9,000)*	*(8,000)*	*65,000*
Dividends declared	*(7,000)*	*-0-*	*(15,000)*
Balance on Dec. 31, Year 2	*$14,000*	*$40,000*	*$70,000*

Instructions

a. Prepare working papers for a consolidated balance sheet for the three companies as of the end of Year 2. Key all working paper entries and explain them.

b. Prepare in good form the liability and stockholders' equity section of the balance sheet, and a statement of consolidated retained earnings and changes in minority interest for Year 2.

10-9 Bohn Company owns a controlling interest in Contex Company and Davis Company. Bohn purchased an 80% interest in Contex at a time when Contex Company reported retained earnings of $500,000. Bohn purchased a 70% interest in Davis at a time when Davis Company reported retained earnings of $50,000.

An analysis of the changes in retained earnings of the three companies during the current year appears below:

	Bohn Company	*Contex Company*	*Davis Company*
Retained earnings balance at beginning of the current year	*$ 976,000*	*$ 843,000*	*$682,000*
Net income	*580,000*	*360,000*	*240,000*
Dividends paid or declared	*(250,000)*	*(200,000)*	*(150,000)*
Retained earnings balance at end of the current year	*$1,306,000*	*$1,003,000*	*$772,000*

Davis Company sells parts to Bohn Company, which after further processing and assembly are sold by Bohn to Contex Company where they become a part of the finished product sold by Contex. Intercompany profits included in inventories at the beginning and end of the current year are estimated as follows:

	Beginning inventory	*Ending inventory*
Intercompany profit in inventory:		
On sales from Davis to Bohn	*$90,000*	*$ 35,000*
On sales from Bohn to Contex	*52,000*	*118,000*

Instructions

a. Compute the consolidated net income for the three companies for the current year.

b. Prepare a statement of consolidated retained earnings for the current year.

10-10 Soha Corporation acquired a 90% interest in the common stock of Moss Corporation at the beginning of Year 1, at a price equal to the book value of the shares at that date. The retained earnings of Moss Corporation at date of acquisition was $15,000. Soha Corporation carries its investment on a cost basis.

The following information, extracted from the accounting records of the two companies, relates to operations during Year 3:

	Soha Corporation	*Moss Corporation*
Net income (including dividend revenues)	*$125,000*	*$66,000*
Dividends paid during Year 3	*60,000*	*30,000*
Retained earnings at the end of Year 3 (after books have been closed)	*375,000*	*95,000*
Intercompany profits on sales made by Moss Corporation to Soha Corporation, included in Soha's inventory:		
At the beginning of Year 3	*15,000*	
At the end of Year 3	*12,000*	

Instructions

a. Prepare a statement of consolidated retained earnings for Year 3, including supporting schedules showing how all figures were derived.

b. Prepare a schedule showing the change in the minority interest in the retained earnings of Moss Corporation during Year 3.

10-11 The pre-closing trial balances of two affiliated companies as of the end of the current year are shown at the top of the next page:

Trial Balances, December 31

	Indy Company Dr	Indy Company Cr	Jery Company Dr	Jery Company Cr
Cash	$ 42,000		$ 23,000	
Receivables	165,000		84,000	
Raw materials inventory	78,000		62,000	
Goods in process inventory	46,000		37,800	
Finished goods inventory	63,400		49,300	
Plant and equipment (net)	950,000		720,000	
Investment in Jery Company (75%)	495,000			
Product development			76,800	
Current liabilities		$ 143,000		$ 115,200
Notes payable				100,000
Sales		1,630,000		1,130,000
Raw material purchases	327,000		373,000	
Direct labor and manufacturing overhead	496,000		426,000	
Administrative and selling expense	532,000		262,200	
Income taxes	101,000		75,000	
Interest and dividend revenues		35,000		1,200
Interest expense	2,400		5,000	
Dividends paid	60,000		40,000	
Retained earnings, Jan. 1		679,800		387,700
Capital stock		870,000		500,000
	$3,357,800	$3,357,800	$2,234,100	$2,234,100

The inventories of the two companies at December 31 of the current year are as follows:

	Indy Company	Jery Company
Raw materials inventory	$50,000	$98,000
Goods in process	39,000	69,000
Finished goods	73,000	83,000

Jery Company sells subassemblies to Indy Company. During the current year such sales amounted to $194,000. The intercompany profit included in the inventories of Indy Company are estimated as follows:

	On Jan. 1	On Dec. 31
Raw materials inventory	$21,000	$13,000
Goods in process inventory	4,600	3,900
Finished goods inventory	8,300	9,100

Indy Company purchased 75% of the outstanding shares of Jery Company for $495,000 twelve years prior to the end of the current year, at a time when the Jery Company had a deficit of $32,000. Indy Company paid an amount in excess of the book value of the underlying net assets in recognition of the value of a new product idea and name which were very promising, but which Jery Company had been unable to exploit because of a lack of capital. At the date of acquisition it was agreed to establish an asset titled Product Development on the books of Jery Company, at a valuation based on the price paid by Indy for its interest in Jery Company. The offsetting credit was to Retained Earnings. This asset was to be amortized to selling expense on a straight-line basis over a 20-year period after date of acquisition. The balance in the Product Development account on Jery Company's books is the unamortized portion of the asset established at date of acquisition. Indy Company also advanced $600,000 to Jery Company on a long-term 5% note, all but $100,000 of which has been paid. Included in the receivables and payables of the two companies is accrued interest on the unpaid balance of this note for the last three months of the current year; except for this accrual, interest has been fully paid on the note.

Assume that Indy and Jery Companies file income tax returns on a consolidated basis. The current year's amortization of product and development cost on Jery's books is not deductible for income tax purposes. After excluding this expense, you may assume that a reasonable estimate of the necessary provision for income taxes on a consolidated basis is 45% of the before-tax consolidated net income (excluding intercompany profits and dividends). The income tax provision and related liability may be allocated between the parent and subsidiary companies on the basis of the respective portions of the consolidated net income attributable to each company.

Instructions

a. Prepare consolidated income statement and balance sheet working papers for the current year. Show all supporting computations in footnotes to the respective working papers.

b. Prepare a statement of consolidated net income for the current year.

c. Prepare a statement of consolidated retained earnings for the current year.

11 CONSOLIDATIONS: INTERCOMPANY TRANSACTIONS IN DEPRECIABLE ASSETS AND LONG-TERM DEBT. PURCHASE VERSUS POOLING OF INTEREST INTERPRETATION OF CONSOLIDATIONS

In this chapter two additional classes of intercompany transactions among affiliated companies and their effect on consolidated financial statements are discussed. The first class of transactions involves the transfer of depreciable assets among affiliates. The second class of transactions involves intercompany holdings of long-term debt securities. Both classes of intercompany transactions may result in gains or losses which produce inconsistencies in the valuation of assets or liabilities in the accounts of affiliated companies over several accounting periods.

In the last section of the chapter the "pooling of interest" interpretation and its impact on consolidated financial statements are discussed.

Intercompany profits on sale of depreciable assets

The general principles applied in eliminating intercompany profits in inventories are also pertinent in dealing with intercompany gains or losses on the sale of depreciable assets among affiliated companies. When one affiliate sells a depreciable asset to another at a price above cost, the selling company records a gain on the transaction and the buying company records the asset at an increased valuation. At the date of the sale the proper consolidating procedure is to eliminate the gain from the valuation of the asset and from the income of the selling affiliate.

In periods after the sale a new element is introduced into the consolidating process. The buying affiliate will presumably depreciate the transferred asset on the basis of the price it paid. As a result depreciation expense on the books of the buying affiliate will be larger than it should be from the viewpoint of the consolidated entity. What happens is that as the revalued services of the asset in question expire and contribute to the revenues of the buying affiliate, some portion of the original gain recorded by the selling affiliate is substantiated; that is, from a consolidated viewpoint the gain (represented by the increase in valuation) is realized period by period throughout the life of the asset as asset services are "sold" to the customers of the buying affiliate. Thus in each period after the sale it will be necessary to eliminate a smaller portion of the original gain. When the asset has been fully depreciated on the books of the buying affiliate the entire gain will have been realized from a consolidated viewpoint, and no further elimination will be necessary in preparing consolidated statements after that date. To illustrate this point, we shall examine the consolidation problem at the date of the intercompany sale of a depreciable asset, and then extend the illustration into subsequent accounting periods.

Consolidation at date of sale

We shall first consider the problem of eliminating intercompany profit on the transfer of a depreciable asset between affiliates *at the date of sale.* P Company owns a 90% interest in S Company acquired at the time S was organized. Assume that S Company sold to the parent for $60,000 a building having a book value on S's books of $40,000. The sale occurred at the end of Year 1 and the asset has a remaining service life of 10 years at that date. Condensed working papers for the consolidated balance sheet as of the end of Year 1 (immediately following the sale) appear on page 342.

In this situation, since the sale of the asset occurred just before the balance sheet date, depreciation of the transferred asset is not at issue. P Company has not depreciated the building on the basis of its cost of $60,000, and therefore consolidated income is overstated by the entire amount of the $20,000 intercompany gain reported by S. When this gain has been eliminated from the net income of S Company, as shown in entry (a), the balance of S's income is then allocated between the controlling and minority interests, entry (d). The purpose of entries (b) and (c) is to restate P's investment on an accrual basis and eliminate the investment account against S's ownership equity accounts.

Elimination of intercompany gain in subsequent periods

Now consider the problem of consolidating P and S Companies' statements one year after the intercompany transfer of the depreciable asset; that is, at the end of Year 2. During Year 2, P Company will depreciate the asset by 10% (assuming straight-line depreciation, no salvage, and a 10-year remaining service life), or $6,000 on the basis of the $60,000 price paid to S Company. The depreciable base of the asset from the consolidated viewpoint, however, is $40,000 (S's book value at date of sale), and consolidated depreciation should be only $4,000. In one sense the depreciation overstatement of $2,000 represents an excessive expense (from a consolidated viewpoint) on P's books. In another sense the fact that P Company has "sold" one year's services of the building to its customers constitutes realization of one-tenth of the $20,000 gain on the intercompany sale by S Company. This reasoning explains why the appropriate elimination on the income statement is to reduce P's depreciation by $2,000 and add the same amount to S's income.

P AND S COMPANIES
Consolidating Balance Sheet Working Papers
as of the end of Year 1

	P Company	S Company	Adjustments and eliminations Dr	Adjustments and eliminations Cr	Consolidated balance sheet
Assets:					
Investment in S—90%	45,000		(b) 27,000	(c) 72,000	
Buildings	200,000	160,000		(a) 20,000	340,000
Accumulated depreciation	(80,000)	(65,000)			(145,000)
Other assets	105,000	55,000			160,000
Totals	270,000	150,000			355,000
Liabilities & Equity:					
Liabilities	74,000	28,000			102,000
Capital stock—P	100,000				100,000
Beginning retained earnings—P	70,000			(b) 27,000	97,000
Net income—P	26,000			(d) 19,800	45,800
Capital stock—S		50,000	(c) 50,000		
Beginning retained earnings—S		30,000	(c) 30,000		
Net income—S*		42,000	(a) 20,000 (d) 22,000		
Minority interest in S				(d) 2,200 (c) 8,000	10,200
Totals	270,000	150,000			355,000

(a) To eliminate $20,000 gain recognized by S Company on sale of building to P. Reduce building valuation and reduce S's net income.

(b) To add to P's investment and beginning retained earnings 90% of the growth in S Company (90% of $30,000) from date of acquisition to the beginning of Year 1.

(c) To eliminate S Company's owners' equity accounts (total: $80,000); eliminate P's investment (90% of $80,000 = $72,000); and establish minority interest as of beginning of Year 1 of $8,000 (10% of $80,000).

(d) To allocate S Company's adjusted net income ($22,000) among controlling interest (90%) and minority interest (10%).

* *Includes $20,000 gain on sale of building to P Company.*

The income statement working papers are illustrated on page 343. Note that the effect of entry (a) is to restate total depreciation to a consolidated-cost basis ($26,000) and to add $2,000 back to S Company's Year 2 net income.

Working papers for the consolidated balance sheet are illustrated on page 344. The elimination of the intercompany profit on the sale of the building is done in two steps, entries (a) and (b), on the balance sheet. Entry (a) removes the $20,000 intercompany gain from the asset account and from the beginning retained earnings of S Company. Entry (b) reduces the accumulated depreciation by $2,000 (the difference between the $6,000 of depreciation taken by P and the $4,000 depreciation on a consolidated-cost basis) and adds this amount to S's income for Year 2. The net effect of these two entries is to reduce consolidated assets by $18,000 at the end of Year 2, eliminate the $20,000 gain recorded by S in Year

P AND S COMPANIES
Working Papers—Consolidated Income Statement
Year 2

	P Company	S Company	Adjustments and eliminations Dr	Adjustments and eliminations Cr	Consolidated income statement
Credits:					
Sales revenues	200,000	100,000			300,000
Debits:					
Depreciation on bldgs.	20,000	8,000		(a) 2,000	26,000
Other expenses	150,000	67,000			217,000
Net income—P	30,000		(b) 24,300		54,300
Net income—S		25,000	(a) 2,000	(b) 27,000	
Minority interest in S net income			(b) 2,700		2,700
Totals	200,000	100,000			300,000

(a) To eliminate $2,000 excess depreciation above cost taken by P on building purchase from S Company. The addition to S Company's income reflects consolidated realization of one-tenth of the original gain of $20,000 recorded by S on the sale of this asset to P.
(b) To allocate S Company's adjusted net income between controlling (90%) and minority (10%) interests.

1 from S's beginning retained earnings, and add $2,000 of the original gain to S's Year 2 net income to reflect the realization during Year 2 of one-tenth of the gain on the intercompany sale. When S Company's revised net income of $27,000 is allocated between the controlling and minority interest, entry (e), the $2,000 realized gain included in S's adjusted income, will be allocated 90% to the controlling interest and 10% to the minority interest. The remainder of the adjusting and eliminating entries are adequately explained at the bottom of the working paper.

In Year 3 these procedures will be repeated. During Year 3, P Company will depreciate another one-tenth of its $60,000 asset cost, making P's expense $2,000 in excess of consolidated depreciation. In effect, by the end of Year 3 another $2,000 of S's originally recorded gain on the asset sale will have been realized through contribution to P's revenues, and only $16,000 of the intercompany markup need be eliminated from the asset accounts. The consolidating entries on the working papers are given below:

Consolidating Entries at the End of Year 3

Balance sheet entry

Accumulated Depreciation..........	4,000	
Beginning Retained Earnings—S......	18,000	
Net Income—S		2,000
Building		20,000

Income statement entry

Net Income—S........	2,000	
Depreciation Expense—P...		2,000

P AND S COMPANIES
Working Papers—Consolidated Balance Sheet
end of Year 2

	P Company	*S Company*	*Adjustments and eliminations*		*Consolidated balance sheet*
			Dr	*Cr*	
Assets:					
Investment in S—90%	*45,000*		*(c) 46,800*	*(d) 91,800*	
Buildings	*200,000*	*160,000*		*(a) 20,000*	*340,000*
Accumulated depreciation	*(100,000)*	*(73,000)*	*(b) 2,000*		*(171,000)*
Other assets	*155,000*	*88,000*			*243,000*
Totals	*300,000*	*175,000*			*412,000*
Liabilities & Equity:					
Liabilities	*74,000*	*28,000*			*102,000*
Capital stock—P	*100,000*				*100,000*
Beginning retained earnings—P	*96,000*			*(c) 46,800*	*142,800*
Net income—P	*30,000*			*(e) 24,300*	*54,300*
Capital stock—S		*50,000*	*(d) 50,000*		
Beginning retained earnings—S		*72,000*	*(a) 20,000*		
			(d) 52,000		
Net income—S		*25,000*	*(e) 27,000*	*(b) 2,000*	
Minority interest in S Company				*(d) 10,200*	
				(e) 2,700	*12,900*
Totals	*300,000*	*175,000*			*412,000*

(a) To remove \$20,000 intercompany gain on sale of building by S to P at the end of Year 1 from P's asset account and from S's beginning retained earnings.

(b) P has depreciated the building by \$6,000, which is \$2,000 in excess of consolidated cost. This entry eliminates the excess depreciation from the accumulated depreciation account and adds \$2,000 to S's net income, reflecting the realization in Year 2 of one-tenth of the original \$20,000 gain recorded by S.

(c) To add to P's investment the parent's share of the growth in S Company from date of acquisition to beginning of Year 2. (S's adjusted retained earnings at the beginning of Year 2 is \$52,000; 90% of \$52,000 = \$46,800.)

(d) To eliminate P's investment (stated now on an accrual basis as of the beginning of Year 2) against S's ownership equity (adjusted) as of the beginning of Year 2, and set forth minority interest at beginning of Year 2 (\$10,200 = 10% of \$102,000).

(e) To allocate S's adjusted Year 2 net income (\$27,000) between the controlling (90%) and minority (10%) interests.

After studying the consolidating procedures in this case during the two periods following the initial sale of a depreciable asset, one can visualize the process for the remainder of the 10-year service life of the asset in question. In each subsequent year one-tenth of the initial gain of \$20,000 will be added back to S Company's net income as a part of the consolidating process, and the amount of the original gain eliminated from retained earnings will be reduced by \$2,000. By the end of the tenth year the gain will be fully realized from the viewpoint of the consolidated entity, and no further consolidating eliminations will be necessary in subsequent years.

It may be useful at this point to compare the depreciable asset and inventory cases. When intercompany profits are eliminated from inventories at the end of each period, the effect is to shift the realization of gross profit as an element of consolidated net income to the next period when, we assumed, the goods were sold to outsiders by the buying affiliate and the intercompany markup was thus validated. In the depreciable asset case, an analagous effect occurs except that the initial gain recorded by the selling affiliate is shifted into more than one subsequent period. From the viewpoint of the consolidated entity, the gain recorded at the time of the original transfer is not recognized; instead it is recognized gradually throughout the remaining service life of the asset as the services of this asset contribute to revenues realized from customers outside the affiliated group.

Intercompany bondholdings

When long-term debt securities of one company are held by an affiliated company, special problems may arise in preparing consolidated statements because of differences between the valuation of the asset on the books of the investor-affiliate and the valuation of the liability on the books of the debtor-affiliate. These discrepancies in asset and liability valuation also result in differences between the interest expense of the debtor-affiliate and the interest revenue of the investor-affiliate. The basic principles to be followed in deriving consolidated information are straightforward, but the proper application of these principles usually requires careful analysis of the data and some attention to working paper procedures.

Bonds acquired from issuing company

When a member of a consolidated group acquires bonds of an affiliate directly from the debtor company at time of issue, the cost valuation assigned to the bond investment is likely to be consistent with the liability recorded by the debtor-affiliate, and offsetting the intercompany asset and liability accounts causes no difficulty. For example, if P Company issues $300,000 of 5%, 20-year bonds at 90, and one-third of the issue is bought by an affiliate, Company S, the consolidation at the date of purchase would be made as follows:

	P Company	*S Company*	*Eliminations*		*Consolidated balance sheet*
			Dr	*Cr*	
Asset:					
Bonds owned		*90,000*		*(a) 90,000*	
Liability:					
Bonds payable	*300,000*		*(a) 100,000*		*200,000*
Discount on bonds	*(30,000)*			*(a) 10,000*	*(20,000)*

The effect of the above entries is to eliminate the $90,000 asset on S's books against one-third of the $270,000 liability on P's books, leaving the $180,000 portion of the debt held outside the consolidated entity to appear on the consolidated balance sheet.

In a published consolidated balance sheet, the $100,000 of bonds held intercompany should be treated as treasury bonds. This puts the reader of the statement on notice that fully authorized bonds are held within the entity and the debt of the consolidated group could be expanded by this amount at any time through sale of the bonds to outsiders, without the formal action usually required to authorize major amounts of long-term debt. An appropriate form of disclosure:

Intercompany Bonds on the Consolidated Balance Sheet

Long-term liabilities:		
5% debenture bonds, due in 19__	*$300,000*	
Less: Bonds held within the consolidated group	*100,000*	
Maturity value of bonds outstanding	*$200,000*	
Less: Discount on bonds outstanding	*20,000*	*$180,000*

If P Company and S Company amortize bond discount on the same basis, the book value of these bonds on the records of the two companies will be consistent and the elimination of the debt may be made in the same manner in all future years. Should S Company ever sell its bonds to outsiders, the entire debt would then be an external one to be reported in full on the consolidated balance sheet, and any gain or loss on the sale would be reflected in S Company's retained earnings.

On the income statement at the end of one year the interest earned by S Company on intercompany bonds would be offset against P's interest expense. Assume, for convenience, that both companies amortize discount on a straight-line basis over the 20 years of bond life. The entries made by P and S Companies to record annual interest on this bond issue would be as follows:

P Company			*S Company*		
Interest Expense	*16,500*		*Bonds Owned*	*500*	
Bond Discount		*1,500*	*Cash or Interest Receivable*	*5,000*	
Cash or Interest Payable		*15,000*	*Interest Revenue*		*5,500*

The appropriate eliminating entry for bond interest on the consolidating income statement working papers is shown at the top of page 347.

The elimination of intercompany interest revenue and expense has no effect on consolidated net income. An intercompany transfer of interest payments does not alter the total net assets of the consolidated entity. The problem is simply to eliminate an equal overstatement of consolidated revenues and expenses.

	P Company	S Company	Eliminations Dr	Eliminations Cr	Consolidated income statement
Revenues:					
Interest revenue		5,500	(a) 5,500		
Expenses:					
Interest expense	16,500			(a) 5,500	11,000

Bonds acquired from outsiders

When a member of a consolidated group acquires bonds of an affiliated company from outsiders, it is unlikely that the price paid will agree with the book value of the debt in the accounts of the issuing company. Bond market prices vary inversely with changes in the market rate of interest, and the yield rate on the bonds at the time of issue may not be the same as the market yield rate at any subsequent date. This situation poses new consolidating issues because we face the problem of eliminating intercompany debt against asset, and expense against revenue, where the amounts differ on the books of the two affiliated companies.

To illustrate, assume that P Company owns 80% of S Company's outstanding shares. At the end of Year 3, S Company has outstanding $400,000 of 4% bonds having 10 years to run, and carried at a book value of $420,000. Because market rates of interest have risen since these bonds were issued, the bonds sell at a discount on January 1 of Year 4, when P Company buys on the open market 60% of the issue (maturity value $240,000) for $225,000. From the viewpoint of the individual companies, P has acquired an investment yielding more than 4%, and S's position remains unchanged; it has outstanding an issue of 4% bonds sold to yield less than 4%. From a consolidated viewpoint, however, there is a difference between the intercompany asset and liability which must be considered:

	100% of issue	60% of issue
Bond liability carried on S's books at	$420,000	$252,000
Bond investment carried on P's books at		225,000
Excess of intercompany liability over related asset		$ 27,000

From the viewpoint of the consolidated entity, the purchase by P Company of 60% of S Company's bond issue for $225,000 in effect canceled $252,000 of debt and produced a net increase in consolidated owners' equity of $27,000. But how should this increase be allocated between the controlling and minority interests? There is no simple, unequivocal answer to this question, since the ultimate disposition of the bonds is uncertain. The two approaches to the issue discussed next make clear the dilemma:

1. Since the affiliated group of companies operate under common control, we might assume that whichever affiliate buys the bonds (in this case, P Company) is acting as an agent for the issuing company. It follows that any gain on the retirement of the bonds should be assigned to the issuing company. In our example this means that the $27,000 increase in owners' equity would be assigned to S Company on consolidated working papers and ultimately 80% of the gain would be allocated to the controlling interest and 20% to the minority stockholders of S. The end accounting result is the same as if P Company had agreed to relinquish the bonds to S upon reimbursement of their $225,000 cost; in that case S would retire $252,000 of debt for $225,000 and have a $27,000 gain.

The major difficulty with this approach is that the assumptions may not square with future events. If, for example, P continues to hold the bonds to maturity, S Company will ultimately pay $240,000 to P Company and the $27,000 consolidated gain should be allocated $12,000 to S and $15,000 to P as follows:

Book value of bond liability on S's books	*$252,000*	*12,000 "gain" to S*
Maturity value of bonds held by P	*240,000*	
Purchase price paid by P	*225,000*	*15,000 "gain" to P*

2. This difficulty suggests a second possible approach; namely, to assume that the purchasing affiliate will hold the bonds to maturity and receive $240,000 from the issuing affiliate. This assumption dictates that $12,000 of the gain be assigned to S Company and $15,000 to P Company. We should note that S Company will in fact record $12,000 ''gain'' on its books during the next 10 years by amortizing $12,000 of bond premium as a reduction of its interest cost on these bonds. Similarly P Company will recognize $15,000 of ''gain'' on its books by amortizing $15,000 of discount on these bonds over the 10-year holding period as an addition to interest revenues.

There are also flaws in this assumption. The maturity value of the bonds is a significant figure only at the maturity date. At the date P Company purchased the bonds, the present value of the payments promised by S Company under the bond contract is reflected in the $225,000 price paid. Furthermore, if S Company were to retire the debt at any time short of maturity, the fair price to reimburse P Company is the current market price of the bonds, not maturity value. Similarly if P were to resell the bonds outside the consolidation, the proceeds would reflect market value, not maturity value.

This basic dilemma cannot be resolved solely on the basis of logic, since it is a product of uncertainty about the ultimate disposition of the bonds held within the affiliated group. In the face of this uncertainty the most reasonable position (in the authors' opinion) is to adopt a consolidated viewpoint and assume that the buying affiliate acts as an agent for the issuing affiliate (approach 1). The consolidated gain or loss will thus be the entire difference between the book value of the liability and the purchase price paid by the buying affiliate. This gain or loss will be allocated to the issuing company at the date of the purchase of the bonds, and this allocation will be adjusted in subsequent periods as premium or discount is amortized by both the purchasing and issuing affiliates.

To illustrate the appropriate consolidating procedures, we shall continue with the example we have just considered, and demonstrate consolidating working papers first at January 1, Year 4, the date the bonds were acquired, and second, at the end of Year 5 after P Company had held the bonds for two years.

Consolidating working papers at date bonds were acquired. The balance sheet working papers on page 350 are based on the following assumptions: P Company acquired an 80% interest in S Company for $320,000 several years ago when S Company had net assets of $400,000, represented by $350,000 in capital stock and $50,000 in retained earnings. Note that P Company paid exactly book value for its investment (80% of $400,000 = $320,000).

The elimination of the intercompany bondholding is made in entry (a). Note that liabilities are reduced by $252,000 ($240,000 face value plus 60% of the $20,000 premium on bonds payable) and assets are reduced by $225,000. The difference of $27,000 is treated as a consolidated gain assigned to S Company, which in entry (b) is allocated $21,600 (80%) to the controlling interest and $5,400 (20%) to the minority interest.

The basis for the elimination of P's investment in S Company, entries (c) and (d), is shown below:

		Total	*80% controlling interest*	*20% minority interest*
Book value of S Company at acquisition		*$400,000*	*$320,000*	*$80,000*
Growth of S since acquisition:				
S's retained earnings now	*$120,000*			
S's retained earnings at date of acquisition	*50,000*	*70,000*	*56,000**	*14,000*
Book value of S at beginning of Year 4, eliminated in entry (d)		*$470,000*	*$376,000*	*$94,000*

* *This $56,000, together with P's $21,600 share of the gain on bond retirement, is added to P's retained earnings to arrive at consolidated retained earnings of $337,600.*

Consolidating working papers after date of bond acquisition. The major consolidating problem on the date intercompany bonds are acquired is simply to allocate between the controlling and minority interests any consolidated gain or loss arising from the debt retirement. This problem remains in subsequent periods (until the bonds are resold by the investing affiliate, or paid by the issuing affiliate) but the eliminations become more complex. The individual companies, in the process of recording effective interest revenues and interest expense, will modify the asset and liability valuations that existed at the time the intercompany bonds were purchased. As a result the initial consolidated gain or loss (measured by the difference between the book value of the debt and the price paid for the bonds) will be altered by the effect of premium and discount amortization on the books of both affiliates.

To illustrate this point we shall carry forward our previous example for two years (Years 4 and 5). Assuming, for convenience, that both affiliates amortize bond

P AND S COMPANIES
Working Papers—Consolidated Balance Sheet
beginning of Year 4

	P Company	S Company	Adjustments and eliminations Dr	Cr	Consolidated balance sheet
Assets:					
Investment in S—80%	320,000		(c) 56,000	(d) 376,000	
S Company bonds owned 60% (at cost)	225,000			(a) 225,000	
Other assets	325,000	920,000			1,245,000
Totals	870,000	920,000			1,245,000
Liabilities & Equity:					
4% bonds payable—S		400,000	(a) 240,000		160,000
Premium on bonds payable		20,000	(a) 12,000		8,000
Other liabilities	110,000	30,000			140,000
Capital stock—P	500,000				500,000
Retained earnings—P	260,000			(c) 21,600 (b) 56,000	337,600
Capital stock—S		350,000	(d) 350,000		
Retained earnings—S		120,000	(d) 120,000		
Gain on retirement of consolidated debt—S			(b) 27,000	(a) 27,000	
Minority interest in S Company				(b) 5,400 (d) 94,000	99,400
Totals	870,000	920,000			1,245,000

(a) To eliminate investment in 60% of S Company bonds against liability on S Company's books, and record consolidated gain on debt retirement.
(b) To allocate gain on retirement of bonds (assigned to S Company) among controlling and minority interests.
(c) To increase P's investment account by 80% of growth in S since date of acquisition. Growth = $70,000 × 80% = $56,000.
(d) To eliminate P's investment account against ownership equity of S Company, and record minority interest of 20%.

discount and premium on a straight-line basis, the changes during this two-year period in the book value of the bond asset and bond liability accounts are shown in the schedule at the top of page 351.

It is clear that the book values of the bonds on S's and P's books are moving toward $240,000, the maturity value. Each year S Company amortizes bond premium, reducing the book value of the 60% of the debt held intercompany by $1,200; and each year P Company amortizes purchase discount, increasing the book value of the bonds owned by $1,500. As a result of these two events the initial difference between the book value of P's asset and S's liability ($27,000) shrinks by $2,700 each year. How should we deal with this shrinkage in the consolidating process?

	60% of bond issue on S Company's books	*Bonds owned—on P Company's books*	*Difference*
Book values at date of acquisition, Jan. 1, Year 4	$252,000	$225,000	$27,000
Amortization of issue premium and purchase discount during Year 4	(1,200)	1,500	(2,700)
Book values at the end of Year 4	$250,800	$226,500	$24,300
Amortization of issue premium and purchase discount during Year 5	(1,200)	1,500	(2,700)
Book values at end of Year 5	$249,600	$228,000	$21,600

We should first note that the $2,700 annual erosion of the original gain or loss on intercompany bond acquisition is reflected on the consolidated income statement. Each year there is a $2,700 difference between interest revenues on P's books and interest expense (applicable to the bonds held intercompany) on S's books:

	Debit (credit)		
	S Company—expense		*P Company (revenues)*
	On all bonds	*60% held by P*	
Interest paid—4% of face value	$16,000	$9,600	$ (9,600)
Purchase discount amortization			(1,500)
Issue premium amortization	(2,000)	(1,200)	
Interest (revenue) or expense	$14,000	$8,400	$(11,100)
Less: Interest expense			8,400
Excess of intercompany revenues over intercompany expense			$ 2,700

In each year after the date of bond acquisition, we should eliminate $11,100 of P's interest revenues and $8,400 of S's interest expense, or $2,700 more revenue than expense, thus reducing total consolidated net income by $2,700. A little thought will show that this $2,700 should be charged against the net income of the issuing company, S Company. At the time the bonds were reacquired within the affiliation, we added $27,000 to S's retained earnings on the grounds that any consolidated gain on bond reacquisition should be credited to the issuing company. Now in each subsequent year the two affiliated companies will recognize $2,700 of the initial gain (S Company by decreasing its liability account $1,200; and P Company by increasing its asset account $1,500) and this $2,700 should be removed each year from total consolidated net income, since the entire $27,000 gain was included as an element of consolidated net income at the time the bonds were reacquired within the affiliation. We remove the $2,700 from S's net income since the original $27,000 gain was credited to S Company.

Intercompany bondholding case, two years later

P AND S COMPANIES
Working Papers—Consolidated Income Statement
Year 5

	P Company	S Company	Adjustments and eliminations Dr	Adjustments and eliminations Cr	Consolidated income statement
Credits:					
Revenues	500,000	400,000			900,000
Interest revenue	11,100		(a) 11,100		
Totals	511,100	400,000			900,000
Debits:					
Cost of goods sold	312,000	276,000			588,000
Other expenses	156,100	84,000			240,100
Interest expense		14,000		(a) 8,400	5,600
Net income—P	43,000		(b) 18,640		61,640
Net income—S		26,000		(a) 2,700 (b) 23,300	
Minority interest in income of S			(b) 4,660		4,660
Totals	511,100	400,000			900,000

(a) To eliminate P's interest revenues from S Company bonds against 60% of interest expense recorded by S Company:

	P Company	60% of S Company
Interest paid (4% of $240,000)	$ 9,600	$9,600
Discount amortization	1,500	
Premium amortization		(1,200)
	$11,100	$8,400

(b) To allocate adjusted net income of S Company ($23,300) between controlling (80%) and minority (20%) interests.

Working papers for the consolidated income statement for Year 5 are shown above. Eliminating entry (a) accomplishes the elimination of the intercompany interest revenue and expense and the adjustment of S's net income by $2,700. S Company's adjusted net income ($23,300) is then allocated between the controlling and minority interests in entry (b).

Working papers for the consolidated balance sheet as of the end of Year 5 are shown on page 353. Some detailed comments on the eliminating entries in this working paper are in order.

The intercompany debt is eliminated and the resulting gain or loss allocated in entry (a). Refer back to the schedule on page 351 to see how the figures in entry (a) were derived. As of the end of Year 5 we find it necessary to offset bonds owned, carried by P at $228,000, against the bond liability of $249,600 (60% of the bonds) on S's books, leaving a difference of $21,600 to be accounted for *at the end of Year 5*. Note however that *at the beginning of Year 4* this difference was $27,000, and *at the beginning of Year 5* it was $24,300. Remember also that the

P AND S COMPANIES
Working Papers—Consolidated Balance Sheet
as of the end of Year 5

	P Company	S Company	Adjustments and eliminations		Consolidated balance sheet
			Dr	Cr	
Assets:					
Investment in S—80%	320,000		(b) 97,840	(c) 417,840	
S Company bonds owned 60% (at cost)	228,000			(a) 228,000	
Other assets	383,000	973,000			1,356,000
Totals	931,000	973,000			1,356,000
Liabilities & Equity:					
4% bonds payable—S		400,000	(a) 240,000		160,000
Premium on bonds payable		16,000	(a) 9,600		6,400
Other liabilities	98,000	33,000			131,000
Capital stock—P	500,000				500,000
Beginning retained earnings—P	290,000			(b) 97,840	387,840
Net income—P	43,000			(d) 18,640	61,640
Capital stock—S		350,000	(c) 350,000		
Beginning retained earnings—S		148,000	(c) 172,300	(a) 24,300	
Net income—S		26,000	(a) 2,700 (d) 23,300		
Minority interest in S Company				(c) 104,460 (d) 4,660	109,120
Totals	931,000	973,000			1,356,000

(a) *To eliminate bonds owned by P Company against 60% of the book value of S Company's liability. Difference: $249,600 − $228,000 = $21,600. Difference at beginning of Year 5: 60% × $418,000 = $250,800 − $226,500 = $24,300 added to S's beginning retained earnings; $2,700 eliminated against S's income.*

(b) *To add to P's investment the growth (adjusted) in S Company to the beginning of Year 5. Retained earnings on Jan. 1, Year 5 = $172,300 − retained earnings at acquisition of $50,000 = $122,300 × 80% = $97,840.*

(c) *To eliminate P's investment against ownership equity of S at beginning of Year 5 and record minority interest as of beginning of Year 5.*

(d) *To allocate S Company's Year 5 adjusted net income ($23,300) between controlling (80%) and minority (20%) interests.*

initial gain of $27,000 was added to total consolidated retained earnings, and in each of the next 10 years consolidated net income will be reduced by $2,700 to cancel out the gradual recognition of intercompany gain by P and S Companies as they amortize purchase discount and issue premium. Remember also that the original gain of $27,000 was credited to S Company, and the $2,700 cancellation each year is charged against S's net income, since S is the issuing company in this case. Now it should be clear that the $24,300 of consolidated gain on debt retirement should be added to S's retained earnings as of the beginning of Year 5 and that $2,700 should be eliminated from S's net income, thus accounting for the $21,600 discrepancy between the bond asset and liability accounts at the end of Year 5. If we look at eliminating entry (a) in journal entry form, we can see how the parts fit together.

Eliminating entry (a)		
Bonds Payable (S Company's books)	*240,000*	
Premium on Bonds Payable (S Company's books)	*9,600*	
Net Income of S Company	*2,700*	
Bonds Owned (P Company's books)		*228,000*
Retained Earnings (S Company's books)		*24,300*
To eliminate intercompany debt on balance sheet working papers.		

The purpose of entry (b) on the balance sheet working papers (page 353) is to adjust P's investment account from a cost to an equity basis in preparation for elimination against S's ownership equity as of the beginning of Year 5. The amount of the adjustment is computed as follows:

Book value of S Company at beginning of Year 5:		
Capital stock	*$350,000*	
Retained earnings, adjusted by entry (a)	*172,300*	*$522,300*
Book value of S Company at date P Company acquired an 80% interest:		
Capital stock	*$350,000*	
Retained earnings	*50,000*	*400,000*
Increase in book value of S Company from date of acquisition to beginning of Year 5		*$122,300*
P Company's share of above increase (80% of $122,300), entry (b)		*$ 97,840*

When P's investment account has been updated by adding the proportionate share of S Company's growth since acquisition, the elimination of the investment and ownership equity accounts, entry (c), is made as follows:

As of the Beginning of Year 5

S Company's ownership equity:			*Consolidated allocation:*	
Capital stock		*$350,000*	*P's investment, 80% controlling interest*	*$417,840*
Retained earnings	*$148,000*			
Adjustment (a)	*24,300*	*172,300*	*Minority interest, 20%*	*104,460*
		$522,300		*$522,300*

Summary comments—intercompany bondholdings

The illustration just completed involved a particular set of facts; the procedures developed in consolidating the statements of P and S Companies can, however, be generalized as follows:

Amount of gain or loss. When one affiliate buys the debt securities of another, the debt is retired from a consolidated viewpoint, and any difference between the valuation of the debt and the purchase price is a consolidated gain or loss. Whether the bonds were originally issued at a discount or a premium and whether the price paid by the buying affiliate is above or below maturity value are irrelevant. For example, if the debt is carried at 90 and purchased at 96, there is a loss of $6 per $100 of bonds repurchased; if the debt is carried at 105 and bought back at 103, there is a gain of $2 per $100 of bonds repurchased.

Allocation of gain or loss. It is usually reasonable to assume that the buying company acts as an agent of the issuing company, since both operate under common control. Therefore any consolidated gain or loss resulting from intercompany bondholdings should be allocated to the issuing company, without regard to whether that company is the parent or subsidiary.

Subsequent adjustment of gain or loss. If one affiliate owns bonds of another and either or both companies amortize premium or discount, there will be a gradual recognition, on the books of the individual companies involved, of the original consolidated gain or loss on bond retirement. This periodic adjustment will show up as a difference between net interest revenue and interest expense to be eliminated in determining total consolidated net income. The appropriate consolidating procedure is to treat this difference as an adjustment of the net income of the company issuing the bonds, since any initial gain or loss at time bonds are reacquired within the affiliation will have been attributed to the issuing company. If the intercompany bonds are held to maturity, the series of annual income adjustments will ultimately exactly cancel the initial consolidated gain or loss recognized.

Alternative method of allocating gain or loss on intercompany bonds. Some accountants prefer to allocate the consolidated gain or loss resulting from intercompany bondholdings on the basis of the maturity value of the bonds. If this approach is followed, any difference between the purchase price of the bonds and their maturity value is charged or credited to the retained earnings of the buying company; any differences between the book value of the intercompany bonds payable and their maturity value is charged or credited to the retained earnings of the issuing company. As a result of these adjustments, the intercompany bond asset and liability accounts are both restated to maturity value and may be offset on consolidated working papers.

On the income statement, any difference between intercompany interest revenues and interest expense caused by variations in the amortization of discount or premium on the books of the holder and debtor companies is similarly allocated between the buying and selling companies. The effect of the amortization of purchase premium or discount is eliminated from the revenues and the income of the buying company; and the effect of the amortization of issuing discount or premium on intercompany bonds is eliminated from expense and the income of the issuing company.

To illustrate, assume that A Company has $100,000 of 5% bonds outstanding, carried as a liability at $104,000. At the beginning of the current year B Company, an affiliate, buys one-half ($50,000 face value) of these bonds at $44,000. The bonds have 10 years to run and both companies amortize premium and discount on a straight-line basis. The appropriate eliminating entries to consolidate the accounts of the two companies at the end of the current year, under the alternative approach, are illustrated below:

Consolidating Entries

Balance sheet working papers

Net Income—A Company......	*200*	
Net Income—B Company......	*600*	
Bonds Payable—A Company...	*51,800*	
Bonds Owned—B Company		*44,600*
Beginning Retained Earnings—A Company......		*2,000*
Beginning Retained Earnings—B Company......		*6,000*
To eliminate intercompany bonds as of the end of the current year, and to adjust beginning retained earnings and net income.		

Income statement working papers

Interest Revenues.............	*3,100*	
Interest Expense..........		*2,300*
Net Income—A Company		*200*
Net Income—B Company		*600*
To eliminate intercompany interest revenues ($2,500 + $600 discount amortization) and interest expense ($2,500 – $200 premium amortization).		

Pooling of interest versus purchase concept

Thus far we have discussed the preparation of consolidated financial statements in situations in which we assumed that the parent company *purchased* its equity interest in a subsidiary. Under certain conditions accountants have adopted an alternative viewpoint, called the *pooling of interest* interpretation, which produces significantly different consolidated results. Whether a given business combination should be interpreted as a purchase or a pooling transaction is often difficult to determine and the entire issue is currently the subject of considerable controversy.[1]

Accountants are generally agreed that the acquisition by one company (B Company) of a substantial proportion of the stock equity of another company (S Company) through an exchange of assets for stock (or debt for stock) is properly inter-

[1] An excellent analysis and review of the controversy has been prepared by Arthur R. Wyatt, "A Critical Study of Accounting for Business Combinations," *Accounting Research Study No. 5,* American Institute of Certified Public Accountants (New York: 1963).

preted as a *purchase*. The important characteristic of this transaction is that a material portion of the original equity interest in S Company is eliminated in the transaction. S Company stockholders obtain cash or other assets in exchange for their former equity interest in S Company.

The pooling of interest interpretation has been proposed to cover the general situation in which one company (B Company) acquires a substantial portion of the stock equity of another company (S Company) through an exchange of equity shares.[2] In this case the important characteristic is that all the equity interests in the individual companies (B and S) continue in the consolidated entity. The former stockholders of S Company now hold B Company stock, which represents an equity interest in the combined net assets of both companies. Any stockholders of S Company not involved in the transaction remain minority stockholders of S Company, with an interest which is in essence unchanged by the pooling transaction.

The accounting distinction between the "purchase" and "pooling" cases centers on the valuation of the net assets of S Company after the combination and the amount of consolidated retained earnings. Under the *purchase* assumption, the net assets of the acquired company (S Company) are valued on consolidated statements at cost or the fair market value of the consideration given in exchange. (The treatment of differences between cost and the book value of the underlying net assets of subsidiaries was discussed in detail in Chapter 8.) In addition, the equity interest of the parent company in the subsidiary's retained earnings at date of acquisition is eliminated from the consolidated balance sheet and only retained earnings subsequent to acquisition are included in consolidated retained earnings.

When a combination is deemed to be a pooling of interest, a new basis of accountability for the subsidiary's net assets does not arise. The net assets of the subsidiary company, if stated in conformity with generally accepted accounting principles, are carried forward to consolidated statements at their book value on S Company's records. Furthermore, the retained earnings (or deficits) of the affiliated companies are combined and reported on consolidated statements without regard to whether they occurred prior to or after the date of acquisition. The stated capital of the consolidated entity may be more or less than the total of the stated capital of the affiliated companies. When the stated capital is larger, the excess is deducted first from the total of any other contributed capital and then from the combined consolidated retained earnings. If the stated capital is smaller, the difference is reported on consolidated balance sheets as capital paid in in excess of stated capital.

Illustration

Before evaluating the pooling of interest concept, we shall illustrate the purchase and pooling principles as applied to a relatively simple situation involving the

[2] The "pooling of interest" idea first received authoritative attention in 1950 with the publication of *Accounting Research Bulletin No. 40,* which later became chap. 7C in *Accounting Research Bulletin No. 43,* the restatement and revision of *ARB's* which appeared in 1953. This pronouncement was subsequently superseded by *ARB 48,* "Business Combinations," issued in 1957. The continuing controversy over purchase versus pooling interpretations, however, presumably led to the commissioning of *Accounting Research Study No. 5* (to which we have already referred) by Arthur Wyatt in 1963.

acquisition of the shares of a subsidiary by a parent company. As a basis for our illustration, assume the following highly condensed balance sheets for B and S Companies at the beginning of Year 1:

	B Company	*S Company*
Assets (details omitted)	*$550,000*	*$228,000*
Liabilities	*$ 50,000*	*$ 28,000*
Capital stock, $100 par value	*300,000*	*100,000*
Additional paid-in capital	*50,000*	
Retained earnings	*150,000*	*100,000*
Total liabilities & capital	*$550,000*	*$228,000*

On January 1, Year 1, B Company acquired a 90% equity interest in S Company. We shall assume two different modes of acquisition: (1) *The purchase assumption:* B Company purchased 90% of S Company's outstanding shares for $216,000, giving S Company shareholders one-year interest-bearing notes in this amount. (2) *The pooling assumption:* B Company exchanged 1,080 shares of its own common stock (current market value $200 per share) for 900 of the 1,000 shares of S Company common stock outstanding.

The working papers to consolidate B and S Companies in Case 1, involving the acquisition of a 90% interest by purchase, are illustrated on page 359. No new feature is introduced here; the net assets of S Company are revalued upward by $40,000 on the basis of the price paid by B Company for its 90% interest, and the elimination of investment against equity accounts is made in the normal fashion.

The pooling of interest interpretation fits Case 2 since none of the stockholders' equity of S Company has been eliminated; all the former shareholders of S Company have an equity interest in some part of the new consolidated entity as follows: Holders of 900 shares of S Company now own 1,080 shares of B Company; holders of 100 shares of S Company (10% minority interest) continue to hold 100 shares in S Company.

The management of B Company faces a choice in recording its investment in 900 shares of S Company. The 90% interest may be recorded at (1) the market value of the shares given in exchange (1,080 × $200 = $216,000); (2) the book value of S's 900 shares (90% of $200,000 = $180,000); or (3) the stated value of shares issued (1,080 × $100 par value = $108,000). The entries made on B Company's books at date of acquisition under these three alternatives are shown below:

	(1) Market value of B shares		*(2) Book value of S shares*		*(3) Stated value of B shares*	
Investment	*216,000*		*180,000*		*108,000*	
Capital Stock		*108,000*		*108,000*		*108,000*
Additional Paid-in Capital		*108,000*		*72,000*		*-0-*

Purchase interpretation: Case 1

B AND S COMPANIES
Consolidating Working Papers—Balance Sheet
as of the beginning of Year 1

	B Company	S Company	Adjusting and eliminating entries Dr	Cr	Consolidated balance sheet
Investment in S	216,000			(b) 216,000	
Other assets	550,000	228,000			778,000
Goodwill			(a) 40,000		40,000
Total net assets	766,000	228,000			818,000
Liabilities	266,000	28,000			294,000
Capital stock—B	300,000				300,000
Additional paid-in capital—B	50,000				50,000
Retained earnings—B	150,000				150,000
Capital stock—S		100,000	(b) 100,000		
Appraisal capital—S			(b) 40,000	(a) 40,000	
Retained earnings—S		100,000	(b) 100,000		
Minority interest—S				(b) 24,000	24,000
Total liabilities	766,000	228,000			818,000

(a) To record goodwill of S Company implied by price paid by B Company for 90% interest:

B paid $216,000 for 90% interest, which implies a value for S Company of ($216,000 ÷ .90)	$240,000
Book value of B Company's net assets at date of acquisition	200,000
Goodwill	$ 40,000

(b) To eliminate B's investment against S Company's ownership equity accounts and establish 10% minority interest.

If B Company had followed alternative (2) or (3) (see page 358) in recording its investment, the eliminating entry would have been as follows:

	Investment in S Company recorded at: (2) Book value		(3) Stated value of shares issued	
Capital Stock—S	100,000		100,000	
Retained Earnings	10,000		10,000	
Additional Paid-in Capital—B	90,000		18,000	
Investment in S		180,000		108,000
Minority Interest—S		20,000		20,000

Note that either of these two eliminations results in the same minority interest ($20,000), the same consolidated retained earnings ($240,000), and the same balance in additional paid-in capital ($32,000) in the consolidated financial statements.

Pooling of interest interpretation: Case 2

B AND S COMPANIES
Consolidating Working Papers—Balance Sheet
as of the beginning of Year 1

	B Company	S Company	Adjusting and eliminating entries Dr	Adjusting and eliminating entries Cr	Consolidated balance sheet
Investment in S—90%	216,000			(b) 216,000	
Other assets	550,000	228,000			778,000
Total net assets	766,000	228,000			778,000
Liabilities	50,000	28,000			78,000
Capital stock—B	408,000				408,000
Additional paid-in capital—B	158,000		(b) 126,000		32,000
Capital stock—S		100,000	(a) 10,000 (b) 90,000		
Retained earnings	150,000	100,000	(a) 10,000		240,000
Minority interest—S				(a) 20,000	20,000
Total liabilities	766,000	228,000			778,000

(a) To establish the 10% minority interest in S Company at book value.
(b) To eliminate B Company's investment account against the stated capital of S Company, and to charge the excess of $126,000 against additional paid-in capital. (If no paid-in capital account existed, consolidated retained earnings would be reduced by the excess of investment over stated capital.)

The choice of entries to record the acquisition of a 90% interest in S Company will affect the individual financial statements of B Company. However, consolidated statements prepared under a pooling of interest interpretation will be the same no matter which approach B Company uses. The working papers to consolidate B and S Companies under the pooling of interest concept and assuming that B Company records its investment in S at $216,000 (the market value of the shares given in exchange) are shown on page 360. The same consolidated results would be obtained if B Company had valued its shares in S Company at book value, or at the stated capital of the 1,080 shares issued in exchange.

In consolidating the statements of affiliated companies under a pooling of interest interpretation, the procedure is designed to carry forward the net assets of the companies on the same basis of accountability as was in effect on the books of the constituent companies, assuming assets and liabilities are stated in conformity with generally accepted accounting principles. In addition the retained earnings balance of the two companies are simply combined, with no elimination of the parent's share of the subsidiary's retained earnings at the date of acquisition.

The stated capital of the consolidated entity may be more or less than the total of the stated capitals of the constituent companies (that is, the stated capital of the parent just prior to affiliation plus the controlling interest in the stated capital of the subsidiary). If the stated capital of the consolidated entity is smaller than the combined stated capital of the affiliates, the difference may appear in the consolidated balance sheet as additional paid-in capital. If it is larger, the excess stated capital should be charged first against consolidated paid-in capital, and next against consolidated retained earnings.

In the example on page 360, note that the stated capital of the consolidated entity is $408,000, while the combined stated capital of the two affiliates was $390,000 ($300,000 capital stock of the parent plus $90,000, the 90% controlling interest in the capital stock of the subsidiary company). The difference of $18,000 ($408,000 – $390,000) is removed from additional paid-in capital, reducing the consolidated additional paid-in capital from the balance of $50,000 on the parent's books prior to affiliation (see page 359) to $32,000 on the consolidated statement.

The two primary differences in the results under the purchase and the pooling of interest interpretations may be seen by comparing the consolidated results in these two cases. In each case B Company gave up economic resources worth $216,000 in exchange for its 90% interest in S. In the purchase case the price was paid in short-term debt; in the pooling case the price was paid in shares of stock having a fair market value of $216,000. Under the purchase interpretation the net assets of B Company were revalued to a basis consistent with a cost of $216,000 for a 90% interest, and no part of S Company's retained earnings were included in consolidated retained earnings at date of acquisition. Under the pooling interpretation the net assets of S Company were carried forward at prior book values, and the consolidated retained earnings figure of $240,000 included $90,000, or 90% of S Company's retained earnings at date of acquisition.

Evaluation of the pooling concept

The pooling of interest interpretation is proposed in those cases where there is a substantial continuity of ownership equity before and after the fusion of the net assets of two or more entities into one economic entity.[3] It is argued that such continuity of ownership calls for continuity in asset valuations rather than the establishment of a new accounting basis for the assets.

Despite its widespread acceptance in practice, there is continued and authoritative opposition to the pooling of interest concept. As is true in many accounting controversies, there are strong practical pressures favoring the pooling approach which are perhaps more important in explaining its acceptance than the merits of the theoretical rationale. The income tax law plays an important role in the controversy. Business combinations involving an exchange of shares are generally tax-free, which means that no taxable gain or loss is recognized at the time of the exchange and any asset revaluations or goodwill recorded at the date of acquisition have no tax status. Thus any increase in net assets recorded at the time of the combination cannot be written off against subsequent taxable income. On the other hand, accounting amortization of increased valuations recognized at the time of combination will depress reported net income and earnings per share figures in subsequent periods. Management does not look with favor on an accounting procedure that would result in recording goodwill or increases in

[3] For a discussion of the factors characterizing a pooling of interest, see *Intermediate Accounting* in this series, pp. 754–756.

tangible assets at the time of combination and lower reported earnings in subsequent periods when the higher values are amortized as non-tax-deductible charges against income.

Those opposed to the pooling concept argue that most if not all business combinations result in an economic exchange, regardless of the kinds of assets or securities exchanged, and there is thus good reason for establishing a new basis of accountability at this time. The accountant is faced with a market transaction between independent parties having generally adverse interests. Such an event produces valid economic evidence in the market values (of the net assets or the shares of stock) established in the negotiations leading up to the consolidation. It is clear that the fair market value of the assets exchanged is a far more significant figure to the new entity than the existing book values of the predecessor corporation. This reasoning has led one authority to conclude that, "No basis exists in principle for a continuation of what is presently known as 'pooling of interests' accounting if the business combination involves an exchange of assets and or equities between independent parties."[4]

Summary

The controversy between the purchase and pooling of interest interpretation arises when two or more companies merge into a single legal or economic entity through an exchange of shares of stock, in such a manner that there is a substantial continuity of ownership equity between the predecessor companies and the new entity. Under a purchase interpretation the net assets of the subsidiary company are revalued on the basis of the fair market value of the shares given in exchange, and only earnings of the subsidiary subsequent to the date of acquisition are included in consolidated retained earnings. Under the pooling interpretation the net assets of the subsidiary company are carried forward at book values and any excess of cost over book value is immediately eliminated, first against additional paid-in capital, and second, against consolidated retained earnings. In addition the retained earnings of both companies (subject to any necessary adjustments related to stated capital) are combined and carried forward as consolidated retained earnings. The minority interest, if any, is the sum of the minority share of stated capital at date of acquisition plus the minority share of retained earnings.

If the valuation of net assets can be established objectively on the basis of the market values of the shares exchanged, logic and theory point to the general relevance and desirability of a "fresh start" in valuation at the time of combination. Practical considerations, such as banker and creditor antagonism to goodwill, management's opposition to the depressing effect on earnings after the consolidation when intangible assets are amortized without income tax benefit, and a desire to combine the retained earnings of all affiliated companies—all these factors favor the pooling assumption. This controversy provides another illustration of the fact that the art of accounting is a product of conflict between pure theory and practical considerations. Practical considerations cannot be ignored since they exert a powerful influence on everything we do. On the other hand, the accountant best serves his function when he siezes every opportunity to incorporate current economic data, when it can be objectively determined, into his financial reporting.

[4] Wyatt, *op. cit.*, p. 105.

Questions

1. How does the process of eliminating intercompany profits on the sale of plant and equipment by one affiliate to another differ from the elimination of intercompany profits on the transfer of inventoriable goods?

2. B Company owns equipment which it purchased some years ago at a cost of $48,000, which has a book value of $18,000. At the beginning of the current year, B Company sold this equipment to C Company, a 75% owned affiliate, for $30,000. The equipment has a remaining service life at the date of sale of three years and an estimated salvage value of $6,000. Describe and explain the eliminating entries relating to this transaction that are necessary to consolidate both the balance sheet and income statement of these companies at the end of the current year.

3. From a consolidated viewpoint, the intercompany profit on the sale of a depreciable asset by one affiliate to another is realized gradually over the life of the asset. Explain.

4. An eliminating entry is made on a consolidated income statement removing $4,200 from the depreciation expense of Company D and adding $4,200 to the net income of Company E. Explain which company is the seller and which the buyer of the depreciable asset to which this adjustment relates.

5. Explain why it is appropriate to treat intercompany bondholdings as treasury bonds on a consolidated balance sheet.

6. Does the elimination of intercompany interest revenue and expense on bonds affect the consolidated net income for the period? Explain.

7. When one affiliate buys the bonds of another at a price which differs materially from book value on the debtor's books, there is a gain or loss from a consolidated viewpoint. Describe two approaches to the treatment of this difference on consolidated statements. What are the assumptions underlying each approach?

8. If the consolidated gain or loss on the intercompany acquisition of bonds is allocated to the issuing company at the date the bonds are purchased by an affiliate, what disposition should be made of this gain or loss (from a consolidated viewpoint) if the bonds were subsequently resold by the purchasing affiliate at its book value?

9. The pooling of interest interpretation of corporate consolidations is considered appropriate under certain conditions. Describe the essential conditions.

10. If the acquisition of a majority of the stock of a subsidiary is made under conditions that may appropriately be interpreted as a pooling of interest, what is the accounting effect as compared with a purchase interpretation?

Short cases for analysis

11-1 A pooling of interest may be described as a business combination of two or more corporations in which the common stockholders of the constituent corporations become the owners of a single corporation which owns the assets and businesses of the constituent corporations either directly or through one or more subsidiaries. It has been suggested that a number of factors should be considered in deciding in any given case whether a pooling of interest (as distinguished from a purchase) interpretation is pertinent; among them are (1) continuity of ownership, (2) continuity of assets, (3) continuity of management, and (4) relative size of the constituent companies.

The owners' equity sections of the balance sheets of two companies, as of the end of the current year, are given below:

	Pappas Company	*Stokes Company*
Capital stock, $100 par value	*$500,000*	*$100,000*
Additional paid-in capital	*80,000*	*50,000*
Retained earnings	*120,000*	*60,000*
Total owners' equity	*$700,000*	*$210,000*

At the date of the above statements, the Pappas Company acquired 80% of the outstanding shares of common stock of Stokes Company through an exchange of shares. Pappas gave four shares of 6%, $50 par value, convertible preferred stock in exchange for each share of Stokes Company common stock acquired. The preferred is convertible into common at any time after one year from date of the exchange, in a ratio of two shares of convertible preferred for one share of Pappas Company common. Stokes Company is a family-owned corporation and its management and board of directors will retire from active participation in the firm's affairs; Pappas Company will appoint a new board and new management, since there is no provision for cumulative voting of shares.

Instructions

a. Discuss the appropriateness of a pooling of interest interpretation in consolidating the statements of these two companies, in relation to the factors mentioned in the first paragraph of the problem. Would you recommend that the pooling or purchase assumption be followed in consolidation?

b. Prepare the owners' equity section of the consolidated balance sheet of Pappas and Stokes Companies as of the date of affiliation, assuming, without regard to your discussion in (a), that a pooling of interest interpretation is applied.

11-2 The condensed balance sheets of Calso and Dine Companies at the end of Year 1 are shown below:

	Calso Company	*Dine Company*
Various assets (details omitted)	*$570,000*	*$330,000*
Liabilities	*$ 70,000*	*$ 30,000*
Capital stock, $100 par value	*400,000*	*200,000*
Additional paid-in capital	*60,000*	*20,000*
Retained earnings	*40,000*	*80,000*
Total liabilities & equity	*$570,000*	*$330,000*

The management of Calso, at the date of the above statements, is negotiating for the acquisition of 80% of the capital stock of Dine Company, either through purchase or through an exchange of shares of stock. The market and book values per share of the two companies at the end of Year 1 are as follows:

	Book value	*Market value*
Calso Company common stock	*$125*	*$160*
Dine Company common stock	*150*	*160*

The alternatives under consideration are: (1) Calso would purchase for cash 1,600 shares of Dine common at $160 per share, a total price of $256,000. (2) Calso would exchange 1,600 of its shares for 1,600 of the shares of Dine stock.

Instructions

a. Assume that Calso purchased an 80% interest for cash. What are the alternative amounts at which total consolidated assets and minority interest might be shown on consolidated statements? Explain.

b. Assume that Calso acquires an 80% interest in Dine through an exchange of shares, and that consolidated statements will be prepared on a pooling of interest basis. Management is then faced with the question of the amount at which to record its investment:

(1) At the fair market value of the shares given in exchange
(2) At the book value of the 80% interest in Dine at date of acquisition
(3) At the stated capital of $100 per share

Assuming a pooling of interest interpretation, determine the amounts of the minority interest, the consolidated retained earnings, and the consolidated additional paid-in capital that would appear on the consolidated balance sheet at date of acquisition, under each of the three alternative methods of recording the investment. Explain any differences in the computed amounts.

c. Assume that you are asked to advise the company with respect to the choice between the purchase interpretation and the pooling of interest interpretation, when the acquisition is made through an exchange of shares. Write a brief statement of the factors that should be considered, and make a recommendation to management.

11-3 The individual and consolidated balance sheet and income statements of X and Y Companies for the current year are given on page 366.

The following additional information is presented for your consideration: X Company purchased its interest in Y Company several years ago. X Company sells products to Y Company for further processing, and also sells to firms outside the affiliated entity. The inventories of Y Company include an intercompany profit at both the beginning and end of the year. At the beginning of the current year, Y Company purchased bonds of X Company having a maturity value of $100,000. These bonds are held as a temporary investment and it is intended that no amortization of purchase premium will be made on either individual or consolidated statements. The bonds are carried by Y Company at cost. Y Company has agreed

X AND Y COMPANIES
Individual and Consolidated Balance Sheets
as of the end of the current year

	X Company	Y Company	Consolidated
Assets:			
Cash and receivables	$ 35,000	$108,000	$ 97,400
Inventories	40,000	90,000	122,000
Plant (net)	460,000	140,000	600,000
Appraisal increase of land			50,000
Investment in Y	245,000		-0-
X bonds owned		103,000	-0-
Total assets	$780,000	$441,000	$869,400
Liabilities & Owners' Equity:			
Current payables	$ 70,000	$ 23,000	$ 53,000
Dividends payable	10,000	8,000	12,400
Mortgage bonds (5%)	200,000	50,000	150,000
Capital stock	300,000	200,000	300,000
Retained earnings (ending)	200,000	160,000	231,000
Minority interest			123,000
Total liabilities & equity	$780,000	$441,000	$869,400

X AND Y COMPANIES
Individual and Consolidated Income Statements
current year

	X Company	Y Company	Consolidated
Sales	$600,000	$400,000	$760,000
Cost of sales	360,000	280,000	403,000
Gross profit	$240,000	$120,000	$357,000
Operating expense	130,000	54,000	184,000
Operating profit	$110,000	$ 66,000	$173,000
Interest revenue	1,800	5,000	1,800
Dividend revenue	11,200	-0-	-0-
Total	$123,000	$ 71,000	$174,800
Interest expense	10,000	3,000	8,000
Provision for income taxes	56,000	34,000	90,000
Nonrecurring loss			3,000
Minority share			10,200
Net income	$ 57,000	$ 34,000	$ 63,600
Dividends	20,000	16,000	24,800
Transfer to retained earnings	$ 37,000	$ 18,000	$ 38,800

to offer X Company the option of reacquiring the bonds at Y's cost, before deciding to dispose of the bonds on the open market.

Instructions

On the basis of the information you can develop from an analysis of the individual and consolidated statements, answer each of the following questions, showing clearly the computations necessary to support your conclusions.

a. Does X Company carry its investment in Y Company on the cost or equity (accrual) basis? Explain the basis for your conclusion.

b. If Y Company's common stock has a stated value of $100 per share, how many shares does X Company own? How did you determine this?

c. The appraisal increase appearing on the consolidated balance sheet represents a revaluation of land owned by Y Company on the basis of the price paid by X Company for its interest in Y. What was the balance of Y Company's retained earnings at the date of acquisition?

d. What is the nature of the nonrecurring loss appearing on the consolidated income statement? Reproduce the consolidating entry from which this figure originated, and explain.

e. What is the amount of intercompany sales during the current year by X Company to Y Company?

f. Are there any intercompany debts other than the intercompany bondholdings? Prepare a schedule of any such debts and demonstrate which company is the debtor and which the creditor in each instance, explaining your reasoning.

g. What is the explanation for the difference between the consolidated cost of goods sold and the combined cost of goods sold of the two affiliated companies? Prepare a schedule reconciling combined and consolidated cost of goods sold, showing the amount of intercompany profit in the beginning and ending inventories of Y Company, and demonstrating how you determined the amount of intercompany profit.

h. Show how the $10,200 minority interest in total consolidated net income was determined.

i. Show how the total minority interest on the balance sheet ($123,000) was determined.

j. Beginning with the $200,000 balance in X Company's retained earnings at the end of the current year, prepare a schedule in which you derive the $231,000 balance of consolidated retained earnings at the end of the current year.

Problems

11-4 The balance sheets of two affiliated companies, A and B, as of the end of Year 4 are presented below:

	A Company	*B Company*
Current assets	*$140,000*	*$ 85,000*
Investment in B Company—80% (cost)	*80,000*	
Plant and equipment	*300,000*	*280,000*
Accumulated depreciation	*(70,000)*	*(45,000)*
Total assets	*$450,000*	*$320,000*
Current liabilities	*$ 60,000*	*$ 90,000*
Capital stock	*300,000*	*100,000*
Beginning retained earnings	*55,000*	*80,000*
Net income—Year 4	*35,000*	*50,000*
Total liabilities & equity	*$450,000*	*$320,000*

A owns 80% of B Company's capital stock, acquired at par value at the date of organization. At the beginning of Year 2, A Company purchased from B Company for $60,000 equipment which B Company had manufactured at a cost of $40,000. A Company has depreciated this equipment on a straight-line basis at the rate of 20% per year.

Instructions

a. Present in journal form the necessary adjusting and eliminating entries to consolidate the balance sheets of these two companies as of the end of Year 4. Be sure to indicate in your account titles which company's accounts are affected by your entries.

b. What is the amount of consolidated net income for Year 4 and the minority interest at the end of Year 4?

11-5 The balance sheets of two affiliated companies as of the end of Year 6 are presented below:

	Pert Company	*Sort Company*
Current assets	*$230,000*	*$175,000*
Investment in Sort Company stock (cost)	*180,000*	
Investment in Pert Company bonds		*52,000*
Other assets	*480,000*	*300,000*
Total assets	*$890,000*	*$527,000*
Current liabilities	*$ 29,500*	*$ 96,000*
6% bonds payable ($100,000 maturity value)	*97,500*	
Capital stock	*400,000*	*200,000*
Beginning retained earnings	*300,000*	*160,000*
Net income	*63,000*	*71,000*
Total liabilities & equity	*$890,000*	*$527,000*

Pert Company owns 90% of the capital stock of Sort Company, acquired at the date of acquisition at par value. At the beginning of Year 2, Sort Company purchased $50,000 face value of Pert Company bonds, due 10 years from that date, for $54,000. The entire bond issue was carried on Pert Company's books at the beginning of Year 2 at $95,000. Pert Company amortizes bond discount on a straight-line basis in the amount of $500 each year. Sort Company amortizes the premium on its bond investment on a straight-line basis at the rate of $400 per year.

Instructions

a. Present in journal form the adjusting and eliminating entries necessary to consolidate the balance sheets of Pert Company and Sort Company as of the end of Year 6. Assume that any consolidated gain or loss resulting from the intercompany bondholdings will be attributed to the issuing company. Be sure to indicate in the account titles which company's accounts are affected by your entries.

b. What is the amount of consolidated net income for Year 6 and the total minority interest at the end of Year 6?

11-6 The financial statements of Avco and Zerco at the end of Year 1 are summarized below:

	Avco	Zerco
Balance sheet data:		
Current assets	$120,000	$120,000
Investment in Zerco—60%	276,000	
Building (net of depreciation)		430,000
Building site		50,000
Total assets	$396,000	$600,000
Current liabilities	$ 90,000	$ 20,000
Bonds payable—5%		400,000
Capital stock	250,000	100,000
Retained earnings—beginning of Year 1	36,000	60,000
Net income	40,000	24,000
Dividends	(20,000)	(4,000)
Total liabilities & equity	$396,000	$600,000
Income statement data:		
Rental revenues	$204,000	$106,000
Income of subsidiary	14,400	
Total revenues	$218,400	$106,000
Rent expense	$106,000	
Depreciation of building		$ 40,000
Other expense	43,400	10,000
Bond interest		20,000
Income taxes	29,000	12,000
Total expenses	$178,400	$ 82,000
Net income	$ 40,000	$ 24,000

Avco purchased a 60% interest in Zerco at the beginning of Year 1, on the basis of an appraisal showing that Zerco's land was worth $200,000 and its building worth $600,000 as of that date. Avco carries its investment in Zerco on an equity basis.

Zerco is depreciating the original cost of the building ($870,000) over a 20-year life, assuming a salvage value at the end of that time of $70,000.

Avco leased the property from Zerco starting in Year 1, and arranged to sub-lease portions of the building to industrial tenants. In consolidated statements Zerco's property will be valued on the basis of the appraised valuation and depreciated accordingly, with no change in the estimated salvage value.

Zerco declared $4,000 in dividends late in December, payable in January. Avco has recorded its share of these dividends as a current receivable.

Instructions

a. Prepare working papers for a consolidated balance sheet as of the end of Year 1 and a consolidated income statement for Year 1.

b. Prepare a statement of consolidated retained earnings for Year 1.

c. In what respects are the consolidated financial statements more useful to a stockholder of Avco than Avco's individual statement? Is there any value in the consolidated statements to the bondholders of Zerco? Why?

11-7 The condensed balance sheets as of the end of Year 2 and income statements for Year 2 of Fort and Greg Companies are shown below:

Balance Sheet Data
end of Year 2

	Fort Company	*Greg Company*
Current assets	*$ 70,000*	*$ 30,000*
Greg Company bonds	*20,000*	
Plant and equipment	*10,000*	*249,500*
Accumulated depreciation	*(2,000)*	*(60,000)*
Investment in Greg Company	*90,000*	
Total assets	*$188,000*	*$219,500*
Bonds payable		*$ 50,000*
Other liabilities	*$ 40,000*	*10,000*
Capital stock	*100,000*	*200,000*
Beginning retained earnings (deficit)	*18,000*	*(50,000)*
Net income	*30,000*	*9,500*
Total liabilities & owners' equity	*$188,000*	*$219,500*

Income Statement Data
Year 2

Sales revenues	*$172,000*	*$121,500*
Interest revenues	*1,000*	
Total revenues	*$173,000*	*$121,500*
Beginning inventory	*$ 20,000*	*$ 10,000*
Purchases	*80,000*	*58,000*
Ending inventory	*(30,000)*	*(20,000)*
Cost of goods sold	*$ 70,000*	*$ 48,000*
Operating expenses	*59,000*	*37,000*
Depreciation expense	*1,000*	*20,000*
Interest expense		*2,500*
Income taxes	*13,000*	*4,500*
Total expenses	*$143,000*	*$112,000*
Net income	*$ 30,000*	*$ 9,500*

Fort Company acquired 80% of the capital stock of Greg Company at the beginning of Year 1, at which time Greg's retained earnings were $10,000. Fort Company carries its investment account on an equity basis and the investment account balance of $90,000 reflects the changes in Greg's retained earnings from the date of acquisition to the beginning of Year 2, as reported on Greg's financial statements. No consolidating adjustments are included in Fort Company's investment account balance. There have been no changes recorded in Fort's investment account during Year 2.

At the beginning of Year 1, Fort Company purchased equipment from Greg Company for $10,000 which had cost Greg Company $12,000 and which was 50% depreciated on Greg's books at the time of sale. Fort Company has depreciated this equipment at the rate of 10% per year.

Fort Company buys all its merchandise from Greg Company. At the end of Year 1 there was an estimated intercompany markup of $8,000 in Fort's ending inventory, and at the end of Year 2 a markup of $17,000.

Fort Company purchased 40% of Greg's bonds at the end of Year 1 at face value. At the time Fort acquired its interest in Greg, it was recognized that land on Greg Company's books was overvalued, but no adjustment of the land value has been made on the books of Greg Company.

Instructions

a. Prepare working papers for a consolidated balance sheet as of the end of Year 2.

b. Prepare working papers for a consolidated income statement for Year 2.

c. Prepare a statement of consolidated retained earnings and changes in minority interest for Year 2.

11-8 Balance sheet and income statement data for two affiliated companies for the current year are given below and on page 372:

Balance Sheet Data
as of the end of the current year

	Park Company	*Site Company*
Cash	*$ 40,000*	*$ 21,000*
Receivables	*92,000*	*84,000*
Inventories	*56,000*	*45,000*
Land	*20,000*	*60,000*
Plant and equipment	*200,000*	*700,000*
Accumulated depreciation	*(80,000)*	*(350,000)*
Investment in Site Company (at cost)	*272,000*	
Advances to Site Company	*100,000*	
Total assets	*$700,000*	*$560,000*
Accounts payable	*$130,000*	*$ 96,500*
Advances payable		*100,000*
Capital stock	*400,000*	*200,000*
Beginning retained earnings	*162,300*	*154,000*
Net income for the year	*29,700*	*17,500*
Dividends	*(22,000)*	*(8,000)*
Total liabilities & owners' equity	*$700,000*	*$560,000*

Income Statement Data
current year

Sales revenues	$600,000	$400,000
Interest revenues	6,700	
Dividend revenues	6,400	
Total revenues	$613,100	$400,000
Cost of goods sold:		
Beginning inventory	$ 30,000	$ 60,000
Purchases of merchandise	360,000	210,000
Ending inventory	(56,000)	(45,000)
Cost of goods sold	$334,000	$225,000
Depreciation expense	20,000	70,000
Selling and administrative expense	207,000	74,000
Interest expense	1,700	6,000
Provision for income taxes	20,700	7,500
Total expenses	$583,400	$382,500
Net income	$ 29,700	$ 17,500

Park Company acquired an 80% interest in Site Company four years prior to the end of the current year at a cost of $272,000. During the negotiations with Site Company, the board of directors of Park Company had an appraisal made of the Site Company properties. The president of Park Company, in a letter to shareholders shortly after the acquisition, stated, "The total price paid to acquire 80% of the outstanding shares of Site Company was greater than the book value of the underlying assets. Of this amount, 25% reflects an undervaluation of a certain portion of Site Company's total plant and equipment.

The estimated service life of the particular undervalued assets mentioned by Park's president is 15 years from the date of their original acquisition by Site Company and no salvage value is contemplated. These assets were one-half depreciated on Site's books at the date Park acquired the shares of Site Company. At the date of acquisition Site Company reported retained earnings of $100,000.

Site Company sells products to Park Company at a negotiated price which has averaged 25% in excess of Site's cost during the current year. All but $5,000 of Park's inventories at the beginning of the year and $15,000 at the end of the current year were products acquired from Site Company. Intercompany sales during the current year amounted to $320,000.

Park Company made an advance of $100,000 to Site Company at the beginning of the current year to finance the acquisition of certain equipment. The advance is due on call, and the contract requires the payment of interest at 6% per year.

Instructions

Prepare consolidating working papers for a balance sheet and income statement for these two companies for the current year.

11-9 Proctor Company owns 80% of the capital stock of Sty Company and carries this investment on its books at cost, $280,000. At the date of acquisition, Sty Company had capital stock of $200,000 and retained earnings of $100,000. The stockholders' equity of the two companies at the end of Year 2 is as follows:

	Proctor Company	Sty Company
Capital stock	$500,000	$250,000 *
Paid-in excess of par value	80,000	25,000 *
Retained earnings, beginning of Year 2	32,000	153,000
Net income—Year 2	25,000	12,000
Dividends declared	(10,000)	(85,000)*
Total stockholders' equity	$627,000	$355,000

* *Stock dividend of $75,000 declared and paid in Year 2.*

At the beginning of Year 1, Sty Company sold equipment to Proctor Company for $24,000, which represented a markup of 20% above the book value of the machine on Sty's books. Proctor Company has taken a total of $4,800 in depreciation on this asset during Years 1 and 2.

At the time Proctor Company purchased its interest in Sty Company, it was determined that certain land on Sty Company's books was incorrectly valued, but no adjustment has been made to reflect this on Sty Company's statement. Any difference between the cost of the investment in Sty and the book value of its net assets is to be attributed to this factor, and the land revalued accordingly on consolidated statements.

Instructions

a. Prepare in journal form the necessary entries to effect the consolidation of these two companies. Show clearly the amount of the minority interest, either as part of your entries or in a separate schedule.

b. Prepare a statement of consolidated retained earnings for Year 2 and a statement explaining the changes in the minority interest during Year 2.

11-10 Condensed financial statements of Pluto and Saturn Companies prepared at the end of Year 3 are given below and on page 374:

PLUTO AND SATURN COMPANIES
Balance Sheets
end of Year 3

Assets	Pluto	Saturn
Cash	$ 14,000	$ 20,000
Receivables	25,000	21,000
Inventories	45,000	50,000
Plant	195,000	260,000
Allowance for depreciation	(35,000)	(40,000)
Other assets	59,600	
Investment in Saturn stock	107,400	
Investment in Saturn bonds	21,000	
Total assets	$432,000	$311,000

Liabilities & Stockholders' Equity

Current liabilities	$ 36,400	$ 49,000
Bonds payable, 5%		100,000
Common stock	350,000	125,000
Retained earnings, Jan. 1	38,000	25,000
Net income	32,600	24,000
Common dividends	(25,000)	(12,000)
Total liabilities & equity	$432,000	$311,000

PLUTO AND SATURN COMPANIES
Income Statements
Year 3

	Pluto	Saturn
Revenues:		
Sales revenues	$460,200	$270,000
Dividend revenues	9,600	
Interest revenues	800	
Total revenues	$470,600	$270,000
Expenses:		
Cost of goods sold:		
Beginning inventory	$ 40,000	$ 60,000
Purchases	355,000	173,000
Ending inventory	(45,000)	(50,000)
Cost of goods sold	$350,000	$183,000
Selling expenses	42,000	28,000
General and administrative expenses	33,000	19,000
Bond interest		5,000
Income taxes	13,000	11,000
Total	$438,000	$246,000
Net income	$ 32,600	$ 24,000

Pluto acquired 80% of Saturn's common stock at the beginning of Year 1 for $107,400. At the date of acquisition, Saturn Company reported a deficit of $12,000, and its net assets were believed to be carried on the books at reasonable valuations. Directors of Pluto noted in the minutes of the meeting in which the acquisition was approved that "the purchase of a controlling interest in Saturn will provide an assured supply of subassemblies and give us the ability to maintain stricter quality control than is possible with an independent contractor."

At the beginning of Year 3, Pluto purchased $20,000 face value of Saturn's 5% debenture bonds at 106. These bonds mature six years from the date of purchase and Pluto intends to hold them to maturity.

Saturn's sales during Year 3 include $40,000 of sales to Pluto. Goods purchased from Saturn and included in Pluto's inventories were $10,000 at the beginning of Year 3 and $15,000 at the end of Year 3. Saturn's cost on sales to Pluto averages 70% of selling price. At the end of Year 3, Pluto owed Saturn $13,300 on open account.

At the beginning of Year 2, Pluto sold sales equipment to Saturn for $60,000, which was Pluto's original cost. The book value of the equipment on Pluto's records at date of sale was $50,000. Saturn recorded the purchase at cost and has depreciated the equipment during Year 2 and Year 3 at the rate of 20% per year, charging selling expenses.

Instructions

a. Prepare consolidating working papers to derive the necessary information for a consolidated income statement for Year 3 and a consolidated balance sheet at the end of Year 3.

b. Prepare an analysis of change in minority interest during Year 3 and a statement of consolidated retained earnings for Year 3.

11-11 The adjusted trial balances of two affiliated companies, as of the end of the current year, are presented below:

	Pepper Company	*Salt Company*
Debits:		
Cash	*$ 18,100*	*$ 20,600*
Receivables	*60,000*	*55,000*
Inventories, Dec. 31	*35,000*	*46,000*
Investment in Salt Co., cost	*100,800*	
Salt Co. bonds	*28,400*	
Plant and equipment	*198,000*	*104,000*
Cost of goods sold	*364,000*	*206,000*
Selling expenses	*78,400*	*24,100*
General and administrative expenses	*46,300*	*18,200*
Interest expense		*2,500*
Dividends paid	*20,000*	*11,000*
Provision for income taxes	*13,800*	*6,200*
Total	*$962,800*	*$493,600*
Credits:		
Cumulative depreciation	*$ 86,000*	*$ 30,000*
Current liabilities	*56,000*	*18,100*
Dividends payable	*5,000*	*5,500*
Bonds payable, 6%		*52,000*
Capital stock (par 100)	*200,000*	*50,000*
Paid-in capital in excess of par	*25,000*	*20,000*
Retained earnings, Jan. 1	*45,500*	*48,000*
Sales	*533,200*	*270,000*
Interest income	*2,200*	
Dividend income	*9,900*	
Total	*$962,800*	*$493,600*

Additional information

Pepper Company acquired a 90% interest in Salt Company several years ago when the retained earnings of the Salt Company were $12,000. The difference between cost and book value was attributed to a manufacturing patent owned by

Salt Company, which had eight years to run at date of acquisition. At the end of the current year, this patent had a remaining life of three years.

The bonds of Salt Company were originally issued at a premium. Their maturity value is $50,000 on December 31, four years from the end of the current year. Pepper Company acquired 60% of the outstanding bonds for $28,000 at the beginning of the current year.

At the beginning of the current year, the inventories of Pepper Company contained items purchased from Salt Company on which Salt Company had made a profit of $1,900. During the current year Salt Company sold goods to Pepper Company for $92,000, of which $21,000 was unpaid at the end of the year. Salt Company made an operating profit of $3,300 on goods remaining in Pepper Company's inventory at year-end.

Salt Company sold certain sales equipment to Pepper Company several years ago at a price which was $9,000 in excess of its book value. Pepper Company has depreciated this property at a rate of 10%. The equipment has six years of service life after the end of the current year.

Pepper Company sold a tract of land to Salt Company several years ago at a profit of $7,000.

Instructions

a. Prepare separate consolidated balance sheet and income statement working papers for the current year.

b. Prepare a statement of consolidated retained earnings for the current year.

11-12 Prior to January 1, Year 1, the stockholders of Big and Little Companies approved the merger of the two companies. On January 1, Year 1, 5,000 shares of Big Company common stock were issued to Little Company stockholders in exchange for the 3,000 shares of Little Company stock outstanding. The December 31, Year 1, balance sheets (after closing) of the two companies are as follows:

BIG COMPANY AND SUBSIDIARY
Balance Sheets
December 31, Year 1

	Big Company	*Little Company*
Cash	$ 36,400	$ 28,200
Notes receivable	22,000	9,000
Accounts receivable	20,900	21,700
Accruals receivable	13,000	3,300
Inventories	81,200	49,600
Plant and equipment	83,200	43,500
Accumulated depreciation	(12,800)	(9,300)
Investment in Little Company	50,000	
Total assets	$293,900	$146,000

Notes payable	*$ 4,000*	*$ 12,000*
Accounts payable	*42,000*	*19,600*
Dividends payable		*4,500*
Accruals payable	*2,600*	*2,100*
Notes receivable discounted	*8,100*	
Capital stock, $10 par value	*120,000*	
Capital stock, $20 par value		*60,000*
Capital in excess of par	*28,500*	*20,000*
Retained earnings	*88,700*	*27,800*
Total liabilities & owners' equity	*$293,900*	*$146,000*

Additional information

(1) Net income for Year 1 (disregard income taxes):

Big Company	*$21,700*
Little Company (including gain on sale of equipment)	*10,200*

(2) On December 31, Year 1, Little Company owed Big Company $16,000 on open account and $8,000 in interest-bearing notes. Big Company discounted $3,000 of Little Company's notes with the First State Bank.

(3) On December 31, Year 1, Little Company accrued interest payable of $120 on notes payable to Big Company: $40 on the notes of $3,000 discounted with the bank and $80 on the remaining notes of $5,000. Big Company did not accrue interest receivable from Little Company.

(4) During Year 1 Big Company sold merchandise, which cost $30,000, to Little Company for $40,000. Little Company's December 31 inventory included $10,000 of this merchandise priced at Little Company's cost.

(5) On July 1 Little Company sold equipment that had a book value of $15,000 to Big Company for $17,000. Big Company recorded $850 depreciation on this equipment during Year 1. The remaining service life of the equipment at the date of sale was 10 years.

(6) Little Company shipped merchandise to Big Company on December 31, Year 1, and recorded an account receivable of $6,000 for the sale. Little Company's cost for the merchandise was $4,800. Because the merchandise was in transit, Big Company did not record the transaction. The terms of the sale were f.o.b. shipping point.

(7) Little Company declared a dividend of $1.50 per share on December 30, Year 1, payable on January 10, Year 2. Big Company made no entry for the declaration.

Instructions

a. Prepare consolidating working papers for the balance sheet as of the end of Year 1, assuming the consolidation is to be accounted for as a pooling of interests. Show beginning retained earnings and Year 1 income separately on the working papers.

b. What figures on the consolidated balance sheet would you expect to differ, if the consolidation had been interpreted as a purchase? (You need not specify the amounts of the differences.)

AICPA adapted

11-13 The trial balances of three affiliated companies, as of the end of the current year, are given below:

ADAM COMPANY AND SUBSIDIARIES
Adjusted Trial Balances
end of current year

Debits:	*Adam Company*	*Seth Company*	*Cain Company*
Cash	$ 82,000	$ 11,000	$ 27,000
Accounts receivable	104,000	41,000	143,000
Inventories	241,000	70,000	78,000
Investment in Seth Company	150,000		
Investment in Cain Company	175,000		
Investments, other	185,000		
Plant and equipment	375,000	58,000	99,000
Accumulated depreciation	(96,000)	(7,000)	(21,000)
Cost of goods sold	820,000	300,000	350,000
Operating expenses	60,000	35,000	40,000
Total	$2,096,000	$508,000	$716,000
Credits:			
Accounts payable	$ 46,000	$ 33,000	$ 24,000
Capital stock, $20 par value	500,000	200,000	100,000
Retained earnings	563,000		12,000
Appropriation for contingency			10,000
Sales	960,000	275,000	570,000
Gain on sale of assets	9,000		
Dividend revenue	18,000		
Total	$2,096,000	$508,000	$716,000

Seth Company was formed by Adam Company on January 1 of the current year. Adam Company purchased 75% of the original capital stock issue at par value for cash and sold the remainder in the open market at par value to raise additional capital.

On July 1 of the current year, Adam Company purchased from stockholders 4,000 shares of Cain Company stock for $175,000. The ownership equity of Cain Company at July 1 was as follows:

Capital stock	$100,000
Retained earnings	36,000
Net income from Jan. 1 to July 1, current year	44,000
	$180,000

The following intercompany sales of certain products were made during the current year:

	Sales	*Gross profit, %*	*Included in purchaser's ending inventory at lower of cost or market*
Adam sold to Cain	*$ 40,000*	*20*	*$15,000*
Seth sold to Cain	*30,000*	*10*	*10,000*
Cain sold to Adam	*60,000*	*30*	*20,000*
	$130,000		*$45,000*

In valuing Cain Company's inventory at lower of cost or market, the portion of the inventory purchased from Adam was written down by $1,900.

On January 2 of the current year, Adam Company sold equipment to Seth Company for $24,000. The equipment had been purchased by Adam two years earlier for $25,000 and was being depreciated on the straight-line method over a 10-year service life. Seth Company continued depreciation on the basis of the remaining useful life, using the same method. Adam Company recorded a gain of $4,000 on the sale.

Cash dividends were paid on the following dates during the current year:

	Adam Co.	*Cain Co.*
June 30	*$22,000*	*$ 6,000*
Dec. 31	*26,000*	*14,000*

Adam Company billed $6,000 to each subsidiary at the end of the year for executive services. The billing was treated as an operating expense and reduction of operating expenses; it had not been paid at year-end.

At year-end Cain Company appropriated $10,000 for a contingent loss in connection with a lawsuit that had been pending for two years.

Instructions

a. Prepare working papers for the consolidated balance sheet and income statement of Adam Company and its subsidiaries for the current year. Revenues and expenses of subsidiaries are to be included in the consolidation as though the subsidiaries had been in the affiliation during the entire year, and preacquisition earnings of Cain Company may be treated as a deduction on the consolidated income statement. Show supporting computations in good form. Ignore income taxes.

b. Prepare a consolidated income statement and statement of consolidated retained earnings in form suitable for publication.

AICPA adapted

12 CONSOLIDATIONS: SPECIAL PROBLEMS

We have now completed our discussion of the fundamental issues of consolidation. Eliminating intercompany debts and profits, analyzing earnings subsequent to acquisition, and interpreting the difference between cost and book value at date of acquisition are problems common to almost all consolidations. In this chapter we shall examine some of the special problems that arise when we encounter more complex subsidiary capital structures, subsidiary stock dividends, and changes in the parent's ownership interest after initial acquisition. In the following chapter we shall consider the consolidation of companies whose structure of affiliation is more complex. These are special and more complicated cases, but in essence they involve only a further application of the principles of consolidation we have discussed in previous chapters.

Subsidiaries having both preferred and common stock

When a subsidiary has both common and preferred stock outstanding, it is necessary to apportion the subsidiary's ownership equity among the various classes of stock. This is true whether the parent owns any of the subsidiary's preferred or not. Apportioning the total subsidiary equity between preferred and common makes it possible to identify the equity in the subsidiary that is associated with the parent's investment. In making the allocation of book values between common and preferred, the rights and priorities of each issue must be studied carefully. The objective is to measure the book value of each type of equity interest.

The book value associated with preferred stock is the stated value or the current call price of the shares outstanding, whichever is higher, plus any cumulative preferred dividends in arrears.[1] Once the book value of preferred stock is determined, the residual ownership equity is then assigned to the common.

Because most preferred stock issues are cumulative and nonparticipating, we shall assume these characteristics in illustrating the general case. When dividends on cumulative preferred are up to date, the book value of the issue is the call price per share times the number of shares outstanding. If there are dividends in arrears, the amount of such dividends should be added to the book value of the preferred and deducted from retained earnings. Any deficit is wholly identified with common; where both a deficit and dividend arrearage exist, the amount of the dividends in arrears should be assigned to preferred and the residual common equity should be reduced by both the amount of the deficit and the unpaid dividends.

To illustrate these principles, assume P Company has two 80% owned subsidiaries, S and T Companies, whose ownership equity at the beginning of Year 1 is as follows:

	Subsidiary S	*Subsidiary T*
Common stock, $100 par	*$100,000*	*$200,000*
6% preferred stock, $50 par value, call price $52.50 per share	*100,000*	*100,000**
Retained earnings (deficit)	*50,000*	*(80,000)*
Total ownership equity	*$250,000*	*$220,000*

* *Cumulative preferred; dividends in arrears of two years; $6 per share on 2,000 outstanding shares.*

The allocation of the ownership equity of these companies between common and preferred stock at the beginning of Year 1 would be as follows:

	Total capital	*Preferred stock*	*Common stock*		
			Total	*Controlling interest*	*Minority interest*
Company S	*$250,000*	*$105,000**	*$145,000*	*$116,000*	*$29,000*
Company T	*220,000*	*117,000†*	*103,000*	*82,400*	*20,600*

* *2,000 shares of preferred at the call price of $52.50.*
† *2,000 shares of preferred at the call price of $52.50, plus $12,000 dividends in arrears.*

The consolidation of P and T Companies will be demonstrated to illustrate the features of this case. The working papers and explanatory notes appear on page 383. The following facts are assumed: P Company acquired an 80% interest in T

[1] See *Intermediate Accounting* in this series for a discussion of the reason for using the higher of stated value or call price. In the absence of a call price, some accountants argue that liquidating value of preferred stock should be used if it is in excess of par or stated value.

for $120,000 on January 1, Year 0, at a time when T Company's deficit was $60,000. During Year 0, T Company suffered a loss of $20,000 and paid no dividends. The book value of P Company's common stock interest at date of acquisition was $103,200, determined as follows:

Total ownership equity—Jan. 1, Year 0.	*$240,000*
Book value of preferred (includes $5,000 call premium and one year's dividend arrearage of $6,000)	*111,000*
Book value applicable to common stock	*$129,000*
Book value of P's 80% interest at acquisition	*$103,200*

At the beginning of Year 1, P Company acquired 40% of the outstanding preferred stock of T Company for $38,000. During Year 1, T Company earned net income of $10,000 and paid no dividends.

P Company carries its investment in both the common and preferred of T Company at cost. The allocation of changes in the ownership equity of T Company from the beginning of Year 0 to the end of Year 1 is shown below:

Book Value of T Company Equity Interests

	Common			*Preferred*		
	Total	*Parent*	*Minority*	*Total*	*Parent*	*Minority*
Jan. 1, Year 0—purchased 80% interest	*$129,000*	*$103,200*	*$25,800*	*$111,000*		*$111,000*
Year 0 loss	*(20,000)*	*(16,000)*	*(4,000)*			
Year 0 preferred dividend (not paid)	*(6,000)*	*(4,800)*	*(1,200)*	*6,000*		*6,000*
Jan. 1, Year 1	*$103,000*	*$ 82,400*	*$20,600*	*$117,000*		*$117,000*
Jan. 1, Year 1—purchase of preferred by parent—40%					*$46,800*	*(46,800)*
Year 1 income	*10,000*	*8,000*	*2,000*			
Year 1 preferred dividends (not paid)	*(6,000)*	*(4,800)*	*(1,200)*	*6,000*	*2,400*	*3,600*
Dec. 31, Year 1	*$107,000*	*$ 85,600*	*$21,400*	*$123,000*	*$49,200*	*$ 73,800*

The preferred equity increases and the common equity decreases each year by the amount of the accumulated but unpaid preferred dividends on the assumption that ultimate profitable operations will enable T Company to make up the dividend arrearage on preferred and resume common dividends. It is possible that preferred stockholders might be induced to accept less than full book value in reorganization proceedings, but this is a possibility not in accord with the going-concern assumption.

Nature of subsidiary's preferred dividends. It should be noted that preferred dividends of a subsidiary, whether declared or in arrears, are in a sense an expense from the viewpoint of the consolidated entity. The subsidiary's preferred dividends constitute a charge against earnings that comes ahead of both the parent com-

COMPANIES P AND T
Consolidating Working Papers—Balance Sheet
December 31, Year 1

	P Company	T Company	Adjustments and eliminations Dr	Adjustments and eliminations Cr	Consolidated balance sheet
Investment in T Company common—80%	120,000			(a) 16,800 (f) 20,800 (g) 82,400	
Investment in T Company preferred—40%	38,000		(c) 8,800 (d) 2,400	(e) 49,200	
Other assets	342,000	250,000			592,000
Excess of cost over book value—common			(a) 16,800		16,800
Excess of book value over cost—preferred				(c) 8,800	(8,800)
Totals	500,000	250,000			600,000
Liabilities	75,000	20,000			95,000
Capital stock—P	300,000				300,000
Beginning retained earnings—P	110,000		(f) 20,800		89,200
Net income—P	40,000			(d) 2,400 (h) 3,200	45,600
Dividends—P	(25,000)				(25,000)
Preferred stock—T		100,000	(e) 123,000	(b) 23,000	
Common stock—T		200,000	(g) 200,000		
Beginning retained earnings—T		(80,000)	(b) 17,000	(g) 97,000	
Net income—T		10,000	(b) 6,000 (h) 4,000		
Outside interest in T: Common (minority)				(g) 20,600 (h) 800	21,400
Preferred				(e) 73,800	73,800
Totals	500,000	250,000			600,000

(a) To reclassify the $16,800 excess of the price paid by P for its 80% interest in T ($120,000) over the book value of P's interest at date of acquisition ($103,200).
(b) To allocate T's dividend arrearage prior to Year 1 ($12,000), the call premium ($5,000), and the Year 1 dividend arrearage ($6,000) to the preferred stock of T Company. Total preferred interest in beginning retained earnings and Year 1 income = $23,000.
(c) To reclassify the $8,800 excess of 40% of the book value of T's preferred stock at the beginning of Year 1 (40% × 117,000 = 46,800) over the price paid by P for its investment ($38,000).
(d) To recognize P's 40% share of the $6,000 undeclared dividend on T's preferred in arrearage at the end of Year 1.
(e) To eliminate P's preferred stock investment against the ownership equity account of T Company, and to establish the 60% outside interest as of the end of Year 1.
(f) To record P's share of the reduction in the book value of T's ownership equity from the beginning of Year 0 (date of acquisition) to the beginning of Year 1. Total reduction is $26,000 (Year 0 loss of $20,000 + $6,000 undeclared preferred dividends); 80% of $26,000 = $20,800.
(g) To eliminate P Company's investment in common against the ownership equity accounts of T Company as of the beginning of Year 1, establishing the amount of the 20% minority interest as of this date.
(h) To apportion the remaining Year 1 net income of T, after provision for $6,000 preferred dividend, between controlling (80%) and minority (20%) interest.

pany and minority common stock interests. Thus before computing the controlling and minority common stock interest in a subsidiary's earnings, the earnings should be reduced by the amount of the subsidiary's preferred dividends accumulated or paid in that period. The result will be that preferred dividends applicable to shares held by outsiders are deducted as a special charge in arriving at consolidated net income.

The net effect of this procedure may be observed by using the figures in the example shown below. The subsidiary's net income per books was $10,000. However, $6,000 of cumulative preferred dividends were allocable to preferred stock during the period, of which 60%, or $3,600, was applicable to preferred shares held outside the consolidated entity. The appropriate allocation of T's net income between the controlling and minority interest is shown in the following schedule:

Common Stock Interest in T Company Net Income

	Total	*Parent's interest*	*Minority interest*
Net income of T Company—Year 1	*$10,000*	*$8,000*	*$2,000*
Preferred dividends of T Company applicable to outsiders (60% of $6,000)	*(3,600)*		
This $3,600 restriction against T Company's net income is divided as follows:			
P Company is credited with 40% of the $6,000 of preferred dividends because it owns 40% of the preferred shares		*2,400*	
The total preferred dividends of $6,000 are charged against the common stock interests in the ratio of common shares owned: 80% to the controlling interest and 20% to the minority interest		*(4,800)*	*(1,200)*
Net income of T Company applicable to common stock interests	*$ 6,400*	*$5,600*	*$ 800*

If P Company had carried its investments in T Company's common and preferred on an equity basis, the two-year history of the investment accounts would appear on P's records as shown at the top of page 385.

The consolidated balance sheet would be the same under either the equity or cost methods. In the consolidating working papers, however, entries (d), (f), and (h) would be unnecessary if P had followed the equity method because the apportionments in these entries would already be reflected on P Company's books. The two working paper entries on page 385 would eliminate the investment accounts and establish the amount of the minority interest.

On P Company's Books—Equity Method

	Investment in		
	Common	Preferred	P's income
Jan. 1, Year 0—purchased common	*$120,000*		
P's share of Year 0 loss plus preferred dividend, 80% of ($20,000 + $6,000)	*(20,800)*		*$(20,800)*
Jan. 1, Year 1—purchased preferred	*$ 99,200*	*$38,000*	
P's share of T Company's Year 1 net income:			
40% of $6,000 preferred dividend undeclared		*2,400*	*2,400*
80% of $4,000 net income after preferred dividend	*3,200*		*3,200*
Investment account balance Dec. 31, Year 1, on equity basis	*$102,400*	*$40,400*	

Elimination of preferred

Preferred stock—T	*123,000*	
Investment in preferred		*40,400*
Minority interest in preferred		*73,800*
Excess of book value over cost		*8,800*

Elimination of common

Common stock—T	*200,000*	
Net income—T	*4,000*	
Excess of cost over book value	*16,800*	
Beginning retained earnings		*97,000*
Investment in T		*102,400*
Minority interest in common		*21,400*

The previous discussion and illustrations involved cumulative nonparticipating preferred. A comparable reasoning applies in handling other types of preferred stock:

1. If preferred is nonparticipating and noncumulative, the entire retained earnings (or deficit) is allocated to the common stock, except for the amount of any call premium.

2. If preferred is fully participating, the retained earnings balance is apportioned between preferred and common according to the terms of the participation clause in the preferred contract. A typical participating provision would call for participation in dividends by preferred in proportion to stated capital. If participating preferred is also cumulative, any dividend arrearage should be allocated to the preferred issue before the remaining retained earnings (or deficit) is apportioned.

Stock dividends by subsidiary

A stock dividend payable in the same class of stock does not change either the total ownership equity of the declaring company or the proportionate ownership interest of any stockholder. Therefore, when a subsidiary transfers amounts from retained earnings to paid-in capital, whether as a result of a stock dividend or otherwise, the transfer has no effect on consolidated financial statements. Stock dividends which occur after a parent has acquired its interest require consideration in consolidations only because they obscure changes in retained earnings since acquisition. For example, if the retained earnings of X Company decreased by $50,000 during a period in which the company had capitalized $90,000 of retained earnings by a stock dividend, the accountant must not be misled by the

P AND Q COMPANIES
Partial Consolidated Working Papers
as of the end of Year 2

	P Company	Q Company	Adjustments and eliminations Dr	Adjustments and eliminations Cr	Consolidated balance sheet
Investment in Q	350,000		(c) 27,000	(b) 80,000 (d) 297,000	
Excess of cost over book value			(b) 80,000		80,000
Common stock—P	250,000				250,000
Beginning retained earnings—P	100,000			(c) 27,000	127,000
Net income—P	50,000			(e) 9,000	59,000
Common stock—Q		120,000	(d) 100,000 (a) 20,000		
Paid-in capital in excess of par		44,000	(a) 44,000		
Retained earnings—Q		166,000	(d) 230,000	(a) 64,000	
Net income—Q		10,000	(e) 10,000		
Minority interest—Q				(d) 33,000 (e) 1,000	34,000

(a) To reverse $64,000 stock dividend declared in Year 1.
(b) To reclassify the amount of P's investment in excess of the book value of P's interest in Q. (P paid $350,000 for an interest having a book value of $270,000.)
(c) To record P's 90% share of Q's $30,000 Year 1 net income earned from date of acquisition to the beginning of the current period.
(d) To eliminate P's investment in Q and establish 10% minority interest in Q as of the end of Year 1.
(e) To allocate Q's Year 2 net income of $10,000 between parent and minority interest.

decrease but should recognize that X Company has accumulated $40,000 of undistributed retained earnings during the period.

If a parent company accounts for its investment on an equity basis, stock dividends may be completely ignored in consolidating the accounts. The parent owns the same proportionate share of the subsidiary before as after the dividend, and it will include in its income this proportion of the undistributed earnings of the subsidiary since date of acquisition.

If a parent carries its investment on a cost basis, the growth in the retained earnings of a subsidiary since acquisition must be measured by adding back to the current retained earnings figure the amount of the stock dividend, and comparing this total with the retained earnings at acquisition. Once the parent's share of growth since acquisition has been added to the investment account, the eliminating entry will cause no problem because it is a matter of no concern whether a given amount of ownership equity is eliminated from paid-in capital or retained earnings.

One way of handling stock dividends in consolidating working papers is simply to reverse the stock dividend entry in a consolidating adjustment, and then proceed in the normal manner. To illustrate, assume that P Company acquired a 90% interest in Q Company for $350,000 at the beginning of Year 1 when Q Company had outstanding 10,000 shares of $10 par value common and $200,000 of retained earnings. During Year 1 Q Company earned $30,000 and declared a 20% stock dividend, capitalizing $32 (fair market value) per share, or $64,000. During Year 2, Q Company earned $20,000 and paid no dividends. The consolidating procedures are illustrated in the partial working papers on page 386.

In this example we know that Q's retained earnings grew by $30,000 during Year 1. If we had known only the balance of retained earnings at the beginning and end of Year 1, we could compute this change as follows:

Q's retained earnings at the end of Year 1	*$166,000*
Add back: Year 1 stock dividend	*64,000*
	$230,000
Q's retained earnings at date of acquisition	*200,000*
Growth in Q's retained earnings during Year 1	*$ 30,000*

When P's 90% interest ($27,000) in this growth has been added to P's investment account, entry (c) on working papers, the following elimination entry might be made, without the necessity of reversing the stock dividend entry:

Common Stock—Q Company	*120,000*	
Paid-in Capital in Excess of Par Value	*44,000*	
Beginning Retained Earnings—Q Company	*166,000*	
Investment in Q		*297,000*
Minority Interest in Q—10%		*33,000*
To eliminate investment in Q Company as of the beginning of Year 2.		

Whether the stock dividend is reversed on consolidating working papers or elimination of the investment is made without reversal, the important factor is to keep the stock dividend in mind in analyzing the change in the subsidiary's retained earnings after date of acquisition.

One theoretical point should be considered. In the above example the consolidated retained earnings at the beginning of Year 2 will be $127,000 (see working papers), including $27,000 of Q's retained earnings. However the total retained earnings of Q Company has actually decreased from $200,000 at acquisition to $166,000 at the beginning of Year 2, as a result of the $64,000 stock dividend, which capitalized $34,000 more than Q Company earned during Year 1. The effect of our consolidating procedure has been to include in beginning consolidated retained earnings $27,000 of Q's earnings that are now a part of Q's paid-in capital. It might be argued that this is improper, since retained earnings capitalized by a subsidiary cannot legally become the basis for a cash dividend to the parent company. But there are many reasons (for example, insufficiency of cash in the subsidiary) why the amount of subsidiary retained earnings included in consolidated retained earnings does not reflect the dividend-paying ability of the parent. The consolidated retained earnings figure should reflect the retained earnings of the affiliated group as an entity, not the maximum amount legally available for parent company dividends. For this reason the Committee on Accounting Procedures of the AICPA has stated ". . . the retained earnings in the consolidated financial statements should reflect the accumulated earnings of the consolidated group not distributed to the shareholders of, or capitalized by, the parent company."[2]

This case should be distinguished from the situation in which a subsidiary has declared postacquisition cash dividends in excess of earnings since date of acquisition. In this latter instance the parent company has in effect recovered in cash a portion of its initial investment, and it is clear that any amount of postacquisition cash dividends in excess of postacquisition earnings should be excluded from consolidated retained earnings and treated as a reduction of the investment account.

Changes in parent's ownership interest in subsidiary

In our previous discussion we have assumed that the parent company gained control of a subsidiary through the purchase of a single block of stock and that the parent's interest does not change. Complicating factors are introduced when a parent company acquires control through several purchases of stock at different times and at varying prices. A parent company's interest in a subsidiary may change as a result of additional purchases or sales of the subsidiary's stock by the parent, or as a result of additional stock transactions by the subsidiary with parties outside the affiliation. The problems that arise in consolidating affiliated companies when such changes in the parent's interest occur are discussed in the following sections.

Serial investment by parent

There are two general cases of serial acquisition of the stock of subsidiaries: (1) A parent company acquires control through a single purchase of stock, and

[2] AICPA, *Accounting Research and Terminology Bulletins (Final Edition),* Bulletin No. 51 (New York: 1961), p. 46.

subsequently purchases additional shares. (2) A parent company acquires control through a series of purchases of the stock of the subsidiary.

Additional investment after control is achieved. Two consolidating problems arise when a parent company increases its investment in a subsidiary after control has been achieved. The first is to determine the parent's share of the earnings of the subsidiary during periods when the parent's percentage interest has changed. The second is to decide how to deal with differences between the prices paid for the various blocks of stock and the book value of the underlying net assets represented by each block.

1. The problem of associating earnings with particular blocks of stock may be solved by a careful analysis of the amount and timing of subsidiary earnings. The earnings included in consolidated retained earnings and net income should be those attributable to the parent's proportionate equity interest during the period when the earnings arose. When a parent's equity interest changes during a fiscal year it may be necessary (in the absence of more precise information) to apportion annual net income on the basis of the number of months during which different percentages of outstanding stock were held by the parent.

2. The problem of interpreting differences between the cost and book value of serial investments is more difficult to resolve. Our previous discussion (in Chapter 8) of the reasons for such differences and their disposition is still pertinent. However, when several stock purchases are made by the parent at different times and at varying prices the accountant may be faced with conflicting evidence as to the fair market value of the subsidiary's net assets. When a parent company acquires substantial control of a subsidiary in a single transaction in which the value of the business as a whole is under consideration by both the buyer and seller, the valuation evidence is relatively clear. On the other hand, it is usually impractical to relate the price paid for small blocks of stock to the value of the subsidiary as a whole. A parent may acquire small blocks of stock when the shares appear to be underpriced in the market. A parent may pay a price for a small block of stock above what management believes the proportionate interest is worth in order to induce a reluctant minority to sell. For these and other reasons the prices paid for small blocks of stock constitute much less satisfactory evidence of value, and the accountant is probably well advised to consider differences between the price paid and underlying book value of such blocks as reconciling items, rather than attempt to use the market prices as a basis for revaluing the overall net assets of the subsidiary.

To illustrate these points, assume the following data for P and W Companies:

	P Company	*W Company*
Common stock, $100 par value	*$400,000*	*$100,000*
Retained earnings—Jan. 1, Year 1	*200,000*	*80,000*
Net income during Year 1—own operations	*60,000*	*25,000*
Net income during Year 2—own operations	*80,000*	*30,000*
Dividends—Dec. 31, Year 2	*(40,000)*	*(15,000)*

P Company acquired common stock of W Company in two blocks as follows:

Jan. 1, Year 1—purchased 700 shares @ $200	*$140,000*
Apr. 1, Year 2—purchased 100 shares @ $220	*22,000*

On P Company's books the effect of the investment in W on P's income and retained earnings will depend on whether the equity method or the cost method is used. The difference in the two approaches are demonstrated in the following schedule:

On P Company's Books

	Cost method		*Equity method*	
	Investment in W	*Retained earnings*	*Investment in W*	*Retained earnings*
Year 1:				
Jan. 1—purchased 700 shares @ $200	*$140,000*	*$200,000*	*$140,000*	*$200,000*
Net income:				
From P's operations		*60,000*		*60,000*
70% of W's income of $25,000			*17,500*	*17,500*
Dec. 31 balances	*$140,000*	*$260,000*	*$157,500*	*$277,500*
Year 2:				
Apr. 1— purchased 100 shares @ $220	*22,000*		*22,000*	
Net income:				
From P's operations		*80,000*		*80,000*
70% of ¼ of W's net income of $30,000			*5,250*	*5,250*
80% of ¾ of W's net income of $30,000			*18,000*	*18,000*
Dividends declared on Dec. 31:				
Company W—$15,000 × 80% . .		*12,000*	*(12,000)*	
Company P—$40,000		*(40,000)*		*(40,000)*
Dec. 31 balances	*$162,000*	*$312,000*	*$190,750*	*$340,750*

The difference between the $190,750 balance of the investment account under the equity method and the $162,000 balance under the cost method represents the parent's share of W Company's earnings from the date of the two stock acquisitions to the end of Year 2. On the next page is an analysis which shows the changes in both the parent's interest and the outside minority interest during the two-year period, and the difference between investment cost and book value on the two acquisition dates.

The consolidating working papers for P and W Companies, assuming that P Company accounts for its investment on a cost basis, are shown on page 393.

P AND W COMPANIES
Analysis of Changes in the Book Value of Parent and Minority Interests and Comparison of Parent's Investment Cost and Book Value

	Book value of W Company's net assets					Parent Company's investment at cost	Excess of cost over book value
	Total	Minority interests		Parent's interest			
		Amount	%	Amount	%		
Jan. 1, Year 1	$180,000	$54,000	30%	$126,000	70%	$140,000	$14,000
Year 1 income	25,000	7,500		17,500			
One-fourth of Year 2 income	7,500	2,250		5,250			
Balance on Apr. 1, Year 2	$212,500	$63,750	30%	$148,750	70%		
Apr. 1, Year 2, purchase of 100 shares @ 220		(21,250)	(10%)	21,250	10%	22,000	750
Totals	$212,500	$42,500	20%	$170,000	80%	$162,000	$14,750
Three-fourths of Year 2 income	22,500	4,500		18,000			
Dividends	(15,000)	(3,000)		(12,000)			
Balance on Dec. 31, Year 2	$220,000	$44,000	20%	$176,000	80%	$162,000	$14,750

Excess of cost over book value	$ 14,750
Parent's investment—equity basis	$190,750
Parent's investment—cost basis	162,000
Growth in parent's interest from date of acquisition to the end of Year 2	$ 28,750

Proof:

Parent's share of Year 1 net income		$17,500
Parent's share of Year 2 net income	$23,250	
Less: Dividends already included in P's income	12,000	11,250
Parent's share of growth in W Company, Years 1 and 2		$28,750

One significant variation in working paper procedure should be noted. In previous illustrations when we were dealing with the cost method, the parent's investment account has been adjusted to an equity basis as of the *beginning* of the period under consideration, and the elimination of the investment against ownership equity accounts has been made as of the *beginning* of the period. Where there are changes in the parent's interest during the current period, it is more convenient to convert the investment account to an equity basis as of the *end* of the year, and make the elimination of the investment as of the end of the year rather than the beginning. Because the change in the parent's interest from 70% to 80% during Year 2 reduced the book value of the minority interest by $21,250, it is simpler to deal with figures representing the minority interest after this adjustment rather than before.

If P Company had accounted for its investment on an equity basis, the investment account balance on P's books would have been $190,750 (see schedule above). The following two eliminating entries would be necessary to consolidate the two companies:

Excess of Cost over Book Value	*14,750*	
Investment in W		*14,750*
To reclassify the excess of P's investment over book value as an intangible asset.		
Capital Stock—W	*100,000*	
Beginning Retained Earnings—W	*105,000*	
Net Income—W	*30,000*	
Dividends—W		*15,000*
Investment in W		*176,000*
Minority Interest—W		*44,000*
To eliminate investment account as of the end of Year 2.		

Revaluation alternative. In the working papers on page 393, the $14,750 excess of the cost of P's investment over book value was treated as an intangible asset on the consolidated balance sheet. As an alternative we might have used the price paid by P for its initial 70% controlling investment as a basis for revaluing the net assets of W at the beginning of Year 1. P Company paid $14,000 in excess of book value for its 70% interest, which implies that W's net assets were undervalued at that date by $20,000 ($14,000 ÷ .70). If specific assets of W were revalued by $20,000 or if goodwill of $20,000 were added to W's assets, the investment account and book value would be consistent as of the beginning of Year 1. On April 1 of Year 2, when P purchased an additional 10% interest for $22,000, the cost of this investment would be $1,250 below the revised book value:

Book value of W's net assets on Jan. 1, Year 1	*$180,000*
Upward revaluation of net assets, based on P's 70% purchase	*20,000*
Revised Jan. 1, Year 1 book value	*$200,000*
Add: Year 1 net income	*25,000*
One-fourth of Year 2 net income—to Apr. 1	*7,500*
Revised book value of W as of Apr. 1, Year 2	*$232,500*
P acquired 10% interest on Apr. 1, Year 2	*$ 23,250*
Price paid by P for 10% interest	*22,000*
Excess of revised book value over P's cost	*$ 1,250*

We are now faced with a dilemma. If the price paid for P's 10% interest on April 1 is valid, it suggests that W's net assets are overvalued at that date by $12,500 ($1,250 ÷ .10). But as of January 1, Year 1 (a year and a half ago) we revalued the net assets of W upward by $20,000 on the basis of the price paid by P for a 70% interest. The 10% purchase constitutes more current information; the 70% purchase is probably better evidence of the value of the business as a whole at that time in view of the size of the acquisition. Furthermore, if we write W's net assets down by $12,500 as of April 1, Year 2, we shall be faced with the prospect either of showing a loss of 70% of this amount on P's books, or of showing $8,750 (70% of $12,500) as excess of cost over book value on the consolidated balance sheet.

P AND W COMPANIES
Consolidating Working Papers—Balance Sheet
(Assuming P carries investment at cost)
as of December 31, Year 2

	P Company	W Company	Adjustments and eliminations Dr	Cr	Consolidated balance sheet
Investment in W—at cost	162,000		(b) 28,750	(a) 14,750 (c) 176,000	
Other assets	600,000	250,000			850,000
Excess of cost over book value			(a) 14,750		14,750
Totals	762,000	250,000			864,750
Liabilities	50,000	30,000			80,000
Capital stock—P	400,000				400,000
Beginning retained earnings—P	260,000			(b) 17,500	277,500
Net income—P	92,000			(b) 11,250	103,250
Dividends—P	(40,000)				(40,000)
Capital stock—W		100,000	(c) 100,000		
Beginning retained earnings—W		105,000	(c) 105,000		
Net income—W		30,000	(c) 30,000		
Dividends—W		(15,000)		(c) 15,000	
Minority interest in W				(c) 44,000	44,000
Totals	762,000	250,000			864,750

(a) To reclassify the excess of cost of P's investment in W over the book value at date of acquisition (see schedule on page 391).
(b) To record P's share of the growth in W's net assets since date of acquisition. Share of Year 1 earnings is added to P's retained earnings; share of Year 2 undistributed net income is added to P's net income. Note that under the cost method, P Company has already included $12,000 of dividends from W in its net income figure of $92,000. (See schedule on page 390 for determination of P's share of Year 1 and Year 2 income.)
(c) To eliminate P's investment account against W's ownership equity account as of the end of Year 2, and establish 20% minority interest at that date.

There is no entirely satisfactory way of resolving this difficulty. We are faced with two acquisitions which give us contradictory evidence as to the value of W's net assets, and no matter which we choose as a basis for revaluation we are confronted with an unexplained difference between cost and book value on the other acquisition. We can, of course, avoid the problem by making no revaluation of W's assets and treating the difference between cost and book value as an intangible asset of the consolidated entity. If we revalue W's net assets on the basis of the original 70% purchase, we should then handle the $1,250 excess of book value over cost on the 10% acquisition in the same way as for any other case where the book value of an investment in a subsidiary exceeds the parent's investment cost (see discussion in Chapter 8). The third alternative, revaluation on the basis of the price paid for the 10% interest acquired on April 1, is procedurally possible but difficult to justify. As with any valuation problem, the accountant should use judgment in choosing the most reasonable interpretation of the evidence.

Control achieved in a series of purchases

A parent company may purchase stock of an affiliated company in a series of transactions, eventually achieving control. Consolidated financial statements will not be prepared until control is achieved and a parent-subsidiary relation exists. Prior to this time the holding company will simply account for its investment, on either the cost or equity basis, as an investment in a nonconsolidated company.

When the purchase is made which results in effective control, consolidated statements are then appropriate. If the parent company has accounted for its investment on a cost basis prior to this time, it will be necessary for purposes of consolidation to recognize as a part of consolidated retained earnings the parent's share of undistributed earnings of the subsidiary relating to each block of stock from the date of acquisition to the balance sheet date.[3] In this respect the procedures do not differ from those previously illustrated in the case where small acquisitions take place after control is achieved in a single purchase.

When control is achieved through a series of stock purchases at varying prices, the problem of interpreting the series of differences between the cost of the parent's investment and the book value of the interest acquired becomes very difficult. In the face of such conflicting evidence, the most reasonable approach is to treat the sum of any excess of cost over book value as a reconciling item to be reported as an intangible asset on the consolidated balance sheet. If the book value of the equity in the subsidiary consistently exceeds the prices paid for the blocks of stock, consideration should be given to a downward revaluation of the subsidiary's net assets, since the alternative is to report such a difference as an element of consolidated paid-in capital, which is difficult to justify.

The following example will illustrate consolidating procedures when control is achieved through a series of acquisitions. Assume that P Company acquires a 90% interest in X Company in the following series of transactions:

Jan. 1, Year 1—30% interest, purchase of 6,000 shares @ $15.....	*$ 90,000*
Oct. 1, Year 2—40% interest, purchase of 8,000 shares @ $20.....	*160,000*
July 1, Year 3—20% interest, purchase of 4,000 shares @ $18....	*72,000*
	$322,000

The elements of the capital of P and X Companies during the three-year period are shown at the top of page 395.

[3] The AICPA Committee on Accounting Procedures considers an alternative procedure acceptable under some circumstances. The committee states: "If two or more purchases are made over a period of time, the (retained earnings) of the subsidiary at acquisition should generally be determined on a step by step basis; however if small purchases are made over a period of time and then a purchase is made which results in control, the date of the latest purchase, as a matter of convenience, may be considered the date of acquisition." *Accounting Research and Terminology Bulletins (Final Edition),* Bulletin No. 51 (New York: 1961), p. 44. Thus if a parent acquired control of a subsidiary by six purchases of 10% of the subsidiary's shares, the committee would condone, as a matter of convenience, treating the total price paid for the six acquisitions as the purchase price of a 60% interest on the date of the last purchase, ignoring the parent's share of the subsidiary's earnings prior to that date. There is, of course, no theoretical basis for this procedure.

	P Company	*X Company*
Capital stock outstanding—$10 par value	*$500,000*	*$200,000*
Retained earnings—beginning of Year 1	*200,000*	*50,000*
Net income from own operations:		
Year 1	*35,000*	*20,000*
Year 2	*45,000*	*40,000*
Year 3	*55,000*	*30,000*
Dividends, declared on Dec. 31:		
Year 1	*(15,000)*	*(10,000)*
Year 2	*(25,000)*	*(15,000)*
Year 3	*(35,000)*	*(20,000)*

An analysis of changes in P's ownership equity in X Company, and the difference between the cost and book value of each of the three investments appears below. Note that when an acquisition occurs during a fiscal year, the net income of the subsidiary for the year has been apportioned by months. At the bot-

P COMPANY AND X COMPANY
Analysis of Changes in Ownership

	Book value of subsidiary net assets				*Parent Company's investment at cost*	*Excess of cost over book value*
	Total	*Minority interest*	*Parent's interest*			
			Dollars	*%*		
Year 1:						
Jan. 1—purchase of 30% interest	*$250,000*	*$175,000*	*$ 75,000*	*30%*	*$ 90,000*	*$15,000*
Net income	*20,000*	*14,000*	*6,000*			
Dividends	*(10,000)*	*(7,000)*	*(3,000)*			
Year 2:						
Net income—9 months	*30,000*	*21,000*	*9,000*			
Balances—Oct. 1, Year 2	*$290,000*	*$203,000*	*$ 87,000*	*30%*		
Oct. 1—purchase of 40% interest		*(116,000)*	*116,000*	*40%*	*160,000*	*44,000*
Net income—3 months	*10,000*	*3,000*	*7,000*	*70%*		
Dividends	*(15,000)*	*(4,500)*	*(10,500)*			
Year 3:						
Net income—6 months	*15,000*	*4,500*	*10,500*			
Balances—July 1, Year 3	*$300,000*	*$ 90,000*	*$210,000*	*70%*		
July 1—purchase of 20% interest		*(60,000)*	*60,000*	*20%*	*72,000*	*12,000*
Net income—6 months	*15,000*	*1,500*	*13,500*	*90%*		
Dividends	*(20,000)*	*(2,000)*	*(18,000)*			
Balances—Dec. 31, Year 3	*$295,000*	*$ 29,500*	*$265,500*	*90%*	*$322,000*	*$71,000*
Excess of cost over book value			*71,000*	←		
Parent's investment—equity basis			*$336,500*			
Parent's investment—cost basis			*322,000*	←		
Growth in parent's interest from date of acquisition to the end of Year 3			*$ 14,500*			

tom of the schedule the comparison between the balance that would appear in the parent's investment account at the end of Year 3 if the equity basis were used and the total cost of the investment shows that P's share of X's undistributed earnings during the three-year period amounts to $14,500. This analytical statement also shows that P Company paid a total of $71,000 in excess of the book value of the three investments at the date the investments were made.

Consolidating working papers, assuming that P Company accounts for its investment in X on a *cost* basis, are illustrated on page 397. Note that an analytical schedule such as that on page 395 provides the necessary data for adjusting entries (a) and (b) on the working papers, and proves the amount of the minority interest ($29,500) at the end of Year 3. As a matter of fact in a relatively simple situation such as this, it would be possible to prepare a consolidated balance sheet directly from the information on the analytical schedule and the individual company statements, without using consolidating working papers.

If P Company had accounted for its investment on an *equity* basis, the balance in the investment account at the end of Year 3 would be $336,500 (as shown on the schedule on page 395), and the preparation of consolidated statements would be quite simple, since P's beginning retained earnings and net income figures would include P's share of X's earnings since acquisition. The $71,000 excess of cost over book value and the $29,500 minority interest are both computed in the schedule on page 395. If P Company began its accounting on an equity basis on October 1 of Year 2 when control was achieved, it would be necessary to make the following adjusting entry at the end of Year 2 on P's books:

Investment in X Company	*19,000*	
Retained Earnings—P		*3,000*
Net Income—Year 2		*16,000*
To accrue in investment account the following interest in X Company's earnings since dates of acquisition:		
30% of Year 1 undistributed net income (30% × 10,000)	*$ 3,000*	
30% of undistributed net income for first nine months of Year 2 (30% × 30,000)	*9,000*	
70% of undistributed net income for last three months of Year 2 (70% × 10,000)	*7,000*	
	$19,000	

The $10,500 of X Company dividends received at the end of Year 2 would be credited to the Investment account, and similar equity method treatment would be followed in subsequent years.

Sale of shares by parent

When a parent company sells a portion of its holdings of subsidiary shares, the resulting change in the parent's equity interest produces changes in the parent's share of subsequent subsidiary earnings and in the difference between the cost and book value of the parent's investment in the subsidiary. These changes must be analyzed in preparing consolidated financial statements. Any gain or loss on the sale of the subsidiary's shares will be included in parent net income. The amount of gain or loss recorded by the parent will differ depending on whether

Cost basis used by P

P COMPANY AND X COMPANY
Working Papers—Consolidated Balance Sheet
end of Year 3

	P Company	X Company	Adjustments and eliminations Dr	Adjustments and eliminations Cr	Consolidated balance sheet
Investment in X	322,000		(b) 14,500	(a) 71,000 (c) 265,500	
Other assets	559,500	340,000			899,500
Excess of cost over book value			(a) 71,000		71,000
Totals	881,500	340,000			970,500
Liabilities	90,000	45,000			135,000
Capital stock—P	500,000				500,000
Beginning retained earnings—P	253,500*			(b) 8,500	262,000
Net income—P	73,000†			(b) 6,000	79,000
Dividends—P	(35,000)				(35,000)
Capital stock—X		200,000	(c) 200,000		
Beginning retained earnings—X		85,000	(c) 85,000		
Net income—X		30,000	(c) 30,000		
Dividends—X		(20,000)		(c) 20,000	
Minority interest—X				(c) 29,500	29,500
Totals	881,500	340,000			970,500

(a) To reclassify excess of cost over book value of P's investment in X.
(b) To record P's share of undistributed earnings of X from dates of acquisition to the end of Year 3 (see schedule on page 395).
(c) To eliminate investment in X and establish 10% minority interest.

* (See analysis of parent's interest on page 395 for figures marked #)

Company P's retained earnings at beginning of Year 1	$200,000
Add: P's net income from own operations Year 1 and Year 2	80,000
P's dividends, Year 1 and Year 2	(40,000)
P's share of X's dividends in Years 1 and 2	13,500 #
	$253,500

† Company P's income from own operations, Year 3	$ 55,000
Add: P's share of X's Year 3 dividends	18,000 #
	$ 73,000

the parent has carried its investment on the cost or equity basis, but the amount of consolidated retained earnings will be the same in either case.

To illustrate these points, we shall assume the following fact situation: P Company holds a 70% interest in Y Company at the end of Year 2, which it acquired in the following series of transactions:

Jan. 1, Year 1—purchased 60% interest	**$90,000**
July 1, Year 1—purchased 20% interest	**25,000**
Apr. 1, Year 2—sold 10% interest	**20,000**

Data concerning changes in the ownership equity accounts of P and Y are given below:

	P Company	Y Company
Capital stock, $50 par value	*$250,000*	*$100,000*
Retained earnings—Jan. 1, Year 1	*80,000*	*40,000*
Net income from own operations:		
Year 1	*26,000*	*14,000*
Year 2 (excluding gain on sale of Y stock)	*28,000*	*12,000*
Gain on sale of Y Company stock:		
If investment recorded on a cost basis	*5,000*	
If investment recorded on an equity basis	*3,800*	
Dividends paid on Dec. 31:		
Year 1		*5,000*
Year 2		*5,000*

An analysis of the changes in the book value of P's interest in Y Company during the two-year period is shown on page 399. The figures on this schedule are self-explanatory, except for the $1,000 adjustment of the excess of cost over book value relating to the sale of 10% of P's interest on April 1, Year 2. This $1,000 can be computed in two different ways. The easiest approach is to note that P purchased its initial 60% interest at a cost $6,000 in excess of book value. The sale of 10% of Y's shares (on a first in, first out basis) is one-sixth of this original purchase, so $1,000 (⅙ of $6,000) of the excess of cost over book value has also disappeared.

There is another way of looking at this computation which perhaps provides a better insight into the reasoning involved. At the time P sells the 10% interest, the book value of Y is $152,000; therefore the book value of the 10% interest is $15,200. This 10% interest cost P $15,000 (⅙ of $90,000). When a parent *buys* additional shares, we can compare the cost of the shares with their book value *at the date of acquisition.* When shares are sold, however, the original cost of the shares and book value at the time of sale are no longer comparable, since the cost relates to an equity interest at an earlier point in time. To determine the appropriate adjustment of the "excess," we must adjust the original cost of the shares sold by the amount of undistributed earnings associated with these shares since date of acquisition:

Original cost of 10% interest (⅙ of $90,000)	*$15,000*
10% of Y's undistributed earnings in Year 1 = 10% of ($14,000 − $5,000)	*900*
10% of Y's undistributed earnings during the first three months of Year 2 = 10% of $3,000	*300*
Adjusted cost of 10% interest in Y on Apr. 1, Year 2	*$16,200*
Book value of 10% interest in Y on Apr. 1, Year 2	*15,200*
Reduction in excess of cost over book value	*$ 1,000*

P COMPANY AND Y COMPANY
Analysis of Changes in Parent's Interest

	Book value of subsidiary net assets				Parent Company's investment at cost	Excess of cost over book value
	Total	Minority interest	Parent's interest			
			Dollars	%		
Year 1:						
Jan. 1—purchase of 60% interest	$140,000	$ 56,000	$ 84,000	60%	$ 90,000	$6,000
Net income—6 months	7,000	2,800	4,200			
Balance—July 1	$147,000	$ 58,800	$ 88,200	60%		
July 1—purchase of 20% interest		(29,400)	29,400	20%	25,000	(4,400)
Net income—6 months	7,000	1,400	5,600	80%		
Dividends	(5,000)	(1,000)	(4,000)			
Year 2:						
Net income—3 months	3,000	600	2,400			
Balance—Apr. 1	$152,000	$ 30,400	$121,600	80%		
Apr. 1—sale of 10% interest		15,200	(15,200)	(10%)	(15,000)	(1,000)*
Net income—9 months	9,000	2,700	6,300	70%		
Dividends	(5,000)	(1,500)	(3,500)			
Balance—end of Year 2	$156,000	$ 46,800	$109,200	70%	$100,000	$ 600
Excess of cost over book value			600			
P's investment—equity basis			$109,800			
P's investment—cost basis			100,000			
P's share of Y's growth since date of acquisition			$ 9,800			
Proof:						
Applicable to Year 2 undistributed income: 70% of ($12,000 − 5,000)			$ 4,900			
Applicable to retained earnings prior to Year 2 (50% of $7,000 + 70% of $2,000)			4,900			
			$ 9,800			

* *See explanation of this figure on page 398.*

The consolidating working papers, assuming P accounts for its investment in Y on an *equity* basis, are shown on page 401. For comparative purposes the consolidating working papers, assuming P accounts for its investment in Y on a *cost* basis are shown on page 402. The resulting consolidated balance sheet is, of course, the same in both cases. We can demonstrate that the total amount included in consolidated retained earnings and income which relates to P's investment in Y is the same under either the cost or equity method (page 400).

Note in the schedule that under the equity method P will include $11,000 more in its own income during the two-year period than under the cost method ($18,500 − $7,500 = $11,000). Of this $11,000, however, $1,200 is attributable to the 10% stock interest sold on April 1 of Year 2, as reflected in the difference between the gain on the sale of the stock reported under the cost method ($5,000) and the gain reported under the equity method ($3,800). In effect, when the cost method is used, the $5,000 gain consists of $3,800 pure gain and $1,200 of un-

	Parent's share of Y	
	Cost method	*Equity method*
Y's income during first six months of Year 1 = $7,000; 60% of $7,000		*$ 4,200*
Y's income during second six months of Year 1 = $7,000; 80% of $7,000		*5,600*
Y's Year 1 dividends (80% of $5,000)	*$ 4,000*	
Y's income during first three months of Year 2 = $3,000; 80% of $3,000		*2,400*
Y's income during last nine months of Year 2 = $9,000; 70% of $9,000		*6,300*
Y's Year 2 dividends (70% of $5,000)	*3,500*	
	$ 7,500	*$18,500*
Gain on sale of 10% interest on Apr. 1, Year 2:		
Cost method ($20,000 − $15,000)	*5,000*	
Equity method ($20,000 − $16,200)		*3,800*
Consolidating adjustment: P's share of Y's undistributed profits since acquisition, adjustment (b) on page 399	*9,800*	
Total credits to consolidated retained earnings and income relating to P's interest in Y	*$22,300*	*$22,300*

recognized growth in the book value of the 10% interest in Y that was sold. This growth is 10% of the $9,000 undistributed profits of Y during Year 1, plus 10% of the $3,000 undistributed profits of Y during the first three months of Year 2.

Sale or purchase of shares by subsidiary—effect on parent's interest

A parent's interest in a subsidiary may change as a result of a share transaction between the subsidiary and outsiders. For example, if a parent owns 8,000 of 10,000 outstanding shares of a subsidiary and the subsidiary issues 2,000 additional shares to outsiders, the parent's interest is reduced from 80% to 66⅔%. Alternatively, if the subsidiary should reacquire 400 of its 10,000 outstanding shares, the parent's interest is increased to 8,000/9,600, or 83⅓%. If shares are sold or reacquired by the subsidiary at exactly their book value, the only effect is a change in the parent's interest in earnings after the date of the transaction. Usually, however, the sale or reacquisition of stock by the subsidiary will be at a figure different from book value, in which case we must account for the increase or decrease in the parent's equity as a result of the subsidiary's stock transaction. This increase or decrease in the parent's equity becomes an element of consolidated retained earnings since it constitutes a growth or decrease in the parent's equity after date of acquisition. The gain or loss may be reported as a special component of consolidated net income in the period in which the subsidiary's stock transaction occurs, or as an unusual adjustment of consolidated retained earnings.

To illustrate the consolidating procedures, we shall assume the following fact

Equity method

P COMPANY AND Y COMPANY
Working Papers—Consolidated Balance Sheet
as of the end of Year 3

	P Company	Y Company	Adjustments and eliminations Dr	Adjustments and eliminations Cr	Consolidated balance sheet
Investment in Y (equity)	109,800			(a) 600 (b) 109,200	
Other assets	332,000	180,000			512,000
Excess of cost over book value			(a) 600		600
Totals	441,800	180,000			512,600
Liabilities	35,500	24,000			59,500
Capital stock—P	250,000				250,000
Beginning retained earnings—P	115,800*				115,800
Net income—P	40,500*				40,500
Capital stock—Y		100,000	(b) 100,000		
Beginning retained earnings—Y		49,000	(b) 49,000		
Net income—Y		12,000	(b) 12,000		
Dividends—Y		(5,000)		(b) 5,000	
Minority interest—Y				(b) 46,800	46,800
Totals	441,800	180,000			512,600

(a) To reclassify excess of cost over book value (see analysis on page 399).
(b) To eliminate investment in Y as of the end of Year 3 and establish amount of 30% minority interest at this date.
* The amount of P's beginning retained earnings and Year 2 net income account was determined as follows:

	Retained earnings	Income
Balance at beginning of Year 1	$ 80,000	
Add: Income from P's own operations—Year 1	26,000	
P's share of Y's Year 1 income	9,800	
Year 2 income from P's own operations		$28,000
Add: Gain on sale of 10% interest in Y		3,800
P's share of Y's Year 2 income		8,700
Totals	$115,800	$40,500

situation: P Company acquired 9,000 shares, a 90% interest in Z Company, on January 1, Year 1, at a cost of $270,000. On July 1, Year 1, Z Company issued an additional 2,000 shares of stock to outsiders for $80,000. P's 90% interest was thus reduced to 9,000/12,000, or 75%, and P's equity in Z was changed since the sale price differed from book value. Ownership equity data for the two companies during Year 1 is shown at the bottom of page 402.

Cost method

P COMPANY AND Y COMPANY
Working Papers—Consolidated Balance Sheet
as of the end of Year 3

	P Company	Y Company	Adjustments and eliminations Dr	Adjustments and eliminations Cr	Consolidated balance sheet
Investment in Y	100,000		(b) 9,800	(c) 600 (d) 109,200	
Other assets	332,000	180,000			512,000
Excess of cost over book value			(c) 600		600
Totals	432,000	180,000			512,600
Liabilities	35,500	24,000			59,500
Capital stock—P	250,000				250,000
Beginning retained earnings—P	110,000*			(a) 900 (b) 4,900	115,800
Net income—P	36,500†		(a) 900	(b) 4,900	40,500
Capital stock—Y		100,000	(d) 100,000		
Beginning retained earnings—Y		49,000	(d) 49,000		
Net income—Y		12,000	(d) 12,000		
Dividends—Y		(5,000)		(d) 5,000	
Minority interest—Y				(d) 46,800	46,800
Totals	432,000	180,000			512,600

(a) To reclassify $900 of gain on sale of 10% interest in Y. This $900 was included in Year 2 income as a part of the $5,000 gain on sale of stock, but it actually represents undistributed profits applicable to this 10% interest during Year 1 (see page 398).
(b) To record P's share of the growth in its present 70% investment since dates of acquisition (see analysis on page 399).
(c) To reclassify excess of cost over book value. (For computation of the $600 excess, see analysis on page 399.)
(d) To eliminate investment in Y as of the end of Year 2, and establish the amount of the 30% minority interest at this date.

* P's retained earnings at beginning of Year 1, $80,000 + Year 1 income, $26,000 + dividends on Y stock, $4,000 = $110,000.

† P's Year 2 income, $28,000 + gain on sale of Y stock, $5,000 + Year 2 dividends on Y stock, $3,500 = $36,500.

	P Company	Z Company
Jan. 1—Capital stock, $20 par value	$350,000	$200,000
July 1—Additional issue by Z:		
Par value—2,000 shares @ $20		40,000
Paid-in capital in excess of par		40,000
Jan. 1—Retained earnings	106,000	80,000
Net income from own operations—Year 1	55,000	24,000
Dividends, Dec. 31, Year 1	(20,000)	(10,000)

An analysis of the changes in P's equity interest in Z Company during Year 1 appears below:

Analysis of Changes in P's Interest in Z Company during Year 1

	Book value of subsidiary net assets				Parent Company's investment at cost	Excess of cost over book value	Parent's gain or (loss)
	Total	Minority	Parent's interest				
			Dollars	%			
Jan. 1, Year 1	$280,000	$28,000	$252,000	90%	$270,000	$18,000	
Net income—6 months	12,000	1,200	10,800				
Balance—July 1, Year 1	$292,000	$29,200	$262,800	90%			
*July 1—Z sells 2,000 shares**	80,000	63,800	16,200	(15%)			$16,200
Balance after sale	$372,000	$93,000	$279,000	75%			
Net income—6 months	12,000	3,000	9,000				
Dividends—Dec. 21	(10,000)	(2,500)	(7,500)				
Balance, Dec. 31, Year 1	$374,000	$93,500	$280,500	75%	$270,000	$18,000	$16,200

Excess of cost over book value	18,000
Parent's investment—equity basis	$298,500
Parent's investment—cost basis	270,000
Total growth in parent's investment in Year 1	$ 28,500
Special gain as result of subsidiary's sale of stock	16,200
Growth in parent's investment related to operations	$ 12,300

* *For explanation of change in minority and parent's interest, see page 402.*

This analysis shows that the total growth in P's equity during Year 1 is $28,500, of which $16,200 arose as a result of the sale of the additional shares by Z. Thus although P's interest was reduced from 90% (9,000/10,000) to 75% (9,000/12,000) as a result of Z's share transaction, P has a 75% interest in a larger collection of net assets, and the book value of P's interest is enhanced by $16,200 as a result of the sale to outsiders at a figure substantially in excess of book value, as demonstrated below:

Book Value of Z Company

	Total	Minority interest		Parent's interest	
		Dollars	Fraction	Dollars	Fraction
Balance after sale of 2,000 shares	$372,000	$93,000	3/12	$279,000	9/12
Balance before sale of 2,000 shares	292,000	29,200	1/10	262,800	9/10
Change in book value of Z Company	+$ 80,000	+$63,800	+3/20	+$ 16,200	−3/20

If P Company used the *cost* method in accounting for its investment in Z, the only transaction recorded during Year 1 would be the receipt of $7,500 in dividends. The $16,200 gain in P's equity would be recorded as a part of the consolidating adjustment to record the growth in P's investment during Year 1. The consolidating working papers are illustrated on page 405.

If P Company used the *equity* method in accounting for its investment in Z, the balance in the investment account at the end of the year would be $298,500, as shown in the following schedule:

P's Books—Equity Method

	Investment in Z	*Retained earnings*	*Net income*	*Special gain*
Balances, Jan. 1, Year 1	*$270,000*	*$106,000*		
P Company's own earnings			*$55,000*	
P's share of Z's earnings:				
First six months—90% of $12,000	*10,800*		*10,800*	
Second six months—75% of $12,000	*9,000*		*9,000*	
Special gain on July 1, Year 1, as result of Z's stock transaction	*16,200*			*$16,200*
Dividends received from Z on Dec. 31, Year 1	*(7,500)*			
Balances, Dec. 31, Year 1	*$298,500*	*$106,000*	*$74,800*	*$16,200*

A comparison of these figures with those on the working papers on page 405 will show that the balances of P's retained earnings, net income, and special gain agree with the consolidated figures. Thus when the equity method is used no consolidating adjustments are required. After reclassifying the $18,000 excess of cost over book value, P's investment may be eliminated against Z's ownership equity accounts and the 25% minority interest of $93,500 will emerge.

Subsidiary transactions in treasury shares

Since a parent's ownership interest is computed as the ratio of the shares owned to the total shares *outstanding*, the existence of treasury shares in a subsidiary poses no special consolidating problems. In consolidating the financial statements, the subsidiary's treasury stock balance should be treated as if the stock were retired, and appropriate reductions made in the Stated Capital, Additional Paid-in Capital, and Retained Earnings accounts of the subsidiary. Consolidation can then proceed in the normal manner.

If, after a parent has acquired its interest in a subsidiary, the subsidiary sells treasury shares or purchases additional treasury shares, the effect for consolidating purposes is the same as if the subsidiary had purchased or sold unissued shares. The parent's percentage interest in the subsidiary will change, and there will be an increase or decrease in the parent's equity if the purchase or sale takes place at a price different from book value per share. A careful analysis of the

Cost method

P COMPANY AND Z COMPANY
Working Papers—Consolidated Balance Sheet
at the end of Year 1

	P Company	Z Company	Adjustments and eliminations Dr	Adjustments and eliminations Cr	Consolidated balance sheet
Investment in Z	270,000		(a) 28,500	(b) 18,000 (c) 280,500	
Other assets	350,000	400,000			750,000
Excess of cost over book value			(b) 18,000		18,000
Totals	620,000	400,000			768,000
Liabilities	121,500	26,000			147,500
Capital stock—P	350,000				350,000
Beginning retained earnings—P	106,000				106,000
Net income—P	62,500			(a) 12,300	74,800
Special gain on investment				(a) 16,200	16,200
Dividends—P	(20,000)				(20,000)
Capital stock—Z		240,000	(c) 240,000		
Additional paid in capital—Z		40,000	(c) 40,000		
Beginning retained earnings—Z		80,000	(c) 80,000		
Net income—Z		24,000	(c) 24,000		
Dividends—Z		(10,000)		(c) 10,000	
Minority interest in Z				(c) 93,500	93,500
Totals	620,000	400,000			768,000

(a) To record growth in P's investment in Z during Year 1, of which $16,200 is the gain in equity as a result of Z's stock transaction and $12,300 relates to operations (see analysis on page 403).
(b) To reclassify excess of cost over book value of investment in Z (see analysis on page 403).
(c) To eliminate investment in Z and establish amount of the 25% minority interest as of the end of Year 1.

changes in the parent's interest as a result of such transactions is necessary in order to consolidate properly the affiliated companies, but the issues and procedures do not differ from those already discussed in this chapter.

Questions

1. When a subsidiary has both common and preferred stock outstanding, is it necessary for consolidation purposes to allocate the subsidiary's ownership equity between the two classes of stock whether or not the parent company owns any of the subsidiary's preferred? Why?

2. Sub Company, an 80% owned subsidiary, has 1,000 shares of $100 par value common stock and 1,000 shares of $100 par value 6% preferred stock outstanding.

The company has suffered severe losses in recent years and has a deficit at the end of the current year of $24,000. Dividends on preferred stock are in arrears for two years. The preferred stock is callable at 105. What is the allocation of Sub Company's ownership equity between the controlling and minority interests?

3. A parent company owns 90% of the common stock of a subsidiary and 60% of the 6% preferred stock. During the current year the subsidiary earned $45,000 before preferred dividends of $12,000. Compute the share of the subsidiary's net income allocable to the parent company and to the minority interest.

4. R Company acquired 75% of the outstanding common stock of S Company at a time when the capital structure of S Company was as follows: Capital stock $100,000, additional paid-in capital $80,000, retained earnings $70,000. R Company accounts for its investment on a cost basis. At the end of the fifth year after date of acquisition, R Company has retained earnings of $240,000 and S Company has retained earnings of $25,000. During the five-year period since acquisition, S Company has declared stock dividends totaling $90,000, of which $50,000 has been added to capital stock and $40,000 to additional paid-in capital. Compute the consolidated retained earnings at the end of the fifth year.

5. T Company acquired an 80% interest in U Company for $190,000 at a time when the book value of U's net assets was $200,000. Several years later, when the book value of U's net assets was $250,000, T Company acquired an additional 10% interest on the open market for $30,000. Compute the excess of cost over book value that should appear on a consolidated balance sheet at the close of the year in which the final 10% interest was acquired, assuming no revaluation of U Company's assets. If the book value of U's net assets at the close of this year was $280,000, compute T's share of U's earnings since acquisition.

6. If a parent company acquires control of a subsidiary through a series of stock purchases, the difference between cost and book value at the date control is achieved may be measured in two ways. Describe each procedure and explain which you believe is preferable and why.

7. On January 1 of the current year, V Company purchased 70% of the outstanding common stock of W Company for $140,000. The book value of W Company's net assets at date of acquisition was $180,000. During the year W Company earned $60,000 and declared dividends of $22,000 on August 15. On September 1 of the current year, V Company sold one-seventh of its holdings of W stock for $23,000. Demonstrate that the consolidated retained earnings at the end of the year will be the same, whether V Company uses an equity or cost method of accounting for its investment in W Company.

8. On January 1 of the current year, P Company acquired 8,000 of the 10,000 outstanding shares of S Company common stock at a cost of $240,000. The book value of S Company's ownership equity on January 1 was $280,000. During the year S Company earned $60,000. On July 1 of the current year S Company sold an additional 2,000 shares of stock to outsiders for $74,000. S Company declared a dividend of $27,000 on December 31 of the current year. Compute the balance of P Company's investment in S at the end of the year, assuming P accounts for its investment on an equity basis.

9. M Company purchased a 75% interest in N Company for $120,000 at a time when the book value of N's ownership equity was $150,000. At a later date, when the book value of N's ownership equity was $200,000, M Company sold 5% of N Company's shares for $16,000. Compute the excess of cost over book value that would appear on a consolidated balance sheet as of the date of the sale of N Company's shares.

10. A parent company purchased 80% of the outstanding shares of a subsidiary at the beginning of Year 1. At the end of Year 3, the parent acquired the remaining 20% of the subsidiary's stock. Explain why it might be reasonable to revalue the net assets of the subsidiary at the beginning of Year 1 on the basis of the price paid by the parent for its 80% interest, and not to revalue the subsidiary's assets at the end of Year 3 on the basis of the price paid for the 20% minority interest.

Short cases for analysis

12-1 Gibbs Company owns several subsidiaries and regularly prepares consolidated financial statements. During Year 1 Gibbs Company purchased all the outstanding shares of Heftner Company for $90,000. At the date of acquisition, Heftner Company had 1,000 shares of $100 par value common stock and retained earnings of $20,000. In consolidated financial statements prepared at the end of Year 1, the excess of the book value of Heftner's net assets over the cost of Gibb's investment was reported on the consolidated statements as additional paid-in capital, $30,000.

During Year 2 the Gibbs Company sold the 1,000 shares of Heftner common for $108,000, at a time when the balance in the Retained Earnings account of Heftner Company was $31,000. Shortly thereafter the controller of Gibbs Company wrote, in a letter to the company's CPA: "The sale of Heftner at a price in excess of our cost produces a gain on our books. However since the sale price was less than the book value of our equity in Heftner, it will produce a loss on the consolidated financial statements. Should this loss, on a consolidated basis, be treated as a charge against consolidated retained earnings or against additional paid-in capital?"

Instructions

Write a reply to the Gibbs Company controller explaining the proper treatment of the various elements involved in the sale of the subsidiary stock.

AICPA adapted

12-2 Plep Company has acquired a 95% interest in Seven Company over a period of years as shown on page 408.

Throughout the six-year period, Seven Company had outstanding 10,000 shares of $10 par value common stock. Plep Company accounts for its investment at cost.

Year	Interest purchased, %	Cost	Seven Company's retained earnings at date of purchase
1	10	$ 13,000	$28,000
2	10	14,000	36,000
3	10	11,000	18,000
4	10	15,000	34,000
5	15	25,000	60,000
	55	$ 78,000	
6	40	75,000	80,000
	95	$153,000	

At the end of Year 5, following the purchase of 15% of the outstanding shares, which gave Plep Company a 55% interest in Seven Company, it was decided to prepare consolidated financial statements. The controller of Plep Company is not sure what figure he should consider to be the acquisition price paid for the 55% interest. He is inclined to argue that his firm has paid $78,000 for its 55% interest in captial and retained earnings as of Year 5, and to prepare consolidated statements on this basis. His assistant, however, contends that the acquisition price should be the sum of the amounts paid for the shares, plus Plep Company's share of Seven Company's earnings prior to the Year 5 purchase.

Instructions

a. Compute and explain the difference in consolidated statements at the end of Year 5 and Year 6 that will result from following the controller's approach or the assistant controller's approach.

b. Which position would you support? Why?

12-3 Caplan Company acquired an 80% interest in Destry Company for $350,000 at the beginning of Year 1. The ownership equity of Destry Company at this date was $390,000, of which $200,000 represented the stated capital of the 2,000 shares of common stock outstanding. Caplan Company accounts for its investment at cost and no entries were made in the investment account during the remainder of Year 1. The capital accounts of the two companies at the end of Year 1 are as follows:

CAPLAN AND DESTRY COMPANIES
Owners' Equity
as of the end of Year 1

	Caplan Company	Destry Company
Common stock, $100 par value	$ 800,000	$220,000
Additional paid-in capital		20,000
Retained earnings	540,000	138,000
Totals	$1,340,000	$378,000

During Year 1, Destry Company declared cash dividends of $40,000 and a 10% stock dividend. By order of the board of directors, the stock dividend was capitalized at $40,000, the approximate market value of the shares at the date of the dividend. Caplan Company declared $20,000 of cash dividends during Year 1.

At the end of Year 1, an accountant on the staff of the controller of Caplan Company prepared the following computation of consolidated net income for the year:

Caplan Company net income		*$110,000*
Destry Company:		
Retained earnings at end of year	*$138,000*	
Retained earnings at beginning of year	*190,000*	
Decline in retained earnings	*$ (52,000)*	
Caplan's share—80% of $52,000		*(41,600)*
Consolidated net income (controlling interest)		*$ 68,400*

When the controller was shown this computation he remarked, "That's an unreasonable result; it can't possibly be right." He was then called to the phone and the accountant was left to ponder the situation and prepare a revised determination of consolidated net income.

Instructions

a. Why is the amount computed by the accountant unreasonable at a glance? What amount would you be willing to support as the consolidated net income for Year 1? Explain any disagreement with the accountant's approach.

b. Prepare a statement of consolidated retained earnings for Year 1, on the basis of the given information.

Problems

12-4 On January 1, Year 1, K Company organized two subsidiaries, L and M Companies. At the date of organization K Company acquired 70% of the common and 50% of the preferred stock of L Company, and 80% of the common and 50% of the preferred stock of M Company, paying par value for all shares acquired. The capitalization of the three companies at the date of acquisition was as follows:

	K Company	*L Company*	*M Company*
Common stock ($10 par value)	*$600,000*	*$250,000*	*$200,000*
7% preferred stock, $100 par value, callable at 104, cumulative		*500,000*	*300,000*
Retained earnings	*395,000*	*-0-*	*-0-*

During the next three years, the operating history of the two subsidiary companies was as follows:

Year 1	*Net income (or loss)*	*$ (75,000)*	*$ 62,000*
	Dividends—common	*-0-*	*-0-*
	Dividends—preferred	*-0-*	*(21,000)*

Year 2	*Net income (or loss)*	*$(60,000)*	*$ 18,000*
	Dividends—common	*-0-*	*-0-*
	Dividends—preferred	*-0-*	*(21,000)*
Year 3	*Net income*	*58,000*	*32,000*
	Dividends—common		*(10,000)*
	Dividends—preferred	*(35,000)*	*(21,000)*
Retained earnings balance, end of Year 3		*$(112,000)*	*$ 39,000*

Instructions

a. Prepare schedules showing the distribution of the stockholders' equity of L and M Companies between the parent and minority interest at the end of Year 3.

b. Prepare in general journal form the necessary eliminating entries to consolidate the balance sheets of K, L, and M Companies, at December 31, Year 3. Include in your entries the establishment of the minority interests at the end of Year 3. The elimination of retained earnings may be made as of the *end* of Year 3, rather than the beginning of the year.

12-5 Financial data for the Gold and Hard Companies as of the end of Year 4 are presented below:

	Gold Company	*Hard Company*
Investment in Hard—9,900 shares	*$133,200*	
Other assets	*408,800*	*$257,000*
Total assets	*$542,000*	*$257,000*
Liabilities	*$ 69,000*	*$ 47,000*
Capital stock—$10 par	*300,000*	*110,000*
Additional paid-in capital		*5,000*
Retained earnings (beginning of Year 4)	*146,000*	*65,000*
Net income (Year 4)	*72,000*	*60,000*
Dividends	*(45,000)*	*(30,000)*
Total liabilities & equity	*$542,000*	*$257,000*

Gold Company purchased 7,000 shares of the capital stock of Hard Company for $14 per share at the beginning of Year 2, at which time Hard Company had 10,000 shares outstanding and retained earnings of $20,000. Gold Company carries its investment on a cost basis. An analysis of the retained earnings of the two companies since date of acquisition is as follows:

	Gold Company	*Hard Company*
Balance—beginning of Year 2	*$ 73,000*	*$ 20,000*
Net income—Year 2	*66,000*	*30,000*
Dividends:		
Cash	*(25,000)*	
10% stock dividend		*(15,000)*
Balance end of Year 2	*$114,000*	*$ 35,000*
Net income—Year 3	*52,000*	*55,000*
Dividends—Year 3	*(20,000)*	*(25,000)*
Balance—end of Year 3	*$146,000*	*$ 65,000*

Both companies regularly declare dividends at the end of the year, payable about the middle of January of the following year. Gold Company has recorded its share of Hard's Year 4 dividend declaration.

Gold Company's current holdings of 9,900 shares of Hard's capital stock were acquired as follows:

	Shares
Original purchase at $14 per share (beginning Year 2)	*7,000*
Stock dividend received at end of Year 2	*700*
Purchased at $15 per share on July 1, Year 3	*1,100*
Purchased at $17 per share at beginning of Year 4	*1,100*
Total shares held at end of Year 4	*9,900*

Instructions

a. Prepare consolidating working papers as of the end of Year 4. Show derivation of eliminating entries in supporting schedules.

b. Prepare a statement of consolidated retained earnings for Year 4.

12-6 The following data were extracted from the books of Cody Company and its subsidiary, Darr Company:

	Jan. 1, Year 1	*Dec. 31, Year 1*	*Dec. 31, Year 2*	*Dec. 31, Year 3*
Books of Cody Company:				
Investment in Darr Company	*$171,000*	*$171,000*	*$146,000*	*$181,000*
Retained earnings	*149,000*	*176,000*	*166,000*	*175,000*
Books of Darr Company:				
Capital stock	*110,000*	*110,000*	*110,000*	*110,000*
Retained earnings	*60,000*	*86,000*	*101,000*	*119,000*

Darr Company has 2,200 shares of $50 par value capital stock outstanding. Cody Company purchased 1,980 shares of Darr on January 1, Year 1; sold 220 shares on January 1, Year 2; and purchased 330 shares on January 1, Year 3. On Cody's books the Investment account was charged with the cost of the stock purchased and credited with the proceeds from the stock sold. No other entries have been made in the Investment account. All dividends received from the subsidiary have been credited to revenues.

At the time Cody Company acquired its original interest in Darr Company, it was agreed that any excess of amounts paid for its interest over the book value of the underlying net assets of Darr Company would be treated in consolidated statements as an intangible asset and amortized at the rate of 10% of the unamortized beginning balance each year. Such amortization has not been recorded on Cody Company's books; it is to be a part of the consolidating adjustments.

Instructions

Prepare schedules showing your determination of the appropriate amount of each of the following items on the consolidated financial statements of Cody and Darr Companies at the end of Years 1, 2, and 3:

a. Unamortized balance of the consolidated intangible asset
b. Consolidated retained earnings
c. Minority interest

AICPA adapted

12-7 Condensed balance sheets of Mola and Win Companies at the end of Year 1 are shown below:

	Mola Company	*Win Company*
Investment in Win Company	$240,000	
Other assets (details omitted)	400,000	$423,000
Total assets	$640,000	$423,000
Liabilities	$ 40,000	$ 30,000
Capital stock, $10 par value	500,000	200,000
Paid-in capital in excess of par		112,000
Retained earnings	100,000	81,000
Total liabilities & owners' equity	$640,000	$423,000

At the beginning of Year 1, Win Company had 8,000 shares of common stock outstanding, and 1,000 shares of treasury stock carried on its books at a cost of $18,000. On January 1, Year 1, Mola Company purchased the 1,000 shares of treasury stock and 11,000 shares of unissued stock directly from Win Company for $20 per share. Negotiations leading up to the purchase indicate that the price paid for the shares reflected unrecorded goodwill of Win Company at the date of acquisition. Win Company's retained earnings balance at the beginning of Year 1 was $56,000; the company paid no dividends during Year 1. Mola Company lost $23,000 during Year 1 and paid no dividends.

Instructions

a. Prepare a schedule showing Win Company's ownership equity balances before and after the purchase of a 60% interest by Mola Company at the beginning of Year 1.

b. Determine the effect of Mola's stock purchase on January 1, Year 1, on the book value per share of Win Company's common stock. If Win Company were to record the goodwill evidenced by Mola's purchase, what would be the book value per share of common immediately after date of acquisition?

c. Prepare working papers to consolidate the balance sheets of the two companies as of the end of Year 1. Show consolidated Year 1 net income as a separate item on the working papers.

12-8 Clifford Company acquired control of Dirk Company on June 30, Year 1, by purchasing in the market 2,800 shares of Dirk's 4,000 issued shares of $100 par value common stock. At that time Dirk Company had 500 shares of its own stock held as treasury shares and carried at par value.

On January 1, Year 3, Clifford acquired an additional 200 shares of Dirk Company from a minority stockholder. On December 31, Year 3, by agreement with the minority stockholders, Clifford acquired the 500 shares held in the treasury of Dirk Company.

The Investment account on Clifford's books shows the following entries recorded at cost:

June 30, Year 1	*2,800 shares of Dirk*	*$394,800*
Jan. 1, Year 3	*200 shares of Dirk purchased from outside interests*	*35,000*
Dec. 31, Year 3	*500 shares of Dirk obtained from Dirk Company*	*90,000*
		$519,800

The analysis below is prepared from the records of Dirk Company:

	Additional paid-in capital	*Retained earnings*
Credits:		
Balance: June 30, Year 1	*$ 74,300*	*$ 43,745*
Earnings from June 30 to Dec. 31, Year 1		*35,306*
Earnings during Year 2		*65,754*
Earnings during Year 3		*51,025*
Premium on sale of treasury shares	*40,000*	
		$195,830
Debits:		
Dividends paid on Dec. 1, Year 1		*$ 35,000*
Dividends paid on Dec. 5, Year 2		*35,000*
Dividends paid on Dec. 15, Year 3		*40,000*
Balance on Dec. 31, Year 3	*$114,300*	*$ 85,830*

Instructions

a. Prepare an analysis of the changes in Clifford Company's interest in Dirk Company from June 30, Year 1, to December 31, Year 3, after the sale of the treasury shares.

b. Prepare in general journal form the eliminating entries necessary for the preparation of consolidated balance sheets as of June 30, Year 1, and as of December 31, Year 3, after acquisition of the treasury stock. Prepare the eliminating entries so that they include the establishment of the amount of the minority interest at each date. Show all supporting computations.

AICPA adapted

12-9 The post-closing trial balances of three affiliated companies as of December 31, Year 4, are shown on the next page:

	Company P	Company S-1	Company S-2
Investment in Company S-1 (acquired Jan. 1, Year 3):			
Common stock (90%)	$200,000		
Preferred stock (40%)	40,000		
Investment in Company S-2 (acquired Jan. 1, Year 4):			
Common stock (70%)	59,300*		
Bonds (face value $10,000)	10,100		
Current assets	50,000	$ 50,000	$ 40,000
Machinery and equipment	40,000	20,000	30,000
Allowance for depreciation:			
Machinery and equipment	(20,000)	(15,000)	(10,000)
Other assets	600	313,000	70,180
Total assets	$380,000	$368,000	$130,180
Current liabilities	$ 20,000	$ 20,000	$ 20,000
Bonds payable, 4%, due Dec. 31, Year 9†			30,000
Premium on bonds payable			180
Capital stock, common, par value $100	300,000	250,000	60,000
Capital stock, preferred, 5%, $100 par, cumulative and nonparticipating		100,000	
Premium on preferred stock		10,000	
Retained earnings (deficit)	60,000	(12,000)	20,000
Total liabilities & owners' equity	$380,000	$368,000	$130,180

* *Cost at date of acquisition was $60,000.*
† *Bonds originally issued on Jan. 1, Year 1.*

Additional information

The investment accounts are carried at cost on P Company's books. On January 1, Year 3, dividends on the preferred stock of S-1 Company were in arrears for Years 1 and 2. Preferred stock has a call and liquidation value of par plus all dividends in arrears. On January 1, Year 4, Company S-1 declared a 25% stock dividend of common on common, charging $50,000 against the Premium on Preferred Stock account.

An analysis of the retained earnings of Companies S-1 and S-2 is as follows:

	Company S-1	Company S-2
Balance, Jan. 1, Year 3	$(10,000)*	$14,000
Net income for Year 3	7,000	7,000
Cash dividends in Year 4:		
On Jan. 1, Year 4	(5,000)	
On Dec. 31, Year 4		(6,000)
Net income (or loss) in Year 4	(4,000)	5,000
Balance, Dec. 31, Year 4	$(12,000)*	$20,000

* *Deficit*

The inventory of Company P includes merchandise purchased from Company S-2 for $5,000. Company S-2 prices goods to Company P at cost plus 25%. The inventory of Company S-2 includes merchandise purchased from Company S-1 for $2,000. Company S-1 sells to Company S-2 at a markup of 10% on selling price.

Current liabilities include the following: Company S-1 owes Company P $1,000; Company S-2 owes Company P $2,000; Company S-1 owes Company S-2 $3,000; and Company P owes Company S-1 $2,000. Company S-2 neglected to amortize premium on bonds payable for Year 4. Issuance and purchase premium on intercompany bonds may be charged or credited to the retained earnings of the respective companies, since P Company intends to hold the bonds to maturity.

Machinery having an estimated service life of 10 years after the date of purchase was bought by Company P from Company S-1 on January 1, Year 3, for $10,000. Company S-1 recorded a gain of $3,000 on the sale of this equipment.

Instructions

a. Prepare working papers for a consolidated balance sheet as of December 31, Year 4.

b. Prepare in good form a consolidated balance sheet as of December 31, Year 4.

AICPA adapted

12-10 The financial position of P Company and its two subsidiaries, North and South Companies, is summarized in the condensed statement on page 416.

P Company acquired its investment in North Company on June 30, Year 4, and has accounted for the investment on an accrual basis. Any difference between the price paid and the underlying book value of the interest in North Company is attributable to an overvaluation of a long-term investment (included in other assets) on North Company's books.

P Company acquired an 80% interest in the common stock of South Company on January 1, Year 4, at a cost of $105,300. At that time dividends on South's preferred stock were three years in arrears. P Company invested in South Company in order to acquire chemical milling facilities which it needed immediately; therefore it was willing to pay more than the book value of an 80% interest in South Company in order to get this productive capacity quickly. At the date of acquisition, it was agreed that the excess cost was to be amortized against P Company's income over a two-year period, but no adjustment has been entered on P Company's records during Year 4.

The bonds of North Company (face value $100,000) were sold at a premium of $6,000 on January 1, Year 1, and mature 12 years later. Premium is amortized on a straight-line basis. P Company bought 60% of the outstanding issue on the open market on July 1, Year 4, for $56,600. Since P Company firmly intends to hold the bonds as an investment to maturity, the gain on retirement should be allocated between P and South Companies in consolidation. P Company amortizes the discount on a straight-line basis over 8½ years.

Included in the ending inventory of P Company are fabricated parts purchased from South Company for $56,000. These parts cost South Company $31,000 to manufacture and $1,000 to ship to P Company.

P Company's engineering department constructed certain facilities for South Company. These were completed on June 30, Year 4, and South Company paid the total price of $40,000 to P Company. The actual cost of construction to P Company was $22,000; the gain of $18,000 is included in P Company's income for Year 1. South Company has charged $2,000 of depreciation on this plant during Year 1.

P, North, and South Companies
Condensed Financial Data
as of end of Year 4

	P Company	*North Company*	*South Company*
Current assets	*$125,000*	*$ 90,000*	*$ 64,000*
Investment in North—70% (accrual)	*189,560*		
Investment in South—80% (accrual)	*105,300*		
Bonds of North Company	*56,800*		
Other assets	*203,340*	*390,000*	*186,000*
Totals	*$680,000*	*$480,000*	*$250,000*
Current liabilities	*$130,000*	*$96,000*	*$ 31,000*
Bonds payable	*80,000*	*104,000*	
6% preferred stock			*50,000*
Common stock	*320,000*	*200,000*	*120,000*
Additional paid-in capital			*20,000*
Retained earnings—beginning of Year 4	*96,250*	*50,000*	*(10,000)*
Net income—Year 1	*85,750**	*45,000*	*51,000*
Dividends (paid Dec. 15, Year 4)	*(32,000)*	*(15,000)*	*(12,000)†*
Totals	*$680,000*	*$480,000*	*$250,000*

* *Includes gain on sale of facilities to South Company, $18,000; share of North Company's Year 1 income, $15,750.*
† *Dividends on preferred stock only, arrears for Years 1, 2, 3, and 4.*

Instructions

a. Prepare working papers for a consolidated balance sheet and statement of retained earnings for Year 4. Key all adjusting and eliminating entries on your working papers and explain, including supporting computations in your explanation of each entry.

b. Prepare a combined statement of consolidated retained earnings and changes in the minority interest in North and South.

c. Show how bonds payable would be presented on the consolidated balance sheet at the end of Year 4.

12-11 Zee Company acquired a controlling interest in Que Company at the beginning of Year 1. The Investment account, which is carried at cost on Zee's books, is shown on the next page:

Investment in Que Company Common Shares

Year 1		*Year 2*	
Jan. 2: 900 shares purchased	*121,500*	*Apr. 1: Sold 200 shares; proceeds*	*30,000*
July 1: 100 shares purchased	*16,000*		

Zee Company has outstanding 25,000 shares of $10 par value common stock. Que Company, since its organization, has had outstanding 1,000 shares of $100 par value common stock. Changes in the retained earnings of the two companies during Years 1 and 2 were as follows:

ZEE AND QUE COMPANIES
Changes in Retained Earnings
during Years 1 and 2

	Zee Company	*Que Company*
Balance at beginning of Year 1	*$180,000*	*$15,000*
Year 1 net income	*25,000*	*30,000*
Dividends declared in December, Year 1	*(20,000)*	*(10,000)*
Balance at end of Year 1	*$185,000*	*$35,000*
Year 2 net income	*35,000*	*46,000*
Dividends declared in December, Year 2	*(25,000)*	*(18,000)*
Balance at end of Year 2	*$195,000*	*$63,000*

At the time Zee Company acquired its initial 90% interest, it was agreed that, for consolidation purposes only, Que Company's assets should be revalued (by establishing a Goodwill account) on the basis of the price paid by Zee for its investment, and that the goodwill thus reported on consolidated statements should be amortized on a straight-line basis over a period of 10 years. No revaluation of assets is to be made on the basis of any subsequent purchase or sale of Que Company's shares by Zee Company. Que Company's net income does not reflect the amortization of goodwill.

Instructions

a. On the basis of the above information and the assumptions given, determine the following amounts as they should appear on consolidated statements as of the end of Year 2:

(1) The balance of Que Company's unrecorded goodwill that would appear on the consolidated balance sheet.

(2) The amount of the minority interest in Que Company.

(3) The controlling interest in consolidated net income for Year 2.

(4) A statement of changes in consolidated retained earnings during Year 2.

b. What is the justification for revaluing Que Company's net assets on the basis of the initial purchase of shares by Zee Company, and failing to change the valuation on the basis of the subsequent purchase and sale of Que's shares by Zee Company?

12-12 The Ace Corporation acquired an 80% interest in the Sellers Company in Year 1 for $800,000. On December 31, Year 4, the following amounts appear on the consolidated balance sheet of the Ace and Sellers Companies:

Minority interest (capital stock and retained earnings)	*$ 200,000*
Consolidated retained earnings	*1,010,000*
Excess of book value over cost of subsidiary company (not subject to periodic amortization)	*300,000*

On October 1, Year 5, the Ace Corporation sold a 10% interest in the Sellers Company for $150,000. The net income, dividends, and depreciation expense reported by each company during Year 5 were as follows:

	Net income	*Dividends*	*Depreciation*
Ace Corporation	*$100,000**	*$40,000*	*$80,000*
Sellers Company	*20,000*	*-0-*	*30,000*

* *Includes gain on sale of Sellers Company shares.*

Instructions

a. Prepare schedules showing the computation of the following amounts as they should appear on a consolidated balance sheet as of December 31, Year 5:

(1) Total minority interest in Sellers (30%)

(2) Consolidated retained earnings

(3) Excess of book value over cost of subsidiary company shares

b. Compute the balance of the Investment in Sellers Company account on Ace Corporation's books, as of December 31, Year 5, assuming Ace Corporation uses the equity method in accounting for its investment.

c. Explain the nature of the Excess of Book Value over Cost account. Discuss the appropriate treatment of this item on the consolidated balance sheet, and defend whatever disposition you recommend.

d. From the information available, compute as many items as you can that would appear on a funds (working capital flow) statement for Year 5, prepared on a consolidated basis.

AICPA adapted

13 CONSOLIDATIONS: INDIRECT AND MUTUAL HOLDINGS

Indirect holdings

Thus far we have confined our consolidation discussion to corporate affiliations that involve what may be described as parent-son relationships. A parent company may exercise control of one or more affiliated companies indirectly through subholding companies. The two general cases of indirect control through subholding companies are illustrated in the diagram below:

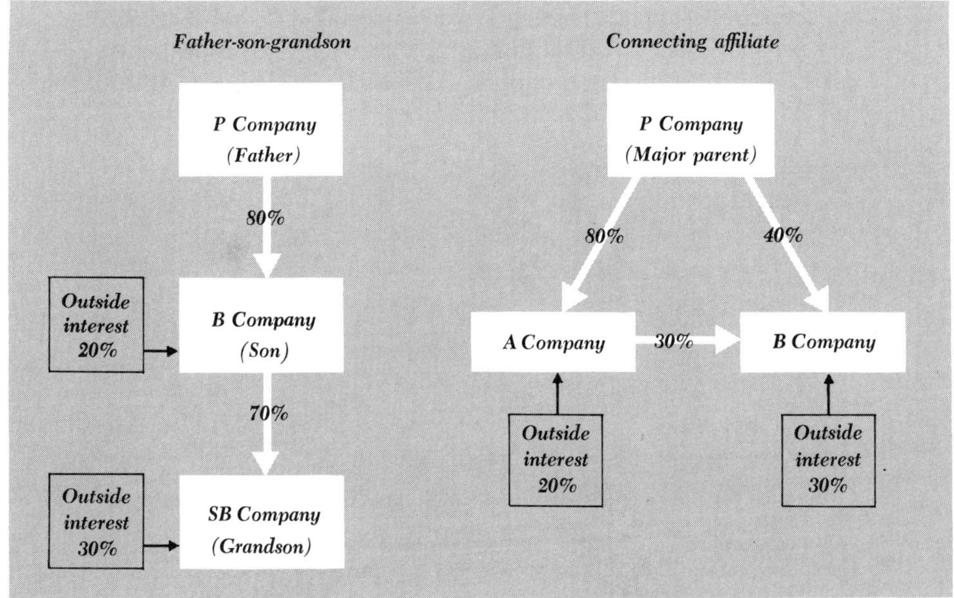

In both the above cases P Company exercises control, either directly or indirectly, over the two affiliates, and consolidated financial statements for the three-company economic entity are appropriate. The left-hand diagram illustrates the situation in which P Company controls B Company, and B is in turn the controlling parent of SB Company. The stockholders of P, through their ownership of 80% of B's stock, exercise effective control over the entire affiliated structure. In the diagram at the right, A Company is a connecting affiliate. P's interest in B Company is in part direct through its 40% stock interest and in part indirect through its 80% stock interest in A Company and A's 30% interest in B.

We face somewhat more complex procedures in consolidating the financial statements of affiliated companies where control is exercised both directly and indirectly. No new theoretical issues are involved. The principles of consolidation which have been discussed in previous chapters are simply applied in handling a more complicated set of data and relationships. Two central problems are the interpretation of the difference between the cost and book value of the holding companies' interest in subsidiaries, and the proper allocation of the growth in the net assets of subsidiaries as a result of operations, after date of acquisition.

The valuation problem

In examining the problem of interpreting the difference between the cost and book value of the direct and indirect interests in subsidiaries, we can distinguish two general cases: (1) A subsidiary becomes a holding company. In this case a parent owns a controlling interest in a son, and *at a later date* the son acquires an equity interest in a grandson. (2) A holding company becomes a subsidiary. In this case a parent acquires a controlling interest in a son which *already owns* an equity interest in what is now a grandson. These two situations may occur in either the parent-son-grandson or the connecting-affiliate framework. Since the problems raised and the analysis required are substantially the same, we shall discuss only the parent-son-grandson case.

Subsidiary becomes a holding company. Suppose P Company acquired 80% of the common stock of B at the beginning of Year 1. Shortly thereafter B Company acquired a 70% interest in Company SB.[1] These relations may be diagrammed as follows:

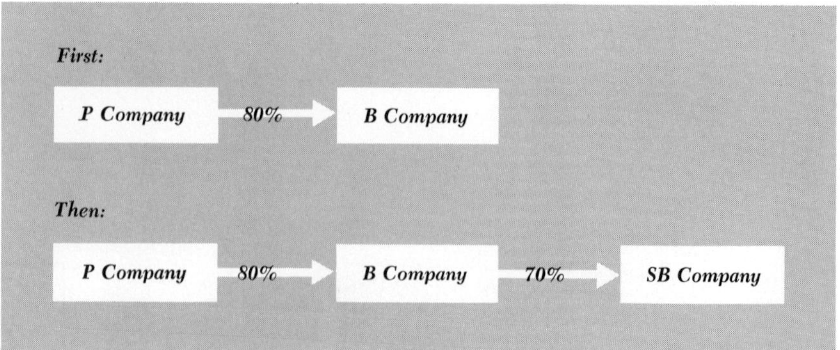

[1] At this stage we shall assume the lapse of only a few days between these acquisitions to avoid the problem of accounting for operations in the interim. In later sections the problem of allocating growth through operations will be fully considered.

Any difference between P's investment in B and the underlying book value of B's net assets is subject to normal interpretation in this case. Furthermore, since B was controlled by P at the time of the acquisition of SB stock, the act of B may be interpreted as the act of P. Any difference between the price paid by B for its interest in SB and the underlying book value of B's equity in SB may be analyzed in the usual manner. To illustrate these points we shall assume the following financial data:

P's Investment in B—80%		*B's Investment in SB—70%*	
Book value of B's net assets at date of acquisition	*$400,000*	*Book value of SB's net assets at date of acquisition*	*$200,000*
Book value of P's interest in B—80%	*$320,000*	*Book value of B's interest—70%*	*$140,000*
Cost of P's investment in B	*300,000*	*Cost of B's investment in SB*	*168,000*
Excess of book value over cost	*$ (20,000)*	*Excess of cost over book value*	*$ 28,000*

Considering first P's investment in B, we note that the book value of P's interest exceeds the cost of P's 80% investment in B Company by $20,000. If we assume that this difference arises because B's net assets are overstated, the evidence implies that the amount of the overstatement is $25,000 ($20,000 ÷ .80). In consolidating P and B, we are thus faced with the necessity of adjusting B's net assets downward. The appropriate consolidating adjustment would be:

Retained Earnings—B Company	*25,000*	
Assets of B, or Allowance for Overvaluation		*25,000*
To reduce the valuation of B's net assets on the basis of the price paid by P Company for an 80% interest.		

After giving effect to this adjustment, the book value of B's net assets would be $375,000 ($400,000 − $25,000); after eliminating the $300,000 investment on P's books against the ownership equity accounts of B, the remaining equity of the minority interest would be $75,000, or 20% of B Company's revised net asset valuation (20% of $375,000 = $75,000).

Now let us look at B's investment in SB Company. The cost of B's investment in SB exceeds the book value of B's 70% interest by $28,000. This difference may be interpreted as evidence of an undervaluation of SB's net assets at the date of acquisition, which suggests that SB's net assets should be revalued upward in consolidation by $40,000 ($28,000 ÷ .70). Alternatively, we might assume that B Company (acting under P's control) paid $28,000 for certain intangible benefits stemming from the affiliation of the two companies.

If we follow the first assumption, the addition of $40,000 to SB's net assets will raise SB's total book value to $240,000. This valuation is consistent with B's 70% investment of $168,000, and the elimination of B's investment account against the ownership equity accounts of SB will leave a minority interest of $72,000, or 30% of $240,000. If we follow the second (purchase of intangibles) assumption, the $28,000 excess of B's cost over book value will be removed from B's investment account, and the remaining $140,000 in B's investment account will eliminate against the equity account of SB, leaving a minority interest of $60,000, or 30% of $200,000. The consolidating entries are illustrated below:

Consolidating Entries Relating to B's Investment in SB

Revaluation Assumption

	Debit	Credit
Assets or Goodwill of SB. . . .	*40,000*	
Appraisal Capital—SB		*40,000*
To record revaluation of SB's net assets.		
Various Ownership Equity Accounts of SB.	*240,000*	
Investment in SB.		*168,000*
Minority Interest in SB —30%		*72,000*
To eliminate investment of B in SB, and establish minority interest.		

Purchase of Intangibles Assumption

	Debit	Credit
Excess of Cost over Book Value of Investment.	*28,000*	
Investment in SB.		*28,000*
To reduce investment to book value.		
Various Ownership Equity Accounts of SB.	*200,000*	
Investment in SB.		*140,000*
Minority Interest in SB —30%.		*60,000*
To eliminate investment of B in SB, and establish minority interest.		

Thus we see that the case in which a subsidiary becomes a holding company really poses no new problems in dealing with differences between investment and book value, other than adding an additional relationship which must be analyzed in the process of consolidation.

Holding company becomes a subsidiary. Now let us consider the case of a parent company which itself becomes a subsidiary. Assume that P Company acquired a 90% interest in C Company at a time when C Company already owns a 60% interest in SC Company. This situation might be diagrammed as follows:

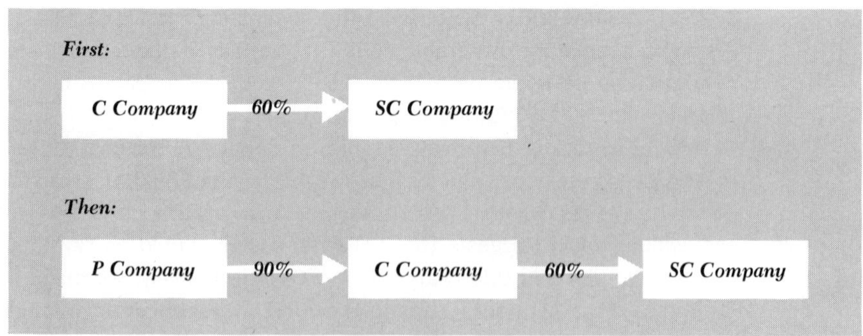

When C acquired its 60% interest in SC the interpretation of any difference between the price paid and the book value of the interest in C's net assets raises no new issues. P's acquisition of a 90% interest in C after this date, however, adds a new complication. In evaluating the net assets of C at the date of acquisition, the management of P will inevitably take into consideration the value of C's investment in SC. Since C has a controlling interest in SC, it is likely that the value of the underlying net assets of C Company will be carefully considered. Thus the price paid by P for its 90% investment in C may well be evidence of the going-concern value of *both* C and SC Companies.

To illustrate these points, we shall assume the following data: C Company acquired its 60% interest in SC for $180,000 at a time when SC's ownership equity was $250,000; C carries its investment on an equity basis. P Company acquired its 90% interest in C at a cost of $514,800 when C's ownership equity had a book value of $542,000. P carries its investment at cost. The condensed balance sheets of the three companies at the date of P's acquisition are shown below:

P, C, AND SC COMPANIES
Condensed Balance Sheets
at date of P's acquisition of 90% interest in C

	P Company	*C Company*	*SC Company*
Assets:			
Investment in C (cost)	$514,800		
Investment in SC (equity)		$222,000	
Other net assets (details omitted)	185,200	320,000	$320,000
Total net assets	$700,000	$542,000	$320,000
Ownership Equity:			
Capital stock	$500,000	$400,000	$200,000
Retained earnings	200,000	142,000	120,000
Total ownership equity	$700,000	$542,000	$320,000

We may analyze the relation between the two controlling investments and the book value of the underlying net assets as follows:

P's Investment in C—90%

Book value of C Company at date of P's acquisition:	
C's own assets	$320,000
Investment in SC (original cost)	180,000
C's 60% share of SC's growth since date of C's acquisition	42,000
Total book value of C at the time of P Company's acquisition	$542,000
Book value of P's 90% interest	$487,800
Price paid by P for 90% interest	514,800
Excess of cost over book value	$ 27,000

C's Investment in SC—60%*

Book value of SC Company	$320,000
Book value of C's 60% interest in SC	$192,000
Balance in C's investment account (equity basis)	222,000
Excess of cost over book value	$ 30,000

* *Since C carries its investment on an equity basis, we can make this comparison as of the current date, rather than as of the date of C's acquisition.*

When we ask ourselves why P was willing to pay $27,000 more than book value for a 90% interest in C Company, there are a number of possible answers. One is that the management of P saw $27,000 of intangible benefits in gaining control of the affiliated enterprises. Another is that P's management believed that the net assets of C were undervalued by $30,000 ($27,000 ÷ .90). It is also possible that P's management found the net assets of C Company (other than the investment in SC) stated at approximately current fair values but concluded that *because the net assets of SC were undervalued,* C's investment in SC was carried at a figure below current fair value.

Let us consider this alternative. Suppose P's preinvestment investigation showed that the net assets of SC were undervalued by $100,000. This implies that C's 60% interest in SC is worth $60,000 more than the underlying book value of SC Company. C carries its investment (on an equity basis) at $222,000, which is $30,000 more than the $192,000 (60% of $320,000) book value of SC at this time. If we revalue SC's net assets upward by $100,000, therefore, we shall also have to restate C's investment account at $252,000 ($222,000 + $30,000) to make it consistent with the valuation of SC. The working papers below show how consolidation would be made under these assumptions.

P, C, AND SC COMPANIES
Condensed Consolidating Working Papers—Balance Sheet
(Assuming revaluation of both S and SC Companies' net assets at the time of P's acquisition of C Company)

	P Company	*C Company*	*SC Company*	*Adjustments and eliminations*		*Consolidated balance sheet*
				Dr	*Cr*	
Investment in C (cost)	*514,800*				*(d) 514,800*	
Investment in SC (equity)		*222,000*		*(b) 30,000*	*(c) 252,000*	
Other assets	*185,200*	*320,000*	*320,000*	*(a) 100,000*		*925,200*
Total net assets	*700,000*	*542,000*	*320,000*			*925,200*
Ownership equity of:						
P Company	*700,000*					*700,000*
C Company		*542,000*		*(d) 542,000*		
SC Company			*320,000*	*(c) 320,000*		
Appraisal capital—C				*(d) 30,000*	*(b) 30,000*	
Appraisal capital—SC				*(c) 100,000*	*(a) 100,000*	
Minority interest in:						
SC Company—40%					*(c) 168,000*	*168,000*
C Company—10%					*(d) 57,200*	*57,200*
Total ownership equity	*700,000*	*542,000*	*320,000*			*925,200*

(a) To revalue net assets of SC Company by $100,000 on the basis of evidence implicit in the price paid by P for its 90% interest in C.
(b) To revalue C's investment in SC by $30,000 on the basis of evidence that SC's net assets are undervalued.
(c) To eliminate C's investment in SC and establish 40% minority interest.
(d) To eliminate P's investment in C and establish 10% minority interest.

Revaluation of the net assets of both SC and C on the basis of P's evaluation and the price paid by P for its investment in C is a perfectly consistent theoretical resolution of the valuation problem. The analysis is useful in focusing attention on the real economic issues management should consider in evaluating an investment in a holding company. Many accountants, however, would be reluctant to make an extensive restatement of the asset values of affiliated companies on the basis of this kind of indirect evidence. An alternative solution, in this event, is to assume that the excess of cost over book value on both P and C's books is a collective intangible asset of the consolidated enterprise. The consolidating working papers illustrating this solution appear below:

P, C, AND SC COMPANIES
Condensed Consolidating Working Papers—Balance Sheet
(Assuming no revaluation of C and SC Companies)

	P Company	C Company	SC Company	Adjustments and eliminations		Consolidated balance sheet
				Dr	Cr	
Investment in C (cost)	514,800				(a) 27,000 (d) 487,800	
Investment in SC (equity)		222,000			(b) 30,000 (c) 192,000	
Other net assets	185,200	320,000	320,000			825,200
Excess of cost over book value—P's investment in C				(a) 27,000		27,000
Excess of cost over book value—C's investment in SC				(b) 30,000		30,000
Total net assets	700,000	542,000	320,000			882,200
Ownership equity of:						
P Company	700,000					700,000
C Company		542,000		(d) 542,000		
SC Company			320,000	(c) 320,000		
Minority interest in:						
SC Company—40%					(c) 128,000	128,000
C Company—10%					(d) 54,200	54,200
Total ownership equity	700,000	542,000	320,000			882,200

(a) To reclassify excess of cost of P's investment in C over book value.
(b) To reclassify excess of cost of C's investment in SC over book value.
(c) To eliminate C's investment in SC and establish 40% minority interest.
(d) To eliminate P's investment in C and establish 10% minority interest.

In summary, when a parent acquires a subsidiary that is itself a holding company, the familiar problem of interpreting the difference between cost and book value appears in a new setting. The source of the difference between cost and book value may be traced to an apparent understatement or overstatement of the net assets of more than one affiliated subsidiary. If it is clear that the price paid for a controlling interest is valid economic evidence on which to base a revaluation of the assets of one or more of the subsidiaries in the affiliated group, it is proper to make the necessary revaluations as a part of the consolidating procedure. If the evidence is not clear, the accountant may be forced to treat the excess of cost over book value as an intangible asset valued at cost on the consolidated balance sheet.

Growth in subsidiaries since acquisition

The second major problem in consolidating affiliated companies where indirect holdings are involved is in properly handling the growth through operations of the subsidiary companies from the various dates of acquisition to the date of the consolidated financial statement. It is likely that original cost will differ from book value and that acquisition dates will vary, and a careful analysis of the data is often required. Again, however, our problem is essentially procedural rather than conceptual.

We can see that we are applying basic principles to more complex data when we note that it is possible to consolidate three or more companies by beginning at the bottom of the control structure and consolidating each subsidiary with its most closely related parent, and then in turn consolidating that combination of companies with the next senior parent, and so on. This procedure, while cumbersome, may be useful in unusually complex situations. In most cases, however, we can more conveniently consolidate all affiliated companies on a single working paper by working from the most junior subsidiary and its parent up through the most senior parent, making all necessary consolidating adjustments and eliminations as we go along.

The procedures do not differ materially whether the parent and subparent use the cost or the equity basis of accounting for their investments. We know that under either approach the consolidated financial statements will be identical. Consolidating procedure when the cost method has been used is simply a matter of adjusting the accounts of the various companies to an equity basis (usually as of the beginning of the current year) before eliminating the investment accounts. Therefore we shall illustrate only the cost method. The student who understands the procedures in this case can readily adapt to situations in which one or more of the affiliated companies have used the equity method.

Father-son-grandson case. Three affiliated companies, P, B, and SB Companies, are related as indicated in the diagram below:

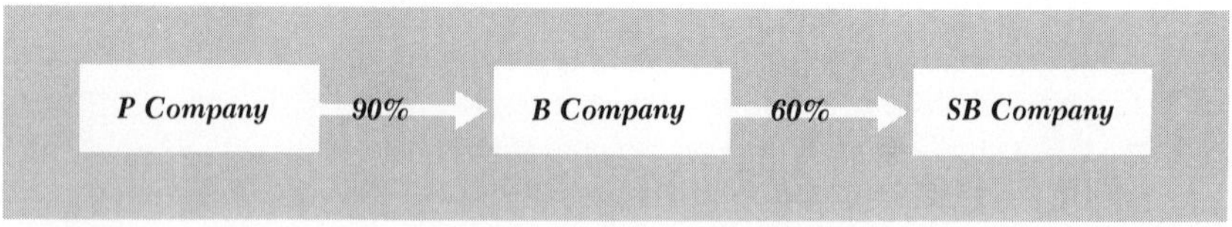

P Company —90%→ *B Company* —60%→ *SB Company*

P acquired a 90% interest in B Company at the beginning of Year 1 for $238,500. At date of acquisition B Company's ownership equity was composed of capital stock, $200,000, and retained earnings, $50,000. P Company thus paid $13,500 more than book value for its investment (90% of $250,000 = $225,000; $238,500 − $225,000 = $13,500), and we shall assume that this excess represents the cost of intangible benefits stemming from the affiliation.

At the beginning of Year 2, B Company acquired a 60% interest in SB Company for $90,000. SB Company had $100,000 of capital stock and $70,000 of retained earnings at this time. It is agreed that SB's net assets are overstated by $20,000 at the date of acquisition and should be written down as a consolidating adjustment. When this is done, 60% of SB's revised ownership equity of $150,000 will exactly equal B's $90,000 investment.

The changes in ownership equity of the three companies during the two-year period from the beginning of Year 1 to the end of Year 2 are shown below:

	P Company	*B Company*	*SB Company*
Capital stock	*$300,000*	*$200,000*	*$100,000*
Retained earnings, beginning of Year 1	*75,000*	*50,000*	*82,000*
Year 1:			
Net income	*40,000*	*30,000*	*(12,000)*
Dividends	*(25,000)*	*-0-*	*-0-*
Retained earnings, end of Year 1	*90,000*	*80,000*	*70,000*
Year 2:			
Net income	*40,000*	*30,000*	*20,000*
Dividends	*(18,000)*	*(5,000)*	*(10,000)*
Retained earnings, end of Year 2	*112,000*	*105,000*	*80,000*

Consolidating working papers for these three companies as of the end of Year 2 appear on page 428. The adjusting and eliminating entries are explained below the working papers. We shall not discuss these entries in detail, but some of the features of the consolidating procedure warrant special comment.

The initial step in the consolidation is to dispose of the differences between the investment accounts and the book value of the underlying interest. In the case of B's investment in SB, the difference led to a downward revaluation of SB's net assets in entry (a). The excess of P's investment over the book value of P's interest in B was treated as an intangible asset and was reclassified in entry (e).

The next step is to recognize the growth through earnings from the date of acquisition to the beginning of Year 2. We start with the most junior company and work up the consolidated structure, since B's share of SB's growth will in turn affect P's share of B's growth. In this case B acquired its 60% interest in SB at the beginning of Year 2, so B's beginning retained earnings figure does not require adjustment. It is necessary, however, to allocate SB's Year 2 net income and dividends between B Company and the minority interest, as shown by entries (b) and (c). The elimination of B's investment in SB as of the beginning of Year 2 completes this phase of the consolidation, entry (d).

Next we move to the top tier of the affiliated structure and consider the relation of P and B Companies. P acquired its interest in B at the beginning of Year 1; therefore P's share of B's growth during Year 1 must be added to P's investment and beginning retained earnings accounts (thus converting these figures to an equity basis as of the beginning of Year 2). Similarly P's 90% interest in B's revised earnings figure (including B's share of SB's Year 2 earnings) and B's dividends are allocated between P Company and the minority interest, entries (h) and (i). The

Cost method

P, B, AND SB COMPANIES
Working Papers—Consolidated Balance Sheet
as of the end of Year 2

	P Company	B Company	SB Company	Adjustments and eliminations Dr	Adjustments and eliminations Cr	Consolidated balance sheet
Assets:						
Investment in B—90%	238,500			(f) 27,000	(e) 13,500	
					(g) 252,000	
Investment in SB—60%		90,000			(d) 90,000	
Other assets	218,500	250,000	205,000		(a) 20,000	653,500
Excess of cost over book value				(e) 13,500		13,500
Total (debits)	457,000	340,000	205,000			667,000
Liabilities & Owners' Equity:						
Liabilities	45,000	35,000	25,000			105,000
Capital stock—P	300,000					300,000
Beginning retained earnings—P	90,000				(f) 27,000	117,000
Net income—P	40,000			(i) 4,500	(h) 32,400	67,900
Dividends—P	(18,000)					(18,000)
Capital stock—B		200,000		(g) 200,000		
Beginning retained earnings—B		80,000		(g) 80,000		
Net income—B		30,000		(c) 6,000		
				(h) 36,000	(b) 12,000	
Dividends—B		(5,000)			(i) 5,000	
Capital stock—SB			100,000	(d) 100,000		
Beginning retained earnings—SB			70,000	(a) 20,000		
				(d) 50,000		
Net income—SB			20,000	(b) 20,000		
Dividends—SB			(10,000)		(c) 10,000	
Minority interest—B				(i) 500	(g) 28,000	
					(h) 3,600	31,100
Minority interest—SB				(c) 4,000	(b) 8,000	
					(d) 60,000	64,000
Total (credits)	457,000	340,000	205,000			667,000

(a) To revalue net assets of SB to a basis consistent with price paid by B for a 60% interest.

Book value of SB at date of acquisition	$170,000
Value implied by payment of $90,000 for 60% interest	150,000
Indicated overvaluation of SB net assets	$ 20,000

(b) To allocate SB's $20,000 Year 2 net income between B (60%) and minority (40%).
(c) To allocate SB's Year 2 dividends ($10,000) between B (60%) and minority (40%).
(d) To eliminate B's investment in SB as of the beginning of Year 2 and establish minority interest (40% of $170,000) at that date.
(e) To reclassify excess of cost of P's investment in B over book value:

Book value of B at date of acquisition	$250,000
90% of book value	$225,000
Price paid by P for 90% interest	238,500
Excess of cost over book value	$ 13,500

(f) To allocate growth in B from date of acquisition to beginning of Year 2 between P and minority:

Book value of B at beginning of Year 2	$280,000
Book value of B at date of acquisition	250,000
Growth	$ 30,000

(Allocated 90% to P and 10% to minority interest.)

(g) To eliminate P's investment in B as of the beginning of Year 2 and establish minority interest at this date.
(h) To allocate B's net income (including B's share of SB's income) between P and minority interest.
(i) To allocate B's dividends between P and minority interest. (Note: P has included $4,500 of dividend revenue in net income; this adjustment eliminates double counting of net income and dividends based on income.)

final step is to eliminate P's investment in B as of the beginning of Year 2, entry (g), and establish the minority interest at this date.

A statement of consolidated retained earnings and change in minority interest for Year 2, based on the data in the working papers, is shown below:

P, B, AND SB COMPANIES
Statement of Retained Earnings and Change in Minority Interests
Year 2

	Consolidated retained earnings	Minority interest in B Company	Minority interest in SB Company
Balance at beginning of Year 2	$117,000	$28,000	$60,000
Net income, Year 2	67,900	3,600	8,000
Dividends, Year 2	(18,000)	(500)	(4,000)
Balance at end of Year 2	$166,900	$31,100	$64,000

If Companies P and B had used the equity method of accounting for their investments, the consolidating procedures would be simplified. B Company's net income would include its 60% share of SB's $20,000 net income for Year 2, and B's investment account balance of $96,000 would eliminate against SB's revised ownership equity of $160,000 as of the end of Year 2, leaving a 40% minority interest of $64,000. Similarly, P's net income would include $32,400 (90% of B's total net income including B's share of SB income) and its investment account of $279,900 would eliminate against B's revised ownership equity of $311,000 as of the end of Year 2, leaving a 10% minority interest of $31,100. It is evident that the use of the equity method often simplifies the consolidation process, since a significant portion of the consolidation has been done when the equity method adjustments of investment accounts have been made. The primary procedural disadvantage of the equity method arises when consolidating adjustments for intercompany transactions and profits make it necessary to revise the equity method adjustments at the time consolidated statements are prepared.

Connecting affiliate case. We shall now demonstrate the consolidating procedures when indirect holdings occur through connecting affiliates, and at the same time use this example to illustrate the consolidation of the income statement in a situation involving indirect holdings. The example involves P, R, and Q Companies, whose affiliation structure is shown in the diagram below:

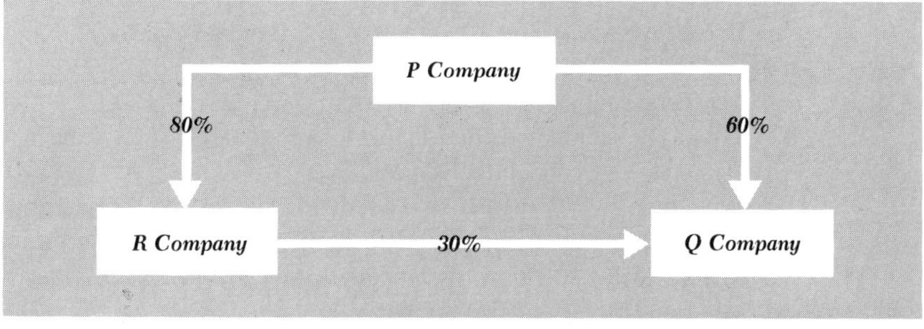

The following data for Companies P, Q, and R form the basis for the illustration:

P, Q, AND R COMPANIES
Balance Sheets (condensed)
end of Year 2

Assets	*P Company*	*R Company*	*Q Company*
Investment in R Company—80% (at cost)	*$180,000*		
Investment in Q Company—60% (at cost)	*252,000*		
Investment in Q Company—30% (at cost)		*$102,000*	
Other assets	*208,000*	*268,000*	*$510,000*
Total assets	*$640,000*	*$370,000*	*$510,000*
Liabilities & Owners' Equity			
Liabilities	*$119,000*	*$110,000*	*$110,000*
Capital stock, $100 par value	*400,000*	*200,000*	*300,000*
Retained earnings, beginning	*90,000*	*50,000*	*80,000*
Net income, Year 2	*56,000*	*30,000*	*50,000*
Dividends, Year 2	*(25,000)*	*(20,000)*	*(30,000)*
Total liabilities & owners' equity	*$640,000*	*$370,000*	*$510,000*

Income Statements
Year 2

	P Company	*R Company*	*Q Company*
Sales revenues	*$350,000*	*$260,000*	*$370,000*
Dividend revenues	*34,000*	*9,000*	*-0-*
Total revenues	*$384,000*	*$269,000*	*$370,000*
Cost of goods sold	*$210,000*	*$160,000*	*$240,000*
Operating expenses	*80,000*	*57,000*	*35,000*
Income taxes	*38,000*	*22,000*	*45,000*
Total expenses	*$328,000*	*$239,000*	*$320,000*
Net income	*$ 56,000*	*$ 30,000*	*$ 50,000*

Additional information:

P Company acquired its 80% interest in R Company for $180,000 at the beginning of Year 1, when R's retained earnings balance was $20,000.

R Company acquired its 30% interest in Q Company for $102,000 at the beginning of Year 1, when Q's retained earnings balance was $30,000.

P Company acquired its 60% interest in Q Company for $252,000 at the beginning of Year 2. As indicated on the financial statements shown above, Q's retained earnings balance at this time was $80,000.

During Year 2, Q Company sold goods for $80,000 to P Company. At the end of Year 2, P Company had on hand some of the stock purchased from Q and it is estimated that $8,000 of intercompany profit applies to the intercompany pur-

P, R, AND Q COMPANIES
Consolidating Working Papers—Income Statement
end of Year 2

	P Company	R Company	Q Company	Adjustments and eliminations Dr	Adjustments and eliminations Cr	Consolidated income statement
Sales revenues	350,000	260,000	370,000	(b) 80,000		900,000
Dividend revenues	34,000	9,000		(a) 43,000		
Totals	384,000	269,000	370,000			900,000
Cost of goods sold	210,000	160,000	240,000	(c) 8,000	(b) 80,000	538,000
Operating expenses	80,000	57,000	35,000			172,000
Income taxes	38,000	22,000	45,000			105,000
Net income—P	56,000			(d) 25,200	(a) 34,000	
				(e) 26,880		74,080
Net income—R		30,000		(d) 12,600	(a) 9,000	
					(e) 33,600	
Net income—Q			50,000		(c) 8,000	
					(d) 42,000	
Minority interest—R				(e) 6,720		6,720
Minority interest—Q				(d) 4,200		4,200
Totals	384,000	269,000	370,000			900,000

(a) To eliminate intercompany dividends.
(b) To eliminate intercompany sales of $80,000 between Q and P Companies.
(c) To eliminate $8,000 intercompany profit in P's ending inventory, on sales from Q to P Company.
(d) To allocate Q's adjusted net income among P (60%), R (30%), and minority interest (10%).
(e) To allocate R's adjusted net income between P (80%) and minority interest (20%).

chases in P's ending inventory. There were no other intercompany transactions other than dividends, which had all been paid prior to the end of Year 2.

Working papers to consolidate the income statement of P, Q, and R Companies appear above. Consolidating working papers for the balance sheet are illustrated on page 432, together with explanatory notes on page 433. The illustrative working papers and supporting notes are for the most part self-explanatory. Some additional comments on the process of consolidating the income statement and balance sheet are in order.

Comments on income statement working papers: The first step in consolidating the income statements of the three companies is to deal with intercompany transactions and profits. Entries (a) and (b) eliminate the duplication resulting from intercompany dividend and sales transactions. Entry (c) eliminates the intercompany profit recorded by Q on goods held in P's ending inventory. Because Q Company's stock is held by both P and R Companies, the allocation of income should begin with Q Company, since any adjustment of Q's income will affect the income of P and R Companies. Q's adjusted income of $42,000 (after removal of the intercompany profit) is allocated 60% to P, 30% to R, and 10% to minority interest. R's net income of $33,600, adjusted for its share of Q's income, may then be allocated between P's controlling interest and the minority interest.

P, R, AND Q COMPANIES
Consolidating Working Papers—Balance Sheet
end of Year 2

	P Company	*R Company*	*Q Company*	*Adjustments and eliminations*		*Consolidated balance sheet*
				Dr	*Cr*	
Investment in R—80%	*180,000*			*(d) 36,000*	*(f) 216,000*	
Investment in Q—60%	*252,000*				*(b) 24,000*	
					(e) 228,000	
Investment in Q—30%		*102,000*		*(c) 15,000*	*(b) 3,000*	
					(e) 114,000	
Other assets	*208,000*	*268,000*	*480,000*		*(g) 8,000*	*948,000*
Goodwill				*(a) 5,000*		*5,000*
Excess of cost over book value				*(b) 27,000*		*27,000*
Totals	*640,000*	*370,000*	*480,000*			*980,000*
Liabilities	*119,000*	*110,000*	*80,000*			*309,000*
Capital stock—P	*400,000*					*400,000*
Beginning retained earnings—P	*90,000*				*(d) 36,000*	*126,000*
Net income—P	*56,000*			*(i) 18,000*	*(h) 25,200*	
				(k) 16,000	*(j) 26,880*	*74,080*
Dividends—P	*(25,000)*					*(25,000)*
Capital stock—R		*200,000*		*(f) 200,000*		
Appraisal capital—R				*(f) 5,000*	*(a) 5,000*	
Beginning retained earnings—R		*50,000*		*(f) 65,000*	*(c) 15,000*	
Net income—R		*30,000*		*(i) 9,000*		
				(j) 33,600	*(h) 12,600*	
Dividends—R		*(20,000)*			*(k) 20,000*	
Capital stock—Q			*300,000*	*(e) 300,000*		
Beginning retained earnings—Q			*80,000*	*(e) 80,000*		
Net income—Q			*50,000*	*(g) 8,000*		
				(h) 42,000		
Dividends—Q			*(30,000)*		*(i) 30,000*	
Minority interest—R				*(k) 4,000*	*(f) 54,000*	
					(j) 6,720	*56,720*
Minority interest—Q				*(i) 3,000*	*(e) 38,000*	
					(h) 4,200	*39,200*
Totals	*640,000*	*370,000*	*480,000*			*980,000*

Comments on the balance sheet working papers: The first step in consolidating balance sheet data is to account for the difference between the cost and book value of the investments. In this example we have assumed that the price paid by P for its 80% interest in R will become the basis for revaluing R's assets through the addition of $5,000 of goodwill. Since P's and R's investment in Q were at different dates, it is difficult to make a consistent interpretation about the valuation of Q's

(a) To record goodwill of R Company implied by price held by P Company for its 80% interest:

Price paid by P for 80% interest in R at beginning of Year 1	*$180,000*
Book value of R at beginning of Year 1 ($220,000)	
80% of book value at beginning of Year 1	*176,000*
Excess of cost of 80% interest over book value	*$ 4,000*
Implied unrecorded goodwill ($4,000 ÷ .80)	*$ 5,000*

(b) To record excess of cost over book value of investment in Q:

	Book value of Q	*Book value of investment*	*Cost*	*Difference*
Beginning of Year 1—R buys 30% interest	*$330,000*	*$ 99,000*	*$102,000*	*$ 3,000*
End of Year 1—P buys 60% interest	*380,000*	*228,000*	*252,000*	*24,000*
Total excess of cost over book value at date of acquisition				*$27,000*

(c) To record R's share of Q's growth from date of acquisition to beginning of Year 2:

Retained earnings of Q, beginning of Year 2	*$80,000*
Retained earnings at date R acquired 30% (beginning of Year 1)	*30,000*
Growth in Q since acquisition	*$50,000*
30% of Q's growth from date of acquisition to beginning of Year 2 (30% of $50,000)	*$15,000*

(d) To record P's share of growth in R from date of acquisition to beginning of Year 2:

R's retained earnings at beginning of Year 2	*$50,000*
R's share of Q's growth, entry (c)	*15,000*
	$65,000
R's retained earnings at beginning of Year 1 when P acquired 80% interest	*20,000*
Growth in R since date of acquisition	*$45,000*
80% of growth in R applicable to P's investment	*$36,000*

(e) To eliminate P and R Companies' investment in Q against Q's ownership equity accounts as of the beginning of Year 2, and to establish minority interest (10%) as of this date.
(f) To eliminate P's investment in R against R's adjusted ownership equity accounts as of the beginning of Year 2, and to establish minority interest (20%) as of this date.
(g) To eliminate $8,000 intercompany profit in P's ending inventory, on sales from Q to P.
(h) To allocate Q's adjusted income ($42,000) among P (60%), R (30%), and minority interest (10%).
(i) To eliminate Q's dividends against income of P and R, and against minority interest.
(j) To allocate R's adjusted net income ($33,600) between P Company (80%) and the minority interest (20%).
(k) To allocate R's dividends of $20,000 between P Company (80%) and the minority interest (20%).

net assets. Therefore the $24,000 excess of P's cost over book value and the $3,000 excess of Q's cost over book value are reclassified in entry (b) as an intangible asset of the consolidated entity.

The next step is to adjust the investment and retained earnings accounts of P and R Companies to an equity basis as of the beginning of Year 2. Again it is advisable to start with Q Company, the subsidiary held by both P and R, since any adjustment of R's retained earnings will affect the amount of R's growth since P's acquisition of R's stock. Entries (c) and (d) bring the investment accounts of P and R to an equity basis as of the beginning of Year 2, and it is then possible to eliminate all investments against the ownership equity accounts of the respective affiliates and establish the amount of the 20% minority interest in R and the 10% minority interest in Q, entries (e) and (f). The remainder of the consolidating entries, (g) through (k), carry forward income adjustments and allocations from the income statement working papers.

A statement of consolidated retained earnings and the changes in minority interest during Year 2, prepared from information in the working papers, is shown below:

P, R, AND Q COMPANIES
Statement of Consolidated Retained Earnings and Changes in Minority Interest
Year 2

	Consolidated retained earnings	Minority interest in	
		R Company 20%	Q Company 10%
Balance at beginning of Year 2	$126,000	$54,000	$38,000
Net income	74,080	6,720	4,200
Dividends	(25,000)	(4,000)	(3,000)
Balance at end of Year 2	$175,080	$56,720	$39,200

Mutual holdings

Mutual (or reciprocal) shareholdings exist whenever two companies own voting shares of each other. The consolidating problems introduced by this type of affiliated relationship may be discussed in terms of four characteristic cases:

Case 1—No outside interests

The following condensed balance sheet data will be used as a basis for the discussion of this case:

P AND S COMPANIES
Condensed Balance Sheet Data
end of Year 1

	P Company	S Company
Net assets:		
Investment in S Company (100%) at cost . . .	$130,000	
Investment in P Company (20%) at cost		$ 90,000
Other net assets (details omitted)	270,000	60,000
Total net assets	$400,000	$150,000
Owners' equity:		
Capital stock, $100 par value	$300,000	$100,000
Retained earnings, end of Year 1	100,000	50,000
Total owners' equity	$400,000	$150,000

The relationship of these two companies may be diagrammed as follows:

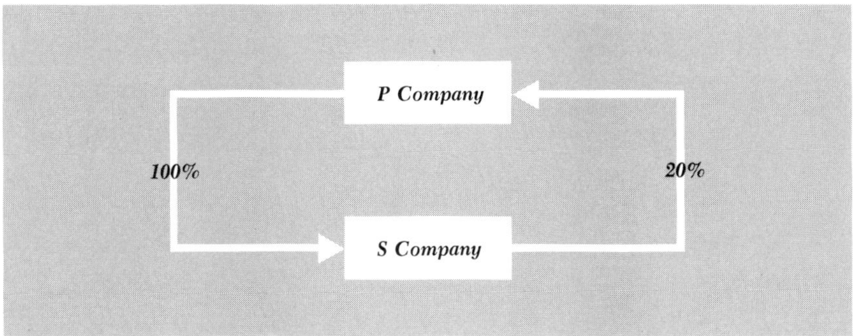

The important feature of this case is that no outside minority interest in S Company exists. The entire consolidated net assets belong to the controlling interest. It is immaterial whether P Company acquired shares in S Company when S already held P Company shares, or whether S Company purchased 20% of P's outstanding shares after P acquired all of S Company's stock. The shares of P Company held within the affiliation are in essence treasury shares. If we assume that P acquired 100% of S's stock when the net assets of S Company were $130,000, the consolidated balance sheet may be prepared directly as follows:

P AND S COMPANIES
Condensed Consolidated Balance Sheet
end of Year 1

Net assets (details omitted)	$330,000
Capital stock, 3,000 shares issued	$300,000
Retained earnings*	120,000
Less: Treasury stock, 600 shares held by S, at cost	(90,000)
Total owners' equity	$330,000

* P's retained earnings plus $20,000 of S's earnings accumulated since acquisition.

It is clear that, from a consolidated viewpoint, only 2,400 of P's shares are outstanding, and the entire consolidated ownership equity is assignable to the controlling interest. Furthermore, any earnings of both companies belong to the controlling interest.

No complication is added if we assume that P acquired its interest in S at more or less than book value. The revaluation of S Company's net assets on the basis of the price paid by P would simply increase or decrease the consolidated net assets by the difference between cost and book value, since P owns 100% of S Company's net assets.

Case 2—Connecting affiliates; no outside interest

The second case involves three companies whose condensed statements are shown at the top of page 436:

P, S, AND T COMPANIES
Condensed Balance Sheet Data
end of Year 1

	P Company	S Company	T Company
Net assets:			
Investment in S, 80% (at cost)*	$160,000		
Investment in S, 20% (at cost)*			$ 40,000
Investment in T, 70% (at cost)†	77,000		
Investment in T, 30% (at cost)†		$ 33,000	
Other net assets	153,000	227,000	90,000
Total net assets	$390,000	$260,000	$130,000
Owners' equity:			
Capital stock, $100 par	$300,000	$200,000	$100,000
Retained earnings	90,000	60,000	30,000
Total owners' equity	$390,000	$260,000	$130,000

*At date S Company was formed.
†At date of investment, T Company's retained earnings balance was $10,000.

The relation among the companies in this affiliation may be diagrammed as follows:

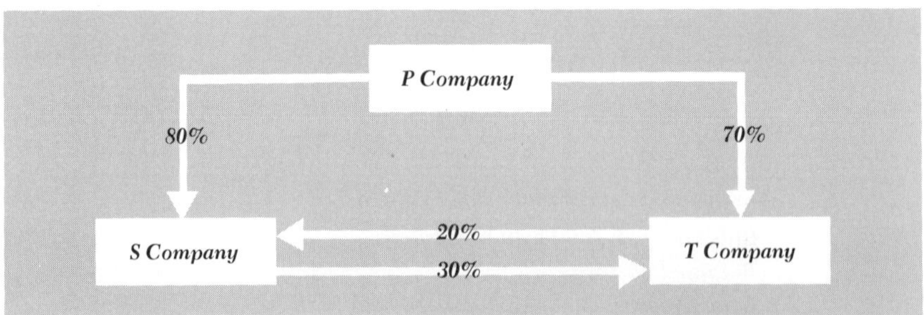

Examination of this situation reveals that it has one important common characteristic with Case 1; namely, that all the stock of S and T Companies is held within the affiliated entity. No outside interest in S and T exists. P Company has simply used T and S Companies as intermediaries to acquire a 100% interest in the net assets of both subsidiary companies. If we assume that all investments were made at book value, a consolidated balance sheet may be prepared directly from the data as follows:

COMPANIES P, S, AND T
Consolidated Balance Sheet
as of the end of Year 2

Net assets (details omitted)	$470,000
Capital stock, 3,000 shares issued and outstanding	$300,000
Retained earnings*	170,000
Total owners' equity	$470,000

*Retained earnings of P, $90,000, plus $60,000 increase in S since acquisition and $20,000 increase in T since acquisition.

The treasury stock issue does not arise in Case 2 because no shares of the parent company are held by either S or T Companies. Also, it is not necessary to allocate changes in the retained earnings of the various companies after acquisition dates, since the controlling interest owns all increases in the net assets of the companies in the affiliated group.

Case 3—Parent and subsidiary with outside interests

The third case involves a parent company and a less than 100% owned subsidiary, whose statements are shown below:

P AND S COMPANIES
Condensed Balance Sheet Data
end of Year 1

	P Company	*S Company*
*Investment in S Company, 80% (at cost)**	*$116,000*	
Investment in P Company, 20% (at cost)†		*$ 72,000*
Other net assets	*204,000*	*88,000*
Total net assets	*$320,000*	*$160,000*
Capital stock ($100 par value)	*$200,000*	*$100,000*
Retained earnings	*120,000*	*60,000*
Total owners' equity	*$320,000*	*$160,000*

** P's interest was acquired several years ago when S's retained earnings were $20,000.*
† S acquired P's stock just prior to preparation of the above statement.

The affiliated relation in this case may be diagrammed as follows:

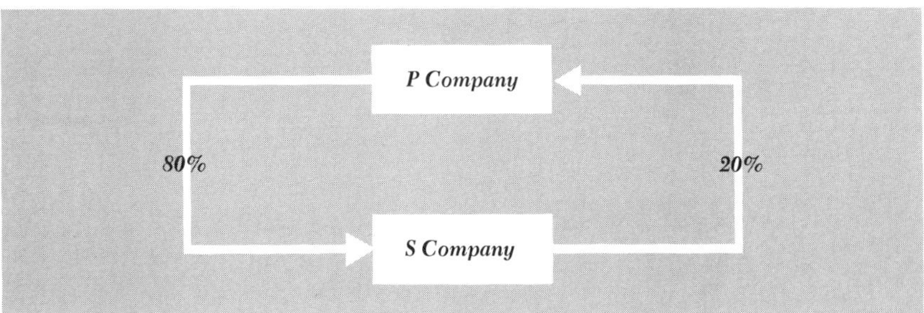

A new feature introduced in this case is the existence of an outside interest in a subsidiary company which owns a reciprocal interest in the parent. What is the status of the share of P held by S Company in this case? There are two possible interpretations. One is that since P controls S Company, the shares of P held by S have a status equivalent to treasury shares. The other is that the minority stockholders of S have a legitimate interest in the net assets and future earnings of P and this interest should be reflected in consolidated statements.

Treasury stock assumption (Case 3). If we regard the shares of P Company held by S Company as treasury shares, held temporarily within the consolidated entity until they are transferred to P or resold to outsiders, the consolidation process is similar to that discussed in Case 1. The net assets of the two companies are combined, and no allocation of P's retained earnings is made to S Company. The treasury shares are valued at cost and treated as a reduction of the consolidated owners' equity. The consolidated balance sheet of P and S Companies at the end of Year 1 would appear as follows based on the working papers immediately following the statement.

P AND S COMPANIES
Condensed Consolidated Balance Sheet
end of Year 1

Other net assets (details omitted)		*$292,000*
Excess of cost of investment in subsidiary over book value		*20,000*
Total net assets		*$312,000*
Minority interest in subsidiary		*$ 32,000*
Capital stock, $100 par, 2,000 shares issued	*$200,000*	
Retained earnings	*152,000*	
	$352,000	
Less: Treasury shares, 400 shares held by S Company, at cost	*72,000*	*280,000*
Total owners' equity		*$312,000*

Case 3: Treasury stock assumption

P AND S COMPANIES
Consolidating Working Papers
end of Year 1

	P Company	*S Company*	*Adjustments and eliminations*		*Consolidated balance sheet*
			Dr	*Cr*	
Investment in S—80%	*116,000*		*(a) 32,000*	*(b) 20,000* *(c) 128,000*	
Investment in P—20%		*72,000*			*72,000*
Other net assets	*204,000*	*88,000*			*292,000*
Excess of cost over book value			*(b) 20,000*		*20,000*
Total	*320,000*	*160,000*			*384,000*
Capital stock—P	*200,000*				*200,000*
Retained earnings—P	*120,000*			*(a) 32,000*	*152,000*
Capital stock—S		*100,000*	*(c) 100,000*		
Retained earnings—S		*60,000*	*(c) 60,000*		
Minority interest—S				*(c) 32,000*	*32,000*
Total	*320,000*	*160,000*			*384,000*

(a) To record P's share of growth in S ($60,000 – $20,000 = $40,000; 80% of $40,000 = $32,000) since date of acquisition.

(b) To establish excess of cost of investment in S over book value. Book value of S at date of acquisition = $120,000; 80% = $96,000. P paid $116,000; therefore, excess is $20,000 ($116,000 – $96,000).

(c) To eliminate investment of P Company against ownership equity accounts of S and to establish 20% minority interest.

There is considerable support for the treasury stock assumption. The Committee on Concepts and Standards of the American Accounting Association has stated, "Shares of the controlling company's capital stock owned by a subsidiary before the date of acquisition of control should be treated in consolidation as treasury stock. Any subsequent acquisition or sale by a subsidiary should likewise be treated in the consolidated statements as though it had been the act of the controlling company."[2] The AICPA's Committee on Accounting Procedures takes a less explicit stand but, in referring to mutual holdings, states, "Shares of the parent held by a subsidiary should not be treated as outstanding stock in the consolidated balance sheet."[3]

Consistent application of the treasury stock interpretation requires that the retained earnings of the parent company be allocated entirely to the controlling interest; the minority interest of the subsidiary is not credited with any portion of the parent's retained earnings. If the parent company declares dividends, there will be a transfer of assets from the parent to the subsidiary, which will be treated as dividend revenue on the subsidiary's books. The minority interest will, of course, share in this direct return on investment. Furthermore, if we assume that the subsidiary purchased P's shares as an agent of the parent company, equity demands that ultimately the subsidiary be reimbursed for its outlays on behalf of the parent. If the subsidiary, instead, resells the stock to outsiders, the problem disappears. So long as the subsidiary retains the shares of P, however, their treatment as treasury stock on consolidated statements precludes any allocation of retained earnings to this reciprocal stock interest.

Conventional assumption (Case 3). It is possible to prepare consolidated financial statements for P and S Companies by treating the reciprocal holdings in the conventional manner. To illustrate this process, let us look one year beyond Year 1 and assume that in Year 2 P Company earned $40,000 and S Company earned $20,000. The working papers to consolidate the balance sheets of the two companies on the assumption that S's interest in P is to be regarded as an independent equity interest are shown on page 440.

These tentative, all-inclusive earnings figures for P Company ($66,667) and S Company ($33,333) include each company's share of the other's earnings, and the duplication may now be eliminated as follows:

	P Company	*S Company*
Tentative all-inclusive earnings	*$ 66,667*	*$ 33,333*
Eliminate 20% of P held by S	*(13,334)*	
Eliminate 80% of S held by P		*(26,666)*
Share of consolidated earnings applicable to the controlling and minority interest	*$ 53,333*	*$ 6,667*
Reported earnings of P Company alone	*40,000*	
P's share of S Company's earnings	*$ 13,333*	

[2] The American Accounting Association, *Accounting and Reporting Standards for Corporate Financial Statements,* "Consolidated Financial Statements" (Madison: 1954), p. 44.
[3] AICPA, *Accounting Research and Terminology Bulletins, Final Edition,* Bulletin No. 51, "Consolidated Financial Statements" (New York: 1961), p. 45.

Case 3: Conventional method

P AND S COMPANIES
Consolidating Working Papers
end of Year 2

	P Company	S Company	Adjustments and eliminations Dr	Cr	Consolidated balance sheet
Investment in S—80%	116,000		(a) 32,000	(b) 20,000 (c) 128,000	
Investment in P—20%		72,000		(d) 1,600 (e) 70,400	
Other net assets	244,000	108,000			352,000
Excess of cost over book value			(b) 20,000 (d) 1,600		21,600
Totals	360,000	180,000			373,600
Capital stock—P	200,000		(e) 40,000		160,000
Beginning retained earnings—P	120,000		(e) 30,400	(a) 32,000	121,600
Net income—P	40,000			(f) 13,333	53,333
Capital stock—S		100,000	(c) 100,000		
Beginning retained earnings—S		60,000	(c) 60,000		
Net income—S		20,000	(f) 20,000		
Minority interest—S				(c) 32,000 (f) 6,667	38,667
Totals	360,000	180,000			373,600

(a) To record P's share of S's earnings from date of acquisition to beginning of Year 2 (80% of \$40,000 = \$32,000).
(b) To establish excess of cost of P's investment in S over book value.
(c) To eliminate P's investment against S Company's ownership equity accounts as of the beginning of Year 2.
(d) To establish excess of the cost of S's investment in P over book value:

Book value of P at end of Year 1	\$320,000
Add: P's share of S's growth since acquisition	32,000
Book value of P at time S acquired 20% interest	\$352,000
20% of book value	\$ 70,400
Cost of investment	72,000
Excess of cost over book value	\$ 1,600

(e) To eliminate S's investment in P against P's ownership equity accounts as of the beginning of Year 2.
(f) To allocate consolidated net income for Year 2. (See explanation on page 441.)

In allocating the earnings of two companies having reciprocal holdings, we must consider a circularity problem. P earned \$40,000, of which S owns 20%. But P owns 80% of S's earnings plus S's share of P's earnings. We are involved in a familiar interdependency of data, which can be most easily resolved through the solution of simultaneous equations as follows:

Let P = the consolidated earnings belonging to P Company, and
S = the consolidated earnings belonging to S Company.
Then $P = \$40{,}000 + .80S$ and $S = \$20{,}000 + .20P$

Substituting the second equation in the first, we get

$$P = \$40{,}000 + .80\ (\$20{,}000 + .20P)$$
$$P = \$40{,}000 + \$16{,}000 + .16P$$
$$.84P = \$56{,}000 \qquad P = \underline{\$66{,}667}$$

Then
$$S = \$20{,}000 + .20\ (\$66{,}667)$$
$$S = \$20{,}000 + \$13{,}333 = \underline{\$33{,}333}$$

This analysis provides the data for entry (f) on the working papers on page 440, allocating S Company's $20,000 net income between the controlling interest ($13,333) and the minority interest ($6,667).

The conventional solution in the example just presented focuses attention on two important points relating to the mutual holding situation:

1. The major new accounting problem in mutual holding situations is the allocation of ownership equity between the controlling and minority interests. The valuation of net assets and the total earnings of the consolidated group are not affected in any particular way by the existence of mutual holdings. The problem of interpreting differences between the cost and book value of investments was resolved in this case by considering the excess in each instance as a consolidated intangible asset. Alternatively, we might have used the price paid by each company for the share of the other as a basis for revaluing the assets of the respective companies without affecting the problem of allocating changes in owners' equity subsequent to the existence of the reciprocal relationship.

2. Under the conventional solution, the use of simultaneous equations to solve the allocation of retained earnings since acquisition results in a series of tentative earnings figures that are not additive. The sum is meaningless since each figure contains a portion of the other. Only when the reciprocal interests have been eliminated from these tentative figures do we have useful information. We can always verify the results by proving that the final allocation adds to the total retained earnings change to be allocated. In the above example, the total Year 2 net income of the two companies was $60,000 ($40,000 for P and $20,000 for S), which was allocated $53,333 to the controlling interest and $6,667 to the minority interest.

Case 4—Connecting affiliates with outside interests

The final case involves the existence of outside interests in connecting affiliates which have mutual stockholdings. An example of this situation is diagrammed below:

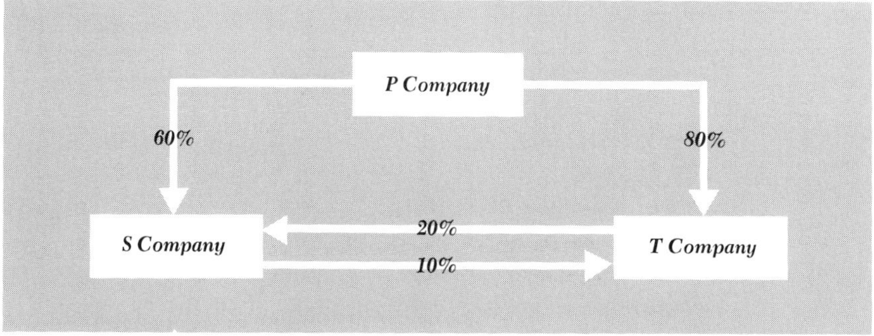

Note in this situation that an outside interest exists in both the subsidiaries and it is necessary to allocate changes in ownership equity to each subsidiary and then in turn between the controlling and minority interests in S and T Companies. As in all other consolidations, any difference between the prices paid for investments in affiliated companies and the book value of the underlying net assets at the date of acquisition must be determined and accounted for. As in any case of reciprocal holdings, the accountant should be cautious in interpreting prices paid by subsidiaries for stock of other subsidiaries *after* control has been established since there is always a question whether these prices are legitimate market values.

The working papers to consolidate the balance sheets of P, S, and T Companies appear on page 443. To simplify the illustration and concentrate on the features peculiar to this case, we shall assume that all investments were made at book value at the date the subsidiary companies were formed. We are thus faced with the problem of allocating the total retained earnings of all three companies, since all retained earnings balances have accumulated since acquisition.

We can resolve the circularity between S and T Companies and make the appropriate allocation through the use of simultaneous equations as follows:

Let P = the retained earnings share of the controlling interest,
S = the retained earnings share of S Company,
T = the retained earnings share of T Company.

Then

$$P = \$127{,}000 + .60S + .80T$$
$$T = \$86{,}800 + .20S$$
$$S = \$56{,}000 + .10T$$

Since P is not involved in the circularity, we need only solve the equations for S and T as follows:

$$T = \$86{,}800 + .20\ (\$56{,}000 + .10T)$$
$$T = \$86{,}800 + \$11{,}200 + .02T$$
$$.98T = \$98{,}000 \qquad T = \underline{\$100{,}000}$$
$$S = \$56{,}000 + .10\ (100{,}000) = \underline{\$66{,}000}$$
$$P = \$127{,}000 + .60\ (\$66{,}000) + .80\ (\$100{,}000)$$
$$P = \$127{,}000 + \$39{,}600 + \$80{,}000 = \underline{\$246{,}600}$$

The allocation of the $246,600 total accumulation of retained earnings in all three affiliates may be determined as follows:

	P Company	*S Company*	*T Company*
Tentative all-inclusive changes	*$246,600*	*$ 66,000*	*$100,000*
Eliminate:			
60% of S held by P.		*(39,600)*	
20% of S held by T.		*(13,200)*	
80% of T held by P.			*(80,000)*
10% of T held by S.			*(10,000)*
Change in retained earnings allocated to controlling and minority interests.	*$246,600*	*$ 13,200*	*$ 10,000*

These data become the basis for entry (a) in the working papers on page 443, in which the retained earnings balances in all three affiliates are debited, and the allocation, as shown above, is made between the controlling interest (P Company) and the minority interests in S and T Companies. The balance of the consolidating entries in the working papers are self-explanatory.

P, S, AND T COMPANIES
Consolidated Working Papers
end of current year

	P Company	*S Company*	*T Company*	*Adjustments and eliminations Dr*	*Adjustments and eliminations Cr*	*Consolidated balance sheet*
Investment in S—60%	*120,000*				*(b) 120,000*	
Investment in S—20%			*40,000*		*(b) 40,000*	
Investment in T—80%	*104,000*				*(c) 104,000*	
Investment in T—10%		*13,000*			*(c) 13,000*	
Other net assets	*203,000*	*243,000*	*176,800*			*622,800*
Totals	*427,000*	*256,000*	*216,800*			*622,800*
Capital stock—P	*300,000*					*300,000*
Retained earnings—P	*127,000*			*(a) 127,000*	*(a) 246,600*	*246,600*
Capital stock—S		*200,000*		*(b) 200,000*		
Retained earnings—S		*56,000*		*(a) 56,000*		
Capital stock—T			*130,000*	*(c) 130,000*		
Retained earnings—T			*86,800*	*(a) 86,800*		
Minority interest—S					*(a) 13,200*	
					(b) 40,000	*53,200*
Minority interest—T					*(a) 10,000*	
					(c) 13,000	*23,000*
Totals	*427,000*	*256,000*	*216,800*			*622,800*

(a) *To allocate total change in retained earnings since date of acquisition among controlling and minority interests (see schedule on page 442).*
(b) *To eliminate investments in S and establish 20% minority interest at date of acquisition.*
(c) *To eliminate investments in T and establish 10% minority interest at date of acquisition.*

Observe that the treasury stock issue does not arise in this case, since the subsidiaries do not own any portion of the parent company. Note also that the computation of P's share of the accumulated retained earnings of the affiliation is not tentative since the reciprocal relation does not extend to the parent.

If we had posed a case where there were changes in retained earnings and also net income for the current year, two sets of simultaneous equations would be necessary, one to resolve the circularity and obtain a beginning consolidated retained earnings figure, the other to resolve the circularity with respect to net income and provide the amount of consolidated net income for the period. The presence of dividends does not complicate the situation, since intercompany dividends may be eliminated from the income of the respective companies prior to any allocation of earnings. From a consolidated viewpoint, the allocation among affiliates is not affected by the amount of dividends distributed.

Other cases

The four typical cases we have discussed do not exhaust the possible mutual relationships among affiliated companies. However, they are sufficient to demonstrate the principles involved in dealing with reciprocal relationships in the consolidating process. Numerous additional situations which might be posed will be found to be simply extensions, combinations, or variations of the four cases discussed in this chapter, and the accountant may apply similar procedures in preparing consolidated financial statements.

Questions

1. P Company owns a 75% interest in Q Company, which in turn owns a 60% interest in SQ Company. If SQ Company earns net income of $50,000 during the current year, explain how this income will be allocated between the controlling and minority interests on consolidated statements.

2. Indirect shareholdings may exist in a parent-son-grandson framework or in a connecting-affiliate framework. Distinguish these two cases.

3. The interpretation of any difference between the price paid for the controlling interest and the underlying book value of the shares at date of acquisition will differ in the parent-son-grandson case depending on the timing of the acquisitions. A special problem of interpretation, not discussed prior to this chapter, arises when a holding company becomes a subsidiary. Explain.

4. P Company owns 80% of S Company, acquired at date of organization, and accounts for its investment on an equity (accrual) basis. At a time when the book value of P Company's assets is $400,000 and the book value of S Company's net assets is $200,000, J Company acquires a 70% interest in P Company at a price which is $56,000 in excess of book value. If J paid a price in excess of the book value of P's shares because the net assets of S Company were believed to be undervalued, determine the current fair value of S Company's net assets as reflected in the price paid by J for the shares of P.

5. P Company acquired a 74% interest in S Company at the beginning of Year 1. At the end of Year 1, S Company acquired an 85% interest in SC Company. Both P and S Companies account for their investment on a cost basis. During Year 2 the three affiliated companies earned the following net incomes: P, $40,000; S, $30,000; SC, $20,000. Assuming none of the companies declared dividends during the year and there are no consolidating adjustments affecting net income, compute the consolidated net income (controlling interest) for Year 2.

6. L Company owns an 80% interest in M Company, which in turn owns 70% of the outstanding shares of N Company. Both L and M Companies account for their investments on an equity basis, and all accruals have been made as of the end of the current year. Net incomes reported by the three companies for the current year are as follows: L, $58,000; M, $25,000; N, $22,000. Assuming no consolidating adjustments affecting net income, what is the consolidated net income (controlling interest) for the current year?

7. Distinguish the case in which affiliated companies own mutual (or reciprocal) shareholdings, from the case in which there is a connecting affiliate. Prepare a diagram illustrating each situation.

8. When there are mutual shareholdings between a parent and a subsidiary, one interpretation which may be used in preparing consolidated statements is that the shares of the parent held by the subsidiary are in essence treasury shares. Explain the reasoning which supports this interpretation.

9. B Company owns 70% of C Company, which in turn owns 15% of the outstanding shares of B Company. Using simultaneous equations, the controller of B Company has computed the following tentative all-inclusive earnings for the two companies for the current year: B Company, $75,000; C Company, $35,250. B Company, which accounts for its investment in C on a cost basis, reported net income of $50,325 for the year. No dividends were declared by either company during the year. On the basis of this information, determine the following:

a. Consolidated net income (controlling interest) for the year (assuming that a share of B's earnings is allocated to C Company)

b. The minority interest in C's earnings for the current year

c. C Company's reported net income for the year

10. D Company owns a controlling interest in both E and F Companies. E Company owns 18% of the outstanding shares of F Company, and F Company owns 12% of the outstanding shares of E Company. Explain why, in this situation, it is not appropriate to consider the shares of F owned by E, and the shares of E owned by F, as treasury stock of the respective issuing companies.

Short cases for analysis

13-1 X Company owns 90% of Y Company, which in turn owns 80% of Z Company. At the close of the current year, the board of directors of X Company was asked to authorize the purchase of 50% of Z Company's stock from Y Company. In discussing this proposed action, one director commented: "I don't see that this purchase will change anything. There will still be a 10% minority interest in Y Company and a 20% minority interest in Z Company. The interests within the affiliated companies will be the same and I suspect the allocation of the income of the various companies between the controlling and minority interests will remain unchanged. Suppose, for example, that each company earns $100,000 next year. Will this purchase we are considering have any effect on the allocation of the $300,000 of combined incomes?"

Instructions

Write an answer to the director's question. Explain why his statement is or is not correct, and then demonstrate the validity of your position by comparing the allocation of the assumed combined net income of $300,000 among the controlling and minority interests under the two different stock ownership situations.

13-2 The condensed balance sheets of Purvis Company and its 51% owned subsidiary Starr Company as of the close of the current year are given on page 446.

PURVIS COMPANY AND SUBSIDIARY
Balance Sheets
end of current year

	Purvis Company	*Starr Company*
Investment in Starr—2,550 shares	*$210,000*	
Investment in Purvis—5,000 shares		*$300,000*
Other assets	*690,000*	*180,000*
Total assets	*$900,000*	*$480,000*
Liabilities	*$180,000*	*$ 85,000*
Capital stock—$50 par value	*550,000*	*250,000*
Retained earnings	*170,000*	*145,000*
Total liabilities & equity	*$900,000*	*$480,000*

At the end of the current year, a stockholder of Purvis Company has offered to sell 610 shares of Purvis Company's common stock for $25,000. The president of Purvis Company, who does not own any shares of either company, has recommended to the Purvis Company board of directors that Starr Company be authorized to acquire these 610 shares. All members of the board of directors are officers of Purvis Company except one outside director, Collins, who is an attorney for a stockholder who owns 30% of the outstanding shares of Purvis Company. Collins objects strongly to the president's proposal, offering to buy the shares for his client, or alternatively asking that Purvis Company buy back the shares as treasury stock.

Instructions

Explain what, in your opinion, is the basis for Collins's objection, pointing out the disadvantage to his client and other outside stockholders of Purvis Company if the president's recommendation were to be accepted.

13-3 Cole Company acquired an 80% interest in Mann Company several years ago when Mann Company had $100,000 of capital stock outstanding and retained earnings of $75,000. At the end of the current year the net assets of the Cole Company were as follows:

Current assets	*$182,000*
Plant and equipment (net of depreciation)	*600,000*
Investment in Mann Company (at cost)	*120,000*
Total assets	*$902,000*
Liabilities	*(192,000)*
Total net assets	*$710,000*

Ana Corporation purchased all the 10,000 outstanding shares of $50 par value common stock of Cole Company at the end of the current year. Cole's shares were selling in the market for $87 and Ana Corporation offered $90 per share, providing a 100% tender of shares was made. Immediately after the purchase was consummated, the controller of Ana Corporation was instructed to prepare a consolidated balance sheet for presentation to the board of directors.

In reviewing the negotiations, the controller had available an analysis given to the board which showed that in appraising Cole Company's position the plant and equipment had been valued at $700,000, and the Mann Company common stock at $210,000. These two revisions of Cole Company's book values explained the basis for the offering of $90 per share. At the end of the current year the Mann Company had retained earnings of $130,000 and stated capital of $100,000.

The controller is puzzled as to how to handle the difference between the cost of Ana's investment in Cole and the underlying book value in preparing consolidated statements. He is not concerned about the income tax implications of his decision, since the data appearing on consolidated statements are not used for tax purposes, and the tax basis of many of the assets of all three companies differs from their book values.

His assistant proposes that all differences between cost and book value in consolidation be treated as intangible assets on consolidated statements. The controller, however, believes that the purchase of 100% of Cole's shares provides sufficiently good evidence to warrant establishing a new accountability for undervalued assets on the books of both Cole and Mann Companies.

Instructions

a. Discuss the alternatives open to the controller in dealing with the excess of cost over book value for purposes of consolidated statements, and make a recommendation of the procedure you would follow.

b. Assuming your recommendation is accepted, present in journal form the adjusting and eliminating entries necessary to effect the consolidation of the three companies at the date of acquisition.

Problems

13-4 Bowman, Keith, and Munson Companies are affiliated firms, each having outstanding 1,000 shares of $100 par value capital stock. Bowman Company acquired a 60% interest in Keith Company, at the beginning of Year 1, for $162,000. Keith Company acquired a 70% interest in Munson Company, at the beginning of Year 2, for $90,000. Both Bowman and Keith Companies account for their investments on a cost basis. A schedule showing the changes in the retained earnings of the three companies appears below:

	Bowman Company	*Keith Company*	*Munson Company*
Retained earnings, Jan. 1, Year 1	$280,000	$150,000	$ 60,000
Net income (loss)—Year 1	60,000	40,000	(20,000)
Dividends—Year 1	(35,000)	(15,000)	-0-
Retained earnings, Jan. 1, Year 2	$305,000	$175,000	$ 40,000
Net income—Year 2	75,000	50,000	18,000
Dividends—Year 2	(40,000)	(20,000)	-0-
Retained earnings, Dec. 31, Year 2	$340,000	$205,000	$ 58,000

Instructions

a. Compute the difference between the cost and book value of Bowman's investment in Keith, and of Keith's investment in Munson, at the date of acquisition.

b. Determine the balance that would appear at the end of Year 2 in Bowman and Keith Companies' investment accounts if the accounting had been on an equity basis during Years 1 and 2.

c. Prepare a schedule showing the allocation of Year 2 consolidated net income among controlling and minority interests.

13-5 Condensed balance sheet information for three affiliated companies as of the end of Year 4 is given below:

	Pitt Company	*Sweet Company*	*Troy Company*
Investment in Sweet Company—80%	*$457,600*		
Investment in Troy Company—75%		*$150,000*	
Other assets	*268,400*	*330,000*	*$390,000*
Total assets	*$726,000*	*$480,000*	*$390,000*
Liabilities	*$ 50,000*	*$ 60,000*	*$ 70,000*
Capital stock	*500,000*	*300,000*	*200,000*
Retained earnings, beginning of Year 4	*143,000*	*100,000*	*96,000*
Net income—Year 4	*58,000*	*50,000*	*64,000*
Dividends—Year 4	*(25,000)*	*(30,000)*	*(40,000)*
Total liabilities & equity	*$726,000*	*$480,000*	*$390,000*

Sweet Company acquired its 75% interest in Troy Company common stock for $150,000 at the beginning of Year 1 when Troy Company was organized. Pitt Company acquired its 80% interest in Sweet Company at the beginning of Year 4, and carries its investment at cost. At the time Pitt Company acquired control of Sweet Company, it was agreed that the price paid by Pitt Company for its interest reflected Sweet Company's unrecorded goodwill. The board of directors of Pitt Company authorized that this goodwill be reflected in full on the consolidated statements as of the beginning of Year 4 and be amortized on a straight-line basis on consolidated statements over the next five years.

Instructions

a. Prepare working papers for a consolidated balance sheet for the three affiliated companies as of the end of Year 4.

b. Prepare a statement of consolidated retained earnings for Year 4, and a statement explaining the changes in minority interests during Year 4.

13-6 At the beginning of Year 1, Pert Company acquired 70% of the outstanding shares of Soll Company for $320,000 and 60% of the outstanding shares of Tass Company for $200,000.

One year later, at the beginning of Year 2, Soll Company purchased from outsiders a 10% interest in Tass Company for $35,000. At the same time Tass Company purchased from outsiders a 20% interest in Soll Company for $100,000.

At the end of Year 2, the three companies had outstanding capital stock having a stated value as follows: Pert Company, $500,000; Soll Company, $300,000; Tass Company, $200,000. An analysis of the retained earnings of the three companies for Years 1 and 2 appears below:

Statement of Changes in Retained Earnings

	Pert Company	*Soll Company*	*Tass Company*
Balance, beginning of Year 1	$250,000	$150,000	$100,000
Year 1 net income	50,000	30,000	20,000
Year 1 dividends paid	(25,000)	(10,000)	(10,000)
Balance, end of Year 1	$275,000	$170,000	$110,000
Year 2 net income	80,000	40,000	30,000
Year 2 dividends paid	(25,000)	(10,000)	(15,000)
Balance, end of Year 2	$330,000	$200,000	$125,000

Instructions

a. Assuming that any excess of investment cost over the book value of the underlying net assets will be treated as an intangible asset of the stock-owning company, compute the total amount of this intangible asset (consolidated goodwill) that should be reported on a consolidated balance sheet at the end of Year 2.

b. Prepare a statement of consolidated retained earnings for Year 2, and a statement of changes in minority interests in Soll and Tass Companies for Year 2. (*Note:* This will require an allocation of the Year 2 net income among the controlling and minority interests. Consider carefully the effect of intercompany dividends in making this allocation. Round all computations to the nearest dollar.)

13-7 Condensed balance sheet data for Jane, Kane, and Lane Companies as of the end of Year 4 is given below:

Assets	*Jane Company*	*Kane Company*	*Lane Company*
Current assets	$ 90,000	$ 83,000	$ 50,000
Investment in Kane—80%	200,000		
Investment in Lane—90%		117,000	
Other assets	110,000	200,000	150,000
Total assets	$400,000	$400,000	$200,000
Liabilities & Capital			
Current liabilities	$100,000	$160,000	$ 60,000
Reserve for contingencies		30,000	
Capital stock	220,000	100,000	50,000
Additional paid-in capital		60,000	
Beginning retained earnings	70,000	40,000	60,000
Net income	20,000	15,000	30,000
Dividends	(10,000)	(5,000)	
Total liabilities & capital	$400,000	$400,000	$200,000

Kane Company acquired its 90% interest in Lane Company on January 1, Year 2, at a cost of $117,000. During Years 2 and 3, Lane Company earned a total of $50,000 and paid dividends of $40,000.

Jane Company acquired its 80% interest in Kane Company on January 1, Year 1, and carries its investment at cost. An analysis of Kane Company's retained earnings since the date of acquisition is as follows:

Balance of retained earnings at beginning of Year 1		*$ 20,000*
Net income, Year 1, 2, and 3		*90,000*
		$110,000
Less: Dividends	*$40,000*	
Approporiation to reserve for contingencies	*30,000*	*70,000*
Balance of retained earnings at end of Year 3		*$ 40,000*

You may assume that any discrepancy between the cost of the investment in Kane and Lane Companies and the book value of that investment represents unrecorded goodwill on the books of the subsidiary, and that such goodwill is not to be amortized on consolidated statements.

Lane Company sells subassemblies to Kane Company. Included in the inventory of Kane Company at the beginning of Year 4 were parts on which Lane had recorded a profit of $8,000; in the inventories of Kane at the end of Year 4 were goods on which Lane had recorded a profit of $3,000.

Instructions

a. Prepare working papers for a consolidated balance sheet at the end of Year 4. Key all working paper entries and show supporting computations.

b. Prepare a statement of consolidated retained earnings for Year 4.

13-8 Condensed financial data for X Company and Y Company as of the end of Year 2 are presented below:

	X Company	*Y Company*
Investment in Y Company—80%	*$192,000*	
Investment in X Company—20%		*$ 75,000*
Other assets	*320,000*	*230,000*
Total assets	*$512,000*	*$305,000*
Liabilities	*$122,000*	*$ 45,000*
Capital stock	*300,000*	*200,000*
Retained earnings, beginning of Year 2	*70,000*	*52,000*
Net income, Year 2	*20,000*	*8,000*
Total liabilities & owners' equity	*$512,000*	*$305,000*

X Company acquired 80% of the outstanding shares of Y Company at the beginning of Year 1 at a cost of $192,000. Y Company reported retained earnings of $20,000 at date of acquisition.

Y Company acquired 20% of the outstanding shares of X Company at the beginning of Year 2 for $75,000.

In consolidated financial statements, the entire amount of Y Company's undervaluation of assets (as indicated by the price paid by X Company for its interest) is to be treated as goodwill not subject to amortization.

Instructions

a. Prepare working papers for a consolidated balance sheet as of the end of Year 2, assuming that the growth in the two companies (through retention of earnings) since date of acquisition is to be allocated between the controlling and minority interest.

b. Prepare a consolidated balance sheet (you need not prepare working papers unless you wish) as of the end of Year 2, treating the shares of X Company held by Y Company as treasury shares.

c. Explain the difference between the resulting consolidated balance sheets prepared under these two different assumptions.

13-9 Financial data for Companies L, M, and N as of the end of Year 4 are given below:

	L Company	*M Company*	*N Company*
Current assets	$ 75,400	$ 68,600	$135,000
Investment in M Company—80%	192,000		
Investment in N Company—60%		122,400	
Investment in N Company—15%	30,600		
Other assets	280,000	190,000	310,000
Total assets	$578,000	$381,000	$445,000
Liabilities	$153,000	$ 83,000	$ 93,000
Capital stock	350,000	200,000	300,000
Retained earnings, beginning of year	60,000	80,000	40,000
Net income, Year 4	45,000	36,000	24,000
Dividends	(30,000)	(18,000)	(12,000)
Total liabilities & equity	$578,000	$381,000	$445,000

L Company acquired an 80% interest in M Company in Year 1 when M Company's retained earnings balance was $13,000. L Company carries its investment at cost, and the price paid for M's stock reflects unrecorded goodwill of M Company at the time of acquisition. On consolidated statements, M Company's goodwill is being amortized in equal annual amounts over a five-year period beginning in Year 2.

L Company and M Company acquired their interest in N Company in a single transaction during Year 2 at a time when N Company had a deficit of $48,000. The price paid by L Company and M Company for the stock of N Company reflects an overvaluation of a nondepreciable asset on the books of N Company. (Assets should be revalued accordingly on consolidated statements.) L and M Companies carry their investment in N Company at cost. N Company's Year 4 dividend was declared near the end of the year and has not been paid as of December 31. Both L and M Companies have recorded their share of the dividend receivable.

During Year 4 N Company sold subassemblies to M Company for the first time since the companies became affiliated. Of total intercompany sales of $75,000 (which cost N Company $45,000), there were $55,000 of goods purchased from N Company in M Company's inventory at the end of year 4.

Instructions

a. Prepare working papers for L, M, and N Companies which provide the necessary data for a consolidated balance sheet at the end of Year 4 and a statement of consolidated retained earnings for Year 4.

b. Prepare a statement of consolidated retained earnings, and a schedule showing the change in minority interests during Year 4.

c. The combined reported net income of L, M, and N Companies is $105,000. The consolidated net income figure (controlling interest) in your solution should be $48,780. Explain briefly why consolidated net income is less than one-half the combined reported income of the affiliated companies. You need not reconcile the two figures in detail; simply explain the major factors that account for the difference.

13-10 Condensed balance sheets for three affiliated companies as of the end of Year 5 are shown below:

	Ande Company	*Bert Company*	*Craf Company*
Current assets	$232,750	$187,000	$196,000
Plant and equipment	486,250	242,000	315,000
Accumulated depreciation	(105,000)	(90,000)	(70,000)
Investment in Bert—70% at cost	296,800		
Investment in Craf—80% at cost		160,000	
Total assets	$910,800	$499,000	$441,000
Current liabilities	$ 74,360	$ 68,000	$ 72,000
Capital stock ($100 par)	425,000	300,000	200,000
Retained earnings, beginning of year	356,520	98,000	142,000
Net income, Year 5	97,420	63,000	47,000
Dividends paid, Year 5	(42,500)	(30,000)	(20,000)
Total liabilities & equity	$910,800	$499,000	$441,000

Ande Company purchased its 70% interest in Bert Company for $296,800 at the end of Year 3, at which time Bert Company reported retained earnings of $54,000 and Craf Company reported retained earnings of $30,000.

Bert Company acquired its 80% interest in Craf Company in Year 1, at the date Craf Company was organized, paying par value for the shares.

At the time Ande Company acquired a controlling interest in Bert Company, it was agreed that the excess of cost over book value represented the value to Ande Company of the intangible benefits of affiliation. The board of directors of Ande Company ordered that this intangible asset be amortized on consolidated financial statements on a straight-line basis during a 10-year period after date of acquisition. No amortization has been recorded on the books of Ande Company.

At the beginning of Year 4, Ande Company sold to Craf Company for $100,000 a depreciable asset which had a book value on Ande's books of $44,000. The asset is being depreciated on Craf's books on a straight-line basis over a period of eight years after date of purchase.

Craf Company sells merchandise to Bert Company. The intercompany markup on goods in the beginning inventory of Bert Company was $12,000; the markup on goods in the ending inventory of Bert Company was $35,000.

Instructions

a. Prepare working papers for the consolidated balance sheet of these three affiliated companies as of the end of Year 5.

b. Prepare a statement of consolidated retained earnings and changes in minority interests during Year 5.

13-11 The balance sheets at the end of Year 5, and income statements for the year for three affiliated companies, Wexel, Xrey, and Yarbo, are shown below:

Balance Sheets
December 31, Year 5

	Wexel Company	*Xrey Company*	*Yarbo Company*
Current assets	$ 25,000	$ 41,550	$ 58,400
Investment in Xrey—80%	108,000		
Investment in Yarbo—75%		90,750	
Investment in Xrey bonds	35,500		
Other assets	300,000	204,700	81,600
Total assets	$468,500	$337,000	$140,000
Current liabilities	$ 39,500	$ 50,800	$ 34,000
5% bonds payable, due Jan. 1, Year 12		100,000	
Premium on bonds		4,800	
Capital stock	350,000	120,000	200,000
Retained earnings, Jan. 1, Year 5	51,000	42,800	(84,000)
Year 5 net income (or loss)	28,000	18,600	(10,000)
Total liabilities & equity	$468,500	$337,000	$140,000

Income Statements—Year 5

	Wexel Company	*Xrey Company*	*Yarbo Company*
Revenues:			
Sales revenues			$276,000
Patent royalties	$88,700		
Interest revenues	2,000		
Rental revenue		$56,000	
Total revenues	$90,700	$56,000	$276,000

Expenses:			
Cost of goods sold			*$ 91,300*
Operating expenses	*$43,700*	*$13,460*	*50,000*
Rent expense		*12,300*	*56,000*
Royalty payments	*11,800*		*88,700*
Interest expense (net)		*4,200*	
Income taxes	*7,200*	*7,440*	*-0-*
Total expenses	*$62,700*	*$37,400*	*$286,000*
Net income (or loss)	*$28,000*	*$18,600*	*$ (10,000)*

Wexel acquired 80% of the outstanding shares of Xrey Company in Year 1, one year after the latter company was formed. Xrey earned $16,000 and paid $5,000 in dividends during its first year of operation. Wexel carries its investment at cost.

Xrey Company acquired a 75% interest in Yarbo Company in Year 2 at the date of Yarbo's organization, by purchasing a partially paid-up subscription contract in a private transaction and making the final payments. Xrey carries its investment on an accrual or equity basis, but the data given above are before any adjustment to reflect Yarbo's Year 5 operations.

On January 1, Year 3, Wexel Company purchased 40% of the 5% bonds of Xrey Company in the open market at a cost of $35,500. Since Wexel intends to hold these bonds to maturity, the board of directors authorized that the discount be amortized for consolidated statement purposes and that the gain on retirement from a consolidated viewpoint be shared by Wexel and Xrey Companies accordingly. The bond premium on Xrey's books is being amortized on a straight-line basis.

The difference between the cost of the investment in Xrey and book value at date of acquisition is to be treated as a revaluation of Xrey's other assets, not subject to amortization. The difference between the cost of the investment in Yarbo and book value is to be treated as an intangible asset on the books of Xrey Company.

Instructions

a. Prepare working papers for the Year 5 consolidated balance sheet and income statement of the three affiliated companies. Support all adjusting and eliminating entries in keyed footnotes to your working papers.

b. After examining the individual financial statements and comparing them with the consolidated results, comment on the position of the minority stockholders in Xrey and Yarbo Companies.

14 REPORTING FOREIGN OPERATIONS

The world of the United States businessman is no longer restricted to the shores of North America. During the twentieth century, United States business has found that it must carry on trade with businesses in foreign lands. Since World War II this trade has expanded with the free world, and now there is even some limited trade with the Soviet Union. American business has also found increasing profit potential in enterprises in other parts of the world. With the increased competitive pressures in many areas in the United States, some companies have turned to foreign investment as a means of achieving increased profitability. At first, foreign investment was restricted to exploitation of the natural resources of other countries; however, in recent years American business has begun to utilize the talents of the labor force of other countries in manufacturing enterprises. Indeed foreign investment has become so great that financial reports of American industry are frequently misleading when the results of foreign operations are not included as a part of the report.

The difficulty of combining the financial representation of foreign operations with domestic operations is that there are two or more currencies used in quantifying the transactions. If the accountant is to prepare meaningful reports, he must restate the money expression of all transactions of each operating unit in terms of a common currency. For American-based companies this means that the foreign currency amounts must be restated in terms of United States dollars.

In preparing his report the accountant may be concerned with any one, or all, of the following types of foreign relationships:

1. Sale of goods by a domestic firm to a foreign buyer with the terms of the transaction stated in terms of the foreign monetary unit.

2. Purchase of goods from a foreign firm by a domestic firm with the terms of the transaction stated in the foreign monetary unit.

3. Branch-office operations with the accounts of the branch kept in terms of the foreign monetary unit.

4. Subsidiary operations with the accounts expressed in monetary units of the foreign country.

The American investor has found the securities of many foreign companies to be very profitable avenues of investment. Many foreign companies' securities are actively traded in the United States stock markets. For these companies the translation of foreign currency balances to dollars is a necessity.

Principles of accounting for foreign activities

Are the principles of accounting for foreign operations different from those accepted by the accountant in accounting for domestic operations? The answer is, of course, no. The principles are the same; that is, the accountant makes the same assumptions. The only additional problem is to find a method of translating transactions, originally expressed in a foreign currency, into terms of the domestic currency without altering the meaning of the data in the process. The purpose of the translation is to permit the aggregation of data in terms of a single monetary unit in order to gain knowledge about the operation of the whole business.

The accounts of the companies must be maintained on a consistent basis both before and after the translation of the money aggregates into terms of the domestic currency. The accountant, therefore, must not permit the effect of price-level changes in either country to affect the accounts unless he adjusts both sets of records on a consistent basis. For this reason the choice of the exchange rate to be used in the translation of each account balance must be chosen with full knowledge and understanding of the effect which the translation will have on the account balance.

Exchange rates

The problem of translating foreign currencies into American dollars is complicated by the selection of an exchange rate which represents the proper relationship between the two currencies. First, the rate of exchange for currencies is not stable. For this reason the accountant cannot determine that the rate of exchange of English pounds and American dollars is 1 pound equals 2.8 dollars and accept this rate for all future conversions of these two currencies. Second, there are multiple exchange rates existing between certain currencies. In such circumstances the problem is to select that exchange rate which will accurately reflect the situation after translation to dollars.[1]

The American Institute of Certified Public Accountants has stated that: "Where more than one foreign exchange rate is in effect, care should be exercised to select the one most clearly realistic and appropriate in the circumstances."[2] This state-

[1] The multiplicity of exchange rates that exist for various currencies can be observed by reference to the International Monetary Fund, *Annual Report on Exchange Restrictions*. The daily fluctuations in free-market rates as exhibited by selling prices, in dollars, for bank transfers in the United States for payment abroad can be observed in *The Wall Street Journal*.

[2] AICPA, *Accounting Research and Terminology Bulletins, Final Edition* (New York: 1961), chap. 12, p. 112.

ment has generally been interpreted to mean that the free market rate of exchange should be used in the conversion. In some cases there is more than one free market exchange rate, and the question arises as to which of these rates is more clearly realistic and appropriate. Professor Hepworth has answered the query in the following manner:

> It is tempting to conclude that since the principal activity of a foreign subsidiary is the manufacture or sale of one general type of commodity, the use of the selling rate (if both buying and selling rates exist) applicable to that class of commodity represents the most satisfactory basis for translating foreign currency net assets into dollars.
>
> On the other hand, it is desirable to consider that the fundamental attribute of value of an asset element (or negative value of a debt) is represented by the present value of the future cash receipts which the asset is capable of producing. If we apply this concept to the problem at hand, it follows that the most satisfactory measure of the dollar value of the foreign currency net assets should be the present value of the future dollar receipts produced thereby. Quite apparently it is impossible to apply such a rigorous theoretical concept in a practical situation. However, this valuation concept would seem to lead to the use of a rate of exchange which was related to the flow of dollar receipts from the foreign subsidiary. In turn, this reasoning would suggest the use of a financial rate as being productive of the most rational results in terms of the dollar value of foreign net assets. On balance, the second argument presented above appears the stronger of the two, and for this reason the use of an exchange rate related to the remittance of earnings from the foreign subsidiary for the purpose of translating foreign currency accounts is recommended.[3]

Domestic company with foreign transactions

When a domestic company buys or sells goods from or to a foreign company, the billing may be handled in foreign or domestic currency. As indicated earlier, the exchange rates between currencies do not remain constant over time; therefore, one party to the transaction may have a gain or loss arising out of the fluctuations in exchange rates. If the billing is in terms of the vendor's domestic currency, then the domestic company realizes no gain or loss. On the other hand, if the billing is made in terms of the foreign currency, then the domestic company may find that in the final settlement a gain or loss has resulted as a result of the fluctuation of the exchange rate. If there has been no change in the exchange rate between the date when the transaction originated and the date when the payment is finally made, there will be no gain or loss to either party to the transaction.

Foreign purchases. When an American company buys goods in the foreign market, the purchase may be billed in terms of the currency of the foreign country or of the United States. As indicated, if the billing is in terms of the American dollar, there will be no exchange gain or loss accruing to the domestic buyer regardless of changes in the exchange rate in the meantime. Remittance will be made to the seller in terms of the American dollar, and any gain or loss resulting from shifts in exchange rates must be recognized by the foreign seller. If the billing is in terms of the foreign currency, the buyer must remit in the foreign currency, and when

[3] Samuel R. Hepworth, *Reporting Foreign Operation,* Bureau of Business Research, University of Michigan (Ann Arbor: 1956), pp. 129–130.

he buys the currency he may find that there has been a change in his obligation. In such situations the buyer must account for this subsequent event. The accountant's problem is one of accounting for this change in the number of dollars required to satisfy the obligation to the seller.

There are two possibilities which should be considered: (1) Add the loss to, or subtract the gain from, the cost of the item purchased; or (2) treat the gain or loss as a revenue or expense of the current period. In considering the first alternative, the accountant should look to accepted accounting principles. In general the criterion cited as the basis for deciding whether to add an outlay to the total cost of some good purchased is: Was the outlay necessary to get the good into the business and to place it in a usable condition? In our example this was not the case. The gain or loss was not a function of the transaction of buying; instead, it was the result of a decision to accept the risk that the exchange rate would change. If the company had desired to avoid this risk, it could have done so by buying some of the foreign currency to be delivered on the day the debt had to be paid. This operation, known as hedging, is used frequently by those who want to avoid the risk of price fluctuation when there is a known commitment to be honored at a particular time. It is clear that, since the company elected to expose itself to this risk, any gain or loss incurred should be considered a part of the period's activity.

The following example illustrates the entries needed to account for transactions between a domestic buyer and a foreign seller. An American company buys goods valued at 10,000 francs from a French firm at a time when 1 franc equals \$.204. Payment for the goods is made when the value of 1 franc is equal to \$.199.

	Billing in Dollars		*Billing in Francs*	
Merchandise	2,040		2,040	
Accounts Payable		2,040		2,040
To record the purchase of merchandise from the French firm for \$2,040, or 10,000 francs.				
Accounts Payable	2,040		2,040	
Cash		2,040		1,990
Exchange Gain or Loss				50
To record payment of the bill to the French firm at a time when 1 franc equals \$.199.				

When the American customer is billed in terms of American dollars, the French firm must recognize the exchange gain. The American firm remits \$2,040, which equals 10,251 francs, a gain of 251 francs for the French firm.

Foreign sales. When a domestic firm sells goods to a foreign firm, the foreign firm may be billed in terms of dollars or in terms of the foreign currency. If the billing is in dollars then no exchange gain or loss accrues to the domestic company; however, if the billing is in terms of the foreign currency, then the gain or loss must be accounted for by the domestic firm. As in the case of the purchase, any gain or loss arising from the transaction should be a revenue or expense of the period and is not an adjustment of the selling price. The domestic firm can sell the foreign currency to be delivered by it on the date that payment is due from the foreign buyer to protect itself from the fluctuations in the exchange rate. Consequently, if the firm accepts the risk, the gain or loss is a proper item to be reflected in the determination of income.

Assume that an American firm sells goods valued at $8,160 to a French firm at a time when the exchange rate is 1 franc equals $.204. Collection of the account is made when 1 franc equals $.200. Entries to record these transactions are:

	Billing in Dollars		*Billing in Francs*	
Accounts Receivable	*8,160*		*8,160*	
Sales		*8,160*		*8,160*
To record the sale of merchandise to a French firm for $8,160, or 40,000 francs.				
Cash	*8,160*		*8,000*	
Exchange Gain or Loss			*160*	
Accounts Receivable		*8,160*		*8,160*
To record the collection of accounts owed by the French firm at a time when 1 franc equals $.200.				

When remittance is in dollars, there is no record in the accounts of the domestic firm that the exchange rate has changed since the billing date. The foreign firm must, however, remit more francs to buy the $8,160 required to satisfy its debt to the American firm. The loss to be recorded by the French firm is 800 francs.

Realized or unrealized exchange gain or loss. In the two situations which we have just examined, we have assumed that the purchase and payment or the sale and collection have taken place within the same accounting period. If this simplifying assumption is removed, what effect does it have on the accounting procedures? The primary question becomes: When is the gain or loss realized? Is it realized when the change in the exchange rate occurs, or is it realized when cash is transferred?

If we look to accepted accounting principles for an answer to this question, we are led to the conclusion that the loss should be recognized as soon as it is determinable but that the gain should not be recognized until the receivable is converted to cash or the payable is paid. The situation in American practice which more closely approximates the exchange gain or loss is the valuation of marketable securities. Here the common approach is to recognize, at statement dates, the loss in value and to indicate market value if the price of the security has appreciated. In *Intermediate Accounting,* the authors made a plea for the valuation of marketable securities at market price. The analogy of marketable securities relates to the receivable or payable in foreign currency because both are money value items and the market provides an impartial arbiter of value of each. In fact, where monetary accounts are to be settled by transfer of a currency other than the domestic one, the accountant has a responsibility to indicate the value of foreign currency to be exchanged.

The AICPA agrees with the principle that the money items should be valued at the domestic dollar equivalent at the date of the financial statements. There is some hesitancy, however, to include the unrealized gains in the determination of income even though it is apparently acceptable to include losses. This position is consistent with the doctrine of conservatism by which the accountant argues that he should recognize all losses as soon as they can be reasonably determined but he should not recognize gains until they are realized. Specifically, the position of the Institute is as follows:

> Realized losses or gains on foreign exchange should be charged or credited to operations.
>
> Provision should be made, ordinarily by a charge against operations, for declines in translation value of foreign net current and working assets (unrealized losses). Unrealized gains should preferably be carried to a suspense account, except to the extent that they may be credited to the account previously charged.[4]

Regardless of the treatment accorded unrealized exchange gains in the determination of income, there seems to be general agreement that the money claims should reflect the expected settlement value at the date of the statement. The disposition on the financial statements of the suspense account referred to by the AICPA is not clear. Since it is not considered a part of the current period's operations, we must assume that it should be included in the balance sheet. Presumably this is one of the items to be included in that nebulous category referred to as the *deferred credit*. In fact it represents an increase in the stockholder's equity; however, there is some question of the propriety of including it there since it is not accepted as a proper element of the current year's operations and it does not constitute capital contribution. Another possibility is to deduct the provision from the receivable balance. The questions then are: What is the purpose of the write-up? How is the provision to be interpreted? Is it in fact a provision for an expected decline in the value of the receivable? Such a presentation would require complete explanation in a footnote. It is difficult to understand why the accounting profession has held so tenaciously to this conservative rule of asset valuation in the face of repeated evidence of the fallacy of its logic.

The application of the rules stated above can be illustrated with the following example. A domestic company sells $8,020 of merchandise to a Mexican company on December 15 when one peso equals $.0802, with payment to be made in Mexican pesos on January 15. In the meantime the domestic company closes its books when the rate of exchange is 1 peso equals $.0810. The remittance is received by the domestic company on January 15 when the peso is equal to $.0812. The journal entries to record this series of events are presented on page 461.

Purchases from foreign companies where the payment is to be made in the foreign currency would be accounted for in a similar manner. Gains occur with declines in the relative value of the foreign currency when money is owed to a foreign company payable in the currency of that country.

[4] AICPA, *op. cit.*, p. 112.

Dec. 15	*Accounts Receivable—100,000 pesos*	*8,020*	
	Sales		*8,020*
	To record the sale of merchandise to a Mexican company, account to be paid in Mexican pesos.		
Dec. 31	*Accounts Receivable—100,000 pesos*	*80*	
	Provision for Exchange Fluctuations		*80*
	To record the unrealized increase in the value of the receivable due to changes in the exchange rate.		
Jan. 15	*Cash*	*8,120*	
	Provision for Exchange Fluctuations	*80*	
	Accounts Receivable		*8,100*
	Exchange Gain or Loss		*100*
	To record the collection of the receivable from the Mexican company remitted in pesos and to recognize the realized exchange gain.		

Inventory on consignment in a foreign country

In the event that a domestic company placed some merchandise in the hands of a foreign company on a consignment basis, there might be problems associated with fluctuating exchange rates different from those encountered when the asset is a money asset. The inventory is not a claim to cash although it is hoped that it will be sold for cash. As a consequence, accepted accounting principles would dictate that the inventory should be carried at cost. If an exchange gain or loss were recognized before the inventory was converted into a monetary asset, then the accountant would have to argue that the inventory is more or less valuable because there has been a change in the relative value of the two currencies. This quite clearly is not the case. The selling price of the inventory may change, but according to accepted practice of American accountants, such changes are not recognized in accounting for assets unless the change results in a permanent decline in the value of the inventory.

The problem which exists and the proposed solution are illustrated by the following example. A United States company ships merchandise, which costs \$9,972 and which is priced at \$14,958, to a Dutch associate with the agreement that the associate will hold the inventory on consignment. Upon sale the associate will remit the selling price less a commission of 10% in Dutch guilders. At the time the inventory is delivered to the associate the exchange rate is 1 guilder equals \$.277. At the end of 30 days the associate reports that one-half of the merchandise has been sold at the agreed price and remits 24,300 guilders (27,000 selling price—2,700 commission). At this time the exchange rate is 1 guilder equals \$.280. At the end of the second 30-day period the associate reports that the remaining goods have been sold at the agreed price and again transmits the 24,300 guilders in full settlement of the consignment. At this time the exchange rate is 1 guilder equals \$.276.

The exchange gain or loss from these transactions might be included as a part

Goods Shipped to Dutch Associate	*9,972*	
Inventory		*9,972*
To record shipment of goods to Dutch associate at time when exchange rate is 1 guilder equals $.277.		

	First Period		*Second Period*	
Cash	*6,804*		*6,707*	
Selling Commission	*756*		*745*	
Exchange Gain or Loss			*27*	
Exchange Gain or Loss		*81*		
Sales		*7,479*		*7,479*
To record sale of merchandise by Dutch associate and remittance of selling price in guilders. For the first period 1 guilder equals $.280; for the second, $.276. (All amounts are rounded to nearest dollar.)				

of sales; however, the above procedure is theoretically preferable in that it reflects more clearly the source of revenue. The selling commission is translated, using either procedure, at the exchange rate at the date the report is received from the associate. The simpler procedure is to convert both sales and expenses at the rate of exchange prevailing on the day of the sale. Unless there are rapid and large changes in the exchange rate, the procedure of separating sales and exchange gains or losses seems unnecessary and may not be practically feasible. The account Goods Shipped to Dutch Associate is closed to Cost of Goods Sold when the associate sells the merchandise.

If the cash is not remitted by the Dutch associate at the time the report of sales is made, a receivable from the associate is created. In the event that there are further fluctuations in the exchange rate prior to the time when the receivable is settled, the resulting exchange gains and/or losses will be recognized at statement dates or at the time the cash is remitted in settlement of the receivable.

Domestic company with foreign investments

Investments in foreign companies may take many forms, and the relationship between the firms varies. There may be home office–branch relationships, investment in securities, or subsidiary relationships created either by buying the stock of a foreign firm or by creating an arm of the domestic company in a foreign country. These relationships, as we have seen, are reported in various ways. The reasons for the variety of reporting practices have been examined at length earlier. When the investment is made in a company located and operating in a foreign country, there is the added uncertainty of government regulation. The problem of reporting foreign operations as a part of a domestic company's total activity is, therefore, quite complex. There appears to be general concern that translation of dollar amounts implies that dollars can be taken out of the foreign operation and used in the United States. When there are restrictions of any kind on the movement of dollars across international boundaries, there is a presumption that combined reports of domestic and foreign operations are misleading.

The American Institute of Certified Public Accountants has taken a rather conservative position on the translation of foreign accounts to American dollars and on the practice of including these balances in the reports of domestic corporations. In *Accounting Research Bulletin No. 43,* the Committee on Accounting Procedures states:

> A sound procedure for United States companies to follow is to show earnings from foreign operations in their own accounts only to the extent that funds have been received in the United States or unrestricted funds are available for transmission thereto. Appropriate provision should be made also for known losses.
>
> Any foreign earnings reported beyond the amounts received in the United States should be carefully considered in the light of all the facts. The amounts should be disclosed if they are significant, and they should be reserved against to the extent that their realization in dollars appears to be doubtful.
>
> As to assets held abroad, the accounting should take into consideration the fact that most foreign assets stand in some degree of jeopardy, so far as ultimate realization by United States owners is concerned. Under these conditions it is important that especial care be taken in each case to make full disclosure in the financial statements of United States companies of the extent to which they include significant foreign items.[5]

When one considers the recommendations of the AICPA, one must wonder why any business is led to invest in foreign assets and further why the investment is accounted for if the situation is so bleak as to make such conservative valuation necessary. Indeed, Professor Hepworth states:

> . . . if relations between the United States and a country in which a subsidiary corporation is domiciled are such as to justify the attaching of any value to the investment in the subsidiary on the records of the parent company, the expression of the financial position and operating results of the subsidiary in dollar figures is appropriate. . . . The existence of a variety of exchange rates, currency devaluations, or restrictions on payment of dollar dividends should be fully disclosed, but the existence of such restrictions should not, per se, be considered as preventing the informative translation of foreign accounts.[6]

Regardless of the manner in which the investment in the foreign corporation is carried, there is a need to reflect the financial position and the results of operations in dollars if the financial report is to include information about the foreign investment. The accountant, therefore, must give consideration to the principles of translating foreign money balances into dollars.

Translation of balance sheet accounts

The translation of foreign account balances into dollars is merely a restatement of the balance in terms of a different currency. If the accounts of the foreign company are to be combined with those of the domestic company, the translation should be executed in a way which will assure compatibility between the domestic and foreign balances. This means that the accepted principles governing accounting practice should be observed in recording the foreign transactions and in translating the balances for statement purposes.

[5] *Ibid.,* pp. 111–112.

[6] Hepworth, *op. cit.,* p. 6.

The AICPA position. The AICPA, in stating the generally accepted principles pertaining to the treatment of foreign exchange in the balance sheet, has set forth the following rules of translation of balance sheet accounts:

1. Cash, accounts receivable, and other current assets should be translated at the rate of exchange prevailing on the date of the balance sheet.

2. Fixed assets, permanent investments, and long-term receivables should be translated into dollars at the rates prevailing when such assets were acquired or constructed.

3. Current liabilities payable in foreign currency should be translated into dollars at the rate of exchange in force on the date of the balance sheet.

4. Long-term liabilities and capital stock stated in foreign currency should not be translated at the closing rate, but at the rates of exchange prevailing when they were originally incurred or issued.

The list of rules for translating balance sheet accounts makes no distinction between monetary and nonmonetary accounts. The distinction is made instead on the basis of whether the balance is classified as current or noncurrent.[7]

The authors' position. The authors contend that a more realistic division of balance sheet accounts, for purposes of translation, is one which groups them by type, monetary and nonmonetary, rather than one which groups them by life, current and noncurrent. The translation rules might then be restated thusly:

1. Cash, accounts receivable, and other monetary assets should be translated at the rate of exchange prevailing on the date of the balance sheet.

2. Inventories, fixed assets, and other cost aggregate assets should be translated at the rate of exchange prevailing when such assets were acquired or constructed.

3. Current and long-term liabilities payable in foreign currency should be translated into dollars at the rate of exchange in force on the date of the balance sheet.

4. Capital stock stated in foreign currency should not be translated at the closing rate, but at the rates of exchange prevailing when it was originally issued or at the date the stock was acquired by the domestic company.

Discussion of differences in positions. The principles of valuation in current accounting practice are that:

1. Monetary accounts should be valued at their cash equivalent, that is, monetary assets at estimated realizable value and liabilities at the dollar claim against assets.

2. Nonmonetary accounts should be carried at unamortized cost, that is, cost

[7] Paul Grady, in *Accounting Research Study No. 7,* "Inventory of Generally Accepted Accounting Principles for Business Enterprises," states:

> The foregoing chapter of *ARB No. 43* has become outmoded in relation to present practice, particularly in the translation of long-term assets and liabilities, due to the prevalence of major currency revaluations and continued substantial inflation in many countries. *Research Report No. 36,* "Management Accounting Problems in Foreign Operations," published by the National Association of Accountants in 1960, is more representative of current practice.

The NAA position is substantially that of the authors expressed in this chapter.

of acquisition less the portion of cost assigned to operations, or in the case of inventories at cost or market, whichever is lower.

The translation of inventory balances as suggested by the AICPA, at the rate in force on the balance sheet date, may result in the recognition of an exchange gain or loss when in fact none has been realized in accordance with accepted accounting practice. Similarly, if long-term receivables and liabilities are translated at the exchange rate prevailing when they were created, the balances do not represent current realizable value or liquidation amount in terms of dollars. These monetary accounts should therefore be translated at the exchange rate prevailing at the date of the balance sheet.

The Institute position with respect to the translation of long-term monetary accounts is presumably predicated on the theory that unrealized gains and losses should not be recognized. This position is not held consistently, however, even in the area of translation of foreign currency balances. For example, there is the recommendation that the inventory be translated at the exchange rate at the date of the balance sheet. Such a procedure will certainly result in the recognition of exchange gains or losses. The question then is: When should exchange gains and losses be realized? American accountants have generally agreed that the creation of a legitimate receivable, upon the transfer of merchandise from the seller to the buyer at a mutually agreeable price, is the appropriate time for recognizing the fact that revenue has been realized. The tentative nature of this revenue is acknowledged by various adjustments at the end of the period, such as the adjustment for anticipated losses from bad debts. In accounting for foreign operations, are not the adjustments for fluctuations in exchange rates mere extensions of this philosophy? Why then should a different standard be applied to account balances stated in terms of a foreign currency when they are translated into balances stated in terms of American dollars? Does such action require acceptance of new principles?

Consistency in the application of accounting principles dictates that the monetary accounts should be translated at the exchange rate prevailing at the balance sheet date, the cost aggregate accounts at the exchange rate prevailing at the date the asset is acquired. Hepworth argues that translation procedures should be adopted which

> . . . restrict the exchange adjustment to what it should logically represent, namely gains or losses caused by changing dollar value of foreign assets and liabilities which represent contractual rights to cash, or to the receipt of cash, or contractual obligations for the disbursement of cash. Only if this is the case does the exchange adjustment have real significance in terms of managerial action and responsibility assignment.[8]

The capital stock and paid-in capital accounts are usually translated at the exchange rate prevailing when the stock was issued, with two exceptions. (1) When the stock is acquired as an investment at a date subsequent to the date when the stock was issued, the exchange rate at the date of acquisition is usually more significant than the exchange rate at the time the stock was originally issued. Similar treatment may also be accorded long-lived cost aggregates. (2) In the event of a

[8] Hepworth, *op. cit.*, p. 11.

sharp devaluation of the currency, a new benchmark is established, and the exchange rate prevailing immediately after the devaluation is more appropriate than the exchange rate at the date of issuance. Again the same treatment is usually accorded cost aggregates. The devaluation case is discussed in detail later.

Translation of income statement accounts

The translation of revenue and expense accounts, like the translation of balance sheet accounts, should be merely a restatement of amounts in terms of a different currency. The income statement depicts revenue and expense flows over time; whereas, the balance sheet reflects status at a point in time. The translated income statement of a foreign affiliate frequently has one account included which is not a translation of a similar foreign balance, the exchange gain or loss.

The AICPA position. The AICPA indicates that the income statement data should be translated at the monthly average rate of exchange when wide fluctuations have occurred or on the basis of a carefully weighted average. In the event of extremely wide fluctuations, there is some reason for departing from the monthly average and accepting an end of the period exchange rate. Specifically, the Institute states:

> Where a major change in an exchange rate takes place during a fiscal year, there may be situations in which more realistic results will be obtained if income computed in foreign currencies is translated for the entire fiscal year at the new rates in effect after such major fluctuation. This procedure would have the practical advantage of making unnecessary a cutoff at the date of the change in the exchange rate. Where dividends have been paid prior to a major change in the exchange rate, out of earnings of the current fiscal year, that portion of the income for the year should be considered as having been earned at the rate at which such dividend was paid irrespective of the rates used in translating the remainder of the earnings.
>
> While the possibility of losses from currency devaluation may ordinarily be considered to be a risk inherent in the conduct of business in foreign countries, the world-wide scope and unprecedented magnitude of devaluations that have occurred in recent years are such that they cannot be regarded as recurrent hazards of business. Accordingly, exchange adjustments arising from extraordinary developments, if so material in amount that their inclusion in the income statement would impair the significance of net income to an extent that misleading inferences might be drawn therefrom, appear to be of such nature that they might appropriately be charged to surplus.[9]

The authors' position. Since revenues and expenses often reflect daily transactions of the enterprise, we find it, at least theoretically, preferable to state that items of revenue and expense should be translated at the exchange rate prevailing at the time the revenue was earned or the cost incurred. Such a proposal may become completely inoperable as the volume of transactions increases. Translation of the revenue and expense amounts, as a matter of expediency, may alternatively be based on simplifying assumptions, such as that transactions occur with a certain degree of regularity each month. The NAA *Research Report No. 36* supports the authors' position on this point also. The report also indicates how workable averages may be derived.

[9] AICPA, *op. cit.*, p. 115.

Discussion of differences. The limitation of the Institute's rule in translation of revenues and expenses is found in the uncertainty of what is meant by "the monthly average rate of exchange." The authors prefer adoption of a rule which is more definite as to what exchange rate should be used in the translation of these accounts. A statement that the income statement data resulting from transactions of the month should be translated at the exchange rate prevailing on the fifteenth or the last date of the month would certainly be simpler to apply. Of course, expirations of costs incurred in prior periods should be translated at the exchange rate prevailing at acquisition date. Depreciation of plant assets, amortization of the cost of other long-lived assets, and, in some cases, inventory costs made a part of cost of goods sold are examples of expenses which would not be translated at the current monthly rate. Dividend payments occur so infrequently that there is no problem of translating these amounts for income statement purposes at the rate prevailing on the date of declaration.

Recognition of exchange gains and losses. As we have seen from the preceding discussion, a logical development of accounting principles requires that the accountant recognize and deal with the exchange gain or loss arising out of foreign operations. The gain or loss arises because there has been a change in the relative value of two currencies. There is some problem of deciding whether the gain or loss is realized or not, and also there is the problem of deciding how to reflect the gain or loss in the financial statements. It was concluded on page 460 that the exchange gain or loss occurred because there were money value assets and liabilities which were stated in terms of a second currency. When the relative values of the two currencies changed, there was a resulting gain or loss which should be recognized as a part of the operating activity for the period but which should be clearly distinguished from the manufacturing and trading profits. The change in the exchange rate is an inherent feature of carrying on operations with foreign interests in terms of the foreign currency. For this reason changes in the exchange rate are considered to be a risk which is incidental to this activity like any other risk which the business faces; therefore, the gain or loss should be considered an integral part of the operation of the foreign branch or subsidiary. The Institute opposes the recognition of exchange gains, as we saw earlier, presumably on the grounds of conservatism.

It is interesting to note the similarities which exist between exchange gains and losses and purchasing power gains and losses, which are discussed in detail in Chapter 15. In both cases there is a change in the value of the domestic dollar expressed in terms of other dollars or goods.

Devaluation and foreign investments

The devaluation of one currency in terms of another is the result of action taken by the government to restate the official rate of exchange between these currencies. The English pound was devalued in terms of the American dollar several years ago when the official exchange rate was changed from 1 pound equals $4.03 to 1 pound equals $2.80. This action made English goods cheaper in terms of American dollars, and the intended effect was to increase exports from England to the United States. Devaluation can thus be defined as an abrupt and substantial reduction in the par value of one currency in terms of other currencies. The changes in exchange rates referred to earlier in the chapter have been the result of free market forces, and they seldom are as large as those which result from a devaluation.

The accounting problems caused by a devaluation relate to the procedure for translating foreign currency aggregates into dollar aggregates. In the case of the assets and liabilities which represent claims to or claims against cash, the problem of translation is the same as for any smaller fluctuation. These accounts should be translated at the exchange rate prevailing at the statement date, which means that the postdevaluation rate will be used.

The more difficult problem involves cost aggregates which represent future service potential rather than dollar claims. Analyzing this problem we ask: What does the dollar aggregate mean? In accounting it is accepted as a measure of the present value of the future revenue to be derived from the use of the asset. It is assumed that the purchase price is a reliable estimate of this amount at the date of purchase and the subsequent amortization of cost represents the expiration of usefulness. Our accounting devices for measurement are rough and there is some question of their adequacy, but this is the accepted interpretation of these dollar figures.

If there is an abrupt and substantial change in the selling price of the commodity which is being produced, there is a corresponding change in the present value of future revenues; therefore, there has been a change in the value of the asset and this should be recognized. Accounting theory dictates, then, that in the event of a devaluation of the foreign currency, the postdevaluation exchange rate should be used to translate the nonmonetary assets and the paid-in capital accounts to dollars instead of the exchange rate prevailing at the date the asset was acquired or the capital was paid in. The American Institute of Certified Public Accountants has taken a different position. As we saw earlier, the Institute does not accept the assumption that long-term liabilities should be treated as monetary accounts; therefore, we would expect a different treatment in this connection. Specifically the official position has been stated as follows:

> *Fixed assets*
>
> Generally, the rule for translation of fixed assets at rates in effect when the asset was acquired or constructed should be followed. One exception to this rule might be with respect to current plant additions when income is translated at post-devaluation rates. Another exception might be with respect to fixed assets acquired with foreign capital, to which reference is made later. When, however, fixed assets are purchased in foreign currencies presumably out of profits which are not restricted as to withdrawal, the United States dollar cost or the dollar equivalent of the foreign currency at the date of purchase should be recognized as the amount at which such assets should be carried.
>
> *Long-term liabilities*
>
> Translation of long-term liabilities presents possibly the greatest deviation from the principles previously stated by the committee. The committee generally has favored translating long-term liabilities at the rates of exchange prevailing when the liability was actually contracted, but recognized that there were exceptions. The purpose was to avoid giving recognition to minor fluctuations in foreign currencies. The argument has been advanced, however and apparently without satisfactory rebuttal, that long-term bonds will be paid off in post-devaluation

currencies and therefore should be translated at post-devaluation rates. The argument may not be compelling in any given instance, but the logic supporting it is convincing for a fall in rates of the breadth and size of the one just witnessed. Accordingly, with respect to long-term bonds, the general rule should be modified to permit translation at post-devaluation rates.

Capital stock
Consideration also should be given to the rates at which capital stock stated in foreign currencies are to be translated; whether they should be translated at historical rates, or at the average of rates applicable to the net assets, or at the post-devaluation rates, would depend on the circumstances in the individual cases.[10]

When one reads this statement he is left wondering what is really recommended. Basically the Institute has reiterated its position with respect to fluctuations in free-market rates except for long-term debt. In addition it has given the accountant some latitude to depart from the earlier prescribed procedure under varying circumstances.

The translation of the revenue and expense accounts following a devaluation is no different from the translation of these accounts under conditions of fluctuating free-market rates of exchange. Accordingly, after the devaluation takes place, the revenue earned and expenses incurred would be translated at the postdevaluation rate.

Again the AICPA has taken a position, in the translation of revenue and expense balances, that almost any procedure is acceptable. There seems to be no clear statement of the objective for the translation of these balances. It will be recalled that earlier in this chapter the assumption was made that the translation of revenue and expense balances should be performed in such a manner as to produce amounts which represent foreign currency balances. In the following statement of the AICPA no similar objective has been set forth.

Operations
In many cases it may be desirable to follow the recommendations of Bulletin No. 4 (now Bulletin No. 43, Chapter 12), which would result in the application of both pre- and post-devaluation rates to operations of a single year. There may, however, be situations in which more realistic results would be obtained if income computed in foreign currencies were to be translated for the entire fiscal year at the post-devaluation rates. This procedure would have the practical advantage of making it unnecessary to cut off at the date of the devaluation. Where dividends have been paid prior to the devaluation date, out of earnings of the current fiscal year, that portion of the income for the year should be considered as having been earned at the pre-devaluation rate irrespective of the rate that may be used in translating the remainder of the earnings accumulated prior to the devaluation date.

There may be cases in which the income statement would present very misleading results if the devaluation exchange rates were used for a large part of the fiscal year, and the loss resulting from the fall in exchange rates were

[10] AICPA—Research Department, *Accounting Problems Arising from Devaluation of Foreign Currencies* (New York: 1962), pp. 6–7.

charged to retained income (surplus). Obviously, the charge to income for the fall in exchange should not be less than the loss applicable to the increase in net current assets since the beginning of the fiscal year during which devaluation took place.[11]

In the calculation of the exchange loss resulting from the devaluation, it is necessary to include not only the net loss in money value accounts but also the loss on the nonmoney value assets. The exchange loss is, therefore, the total decline in the net foreign currency assets. The disclosure of the loss in the financial statements depends upon the accountant, whether he espouses the operating or the all-inclusive concept of net income. In any event the magnitude and cause of the loss must be fully disclosed if the statements are to present a fair presentation of the affairs of the company.

Effect of exchange restrictions

Once we have found an acceptable method of translating foreign currency balances into dollars, then the policy question must be answered: When is translation appropriate? There are at least three aspects of this question.

1. Should we make any attempt to translate foreign currency balances into dollars when there are restrictions on the convertibility of foreign currency into dollars?

2. Should we include any unremitted foreign earnings in the accounts of the domestic company when there are convertibility restrictions?

3. Should we include, in consolidated statements of American companies, the accounts of foreign subsidiaries located in countries where currency restrictions exist?

In answering these questions, we must remember that there are two elements of currency convertibility restriction. There may be a restriction on the convertibility of capital or there may be a restriction on the remittance of earnings. Of course, both types of restriction might be imposed by any one country.

In answer to the first question, the currency restriction does not prevent translating the accounts. This is not to say that the translated accounts should become a part of the accounting report; on the other hand, there is no reason to forego the information which can be gained from accounts stated in terms of dollars.

The second and third questions raise more difficult problems because of the impact of the foreign operations on the activities of the domestic corporation. Within the domestic economy there are contractual provisions and laws which restrict (1) the declaration and payment of cash dividends and (2) the withdrawal of assets comprising contributed capital in certain circumstances. For example, a loan agreement may include a restrictive provision related to the payment of dividends, state law in certain circumstances may prohibit the payment of dividends even though the corporation earned a profit, and in all states there are laws which prohibit the corporation from distributing assets which represent contributed capital. Restrictions such as these do not cause the accountant to omit unremitted earnings of domestic subsidiary companies in the report of combined

[11] *Ibid.*, p. 6.

earnings for the period. Similar restrictions on the withdrawal of funds from a foreign country are not sufficient cause for omitting the earnings on foreign investments from combined statements of income. The principal obligation of the accountant for complete and adequate disclosure would be fulfilled if he indicated the degree of restriction existing at the date of the financial statements.

Certainly the position taken here is not intended to condone the translation of foreign accounts in any and all cases regardless of the circumstances. In situations where the relationship between the United States and the foreign country has reached such a state that no trade or financial transactions are permitted between the citizens of the two countries, then there is reason to forego the translation of the foreign balances, and certainly there is doubt as to whether any combination of accounts should be permitted in this case. As a matter of fact the investment in the foreign country might be written off as a loss. If no transactions are permitted, there is no need to look for further restriction; however, the mere fact that a restriction does exist does not mean that the investment has no value.

Professor Hepworth argues that:

> The existence of restrictions on the convertibility of the foreign currency for the purpose of transmitting *Capital* to the United States should have no necessary impact on the recognition of unremitted foreign income. Disclosure of the existence of such restrictions on the statement of the parent corporation is appropriate, although when the restrictions relate exclusively to the remittance of capital, it would not appear that disclosure of such restrictions is mandatory. The existence of restrictions on the remittance of current earnings should not, as a general rule, cause the recognition of unremitted foreign earnings to be improper. It has been pointed out that the degree of restriction on the remittance of foreign earnings may vary widely, and it is apparent that particular situations may exist which may justify modification of the general principle cited above. Consistent treatment of domestic and foreign subsidiary earnings represents a much more important consideration than observance of consistency over time or insistence on conservatism as the most important reporting objective. Disclosure of restrictions on the remittance of current earnings in the statements of the parent corporation which include recognition of such earnings should be considered essential as a part of adequate reporting.[12]

Home office and branch operations

The accounting procedures usually employed in accounting for branch operations have already been discussed in some detail in Chapter 7. The purpose of reviewing a portion of this material here is to illustrate the accounting technique of recording these transactions when two or more currencies are involved.

Illustration. The Cascades Manufacturing Company decides to open a branch to sell its products and similar local products in the Philippines. During the first year the following transactions occurred (all amounts rounded to nearest whole unit):

(1) The home office sends the Philippine branch a draft for 25,000 pesos, which it purchases when the exchange rate is 1 peso equals $.25.

[12] Hepworth, *op. cit.,* p. 128. For the AICPA position see p. 463.

(2) Merchandise which cost $20,000 is shipped to the foreign branch when the exchange rate is $.26.

(3) The branch buys local goods on account at a cost of 12,000 pesos and furniture and fixtures for 15,000 pesos when the exchange rate is $.24.

(4) Sales totaling 62,000 pesos are made to customers on account.

	Home Office Books (in dollars)			*Branch Books (in pesos)*		
(1)	*Branch—Current*	*6,250*		*Cash*	*25,000*	
	Cash		*6,250*	*Home Office—Current*		*25,000*
	To record deposit of cash with branch.			*To record receipt of cash from home office.*		
(2)	*Branch—Current*	*20,000*		*Merchandise*	*76,923*	
	Inventory		*20,000*	*Home Office—Current*		*76,923*
	To record shipment of merchandise to branch.			*To record receipt of merchandise from home office.*		
(3)				*Merchandise*	*12,000*	
				Furniture and Fixtures	*15,000*	
				Accounts Payable		*27,000*
				To record purchase of merchandise and furniture and fixtures on account.		
(4)				*Accounts Receivable*	*62,000*	
				Sales		*62,000*
				To record sales of merchandise.		
(5)				*Cash*	*60,000*	
				Accounts Receivable		*60,000*
				To record collection of accounts.		
(6)				*Accounts Payable*	*25,000*	
				Cash		*25,000*
				To record payment of accounts.		
(7)				*Expenses*	*5,000*	
				Cash		*5,000*
				To record expenses for the period.		
(8)	*Cash*	*1,620*		*Home Office—Current*	*6,000*	
	Branch—Current		*1,620*	*Cash*		*6,000*
	To record remmittance from branch.			*To record remittance of cash to home office.*		
(9)				*Cost of Goods Sold*	*50,923*	
				Merchandise		*50,923*
				To record cost of goods sold.		
(10)				*Depreciation*	*1,500*	
				Allowance for Dep.		*1,500*
				To record depreciation.		

CASCADES MANUFACTURING COMPANY
Translation of Philippines Branch Accounts from Pesos to Dollars

	Trial balance per books (pesos)		Translation rate	Trial balance after translation (dollars)	
	Dr	Cr		Dr	Cr
Cash	49,000		.25[a]	12,250	
Accounts receivable	2,000		.25[a]	500	
Inventory:					
From home office	26,000		.26[d]	6,760	
Purchased	12,000		.24[e]	2,880	
Furniture and fixtures	15,000		.24[e]	3,600	
Allowance for depreciation		1,500	.24[e]		360
Accounts payable		2,000	.25[a]		500
Home office		95,923	Branch[f]		24,630
Sales		62,000	.25[b]		15,500
Cost of goods sold	50,923		.26[d]	13,240	
Expenses	5,000		.25[b]	1,250	
Depreciation	1,500		.24[e]	360	
Totals	161,423	161,423		40,840	40,990
Exchange adjustment				150	
Totals				40,990	40,990

[a] Current rate
[b] Average rate for the period
[c] Beginning rate
[d] Rate at date inventory received from home office
[e] Rate on date of purchase of furniture and inventory
[f] Balance of the branch account, in dollars, in the home office accounts

(5) Collections on account total 60,000 pesos.

(6) Payments to creditors total 25,000 pesos.

(7) Expenses of the branch total 5,000 pesos.

(8) A draft for 6,000 pesos is sent to the home office. The draft is sold when the exchange rate is $.27.

(9) The branch inventory at the end of the period is priced at 38,000 pesos. The branch uses the fifo method of inventory pricing.

(10) The furniture and fixtures are expected to have a 10-year life with no salvage value. A full year's depreciation is charged.

(11) The average exchange rate and the year-end exchange rate are 1 peso equals $.25.

Translation of foreign account balances into dollars has been carried out in accordance with the procedure preferred by the authors; monetary balances translated at the exchange rate prevailing at the date the statements are prepared; cost aggregate balances, at the exchange rate prevailing when the cost was incurred.

The AICPA position is that the inventory balance should be considered a monetary account.

Branch financial statements may be prepared in terms of dollars from the converted data presented on page 473. The exchange adjustment, having a debit balance, is treated as an additional expense on the income statement. The figure represents the net realized exchange loss for the period. A credit balance in this account is considered a gain from exchange rate fluctuations and it is treated as additional revenue.

The income statement of the Philippines branch of the Cascades Manufacturing Company is presented below in terms of dollars.

CASCADES MANUFACTURING COMPANY
Philippines Branch
Income Statement
for the year ended December 31, 19__

Sales		*$15,500*
Less:		
Cost of goods sold	*$13,240*	
Expenses	*1,250*	
Depreciation	*360*	
Exchange adjustment	*150*	*15,000*
Net income		*$ 500*

The balance sheet in terms of dollars for the branch would appear as follows:

CASCADES MANUFACTURING COMPANY
Philippines Branch
Balance Sheet
December 31, 19__

Cash		*$12,250*	*Accounts payable*	*$ 500*
Accounts receivable		*500*		
Inventory		*9,640*	*Home office*	*25,130*
Furniture and fixtures	*$3,600*			
Less: Accumulated depreciation	*360*			
		3,240		
Totals		*$25,630*	*Totals*	*$25,630*

Combined statements of the home office and branch can be prepared by adding the asset and liability balances together and by offsetting or eliminating the home office account on the branch statements against the branch account on the home office statements.

The entries required to close the home office and branch accounts at the end of the period are as follows:

Home Office Books (in dollars)			*Branch Books (in pesos)*		
			Sales	62,000	
			Cost of Goods Sold		50,923
			Expenses		5,000
			Depreciation		1,500
			Income Summary		4,577
			To close branch operating accounts for the year.		
Branch—Current	500		*Income Summary*	4,577	
Income of Branch		500	*Home Office—Current*		4,577
To record profit of branch in home office books.			*To close out profit to home office account.*		

Accounting for the foreign subsidiary

The basic criteria for determining whether consolidated statements should be prepared as discussed in Chapter 8 are (1) the degree of control exercised by the parent over the subsidiary and (2) the compatibility of the operations of the two entities. In the opinion of the authors, these same criteria should be used as the basis for the decision when there is a domestic parent and a foreign subsidiary.

The AICPA has taken the following position:

> In view of the uncertain values and availability of the assets and net income of foreign subsidiaries subject to controls and exchange restrictions and the consequent unrealistic statements of income that may result from the translation of many foreign currencies into dollars, careful consideration should be given to the fundamental question of whether it is proper to consolidate the statements of foreign subsidiaries with the statements of United States companies.[13]

The crucial question which must be answered before a definitive position can be taken with respect to the preparation of consolidated statements for a domestic parent and its foreign subsidiary, assuming it meets the standard criteria in all other respects, is: Do the exchange restrictions imposed by the foreign government reduce the degree of control by the parent to the point where consolidation of the companies is not appropriate? On page 470 the authors conclude that restrictions imposed by a foreign government on the movement of capital or money out of the country are generally not sufficient grounds for refusing to prepare consolidated statements. It is only when substantially all trade and financial transactions are prohibited that the accountant is justified in refusing to translate foreign account balances and include them as part of the statements of the parent.

[13] AICPA, *Accounting Research and Terminology Bulletins, Final Edition,* p. 112.

In his study Professor Hepworth states:

> The accounts of foreign subsidiaries should be included in financial statements in situations in which substantial stock ownership exists and the activities of the foreign corporation are reasonably closely related to those of the American parent company. Exceptions to this general principle may certainly exist in particular circumstances which may cause exclusion from consolidation to represent desirable reporting procedure, but exclusion should be considered preferable only in situations in which the absence of effective control and/or lack of an adequate degree of homogeneity of operations can be clearly demonstrated. In other words, the burden of proof would seem to fall on those favoring exclusion of a foreign subsidiary's accounts from consolidation, rather than the opposite situation which appears to exist at the present time. Perhaps what is called for is not so much concern as to the inclusion or exclusion of foreign subsidiaries from consolidation but, rather, a more general recognition of the nature of consolidated statements as being distinctly supplementary to the financial reports of the separate constituent entities.[14]

Translation of account balances

The accounts of the foreign subsidiary, like the accounts of the foreign branch, are usually kept in terms of the currency of the country in which the subsidiary is domiciled. In order to prepare statements for foreign companies which can be compared and combined with the American counterpart, the account balances must be translated into equivalent dollars. This translation is similar to that which has been illustrated for the branch operation. The monetary accounts are translated at the exchange rate prevailing at the statement date, and the cost aggregate accounts at the rates prevailing when the costs were incurred. The intercompany accounts present some special problems when the intention is to prepare consolidated statements including the foreign subsidiary.

Parent's investment and subsidiary's equity. The parent's investment in the subsidiary is a cost aggregate account using the cost method of accounting for investments. The account is carried in dollars since it is a part of the assets of the parent company. The significant factor here is that this cost aggregate represents an ownership interest in the subsidiary, reflected in the accounts of the subsidiary as paid-in capital and earnings retained in the business. In translating the subsidiary's accounts into dollars, the capital stock and paid-in capital accounts are translated at the exchange rate prevailing when the stock was acquired by the parent company. The retained earnings balance would be translated in parts. The balance of this account existing at the date of the investment would be translated at the exchange rate prevailing on the date of the investment. Additions since that date would be the difference between the foreign earnings translated into dollars and the dividends distributed by the subsidiary translated into dollars. Appropriations of retained earnings would be translated at the rate in effect on the date of the appropriation and deducted from the dollar balance of retained earnings. This procedure is simplified by accepting the dollar cost recorded in the investment account as the equivalent of the acquired portion of the stock equity at the date

[14] Hepworth, *op. cit.*, pp. 171–172.

of acquisition, translated into dollars. The earnings retained in the business subsequent to the acquisition are frequently accumulated in dollars as well as in the foreign currency. This procedure eliminates the difficult task of translating past balances at the various exchange rates prevailing when the capital was accumulated. Each year, therefore, the earnings retained by the subsidiary since the date of acquisition will be comprised, in the translated account balances, of the retained earnings balance at the end of the previous year stated in dollars and the earnings retained in the company for the current year in terms of dollars.

Any exchange gains or losses arising from the monetary accounts are considered to be realized and are used in determining the dollar profit or loss of the subsidiary for the period. No exchange gains or losses are recognized in connection with the other assets since they are carried at cost, being translated at the exchange rate prevailing when they were acquired.

Intercompany transactions. Intercompany transactions are recorded by the parties to the transaction just as those between two unrelated enterprises. Usually, however, all intercompany transactions are entered into with the understanding that final settlement will be made in terms of one of the currencies. The simpler procedure might well be to require all debts between the companies to be satisfied in terms of dollars. In this way all exchange fluctuations would be restricted to the accounts of the foreign subsidiary. An agreement such as this might meet with some resistance where there are other stockholders of the subsidiary company. If the parent owns 100% of the stock of the subsidiary, there would of course be no problem. The balance of any intercompany payables and receivables must of course be stated at the same total dollar amount. This requirement is not peculiar to parent and subsidiary relations, but it needs emphasis here to stress that accounting practice must be consistent when the accounts of two or more companies are to be combined into a consolidated statement.

Similarly, any intercompany sales and purchases must be stated in terms of the same number of dollars. When the subsidiary sells items to the parent, the selling price must be translated into dollars at the same exchange rate that is used by the parent in translating the purchase price into dollars. The process of eliminating such transactions for consolidated statement purposes make such a procedure essential.

Illustration. The National Company and its 100% owned German subsidiary report their financial status and operating results yearly on December 31. The subsidiary prepares its report in terms of deutsche marks and submits these reports and a pre-closing trial balance to its American parent each year. The American parent then translates the German mark to dollars based on the selling prices of bank transfers and using the December 31 rate as the current exchange rate. In the translation process, the National Company employs the techniques previously discussed; however, the operating data have been converted at the average exchange rate for the year, rather than at a monthly exchange rate. The justification of this procedure is that the fluctuation has been so minor in recent years that the benefit from using monthly averages cannot be justified in terms of added effort.

The trial balance of the German subsidiary and additional data concerning the translation are presented on page 478.

THE NATIONAL COMPANY
German Subsidiary
Trial Balance
December 31, 1966

	Deutsche marks		Translation rates	Dollars	
	Dr	Cr		Dr	Cr
Cash	40,000		.24	9,600	
Accounts receivable	110,000		.24	26,400	
Allowance for uncollectible accounts		15,000	.24		3,600
Merchandise inventory, Jan. 1	90,000		23,850	23,850	
Land	40,000		.30	12,000	
Building	560,000		.30	168,000	
Accumulated depreciation		56,000	.30		16,800
Furniture and fixtures	105,000		.30	31,500	
Accumulated depreciation		57,500	.30		17,250
Accounts payable		60,000	.24		14,400
Accounts payable to parent		100,000	25,000		25,000
Capital stock		500,000	150,000		150,000
Retained earnings		78,200	21,114		21,114
Sales		900,000	.25		225,000
Purchases	700,000		.25	175,000	
Expenses	80,000		.25	20,000	
Dividends	20,000		.24	4,800	
Depreciation expense	21,700		.30	6,510	
Totals	1,766,700	1,766,700		477,660	473,164
Exchange adjustment					4,496
Totals				477,660	477,660

Additional data

(1) Merchandise inventory, December 31, acquired throughout the period—105,000 marks, was translated to $26,250.

(2) Official exchange rates for one deutsche mark:

Date of investment	$.30
Beginning of year	.26
Average for year	.25
End of year	.24

(3) All plant assets were acquired at the time the investment was made by the parent company.

(4) Merchandise inventory, January 1—90,000 marks, translated to $23,850.

(5) Dividends to parent were paid on December 31.

(6) The subsidiary purchased merchandise, included in purchases, from the parent at a cost of $25,000, translated to 100,000 marks on the day of purchase. Payment is to be in dollars.

Particular attention should be given to the translation of the amount owed to the parent. All intercompany payables and receivables are to be satisfied in dollars; therefore, the liability to the subsidiary is $25,000. This means that the deutsche marks required to satisfy this debt will be in excess of 100,000 as indicated in the trial balance. Whenever receivable or payable balances must be settled in dollars, the translated figure should be the required dollar amount.

Consolidated statements for parent and foreign subsidiary. Working papers to consolidate National Company and its German subsidiary on the equity basis follow.

THE NATIONAL COMPANY AND GERMAN SUBSIDIARY
Consolidated Balance Sheet Working Paper (Equity Basis)
for the year ended December 31, 1966

	Parent company	Subsidiary company	Eliminations Dr	Eliminations Cr	Consolidated balance sheet
Cash	120,000	9,600			129,600
Accounts receivable	330,000	26,400			356,400
Allowances for uncollectible accounts	(45,000)	(3,600)			(48,600)
Merchandise inventory, Dec. 31	315,000	26,250			341,250
Account receivable from subsidiary	25,000			(b) 25,000	
Investment in subsidiary (equity basis)	196,700			(a) 196,700	
Land	120,000	12,000			132,000
Building	1,680,000	168,000			1,848,000
Accumulated depreciation	(168,000)	(16,800)			(184,800)
Furniture and fixtures	315,000	31,500			346,500
Accumulated depreciation	(172,500)	(17,250)			(189,750)
Totals	2,716,200	236,100			2,730,600
Accounts payable	180,000	14,400			194,400
Accounts payable to parent		25,000	(b) 25,000		
Notes payable	450,000				450,000
Capital stock—parent	1,450,000				1,450,000
Retained earnings, Jan. 1, parent	285,604				285,604
Net income—parent	350,596				350,596
Capital stock—subsidiary		150,000	(a) 150,000		
Retained earnings, Jan. 1, subsidiary		21,114	(a) 21,114		
Net income—subsidiary		30,386	(a) 30,386		
Dividends—subsidiary		(4,800)		(a) 4,800	
Totals	2,716,200	236,100	226,500	226,500	2,730,600

(a) To eliminate investment by parent and equity of subsidiary represented therein.
(b) To eliminate intercompany accounts.

THE NATIONAL COMPANY AND GERMAN SUBSIDIARY
Consolidated Income Statement Working Paper (Equity Basis)
for the year ended December 31, 1966

	Parent company	Subsidiary company	Eliminations		Consolidated income statement
			Dr	Cr	
Credits:					
Sales	2,700,000	225,000	(b) 25,000		2,900,000
Earnings of German subsidiary	30,386		(a) 30,386		
Exchange gain		4,496			4,496
Total	2,730,386	229,496			2,904,496
Debits:					
Cost of goods sold	2,055,000	172,600		(b) 25,000	2,202,600
Expenses	259,690	20,000			279,690
Depreciation expense	65,100	6,510			71,610
Net income—parent	350,596		(c) 30,386	(a) 30,386	350,596
Net income—subsidiary		30,386		(c) 30,386	
Total	2,730,386	229,496	85,772	85,772	2,904,496

(a) To eliminate share of subsidiary's earnings included in parent company net income.
(b) To eliminate intercompany purchases and sales, item (6) of additional data.
(c) To allocate subsidiary net income to parent.

Once the accounts of the foreign subsidiary have been translated into dollars, the procedure for consolidating the two companies is identical with that employed for the consolidation of a parent and a domestic subsidiary. The parent company may elect to carry its investment in the subsidiary at cost or at cost plus its share of the earnings of the subsidiary earned since the date of acquisition of the investment. When investments in foreign subsidiaries are carried on the equity basis, the income stated in terms of dollars is added to the investment account, as illustrated below for the National Company.

Investment: Equity Basis	*30,386*	
Earnings of German Subsidiary		*30,386*
To record the parent's share of the subsidiary's earnings for the year.		

Also, when the equity method is used, any dividends received from the subsidiary are deducted from the investment. The entry to record the dividend paid would be:

Cash	*4,800*	
Investment: Equity Basis		*4,800*
To record receipt of cash dividend for German subsidiary. The investment account is carried at cost plus parent's share of undistributed earnings.		

Questions

1. What is the difficulty of reporting on foreign operations carried on by a domestic company? How can this difficulty be overcome?

2. Where more than one exchange rate exists between two currencies at a given date, how should one select the most appropriate rate to use in the translation of foreign account balances to dollars?

3. What disposition should be made of gains and losses arising from fluctuations in the exchange rate between two currencies when there are fixed commitments in terms of one of the currencies?

4. An American company has an account receivable of 10,000 pounds which is to be satisfied in pounds. At the time the receivable arose, the exchange rate between dollars and pounds was 1 pound equals 2.8 dollars. At the date the receivable is collected the exchange rate is 1 pound equals 2.76 dollars. Make the entry to record the collection of the receivable by the American firm.

5. When should exchange gains and losses be recognized?

6. When a domestic company holds real goods in a foreign country, should exchange gains and losses be shown when there are fluctuations in the exchange rate?

7. Why is there concern about preparing consolidated statements for a domestic parent company and a foreign subsidiary?

8. Contrast the AICPA position and the authors' position on the translation of balance sheet accounts.

9. What is the disagreement between the AICPA and the authors over the translation of income statement data?

10. What is meant by the term *devaluation* when used in discussing the currency of a country?

11. What additional accounting problem is raised when there is a devaluation of one currency in terms of another?

12. What effect do exchange restrictions have on reporting foreign operations of subsidiaries of domestic corporations?

Short cases for analysis

14-1 Mr. Fox, president of Fox Enterprises, Inc., is concerned about the consolidation of the parent company and its foreign subsidiaries. His concern is over the procedure recommended by the AICPA for the translation of inventory and plant asset account balances from foreign currencies into United States dollars.

Instructions

a. What is the AICPA position on the translation into dollars of foreign currency balances of plant assets held by foreign branches or subsidiaries and of inventory purchased by a foreign branch in the foreign currency?

b. In your opinion, is such a position justified? Explain your position using accounting principles underlying accounting in the United States as the basis of your argument.

14-2 On January 1 the Heath Corporation opened a manufacturing and selling branch in a foreign country. You are concerned with preparing financial statements for the Heath Corporation at December 31, the end of the accounting period. You find the following accounts in the trial balance of the branch. In addition you learn that all current transfers of funds are executed at the free-market rate.

(1) Sales
(2) Remittances from home office
(3) Accounts receivable, trade
(4) Office equipment (purchased in the United States and paid for in United States dollars)
(5) Factory building
(6) Inventory of finished goods, December 31
(7) Mortgage payable on factory building (due December 31, 1987)
(8) Inventory of finished goods, January 1 (shipped from home office)
(9) Notes payable to bank (due January 31 of the following year)
(10) Accumulated depreciation on the factory

Instructions

a. Following the AICPA recommendations, indicate at which of the following exchange rates each account would be converted into United States dollars.

(1) The official rate of currency exchange at the date of payment, acquisition, or entry
(2) The official rate of currency exchange at December 31
(3) The free-market rate at the date of acquisition, entry, or payment
(4) The free-market rate at December 31
(5) An average rate of official currency exchange for the year
(6) The average free-market rate for the year or for each month of the year
(7) None of the above (If you use this answer, indicate what rate you would use.)

b. What differences would there be in your answer if instead of adopting the

AICPA position you followed the approach suggested in the text? Explain why these differences would exist.

AICPA adapted

14-3 The Intercontinental Corporation, with its home office in the United States and branches in foreign countries, prepares consolidated financial statements which reflect the assets and liabilities and the operating results in such locations. The accounts of the foreign branches are kept in the respective currencies of the countries in which they are situated.

Instructions

a. Explain the basis of translating the statements prepared in foreign currencies for purposes of consolidation with that of the home office, with respect to each of the following items:

Accounts receivable—trade debtors	Accrued payroll
Sales	Depreciation of building
Factory building	Home office account

b. Explain the nature of any difference between the debits and credits of a foreign branch trial balance after it has been translated to the currency of the home office.

AICPA adapted

14-4 **a.** The ABC Manufacturing Corporation during the current year opened a manufacturing and selling branch in X Country. At the year-end, the official rate of currency exchange with Country X was 12 to $1, and the unofficial free-market rate was 15 to $1. In combining the statements of the branch with those of the parent at year-end, how would the following branch accounts be translated for use in the combined balance sheet?

(1) Accounts receivable
(2) Fixed assets
(3) Inventories
(4) Short-term debt
(5) Long-term debt

b. How is the gain or loss resulting from the translation of the foreign currency into United States currency reflected in the balance sheet of ABC Manufacturing Corporation at year-end?

c. On June 30, 1966, ABC sold merchandise costing $75,000 to Z located in Y Country, taking a note payable in Y currency, which at the official rate of exchange on the date of sale had a fair-market value of $100,000. On December 31, 1966, the note was worth $75,000 because of a change in the rate of exchange. On March 15, 1967, the note was paid in full and, when immediately converted to United States dollars, ABC received $125,000. What journal entries are required at June 30, 1966, December 31, 1966, and March 16, 1967? Explain.

AICPA adapted

Problems

14-5 Artisans, Inc., is an American importer of foreign-made gift items. The following purchases were made from an exporter in Norway:

Date	*Norwegian kronen*	*Exchange rate of kronen on date of sale*
Feb. 16	*8,331.0*	*$.2777*
Apr. 28	*9,740.5*	*.2783*
July 17	*6,940.0*	*.2776*
Oct. 12	*12,260.5*	*.2769*

The bills for the above purchases were paid as follows:

Date	*Exchange rate of 1 kronen on date of payment*
Mar. 7	*$.2779*
May 25	*.2778*
Aug. 14	*.2775*
Nov. 5	*.2773*

Instructions

Record the above transactions on the books of both the buyer and seller in general journal form assuming (1) that all billings were made in terms of Norwegian kronen and (2) that all billings were made in terms of United States dollars.

14-6 Domestic Corp. is interested in establishing a market for its product in western Europe. After a series of unsuccessful attempts to get foreign companies to stock the item, Domestic decided to try to create consumer demand by placing the goods in a French dealer's hands on a consignment agreement. The agreement called for the dealer to stock the goods and to remit to Domestic Corp. the advertised price of the goods less a 15% commission within 30 days after sale. The dealer is to pay for the goods in francs.

The following transactions occurred during the last quarter of the Domestic Corp.'s accounting period. The consignment inventory is maintained on a fifo basis.

Consignment Shipments

Date	*Cost, dollars*	*Exchange rate of 1 franc*	*Selling price, francs*
Oct. 5	*$ 7,680*	*$.2040*	*64,000*
Nov. 10	*11,040*	*.2044*	*92,000*
Dec. 12	*12,636*	*.2042*	*105,300*

Reported Sales

Date	*Selling price, francs*	*Exchange rate of 1 franc*
Oct. 31	*41,600*	*$.2043*
Nov. 30	*67,500*	*.2043*
Dec. 31	*91,400*	*.2039*

Receipt of Remittance

Date	*Francs*	*Exchange rate of 1 franc*
Nov. 20	*35,360*	*$.2044*
Dec. 20	*57,375*	*.2041*

Instructions

Prepare journal entries on the books of Domestic Corp. to account for the transactions with the foreign dealer for the three-month period. Also make any year-end adjustments necessary relative to these transactions. Assume that exchange gains and losses are to be separated from sales.

14-7 XYZ Company of Seattle and its Vancouver, B. C., branch report balances as follows at December 31, 1967.

Accounts	*Seattle*	*Vancouver*
Current assets	*$ 75,000*	*$ 45,000*
Fixed assets, net	*150,000*	*100,000*
Prepaid expenses	*5,000*	*3,000*
Vancouver	*100,000*	
Expenses	*65,000*	*35,000*
Cost of sales	*375,000*	*105,000*
Total assets	*$770,000*	*$288,000*
Current liabilities	*$ 25,000*	*$ 33,000*
Seattle		*105,000*
Sales	*400,000*	*150,000*
Shipments a/c Vancouver	*95,000*	
Capital stock	*100,000*	
Surplus	*150,000*	
Total liabilities & equity	*$770,000*	*$288,000*

Additional information

(1) A remittance of $10,000 Canadian was mailed December 27, 1967, from Vancouver but was not received and entered in Seattle until January 3, 1968.

(2) The Canadian fixed assets were acquired in 1957.

(3) Depreciation has been charged on the Vancouver books at 5% per annum; assume that none was charged in the year of acquisition.

(4) Seattle ships on order direct to Vancouver's customers; no inventory is carried at Vancouver except $6,000 worth of samples and display stock, included in current assets at an arbitrary figure of 150% of current year's cost. Other billings on account of Vancouver shipments are at Seattle cost. No changes have occurred in the Vancouver stock during the year. Vancouver sells Seattle products exclusively and makes no outside purchases.

(5) The free rate for Canadian dollars in terms of American currency is:

1957 average	*$1.00*
1962 average	*.88*
1967 average	*.92*
Dec. 31, 1967	*.88*

Instructions

Prepare a work sheet showing a combined income statement and a combined balance sheet.

14-8 The Wiend Corporation acquired The Dieck Corporation on January 1, 1965, by the purchase at book value of all outstanding capital stock. The Dieck Corporation is located in a Central American country whose monetary unit is the peso. The Dieck Corporation's accounting records were continued without change; a trial balance, in pesos, of the balance sheet accounts at the purchase date follows:

THE DIECK CORPORATION
Trial Balance (in pesos)
January 1, 1965

	Debit	*Credit*
Cash	*3,000*	
Accounts receivable	*5,000*	
Inventories	*32,000*	
Machinery and equipment	*204,000*	
Allowance for depreciation		*42,000*
Accounts payable		*81,400*
Capital stock		*50,000*
Retained earnings		*70,600*
Totals	*244,000*	*244,000*

The Dieck Corporation's trial balance, in pesos, at December 31, 1966, appears on page 487.

The following additional information is available:

(1) All The Dieck Corporation's export sales are made to its parent company and are accumulated in the account, Sales—Foreign. The balance in the account, Due from The Wiend Corporation, is the total of unpaid invoices. All foreign sales are billed in United States dollars. The reciprocal accounts on the parent company's books show total 1966 purchases as $471,000 and the total of unpaid invoices as $70,500. The inventory was acquired uniformly throughout the year.

THE DIECK CORPORATION
Trial Balance (in pesos)
December 31, 1966

Cash	*25,000*	
Accounts receivable	*20,000*	
Allowance for bad debts		*500*
Due from The Wiend Corporation	*30,000*	
Inventories, Dec. 31, 1966	*110,000*	
Prepaid expenses	*3,000*	
Machinery and equipment	*210,000*	
Allowance for depreciation		*79,900*
Accounts payable		*22,000*
Income taxes payable		*40,000*
Notes payable		*60,000*
Capital stock		*50,000*
Retained earnings		*100,600*
Sales—domestic		*170,000*
Sales—foreign		*200,000*
Cost of sales	*207,600*	
Depreciation	*22,400*	
Selling and administration expenses	*60,000*	
Gain on sales of assets		*5,000*
Provision for income taxes	*40,000*	
Totals	*728,000*	*728,000*

(2) Depreciation is computed by the straight-line method over a 10-year life for all depreciable assets. Machinery costing 20,000 pesos was purchased on December 31, 1965, and no depreciation was recorded for this machinery in 1965. No other depreciable assets have been acquired since January 1, 1965, and no assets are fully depreciated.

(3) Certain assets that were in the inventory of fixed assets at January 1, 1965, were sold on December 31, 1966. For 1966 a full year's depreciation was recorded before the assets were removed from the books. Information regarding the sale follows:

	Pesos
Cost of assets	*14,000*
Accumulated depreciation	*4,900*
Net book value	*9,100*
Proceeds of sale	*14,100*
Gain on sale	*5,000*

(4) Notes payable are long-term obligations that were incurred on December 31, 1965.

(5) No entries have been made in the Retained Earnings account of the subsidiary since its acquisition other than the net income for 1965. The Retained Earnings account at December 31, 1965, was converted to $212,000.

(6) The prevailing rates of exchange appear on page 488.

	Dollars per peso
Jan. 1, 1965	*2.00*
1965 average	*2.10*
Dec. 31, 1965	*2.20*
1966 average	*2.30*
Dec. 31, 1966	*2.40*

Instructions

Prepare a work sheet to convert the December 31, 1966, trial balance of The Dieck Corporation from pesos to dollars. The work sheet should show the unconverted trial balance, the conversion rate, and the converted trial balance.

AICPA adapted

14-9 The Harrison Corporation opened a branch in West Germany on January 1. The transactions relative to the branch operation are summarized below:

Remittances to branch:
Draft for 15,900 deutsche marks, exchange rate $.2516
Draft for 20,000 deutsche marks, exchange rate $.2508
Shipments to branch:
Merchandise cost $14,500, exchange rate $.2516
Merchandise cost $16,000, exchange rate $.2520
Purchases by branch on account:
Merchandise cost 24,800 deutsche marks, exchange rate $.2520
Fixed assets cost 4,800 deutsche marks, exchange rate $.2518
Merchandise cost 18,000 deutsche marks, exchange rate $.2510
Sales:
On account 106,000 deutsche marks
Cash 8,000 deutsche marks
Collections:
On account 104,000 deutsche marks
Expenses:
On account 14,000 deutsche marks
Cash payment 4,500 deutsche marks
Purchases by home office for branch:
Fixed assets 6,500 deutsche marks, exchange rate $.2512
Remittances from branch:
Draft for 14,000 deutsche marks, exchange for dollars at $.2514
Draft for $2,000 purchased at exchange rate of $.2508
Branch payment:
Purchase accounts 30,000 deutsche marks
Fixed asset acquisition 4,800 deutsche marks
Expenses 13,000 deutsche marks
Ending inventory:
Merchandise costing 78,000 deutsche marks, of which 60,000 purchased when exchange rate was $.2520 and 18,000 purchased when exchange rate was $.2510

Depreciation:

Fixed assets are estimated to have a 10-year life; the straight-line method is used; and a half-year's depreciation is charged in year of acquisition.

Exchange rates:

Average rate for the year is $.2514

Year-end rate is $.2512

Instructions

a. Prepare journal entries to record the year's transactions on the books of the home office and the branch.

b. Prepare a pre-closing trial balance for the branch and translate West German marks to dollars.

c. Prepare closing entries for the year on both the home office and branch books.

14-10 The trial balances of Southern Company and its wholly owned Canadian subsidiary, Northwest, Ltd., are presented below:

Trial Balances
December 31

	Southern Company U.S. dollars		*Northwest, Ltd. Canadian dollars*	
	Dr	*Cr*	*Dr*	*Cr*
Cash	$ 50,000		$ 40,000	
Accounts receivable	80,000		30,000	
Allowance for uncollectibles		$ 5,000		$ 2,000
Merchandise inventory	100,000		50,000	
Prepaid expenses	10,000			
Land	300,000		100,000	
Building	3,500,000		2,700,000	
Accumulated depreciation		375,000		250,000
Furniture and fixtures	500,000		300,000	
Accumulated depreciation		75,000		40,000
Investment in common stock of Northwest, Ltd.	2,200,000			
Accounts payable		90,000		50,000
Accounts payable to parent				10,000
Capital stock—par value		4,000,000		1,500,000
Capital paid-in in excess of par value		1,500,000		500,000
Retained earnings		1,095,575		678,000
Sales		5,000,000		2,200,000
Purchases	4,700,000		1,550,000	
Expenses	500,000		300,000	
Depreciation	80,000		60,000	
Dividends	120,000		100,000	
Exchange gain or loss	575			
Totals	$12,140,575	$12,140,575	$5,230,000	$5,230,000

Additional data

Merchandise inventory of Northwest, Ltd., at December 31, $60,000; acquired at average exchange rate of the last quarter.

Merchandise inventory of Southern Company at December 31, $80,000.

All plant assets were held by subsidiary at the date the investment by Southern Company was made.

Investment in stock of subsidiary is carried on the equity basis. Earnings of the subsidiary since acquisition have totaled 240,000 Canadian dollars, translated to 228,000 United States dollars.

Purchases totaling 125,000 Canadian dollars were acquired from the parent. The billing price to the subsidiary was 125% of cost and all billings were made to the subsidiary in Canadian dollars. The parent kept its records in terms of American dollars with a memorandum of the billing price. When accounts were settled, the difference between the billing price in American dollars and the American dollars received when the Canadian currency is converted were charged or credited to exchange gain or loss. At December 31 all accounts have been settled except for an amount of 10,000 Canadian dollars recorded on the parent's books at 9,200 United States dollars. Of the goods purchased by Northwest from Southern 20% are held in the ending inventory.

Dividends were paid by the subsidiary on December 31.

Beginning inventory of subsidiary was acquired during the last quarter of the prior year and the fifo inventory method is used.

Official exchange rates for the Canadian dollar are:

At date of investment	*$.986*
Beginning of the year	*.934*
Average for the year	*.930*
Average for the last quarter	*.925*
End of the year	*.920*
Average for the last quarter of prior year	*.935*

Instructions

Prepare consolidated statement working papers to show the consolidation of Southern Company and Northwest, Ltd. Also include your schedule showing the conversion of the subsidiary accounts from Canadian to American dollars.

14-11 Trial balances as of December 31, 1966, of the Parent Company and its two subsidiaries appear on page 491.

Additional data

In April, 1966, the Mexican peso was devalued from U.S. $.12, the prevailing rate of exchange on December 31, 1965, to $.08, which was also the prevailing rate of exchange on December 31, 1966. All sales by parent to subsidiary are made at regular selling prices.

	Parent company, dollars		Domestic subsidiary, dollars		Mexican subsidiary, pesos	
	Dr	Cr	Dr	Cr	Dr	Cr
Cash	$ 10,000		$ 1,500		10,000	
Accounts receivable—trade	30,000		8,000		35,000	
Accounts receivable—merchandise in transit to domestic subsidiary	4,000					
Inventories	20,000				83,000	
Investments at cost:						
Domestic subsidiary: 900 shares acquired Dec. 31, 1965	9,000					
Foreign subsidiary: 1,000 shares acquired Dec. 31, 1965	12,000					
Fixed assets	45,000		3,500		175,000	
Goodwill			2,000			
Cost of sales	300,000		15,000		300,000	
Depreciation	3,000		200		7,000	
Taxes	15,000		400		15,000	
Selling expenses	42,000		2,400		27,000	
Administrative and general expenses	35,000		2,000		18,000	
Dividends declared			1,000			
Sales—trade		$400,000		$21,000		381,000
Sales—domestic subsidiary		10,000				
Accounts payable—trade		25,000				7,000
Dividend payable				1,000		
Long-term debt due Jan. 1, 1970						100,000
Accumulated depreciation		15,000		2,000		75,000
Capital stock		50,000		10,000*		100,000*
Retained earnings, Jan. 1, 1966		25,000		2,000		7,000
Totals	$525,000	$525,000	$36,000	$36,000	670,000	670,000

* 1,000 shares issued and outstanding.

Instructions

a. Prepare a working trial balance in United States dollars for the Mexican subsidiary.

b. Prepare working papers for consolidated statements.

AICPA adapted

PRICE-LEVEL CHANGES

PART FOUR

15 CHANGING PRICE LEVELS AND FINANCIAL REPORTING

Money serves three major functions in our economy: (1) as a medium of exchange, (2) as a store of purchasing power, and (3) as a standard of value. It is the third function with which we are primarily concerned in accounting. The dollar, when used to describe the value of commodities or services, is a measuring rod of economic size, as the yardstick is a measuring rod of physical size. Unlike the yardstick, the dollar has no prescribed economic length. The economic "length" of the dollar is its ability to command goods and services. As the economy experiences periods of inflation (rising price level) and deflation (declining price level), the number of dollars required to command a given quantity of goods or services changes.

In using the dollar as a unit of economic measurement, the accountant appears to assume that the ability of the dollar to command goods and services is unchanging over time. This assumption clearly is not in accord with economic reality in the United States or in most other countries. When he employs a changing measuring rod to express unlike commodities and services in terms of a common denominator, the accountant in fact adds together quantities which are not measured by the same standard. As we have seen (in Chapter 14) there is reluctance to add together Canadian and United States dollars. It is similarly misleading to add 1958 and 1966 dollars if the length of the dollar has changed significantly.

An index of prices is commonly used as a measure of the "economic length" of the dollar. A price index is a weighted-average relation between money and a given set of goods and services. For example, if we say that it now takes $550 to acquire certain goods and services whereas two years ago it required only $500, we imply that the economic length of the dollar is decreased by 10%. Although the physical quantities and quality of goods and services are the same in two periods, we might express the aggregate in dollars as $500 in one period and as $550 two years later. In order to combine quantities of real goods into meaningful aggregates, it is necessary for them to be measured in terms of a common measuring rod, *dollars of equal purchasing power.*

The problem of constructing a price index which measures the change in the economic length of the dollar is complex. There are problems of excluding price changes which reflect payment for improved technology. There is the practical problem of determining what the prices of the items included in the index are. In addition there are the problems of determining the economic importance of (that is, assigning relative weights to) the items and of deciding which average (arithmetic mean, geometric mean, or median) is appropriate. The calculation of a simple index in which the major problems are resolved by assumption is illustrated below:

Calculation of a Simple Price Index for Period 1

Commodity	*Relative weights*	*Base-period unit price*	*Period 1 unit price*	*Base-period amount*	*Period 1 amount*
Wheat	100	$2.00	$2.20	$200	$220
Corn	70	1.50	1.40	105	98
Lead	30	3.00	3.00	90	90
Copper	50	4.50	4.70	225	235
Zinc	20	3.20	2.90	64	58
				$684	$701

Price index = $701/$684 = 102.5
(Calculation rounded to nearest 1⁄10 of 1%)

From this illustration it is easy to see that individual prices did not change in the same direction or in the same degree as the price level. The price index reflects the weighted-average change in the prices of goods and services during the interval over which the index applies. The weights (usually assigned in terms of quantities purchased) represent an attempt to allow for the fact that some goods or services are of greater importance than others.

Measures of general price changes

There are several indices of price change which are computed regularly by departments of the United States government. The more widely used ones are described below:

1. *The Consumer Price Index* measures the average change in the retail prices of approximately 300 goods and services purchased by wage and clerical–worker families in the United States. The goods and services are similar in quality and quantity in consecutive periods except for changes necessitated because some items are no longer available.

2. *The Wholesale Price Index* measures average changes in prices of approximately 2,200 commodities sold in primary markets. The index includes fabricated parts as well as raw materials. There are subindices of this index which relate to individual industries, commodities, and product classes.

3. *The 22 Commodity Spot Price Index* measures daily the average change in price of 22 primary materials, including 9 foodstuffs and 13 raw materials. These commodities contain very little labor cost and are very sensitive to changes in economic conditions.

4. *The Composite Construction Cost Index* is a combination of various construction cost indices weighted as to the relative importance of the major classes of construction. Unlike the indices of commodity prices, described above, which are indices of output, this index is a measure of the relative change in cost of the units of input, that is, wage rates and materials cost.

5. *The GNP Implicit Price Deflator* measures the relationship between the total value of all goods and services produced in a given year expressed in current dollars and those same goods and services expressed in dollars of a base year. This index is the most comprehensive one we have at the present time.

The Consumer Price Index and the GNP Implicit Price Deflator have moved in the same direction and by approximately the same magnitude over the period since World War II. The Consumer Price Index is reported monthly whereas the Deflator is reported quarterly. Because of its timeliness (and its known past relation to the Deflator), the Consumer Price Index is often used as a current measure of the change in average prices or in the general purchasing power of the dollar in spite of the fact that it is not so comprehensive as the Implicit Price Deflator. AICPA's *Accounting Research Study No. 6* concludes that the GNP Implicit Price Deflator is a reliable index of general price-level change in the United States, at least since 1945.

Measures of specific price changes

There are also indices of average price change for many specific groups of goods and services. There are subindices of the Consumer Price Index; for example, price indices for food, housing, clothing, durable goods, nondurable goods, and services are computed. The Wholesale Price Index also has many subindices of specific industries, commodities, and products. As indicated, the Composite Construction Cost Index is a combination of various construction indices, such as residential building, except farm; farm buildings; nonresidential building; public utilities; military facilities; highways; and many others.

There are, therefore, many different measures of the change in the command of the dollar over goods and services. If the accountant wishes to depart from the use of the dollar as a standard unit of measure, which of these many indices of change in the value of money is most appropriate in translating all dollars to a common base?

Structural price changes versus general price changes

The pattern of price changes is such that we find it difficult to know exactly whether there has been a shift in the relative value of products or whether there has been a general change in prices and a corresponding change in the value of money. The example on page 496 shows a general increase of 2.5% in the prices of all commodities included in the sample; however, some of the prices increased more than 2.5%, some decreased, and one remained unchanged. We would say in this case that the average price level (in terms of these particular commodities) rose by 2.5% and the value or purchasing power of money decreased by 2.5%. The measuring rod is shorter in period 1 than in the base period by 2.5%. If the price changes had been such that the increases in price were offset by the decreases, there would have been no change in the value of money but the relative value of the individual commodities would have changed. The significant thing to note is that the price change of any particular commodity may reflect a change in its real value relative to all other goods. The change may be affected by a general change in the price level, however.[1] For this reason we find it extremely difficult to isolate price changes of particular goods and state that they are structural or general, in spite of the following definition:

> A change in the structure of prices involves a change in the prices of certain goods and services relative to the prices of other goods and services, with, therefore, a change in the real economic value of both sets of goods and services. A change in the general price level involves only a proportional change in the prices of all goods and services. If there is a change only in the general price level, this does not in itself imply a change in the value of any good or service, but does imply a change in the value of money and of obligations expressed in terms of a certain amount of money.[2]

Consider the case of Wilson Corporation. The company acquired a tract of land in 1960 for a total price of $100,000. Just recently Wilson received an offer of $400,000 for the land. The price level during this period has risen from 90 to 120; therefore, in terms of current dollars the land cost $133,333 ($100,000 × 120/90). At what dollar amount should Wilson Corporation carry the land on its balance sheet? In terms of currently accepted accounting principles, the land would be carried at historical cost, $100,000. There is evidence, however, that its current-dollar value is $400,000; therefore, Wilson, in effect, has $400,000 invested in the land at this time as a result of the decision not to sell but to use the land in its business. The historical cost of the land expressed in terms of the current dollar is $133,333.

In many instances specific evidence of the market value of a particular asset is not available. Adams Company has a building which cost $500,000 to construct 10 years ago. The life of the building has been estimated to be 50 years with no salvage value at that time. During the past 10 years the index of nonresidential construction cost has increased from 80 to 150 while the general price level, as measured by the Consumer Price Index, has changed from 100 to 115. The cost to construct this building today might be estimated as $937,500 ($500,000 × 150/80); as measured by the current dollar the building has a cost of $575,000 ($500,000 × 115/100). The accumulated depreciation in each case would be 20% of the carrying value of the asset, assuming that the estimated life is correct and that the straight-line method of depreciation is the appropriate means of

[1] See chap. 3 of *Intermediate Accounting* in this series for a discussion of this point.

[2] John E. Kane, "Structural Changes and General Changes in the Price Level in Relation to Financial Reporting," *The Accounting Review*, vol. 26, October, 1951, p. 496.

allocating the cost of the building between time periods. The unamortized cost of the building would thus be in terms of historical cost $400,000 ($500,000 − .20 × $500,000); current nonresidential construction cost $750,000 ($937,500 − .20 × $937,500); or current purchasing power of the dollar, $460,000 ($575,000 − .20 × $575,000).

A specific price index measures changes in the structure of prices and a general index measures changes in the general level of prices. The choice among the three amounts (historical cost, replacement cost, and cost expressed in current dollars) as a dollar measure of the building rests on the accountant's criteria for measuring business position and performance.

There is agreement that one of the accountant's most important functions is to measure the accomplishments (revenues) and efforts (expired costs) of a business during specified periods of time. Matching these two aggregates provides a measure of the success (profit) of the entity for the period. Simultaneously, and partly as a result of the double-entry system, the accountant measures financial position at the beginning and end of the period. He assumes that revenue (represented by an increase in the quantity A − L) and expenses (represented by a decrease in the quantity A − L) incurred in earning this revenue are the variables in measuring the success of the endeavor. In an attempt to provide an objective appraisal of business activity, the point of sale has been generally accepted as the appropriate time for recognizing revenue, and expenses of earning this revenue are stated in terms of cost to the enterprise. Both these items are based on market transactions measured in terms of dollars at the transaction date. Thus has evolved the assumption (implicit in the accounting process) that the length of the dollar, as a standard of measure, is constant over time.

The American Accounting Association in its 1957 restatement of standards of corporate reporting made the following statement:

> It has sometimes been suggested that the current or anticipated replacement cost of specific types of assets be used as a means of measuring the current dollar costs of capital "consumed." This, however, would represent a departure from recorded historical cost and thereby would destroy to a considerable degree the objectivity of accounting. The cost of "consuming" existing capital should be determined irrespective of the intention to replace in kind, to replace with a different type of capital, or not to replace at all. This conclusion appears to rule out, in the determination of income for periodic reporting to stockholders and other non-management groups, the use of either replacement costs or a price index specific to the particular kinds of assets "consumed" by a given corporation.
>
> In contrast, the adjustment of historical dollar costs—the restatement of these costs in current dollars of equivalent purchasing power as measured by a *general* price index—is independent of estimated replacement costs or replacement policy. It differs from the conventional original dollar cost concept only in that it recognizes changes in the value of the dollar and reflects these changes in the amortization of costs and in the determination of periodic income. Its application is independent of possible or probable future price changes, either upward or downward, since only past changes in the value of the dollar are reflected in the adjusted figures.

> The use of a measure of overall price levels as a basis for such adjustment is entirely consistent with the fact that initial investment is made as an alternative to all other possible business uses of funds and as recovered again becomes "free" for reinvestment or any other proper business use.[3]

The Committee on Accounting Procedures of the American Institute of Certified Public Accountants has given consideration at various times to the problem of the changing value of the dollar. The committee has been primarily concerned with the effect of inflation on the balance sheet valuation of fixed assets, particularly as related to the annual depreciation charge which is used in the determination of net income. On the basis of its formal pronouncements in *ARB 43,* the committee has apparently considered only the possibility of using replacement costs in accounting for depreciable assets. Specifically it states "an attempt to recognize current prices in providing depreciation, to be consistent, would require the serious step of formally recording appraised current values for all properties and continuous and consistent depreciation based on the new values." In 1961 the committee rejected this possibility with the following statement:

> Any basic change in the accounting treatment of depreciation should await further study of the nature and concept of business income.
>
> The immediate problem can and should be met by financial management. The committee recognizes that the common forms of financial statements may permit misunderstanding as to the amount which a corporation has available for distribution in the form of dividends, higher wages, or lower prices for the company's products. When prices have risen appreciably since original investments in plant and facilities were made, a substantial proportion of net income as currently reported must be reinvested in the business in order to maintain assets at the same level of productivity at the end of a year as at the beginning.
>
> Stockholders, employees, and the general public should be informed that a business must be able to retain out of profits amounts sufficient to replace productive facilities at current prices if it is to stay in business. The committee therefore gives its full support to the use of supplementary financial schedules, explanations or footnotes by which management may explain the need for retention of earnings.[4]

The accounting conventions which are challenged here, the stable money assumption and the realization convention and/or the cost assumption, need to be considered separately. The remaining portion of this chapter is devoted to a re-evaluation of the usefulness of the assumption that the length of the monetary unit is stable and a demonstration of how financial statements would be changed if accountants were to abandon this assumption. The succeeding chapter evaluates the usefulness of the realization convention and the cost assumption.

[3] Committee on Concepts and Standards Underlying Corporate Financial Statements, American Accounting Association, "Price Level Changes and Financial Statements," *Accounting and Reporting Standards for Corporate and Financial Statements* (Columbus, Ohio: 1957), p. 24.

[4] AICPA, *Accounting Research and Terminology Bulletins, Final Edition* (New York: 1961), p. 69.

Changing price levels and the assumption of a stable monetary unit

One problem the accounting profession faces at the present time is whether or not the assumption that the length of the monetary unit is unchanging should be abandoned. George O. May, a leader in the development of accounting in the United States, has stated:

> It has been said that the proposal here put forward contemplates a departure from the accepted manner of using the monetary unit as the unit of accounting. It has even been suggested . . . that the proposal involves the *adoption* of an elastic yardstick. But the yardstick used has always been elastic and its usefulness has been impaired (though not destroyed) by that fact. Today a natural elasticity has been supplanted by an artificial and purposive elasticity which goes much further towards destroying the appropriateness of the monetary unit for secondary employment in accounting in the same way as in the past.
>
> The proposal does not contemplate discontinuance of the use of the yardstick. It is intended only to use the yardstick intelligently with a frank recognition of its defects, rather than to close one's eyes to its shortcomings.[5]

The restatement of all dollar measurements in terms of a common unit does not involve the alteration of any other of the presently accepted accounting conventions. The effect of making this change is to allow the accountant to report that all quantities are measured with a standard measuring rod. The result is to achieve a more meaningful aggregation of data, an aggregate in which the different elements are converted to a common denominator before they are combined.[6]

In *Accounting Research Study No. 7,* Paul Grady asserts:

> The APB has already agreed in the 1961 resolution that, under prevailing conditions, the assumption in accounting that fluctuations in the value of the dollar may be ignored is unrealistic. If the Board agrees with the findings in *ARS No. 6* that a reliable index number series is available, at least, since 1945, it would seem that the only remaining question is whether business entities have an accountability for changes in capital resources and results of operations in terms of current purchasing power dollars as well as in historical or nominal dollars.

Mr. Grady feels that if the APB accepts the idea that businesses do have accountability for reporting in terms of current dollars the extent of inflation in the future will determine when such accountability becomes mandatory.

Conversion of recorded dollar cost

The procedure for converting historical-dollar costs to costs expressed in terms of the current purchasing power of the dollar is mathematically a simple process.

[5] G. O. May, *Business Income and Price Levels—An Accounting Study* (Privately printed, 1949), pp. 72–73.

[6] In *Accounting Research Study No. 6,* "Reporting the Financial Effects of Price-level Changes," the Staff of the Accounting Research Division of the AICPA has discussed the effect of changing prices on financial statements and has discussed in detail the procedures for translating the data to a common base.

As a matter of fact, it is quite similar to the translation of foreign currency balances to dollars discussed in detail in Chapter 14. The technique is to translate all dollar amounts to the base period—the period from which change is measured by the index. The base-period dollars can then be restated in terms of current-period dollars by multiplying the restated dollars by the price index for the current period.

Plant accounts. The mathematical technique of conversion of historical-dollar cost to current-dollar equivalent is illustrated first in connection with the plant accounts. The effect of price change is more apparent in the case of these assets because of the long holding period between time of purchase and retirement.

Assume that the Plant account is composed of the following dollar aggregates originating in the years indicated. The base period for the index is the period 1955–1957 and the price index for the current year, 1967, is 150.

Acquisition date	*Price index, 1955-57 base*	*Acquisition cost*
1948	*50*	*$1,200*
1956	*100*	*800*
1964	*140*	*1,400*

The useful life of the plant is estimated to be 40 years, with no net salvage at the end of that time. Using the indicated price index as a measure of the change in length of the measuring rod, the plant cost can be converted into 1967 dollars as follows:

Acquisition date	*Price index*	*Acquisition cost*		
		Recorded cost (mixed dollars)	*Base-period dollars**	*1967 dollars*†
1948	*50*	*$1,200*	*$2,400*	*$3,600*
1956	*100*	*800*	*800*	*1,200*
1964	*140*	*1,400*	*1,000*	*1,500*
		$3,400	*$4,200*	*$6,300*

* *Recorded cost divided by the price index of the year of acquisition*
† *Base-period dollars multiplied by 150, the price index in the current year, 1967*

Note the increase in the dollar aggregate representing the gross plant investment. The plant cost expressed in 1967 dollars does not represent current value; it reflects the market value at the time of purchase expressed in terms of current dollars. Historical cost expressed in 1967 dollars does not purport to represent the current market price of the asset or its 1967 replacement cost.

We should also note that the base-period-dollar column is also stated in terms of common dollars, 1955–1957 dollars. The restatement of these dollars in terms of 1967 dollars simply expresses the original costs in terms of the measuring unit currently in use, and thus the measuring unit most susceptible to valid interpretation by the reader of financial statements.

If we convert the original plant cost to the current-dollar equivalent, to be consistent we must also convert the related accumulated depreciation. The depreciation rate is 2.5% per year and it is assumed for simplicity that the additions were made at the beginning of each year. The balance of the Accumulated Depreciation account can be derived as follows:

Acquisition date	*Plant cost*	*Years in use*	*Plant cost depreciation, %*	*Accumulated depreciation*
1948	*$1,200*	*20*	*50*	*$600*
1956	*800*	*12*	*30*	*240*
1964	*1,400*	*4*	*10*	*140*
	$3,400			*$980*

The accumulated depreciation may be converted to current-dollar aggregates by using the same techniques which were used in the conversion of acquisition cost.

Acquisition date	*Price index*	*Accumulated depreciation based on acquisition cost*		
		Recorded cost (mixed dollars)	*Base-period dollars**	*1967 dollars†*
1948	*50*	*$600*	*$1,200*	*$1,800*
1956	*100*	*240*	*240*	*360*
1964	*140*	*140*	*100*	*150*
		$980	*$1,540*	*$2,310*

* *Recorded cost divided by the price index of the year of acquisition*
† *Base-period dollars multiplied by 150, the price index in the current year, 1967*

The effect of inflation on the value of money is clearly demonstrated. The net book value of plant expressed in terms of common dollars has increased from $2,420 ($3,400 – $980) to $3,990 ($6,300 – $2,310). This is an increase in total assets and in common stock equity of $1,570. Although this is a significant change, the total effect on earnings and the rate of return on common stock equity may well be more pronounced. Assume that our hypothetical company had total stock equity of $4,500 and net income for 1967 of $450 before conversion. The depreciation charge for 1967 is increased from $85 ($3,400 × .025) to $157.50 ($6,300 × .025). The increase in depreciation causes a similar reduction in net income from $450 to $377.50, or a 16.1% reduction in net income. The rate of return on common stock equity is therefore reduced from 10% ($450/$4,500) to 6.2% ($377.50/$6,070), a reduction of 38% in return on investment.

For several years the Indiana Telephone Company has prepared supplementary financial statements reflecting the effect of inflation on plant cost. Their financial statements for 1959 revealed the following results: Net income, after payment of preferred dividends of $62,704 and using traditional accounting procedures, totals $450,216; after adjustment of depreciation charges to a common-dollar basis, net income is $332,931. The common stock equity before adjustment for the effect of inflation on plant assets totals $2,954,134; after adjusting plant assets, the stock equity totals $4,578,067. The rate of return on common stock equity therefore declined from 15.2% ($450,216/$2,954,134) to 7.3% ($332,931/$4,578,067).

In the notes to financial statements of Indiana Telephone Company, Note (1) related to "Property cost consumed in current year's operations" states:

> This represents the cost of plant capacity consumed during the period indicated and received by telephone users in the form of service for which they pay rates presumably sufficient to cover such cost, including a fair return on the property.
>
> Since the dollars of revenue from customers in a given period are current dollars as of that period, the cost of property currently consumed should also be expressed in current dollars.
>
> . . . .
>
> The additional cost of plant consumed in operations, resulting from the adjustments made to state such costs on the basis of current cost of plant, is not allowable for Federal income tax under the present Internal Revenue Code. Therefore, the Federal income tax for the year 1959 is stated in Column B in the same amount as it is stated in Column A. If this additional amount of $117,285.26 were allowable as a deduction for tax for the year 1959, it would result in a reduction of $60,988.34 in Federal income tax for that year.

The independent certified public accountants' opinion on these statements is interesting in that it is a departure from the typical opinion paragraph.

> In our opinion the above described statements present fairly the financial position of the corporation at the end of the stated years and the results of its operations for the stated periods in conformity with generally accepted accounting methods applied on a consistent basis. However, such accounting methods show allowances for plant consumed in current operations expressed in dollars as recorded at the respective dates of acquisition and construction, but do not recognize the effect of changing price levels on the value of the dollars.
>
> Under Column B are shown the data of the financial position as of December 31, 1959, and the results of operation for the year 1959 after conversion of the recorded dollars of plant cost of varying dates of acquisition, and the related current and accumulative allowances for plant consumed in operations, expressed in dollars as recorded at the respective dates of acquisition and construction, converted to the common denominator of the current dollar. The conversions referred to are based upon indexes and methods determined by a professional engineer. The indexes and methods used have been reviewed

by us and in our opinion result in reasonably accurate conversion. Thus the financial results are more fairly presented.[7]

Inventory accounts. The effect of price-level changes on the inventory accounts varies widely, depending upon the method used in determining the flow of costs. The fifo method generally produces an inventory valuation which is expressed in terms of near-current dollars, because items comprising the ending inventory are usually held in stock for relatively short periods of time. The change in the level of prices in the United States has not been so rapid as to make the conversion of fifo inventory valuations essential to the preparation of meaningful financial statements in terms of current dollars. Some accountants contend that the fifo pricing procedure produces near-current-dollar values for the position statement, but that cost of goods sold is stated in mixed dollars. This is true, but one must look at the history of price-level changes in the United States to determine the significance of this factor. The period during and immediately following World War II, probably the period of greatest price-level change since 1929, witnessed general price-level changes of about 10% per year. During the decade of the 1950s and early 1960s, prices have increased about 2 to 3% per year. Since the inventory turnover period is usually rather short, the effect of general price changes on the cost of goods sold assigned to the determination of the year's income can hardly be considered large in relation to the comparative effect on the valuation of long-lived plant assets and related depreciation charges.

The lifo method produces an inventory valuation which is expressed in terms of dollars and prices of prior periods. The cost of goods sold under this procedure, however, is expressed in terms of the price level and prices prevailing when the most recent purchases were made. The lifo method does not accomplish the same result as that achieved by the procedure of converting historical-dollar cost to current-dollar cost for two reasons: (1) Where there are changes in the price of specific goods purchased which differ in size or direction from changes in the general price level, the cost of goods sold under the lifo method will be expressed in terms of mixed dollars, not common dollars; (2) in addition, the lifo method makes no provision for restating the ending inventory balance in terms of current dollars.

The procedure for converting the inventory cost to current dollars, whether the lifo or fifo method is used, is the same as that used to convert plant costs. Each layer of cost must be identified as to when it was added. The historical-dollar cost is then converted first to base-year dollars and then to current dollars, using a general price index. When applied to two identical operations, this procedure will not necessarily produce the same inventory balance nor the same cost of goods

[7] Indiana Telephone Company, Annual Report, 1959. The accountant in this case appears to have used a combination of a specific price index of construction costs and the index of wholesale prices. The construction cost index was apparently used to restate costs to a base year and the wholesale price index, as a measure of general price change, was used to restate the base-year data to later current-year dollar equivalents. In terms of our prior discussion in this chapter, the use of a general price index in converting original costs to current dollars would be appropriate. For purposes of discussion and illustration we have assumed, in the context of this chapter, that the current-dollar figures quoted are derived through the use of a general price index.

sold figure, where the lifo method is used in one and the fifo method in the other. The reason for the divergence is that the actual price changes at which goods were acquired may differ significantly from the change in the general price level. Therefore, the current-dollar cost of a fifo inventory stated in terms of 1948 prices may be quite different from the current cost of an identical inventory, in terms of physical units, stated in terms of 1967 prices. As a result, differences in income resulting from the use of different methods of valuing inventory will not be eliminated by the process of expressing accounting data in current dollars.

Inflation and monetary accounts[8]

Although managers and accountants readily recognize that asset costs and expenses are distorted when cost aggregates are not measured in terms of the same standard, the fact that a company may suffer losses through holding money or claims to money during inflationary periods is not so well understood. Many foreign managers appear to be better informed on this score. They have seen the effect of rapidly rising prices on the firm's ability to use its cash to acquire goods and services. In a country where inflation does not proceed at anything approaching the rate experienced in foreign countries, the effect of inflation on monetary assets is less noticeable but no less real. It is sometimes suggested that plant assets and depreciation may be understated in terms of current dollars but that the monetary accounts are automatically stated in current dollars. It is true that the monetary accounts are expressed in dollars as of the date of the balance sheet because these accounts reflect dollars or claims to or against dollars which represent current purchasing power. The effect of holding dollars over time, however, is not reflected in traditional accounting statements and this may be the more important piece of information. Consider the following case history of John Doe.

In 1950 John worked for All American Corporation. He was making a good salary and found that he was able to save $1,000 each year. He invested this money on January 1 of each year, beginning in January, 1950, in a savings account paying 3% interest compounded annually. On January 1, 1960, John, in reviewing the past 10 years, boasted proudly, "I invested $1,000 a year for 10 years and now I have $11,464." John was indeed very proud of his accomplishment until he told his story to an accountant, who informed him that in terms of purchasing power he had earned only $204 on his investment of $10,000 instead of $1,464 as John thought. John was rightfully disturbed and demanded an explanation. The accountant explained that John should be interested, not in dollars, but in command over goods and services. He then made the calculation for John shown on page 507.

The accountant explained that in 1960, $1,278 was required to purchase the same goods that could have been purchased for $1,000 in 1950; $1,189 was required to equal purchasing power of $1,000 in 1951; and in total $11,260 was required to purchase goods equivalent to those that could have been purchased for a total of $10,000 over the past 10 years.

In this case John has earned a small "real" profit on his savings. Every saver is not so fortunate. The loss which might occur as a result of holding cash or other

[8] The term *monetary accounts* as used refers to assets representing money or claims to money (cash, marketable securities, receivables) and all liabilities, since they require disbursement of a fixed quantity of dollars.

1974

DECEMBER

16

MONDAY

Deposit date	Amount of deposit	Conversion* multiplier	1960 dollars required to command same goods and services as original deposit
1950	$ 1,000	114.4/ 89.5	$ 1,278
1951	1,000	114.4/ 96.2	1,189
1952	1,000	114.4/ 98.1	1,166
1953	1,000	114.4/ 99.0	1,156
1954	1,000	114.4/100.0	1,144
1955	1,000	114.4/101.2	1,130
1956	1,000	114.4/104.6	1,094
1957	1,000	114.4/108.4	1,055
1958	1,000	114.4/110.8	1,032
1959	1,000	114.4/112.6	1,016
	$10,000		$11,260

* *Based on GNP Implicit Price Deflators reported in* Economic Report of the President, *January, 1963, Table C-6, p. 178.*

monetary accounts during a period of inflation is vividly portrayed in the case of Standard Oil Company of New Jersey's Hungarian subsidiary immediately after World War II. On July 1, 1945, 635 pengos was equal to one United States dollar. One year later, on July 1, 1946, 45,000,000,000,000,000 pengos equaled one dollar and on July 30, 1946, 30 days later, 4,600,000,000,000,000,000,000,000,000,000 pengos equaled one dollar. There is little doubt that a person or firm holding pengos during this period suffered a real loss.[9]

A much more modest degree of inflation has the same effect on a business holding cash and claims to cash as it does on John's savings account; however, the business may be able to offset a portion, if not all, of the loss from holding monetary assets by borrowing money on fixed-dollar contracts. In this way the firm loses purchasing power by holding monetary assets but gains by paying off contracts in dollars having less purchasing power than was present when the dollars were originally borrowed.

W. A. Paton, Jr., observes that, of 52 companies surveyed, 20 "show an increasing ratio between short-term monetary liabilities and monetary assets, a tendency to move toward the 'neutral position.'"[10] This suggests that an "acid test" or quick asset ratio of 1 to 1 is highly preferable, from the point of view of the effects of inflation, to one which indicates a higher proportion of monetary assets. The loss resulting from a decline in the purchasing power of the monetary unit is as real as any other loss. A well-informed manager may decide on other grounds that

[9] See Lloyd Paxon, "How a Large Oil Company Adjusted Its Accounts during Postwar Inflation behind the Iron Curtain," *The Journal of Accountancy,* August, 1951, pp. 190–196. Paxon quotes a study which concludes with the observation that to purchase one streetcar ticket in the latter days of the inflation would require an amount equivalent to the total gross rental income from all the real property in Budapest (a city of over 1 million population) for a period of 50,000 years.

[10] William A. Paton, Jr., *A Study in Liquidity* (University of Michigan, Ann Arbor: 1958), p. 99.

an acid test ratio of 1 to 1 is not feasible; however, if this is the case he should be aware of the potential cost of his decision, which includes the loss from holding money and claims to receive money in excess of claims to pay money in an inflationary period.

The following illustration will indicate one procedure for ascertaining the loss from holding monetary assets during a period of inflation. The increases and decreases in all monetary assets (cash, marketable securities, receivables) and all current liabilities grouped together for Smith Company are shown in the accompanying table. These data indicate that the net monetary asset position of Smith Company has improved substantially during 1967. The quick ratio increased from 1.6 to 3.18 to 1. When these mixed dollars are converted to common dollars the improvement is not so marked.

	Monetary assets		*Current liabilities*	
	Increases	*Decreases*	*Decreases*	*Increases*
1967				
Balance, Jan. 1	*$ 40,000*			*$ 25,000*
Quarter ending				
Mar. 31	*31,000*	*$ 25,000*	*$ 25,000*	*33,000*
June 30	*44,000*	*33,000*	*33,000*	*48,000*
Sept. 30	*60,000*	*48,000*	*48,000*	*20,000*
Dec. 31	*40,000*	*20,000*	*20,000*	*28,000*
Balance, Dec. 31		*89,000*	*28,000*	
	$215,000	*$215,000*	*$154,000*	*$154,000*
1968				
Balance, Jan. 1	*$ 89,000*			*$ 28,000*

The procedure for conversion of the monetary accounts is the same as that used for conversion of the nonmonetary accounts. We have assumed that the increases and decreases in the accounts have occurred uniformly during each

Conversion of Monetary Assets

	Original-transaction dollars	*General price index*	*Base-period dollars*	*Year-end general price index*	*Year-end dollars*
Balance, Jan. 1	*$40,000*	*80*	*$50,000*	*125*	*$ 62,500*
Net change:					
Increase (decrease):					
1st quarter	*6,000*	*100*	*6,000*	*125*	*7,500*
2d quarter	*11,000*	*110*	*10,000*	*125*	*12,500*
3d quarter	*12,000*	*120*	*10,000*	*125*	*12,500*
4th quarter	*20,000*	*125*	*16,000*	*125*	*20,000*
Balance, Dec. 31	*$89,000*		*$92,000*		*$115,000*

quarter so that the index for each quarter applies to all dollar amounts of the quarter. The year-end price level is unchanged from the fourth-quarter index. The monetary asset balance required at the end of the year to avoid a reduction in the purchasing power of the dollars that Smith Company holds would have been $115,000. The actual balance was $89,000; therefore, as a result of holding monetary assets, the company suffered a purchasing power loss of $26,000.

Similar computations should be made for the current liabilities to measure the purchasing power gain resulting from borrowing money on fixed-dollar contracts. The gain from borrowing on fixed-dollar contracts can be computed by comparing the fixed dollars actually owed with the purchasing power equivalent owed. The gain of $16,942 ($44,942 – $28,000) on current liabilities should be offset against the loss of $26,000 from holding monetary assets to determine the effect of inflation on the net monetary asset position.

Conversion of Current Liabilities

	Original-transaction dollars	General price index	Base-period dollars	Year-end general price index	Year-end dollars
Balance, Jan. 1	$25,000	80	$31,250	125	$39,063
Net change:					
Increase (decrease):					
1st quarter	8,000	100	8,000	125	10,000
2d quarter	15,000	110	13,636	125	17,045
3d quarter	(28,000)	120	(23,333)	125	(29,166)
4th quarter	8,000	125	6,400	125	8,000
Balance, Dec. 31	$28,000		$35,953		$44,942

Careful management of monetary items to avoid losses due to erosion of the purchasing power of the dollar may be equally as important as the protection of these assets from loss by theft or efforts to avoid loss of inventory or plant assets through obsolescence or deterioration.

Long-term liabilities. The effect of inflation on long-term liabilities is similar to the effect on current debts; that is, upward changes in the price level mean that the repayment of the debt will be made in dollars of lesser purchasing power. For this reason, long-term debt may also serve as a hedge against loss from inflation as a result of holding dollars or fixed-dollar claims. In the case of long-term liabilities, there is the question of when to realize the purchasing power gains and losses. The gains and losses on current items are usually considered part of the current period's operations by those who argue for price-level adjustments. The gains and losses on long-term monetary items have caused more difficulty. Since payment may be deferred for several periods, the direction of price-level change at any time short of due date may be reversed and the ultimate retirement of the debt may come at a time when the purchasing power of the dollar is greater than it was when a purchasing power gain was recognized in a previous period. In this event recognition of the subsequent decline in the price level (that is, the increase in the purchasing power of the dollar) would require the recognition of a loss in that period, which is in fact cancellation of a gain recognized in a prior period. Some accountants hold, therefore, that recognition of purchasing power gains and losses on long-term debt before retirement is not in accord with accepted accounting principles. Such a position seems unnecessarily conservative. A compromise approach is to separate the gains and losses on current and long-term liabilities and to label the latter "unrealized gains (losses) on long-term liabilities."

Accounting without the stable monetary assumption

To illustrate one technique of accounting for business transactions when the assumption of a stable monetary unit is abandoned, the following simplified yet comprehensive example is presented. In order to emphasize the essential points in the discussion, we have exaggerated the changes in the general price index. To simplify the illustration, large numbers of individual transactions have been combined.

The Monson Company began operations on January 2, 1967, with the sale of 55,000 shares of $10 par value common stock at par.

(1) The company acquired land and building for $150,000.

(2) A 6% mortgage for $100,000, due in annual payments of $5,000 each, was signed and $50,000 in cash was delivered to close the deal. The purchase price was allocated one-fourth to land and three-fourths to building. The building had an expected life of 25 years.

(3) $60,000 of merchandise, 6,000 units, was acquired on account.

(4) Equipment was acquired for $125,000 cash, estimated life 10 years, no salvage.

(5) Sales amounting to $125,000 were made on account.

(6) Expenses totaling $30,000 were incurred and paid.

(7) Accounts payable totaling $50,000 were paid.

(8) Accounts receivable totaling $105,000 were collected.

(9) Annual payment on mortgage plus interest for one year was paid.

(10) Merchandise sold cost $50,000.

The journal entries to record the transactions of Monson Company for the first year of operation are presented on page 511 in terms of dollars at date of transaction, in terms of base-year dollars (the year the price index equals 100), and in terms of current-year dollars (price index equals 140). The price index indicated to the left of the transaction is the assumed general price index at the time of the transaction. The price index at year-end was 140.

The working paper on page 513 for Monson Company includes (1) trial balance columns for actual dollars, base-period dollars, and current dollars; (2) income statement columns; (3) balance sheet columns; and (4) a column for monetary gains and losses. Note particularly that all figures carried forward to the statement columns are the current-dollar figures from the trial balance, except for the monetary items, in which case the actual balances are included on the balance sheet. The difference between the actual balance and the current-dollar balance is the monetary gain or loss for the period. The gains or losses on current items are considered realized; those on noncurrent items are unrealized.

The retained earnings of Monson Company at the end of the first year would be composed of the profit for the year, with revenues and expenses stated in cur-

General price index		Actual dollars		Base-year dollars		Current-year dollars	
110	(1) Cash	550,000		500,000		700,000	
	Common Stock		550,000		500,000		700,000
115	(2) Land	37,500		32,609		45,653	
	Building	112,500		97,826		136,956	
	Cash		50,000		43,478		60,869
	Mortgage Payable		100,000		86,957		121,740
120	(3) Merchandise	60,000		50,000		70,000	
	Accounts Payable		60,000		50,000		70,000
125	(4) Equipment	125,000		100,000		140,000	
	Cash		125,000		100,000		140,000
125	(5) Accounts Receivable	125,000		100,000		140,000	
	Sales		125,000		100,000		140,000
120	(6) Expenses	30,000		25,000		35,000	
	Cash		30,000		25,000		35,000
130	(7) Accounts Payable	50,000		38,462		53,847	
	Cash		50,000		38,462		53,847
130	(8) Cash	105,000		80,769		113,077	
	Accounts Receivable		105,000		80,769		113,077
140	(9) Mortgage Payable	5,000		3,571		5,000	
	Interest Expense	6,000		4,286		6,000	
	Cash		11,000		7,857		11,000
	(10) Depreciation	17,000		13,913		19,478	
115	Acc. Depr.: Bldg.		4,500		3,913		5,478
125	Acc. Depr.: Eqpt.		12,500		10,000		14,000
120	(11) Cost of Goods Sold	50,000		41,667		58,333	
	Merchandise		50,000		41,667		58,333

rent dollars, less the loss from holding net current monetary assets. The gain resulting from the long-term liability is not considered realized at the end of Year 1 and would be shown as a separate element in the owners' equity section of the balance sheet.

The year-end closing entries, in terms of current dollars, required (1) to recognize the loss on monetary accounts and adjust these accounts to their actual-dollar balance and (2) to close the nominal accounts to Retained Earnings are illustrated on page 512.

	Current year	
(a) Mortgage Payable	*21,740*	
Accounts Payable	*6,153*	
Realized Loss on Monetary Accounts	*124,131*	
Cash		*123,361*
Accounts Receivable		*6,923*
Unrealized Gain on Long-term Liability		*21,740*
(b) Retained Earnings	*102,942*	
Sales	*140,000*	
Cost of Goods Sold		*58,333*
Expenses		*35,000*
Depreciation		*19,478*
Interest Expense		*6,000*
Realized Loss on Monetary Accounts		*124,131*

Using accepted accounting principles, entry (a) above is not necessary and of course there is no loss on monetary accounts to close in the corresponding entry (b).

Comparative financial statements

During periods of changing price levels, the usefulness of comparative statements and accounting data is substantially improved if the dollar aggregates are converted to common units of measure. What does it mean to compare operating data showing growth in total revenues and net income or financial position over time if the unit of measure used in accumulating the data being compared is not comparable? Judgments made on the basis of such data may be in error because the facts are misinterpreted.

The procedure for translating comparative financial data to common dollars is essentially the same as that discussed for translation of other dollar aggregates to a common base: all data are expressed in dollars with the purchasing power equivalent of dollars of the current period. The thing which may seem unusual about the translation of prior-year account balances to current dollars is the fact that the monetary accounts of prior years must also be converted to current dollars for inclusion in comparative statements. In other words, how many 1967 dollars equal the purchasing power of the 1957 dollars held as cash at December 31, 1957? In statements of the current year, actual balances of monetary accounts will be reported. However, when we compare operations and financial position of 1967 with these same data for 1957, all data should be measured with the same yardstick. This means that the monetary account balances, like all other account balances of prior periods, 1957 in this illustration, must be stated in terms of 1967 dollars. The number of 1967 dollars required to equal the purchasing power of the 1957 dollar balance should be the balance of each account (monetary or nonmonetary) to be included on comparative financial statements of the years 1967 and 1957.

The translation of the Retained Earnings account to a current-dollar equivalent presents the same problems as the translation of any other account balance; all changes must be identified as to date of change, and the index prevailing at that

MONSON COMPANY
December 31, 1967

	Trial balance						Income statement		Balance sheet		
	Actual dollars Index = various		Base-year dollars Index = 100		Current dollars* Index = 140		Current dollars		Current dollars		Monetary† gain or (loss)
	Dr	Cr	Dr	Cr	Dr	Cr	Dr	Cr	Dr	Cr	
Cash	389,000		365,972		512,361				389,000		(123,361) (1)
Accounts receivable	20,000		19,231		26,923				20,000		(6,923) (2)
Merchandise	10,000		8,333		11,667				11,667		
Land	37,500		32,609		45,653				45,653		
Building	112,500		97,826		136,956				136,956		
Accumulated depreciation		4,500		3,913		5,478				5,478	
Equipment	125,000		100,000		140,000				140,000		
Accumulated depreciation		12,500		10,000		14,000				14,000	
Accounts payable		10,000		11,538		16,153				10,000	6,153 (3)
Mortgage payable		95,000		83,386		116,740				95,000	21,740 (4)
Common stock		550,000		500,000		700,000				700,000	
Sales		125,000		100,000		140,000		140,000			
Cost of goods sold	50,000		41,667		58,333		58,333				
Expenses	30,000		25,000		35,000		35,000				
Depreciation	17,000		13,913		19,478		19,478				
Interest expense	6,000		4,286		6,000		6,000				
Totals	797,000	797,000	708,837	708,837	992,371	992,371	118,811	140,000			
Net income							21,189			21,189	
Totals							140,000	140,000			(102,391)
Realized loss on monetary accounts									124,131		(124,131) (1 + 2 − 3)
Unrealized gain on long-term liability										21,740	21,740 (4)
Totals									867,407	867,407	102,391

*The current-dollar amount is obtained by multiplying the base-year dollar balances by the year-end index of 140.

† The monetary gain (or loss) results from holding cash and fixed-dollar receivables or from owing fixed-dollar payables during periods when the general price level is shifting. The amount of the gain (or loss) on monetary accounts is the difference between the actual dollar balance in the account and the current-dollar trial balance figure. The current-dollar figure in the trial balance columns is a restatement of net cash inflows and outflows at an amount which is equivalent (in current general purchasing power) to the dollars originally received and paid out. The gain on holding long-term debt during a period of general price increases is considered unrealized, for reasons discussed on pp. 509 to 510.

date is used in the translation. Frequently we do not make a detailed translation of the Retained Earnings account; instead the account is treated as a balancing amount. If all other account balances have been translated to current-dollar balances, then the Retained Earnings account balance will reflect the current-dollar equivalent of the layers comprising the balance.

The following data for Hoffmann's, Inc., will be used to illustrate the procedure for preparing comparative income statements and balance sheets for two periods 10 years apart stated in terms of a common measuring unit, 1967 dollars.

HOFFMANN'S, INC.
Comparative Balance Sheets
as of December 31
(unadjusted book figures)

	1967	1957
Assets		
Cash	$ 65,000	$ 20,000
Accounts receivable	42,000	18,000
Inventories, at average cost	90,000	36,000
Land	40,000	40,000
Building	600,000	300,000
Accumulated depreciation: Building	(115,000)	(13,750)
Equipment	190,000	70,000
Accumulated depreciation: Equipment	(63,750)	(7,750)
Total assets	$848,250	$462,500
Liabilities & Equity		
Current liabilities	$ 57,000	$ 25,000
Bonds payable	450,000	200,000
Common stock: Par value	200,000	200,000
Retained earnings	141,250	37,500
Total liabilities & equity	$848,250	$462,500

HOFFMANN'S, INC.
Comparative Income Statements
for the years ended December 31
(unadjusted book figures)

	1967		1957	
Sales		$400,000		$200,000
Expenses:				
Cost of goods sold	$210,000		$100,000	
Selling and general expenses	50,000		50,000	
Depreciation	24,500		7,500	
Interest	22,500		5,000	
Taxes	42,860	349,860	14,000	176,500
Net income to common stockholders		$ 50,140		$ 23,500
Common stock dividends		20,000		10,000
Retained earnings		$ 30,140		$ 13,500

Additional information

(1) Hoffmann's, Inc., was organized in 1953 when the capital stock was sold for par value. The land was purchased at a cost of $40,000, the original building at a cost of $100,000, and the original equipment at a cost of $30,000.

(2) The second building was constructed at a cost of $200,000 in 1957 and additional equipment was purchased at a cost of $40,000. $200,000 of 5% 20-year bonds were sold to finance this acquisition partially.

(3) The last addition to the building was constructed at a cost of $300,000 in 1964 and the remaining equipment, costing $120,000, was purchased then. Additional 5% bonds with a par value of $250,000 were sold at par to finance this addition.

(4) The buildings have a 40-year life and the equipment a 20-year life. The company uses the straight-line method of depreciation, taking one-half year's depreciation in the year of acquisition.

(5) Assume that revenues, expenses, taxes, interest, and dividends are earned or paid evenly over the accounting period.

(6) The inventory is assumed to have been acquired when the average index for the year prevailed. The cost of goods sold is also assumed to have been purchased evenly throughout the period.

(7) Applicable general price indices were as follows:

1953 average	80
1957 average	100
1964 average	120
1967 average	150
1967 year-end	160

The work sheets presented here are used as a convenient method of data accumulation. Each dollar aggregate in the mixed-dollar column is translated to base-year dollars by dividing it by the general price index prevailing when the dollars were used or available for use. The base-year data are in turn translated to current-year data by multiplying each base-year-dollar amount by the general price index at the end of the current year. The Retained Earnings account is the exception. In order to simplify the illustration, changes in the Retained Earnings account have not been enumerated. As a result this account balance is ascertained, for the base year, by inserting an amount which will cause the credits to equal the debits (A = L + OE). The retained earnings balance in the current-year columns can be obtained by multiplying the base-year amount by the general price index prevailing at the end of 1967.

Based on these statements, we can see that changes in the value of the dollar are significant for comparative statements of financial position and income determination. Comparative statements which have not been adjusted for the effect of price-level changes can be the basis for erroneous decisions which depend on information about the growth of the enterprise in terms of dollars committed to the enterprise and growth of the sales and net income or operating data. For example, Hoffmann's sales volume has not doubled over the 10-year period; instead it has increased by only 33⅓%. Net income has increased by only 17⅝%; and the rate of return on common stock equity for 1967 has declined from 14.7 to 6.2%

HOFFMANN'S, INC.
Price Level Adjustment Work Sheet for Comparative Balance Sheets

	Mixed dollars		Base-year dollars*		Current-year dollars†	
	1967	1957	1967	1957	1967	1957
Assets						
Cash	(a) 65,000	(d) 20,000	40,625	20,000	65,000	32,000
Accounts receivable	(a) 42,000	(d) 18,000	26,250	18,000	42,000	28,800
Inventories	(b) 90,000	(d) 36,000	60,000	36,000	96,000	57,600
Land	(e) 40,000	(e) 40,000	50,000	50,000	80,000	80,000
Building:						
1953	(e) 100,000	(e) 100,000	125,000	125,000	200,000	200,000
1957	(d) 200,000	(d) 200,000	200,000	200,000	320,000	320,000
1964	(c) 300,000		250,000		400,000	
Total	600,000	300,000	575,000	325,000	920,000	520,000
Accumulated depreciation:						
1953	(e) (36,250)	(e) (11,250)	(45,313)	(14,063)	(72,500)	(22,500)
1957	(d) (52,500)	(d) (2,500)	(52,500)	(2,500)	(84,000)	(4,000)
1964	(c) (26,250)		(21,875)		(35,000)	
Total	(115,000)	(13,750)	(119,688)	(16,563)	(191,500)	(26,500)
Equipment:						
1953	(e) 30,000	(e) 30,000	37,500	37,500	60,000	60,000
1957	(d) 40,000	(d) 40,000	40,000	40,000	64,000	64,000
1964	(c) 120,000		100,000		160,000	
Total	190,000	70,000	177,500	77,500	284,000	124,000
Accumulated depreciation:						
1953	(e) (21,750)	(e) (6,750)	(27,188)	(8,438)	(43,500)	(13,500)
1957	(d) (21,000)	(d) (1,000)	(21,000)	(1,000)	(33,600)	(1,600)
1964	(c) (21,000)		(17,500)		(28,000)	
Total	(63,750)	(7,750)	(65,688)	(9,438)	(105,100)	(15,000)
Total assets	848,250	462,500	743,999	500,499	1,190,400	800,800
Liabilities & Equity						
Current liabilities	(a) 57,000	(d) 25,000	35,625	25,000	57,000	40,000
Bonds payable	(a) 450,000	(d) 200,000	281,250	200,000	450,000	320,000
Common stock, par value	(e) 200,000	(e) 200,000	250,000	250,000	400,000	400,000
Retained earnings‡	141,250	37,500	177,124	25,499	283,400	40,800
Total liabilities & equity	848,250	462,500	743,999	500,499	1,190,400	800,800

Key to index numbers for adjustment to base year:

- (a) 1967 year-end 160
- (b) 1967 average 150
- (c) 1964 average 120
- (d) 1957 average 100
- (e) 1953 average 80

* *Divide mixed-dollar amounts by general price index indicated by key letter to obtain base-year dollar equivalent.*

† *Multiply base-year amount by 160, 1967 year-end price index, to obtain current-year dollars.*

‡ *Retained earnings is a balancing figure in this illustration because we have not provided information about the earnings which were added to the account each year during the 10-year interval.*

HOFFMANN'S, INC.
Price Level Adjustment Work Sheet for Comparative Income Statements

	Mixed dollars		*Base-year dollars*°		*Current-year dollars*†	
	1967	*1957*	*1967*	*1957*	*1967*	*1957*
Sales	*(b) 400,000*	*(d) 200,000*	*266,667*	*200,000*	*426,667*	*320,000*
Less expenses:						
Cost of goods sold	*(b) 210,000*	*(d) 100,000*	*140,000*	*100,000*	*224,000*	*160,000*
Selling and general expenses	*(b) 50,000*	*(d) 50,000*	*33,333*	*50,000*	*53,333*	*80,000*
Depreciation:						
1953	*(e) 4,000*	*(e) 4,000*	*5,000*	*5,000*	*8,000*	*8,000*
1957	*(d) 7,000*	*(d) 3,500*	*7,000*	*3,500*	*11,200*	*5,600*
1964	*(c) 13,500*		*11,250*		*18,000*	
Total	*24,500*	*7,500*	*23,250*	*8,500*	*37,200*	*13,600*
Interest	*(b) 22,500*	*(d) 5,000*	*15,000*	*5,000*	*24,000*	*8,000*
Taxes	*(b) 42,860*	*(d) 14,000*	*28,573*	*14,000*	*45,717*	*22,400*
Total	*349,860*	*176,500*	*240,156*	*177,500*	*384,250*	*284,000*
Net income	*50,140*	*23,500*	*26,511*	*22,500*	*42,417*	*36,000*
Dividends	*(b) 20,000*	*(d) 10,000*	*13,333*	*10,000*	*21,333*	*16,000*
Earnings retained	*30,140*	*13,500*	*13,178*	*12,500*	*21,084*	*20,000*

Key to index numbers for adjustment to base year:
(a) 1967 year-end 160
(b) 1967 average 150
(c) 1964 average 120
(d) 1957 average 100
(e) 1953 average 80

° *Divide mixed-dollar amounts by general price index indicated by the key letter to obtain base-year dollar equivalent.*
† *Multiply base-year amounts by 160, 1967 year-end price index, to obtain current-year dollars.*

as a result of adjusting for price-level changes. Similarly, monetary assets have not tripled; in terms of purchasing power, these assets have increased by only 75%. In terms of purchasing power, the liabilities of Hoffmann's, Inc., have increased by only \$147,000 (\$360,000 to \$507,000) not by \$282,000 (\$225,000 to \$507,000), as indicated in the unadjusted statements.

Questions

1. What functions does money serve in our economy?
2. What does the accountant assume about money as a standard of value?
3. What are some of the major problems of constructing an index which will accurately reflect changes in the economic length of the dollar?
4. Distinguish between a specific price index and a general price index.
5. If the accountant does recognize that the dollar is a changing unit of measure, does this mean that other presently accepted accounting conventions, assumptions, or postulates will have to be modified?

6. How is the translation of dollar cost to be accomplished?

7. Illustrate the translation technique by translating the cost of a building, $100,000, acquired when the general price index was 80 to current-year dollars when the general price index is 170.

8. Why have accountants been primarily concerned with plant assets when they discuss the problem of an unstable monetary unit on accounting data?

9. The monetary assets and liabilities are stated in terms of current dollars at all times because the amount owed or claimed is to be settled in dollars. Is there then any special problem of accounting for monetary items during periods of changing price levels?

10. What action might a firm take to reduce the loss from inflation on the monetary accounts?

11. Why do some accountants who favor accounting for price-level changes object to recognizing purchasing power gains and losses on long-term debt as the price level changes?

12. Why is it important to restate comparative statements in terms of a common unit of measure?

Short cases for analysis

15-1 McAdams of Adams-Baker posed the following situations and asked for your opinion:

a. In considering the merits of using price indices for the purpose of converting the accounting data as reflected in the conventional historical cost accounts, some people have suggested that these price-level adjustments should be confined to the fixed assets and related depreciation. What can be said in favor of such a proposal? Against it?

b. The price index rose from 125 to 175 during the previous year and from 175 to 225 during the current year. The dollar sales during the previous year were $240,000 and during the current year were $300,000.

(1) For comparative income statement purposes, convert the sales figures for both years to the price level existing at the end of the current year. Assume that sales were made uniformly throughout both years and that the change in price level was also uniform.

(2) What additional information is revealed by a comparison of the converted figures? How do you interpret them?

AICPA adapted

15-2 Mr. Alexander, a staunch advocate of the lifo method of inventory valuation, argues that there is no reason to be concerned over the development of new techniques for handling changes in the purchasing power of the dollar as far as inventories are concerned. He argues that lifo adequately reflects the impact of inflation on the income statement and that the balance sheet is of practically no importance as a financial statement anyway.

Instructions

a. Compare the lifo inventory valuations and the cost of goods sold, using unadjusted historical dollar cost and adjusted cost for a four-year period, based on the following data:

Purchases, which are acquired uniformly throughout the period, and end-of-year quantities are shown in the schedule below:

	1st year		*2d year*		*3d year*		*4th year*	
	Units	*Price per unit*	*Units*	*Price per unit*	*Units*	*Price per unit*	*Units*	*Price per unit*
Beginning quantity	1,000	$2.00						
Purchases	10,000	2.12	12,000	$2.25	14,000	$2.48	14,000	$2.73
Ending quantity	1,200		1,200		1,200		800	

The price index for this period indicated the following changes in the general purchasing power of the dollar:

Beginning of 1st year	100	*Average for 3d year*	127
Average for 1st year	105	*End of 3d year*	133.1
End of 1st year	110	*Average for 4th year*	139.8
Average for 2d year	115.5	*End of 4th year*	146.4
End of 2d year	121		

b. Draft a reply to Alexander based on your calculations using the above data.

15-3 You have just finished an elaborate explanation of the effect of inflation on financial statements prepared on the basis of recorded dollar cost. Mr. Ryan, president of Industrial Machines Co., says, "Now, that's all right Mr. CPA, but the procedures you are espousing are going to reduce my reported net income, increase my net investment, and decrease my rate of return on net investment. You have indicated that the balance sheet will still not indicate the value of my business, my income tax liability to the Federal and state governments will not be reduced, and your fee will be increased because of a more complex audit assignment. Now this just doesn't make sense to me. I understand thoroughly that if I had buried $1,000 in 1940 and in turn elected to uncover it and spend it today that I could buy much less in terms of commodities. But you see, Mr. CPA, this is not the way business is. We do not bury money; as a matter of fact, we attempt to hold a minimum amount of cash. Our money is invested in real commodities and these commodities are being used to make more money for us. Now why should I adopt accounting procedures which only result in making me look like a less efficient manager and you like a more valuable auditor?"

Instructions

Draft a reply to Ryan pointing out the difference in the information which will be provided if the statements are prepared under the present assumption that the monetary unit is stable or if they are prepared with full recognition that the purchasing power of the monetary unit is not constant over time.

15-4 The Hampton Stores, Inc., has followed a policy of maintaining a high current asset position relative to operations when compared to their more important competitors. Mr. Jones, the president, has stated on many occasions that such a position is justified because the company needs to be in a position to take advantage of any opportunity to buy out small operations which will fit into the long-range plans for growth of Hampton Stores. Recently he has become concerned because he has heard so much discussion of the effect of inflation on cash holdings and fixed-dollar income investments. Presented below are the comparative balance sheets of Hampton Stores, Inc., for the past five years:

HAMPTON STORES, INC.
Comparative Balance Sheets
for the years ended

	1962	1963	1964	1965	1966
Cash	$100,000	$130,000	$150,000	$ 180,000	$ 200,000
Marketable securities	400,000	470,000	550,000	620,000	710,000
Accounts receivable	80,000	80,000	90,000	90,000	100,000
Inventory	120,000	120,000	130,000	140,000	150,000
Other assets	10,000	8,000	10,000	10,000	10,000
Total assets	$710,000	$808,000	$930,000	$1,040,000	$1,170,000
Accounts payable	$ 40,000	$ 30,000	$ 30,000	$ 40,000	$ 50,000
Other current liabilities	10,000	8,000	10,000	10,000	10,000
Capital stock	300,000	300,000	300,000	300,000	300,000
Retained earnings	360,000	470,000	590,000	690,000	810,000
Total liabilities	$710,000	$808,000	$930,000	$1,040,000	$1,170,000

One of the more reliable indices of changes in the purchasing power of the dollar indicated the relative value of the dollar at the end of the respective years with the base year 1962 at 100.0 as follows: 1963, 110.0; 1964, 121.0; 1965, 133.1; 1966, 146.4.

Instructions

a. Compute the gain or loss accruing to Hampton Stores over the past four years, as a result of the decision relating to current assets, arising from the changing purchasing power of the dollar. Assume that any change in the monetary account balances occurred on the last day of the year.

b. What is the effect of the stated assumption in part (a) on your answer? Explain.

c. How might Jones accomplish his objective of expansion at less cost to Hampton Stores, Inc.? What are the limiting factors of your suggestions?

15-5 Mr. Stewart comes to his CPA after the completion of the audit of Stewart Enterprises and asks for a more complete explanation of the item, "Inflation loss on monetary items." He explains that there has been no loss of anything because the CPA has shown the same balances for cash and receivables and current liabilities that his ledger shows for the end of the year. Furthermore, there has been no write-off of monetary assets during the past year for any reason, not even for bad debts. The collection record of the credit department has been better in the last 18 months than it ever has and this is all due to new practices instituted by Mr. Rogel.

Furthermore, the cash, receivable, and current liability balances reflected on last year's statements have been changed from those which were certified to last year. "What's the matter, old man, have you gone off your debits and credits? How can this be?"

Instructions

Explain to Stewart the adjustments which must have been made in preparing the comparative balance sheets and the income statement. Include in your explanation a discussion of the effect of inflation on the purchasing power of the monetary unit. Be prepared for the comment by Stewart that, "Well, this is all OK, but you see, these balances are not constant. They are continually revolving. You see, cash which we collected yesterday may be paid to a creditor today. Surely inflation is not proceeding at such a rapid rate that my money loses value overnight. If this is the case we had better see what we can do about a change in administration in the White House."

Problems

15-6 Mr. Dodson has come to you as his CPA and asked for an explanation of the effect of inflation on his business, Dodson's Stores. Since he owns no long-lived assets except for a small amount of store fixtures, he has felt that he was isolated from the damaging effects of inflation. He has read about industries which employ a large amount of depreciable equipment being unable to replace their equipment because of rising prices. Only recently, however, has he read much about the effect of inflation on monetary accounts. You are given the following summary of his monetary accounts and are told that transactions have occurred uniformly during each quarter:

	Monetary assets		*Liabilities*	
Balance, Jan. 1	*$ 100,000*			*$ 40,000*
1st quarter	*200,000*	*$ 80,000*	*$ 80,000*	*100,000*
2d quarter	*300,000*	*120,000*	*120,000*	*400,000*
3d quarter	*700,000*	*450,000*	*450,000*	*400,000*
4th quarter	*300,000*	*400,000*	*400,000*	*200,000*
Balance, Dec. 31		*550,000*	*90,000*	
	$1,600,000	*$1,600,000*	*$1,140,000*	*$1,140,000*
Balance	*$ 550,000*			*$ 90,000*

The following index numbers are assumed to apply in this situation:

Jan. 1	*120*	*3d quarter average*	*140*
1st quarter average	*125*	*4th quarter average*	*150*
2d quarter average	*130*	*Dec. 31*	*155*

Instructions

Compute the gain or loss on the monetary accounts for the year.

15-7 To obtain a more realistic appraisal of his investment, Martin Arnett, your client, has asked you to adjust certain financial data of the Glo-Bright Company for price-level changes. On January 1, 1964, he invested $50,000 in the Glo-Bright Company in return for 10,000 shares of common stock. Immediately after his investment the trial balance appeared as follows:

	Debit	*Credit*
Cash and receivables	*$ 65,200*	
Merchandise inventory	*4,000*	
Building	*50,000*	
Accumulated depreciation: Building		*$ 8,000*
Equipment	*36,000*	
Accumulated depreciation: Equipment		*7,200*
Land	*10,000*	
Current liabilities		*50,000*
Capital stock, $5 par		*100,000*
Totals	*$165,200*	*$165,200*

Balances in certain accounts as of December 31 of each of the next three years were as follows:

	1964	*1965*	*1966*
Sales	*$39,650*	*$39,000*	*$42,350*
Inventory	*4,500*	*5,600*	*5,347*
Purchases	*14,475*	*16,350*	*18,150*
Operating expenses	*10,050*	*9,050*	*9,075*

Assume the 1964 price level as the base year and that all changes in the price level take place at the beginning of each year. Further assume that the 1965 price level is 10% above the 1964 price level and that the 1966 price level is 10% above the 1965 level.

The building was constructed in 1960 at a cost of $50,000 with an estimated life of 25 years. The price level at that time was 80% of the 1964 level.

The equipment was purchased in 1962 at a cost of $36,000 with an estimated life of 10 years. The price level at that time was 90% of the 1964 level.

The lifo method of inventory valuation is used. The original inventory was acquired in the same year that the building was constructed and was maintained at a constant $4,000 until 1964. In 1964 a gradual buildup of the inventory was begun in anticipation of an increase in the volume of business.

Arnett considers the return on his investment as the dividend he actually receives. In 1966 Glo-Bright paid cash dividends in the amount of $8,000.

On July 1, 1965, there was a reverse stock split of the company's stock in the ratio of 1 for 10.

Instructions

a. Compute the 1966 earnings per share of common stock in terms of 1964 dollars and in terms of mixed dollars (accepted accounting practice).

b. Compute the percentage return on the original investment by Arnett for 1966 in terms of 1964 dollars and in terms of mixed dollars (accepted accounting practice).

c. How would the 1966 income statement adjusted to 1964 dollars be translated to 1966 dollars?

d. Would the rate of return calculated using 1966 dollars be different from that computed using 1964 dollars?

AICPA adapted

15-8 The financial statements for Hazlet's, Inc., appear below and on page 524:

HAZLET'S, INC.
Balance Sheet
December 31
(unadjusted book figures)

Cash	*$ 60,000*
Accounts receivable	*50,000*
Inventories—fifo cost	*70,000*
Land	*40,000*
Building	*100,000*
Accumulated depreciation	*(10,000)*
Equipment	*100,000*
Accumulated depreciation	*(37,500)*
Total assets	*$372,500*
Current liabilities	*$ 80,000*
Bonds payable—4%	*100,000*
Common stock	*150,000*
Retained earnings	*42,500*
Total liabilities	*$372,500*

Other data

(1) The land and building were acquired when the price index was 80. The building is estimated to have a useful life of 50 years.

(2) One-half of the equipment was acquired when the price index was 80, one-fourth when it was 100, and the final one-fourth when it was 120. All the equipment is assumed to have a 10-year life.

HAZLET'S, INC.
Income Statement
for the year ended December 31
(unadjusted book figures)

Sales		*$500,000*
Expenses and taxes:		
Cost of goods sold	*$350,000*	
Selling and general expenses	*80,000*	
Depreciation	*12,000*	
Interest	*4,000*	
Income taxes	*24,000*	*470,000*
Net income to common stockholders		*$ 30,000*
Dividends		*20,000*
Earnings retained in the business		*$ 10,000*

(3) The beginning inventory cost was $80,000 and was acquired when the price index was 145. The ending inventory was acquired when the price index was 170.
(4) All operating revenues and expenses, excluding depreciation, are assumed to have been incurred uniformly throughout the year.
(5) Dividends were declared on December 31 payable the following January 15.
(6) The bonds and stock were issued at the time the land and building were acquired. Bond interest is payable at midyear and year-end.
(7) The price index at the beginning of the year was 150, the average for the year was 160, and the index at the end of the year was 175.

Instructions

Prepare financial statements for Hazlet's at December 31 with all dollar amounts stated in terms of the purchasing power equivalent of the dollar at December 31. Ignore the calculation of purchasing power gains or losses on monetary accounts for this problem.

15-9 The controller's department of Davison, Inc., has prepared the following statements for the first two years of operations:

DAVISON, INC.
Comparative Balance Sheet
(historical cost)

Assets	*Beginning of first year*	*End of first year*	*End of second year*
Cash	*$ 180,000*	*$ 170,000*	*$ 315,000*
Accounts receivable	*120,000*	*120,000*	*150,000*
Inventories—fifo cost	*375,000*	*450,000*	*300,000*
Land	*100,000*	*100,000*	*100,000*
Plant and equipment	*450,000*	*600,000*	*600,000*
Less: Accumulated depreciation	*-0-*	*(45,000)*	*(105,000)*
Total assets	*$1,225,000*	*$1,395,000*	*$1,360,000*

Liabilities			
Current	*$ 150,000*	*$ 270,000*	*$ 150,000*
Long-term	*525,000*	*525,000*	*450,000*
Total	*$ 675,000*	*$ 795,000*	*$ 600,000*
Stockholders' equity			
Capital stock	*$ 550,000*	*$ 550,000*	*$ 635,000*
Retained earnings	*-0-*	*50,000*	*125,000*
Total	*$ 550,000*	*$ 600,000*	*$ 760,000*
Total liabilities & stockholders' equity	*$1,225,000*	*$1,395,000*	*$1,360,000*

DAVISON, INC.
Comparative Income Statement
(historical cost)

	First year	*Second year*
Sales	*$1,200,000*	*$1,500,000*
Operating expenses:		
Cost of goods sold	*$ 675,000*	*$ 850,000*
Depreciation	*45,000*	*60,000*
Selling and administrative expenses	*360,000*	*400,000*
Income taxes	*55,000*	*85,000*
Total operating expenses	*$1,135,000*	*$1,395,000*
Net income from operations	*$ 65,000*	*$ 105,000*
Dividends to common stockholders	*15,000*	*30,000*
Earnings retained in the business	*$ 50,000*	*$ 75,000*

Additional data

(1) The applicable index numbers for the period as a measure of the general purchasing power of the dollar were:

Beginning of the first year	*120*	*Average for the second year*	*150*
End of the first year	*140*	*End of the second year*	*165*
Average for the first year	*132*		

(2) All revenue and expenses, except depreciation and beginning inventory, were earned or incurred evenly throughout the year. The ending inventory is assumed to have been acquired at the average price level for each year.
(3) Acquisitions of plant and equipment subsequent to the opening of business took place at the end of the first year. The average depreciation rate for these assets is 10% per year.
(4) Dividends are declared and paid at the end of each year.
(5) Additional stock was sold at beginning of second year.

Instructions

Prepare comparative income statements and comparative balance sheets for the first and second years of operations of Davison, Inc., stated in terms of the end of the second-year dollars.

15-10 The following data was taken from the ledger of Nelson's, Inc.:

NELSON'S, INC.
Comparative Balance Sheets

	Beginning of the year	*End of the year*
Cash	$100,000	$170,000
Accounts receivable	90,000	118,000
Inventories—lifo cost	48,000	44,000
Land	100,000	100,000
Buildings	300,000	300,000
Accumulated depreciation	(45,000)	(52,500)
Equipment	200,000	200,000
Accumulated depreciation	(90,000)	(110,000)
Total assets	$703,000	$769,500
Accounts payable	$ 60,000	$ 80,000
Other current liabilities	20,000	30,000
Common stock	500,000	500,000
Retained earnings	123,000	159,500
Total liabilities & equity	$703,000	$769,500

NELSON'S, INC.
Income Statement
for the year

Sales		$900,000
Expenses and taxes:		
Cost of goods sold	$554,000	
Selling and administrative expenses	180,000	
Depreciation	27,500	
Income taxes	62,000	823,500
Net income		$ 76,500
Dividends		40,000
Earnings retained in the business		$ 36,500

Additional data

(1) The land, buildings, and one-half of the equipment were acquired when the price level was 60. All the common stock was issued at the same time.
(2) The remainder of the equipment was acquired when the price level was 90.
(3) The estimated useful life of the building is 40 years and of the equipment 10 years. There is no estimated salvage value for any of the depreciable assets.
(4) The beginning inventory was accumulated as follows:

	Cost	*Price level*
Beginning inventory	$30,000	60
Additional layer	2,000	80
Additional layer	6,000	90
Final layer	10,000	110

(5) All sales and operating expenses and taxes have been incurred by the business uniformly throughout the year. Collections and payments have also been spread uniformly over the year. The dividends were declared and paid at the end of the year.

(6) The price index was 120 at the beginning of the year, 125 on average during the year, and 132 at the end of the year.

Instructions

Prepare financial statements for Nelson's, Inc., at the end of the year stated in terms of the purchasing power of the dollar prevailing at the end of the year. Include any purchasing power gain and/or loss incurred on the monetary accounts as an adjustment of Net Income after taxes but before dividends to common stockholders.

15-11 John Witsoe comes to you with a trial balance taken from his ledger at December 31, 1966. He explains that he has heard quite a bit about the impact of inflation on financial statements of business. He does not understand what all this means but he asks you to prepare his statements for the year on a comparative basis with one set based on traditional accounting procedures and the other based on the notion that the accounts should be adjusted for general changes in the purchasing power of the dollar. His trial balance, together with other data about the assets, is presented below:

WITSOE AND CO.
Trial Balance
December 31, 1966

Cash	$ 40,000	
Accounts receivable	30,000	
Inventory—lifo cost	23,000	
Land	80,000	
Building	200,000	
Accumulated depreciation		$ 42,000
Equipment	140,000	
Accumulated depreciation		59,500
Accounts payable		36,000
Bonds payable, 5%		100,000
Capital stock		200,000
Retained earnings		68,400
Sales		810,000
Sales returns, allowances, and discounts	10,000	
Purchases	479,500	
Salaries and wages	60,000	
Selling expenses	120,000	
General expenses	40,000	
Depreciation	14,000	
Dividends	20,000	
Interest charges	5,000	
Income tax charges	54,400	
Totals	*$1,315,900*	*$1,315,900*

Other data

The land was acquired in July, 1954, the building was constructed under contract dated July 1, 1955, was occupied July 1, 1956, and is assumed to have a 50-year life.

The equipment was acquired as follows and is assumed to have a 10-year life.

$30,000 in July, 1956
40,000 in July, 1961
20,000 in July, 1964
50,000 in July, 1966

The capital stock was issued in July, 1954.

The inventory is composed of layers added as follows:

$10,000 in 1956
2,000 in 1958
4,000 in 1961
6,000 in 1964
1,000 in 1965

All sales, purchases, and expenses are assumed to have been incurred uniformly throughout the year. Interest is paid semiannually, June 30 and December 31, and dividends and income taxes were paid on December 31. The ending inventory at lifo cost was $24,000.

The applicable general price indices are as follows:

Average for the year	*1954*	*60*
	1955	*70*
	1956	*75*
	1958	*80*
	1961	*100*
	1964	*110*
	1965	*120*
	1966	*130*
Beginning of	*1966*	*125*
End of	*1966*	*140*

Instructions

a. Prepare a balance sheet and income statement for Witsoe and Company using conventional accounting concepts.

b. Prepare a balance sheet and income statement for Witsoe and Company using adjusted dollar amounts to reflect changes in the purchasing power of the dollar. Ignore purchasing power gains and losses resulting from holding money and money claims.

15-12 The comparative balance sheet of Madison, Inc., for the Years 1 and 2 and the income statement for Year 2 are given on page 529:

MADISON, INC.,
Comparative Balance Sheet

Assets	*Year 1*	*Year 2*
Current assets:		
Cash	*$ 60,000*	*$ 97,600*
Receivables	*80,000*	*100,000*
Inventories	*120,000*	*135,100*
Total current assets	*$260,000*	*$332,700*
Plant and equipment:		
Land	*27,000*	*27,000*
Buildings	*360,000*	*360,000*
Accumulated depreciation: Buildings	*(12,000)*	*(24,000)*
Equipment	*180,000*	*180,000*
Accumulated depreciation: Equipment	*(18,000)*	*(36,000)*
Total assets	*$797,000*	*$839,700*
Liabilities		
Current liabilities	*$ 90,000*	*$115,700*
Long-term liabilities—6%	*150,000*	*150,000*
Stockholders' equity:		
Capital stock	*450,000*	*450,000*
Retained earnings	*107,000*	*124,000*
Total liabilities & stockholders' equity	*$797,000*	*$839,700*

MADISON, INC.,
Statement of Income
Year 2

Sales		*$600,000*
Cost and expenses:		
Cost of goods sold	*$370,000*	
Services purchased	*108,000*	
Depreciation on buildings and equipment	*30,000*	
Taxes	*42,000*	
Interest on long-term debt	*9,000*	*559,000*
Net income		*$ 41,000*

Madison, Inc., was organized at the beginning of Year 1, when an index of the general price level stood at 100. Prices remained steady during Year 1, and at the end of Year 1 the index remained at 100. During Year 2, however, prices rose steadily, and the index of the general price level stood at 120 at the end of Year 2.

A summary of the transactions of Madison, Inc., during Year 2, and the price index at the time the transaction occurred is given below and on page 530:

Transaction	*Price index*
Sales on account of $96,000	*100*
Sales on account of $330,000	*110*
Sales on account of $174,000	*116*

Merchandise purchased on account for $112,000	*112*
Merchandise purchased on account for $161,000	*115*
Merchandise purchased on account for $112,100	*118*
Services purchased on account—$39,600	*100*
Services purchased on account—$22,400	*112*
Services purchased on account—$46,000	*115*
Receivables collected—$88,800	*100*
Receivables collected—$259,200	*108*
Receivables collected—$232,000	*116*
Current liabilities paid—$255,000	*102*
Current liabilities paid—$212,400	*118*
Depreciation on building—$12,000	*100*
Depreciation on equipment—$18,000	*100*
Taxes ($42,000), interest ($9,000), and dividends ($24,000) were recognized and paid in cash at year-end	*120*
Inventory of merchandise at end of year is $135,100, determined on a first in, first out basis	

Instructions

On the basis of this information, prepare a balance sheet and income statement for Madison, Inc., in terms of current dollars, adjusting all transactions for changes in the general price level. Present these statements in comparative form, showing the unadjusted statements and the adjusted statements for Year 2.

15-13 Mr. Zopp presents you with two sets of financial statements for his business, Zopp's, Inc., which have been prepared in accordance with generally accepted accounting procedures. He explains that he is concerned because although his financial statements have indicated a record of steady growth over the past ten years, an acquaintance, the controller of a large national firm, has told him that there has probably been little or no growth when the effects of inflation over the past years are considered.

ZOPP'S, INC.
Comparative Balance Sheets
December 31

	1966	*1956*
Cash and receivables	*$300,000*	*$200,000*
Inventory—fifo	*200,000*	*50,000*
Land	*50,000*	*50,000*
Plant and equipment	*200,000*	*150,000*
Less: Accumulated depreciation	*(100,000)*	*(50,000)*
Total assets	*$650,000*	*$400,000*
Current liabilities	*$100,000*	*$ 50,000*
Mortgage payable	*100,000*	*100,000*
Common stock	*300,000*	*200,000*
Retained earnings	*150,000*	*50,000*
Total liabilities & equity	*$650,000*	*$400,000*

ZOPP'S, INC.
Comparative Income Statements
for the year ended December 31

	1966	*1956*
Sales	*$1,000,000*	*$500,000*
Less: Expenses and taxes:		
Cost of goods sold	*$ 800,000*	*$400,000*
Depreciation	*8,000*	*4,000*
Selling and administrative expenses	*80,000*	*40,000*
Taxes	*50,000*	*22,000*
Total	*$ 938,000*	*$466,000*
Net income	*$ 62,000*	*$ 34,000*
Dividends	*50,000*	*30,000*
Income retained in the business	*$ 12,000*	*$ 4,000*

Additional data

(1) All revenue and expenses and taxes, except for depreciation, are earned or incurred evenly throughout each of the years.

(2) The beginning inventory of $180,000 for 1966 was acquired when the price level was 150; the beginning inventory of $55,000 for 1956 was acquired when the index was 90.

(3) The land and all the plant and equipment owned in 1956 was acquired when the index was 70. The additions to plant and equipment were made on July 1, 1964, when the index was 140.

(4) The mortgage was executed on the date the original plant and equipment were purchased.

(5) The original common stock of 200,000 was issued when the index was 70 and the additional stock was issued June 30, 1964.

(6) Dividends were declared and paid on June 30 and December 31 for one-half of the total dividend paid in each year.

(7) The index of general purchasing power of the dollar was:

	1966	*1956*
Beginning of year	*160*	*100*
Average for year	*170*	*110*
End of year	*175*	*120*

Instructions

Prepare a comparative balance sheet and a comparative income statement for Zopp's, Inc., stating all dollar aggregates in terms of dollars of uniform purchasing power.

16 REPLACEMENT COST AND FINANCIAL REPORTING

In the preceding chapter we noted the importance of income determination in the development of accounting conventions. Under the presently accepted concept of income (revenues minus the cost of goods and services consumed) the accountant reports as income a variety of elements. These elements involved in measuring income may include (1) changes in the level of average prices, (2) changes in prices of specific goods and services, and (3) excesses of selling prices over the current cost of providing the service. Moreover, the balance sheet reflects cost aggregates which are measured in dollars of different significance and may include identical physical items valued at different unit costs.

The arguments for accounting for the effect of changes in the length of the dollar as a unit of measurement were presented in Chapter 15 along with the appropriate procedures. The question now raised is: Should changes in the prices of specific goods and services between the time they are acquired and the time they are consumed be isolated and distinguished from what might be called pure operating income? We shall call these price changes *holding gains and losses*. In attempting to answer this question, we must face at least two important considerations: (1) timeliness of revenue and cost data incorporated in income determination, and (2) the effect of specific price changes on a firm's financial position. Where assets are acquired and consumed in producing revenues in one accounting period, the importance of distinguishing between holding gains and operating income may be negligible. In terms of complete information, however, disclosure of holding gains and losses as a separate item on the income statement may be desirable. Under present accounting conventions, when assets are acquired in one period and their usefulness expires in later periods, holding gains or losses will be reflected in reported income in the period when the usefulness of the asset expires. The result is that holding gains and losses are not disclosed; they are reflected in income in the year in which the asset services are used rather than in the period in which the specific price change occurs. During the holding period, the asset is reported on the balance sheet at its acquisition cost, which may be more or less than the replacement cost of the asset at the statement date. The question arises whether statements which do not report changes in value of assets (as represented by specific price changes) are as useful as statements in which an attempt (however imperfect) is made to report these changes.

Professor Paton has written on this issue:

> The crux of accounting theory and accounting practice . . . is valuation. . . . The problem facing the accountant is that of periodic revaluation—that is, it is his business to register the flow of values into the particular business enterprise and to follow these values as, attaching to manifold structures, commodities, services, and rights, they become affected by the business process and all attendant circumstances. The allocation of the value data of the particular enterprise to particular periods of time in terms of essential statements, income sheet and balance sheet, is the essence of accounting, and this involves revaluation at almost every point.[1]

Professors Sprouse and Moonitz state, in *Accounting Research Study No. 3:*

> The existence of an asset (future economic services) is independent of the means by which it was acquired although the means (e.g., for cash or for debt) may be used as a measure of the size of the services acquired. Subsequent to acquisition, events may demonstrate that acquisition cost or other initial basis no longer represents a useful measure of future benefits for a particular asset. As obvious examples, oil or other valuable natural resources may be discovered on enterprise land holdings acquired initially for other purposes or unforeseen obsolescence of a product or process may occur. In cases of this type and of others in which initial basis is no longer a useful or representative measure a different basis should be adopted.[2]

Illustration of accounting for replacement cost

A highly simplified illustration of the technique of accounting for replacement cost is presented here to provide a working knowledge of the principles and procedures involved. The transactions are limited to those which highlight the problems of accounting for replacement costs and the changes in prices are exaggerated for emphasis.

[1] W. A. Paton, "Valuation of Inventories," *The Journal of Accountancy,* December, 1922, p. 433.

[2] R. T. Sprouse and M. Moonitz, "A Tentative Set of Broad Accounting Principles for Business Enterprises," *Accounting Research Study No. 3,* American Institute of Certified Public Accountants (New York: 1962), p. 26.

X Company began business in period 1 with the following assets and capital:

X COMPANY
Balance Sheet
beginning of period 1

Cash	$ 10,000	Capital stock	$125,000
Inventory (1,000 units @ $5)	5,000		
Land	10,000		
Building	100,000		
Total	$125,000	Total	$125,000

	Accepted accounting principles		Replacement cost	
Inventory	30,000		30,000	
Liabilities		30,000		30,000
Accounts Receivable	75,000		75,000	
Sales		75,000		75,000
Inventory			19,000	
Unrealized Holding Gain				19,000
To write inventory up to replacement cost at date of sale.				
Cost of Goods Sold	30,000		45,000	45,000
Inventory		30,000		
Unrealized Holding Gain			15,000	
Realized Holding Gain				15,000
To recognize portion of holding gain realized through sale of 5,000 units of inventory, assuming lifo method of inventory valuation.				
Inventory			3,000	
Land			10,000	
Building			100,000	
Unrealized Holding Gain				113,000
The nonmonetary assets are written up to reflect cost of replacement at statement date.				
Depreciation	10,000		20,000	
Accumulated Depreciation		10,000		20,000
Unrealized Holding Gain			10,000	
Realized Holding Gain				10,000

X Company uses the lifo method of accounting for its inventory and the straight-line method of depreciating its building, which has a 10-year service life. During period 1, the following events occurred.

(1) Purchased 5,000 units of merchandise for $6 per unit on credit.
(2) Sold 5,000 units for $15 each at a time when replacement cost was $9.
(3) Construction costs and land costs doubled during the period. Replacement cost of the inventory was $12 per unit at the end of period 1.

These transactions for X Company are summarized in journal entry form on page 534 assuming (1) accepted accounting practice and (2) adoption of replacement cost accounting.

The income statement for period 1 and the balance sheet at the end of period 1 are presented below for X Company, using the data developed in accordance with both accepted accounting principles and replacement cost techniques.

X COMPANY
Income Statement
for period 1

	Accepted accounting principles	*Replacement cost*
Sales	$75,000	$75,000
Less: Cost of goods sold	30,000	45,000
Gross margin	$45,000	$30,000
Depreciation	10,000	20,000
Operating income	$35,000	$10,000
Realized holding gains		25,000
Net income	$35,000	$35,000

X COMPANY
Balance Sheet
end of period 1

	Accepted accounting principles	*Replacement cost*
Assets		
Cash	$ 10,000	$ 10,000
Accounts receivable	75,000	75,000
Inventory	5,000	12,000
Land	10,000	20,000
Building (net of accumulated depreciation)	90,000	180,000
Total assets	$190,000	$297,000
Liabilities & Equity		
Liabilities	$ 30,000	$ 30,000
Capital stock	125,000	125,000
Retained earnings	35,000	35,000
Unrealized holding gains		107,000
Total liabilities & equity	$190,000	$297,000

Accepted conventions

Accountants have generally conceded that revenue may be *earned* during the process of producing a product or of providing a service, but they have held that revenue is not *realized* until (1) there is objective evidence of the marketable value of the output and (2) the earning process is substantially complete.[3]

> The realization of revenue from sales therefore marks the time and measures the amount of (1) recapture of costs previously advanced in productive efforts, and (2) capture of additional assets (income) representing amount of compensation for capital service rendered, responsibility taken, and risk assumed in the process of production. Inventories and plant are not "values," but cost accumulations in suspense, as it were, awaiting their destiny.[4]

Income, measured in accordance with accepted accounting principles, is the excess of revenue realized (the value of goods and services transferred) over the market value at date of acquisition of goods and services consumed in earning the revenue. Is this measure of income a useful one? In answer to this question, we can expect a loud chorus of affirmative opinion.

Is this the *most* useful measure of income we can devise? The answer here is likely to be given with less certainty. If we ask for what purpose is income determined, we will find agreement that income is measured to determine whether, and by how much, a firm has improved its position during a given time period, and to provide a basis for making judgments about the future. If this is the case, then is a composite measure of the realized improvement in position the best information the accountant can produce? Might we not argue that a measure of success or failure in operations, distinguished from gains or losses from holding resources, provides better decision-making information? It is true that each aspect of business is an integral part of the complete operation, but if the source of income or lack of it could be traced with greater precision and if the effect of changes in specific prices were disclosed as soon as information could be objectively measured, we might provide both outsiders and managers with better decision-making data.

Enterprises provide service to their customers by manufacturing goods and/or by making goods or services available to customers at the time and place that they are desired. Net income (the excess of revenue over expenses of providing the service) is the enterprise's compensation for the service performed. There may be reason to argue that the net income from *operations* is the difference between selling price and the cost of providing the service at the time sale takes place. The reason for making such an argument is that the cost of acquiring the factors required to provide the service at the time of sale represents the outlay which would be required at this point. The income from the sale is therefore the excess of selling price over the current value or cost of the resources consumed. This is the income resulting from operations.

There may well be other sources of income to the enterprise. Income is certainly derived from buying resources when they are cheap and using them when they are more costly. This income is the result of *holding* resources over time while

[3] See discussion in chap. 3 of *Intermediate Accounting* in this series.

[4] W. A. Paton, and A. C. Littleton, *An Introduction to Corporate Accounting Standards*, American Accounting Association (Iowa City, Iowa: 1940), p. 14.

they become relatively more valuable. There is also the possibility that the goods will become relatively less valuable over time, in which case a loss from holding the resources may result. When the firm takes a position in resources, it must accept the risk which accompanies such action. The reward for accepting such risks may come in many ways: operating efficiency, better service to the customer, and change in the cost of the resources. At the present time little or no attempt is made to analyze the annual income figure as to source.

There are accountants who believe that the gain or loss arising from holding an investment in inventory and plant assets during periods of specific price change can be identified. As the current market price of these items fluctuates, the firm benefits if prices rise, or suffers a loss if prices fall. This gain or loss is the result of conscious or involuntary decisions to invest in and hold particular goods; it may have little to do with the producing or service activity which is the major purpose of a firm's existence. While an individual firm may have limited control over these gains and losses once inventory or plant is acquired, the effect of price change is often an important element of periodic income. Since these gains and losses are the result of holding assets and of timing purchases and sales in relation to price changes, a case can be made that accountants should attempt to disclose separately the amount of such gains and losses in financial statements.

The total income of the firm is not changed by the adoption of replacement cost accounting. Income remains the difference between outlays for goods and services and receipts from the sale of products or services. The main changes relate to the reported source of income and possibly to the period when the income is reported. If there is no change in the realization convention, that revenue is *realized* only when there is objective evidence of marketable value of the output and the earning process is substantially complete, then there is no change in the periodic income reported. The only change is that income from operations is the result of deducting the replacement cost of resources consumed from revenues realized, and income from holding resources is the difference between replacement cost and acquisition cost of the resources consumed. The change in the carrying value of the assets remaining on hand at the end of the period is considered to be unrealized until the resources are consumed. This procedure has been demonstrated in the highly simplified example on page 535.

There are some accountants who would support recognition of the total gain or loss derived from holding resources during a period as part of the income for that period. Such a position requires a modification of the presently accepted realization convention. In order to allow this practice the convention would have to be amended to include specific provisions for holding gains. The modification would need to state that holding gains and losses are *realized* when: (1) there is objective evidence of the replacement cost of the resource; (2) the earning process constitutes holding resources for a period of time; and (3) the earning process is completed when the resource is consumed or at the end of the accounting period, whichever occurs first.

In order to conform more closely with presently accepted accounting principles, in this chapter we have chosen to recognize holding gains or losses as a part of periodic income only to the extent that the asset is consumed in the current period. In order to apply this technique consistently when the replacement cost of inventory declines, we do not consider the total reduction in inventory value a loss applicable to the current period. Only that portion of the loss which is directly related to the goods sold during the period is considered realized. This is a departure from accepted practice in the application of the lower of cost or market rule; however, this departure seems justified in order to permit consistent application of the techniques being discussed.

Advantages and disadvantages of replacement cost

The primary advantage of measuring assets and expired asset services in terms of replacement cost is that it gives the user of accounting data additional and more relevant information about the economic resources of a business and the value, in terms of replacement cost, of resources consumed during any given period. The historical cost of economic resources simply reflects their unamortized acquisition price at some point in the past. When assets have been acquired at various times and at various prices, an aggregation of historical costs at acquisition date is meaningless as a basis for current decisions.

The main disadvantage of adopting replacement cost as a basis of asset valuation is the lack of objective, verifiable information about the cost of replacing complex assets, such as buildings, manufactured inventory, and land. In the case of purchased inventory there may be readily available market quotations which can be relied upon for replacement cost. Such data are not available, however, for factory overhead, which is frequently a large part of the cost of manufactured inventories. Similarly there is no ready stock of steel plants or textile plant buildings which will allow us to state that replacement cost of a particular building is precisely X dollars. There are indices of specific price change, as we have already noted. These indices have certain limitations, which were discussed in Chapter 15; in addition, there is the eternal question of whether we should use the cost of replacing the exact facility or the cost of replacing the capacity to produce.

Many accountants, who favor replacement cost, state that of course we are concerned with the capacity to produce. How do we determine this? Consider the relatively simple case of an office building. The building at 740 Main Street was constructed in 1939. The composite index of nonresidential construction cost has risen from 60 to 140. The subindices have varied widely in their movements; some have declined, others have risen, and still others remain unchanged. The building materials used in construction are not now generally used for this type building; lighting, heating, and air-conditioning facilities have undergone major technological changes and the older type equipment is no longer available. Is a calculation of replacement cost useful in this instance? Some concept of current cost would probably be more useful than historical cost, but what is it? The determination of appropriate replacement cost data may well be a major barrier to the adoption of this technique.

The advantages claimed for replacement cost, if this major problem can be solved, are cited below for the two principal types of assets involved: (1) inventory and (2) long-lived tangible assets. Since intangible assets are seldom carried in financial reports at the present time, it seems unnecessary in the present discussion to consider the problems of ascertaining replacement cost for these items.

Inventory. The use of replacement cost in pricing the inventory may accomplish the avowed objectives of both the lifo and fifo methods of inventory valuation. Regardless of the actual flow of goods, the replacement cost of an inventory item is the same. The cost of goods sold is measured at current replacement cost, which accomplishes the avowed purpose of the lifo method of inventory valuation. In addition, the inventory on hand is valued at current replacement cost, which approximates the valuation obtained under the fifo method. As discussed in *ARS 3*, the method is consistent with and is based upon the rationale in support of the lower of cost or market valuation of inventory.[5] The portion of the holding gain which is realized in a given period will, however, depend upon the method of inventory valuation used. In the event that prices have risen consistently over a period of years, adoption of the lifo method will cause a continuing increase in the balance of unrealized holding gains. The amount of the holding gain realized in a given period, under these circumstances, will be greatest if we assume that the oldest goods are sold first, that is, if we adopt fifo.

Long-lived tangible assets. The valuation of long-lived tangible assets at replacement cost clearly reflects the advantage or disadvantage accruing to a firm or department because it acquired the facilities at a cost substantially different from that existing at the time of use. The operating income then becomes a measure of the profitability of manufacturing and selling operations for the period, uninfluenced by the timing of acquisitions. The timing of acquisitions will influence the overall net income, but the sources of the total dollar net income will be identified.

Determination of replacement cost

In cases where there is an active market for the items included among the assets, replacement cost can be defined as the current market quotation at usual terms for the quantity of goods normally purchased. Replacement cost of manufactured inventory, either work-in-process or finished goods, would be composed of the replacement cost of raw materials, labor hours priced at prevailing wage rates, and overhead costs accumulated at current prices.

In the case of manufactured inventories and long-lived tangible assets, indices of price changes for specific types of assets could be established as a means of objectively estimating replacement costs. Certain indices of specific price changes are now calculated as components of general price indices and others could be developed if replacement cost valuation became an accepted accounting convention. Indices of specific price changes are subject to the same limitations discussed in connection with general price indices; whether these limitations are sufficiently serious to cause rejection of the idea of substituting replacement cost for historical cost in asset valuation is an important element of the controversy about this departure from accepted practice.

Determination of holding gains and losses

The holding gain or loss resulting from changes in the prices (replacement costs) of assets is measured for the time the asset is held during an accounting period. The gain or loss is the difference between the acquisition cost or value at the date of acquisition or beginning of the period, whichever occurs later, and the replacement cost at the date of expiration of usefulness or the end of the period, whichever occurs first. All expirations of asset services are charged to expense accounts at replacement cost.

[5] *Accounting Research Study No. 3,* p. 31.

Inventories. The determination of the holding gain on inventory in a retail store is illustrated, on the basis of the summarized data:

Beginning inventory, Jan. 1	*500 units @*	*$20 per unit*
Purchases, Jan. 1	*4,600 units @*	*$20 per unit*
Sales, Jan.-Apr.	*3,100 units*	
Purchases, May 1—price changed Jan. 2	*6,900 units @*	*$26 per unit*
Sales, May-Sept.	*7,600 units*	
Purchases, Oct. 1—price changed May 2	*4,800 units @*	*$24 per unit*
Sales, Oct.-Dec.	*3,600 units*	
Replacement cost, Dec. 31—price changed Dec. 1; one-half of sales for the Oct.-Dec. period occurred before Dec. 1		*$22 per unit*

Period	*Units*	*Inventory value or cost**	*Replacement cost*	*Holding gain (loss)*
Jan.-Apr.:				
Beginning inventory	500	$ 10,000	$ 13,000	
Purchases	4,600	92,000	119,600	
	5,100	$102,000	$132,600	$30,600
Cost of goods sold	3,100		80,600	
Ending inventory	2,000		$ 52,000	
May-Sept.:				
Beginning inventory	2,000	$ 52,000	$ 48,000	
Purchases	6,900	179,400	165,600	
	8,900	$231,400	$213,600	(17,800)
Cost of goods sold	7,600		182,400	
Ending inventory	1,300		$ 31,200	
Oct.-Nov.:				
Beginning inventory	1,300	$ 31,200	$ 31,200	
Purchases	4,800	115,200	115,200	
	6,100	$146,400	$146,400	
Cost of goods sold	1,800		43,200	
Ending inventory	4,300		$103,200	
Dec. 1-31:				
Beginning inventory	4,300	$103,200	$ 94,600	(8,600)
Cost of goods sold	1,800		39,600	
Ending inventory	2,500		$ 55,000	
Holding gain on inventory for the year		-0-	-0-	$ 4,200

* *The beginning inventory is stated in terms of the replacement cost at the end of the preceding period. Purchases are stated at acquisition cost.*

It should be noticed that each element of cost of goods sold reflects replacement cost at the date of sale. If we eliminate the simplifying assumption of the illustration, that price changes occur on stated dates, then we are faced with the practical problem of how to apply the technique in a complex business situation. A practical solution might be to determine replacement cost of the nonmonetary assets at the end of each accounting period (monthly, quarterly, or annually). This price can then be presumed to apply to all transactions involving these assets during the period. In other words, we could assume that the price change occurred immediately after the start of each period and that it changed to the replacement cost prevailing at the end of the period. Other practical solutions can be found and each has its own particular merits. The point is merely that some practical solution would need to be found for identifying the replacement cost and the goods to which it is applicable.

Long-lived tangible assets. The principle of determining holding gains and losses is the same for long-lived tangible assets as it is for inventories. The fact that the cost of long-lived tangible assets is allocated by depreciation rather than by association with particular product sales does not change the basic process.

The procedure is illustrated in the following example. An asset acquired at a cost of $100,000 is assumed to have a 25-year life and to have no salvage value at the end of that time. The straight-line method of depreciation is considered appropriate as a means of allocating the asset's cost between periods. Assume that the specific price index for assets of this type was 120 at date of acquisition, rose to 140 at the end of the first year, and climbed to 175 at the end of the second year.

First Year

Acquisition cost	*$100,000*
Replacement cost at end of first year ($100,000 × 140/120)	*116,667*
Depreciation charge for the first year at year-end value ($116,667 × 4%)	*4,667*
(This calculation assumes that the price of the asset changed immediately after the beginning of the year. The replacement cost to be associated with revenue is that prevailing at the date the revenue is earned.)	
Accumulated depreciation	*4,667*
Holding gain for the first year ($116,667 − $100,000)	*16,667*
(Change in net asset value at the beginning of the year. This means that net asset value at the end of the year before depreciation for the current year should be compared with the beginning value.)	

It is unlikely that an index of specific asset prices would change from 120 to 140 immediately after the end of the year. A more realistic assumption is that the index increased gradually over the entire period. In this case (a gradual change from 120 to 140), the accountant might well conclude that replacement cost depreciation should be measured on the basis of the average replacement cost during the period, as reflected by an average price index of 130. In this case replacement cost depreciation would be calculated as shown on page 542.

Replacement cost at midyear ($100,000 × 130/120)		*$108,333*
Depreciation cost for first year at average value ($108,333 × 4%)		*4,333*
Replacement cost at end of first year ($100,000 × 140/120)		*116,667*
Accumulated depreciation at midyear		*4,333*
Accumulated depreciation at year-end ($4,333 × 140/130)		*4,667*
Holding gain for the first year:		
Gain for first half ($108,333 − $100,000)	*$8,333*	
Gain for second half [($116,667 − $4,667) − ($108,333 − $4,333)]	*8,000*	*16,333*

Second Year

Beginning year asset value		*$116,667*
Beginning year accumulated depreciation		*4,667*
Beginning year net value		*$112,000*
Replacement cost of asset at end of second year ($116,667 × 175/140)		*$145,833*
Replacement cost of accumulated depreciation at end of second year ($4,667 × 175/140)		*5,833*
Replacement cost of net asset value at end of year		*$140,000*
Holding gain ($140,000 − $112,000)		*$ 28,000*
Depreciation charge for second year at year-end value ($145,833 × 4%)		*$ 5,833*
Accumulated depreciation charge ($145,833 × 8%)		*11,667*
Depreciation charge for second year at average asset value ($116,667 × 157.5/140 × 4%)		*5,250*
Holding gain for the second year, with depreciation at midyear value:		
Gain for first half ($112,000 × 157.5/140 − $112,000)	*$14,000*	
Gain for second half [($145,833 − $11,667) − ($126,000 − $5,250)]	*13,417*	*27,417*

Illustration of replacement cost techniques

The Madison Company has decided that the practical problems of accounting for replacement cost of its nonmonetary assets can be solved. For the year ending December 31, 1966, and all prior years, the accounts have been kept in accordance with generally accepted accounting principles. For the purposes of our discussion it is assumed in this illustration that the general price level remains unchanged. This simplifying assumption will be removed in a later illustration.

The balance sheet for Madison Company as of December 31, 1966, and operating data for the year 1967 are presented on page 543. (All amounts are rounded to the nearest dollar throughout this illustration.)

MADISON COMPANY
Balance Sheet
December 31, 1966
(assets carried at cost)

Assets

Cash		*$ 50,000*
Inventory (1,200 units @ $48)		*57,600*
Land		*70,000*
Building	*$125,000*	
Less: Accumulated depreciation	*41,667*	*83,333*
Equipment	*$ 32,000*	
Less: Accumulated depreciation	*16,000*	*16,000*
Total assets		*$276,933*

Liabilities & Equities

Current payables	*$ 30,000*
Capital stock	*200,000*
Retained earnings	*46,933*
Total liabilities & equities	*$276,933*

Additional data

(1) Sales at $100 per unit for cash were:

1st quarter	$100,000
2d quarter	125,000
3d quarter	90,000
4th quarter	180,000

(2) Purchases of inventory for cash were:

	Units	*Acquisition cost*	*Replacement cost at end of quarter*
1st quarter	*1,000*	*$60*	*$62*
2d quarter	*2,000*	*64*	*63*
3d quarter	*2,500*	*60*	*60*
4th quarter	*1,000*	*68*	*65*

(3) Expenses other than depreciation and taxes were:

1st quarter	$10,000
2d quarter	11,500
3d quarter	4,750
4th quarter	14,000

(4) Inventory cost has been computed using the lifo method. The replacement cost of the inventory at December 31, 1966, is $61 per unit.

(5) Land value has remained unchanged.

(6) The industrial construction cost index rose from 100 at the date the building was acquired to 120 at January 1, 1967, and reached 140 at December 31, 1967. The change during 1967 occurred uniformly each quarter.

(7) The index of equipment cost rose from 100 at the date the equipment was acquired to 125 at January 1, 1967, and reached 135 at December 31, 1967. The change during 1967 occurred uniformly each quarter.

(8) The income tax rate is assumed to be 50% of net income including realized holding gains and losses. No payments have been made on the tax bill for the year.

(9) Current payables remain at $30,000 throughout the year.

(10) The estimated life of the building is 50 years and of the equipment 25 years. The straight-line method of depreciation is used and salvage value is assumed to be zero for both the building and the equipment.

(11) Holding gains and losses are realized only for the assets consumed during the period.

The journal entry required to restate the December 31, 1966, asset balances in terms of replacement cost at that date is:

Inventory	15,600	
Building	25,000	
Equipment	8,000	
Accumulated Depreciation—Building		8,333
Accumulated Depreciation—Equipment		4,000
Unrealized Holding Gain		36,267

The December 31, 1966, balance sheet, with nonmonetary assets stated at replacement cost, would appear as follows:

MADISON COMPANY
Balance Sheet
December 31, 1966
(nonmonetary assets carried at replacement cost)

Assets

Cash		$ 50,000
Inventory (1,200 units @ $61)		73,200
Land		70,000
Building	$150,000	
Less: Accumulated depreciation	50,000	100,000
Equipment	$ 40,000	
Less: Accumulated depreciation	20,000	20,000
Total assets		$313,200

Liabilities & Equities

Current payables	$ 30,000
Capital stock	200,000
Unrealized holding gains	36,267
Retained earnings	46,933
Total liabilities & equities	$313,200

The journal entries required to record the transactions for Madison Company are presented below using both accepted accounting principles and replacement

			Accepted accounting principles		Replacement cost	
1st Quarter						
Cash			100,000		100,000	
Sales				100,000		100,000
Inventory			60,000		60,000	
Cash				60,000		60,000
Expenses			10,000		10,000	
Cash				10,000		10,000
Inventory					3,200	
Building					6,250	
Equipment					800	
Accumulated Depreciation—Building						2,083
Accumulated Depreciation—Equipment						400
Unrealized Holding Gain						7,767
Inventory:						
2,200 units × $62		$136,400				
Less: Beginning inventory	$73,200					
Purchases	60,000	133,200				
Holding gain		$ 3,200				
Building:						
$150,000 × 125/120		$156,250				
Less: Beginning valuation		150,000				
Holding gain		$ 6,250				
Accumulated depreciation ($156,250 × 33.333%)		$ 52,083				
Equipment:						
$40,000 × 127.5/125		$ 40,800				
Less: Beginning valuation		40,000				
Holding gain		$ 800				
Accumulated depreciation ($40,800 × 50%)		$ 20,400				
Depreciation Expense			945		1,189	
Accumulated Depreciation—Building				625		781
Accumulated Depreciation—Equipment				320		408
Cost of Goods Sold			60,000		62,000	
Inventory				60,000		62,000
Replacement cost of inventory at end of each quarter is assumed to apply to goods sold during that quarter.						
Unrealized Holding Gain					2,244	
Realized Holding Gain						2,244
($1,189 − $945) + ($62,000 − $60,000).						
Income Tax Expense			14,528		14,528	
Income Tax Payable				14,528		14,528
Sales			100,000		100,000	
Realized Holding Gain					2,244	
Cost of Goods Sold				60,000		62,000
Expenses				10,000		10,000
Depreciation				945		1,189
Income Tax Expense				14,528		14,528
Retained Earnings				14,527		14,527

MADISON COMPANY
Income Statement
for the quarter ended March 31, 1967

	Accepted accounting principles		Replacement cost	
Sales		$100,000		$100,000
Cost of goods sold	$60,000		$62,000	
Expenses	10,000		10,000	
Depreciation	945	70,945	1,189	73,189
Net operating income		$ 29,055		$ 26,811
Realized holding gain				2,244
Net income before tax		$ 29,055		$ 29,055
Income tax expense		14,528		14,528
Net income		$ 14,527		$ 14,527

MADISON COMPANY
Balance Sheet
March 31, 1967

	Accepted accounting principles		Replacement cost	
Assets				
Cash		$ 80,000		$ 80,000
Inventory		57,600		74,400
Land		70,000		70,000
Building	$125,000		$156,250	
Less: Accumulated depreciation	42,292	82,708	52,864	103,386
Equipment	$ 32,000		$ 40,800	
Less: Accumulated depreciation	16,320	15,680	20,808	19,992
Total assets		$305,988		$347,778
Liabilities & Equities				
Current payables		$ 30,000		$ 30,000
Income tax payable		14,528		14,528
Capital stock		200,000		200,000
Unrealized holding gain				41,790
Retained earnings		61,460		61,460
Total liabilities & equities		$305,988		$347,778

cost as a basis of valuation for inventory and plant assets. The transactions are grouped by quarters to allow the preparation of quarterly statements.

In the illustration for the second quarter, we find it necessary to debit Realized Holding Loss and credit Unrealized Holding Gain. The reason for this rather peculiar journal entry can be found by analyzing the details of the holding gains and losses for the period (bottom of page 548).

			Accepted accounting principles		Replacement cost	
2d Quarter						
Cash			125,000		125,000	
Sales				125,000		125,000
Inventory			128,000		128,000	
Cash				128,000		128,000
Expenses			11,500		11,500	
Cash				11,500		11,500
Building					6,250	
Equipment					800	
Inventory						800
Accumulated Depreciation—Building						2,115
Accumulated Depreciation—Equipment						408
Unrealized Holding Gain						3,727
Inventory:						
3,200 units @ $63		$201,600				
Less: Beginning inventory	$ 74,400					
Purchases	128,000	202,400				
Holding loss		$ (800)				
Building:						
$156,250 × 130/125		$162,500				
Less: Beginning valuation		156,250				
Holding gain		$ 6,250				
Accumulated depreciation ($162,500 × 33.833%)		$ 54,979				
Equipment:						
$40,800 × 130/127.5		$ 41,600				
Less: Beginning valuation		40,800				
Holding gain		$ 800				
Accumulated depreciation ($41,600 × 51%)		$ 21,216				
Depreciation Expense			945		1,229	
Accumulated Depreciation—Building				625		813
Accumulated Depreciation—Equipment				320		416
Cost of Goods Sold			80,000		78,750	
Inventory				80,000		78,750
Realized Loss (see explanation p. 550)					966	
Unrealized Holding Gain						966
($1,229 − $945) + ($78,750 − $80,000).						
Income Tax Expense			16,278		16,278	
Income Tax Payable				16,278		16,278
Sales			125,000		125,000	
Cost of Goods Sold				80,000		78,750
Expenses				11,500		11,500
Depreciation				945		1,229
Realized Holding Loss						966
Income Tax Expense				16,278		16,278
Retained Earnings				16,277		16,277

MADISON COMPANY
Income Statement
for the quarter ended June 30, 1967

	Accepted accounting principles		Replacement cost	
Sales		$125,000		$125,000
Cost of goods sold	$80,000		$78,750	
Expenses	11,500		11,500	
Depreciation	945	92,445	1,229	91,479
Net operating income		$ 32,555		$ 33,521
Realized holding loss				966
Net income before tax		$ 32,555		$ 32,555
Income tax expense		16,278		16,278
Net income		$ 16,277		$ 16,277

MADISON COMPANY
Balance sheet
June 30, 1967

Assets	Accepted accounting principles		Replacement cost	
Cash		$ 65,500		$ 65,500
Inventory		105,600		122,850
Land		70,000		70,000
Building	$125,000		$162,500	
Less: Accumulated depreciation	42,917	82,083	55,792	106,708
Equipment	$ 32,000		$ 41,600	
Less: Accumulated depreciation	16,640	15,360	21,632	19,968
Total assets		$338,543		$385,026
Liabilities & Equities				
Current payables		$ 30,000		$ 30,000
Income tax payable		30,806		30,806
Capital stock		200,000		200,000
Unrealized holding gain				46,483
Retained earnings		77,737		77,737
Total liabilities & equities		$338,543		$385,026

Analysis of Holding Gains and Losses for Second Quarter

Beginning inventory at replacement cost		$ 74,400
Purchases at cost		128,000
Total available		$202,400
Replacement cost of goods available—3,200 @ $63		201,600
Holding loss		$ 800
Holding loss composed of:		
Beginning inventory at prices as of Mar. 31: 1,200 × $62		$ 74,400
Beginning inventory at prices as of June 30: 1,200 × $63		75,600
Holding gain		$ 1,200
Purchases at cost	$128,000	
Purchases at prices as of June 30: 2,000 × $63	126,000	
Holding loss		2,000
Net holding loss		$ 800
Cost of goods sold: 1,250 × $64	$ 80,000	
Replacement cost: 1,250 × $63	78,750	
Realized holding loss	$ 1,250	

			Accepted accounting principles		Replacement cost	
3d Quarter						
Cash			90,000		90,000	
Sales				90,000		90,000
Inventory			150,000		150,000	
Cash				150,000		150,000
Expenses			4,750		4,750	
Cash				4,750		4,750
Unrealized Holding Gain					1,361	
Building					6,250	
Equipment					800	
Inventory						5,850
Accumulated Depreciation—Building						2,145
Accumulated Depreciation—Equipment						416
Inventory:						
4,450 units @ $60		$267,000				
Less: Beginning inventory	$122,850					
Purchases	150,000	272,850				
Holding loss		$ 5,850				
Building:						
$162,500 × 135/130		$168,750				
Less: Beginning valuation		162,500				
Holding gain		$ 6,250				
Accumulated depreciation ($168,750 × 34.333%)		$ 57,937				
Equipment:						
$41,600 × 132.5/130		$ 42,400				
Less: Beginning valuation		41,600				
Holding gain		$ 800				
Accumulated depreciation ($42,400 × 52%)		$ 22,048				
Depreciation Expense			945		1,268	
Accumulated Depreciation—Building				625		844
Accumulated Depreciation—Equipment				320		424
Cost of Goods Sold			54,000		54,000	
Inventory				54,000		54,000
Unrealized Holding Gain					323	
Realized Holding Gain						323
($1,268 − $945) + ($54,000 − $54,000).						
Income Tax Expense			15,153		15,153	
Income Tax Payable				15,153		15,153
Sales			90,000		90,000	
Realized Holding Gain					323	
Cost of Goods Sold				54,000		54,000
Expense				4,750		4,750
Depreciation				945		1,268
Income Tax Expense				15,153		15,153
Retained Earnings				15,152		15,152

MADISON COMPANY
Income Statement
for the quarter ended September 30, 1967

	Accepted accounting principles		Replacement cost	
Sales		*$90,000*		*$90,000*
Cost of goods sold	*$54,000*		*$54,000*	
Expenses	*4,750*		*4,750*	
Depreciation	*945*	*59,695*	*1,268*	*60,018*
Net operating income		*$30,305*		*$29,982*
Realized holding gain				*323*
Net income before tax		*$30,305*		*$30,305*
Income tax expense		*15,153*		*15,153*
Net income		*$15,152*		*$15,152*

MADISON COMPANY
Balance Sheet
September 30, 1967

Assets	Accepted accounting principles		Replacement cost	
Cash		*$ 750*		*$ 750*
Inventory		*201,600*		*213,000*
Land		*70,000*		*70,000*
Building	*$125,000*		*$168,750*	
Less: Accumulated depreciation	*43,542*	*81,458*	*58,781*	*109,969*
Equipment	*$ 32,000*		*$ 42,400*	
Less: Accumulated depreciation	*16,960*	*15,040*	*22,472*	*19,928*
Total assets		*$368,848*		*$413,647*
Liabilities & Equities				
Current payables		*$ 30,000*		*$ 30,000*
Income tax payable		*45,959*		*45,959*
Capital stock		*200,000*		*200,000*
Unrealized holding gains				*44,799*
Retained earnings		*92,889*		*92,889*
Total liabilities & equities		*$368,848*		*$413,647*

The $1,250 holding loss, which is realized as a result of the sale of 1,250 units, is in fact a realization of a portion of the unrealized loss resulting from holding the 2,000 new units during the second quarter. Since the unrealized holding loss has been netted against the unrealized holding gain, we must reflect the reduction in the unrealized holding loss by increasing the net balance of unrealized gains and losses by crediting the account. The entry, then, is a product of the bookkeeping system and it does not imply that the realization of a holding loss creates an unrealized holding gain.

			Accepted accounting principles		*Replacement cost*	
4th Quarter						
Cash			180,000		180,000	
Sales				180,000		180,000
Inventory			68,000		68,000	
Cash				68,000		68,000
Expenses			14,000		14,000	
Cash				14,000		14,000
Inventory					14,750	
Building					6,250	
Equipment					800	
Accumulated Depreciation—Building						2,177
Accumulated Depreciation—Equipment						424
Unrealized Holding Gain						19,199
Inventory:						
4,550 units @ $65		*$295,750*				
Less: Beginning inventory	*$213,000*					
Purchases	*68,000*	*281,000*				
Holding gain		*$ 14,750*				
Building:						
$168,750 × 140/135		*$175,000*				
Less: Beginning valuation		*168,750*				
Holding gain		*$ 6,250*				
Accumulated depreciation ($175,000 × 34.833%)		*$ 60,958*				
Equipment:						
$42,400 × 135/132.5		*$ 43,200*				
Less: Beginning valuation		*42,400*				
Holding gain		*$ 800*				
Accumulated depreciation ($43,200 × 53%)		*$ 22,896*				
Depreciation Expense			945		1,307	
Accumulated Depreciation—Building				625		875
Accumulated Depreciation—Equipment				320		432
Cost of Goods Sold			116,000		117,000	
Inventory				116,000		117,000
Unrealized Holding Gain					1,362	
Realized Holding Gain						1,362
($1,307 − $945) + ($117,000 − $116,000).						
Income Tax Expense			24,528		24,528	
Income Tax Payable				24,528		24,528
Sales			180,000		180,000	
Realized Holding Gain					1,362	
Cost of Goods Sold				116,000		117,000
Expense				14,000		14,000
Depreciation				945		1,307
Income Tax Expense				24,528		24,528
Retained Earnings				24,527		24,527

MADISON COMPANY
Income Statement
for the quarter ended December 31, 1967

	Accepted accounting principles		*Replacement cost*	
Sales		$180,000		$180,000
Cost of goods sold	$116,000		$117,000	
Expenses	14,000		14,000	
Depreciation	945	130,945	1,307	132,307
Operating net income		$ 49,055		$ 47,693
Realized holding gain				1,362
Net income before tax		$ 49,055		$ 49,055
Income tax expense		24,528		24,528
Net income		$ 24,527		$ 24,527

MADISON COMPANY
Balance Sheet
December 31, 1967

Assets	*Accepted accounting principles*		*Replacement cost*	
Cash		$ 98,750		$ 98,750
Inventory		153,600		178,750
Land		70,000		70,000
Building	$125,000		$175,000	
Less: Accumulated depreciation	44,167	80,833	61,833	113,167
Equipment	$ 32,000		$ 43,200	
Less: Accumulated depreciation	17,280	14,720	23,328	19,872
Total assets		$417,903		$480,539
Liabilities & Equities				
Current payables		$ 30,000		$ 30,000
Income tax payable		70,487		70,487
Capital stock		200,000		200,000
Unrealized holding gains				62,636
Retained earnings		117,416		117,416
Total liabilities & equities		$417,903		$480,539

Replacement cost and changing general price levels

In the preceding discussion, the determination of holding gains and losses has been illustrated in cases in which the general level of prices has been assumed constant. This situation seldom prevails; therefore, we must give consideration to the determination of holding gains and losses when the general price level is changing. In effect this involves a combination of the procedures developed in this and the preceding chapter.

In Chapter 15 we observed that indices of general price-level changes are con-

MADISON COMPANY
Reconciliation of Unrealized Holding Gains
December 31, 1967

	Acquisition cost	*Replacement cost*	*Holding gain*
Inventory (replacement cost @ $65 per unit):			
Beginning inventory: 1,200 units @ $48	*$ 57,600*	*$ 78,000*	
1st layer: 750 units @ $64	*48,000*	*48,750*	
2d layer: 800 units @ $60	*48,000*	*52,000*	
	$153,600	*$178,750*	*$25,150*
Building	*$125,000*	*$175,000*	
Less: Accumulated depreciation	*44,167*	*61,833*	
Net book value	*$ 80,833*	*$113,167*	*32,334*
Equipment	*$ 32,000*	*$ 43,200*	
Less: Accumulated depreciation	*17,280*	*23,328*	
Net book value	*$ 14,720*	*$ 19,872*	*5,152*
Unrealized holding gains			*$62,636*

sidered indications of change in the size (value) of the dollar as a measuring unit. Replacement cost data are expressed in terms of the ability of a dollar to command particular goods, not goods and services in general. In order to compare acquisition cost and replacement cost, it is necessary to have both measures stated in terms of the same measuring unit. For purposes of determining holding gains and losses, acquisition cost must be translated into current dollars. The difference between acquisition cost or replacement cost at the end of the preceding period restated in current dollars and replacement cost at the end of the current period is the holding gain or loss for the period.

Referring to the example of Wilson Corporation, discussed in Chapter 15, we can illustrate this principle. A tract of land was acquired for $100,000 in 1960 when the index of general prices was 90. The price level currently stands at 120. Wilson has in his possession a bona fide offer of $400,000 for the land. The acquisition cost of the land in terms of current dollars is $133,333. Wilson Corporation therefore has a holding gain of $266,667 accumulated since 1960. Assume that Wilson also had an opportunity to sell the land for $400,000 on last December 31 when the general price index stood at 110. The replacement cost at the end of last year expressed in terms of current dollars is $436,364 ($400,000 × 120/110); therefore, during the current period Wilson Corporation suffered a holding loss of $36,364 ($436,364 – $400,000). As of last December 31 the total accumulated holding gain resulting from the investment in land was $277,778 ($400,000 – $100,000 × 110/90) or in terms of current dollars $303,031 ($277,778 × 120/110). Should Wilson Corporation decide to sell the land rather than recognize a gain of $300,000 ($400,000 – $100,000) in the current year, the loss of $36,364 from holding the asset during the year should be reflected. Thus, we can begin to see some of the benefits of a more careful analysis of business operations.

MONSON COMPANY
Journal Entries for the Year 1967

General price index		Accepted accounting principles		Current-year dollars		Replacement cost	
110	(1) Cash	550,000		700,000		700,000	
	Common Stock		550,000		700,000		700,000
115	(2) Land	37,500		45,653		45,653	
	Building	112,500		136,956		136,956	
	Cash		50,000		60,869		60,869
	Mortgage Payable		100,000		121,740		121,740
120	(3) Merchandise	60,000		70,000		70,000	
	Accounts Payable		60,000		70,000		70,000
125	(4) Equipment	125,000		140,000		140,000	
	Cash		125,000		140,000		140,000
125	(5) Accounts Receivable	125,000		140,000		140,000	
	Sales		125,000		140,000		140,000
120	(6) Expenses	30,000		35,000		35,000	
	Cash		30,000		35,000		35,000
130	(7) Accounts Payable	50,000		53,847		53,847	
	Cash		50,000		53,847		53,847
130	(8) Cash	105,000		113,077		113,077	
	Accounts Receivable		105,000		113,077		113,077
140	(9) Mortgage Payable	5,000		5,000		5,000	
	Interest Expense	6,000		6,000		6,000	
	Cash		11,000		11,000		11,000
	Year-end (a)						
	Realized Loss on Monetary Accounts			124,131		124,131	

		Accounts Payable			6,153		6,153	
		Mortgage Payable			21,740		21,740	
		Cash				123,361		123,361
		Unrealized Gain on Long-term Liabilities				21,740		21,740
		Accounts Receivable				6,923		6,923
		Year-end (b)						
		Merchandise					14,000	
		Building					13,044	
		Unrealized Holding Loss					609	
		Land						5,653
		Equipment						22,000
	(10)	*Depreciation*	17,000		19,478		17,800	
115		*Accumulated Depreciation—Building*		4,500		5,478		6,000
125		*Accumulated Depreciation—Equipment*		12,500		14,000		11,800
	(11)	*Cost of Goods Sold*	50,000		58,333		70,000	
120		*Merchandise*		50,000		58,333		70,000
		Year-end (c)						
		Unrealized Holding Loss					9,989	
		Realized Holding Gain						9,989
		Closing entry						
		Sales	125,000		140,000		140,000	
		Realized Holding Gain					9,989	
		Retained Earnings		22,000	102,942		102,942	
		Expenses		30,000		35,000		35,000
		Interest Expense		6,000		6,000		6,000
		Depreciation		17,000		19,478		17,800
		Cost of Goods Sold		50,000		58,333		70,000
		Realized Loss on Monetary Accounts				124,131		124,131

Techniques for recognition of changing general price levels

In Chapter 15 we examined the affairs of Monson Company for 1967, its first year of operations, in terms of the impact of changing general price levels on the financial data. We shall continue the Monson Company illustration here so that the relationship of these two topics, changing general price levels and changing specific prices, can be examined as a unit. Many of the practical problems, such as calculation of price indices and determination of replacement costs, are assumed away in this illustration as they have been in the earlier illustrations. The purpose of the illustration is to demonstrate how we might deal with the data in the accounts and statements if we can solve the practical problems of getting the data. In addition, the effect of the proposed changes on financial reporting can be analyzed.

The journal entries to record the activities for Monson Company for the year 1967, which were presented in Chapter 15 are reproduced on pages 554 and 555. We have added the journal entries which would have to be made using "replacement cost." The following additional data are needed to present the same transactions using the principles of replacement cost:

(1) Replacement cost of merchandise at the end of the year is $14 per unit of services $35,000. The price change occurred immediately after the purchase.
(2) The market value of the land is estimated to be $40,000.
(3) The index of nonresidential construction cost has risen from 112.5 to 150.
(4) The index of equipment cost has declined from 125 to 118.

In the above series of journal entries, there are three complete recordings of the financial affairs of Monson Company for 1967. Note that transactions numbered (1) through (9) are exactly the same for "current-year dollars" and "replacement cost." This is consistent with the earlier discussion in this chapter, in that transactions using replacement cost are recorded at actual-dollar cost or, if we account for general price-level changes, at the current-dollar equivalent. Year-end entry (a) adjusts the current-dollar equivalent of the money accounts to the actual dollar balance at the end of the period. The gain or loss arising from the changing purchasing power of the dollar is considered realized for the investment in current monetary assets and contractual obligations to pay, within the next accounting period, a stated sum of dollars. The gain or loss on long-term commitments to pay a given sum of dollars is considered to be unrealized until the obligation matures. Year-end entry (b) reflects the revaluation of nonmonetary assets from cost or current-dollar equivalent to replacement cost and the accompanying holding gain or loss for the period. Entries (10) and (11) then reflect the amortization of the carrying value of nonmonetary assets for the portion of the asset's usefulness which expired during the current period. Year-end entry (c) reflects the recognition of the realized portion of the holding gain or loss (the difference between cost or current-dollar equivalent and replacement cost of expenses representing amortization of assets held during a period when the specific price of the asset changed).

The financial statements for Monson Company are illustrated for 1967 on a comparative basis for each of the three methods of accounting: (1) accepted accounting principles, (2) recognition of changing general price levels (current-year dollars), and (3) recognition of changing general price levels and replacement cost of the nonmonetary assets (replacement cost).

MONSON COMPANY
Balance Sheet
December 31, 1967

	Accepted accounting principles	Current-year dollars	Replacement cost
Assets			
Cash	$389,000	$389,000	$389,000
Accounts receivable	20,000	20,000	20,000
Merchandise	10,000	11,667	14,000
Land	37,500	45,653	40,000
Building	112,500	136,956	150,000
Less: Accumulated depreciation	(4,500)	(5,478)	(6,000)
Equipment	125,000	140,000	118,000
Less: Accumulated depreciation	(12,500)	(14,000)	(11,800)
Total assets	$677,000	$723,798	$713,200
Liabilities & Equities			
Accounts payable	$ 10,000	$ 10,000	$ 10,000
Mortgage payable	95,000	95,000	95,000
Common stock	550,000	700,000	700,000
Unrealized holding loss			(10,598)
Unrealized gain on long-term debt		21,740	21,740
Retained earnings	22,000	(102,942)	(102,942)
Total liabilities & equities	$677,000	$723,798	$713,200

MONSON COMPANY
Income Statement
for the year ended December 31, 1967

	Accepted accounting principles	Current-year dollars	Replacement cost
Sales	$125,000	$ 140,000	$ 140,000
Less expenses:			
Cost of goods sold	$ 50,000	$ 58,333	$ 70,000
Expenses	30,000	35,000	35,000
Depreciation	17,000	19,478	17,800
Interest expense	6,000	6,000	6,000
Total expenses	$103,000	$ 118,811	$ 128,800
Net operating income	$ 22,000	$ 21,189	$ 11,200
Realized loss on current monetary accounts		(124,131)	(124,131)
Realized gain on holding nonmonetary assets			9,989
Net income (loss)	$ 22,000	$(102,942)	$(102,942)

These statements reflect clearly the different information which may be obtained from the same basic data. In the statement headed "current-year dollars," we have accepted the fact that general price levels change. These changes are accounted for with the result that the large net working capital position resulted in a significant loss to the company. This loss was caused by the fact that the dollars held lost a portion of their ability to command goods and services. In the statement headed "replacement cost," we have accepted the indicated cost of replacing the nonmonetary assets as the dollar amount to be accounted for. The portion of the change in replacement cost reflected in the income statement as cost of goods sold and depreciation is considered a realized gain from holding nonmonetary assets. This portion is realized because it has been sold to customers as goods and/or services. The remaining increase or decrease in the carrying value of these assets is considered unrealized because the service potential of the assets has not been consumed.

The change in net operating income reflected on the income statements is the result of changing the asset carrying values which are to be amortized or written off as the usefulness of the asset expires. Note the difference in net operating income between "current-year dollars" and "replacement cost" and the similarity of the figure labeled "net loss" for these two methods. The "current-year dollar" figures have replaced the "accepted accounting principles" figures used in our earlier illustration in the determination of holding gains and losses, both realized and unrealized.

We do not have to accept both price-level adjustment accounting and replacement cost accounting in order to implement one or the other. Either or both modifications of accepted accounting principles can be implemented. We should keep in mind that each of these techniques is a separate and distinct means of gaining additional information about the firm from the accounting system.

To illustrate the fact that each can be adopted without the other, we need only to demonstrate the acceptance of replacement cost for Monson Company while ignoring the changes in the general price level. In Chapter 15 we have accounted for the changes in the general price level while ignoring changes in replacement cost for Monson. The journal entries to account for replacement cost changes alone are compared on pages 559 and 560 with those resulting from the application of accepted accounting principles.

The financial statements based on the above transactions are presented on page 561.

We should note particularly that the asset section of the balance sheet using replacement cost is identical whether we account for changes in the general price level or not. The difference is to be found in the composition of the stockholders' equity. In addition, the reported net income obtained by using replacement cost without accounting for general price-level changes is different from that obtained when these changes are accounted for. The difference can be found in sales, expenses, and the data following net operating income. From this comparison we can see that adoption of replacement cost without recognition of general price-level changes results in treating general price-level changes related to nonmonetary assets as holding gains or losses and ignores the effect of these changes on the remaining affairs of the firm.

	Accepted accounting principles		Replacement cost	
(1) Cash	550,000		550,000	
Common stock		550,000		550,000
(2) Land	37,500		37,500	
Building	112,500		112,500	
Cash		50,000		50,000
Mortgage Payable		100,000		100,000
(3) Merchandise	60,000		60,000	
Accounts Payable		60,000		60,000
(4) Equipment	125,000		125,000	
Cash		125,000		125,000
(5) Accounts Receivable	125,000		125,000	
Sales		125,000		125,000
(6) Expenses	30,000		30,000	
Cash		30,000		30,000
(7) Accounts Payable	50,000		50,000	
Cash		50,000		50,000
(8) Cash	105,000		105,000	
Accounts Receivable		105,000		105,000
(9) Mortgage Payable	5,000		5,000	
Interest Expense	6,000		6,000	
Cash		11,000		11,000
Year-end (a)				
Merchandise			24,000	
Land			2,500	
Building			37,500	
Expenses			5,000	
Unrealized Holding Gain				62,000
Equipment				7,000

(continued)

	Accepted accounting principles		Replacement cost	
Inventory:				
6,000 units @ $14 . . . . $ 84,000				
Less: Purchases 60,000				
Holding gain . . . . $ 24,000				
Building:				
$112,500 × 150/112.5 . . . . $150,000				
Cost 137,500				
Holding gain . . . . $ 2,500				
Equipment:				
$125,000 × 118/125 . . . . $118,000				
Cost 125,000				
Holding loss . . . . $ 7,000				
Land:				
Replacement cost . . . . $ 40,000				
Cost 37,500				
Holding gain . . . . $ 2,500				
(10) Depreciation	*17,000*		*17,800*	
Accumulated Depreciation—Building		*4,000*		*6,000*
Accumulated Depreciation—Equipment		*12,500*		*11,800*
(11) Cost of Goods Sold	*50,000*		*70,000*	
Merchandise		*50,000*		*70,000*
Year-end (b)				
Unrealized Holding Gain			*25,800*	
Realized Holding Gain . . . . ($17,800 – $17,000) + ($70,000 – $50,000) + ($35,000 – $30,000).				*25,800*
Closing entry				
Sales	*125,000*		*125,000*	
Realized Holding Gain			*25,800*	
Cost of Goods Sold		*50,000*		*70,000*
Expenses		*30,000*		*35,000*
Depreciation		*17,000*		*17,800*
Interest Expense		*6,000*		*6,000*
Retained Earnings		*22,000*		*22,000*

MONSON COMPANY
Income Statement
for the year ended December 31, 1967

	Accepted accounting principles	*Replacement cost*
Sales	*$125,000*	*$125,000*
Less expenses:		
Cost of goods sold	*$ 50,000*	*$ 70,000*
Expenses	*30,000*	*35,000*
Depreciation	*17,000*	*17,800*
Interest expense	*6,000*	*6,000*
Total expenses	*$103,000*	*$128,800*
Net operating income	*$ 22,000*	*$ (3,800)*
Realized holding gain		*25,800*
Net income	*$ 22,000*	*$ 22,000*

MONSON COMPANY
Balance Sheet
December 31, 1967

Assets	*Accepted accounting principles*	*Replacement cost*
Cash	*$389,000*	*$389,000*
Accounts receivable	*20,000*	*20,000*
Merchandise	*10,000*	*14,000*
Land	*37,500*	*40,000*
Building	*112,500*	*150,000*
Less: Accumulated depreciation	*(4,500)*	*(6,000)*
Equipment	*125,000*	*118,000*
Less: Accumulated depreciation	*(12,500)*	*(11,800)*
Total assets	*$677,000*	*$713,200*
Liabilities & Equities		
Accounts payable	*$ 10,000*	*$ 10,000*
Mortgage payable	*95,000*	*95,000*
Common stock	*550,000*	*550,000*
Unrealized holding gain		*36,200*
Retained earnings	*22,000*	*22,000*
Total liabilities & equities	*$677,000*	*$713,200*

Summary

In these two chapters (15 and 16) we have illustrated the procedure which might be used if the accountant should modify his assumptions regarding the stability of the measuring unit and adherence to the cost principle. The authors have attempted to indicate what additional information may be available under certain circumstances and how we might change accounting procedures to get the information. Some of the questions which might be raised and which we have not answered are: (1) Is the additional information useful to management, stockholders, or other users of financial information? (2) Do the revised statements present more fairly the affairs of the enterprise? (3) Is the information included in the statements more realistic or a better representation of the activities of the enterprise than the information which is currently available? (4) Can the information be obtained in a manner which removes the possibility of fraudulent manipulation? There are undoubtedly additional questions to be considered before a major change in accepted accounting principles can be expected. Our purpose here has been to explore means of accounting for the affairs of a firm if the accounting system is modified to report a different type of information or to report additional information.

Questions

1. Why is it desirable to separate holding gains and losses from operating income?
2. Why is replacement cost used as an indicator of value?
3. When is income considered realized under accepted accounting conventions?
4. In what ways would the realization convention have to be changed to allow recognition of holding gains and losses in the period the assets are held?
5. What are the primary advantages and disadvantages of adopting replacement cost?
6. If replacement cost accounting is adopted, will this remove the differences which currently exist between firms where one uses the fifo method of valuing inventory and the other uses the lifo method?
7. How are holding gains and losses determined?
8. XYZ Company acquired a building at a cost of $500,000 on the first day of the year when the nonresidential construction index was 125. At the end of the year the index was 180. Compute the net replacement cost of the building at the end of the year and the depreciation charge for the year, assuming a 40-year life and no net salvage value.
9. Why is it necessary or even desirable to separate general price-level changes and specific price-level changes?
10. What is the difference between the information obtained when general and specific price changes are accounted for and when only specific price changes are accounted for?

Short cases for analysis

16-1 The controller of Witsoe Corporation asks you to come to a board of directors meeting to explain some accounting problems to the members of the board. He indicates that the questions will be concerned with the problems of depreciation and inventories. As the auditor of the firm, you are fully aware that the corporation has used the straight-line method of depreciation for many years and that they have consistently used the lower of fifo cost or market value in accounting for the inventory.

At the board meeting the following questions are raised:

1. What is the objective of calculating depreciation based on replacement cost and of determining the cost of the inventory in accordance with the principles of the lifo method?

2. Is there some accounting assumption which is responsible for the development of these methods?

3. What effect would the adoption of the methods have on the financial statements?

4. What are the pros and cons of modifying financial statements for changes in the level of prices?

Instructions

Draft responses to these questions which are devoid of technical jargon and which would permit a group of listeners to understand the problems presented and the likely effect on financial statements.

16-2 X and Y are firms with identical operating characteristics. Their plants, sale volume, and other indicators of size are identical. Firm X has maintained its inventory on a fifo basis and Firm Y has used the lifo method. In all other respects the firms are identical.

The following facts are ascertained about the affairs of the two firms:

	Firm X	*Firm Y*
Beginning inventory year 10:		
2,000 units @ $20 per unit	*$ 40,000*	
2,000 units @ $5 per unit		*$ 10,000*
Purchases:		
12,000 units @ $25 per unit	*300,000*	*300,000*
Cost of sales:		
2,000 units @ $20 per unit	*(40,000)*	
9,000 units @ $25 per unit	*(225,000)*	
11,000 units @ $25 per unit		*(275,000)*
Net income	*60,000*	*50,000*
Retained earnings, beginning of year	*150,000*	*120,000*

Instructions

a. Explain why the differences exist in the net income and retained earnings figures.

b. Assume that the replacement cost of the inventory at the end of Year 10 is $27.50 per unit. Using replacement cost data, indicate what changes would be made in the financial statements.

c. Explain why any differences remain on the financial statements when replacement costs are used to account for inventories. Would these differences exist if all holding gains and losses were realized in the period in which price changes occur? Explain.

d. In which company will the unrealized gain account accumulate to the greatest extent if prices continue to rise, or will the balance be the same? Explain.

16-3 Southern Textiles Company has employed you to review the effect on net income of adopting replacement cost for plant asset valuation. You find the following information:

Plant Assets at Cost

Land	*$ 20,000*
Building	*300,000*
Equipment	*250,000*
Total	*$570,000*

The land, building, and one-half of the equipment were acquired five years ago. The remaining portion of the equipment was acquired at the beginning of the current year. The straight-line method of depreciation is used. The building has an estimated 25-year life and the equipment a 10-year life. None of the depreciable assets is assumed to have any salvage value.

The replacement cost of the land is estimated to be $30,000 at the end of the current year. The index of construction cost was 100 when the building was acquired. At the beginning of the current year it was 150 and at the end of the year it was 175. The replacement cost of the original purchase of equipment was $300,000 at the beginning of the year. The replacement cost of the equipment at the end of the year was $330,000 for the original purchase and 170,000 for the last purchase.

Instructions

a. Show the effect on the depreciation charge for the current year of adopting replacement cost, with depreciation computed on the year-end asset value.

b. Compute the depreciation charge and the asset and associated accumulated depreciation account balances if the depreciation were computed on the average value of the asset during the year.

c. What would be the difference between statements prepared using the method required under (*a*) and that required under (*b*)?

16-4 DIDCO acquired a tract of land in 1960 at a total cost of $500,000. At that time the general price level stood at 80. On December 31, 1966, when the general price level was 140, DIDCO had a firm offer for the land of $1,000,000. The offer was refused. On December 31, 1967, DIDCO received another offer of $1,350,000 for the land; at this time the general price index was 180. The offer was accepted and the transaction was completed on January 2, 1968. Mr. Davis, president, asks you if he is correct in saying that he made a $350,000 profit during 1967. He explains that he realizes that the total appreciation covered a period of almost eight years, but he feels a strict average over the eight-year period ignores the fact that some evidence of market value existed one year previously.

Instructions

Explain to Davis as completely as you can the situation as you understand it, including recognition of general price-level changes as well as replacement cost information. Indicate how your proposal is different from or in accord with generally accepted accounting practice.

Problems

16-5 Econo Corporation began operations for period 1 with the following assets and capital:

ECONO CORPORATION
Balance Sheet
beginning of period 1

Cash	*$ 15,000*	*Capital stock*	*$121,000*
Inventory (3,000 units @ $8)	*24,000*		
Land	*12,000*		
Building	*50,000*		
Equipment	*20,000*		
Total	*$121,000*	*Total*	*$121,000*

Econo uses the fifo method of accounting for the inventory and the straight-line method of accounting for the depreciation of its building and equipment. The building is estimated to have a 20-year service life and the equipment a 10-year life. Neither of these assets is assumed to have any salvage value at the end of its estimated useful life.

Information about the transactions of period 1 is as follows:

(1) 20,000 units of merchandise were purchased on credit at a price of $10 per unit.
(2) 15,000 units of merchandise were sold at $16 per unit for cash at a time when the replacement cost was $12 per unit.
(3) 16,000 units of merchandise were purchased on credit at a price of $13 per unit.
(4) 18,000 units of merchandise were sold at $18 per unit for cash at a time when the replacement cost was $14 per unit.
(5) Replacement cost of land, buildings, and equipment increased by 50% during the year. Replacement cost of the inventory at year-end was $15 per unit.
(6) $400,000 was paid to creditors.

Instructions

Prepare journal entries to record the transactions of Econo Corporation for the period using (1) accepted accounting practice and (2) replacement cost procedures.

16-6 The balance sheet as of the end of Year 9 and the transaction data for Year 10 for Boone Company are presented below:

BOONE COMPANY
Balance Sheet
end of Year 9

Assets		
Cash		*$ 75,000*
Accounts receivable		*105,000*
Inventories at lifo cost (5,000 units @ $16)		*80,000*
Land		*30,000*
Building	*$120,000*	
Less: Accumulated depreciation	*27,000*	*93,000*
Equipment	*$150,000*	
Less: Accumulated depreciation	*67,500*	*82,500*
Total assets		*$465,500*
Liabilities & Equity		
Current liabilities		*$ 60,000*
Capital stock		*350,000*
Retained earnings		*55,500*
Total liabilities & equity		*$465,500*

Transaction data

(1) Purchased 40,000 units of merchandise for $21 each on credit.
(2) Sold 39,000 units for $36 each on credit.
(3) Other expenses of $500,000 were incurred and paid for.
(4) Current liabilities paid totaled $780,000.
(5) Accounts receivable collected totaled $1,400,000.
(6) The replacement cost of the inventory at the end of the year was $20 per unit.
(7) The land had an appraised value of $48,000 at year-end. The index of nonresidential construction cost stood at 180 at year-end. The index had been 120 at the date the building was acquired. The replacement cost of the equipment is $225,000, which represents its gross value at year-end.

Instructions

Prepare an income statement and a balance sheet for Boone Company, reporting on the affairs of the firm for Year 10 using replacement cost data.

16-7 The controller of the Western Sales Company has become concerned about what he terms the inadequacy of presently accepted accounting practice. He asks you to prepare statements as of December 31 for Years 1 through 3 which will allow him to compare the effect of replacement cost and accepted accounting practice in financial information. He provides you with the following statement and information:

WESTERN SALES COMPANY
Balance Sheet
December 31, Year 0

Assets

Cash		*$ 80,000*
Accounts receivable		*112,500*
Inventory (2,000 units at $40 each)		*80,000*
Land		*60,000*
Building	*$200,000*	
Less: Accumulated depreciation	*40,000*	*160,000*
Equipment	*$300,000*	
Less: Accumulated depreciation	*100,000*	*200,000*
Total assets		*$692,500*

Liabilities & Equities

Current payables	*$ 50,000*
Income taxes payable	*75,000*
Capital stock	*450,000*
Retained earnings	*117,500*
Total liabilities & equities	*$692,500*

Additional data

(1) As of December 31 of each year accounts receivable total 15% of the year's sales, accounts payable total 10% of the year's purchases, and the income tax liability for the year just ended is paid on April 15 of the succeeding year, the tax rate is assumed to be 50% of net income including realized holding gains and losses.

(2) Sales for the three years were:

	Units	*Price per unit*
Year 1	*10,000*	*$ 80*
Year 2	*12,000*	*90*
Year 3	*13,000*	*100*

(3) Purchases for the three years were:

	Units	*Acquisition cost*	*Replacement cost at end of year*
Year 1	*12,000*	*$60*	*$65*
Year 2	*10,000*	*68*	*75*
Year 3	*14,000*	*80*	*75*

(4) Expenses other than depreciation and income taxes were:

Year 1	*$ 80,000*
Year 2	*95,000*
Year 3	*105,000*

(5) Inventory is priced using the last in, first out method. Replacement cost of the inventory at the end of Year 0 is $58 per unit.
(6) The land value has increased $5,000 each year, based on an independent real estate appraisal.
(7) The industrial construction index has risen from 80 at the date the building was acquired to 110 at the end of Year 0, 115 at the end of Year 1, 125 at the end of Year 2, and 140 at the end of Year 3.
(8) The index of equipment cost has risen from 100 at the date the equipment was acquired to 120 at the end of Year 0, 140 at the end of Years 1 and 2, and 150 at the end of Year 3.
(9) The estimated life of the building is 40 years and of the equipment 20 years. The straight-line method of depreciation is used and salvage value is assumed to be zero for both buildings and equipment.
(10) Holding gains and losses are considered to be realized for assets or portions of assets whose usefulness expires during the period.

Instructions

Prepare comparative financial statements for Years 1, 2, and 3 using (1) accepted accounting principles and (2) replacement cost. (The preparation of journal entries may be beneficial in accumulating the data. Round all amounts to the nearest dollar.)

16-8 The following data are presented for Addison, Inc., for the first year of operation:

ADDISON, INC.
Balance Sheet
at beginning of operations

Assets

Cash	*$ 20,000*
Inventory, fifo cost (5,000 units @ $10)	*50,000*
Land	*10,000*
Building	*60,000*
Equipment	*40,000*
Total assets	*$180,000*

Liabilities & Equities

Mortgage payable	*$ 30,000*
Capital stock	*150,000*
Total liabilities & equities	*$180,000*

Transaction data

(1) Cash sales of the period totaled $600,000 (30,000 @ $20).
(2) Purchases on account totaled 416,000 (32,000 @ $13).
(3) Other cash expenses totaled $100,000.
(4) The building has an estimated useful life of 30 years and the equipment 20 years. Neither asset is expected to have any salvage value at the end of its useful life.

(5) Payments of $400,000 were made to creditors when the general price index was 140.

(6) The income tax rate is assumed to be 48% of reported income including realized holding gains and losses and purchasing power gains and losses on monetary assets.

(7) The general price index was 120 at the beginning of the year, 132 at midyear, and 144 at year-end.

(8) At year-end the replacement cost of the inventory was $15 per unit, the land $15,000, and the equipment $46,000. The index of nonresidential construction was 140 at the beginning of the year and 200 at year-end.

(9) Purchases, other services, and sales transactions are assumed to have been uniformily incurred over the year.

Instructions

a. Prepare comparative financial statements for Addison, Inc., using both general price-level adjustments and replacement cost, using only replacement cost, and using generally accepted accounting principles.

b. What are the main differences and similarities? Why do they exist?

16-9 The controller of Madison, Inc., has become concerned about the impact of replacement cost on the financial statements of his company. He requests that you give him a set of comparative statements showing (1) accepted accounting practice, (2) adjustments for changes in the general price level, and (3) adjustments for adoption of replacement cost.

The basic data for this problem are presented as Problem 15-12 on page 529. The additional information required to complete this problem is presented below:

Additional data

(1) Replacement cost of merchandise at the end of the year is $168,875. Replacement cost of the merchandise sold during the year was $462,500.

(2) The market value of land, based on appraisal, at the end of the year is $30,000.

(3) The index of nonresidential construction cost has risen to 140 at year-end. The index was 90 at the date the building was acquired.

(4) The index of equipment cost stands at 110 at year-end. The index was 100 at the date the equipment was acquired.

(5) Replacement cost of services followed the general price level during the year.

16-10 The balance sheet as of the end of Year 6 for Kanès Company and the transaction data for Year 7 are given on page 570.

Kanes Company was organized at the beginning of Year 1, when the general price index was 80. The land, plant, and equipment were acquired at that time. The bonds payable were issued later when the index was 100. The inventory was acquired when the index was 118 and the index was 150 at the end of Year 6. The index continued to rise and by the end of Year 7 it was 180.

KANES COMPANY
Balance Sheet
Year 6

Assets		
Cash		*$ 60,000*
Receivables		*90,000*
Inventories (23,600 units @ $6)		*141,600*
Land		*24,000*
Plant and equipment	*$180,000*	
Less: Accumulated depreciation	*36,000*	*144,000*
Total assets		*$459,600*
Liabilities & Equities		
Accounts payable		*$ 45,000*
Bonds payable—6%		*105,000*
Capital stock		*260,000*
Retained earnings		*49,600*
Total liabilities & equities		*$459,600*

Kanes Company's transactions during Year 7 are summarized below and the index prevailing at the time of the transaction is also provided. All merchandise was sold for $20 per unit.

Transaction	*General price index*
Sales on account of $170,500	*155*
Sales on account of $280,500	*170*
Sales on account of $416,500	*175*
Merchandise purchased on account (14,000 units @ $8) $112,000	*160*
Merchandise purchased on account (17,200 units @ $8) $137,600	*172*
Merchandise purchased on account (15,575 units @ $10) $155,750	*178*
Services purchased on account, $224,400	*165*
Services purchased on account, $212,280	*174*
Receivables collected, $497,280	*168*
Receivables collected, $344,960	*176*
Accounts payable paid, $384,750	*171*
Accounts payable paid, $405,840	*178*
Taxes ($25,400), interest ($6,300), and dividends ($20,000) were recognized and paid in cash at year-end	*180*
Inventory of merchandise at end of year is $168,800, determined on a last in, first out basis.	

The replacement cost of the inventory was $12 per unit at the end of the year. The land was appraised at $30,000 and the plant and equipment at a gross value of $400,000.

Instructions

Prepare financial statements for Kanes Company for Year 7 adjusted for changes in the general price level and giving effect to replacement cost. Distinguish clearly the gains and losses resulting from general price-level changes and changes in replacement cost.

PART FIVE

PRESENT-VALUE CONCEPTS

17 REVIEW OF COMPOUND INTEREST FUNDAMENTALS

The underlying principles of accumulating and discounting sums of money due at varying points in time through the use of compound interest formulas and tables are summarized in this chapter. In the next two chapters we shall consider some accounting applications which call for an understanding of present and future values and the ability to compute them. Students who have a good grasp of the mathematics of compound interest may skip this chapter and proceed immediately to the discussion of accounting applications. This chapter is designed to provide a review for those who need to refresh their understanding and an introduction to the subject for those whose prior background is inadequate.

Why is compound interest important?

Compound interest concepts have a wider application in business and economic analysis than many people imagine.

In the first place, such concepts are fundamental in evaluating investment and borrowing decisions. All business organizations are at some time faced with two basic types of decisions: (1) committing present funds in the expectation of realizing periodic benefits in future periods; (2) receiving present funds in return for a promise to pay or deliver resources at some future time. These "investment-and-return" and "borrowing-and-repayment" situations have an important common characteristic: The difference in the *timing* of the receipts and payments has an important effect on the worth of the various commitments and thus on the value of the resulting assets and liabilities. Consequently investment and borrowing decisions should be made only after a careful analysis of the relative values of the cash outlays and inflows in prospect. Measuring these values involves the use of compound interest formulas. The accountant, as an adviser to decision makers, must not only be able to make value measurements but must also understand their implications.

Even in his role as an economic historian, the accountant will encounter a number of situations where an objective measure of what has happened is dependent on a present evaluation of future prospects. An installment account receivable, for example, represents a series of future cash inflows. The proceeds of a bond issue reflect the present value of the corporate promise to make a series of future payments of principal and interest. To deal effectively with financial reporting problems, the accountant should understand and be able to measure the present value of prospective cash inflows and outflows. This measurement requires an understanding of compound interest.

The relative significance of simple and compound interest

Interest is fundamentally the growth in a principal sum representing the price charged for the use of money for a given time period. Our concept of economic earnings (whether in the form of interest or some other kind of return on investment) is periodic. Economic activity is carried on during specifiable time periods and we think of return on investment in terms of return per month, per quarter, or per year.

Simple interest is the return on (or growth of) a principal sum for one time period. We may also think of simple interest as a return for more than one time period if we assume that the interest (growth) itself does not earn a return, but this kind of situation occurs rarely in the real world. Simple interest is usually applicable only to short-term investment and borrowing transactions involving a time span of one year or less.

Compound interest is the return on (or growth of) a principal sum for two or more time periods, assuming that the growth in each time period is added to the principal sum at the end of the period and earns a return in all subsequent periods. Many important investment and borrowing transactions involve more than one time period. This is particularly true in a capitalistic economy where large amounts of long-lived capital are employed productively and financed over long periods of time. Businessmen think about and evaluate such investment opportunities in terms of a series of periodic returns, each of which may be reinvested in turn to yield future returns. The growth of capital through the reinvestment of earnings is thus a common feature of the economic scene and must be taken into account in attaching a value to cash inflows and outflows which are spread over time in varying patterns. Fortunately the accumulation and reinvestment of earnings at periodic intervals is sufficiently analogous to the financial process of compound interest that formulas developed to deal with annuities and actuarial computations are applicable to the valuation problems faced by the accountant.

Simple interest formulas[1]

The basic components of the computation of simple interest I_s are the principal amount p_s, the rate of interest r, and the time t. The basic formula is:

[1] The subscript s is used to distinguish symbols for simple interest from symbols relating to compound interest used in later sections of this chapter.

$$I_s = p_s \times r \times t \qquad \text{or} \qquad I_s = p_s rt$$

Formula for simple interest	I_s

It is assumed that the interest rate and time are expressed in common units; that is, if r is an annual rate then t is expressed in years. Interest rates are expressed in terms of annual rates unless otherwise stated.

The *amount* to which a principal sum will accumulate at interest during a given time period, designated by the symbol a_s, is simply the principal sum plus the interest; this may be expressed:

$$\textit{Amount} = \textit{principal} + \textit{interest}$$
$$a_s = p_s + (p_s rt)$$
or
$$a_s = p_s(1 + rt)$$

Formula for amount at simple interest	a_s

Example 1. Find the interest due on a loan of \$1,000 for two months at 6%.

Solution $\quad I_s = p_s rt = \$1,000 \times .06 \times 1/6 = \$10$

Example 2. To what amount would \$1,000 accumulate in three months if invested at 6% annual interest?

Solution
$$a_s = p_s(1 + rt) = \$1,000\,[1 + (.06 \times 1/4)]$$
$$= \$1,000\,(1.015) = \$1,015$$

If we wish to know the present value p_s of a future sum that includes simple interest, the formula for determining the amount of the future sum a_s may be adapted by simply solving for the principal amount p_s, as follows:

We know that $\quad a_s = p_s(1 + rt)$

Solve for p_s $\quad p_s = \dfrac{a_s}{1 + rt}$

Formula for present value at simple interest	p_s

Example 3. Able has the prospect of receiving \$1,030 at the end of six months. What is the present value of this prospect if money is worth 6% per year?

Solution $\quad p_s = \dfrac{a_s}{(1 + rt)} = \dfrac{\$1,030}{(1 + .06 \times 1/2)} = \dfrac{\$1,030}{1.03} = \$1,000$

We can diagram the simple interest relationships just described as follows:

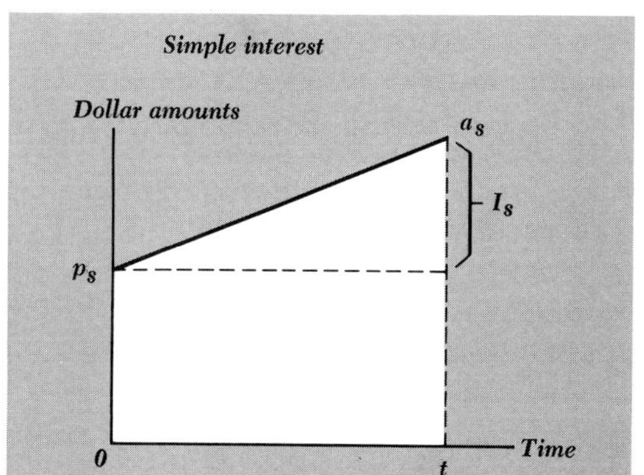

Formulas
$I_s = p_s rt$
$a_s = p_s(1 + rt)$
$p_s = \dfrac{a_s}{1 + rt}$

Compound interest

Amount of a principal sum at compound interest

Suppose that, knowing only simple interest formulas, we wished to determine the amount to which \$100,000 would accumulate at 6% annual interest for three years, assuming that the interest at the end of each period is added to the principal and in turn earns interest. We might compute this amount (which we shall designate a) as follows:

	p_s	r	t	a_s
Amount at end of 1st year:	\$100,000 (1 +	.06 ×	1) =	\$106,000.00
Amount at end of 2d year:	\$106,000 (1 +	.06 ×	1) =	\$112,360.00
Amount at end of 3d year:	\$112,360 (1 +	.06 ×	1) =	\$119,101.60

On the basis of the formulas previously developed, we can designate each of the above three terms as follows:

Amount at end of 1st year: $p_s(1 + rt)$
Amount at end of 2d year: $p_s(1 + rt)(1 + rt)$, or $p_s(1 + rt)^2$
Amount at end of 3d year: $p_s(1 + rt)(1 + rt)(1 + rt)$, or $p_s(1 + rt)^3$

The answer obtained above could therefore have been obtained directly as follows:

$$a = p_s(1 + rt)^3 = \$100{,}000\,(1 + .06 \times 1)^3 = \$100{,}000\,(1.06)^3$$
$$= \$100{,}000\,(1.191016) = \$119{,}101.60$$

Simplifying the formula. The general situation in which a sum of money is accumulated at compound interest is outlined in the diagram below:

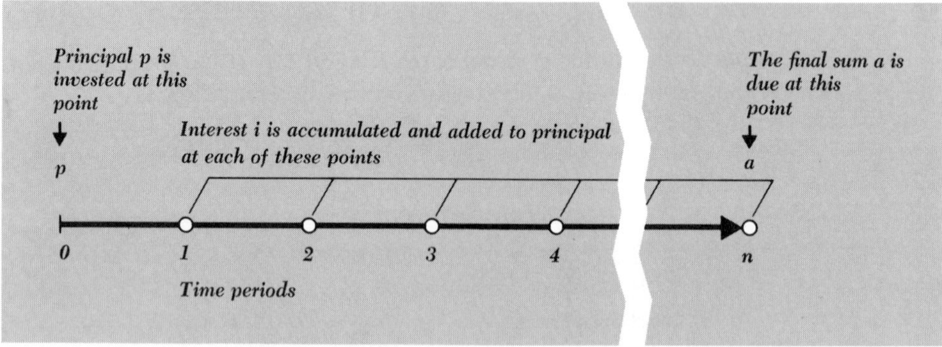

To develop a general formula that will enable us to deal with the entire class of fact situations which fit the above picture, it is useful to define the following symbols:

$i =$ the rate of interest *per time period.* (Note that this is merely the substitution of the single term i for the multiplied term rt used in simple interest formulas. For example, if i is the interest rate per year, $i = r \times 1$; if i is the interest rate per quarter, then $i = r \times 1/4$; etc.)

p = the principal sum which accumulates at i interest per period, compounded once each period.

n = the number of periods during which the principal sum accumulates at interest.

a = the amount to which a principal sum accumulates at compound interest.

Using these symbols, the formula for determining the amount a of a principal sum p at compound interest of i rate per period for n periods becomes:

$a = p(1 + i)^n$	Formula for the amount of a single sum p for n periods at i interest per period	a

Example 4. If $10,000 is invested for three years at 5% interest per year, compounded annually, how much will be accumulated by the end of the third year?

Solution $a = p(1 + i)^n = \$10{,}000\,(1.05)^3 = \$10{,}000\,(1.1576) = \$11{,}576$

Amount of $1. It will also be useful to define the following symbol:

$a_{\overline{n}|i}$ = the amount to which $1 will accumulate at i rate of interest per period for n periods, assuming that i is compounded (that is, added to the principal) once each period. This symbol is read "small a angle n at i." The amount to which $1 will accumulate at 3% interest compounded annually for 12 years would be stated "small a angle 12 at 3%" and would be written $a_{\overline{12}|3\%}$.

The advantage of defining an amount at compound interest in terms of $1 is that the result may then be multiplied by *any* principal sum to obtain a desired accumulation. The formula for $a_{\overline{n}|i}$ is $1 $(1 + i)^n$; since the principal of $1 is always understood and multiplication by 1 has no effect on the result, the $1 may be omitted and the formula written simply:

$a_{\overline{n}\|i} = (1 + i)^n$	Formula for amount of $1 at i compound interest for n periods	$a_{\overline{n}\|i}$

Note in particular that the symbols a and $a_{\overline{n}|i}$ are two distinct terms. The symbol a represents *any* dollar amount due or payable at some future date. The symbol $a_{\overline{n}|i}$ is the *specific* amount to which $1 will accumulate in n periods at i rate of interest per period.

Table for amount of $1. The amount of $1 can be computed for any given values of n and i by the process of repeated multiplication, or by using logarithms. However, tables have been constructed which make it possible to evaluate $a_{\overline{n}|i}$ by simply referring to the appropriate line and column in the table. An extract from such a table appears on page 578. (More complete tables appear in an appendix.)

The amount of $1 for any number of periods n and varying rates of interest i may be determined simply by finding the appropriate line and column in the above table. For example: $a_{\overline{7}|6\%} = 1.5036$. The value given in the table may be multi-

Table for $a_{\overline{n}|i}$ = Amount of \$1 at Compound Interest = $(1 + i)^n$

n = number of periods	i = interest rate per period				
	2%	3%	4%	6%	8%
1	1.0200	1.0300	1.0400	1.0600	1.0800
2	1.0404	1.0609	1.0816	1.1236	1.1664
3	1.0612	1.0927	1.1249	1.1910	1.2597
4	1.0824	1.1255	1.1699	1.2625	1.3605
5	1.1041	1.1593	1.2167	1.3382	1.4693
6	1.1262	1.1941	1.2653	1.4185	1.5869
7	1.1487	1.2299	1.3159	1.5036	1.7138
8	1.1717	1.2668	1.3686	1.5938	1.8509

plied by any principal sum to obtain the amount to which that sum will accumulate at compound interest. For example, \$10,000 will accumulate in six years at 8% interest per year to

$$\$10{,}000\ (1.5869) = \$15{,}869$$

Note that i and n are related, since i is defined as the interest rate *per time period,* and there are n specified time periods. When interest is expressed in terms of an annual rate but the compounding period is less than one year, it is necessary to convert the annual rate r into the rate per compounding period i by dividing the annual rate by the number of interest periods per year, and to adjust n by multiplying the number of years by the number of compounding periods per year. To illustrate, if we want to know the amount to which \$1 will accumulate in five years at 6% annual interest compounded *quarterly,* we interpret $i = .06 \div 4 = .015$; and $n = 4 \times 5 = 20$. We would thus read the result from a table: $a_{\overline{20}|1\frac{1}{2}\%}$.

Example 5. Baker invested \$10,000 four years ago. During the first two years his investment earned 6% compounded semiannually. During the last two years it earned 8% compounded quarterly. How much does Baker have at the end of the fourth year?

Solution. At the end of the second year Baker had

$$\$10{,}000 \times a_{\overline{4}|3\%} = \$10{,}000\,(1.1255) = \$11{,}255$$

During the last two years this amount (\$11,255) grew at the rate of 8% compounded quarterly and became

$$\$11{,}255 \times a_{\overline{8}|2\%} = \$11{,}255\,(1.1717) = \$13{,}187$$

Present value of a future amount

Because many business decisions are based on the present worth of a prospective inflow or outflow of cash, the concept of present value is more widely applicable in accounting than the concept of accumulation. The general situation involving the determination of the present value of a future sum is shown on the following time diagram:

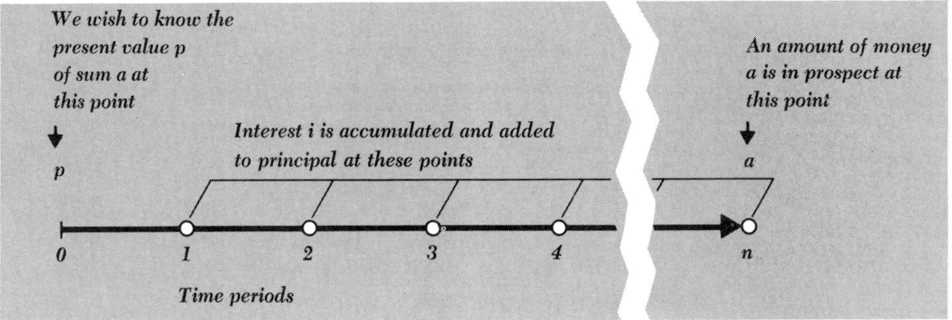

From this diagram we see that finding the present value of a future sum is simply a reversal of the process of finding the amount to which a present sum will accumulate. As in the case of simple interest, the formula for present value may be derived from the formula we have already developed for the amount of any principal sum:

We know that $a = p(1 + i)^n$

If we solve for p by dividing both sides of the equation by $(1 + i)^n$, we get

$$p = \frac{a}{(1 + i)^n} \quad \text{or} \quad \frac{1}{(1 + i)^n} \times a$$

Formula for present value of any future amount a	p

Present value of $1. It is clear that we can determine the present value p of any future amount a by dividing the amount by $(1 + i)^n$. However, since multiplication is usually an easier arithmetic process than division, it will be useful for computational purposes to define the following symbol:

$p_{\overline{n}|i}$ = the present value of $1 due in n periods at i rate of interest per period, assuming that i is compounded at the end of each period. This symbol is read "small p angle n at i." The present value of $1 due in 18 years at 4% annual interest would be stated "small p angle 18 at 4%" and would be written $p_{\overline{18}|4\%}$.

The formula for the present value of $1 is:

$$p_{\overline{n}|i} = \frac{1}{(1 + i)^n}$$

Formula for present value of $1 due in n periods at i rate of interest per period	$p_{\overline{n}\|i}$

Tables for present value of $1. It is apparent that tables evaluating $1/(1 + i)^n$ at varying rates of interest and for different n's would be useful. An extract from such a table appears on page 580. (More extensive tables appear in an appendix.)

The present value of $1 for a given value of n and i may be read directly from the appropriate line and column of the above table. For example, $p_{\overline{7}|4\%} = .7599$. This value may be multiplied by any future amount due in seven periods to determine its present value at 4%.

Table for $p_{\overline{n}|i}$ = *Present Value of \$1 at Compound Interest* = $\frac{1}{(1+i)^n}$

n = number of periods	i = interest rate per period				
	2%	3%	4%	6%	8%
1	.9804	.9709	.9615	.9434	.9259
2	.9612	.9426	.9246	.8900	.8573
3	.9423	.9151	.8890	.8396	.7938
4	.9238	.8885	.8548	.7921	.7350
5	.9057	.8626	.8219	.7473	.6806
6	.8880	.8375	.7903	.7050	.6302
7	.8706	.8131	.7599	.6651	.5835
8	.8535	.7894	.7307	.6274	.5403

Example 6. Find the present value of the following future amounts:

(1) The present value of \$1,200 due in four periods at 6%.

Solution $\$1{,}200 \times p_{\overline{4}|6\%} = \$1{,}200\,(.7921) = \$950.52$

(2) The present value of \$20,000 due in four years at 6% annual interest compounded semiannually.

Solution $\$20{,}000 \times p_{\overline{8}|3\%} = \$20{,}000\,(.7894) = \$15{,}788$

Relation of amounts and present values to n and i. In dealing with computations of accumulations and present values, it is useful to have some general idea of relationships as a basis for verifying the reasonableness of results. We can reason, for example, that $a_{\overline{n}|i}$ should grow larger for increasing rates of interest i and for increasing numbers of periods n, since the longer a principal sum accumulates the larger it grows, and the higher the rate of interest the larger the future amount. The reverse situation is true of present values. The longer the time period n or the higher the rate of interest i, the smaller will be the present value of any future sum. This squares with our intuition that a far-distant prospect is worth less than one in the near future, and that the higher the rate of interest that can be earned on a present-dollar amount, the less valuable is the prospect of receiving an amount of money in the future.

Compound interest and compound discount. The terms *compound interest* or *compound discount* are sometimes used to describe the excess of the amount to which an investment will grow at compound interest over the original investment (principal). Compound interest or discount may thus be defined in general as $a - p$.

If we express the concepts of compound interest I and compound discount D in terms of \$1, then we may define the following terms:

$$I_{\overline{n}|i} = (1+i)^n - 1 = a_{\overline{n}|i} - 1$$

$$D_{\overline{n}|i} = 1 - \frac{1}{(1+i)^n} = 1 - p_{\overline{n}|i}$$

***Example* 7.** Illustrate the fact that the amount of compound interest I and the amount of compound discount D are the same for any given principal sum p which will grow to a given amount a.

Solution. Assume a given amount $1,000 which, if invested at 4% interest for six years, will grow to $1,265. Compound interest and compound discount should therefore be

$$a - p = \$1,265 - \$1,000 = \$265$$

To find I: $I = \$1,000\ I_{\overline{6}|4\%} = \$1,000\,(a_{\overline{6}|4\%} - 1) = \$1,000\,(1.2653 - 1)$
$= \$1,000\,(.2653) = \$265$

To find D: $D = \$1,265\ D_{\overline{n}|i} = \$1,265\,(1 - p_{\overline{6}|4\%}) = \$1,265\,(1 - .7903)$
$= \$1,265\,(.2097) = \$265$

Tables are not normally constructed for values of I and D at $1, since these quantities can always be obtained from tables for a and p by a simple process of subtraction.

Annuities

Cases involving the accumulation of a single principal sum or the present value of a single future amount do not occur as frequently in business as do situations in which a series of dollar amounts are to be paid or received periodically. Borrowings to be repaid in installments, investments that will be partially recovered at regular intervals, cost savings that occur repeatedly—all are common business events.

It is possible to deal with cases involving periodic receipts or payments by repeating the process of computing the amount or present value of each individual sum and adding to obtain the desired result for the whole series. Fortunately, in certain standard cases, we can greatly simplify the arithmetic by using annuity formulas and tables. The formulas for computing the amount or present value of a series of regular payments or receipts were first developed in the insurance field. Insurance companies commonly agree, in return for a series of premiums or the deposit of a fixed sum, to pay to the insured a regular annual amount so long as he lives. These contracts are known as *annuities,* and the mathematics necessary for the insurance companies to set the terms of such contracts were worked out by experts who came to be known as *actuaries.* Today the annuity principle has far wider application than in the field of insurance, although the original insurance terminology is still commonly employed.

A standard investment situation involving a series of equal payments or receipts (usually called *rents*) at regular time intervals is called an *annuity.* The regular time intervals between rents are assumed to be equal in length, but they may be any period, such as a month, a half-year, a year, etc. It is also assumed in a standard annuity that interest is compounded once each time period.[2]

[2] It is possible to compute amounts and present values when interest is compounded more frequently than rents are received by determining the effective rate of interest for each rental period. Similarly, we can handle cases in which rents are received more frequently than compounding periods by computing an effective rent per compounding period. These situations occur rarely, however, and are not discussed here.

Kinds of standard annuity situations

A number of different standard annuity situations may be identified and will be discussed in the sections that follow:

Ordinary annuity. An ordinary annuity is one in which equal periodic rents occur *at the end* of each period.

Annuity due. An annuity due is an annuity in which the equal rents occur *at the beginning* of each period, and interest continues for one period after the last rent.

Open-end annuity. An open-end annuity is one which remains invested at a given rate of interest for more than one period after the last rent.

Deferred annuity. A deferred annuity is an annuity in which the rents begin two or more periods after the initial investment is made.

Computing amounts of annuities

Amount of an ordinary annuity. The amount of an annuity is the sum of the periodic rents and the compound interest that accumulates on these rents. If we designate the amount of an ordinary annuity as A, the equal periodic rents as R, and the number of time periods as n, a general ordinary annuity situation might be diagrammed as follows:

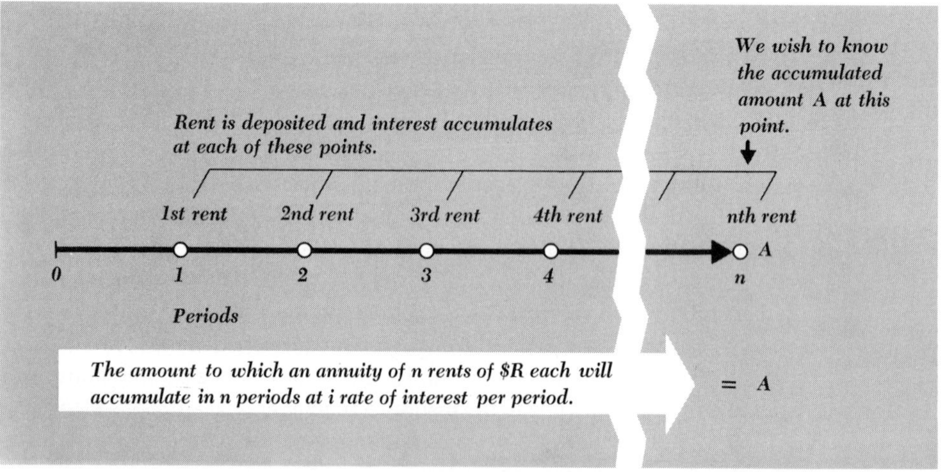

Formula for the amount of an ordinary annuity. We might compute the amount of an ordinary annuity by summing the accumulated amounts of the individual rents. For example, the amount of an annuity of $1 per period for four periods at 6% interest might be determined as follows:

The first rent accumulates at 6% for three periods and grows to $\$1\ (a_{\overline{3}|\,6\%}) = \$1\ (1.1910)$	$1.191
The second rent accumulates at 6% for two periods and grows to $\$1\ (a_{\overline{2}|\,6\%}) = \$1\ (1.1236)$	1.124
The third rent accumulates at 6% for one period and grows to $\$1\ (a_{\overline{1}|\,6\%}) = \$1\ (1.06)$	1.060
The fourth rent is due at the end of the annuity period	1.000
Amount of ordinary annuity of $1 for four periods at 6%	$4.375

For future reference let us define the following symbol:

$A_{\overline{n}|i}$ = the amount to which an ordinary annuity of $1 per period will accumulate in n periods at i rate of interest per period. This symbol is read "capital A angle n at i"; for example, the amount to which an annuity of $1 will accumulate in four periods at 6% is stated "capital A angle 4 at 6%" and is written $A_{\overline{4}|6\%}$.

We can derive a formula for arriving at the amount of an annuity of $1 ($A_{\overline{n}|i}$) by examining the relationship between compound interest and an annuity of the amounts of the interest. To illustrate, assume the sum of $1 was invested for four periods at 6% interest. We know that the accumulated amount at the end of the fourth period would be: $a_{\overline{4}|6\%} = \$1.2625$. If we subtract the original principal of $1 from this amount, we get the amount of compound interest on $1 for four periods at 6%; that is,

$$I_{\overline{4}|6\%} = (a_{\overline{4}|6\%} - 1) = (1.06)^4 - 1 = \$1.2625 - 1 = \$0.2625$$

Now examine the diagram below of just *the annuity of the 6% interest* on $1:

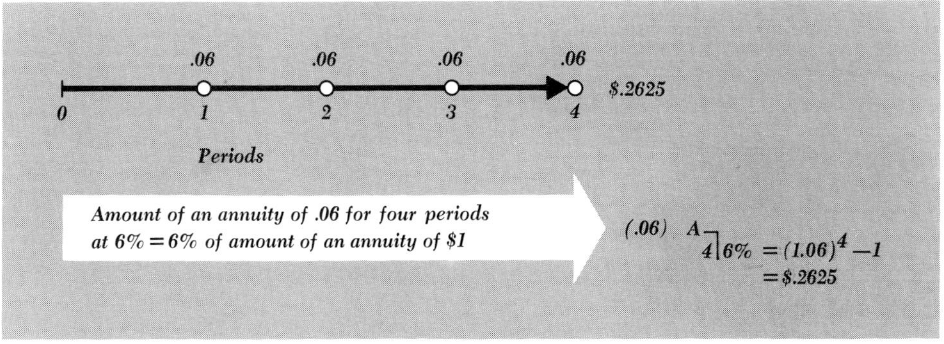

Observe that the amount of compound interest on $1 is nothing more than the amount of an annuity of 6 cents per period for four periods at 6%. Furthermore, note that if we divide both sides of the above equation by the interest rate (6% in this case), we can convert the equation to one that will give us the *amount of an annuity of $1* per period for four periods at 6%: (We know from our previous computation that this amount should be $4.375.)

Divide by 6%: $$\frac{.06\,A_{\overline{4}|6\%}}{.06} = \frac{(1.06)^4 - 1}{.06}$$

Therefore $$A_{\overline{4}|6\%} = \frac{(1.06)^4 - 1}{.06} = \frac{.2625}{.06} = \underline{\underline{\$4.375}}$$

The reasoning we have applied to the specific case of an annuity of $1 for four periods at 6% can now be generalized for any n and any i as follows:

$$A_{\overline{n}|i} = \frac{(1+i)^n - 1}{i}$$

Formula for amount of annuity of $1 for n periods at i interest per period	$A_{\overline{n}\|i}$

The formula for the amount of *any* annuity of R dollars per period may be stated:

$$A = R\,(A_{\overline{n}|i}) = R\left(\frac{(1+i)^n - 1}{i}\right)$$

Formula for amount of annuity of \$$R$ for n periods at i interest per period	A

Tables for the amount of an annuity of \$1. Tables for the amount of an annuity of \$1 for varying periods and interest rates appear in an appendix. An extract from these tables appears below:

Table for $A_{\overline{n}|i}$ = *Amount of Annuity of \$1* = $\dfrac{(1+i)^n - 1}{i} = \dfrac{a_{\overline{n}|i} - 1}{i}$

n = number of periods	*i = interest rate per period*				
	2%	*3%*	*4%*	*6%*	*8%*
1	1.0000	1.0000	1.0000	1.0000	1.0000
2	2.0200	2.0300	2.0400	2.0600	2.0800
3	3.0604	3.0909	3.1216	3.1836	3.2464
4	4.1216	4.1836	4.2465	4.3746	4.5061
5	5.2040	5.3091	5.4163	5.6371	5.8666
6	6.3081	6.4684	6.6330	6.9753	7.3359
7	7.4343	7.6625	7.8983	8.3938	8.9228
8	8.5830	8.8923	9.2142	9.8975	10.6366

By multiplying the values found in the appropriate line and column of the above table by the dollar amount of any rents involved in an ordinary annuity, the accumulated sum of the rents and compound interest to the date of the last rent may be readily obtained.

Example 8. Given periodic rents, compute amount. Reed plans to deposit \$10,000 at the end of each year for six years in a savings account that will earn interest at the rate of 4% compounded annually. How much will he have in the fund at the end of the sixth year?

Solution

$$\text{Amount} = R\,(A_{\overline{n}|i}) = \$10{,}000\,(A_{\overline{6}|4\%}) = \$10{,}000\,(6.6330) = \$66{,}330$$

Example 9. Given desired amount, compute periodic rents. Smith can invest funds to earn an annual return of 8% compounded semiannually. How much should he deposit (to the nearest dollar) at the end of each six-month period if he wishes to accumulate a fund of \$12,000 by the end of four years?

Solution. First convert the formula for the amount of an annuity into a formula for the rent:

$$\text{Amount} = \text{rent}\,(A_{\overline{n}|i})$$

Solve for rent:

$$R = \frac{A}{A_{\overline{n}|i}}$$

Using the data from the example,

$$n = 4 \times 2 = 8 \qquad i = .08 \div 2 = .04$$

$$R = \frac{\$12{,}000}{A_{\overline{8}|4\%}} = \frac{\$12{,}000}{9.2142} = \$1{,}302$$

The accuracy of the computation in Example 9 is demonstrated in the following tabulation. (All amounts are rounded to the nearest dollar.)

Years	*Periods*	*Interest on balance in fund (4%)*	*Deposit at end of period*	*Total increase in fund during period*	*Balance in fund at end of period*
1	1	-0-	$1,302	$1,302	$ 1,302
	2	$ 52	1,302	1,354	2,656
2	3	106	1,302	1,408	4,064
	4	163	1,302	1,465	5,529
3	5	221	1,302	1,523	7,052
	6	282	1,302	1,584	8,636
4	7	345	1,302	1,647	10,283
	8	411	1,306*	1,717	12,000

* *Because the annual deposit was rounded to the nearest dollar and because interest computations were similarly rounded, it is necessary to assume the addition of $4 to the final deposit to compensate for these cumulative errors. Computations to the nearest dollar are sufficiently accurate for most accounting purposes; the slight rounding error causes no difficulty and is a cheap price to pay for the saving in computational time. Accuracy to the penny may be obtained, when necessary, by using annuity tables which carry results to more places to the right of the decimal point.*

Amount of an annuity due. A number of investment situations involve deposits or withdrawals at the beginning of each period rather than at the end. An annuity which involves equal periodic rents R at the beginning of each period is known as an *annuity due,* and the general case may be diagrammed as follows:

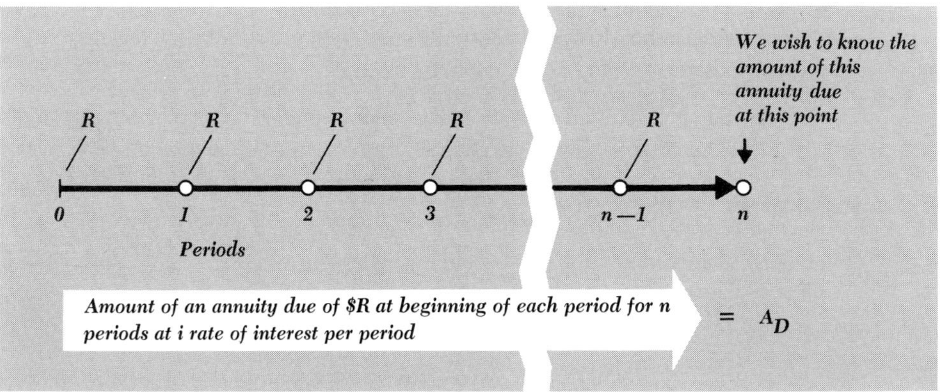

We could compute the amount of an annuity due by taking each rent and accumulating it at i for the number of periods involved. Since tables are available for the amount of an ordinary annuity, however, we should like to be able to use these tables in working with annuity due situations. We can do this by converting the annuity due situation into an ordinary annuity in such a way that we can compute the amount of the adjusted ordinary annuity and then adjust this amount in some simple fashion to arrive at the amount of the desired annuity due. Let us revise the above diagram of an annuity due by adding one period at the beginning and adding one rent at the end and see if we cannot accomplish our objective:

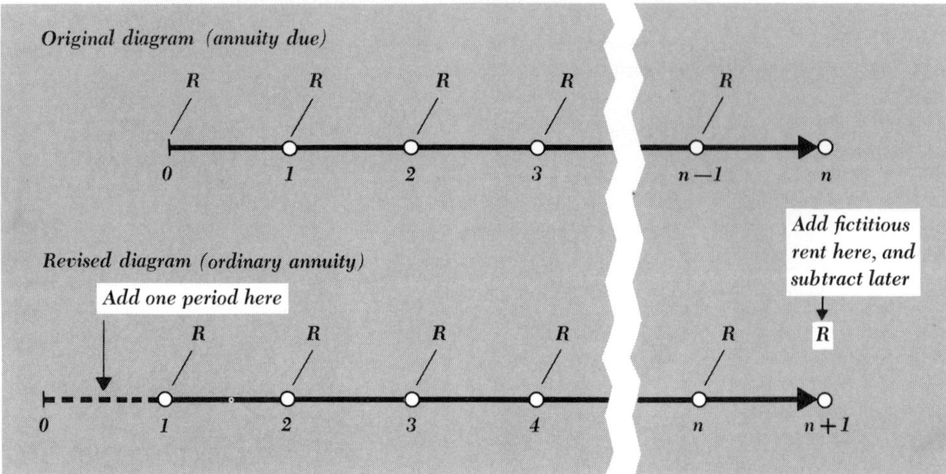

We now have a diagram of an ordinary annuity, which has been altered from the annuity due by the addition of one period at the beginning and the addition of a fictitious rent at the end. If we compute the amount of this ordinary annuity, what damage have we done to the annuity due amount which we want to obtain? Adding the extra period at the beginning of the time span does not affect the amount that will be accumulated, since there is no deposit at time 0 and therefore no interest will be earned during this period. The addition of the fictional rent at the end of the last period will be easy to adjust for, since this rent occurs at the end of the time span and therefore does not earn interest; we can simply deduct this one added rent from the amount of an ordinary annuity for $n + 1$ periods to arrive at the amount of an annuity due for n periods.

Using the symbol A_D to represent the amount of an annuity due, we can express the above demonstrated relationship as follows:

$A_{D\overline{n}|i} =$ the amount of an annuity due involving equal rents of $1 at the beginning of each period for n periods at i rate of interest per period. This symbol may be read "capital A sub D angle n at i."

When we are dealing with a series of rents of $1 each, we can arrive at the amount of an annuity due by computing the amount of an ordinary annuity of $1 for $n + 1$ periods and subtracting $1 from the result.

Thus	$A_{D\overline{n}|i} = (A_{\overline{n+1}|i} - 1)$	Formula for amount of annuity due of $1 for n periods at i rate of interest per period	$A_{D\overline{n}|i}$

When faced with a problem involving *any* series of rents R, we can determine the amount of an annuity due by computing the amount of an ordinary annuity of $\$R$ rents for $n + 1$ periods and subtract one rent:

$$A_D = R\,(A_{D\overline{n}|i}) = R\,(A_{\overline{n+1}|i}) - R = R\,(A_{\overline{n+1}|i} - 1)$$

Formula for amount of annuity due of $\$R$ for n periods at i rate of interest per period	A_D

Alternative approach to find amount of annuity due. Another way of finding the amount of an annuity due is based on a fact already noted: The difference between an annuity due and an ordinary annuity of the same number of rents is that each rent of an annuity due earns interest for one more period. Therefore, if we increase the amount of an ordinary annuity of the same number of rents by the amount of the interest on all the rents for one additional period, we have the amount of an annuity due. This relationship may be expressed in the following alternative formula:

$$A_{D\overline{n}|i} = (A_{\overline{n}|i})\,(1 + i)$$

Alternative formula for amount of an annuity due of $1 rents

When annuity tables are available, this device of adding one period, subtracting one rent, and working with an ordinary annuity is usually a simpler way of computing the amount of an annuity due.

Example 10. Given rents, find amount of annuity due. Danby plans to deposit $1,000 in a savings account on January 1 and July 1 of each year for three years. How much (to the nearest dollar) will he have on deposit on December 31 of the third year if the fund earns interest at an annual rate of 6% compounded semiannually?

Solution. Since interest is compounded semiannually,

$$n = 2 \times 3 = 6 \text{ periods} \qquad \text{and} \qquad i = 6\% \div 2 = 3\%$$

$$A_D = R\,(A_{D\overline{6}|3\%}) = R\,(A_{\overline{n+1}|i} - 1) = \$1{,}000\,(A_{\overline{7}|3\%} - 1)$$
$$= \$1{,}000\,(7.6625 - 1) = \$1{,}000\,(6.6625) = \$6{,}663$$

Using the alternative approach,

$$A_D = R\,(A_{D\overline{n}|i}) = R\,(A_{\overline{n}|i})\,(1 + i) = \$1{,}000\,(A_{\overline{6}|3\%})\,(1.03)$$
$$= \$1{,}000\,(6.4684)\,(1.03) = \$6{,}663$$

Example 11. Given amount of an annuity due, find periodic rents. Egbert has signed a note for $9,000 due in five years. He wishes to invest an equal amount at the beginning of each of the next five years so that he will have enough to pay off the debt at the end of the fifth year. If he can earn 4% on his investment, how much (to the nearest dollar) should be deposited at the beginning of each year?

Solution. First convert the formula for the amount of an annuity due into a formula for the rents:

$$A_D = R\,(A_{D\overline{n}|i})$$

Therefore

$$R = \frac{A_D}{A_{D\overline{n}|i}} = \frac{A_D}{(A_{\overline{n+1}|i} - 1)}$$

Using the data from the problem ($n = 5$; $i = 4\%$),

$$R = \frac{\$9{,}000}{A_{\overline{6}|4\%} - 1} = \frac{\$9{,}000}{(6.6330 - 1)} = \frac{\$9{,}000}{5.6330} = \$1{,}598$$

The accuracy of the computation on Example 11 may be demonstrated in tabular form as follows:

Period	Amount deposited	Interest on fund balance (4%)	Total increase in fund during period	Fund balance
0	$1,598	-0-	$1,598	$1,598
1	1,598	$ 64	1,662	3,260
2	1,598	130	1,728	4,988
3	1,598	200	1,798	6,786
4	1,598	271	1,869	8,655
5	-0-	346	346	9,001*

* *Error of $1 due to rounding of deposits and interest to the nearest dollar.*

Amount of an open-end annuity. An open-end annuity is one in which a series of rents is left to accrue interest for one or more periods after the date of the last rent. If we designate the number of annuity periods as n and the number of open-end periods as m, an open-end annuity involving four annuity periods and three open-end periods may be diagrammed as follows:

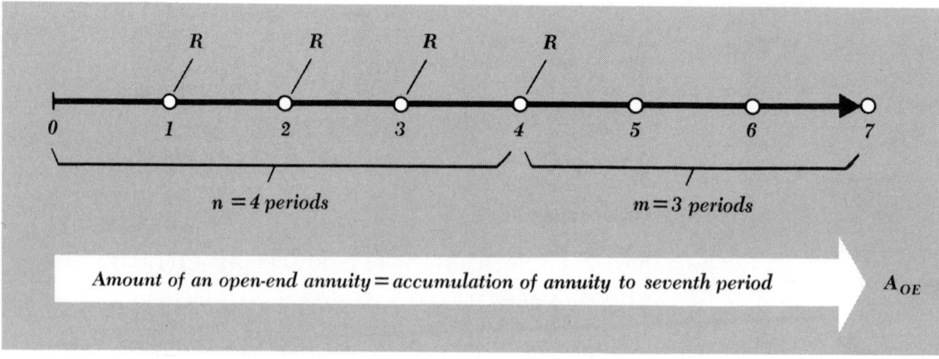

Two computational approaches may be used in determining the amount of an open-end annuity (A_{OE}):

Method 1 is to compute the amount of the annuity to the date of the last rent (n periods) and then accumulate this sum at interest for the open-end period (m periods) during which no rents are paid. The problem is thus a combination of finding the amount of an annuity and the amount of a principal sum during the open-end period.

Method 2 is to assume that rents are paid during the entire period of the open-end annuity (the annuity period n and the open-end period m) and then adjust the result. We first compute the amount of this enlarged annuity ($n + m$ periods) and then deduct the amount of the annuity of rents (for m periods) that do not in fact exist. This second approach involves an easier set of computations, since subtraction is simpler than multiplication.

Example 12. Find amount of an open-end annuity. Firman plans to invest $1,000 at the end of each year for the next three years and to leave this sum invested for two more years. If the fund earns a return of 6% compounded annually during the entire five-year period, what amount (to the nearest dollar) will be accumulated at the end of the fifth year?

Solution (Method 1). This approach to the solution may be diagrammed as follows:

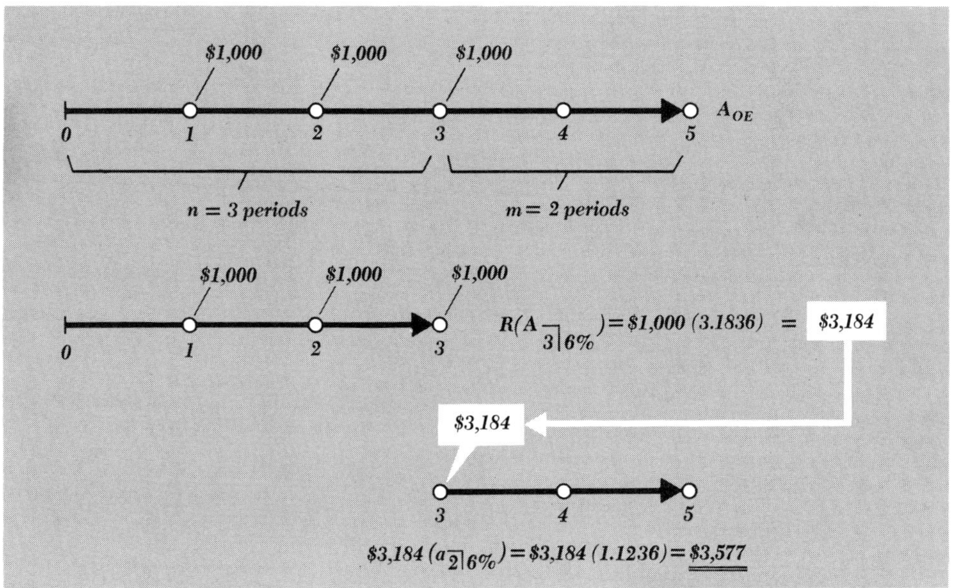

Computation summarized:

$$A_{OE} = R\,(A_{\overline{n}|i})\,(a_{\overline{m}|i}) = \$1{,}000\,(A_{\overline{3}|6\%})\,(a_{\overline{2}|6\%})$$
$$= \$1{,}000\,(3.1836)(1.1236) = \underline{\underline{\$3{,}577}}$$

(Method 2). This approach to the solution may be diagrammed as shown on page 590.

Computation summarized:

$$A_{OE} = R\,(A_{\overline{n+m}|i} - A_{\overline{m}|i}) = \$1{,}000\,(A_{\overline{5}|6\%} - A_{\overline{2}|6\%})$$
$$= \$1{,}000\,(5.6371 - 2.0600) = \$1{,}000\,(3.5771) = \underline{\underline{\$3{,}577}}$$

It is apparent from this example that Method 2 avoids an extra, rather complicated multiplication, and is therefore a simpler method of finding the amount of an open-end annuity.

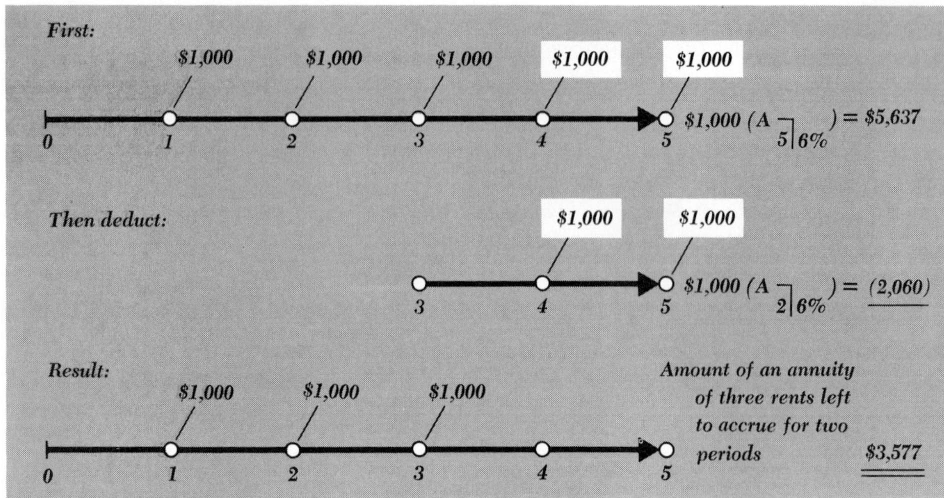

Computing the present value of annuities

Present value of an ordinary annuity. The present value of an ordinary annuity P is the amount which, if invested now to earn compound interest at a rate i per period, would be just sufficient to allow for the withdrawal of equal rents R at the end of each of n periods.

The concept of the present value of an annuity, which is applicable to a wide variety of business decisions in which a present investment is to be made in contemplation of a series of future returns, is illustrated in the graph below, for a situation in which $n =$ five periods.

Graph Showing the Present Value of an Annuity of R Rents for Five Periods

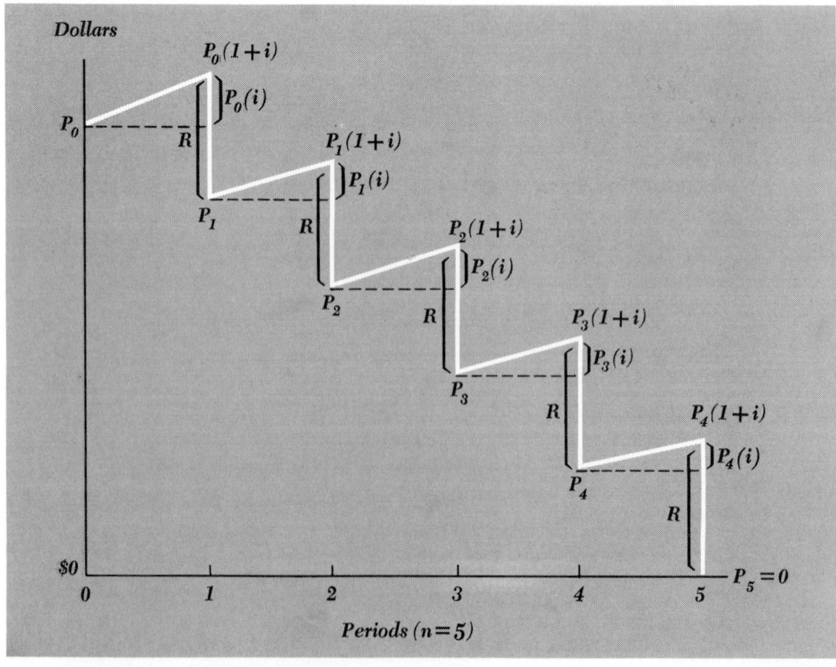

In this graph, P_0 is the present value of the annuity at period zero, P_1 the present value at the end of period 1 after the withdrawal of R, etc. Note that during each period the present value grows by an amount equal to the present value at the beginning of the period multiplied by the interest rate i and at the end of each period it is decreased by the withdrawal of the rent R. The withdrawal of the last rent at the end of the fifth period reduces the present value to zero at that point. Observe that the amount of growth in each period decreases as the present value declines over the life of the annuity.

Formula for the present value of an ordinary annuity. It is apparent that the present value of an annuity is the sum of the present values of each of the individual rents. For example, the present value of an annuity of \$1 per period for four periods at 6% might be computed as follows:

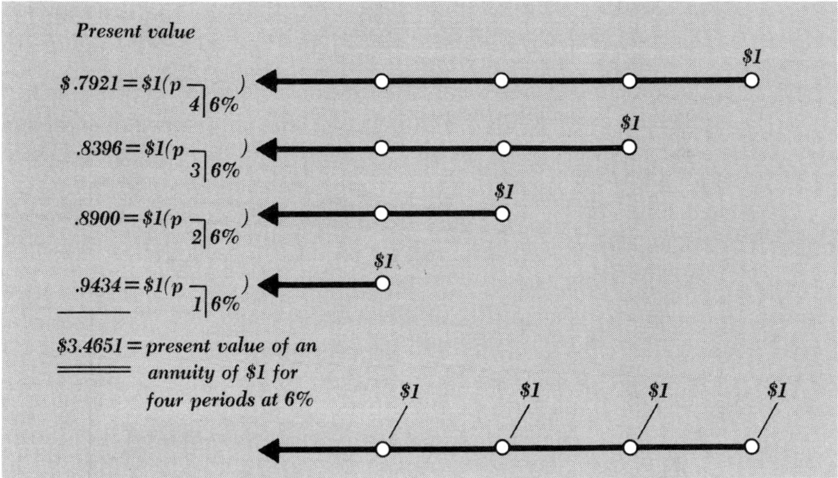

This computation tells us that if \$3.47 were invested at 6% interest for four periods, it would be possible to withdraw \$1 at the end of each period.

We can develop a formula for the present value of an annuity in a manner comparable to that used in deriving a formula for the amount. First it is useful to define the following symbol:

$P_{\overline{n}|i}$ = the present value of an ordinary annuity of n rents of \$1 at the end of each of n periods at i rate of interest per period. This symbol may be read "capital P angle n at i."

It has previously been shown (see page 580) that the compound discount on \$1 is computed as

$$D_{\overline{n}|i} = 1 - p_{\overline{n}|i} \qquad \text{or} \qquad 1 - \frac{1}{(1+i)^n}$$

Thus the compound discount on \$1 due in four periods at 6% in our present example is:

$$D_{\overline{4}|6} = 1 - \frac{1}{(1.06)^4} = 1 - .7921 = .2079$$

Now we observe that the compound discount on \$1 for n periods at i rate of interest is equivalent to the present value of an ordinary annuity whose rents are the amounts of periodic interest on \$1 (\$1 $\times$ i) each period discounted at the same i interest rate. We can diagram the compound discount on the \$1 annuity in our example as follows:

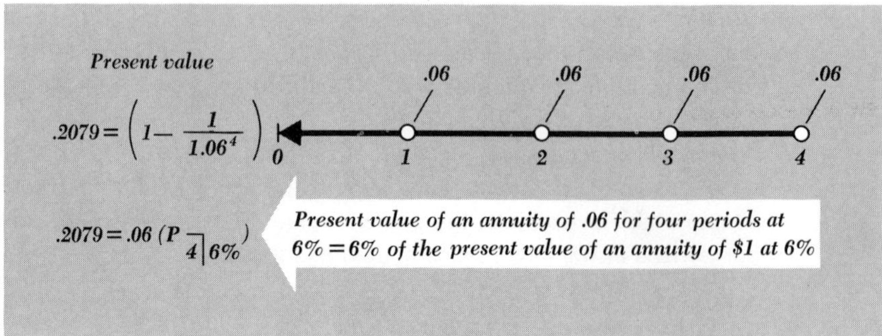

If the compound discount on \$1 at 6% is 6% of the present value of an annuity of \$1, we can arrive at the formula for the present value of an annuity of \$1 per period by dividing the formula for compound discount by the rate of interest (6% in this case):

Divide by 6%:
$$\frac{.06\,(P_{\overline{4}|6\%})}{.06} = \frac{\left(1 - \frac{1}{(1.06)^4}\right)}{.06}$$

Therefore:
$$P_{\overline{4}|6\%} = \frac{\left(1 - \frac{1}{(1.06)^4}\right)}{.06} = \frac{.2079}{.06} = \underline{\underline{\$3.47}}$$

The reasoning we have applied to the specific case of an annuity of \$1 for four periods at 6% may now be generalized into a formula for the present value of an annuity of \$1 per period for *any* n and *any* i, as follows:

$$P_{\overline{n}|i} = \frac{\left(1 - \frac{1}{(1+i)^n}\right)}{i} = \frac{(1 - p_{\overline{n}|i})}{i} = \frac{D_{\overline{n}|i}}{i}$$

Formula for present value of an annuity of \$1 for n periods at i rate of interest per period	$P_{\overline{n}\|i}$

The formula for the present value of *any* annuity of R dollars per period may be stated:

$$P = R\,(P_{\overline{n}|i}) = R\left[\frac{1 - \frac{1}{(1+i)^n}}{i}\right]$$

Formula for present value of an annuity of \$$R$ for n periods at i rate of interest per period	P

Tables for the present value of an ordinary annuity. Tables for the present value of an annuity of \$1 per period for various numbers of periods and varying rates of interest i appear in an appendix. An extract from these tables follows:

Table for $P_{\overline{n}|i}$: Present Value of an Ordinary Annuity of \$1 $= \dfrac{1 - \dfrac{1}{(1+i)^n}}{i}$

n = periods	*i = interest rate per period*				
	2%	*3%*	*4%*	*6%*	*8%*
1	0.9804	0.9709	0.9615	0.9434	0.9259
2	1.9416	1.9135	1.8861	1.8334	1.7833
3	2.8839	2.8286	2.7751	2.6730	2.5771
4	3.8077	3.7171	3.6299	3.4651	3.3121
5	4.7135	4.5797	4.4518	4.2124	3.9927
6	5.6014	5.4172	5.2421	4.9173	4.6229
7	6.4720	6.2303	6.0021	5.5824	5.2064
8	7.3255	7.0197	6.7327	6.2098	5.7466

By multiplying the value in the appropriate line and column of the above table by the dollar amount of the equal periodic rents R involved in any ordinary annuity, the present value of the rents can be easily computed.

Example 13. Given rents, determine present value. Gange has arranged to buy a certain property by paying \$1,000 at the end of each six-month period for the next four years. What present cash payment (to the nearest dollar) would be equivalent to these future installments if money is worth 6% annually?

Solution $n = 4 \times 2 = 8 \qquad i = .06 \div 2 = 3\%$ per period

$$P = R\,(P_{\overline{n}|i}) = \$1{,}000\,(P_{\overline{8}|3\%}) = \$1{,}000\,(7.0197) = \underline{\underline{\$7{,}020}}$$

Example 14. Given present value, find periodic rent. Hersh has \$10,000 saved to finance his son's education. If this money can be invested to earn 4% annually, what equal amounts (to the nearest dollar) can his son withdraw at the end of each of the next five years if he plans to exhaust the fund at the end of the fifth year?

Solution. We must first solve the general equation for the rent R:

$$P = R\,(P_{\overline{n}|i})$$

Solve for R:

$$R = \frac{P}{P_{\overline{n}|i}}$$

Now substituting the data given in the example,

$$R = \frac{\$10{,}000}{P_{\overline{5}|4\%}} = \frac{\$10{,}000}{4.4518} = \underline{\underline{\$2{,}246}}$$

The table on page 594 demonstrates the accuracy of the computation in Example 14.

Present value of an annuity due. Present value applications frequently involve an annuity due situation where a withdrawal or a payment on a debt is to be made

Period	Interest on fund balance during period (4%)	Withdrawal from fund at end of period	Net decrease in fund during period	Fund balance at end of period
0				$10,000
1	$400	$2,246	$1,846	8,154
2	326	2,246	1,920	6,234
3	249	2,246	1,997	4,237
4	169	2,246	2,077	2,160
5	86	2,246	2,160	-0-

at the beginning of each period. The problem of finding the present value of an annuity due for four periods might be diagrammed as follows:

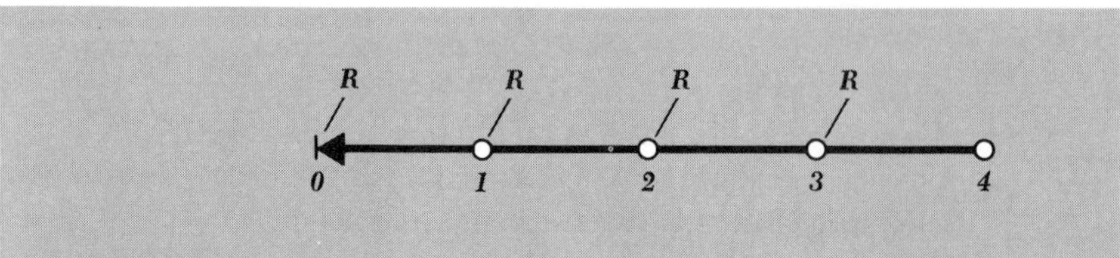

We could compute the present value of an annuity due by simply adding together the present values of each of the periodic rents. However we should like to be able to use the present value tables for ordinary annuities to simplify the computational task. A little adjustment of the above annuity due picture will demonstrate a way of converting from the annuity due situation to an ordinary annuity in such a manner that we can easily adjust the present value of the ordinary annuity back to fit the annuity due situation.

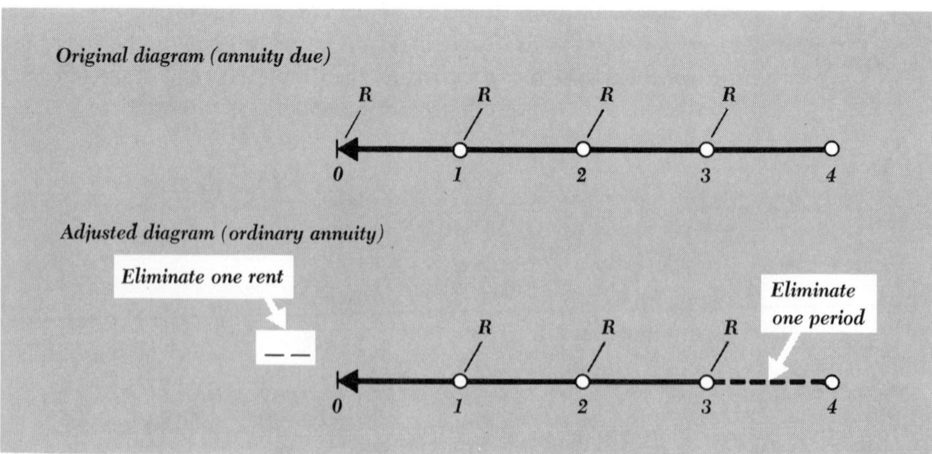

Now we have a picture of an ordinary annuity involving one less period and one less rent. Eliminating the period at the end of the time span does not change the present value, because the present value of an annuity due is zero during its final period after the last withdrawal. The elimination of the initial rent can easily be compensated for in our computation because this rent has a present value exactly equal to the amount of the rent, since it will not earn interest. Thus we can convert the present value of an annuity due of n periods to the present value of an ordinary annuity of $n - 1$ periods plus one additional rent. This relationship may be expressed as follows:

Let $P_{D\overline{n}|i}$ = the present value of an *annuity due* involving equal rents of $1 at the beginning of each of n periods at i rate of interest per period. This symbol may be read "capital P sub D angle n at i."

Then $P_{D\overline{n}|i} = (P_{\overline{n-1}|i} + 1)$

Formula for present value of annuity due of $1 for n periods at i rate of interest per period	$P_{D\overline{n}|i}$

And $\quad P_D = R\,(P_{D\overline{n}|i}) = R\,(P_{\overline{n-1}|i} + 1)$

Formula for present value of annuity due of $$R$ for n periods at i rate of interest per period	P_D

Alternative approach to find present value of an annuity due. The present value of an annuity due of n periods is larger than the present value of an ordinary annuity of the same n periods by the interest on each of the rents for one period. This is true because each type of annuity (given n) involves the same number of rents but the rents in the case of the annuity due are each one period closer in time. Therefore we can derive an alternative formula for the present value of an annuity due:

$$P_{D\overline{n}|i} = (P_{\overline{n}|i})(1 + i)$$

Alternative formula for present value of an annuity due of $1 for n periods	$P_{D\overline{n}|i}$

Example 15. Given rents; determine present value of annuity due. Jenks has signed a rental agreement promising to pay $1,000 at the beginning of each of the next four years. He wishes to settle this lease obligation by making a lump-sum payment now. If money is worth 6% annually, how much (to the nearest dollar) is required to settle the lease?

Solution $\qquad (n = 4 \qquad i = 6\%)$

$$P_D = R\,(P_{D\overline{n}|i}) = R\,(P_{\overline{n-1}|i} + 1) = \$1{,}000\,(P_{\overline{3}|6\%} + 1)$$
$$= \$1{,}000\,(2.6730 + 1) = \$1{,}000\,(3.6730) = \underline{\underline{\$3.673}}$$

Alternative solution

$$P_D = R\,(P_{D\overline{n}|i}) = R\,(P_{\overline{n}|i})(1 + i) = R\,(P_{\overline{4}|6\%})(1.06)$$
$$= \$1{,}000\,(3.4651)(1.06) = \underline{\underline{\$3{,}673}}$$

It is apparent that the first approach is easier because it avoids one rather complex multiplication.

Example 16. Given present value of annuity due; find rents. Knox owes $10,000, with interest at 2% semiannually. He wishes to pay this debt by making a series of five equal semiannual payments beginning immediately and each six months thereafter. Compute the necessary payments to the nearest dollar.

Solution. First we must solve the general annuity due equation for R:

$$P_D = R\,(P_{D\overline{n}|i})$$

Solve for R:

$$R = \frac{P_D}{P_{D\overline{n}|i}}$$

Now substituting the data given in the example ($n = 5$; $i = 2\%$):

$$R = \frac{\$10{,}000}{P_{D\overline{n}|i}} = \frac{\$10{,}000}{P_{D\overline{5}|2\%}} = \frac{\$10{,}000}{(P_{\overline{n-1}|i} + 1)} = \frac{\$10{,}000}{(P_{\overline{4}|2\%} + 1)}$$

$$= \frac{\$10{,}000}{(3.8077 + 1)} = \frac{\$10{,}000}{4.8077} = \underline{\underline{\$2{,}080}}$$

We may demonstrate the accuracy of the computation in Example 16 in the following tabular form:

Year	*Period*	*Interest at 2% on unpaid balance of note*	*Payment on debt during period*	*Decrease in debt during period*	*Balance of debt after payment*
	0	*-0-*	*2,080*	*2,080*	*7,920**
1	*1*	*158*	*2,080*	*1,922*	*5,998*
	2	*120*	*2,080*	*1,960*	*4,038*
2	*3*	*81*	*2,080*	*1,999*	*2,039*
	4	*41*	*2,080*	*2,039*	*-0-*
3	*5*	*-0-*	*-0-*	*-0-*	*-0-*

* *$10,000 original debt less initial payment of $2,080.*

Present value of a deferred annuity. When the first rent of an annuity occurs two or more periods after the initial investment is made, this situation is known as a *deferred annuity.* There is no new problem involved in computing the *amount* of a deferred annuity, since nothing accumulates until the first rent occurs. The deferral period *does* have an effect on the computation of *present value,* however, because the original investment or deposit will accumulate at interest for the deferral period prior to the first withdrawal or payment.

If we designate the number of annuity periods as n and the number of deferral periods as m, the present value of a deferred annuity P_{def}, involving four annuity periods and two deferral periods, might be diagrammed as shown on page 597.

Computing the present value of a deferred annuity is analogous to the computation of the amount of an open-end annuity, and two similar approaches to the solution are possible:

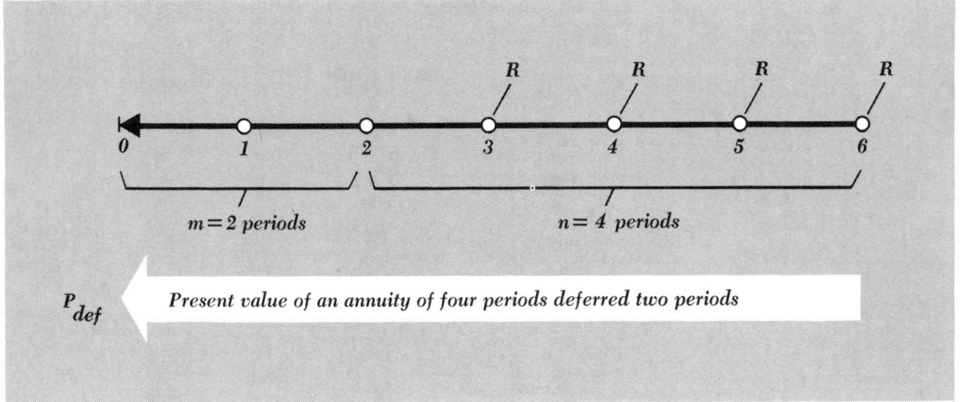

Method 1 is to compute the present value of the series of rents as of one period prior to the initial rent (n periods); then discount this present value back to the date of the original deposit or investment (m periods).

Method 2 is to compute the present value of a series of rents over the entire number of periods from the initial deposit to the last rental ($n + m$ periods); then subtract the present value of the nonexistent rents during the deferral period (m periods).

Example 17. Given rents, compute present value of a deferred annuity. Larsen plans to take a trip around the world beginning four years from now. He figures that to finance his trip he will need $10,000 at the beginning of the trip and $10,000 at the end of the fifth year. How much must he invest today at 6% in order to have sufficient funds for his trip?

Solution (Method 1). This problem may be diagrammed as follows:

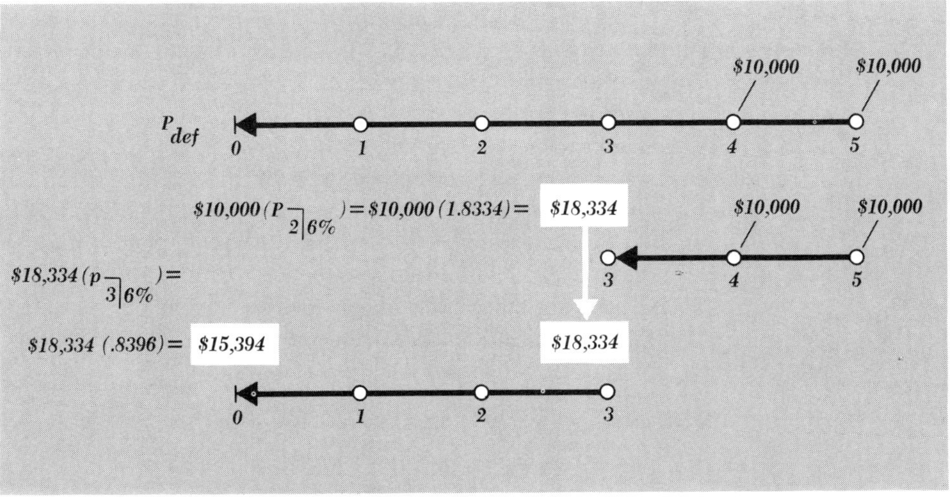

Computation summarized:

$$P_{\text{def}} = R\,(P_{\overline{n}|i})\,(p_{\overline{m}|i}) = \$10{,}000\,(P_{\overline{2}|6\%})\,(p_{\overline{3}|6\%})$$
$$= \$10{,}000\,(1.8334)\,(.8396) = \underline{\underline{\$15{,}394}}$$

(Method 2). The reasoning behind this approach to the solution of Example 17 is indicated in the following diagram:

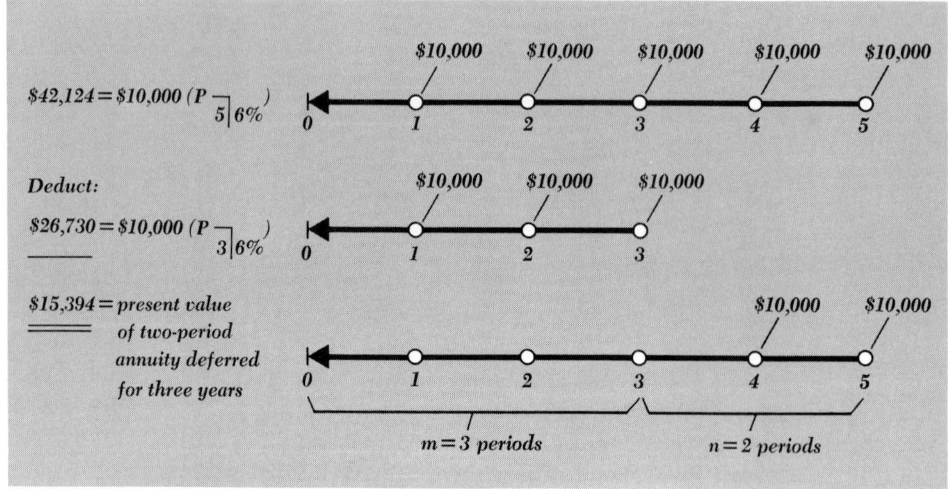

Computation summarized:

$$P_{\text{def}} = R\,(P_{\overline{n+m}|i} - P_{\overline{m}|i}) = \$10{,}000\,(P_{\overline{5}|6\%} - P_{\overline{3}|6\%})$$
$$= \$10{,}000\,(4.2124 - 2.6730) = \$10{,}000\,(1.5394) = \underline{\underline{\$15{,}394}}$$

From a computational standpoint, Method 2 is preferable because it avoids one rather lengthy multiplication.

Comparing values over time

Since money can be readily invested to earn a return, there is a universal service charge (interest) for its use and any given amount of money available on a stated date has a different value at all other points in time. In essence the compound interest procedures discussed in this chapter are nothing more than a means of moving money inflows and outflows forward and backward in time on a basis that enables us to compare values in equivalent terms.

For example, if we are given a choice between $10,000 in two years or $15,000 in eight years, the optimal decision is not obvious. These two sums of money can no more be subtracted in a meaningful sense than we could subtract n apples from m automobiles and get useful results. Assuming that money is worth 8% per annum, we can compare these sums at any point in time only by measuring their value at that point. If we choose *now* (time point zero), the appropriate analysis would show that the $10,000 in two years is preferable:

$$\$10{,}000\,(p_{\overline{n}|i}) = \$10{,}000\,(p_{\overline{2}|8\%}) = \$10{,}000\,(.8573) = \underline{\underline{\$8{,}573}}$$

$$\$15{,}000\,(p_{\overline{8}|8\%}) = \$15{,}000\,(.5403) = \underline{\underline{\$7{,}105}}$$

We can reach the same decision by comparing values at the end of eight years:

$$\$10{,}000\;a_{\overline{6}|8\%} = \$10{,}000\,(1.5869) = \underline{\underline{\$15{,}869}}$$

$15,000 at the end of eight years is equivalent to $\underline{\underline{\$15{,}000}}$

The \$10,000 in two years is still shown to be preferable to \$15,000 in eight years since, if invested at 8%, \$10,000 would grow to \$15,869 by the end of eight years. We could choose any other point in time and make a similar comparison without changing the validity of the decision in favor of the \$10,000.

Summary of Value Relationships

The value relationships discussed thus far may be summarized in terms of the following diagram of an assumed set of equal cash flows R:

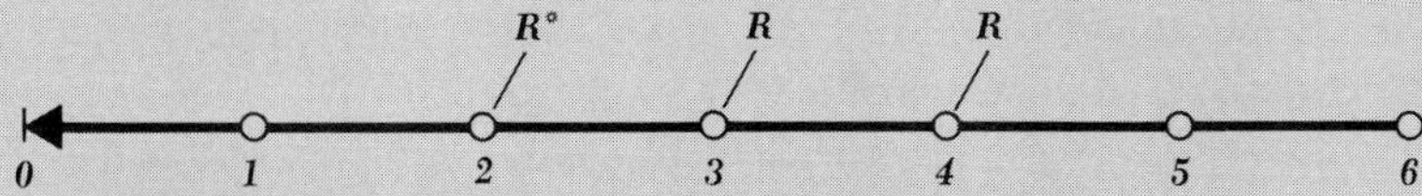

Problem	Value situation	Formula
(1) Find the value of R* at time point 0.	Present value of a single sum. $n = 2$	$p = R^*(p_{\overline{n}\vert i})$ $\quad p_{\overline{n}\vert i} = \dfrac{1}{(1+i)^n}$
(2) Find the value of R* at time point 6.	Amount of a single sum. $n = 4$	$a = R^*(a_{\overline{n}\vert i})$ $\quad a_{\overline{n}\vert i} = (1+i)^n$
(3) Find the value of all R's at time point 1.	Present value of an ordinary annuity. $n = 3$	$P = R(P_{\overline{n}\vert i})$ $P_{\overline{n}\vert i} = \dfrac{1 - \dfrac{1}{(1+i)^n}}{i} = \dfrac{1-p}{i}$
(4) Find the value of all R's at time point 4.	Amount of an ordinary annuity. $n = 3$	$A = R(A_{\overline{n}\vert i})$ $A_{\overline{n}\vert i} = \dfrac{(1+i)^n - 1}{i} = \dfrac{a-1}{i}$
(5) Find the value of all R's at time point 2.	Present value of an annuity due. $n = 3$	$P_D = R(P_{D\overline{n}\vert i})$ $P_{D\overline{n}\vert i} = (P_{\overline{n-1}\vert i} + 1)$ or $(P_{\overline{n}\vert i})(1+i)$
(6) Find the value of all R's at time point 5.	Amount of an annuity due. $n = 3$	$A_D = R(A_{D\overline{n}\vert i})$ $A_{D\overline{n}\vert i} = (A_{\overline{n+1}\vert i} - 1)$ or $(A_{\overline{n}\vert i})(1+i)$
(7) Find the value of all R's at time point 0.	Present value of a deferred annuity. $n = 3;\ m = 1$	$P_{\text{def}} = R(P_{\overline{m+n}\vert i} - P_{\overline{m}\vert i})$ or $= (P_{\overline{n}\vert i})(p_{\overline{m}\vert i})$
(8) Find the value of all R's at time point 6.	Amount of an open-end annuity. $n = 3;\ m = 2$	$A_{OE} = R(A_{\overline{m+n}\vert i} - A_{\overline{m}\vert i})$ or $= R(A_{\overline{n}\vert i})(a_{\overline{m}\vert i})$

Finding an unknown rate of interest (yield)

It is sometimes useful to be able to estimate the rate of interest involved in an annuity contract when the number of periods, the number of rents, and either the present value or amount of the annuity are known. Actually computing the yield rate of an annuity is a rather involved mathematical problem, since the unknown i appears within the exponential element $(1 + i)^n$ in the annuity equation. Fortunately there are several means of approximating the value of i with sufficient accuracy for most decision-making purposes.

Estimating i when rents are equal. If we are dealing with an annuity situation involving equal rents and tables are available, the easiest way to approximate i is to interpolate between two values of $A_{\overline{n}|i}$ or $P_{\overline{n}|i}$ in the annuity tables. The procedure can best be demonstrated by an illustration:

Example 18. Find i, given present value and rent. If $14,600 is invested at the present, a company can anticipate an annual cost saving of $4,000 in each of the next four years. If the cost is assumed to occur at the end of each year, what is the yield rate of return on this investment?

Solution. Note the "knowns" in this problem. We know the present value of the annuity of cost savings ($P = \$14{,}600$), the rent ($R = \$4{,}000$), and the number of periods ($n = 4$). If we put these known factors into the general equation for the present value of an ordinary annuity, we have:

$$P = R\,(P_{\overline{n}|i})$$

Therefore:

$$\$14{,}600 = \$4{,}000\,(P_{\overline{4}|i})$$

Now solve this equation for the factor $P_{\overline{4}|i}$:

$$P_{\overline{4}|i} = \frac{\$14{,}600}{\$4{,}000} = 3.65$$

What we have established is that the present value of an annuity of $1 per year for four periods at some unknown rate of interest is equal to $3.65. If we can find this value for $P_{\overline{4}|i}$ in a set of annuity tables, we can determine the rate i which will satisfy this valuation. Suppose we go to the table on page 593 which shows the present value of an annuity of $1 for varying n and i, enter the table at the line $n = 4$, and follow across until we locate a value close to 3.65.

We find that the value $P_{\overline{4}|i} = 3.65$ falls between two present values appearing in the table:

$$\left.\begin{array}{r} \left.\begin{array}{r} P_{\overline{4}|3\%} = 3.72 \\ P_{\overline{4}|i} = 3.65 \end{array}\right\} .07 \text{ difference} \\ P_{\overline{4}|4\%} = 3.63 \end{array}\right\} .09 \text{ difference}$$

It is clear that the unknown yield rate lies between 3% and 4%. The difference between 3.72 (the value of P at 3%) and 3.63 (the value of P at 4%) is .09. The difference between 3.72 and 3.65 (the value of P at i%) is .07. By interpolation, we may estimate that the yield rate of interest on the investment we are considering is 3% plus 7/9 of the difference between 3% and 4%. The approximate effective or yield rate would be computed as follows:

$$i = 3\% + \tfrac{7}{9}\,(4\% - 3\%) = 3.8\% \text{ approximate rate of return}$$

For many decision-making purposes exact interpolation is not necessary; it is sufficient to know that the yield rate is between 3% and 4%, or that it is slightly more than 3½%.

If we know the rents R, the number of periods n, and the amount A to which a series of rents will accumulate, a similar procedure using values of $A_{\overline{n}|i}$ from annuity tables of amounts will provide an estimate of the effective rate of interest i.

Estimating *i* when rents are unequal. If we are faced with a situation in which future inflows or outflows are not equal, we can no longer use annuity tables to approximate i. We can, however, use a relatively simple trial-and-error approach which will give us a usable approximation of i. An example will illustrate the method:

Example 19. Given unequal rents, find i. By investing $5,100 immediately, Company A may expect to realize additional income of $1,000 at the end of the first year, $2,000 at the end of the second year, and $3,000 at the end of the third year. What rate of return would the company earn on this investment?

Solution. An answer requires that we solve for i in the following equations:

$$5{,}100 = \frac{1{,}000}{(1+i)} + \frac{2{,}000}{(1+i)^2} + \frac{3{,}000}{(1+i)^3}$$

or

$$0 = -5{,}100 + \frac{1{,}000}{(1+i)} + \frac{2{,}000}{(1+i)^2} + \frac{3{,}000}{(1+i)^3}$$

Solution for i by ordinary mathematical means is very difficult, since i appears in expressions raised to varying powers. We can estimate the yield rate with satisfactory accuracy, however, by computing the present value of the prospective cash flows at different rates of interest i on a trial-and-error basis until we find a rate which makes the present value of the entire prospect equal to zero.

Suppose on our first trial we compute the present value at 8%:

Time period	*Cash flow*	*Present value of $1 at 8%*	*Present value of investment at 8%*
0	−$5,100	1.0000	−$5,100
1	+ 1,000	.9259	+ 926
2	+ 2,000	.8573	+ 1,715
3	+ 3,000	.7938	+ 2,381
	+$ 900		−$ 78

Since the present value of this investment prospect is negative at 8%, we know that the actual yield rate is lower than 8%, because the present value of future inflows increases as the rate of discount decreases.

Therefore, on the next trial we select 6% as the interest rate:

Time period	*Cash flow*	*Present value of $1 at 6%*	*Present value of investment at 6%*
0	*−$5,100*	*1.0000*	*−$5,100*
1	*+ 1,000*	*.9434*	*+ 943*
2	*+ 2,000*	*.8900*	*+ 1,780*
3	*+ 3,000*	*.8396*	*+ 2,519*
	+$ 900		*+$ 142*

The net present value is positive at 6%. We now know that the actual yield rate of return i lies between 6% and 8%. By interpolation, we can approximate the yield rate as follows:

$$i = 6\% + \frac{142}{142 + 78}(8\% - 6\%) = 6\% + \frac{142}{220}(2\%) = 6\% + 1.3\% = 7.3\%$$

The trial-and-error process may be shown graphically by plotting the relation between net present values and varying rates of return, using the known present values at three interest rates: 0%, 6%, and 8%. If the interest rate were 0, the net present value would be $900; the net present value at 6% is a positive $142, and at 8%, a negative $78.

Net Present Values at Various Interest Rates

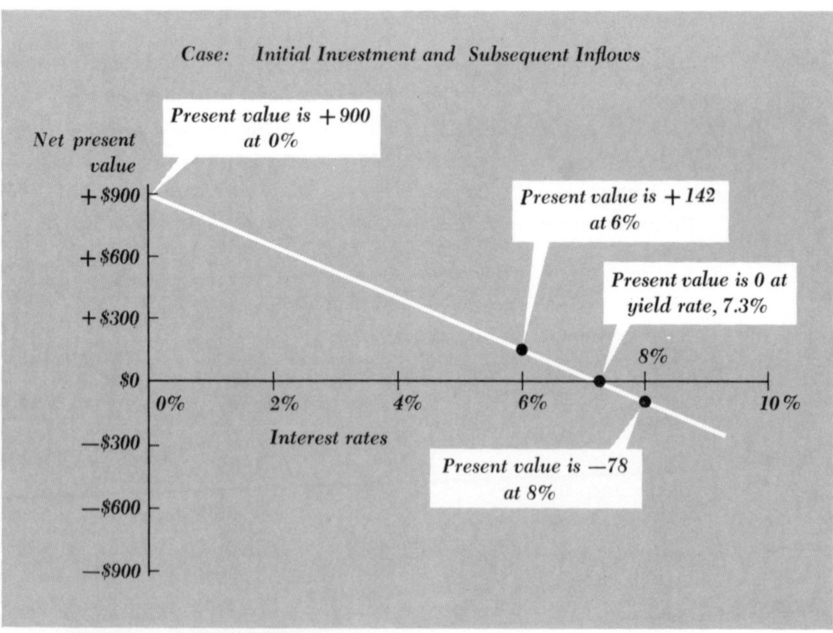

This graph simply shows that as the rate of interest rises, the present value of a prospect involving an initial cash outlay and a series of positive inflows greater than the initial investment falls, and that the present value is exactly zero at the yield rate of interest i.

The borrowing case. If we are dealing with a situation involving the immediate *receipt* of funds and the *subsequent repayment* of the funds borrowed, the same general relationship holds and the same computational approach may be used to approximate i. The curve of present value in relation to the yield rate is reversed, however, because the present value of the initial cash receipt is positive, and the present value of the subsequent repayments is negative. This relationship is indicated on the accompanying diagram:

Net Present Values at Various Interest Rates

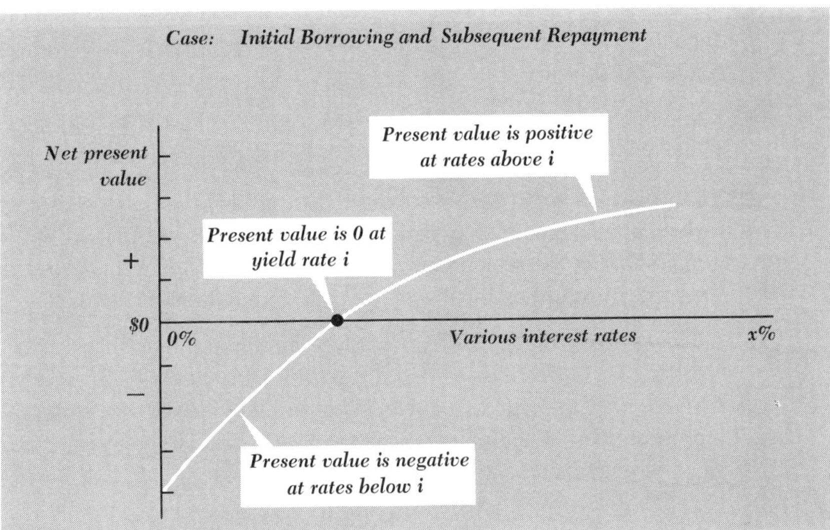

Note in this case that at 0% interest the net present value will be negative, which is another way of saying that the sum of the repayments exceeds the amount borrowed. As the rate of interest increases, the net present value of the entire borrowing opportunity rises because the present value of the negative repayments becomes smaller, until net present value reaches $0 at the yield rate. Once the present values at rates on either side of the yield rate have been computed, the yield rate may be estimated by interpolation.

Questions

1. A knowledge of compound interest formulas and computations is useful to the accountant both in his role as an economic historian, and as a decision analyst. Distinguish these two applications and give examples of situations in which compound interest computations are useful.

2. Distinguish simple and compound interest. Why is simple interest relatively less important?

3. Draw a freehand graph of the periodic value of a sum accumulating at simple interest, and another graph of a sum accumulating at compound interest. The vertical axis should represent dollars and the horizontal axis time. Explain why the graphs differ.

4. What is the relation between n and i in compound interest formulas?

5. Compound discount D and compound interest I are always equal. Why?

6. Distinguish an ordinary annuity, annuity due, open-end annuity, and deferred annuity.

7. Jedlo Company is negotiating for a fire insurance policy. They are offered the choice of paying for the policy in annual premiums of $2,240, in one three-year premium of $5,600, or in one five-year premium of $8,960. Assuming that all premiums are payable in advance, that the company plans to continue the insurance for at least five years, and that money is worth 6% per year, which alternative would you advise?

8. Kemp has arranged to settle a debt of $10,000 by paying $1,300 per year for nine years. What effective rate of interest is Kemp paying under this arrangement?

9. An investment of $12,000 is expected to produce out-of-pocket cost savings of various annual amounts totaling $15,000 over a five-year period. Draw a freehand graph showing the relation between the present value of this investment and the yield rate of return on the investment. Be sure to label all elements of your graph.

10. An investment situation which involves an initial outlay followed by a series of returns has a present value that *decreases* as the yield rate of return is increased. A borrowing situation involving an initial receipt followed by a series of outlays has a present value which *increases* as the yield rate of interest is increased. Explain why the relationships are reversed in these cases.

Short cases for analysis

17-1 A college is planning to build a dormitory. The construction cost is to be paid from the proceeds of a serial note issue. The notes are of equal amounts and include a provision for interest at an annual rate of 4% payable annually. It is expected that receipts from students for room and board in excess of out-of-pocket operating expenses will provide for the payments of principal and interest on the notes.

The business manager of the college has estimated that net receipts available for payment of principal and interest will be $45,000 per year. The dormitory is expected to cost $342,000 to construct.

Instructions

a. Assuming that interest and principal payments are to be made at the end of each year, determine whether the debt can be paid off in 10 years.

b. If there is a 10% increase in the actual cost of construction over the $342,000 estimate and receipts do not change, can the indebtedness and interest be paid off in 10 years? Show computations to support your answer.

17-2 For each of the four cases described write a formula for the computation of the amount required. You need not solve the formula numerically; simply formulate the solution:

Example. Find the amount A to which \$100 will accumulate in seven years if it is deposited in a savings account that earns 3% annually during the first three years and 4% annually during the next four years:

Solution $100\,(a_{\overline{3}|3\%}) = X \qquad X\,(a_{\overline{4}|4\%}) = A$

or $(100\,a_{\overline{3}|3\%})\,(a_{\overline{4}|4\%}) = A$

Case 1. Crockett owed various debts totaling \$8,450. On May 1 he arranged with a finance company to have the debts paid and to repay the finance company over a period of 48 months by a series of equal monthly payments which would be applied first to interest and then to principal until the loan was retired. The finance company charges interest of 12% compounded monthly. What monthly payments R will be required?

Case 2. Senner deposited \$100 in a savings account in his daughter's name on the day his daughter was born, and \$200 on each birthday thereafter until she reached the age of twenty-one, at which time he added a final deposit of \$2,100. If the fund earned interest at 4% compounded annually, how much A would be in the account on the daughter's twenty-second birthday?

Case 3. Mohr has an opportunity to acquire a piece of property. If he owned the property, he could expect to rent it as a parking lot for \$2,000 per year for 10 years, rent payable each year in advance. Property taxes on the property are \$400 per year, payable at the end of each year. At the end of the tenth year Mohr believes he can sell the property for \$28,000. Mohr would not undertake this investment unless he could earn a return of 10% on his investment. Determine the maximum amount M Mohr should offer for the property.

Case 4. Kingsley Company has an issue of preferred stock which must be retired at the end of 20 years. There are 80,000 shares outstanding which must be called at a price of \$105 per share. The company wishes to plan for this retirement by investing an equal annual amount R at the end of each of the first 10 years, and an equal annual amount twice as large at the end of each of the last 10 years, with the objective of having a fund sufficient to retire the preferred at the end of 20 years. The treasurer estimates that the fund can be invested to earn an annual return of 5%, and he wishes to determine the amount of the necessary annual investments during the first and second 10-year periods.

17-3 At the end of this problem appear the first three lines from the 2% columns of several tables of compound interest values. For each of the following five items you are to select from among these fragmentary tables the one from which the amount required can be obtained *most directly* (assuming that complete tables are available in each instance).

a. The amount to which a single sum would accumulate at compound interest by the end of a specified period (interest compounded annually)

b. The amount which must be appropriated at the end of each of a specific number of years in order to provide for the accumulation, at annually compounded interest, of a certain sum of money

c. The amount which must be deposited in a fund which will earn interest at a specified rate, compounded annually, in order to make possible the withdrawal of certain equal sums annually over a specified period starting one year from the date of the deposit

d. The amount of interest which will accumulate on a single deposit by the end of a specified period (4% interest compounded semiannually)

e. The amount, net of compound discount, which if paid now would settle a debt of a larger amount due at a specified future date

Partial Tables

Periods	*Table A*	*Table B*	*Table C*	*Table D*	*Table E*	*Table F*
0	1.0000		1.0000			
1	.9804	1.0200	1.0200	1.0000	.9804	1.0200
2	.9612	2.0604	1.0404	.4950	1.9416	.5150
3		3.1216		.3268	2.8839	.3468

Instructions

List the numbers 1 through 5 on your answer sheet. Beside each number print the capital letter which identifies the table you would use in obtaining most directly the amount required. Then explain your reasoning.

AICPA adapted

Problems

17-4 The following exercises are designed to test your understanding of the use of compound interest tables and formulas.

a. Determine i and n in each of the following cases:

(1) 6% per year, for five years, compounded semiannually

(2) 5% per year, for six years, compounded quarterly

(3) 9% per year, for three years, compounded monthly

b. Write the appropriate symbol for and compute each of the following to the nearest dollar, using the appropriate tables in the Appendix. (In each case the interest rate stated is an annual rate.)

(1) The amount to which $100 will accumulate in five years at 4%, compounded annually

(2) The present value of $1,000 due in six years at 6%, compounded semiannually

(3) The amount of $2,000 accumulated for four years at 8%, compounded quarterly

(4) The present value of an annuity of $100 every six months for 10 years, at 5%, compounded semiannually

(5) The amount of an annuity of $600 every three months for six years at 6%, compounded quarterly

(6) The present value of an annuity of $3,000 per year for 30 years at 3%, compounded annually

(7) The present value of $10,000 due in 10 years at 8%, compounded quarterly

(8) The amount of an annuity of $5,000 per year for three years at 6% interest, compounded monthly

17-5 a. Find the interest rate i (by interpolation) in each of the following cases:
(1) $P_{\overline{8}|i} = \$6.00$
(2) $A_{\overline{11}|i} = \$13.034$

b. Find the yield rate of interest on an initial investment of $12,000 which is expected to produce a return of $3,000 the first year, $4,000 the second year, and $8,000 the third year. Draw a graph showing the relationship between the present value of these prospective returns and various yield rates of return.

c. Find the yield rate of interest involved in borrowing $20,000, to be repaid $5,000 at the end of the first year, $8,000 at the end of the second year, and $12,000 at the end of the third year. Draw a graph showing the relationship between the present value of this borrowing and various effective rates of interest.

17-6 Compute the following, rounding all answers to the nearest dollar.

a. Using only the table for $a_{\overline{n}|i}$ (but any formulas you wish), compute the amount to which an annuity of $2,000 each six months will accumulate in 10 years at 5% interest compounded semiannually.

b. Using only the table for $p_{\overline{n}|i}$ (but any formulas you wish), compute the present value of an annuity of $10,000 per quarter for seven years at 8% interest compounded quarterly.

c. Compute by two different methods the amount of an open-end annuity in which $3,000 is deposited at the end of each of the first five years and left invested for five additional years at 3% interest compounded annually.

d. Compute by two different methods the present value of an annuity of 10 annual rents, the first rent of which begins six years after the starting date. The annuity earns interest of 6% annually, and withdrawals of $4,000 are to be made at the end of each of the 10 years.

e. Compute by two different methods the amount of an annuity due of $1,200 per year for 10 years at 6% interest compounded annually.

f. Compute by two different methods the present value of an annuity due of $5,000 per year for 17 years at 5% interest compounded annually.

17-7 Compute the following, rounding all amounts to the nearest dollar.

a. Compute the semiannual deposit necessary to accumulate a fund of $20,000 at the end of four years, if the fund earns interest at the annual rate of 6% compounded semiannually. Prepare a schedule showing the accumulation for the four-year period.

b. If $10,000 is invested at the beginning of Year 1, to earn 5% annually, what equal amount may be withdrawn from the fund at the end of each year for five years? Compute the amount and construct a schedule showing that the fund will be exhausted at the end of five years.

c. If $50,000 is invested now to earn an annual return of 4%, what equal amount can be withdrawn at the end of the third year and for each of the next three years? Compute the amount and prepare a schedule showing that the fund will be exhausted at the end of six years.

17-8 Carl Jones has just accepted a position with a state agency. The state has a retirement pension plan which calls for joint contributions by the employee and employer; however, the retirement fund earns a very low rate of return. Jones, who is 10 years from retirement age of 65, expects to contribute $600 per year to the plan, and after 10 years of contributions to be eligible to receive approximately $1,000 per year for life.

Jones is uncertain whether he should accept the plan. Since the retirement plan is optional, he is considering the alternative of investing annually an amount equal to his contribution under the plan, with the idea that the higher rate of earnings on such an investment might well more than offset the loss of his employer's contribution. Jones is firmly convinced that he can invest $600 per year to earn a return of 8% annually for the next 10 years and also after his retirement. After his retirement, Jones would plan to exhaust his investment fund by withdrawing an equal amount each year from his investment for a period of 15 years, which is his life expectancy at age 65.

Instructions

Assuming that Jones can carry out his investment plan and that he will realize earnings on his investment at the expected rate, prepare a schedule showing whether he is likely to be better or worse off if he accepts his employer's pension plan. How would you advise Jones with respect to this decision?

AICPA adapted

17-9 Paul Bunyan is considering the purchase of a stand of timber which he plans to cut and sell to lumber manufacturing firms. A cruise of the acreage at the time of the prospective purchase indicates that it contains 29,199,000 board-feet of merchantable timber. Bunyan is advised by forestry experts that a stand of this type will exhibit an average growth factor of 4% per year, which as a rough estimate may be computed as applying to the uncut balance at the beginning of each year. Bunyan plans to cut the tract in equal annual quantities during each of the next 10 years. Bunyan estimates that standing timber will be worth an average of $20 per thousand board-feet during the next five years and $22 per thousand board-feet during the following five-year period. The amount he receives in excess of these prices at the mill will be just sufficient to cover the cost of cutting and hauling. The land is expected to be worth $10,000 at the end of 10 years after all timber has been cut.

Instructions

a. Compute the amount (in board-feet) that Bunyan may expect to cut from this tract in each of the 10 years after purchase. (Round to the nearest thousand board-feet.)

b. If Bunyan expects to earn a return of 10% on his investment, what is the maximum price he should offer for the timber tract at this time?

17-10 Mr. Davee owns a piece of property having a fair market value of $300,000. He has decided to give this property to his two sons, John and Douglas, provided they will guarantee him an income for life. An agreement is signed whereby the sons will pay Davee $10,000 at the end of each year for the first five years, and $15,000 per year thereafter for the rest of his life. A Federal gift tax will be levied on this transaction, based on the present value of the gift computed on a 3% basis. According to actuarial tables prepared by the Treasury Department, Davee has a life expectancy at the time of the gift of nine years.

Instructions

Compute to the nearest dollar the present value of the gift for tax purposes.

17-11 Mr. Doake is forced to retire early because of a disability. He is entitled to a retirement pension, and has the option of taking a lump-sum settlement of $30,000 or an annual annuity for life. The annuity would be determined on the basis of a life expectancy of 20 years and an interest rate of 4% compounded annually. Doake has observed that real estate investments have earned 5% over a long period, and he therefore decided to take the lump-sum settlement and invest it in a duplex.

The property appears to have the following prospects:

	Prospective annual rental receipts at beginning of each year	*Prospective annual outlays for taxes, repairs, etc., as of the end of each year*
First 10 years	*$4,800*	*$2,000*
Eleventh to twentieth year	*3,600*	*2,200*
Resale value of lot at end of 20 years	*6,000*	

Instructions

Compute to the nearest dollar.

a. What amount should Doake offer for the property, assuming that his appraisal of the prospects is accurate and that he expects a 5% return?

b. If he should be able to purchase the property for exactly $30,000, would he earn a return of more than or less than 5% on his investment, again assuming that his estimates are accurate? Explain.

c. If Doake had chosen to take the annuity option rather than the lump sum, what would have been his annual pension?

d. Doake's wife has a life expectancy of 30 years at the time of his retirement. Suppose he had selected an option whereby he would receive a given annuity during his lifetime, and at his death his wife would receive one-half this amount for the remainder of her life. Compute the annual amount Doake would receive, based on life expectancies.

17-12 Kovart Company is offering for sale a piece of land adjacent to its plant. The land has a book value of $30,000. The company has received three offers from prospective purchasers, as described below:

(1) A offers $11,000 in cash and a non-interest-bearing note in the amount of $50,000 due at the end of three years.

(2) B offers $12,250 in cash and a note for $45,000 due at the end of three years, with interest of 3% payable annually at the end of each year.

(3) C can pay nothing down, but offers $10,000 per year for five years, each annual obligation to be evidenced by a note bearing simple interest at 10% per annum, payable when each note falls due.

The risk element is considered to be comparable in each of the three cases so there is no basis for a choice among the offers on that score. The controller of Kovart Company estimates that he could discount any of the notes involved at the bank at 6%.

Instructions

a. Prepare an analysis showing which offer the company should accept, assuming that money is worth 6% per year.

b. Prepare a journal entry to record the sale of the land to the person making the best offer.

17-13 The state highway department has decided to build a toll bridge across a river between two towns. The construction contract is won by the Neilsen Company with a bid of $2 million to complete the bridge by the end of the current year. The Neilsen Company agrees to accept the state's 20-year, 4% bonds (with interest payable annually) in payment for the bridge when construction is completed. The highway department plans to provide for a schedule of toll rates that will produce revenues sufficient to cover interest, operating costs, and an annual deposit in a sinking fund to retire the bonds at maturity.

Engineers estimate that the ratio of automobiles to trucks will be 10 to 1, and that tolls of 25 cents for automobiles and 50 cents for trucks can be established. The cost of collecting tolls and maintaining the bridge is estimated to be $30,000 per year.

Instructions

Determine (to the nearest thousand) the number of automobile and truck tolls that must be collected annually in order to meet annual sinking fund, interest, and maintenance costs. Assume that the sinking fund will earn 4% compounded annually.

AICPA adapted

17-14 Christy Company has a $100,000 debt which is to be repaid in 28 equal semiannual installments of $5,000 each plus a final twenty-ninth payment, six months later, sufficient to retire the principal of the debt and interest at an annual rate of 5%, compounded semiannually. Payments are applied first to interest and any remaining portion to the reduction of the principal.

Instructions

Round all computations to the nearest dollar.

a. Compute the amount of the final twenty-ninth payment.

b. Compute the unpaid principal balance of the loan at the end of the fifth year, just after the tenth semiannual installment has been paid.

c. Compute the amount of interest expense incurred in connection with this debt during the sixth year it is outstanding, that is, the sum of the interest elements in the eleventh and twelfth payments on this debt.

d. Of the tenth payment of $5,000, how much applied to reduction of the principal of the debt and how much was interest expense? Show computations.

AICPA adapted

17-15 **a.** Oredin Company has made annual payments of $2,500 into a fund at the close of each year for the past nine years. The fund balance immediately after the ninth payment totaled $26,457. The controller asks you to determine how many more $2,500 annual payments will be required to bring the fund to $50,000, assuming that the fund continues to earn interest at 4% compounded annually.

Instructions

Compute the number of full payments required and the amount of the final payment (to the nearest dollar) if a full $2,500 is not required.

b. Oredin Company wishes to provide for the retirement of an obligation of $200,000 due on July 1, Year 8. The company plans to deposit $20,000 in a special fund each July 1 for eight years, starting July 1, Year 1. The company wishes to deposit on July 1, Year 0, an amount which, with accumulated interest at 4% compounded annually, will bring the fund up to $200,000 at the maturity of the obligation.

Instructions

Compute (to the nearest dollar) the amount to be deposited on July 1, Year 0.

AICPA adapted

18 COMPOUND INTEREST APPLICATIONS: VALUATION OF ASSETS AND LIABILITIES

In *Intermediate Accounting,* the following definitions were employed:

Assets: expected future economic benefits, the rights to which have been acquired by the entity as a result of some current or past transaction.

Liabilities: obligations, resulting from past or current transactions, to convey cash or other assets or to perform services in the future.

These definitions embody the idea that assets and liabilities are rights in and obligations to convey resources *in the future* and that their ultimate worth is the present value of expected future economic events. A businessman who buys an asset recognizes these facts and decides to make the purchase because in some sense he believes the present value of the future benefits is equal to or greater than the purchase price. Similarly, anyone who incurs an obligation should do so on the basis of a determination that what he receives now is worth as much or more than the present value of the future obligation he undertakes. Because these rational forces are at work in a competitive economy, the accountant is justified in assuming that the initial cost of an asset is good objective evidence of its value at that time and that the proceeds of a debt transaction represent the value of the liability at the time it is incurred. In following this procedure the accountant is relying on *indirect evidence* (that is, the cost incurred or the proceeds of a debt) of the present value of future events. There are numerous occasions, however, where businessmen and accountants find it useful to employ *direct valuation* (that is, to estimate the present value of future expected economic events). Such estimates are obviously useful in making business investment decisions. Direct valuation is also applicable to a number of problems faced by accountants in establishing valuations for financial reporting purposes.

In this chapter we shall discuss direct valuation applications in the area of financial reporting. In the next chapter the use of direct valuation in analyzing investment decisions will be considered.

Direct valuation under conditions of certainty

A basic problem in dealing with future events is that they are surrounded by some degree of uncertainty, ranging from an almost complete inability to predict what will happen to relative certainty as to the probable course of events. For example, when an accountant examines an account receivable from a customer having a good credit rating, he is reasonably sure what this means in terms of a future cash inflow. At the other extreme, the accountant who observes an investment of $100,000 in market research knows the results that will flow from this expenditure are highly uncertain. The problem of valuation has and always will be one of dealing with uncertainty.

If we were faced with a business situation involving complete certainty, we could value assets and liabilities and measure periodic income with a highly satisfying degree of accuracy. This point is worth illustrating since the case of certainty is an important step on the road to a thorough understanding of the role of uncertainty in asset and liability valuation and income measurement.

Illustration. Suppose we examine a hypothetical situation in which future events are perfectly predictable. Mr. Fortell has a contract to furnish equipment to User Company for a period of three years, at an annual rent of $10,000 at the end of each year. Fortell can buy the equipment by paying $8,107 in cash now and giving a note for $20,000 due at the end of three years, with interest at 5%. User Company agrees to pay all operating costs and maintenance (including property taxes) on the equipment during the period and to purchase the used equipment at the end of the three-year period for $1,000. We shall assume that Fortell has entered into this business arrangement because he is satisfied, given the risks involved, with a 10% return on his investment during the three-year period. We shall also assume (in order to avoid having to liquidate the business at the end of the three-year period) that Fortell can invest any idle cash during the period to earn a 10% return. We can diagram Fortell's prospects as follows:

Assets

$25,620 = present value of rent and salvage value

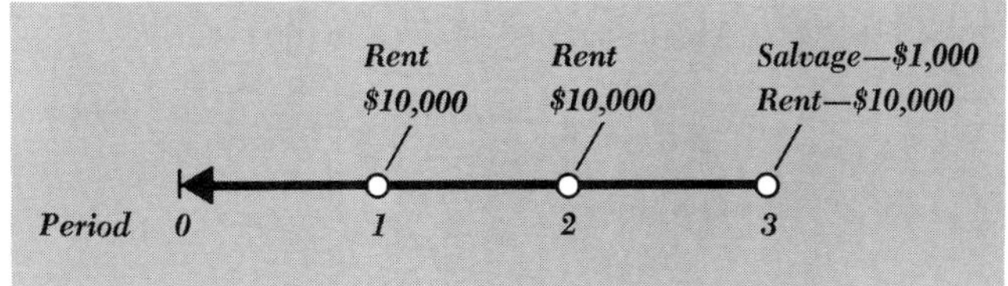

Computation:

Present value of rent = 10,000 ($P_{\overline{3}\rceil 10\%}$) = 10,000 (2.4869)........	$24,869
Present value of salvage = 1,000 ($p_{\overline{3}\rceil 10\%}$) = 1,000 (.7513)........	751
	$25,620

Liabilities

$17,513 = present value of debt

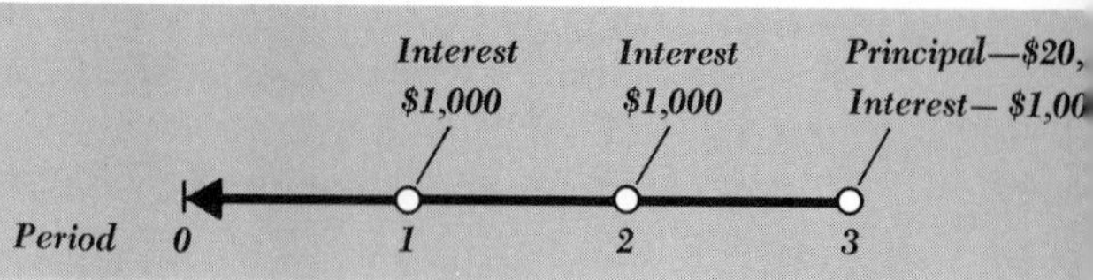

Computation:

Present value of principal $= 20{,}000\,(p_{\overline{3}|10\%}) = 20{,}000\,(.7513)$	$15,026
Present value of interest $= 1{,}000\,(P_{\overline{3}|10\%}) = 1{,}000\,(2.4869)$	2,487
	$17,513

$8,107 = owners' equity (assumed cash down payment on the equipment)

Fortell's balance sheet at the start of business would be:

FORTELL RENTAL COMPANY
Balance Sheet (Direct Values @ 10%*)
beginning of first year

Assets		***Liabilities & Owners' Equity***	
Equipment	*$25,620*	*Liabilities*	*$17,513*
		Fortell, capital	*8,107*
Totals	*$25,620*	*Totals*	*$25,620*

* *For an explanation of the use of 10% as the discount rate, see the discussion below.*

Fortell's case is one of relative certainty in which assets and liabilities can be valued precisely on the basis of future prospects discounted on a 10% return basis. Let us continue the illustration and see how we should record Fortell's transactions during the three-year period, assuming that events take place as expected.

Equipment. Consider first the asset, equipment. It is clear that the value of this asset will grow at the rate of 10% each year and that at the end of each year Fortell will receive $10,000 worth of benefits (rent revenues) from the use of the asset. In addition he will receive $1,000 salvage at the end of the third year. This series of events is summarized in the following table:

Three-year History of Equipment

	Year 1	*Year 2*	*Year 3*
Asset balance at beginning of year	*$25,620*	*$18,182*	*$10,000*
Add: Growth in value at 10%	*2,562*	*1,818*	*1,000*
	$28,182	*$20,000*	*$11,000*
Less: Value of benefits yielded (revenue)	*(10,000)*	*(10,000)*	*(10,000)*
Sale at end of third year			*(1,000)*
Asset balance at end of year	*$18,182*	*$10,000*	*$ -0-*

Note that in Year 1 the value of equipment declines by $7,438 ($25,620 − $18,182), which may be thought of as a precise measure of depreciation. In order to maintain his investment, Fortell must recover $7,438 out of revenues to compensate him for the value of asset services expired during the period. Similarly, depreciation in the second year is $8,182 ($18,182 − $10,000), and in the third year is $9,000 ($10,000 − $1,000 salvage).

On the basis of this analysis we can schedule the following journal entries for the three-year period:

	Year 1		Year 2		Year 3	
(1) Journal entries to record receipt of revenues:						
Cash...........	10,000		10,000		10,000	
Rent Revenues		10,000		10,000		10,000
(2) Journal entries to record depreciation of equipment:						
Depreciation						
Expense........	7,438		8,182		9,000	
Equipment ...		7,438		8,182		9,000

° *Alternatively, the credit might be made to a contra-asset account: Accumulated Depreciation on Equipment.*

Liability—notes payable. The note obligation incurred by Fortell in payment for the equipment was valued on a 10% basis. Therefore this liability will grow at the rate of 10% per year and will be reduced by the interest payments of $1,000 at the end of each year and the $20,000 payment of principal at the end of the third year. The series of transactions is summarized in the following schedule:

Three-year History of Liability (Note Payable)

	Year 1	Year 2	Year 3
Liability balance at beginning of year....	$17,513	$18,264	$19,090
Add: Growth in value of debt at 10%.....	1,751	1,826	1,910°
	$19,264	$20,090	$21,000
Less: Payment on debt:			
Interest payments (5% of $20,000)......	(1,000)	(1,000)	(1,000)
Payment of principal...............			(20,000)
Liability balance at end of year.........	$18,264	$19,090	$ -0-

° *$1 added to compensate for rounding errors.*

The growth in the value of Fortell's debt each year represents the effective interest expense on this liability. It may seem a bit odd to record interest expense at a 10% rate when the note contract calls for interest payments at 5% of the face amount. Remember, however, that this note was given in payment for an asset, which Fortell valued on a 10% basis. The effective cost of the note would be 5% only if Fortell received $20,000 in exchange. Since he received (at present value) only $17,513 of assets in exchange for the liability, the debt has a higher effective cost than 5%. From Fortell's viewpoint the interest payments of $1,000 and the payment of $20,000 at maturity are simply future prospective cash outflows which are directly valued on the basis of a 10% return on investment.

The journal entries to record the accrual of interest and the payments on the debt would be as follows:

	Year 1		Year 2		Year 3	
(3) Journal entries to record accrual of interest:						
Interest Expense	*1,751*		*1,826*		*1,910*	
Liability		*1,751*		*1,826*		*1,910*
(4) Journal entries to record payments on the liability:						
Liability	*1,000*		*1,000*		*21,000*	
Cash		*1,000*		*1,000*		*21,000*

Cash receipts and disbursements. Fortell will accumulate cash during the first two years to meet the maturity amount of his note ($20,000) at the end of the third year. Some of the cash accumulated will represent a recovery of his original investment in equipment (measured by depreciation), and some will represent earned income. Since Fortell's entire set of prospects was valued on a 10% return basis, we will destroy the consistency of our illustration if we allow Fortell to accumulate idle cash balances. Implicit in the assumption that any series of future benefits have a present value at 10% is the corollary assumption that any amount of cash recovered from the investment can be reinvested to earn a 10% return. This concept and its consequences will be explored in more detail in Chapter 19. At present we can deal with the problem simply by assuming that Fortell can invest any amounts of idle cash to earn a return of 10%, which enables Fortell to maintain intact the value of his original capital and retained earnings. Following this assumption, a summary of Fortell's cash account appears below:

Three-year History of Cash

	Year 1	Year 2	Year 3
Balance of cash at beginning of year	*$ -0-*	*$ 9,000*	*$18,900*
Add: Rental receipts (1)[°] *. . . . .*	*10,000*	*10,000*	*10,000*
Interest at 10% on investment of cash balances at beginning of year (5)	*-0-*	*900*	*1,890*
Sale of equipment to lessee (6)			*1,000*
	$10,000	*$19,900*	*$31,790*
Less: Payments on debt (4)	*(1,000)*	*(1,000)*	*(21,000)*
Balance of cash at end of year	*$ 9,000*	*$18,900*	*$10,790*

° *Journal entries.*

On the basis of this analysis, we can now schedule the remaining two sets of journal entries necessary to complete the three-year picture:

	Year 1		Year 2		Year 3	
(5) Journal entries to record interest on investment of idle cash:						
Cash	-0-		900		1,890	
Interest Revenues		-0-		900		1,890
(6) Journal entries to record sale of equipment:						
Cash	-0-		-0-		1,000	
Equipment		-0-		-0-		1,000

FORTELL RENTAL COMPANY—GENERAL LEDGER
Summary of Transactions during Three-year Period

Cash

	Ref	Debit	Credit	Balance
Year 1	(1)	10,000		10,000
	(3)		1,000	9,000
Year 2	(1)	10,000		
	(3)		1,000	
	(5)	900		18,900
Year 3	(1)	10,000		
	(3)		21,000	
	(5)	1,890		
	(6)	1,000		10,790

Equipment

	Ref	Debit	Credit	Balance
Balance		25,620		25,620
Year 1	(2)		7,438	18,182
Year 2	(2)		8,182	10,000
Year 3	(2)		9,000	1,000
	(6)		1,000	-0-

Liabilities

	Ref	Debit	Credit	Balance
Balance			17,513	17,513
Year 1	(3)		1,751	
	(4)	1,000		18,264
Year 2	(3)		1,826	
	(4)	1,000		19,090
Year 3	(3)		1,910	
	(4)	21,000		-0-

Fortell—Capital

	Debit	Credit	Balance
Balance		8,107	8,107
Year 1 (Income)*		811	8,918
Year 2 (Income)*		892	9,810
Year 3 (Income)*		980	10,790

*Revenues − expenses = 10% on capital investment at beginning of year. Income in the third year lacks $1 of being 10% of beginning capital because of rounding errors.

Revenues

	Ref	Debit	Credit	Balance
Year 1				
(Rent)	(1)		10,000	10,000
Year 2				
(Rent)	(1)		10,000	
(Interest)	(5)		900	10,900
Year 3				
(Rent)	(1)		10,000	
(Interest)	(5)		1,890	11,890

Expenses

	Ref	Debit	Credit	Balance
Year 1				
(Depreciation)	(1)	7,438		
(Interest)	(3)	1,751		9,189
Year 2				
(Depreciation)	(1)	8,182		
(Interest)	(3)	1,826		10,008
Year 3				
(Depreciation)	(1)	9,000		
(Interest)	(3)	1,910		10,910

FORTELL RENTAL COMPANY
Three-year Income Statement—Direct Valuation

	Year 1	Year 2	Year 3
Revenues:			
Rental revenues	$10,000	$10,000	$10,000
Interest revenues		900	1,890
Expenses:			
Depreciation expense	(7,438)	(8,182)	(9,000)
Interest expense	(1,751)	(1,826)	(1,910)
Net income	$ 811	$ 892	$ 980

Financial statements. The record of Fortell's activities during the three-year period is summarized in the general ledger accounts on page 617 which show the effect of the journal entries previously described.

Fortell Company's income statement for the three-year period appears above. Note that net income as measured by the difference between revenues and expenses is exactly equal to a 10% return on the capital invested in the business during each year. This is not surprising, since the values of assets, the liability, and thus owner's equity were measured on the assumption that Fortell would earn a 10% return on his investment, and we are dealing with a case of perfect certainty in which expectations are exactly realized.

The balance sheets for the three-year period, shown below, are prepared on the basis of figures in the general ledger accounts:

FORTELL RENTAL COMPANY
Comparative Balance Sheets—Direct Valuation
three-year period

	Year 0	Year 1	Year 2	Year 3
Assets				
Cash (invested at 10%)	-0-	$ 9,000	$18,900	$10,790
Equipment (net of depreciation)	$25,620	18,182	10,000	-0-
Total assets	$25,620	$27,182	$28,900	$10,790
Liabilities & Owners' Equity				
Notes payable	$17,513	$18,264	$19,090	-0-
Fortell, original capital	8,107	8,107	8,107	$ 8,107
Retained earnings	-0-	811	1,703	2,683
Total liabilities & owner's equity	$25,620	$27,182	$28,900	$10,790

The first notable feature of these balance sheets is that under these circumstances (assumed certainty) the position statement becomes a very valuable financial document. At any given point in the three-year period, Fortell's balance sheet reflects exactly what his business is worth on a 10% return basis. He can sell the business at the end of any year for the book value of the owners' equity with full assurance that both he and the buyer are receiving full value. A second feature is that the rate of return earned on owners' equity is exactly 10% each year. If it were possible to value assets and liabilities on the basis of known future prospects, net income would be a rather uninteresting figure; it would always be the rate of interest used in valuation multiplied by the owners' equity at the beginning of the year. As a matter of fact, we could measure net income without ever looking at the details of revenues and expenses.

Results under indirect valuation. It is instructive to compare the results achieved under an "ideal" valuation of assets, liabilities, and measurement of income with the results that would be reported if we used ordinary accounting procedures. Assuming that we started from the same original balance sheet at the beginning of Year 1, the three-year income statement of Fortell would appear as follows:

FORTELL RENTAL COMPANY
Three-year Income Statement—Ordinary Accounting Procedures

	Year 1	Year 2	Year 3
Revenues:			
Rent revenues	$10,000	$10,000	$10,000
Interest earned on invested cash	-0-	900	1,890
Expenses:			
*Depreciation expense**	(8,207)	(8,207)	(8,206)
Interest expense†	(1,829)	(1,829)	(1,829)
Net income or (loss)	$ (36)	$ 864	$ 1,855

* *Depreciation on a straight-line basis is computed as: cost less salvage divided by three-year service life: $25,620 – $1,000 = $24,620/3 = $8,207.*
† *Interest is the $1,000 paid each period plus amortization of discount: $1,000 + 1/3($20,000 – $17,513) = $1,000 + $829 = $1,829.*

Although the pattern of periodic income differs, the total three-year income is the same under either the direct valuation or the ordinary accounting (indirect valuation) approach.

Period	Net income: Direct valuation	Net income: Indirect valuation
1	$ 811	$ (36)
2	892	864
3	980	1,855
Total three-year income	$2,683	$2,683

This feature of our illustration simply reflects the fact that the lifetime income of a business is easily measured; it is the difference between the original investment and the final liquidating value of the business (taking into account any withdrawals by the owner). In this example the business is completely liquid at the end of the third year, so there is no valuation problem at that time.

We might ask, however, why the *pattern* of periodic income is so different under these two approaches, even though the valuation at the beginning and the end of the three-year period was identical. The answer is that the straight-line averaging of depreciation and interest costs is a cost allocation process that does not take into account the present value of the asset services and the payment obligations at intermediate dates. The reason for this effect will become evident from our discussion of more realistic valuation problems in the latter part of this chapter.

The accountant's valuation problem. The case of perfect certainty, just illustrated, points up the fact that whenever future events are uncertain, the measurement of income and the valuation of assets and liabilities are correspondingly uncertain. In response to the need for objective reporting in an uncertain world, the accountant bases his record of financial position and operating results on past exchanges which have produced indirect evidence of value, plus a direct valuation of the limited scope of future events that he can foresee with some assurance. At any given time it is likely that the accountant will fail to foresee and value some future prospects as an asset, and to foresee and value some future obligations as a liability. Furthermore, accounting valuations based on indirect evidence (past exchanges at market price) inevitably become outdated and no longer a good approximation of direct valuation. To a large extent these errors are inevitable in the light of the practical difficulties facing the accountant.

On the other hand, investors and managers frequently make direct valuation estimates of future events and use them as a basis for their decisions. The accountant must understand the power and the limitations of the direct valuation process if he is to perform well as an analyst of quantitative data for decision-making purposes. Furthermore, the accountant should constantly assess the shortcomings of his art and attempt to move the data he develops closer to the ideal wherever progress is feasible without destroying the benefits of objectivity. An understanding of the direct valuation process helps explain the gap between ideal valuations and measures that are practically feasible; it also provides a basis for intelligent consideration of the means by which this gap may be narrowed.

Direct valuation and bond issues

Bond contracts are a good example of liabilities (to the issuer) and assets (to the investor) involving future events that can be foreseen accurately and evaluated objectively. From the viewpoint of the issuing corporation, a bond contract embodies two distinct obligations: (1) to pay the face amount of the bonds at maturity; and (2) to pay interest periodically, in amounts specified in the contract, until maturity. Both the issuing company and investors assume that the terms of the contract will be carried out exactly in future periods. The only element of uncertainty is the risk that the debtor may default, and the adverse value of this risk is established by the bond buyer in the *yield* (or effective) rate of interest used in pricing the bond. When a bond contract is offered in the market, investors bid at prices which reflect a direct valuation of both elements of the bond obligation at the yield rate of interest (which usually differs from the *nominal* interest promised in the bond contract).

Determining bond prices. Assume that X Corporation has decided to issue \$100,000 in 5%, five-year bonds, interest payable semiannually.[1] The price at which these bonds can be sold will be determined by the yield rate at which buyers are willing to invest, and is equal to the present value of the stream of future payments promised in the bond contract discounted at the yield rate of interest. The bond contract may be diagrammed as follows:

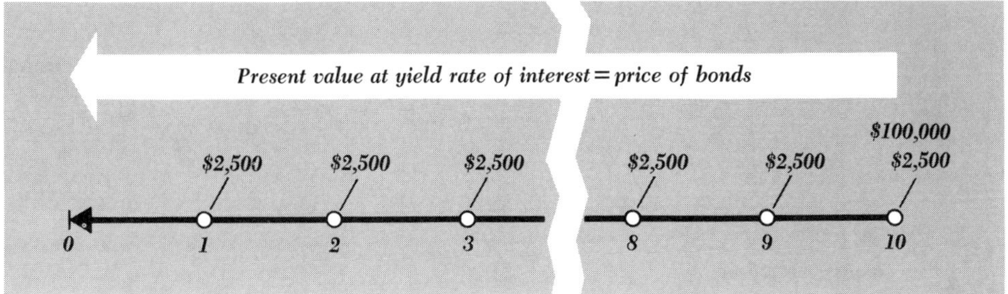

The present value of this contract, computed under two different assumptions as to the yield rate of interest, is demonstrated below:

1. Assume bonds are sold to yield 6% (3% semiannually):

Present value of maturity amount	
\$100,000 ($p_{\overline{10}|3\%}$) = \$100,000 (.7441)	\$74,410
Present value of interest payments	
\$2,500 ($P_{\overline{10}|3\%}$) = \$2,500 (8.5302)	21,325
Price = present value of bond contract @ 3% semiannual yield	\$95,735

2. Assume bonds are sold to yield 4% (2% semiannually):

Present value of maturity amount	
\$100,000 ($p_{\overline{10}|2\%}$) = \$100,000 (.82034)	\$ 82,034
Present value of interest payments	
\$2,500 ($P_{\overline{10}|2\%}$) = \$2,500 (8.9826)	22,457
Price = present value of bond contract @ 2% semiannual yield	\$104,491

Thus the same bond contract promising 5% nominal interest (2½% semiannually) will sell for \$95,735 if the effective interest rate is 6% (3% semiannually) and for \$104,491 if the effective interest rate is 4% (2% semiannually).[2] In the

[1] Bond issues as small as \$100,000 seldom if ever occur in the real world. This is a convenient figure to use in discussing principles, however, and adding a few more zeros provides no additional insight into the concepts.

[2] Stated interest rates are always annual rates unless otherwise specified (as in the case of *2% semiannually,* above). Strictly speaking, 2% interest compounded semiannually is equivalent to an annual rate of 4.04%, not 4%, since compounding twice a year has the effect of allowing interest to run during the second half of the year on interest accumulated at the end of the first half. As a practical matter, however, a 4% annual yield and 2% semiannual yield are often spoken of as equivalents. In computing bond prices, the compounding period is determined by the intervals between interest payments, and the yield rate *per compounding period* is the true effective rate on the bond issue.

first case the bonds sell at a *discount* of \$4,265 (\$100,000 – \$95,735) and in the second at a *premium* of \$4,491 (\$104,491 – \$100,000), in relation to maturity or face amount. The practice of establishing fixed terms for long-term debt issues and allowing the market price of bonds to determine the effective interest rate is a convenient means of letting market forces work through variations in bond prices rather than changes in the bond contract. Bonds will sell at a premium over maturity value whenever the yield rate is lower than the nominal interest; they will sell at a discount whenever the yield rate is higher than the nominal interest. Thus there is an inverse relation between bond prices and yield rates: The higher the bond price the lower the yield rate, and vice versa.

Alternative method of computing bond prices. Another, and often simpler, approach may be used to compute bond prices. Note that when the yield and nominal interest rates coincide a bond will sell at face value, and there is no discount or premium. The amount of discount or premium on a bond issue, therefore, is an amount sufficient to compensate the bond owner for the difference between the return he demands (yield) and the return specified in the contract (nominal).

If an investor demands a yield rate higher than the nominal rate, he deducts from the face value of the bonds the present value (at the yield rate) of a series of payments equal to the excess of the interest on the principal amount at the yield rate and the interest on the principal amount at the nominal rate. This discount exactly compensates the investor for the fact that he is scheduled to receive periodic interest payments that are less than the return he demands, and gives him an investment which earns the yield rate of interest.

On the other hand, if the nominal rate is higher than the yield rate demanded by the investor, he will receive periodic payments higher than those he demands. He is willing to pay a premium for these excess payments equal to their present value (at the yield rate), thus arranging an investment which will yield him the return he desires.

Since the position of the issuing corporation is exactly the reverse of that of the investor, the premium or discount on a bond issue rearranges the bond contract so that the issuing corporation incurs an interest cost on the amount it borrows exactly equal to the yield rate.

Following this reasoning, an alternative bond price computation may be illustrated by using the data from the previous example (\$100,000 of five-year, 5% bonds, interest payable semiannually) as shown on page 623.

The computational advantage of this approach is that it requires only one reference to annuity tables and only one multiplication to find the amount of discount or premium.

Recording interest revenue and expense. When the proceeds and yield rate of a bond issue have been established, the proper accounting for interest expense (to the issuer) and interest revenue (to the investor) might well take into account the effective rate of interest and the actual values established in the transaction. The terms of the bond contract will govern the actual cash flows at various dates, but the economic realities should control the accountant's record of what has and will probably happen.

Alternative Computation of Bond Price

		If bonds are sold to yield		
		3% semi-annually	2½% semi-annually	2% semi-annually
Maturity amount promised in contract		$100,000	$100,000	$100,000
Discount:				
Semiannual interest promised in contract (2½% of 100,000)	$2,500			
Semiannual interest demanded by investor (3% of 100,000)	3,000			
Difference (deficiency)	$ (500)			
Present value of deficiency at yield rate = $500(P_{\overline{10}|3\%}) = $500(8.5302)$		(4,265)		
Face Value: No difference between yield and nominal interest			-0-	
Premium:				
Semiannual interest promised in contract (2½% of 100,000)	$2,500			
Semiannual interest demanded by investors (2% of 100,000)	2,000			
Difference (excess)	$ 500			
Present value of excess at yield rate = $500(P_{10|2\%}) = $500(8.9826)$				4,491
Price at which bonds are issued		$ 95,735	$100,000	$104,491

Bonds sold at a discount. The actual history of a bond issue may be demonstrated in a simplified example. Assume an issue of $100,000 of 5%, four-year bonds (interest payable annually) sold to yield 6%. The price (and proceeds) of the bond issue would be computed:

Present value of maturity amount	
$100,000 ($p_{\overline{4}|6\%}$) = $100,000 (.7921)	$79,210
Present value of interest payments	
$5,000 ($P_{\overline{4}|6\%}$) = $5,000 (3.4651)	17,326
Price of bonds to yield 6%	$96,536

Note that the bond liability is composed of two elements: the present value of the amount promised at maturity and the present value of the interest payments. The four-year history of the total debt and of these two elements is shown in the table on page 624.

It would be possible to account for bond liabilities in two accounts, reflecting the change in the value of the two elements of the bond contract. These bonds would then be reported on the balance sheet (at the end of the second year, for example) as follows:

Long-term liabilities:
Bonds payable ($100,000, 5% bonds due in two years):
Maturity amount (present value) *$89,001*
Interest payments (present value) *9,167* *$98,168*

Because businessmen commonly think of bonds in terms of maturity value plus premium or minus discount, however, accountants would be more likely to report the debt on the balance sheet (at the end of the second year):

Long-term liabilities:
5% bonds payable, due in two years *$100,000*
Less: Unamortized bond discount *1,832* *$98,168*

In published financial statements, one often will find bond liabilities reported at maturity value and bond discount shown among the assets as a deferred charge. This procedure has no theoretical foundation.

Four-year History of $100,000, 5%, Four-year Bonds Sold to Yield 6%

	Present value of total debt	Present value of maturity amount	Present value of interest payments	Actual annual interest expense or revenue
First year:				
Present value at issue date	$ 96,536	$ 79,210	$17,326	
Growth of debt at 6%	5,792	4,753	1,039	$ 5,792
Interest payment	(5,000)		(5,000)	
Value at end of first year ...	$ 97,328	$ 83,963	$13,365	
Second year:				
Growth of debt at 6%	5,840	5,038	802	5,840
Interest payment	(5,000)		(5,000)	
Value at end of second year	$ 98,168	$ 89,001	$ 9,167	
Third year:				
Growth of debt at 6%	5,890	5,340	550	5,890
Interest payment	(5,000)		(5,000)	
Value at end of third year	$ 99,058	$ 94,341	$ 4,717	
Fourth year:				
Growth of debt at 6%	5,942*	5,659*	283	5,942
Interest payment	(5,000)		(5,000)	
Value at end of fourth year	$100,000	$100,000	$ -0-	$23,464

* *$1 deducted to compensate for errors in rounding to nearest dollar.*

In theory, bond interest expense is the periodic growth in the present value of the bond liability at the yield rate, as demonstrated in the right-hand column of the table on page 624. The payment of nominal interest simply reduces the liability. The net change in the present value of the liability during any period is the difference between the nominal interest payment and interest expense.

In practice, the bond liability is carried at maturity value and bond discount appears in a separate account. Interest expense on bonds is therefore recorded in an entry which reflects the combined process of growth in the liability and reduction through payment of nominal interest. The net increase in the bond liability is produced indirectly through a reduction in the contra-liability account, Discount on Bonds Payable. The data for the appropriate journal entries may be developed in a bond amortization table, illustrated below:

Interest Expense and Discount Amortization
$100,000 of 5%, Four-year Bonds, Interest Payable Annually
Sold at $96,536, to Yield 6%

Date	*(1) Effective interest (6% of book value) (1)*	*(2) Interest payment (5% of face value) (2)*	*(3) Discount amortization (1) − (2)*	*(4) Book value of bonds (4) + (3)*
At issue date				*$ 96,536*
End of 1st year	*$5,792*	*$5,000*	*$792*	*97,328*
End of 2d year	*5,840*	*5,000*	*840*	*98,168*
End of 3d year	*5,890*	*5,000*	*890*	*99,058*
End of 4th year	*5,942°*	*5,000*	*942*	*100,000*

° $1 deducted to compensate for rounding errors.

The journal entries to record the issuance of these bonds and the periodic interest payments on an effective rate basis, both for the issuing corporation and from the viewpoint of the owner of the bonds, are shown below:

Date	*Books of issuer*			*Books of investor*		
Issue date	*Cash . . . .*	*96,536*		*Investment in Bonds . . .*	*96,536*	
	Discount on Bonds . . .	*3,464*		*Cash . . . .*		*96,536*
	Bonds Payable		*100,000*			
End of 1st year—interest payment	*Interest Expense . . . . .*	*5,792*		*Cash . . . .*	*5,000*	
	Bond Discount		*792*	*Investment in Bonds . . .*	*792*	
	Cash		*5,000*	*Interest Revenue*		*5,792*
End of 2d year—interest payment	*Interest Expense . . . . .*	*5,840*		*Cash . . . .*	*5,000*	
	Bond Discount		*840*	*Investment in Bonds . . .*	*840*	
	Cash		*5,000*	*Interest Revenue*		*5,840*

These entries demonstrate why the process of recording the growth of the bond liability between issue date and maturity is called "amortizing bond discount." The book value of the bonds at any time is the difference between maturity amount and the bond discount, which gradually disappears as the bonds approach maturity.

Bonds sold at a premium. When a bond contract promises periodic interest payments at a rate larger than the market rate for comparable securities, the bonds will sell for a premium and effective interest cost (or revenue) each period will be smaller than the interest payments. To illustrate, assume the same $100,000, 5%, four-year bond issue used in the previous example, except that interest is paid semiannually and the bonds are sold to yield 4%. The issue price of these bonds may be computed under either of the alternative methods previously discussed:

Computation of Bond Price

First approach		*Second approach*	
Present value of maturity amount:		*Maturity amount . . . .*	*$100,000*
$100,000($p_{\overline{8}|2\%}$) = $100,000(.85349)	*$ 85,349*	*Present value of excess of interest payments ($2,500) over yield interest ($2,000) at effective rate of 2%:*	
Present value of interest payments:			
$2,500($P_{\overline{8}|2\%}$) = $2,500(7.3255)	*18,314*	*$500($P_{\overline{8}|2\%}$) = $500(7.3255) . . . .*	*3,663*
Issue price of bonds	*$103,663*	*Issue price of bonds . . . .*	*$103,663*

In the premium case, as in the discount situation, periodic interest expense is determined by multiplying the semiannual yield rate by the present value of the bonds at issue date and at the beginning of each period thereafter. A schedule of the semiannual interest expense (or revenue) and premium amortization on these bonds appears below:

Interest Expense and Premium Amortization
$100,000 of 5%, Four-year Bonds, Interest Payable Semiannually
Sold at $103,663, to Yield 4%

Year	*Period*	*(1) Effective interest (2% of book value)*	*(2) Interest payment (2½% of face value)*	*(3) Premium amortization (2) − (1)*	*(4) Book value of bonds (4) − (3)*
0	0				$103,663
1	1	$2,073	$2,500	$427	103,236
	2	2,065	2,500	435	102,801
2	3	2,056	2,500	444	102,357
	4	2,047	2,500	453	101,904
3	5	2,038	2,500	462	101,442
	6	2,029	2,500	471	100,971
4	7	2,019	2,500	481	100,490
	8	2,010	2,500	490	100,000

The journal entries to record the issue of these bonds, the periodic interest payments, and the effective interest expense (or revenues) during the first two semiannual periods are illustrated below:

Date	*Books of issuing company*			*Books of investor*		
Issue date	*Cash*	*103,663*		*Investment in Bonds*	*103,663*	
	Bond Premium		*3,663*	*Cash*		*103,663*
	Bonds Payable		*100,000*			
End of 1st 6-month interest payment	*Interest Expense*	*2,073*		*Cash*	*2,500*	
	Bond Premium	*427*		*Investment in Bonds*		*427*
	Cash		*2,500*	*Interest Revenues* . . .		*2,073*
End of 2d 6-month interest payment	*Interest Expense*	*2,065*		*Cash*	*2,500*	
	Bond Premium	*435*		*Investment in Bonds*		*435*
	Cash		*2,500*	*Interest Revenue*		*2,065*

Effective interest versus straight-line average interest. When interest expense (or revenue) is measured on an effective rate basis, interest expense each period is equal to the yield rate on the present value of the liability at the beginning of the period. Periodic interest expense on bonds sold at a discount will thus increase in each period as the value of the liability grows; and periodic interest expense on bonds sold at a premium will decrease each period as the liability declines to maturity amount. In contrast, if bond discount or premium is amortized on a straight-line average basis, the interest expense is the same in each period despite changes in the book value of the debt. This relationship is demonstrated in the two charts below, using data from the previous two examples:

Chart of Bond Value and Bond Interest Expense (Revenue)

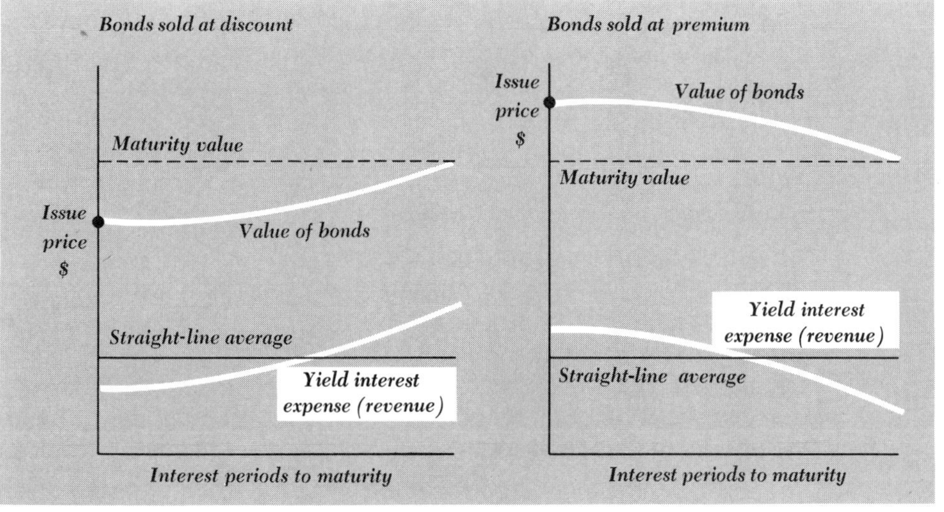

The effect of straight-line averaging when bonds are issued at a discount is to overstate interest expense (revenue) in the early stages of bond life and understate it in the latter stages. The reverse situation is true when bonds are issued at a premium. Whether these errors are sufficiently material to warrant the use of the more complex effective rate method in accounting for bond issues is a matter for judgment in any given situation. The issue of uncertainty which plagues the accountant in other areas is not significant in the bond case. In the real world businessmen buy and sell bonds not on the basis of straight-line averages but on the basis of yield rates of return; and this is a situation in which the accountant can easily make his record conform to economic reality.

Callable bonds. Most bond issues provide for redemption prior to maturity at the option of the issuer. The *call provision* is put in the contract to protect the issuer, who may want to retire the debt prior to the originally stated maturity. The calling of bonds is usually a disadvantage to the investor because the issuer is most likely to call if interest rates have fallen, in which case the investor is faced with the necessity of reinvesting at a lower return. For this reason investors usually insist that a *call premium* over and above face value be paid if bonds are redeemed prior to maturity. In some cases bond contracts provide for a series of optional call dates, with a declining call provision applicable to call dates nearer to maturity.

The existence of a call provision creates some uncertainty as to the effective yield of a bond issue, since the optional redemption creates two (or more) possible debt contracts, depending on whether the bonds are called (and when) or allowed to run to maturity. In bidding on bond issues, the buyer should compute the price (at the desired yield rate) under both options and offer the lower price if he wants to be assured of a given yield on his investment.

If a callable bond sells at a discount, the value of the bond for its full life will always be smaller than its value assuming the call takes place, without regard to the existence of amount of any call premium. If a callable bond is issued at a premium, however, the relative value of the bond at issue date depends on the timing of the potential call and the amount of any call premium. If there is no call premium, the value of the bond to call date will always be lower than the value to maturity.

To illustrate, assume the case of a $100,000, 20-year, 4% bond, interest payable annually, and callable at 105. The price of this bond to yield 3% depends on the timing of the call, as indicated in the following computations.

	At the end of 5 years	At the end of 15 years
1. Assuming the bonds will be called:		
Present value of call price ($100,000 + $5,000):		
$105,000 ($p_{\overline{5}\rceil 3\%}$) = $105,000 (.8626)	$ 90,573	
$105,000 ($p_{\overline{15}\rceil 3\%}$) = $105,000 (.6419)	...	$ 67,400
Present value of interest payments:		
$4,000 ($P_{\overline{5}\rceil 3\%}$) = $4,000 (4.5797)	18,319	
$4,000 ($P_{\overline{15}\rceil 3\%}$) = $4,000 (11.9379)	...	47,752
Present value of bonds to yield 3% to call date	$108,892	$115,152

2. Assuming the bonds will be allowed to run to maturity:

Present value of maturity amount:	
$100,000 ($p_{\overline{20}|3\%}$) = $100,000 (.5537)	$ 55,370
Present value of interest payments:	
$4,000 ($P_{\overline{20}|3\%}$) = $4,000 (14.8775)	59,510
Present value of bonds to yield 3% to maturity	$114,880

If the bonds are callable at the end of the fifth year, an investor would want to bid only $108,892, the value to call date, to assure himself a 3% return on his investment. If he bid $114,880 and the bonds were called in five years, his yield would be less than 3% since the $5,000 call premium would not compensate him for the failure to receive expected $4,000 interest payments during the last 10 years. On the other hand, if the bonds were callable in 15 years, the investor should bid $114,880 (the price to yield 3% to maturity), but in this case he would find a call to his advantage, since the present value at 3% assuming a 15-year call is $115,152.

The existence of a call provision creates an accounting problem since the accounting for interest will differ depending on whether the bonds are called or are allowed to run to maturity. Some accountants urge a conservative practice of amortizing bond premium to the date of the call, to avoid possible overstatement of the bonds. Here, as in other cases, however, the objective is to record values on the basis of the expectation that is most probable—not on the basis of possible events that will produce minimal valuations. Showing a gain or loss at the time of an unexpected call is preferable to an arbitrary approach which results in a misstatement of interest throughout the life of a bond which is not expected to be called.

Issuing bonds between interest dates. It is often necessary to value bonds at a time other than the date the bond contract starts to run. For example, bonds may be sold by the debtor corporation some time after the legal date of issue, and bonds are bought and sold in the market at any time. The process of computing the value of a bond *on any interest date* is essentially the same as at date of issue. The value of the bond is the sum of the present values of the maturity amount and the remaining future interest payments discounted at the yield rate of interest. If a 10-year bond, with interest payable annually, is to be valued at the end of the seventh year (three years prior to maturity), the future obligation would be discounted at the yield rate for three years.

The problem of finding the value of a bond at a date *other* than an interest date is more complicated. To illustrate, assume a three-year, 5% bond issue, interest payable annually, officially issued on January 1, 1968. Suppose that not all bonds were sold at that time, and on March 1, 1968, the debtor corporation wishes to sell $100,000 of these bonds. The pattern of change in the value of these $100,000 of bonds during 1968 is shown in the two diagrams on page 630. In Case A it is assumed that the bonds are sold at a discount to yield 6%; in Case B that the bonds are sold at a premium to yield 4%.

Change in Value of Bonds between Interest Dates
$100,000 of 5%, Three-year Bonds, Dated January 1, 1968
Value on March 1, 1968

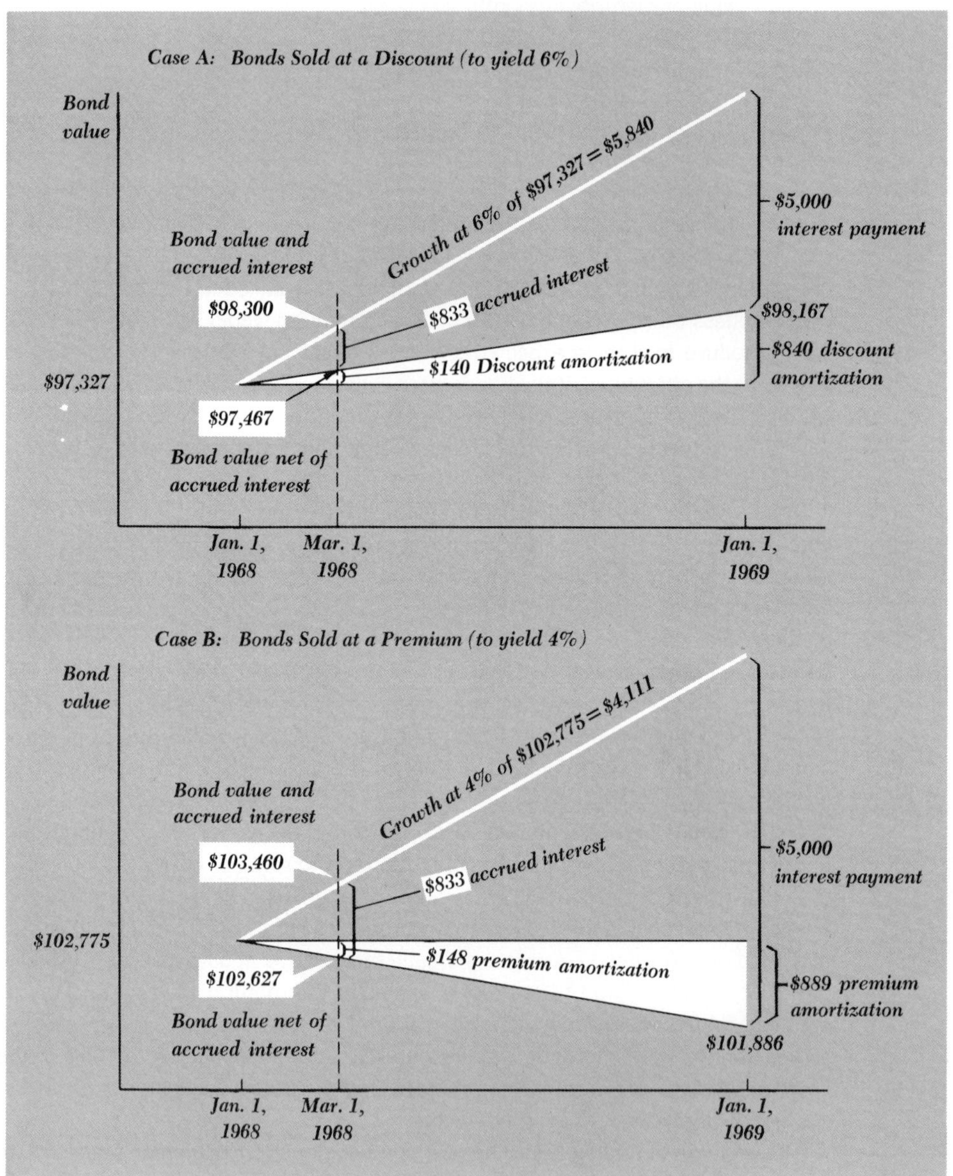

The computation of the value of these bonds at the beginning and end of 1968 is shown at the top of the next page.

The path of the change in the value of the bonds during 1968 follows a sawtooth shape, as indicated in the diagrams. The debt grows at the yield rate of interest during the year and is reduced at the end of the interest period by the interest payment.

	Value at Jan. 1, 1968 (three periods from maturity)	Value at Jan. 1, 1969 (two periods from maturity)
Case A (discount):		
Present value: \$100,000 – (\$6,000 – \$5,000) $P_{\overline{n}\rceil 6\%}$*:*		
At Jan. 1, 1968: \$100,000 – (\$1,000)(2.6730)	*\$ 97,327*	
At Jan. 1, 1969: \$100,000 – (\$1,000)(1.8334)		*\$ 98,167*
Case B (premium):		
Present value: \$100,000 + (\$5,000 – \$4,000)($P_{\overline{n}\rceil 4\%}$*):*		
At Jan. 1, 1968: \$100,000 + (\$1,000)(2.7751)	*102,775*	
At Jan. 1, 1969: \$100,000 + (\$1,000)(1.8861)		*101,886*

To find the price of a bond with accrued interest between interest dates, we simply find the present value at the last preceding interest date and add to that present value the growth in value for the partial period at the yield rate of interest. Subtracting the accrued interest (face amount times nominal interest rate) for the partial period gives us the value of the bond net of accrued interest. The computations applicable to the diagram are given below:

Case A		*Case B*	
Value of bond, Jan. 1, 1968	*\$97,327*	*Value of bond, Jan. 1, 1968*	*\$102,775*
Add: Growth at 6% for two months:		*Add: Growth at 4% for two months:*	
⅙(\$97,327 × 6%) = ⅙(5,840)	*973*	*⅙(102,775 × 4%) = ⅙(4,111)* . . .	*685*
Value of bond and accrued interest at Mar. 1, 1968	*\$98,300*	*Value of bond and accrued interest at Mar. 1, 1968*	*\$103,460*
Less: Accrued interest for two months (⅙)(\$100,000)(5%)	*833*	*Less: Accrued interest for two months ⅙(\$100,000)(5%)*	*833*
Value of bond at Mar. 1, 1968, net of accrued interest	*\$97,467*	*Value of bond at Mar. 1, 1968, net of accrued interest*	*\$102,627*

An alternative method of computing bond values between interest dates is based on a straight-line apportionment of the discount or premium amortization during the full interest period. That this approach gives the same results as before is demonstrated at the top of page 632.

The entries to record the issue of these bonds or an investment in them, as of March 1, 1968, and the payment (or receipt) of the first interest payment on January 1, 1969, are also shown on page 632.

The amortization of bond discount between March 1, 1968, and January 1, 1969, represents the net growth in bond value for the 10-month period at \$70 per month (\$840 ÷ 12). Interest expense (or revenue) of \$4,867 is equal to the interest on the value of the bonds at January 1, 1968 (\$97,327), at the yield rate of 6% for 10 months: \$97,327 (6%) (10/12) = \$4,867.

The journal entries for the case in which bonds were issued at a premium are given at the bottom of page 632.

Case A (discount)		*Case B (premium)*	
Value of bond at Jan. 1, 1968	*$97,327*	*Value of bond at Jan. 1, 1968*	*$102,775*
Value of bond at Jan. 1, 1969	*98,167*	*Value of bond at Jan. 1, 1969*	*101,886*
Amortization of bond discount during the year	*$ 840*	*Amortization of bond premium during the year*	*$ (889)*
Price at Jan. 1, 1968	*$97,327*	*Price at Jan. 1, 1968*	*$102,775*
Add: Two months' amortization of discount: 1/6($840)	*140*	*Less: Two months' amortization of premium: 1/6($889)*	*(148)*
Bond value net of accrued interest at Mar. 1, 1968	*$97,467*	*Bond value net of accrued interest at Mar. 1, 1968*	*$102,627*
Add: Accrued interest for two months: 1/6($100,000)(5%)	*833*	*Add: Accrued interest for two months: 1/6($100,000)(5%)*	*833*
Price of bond with accrued interest at Mar. 1, 1968	*$98,300*	*Price of bond with accrued interest at Mar. 1, 1968*	*$103,460*

Journal Entries—Case A (Discount)
Issue of Bonds between Interest Dates

Date	*Books of issuing company*			*Books of investor*		
Mar. 1, 1968	*Cash*	*98,300*		*Bond Investment*	*97,467*	
Bonds	*Bond Discount*	*2,533*		*Interest Receivable*	*833*	
issued	*Interest Payable*		*833*	*Cash*		*98,300*
	Bonds Payable		*100,000*			
Jan. 1, 1969	*Interest Payable*	*833*		*Cash*	*5,000*	
Payment	*Interest Expense*	*4,867*		*Bond Investment*	*700*	
of	*Bond Discount*		*700*	*Interest Receivable*		*833*
interest	*Cash*		*5,000*	*Interest Revenue*		*4,867*

Journal Entries—Case B (Premium)
Issue of Bonds between Interest Dates

Date	*Books of issuing company*			*Books of investor*		
Mar. 1, 1968	*Cash*	*103,460*		*Bond Investment*	*102,627*	
Bonds	*Bond Premium*		*2,627*	*Interest Receivable*	*833*	
issued	*Interest Payable*		*833*	*Cash*		*103,460*
	Bonds Payable		*100,000*			
Jan. 1, 1969	*Interest Payable*	*833*		*Cash*	*5,000*	
Interest	*Interest Expense*	*3,426*		*Bond Investment*		*741*
payment	*Bond Premium*	*741*		*Interest Receivable*		*833*
	Cash		*5,000*	*Interest Revenue*		*3,426*

The amortization of bond premium between March 1, 1968, and January 1, 1969, represents the net decline of $741 (10/12 of $889) in bond value for the 10-month period. Interest expense (or revenue) of $3,426 is equal to interest on the January 1, 1968, value of the bonds at the yield rate of 4% for 10 months: ($102,775) (4%) (10/12) = $3,426.

Serial bonds. A serial bond contract provides for the redemption of the principal amount in installments throughout the life of the issue. As in the case of regular bonds, the price of a serial bond is the present value at the yield rate of the future payments of principal and interest promised in the contract. Sometimes different yield rates are applicable to different maturities of a serial bond issue since long- and short-term interest rates often differ. In this case each maturity of the serial bond may be treated as a separate debt contract.

In some cases, however, it is more convenient to view a serial bond issue as if it were a single debt and to account for it in terms of an average yield rate of interest. To illustrate, assume an $800,000, 5%, five-year serial bond issue calling for payment of the principal at $200,000 per year, starting at the end of the second year. The contractual payments involved in this debt issue may be summarized:

	Payments at the end of				
	Year 1	*Year 2*	*Year 3*	*Year 4*	*Year 5*
Payments on principal....	*-0-*	*$200,000*	*$200,000*	*$200,000*	*$200,000*
Interest payments........	*$40,000*	*40,000*	*30,000*	*20,000*	*10,000*
Total payments..........	*$40,000*	*$240,000*	*$230,000*	*$220,000*	*$210,000*

The price of this bond issue, to yield 6%, would be computed as follows:

$40,000 ($p_{\overline{1}|6\%}$) = $40,000 (.9434)	$ 37,736
$240,000 ($p_{\overline{2}|6\%}$) = $240,000 (.8900)	213,600
$230,000 ($p_{\overline{3}|6\%}$) = $230,000 (.8396)	193,108
$220,000 ($p_{\overline{4}|6\%}$) = $220,000 (.7921)	174,262
$210,000 ($p_{\overline{5}|6\%}$) = $210,000 (.7473)	156,933
Present value of serial bonds at 6%	$775,639

If this issue of serial bonds were sold to yield 6%, the accounting record of interest expense on an effective rate basis might be summarized as shown in the table on page 634.

Long-term leases

Asset services may be acquired by outright purchase or by renting the asset from the owner under a lease agreement. In the post-World War II period, there has been a rapid expansion of leasing in a variety of forms. Today lease contracts are an important means of financing the use of long-lived business assets of all kinds. Under a lease contract the lessee (one who acquires the use of leased property) gets valuable property rights from the lessor (the owner) in exchange for undertaking an obligation to make rental payments in the future.

Interest Expense and Discount Amortization—Serial Bonds
$800,000 of Serial Bonds, Interest at 5% Annually
Sold (to Yield 6%) for $775,639

Period	(1) Effective interest expense (6% of book value)	(2) Interest payment (5% of face value)	(3) Discount amortization (1) − (2)	(4) Bond redemption	(5) Book value of bond issue +(3) − (4)
0					$775,639
1	$46,538	$40,000	$6,538	-0-	782,177
2	46,931	40,000	6,931	$200,000	589,108
3	35,346	30,000	5,346	200,000	394,454
4	23,667	20,000	3,667	200,000	198,121
5	11,879*	10,000	1,879	200,000	-0-

* *$8 deducted to compensate for rounding errors.*

Valuation of a leasehold. The nature of lease rights and obligations may be demonstrated by first considering the case of a lease which is paid in advance in a single payment. Assume that W Company leases certain property for 10 years, agreeing to an annual rent of $10,000 at the beginning of each year. The company then decides to pay the full amount of rental at the beginning of the lease period, and the lessor agrees to accept an amount equal to the future rents discounted at 5%. The single payment would be computed as follows:

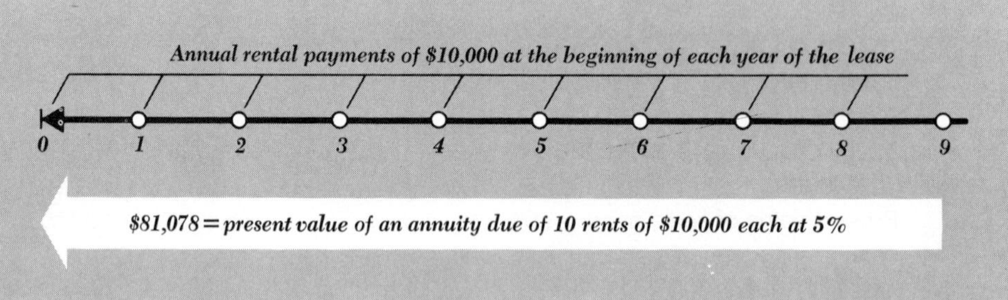

$$P_D = R(P_{D\overline{10}|5\%}) = \$10{,}000\,(P_{\overline{n-1}|5\%} + 1) = \$10{,}000\,(P_{\overline{9}|5\%} + 1)$$
$$= \$10{,}000\,(7.1078 + 1) = \$10{,}000\,(8.1078) = \$81{,}078$$

The journal entries on the books of the lessee to account for this leasehold on a present value basis are summarized in the schedule on page 635.

The asset Leasehold represents the value (and original cost) of the right to occupy and use this property for the next 10 years. At the beginning of each year, the $10,000 advance rent is recorded as a short-term prepaid expense which is then amortized monthly. The value of the asset increases at the rate of 5% to the end of each period, representing the amount earned in that year by paying the lease rentals in advance. The pattern of entries in the above schedule will be re-

Period		Accounts debited or (credited)				
Period		*Asset—leasehold*	*Rent expense*	*Interest earned*	*Cash*	*Short-term prepayment*
	First year:					
0	*Paid lease rental in advance*	*81,078*			*(81,078)*	
0	*Record prepaid rent for first year*	*(10,000)*				*10,000*
		71,078				
0-1	*Amortize prepaid rent monthly during first year*		*10,000*			*(10,000)*
0-1	*Growth in value of leasehold at 5%*	*3,554*		*(3,554)*		
1	*Leasehold value at end of first year*	*74,632*				
	Second year:					
1	*Record prepaid rent for second year*	*(10,000)*				*10,000*
		64,632				
1-2	*Amortize prepaid rent monthly during second year*		*10,000*			*(10,000)*
1-2	*Growth in value of leasehold at 5%*	*3,232*		*(3,232)*		
2	*Value of leasehold at end of second year*	*67,864*				

peated in each of the 10 years, at the end of which time the Leasehold asset will have been completely amortized.

If a straight-line approach were used in amortizing the asset Leasehold, the periodic assignment of cost would be distorted, and the distinction between the rental cost and the benefits (interest) that result from the financial arrangement of paying the lease rentals in advance would be obscured. This is illustrated in the schedule on page 636.

This leasehold might be accounted for on the books of the lessor on a present-value basis in a similar manner, except that rental revenues are involved. The landlord's asset is the property, and the receipt of 10 years' rent in advance creates a deferred liability. The entries for the first year on the lessor's books are also shown on page 636.

Leases—periodic payments. Assume now a situation involving the same lease contract except that W Company does *not* pay the rentals in a single advance payment. How does this change in assumption affect the position of W Company? The company still has a valuable right—the right to use the property for the next 10 years. This right was acquired by incurring a contractual obligation to pay $10,000 in rent at the beginning of each of the next 10 years. One view of this

Comparison of Present Value and Straight-line Amortization

Period	Present-value method			Straight-line method
	Rent expense	Interest revenue	Expense (net)	Average rent expense*
1	$10,000	$3,554	$ 6,446	$8,108
2	10,000	3,232	6,768	8,108
3	10,000	2,893	7,107	8,108
4	10,000	2,538	7,462	8,108
5	10,000	2,165	7,835	8,108
6	10,000	1,773	8,227	8,108
7	10,000	1,362	8,638	8,108
8	10,000	930	9,070	8,108
9	10,000	475	9,525	8,108
10	10,000	-0-	10,000	8,106†
			$81,078	$81,078

* *Leasehold cost $81,078 ÷ 10 = $8,108.*
† *$2 deducted to compensate for rounding errors.*

Cash	*81,078*	
Lease Deposit Liability		*81,078*
To record receipt of advanced payment.		
Lease Deposit Liability	*10,000*	
Rent Revenues		*10,000*
To record assignment of first year's rental revenue.		
Interest Expense	*3,554*	
Lease Deposit Liability		*3,554*
To record growth in value of deferred rents.		

transaction is that W Company has purchased an asset (lease rights) at a cost represented by the present value of the future lease payments it is obligated to make.

If we were to adopt this view, the accounting entries on the books of W Company for the first, ninth, and tenth years of the lease would be as illustrated in the schedule on page 637. Note on this schedule that the values of the asset and liability change in the typical sawtooth pattern; each is decreased at the beginning of the year by the amount of the rent ($10,000) and increased during the year by the growth in value at 5%, the rate used in measuring present values. In this instance, in contrast to the case of the purchased leasehold, the interest earned on the asset Lease Rights is offset by the interest expense accruing on the account Lease Liability. Thus the effective net charge against revenues each period is the full amount of the periodic rent of $10,000, unreduced by any interest-earning factor since the company does not have a *net* investment in the leased property.

Opinion No. 5, Accounting Principles Board. The view that lease rights and lease obligations should be capitalized and reported on the balance sheet has substantial

Accounting History of a Lease
First, Ninth, and Tenth Years
(Assume: 10-year lease; rents of $10,000 at beginning of each year; valued on a 5% basis)

	Accounts debited or (credited)					
	Lease rights— (asset)	*Lease liability*	*Interest expense (revenue)*	*Prepaid rent*	*Rent expense*	*Cash*
First year:						
Sign lease agreement	81,078	(81,078)				
1st rental payment		10,000				(10,000)
1st year's rent	(10,000)			10,000		
	71,078	(71,078)				
Amortization of rent during 1st year				(10,000)	10,000	
Growth in value of lease rights at 5%	3,554		(3,554)			
Growth in value of liability at 5%		(3,554)	3,554			
Balance at end of first year	74,632	(74,632)				
Ninth year:						
Balances at beginning of ninth year	19,525	(19,525)				
9th rental payment		10,000				(10,000)
9th year's rent	(10,000)			10,000		
	9,525	(9,525)				
Amortization of rent during 9th year				(10,000)	10,000	
Growth in value of lease rights at 5%	475		(475)			
Growth in value of liability at 5%		(475)	475			
Balances at end of 9th year	10,000	(10,000)				
Tenth year:						
10th rental payment		10,000				(10,000)
Amortization of rent during 10th year	(10,000)				10,000	
Balances at end of 10th year	-0-	-0-				

authoritative support but it is not the official position of the accounting profession. The Accounting Principles Board in September, 1964, stated, "The rights and obligations under leases which convey merely the right to use property, without an equity in the property accruing to the lessee, fall into the category of pertinent information which should be disclosed in schedules and notes rather than by recording assets and liabilities in the financial statements."[3]

[3] Accounting Principles Board of the AICPA, Opinion No. 5, *Reporting of Leases in Financial Statements of Lessee* (New York: September, 1964).

The board *did* take the position that lease rights and lease obligations should be reported as assets and liabilities when the lease contract is essentially equivalent to the installment purchase of the property. Two criteria for determining when lease rights and obligations should be capitalized were suggested by the board: (1) If the initial term of the lease is materially less than the useful life of the property and the lessee has the option to renew the lease for the remaining useful life of the property at substantially less than fair rental value; or (2) if the lessee has the right during or at the end of the lease to acquire the property at a price which appears to be substantially less than the probable fair value of the property at the time it may be acquired.

Thus the procedures for valuing and accounting for lease rights and obligations, illustrated in this chapter, are not standard practice at this time. Obtaining the right to use property by leasing, however, continues to grow in importance. During the past decade the accounting profession has made significant progress in moving toward a more complete disclosure of and accounting for lease obligations. The full recognition of the nature of lease rights as assets and of lease obligations as liabilities may well become the generally accepted view in the future. The student who understands the process of measuring the value of lease obligations and rights and who is fully aware of the impact of leases on financial position will be well prepared for this development.

Choosing an appropriate interest rate. In the case of the leasehold purchased for a single payment, the effective interest rate in the contract is known (since it is set by the parties) or can be computed from the terms of the contract. In valuing a contract that calls only for periodic payments, however, computations of present value will be based on an estimate of an appropriate interest rate. If it is possible to estimate the original value of the property and its residual value at the end of the lease period, the interest implicit in the contract can be computed. If there is not enough information to determine the interest rate implicit in the transaction, it is necessary to impute a reasonable rate on the basis of the market rate of interest the company is paying for similar types of credit. Since leases typically are considered a higher risk method of financing, one authority has suggested that ½ to 1% be added to the market rate for loans to arrive at an estimated rate.[4] The effect of minor variations in the rate of interest chosen to measure the present value of the lease asset and liability is probably not material when one considers that the alternative is to omit both the asset and the liability from the record. The table on page 639 shows the difference in the present value of rentals involved in the lease of property having an initial value of $1,000,000 and a residual value of zero at the end of the lease period.[5]

Depreciation and the interest factor

The transition from the case of leasing property to the problem of accounting for the outright purchase and use of property is not great. In essence, when a company buys a long-lived depreciable asset it pays in advance for a "bundle" of asset services to be realized periodically over the life of the asset. If a firm expects to

[4] John H. Myers, "Reporting of Leases on Financial Statements," *Accounting Research Study No. 4,* AICPA (New York: 1962), p. 46.
[5] *Ibid.,* p. 47.

Present Value of Rentals on \$1,000,000 Property for Various Periods and at Various Interest Rates

Lease period years	Annual rental*	Present value assuming an interest rate of				
		4%	5%	5½%	6%	7%
5	\$234,176	\$1,042,512	\$1,018,861	\$1,000,000	\$986,436	\$960,170
20	83,679	1,137,229	1,042,829	1,000,000	959,795	886,469
50	59,061	1,268,769	1,078,221	1,000,000	930,918	815,092

* Computed to amortize \$1,000,000 in the lease period at 5½%.

earn a return on this investment, it should pay no more for the asset than the present value of the stream of future services, discounted at the desired rate of return.

To illustrate, assume that Y Company is considering a machine which it plans to rent to a customer for five years at \$10,000 per year, and then expects to sell for \$6,000 at the end of the fifth year. If the company expects to earn a return of 10% (before income taxes) on this investment, it should pay no more than \$41,633 for the equipment (the present value of the expected rents and salvage value), computed as follows:

$$
\begin{aligned}
P &= \$10{,}000\,(P_{\overline{5}|10\%}) + \$6{,}000\,(p_{\overline{5}|10\%}) \\
&= \$10{,}000\,(3.7908) + \$6{,}000\,(.6209) = \$37{,}908 + \$3{,}725 = \underline{\underline{\$41{,}633}}
\end{aligned}
$$

Annuity method of depreciation. Suppose that Y Company purchased the machine discussed above for \$41,633. It would be possible to depreciate this equipment on the assumption that the initial cost represented the present value of five years of asset services and an expected salvage value of \$6,000 at the end of the fifth year. This approach to depreciation is known as the *annuity method* and the annual depreciation of \$10,000 (which we already know in this case) would be computed as follows:

$$
\begin{aligned}
\text{Depreciation} &= \frac{\text{cost} - \text{present value of salvage}}{P_{\overline{n}|i}} = \frac{\$41{,}633 - \$6{,}000\,(p_{\overline{5}|10\%})}{P_{\overline{5}|10\%}} \\
&= \frac{\$41{,}633 - \$6{,}000\,(.6209)}{P_{\overline{5}|10\%}} = \frac{\$37{,}908}{3.7908} = \$10{,}000
\end{aligned}
$$

Having determined that the purchase price of the equipment less salvage value is the equivalent of an annuity of \$10,000 in asset services each year for five years, the accounting for this asset during its service life would be as summarized in the table at the top of page 640.

Each year \$10,000 would be charged to depreciation expense, interest revenue would be credited with the return on investment of 10%, and the difference would be credited to accumulated depreciation, reducing the book value of the asset to salvage value (\$6,000) by the end of the fifth year.

Note that under the annuity method of depreciation the total charge to depreciation expense (\$50,000) is larger than the original depreciable cost of the asset

Annuity Method of Depreciation

Period	*Interest on investment at 10%*	*Annual depreciation expense*	*Credit to accumulated depreciation*	*Book value of asset: Cost less accumulated depreciation*
At acquisition				*$41,633*
1	*$ 4,163*	*$10,000*	*$ 5,837*	*35,796*
2	*3,580*	*10,000*	*6,420*	*29,376*
3	*2,938*	*10,000*	*7,062*	*22,314*
4	*2,231*	*10,000*	*7,769*	*14,545*
5	*1,455*	*10,000*	*8,545*	*6,000*
	$14,367	*$50,000*	*$35,633*	

($41,633 − $6,000 = $35,633) by an amount equivalent to interest at 10% on the unrecovered investment in asset services. The net charge against revenues over the service life of the asset, however, is equal to depreciable cost because of the offset of interest earned on the investment against the depreciation charge. This point is demonstrated in the following comparison between the income of Y Company under the annuity method of depreciation and under the straight-line method:

Y COMPANY
Income Statement for Five Years
(Assuming annuity method of depreciation)

	Year 1	*Year 2*	*Year 3*	*Year 4*	*Year 5*
Rent revenues	*$10,000*	*$10,000*	*$10,000*	*$10,000*	*$10,000*
Interest earnings	*4,163*	*3,580*	*2,938*	*2,231*	*1,455*
Total revenues	*$14,163*	*$13,580*	*$12,938*	*$12,231*	*$11,455*
Depreciation expense	*10,000*	*10,000*	*10,000*	*10,000*	*10,000*
Net income	*$ 4,163*	*$ 3,580*	*$ 2,938*	*$ 2,231*	*$ 1,455*

Y COMPANY
Income Statement for Five Years
(Assuming straight-line method of depreciation)

Rent revenues	*$10,000*	*$10,000*	*$10,000*	*$10,000*	*$10,000*
Depreciation expense:					
$\frac{\$41,633 - \$6,000}{5}$	*7,127*	*7,127*	*7,127*	*7,127*	*7,125°*
Net income	*$ 2,873*	*$ 2,873*	*$ 2,873*	*$ 2,873*	*$ 2,875*

° *Adjusted by $2 to compensate for rounding.*

A comparison of the effect of these two methods of depreciation on the rate of return on Y Company's investment will illustrate one of the strongest arguments for the use of the annuity method of depreciation.

Year	*Annuity method*			*Straight-line method*		
	Asset value at beginning of year	*Net income*	*Rate of return, %*	*Asset value at beginning of year*	*Net income*	*Rate of return, %*
1	$41,633	$4,163	10	$41,633	$2,873	6.9
2	35,796	3,580	10	34,506	2,873	8.3
3	29,376	2,938	10	27,379	2,873	10.5
4	22,314	2,231	10	20,252	2,873	14.0
5	14,545	1,455	10	13,125	2,873	21.9
6	6,000			6,000		

Historically, the increasing rate of return resulting from the use of straight-line depreciation was a factor in the early objections by the public utility industry to depreciation accounting. The reason for this position is evident. In an industry typified by large initial capital investment in depreciable assets, recording depreciation on a straight-line basis could produce increasing rates of return on investment even in the face of little change in revenues or costs. Since public utility selling prices are regulated on the basis of rate of return on investment, the use of straight-line depreciation had obvious disadvantages.

The primary argument against the annuity method of depreciation, other than its relative complexity, is that it produces a pattern of net charges against revenue (depreciation net of interest earnings) that is smaller in early years of service life and larger in later years. Income tax considerations, which make it advantageous from a tax standpoint to depreciate assets as rapidly as possible, represent an insuperable barrier to the acceptance of this method in practice. Some accountants raise a theoretical argument against the annuity method because of the inclusion of an implicit interest factor in depreciation costs allocated to production. As we shall see in the next chapter, however, this way of thinking about depreciation is very useful for decision-making purposes, since interest on investment is an economic factor that cannot be ignored.

Sinking-fund method of depreciation. This is another in the family of depreciation methods that takes into account interest on investment as a factor influencing the pattern of allocating asset cost to expense. The term *sinking fund* describes the rationale of the method: Depreciation expense in each period is measured by the increase in a sinking fund (deposit + interest) which, if invested at a given rate of interest each period, will accumulate to the depreciable cost of the asset at the date of retirement.

To illustrate the method, assume the same facts as before: an asset purchased for $41,633, estimated service life five years, estimated salvage value $6,000, appropriate interest rate 10%. On the basis of these data, the sinking-fund deposit necessary to accumulate to $35,633 (cost minus salvage value) in five years would be computed as shown on page 642.

$$\text{Sinking-fund deposit} = \frac{\text{cost} - \text{salvage}}{A_{\overline{n}|i}} = \frac{\$41{,}633 - \$6{,}000}{A_{\overline{5}|10\%}}$$

$$= \frac{\$35{,}633}{6.1051} = \underline{\underline{\$5{,}837}}$$

Since we are assuming the accumulation of a fund at retirement in this case, it is not necessary to determine the present value of the estimated salvage proceeds of $6,000; the assumed fund to be accumulated is simply reduced by this amount. A summary of the depreciation entries under the sinking-fund method for the five-year period appears below. The hypothetical fund balance is shown in the Accumulated Depreciation column.

Sinking-fund Method of Depreciation

Period	*Assumed deposit in fund each period*	*Interest at 10% on fund balance*°	*Depreciation expense (deposit + interest) (debit)*	*Accumulated depreciation (credit)*	*Book value of asset*
0					$41,633
1	$5,837	-0-	$5,837	$ 5,837	35,796
2	5,837	$ 583	6,420	12,257	29,376
3	5,837	1,225	7,062	19,319	22,314
4	5,837	1,932	7,769	27,088	14,545
5	5,837	2,708	8,545	35,633	6,000

° *Minor adjustments made in rounding to even dollar amounts.*

Under the sinking-fund method of depreciation, the amount in the Depreciation Expense column will be both debited to Depreciation Expense and credited to Accumulated Depreciation in each of the five years. The book value of the asset will thus be reduced to salvage value ($6,000) at the end of the fifth year.

Annuity and sinking-fund methods compared. The idea of depreciation as an accumulating fund for replacement is at odds with the concept of depreciation as a process of cost allocation. For this reason most accountants reject the sinking-fund approach as a faulty way of thinking about depreciation. Despite this conceptual weakness, however, the net effect of the two depreciation methods is strikingly similar, as can be seen from the following summary:

Period	*Annuity method*		*Sinking-fund method*	*Credit to accumulated depreciation under both methods*
	Charge to depreciation expense	*Credit to interest earned*	*Charge to depreciation expense*	
1	$10,000	$ 4,163	$ 5,837	$ 5,837
2	10,000	3,580	6,420	6,420
3	10,000	2,938	7,062	7,062
4	10,000	2,231	7,769	7,769
5	10,000	1,455	8,545	8,545
	$50,000	$14,367	$35,633	$35,633

The relation between the net results obtained under the two methods may be visualized from the following diagram:

Comparison of Depreciation under Annuity and Sinking-fund Methods

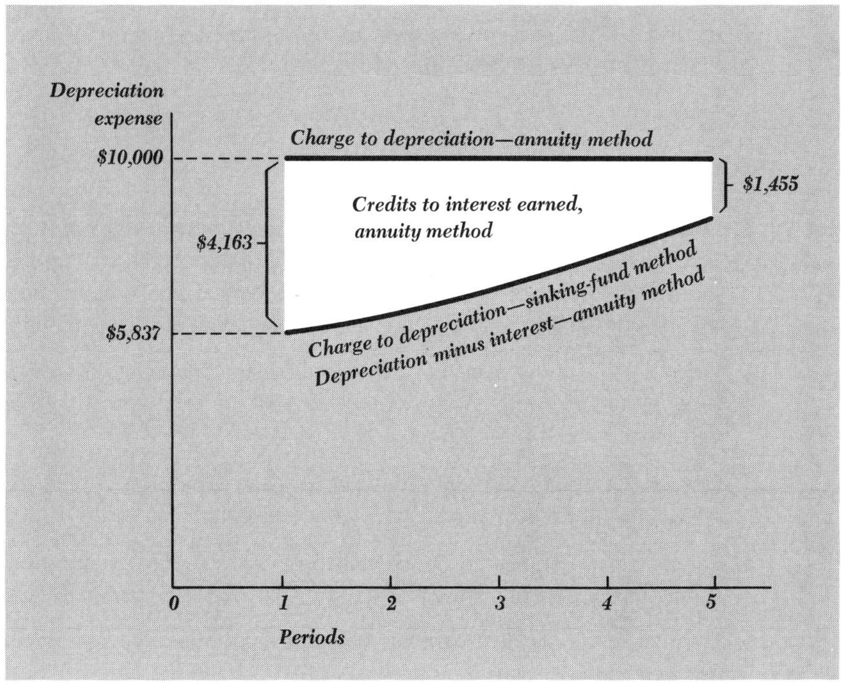

This diagram shows that the net charge against revenues under the sinking-fund method will be the same as under the annuity method *unless* depreciation becomes a part of the cost of production and the valuation of inventories. In this latter event a somewhat larger amount of depreciation will be capitalized in inventories under the annuity method, since interest on investment is included as an element of the depreciation charge. Because it avoids the inclusion of implicit interest on investment as an element of depreciation expense and yet has essentially the same effect on the rate of return on investment as the annuity method, the sinking-fund method of depreciation is actually used by a few public utility companies.

Summary—present-value depreciation methods. Neither the annuity nor sinking-fund method of depreciation is found to any significant extent in practice. They are thus not important if one is concerned simply with how things are done in the business world. An understanding of the present-value approach to depreciation and its effect on net income and the rate of return on investment, however, provides an invaluable insight into the nature of an investment in depreciable assets and the accounting problem of measuring the cost of asset services and the recovery of this cost through revenues. Because the annuity method of depreciation produces a rational picture of the results of using depreciable assets in a profit-making venture, it constitutes a standard against which to judge other measures of depreciation. For example, in a "seasoned" firm where some of the assets are being replaced each year, the errors inherent in straight-line depreciation may tend to cancel out. The exaggerated rate of return on older assets may be offset by the understated rate of return on new assets and net income under the straight-line method may be roughly the same as if the annuity method were used. Furthermore, if it is true that the value of asset services tends to be higher in early years than later, the decline in benefits through service life may offset the tendency of the straight-line method to overstate the charge against revenues in the early stages of service life and to understate it in later years.[6]

Questions

1. Because future events are uncertain, the measurement of income and the valuation of assets and liabilities is also uncertain. Under conditions of perfect certainty, the measurement of income is a relatively simple and precise process. Explain the relation between income and net asset valuation under conditions of certainty.
2. When a company issues $50 million of 20-year, 5% bonds, the effective interest rate on the borrowing is not established until the proceeds of the bond issue are determined. Explain this statement.
3. Company A issues 4% bonds to yield 5%; Company B issues 5% bonds to yield 4½%. Which of these bonds is issued at a discount? Explain.
4. Compute the issue price of $1 million of 6%, 10-year bonds, interest payable semiannually, sold at a price to yield 2½% semiannually, by two different methods.
5. In published financial statements bond discount often appears among the assets under a caption "deferred charges." What are the theoretical objections to this treatment?
6. Company B issues bonds at a premium at the same time as Company A issues bonds at a discount. Both companies amortize premium and discount on a straight-line basis. An accountant remarks: "One of these companies has overstated net income; the other has understated net income in the first year of the bond issue." Assuming that he is referring only to the effect of interest expense on net income, specify which company has overstated and which has understated net income, and explain your reasoning.
7. Is a call feature entered in a bond contract for the benefit of investors or the issuing corporation? If an investor has computed a bid price on a bond issue at a price which yields him a satisfactory return, and then discovers that the bonds are callable at 104 prior to maturity, should this discovery affect the amount of his bid? Why?
8. If a company acquires the right to occupy and use property under a long-term lease, it may be argued that the company has a valuable property right that should appear on its balance sheet. If this argument were accepted, explain how you would arrive at a defensible valuation for the asset, and where the offsetting credit would appear on the balance sheet.

[6] For an excellent discussion of this point, see Hector R. Anton, "Depreciation, Cost Allocation and Investment Decisions," *Accounting Research,* vol. 7, April, 1956, pp. 117–134.

9. The annuity method of depreciation is a method of measuring the cost of using a long-lived asset which includes the factor of interest on investment as an element of periodic depreciation expense. Explain this statement.

10. Compare the annuity and sinking-fund methods of depreciation in terms of their effect on net income over the service life of a depreciable asset.

Short cases for analysis

18-1 A particular item of manufacturing equipment costs $100,000 and has an expected service life of 10 years. Doerr Company leases a similar piece of equipment at the beginning of Year 1. The lease contract calls for lease rentals of $20,000 per year, at the beginning of each year, for five years. At the end of the fifth year, Doerr Company has an option to renew the lease for another five-year period, paying reduced lease rentals of $2,000 per year at the beginning of each year. Doerr Company is to pay all insurance, property taxes, and maintenance on the property during the lease.

The controller of the Doerr Company has consulted the company's CPA about the proper accounting for this lease. Both are agreed that the lease rights and lease liability should be recorded as a long-term asset and liability, respectively, valued at the beginning of Year 1 at $92,112, which is the present value of the rental payments at 8%, the company's estimated cost of capital. A disagreement arises, however, over the subsequent accounting for the asset and liability accounts. The controller argues that the lease rights account should be amortized so that an effective rental expense of $20,000 per year is charged during the first five years of the lease, and $2,000 per year in each of the next five years. The CPA argues that this lease contract is in effect an installment purchase arrangement, since the lease rentals during the last five years are clearly below the fair market value of the asset services during that period. The CPA suggests that the $92,112 lease rights account be amortized over a 10-year period on the sum of the years' digits basis, and that the liability be accounted for on the assumption that interest accrues at the rate of 8% and payments of $20,000 are made on the debt during each of the first five years, and $2,000 during each of the next five years. The CPA states, "You are paying off the liability at a faster rate during the first five years, but the services of the equipment will be used up over a 10-year period, and there is no necessary relation between the annual cost of the asset services and the rate at which the lease liability is being extinguished."

Instructions

a. Demonstrate that $92,112 is the appropriate valuation of the lease rights and lease liability accounts.

b. Prepare comparative journal entries to account for the lease during the first year, demonstrating the difference between the accounting procedures proposed by the controller and the CPA.

c. Evaluate the arguments of the controller and the CPA, and write a statement explaining which position you would support.

18-2 Pledin Manufacturing Company has two production departments, A and B. Each department uses machine tools which are identical in all essential characteristics. The machine tools in Department A are leased by Pledin Company for a three-year period at an annual rental of $10,000, payable at the end of each year. The tools in Department B were purchased outright for $28,640, including delivery and installation, and have an estimated service life of three years and an estimated salvage value of $1,000 at the end of the three-year period.

Instructions

a. Compute the annual depreciation expense on the machine tools in Department B on (1) the straight-line basis, and (2) the annuity basis, using a 4% interest rate.

b. The foreman in each department receives a bonus each year based for the most part on the average unit cost of product processed in his respective department; the lower the average cost the higher the bonus amount. A fixed bonus amount is divided between the two foremen on the basis of their relative performance in minimizing costs. If you were the foreman of Department A, which method of depreciation would you like to see used in depreciating the machine tools in Department B? Why? Could your position be sustained on the grounds of accounting theory as well as mere expediency with respect to your bonus situation? Explain.

18-3 Shortly before January 1, Year 1, the board of directors of the Ultramodern Corporation authorized the issuance of $100,000 of 5-year, 5% bonds to be priced to yield 4%. Interest is payable annually on December 31 of each year. The bonds were sold on January 1, Year 1.

The controller of Ultramodern has decided to account for this bond issue on a present-value basis and to report the bond liability in two separate accounts, one representing the liability for the principal of the bonds due in five years, the other representing the obligation for the future interest payments promised under the bond contract.

Instructions

a. What was the amount of cash (to the nearest dollar) received by the Ultramodern Corporation at the date of the bond issue?

b. Prepare a schedule showing the balances in the two long-term liability accounts and the bond interest expense account at the end of Year 1 and Year 2.

c. Draw two freehand graphs which will indicate the trend of the balances in each of the two liability accounts during the five-year life of the bonds. Show time in years on the horizontal axes and dollars on the vertical axes of your graphs.

Problems

18-4 Three situations involving the issuance of bonds are described below:

Case A W Company issued $1,000,000 in 10-year, 5% bonds on January 1, Year 1. The bonds were sold to yield 4%; interest is payable semiannually.

Case B X Company issued $1,000,000 in 20-year, 3% bonds. Interest is payable semiannually on July 1 and January 1. The bonds were sold on March 1 of Year 1 to yield 5%.

Case C Y Company issued $1,000,000 in 6%, four-year serial bonds on January 1, Year 1. Interest is payable annually, and the bonds are to be retired by payments of $250,000 on principal at the end of each year. The bonds were sold to yield 4%.

Instructions

For each of the above cases compute to the nearest dollar (*a*) the proceeds of the bond issue; (*b*) the interest expense (on an effective yield basis) for the first and second years.

18-5 Mr. Kydd has just purchased an ocean-going ship, paying $14,500 in cash and signing a three-year non-interest-bearing note for the balance of $100,000. Kydd does not like boating since he is subject to seasickness. However, he has an opportunity to rent his boat to a group of men who are expert divers and who need a ship to undertake a three-year search for buried treasure off the western coast of the United States.

The divers offered Kydd his choice of a 40% share in any treasure discovered, or a firm lease contract calling for payments to Kydd of $30,000 per year at the end of each of three years. Being a conservative person by nature, Mr. Kydd chose to take the lease contract. Kydd has formed a company, called the Kydd Ship Rental Company, whose sole asset is the ship. The lease contract gives the divers the option of buying the ship for $20,000 at the end of the three-year period, and it is expected that they will exercise their option.

Instructions

a. Prepare in columnar form a series of projected balance sheets for the Kydd Ship Rental Company as of the beginning of Year 1, and as of the end of each of the next three years. Kydd expects a return of 10% on his investment, and desires that assets and liabilities shall be valued and accounted for on this basis. You may assume that any idle funds can be invested on a short-term basis to earn an annual return of 10%.

b. Prepare in columnar form the projected annual income statements for the Kydd Ship Rental Company for the three years of this rental contract. Depreciation on the ship is to be recorded on the sinking-fund method, using a 10% interest rate.

c. Prove that the net income reflected in your income statements represents a 10% return on Kydd's investment.

d. Explain how the statements in (*a*) and (*b*) differ from those prepared in accordance with conventional accounting procedures.

18-6 Donald Rodgers buys a $20,000, 5% bond, having semiannual coupons, on a 4% yield basis two years and four months before the maturity of the bond. He plans to hold the bond to maturity and intends to account for interest revenue on a yield basis.

Instructions

Carry all computations to the nearest cent.

a. Prepare a table of amortization of bond discount or premium showing the history of this bond from purchase date to maturity.

b. Prepare the journal entries on Rodgers's books to record the purchase of the bonds and the receipt of the first and second interest coupons.

c. What is the book value of the bond after Rodgers has recorded the second interest payment?

18-7 On January 1, 1965, the Proctor Company issued 20-year, 5% bonds having a face value of $500,000, at a price to yield 3% semiannually. Interest is payable on July 1 and January 1.

The bond contract provided that the issuer may call any or all of the bonds on any interest date at a price of 104 plus accrued interest. At the time of issue the Proctor Company had no definite intention with respect to the call, but on July 1, 1968, the company called bonds having a face value of $100,000.

Instructions

Round all computations to the nearest dollar.

a. Prepare the journal entry to record the issuance of the bonds.

b. Prepare an amortization schedule for the period from January 1, 1965, to July 1, 1968.

c. Prepare the journal entries to record payment of bond interest and the retirement of bonds by call on July 1, 1968.

18-8 The Byway Plastic Company purchased a major item of plastic processing equipment for $100,000. The freight and installation costs on this equipment were $9,745. The equipment had an estimated service life of 10 years and an estimated salvage value at the end of that time of $12,000.

At the end of the second year of service life, an auxiliary unit of machinery, costing $12,416, was added to the original equipment. The service life of this addition will not extend beyond that of the original equipment, and there is no change in the estimated salvage value as a result of the addition.

Instructions

Prepare depreciation schedules for this equipment for the first three years of service life, using a 6% interest rate, under (*a*) the annuity method of depreciation, and (*b*) the sinking-fund method of depreciation.

In connection with each method, prepare the appropriate journal entry to record depreciation for the *third year*. Show all supporting computations, which may be rounded to the nearest dollar. (*Hint:* It will be necessary to make a revised depreciation computation at the end of the second year to take the addition into account.)

18-9 John Auxier received a five-year franchise to operate a cargo-passenger plane route into a remote mining area. Auxier agreed to maintain in operation two used airplanes which he acquired at a cost of $126,142 at the beginning of Year 1. The mining company agreed to pay Auxier a fee of $55,000 per year for five years for operating the route, and to purchase the two planes for $20,000 at the end of the five-year period. Auxier estimates that his operating expenses, other than depreciation, will amount to $25,000 per year. Auxier is able to secure short-term credit from suppliers sufficient to take care of his working capital needs. At the beginning of the first year of operation under the franchise, his position statement is:

AUXIER FLYING SERVICE
Balance Sheet
at beginning of Year 1

Current assets	*$ 20,000*	*Current liabilities*	*$ 20,000*
Planes	*126,142*	*Auxier, capital*	*126,142*
Totals	*$146,142*	*Totals*	*$146,142*

Since he expects to liquidate his business at the end of the five-year period, Auxier plans to withdraw from the business at the end of each year all earnings plus an amount equal to that year's decrease in the book value of the planes due to accumulated depreciation.

Instructions

a. Prepare schedules showing for the five-year period the percentage relationship between Auxier's capital at the beginning of each year and his reported net income for the year (in other words, determine the yearly rate of return on invested capital) under each of the following assumptions: (Round computations to the nearest dollar and nearest 1/10 of 1%.)

(1) That depreciation is computed on the annuity basis (using a rate of 10% as the value of money).

(2) That depreciation is computed on a straight-line time basis.

(3) That depreciation is computed on the sum of the years' digits method.

b. Explain the reason for the differences in the computed rates of return on capital investment in (*a*).

18-10 Wattles Company purchased automatic processing equipment for $64,000 at the beginning of the current year. Freight and installation amounted to $639. This equipment is expected to give the company a competitive advantage for a period of about three years, by which time management expects that all companies in the industry will have converted to the same type of equipment. On this basis, the production manager estimates that the services of the equipment will be worth about twice as much during the first three years of its life as during the last two years. It is expected that the machine will be scrapped at the end of five years and a net salvage of $3,000 realized at that time.

Instructions

a. Assuming that the company uses the annuity method of depreciation and expects a 10% rate of return, compute the depreciation charge that should be made during the first three years and during the last two years of service life.

b. Prepare a schedule showing the depreciation charge each year and the reduction in the book value of the machine to demonstrate that the book value of the asset will be reduced to $3,000 at the end of the fifth year.

18-11 Kylent Corporation leased a building on January 1, 1960. The lease agreement provided for annual rents of $4,000 for the first five years, $5,000 for the next five years, and $6,000 for the third five-year period, with rents payable annually in advance. There was no option to renew the lease after 15 years.

On December 31, 1966, the Kylent Corporation found it necessary to acquire larger properties because of expanded operations, and the lease was assigned to Orlando Realties. It was agreed that a fair rental value for the next three years would be $8,000 per year, and for the last five years of the lease, $10,000 per year. Orlando Realties paid a lump sum for the lease rights on the basis of the present value of these revised rents discounted at 4%.

Instructions

Round all computations to the nearest dollar.

a. Assume that Kylent Corporation purchased the entire 15-year leasehold on January 1, 1960, by paying a lump sum in cash equal to the present value of all rents on a 4% discount basis. Give the journal entries to record the purchase of the leasehold and the lease expense for the first year.

b. Continuing the assumption in (*a*), give the appropriate journal entry to record the assignment of the leasehold to Orlando Realties.

c. Assume the Kylent Corporation *did not* pay a lump sum in cash for the leasehold on January 1, 1960. What entry should be made at the time the lease was signed? What entries should be made to record lease payments and rental expense in each of the first two years?

d. Continuing the assumption in (*c*), give the appropriate journal entry to record the assignment of the lease to Orlando Realties, assuming that Orlando Realties will take over Kylent's obligation to make all future lease rental payments, and that Orlando pays a lump sum equal to the present value of the *increased* rental value, at 4%.

18-12 On January 1, Year 1, the Jordan Company acquired by leasing a piece of land which they expected to use later as the location of a branch outlet. The lease agreement called for annual rental payments of $12,000 per year, payable at the end of each year, for 10 years.

The intangible property rights acquired and the liability incurred under this lease were recorded by Jordan at a valuation determined on a 4% per annum discount basis. The growth and amortization of the asset and liability accounts during the first three years were accounted for in accordance with theoretical valuation procedures.

On January 1, Year 3, it became apparent that the property had grown too valuable as parking space to warrant use as a branch store site. Accordingly, the Jordan Company subleased the land to Aceparkers (a reputable firm) for the remaining eight years of the original lease agreement. The sublease called for payments by

Aceparkers to Jordan of $60,000 per year, the first payment to be made on December 31, Year 3.

On the basis of this transaction, the board of directors of Jordan Company authorized an immediate revaluation of the lease rights (asset) account to reflect its present value on a 4% basis, since the receipts under the sublease are well protected by the established credit and earning power of Aceparkers.

Instructions

Round all computations to the nearest dollar.

a. Assuming that no entries have been made during the year, present all the journal entries relating to the lease asset and liability accounts as of the end of Year 2.

b. What journal entry would you recommend be made to revalue the lease asset account as of January 1, Year 3, in accordance with the evidence reflected in the sublease?

c. Present the journal entries necessary at December 31, Year 3, to record the receipt and payment of annual lease and sublease rentals by the Jordan Company, and the amortization of the lease accounts on a theoretical basis.

d. If you had been a member of the board of directors, would you have favored the revaluation? Explain why you do or do not think the revaluation increase should be recognized on the records of the Jordan Company as of January 1, Year 3.

18-13 The Mystro Company issued five-year, 5% debenture bonds for cash on January 1, Year 1. On December 31, Year 1, the following entry was made on the books of the corporation, reflecting interest expense on an effective cost basis.

Bond Interest Expense		*20,815.96*	
Premium on Bonds Payable		*4,184.04*	
Cash			*25,000.00*
To record semiannual interest expense for last half of Year 1:			
Bond interest		*$25,000.00*	
Less: Premium at June 30, Year 1	*$40,798.00*		
Premium at Dec. 31, Year 1	*36,613.96*	*4,184.04*	
Total interest cost		*$20,815.96*	

Instructions

On the basis of the above information, determine and present the journal entry that must have been made by Mystro Company when the bonds were issued on January 1, Year 1.

19 DIRECT VALUATION AND INVESTMENT DECISIONS

Most investment decisions require a comparative evaluation of the cash outlays (or their equivalent) necessary to acquire productive resources and the expected future incremental cash inflows (or their equivalent) that represent the economic reward for having made the investment. Most investment decisions also involve a choice among alternative investment opportunities. In many business situations these choices are made on the basis of intuitive judgment; perhaps because the decision maker has faith in his intuition, perhaps because the decision depends on factors of emotion and attitude that cannot be reduced to meaningful quantitative terms. There is a broad class of business situations, however, where it is possible to measure and evaluate systematically in quantitative terms the major economic consequences of alternative investment opportunities. It is with these cases that this chapter is concerned.

In measuring income *after the fact of investment,* the major task facing the accountant is to measure realized revenues and expired costs in order to isolate the amount that represents a return over and above the recovery of past investment and costs incurred. We must shift our thinking somewhat in analyzing investment decisions *before the fact.* In the first place, we can concentrate on future expenditures and benefits; any cost already incurred is sunk and cannot be changed by a present decision unless some portion of the past cost can be recovered by selling the asset in question. Furthermore, in evaluating future receipts and outlays we need be concerned only with their amount and timing and not with their ultimate association as costs and revenues.

It is important to recognize, however, that when we compute the present value of future expenditures and receipts, we are automatically reflecting in the valuation figures the prospect of earning a standard income, that is, a return on the investment. Because the present value at i rate of interest is an amount which if invested to generate the expected net inflows would produce a return of $i\%$ on the investment, it is possible to use the present values of two or more investment proposals as a valid indirect means of comparing the size of the future income streams that would result. This is the feature that makes direct valuation an important tool in sorting out the good fruit from the bad in the orchard of investment opportunities. The term *capital budgeting* is often used to describe the entire process of measuring and evaluating prospective investment proposals.

Methods of analysis

Evaluating investment proposals

To evaluate the merits of an investment proposal, we may compare the value of the required expenditures with the value of prospective benefits. Since outlays and inflows are typically spread out in time, the logical way to bring these economic events into focus at a single point in time is to compute the net present value at the time of the decision. Alternatively, we may compute the yield rate of return that makes the net present value of the investment prospect equal to zero.

The use of either of these procedures is predicated on two fundamental assumptions: (1) That the objective in making business investments is to realize an optimal or at least satisfactory return on the investment; and (2) that if two or more alternative investment opportunities are under consideration, management should select the one likely to lead to the highest return on investment.

The general term *investment decision* encompasses two general situations. A *conventional investment* is one in which there is an immediate net outlay followed by net cash inflows for one or more periods. A *conventional loan* situation is one in which there is an immediate net cash inflow followed by net cash outflows for one or more periods. In the investment situation our objective is to maximize present value, that is, to choose the investment having the largest net present value. In the loan situation the objective is reversed; that is, to choose the loan having the smallest present value.

Some investment and loan situations involve *nonconventional* patterns of cash flows, for example, an immediate net cash outlay followed by a number of net inflows interspersed with periods in which additional net cash outlays occur. A simple example of such a nonconventional investment is the purchase of a machine which is expected to produce annual benefits for a period of six years but to require a major overhaul at the end of three years. This investment involves an immediate outlay, two years of net receipts, one year of net outflow (the year of the overhaul), and three more years of net inflow. Nonconventional investments cause some computational difficulties, but in general they may be evaluated on the same net present value basis as conventional investment or loan situations.[1]

Evaluating investments by the yield method. The *yield method* of evaluating an

[1] One of the interesting technical quirks of nonconventional investments is that they may have more than one yield rate. The problem of dual yield rates is discussed by James H. Lorie and Leonard J. Savage, "Three Problems in Rationing Capital," *Journal of Business*, October, 1955, pp. 229–239.

investment proposal requires that we compute the effective interest rate (yield rate) that will exactly equate the present value of the inflows and the present value of the outflows expected. The yield rate is the rate of return on the investment that would be realized if the investment proposal were accepted and benefits occurred exactly in the amounts and at the time expected.

Once the yield rate on an investment has been computed, the investment is evaluated either by comparing its yield with that of alternative investment opportunities or by comparing it with some standard of minimum yield requirements. Management should prefer the investment situation promising the highest yield rate; faced with a borrowing situation, the choice should be the proposal with the lowest effective rate.

In a conventional investment or loan situation where an initial outlay is followed by constant periodic returns (or an initial inflow is followed by constant periodic repayments), the yield rate may be computed by the use of annuity tables and interpolation between given rates in such tables, as demonstrated in Chapter 17. When the periodic returns or repayments are unequal in amount, the most feasible approach is to compute the present value of the investment flows at an estimated yield rate and then proceed by trial and error to find the yield rate of interest that will make the present value of the entire investment proposal equal zero. This procedure was also described and illustrated in Chapter 17. Fortunately, given a schedule of cash flows, computers may be programmed to find the yield rate on conventional investment and loan situations.

The net present value method. A second approach in evaluating an investment proposal is to compute the net present value, at a chosen interest rate, of all inflows expected from the investment and all outlays required. The excess of the present value of proceeds over the present value of outlays is known as the *net present value* of the investment proposition; this quantity may be either positive or negative in sign. A positive net present value means that the investment proposal will yield a return higher than the chosen rate; if the net present value is negative, a yield rate smaller than the chosen rate is indicated. A net present value of zero at the chosen discount rate indicates that the company could borrow funds at that interest rate, make the investment, and realize from the investment cash proceeds exactly sufficient to pay off the loan and interest. Stated another way, a zero net present value indicates that the yield rate of return and the chosen discount rate are identical.

It is evident that the choice of an appropriate rate of discount is crucial to the net present value method, since a given investment proposal may have a positive or negative net present value depending on the interest rate used to discount cash flows. In general, the interest rate chosen should be the minimum rate of return that the company is willing to accept for an investment, given the degree of risk involved. At the margin this minimum rate should be the *cost of capital,* which is defined as the cost (expressed as a yield rate) of obtaining the necessary investment funds, whether through borrowing, additional equity investment, or retention of earnings. Some firms use an arbitrary "desired rate" in computing net present value, usually set somewhat above the cost of capital as a safety margin to allow for overoptimism in estimating the potential benefits to be realized from any given investment. Determining the cost of capital for any given firm is difficult; some accepted means of approximation are discussed in a later section of this chapter. In the examples that follow we shall simply assume an appropriate cost of capital rate for purposes of computing net present value.

Frequency of flows and compoundings. When present values are computed using tables containing values of $P_{\overline{n}|i}$ or $p_{\overline{n}|i}$ and both i and n are expressed in terms of years, there is an assumption inherent in the use of these values that the inflows and outflows occur in lump sums at the end of the year. This is to some extent unrealistic since in many business investment situations the inflows and outflows occur at intervals more frequent than one year. For example, rents may be paid monthly or factory wages may be paid weekly. It is possible to construct tables for the present value of amounts received monthly with interest compounded monthly. As might be expected, present values under this assumption are slightly higher than present values if cash flows and compounding are assumed to occur at one-year intervals. This is demonstrated in the following table:

Present Value of $1 per Year for n Years at i Rate of Interest Annually If Receipts and Frequency of Compounding Are Yearly and Monthly

Number of years, n	Rate of interest per year, i					
	6%		10%		15%	
	Yearly	Monthly	Yearly	Monthly	Yearly	Monthly
5	$ 4.212	$ 4.327	$3.791	$3.962	$3.352	$3.577
10	7.360	7.560	6.145	6.421	5.019	5.355
15	9.108	9.977	7.606	7.949	5.847	6.239
20	11.470	11.782	8.514	8.897	6.259	6.679

It would appear that unless the service life of the investment is long or the discount rate is high, the difference between present values on a monthly basis and present values on an annual basis is not sufficiently large to affect any but the very marginal decisions. Since business decisions depend on estimates of future flows which may themselves be subject to error and which tend to err on the side of optimism, the assumption of annual receipts and annual compounding is probably sufficiently precise for most business purposes.[2]

[2] A means is also available for computing amounts and present values under the assumption of *continuous compounding*. The idea of continuous compounding is somewhat difficult to grasp, but the assumption is fairly realistic in dealing with many business situations where cash flows occur at frequent intervals. The formula for the present value of $1 in n periods with interest (at the annual rate i) compounded continuously is $\frac{1}{e^{ni}}$ where e (2.71828) is the base of the natural or Naperian system of logarithms. Correspondingly, the formula for the present value of an annuity of $1 per period for n periods, assuming the $1 is received continuously throughout the year, is $\frac{1 - \frac{1}{e^{ni}}}{i}$. Since tables for the value of e raised to various powers are readily available and the concept of continuity lends itself readily to the operations of the calculus, the assumption of continuous compounding and cash flows sometimes simplifies calculations in complex analyses.

Comparison of yield and net present value methods

The choice between the yield and net present value methods is not entirely a matter of computational preference. There are situations where each method gives a different answer because each involves a different basic assumption as to the earnings on the reinvestment of funds recovered from a capital investment. This point is best demonstrated by considering two general classes of investment decisions and some simple examples.

Accept or reject decisions. The simplest investment decision is one in which the question at issue is whether to accept or reject a given investment proposal. It is typified by such decisions as whether to buy new equipment or not, whether to move into a new territory or not, whether to buy out an existing firm or not.

Under the yield method of evaluation, the decision rule is to accept the investment if the yield rate is above the cost of capital and to reject it otherwise. Under the net present value approach, the decision rule is to accept the investment if the net present value (computed at the cost of capital rate) is zero or larger and to reject it if the net present value is less than zero.

Example. Company A has a cost of capital of 8%. By investing \$12,450 in new materials-handling equipment, the company estimates that it can save \$3,000 annually in wage cost for each of the next five years. Should the company buy the equipment?

Solution (Yield method). The yield rate of return on this investment is computed by solving for i: $P = R\,(P_{\overline{5}|i})$.

Substituting,

$$\$12{,}450 = \$3{,}000\,(P_{\overline{5}|i}) \qquad P_{\overline{5}|i} = \$12{,}450/\$3{,}000 = 4.15$$

From annuity tables, we can determine that:

$$P_{\overline{5}|7\%} = 4.05 \qquad \text{and} \qquad P_{\overline{5}|6\%} = 4.21$$

Therefore, we know that the unknown yield rate i is between 6% and 7%. The investment should therefore be rejected since its expected yield is less than the company's 8% cost of capital. (By interpolation, we could compute the yield rate to be approximately 6% + $^6/_{16}$ (1%) = 6.38%, but this degree of precision is not necessary to reach a proper decision.)

Solution (Net present value method). The net present value at 8% of all elements of the investment proposal is

	Present value at 8%
Initial outlay	−\$12,450
Cost savings: \$3,000 ($P_{\overline{5}|8\%}$) = \$3,000 (3.9927)	+ 11,978
Net present value of investment at 8%	−\$ 472

Since the net present value is negative, this means that it would not be profitable to undertake this investment if capital funds cost 8% or if 8% is the minimum rate of return we will accept on an investment of this type. We should reject the investment since its cost is greater than its present value at the cost of capital.

Mutually exclusive investments. Management is often faced with a choice between investments where accepting one proposal automatically results in rejecting the other. In this case the question is not only "Is the proposal worth undertaking?" but also "Which of the two (or more) alternatives is preferable?" The two investment proposals are usually alternative ways of gaining the same objective, and both may be profitable in relation to the cost of capital; since only one project can be accepted, the problem is to determine which proposal is most desirable.

The object of present-value analysis is to rank the two (or more) mutually exclusive investments in terms of their yield rate or net present value. The decision rule is to choose the one having the highest yield, or the highest present value.

Ranking mutually exclusive investment proposals is more complex than evaluating simple accept or reject decisions. The size of the initial investment may differ among the proposals, or the length of the time over which benefits are expected to continue may be different.

In these cases we must be careful to see that the data we use are actually comparable. Furthermore, we shall find that in some instances the present value and yield methods give contradictory results, and we must understand the source of the conflict to interpret the quantitative answers properly.

To illustrate these points in concrete terms, we shall consider three cases of investment decisions involving two mutually exclusive investment proposals:

Case 1—Same initial outlay and same period of return. Assume that Z Company is faced with the choice between two mutually exclusive investments of $10,000. Investment A is expected to produce net benefits of $2,400 the first year and $11,520 the second. Investment B is expected to produce $10,500 the first year and $2,500 the second. The company's cost of capital is 10%. Following the yield and net present value methods, we would rank these two investment proposals as follows:

Investment	*Outlay*	*Proceeds*		*Yield method*		*Net present value method*	
	Year 0	*Year 1*	*Year 2*	*Yield, %*	*Rank*	*NPV at 10%*	*Rank*
A	−$10,000	+$ 2,400	+$11,520	20	2	+$1,702	1
B	− 10,000	+ 10,500	+ 2,500	25	1	+ 1,612	2

Here is a situation in which the two methods yield contradictory rankings and therefore point to different investment decisions. The yield method tells us that investment B carries the higher yield and is thus presumably preferable. The net present value method indicates a preference for investment A, which has a higher present value at the 10% cost of capital. Which is the better guide?

In order to answer this question and interpret the results, we must understand why the rankings are reversed. The answer lies in a different basic assumption implicit in the two analytical methods:

Method	Implicit assumption
Yield method	That all net cash inflows from either project can be reinvested at the *yield rate* of return on that project
Net present value method	That all net cash inflows can be reinvested at the *cost of capital,* that is, the rate used in computing net present value

It is now evident why the two methods are at odds in this particular case. Under investment B a greater amount of cash is released at the end of Year 1, which under the yield method is assumed to be reinvested to yield 25% and under the present value method is assumed to be reinvested to yield only 10%. We can demonstrate this point by looking at the incremental cash flows under the two investments:

Cash Flows in Years 0, 1, and 2

Investment	*Year 0*	*Year 1*	*Year 2*
A	−$10,000	+$ 2,400	+$11,520
B	− 10,000	+ 10,500	+ 2,500
Incremental cash flows			
(A − B)	-0-	−$ 8,100	+$ 9,020

Note that if we choose investment A over investment B we give up $8,100 at the end of the first year in exchange for an additional inflow of $9,020 at the end of Year 2. This incremental investment promises a return of 11.3%

$$\left(\frac{9{,}020 - 8{,}100}{8{,}100} = \frac{920}{8{,}100} = 11.3\%\right)$$

which is clearly advantageous for a firm whose cost of capital is 10%. On the other hand, it is true that if the firm had other investment opportunities which would enable it to reinvest the $8,100 at the end of Year 1 to earn 25% (the yield method assumption), then the $8,100 would grow to $10,050 ($8,100 × 1.25) and investment B would be preferable.

This analysis suggests that the appropriate way to use the yield method in comparing two mutually exclusive alternative investment opportunities is to compute the yield on the *incremental* cash flows and compare this yield with alternative investment opportunities. In effect we say to ourselves, "Investment A gives us everything that investment B does except that we are short $8,100 at the end of Year 1 and gain $9,020 at the end of Year 2.[3] Is this an advantageous or disadvantageous differential in terms of yield rate of return?" If more than two alternatives are under consideration, we will have to make an incremental analysis by pairs, carrying into competition the better-ranking investment proposal in each case until one emerges victorious.

It is clear that a simple comparison of the yields of two or more investments produces confusing information because different yield rates imply different rates of return on the reinvestment of recovered capital during the life of the investment. Some capital budgeting authorities suggest that the long-run average rate of return which a firm may expect to realize from reinvestment is roughly approximated by the cost of capital. Since reinvestment at the cost of capital is implicitly assumed in the net present value method, this reasoning leads to the conclusion

[3] We might, of course, have reversed the comparison and subtracted the flows from investment B from those of investment A without changing the results. In this case we would be comparing incremental proceeds of $8,100 at the end of Year 1 with a shortage of $9,020 at the end of Year 2, and the question is whether we could invest the $8,100 excess for a year to yield more than $9,020 at the end of Year 2.

that the net present value method is superior to the yield method in evaluating mutually exclusive investment opportunities.[4] Another way of resolving the conflict is to compute the yield rate on incremental cash flows and compare this yield with the cost of capital; this approach will always indicate the same investment decision as the net present value method.

Case 2—Different initial outlays; same period of return. Suppose that Company Z has the choice of investing $10,000 or $25,000 in a project under the condition that one investment precludes the other. The cost of capital is still assumed to be 10%. The investment prospects analyzed under both the yield and net present value methods are summarized below.

Investment	*Year 0*	*Year 1*	*Year 2*	*Yield method*		*Net present value method*	
	(Outlay)	*(Proceeds)*	*(Proceeds)*	*Rate, %*	*Rank*	*NPV at 10%*	*Rank*
C.	−$10,000	+$ 2,400	+$11,520	20	1	+$1,702	2
D.	− 25,000	+ 10,000	+ 23,000	18	2	+ 3,098	1
Incremental returns (D − C).	−$15,000	+$ 7,600	+$11,480				

The basic difference between this case and Case 1 is that here there is a substantial difference in the initial outlay required under the two alternative investment proposals. Once more we note that the ranking of the two investments under the yield method is the opposite of the ranking under the net present value method, and the question of which investment should be selected is in doubt.

In comparing investment C with D on an incremental cash flow basis, we see that the basic issue is: Investment D promises everything that investment C does except that in D we must invest $15,000 more in the expectation of receiving $7,600 at the end of Year 1 and $11,480 at the end of Year 2. Is this additional investment worthwhile? We can analyze the incremental investment situation in two ways:

Incremental cash flows	*Amount*	*Net present value at 10%*		*Present value at approximate yield rate, 16%*°	
		$p_{\overline{n}|10\%}$	*Present value*	$p_{\overline{n}|16\%}$	*Present value*
Assumed additional investment.	−$15,000	1.0000	−$15,000	1.0000	−$15,000
Year 1 proceeds.	+ 7,600	.9091	+ 6,909	.8621	+ 6,551
Year 2 proceeds.	+ 11,480	.8264	+ 9,487	.7432	+ 8,532
Net present value			+$ 1,396		+$ 83

° *16% rate was determined by trial and error.*

[4] See H. Bierman and S. Smidt, *The Capital Budgeting Decision,* The Macmillan Company (New York:1961), p. 39.

The incremental cash flows of investment D over investment C yield a return of 16+% (present value would be zero at the exact yield), which is a favorable prospect to a firm whose cost of capital is 10%. The net present value of the incremental returns at 10% is $1,396, which also points to investment D as the proper choice. Unless Company Z has alternative opportunities to invest $15,000 at a yield in excess of 16% over the next two years, the evidence supports the ranking of the net present value method. It is evident that the yield of the incremental cash flows is more useful information than a simple comparison of the yield of two investments. But if the assumption of reinvestment at the cost of capital is reasonable, the net present value method gives an immediate answer that can only be confirmed by incremental analysis.

Net present value index. The net present value method is sometimes criticized because it does not reflect the relative size of alternative investments. A net present value of $1,000 may result from an investment of $10,000 or $1 million. To meet this objection, some writers have suggested that a *net present value index* be computed, relating the present value of the cash inflows to the present value of the cash outlays. It is claimed that such an index, or proceeds per dollar of investment, would provide a better basis for comparing two investments of different size.

If we had computed a net present value index as a basis for comparing investments C and D, the results would have been:

		Net present value index
Investment C:	$\frac{\text{PV of proceeds}}{\text{Initial investment}} = \frac{\$11{,}702}{\$10{,}000}$	1.17
Investment D:	$\frac{\text{PV of proceeds}}{\text{Initial investment}} = \frac{\$28{,}098}{\$25{,}000}$	1.12

In this case the net present value index agrees with the yield method and ranks investment C ahead of investment D. But how useful is this ranking? Investment C has a slightly higher net present value per dollar invested, but if we assume that the firm can secure additional funds at the cost of capital, investment D is preferable. So long as this assumption is valid, we shall not go wrong in choosing among mutually exclusive investments by selecting the proposal having the largest net present value, without regard to the net present value index.

The primary value of the net present value index is that it provides an indication of the relative desirability of any given investment opportunity. As an extreme example, the index would show that an investment of $200 having a net present value of $100 is relatively more desirable than an investment of $200,000 having a net present value of $500. One technical objection to the index approach is that it is often difficult to distinguish between an investment outlay and an expense outlay which should be netted against gross proceeds to arrive at a measure of the net benefits to be realized.[5] For example, is the cost of machinery maintenance a part of the investment or an expense incurred in generating revenues?

Case 3—Unequal periods of benefits. When the period of time over which benefits are expected to be received from two mutually exclusive investments differs, a new area of comparability must be considered. This problem arises frequently

[5] *Ibid.*, p. 47.

in connection with equipment replacement decisions, where the new equipment has a life that extends beyond that of the old, or in refunding debt where the new debt matures later than the old. To illustrate the problem, assume that Company Z has a choice between the following two mutually exclusive investment opportunities:

Investment	*Initial outlay*	*Yearly net cash inflows*	*Life, years*	*Yield method*		*Net present value method*		
				Rate, %	*Rank*	*NPV at 10% of inflows*	*NPV at 10%°*	*Rank*
E.	$2,689	$1,000	5	25	1	$3,791†	$1,102	2
F.	4,193	1,000	10	20	2	6,145†	1,952	1

° *Present value at 10% of cash inflows minus the initial investment.*
† *$1,000($P_{\overline{5}|10\%}$) = $3,791; $1,000($P_{\overline{10}|10\%}$) = $6,145.*

Once more we can resolve the conflict between the rankings produced by the yield and net present value methods by looking at incremental cash flows. Comparing investment F with investment E, we note

	Investment F	Investment E	Difference
Initial outlay	$4,193	$2,689	−$1,504
Return per year for first five years	1,000	1,000	-0-
Return per year for next five years	1,000	-0-	+1,000

The decision centers on the merits of making an outlay of $1,504 now in order to receive a series of five annual returns of $1,000 each in Years 6 to 10. The present value at 10% of a five-year annuity of $1,000 deferred for five years may be computed as follows:

$$P_{\text{def}} = \$1{,}000\,(P_{\overline{10}|10\%} - P_{\overline{5}|10\%}) = \$1{,}000\,(6.1446 - 3.7908)$$
$$= \$1{,}000\,(2.3538) = \underline{\underline{\$2{,}354}}$$

Investment F is preferable since, if money is worth 10%, the investment now of $1,504 to obtain a future return having a present value of $2,354 is clearly advantageous. We can determine that the actual yield on the incremental investment is between 16% and 17%, as follows:

$$P_{\text{def}} = \$1{,}000\,(P_{\overline{10}|i} - P_{\overline{5}|i}) \qquad \$1{,}504 = \$1{,}000\,(P_{\overline{10}|i} - P_{\overline{5}|i})$$
$$(P_{\overline{10}|i} - P_{\overline{5}|i}) = \$1{,}504/1{,}000 = \underline{1.504}$$

By trial at 16% and 17%, we note:

$$(P_{\overline{10}|16\%} - P_{\overline{5}|16\%}) = (4.8332 - 3.2743) = \underline{1.5589}$$
$$> 1.5040$$
$$(P_{\overline{10}|17\%} - P_{\overline{5}|17\%}) = (4.6586 - 3.1993) = \underline{1.4593}$$

Since 1.5040 lies between 1.5509 and 1.4593, the yield rate is between 16% and 17%.

Equivalent average annual cash flows. One difficulty with the above analysis is that investments E and F may not be strictly comparable. If we choose investment E we may have to make a new investment at the end of the five-year period, and thus the relative advantage or disadvantage of E and F depends on what the firm will do at the end of five years. For example, if E and F are manufacturing machines, we shall have to replace E at the end of five years, and F only at the end of 10 years.

One way of dealing with this problem is to convert the two investments into equivalent average annual cash flows. The net present value of investment E is $1,102 and of investment F is $1,952. To convert these into equivalent cash flows, we would find the average annual annuity for five years and 10 years, respectively, which has these present values. The computation is shown below:

Investment E—Average annual cash flow R:

$$\text{NPV} = R\,(P_{\overline{5}|10\%}) \qquad 1{,}102 = R\,(3.791) \qquad R = \$1{,}102/3.791 = \$291$$

Investment F—Average annual cash flow R:

$$\text{NPV} = R\,(P_{\overline{10}|10\%}) \qquad 1{,}952 = R\,(6.145) \qquad R = \$1{,}952/6.145 = \$318$$

This analysis still indicates a preference for investment F, since this investment promises equivalent average cash flows for 10 years in excess of the equivalent average annual cash flows expected from E for five years.

Equalizing terminal lives. Another approach in dealing with investments having unequal lives is to attempt to estimate what will happen at the end of the life of the investment having the shorter duration. For example, suppose in this case that at the end of five years it is estimated that we might repeat investment E to produce another five years of cash inflows of $1,000, at a *lower* cost of $2,200. We now have two investment alternatives with equal 10-year lives, and a comparison would be as follows:

	Net present value at 10%	
	Investment E	Investment F
Initial outlay	−$2,689	−$4,193
First five years of returns: $1,000 ($P_{\overline{5}|10\%}$)	+ 3,791	+ 3,791
Additional outlay at end of five years:		
$2,200 ($p_{\overline{5}|10\%}$) = $2,200 (.6209)	− 1,366	
Returns of $1,000 for next five years:		
$1,000 ($P_{\overline{10}|10\%} - P_{\overline{5}|10\%}$)	+ 2,354	+ 2,354
Net present value at 10%	+$2,090	+$1,952

Under these altered circumstances (the assumption that the repeat of investment E could be made at a lower cost), investment E proves to be preferable, since the present value of the entire 10-year pattern of investment and reinvestment is higher.

Sometimes the estimated lives of the two investments may be equalized by assuming a residual value at the terminal date of the shorter investment for the longer-lived investment. For example, in this illustration if it were possible to estimate a residual value for investment F at the end of five years, we could compare the present values of the two investment alternatives (including the present value of the estimated residual salvage value of F) on a five-year basis.

Summary—net present value versus yield method. Either of these two direct valuation approaches to investment evaluation may be used in analyzing accept or reject decisions. The investment should be accepted if it has a positive net present value at the cost of capital rate or if the indicated yield rate is in excess of the cost of capital.

The two methods may produce different rankings of mutually exclusive investment opportunities because there are different assumptions implicit in each method as to the rate at which funds recovered from any given investment can be reinvested. Reinvestment at the cost of capital is assumed in the net present value method; reinvestment at the indicated yield rate is assumed in the yield method. The proper choice between methods rests on the question of which assumption about reinvestment is most closely in accord with the facts in any given case. If the assumption that reinvested proceeds will earn at the cost of capital rate is not reasonable, the best approach in evaluating two investments is to compute the yield rate on the incremental cash flows in one investment as compared with the other. If the cost of capital is a good approximation of the reinvestment rate, this procedure is not necessary, since the net present value method will rank the investments properly and is a simpler and more direct analytical process.

Income taxes and investment decisions

Since income tax rates are always less than 100%, one might assume that maximizing before-tax values will automatically maximize after-tax values. This reasoning is not valid in analyzing investment decisions because income taxes have a direct bearing on the amount and timing of net cash inflows and outflows. Cash proceeds representing revenues are reduced by income taxes, and cash outlays representing deductible expenses are also reduced by the tax savings relating to them. The timing of tax benefits and detriments may be quite different from that of the cash outlays. For example, if some part of an expenditure in period zero is deductible for income tax purposes in period 5, the outlay in period zero and the tax benefit in period 5 must be considered in scheduling the pertinent cash flows. There are no simple procedural rules of thumb to be followed in dealing with the income tax impact on cash flows. Because income taxes are affected by many factors (progressive rates, loss carry-overs, state taxes, short- and long-term gains and losses, exchanges of property, etc.) the tax impact on each investment decision is to some extent an individual problem.

Income taxes affect not only cash flows but rates of return. After-tax earnings rates are relevant in comparing the after-tax yield or the after-tax net present value of various investment proposals. The effect of income taxes on the cost of capital is discussed in the next section of this chapter. Following this discussion are several illustrations which demonstrate how income tax factors should be incorporated into investment decision analysis.

The cost of capital

It is clear from the discussion thus far that some defensible notion of the cost of capital (expressed as a rate of return on investment) is essential in evaluating investment proposals. Unfortunately, as in the case of many other costs, we can describe the cost of capital theoretically but have a great deal of trouble in measuring it. In this brief discussion we can only suggest some of the reasons for the difficulty and outline a generally accepted way of approximating the cost of capital.

The funds to finance business investments may come from a variety of sources: an increase in current liabilities, short-term borrowing, long-term borrowing, sale of marketable securities or other business assets, issuance of capital stock, or the retention of funds generated by operations. Funds from each of these sources have a *cost* in the sense that some rate of return is required to compensate the owners of the business for the economic disadvantage of acquiring and investing the funds. Thus there are a number of different "costs of capital" in existence at any given time, depending on the capital source. In some cases the cost will be explicit. For example there may be a fixed contractual payment of interest (as in the case of bonds) or dividends (as in the case of preferred stock). A large part of the available investment funds in most firms, however, is derived from internal sources or from additional injections of capital by residual equity holders. In these cases the cost of capital is an implicit cost—a rate of return necessary to maintain the value of the stockholders' equity at its current level. The extreme difficulty of measuring the cost of capital in this latter case is obvious. One writer has noted that the "problems of measuring capital costs are much the same as the problems that arise in trying to appraise the going value of a business enterprise . . . ."[6] This suggests that we can hope to arrive at only very rough measures of the cost of capital. However, estimates of the value of businesses are made every day, and decisions involving large sums of money are based on such estimates. Similarly, some notion of the cost of capital, however rough, is necessary to pull investment decision making out of the "seat of the pants" category and into the realm of scientific management.

The cost of debt and preferred stock. The cost of either short- or long-term debt is the current effective interest rate incurred in borrowing funds. Since interest is deductible for income tax purposes, any after-tax investment analysis should take into account the after-tax cost of interest. For example, if the effective rate of interest is 5% and the corporation is subject to income taxes at 48%, the after-tax cost of borrowing is 2.6% (52% of 5%).

Many elements of short-term liabilities do not have an explicit interest cost, for example, accounts payable or accrued taxes. It is unrealistic to assume, however, that such financing is "free." Therefore, in measuring the cost of this form of capital we can do one of two things: (1) Assume that the same interest rate applies as in the case of short-term borrowing having an explicit cost; (2) offset any increase in non-interest-bearing liabilities against the increase in current assets required by a proposed investment, and consider only the net amount as a cash outlay or borrowing in evaluating an investment proposal.

Since preferred stock dividends are not deductible for income tax purposes, the cost of financing through an issue of preferred stock is simply the rate of dividend promised in the contract.

The cost of common stock capital. The cost of acquiring funds from common stockholders may be measured by the rate of return required by equity holders

[6] D. Durand, "The Cost of Debt and Equity Funds for Business," *The Management of Corporate Capital,* Ezra Solomons (ed.), The Free Press of Glencoe (New York:1959), p. 91.

in order to commit funds to the business. The buyer of a share of common stock will receive the dividends declared on his share plus the price at which he sells the share when he disposes of it. Presumably the market price of common stock at any given time reflects the consensus of the market as to the future course of dividends and stock prices, discounted at the rate of return required to justify the investment of funds in a security of comparable risk. Since a stockholder who sells his stock gives up all future dividends into the indefinite future, we can think of the market value of the stock at any time as a consensus of the present value of all future dividends in perpetuity. In theory, then, the cost of common stock capital is the rate of discount that equates the present price a corporation could receive for its shares (market price less issue costs per share) with future expected dividends in perpetuity.

This is the concept of the cost of common stock capital; how can it be measured? For all corporations whose stock is listed on national exchanges and for a large number of companies whose stock is sold over-the-counter, the current market price of the shares at any given time is known. The stream of expected future dividends in perpetuity is, of course, the unknown. If we assume that the present dividend will continue indefinitely, the cost of capital is simply equal to the yield rate on the stock. That is, if the stock sells for \$100 and pays \$5 per year in dividends, the cost of capital would be estimated: Dividend/price = 5%.

Realistically, investors normally expect changes in future dividend rates. It can be shown mathematically that the rate at which the market discounts future dividends in perpetuity can be approximated by the following equation, which requires that we know or estimate D, the current dividend per share; P, the current market price per share; and g, the expected annual percentage rate of increase in future dividends:[7]

$$i \text{ (cost of capital)} = \frac{D}{P} + g$$

For example, if the common stock of a company now sells for \$100 and pays a dividend of \$5 and investors expect that dividends will grow in the future at an average rate of 4% per year, the cost of shareholder capital for this corporation would be estimated:

$$i = \frac{\$5}{\$100} + .04 = .05 + .04 = 9\%$$

Stated another way, this approach simply implies that a stockholder who pays \$100 for a share of stock and who receives \$5 in dividends the first year and dividends in all subsequent years that increase at the average annual rate of 4% will earn an average return of approximately 9% on his investment.

This formulation provides a conceptual basis for thinking about the cost of capital, but most analysts use more rough-and-ready factors in measuring the cost of equity capital. Some writers suggest that the ratio of earnings per share to market price is a reasonable approximation to the cost of equity capital since earnings will either be paid out in dividends or will be reinvested in the company and reflected in future increases in the market price of stocks. Therefore, a concept

[7] M. J. Gordon and E. Shapiro, "Capital Equipment Analysis: The Required Rate of Profit," *Management Science*, October, 1956, p. 106.

of the cost of equity capital that may be useful in analyzing a proposed investment because it is more susceptible of objective estimate is:[8]

$$i = \frac{\text{expected average per-share future earnings (assuming the proposed investment is not made)}}{\text{current market price per share}}$$

Obviously, expected average future earnings is by no means a known quantity, but it is an unambiguous concept and does not have the weakness of the current year's per-share earnings figure, which may be unrepresentative for a wide variety of reasons. Note that i measured in this way is simply the inverse of the price-earnings ratio. It is therefore not necessary to project an earnings pattern indefinitely into the future. If one can estimate with some confidence that the average future price-earnings ratio for the common stock of a particular company is likely to be about 15 to 1, an estimate of $i = 6.7\%$ is reasonable.

Measuring the average cost of capital. Since the factors that go to make up the cost of capital are uncertain and the rate is based on rough estimates, there is little point in undue concern about minor factors affecting the accuracy of the computation.

It is tempting to assume that the cost of capital for each investment proposal should be related to the cost of the particular form of financing used to supply the funds. In some cases the marginal cost of capital by specific source may be appropriate, but there are obvious difficulties in this approach. In many firms the source of funds for the composite of new capital investment that will be undertaken in any given year is general and not specific. Furthermore, an investment this year financed by debt may mean that next year's investment will require new stock issues, leaving the question, Which investment caused the need for additional equity funds? For general investment decision making, therefore, it is usually assumed that there are a series of desirable investment opportunities and a series of alternative ways by which funds can be raised, and that the cost of capital appropriate to the decision is a weighted average of the cost to this firm of obtaining capital from all sources.

In setting the weights for the purpose of measuring an average cost of capital, a company may use the ratio of the current market value of debt and capital issues to the market value of all securities issued by the company, or it may assume some long-run relationship that it considers normal for the firm considering managerial financing policy. To illustrate, assume that Company G has outstanding \$100 million of bonds, currently selling at 101 to yield 5%; 1 million shares of 6% preferred stock currently selling at 86 to yield 7%; and 10 million shares of common stock selling for \$50. The weights used in determining the average cost of capital might be either of the sets of percentages shown at the top of page 667.

In estimating the cost of capital, the proportions considered by management to be normal might well be preferred over the actual weights at the moment, since these weights reflect the long-run average expected sources of capital. On the other hand, if the company should increase its long-term debt to 30% of its total capitalization, both the effective interest rate on debt might rise and the price-

[8] Ezra Solomons, "Measuring a Company's Cost of Capital," *Journal of Business,* October, 1955.

Weights of Sources of Long-term Capital

Source of capital	Current actual market value		Managerial estimate of "normal," %
	Dollars	%	
Long-term debt.....	$101,000,000	15	30
Preferred stock.....	86,000,000	12	10
Capital stock / Retained earnings	500,000,000	73	60
Total..........	$687,000,000	100	100

earnings ratio of common stock might fall because of the higher risk inherent in a larger debt position. These factors should be taken into account in any cost of capital estimate.

Assume, for purposes of illustration, that we accept management's estimates. The average long-run cost of capital for Company G might then be estimated as follows:

Source of funds	Long-run proportion of new funds, %	Before-tax cost of funds, %	After-tax cost of funds, %*	Weighted total,†
Long-term borrowing..............	30	5.0	2.5	.0075
Preferred stock....................	10	7.0	7.0	.0070
Common stock and retained earnings...	60	12.5‡	12.5	.0750
				.0895
Weighted average cost of capital......				8.95%

* Assuming a 50% income tax rate.
† After-tax cost of funds weighted by the long-run proportion of new funds.
‡ Assuming the expected average price-earnings ratio on common stock to be 8 to 1.

This estimate indicates that management should in general not accept investment proposals whose net present value at 9% is negative.

Estimating the opportunity (lending) rate. Thus far we have discussed the cost of capital only from the standpoint of the *source* of funds. There is also an opportunity cost of capital (sometimes known as the "lending" rate) which is the rate of return that can be earned on alternative investments having a similar degree of risk. In concept the lending rate applies to external investments, that is, investments outside the firm in marketable securities or independent ventures. In practice, however, an opportunity cost of capital may be thought of in terms of competing projects within the firm. All projects proposed for investment are not subject to the same degree of risk. For example, the result of an investment to retire an existing preferred stock issue is much less uncertain than an investment in a research project to develop possible new products. Therefore, it may be reasonable in some cases to use different cost of capital rates in evaluating competing investment proposals to allow for differences in the degree of risk and uncertainty surrounding the estimates of expected benefits. The higher the risk, the higher the cost of capital rate that should apply.

Analyzing investment proposals

Lease or buy decisions

Since leasing is a common way to finance assets, the choice between buying an asset or leasing it is a common investment decision. The typical choice is between an immediate outlay to purchase plus periodic expenses, as compared with periodic rents plus periodic expenses. It is clear that any periodic expenditures common to both ownership and rental may safely be ignored since these costs cannot affect the decision.

Illustrative case. We shall consider first the lease versus buy decision, ignoring income tax factors, and then add this complexity and observe its effect. Assume that Company K is considering whether to lease or buy a small computer. The company estimates its cost of capital at 8%. The computer costs $100,000 and is expected to have a service life of five years. The company can buy a maintenance contract for $3,000 per year and property taxes, insurance, etc., are expected to run an additional $2,000 per year. At the end of five years it is expected that the computer can be sold for $15,000. Alternatively, the company can lease the computer under an arrangement whereby all costs of maintenance, insurance, etc., are included in the annual lease rental charge of $28,000 at the end of each year.

Solution—present value approach (ignoring income taxes). Since the benefits from the use of the computer are presumably equal in either case, they can be ignored and we have in essence a minimum cost problem. Company K should choose the alternative having a minimum cost, measured by its present value at 8%, the cost of capital. We can diagram the problem as follows:

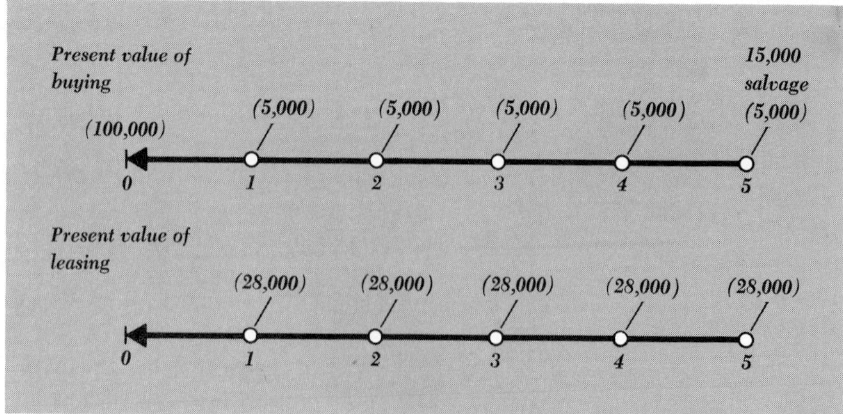

The computation of the net present value of the two alternatives at an 8% cost of capital follows:

	Net present value at 8%
Cost of buying:	
Period 0: Outlay of	$-\$100{,}000$
Period 1–5: $5,000 $(P_{\overline{5}|8\%}) = 5{,}000\,(3.9927)$	$-\quad 19{,}964$
Period 5: Salvage of $15,000 $(p_{\overline{5}|8\%}) = 15{,}000\,(.6806)$	$+\quad 10{,}209$
Cost of buying (net present value at 8%)	$-\$109{,}755$
Cost of leasing:	
Period 1–5: Annual cost of $28,000 $(P_{\overline{5}|8\%}) = 28{,}000\,(3.9927)$	$-\$111{,}796$

Since the economic cost of buying is less than the cost of rental, in the absence of other considerations, the company is better off to buy the computer.

Before-tax solution—alternative approach. A second way of analyzing the alternatives is based upon what we know about the annuity method of depreciation. Since annuity method depreciation includes the factor of interest on investment, it is possible to compare the annual rental cost with the annual depreciation under the annuity method of depreciation plus current operating costs to reach a decision. What we are doing is computing the equivalent *annual* cost of buying, *including interest at 8%* on our investment:

Cost to lease (annual rental)		$28,000
Equivalent annual cost of buying:		
$\dfrac{\text{Cost} - \text{present value of salvage}}{P_{\overline{5}|8\%}}$		
$\dfrac{\$100{,}000 - 15{,}000\,(.6806)}{3.9927} = \dfrac{\$89{,}776}{3.9927}$	$22,488	
Add: Annual cost of property taxes, insurance, maintenance	5,000	27,488
Equivalent annual advantage of buying		$ 512

Income tax factors. Now let us see what effect income taxes have on the buy or lease decision discussed above. If we assume that Company K is subject to a 50% income tax, how does this affect the analysis?

In the first place the out-of-pocket rental and operating expenses are fully deductible, and therefore their effective annual cost is only one-half as large on an after-tax basis. In addition, however, the depreciation of the original cost of the computer will be deductible for income tax purposes and will thus (assuming adequate revenue) produce a tax saving equal to 50% of annual depreciation over the five-year period. Note that while depreciation is *not* a factor in the investment decision (since the relevant cash flow is represented by the initial outlay), its income tax effect *is* a factor since this produces periodic out-of-pocket savings (income taxes) over the life of the asset. Assuming straight-line depreciation in this case, the annual tax savings would amount to one-half of the annual depreciation of $17,000 per year.

A second factor that would be changed is the cost of capital. We have assumed a before-tax cost of capital for this firm of 8%. The after-tax cost of capital would be smaller. For purposes of this illustration, we shall assume an after-tax cost of capital of 6%. The appropriate comparative analysis is demonstrated on page 670.

Period	Explanation	Net present value at 6%
Cost of buying (after income taxes):		
0	Initial outlay	$-\$100,000$
1–5	Five-year maintenance, etc.: 50%($5,000)($P_{\overline{5}\rceil 6\%}$) = $2,500(4.2124)	$-\ \ 10,531$
	Tax savings: Annual depreciation $= \dfrac{\$100,000 - \$15,000}{5}$ $= \$17,000$	
	Annual tax savings = 50% of $17,000 = $8,500	
	Present value = $8,500($P_{\overline{5}\rceil 6\%}$) = $8,500(4.2124)	+ 35,805
5	Salvage in fifth year: $15,000($p_{\overline{5}\rceil 6\%}$) = $15,000(.7473)	+ 11,210
	Net present value of cost of buying computer (after taxes)	−$ 63,516
Cost of leasing (after income taxes):		
1–5	Annual rental of $28,000 less 50% tax deduction = $14,000	
	$14,000($P_{\overline{5}\rceil 6\%}$) = $14,000(4.2124)	−$ 58,974

The existence of a 50% tax on net income changes the relative advantage in this situation to favor the alternative of leasing the computer. The effect of the income tax is to cut the cost of leasing almost in half; however, because of the differences in the after-tax cost of capital, the timing of the initial expenditure, the recovery of salvage value, and the tax savings from depreciation, there is not a corresponding 50% reduction in the cost of buying.

Bond refunding decisions

If the market rate of interest drops during the time that a firm has an issue of bonds outstanding, it may be desirable to call the old bonds and simultaneously issue new bonds at the lower rate of interest, a process known as *refunding* the old bond issue. If the only cost involved in connection with a bond issue were the interest payments, the refunding decision could be made by simply comparing the interest rates on the bonds. For example, if a company had outstanding an issue of 5% bonds and it became possible to refund the debt and issue new 4% bonds, it would be advantageous to do so. The existence of call premiums, bond issue costs, and income tax deductions for unamortized bond discount and issue costs on the old bonds, however, complicates the analysis. An example will illustrate the factors that must be considered.

Illustrative case. Just prior to an interest date, R Company has outstanding $1 million of 20-year, 6% bonds (interest payable annually) due nine years from current date. These bonds were originally issued at a discount; unamortized bond discount of $30,000 and unamortized issue costs of $6,000 appear on the books at this time. The bonds are callable at 104 on any interest date. The company is offered an opportunity to borrow $1 million at 5% for nine years; issue costs on the new bonds will be $27,000.

Let us first consider this investment decision without taking income tax factors into account.

Solution—ignoring income tax factors. We can diagram the two alternatives facing R Company as follows:

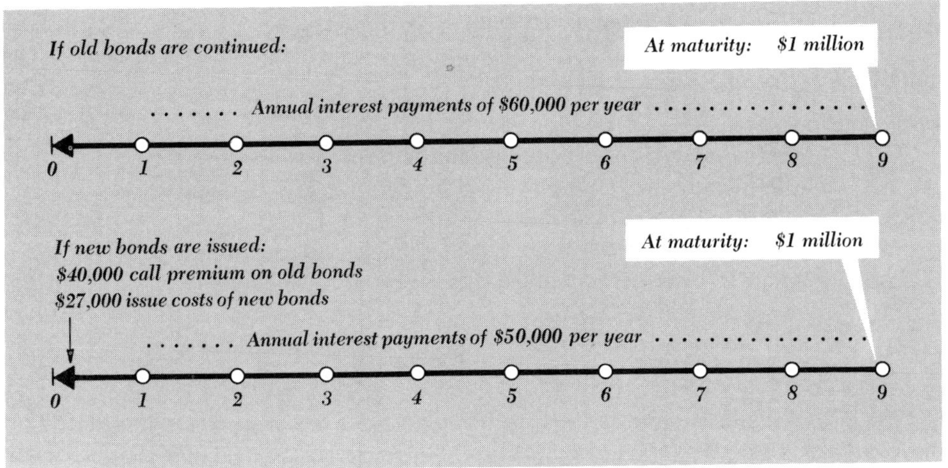

There are two notable omissions from these diagrams of decision factors: (1) The interest payment on the old bonds ($60,000) at period zero (interest date of the call) is omitted because this expenditure will be required whether we call the bonds or not. (2) The unamortized bond discount ($30,000) and issue costs ($6,000) on the old bonds are ignored. These costs will be charged to expense throughout the life of the old bonds or written off immediately if we refund, but they are not factors in the before-tax analysis of the refunding decision. The reason is that these costs are sunk and will not be changed in any way by the decision to refund or not to refund. For decision-making purposes, only cash outlays that are changed by the decision are relevant. The tax impact of these costs will have to be considered when we bring in income tax factors, but for the moment they can be safely omitted from the decision analysis.

We should like to choose the alternative that has the lowest present value at the present cost of borrowing, 5%. We could do this by comparing the present value of the two prospective cost streams in the above diagrams, but we can simplify the task somewhat by first determining the incremental cash flows and looking at the present value of these incremental elements.

The change in cash flows, depending on whether we refund or continue the old bonds, may be summarized as shown on page 672.

Therefore we conclude that R Company will be $4,078 better off if it refunds the bond issue at this time.

Solution—including income tax factors. If we now add the factor of income taxes to our analysis (assuming a 50% income tax rate) a number of elements are changed. First, the after-tax interest savings drops from $10,000 to $5,000. Second, we must consider the tax deductibility of a number of items. If the bonds are refunded, the unamortized bond discount, issue costs, and the call premium on the old issue may be deducted immediately for tax purposes, while the issue costs on the new bonds will be written off over the next nine years. If we do not refund, there will be no call premium, and unamortized bond discount and issue costs on the old issue will be written off for tax purposes over the nine-year period, thus producing an annual out-of-pocket tax saving which is a factor in the decision.

Before-tax Analysis of Bond Refunding

Period	Explanation	Change in cash outlay if bonds are refunded
0	Pay off the old bonds with the proceeds of the new issue—no net cost. In addition we must pay a call premium of $40,000 and issue costs on the new bonds of $27,000	−$67,000
1–9	There will be an annual interest saving of $10,000, the difference between interest on the old bonds ($60,000) and interest on the new bonds ($50,000)	+ 10,000
9	In either case we will have to pay $1 million at maturity, so there is no change	-0-

The issue thus boils down to the question whether it is worthwhile to invest $67,000 now in order to save $10,000 in annual interest costs during the next nine years:

Present cost of refunding (before income taxes)	−$67,000
Present value of before-tax savings over nine years:	
$\$10{,}000(P_{\overline{9}|5\%}) = \$10{,}000(7.1078)$	+ 71,078
Present value of advantage of refunding (at 5%)	+$ 4,078

For simplicity we shall assume straight-line amortization for tax purposes in all cases.

The general approach of the analysis is the same but the comparison of incremental cash flows is altered somewhat:

After-tax Analysis of Bond Refunding

Period	Explanation		Incremental cash flows if bonds are refunded
0	Call premium ($40,000) and new issue costs ($27,000)	−$67,000	
0	Tax saving (50%) resulting from immediate deduction of unamortized bond discount ($30,000), issue costs ($6,000), and call premium ($40,000) on the old bond issue: 50%($30,000 + $6,000 + $40,000)	+ 38,000	−$29,000
1–9	Cash outlay for interest less tax saving on deduction of total interest cost (including discount and issue cost amortization:		
	On old bonds (annual cash cost):		
	Annual after-tax interest cost: 50%($60,000)	$30,000	
	Tax saving on amortization of discount and issue costs: $50\%\left(\dfrac{\$30{,}000 + \$6{,}000}{9}\right)$	(2,000)	
		$28,000	
	On new bonds (annual cash cost):		
	Annual after-tax interest cost: 50%($50,000)	$25,000	
	Tax saving on amortization of issue costs: 50%($27,000/9)	(1,500)	
		$23,500	+ 4,500

In essence, then, the choice is whether to invest $29,000 now in order to save $4,500 each year for the next nine years. If we compare present values at an after-tax cost of capital of 2½% (50% of 5%), we get:

Immediate cost of refunding (net of income taxes)	−$29,000
Present value of after-tax savings:	
$4,500 $(P_{\overline{9}|2\frac{1}{2}\%})$ = $4,500 (7.9709)	+ 35,869
Present value of the *advantage* of refunding	+$ 6,869

In this case the decision remains the same after tax as before, but the size of the advantage increases from $4,000 to almost $7,000.

Different terminal lives of debt. In this example the life of the new bonds was assumed to be exactly equal to the remaining life of the old. Our analysis might be affected, however, if the new bonds had a life of, say, 20 years, since the question then arises whether there is any interest saving during the last 11 years beyond the terminal life of the present debt issue. If we assumed that the company could borrow at 5% at the end of nine years, the same analysis would apply, since Company R will be in roughly the same position at the end of nine years whether it refunds or not. If the bonds were refunded, the company would have a $1 million debt at 5%; if the old bonds were continued, the company could presumably borrow $1 million at 5% at the end of nine years. If the company could expect to borrow $1 million nine years from now at a rate higher or lower than 5%, however, this would affect our comparison since the decision not to refund now would carry with it the implication of having to borrow $1 million at a different interest cost than 5% at the end of nine years. The easiest way to handle this would be to extend the analysis over a 20-year period and assume a new 11-year borrowing at the end of nine years at the effective rate expected at that time.

Property replacement decisions

The issue of when it is desirable to replace existing depreciable property with new is a universal business problem. A variety of analytical approaches to the problem have been expounded and the decision factors are often quite complicated. The objective of this discussion is to outline the basic elements of the replacement decision and some of the issues that arise in analyzing replacement proposals. It is easy to make an invalid analysis by failing to separate the bookkeeping impact of the removal of old equipment and changes in depreciation charges from the incremental factors that are relevant to the decision.

In the replacement decision, as in previous cases, the basic comparison is between an investment in exchange for future benefits (either increased revenues, cost savings, or both). Often intangible benefits are difficult to express in dollar terms and the decision finally turns on subjective factors after considering the economic advantage or disadvantage. The major analytical problem is to assemble the pertinent data properly for analytical purposes.

Illustrative replacement case. T Company presently owns certain equipment which cost new $118,000 and is carried at a book value (net of $78,000 accumulated depreciation) of $40,000. The company has used straight-line depreciation on this equipment for both book and tax purposes. The equipment has a current disposal value of $10,000, an estimated remaining service life of five years, and an estimated salvage value at the end of five years of $1,000. The company has been approached by the representative of a manufacturer of new improved equipment. New equipment can be purchased for $208,000. Engineers estimate that the new equipment will have a service life of eight years. The new equipment is expected to produce average annual cash cost savings of $45,000 a year for the next five years, and its residual value at the end of five years is estimated to be $58,000. (Note that this residual estimate is necessary to enable us to make a five-year comparison, since the actual expected service life of the new equipment extends beyond the remaining life of the old asset.) We shall assume that this new equipment will be depreciated from $208,000 to its residual value at the end of five years ($58,000) on a sum of the years' digits basis for both book and tax purposes. The company's average income tax rate is 40%.

Solution—ignoring income taxes. Forgetting about income tax factors for the moment, the investment decision is to choose between keeping the old machine or buying the new. We can evaluate these alternatives by determining incremental costs of buying the new equipment and measuring their net present value. We shall assume a before-tax cost of capital of 15%.

Equipment Replacement Analysis—Ignoring Income Taxes

If company buys new equipment:

Period	Explanation		New present value of incremental cash flow
0	Receipt of disposal value of the old machine......	+$ 10,000	
	Cost of new equipment........................	− 208,000	−$198,000
1–5	Receipt of $45,000 annual cost savings:		
	Present value = $\$45{,}000(P_{\overline{5}\vert 15\%}) =$ $45,000(3.3522)........................		+ 150,849
	Receipt of benefits of residual value of new machine:		
	$\$58{,}000(p_{\overline{5}\vert 15\%}) = \$58{,}000(.4972)$...........	+$ 28,838	
5	Failure to receive ultimate salvage value of old machine: $\$1{,}000(p_{\overline{5}\vert 15\%}) = \$1{,}000(.4972)$........	− 497	+ 28,341
	Net present value of the *disadvantage* of buying new equipment..................................		−$ 18,810

This analysis indicates that the company will be worse off by about $18,810 if they choose to buy the new equipment. Note that the book value of the old machine ($40,000) is completely irrelevant since this is a sunk cost that cannot be changed by the decision to replace. The opportunity cost of continuing to use the old machine is represented by its $10,000 disposal value at the present time, because this is what Company T gives up by continuing the old machine in service.

Solution—including income tax factors. If income tax factors are now added to our analysis, we must consider some new elements as relevant to the decision. We can summarize the analysis as follows (assuming a 10% after-tax cost of capital and a marginal income tax rate of 40%):

The after-tax analysis also points to a decision not to buy the new equipment. The negative present value of $11,716 is not so large as the negative present value

Equipment Replacement Analysis—Including Income Tax Factors

Period	Explanation		Net present value of incremental cash flows	
0	Cost of the new equipment		−$208,000	
	Receipt of disposal value of old machine		+ 10,000	
	Receipt of tax savings from the deductible loss on the old machine:			
	Book value ($118,000 − $78,000)	$40,000		
	Disposal value	10,000		
	Tax loss	$30,000		
	Tax saving @ 40% income tax rate	40%	+ 12,000	−$186,000
1–5	Cost savings:			
	Receipt of benefits for five years of the annual operating cost savings (net of taxes):			
	Annual cost savings $45,000			
	Tax on savings @ 40% 18,000			
	Net annual saving $27,000 $(P_{\overline{5}\rvert 10\%})$ = $27,000 (3.7908)			+ 102,352

Income tax effect of additional depreciation:

Year	Depreciation on equipment: Old*	Depreciation on equipment: New†	Additional depreciation	Tax saving, 40%	$p_{\overline{n}\rvert 10\%}$	Present value at 10%
1	$7,800	$50,000	$42,200	$16,880	.9091	$15,346
2	7,800	40,000	32,200	12,880	.8264	10,644
3	7,800	30,000	22,200	8,880	.7513	6,672
4	7,800	20,000	12,200	4,880	.6830	3,333
5	7,800	10,000	2,200	880	.6209	546
						$36,541

* Book value ($40,000) − salvage ($1,000) ÷ 5 = $7,800 depreciation.
† Depreciable cost = $208,000 − $58,000 = $150,000. Sum of digits from 1–5 = 15. Depreciation = $150,000/15 = $10,000 times years of remaining service life.

Period	Explanation		Net present value of incremental cash flows
1–5	Income tax effect of additional depreciation (above)		+ 36,541
5	Receipt of residual value of new machine at end of five years:		
	$58,000 $(p_{\overline{5}\rvert 10\%})$ = $58,000 (.6209)	+$ 36,012	
	Less: Failure to receive salvage value of old equipment:		
	$1,000 $(p_{\overline{5}\rvert 10\%})$ = $1,000 (.6209)	− 621	+ 35,391
	Net present value of *disadvantage* of buying new machine		−$ 11,716

of $18,810 in the before-tax analysis, but the conclusion must be that the new equipment will not produce a 10% after-tax return on the additional investment.

Summary—replacement decisions

The basic principles in dealing with equipment replacement may be summarized as follows:

1. Increased revenues or cost savings are independent of the effect of depreciation charges, and their present value (net of income taxes) should be treated separately. If savings can reasonably be projected at an average annual amount, it is possible to evaluate their present value by using annuity tables. The projected savings may differ materially year by year, however, in which case it will be necessary to compute the present value of the savings for each future year.

2. Except for the income tax impact, depreciation on either the old or new asset is not a factor in the replacement decision. Depreciation is deductible for tax purposes, however, and therefore produces an income tax saving that must be taken into account as an element of the differential cash flows.

3. The book value of present equipment is irrelevant except for its effect on the tax loss from present retirement. The present value, and opportunity cost, of the old equipment is the amount of present disposal value that is foregone by continuing the asset in service. Losses on the disposal of depreciable assets are deductible against ordinary income from other sources. In general, gains on the sale of real estate are taxed at capital gain rates (not in excess of 25%) while gains on the sale of personal property are taxed as ordinary income with some exceptions.[9]

4. If the new asset produces benefits beyond the terminal life of the old asset, the choice facing the decision maker is to replace now or to replace at a later date. There are several possible ways of dealing with this complication: (*a*) Estimate the residual value of the new equipment at the end of the service life of the old equipment, and make the comparison over the remaining life of the present asset. This is the approach followed in the previous illustration. (*b*) Make the comparison over the life of the new asset, and assume replacement of the old asset at the end of its service life. In this case it may be necessary to assume a residual value for the delayed replacement asset at the end of the service life of the current contender. For example, if the presently owned asset will last three years and the contending replacement eight years, it is necessary to assume replacement of the old asset at the end of three years and a residual value for that replacement five years later in order to have a common terminal date (at the end of eight years) for the series of investment proposals under consideration. (*c*) Assume an infinitely continuous replacement cycle and determine present values on the basis of perpetuity formulas. This approach is theoretically satisfying, but it requires estimates of benefits and expenditures too far into the future to be practical in most cases. It has been applied, however, in determining the optimal timing of the replacement of standard items of equipment (such as trucks). For example, such an analysis might indicate that the optimal decision rule is to drive a new truck for three years and then replace it. The cost savings in this case are expenditures for repairs and maintenance, which can be estimated on a recurring basis with reasonable accuracy.

Questions

1. A taxicab company is considering a proposal to install small television sets in each of its cabs, for customer viewing. An analysis of expected increased fare revenues in relation to the cost of this investment indicates that a return of 10% on the investment is likely. What are some of the nonquantitative factors that should be considered in reaching a decision on this investment proposal?

[9] See Section 1245 of the Internal Revenue Code.

2. A salesman has just made a presentation to Argo Company, demonstrating a new piece of equipment that makes Argo's present equipment obsolete. The production manager of Argo comments, "Unfortunately, we just completed an overhaul of our old equipment at a cost of $15,000. We can't afford to throw this investment away and buy new equipment at this time." Discuss the probable validity of the production manager's conclusion.

3. Distinguish a *conventional* investment or loan situation from an investment and loan situation which may be described as *nonconventional.*

4. Distinguish the *yield* and *net present value* methods of analyzing a given investment proposal.

5. The controller of a company has analyzed the net present value of a proposed investment using ordinary annuity tables. His assistant points out to him that the results are not very precise because the cash flows involved will be received or paid in weekly rather than yearly intervals. The assistant shows the controller a set of present-value annuity tables which assume weekly rents and compounding. Explain whether you would expect the values in the assistant's tables to be larger or smaller than those in the tables the controller used, and why.

6. Explain why the yield method and the net present value method may provide different answers in choosing between two mutually exclusive investment opportunities.

7. Evaluating alternative investment opportunities by the use of the net present value method, using the long-run cost of capital as the discount rate, will always produce a valid comparison. Explain this statement and why you agree or disagree with it.

8. What are the advantages and disadvantages of using a net present value index in evaluating two or more alternative investment opportunities?

9. Explain two different ways of analyzing an investment situation which involves mutually exclusive investments whose terminal lives differ.

10. What effect does the existence of a tax on income have on the evaluation of alternative investment opportunities?

11. What is the cost of capital? Explain how, given access to a company's financial statements, the long-run average cost of capital might be estimated for the firm.

Short cases for analysis

19-1 The Arrow Company is considering the installation of certain equipment to replace present facilities which are obsolete. Two brands of equipment are under consideration, both of which have a prospective service life of four years. One type of equipment (Model J) has a considerably higher prospective salvage value because one element of the machine can be removed and used in alternative service. The other type of equipment (Model K) is more readily installed and will produce considerable savings in installation and break-in costs. The controller of the company has prepared the following analysis for use of the purchasing committee.

	Original investment	*Net out-of-pocket cost savings*				*Yield rate of return, %*
		Year 1	*Year 2*	*Year 3*	*Year 4*	
Model J	*$19,760*	*$ 3,000*	*$3,000*	*$3,000*	*$18,000*	*10*
Model K	*22,700*	*20,000*	*2,000*	*2,000*	*2,000*	*10*

One of the directors, after studying this analysis, argues strongly for Model K on the grounds that the investment will be paid back in approximately two years, versus four years for Model J. Another director argues for Model J on the grounds that it will produce a higher average return on investment. He produces on his scratch pad the following figures:

	Original cost	*Annual depreciation (cost ÷ 4)*	*Average return (cash flow ÷ 4)*	*Rate of return: average return − depreciation ÷ total investment*
Model J	*$19,760*	*$4,940*	*$27,000/4 = $6,750*	$\frac{\$6,750 - \$4,940}{\$19,760} = 9\%$
Model K	*22,700*	*5,700*	*26,400/4 = 6,500*	$\frac{6,500 - 5,700}{22,700} = 3.5\%$

The controller states, "I don't see any basis for choosing one model over another. Our cost of capital is about 6%, and any investment that promises a yield of 10% is a good deal. The foreman says that he gets along well with the representatives of J Company so I move we buy their machine."

Instructions

a. Evaluate the analyses of the controller and the two directors, ignoring income tax factors. You may assume that all figures are correct and all computations are accurately made; you need not verify these. You should explain clearly why you agree or disagree with the position taken and your reasons for rejecting any or all of their arguments.

b. State which investment you would recommend, and explain the basis for your preference, including any supporting computations.

c. Draw a freehand graph showing the general relation between the net present value of the investment in Model K and various yield rates below and above 10%. Be sure to label clearly the axes on your graph.

19-2 Citizen's Bank carries a substantial portfolio in securities. The bank follows the usual practice of national banks in accounting for discount or premium: When bonds are acquired at a cost above maturity value the premium is amortized to the call or maturity date; when bonds are acquired below maturity value, only the amount of interest received is taken into revenue each year and the discount is treated as a gain in the year the bond is redeemed.

At the beginning of the current year, the bank's investment department has an opportunity to buy at a substantial discount certain government bonds carrying a low coupon. The investment officer believes these bonds are a good investment because the yield is attractive if the bonds are held to maturity. At a board of directors meeting, however, one of the directors opposed the investment because "the benefits of such an investment would not show up in the income statement for a number of years, and we would simply be penalizing ourselves in terms of current earnings."

The investment officer's proposal is to buy \$100 million of 10-year bonds carrying coupons at an annual 2% rate, interest payable semiannually, at a present cost of \$68 million. Interest received would be subject to income taxes of 50%, and the discount would be taxed at 25% at the end of the 10-year period. "These bonds are very attractive from a yield viewpoint," he argued.

Instructions

a. The highest annual after-tax yield the bank can obtain on a comparable investment is 3.7%. Make an estimate of the annual after-tax yield rate on these bonds to determine whether the investment is attractive from a yield viewpoint.

b. The primary argument for the accounting procedure followed by national banks is that it is conservative. Discuss.

c. Assume that the bank should decide to accrue the bond discount on a straight-line basis and provide for future income taxes on the basis of a straight-line accrual. Illustrate the appropriate journal entry to record the first semiannual receipt of interest.

d. Let X represent the price the bank would pay for the bonds if a 5% annual after-tax yield (2½% semiannually) were required. Formulate a solution for X. (You need not solve.)

19-3 Lorie-Savage owns an oil well which, without further capital expenditures, will produce oil and return a cash flow from oil revenues of \$10,000 in each of the next two years, at the end of which time it will be dry. The controller, Mr. Astute, has discovered that if the company invests \$1,600 in a large pump, the company can pump out all the oil within the next year, thereby realizing \$20,000 then and nothing the following year.

Astute reasoned that on a differential cash flow basis the \$1,600 investment will increase cash flow \$10,000 in the first year and decrease it in the second year by \$10,000. In order to determine the yield on this investment, he set up the following equation:

$$\$1{,}600 = \frac{10{,}000}{(1+i)} - \frac{10{,}000}{(1+i)^2}$$

He solved this for i, and arrived at two answers: $i = 25\%$ and $i = 400\%$.

Astute is puzzled by these results. There is another type of pump available costing \$2,500 that will do the same job, and when Astute put the alternative \$2,500 investment in his equation he found that the yield rate on the new pump would be 100%. At this point he is even more confused, since he is faced with the unlikely conclusion that paying more for the pump removes the dilemma.

Instructions

a. Prove by computation that the respective yields mentioned above are actually 25%, 400%, and 100%.

b. Make an analysis of the above situation that will provide Astute with some basis for reaching a decision on the problem facing him.

Problems

19-4 The Ericka Company has decided to surface a vacant lot next to one of its retail outlets, to serve as a parking lot for customers. Management is considering the following bids involving two different qualities of surfacing for a parking area of 10,000 square yards:

Bid A. A surface which costs $5.55 per square yard to install. This surface has a probable useful life of 10 years and will require annual maintenance in each year except the last year, at an estimated cost of 2 cents per square yard.

Bid B. A surface which costs $3.00 per square yard to install. This surface will have to be replaced at the end of five years. The annual maintenance cost on this surface is estimated at 10 cents per square yard, for each year but the last year of its service.

Instructions

Prepare a computation showing which bid should be accepted by the company. You may assume that the cost of capital is 10%, that the annual maintenance expenditures are incurred at the end of each year, and that prices are not expected to change during the next 10 years. On the basis of your analysis, make a recommendation to the management of the Ericka Company.

19-5 In the following three cases, ignore income tax factors.

Case A. Dennis Company is considering the purchase of a machine that is expected to produce out-of-pocket operating cost savings as follows: Period 1, $10,000; period 2, $6,000; period 3, $4,000; period 4, $2,000.

Instructions

Assuming a cost of capital of 8%, what is the maximum amount the Dennis Company could pay for this equipment and expect to earn a return equal to the cost of capital?

Case B. Ehrhardt Company has an opportunity to invest $20,000 in new equipment. The equipment is expected to have a service life of 15 years and to produce a net return of $3,000 per year.

Instructions

Advise the company, using net present value analysis, whether they should accept or reject this opportunity if the cost of capital is (*a*) 5%, (*b*) 10%, (*c*) 15%. Compute the expected yield rate of return on this investment. Do the yield and net present value methods give contradictory results in this case? Explain.

Case C. Faber Company is considering the following two mutually exclusive investment opportunities:

Proposal	*Investment period 0*	*Net cash inflows*			*Yield, %*
		Period 1	*Period 2*	*Period 3*	
X.	*$ (16,300)*	*$ 10,000*	*$ 6,000*	*$ 5,000*	*16*
Y.	*(153,100)*	*100,000*	*56,000*	*30,000*	*13*

Instructions

Assuming that the company's cost of capital is 10%, compute the net present value of each investment and the net present value of the incremental cash flows. Compute also the yield rate of return on incremental cash flows. Which investment would you advise management to choose?

19-6 The Bookwalter Company finds it necessary to borrow $5 million to finance the development of a new product. Investment bankers have presented two proposals for management's consideration, and the controller has come to you for advice.

The first proposal is to issue $5 million in 20-year, 3½% bonds at face value. Interest would be paid annually. The bankers point out that this favorable rate may be obtained only if the corporation will agree to set up a sinking fund and deposit equal annual payments sufficient to liquidate the debt at maturity. It is estimated that sinking-fund deposits would earn a return of 3% annually.

The second proposal is to issue 20-year serial bonds. Under this arrangement equal portions of the issue would be retired at the end of each year, and it is estimated that such an issue could be sold at face value if annual interest payments at the rate of 4% were provided in the bond contract.

Instructions

a. Prepare a schedule showing a comparison of the cash outlays under the two proposals.

b. Prepare an analysis of comparative yields or present values and a report to the controller stating your recommendation and explaining your position. Round all computations to the nearest dollar, and ignore income tax considerations.

19-7 Bingham Company is faced with a choice between two different kinds of pattern molds which it uses to produce a standard product. Mold E costs less but has a shorter service life. Mold F will last longer but has a higher initial cost and higher operating costs. Bingham Company estimates its after-tax cost of capital at 6%. The expected cash flows after taxes are shown below:

Mold	*Initial cost*	*Expected net cash inflows*			
		Period 1	*Period 2*	*Period 3*	*Period 4*
E.	*$20,000*	*$16,000*	*$16,000*		
F.	*24,000*	*10,000*	*10,000*	*$10,000*	*$10,000*

Instructions

On the basis of the above information, prepare an analysis that will show whether the Bingham Company should buy mold E or mold F. In your analysis use two different approaches in handling the problem of unequal service lives and explain why your recommendation is the same (or why it differs) under each of the two approaches.

19-8 Aberle Company issued $1 million in 10-year, 5% bonds (interest payable annually) at a price to yield 5%. At the beginning of the fifth year after the issue date, the company is considering a proposal to call these bonds at 104. If the bonds are called they will be called on an interest date at the end of the fourth year, and the first interest payment on the new bonds will be made at the end of the fifth year after the issuance of the old bonds. The call will be financed for the most part by a new $1 million issue of six-year, 3% bonds (interest payable annually), which the company expects to sell at a price to yield 4%. It will cost $8,000 to accomplish the call and new issue. Interest cost on the new bond issue will be deducted, for income tax purposes, on a straight-line average basis. It may be assumed that the issue costs on the new bonds and the call premium on the old bonds are deductible for tax purposes immediately in the year they are incurred.

Instructions

Assume that the Aberle Company is subject to a marginal income tax rate of 50%. Prepare an analysis that will show whether or not it is advisable to refund the old bond issue. Write a brief statement of your recommendation, explaining your conclusion.

19-9 The Logworth Paper Company is considering the advisability of buying computerized process control equipment. The equipment installed can be purchased for $170,000. The sales engineer estimates that the service life of the equipment is five years. The same machine can be rented for $40,000 per year, payable annually in advance.

If the machinery is purchased, it is expected to have a salvage value of $20,000 at the end of the five-year service life. The Logworth Paper Company will depreciate the equipment for tax purposes on a sum of the years' digits basis.

If the equipment is rented, the computer company will pay all taxes, insurance, repairs, and maintenance. If the equipment is purchased, a service contract covering repairs and maintenance can be purchased at a cost of $2,000 per year, payable each year in advance. Property taxes on an owned machine will amount to $1,000 per year payable at year-end, and insurance would be $300 per year payable annually at the beginning of each year.

Instructions

a. Prepare an analysis showing whether the company should rent or buy the equipment, ignoring income taxes and assuming a 5% cost of capital. Make the same analysis assuming a 10% cost of capital. How is the decision affected by the higher cost of capital? Why?

b. Assume that the company is subject to income taxes at a marginal rate of 50% and has a 10% after-tax cost of capital. Prepare an after-tax analysis of the investment decision assuming that tax benefits occur at the end of the year. In what way does the income tax factor affect the decision? Why?

19-10 The budget committee of the Ambrose Company has received a proposal to purchase special-purpose equipment, at a cost of $280,000, to process materials now being manufactured on an assembly-line basis.

The new equipment will require two men to operate it, at an annual cost in wages of $18,000. Annual operating costs other than depreciation are estimated to be $12,000. Because of obsolescence, it is estimated that the new equipment will last four years, at which time it will have a salvage value of $40,000; however, the minimum service life for tax purposes is seven years and the company will depreciate the new equipment on its tax returns on a seven-year sum of the years' digits basis, ignoring potential salvage value in the depreciation computation.

Removal of the present hand-assembly operation will cost $20,000 over and above the disposal value of the machinery. The present machinery has a book value of $48,000 and is being depreciated over the remaining four years of its service life at $12,000 per year for both book and tax purposes.

If the new equipment is purchased, the company will be able to use a part of its present space for another operation, which is now conducted in space leased at a cost of $3,000 per year, payable at the beginning of each year. The lease can be canceled at any time by paying a penalty equal to the rent for one year beyond the cancellation date.

Eliminating the old process will result in a reduction in present operating costs (other than depreciation) of $48,000 in the first year (because of termination payments to employees) and $120,000 in each of the next three years. These reductions do not take into account the cost of operating the new equipment.

Instructions

a. Prepare an analysis showing whether or not the replacement is advisable, assuming a 20% before-tax cost of capital and ignoring income tax factors completely.

b. Prepare an analysis showing whether or not the replacement is advisable, assuming a 10% after-tax cost of capital and taking into account all income tax factors. A tax rate of 50% may be assumed.

c. Write a brief explanation of any difference in your results in (*a*) and (*b*).

19-11 The Allen Company has offered to lease a plant to the Baugh Corporation for 10 years at $1,800,000 per year, rents payable at the beginning of each year. The lease contract provides that all maintenance and repairs are to be paid by the Allen Company.

The Baugh Corporation can purchase an identical plant for $11 million. However, in order to buy the plant it will be necessary for the company to raise $10 million from the sale at face value of 10-year bonds, bearing interest at 4%, payable annually. It is estimated that repair and maintenance of the plant will cost

$600,000 per year. The plant is expected to have a service life of 10 years, and a salvage value at the end of the 10-year period of $500,000. The Baugh Corporation will use the straight-line method of depreciation both on its books and for tax purposes. Baugh Corporation is subject to combined Federal and state income taxes of 60% of taxable income.

Instructions

a. Assuming that money is worth 5% after taxes to the Baugh Corporation, determine on the basis of after-tax cost whether the plant should be leased or purchased. Show supporting computations (rounded to the nearest dollar) in an orderly schedule.

b. Without regard to your answer in (*a*), assume that the Baugh Corporation leases the property and wishes to show the value (on a 5% basis) of the lease rights and the lease obligation on its financial statements. Prepare the necessary journal entries to record the lease during the first two years of its existence.

19-12 Elmira Electric Company plans to issue $53 million of first mortgage bonds due 30 years from issue date. The company has received bids from underwriters as follows:

(1) Underwriter A offers for itself and others for 3½% coupon bonds a price of 101.913; Elmira Electric Company to receive $54,013,890.

(2) Underwriter B offers for itself and others for 3.3% coupon bonds a price of 100.217, Elmira Electric Company to receive $53,115,010.

Interest on the bonds is to be payable annually. The legal, accounting, and other issue costs will amount to $300,000. Elmira has outstanding a $16 million issue of three-year, 5% notes due shortly. These notes are renewable for an additional three years.

After awarding the issue to Underwriter A for offer (1), the president of Elmira Electric Company issued the following announcement: "The management has recommended and the directors have approved the sale of $53 million in 30-year, first mortgage, 3½% bonds to Underwriter A, who bid 101.913. Management gave long and serious consideration to an offer from Underwriter B carrying a 3.3% coupon. Although this would mean an interest saving over the 30-year life of the bonds, the premium offered amounted to only $115,010 as compared with a premium of $1,013,890 in the offer accepted. The receipt of nearly $900,000 in additional money at this time would be a great advantage to the company in further reducing certain short-term notes outstanding after the completion of this debt issue. Management is of the opinion that this advantage more than offsets the interest savings under the lower coupon rate."

Instructions

Assuming you had been asked to advise management in awarding the bid, what decision would you have recommended, and why?

a. Ignoring income taxes.

b. Assuming that the company is subject to a 50% marginal income tax rate and that premium will be amortized for tax purposes on a straight-line basis.

19-13 The Gercken Company sells computer services to its clients. The company completed a feasibility study and decided to obtain an additional computer on January 1, Year 1.

The new computer will cost $230,000. Maintenance, property taxes, and insurance will be $20,000 per year. If the computer were rented, the annual rent would be $85,000 plus 5% of annual billings. The rental price includes maintenance, and the Gercken Company will not pay insurance or property taxes on the rental computer.

It is estimated that the company will find it necessary to replace the computer at the end of three years with one which is larger and more advanced. The used computer is expected to have a resale value of $110,000 at the end of the three years. Gercken Company will depreciate the computer on a straight-line basis for both financial reporting and income tax purposes. The income tax rate is 50%.

The estimated annual billing for the services of the new computer will be $220,000 during the first year and $260,000 during each of the second and third years. The estimated annual expense of operating the computer is $80,000 in addition to the expenses mentioned previously. An additional $10,000 of start-up expenses will be incurred during the first year.

The company will pay cash if the computer is purchased. If it is rented, the $230,000 purchase price can be otherwise invested to earn a return of 15% after taxes. If the computer is purchased, it may be assumed that the amount of the investment recovered during each of the three years can be reinvested immediately at a 15% rate of return. Each year's recovery of investment in the computer will have been reinvested for an average of six months by the end of the year.

The present value of $1.00 received in a uniform stream throughout the year, discounted at 15% is: 0–1 years, $.93; 1–2 years, $.80; 2–3 years, $.69.

Instructions

a. Prepare a schedule comparing the estimated annual income from the new computer under the purchase plan and under the rental plan. The comparison should include a provision for the opportunity cost of the average investment tied up in the computer during each year under the purchase plan.

b. Prepare a schedule showing the annual cash flows under the purchase plan and under the rental plan.

c. Prepare a present value analysis of the cash flows under the purchase plan and under the rental plan.

d. Discuss the difference between your results in (*a*) and (*c*). Prepare a recommendation as to how the computer should be financed, explaining your position.

AICPA adapted

19-14 Craig Webb is subject to a marginal income tax rate of 60% on dollars added to his present income, and is therefore very much interested in municipal bonds, which yield tax-free income. A broker informs Webb that he can obtain municipal bonds which meet his safety requirement and yield approximately 4%.

Prior to the time Webb had made a firm decision to invest, however, he was approached by a representative of the Scapoose Oil Company. The company has under option a location for a super service station. They estimate the land will cost $50,000 and the station and improvements $400,000. The oil company representative proposes that Webb buy the property, with the understanding that Scapoose Oil Company will lease it back from Webb for 10 years, with the option to buy the property from Webb at the end of 10 years for $100,000 in cash. Since the property is almost certain to have a value substantially in excess of $100,000 at this time, the representative points out that Webb can look upon the option as equivalent to a guaranteed repurchase.

The oil company representative states that he has made arrangements with a financial institution to have a responsible person, such as Webb, buy the property, paying $49,890 down and borrowing the remaining $400,110 under a loan agreement that will provide for equal annual payments to cover interest at 4% and reduction of the principal to $100,000 at the end of the 10-year period. At that time, he states, Webb could pay off the loan with the $100,000 received from the Scapoose Oil Company.

The oil company would agree to pay an annual lease rental of $47,000 per year for the 10-year period at the end of each year, and to take care of all maintenance and property taxes. Thus Webb would have $47,000 per year clear of all expenses (other than interest on the loan) and the oil company representative states that this would result in a yield of more than 12% on his investment.

Webb asks for some time to think over the proposition. The next day he outlines the proposal to Mr. Callahan, a CPA who has previously consulted with Webb on tax matters, and asks his advice. After making some computations, Callahan tells Webb that payments of $41,000 per year will take care of the loan, and therefore the net cash inflow to Webb each year on his investment of $49,890 will be $6,000 per year ($47,000 lease receipts minus $41,000 loan payments), which on the surface supports the oil company representative's claim of a return of more than 12%. However, he asks for a few days to consider the tax implications. Webb agrees to call back at the end of the week for Callahan's advice.

Instructions

a. Show how Callahan arrived at the figure of $41,000 for the loan payments.

b. Callahan figures that Webb will be able to deduct depreciation and interest from his lease receipts in computing taxable income, and realizes that Webb has three depreciation methods open to him: straight-line, double-declining balance, and sum of the years' digits. He feels that in any case the asset could not be depreciated below its $100,000 recovery value at the end of 10 years. He decides to prepare a schedule of income (or loss) after taxes, assuming the use of the sum of the years' digits method, for each of the 10 years. Callahan knows that Webb has other income and that any taxable loss will thus produce marginal tax savings of approximately 60%.

As Callahan, prepare the necessary analysis to arrive at a recommendation to Webb as to whether he should accept or reject this proposal. All computations may be rounded to the nearest dollar.

PART SIX

BUSINESSES IN FINANCIAL DIFFICULTIES

20 BANKRUPTCY AND THE STATEMENT OF AFFAIRS

At this point in the study of accounting, our emphasis changes from the going concern to the liquidating concern. The major shift involved is one of a different objective and therefore of different assumptions and concepts. When we account for the affairs of a going concern, we are primarily interested in the allocation of cost into expired and unexpired portions and the determination of the results of operations for the current or most recent period. The valuation of assets is considered to be the unamortized cost of those assets and the liabilities are those which we expect the corporation to pay in the normal course of business, assuming continued and profitable operations.

When we account for the affairs of a liquidating concern, we are interested in the realizable value of the assets and the legally enforceable liabilities which must be paid if the concern ceases operations. The operating characteristics are of secondary or no importance; the expected realizable value of the assets and the legal claims against those assets are of primary importance. In essence, the focal point of the accountant's work is shifted from that of economic relationships to detailed considerations of legal relationships; for example, from the matching of revenue and related costs to the matching of assets with the legal claims against those assets in terms of preferred, secured, partially secured, and unsecured creditors. The emphasis is shifted from the affairs of a solvent business to the affairs of an insolvent business.

Insolvency defined

What do we mean by the term *insolvency?* If we speak of a person being insolvent, we mean that he cannot pay the bills which he has accumulated. We have related this definition to business affairs and concluded that a business is insolvent when it cannot meet its currently maturing liabilities with the cash resources immediately available. Such cases of insolvency usually arise from excessive investment in inventory or plant financed with credit, in anticipation of increased sales which do not materialize, or from excessive credit extended to customers. In other words, the business is desperate for cash to pay off currently maturing liabilities even though the realizable cash value of the assets may be in excess of the debts owed.

The legal use of the term *insolvency* is subject to a more precise definition than that used by the layman. The National Bankruptcy Act defines insolvency as follows: "A person shall be deemed insolvent within the provisions of this act whenever the aggregate of his property . . . shall not, at a fair valuation, be sufficient in amount to pay his debts."[1] The nebulous part of this definition is the meaning attached to "fair valuation." The courts have interpreted this phrase in different ways, and usually each case is considered on the basis of its own peculiar facts. The limits of the term seem to range from "value to a going business" at one extreme to "value realized at forced sale" at the other.

The question of fair value is not of immediate importance to us as accountants; more important is a clear distinction between (1) a firm which cannot meet maturing obligations temporarily and is legally solvent and (2) a firm which is able to meet maturing obligations temporarily but has liabilities exceeding the fair value of its assets and is therefore legally insolvent.

The distinction must be made in order to assure fair and equal treatment of the various categories of creditors. As long as the firm is solvent, even though it may not be able to meet currently maturing obligations, the creditors are usually not allowed to take over control of the firm's assets. On the other hand, when a firm becomes insolvent in the eyes of the law, then the creditors may organize and assume control of the insolvent's assets in order to protect their individual interests.

Nonjudicial procedures available to debtors in financial distress

A business which is not able to pay its debts as they mature may attempt to clear its financial difficulties with its creditors without recourse to legal action. These procedures are usually simple and involve a meeting of the creditors with the debtor. The possible courses of action which are available are (1) extension of time for payment, (2) a composition agreement, (3) control of the debtor's business by a creditor committee, or (4) voluntary assignment of assets.

Extension of time for payment. In cases where a business is unable to pay its maturing obligations currently but has sufficient resources to pay the creditors eventually, additional time for payment may be granted by the creditors. Such an arrangement frees the business from the immediate pressure of paying its bills. Voluntary arrangements of this kind allow the business to continue to operate without the impediments of more restrictive creditor control and also permit orderly realization of assets without the pressure of a forced sale. From the standpoint of the debtor, such an arrangement usually allows for the continuation rather than the liquidation of the business. From the standpoint of the creditor, he may have secured a valuable customer if the debtor is able to solve his financial problems. Extensions of time are usually feasible only when there exists a relatively small group of creditors. This procedure is, therefore, usually limited to small businesses.

[1] *11 U.S. Code (1964), Sec. 1.*

Composition agreements. A composition agreement is one in which substantially all the creditors agree to accept a proportionate part of their total claims against the debtor as full payment. The composition payment is frequently part cash, with the remainder being covered by notes payable. The creditors thus allow the debtor to keep some portion of his assets. In such cases the debtor is usually insolvent in the legal meaning of the term and the creditors enter into a composition agreement in order to avoid excessive delays and legal proceedings, which might result ultimately in a lower proportionate part of the debt being paid. The debtor is frequently able to continue in operation as a result of such an agreement, whereas if legal proceedings had been initiated he would have had to liquidate the business. Again, the composition agreement is usually found only when there is a small group of creditors.

In order for the composition agreement to be binding on the creditors, the debtor must have made full and complete disclosure of all his assets and he must not have entered into any recent preferential agreement with any creditor. If these conditions are not met by the debtor, the creditors may void the agreement, keeping all payments received, and prosecute the debtor to the limit of the bankruptcy law to obtain all possible recovery of their individual claims. If a few creditors with small claims refuse to enter into the composition agreement, they may be paid in full or in a relatively larger proportion to their claims by consent of the creditors entering into the agreement.

Control by creditor committee. This is another form of cooperation between the debtor and the creditors. In this case, by agreement between the parties, a committee composed of the creditors assumes the responsibility for managing the business and paying its debts. Frequently the agreement provides for the extension of time for the payment of debts; in rare cases the creditors may put additional capital into the business if in their opinion a good possibility exists for successful operation under supervision of competent management.

The agreement establishing control by the creditor committee usually provides for the return of any assets or of the operating business to the owner when the claims of the creditors have been satisfied. The creditor committee usually has all the powers of management: that is, to replace personnel, to supervise or effect a reorganization or, if rehabilitation of the business seems impossible or unwise, to liquidate the business. In general, creditor committees attempt to manage the business so as to cause a minimum number of changes. Their function is not to remake the business or change its character but merely to see that their claims are paid as expeditiously as possible without doing unnecessary damage to the debtor.

Voluntary assignment of assets. Under many state laws, an insolvent business may voluntarily assign all assets to a trustee for the benefit of creditors. The trustee must then convert the assets into cash for the benefit of the creditors and distribute the cash pro rata among them. Any assets remaining after all liabilities have been satisfied are returned to the assigner. The trustee in a voluntary assignment is required under most state statutes to file reports with a court. These reports constitute an inventory of the assets held and a report of the results of the realization on the assets and distribution of cash to the creditors. The trustee frequently must serve under bond and publish the appropriate notices of the assignment. It is important to note that this arrangement can only be entered into by mutual agreement between the parties, since the assignment of assets to a trustee constitutes an act of bankruptcy; therefore, a dissatisfied creditor who does not want to participate in the assignment may file a petition in bankruptcy against the creditor. One of the acts of bankruptcy as defined by the bankruptcy law is that the insolvent has "made a general assignment for the benefit of his creditors; or, while insolvent, a receiver or a trustee has been appointed or put in charge of his property."

Judicial procedures available to the insolvent business

If the insolvent is unable to work out a satisfactory agreement with his creditors, he may turn to the courts for help or dissatisfied creditors may seek a more satisfactory settlement through the courts. The judicial procedures are (1) equity receiverships and (2) bankruptcy proceedings under the National Bankruptcy Act.

The National Bankruptcy Act of 1898, as amended in 1933 and 1934 and as amended and revised by the Chandler Act in 1938, is composed of fourteen chapters. The first seven chapters cover bankruptcy and the next six chapters pertain to the relief of debtors, with the final chapter devoted to Maritime Commission liens. It is significant that these last chapters were added to the law during the great depression in the United States and the object of these chapters seems to be the preservation and/or the rehabilitation of insolvent businesses. The chapters dealing with the relief of debtors are:

Chapter VIII	
Sec. 75	Agricultural Compositions and Extensions
Sec. 77	Reorganizations of Railroads Engaged in Interstate Commerce
Chapter IX	Composition of Indebtedness to Local Taxing Agencies
Chapter X	Corporate Reorganizations
Chapter XI	Arrangements
Chapter XII	Real Property Arrangements by Persons Other Than Corporations
Chapter XIII	Wage Earner's Plans

The sections of the act which are of greatest concern to accountants are Chapters I to VII (bankruptcy), Chapter X (reorganizations), and Chapter XI (arrangements). The discussion of procedures available to insolvents or debtors will therefore be limited to a discussion of these sections of the act.

Equity receivership. A distinction should be made between a voluntary assignment of assets and an equity receivership. In the former the court is not involved in the proceedings and in the latter the receivership comes under the jurisdiction of a state or Federal court which appoints the receiver. In either case, the creation of a receivership for an insolvent is an act of bankruptcy and the creditors may avail themselves of the procedures available under the act.

The procedures to be followed in an equity receivership are generally as follows:

The property of the debtor is brought before the court and a receiver is appointed to take charge of the property and the business. Since the receiver is an appointee of the court, he is subject to the orders of the court but he also has the protection of the court. The appointment of a receiver has the effect of immediately bringing the property of the debtor under the control of the court. The creditors are thus prevented from employing any legal procedures which would result in inequities among the several creditors. The receiver is then charged with the responsibility of rehabilitating the business in an attempt to restore its solvency. If solvency is restored, the business is returned to its owner. If solvency cannot be restored, the court may then permit the receiver to proceed with (1) a reorganization of the business which results in reducing or eliminating the equity of the debtor or (2) a liquidation of the business, paying the creditors in proportion to their claims against the business. During the time the business is in the hands of the receiver, the creditors' rights and claims remain unchanged, but the payment of their claims is delayed until rehabilitation, reorganization, or liquidation is effected.

Equity receiverships may take many years to reach a conclusion. The various groups of creditors and owners form protective committees, which may mean that there are many conflicts and the proceedings may go on for years. The expenses of receiverships are frequently very great and at the end of the proceeding a complete reorganization may be effected in which the securities of the new corporation are exchanged for the claims of the various types of creditors. Since there are faster, more efficient, and less expensive procedures available under the National Bankruptcy Act, the use of court-appointed receivers has become less popular as a means of satisfying the creditors of an insolvent business.

Just as business management must maintain complete and accurate records, so must the receiver. The receiver's records are for the information of the creditors, courts, and owners and these records should provide a complete accounting of the receiver's actions. The detailed accounting procedures which a receiver follows are discussed fully in Chapter 21.

Bankruptcy proceedings. Bankruptcy proceedings begin with the filing of a petition with a Federal court asking that the named person or business be adjudged bankrupt. The act provides for both voluntary and involuntary petitions instituting bankruptcy proceedings.

A petition seeking to be adjudged a *voluntary* bankrupt is allowed " any person, except a municipal, railroad, insurance, or banking corporation or a building and loan association." The amount of money owed by the debtor is immaterial in a voluntary proceeding. [Sec. 22]

A person's or firm's creditors may file a petition asking that the person or firm be adjudged an *involuntary* bankrupt. "Any natural person, except a wage earner or farmer, and any moneyed, business, or commercial corporation, except a building and loan association, a municipal, railroad, insurance or banking corporation, owing debts to the amount of $1,000 or over may be adjudged an involuntary bankrupt . . . and shall be subject to the provisions and entitled to the benefits of this Act." It is interesting to note that a partnership may be adjudged bankrupt separately from its partners or jointly with any or all of its partners. [Sec. 22]

Earlier in the chapter, we noted the definition of insolvency as stated by the National Bankruptcy Act. Insolvency alone, however, is not sufficient grounds for the creditors to file a petition asking that a debtor be adjudged an *involuntary* bankrupt. In addition to being insolvent, the debtor must have committed an *act* of bankruptcy within four months preceding the filing date of the petition. An act of bankruptcy is considered to have taken place if the debtor has:

(1) conveyed, transferred, concealed, removed, or permitted to be concealed or removed any part of his property, with intent to hinder, delay or defraud his creditors or any of them; or
(2) transferred, while insolvent, any portion of his property to one or more of his creditors with intent to prefer such creditors over his other creditors; or
(3) suffered or permitted, while insolvent, any creditor to obtain a lien upon any of his property through legal proceedings and not having vacated or discharged such lien within thirty days from the date thereof or at least five days before the date set for any sale or other disposition of such property; or
(4) made a general assignment for the benefit of his creditors; or
(5) while insolvent or unable to pay his debts as they mature, procured, permitted, or suffered voluntarily or involuntarily the appointment of a receiver or trustee to take charge of his property; or
(6) admitted in writing his inability to pay his debts and his willingness to be adjudged a bankrupt. [Sec. 21]

After the voluntary or involuntary petition has been filed indicating the grounds for the petition, the court may appoint a *receiver* or *marshal* who has the duty of taking charge of the property of the debtor to protect it against loss during the term of the bankruptcy proceeding. When the debtor is adjudged bankrupt, the creditors appoint one to three *trustees* who are charged with liquidating the debtor's property and with using the money so derived to satisfy the claims of the creditors in accordance with their individual rights. A *referee* is appointed by the court to review all activities of the trustees as well as the list of properties prepared by the debtor to assure the completeness of the list.

Creditors of the bankrupt must submit a proof of claim to the court in order to substantiate their claim against the debtor. The proof of claim must set forth the claim, the consideration given for the claim, what securities are held for the claim, what payments if any have been made on the claim, and a statement that the claim is just and is owed by the bankrupt to the creditor. All claims must be filed within six months after the first meeting of the creditors unless the court grants an extension for good and just reasons. Creditors who have been pledged specific assets as security for their claims are known as *secured creditors.* Creditors who are entitled under the law to priority in payment over general creditors are known as *creditors with priority.* A creditor who receives a transfer of property from a debtor while the debtor is insolvent and within four months before the filing of a petition in bankruptcy is known as a *preferred creditor* if the transfer enables the creditor to receive more than his pro rata share of the debtor's assets. The preference may be void and the property recovered by the trustee if the preferred creditor has, at the time of the transfer, reasonable cause to believe that the debtor is insolvent. [Sec. 93]

The trustee in a bankruptcy proceeding must follow a very definite pattern in the distribution of the cash derived from the sale of assets. The cash derived from the sale of unpledged assets is held for distribution to the creditors with priority and then to the unsecured or general creditors. The cash derived from the sale of pledged assets is first distributed to the creditor to whom the asset was pledged, with any remaining cash being added to that derived from unpledged assets. This cash is then available for distribution to creditors with priority and the unsecured group. If the cash derived from the pledged assets is not adequate to pay the secured creditors in full, the unpaid balance is considered as an unsecured claim and the creditors then share pro rata in the distribution of cash after the payment to creditors with priority.

The claims against a bankrupt which have priority and which are to be paid in full and the order in which they shall be paid are itemized in the act as follows:

(1) the actual and necessary costs and expenses of preserving the estate subsequent to filing the petition; including filing fees paid by creditors, costs and expenses of recovering property transferred to a preferred customer, costs and expenses of administration, including trustees fees and one reasonable attorney's fee;
(2) wages, not to exceed $600 to each claimant, which have been earned within three months before the date of the commencement of the proceeding, due to workmen, servants, clubs, traveling or city salesmen on salary or commission basis, whole or part time, whether or not selling exclusively for the bankrupt;
(3) costs and expenses incurred by creditors successful in establishing the confirmation of an arrangement or wage-earner plan or in having the bankrupt's discharge refused, revoked or set aside, and costs or expenses of creditors' resulting in the conviction of any person guilty of an offense under this act;
(4) taxes legally due and owing by the bankrupt to the United States or any State or subdivision thereof;
(5) debts owing to any person, including the United States, who by the laws of the United States is entitled to priority, and rent owing to a landlord who is entitled to priority by applicable state law. [Sec. 104]

When all claims having priority have been paid in full, the referee will declare that a *dividend* may be paid to all unsecured creditors. Dividends are an equal percentage of all allowed unsecured claims and are paid as money becomes available in excess of that required to pay creditors with priority. Upon payment of the final dividend, the unpaid balance of the unsecured claims should be treated as a loss by the creditors. [Sec. 105]

A discharge in bankruptcy is a means of securing release from the burden of many past obligations, whether paid in full or in part. There are some obligations, however, which the person in financial difficulty cannot avoid even though he is adjudged a bankrupt. Such debts are:

(1) taxes levied by the United States, or any State, county, district, or municipality;
(2) liabilities for obtaining money or property by false pretenses or false representations, or for willful and malicious injuries to the person or property of another, or for alimony due or to become due or for maintenance or support of wife or child, etc;
(3) debts which have not been duly scheduled in time for proof and allowance if the creditor had no notice or knowledge of the proceedings in bankruptcy;

(4) debts which were created by bankrupt's fraud, embezzlement, misappropriation or defalcation while acting as an officer or in any fiduciary capacity;
(5) debts for wages which have been earned within three months before the date of commencement of the proceedings in bankruptcy due to workmen, servants, clubs, or traveling or city salesmen, on salary or commission basis;
(6) debts for money received or retained by an employer from his employee to secure faithful performance by such employee of the terms of contract of employment. [Sec. 35]

The adjudication of any person as a bankrupt, except a corporation, shall operate as an application for a discharge and a corporation may, within six months after its adjudication, file an application for a discharge in the court in which the proceedings are pending. After the bankrupt has been examined, the court shall issue an order fixing the time for filing objections to the bankrupt's discharge. Upon expiration of the time fixed, the court will discharge the bankrupt if no objection has been filed. If objections have been filed the count will give the bankrupt and the objecting parties a reasonable opportunity to be heard. [Sec. 32]

The court will grant the discharge unless it is satisfied that the bankrupt has been guilty of

(1) committing an offense* punishable by imprisonment,
(2) failing to maintain a proper record of the business transactions,
(3) obtaining credit by making false statements regarding his financial condition,
(4) removing any property with intent to defraud creditors,
(5) refusing to obey any lawful order of the court, or
(6) failure to explain satisfactorily any losses or deficiences of assets. [Sec. 32]

* The offenses referred to here include (1) concealing from an officer of the court, charged with control or custody of property, any property belonging to the estate of the bankrupt; (2) making false oath or account in any proceeding under the Act; (3) presenting any false claim against the estate of the bankrupt; (4) receiving any material amount of property from bankrupt after the filing of a proceeding under this Act; (5) receiving any compensation for acting in any proceeding under this Act; (6) transferring property of the bankrupt while an agent or officer of the bankrupt with the intent to defeat the Act; (7) concealing, destroying, mutilating, falsifying or making any false entry affecting or relating to the property of a bankrupt; (8) withholding any document affecting or relating to the property or affairs of a bankrupt. These offenses are also punishable by fine and/or imprisonment and apply not only to the bankrupt but to any other person committing, advising or assisting in such offenses.

The act also provides that a discharge will not be allowed if the debtor has been granted a discharge under the provisions of the act within the preceding six years. A discharge may also be refused if the bankrupt fails to appear at the hearing upon his application for discharge, or, having appeared, refuses to submit himself to examination. [Sec. 32]

Statement of affairs

The statement of affairs is a statement of financial condition as of a given date which presents the financial position of a business and the status of the creditors with respect to their claims against the assets. A typical balance sheet prepared on the basis of the going-concern concept is usually not appropriate for an insolvent business facing bankruptcy or liquidation. The more important concept of financial position for an insolvent business is one which presents the realizable value of the assets and portrays the liabilities and ownership equities in the order in which the claims against the assets will be liquidated. The realizable value of the assets is frequently interpreted to mean the cash value of the assets as they are severed from the business through forced sale or abandonment. The concept of "value in use" is of no concern if in fact the continued use of the assets is severely restricted.

The statement of affairs is used by the creditors in their meetings to decide upon a course of action with respect to the insolvent. Generally the accountant prepares the statement under the direction of the courts or with the advice of legal counsel. As a matter of fact, the accountant may also be forced to rely heavily upon various appraisers in an attempt to ascertain reliable data for the valuation of the assets held by the insolvent.

In addition to accounting for and valuing all known assets and ordering, in terms of priority of claim, all liabilities at book value, the accountant must include obligations expected to be incurred and assets accruing to the insolvent during the course of the liquidation. These claims and assets are usually excluded from the traditional balance sheet.

Classification of assets. The classification of assets on the statement of affairs is different from that found on the traditional balance sheet. Instead of the common classification of current, noncurrent, and other, the assets are classified in groups and in the following order:

1. ***Assets pledged with fully secured creditors.*** These are pledged assets with a realizable value expected to exceed the claims which they secure.
2. ***Assets pledged with partially secured creditors.*** These are pledged assets with the realizable value expected to be less than the amount of related claims.
3. ***Free assets.*** These are assets which have no direct relation with individual liabilities but are available to pay the claims of creditors with priority and unsecured creditors.

Classification of liabilities and capital. The classification of liabilities on the statement of affairs also differs from that on the traditional balance sheet. On the statement of affairs the liabilities are classified as to their legal priority and secured status, whereas on the balance sheet they are usually classified on the basis of maturity date. The following groups and order are frequently found on the statement of affairs:

1. ***Liabilities with priority.*** These are the creditors' claims which must be paid before anything may be paid to the unsecured creditors under the terms of the National Bankruptcy Act. These claims were discussed on page 695.

2. ***Fully secured liabilities.*** These liabilities are secured by assets pledged to the payment of these claims, and the realizable value of the assets is expected to exceed the amount of the claims.

3. ***Partially secured liabilities.*** These liabilities are also secured by assets pledged to the payment of these claims but the expected realizable value is less than the amount of the claims.

4. ***Unsecured liabilities.*** These liabilities have no legal priority and are not secured by pledged assets. This category also includes the portion of the partially secured liabilities which is in excess of the realizable value of the pledged assets.

5. ***Capital accounts.*** These balances are listed last in the book value column, following the liabilities, in order to provide balance for the book value columns and to indicate the extent to which the owners participate in the loss.

Preparation of statements of affairs illustrated. The partially adjusted financial data at book value as of April 5, 1967, and some additional data for the Jamestown Corporation are presented below as the basis for the preparation of a statement of affairs.

JAMESTOWN CORPORATION
Account Balances
April 5, 1967

	Debit	*Credit*
Cash	$ 3,000	
Marketable securities	30,000	
Accounts receivable, less allowance for bad debts	105,000	
Inventory, raw material	60,000	
Inventory, work in process	20,000	
Inventory, finished goods	90,000	
Land	19,500	
Buildings, less accumulated depreciation	135,000	
Machinery, less accumulated depreciation	180,000	
Goodwill	30,000	
Prepaid expenses	7,500	
Accounts payable		$120,000
Notes payable		202,500
Accrued wages		22,500
Mortgages payable		195,000
Common stock		150,000
Deficit		(10,000)
Totals	$680,000	$680,000

Additional data

1. Cash includes a $750 travel advance which has been expended.

2. Accounts receivable of $60,000 have been pledged in support of bank loans of $45,000. Credit balances of $7,500 have been netted in the accounts receivable total. Pledged receivables are estimated to realize $60,000. Unpledged receivables are expected to realize $42,500.

3. Marketable securities consist of government bonds costing $15,000 and 750 shares of Bartlett Company common stock. The market value of the bonds is $15,000 and the common stock is $18 per share. The bonds have accrued interest of $300 which is not recorded. These securities have been pledged as collateral for a $30,000 bank loan.

4. Appraised value of raw materials is $45,000, work in process is $4,000, and finished goods is $75,000. For an additional cost of $25,000, the raw materials and work in process would realize $87,500 as finished goods.

5. The appraised value of fixed assets is: land, $37,500; buildings, $165,000; machinery, $112,500.

6. Prepaid expenses will be exhausted during the liquidation period.

7. Accounts payable include $22,500 withheld payroll taxes. Creditors with claims of $9,000 have been reassured by the president that they would be paid. The unrecorded employees' payroll taxes amount to $750.

8. The wages payable do not exceed the limitations imposed by the National Bankruptcy Act.

9. Mortgages payable consist of $150,000 on land and buildings, and a $45,000 chattel mortgage on machinery. Total unrecorded accrued interest for these mortgages amounts to $3,600.

10. Estimated legal fees and expenses in connection with the liquidation are $15,000.

11. Probable judgment on a pending damage suit is $75,000.

12. The audit fee for the year ended December 31, 1966, was $7,500 but a bill has not been submitted and the liquidation work will probably cost $1,500.

Deficiency account. Frequently the statement of affairs is accompanied by a deficiency account which shows the estimated gains and losses on the realization of assets and the additional costs associated with unrecorded liabilities. The deficiency account indicates why it is impossible to pay all the creditors; in other words, it indicates how the capital contributed to the enterprise has been exhausted. A statement of estimated deficiency to the unsecured creditors of Jamestown Corporation appears on page 702. It is based on the statement of affairs on pages 700–701.

The statement shows clearly the total estimated loss from liquidation, the amount of the loss borne by the stockholders, and the deficiency to the creditors as a result of insolvency. The statement of affairs shows the deficiency to creditors as a total amount, but the advantage of the deficiency statement is that it shows the sources of the deficiency.

Items of special interest

Since the statement of affairs is used much less frequently than the basic financial statements of a going concern, we need to consider some of the unique characteristics of the statement.

Book value columns. The "book value" columns contain the balance of each asset and liability as it would appear on a balance sheet at that date. In the case of assets or liabilities which have related valuation accounts, such as plant assets or accounts receivable, the book value is usually shown as the net balance. The gross cost and related depreciation allowances of plant assets are of practically no value to the user of the statement of affairs. If the allowance for depreciation

JAMESTOWN CORPORATION
Statement of Affairs
April 5, 1967

Book value	*Assets*		*Appraised value*	*Estimated amount available*	*Loss (or gain) on realization*
	Assets pledged with fully secured creditors:				
$ 60,000	*Accounts receivable*		$ 60,000		
19,500	*Land*		37,500		$ (18,000)
135,000	*Buildings*		165,000		(30,000)
180,000	*Machinery*		112,500		67,500
	Total		$375,000		
	Less: Fully secured claims (contra)		243,600	$131,400	
	Assets pledged with partially secured creditors:				
30,000	*Marketable securities*		$ 28,500		1,500
	Accrued interest		300		(300)
	Total (deducted contra)		$ 28,800		
	Free assets:				
3,000	*Cash*		$ 2,250	2,250	750
45,000	*Accounts receivable* . . . $45,000				
	Add: Credit balances . . 7,500	$52,500	42,500	42,500	10,000
60,000	*Raw materials*				
20,000	*Work in process expected to realize*	$87,500			
	Less: Cost to complete	25,000	62,500	62,500	17,500
90,000	*Finished goods*		75,000	75,000	15,000
30,000	*Goodwill*				30,000
7,500	*Prepaid expenses*				7,500
	Estimated amount available			$313,650	$101,450
	Liabilities with priority (contra)			62,250	
	Estimated amount available for unsecured creditors			$251,400	
	Estimated deficiency on unsecured liabilities			64,800	
$680,000				$316,200	

or bad debts were included, it would be deducted immediately from the asset by the reader. The purpose of the "book value" columns is merely to show that all account balances have been included. The proof is in the balancing of the two columns; note that in the illustration the balancing figure is $680,000. The focus of the statement is the estimated realizable value of the asset, not its book value.

In the case of items which would not have appeared on a balance sheet or which have not been recorded, there will be no book value figure. Items of this type are

Book value	Liabilities & Capital		Amount unsecured
	Liabilities with priority:		
$ 22,500	Withheld taxes payable	$ 22,500	
	Employee payroll taxes payable	750	
22,500	Accrued wages	22,500	
	Estimated liquidation costs	15,000	
	Auditors liquidation service fee	1,500	
	Total (contra)	$ 62,250	
	Fully secured creditors:		
45,000	Notes payable	$ 45,000	
195,000	Mortgages payable	195,000	
	Accrued interest payable	3,600	
	Total (contra)	$243,600	
	Partially secured creditors:		
30,000	Notes payable	$ 30,000	
	Less: Appraised value of pledged accounts and collateral (contra)	28,800	$ 1,200
	Unsecured creditors:		
97,500	Accounts payable		97,500
127,500	Notes payable		127,500
	Accounts receivable credit balances (contra)		7,500
	Unbilled auditor's fees		7,500
	Estimated liability on damage suit pending		75,000
	Capital:		
150,000	Common stock		
(10,000)	Deficit		
$680,000	Total unsecured liabilities		$316,200

fully depreciated assets that have some liquidation value, accrued interest which has not been recorded, expected expenses of liquidation, and claims which have been considered contingent but which may evolve ultimately into a claim against the assets in liquidation. The "book value" column is left blank in these cases. If some figure were inserted, the balance would be destroyed. Items of this kind in the illustration are: (1) the accrued interest of $300 on marketable securities, (2) the employer payroll taxes payable of $750, (3) the estimated liquidation costs

JAMESTOWN CORPORATION
Statement of Estimated Deficiency to Unsecured Creditors
April 5, 1967

Estimated losses on realization:		
On machinery		*$ 67,500*
On marketable securities		*1,500*
On accounts receivable		*10,000*
On unrecorded expenditures		*750*
On raw materials and work in process inventory		*17,500*
On finished goods inventory		*15,000*
On goodwill		*30,000*
On prepaid expenses		*7,500*
		$149,750
Estimated gains on realization:		
On land	*$18,000*	
On buildings	*30,000*	
On accrued interest revenue	*300*	*48,300*
Net loss on realization		*$101,450*
Unrecorded expenses:		
Accrued interest expense	*$ 3,600*	
Employer payroll taxes	*750*	
Audit fee for preceding year	*7,500*	
Estimated liability for damage suit	*75,000*	*86,850*
		$188,300
Liquidation expenses:		
Legal fees and liquidation costs	*$15,000*	
Liquidation accountants' fees	*1,500*	*16,500*
Total estimated losses and costs of liquidation		*$204,800*
Less: Stockholders' equity:		
Common stock	*$150,000*	
Less: Deficit	*10,000*	*140,000*
Estimated deficiency to unsecured creditors		*$ 64,800*

of $15,000 and auditors' expenses of $1,500, (4) the accrued interest on the mortgage payable of $3,600, (5) the unbilled audit fee of $7,500, and (6) the contingent liability of $75,000.

Accrued interest. The interest accrued on investments or on outstanding obligations is always added to the asset value or to the liability and treated as a part of the asset or liability. For example, the interest accrued on a pledged asset is also pledged to the payment of the secured creditor. Note, for example, the treatment of the accrued interest on the marketable securities, which are assets pledged with partially secured creditors. The interest is also pledged and the liquidation value of these assets will go toward the partial payment of the notes payable. Also note the treatment of the interest accrued on the mortgage payable. The mortgage is a fully secured obligation and the accrued interest is also fully secured to the extent that pledged assets are available. In the illustration both are fully secured.

Liabilities with priority. The liabilities with prior claim against the unsecured assets are itemized at the top of the right side of the statement of affairs. The amounts are not extended into the column headed "amount unsecured" for the reason that these amounts will be deducted from the free assets prior to allowing a deduction for any other unsecured creditor. These amounts have a prior claim against the assets; therefore, they should not be considered with the other unsecured claims.

Capital accounts. The capital accounts are included so that the book value amounts can be added into the "book value" credit column to achieve balance. No amounts are extended to the "amount unsecured" column, however, since the owners have a claim against only those assets which remain after the creditors have been fully satisfied.

In cases where the stock has been sold at a discount and the stockholders are being assessed for this deficiency, the discount is usually shown on the asset side of the statement of affairs. The estimated amount of cash to be realized by assessment will increase the total free assets available to unsecured creditors. Similar treatment would be accorded any anticipated contributions by partners, whether the contribution was voluntary or required by law.

In the rare situation where an assessment against the outstanding stock is likely to produce more assets than are required to pay all creditors in full, only the portion of the assessment required to pay the creditors would be extended to the "estimated amount available" column. The entry on the statement of affairs would probably appear as follows:

Book value	*Assets*	*Appraised value*	*Estimated amount available*	*Loss (or gain) on realization*
$50,000	*Discount on common stock*			
	Estimated amount collectible	*$47,000*		
	Estimated amount required to pay creditors in full		*$33,000*	*$17,000*

Assets requiring outlays prior to realization. In the case of a manufacturing concern, the realizable value of the inventory may be increased by the incurrence of additional costs. This cost is incurred to bring the raw material and work in process to a more salable state. In deciding on the wisdom of incurring these additional costs, the trustee must be reasonably assured that the increase in realizable value is greater than the outlay required to bring the asset to this state. Where this is the case, the asset is shown on the statement of affairs at its estimated realizable value in the completed state and the cost of completion is deducted from this amount prior to extending the expected realizable value to the "estimated amount available" column. In the illustration, the raw material inventory with book value of $60,000 had a realizable value of $45,000 and the work in process inventory with a book value of $20,000 had a realizable value of $4,000. By expending $25,000, these two inventories can be converted to finished goods with an estimated realizable value of $87,500. The realizable value is increased by $38,500 with the outlay of $25,000, for a net increase of $13,500 in the realizable value of the assets. Note on the statement of affairs that the $87,500 is shown with the $25,000 deducted, indicating appraised value of $62,500.

Rule of offset. As in accounting for a going concern, there is a general rule against offsetting assets and liabilities. Occasionally, advances by customers to a going concern will be considered as offsets against accounts receivable, if the amount involved is small. This practice is not permitted in preparing a statement of affairs, however. The amount of the deficiency would be unchanged by such offsetting of assets and liabilities, but the distribution of the assets among the creditors would not be the same. The customers who had advanced the money would be given preferential treatment. Such treatment is enough to deny discharge to the bankrupt; therefore, the accountant must be careful to classify all assets and liabilities properly. The reclassification is handled in the illustration by adding an amount equal to the credit balances to the accounts receivable balance in the "appraised value" column with no change in the "book value" column, and by adding an equal sum in the "amount unsecured" column on the liability side, again with no entry in the "book value" column.

Reserve accounts. The use of the term *reserve* in present-day accounting is restricted in most cases to appropriations of retained earnings. When a statement of affairs is being prepared, special attention should be devoted to accounts bearing the label "reserve." This title has been used to indicate valuation accounts, estimated liabilities, or appropriations of retained earnings and it is essential in preparing a statement of affairs that the account be properly classified.

Prepaid expenses. In many cases prepaid expenses have a realizable value at the date the petition in bankruptcy is filed or at the date the statement of affairs is prepared. These values are seldom extended to the "estimated amount available" column, however, because in many cases the value expires prior to the time final liquidation is completed. In a great many cases this account represents unexpired insurance. Although there are short-term cancellation rates for most insurance policies, these policies are seldom canceled because the trustee feels that the protection against loss afforded by the policy is more valuable than the amount which might be added to free assets. There are exceptions; however, each case should be examined on its merits. In the illustration it was assumed that the value of the prepaid expense item would expire prior to the final liquidation of the enterprise.

Interperiod allocation of income taxes. In cases where the insolvent has followed the practice of allocating the tax expense between periods, there may be a deferred tax liability or a prepaid tax account on the books. In both cases it is assumed that future profitable operations will be necessary before the deferred liability becomes payable or before the prepaid tax can be used to reduce a tax liability. Since the corporation is now insolvent or is fearing insolvency, the possibility for future profitable operations is probably remote; therefore, the asset, prepaid taxes, may have no realizable value and the deferred liability will probably never become due and payable.

Both these accounts should be listed on the statement of affairs and the balance included in the "book value" column, but in the case of the asset no value is carried to the "estimated amount available" column and in the case of the liability no claim is carried to the "amount unsecured" column.

Interests in affiliated organizations. A parent-subsidiary relationship means that the parent company owns a controlling stock interest in the subsidiary. Such affiliated companies are considered separate entities in the eyes of the law. In the event that the parent becomes insolvent, this does not mean that the subsidiary is also insolvent. The investment in the stock of the subsidiary is considered an asset of the parent, to be liquidated if necessary in order to satisfy the claims of the creditors; however, the assets of the subsidiary are separate and distinct from those of the parent and are not considered assets of the parent in the event of a bankruptcy proceeding. Similarly, if the subsidiary becomes insolvent, only the assets of the subsidiary can be used to satisfy the claims of the creditors. Occasionally exceptions to this principle may be encountered, as in the recent case in which American Express Company offered to make partial payment of the claims against an insolvent subsidiary. Usually the parent merely loses its investment in the subsidiary because it stands in the position of a residual owner. The parent is not legally responsible for the debts of the subsidiary.

If there is a home office–branch relationship, separate entities do not exist in the eyes of the law. In this case the assets of both the home office and the branch are realized if necessary to satisfy the claims of the creditors. The test of whether the assets are considered joint or separate depends on whether there is only one entity or whether there are actually two or more separate legal entities.

Amount payable to unsecured creditors. The estimated amount to be paid to creditors without priority or security is obtained by dividing the free assets by the total amount of the unsecured claims. The percentage so obtained is the percentage of each claim which will be paid. For example, in the illustration of the Jamestown Corporation, the estimated free assets after deducting the liabilities with priority are $251,400 and the unsecured claims are $316,200. Each creditor will receive 79.5% ($251,400/$316,200) of his claim, or 79.5 cents on the dollar.

Uses of the statement of affairs by a going concern

Although the statement of affairs has been discussed as a statement for bankruptcy purposes, the information contained on the statement is often useful for other purposes. Frequently businesses which have valued inventory at lifo cost or are using valuable though fully depreciated plant assets will prepare statements similar to the statement of affairs as a basis for a loan application. The emphasis of such a statement is to show the excess of realizable value of the assets over the claims of creditors, rather than the deficiency as indicated earlier. Similar statements may also be used by management for the purposes of internal management and planning. When prepared for a going concern, the statement of affairs more nearly represents a statement of financial condition than does the traditional balance sheet.

Questions

1. What are some of the basic differences between the accountant's work for a going concern and that for a liquidating business?
2. In discussing insolvency the legal definition is cited. In this definition the "fair value" of assets relative to debts is a crucial element in determining insolvency.

What is the difference, if any, between "value to a going business" and "value at forced sale"?

3. Distinguish between the following designations of groups of creditors as the terms are used in bankruptcy proceedings.
   a. Secured creditors
   b. Creditors with priority
   c. Preferred creditors

4. For what purposes can the statement of affairs be used:
   a. For the business facing liquidation?
   b. For the going concern?

5. What is the purpose of the deficiency account or the statement of estimated deficiency?

6. What is the purpose of the "book value" columns on the statement of affairs and what items are included therein?

7. Indicate how the following data would be reported on the statement of affairs and give the reasons for this reporting practice:

   XYZ Company has (1) a raw materials inventory with a book value of $40,000 and an estimated realizable value of $38,000, (2) a work in process inventory with a book value of $70,000 and an estimated realizable value in the present state of $10,000. By incurring costs of $30,000 to convert both of these inventories to finished goods, the realizable value of this inventory is estimated to be $105,000.

8. Indicate how the following data would be reported on the statement of affairs:
   a. Accounts payable balance $56,000, net of $15,000 advanced to certain creditors
   b. Reserve for Federal income taxes $8,000
   c. Reserve for general contingencies $100,000
   d. Liquidation costs, estimated to total $25,000, not recorded at the date the statement of affairs is prepared
   e. Retained earnings balance $72,000

9. a. R. S. Corporation has a deferred Federal income tax liability amounting to $120,000. The corporation is being liquidated in accordance with the provisions of the National Bankruptcy Act. How will this liability be reported on the statement of affairs? Why?
   b. Spear Company has filed a petition for relief from its debts under the provisions of the National Bankruptcy Act. At the time of the petition, Spear has included in its accounts a prepaid tax account in the amount of $30,000. The prepayment represents income taxes paid to the Federal government before the income was recognized for accounting purposes. No taxes have been paid by Spear during the preceding four years; therefore, there is no possibility of relief from the operating loss provision of the Internal Revenue Code. How will this asset be reported on the statement of affairs? Why?

10. When there are affiliated companies which have separate identity in the eyes of the law, what is the effect on the parent if the subsidiary company should be declared a bankrupt? What is the effect on the subsidiary if the parent should be declared a bankrupt?

Short cases for analysis

20-1 The ABC Company, Inc., a retail jewelry company, has been operating at a loss for several years, and it has no new sources of capital. A creditors' committee wishes to determine the loss to the creditors should the ABC Company, Inc., be placed in bankruptcy. You have been asked to review the books and records of the company.

Instructions

a. List the section and column headings of each statement you would prepare for the guidance of the creditors' committee. Include a brief description of the data which you would include in each section of the statement.

b. List the data you would require in order to prepare the statements.

AICPA adapted

20-2 **a.** On January 2, 1966, Richard Retailer purchased 20 television sets on credit, executing trust receipts which stated that title remained in the finance company to secure payment of the price. The Uniform Trust Receipts Act was in force and it required the filing of a statement that trust receipt financing was contemplated. That provision of the act was complied with on January 3, 1966. On August 15, 1966, Richard Retailer became bankrupt and the finance company claimed the remaining television sets on hand. The trustee in bankruptcy also claimed the television sets, stating that the finance company had a "voidable preference."

(1) What is meant by the term "preference" under the National Bankruptcy Act? Explain.

(2) Who will prevail in the above case, the finance company or the trustee? Explain.

(3) Suppose, instead of selling on credit via trust receipts financing, the manufacturer had sold the 20 sets for fair market value to Richard Retailer one week before bankruptcy. Could this transaction be set aside as a preference? Explain.

b. List and explain six acts of bankruptcy.

AICPA adapted

20-3 Mr. Schaeffer, of Rogers Manufacturing Company, has recently seen a statement of affairs prepared for Johnson-Smith, Inc. In his opinion this statement appears to be a good substitute for the traditional balance sheet. At least it has overcome the objection that balance sheets do not present the "value" of the assets, as on this statement there is a column headed "appraised value."

Instructions

a. Explain to Schaeffer the difference between a statement of affairs and a balance sheet.

b. Schaeffer also has several questions about the presentation of various facts on the statement of affairs. Illustrate and/or explain to him how the following items should be handled:

(1) John Stokes has been an employee of Johnson-Smith, Inc., Manufacturing Company for several years. His salary of $325 per month had not been paid for the five months prior to the time the company filed a petition for voluntary bankruptcy.

(2) Johnson-Smith, Inc., has an accumulated deficit of $58,000 included with the assets.

(3) Contingent liabilities of $50,000.

(4) What is the difference between a preferred liability or a "liability having preference" and a secured liability?

(5) Stock discount of $25,000, of which $13,500 is believed collectible provided attorney fees of $1,000 are spent in suit; the deficiency to unsecured creditors before consideration of the discount is estimated at $10,000.

(6) Building with a book value of $42,500 (cost $50,000 less reserve for depreciation, $7,500), which is mortgaged for $25,000. Interest at 6% for six months is unpaid on the mortgage. It is estimated that the building can be sold for $45,000 under present conditions.

(7) Trade receivables of $100,000 with an allowance for doubtful accounts of $10,000. Half of the accounts, after deducting the allowance, are good but of the other half, a loss of one-third is expected.

(8) Notes receivable discounted of $10,000, of which one-fourth will probably be dishonored when presented for payment.

Problems

20-4 A receiver is appointed for ABC Corporation, on November 1, at which time the following trial balance was prepared from the general ledger:

Trial Balance
November 1

Cash	$ 66,000	
Notes receivable	114,000	
Accounts receivable	438,000	
Inventory of merchandise	291,000	
Investments—cost	60,000	
Plant and equipment	1,040,000	
Accumulated depreciation		$ 170,000
Notes payable		210,000
Accounts payable		960,000
Capital stock—par value $20		300,000
Retained earnings		369,000
Totals	$2,009,000	$2,009,000

Additional data

(1) Accrued expenses, not recorded as of this date, amount to $20,100, of which $6,600 is for property taxes and $7,200 is for wages for the past month. (Not more than $600 is owed to any one employee.)

(2) The investments have a market value of $69,000 and have been pledged as collateral on a note for $60,000.
(3) Accounts receivable of $180,000 have been assigned as security for the remainder of the notes payable.
(4) It is estimated that 95% of the notes receivable, 95% of the assigned accounts receivable, and 75% of the remaining accounts receivable will be collected. A quick sale of the inventory will realize $180,000 and of the plant $330,000. The corporation also owns a patent not recorded on the books which is expected to realize $12,000.

Instructions

Prepare a statement of affairs and a deficiency account.

20-5 The following balance sheet was prepared for Nelson, Inc., at the close of business on November 30 in support of a claim by the company that it was insolvent.

NELSON, INC.
Balance Sheet
November 30

Assets		
Cash		$ 3,600
Accounts receivable:		
Good	$ 7,000	
Doubtful (estimated to realize 50%)	1,000	
Bad	1,800	9,800
Notes receivable:		
Secured	$ 5,000	
Unsecured (estimated value $1,600)	2,000	7,000
Inventories (estimated value $60,000)		70,000
Store furniture (estimated value $600)		1,500
Bonds (at market value):		
Company J	$ 6,000	
Company K—pledged to banks for loans	15,000	
Company L—pledged to trade creditors on notes payable	11,000	32,000
Deficit		58,000
Total assets		$181,900
Liabilities & Capital		
Accounts payable		$ 71,100
Notes payable:		
Banks	$12,000	
Trade creditors	48,000	60,000
Accrued wages		800
Capital stock		50,000
Total liabilities & capital		$181,900

Instructions

You have been asked by the bank to prepare a statement of affairs and an estimated deficiency account for Nelson, Inc., as of November 30.

20-6 The Thompson Corporation has been forced into bankruptcy as of April 30. The following trial balance was prepared by the bookkeeper as of April 30 from the books of account:

	Debit	Credit
Cash	$ 2,700	
Accounts receivable	39,350	
Notes receivable	18,500	
Inventories:		
Raw materials	19,600	
Work in process	35,100	
Finished machines	12,000	
Supplies	6,450	
Tools	14,700	
Prepaid expenses	950	
Plant and property:		
Land	20,000	
Buildings	75,000	
Machinery	80,900	
Note payable to the Pacific National Bank		$ 15,000
Notes payable to suppliers		51,250
Accounts payable		52,000
Accrued salaries and wages		8,850
Accrued property taxes		2,900
Employees' taxes withheld		1,150
Accrued wage taxes		600
Accrued interest on bonds		1,800
First mortgage bond payable		90,000
Allowance for depreciation—buildings		33,750
Allowance for depreciation—machinery		32,100
Common stock, $100 par value		75,000
Deficit		(39,150)
Totals	$325,250	$325,250

Additional information

(1) Of the total accounts receivable, $10,300 are believed to be good. The other accounts are doubtful, but it seems probable that 20% of these will be ultimately collected.

(2) A total of $15,000 of the notes receivable of which all except $2,500 appear to be good have been pledged to secure the note payable to the Pacific National Bank. Interest of $800 is accrued on the $12,500 of collectible notes pledged and $300 is accrued on the $15,000 payable to the bank. The remaining notes receivable are not considered collectible.

(3) The finished machines are expected to be sold for a third more than their cost, but expenses in connection with their disposition will equal 20% of their sales price. Work in process can be completed at an additional cost of $15,400, of which $3,700 would be material used from the raw material inventory. The work in process, when completed, will probably sell for $40,000 and the sell-

ing cost will be 20% of the sales price. The raw material not used will realize $8,000. Most of the value of the tools consists of special items. After completion of work in process, the tools should sell for $3,000. The supplies inventory which will not be needed to complete work should sell for $1,000.

(4) Land and buildings are mortgaged as security for bonds. They have an appraised value of $95,000. The company recently purchased $20,000 of machinery on a conditional sales contract. They still owe $12,000 principal on this contract, which is included in the notes payable. These machines have a current used value of $10,000. Depreciation taken on these machines amounts to $1,800. The remaining machinery is believed to be salable at $10,000 but cost of selling it may be $1,000.

Instructions

a. Prepare a statement of affairs showing clearly the estimated deficiency to unsecured creditors.

b. Indicate clearly the causes of the deficiency.

c. Compute the percentage of probable payments to the $52,000 accounts payable. Do not assume any expense of liquidation other than that itemized above.

AICPA adapted

20-7 The Nevin Corporation advises you that it is facing bankruptcy proceedings. As the company's CPA, you are aware of its condition.

The balance sheet of the Nevin Corporation at June 30 and supplementary data are presented below:

Assets	
Cash	*$ 2,000*
Accounts receivable, less allowance for bad debts	*70,000*
Inventory, raw material	*40,000*
Inventory, finished goods	*60,000*
Marketable securities	*20,000*
Land	*13,000*
Buildings, less allowance for depreciation	*90,000*
Machinery, less allowance for depreciation	*120,000*
Goodwill	*20,000*
Prepaid expenses	*5,000*
Total assets	*$440,000*

Liabilities & Capital	
Accounts payable	*$ 80,000*
Notes payable	*135,000*
Accrued wages	*15,000*
Mortgages payable	*130,000*
Common stock	*100,000*
Retained earnings (deficit)	*(20,000)*
Total liabilities & capital	*$440,000*

Supplementary data

(1) Cash includes a $500 travel advance which has been spent.

(2) Accounts receivable of $40,000 have been pledged in support of bank loans of $30,000. Credit balances of $5,000 are netted in the accounts receivable total. All accounts are expected to be collected except those for which an allowance has been set up.

(3) Marketable securities consist of government bonds costing $10,000 and 500 shares of Bartlett Company stock. The market value of the bonds is $10,000 and the stock is $18 per share. The bonds have accrued interest due of $200. The securities are collateral for a $20,000 bank loan.

(4) Appraised value of raw materials is $30,000 and finished goods is $50,000. For an additional cost of $10,000, the raw materials would realize $70,000 as finished goods.

(5) The appraised value of fixed assets is: land, $25,000; buildings, $110,000; machinery, $75,000.

(6) Prepaid expenses will be exhausted during the liquidation period.

(7) Accounts payable include $15,000 withheld payroll taxes and $6,000 to creditors, who had been reassured by the president that they would be paid. There are unrecorded employer's payroll taxes in the amount of $500.

(8) Wages payable are not subject to any limitations under bankruptcy laws.

(9) Mortgages payable consist of $100,000 on land and buildings, and a $30,000 chattel mortgage on machinery. Total unrecorded accrued interest for these mortgages amounts to $2,400.

(10) Probable judgment on a pending damage suit is $50,000.

(11) Estimated legal fees and expenses in connection with the liquidation are $10,000.

(12) You have not submitted an invoice for $5,000 for last year's audit, and you estimate a $1,000 fee for liquidation work.

Instructions

a. Prepare a statement of affairs.

b. Compute the estimated settlement per dollar of unsecured liabilities.

AICPA adapted

20-8 The Taylor Corporation is facing bankruptcy proceedings, and the creditors have organized a committee. The chairman of the creditors' committee has employed you to advise him as to what payments the creditors can expect on their claims against Taylor Corporation. You are provided with the balance sheet on page 713, which was prepared by the corporation's bookkeeper.

Your analysis of the corporation's accounts disclosed the following:

(1) Taylor started business April 1, 1961, with authorized capital of $50,000, represented by shares of $100 par value. Of the 500 authorized shares, 375 were fully paid at par and 125 were subscribed at par, payment to be made on call.

TAYLOR CORPORATION
Balance Sheet
as of March 31, 1966

Assets

Cash		$ 2,000
Notes receivable	$ 4,640	
Less: Notes receivable discounted	4,640	
Accounts receivable		4,000
U.S. Treasury bonds		10,000
Inventories:		
Finished goods	$15,000	
Work in process	4,500	
Raw materials	6,000	25,500
Total current assets		$ 41,500
Subscriptions to common stock		12,500
Investments		2,300
Property and equipment:		
Real estate	$45,000	
Factory equipment	24,000	
Total	$69,000	
Less: Accumulated depreciation	20,000	49,000
Total assets		$105,300

Liabilities

Current:		
Notes payable to:		
Manufacturers' Trust Co.	$10,000	
Alex Smith	25,000	$ 35,000
Accounts payable		24,000
Accrued liabilities:		
Salaries and wages	$ 992	
Property taxes	460	1,452
Total current liabilities		$ 60,452
Long-term liabilities:		
First mortgage on real estate	$15,000	
Second mortgage on real estate	20,000	35,000
Total liabilities		$ 95,452

Capital

Capital stock—authorized, subscribed, and issued shares, par $100 per share	$50,000	
Less: Deficit	(40,152)	9,848
Total liabilities & capital		$105,300

(2) The Manufacturers' Trust Company holds $10,000 of U.S. Treasury bonds as security for its $10,000 loan; it also holds the first mortgage of $15,000 on the company's real estate, interest on which is paid through March 31, 1966.

(3) The real estate includes land, which cost $5,000, and a building erected thereon at a cost of $40,000. Of the reserve for depreciation, $5,000 is applicable to the building and $15,000 to the factory equipment. The realizable value of the real estate is estimated to be $30,000.
(4) The note payable to Alex Smith is secured by a chattel mortgage on factory equipment and inventory. Interest on the note has been paid through March 31, 1966.
(5) Alex Smith holds the second mortgage on the real estate.
(6) The notes receivable, $4,640, which were discounted though not yet due, are deemed uncollectible.
(7) Of the accounts receivable of $4,000, $1,000 is considered uncollectible.
(8) Inventories are valued at cost; finished goods are expected to yield 110% of cost. Goods in process cost $4,500 and have a realizable value, if scrapped, of $900. It is estimated, however, that the work in process can be completed as finished goods by the use of $1,200 of raw material and an expenditure of $1,400 for labor and other costs. These goods can also be sold at a price equal to 110% of their cost. The raw material deteriorates rapidly and it is expected that only 25% of this cost will be realized.
(9) The factory equipment, which cost $24,000 on April 1, 1961, is considered to have a realizable value of $5,000 at March 31, 1966.
(10) The subscription to the capital stock for 125 shares at par is due from Wyman Taylor, president of the company, and is fully collectible.
(11) Investments include 15 shares of the common stock of the Magson Company, acquired at a cost of $1,500, which have a market value of $3,390 at March 31, 1966; and 20 shares of treasury stock carried at cost.
(12) Expenses of liquidation and accruals not mentioned need not be considered.

The creditors' committee has called for the payment of the capital stock subscription and has decided to have the goods in process converted into finished goods. Completion of goods in process can be accomplished so quickly that no further expenses, other than those already mentioned, will be incurred.

Instructions

a. Prepare a statement of affairs for Taylor Corporation at March 31, 1966.

b. Prepare a statement of deficiency to unsecured creditors, including explanations where necessary.

c. Prepare a statement of estimated amounts available for each class of creditors, showing ratio of assets available to original claim.

AICPA adapted

20-9 The Hardin Corporation is in financial difficulty because of low sales. Its stockholders and principal creditors want an estimate of the financial results of the liquidation of the assets and liabilities and the dissolution of the corporation. The corporation's trial balance appears on page 715.

HARDIN CORPORATION
Post-closing Trial Balance
December 31, 1966

	Debit	Credit
Cash	$ 1,000	
Accounts receivable	20,500	
Allowance for bad debts		$ 350
Inventories	40,000	
Supplies inventory	3,000	
Downhill Railroad, 5% bonds	5,000	
Accrued bond interest receivable	750	
Advertising	6,000	
Land	4,000	
Building	30,000	
Accumulated depreciation—building		5,000
Machinery and equipment	46,000	
Accumulated depreciation—machinery and equipment		8,000
Accounts payable		26,000
Notes payable—bank		25,000
Notes payable—officers		20,000
Payroll taxes payable		800
Wages payable		1,500
Mortgage payable		42,000
Mortgage interest payable		500
Capital stock		50,000
Retained earnings	29,100	
Reserve for product guarantees		6,200
Totals	$185,350	$185,350

The following information has been collected in anticipation of a meeting of the stockholders and principal creditors to be held on January 2, 1967:

(1) Cash includes a $300 protested check from a customer. The customer stated that he would have funds to honor the check in about two weeks.

(2) Accounts receivable include accounts totaling $10,000 that are fully collectible and have been assigned to the bank in connection with the notes payable. Included in the unassigned receivables is an uncollectible account of $150. The Allowance for Bad Debts account of $350 now on the books will adequately provide for other doubtful accounts.

(3) Purchase orders totaling $9,000 are on hand for the corporation's products. Inventory with a book value of $6,000 can be processed at an additional cost of $400 to fill these orders. The balance of the inventory, which includes obsolete materials with a book value of $1,200, can be sold for $10,500.

(4) In transit at December 31 but not recorded on the books was a shipment of defective merchandise being returned by a customer. Mr. Hardin, president of the corporation, had authorized the return and the refund of the purchase price of $250 after the merchandise had been inspected. Other than this

return, Hardin knows of no other defective merchandise that would bear upon the appropriated Reserve for Product Guarantees account. The merchandise being returned has no salvage value.

(5) The supplies inventory is comprised of advertising literature, brochures, and other sales aids. These could not be replaced for less than $3,700.

(6) The Downhill Railroad bonds are recorded at par value. They were purchased in 1960 for $600, and the adjustment to par value was credited to Retained Earnings. At December 31, 1966, the bonds were quoted at 18% of par value without accrued interest.

(7) The Advertising account represents the future benefits of a 1966 advertising campaign and contains 10% of certain advertising expenditures. Hardin stated that this was too conservative and that 20% would result in a more realistic measure of the market that was created.

(8) The land and building are in a downtown area. A firm offer of $50,000 has been received for the land, which would be used as a parking lot; the building would be razed at a cost of $12,000 to the buyer. Another offer of $40,000 was received for the real estate, which the bidder stated would be used for manufacturing that would probably employ some Hardin employees.

(9) The highest of the offers received from used machinery dealers was $18,000 for all the machinery and equipment.

(10) One creditor, whose account for $1,000 is included in the accounts payable, confirmed in writing that he would accept 90 cents on the dollar if the corporation paid him by January 10.

(11) Wages payable include year-end adjustments of $325 payable to certain factory employees for their overtime during the busy season. All wages meet the test of liabilities with priority.

(12) The mortgage payable is secured by the land and building. The last two monthly principal payments of $200 each were not made.

(13) Estimated liquidation expenses amount to $3,200.

(14) For income tax purposes, the corporation has net operating loss carry-overs for 1961 of $10,000; 1962, $12,000; and 1963, $8,000. (The tax rate is 50%.)

Instructions

a. Prepare a statement of affairs.

b. Compute the estimated settlement per dollar of unsecured liabilities.

AICPA adapted

20-10 The A Corporation of New York, with a branch in Philadelphia, has a wholly owned subsidiary, the B Corporation, which was forced into bankruptcy on June 30, 1967. The creditors of A Corporation formed a committee, following the application of the company's balance of cash on deposit with the Dexter National Bank against its loan to A Corporation.

The following trial balances after closing, June 30, 1967, and other data were furnished to the committee by the company:

A CORPORATION (NEW YORK BOOKS)

Cash—New York Trust Co.	$ 1,524	Notes payable—Dexter National Bank, Philadelphia	$20,000
Securities, at cost (pledged)	14,650	Loans payable—secured, per contra	12,500
Furniture and fixtures	1,000	Capital stock	25,000
Capital stock—B Corp.	7,500		
Advances—Phila. branch	15,680		
Advances—B Corp.	14,640		
Deficit—per books	2,506		
Total	$57,500	Total	$57,500

The pledged securities have a market value of $5,200 and the furniture and fixtures of A Corporation an appraised value of $300.

PHILADELPHIA BRANCH (PHILADELPHIA BOOKS)

Cash—Dexter National Bank, Philadelphia, per bank statement	$ 1,580	Accounts payable	$19,060
Accounts receivable	10,000	Wages payable	1,550
Merchandise inventory, June 30, 1967	9,500	Taxes payable	800
Furniture and fixtures	7,500	Due to A Corp.	15,680
Profit and loss	8,510		
Total	$37,090	Total	$37,090

The sale of the branch assets should realize the following: accounts receivable, $6,200; merchandise, $4,675; furniture and fixtures, $2,500.

The cost of liquidation for New York and Philadelphia should be about $4,000. Receiver and trustee administrative expenses are estimated at $5,000. Checks for $4,520 to merchandise creditors, on which payment was stopped when the bank applied cash on deposit against its loan, have not been adjusted on the above trial balance.

B CORPORATION—ALLEGED BANKRUPT
(assets are at estimated realizable value)

Accounts receivable	$ 5,582	Overdraft—Camden bank	$ 1,600
Land and building	9,860	Loan payable—Camden bank	7,000
Merchandise inventory, June 30, 1967	7,500	Store wages payable	540
Furniture and fixtures	1,230	Office salaries payable	200
John Doe, president—loan account	300	Executive salaries payable—president	1,800
Deficit	34,388	Mortgage payable	12,000
		Mortgage interest accrued	240
		Real estate taxes payable	530
		Accounts payable	12,810
		A Corporation	14,640
		Capital stock	7,500
Total	$58,860	Total	$58,860

The salary of John Doe, the president, is $6,000 per annum. The store wages and office salaries are for the two weeks ending June 30, 1967. The A Corporation is guarantor on the B Corporation mortgage on B Corporation's land and building.

Instructions

Having engaged your services, the committee has instructed you to prepare, from the above information, statements showing

a. The probable amount which should be available for unsecured claims against B Corporation.

b. The probable amount which should be available for creditors of A Corporation in the event of liquidation. (Round all calculations to the nearest dollar.)

AICPA adapted

20-11 The Sellow Furniture Company, Inc., has been finding it more and more difficult to meet its obligations. Although its sales volume appeared to be satisfactory and it was showing a profit, the requirements for capital to carry inventory and time contracts were greater than the company could provide. Finally, after pledging all its installment accounts, it found itself unable to meet the bills falling due on October 10, 1967. It is the opinion of the management that if it could obtain an extension of time in which to pay its obligations, it could meet its liabilities in full. The corporation has arranged for a meeting of creditors to determine if the company should be granted an extension or be forced into bankruptcy.

The trial balance for the current year as of September 30, 1967, is shown on page 719.

Upon further investigation you discover the following additional data:

(1) Depreciation, bad debts, prepaid and accrued items had all been adjusted as of September 30, 1967.

(2) All installment contracts had been pledged with the bank on September 30, 1967; the bank had deducted its interest to date and had increased the company loan to equal 75% of face amount of the contracts in accordance with a loan agreement. It was estimated that a forced liquidation would result in a loss of $40,000 from the face amount of the contracts.

(3) It was estimated that 30-day accounts receivable not pledged would provide $16,500 on a liquidation basis.

(4) It was estimated that since January 1, 1967, the company had made a gross profit of 33⅓%, but that the inventory on hand would provide only $100,000 on a forced liquidation basis.

(5) Cancellation of the insurance would provide $990.

(6) All autos and trucks were covered by a chattel mortgage, and their total market value was $8,000.

(7) The store had been remodeled in 1966 and the furniture and equipment had been acquired on contract. Because of its special utility, it was estimated that on a forced sale no more than $5,000 could be expected.

(8) The land and buildings were subject to a 6% first mortgage on which interest had been paid to July 30, 1967. It was estimated the property could be sold for $75,000.

	Debit	Credit
Cash on hand	$ 500	
Cash in bank	1,620	
Installment contracts pledged	215,000	
Allowance for uncollectible contracts		$ 13,440
Accounts receivable—30-day	30,830	
Allowance for bad debts		1,050
Inventories—Jan. 1, 1967	151,150	
Unexpired insurance	1,490	
Autos and trucks	22,380	
Accumulated depreciation—autos and trucks		14,960
Furniture and equipment	12,500	
Accumulated depreciation—furniture and equipment		2,140
Buildings	89,760	
Accumulated depreciation—building		7,530
Land	10,240	
Organization expense	880	
Trade accounts payable		132,100
Contract payable—furniture and equipment		5,800
Chattel mortgage on autos and trucks		10,000
Bank loan—secured by installment contracts		161,250
Taxes payable		14,220
Accrued salaries and wages		4,680
Accrued interest		10,990
Notes payable—stockholder		100,000
First mortgage		49,000
Capital stock		100,000
Deficit	55,290	
Sales		708,900
Purchases	527,630	
Expenses and miscellaneous income (net)	216,790	
Total	$1,336,060	$1,336,060

(9) The notes payable to stockholders had not been subordinated to general creditors. The notes carried a 6% rate of interest, but no interest had been paid since December 31, 1965.

(10) Since prior income tax returns disclosed a large available net operating loss carry-over, no current income tax need be considered.

(11) The cost of liquidation proceedings was estimated to be $5,000.

(12) There appeared to be no other values on liquidation and no unrecorded liabilities.

Instructions

a. Prepare a statement of affairs.

b. Prepare a statement of estimated deficiency to unsecured creditors.

c. Compute the estimated percentage of recovery by the unsecured creditors if the company were to be forced into bankruptcy.

AICPA adapted

20-12 The Adams-Story Partnership, of which Adams is manager, has had difficulty in meeting its obligations as the debts matured. If the business is dissolved it will require six months. The bookkeeper prepared the following trial balance.

ADAMS-STORY PARTNERSHIP
Trial Balance
April 15

Cash in banks	$ 20,000	
Accounts receivable	100,000	
Allowance for bad debts		$ 4,000
Notes receivable	58,000	
Notes receivable discounted		12,000
Raw materials	9,000	
Work in process	20,000	
Finished goods	15,000	
Prepaid insurance	1,200	
Property held in trust	18,000	
Machinery and equipment, cost	9,000	
Land	12,000	
Building	33,000	
Accumulated depreciation		6,000
Interest receivable on notes	700	
Payroll taxes payable		200
Real estate taxes		1,200
Wages payable		3,450
Notes payable		60,000
Accounts payable		125,700
Mortgage payable, 4%		40,000
Equipment contract payable (purchased on a conditional sales contract)		6,400
Interest payable		1,000
Adams, capital		15,975
Story, capital		1,975
Trust principal		18,000
Totals	$295,900	$295,900

An analysis of the accounts revealed the following:

(1) Cash in First Bank, $8,000; in Second Bank, $12,000.

(2) Of the accounts receivable, 60% are good and fully collectible; 30% are doubtful and considered to be only 80% collectible; the remaining 10% are worthless.

(3) All notes are good and are pledged as security on notes payable to the Factor House of $50,000 with accrued interest of $500.

(4) Of the notes which were discounted at the Manning Bank, it is estimated that one, amounting to $2,000, will not be paid at maturity or thereafter.

(5) All finished goods will be sold for 20% less than their cost. Work in process cannot be sold until finished and can be completed by incurring labor and

material costs of $9,000, of which $3,000 will be from raw material inventory. The balance of the raw material inventory will realize $5,000.

(6) The prepaid insurance, which expires October 15, has a short-term cancellation value on April 15 of $900.

(7) Property held in trust is in the form of stocks and bonds with realizable value of $24,000. The partnership is entitled to a fee of $600 per year, payable April 15, for their services. Cash was not available in the trust for the payment; therefore the fee was not recorded.

(8) The machinery and equipment, with a book value of $8,000, will realize $5,000.

(9) The land and building may be sold for $38,000; however, the mortgage holder has indicated a willingness to cancel the debt and assume all encumbrances for the surrender of title to the real estate. Interest on the mortgage was paid on January 15.

(10) The wages and commissions were last paid in full on December 31. Commission salesmen were dismissed on February 15. Accrued wages in the trial balance are:

Burke, bookkeeper (to Apr. 15)	$1,400
Commission salesman (to Feb. 15)	300
Adams, manager (to Apr. 15)	1,750
	$3,450

(11) The remaining note payable of $10,000 and interest of $100 are unsecured.

(12) The estimated administrative expenses are $3,000.

(13) While Adams has personal liabilities which are approximately equal to his personal assets, Story's personal assets exceed his personal liabilities by $2,800.

Instructions

a. Prepare a statement in good form showing the estimated deficiency, if any, to unsecured creditors.

b. Prepare a statement showing the estimated amount available for each class of creditors.

AICPA adapted

21 RECEIVERSHIP ACCOUNTS

Receivership in equity

When the creditors of a business find that they need protection from the wanton distribution of the assets of a debtor, they may apply to the state or Federal court for a receiver in equity to be appointed. The court in turn will appoint a person designated as a receiver to take charge of the assets of the debtor. Control over the business is thus removed from the debtor and placed in the hands of the receiver until his duties are completed. The receiver acts in a fiduciary capacity, operating under the laws governing such persons and under the instructions of the court having jurisdiction in the case.

The receiver may be appointed to liquidate the business or to make an acceptable settlement with the creditors, or he may be appointed to attempt to restore the financial solvency of the business. If the creditors can be satisfied without liquidating the business, the assets remaining after the settlement will be returned to the owner. The function of the receiver is to assume control of the assets, convert some or all of them into cash, make complete or partial settlement with the creditors, and make interim and final reports to the courts. Major decisions and contracts are made or entered into only with the advice and consent of the court. The court directs the activities of the receiver in many ways; however, he is at liberty to make the day-to-day decisions and to expedite routine matters. Nevertheless, the receiver is acting in a fiduciary capacity and for this reason he is responsible for the safekeeping of the assets as long as they remain under his control. He, therefore, usually finds it desirable to set up a separate set of books to account for the activities during his administration. The accounts established are those necessary to provide for a complete accounting to the courts, creditors, owners, and other interested parties of all of his activities. The records kept by the receiver are not substitutes for the corporate records but are in addition to these records.

The accounts of the receiver should make provision for recording the assets and related valuation accounts at book value at the time that he is appointed. In general the receiver is not responsible for the liabilities owed by the firm at the time of his appointment; therefore, no accounts need be set up for them. Liabilities which are incurred by him are his responsibility and are entered in his records, however. An accountability account is set up to make the receiver's books balance and to indicate the net book value of the assets for which he is accountable. The accountability account is frequently designated by the name of the company followed by the words "in receivership."

On the firm's books, the asset and related valuation accounts are closed when they are turned over to the receiver and an account, including the receiver's name followed by the word "receiver," is opened for the book value of the accounts closed. The new account is a type of receivable indicating that the receiver is indebted to the firm in the amount of these particular assets. No change is made in the liability or capital accounts since they are not disturbed by the transfer of assets.

No special system of accounting is prescribed by the courts; any system is acceptable which will provide the information required by the interested parties. The only requirement is that the receiver be able to offer a full and complete account of his activities with regard to the assets of the firm in receivership during the period he is acting in a fiduciary capacity. The receiver should be able to prove that he has acted prudently and has faithfully fulfilled the responsibilities of his position.

Receivership accounting

The problem of dual accounting for the same transactions arises after the receiver has assumed control of the assets of the firm. He must make entries in his accounts for any change in the assets over which he has control and for any liabilities incurred by him in carrying out his duties as receiver. Similarly, the corporation must make entries for any changes in the liabilities which existed prior to assumption of control by the receiver. Some transactions must be recorded on both sets of books; for example, entries to record the payment by the receiver of liabilities existing prior to the appointment of the receiver must be recorded by the receiver to show disbursement of cash for which he is accountable and they must also be recorded by the firm to show the reduction of the liabilities and the receiver's accountability.

In cases where the receiver is charged only with the liquidation of the enterprise and there is no problem of continuing operations, the accounting problems are usually rather simple. The only events which must be recorded are those related to the conversion of the assets into cash, the payment of the liabilities, and the recognition of any gains or losses arising from the liquidation. After all the assets have been realized and all claims settled, the receiver renders his final report and returns any cash remaining to the owner.

The receiver may also be charged with operating the enterprise for a period of time pending eventual liquidation or rehabilitation of the firm as a going concern.

The objective in the case of planned liquidation after a period of operation is of course to secure the maximum amount for the assets. The accounting problems under either of these alternatives are essentially the same. The additional complication is that the receiver must account for the added activities of operating the business.

Generally when the receiver is charged with operating the enterprise for a period of time, the transactions are recorded only on the books of the receiver at the time of occurrence. He then submits operating reports periodically as directed by the courts and these reports are summarized into entries to be made on the books of the corporation. The problem of transferring the information for the purpose of permitting the debtor to record each transaction is extremely time-consuming and seldom serves any useful purpose. The profit or loss arising from operations results in an increase or decrease in the receivable from the receiver. In order to obtain a complete report on the affairs of the firm in receivership, the events which have been recorded on the firm's books must be combined with the events which have been recorded by the receiver.

Basic procedures illustrated: ***1. Establishment of receivership for Jones Company, J. C. Smith, receiver.*** The receiver records the assets but not the liabilities of the firm; therefore, the entry to establish the receivership on the receiver's books, assuming hypothetical dollar amounts, is as follows:

Cash	5,400	
Accounts Receivable	15,500	
Merchandise Inventory	29,800	
Furniture and Fixtures	8,700	
Allowance for Bad Debts		1,750
Accumulated Depreciation		5,340
Jones Co., in Receivership		52,310
To set up accounts for Jones Co. receivership.		

The firm must make a similar entry to indicate the fact that the assets have been surrendered to the receiver. The following entry would be made on the firm's books:

J. C. Smith, Receiver	52,310	
Accumulated Depreciation	5,340	
Allowance for Bad Debts	1,750	
Cash		5,400
Accounts Receivable		15,500
Merchandise Inventory		29,800
Furniture and Fixtures		8,700
To record the fact that the assets of the business have been turned over to a court-appointed receiver.		

In the first entry the liability to the firm by the receiver has been recognized by the credit to the receivership account. Also, in the second entry the receivable from the receiver has been recorded by the firm by the creation of a receiver's account. These two accounts are self-balancing. Any entry which affects the balance in one of these accounts must be recorded on the books of the other party to the receivership.

2. Payment of liability of Jones Company existing at the date receiver is appointed. Since the receiver does not record the existing liabilities of the debtor on his books, the entry to record the payment of the debt creates some problems. Liabilities of this kind are generally paid only upon order of the court. The payment of this liability reduces the assets for which the receiver is responsible and accordingly reduces the accountability of the receiver. The receiver has the choice of making an entry which will reduce his accountability account directly or he may set up additional temporary accounts to aid in the preparation of his reports at a later date. These temporary accounts are similar to the nominal accounts used to record activities of the period for a going concern. They are closed at the end of the accounting period to the accountability account to arrive at the results of the continued operation. In this case they represent the increase or decrease in the assets for which the receiver is responsible. Assume in the present illustration that Smith pays a bill of Jones Company for $8,000 which was owed prior to appointment of Smith as receiver and that Smith used temporary accounts to reflect changes in his accountability. The following entry would be made by Smith:

Accounts Payable Paid	*8,000*	
Cash		*8,000*
To record the payment of an account owed by Jones at the date the receivership was created.		

Jones Company would make the following entry on its books:

Accounts Payable	*8,000*	
J. C. Smith, Receiver		*8,000*
To record the payment of the bill to ABC Corp. by Smith, the receiver.		

Since the firm is not particularly interested in preparing a report of the activity for the period, there is no need for temporary accounts in the ledger of the debtor. The payment of the debt is therefore credited directly to the receivable from the receiver, indicating the fact that the receiver has been relieved of a portion of his accountability.

3. Realization of assets taken over by the receiver. When the assets which have been taken over by the receiver are sold to obtain cash for the purpose of settling with the creditors, a gain or loss usually will be realized on the conversion. A gain represents an increase in the accountability of the receiver and a loss represents a decrease. As indicated in the preceding illustration, the receiver typically uses temporary accounts to reflect changes in his accountability during the period. In the event that assets are realized at an amount different from their book value, the difference is shown in a temporary account. Assume that $10,000 of the inventory is sold for $7,800. The entry to record the conversion is as follows:

Cash	*7,800*	
Loss on Sale of Assets	*2,200*	
Merchandise Inventory		*10,000*
To record the sale of a portion of the inventory at a loss of $2,200.		

Jones Company needs to reduce the receivable from Smith by the amount of the loss, in this case $2,200. The loss represents a reduction in the ownership equity of Jones Company just as it would if the company were a going concern. Assuming the owners' equity is reduced immediately and that a deficit already existed, the entry would be as follows:

Accumulated Deficit	*2,200*	
J. C. Smith, Receiver		*2,200*
To record a loss on the liquidation of $10,000 of the merchandise inventory in the process of settling creditors' claims by the receiver.		

Although in both this illustration and the preceding one, entries have been made on both sets of books simultaneously, this duplication of record keeping may be avoided. As will be shown in the extended illustration, the firm in receivership may choose to make the entries in summary form at the end of each period when the receiver's report is received.

4. Changes in liabilities or assets existing at the date the receivership is established. Accruals relating to liabilities existing at the time the receiver is appointed should be recorded on the books of the debtor. The receiver is responsible for seeing that the creditors receive equitable treatment; however, he is not responsible for keeping records of liabilities which existed at the time he was appointed. A typical example of such accruals is the accrual of interest on bonds or notes payable which were issued prior to the appointment of the receiver. The accrued interest will be paid by the receiver under the same conditions that the original liability will be discharged.

Since assets are recorded on the receiver's books, any changes in asset values will also be recorded by the receiver. These same changes may be recorded by the debtor. The important point is that the receiver is charged with the protection of the assets and he must keep complete records of the items over which he is acting as custodian. The receiver's report may be a sufficient record for the debtor; therefore, there is no requirement that he keep up with the changes which occur in the assets.

5. Incurrence and payment of liabilities by the receiver subsequent to his appointment. The receiver is frequently authorized by the courts to incur any necessary obligations in order to satisfy more effectively the demands of the creditors. In carrying out his duties, the receiver records these liabilities on his books to distinguish them from the liabilities existing at the date of his appointment. These transactions are recorded by the receiver as a debit to an asset or an expense account and a credit to a liability account, probably Accounts Payable. When the account is paid the entry is to debit Accounts Payable and credit Cash. No change is made in the receivership account and no entries are required on the books of the debtor. The transaction is recorded as it would have been under any ordinary circumstances except that it is recorded by the receiver in the accounts he keeps for the debtor.

6. Operating transactions. When the receiver is so instructed by the courts, he may operate the business for the debtor for a period of time. The purpose of operating the business may be to attempt to save it for the owners or to minimize the loss to the creditors. The receiver is charged with accounting for these transactions in the normal manner. The account classification usually parallels that used by the corporation. No entries need to be made by the insolvent until the periodic reports are submitted by the receiver. When the insolvent company receives the operating results as reported by the receiver, then the profit or loss is recorded in the corporation's accounts and the accountability account is adjusted to reflect the change which has occurred as a result of the operations of the period.

7. Termination of the receivership relationship. The receivership will be terminated when the assets have been realized and an equitable distribution has been made to the creditors or when the firm has been restored to solvency. In either situation the receiver closes his books by closing the accountability account against any assets or losses which remain on the books. Any unpaid liability accounts on the books of the receiver would also be transferred to the debtor through the accountability account. The corporation will also record the termination of the receivership by making entries to show the effect of the receiver's report and by closing the accountability account. If the corporation has been liquidated, the losses are closed to the capital accounts. If the business has been restored to good health, then operations will proceed as usual and the accounts will be kept as they would be for any other solvent corporation.

Statements prepared by receiver. If the receiver is operating the firm for a period of time, it will be necessary for periodic statements of financial position and of operations to be prepared. The information required for these statements includes data on both sets of accounts. The work sheet is a convenient device for combining and adjusting the data in the two sets of accounting records. The working paper usually includes columns for the unadjusted trial balance of the receiver's ledger and of the corporation's ledger. In addition columns are provided for adjustments to both sets of accounts and columns for eliminating the duplicated items. Finally, the work sheet includes columns for balance sheet data and for income statement data. The formal statements are prepared from the last two sets of columns on the work sheet.

The balance sheet may be prepared in the conventional format. The income statement is frequently divided so that the results of the receiver's activities are clearly separate and distinct from those of the debtor. The reason for this separation is merely to identify the particular results with the party responsible for them. In general the greater part of the revenue and expense items result from the actions of the receiver. Therefore, they usually appear first on the statement followed by the items attributable to the debtor. The work sheet and illustrative statements will follow the illustration.

Illustration

Information available. The Tyler Trading Company is on the verge of insolvency and J. Thompson has been appointed by the court as a receiver in equity to take legal possession of the company's assets as of February 1, 1966. On January 31, 1966, the accounts were closed and the following trial balance was prepared:

TYLER TRADING COMPANY
Trial Balance
January 31, 1966

Cash	$ 48,000	
U.S. government bonds	25,000	
Notes receivable	90,000	
Notes receivable discounted		$ 10,000
Accrued interest on notes receivable	3,000	
Accounts receivable	138,000	
Allowance for bad debts		7,500
Inventory	174,200	
Subscriptions receivable: Common stock	20,500	
Buildings	121,400	
Accumulated depreciation		56,540
Prepaid insurance	1,400	
Deficit	47,040	
Notes payable		127,500
Accrued interest on notes payable		9,800
Accounts payable		296,000
Mortgage payable on building		60,000
Accrued interest on mortgage payable		1,200
Common stock		100,000
Totals	$668,540	$668,540

The transactions occurring during the period of the receivership are summarized below:

(a) On February 1, 1966, the receiver opens a set of books for Tyler Trading Company, taking over all the assets listed in the trial balance. All receivable and valuation accounts are designated as *old* to distinguish them from receivables which will arise during the period of receivership. The allowance for bad debts is applicable only to the accounts receivable and not to notes receivable, which are believed to be collectible in full.

(b) Merchandise was purchased on account at gross prices $110,000.

(c) Sales on account at gross prices amounted to $260,000.

(d) Selling expenses of $33,000 and general expenses of $13,000 were incurred by the receiver on account.

(e) Cash collections on accounts receivable—old totaled $104,500 net of discounts of $2,000 and accounts totaling $3,500 were written off.

(f) Cash collected on notes receivable—old of $79,000 totaled $70,910, with

$8,090 written off as a loss. In addition cash was collected representing interest on this note of $4,400 including an accrual of $3,000 recorded as of January 31, 1966.

(g) The maker of the non-interest-bearing note receivable discounted paid only $7,500 at maturity. Receiver was required to pay the unpaid portion of $2,500 plus protest fee of $25.

(h) Liabilities incurred prior to appointment of receiver were paid as follows:

Accounts payable—old (retired at 10% discount)	*$ 45,000*
Accounts payable—old (retired at face amount)	*210,000*
Notes payable—old	*65,200*
Interest on notes payable, including accrual of $9,800	*11,000*
Interest on mortgage payable, including accrual of $1,200	*2,600*

(i) Cash collections on subscriptions receivable: Common stock amounted to $19,500. The balance of $1,000 is uncollectible and is written off.

(j) Securities considered worthless on February 1, 1966, were sold for $4,700. These securities were not included on the balance sheet nor in the receiver's accounts.

(k) Receiver's certificates were issued in the amount of $120,000, with interest at 4½% of par value.

(l) Cash collected on accounts receivable—new totaled $214,400 net of discounts of $10,600.

(m) Interest of $500 was collected on United States government bonds.

(n) Accounts payable of $124,000 were paid after deducting applicable discounts of $2,000.

(o) Interest on receiver's certificates of $2,700 and principal of $40,000 were paid.

(p) Receiver's expenses of $8,000 were paid.

(q) The following data were accumulated at January 31, 1967, as the basis for adjusting the accounts:

Merchandise inventory	*$120,000*
Depreciation of buildings	*3,600*
Accrued taxes	*3,700*
Accrued interest on notes receivable	*300*
Estimated bad debts on new accounts	*800*
Insurance expired	*300*
Interest accrued on old note payable	*2,800*
Interest accrued on old mortgage payable	*1,200*
Interest accrued on receiver's certificates	*900*

(r) At the close of business on January 31, 1967, the receivership was terminated and the assets and unpaid liabilities arising during the year were turned over to Tyler Trading Company.

Journal entries to record transactions of the receivership. The following journal entries would be made by the receiver and Tyler Trading Company, as indicated, to record the affairs of the company during the period of the receivership.

Receiver's Books

		Debit	Credit
(a)	*Cash*	*48,000*	
	U.S. Government Bonds	*25,000*	
	Notes Receivable	*90,000*	
	Accrued Interest on Notes Receivable	*3,000*	
	Accounts Receivable—Old	*138,000*	
	Inventory	*174,200*	
	Subscriptions Receivable: Common Stock	*20,500*	
	Buildings	*121,400*	
	Prepaid Insurance	*1,400*	
	Notes Receivable Discounted		*10,000*
	Allowance for Bad Debts		*7,500*
	Accumulated Depreciation		*56,540*
	Tyler Trading Company, in Receivership		*547,460*
	To open receiver's books.		
(b)	*Purchases*	*110,000*	
	Accounts Payable		*110,000*
	To record purchases of merchandise on account.		
(c)	*Accounts Receivable*	*260,000*	
	Sales		*260,000*
	To record sales on account.		
(d)	*Selling Expenses*	*33,000*	
	General Expenses	*13,000*	
	Accounts Payable		*46,000*
	To record expenses incurred.		
(e)	*Cash*	*104,500*	
	Sales Discounts	*2,000*	
	Allowance for Bad Debts	*3,500*	
	Accounts Receivable—Old		*110,000*
	To record collection of receivables and write-off of uncollectible accounts.		
(f)	*Cash*	*70,910*	
	Loss on Uncollectible Notes	*8,090*	
	Notes Receivable		*79,000*
	To record collection of notes.		

	Account	Debit	Credit
	Cash	*4,400*	
	Accrued Interest on Notes Receivable		*3,000*
	Interest Revenue		*1,400*
	To record collection of interest.		
(g)	*Notes Receivable Discounted*	*10,000*	
	Notes Receivable		*10,000*
	To record maturity of discounted note.		
	Accounts Receivable—Old	*2,525*	
	Cash		*2,525*
	To record payment of balance of discounted note when maker was unable to make full payment.		
(h)	*Accounts Payable Paid*	*260,000*	
	Notes Payable Paid	*65,200*	
	Interest Paid	*1,200*	
	Interest Accrued on Note Payable Paid	*9,800*	
	Interest Paid	*1,400*	
	Interest Accrued on Mortgage Payable Paid	*1,200*	
	Discount on Accounts Payable		*5,000*
	Cash		*333,800*
	To record payment of prior liabilities.		
(i)	*Cash*	*19,500*	
	Bad Debt Expense	*1,000*	
	Subscriptions Receivable: Common Stock		*20,500*
	To record collection of common stock subscriptions.		
(j)	*Cash*	*4,700*	
	Gain on Sale of Securities		*4,700*
	To record sale of securities considered worthless for $4,700.		
(k)	*Cash*	*120,000*	
	Receiver's Certificates Payable		*120,000*
	To record sale of 4½% receiver's certificates.		
(l)	*Cash*	*214,400*	
	Sales Discount	*10,600*	
	Accounts Receivable—New		*225,000*
	To record collection of new accounts.		

		Debit	Credit
(m)	*Cash*	*500*	
	Interest Revenue		*500*
	To record collection of interest on government bonds.		
(n)	*Accounts Payable*	*124,000*	
	Purchase Discounts		*2,000*
	Cash		*122,000*
	To record payment of accounts payable.		
(o)	*Receiver's Certificates Payable*	*40,000*	
	Interest Expense	*2,700*	
	Cash		*42,700*
	To record retirement of portion of receiver-created debt and interest payment for six months.		
(p)	*Receiver's Expenses*	*8,000*	
	Cash		*8,000*
	To record payment of receiver's expenses.		
(q)	*Depreciation Expense*	*3,600*	
	Tax Expense	*3,700*	
	Accrued Interest on Note Receivable	*300*	
	Bad Debt Expense	*800*	
	Insurance Expense	*300*	
	Interest Expense	*900*	
	Accumulated Depreciation		*3,600*
	Taxes Payable		*3,700*
	Interest Revenue		*300*
	Allowance for Bad Debts		*800*
	Prepaid Insurance		*300*
	Accrued Interest on Receiver's Certificates		*900*
	To adjust books at end of year.		
	Merchandise Inventory	*120,000*	
	Purchase Discounts	*2,000*	
	Cost of Goods Sold	*162,200*	
	Purchases		*110,000*
	Merchandise Inventory		*174,200*
	To adjust inventory and cost of goods sold.		
Closing entries			
	Sales	*260,000*	
	Interest Revenue	*2,200*	
	Discount on Accounts Payable	*5,000*	
	Gain on Sale of Securities	*4,700*	
	Income Summary		*271,900*
	To close accounts with credit balances.		

	Dr.	Cr.
Income Summary	*249,890*	
General Expenses		*13,000*
Selling Expenses		*33,000*
Sales Discounts		*12,600*
Loss on Uncollectible Notes		*8,090*
Bad Debts		*1,800*
Interest Expense		*3,600*
Receiver's Expense		*8,000*
Depreciation Expense		*3,600*
Tax Expense		*3,700*
Cost of Goods Sold		*162,200*
Insurance Expense		*300*
To close accounts with debit balances.		
Income Summary	*22,010*	
Tyler Trading Company, in Receivership		*22,010*
To close Income Summary to Accountability account.		
Tyler Trading Company, in Receivership	*338,800*	
Accounts Payable Paid		*260,000*
Notes Payable Paid		*65,200*
Interest Paid		*1,200*
Interest Accrued on Notes Payable Paid		*9,800*
Interest Paid		*1,400*
Interest Accrued on Mortgage Payable Paid		*1,200*
To close temporary accounts for payment of prior liabilities.		

Tyler Trading Company Books

		Dr.	Cr.
(a)	*J. Thompson, Receiver*	*547,460*	
	Notes Receivable Discounted	*10,000*	
	Allowance for Bad Debts	*7,500*	
	Accumulated Depreciation	*56,540*	
	Cash		*48,000*
	Notes Receivable		*90,000*
	Accrued Interest on Notes Receivable		*3,000*
	Accounts Receivable		*138,000*
	Inventory		*174,200*
	Subscriptions Receivable: Common Stock		*20,500*
	U.S. Government Bonds		*25,000*
	Buildings		*121,400*
	Prepaid Insurance		*1,400*
	To charge receiver with assets taken over.		

(h)	*Accounts Payable*	*260,000*	
	Notes Payable	*65,200*	
	Accrued Interest on Notes	*9,800*	
	Interest Expense	*1,200*	
	Accrued Interest on Mortgage Payable	*1,200*	
	Interest Expense	*1,400*	
	J. Thompson, Receiver		*338,800*
	To record liquidation of prior liabilities.		
(q)	*Interest Expense*	*4,000*	
	Interest Accrued on Notes Payable		*2,800*
	Interest Accrued on Mortgage Payable		*1,200*
	To record accrued interest.		
Closing entries			
	J. Thompson, Receiver	*22,010*	
	Income Summary		*22,010*
	To record net income before interest expense as shown by the receiver's books.		
	Income Summary	*6,600*	
	Interest Expense		*6,600*
	To close Interest Expense to Income Summary.		
	Income Summary	*15,410*	
	Deficit		*15,410*
	To close Income Summary to Deficit.		

Termination of the receivership. On January 31, 1967, the receivership is terminated and the assets are transferred to Tyler Trading Company.

Receiver's Books

Accounts Payable	*32,000*	
Receiver's Certificates Payable	*80,000*	
Accumulated Depreciation	*60,140*	
Allowance for Bad Debts	*4,800*	
Taxes Payable	*3,700*	
Accrued Interest on Receiver's Certificates	*900*	
Tyler Trading Company, in Receivership	*230,670*	
Cash		*77,885*
Notes Receivable		*1,000*
Accrued Interest on Notes Receivable		*300*
Accounts Receivable—Old		*28,000*
Accounts Receivable—New		*37,525*

Inventory		*120,000*
U.S. Government Bonds		*25,000*
Buildings		*121,400*
Prepaid Insurance		*1,100*
To transfer assets held by receiver and liabilities created by receiver to Tyler Trading Company.		

Tyler Trading Company's Books

Cash	*77,885*	
Notes Receivable	*1,000*	
Accrued Interest on Notes Receivable	*300*	
Accounts Receivable	*65,525*	
Inventory	*120,000*	
U.S. Government Bonds	*25,000*	
Buildings	*121,400*	
Prepaid Insurance	*1,100*	
Accounts Payable		*32,000*
Receiver's Certificates Payable		*80,000*
Accumulated Depreciation		*60,140*
Allowance for Bad Debts		*4,800*
Taxes Payable		*3,700*
Accrued Interest of Receiver's Certificates		*900*
J. Thompson, Receiver		*230,670*
To take up assets and liabilities held by the receiver at the termination of the receivership.		

The fact should be noted that the two entries to terminate the receivership are practically duplicates except for the reversal of the debits and credits. The two accountability accounts have identical balances, indicating that the books have been kept in agreement during the term of the receivership. Also the designation of old and new can be dropped from the accounts receivable balances because now that they are being taken over by the company this designation is no longer necessary.

Working papers. The accountant may find working papers to be an aid in the preparation of financial statements for the company in receivership. The need for working papers arises because there are two sets of books with accounts related to the financial affairs of the company in receivership. The working paper is not essential; however, in many cases it simplifies the accumulation of the data. The working paper technique is demonstrated for Tyler Trading Company on pages 736 and 737.

In addition to the financial statement working papers, the accountant may also find it convenient to prepare a working paper for the reconciliation of the accountability accounts. This working paper is most helpful when the nominal accounts have been closed and the receivership is to be terminated or when the receiver wants to establish the accuracy of the bookkeeping. The resulting figures may be

TYLER TRADING COMPANY, IN RECEIVERSHIP
Working Papers
January 31, 1967

	Receiver's trial balance		Tyler Trading trial balance		Eliminations		Income statement		Balance sheet	
	Dr	Cr	Dr	Cr	Dr	Cr	Dr	Cr	Dr	Cr
Cash	77,885								77,885	
Notes receivable	1,000								1,000	
Accrued interest on notes	300								300	
Accounts receivable—old	28,000								28,000	
Accounts receivable—new	37,525								37,525	
Inventory	120,000								120,000	
U.S. government bonds	25,000								25,000	
Buildings	121,400								121,400	
Prepaid insurance	1,100								1,100	
Accounts payable		32,000								32,000
Receiver's certificates payable		80,000								80,000
Accumulated depreciation		60,140								60,140
Allowance for bad debts		4,800								4,800
Taxes payable		3,700								3,700
Accrued interest on certificates		900								900
Accrued interest on mortgage				1,200						1,200
Notes payable				62,300						62,300
Mortgage payable				60,000						60,000
Accounts payable				36,000						36,000
Accrued interest on notes				2,800						2,800

Deficit			47,040						47,040	
Sales		260,000						260,000		
Interest revenue		2,200						2,200		
Discounts on accounts payable		5,000						5,000		
Gain on sale of securities		4,700						4,700		
General expenses	13,000						13,000			
Selling expenses	33,000						33,000			
Sales discounts	12,600						12,600			
Loss on uncollectible notes	8,090						8,090			
Bad debts	1,800						1,800			
Interest expense	3,600		6,600				10,200			
Receiver's expense	8,000						8,000			
Depreciation expense	3,600						3,600			
Tax expense	3,700						3,700			
Cost of goods sold	162,200						162,200			
Insurance expenses	300						300			
Accounts payable paid	260,000					260,000				
Notes payable paid	65,200					65,200				
Interest paid	2,600					2,600				
Interest accrued on notes paid	9,800					9,800				
Interest accrued on mortgage paid	1,200					1,200				
Tyler Trading Company, in receivership		547,460			547,460					
J. Thompson, receiver			208,660			208,660				
	1,000,900	1,000,900	262,300	262,300	547,460	547,460	256,490	271,900		
Net income							15,410			15,410
							271,900	271,900	459,250	459,250

used to prepare a balance sheet; however, this working paper does not show revenue and expense figures. This particular working paper is most useful when the receiver has not been required to operate the business. The post-closing working papers for Tyler Trading Company is illustrated below:

TYLER TRADING COMPANY, IN RECEIVERSHIP
Post-closing Working Papers
January 31, 1967

	Receiver's books	Tyler's books	Elimination	Combined balances
Debits				
Cash	77,885			77,885
Notes receivable	1,000			1,000
Accrued interest on notes	300			300
Accounts receivable—old	28,000			28,000
Accounts receivable—new	37,525			37,525
Inventory	120,000			120,000
U.S. government bonds	25,000			25,000
Buildings	121,400			121,400
Prepaid insurance	1,100			1,100
Deficit		31,630		31,630
J. Thompson, receiver		230,670	230,670	
Totals	412,210	262,300	230,670	443,840
Credits				
Accounts payable	32,000	36,000		68,000
Receiver's certificates payable	80,000			80,000
Accumulated depreciation	60,140			60,140
Allowance for bad debts	4,800			4,800
Taxes payable	3,700			3,700
Accrued interest on certificates	900			900
Accrued interest on mortgage		1,200		1,200
Accrued interest on notes		2,800		2,800
Notes payable		62,300		62,300
Mortgage payable		60,000		60,000
Capital stock		100,000		100,000
Tyler Trading Company, in receivership	230,670		230,670	
Totals	412,210	262,300	230,670	443,840

Financial statements. The financial statements of Tyler Trading Company as prepared from working papers are illustrated on page 739. Although the company is in receivership, the statements are presented from the point of view of a going concern. Indeed in the case of Tyler Trading Company this approach is quite realistic. If there is little or no likelihood of the company becoming solvent, a statement of affairs would be more appropriate.

TYLER TRADING COMPANY, IN RECEIVERSHIP
J. Thompson, Receiver
Balance Sheet
January 31, 1967

Assets		
Current assets:		
Cash		$ 77,885
U.S. government bonds		25,000
Notes receivable		1,000
Accrued interest on notes		300
Accounts receivable	$65,525	
Less: Allowance for bad debts	4,800	60,725
Inventory		120,000
Prepaid insurance		1,100
Total current assets		$286,010
Plant and equipment:		
Buildings	$121,400	
Less: Accumulated depreciation	60,140	61,260
Total assets		$347,270

Liabilities & Stockholders' Equity		
Current liabilities:		
Accounts payable		$ 68,000
Notes payable		62,300
Accrued interest payable		4,900
Taxes payable		3,700
Total current liabilities		$138,900
Long-term liabilities:		
Receiver's certificates	$ 80,000	
Mortgage payable	60,000	140,000
Total liabilities		$278,900
Stockholders' equity:		
Common stock	$100,000	
Less: Deficit	31,630	68,370
Total liabilities & stockholders' equity		$347,270

TYLER TRADING COMPANY
J. Thompson, Receiver
Income Statement
for the year ended January 31, 1967

Revenues:		
Gross sales		$260,000
Less: Cash discounts		12,600
Net sales		$247,400
Other revenue:		
Interest revenue	$ 2,200	
Gain on liability settlement	5,000	
Gain on sale of securities	4,700	11,900
Total revenue		$259,300

(continued)

Cost of goods sold:			
Beginning inventory		$174,200	
Purchases	$110,000		
Less: Purchase discounts	2,000	108,000	
Goods available for sale		$282,200	
Less: Ending inventory		120,000	162,200
Gross profit			$ 97,100
Operating expenses:			
General expenses		$ 13,000	
Selling expenses		33,000	
Bad debts		1,800	
Loss on uncollectible note		8,090	
Receiver's expenses		8,000	
Depreciation expense		3,600	
Tax expense		3,700	
Insurance expense		300	71,490
Operating income			$ 25,610
Less: Interest expense			10,200
Net income			$ 15,410

Questions

1. What is the function of the receiver? What purpose should his accounting records serve?
2. What is meant by the term *accountability accounting?*
3. A. Smyth was appointed receiver for Abrams, Inc., on April 1. A trial balance of the ledger of Abrams, Inc., revealed the following:

Trial Balance
April 1

Cash	$ 100	
Accounts receivable	20,400	
Allowance for bad debts		$ 6,700
Inventory	32,300	
Accounts payable		14,000
Bank loan		30,000
Owners' equity		2,100
Totals	$52,800	$52,800

Make the journal entries necessary to create the receivership on the books of both the company and the receiver.

4. When the receiver pays liabilities existing at the date the receivership is created, he frequently debits accounts such as Accounts Payable Paid or Notes Payable

Paid. Why are these accounts used? Why is this procedure preferable to one which debits the Accountability account?

5. Assume that the receiver is able to get the trade creditors with a total claim of $14,000 to settle for 50 cents on the dollar. What entries would be made by the receiver and the bankrupt?

6. In the discussion of receivership accounting, there are frequent illustrations of dual recording of a given transaction. Is this practice necessary? What purpose does it serve?

7. Record the following data in the receiver's books in journal entry form:
 a. Inventory belonging to the bankrupt valued at $7,000 was discovered by the receiver after his books were opened.
 b. Plant assets carried by the receiver at $10,000 were sold for $13,000.
 c. Interest accrued on the first mortgage amounted to $3,000 for the six-month period just ended.
 d. The receiver incurred $6,000 of costs in carrying out his duties during the first year. These activities had the approval of the court.

8. The trial balance for W. Peabody, receiver for the Sandhills Company, which has been declared insolvent, appears as follows:

Trial Balance

Cash	*$ 500*	
Accounts receivable	*26,400*	
Allowance for bad debts		*$ 8,000*
Inventory	*15,000*	
Sandhills Company, in receivership		*33,900*
Totals	*$41,900*	*$41,900*

The following transactions occurred during the succeeding six months:

(1) Merchandise was purchased for $20,000 cash. Inventory at the end of the period is $12,000.
(2) Sales for cash total $37,000.
(3) Expenses incurred and paid total $9,000.
(4) Accounts receivable of $16,000 were collected.
(5) Accounts receivable totaling $9,500 were written off. The balance of the receivables are considered fully collectible.

Record these transactions on the receiver's books in general journal form and close the accounts at the end of the period.

9. The receiver has requested the court's permission to settle with the unsecured creditors of the bankrupt by paying them 50 cents for each dollar claimed. The court grants the request and approves the payment of $8,000 to the receiver as compensation for his services. Upon payment of these claims the receivership is to be closed. The creditors' claims total $80,000 at the present time. The receiver's trial balance at the time of the court order appears on page 742.

Trial Balance

Cash	*$ 48,000*	
Loss on realization of assets	*77,500*	
Gain on realization of assets		*$ 2,400*
Mortgage payable paid	*100,000*	
Accrued interest on mortgage paid	*9,000*	
Receivership account		*232,100*
Totals	*$234,500*	*$234,500*

The bankrupt's trial balance at this time appears as follows:

Trial Balance

Receiver's account	*$232,100*	
Accounts payable		*$ 80,000*
Mortgage payable		*100,000*
Accrued interest payable		*3,000*
Capital		*49,100*
Totals	*$232,100*	*$232,100*

Record in journal entry form the termination of the receivership relationship and the liquidation of the company.

10. What information should be revealed by the financial statements prepared by the receiver? How is the Accountability account handled on a combined balance sheet?

Short case for analysis

21-1 John Adams has recently been appointed as a receiver for Jones Enterprises. He has practically no knowledge of receivership accounting and he has come to you for advice. He does have a fair knowledge of commercial accounting and asks you to relate your remarks to the things he understands.

Instructions

Prepare illustrative entries to record the following events and explain how they differ from those entries which might be made in commercial accounting. Explain to Adams why the difference is necessary.

a. Establishment of receivership
b. Payment of liabilities existing at the date the receivership is established
c. Realization of assets
d. Changes in assets or liabilities existing at the date the receivership began
e. Incurrence of liabilities by receiver
f. Operating transactions
g. Termination of receivership

Problems

21-2 George Perkins, Inc., has recently filed a petition in bankruptcy and Henry Smith has been appointed receiver by the court. The trial balance of George Perkins, Inc., prepared from the general ledger as of the date the receiver takes over, appears below.

Trial Balance
March 10

Cash	*$ 600*	
Accounts receivable	*28,600*	
Inventory	*40,000*	
Furniture and fixtures (net)	*6,000*	
Accounts payable		*$30,000*
Notes payable		*25,000*
Capital stock		*25,000*
Deficit	*4,800*	
Totals	*$80,000*	*$80,000*

The receiver discovered securities with a market value of $2,000 which had been presumed to be valueless and had been written off as a loss. The receiver realized $50,000 on all the assets including the securities and incurred liabilities of $5,000 during the liquidation. The receiver's fee of $8,000 is approved by the court, liabilities incurred by the receiver are paid, and the remaining cash is distributed pro rata among the remaining creditors as they are all unsecured claims.

Instructions

Prepare all the entries in the receiver's accounts required to account for the activity of the receiver, including opening and closing entries.

21-3 The following trial balance was taken from the books of Jason Corporation, In Receivership and Henry Beagle, Receiver at the close of business on December 31.

Trial Balance
December 31

Cash	*$ 40,000*	
Accounts receivable—old	*15,000*	
Accounts receivable—new	*80,000*	
Marketable securities	*20,000*	
Raw materials	*78,000*	
Work in process	*99,500*	
Finished goods	*116,000*	
Prepaid expenses	*2,400*	
Plant assets—net	*190,000*	
Accounts payable		*$ 70,000*
Notes payable—old		*24,000*
Accrued interest payable—old		*150*
Notes payable—new		*40,000*
Mortgage payable—old		*120,000*
Accrued interest on mortgage		*2,200*
Capital stock		*225,000*
Retained earnings		*66,190*
Sales		*800,000*

Sales returns and discounts	6,000	
Purchases	210,000	
Purchase returns and discounts		2,000
Labor cost	215,000	
Other factory costs	100,000	
Salaries	40,000	
General and selling expenses	90,000	
Bad debts	4,000	
Interest expense	10,640	
Receiver's expense and fees	15,000	
Tax expense	18,000	
Accounts payable paid	85,000	
Interest paid	8,640	
Interest accrued on notes paid	150	
Interest accrued on mortgage paid	2,200	
Jason Corporation, in receivership		524,890
Henry Beagle, receiver	428,900	
Totals	$1,874,430	$1,874,430

The ending inventories were raw materials, $28,000; work in process, $49,500; and finished goods, $36,000.

Instructions

a. Prepare a working paper showing accounts properly classified between receiver's books and corporation's books, elimination entries, cost of goods sold, net income or loss, and a year-end balance sheet.

b. Prepare any entries necessary to close the books for the year for both the corporation and the receiver.

21-4 The following trial balance was prepared from the books of the Adamson Corporation, In Receivership and J. Nagle, Receiver as of March 31, the end of the receivership period.

Trial Balance
March 31

Cash	$ 48,000	
Accounts receivable—old	3,000	
Accounts receivable—new	38,000	
Inventory	91,500	
Equipment (net)	16,250	
Accounts payable—old		$ 4,000
Accounts payable—new		29,000
Notes payable—new 6%		40,000
Bonds payable—old 5%		50,000
Capital stock		80,000
Retained earnings	37,850	
Sales		320,000

Purchases	*180,000*	
Selling and administrative expenses	*69,000*	
Accounts payable paid	*130,000*	
Bond interest expense	*2,500*	
Bond interest paid	*2,500*	
Note interest expense	*2,400*	
Receiver's expenses and fees	*10,000*	
J. Nagle, receiver	*93,650*	
Adamson Corporation, in receivership		*226,150*
Bad debts	*24,500*	
Totals	*$749,150*	*$749,150*

Instructions

Prepare all entries necessary to close the corporation's and the receiver's books and to transfer the control of the business from the receiver to the owners.

21-5 The following trial balance was prepared by the bookkeeper for McKellips, Inc., on September 30:

Trial Balance
September 30

Cash	*$ 22,000*	
Accounts receivable	*189,700*	
Inventory	*362,500*	
Plant assets—net	*195,000*	
Accounts payable		*$492,000*
Capital stock		*200,000*
Retained earnings		*77,200*
Totals	*$769,200*	*$769,200*

The creditors of the company were pressing for settlement of their claims and the company applied to the court for a receiver to liquidate or operate the business until it was in better financial condition. John Hughes was appointed receiver and he took charge of the business on October 1.

During the following six months, Hughes collected $156,000 of the old receivables and wrote off the remainder. He made sales of $506,000 on account and collected $462,000 of the accounts; of the balance, only one account of $800 was considered uncollectible. He paid off all the old creditors, incurred a total of $82,560 of expenses of which $50,000 were paid for (and charged off $12,600 of depreciation during his administration). At the end of six months Hughes requested that he be relieved of his responsibility and be paid $15,000 for his services. An audit by a CPA firm revealed that all balances were correct and that a physical inventory of the merchandise indicated it was all in salable condition and had a value, at cost, of $66,450. The court ordered the $1,500 fee of the CPA to be paid by the receiver and authorized the payment of the receiver's fee. All assets and unpaid liabilities were returned to the owners following the payment of the above claims.

Instructions

a. Prepare all journal entries required to account for the receiver's actions during the period of his receivership on the receiver's books.

b. Prepare a balance sheet for the company on the day it was returned to its owners.

21-6 The following trial balances were taken from the books of Foster Fulp, Inc., In Receivership and J. T. White, Receiver at December 31.

Trial Balances
December 31

	Foster Fulp, Inc.		*J. T. White, Receiver*	
	Dr	*Cr*	*Dr*	*Cr*
Cash			*$ 21,600*	
Accounts receivable			*49,000*	
Inventory			*143,400*	
Land and building (net)			*146,000*	
Equipment (net)			*68,600*	
Accounts payable				*$ 38,750*
Note payable—old		*$ 60,000*		
Accrued interest payable		*200*		
Capital stock		*150,000*		
Retained earnings		*103,450*		
Sales				*490,000*
Purchases			*320,000*	
General and selling expense			*58,200*	
Interest expense	*$ 3,600*			
Accrued wages paid			*4,300*	
Accrued interest paid			*200*	
Interest paid			*3,400*	
Accounts payable—old paid			*98,600*	
Bad debts			*32,000*	
Foster Fulp, Inc., in receivership				*416,550*
J. T. White, receiver	*310,050*			
Totals	*$313,650*	*$313,650*	*$945,300*	*$945,300*

The ending inventory as determined by physical count was $68,500 at December 31. All other year-end adjustments have been made.

Instructions

a. Prepare a work sheet showing the income statement and the balance sheet for Foster Fulp, Inc., In Receivership at December 31.

b. Make all entries necessary to close both sets of books assuming that the receiver is relieved of his obligations and the assets are returned to Foster Fulp, Inc.

21-7 John Burton Company finds itself in a position where it is forced to liquidate, because of its inability to borrow money or to obtain an extension of credit from its suppliers. The company files a petition for voluntary bankruptcy and the court appoints J. F. Hillman as receiver to handle the liquidation. A trial balance of the company's general journal ledger is presented below:

Trial Balance
July 31

	Dr	Cr
Cash	$ 3,200	
Accounts receivable	8,640	
Materials and supplies	12,960	
Contracts in process	51,200	
Completed contracts	11,200	
Prepaid expenses	7,475	
Land and buildings	68,000	
Accumulated depreciation		$ 22,500
Plant equipment	36,160	
Accumulated depreciation		24,300
Accumulated deficit	53,915	
Accounts payable		82,750
First mortgage, land and building		27,200
Interest on mortgage		368
Notes payable		19,680
Salaries and wages payable		3,760
Taxes payable		192
Capital stock—par value $50		72,000
Totals	$252,750	$252,750

The trustee is aware at the time of his appointment that the account "completed contracts" is composed entirely of charges representing allowances to customers for unsatisfactory work and excess materials which were purchased for a specific job. The realizable value of these items is zero.

The receiver's cash account at September 30 is summarized below.

At this time all the assets to be realized have been disposed of and all liabilities to be liquidated have been paid. The receiver is thereby ordered by the court to distribute the remaining cash to the owners and to close the accounts.

Debits

Balance, July 31	$ 3,200
Sale of land and building	46,640
Sale of plant equipment	24,270
Sale of materials and supplies	11,060
Collections of accounts receivable	4,390
Collection from customers on partially completed contracts	49,824
Cash realized from sale of prepaid expenses	6,230
Total	$145,614

Credits

Mortgage:	
Principal	*$ 27,200*
Interest	*400*
Salaries and wages	*3,760*
Taxes	*192*
Accounts payable	*82,750*
Notes payable	*19,680*
Liquidation expenses	*4,710*
Balance, Sept. 30	*6,922*
Total	*$145,614*

Instructions

Prepare in general journal form all the entries necessary to record the activity of the receiver during the period of the receivership on the receiver's books.

21-8 The Wilford Manufacturing Company has been adjudged insolvent and a court-appointed receiver took charge of the business on June 15, at which time the following trial balance was prepared:

Trial Balance
June 15

	Dr	*Cr*
Cash on hand	*$ 1,200*	
Receivables	*2,100*	
Finished goods	*150,000*	
Materials and supplies	*22,500*	
Goods on consignment	*330,000*	
Unexpired insurance	*1,200*	
Machinery and equipment	*760,950*	
Accounts payable		*$ 165,000*
Bank overdraft		*1,500*
Notes payable—bank		*207,000*
Notes payable—Adams, Inc.		*375,000*
City taxes accrued		*6,000*
Mortgage on machinery		*150,000*
Accrued interest on mortgage		*4,500*
Accumulated depreciation		*10,950*
Capital stock—preferred		*150,000*
Capital stock—common		*150,000*
Retained earnings		*48,000*
Totals	*$1,267,950*	*$1,267,950*

The receiver has not kept a set of accounts during the first six months of his tenure; at the direction of the court you are hired to set up a set of books and record the transactions for the period.

On December 15 you undertake to record the activities of the past six months and obtain the following facts from the checkbook and from correspondence:

(1) Cash receipts:

Collection of accounts receivable	*$ 1,500*
Rebate upon cancellation of insurance	*150*
Proceeds from cash surrender value of life insurance on life of manager	*1,500*
Sales of finished goods during receivership	*112,500*
Rent on portion of building sublet	*1,500*
Unclaimed wages	*750*
Sale of all remaining goods and supplies	*37,500*
Sale of all machinery and equipment owned	*300,000*
	$455,400

(2) Cash disbursements:

City taxes paid	*$ 6,000*
Interest on city taxes	*600*
Mortgage	*150,000*
Interest on mortgage	*7,500*
Labor, materials, and other operating and general expenses during receivership	*61,000*
	$225,100

(3) Of the inventory of finished goods on hand June 15, $90,000 was sold and $13,500 of materials and supplies were used.

(4) The accounts payable were understated by $15,000 on June 15 and included one item for $7,500 which is in dispute. Proper claims have been filed for all other liabilities except for one account payable totaling $10,500 for which no claim has been filed.

(5) The merchandise on consignment was pledged as collateral for the loan from Adams, Inc., and it was accepted at book value in partial settlement of their claim.

(6) Receiver's fees and expenses to date total $8,500.

Instructions

Prepare the journal entries on receiver's books to record the activity of the receiver for the six-month period.

AICPA adapted

21-9 Aldous-Barker Company is facing financial difficulty because of maturing debt obligations. The bookkeeper has prepared the post-closing trial balance as of December 31 shown on page 750.

Trial Balance
December 31

Cash	*$ 25,000*	
Accounts receivable	*150,000*	
Allowance for uncollectibles		*$ 10,000*
Notes receivable	*82,000*	
Notes receivable discounted		*15,000*
Raw materials	*13,000*	
Work in process	*32,000*	
Finished goods	*19,500*	
Prepaid insurance	*1,800*	
Machinery and equipment—cost	*24,000*	
Building—cost	*50,000*	
Land	*16,000*	
Accumulated depreciation—building		*4,000*
Accumulated depreciation—machinery and equipment		*5,000*
Interest receivable	*2,100*	
Payroll taxes payable		*300*
Real estate taxes		*1,800*
Wages payable		*4,750*
Notes payable—non-interest-bearing		*90,000*
Accounts payable		*180,400*
Mortgage payable, 6%		*60,000*
Equipment contract payable		*20,000*
Interest payable on mortgage		*1,800*
Aldous, capital		*18,600*
Barker, capital		*3,750*
Totals	*$415,400*	*$415,400*

The partners decide to liquidate the partnership and file a petition of voluntary bankruptcy. The court appoints James Cannon, CPA, as receiver, to assume his responsibilities on January 2.

During the course of the receivership the following transactions occur:

(1) Realization of receivables:

Collection of accounts	$135,000
Accounts written off as uncollectible	15,000
Collection of notes and interest	64,000
Notes written off as uncollectible	5,000
Interest written off as uncollectible	500

The discounted note is paid at maturity.

(2) Realization of inventory and prepayments: Work on the in-process inventory was continued, using $4,000 of the raw materials and incurring $18,000 in other costs including labor cost. The liability thus created was paid from the proceeds of the sale of finished product, which totaled $68,000. The remainder of the raw materials was sold for $5,000. The insurance policy was canceled, resulting in a refund of $450.

(3) Realization of plant assets: The machinery and equipment were returned to the vendor, who was holding a conditional sales contract in full satisfaction of that indebtedness. The land and building were sold for $64,000.
(4) Aldous is personally bankrupt, and Barker has only $5,000 which is available for creditors of the partnership.
(5) The receiver's commission and expenses were $12,000 as approved by the court.
(6) The court approved the receiver's actions and ordered the payment of liabilities with those having priority being paid in full, with those being secured being paid to the extent of the proceeds from the sale of pledged assets, and with the unsecured creditors sharing the remaining resources after the payment of $5,000 by Barker to the partnership.

Instructions

Record all the receiver's activities in general journal form on the receiver's books only.

21-10 D. C. Richardson has been acting as a court-appointed receiver of Maddox, Inc., for the past year. At the end of the year, in the process of preparing financial statements for the court, he discovers that the Accounts Payable account in his accounts has a debit balance. He cannot understand this and he brings his trial balance to you to ask for help.

Trial Balances

	Maddox, Inc.		*D. C. Richardson, Receiver*	
	Dr	*Cr*	*Dr*	*Cr*
Cash			$116,700	
Inventory			168,000	
Receivables—old			40,000	
Accounts payable—old		$ 90,000		
Accounts payable—new			60,000	
Accrued interest payable		700		
Accrued salaries payable		9,500		
Note payable—old, 6%		150,000		
Capital stock		200,000		
Retained earnings	$ 60,000			
Sales				$200,000
Purchases			125,000	
Other expenses			50,000	
Salaries			21,500	
Interest expense			9,000	
Maddox, Inc., in receivership				390,200
D. C. Richardson, receiver	390,200			
Totals	$450,200	$450,200	$590,200	$590,200

Additional data

A physical inventory of the goods on hand at the end of the year totals $32,500. It is estimated that only 40% of the receivables unpaid at the end of the year will be collected. No entries have been made on the books of the corporation since the receiver took over the affairs of the business. All sales of assets have been made for cash and all bills incurred by the receiver have been paid. The liabilities having priority have been paid by the receiver.

Instructions

a. Indicate the errors which have been made in recording the transactions by the receiver and explain what he should have done.

b. Make any entries necessary to correct the accounts.

c. Prepare financial statements for the court at the end of the receiver's first year.

21-11 At the meeting of the creditors of Sellow Furniture Company, Inc., the creditors decided to force the company into bankruptcy proceedings. Accordingly, a petition was filed with the court and J. Hansen was appointed receiver. The trial balance prepared by the bookkeeper of Sellow presented below was given to Hansen as the basis for his take-over of the company.

Trial Balance
September 30, 1967

Cash on hand	$ 500	
Cash in bank	1,620	
Installment contracts pledged	215,000	
Allowance for uncollectible contracts		$ 13,440
Accounts receivable—30-day	30,830	
Allowance for uncollectible accounts		1,050
Inventories—Jan. 1, 1967	151,150	
Unexpired insurance	1,490	
Autos and trucks	22,380	
Accumulated depreciation—autos and trucks		14,960
Furniture and equipment	12,500	
Accumulated depreciation—furniture and equipment		2,140
Buildings	89,760	
Accumulated depreciation—buildings		7,530
Land	10,240	
Organization expense	880	
Trade accounts payable		132,100
Contract payable—furniture and equipment		5,800
Chattel mortgage on autos and trucks		10,000
Bank loan—secured by installment contracts		161,250
Taxes payable		14,220
Accrued salaries and wages		4,680

Accrued interest (stockholder note $10,500; interest for past 21 months; and chattel mortgage $490)		*10,990*
Notes payable—stockholder		*100,000*
First mortgage on land and buildings		*49,000*
Capital stock		*100,000*
Retained earnings	*55,290*	
Sales		*708,900*
Purchases	*527,630*	
Expenses and miscellaneous income (net)	*216,790*	
Totals	*$1,336,060*	*$1,336,060*

Hansen was informed that the adjustments for depreciation, bad debts, prepaid and accrued items had been made as of September 30, 1967. In addition, all installment contracts had been pledged with the bank on September 30, 1967. The bank had deducted interest owed to date and had increased the loan to the company to 75% of the face amount of the contracts in accordance with the loan agreement. The cost of the ending inventory as determined by a physical count was $207,000.

The proceeds realized from the liquidation of the assets were:

Installment contracts pledged	*$172,500*
Accounts receivable—30-day	*14,400*
Inventories	*128,000*
Short-term cancellation of insurance	*650*
Autos and trucks	*9,250*
Furniture and equipment	*6,000*
Land and buildings	*72,000*

The liquidation expenses and receiver's fees totaled $18,000, $6,000 of which had been paid during the process of liquidation. The notes payable to stockholders were not subordinated to the claims of the general creditors.

The court approved the receiver's activities and authorized the payment of cash to the creditors in accordance with the plan submitted to pay the priority claims and the partially secured claims to the extent covered by the security and to divide the remaining assets among the unsecured creditors pro rata on the basis of their claims.

Instructions

Make general journal entries required on the books of Sellow Furniture Company, Inc., and J. Hansen, Receiver, to record the receiver's activities and to close the accounts on both sets of books. (Round all calculations to the nearest dollar.)

AICPA adapted

21-12 On February 28 the court appointed J. C. Smith, receiver, to take over the affairs of King Corp., which had been unable to pay its obligations. The following trial balance was prepared from the general ledger:

Trial Balance
February 28

Cash	$ 33,000	
Notes receivable	57,000	
Accounts receivable	219,000	
Inventory of merchandise	145,500	
Investments cost	30,000	
Plant and equipment	520,000	
Accumulated depreciation		$ 85,000
Notes payable		105,000
Accounts payable		480,000
Capital stock—par value $10		150,000
Retained earnings		184,500
Totals	$1,004,500	$1,004,500

The following facts were discovered and transactions completed by the receiver during the subsequent six-month period:

Accrued liabilities existing, but unrecorded, at February 28 totaled $16,800.

Transactions relating to operations are summarized as follows:

Sales on account	$130,000
Purchases on account	55,000
Selling and general expenses incurred and paid in cash	23,000
Reductions in receivables:	
Old accounts:	
Collections	195,000
Sales returns	12,000
Written off	10,000
Sales discount	2,000
New accounts:	
Collections	82,000
Sales returns	3,000
Sales discounts	1,400
Estimated uncollectible	2,000
Old notes:	
Collections	52,000
Written off	5,000
Reductions in liabilities:	
Old accounts:	
Paid	205,000
Signed notes	275,000
Old notes:	
Paid	20,000
Extended	85,000
New accounts:	
Paid	35,000

Other transactions:

Sold investments for $37,500 cash.
Received dividends on investments of $2,600.
Collected interest on notes receivable of $40.
Paid interest on notes payable of $2,800, including beginning accrual of $300.
Paid receiver's expenses of $6,800.

The following data were accumulated on August 31 for the purpose of adjusting the accounts at that date:

Merchandise inventory—cost	*$78,500*
Depreciation of plant assets	*3,000*
Accrued taxes	*2,600*
Accrued interest payable	*1,400*

Instructions

a. Record the transactions required on the books of King Corp. and J. C. Smith, Receiver, to establish the receivership, to record transactions occurring during the period, and to adjust and close the books on August 31.

b. Prepare a balance sheet as of August 31 and an income statement for the period ending August 31 for King Corp.

22 REALIZATION AND LIQUIDATION STATEMENTS, REORGANIZATION, AND ARRANGEMENTS

Realization and liquidation statements

The realization and liquidation statement is prepared periodically by or for the trustee or receiver in bankruptcy to report on his operation of the business and his progress in the realization of assets and liquidation of liabilities. It is in fact a summary of: (1) the financial position of the bankrupt at the beginning of the particular reporting period, with the exception of the cash balance and the owner's equity; (2) the assets acquired and the liabilities incurred during the period; (3) the proceeds from the sale of assets and the payments of liabilities as a result of the receiver's activities; (4) the financial position of the bankrupt at the end of the reporting period, again with the exception of cash and owners' equity; and finally (5) the gain or loss resulting from the receiver's activities.

To include all this information on one statement is a major task and one quite different from preparing traditional financial statements, although much of the same information is found on the balance sheet and income statement. The realization and liquidation statement may take many forms, and frequently the particular form it takes is dictated by the court. The more common form resembles an ordinary ledger account. As a matter of fact, the statement is frequently referred to as the realization and liquidation account. A typical presentation would be developed according to the following outline:

BANTER COMPANY, IN RECEIVERSHIP
Harry Candle, Receiver
Statement of Realization and Liquidation
for the month ended May 31, 19__

Assets to be realized: All assets, except for cash, listed at their carrying (book) values at the beginning of the period		Liabilities to be liquidated: All liabilities known to exist at the beginning of the period, listed at their liquidation amount
Assets acquired: All assets, except for cash, discovered or acquired during the period listed at cost or estimated fair value		Liabilities incurred: All liabilities discovered or incurred during the period, listed at liquidation amount
Supplementary charges: All expenses of the period, except for asset expirations and realization losses		Supplementary credits: All revenues of the period, except for gains on asset realization and liability liquidation
Liabilities liquidated: All liabilities which are settled during the period		Assets realized: Proceeds from the realization of the various assets
Liabilities not liquidated: All liabilities known to exist at the end of the period, listed at their liquidation amount		Assets not realized: All assets, except for cash, not realized during the period, listed at their carrying value at the end of the period
Net gain: A net gain will have resulted if the balance on the right side is greater than that on the left. A net gain is composed of (1) the difference between the supplementary charges and credits, (2) the difference between the realization proceeds and the carrying value of the realized assets, and (3) the difference between the outlays to liquidate liabilities and their indicated liquidation amount	or	Net loss: A net loss will have resulted if the balance on the left side is greater than that on the right. A net loss is composed of the same elements as a net gain, except that the charges and losses exceed the credits and gains
Balance: Total of left column		Balance: Total of right column

If one thinks of the left column as the debit column and the right column as the credit column, the ledger account organization becomes apparent. The beginning asset balance and the cost of assets acquired during the period are found in the left column. The proceeds realized from the disposition of assets and the book value of the assets remaining are found in the right column. We should note that it is not necessary for the asset values in the two columns to be equal, as for debits and credits in the typical ledger account. The difference between these two totals is the gain or loss resulting from the disposition of the assets, and it is reflected in the net gain or loss at the bottom of the statement. A similar analysis can be made of the liabilities.

Note that the realization and liquidation statement contains no gain and loss accounts and that only limited information is given about revenues and expenses. For this reason the cause of the net gain or loss, the balancing figure, is not readily apparent. The statement follows this pattern because the court requires that only the net change, gain or loss, be reflected. The fiduciary status of the trustee places him in the position of protecting the asset values rather than in the position of actively seeking a profit. The report is concerned, therefore, with the status of the estate rather than with the results of operations.

The information to be presented in the realization and liquidation statement should first be recorded in ledger accounts in an orderly manner, using the double-entry system. The desired information can then be selected from the ledger and used in the preparation of the statement. This approach is of course a familiar one for the accountant. His system of accounts is a means of classification which permits him to accumulate data in meaningful aggregates for use in reporting. The same procedure will be helpful in the preparation of a realization and liquidation statement.

Anatomy of the realization and liquidation statement

The information needed in the preparation of the realization and liquidation statement may be classified in five ledger control accounts: (1) cash, (2) all other assets, (3) all monetary claims against the assets, (4) owners' equity, and (5) profit and loss summary. The statement usually includes details derived from the subsidiary ledgers supporting control accounts (2) and (3), together with the balance of control account (5). It is usually supplemented by separate schedules for cash and owners' equity.

The ledger detail necessary to produce the statement varies depending upon the information the receiver is required to show. In general the function of the statement is to recapitulate the receiver's activities for the period. This means that the proceeds received from the realization of assets, the resources used in satisfying obligations, and the transactions of the receiver which consume resources or place claims against the resources should be included in the statement. There seems to be a general feeling that full disclosure of gains and losses is not necessary; however, it is desirable for the receiver or the preparer of the statement to be fully cognizant of all such facts when the statement is prepared.

Illustration

The basic procedures used in the preparation of the conventional realization and liquidation statement are illustrated with the following example:

The Specialty Shops Company was unable to meet its obligations. As a result John Mann was appointed receiver on February 5. The trial balance on page 759 was taken from the books as of that date.

In the period from February 5 to April 30, the receiver's actions resulted in the following:

1. An audit of the accounts receivable disclosed an additional $423 of accounts receivable which had not been brought on the books.

Trial Balance

Cash	*$ 764*
Accounts receivable	*5,928*
Merchandise	*16,536*
Prepayment of expenses	*704*
Fixtures, at cost	*12,342*
Total	*$36,274*
Accounts payable	*$15,987*
Notes payable	*3,500*
Accrued wages, taxes, etc.	*1,275*
Accrued rent	*600*
Accumulated depreciation	*3,803*
Capital stock	*10,000*
Retained earnings	*1,109*
Total	*$36,274*

2. Merchandise costing $8,310 was sold for $9,108 cash.

3. A portion of the fixtures, which cost $5,376 and had accumulated depreciation credits of $942, was sold.

4. Accounts receivable totaling $1,882 were collected. Other accounts amounting to $741 were determined to be worthless.

5. Claims were approved and paid for $903 of the wages and taxes which were accrued at February 5. Wage claims for $125 which were unrecorded on February 5 were also approved and paid. Other claims remain unpaid.

6. Expenses for wages and supplies used in liquidating the business to April 30 amounted to $1,245. (Fees for the receiver need not be considered.)

7. Rent under leases has continued to accrue in the amount of $900. Interest of $70 accrued on notes payable.

8. Cash receipts and cash disbursements show the following:

Cash Receipts

Collection of accounts	*$ 1,882*
Sales of merchandise	*9,108*
Sale of fixtures	*1,000*
Total	*$11,990*

Cash Disbursements

Accrued wages and taxes	*$ 1,028*
Expenses of the receivership	*1,245*
Total	*$ 2,273*

The activities of the receiver for the period February 5 through April 30 are summarized in the following ledger accounts:

Cash

Balance, Feb. 5	764	*Accrued wages and taxes*	1,028
Sales of merchandise	9,108	*Expenses of the receivership*	1,245
Sale of fixtures	1,000		
Collection of accounts	1,882	*Balance*	10,481

Other Assets

Assets to be realized:		*Assets realized:*	
Accounts receivable	5,928	*Sales of merchandise*	8,310
Merchandise	16,536	*Sale of fixtures*	4,434
Prepayment of expenses	704	*Collection of accounts*	1,882
Fixtures (net)	8,539	*Write-off of bad accounts*	741
Assets discovered:		*Assets not realized:*	
Accounts receivable	423	*Accounts receivable*	3,728
		Merchandise	8,226
		Prepayment of expenses	704
		Fixtures (net)	4,105

Liabilities

Liabilities liquidated:		*Liabilities to be liquidated:*	
Accrued wages, taxes, etc.	1,028	*Accounts payable*	15,987
Liquidating wages and supplies	1,245	*Notes payable*	3,500
		Accrued wages, taxes, etc.	1,275
		Accrued rent	600
Liabilities to be liquidated:		*Liabilities discovered:*	
Accounts payable	15,987	*Accrued wages*	125
Notes payable	3,500	*Liabilities incurred:*	
Interest payable	70	*Liquidating wages and supplies*	1,245
Accrued rent	1,500	*Accrued rent*	900
Accrued wages	372	*Accrued interest*	70

Profit and Loss

Loss on sale of fixtures	3,434	*Gain on sale of merchandise*	798
Loss from bad debts	741	*Assets acquired*	423
Liquidating wages and supplies	1,245		
Additional wages	125		
Lease accruals	900		
Accrued interest	70	*Net loss*	5,294

Owners' Equity

Net loss	5,294	*Capital stock*	10,000
		Retained earnings	1,109
Ending balance:			
Capital stock	10,000		
Deficit	(4,185)		

The following realization and liquidation statement for The Specialty Shops Company includes all the information shown above in the accounts. This is a slight departure from the usual form but provides a more complete explanation of the statement than can be achieved by omitting information about the realization gains and losses. The loss indicated in the following statement consists of the loss on realization of $5,592 plus the unrecorded accrued wage of $125 less the unrecorded receivable of $423, for a net change in owners' equity of $5,294. In this particular statement, the loss can be substantiated by deducting the supplementary credits from the supplementary debits.

THE SPECIALTY SHOPS COMPANY, IN RECEIVERSHIP
John Mann, Receiver
Statement of Realization and Liquidation
for the period February 5 to April 30

Debits		*Credits*	
Assets to be realized:		*Liabilities to be liquidated:*	
Accounts receivable	$ 5,928	Accounts payable	$15,987
Merchandise	16,536	Notes payable	3,500
Prepaid expenses	704	Accrued wages, taxes, etc.	1,275
Fixtures (net)	8,539	Accrued rent	600
	$31,707		$21,362
Assets discovered:		*Liabilities discovered:*	
Accounts receivable	423	Accrued wages	125
Supplementary charges:		*Liabilities incurred:*	
Loss on sale of fixtures	3,434	Liquidating expenses	1,245
Loss from bad debts	741	Accrued rent	900
Liquidating expenses	1,245	Accrued interest	70
Lease accruals	900	*Assets realized:*	
Interest expense	70	Accounts receivable	2,623
Liability discovered	125	Merchandise	8,310
Liabilities liquidated:		Fixtures	4,434
Accrued wages, taxes, etc.	1,028	*Supplementary credits:*	
Liquidating expenses	1,245	Gain on sale of merchandise	798
Liabilities not liquidated:		Discovered accounts receivable	423
Accounts payable	15,987	*Assets not realized:*	
Notes payable	3,500	Accounts receivable	3,728
Interest payable	70	Merchandise	8,226
Accrued rent	1,500	Prepaid expenses	704
Accrued wages	372	Fixtures (net)	4,105
		Net loss	5,294
Total	$62,347	Total	$62,347

Supplementary schedules should be prepared to explain the changes in cash and owners' equity. Such schedules in this illustration would be recapitulations of the ledger accounts which were included earlier. The statement presented above overcomes one of the limitations usually found in conventional realization and liquidation statements in that the gains and losses are fully explained. In addition, the statement presents clearly the causes for the changes in the assets and liabilities which occurred between the beginning and the end of the period.

The statement in more traditional form would appear as follows:

THE SPECIALTY SHOPS COMPANY, IN RECEIVERSHIP
John Mann, Receiver
Statement of Realization and Liquidation
for the period February 5 to April 30

Debits		*Credits*	
Assets to be realized:		*Liabilities to be liquidated:*	
Accounts receivable	$ 5,928	Accounts payable	$15,987
Merchandise	16,536	Notes payable	3,500
Prepaid expenses	704	Accrued wages, taxes, etc.	1,275
Fixtures (net)	8,539	Accrued rent	600
	$31,707		$21,362
Assets discovered:		*Liabilities discovered:*	
Accounts receivable	423	Accrued wages	125
Supplementary charges:		*Liabilities incurred:*	
Liquidating expenses	1,245	Accrued rent	900
Lease accruals	900	Accrued interest	70
Interest expense	70		
		Assets realized:	
Liabilities liquidated:		Accounts receivable	1,882
Accrued wages, taxes, etc.	1,028	Merchandise	9,108
		Fixtures	1,000
Liabilities not liquidated:			
Accounts payable	15,987	*Assets not realized:*	
Notes payable	3,500	Accounts receivable	3,728
Interest payable	70	Merchandise	8,226
Accrued rent	1,500	Prepaid expenses	704
Accrued wages	372	Fixtures (net)	4,105
		Net loss	5,592
Total	$56,802	Total	$56,802

The net loss reported in the first statement shown on page 761 is the difference between the supplementary charges and credits. Here the differences between the proceeds from realization and the assets' book values and the difference between the outlays for liquidation and the liabilities' book values are reflected as either supplementary charges or credits. In the second statement, the assets realized are shown at the realization value and the liabilities liquidated at the liquidation amount. The differences between the proceeds and book values or disbursements and book values are reflected in the balancing figure net loss. The net loss is larger in the latter statement because the discovered asset and liability are treated as adjustments of the owners' equity, whereas in the former they were shown as supplementary credits and charges, respectively, in computing the net loss.

In many cases other financial statements are prepared for the courts; for example, beginning and ending balance sheets and a statement of gains and losses resulting from the receiver's actions. The April 30 balance sheet for The Specialty Shops Company is presented below:

THE SPECIALTY SHOPS COMPANY, IN RECEIVERSHIP
John Mann, Receiver
Balance Sheet
April 30

Assets		*Liabilities*		
Cash	*$10,481*	*Accounts payable*		*$15,987*
Accounts receivable	*3,728*	*Notes payable*		*3,500*
Merchandise	*8,226*	*Interest payable*		*70*
Prepaid expenses	*704*	*Accrued wages*		*372*
Fixtures (net)	*4,105*	*Accrued rent*		*1,500*
		Total liabilities		*$21,429*
		Owners' Equity		
		Capital stock	*$10,000*	
		Deficit	*(4,185)*	*5,815*
Total	*$27,244*	*Total*		*$27,244*

The income statement prepared by the receiver may take many forms. If he is operating the business with the intention of returning it to a solvent position, the customary form of income statement prepared for a going concern is appropriate. If he is fighting a holding action or is proceeding with an order of liquidation of the firm, then a less orthodox form of statement might be used. In the case of The Specialty Shops Company, the form on page 764 is suggested as one alternative.

The change in form of the income statement reflects the difference in purpose for which the statement is to be used. Although some merchandise was sold, the problem of matching revenue and expired costs is of little significance since the operation is almost wholly one of liquidation.

Bookkeeping and the realization and liquidation statement

The realization and liquidation statement, as indicated earlier, is prepared by the trustee or receiver as a report of his administration of the business. The recording procedures generally followed by receivers have been described in Chapter 21. These procedures develop the information in the accounts which is necessary for the preparation of the report.

Old and new accounts. We saw earlier that it was desirable for the receiver to

THE SPECIALTY SHOPS COMPANY, IN RECEIVERSHIP
John Mann, Receiver
Statement of Gains and Losses from Receiver's Activities
for the period February 5 to April 30

	Book value	Realization proceeds	Gain or (loss)
Gains and losses on asset realization:			
Accounts receivable	$ 2,623	$ 1,882	$ (741)
Merchandise	8,310	9,108	798
Fixtures	4,434	1,000	(3,434)
Loss on realization	$15,367	$11,990	$(3,377)
Liquidating expenses:			
Lease accruals		$ 900	
Interest accrual		70	
Miscellaneous		1,245	(2,215)
Loss from receiver's activities			$(5,592)
Other income:			
Accounts receivable discovered		$ 423	
Less: Accrued wages discovered		125	298
Net loss for the period			$(5,294)

make a distinction between the receivables existing at the time of his appointment and the receivables arising from his activity. The reason for this is that the receiver has a different responsibility for the two categories of accounts. He is responsible only for exercising diligent effort in the collection of the old accounts; however, he is responsible for examination of the credit risk in extending new credit.

We also indicated that the receiver seldom took the existing liabilities on to his books when he took charge of the affairs of the company. This was true despite the fact that he was responsible for paying these creditors in accordance with court order. Any liabilities which are incurred by the receiver are recorded on the receiver's books. This separation is important because of the priority of the creditors' claims which arise from dealings with the receiver. In spite of these separations for record-keeping purposes, all liability accounts are included in the realization and liquidation statement.

Accrued interest and other payables. There is a general rule that interest, rent, and other such contractual accruals follow the contract creating the liability. For example, interest accrued on a note which was signed by the firm before the receiver was appointed is generally considered an old payable and the entry to record the accrual would be made on the firm's books rather than on the receiver's. Interest on a contract entered into by the receiver is a new payable and would be recorded by the receiver.

Regardless of whether the interest arises out of an old or new contract, it is generally shown on the realization and liquidation statement as a "supplementary charge" and as a "liability incurred." This treatment is desirable since the statement presents a total picture of the enterprise, which means that the firm's and the receiver's accounts must be combined for statement purposes. Payment of these liabilities is accordingly reported as a "liability liquidated."

Accruals involving revenue are reported in a similar manner. The accrual is reported as a "supplementary credit" and the collection is shown as a part of "assets realized."

Purchases and sales of product. In circumstances where the receiver is carrying on the operations of the firm, the results of operations must be reflected in the realization and liquidation statement. The transactions which most often raise questions are those of purchases and sales. A purchase of inventory is usually shown on the debit side of the statement as a "supplementary charge" with an increase in "liabilities incurred." This transaction might alternatively be shown as an "asset acquired" and as a "liability incurred."

The sale of merchandise also presents alternatives in record keeping. Frequently the transaction will be shown as an increase in "assets acquired" and as a "supplementary credit." Another procedure is to show the increase in "assets acquired" on the debit side and include sales on the credit side as an "asset realized." The particular approach to be followed is usually left to the accountant. The authors prefer to show the debit for purchases as a "supplementary charge" and the credit for sales as a "supplementary credit," especially in situations where operations are likely to continue over an extended period of time.

Depreciation and other asset write-offs. The reporting of depreciation, bad debts, and other asset write-offs is another problem to be considered by the receiver, especially in situations where he is carrying on continuous operations. In general these write-offs do not appear in the realization and liquidation statement. These asset write-offs are considered losses on the realization of assets; therefore, when the traditional form of the realization and liquidation statement is used, the carrying value of the asset is merely reduced. There is no indication on the face of the statement that the write-off has occurred. The loss becomes a part of the net gain or loss for the period.

Purchase and sales discounts. When discount terms are accepted by customers or when discount terms offered to the company or receiver are accepted, a reporting problem is created. There are two alternatives: (1) The sales discount may be included as a "supplementary charge" with the receivable being listed under "assets realized" at the gross amount; or (2) the discount may be ignored with the net amount collected being included under "assets realized." Purchase discounts should be handled similarly; for example, (1) the purchase discount may be included as a "supplementary credit" with the liability being listed under "liabilities liquidated" at the gross amount; or (2) the discount may be ignored with the net payment being included under "liabilities liquidated."

Composition agreements with creditors. A composition agreement with the creditors is usually the result of a meeting with all the creditors at which they agree to accept a stated percentage of the claim against the bankrupt in full settlement, and the receiver agrees that the bankrupt will pay this percentage of the amount owed to each creditor. In effect, this results in liquidation of the original obligations and in the incurrence of new debts payable to the same persons but for lesser amounts. Transactions of this type are handled on the realization and liquidation statement by including the original obligations under "liabilities liquidated," entering the new debts under "liabilities incurred," and reporting the difference as a composition gain under the "supplementary credit" caption.

An acceptable alternative to the above procedure would be to omit the composition gain as a specific entry on the statement. The gain would, of course, be reflected in the final realization gain or loss figure, but it would not be separately identifiable on the face of the statement. The first alternative is preferable since in many liquidations the composition agreement is a rather significant transaction.

Illustration of a realization and liquidation statement for an operating receivership

In the previous chapter, the receiver's accounts for Tyler Trading Company were examined and the recording process was reviewed. Tyler Trading Company was able to operate profitably under the guidance of the receiver and orthodox financial statements, balance sheet and income statement, were illustrated for this company. If the receiver had been requested to prepare a realization and liquidation report for the courts, the statement on page 767 with accompanying schedules on page 768 would probably have been prepared.

Explanation of special problems. The asset expirations in this illustration have been handled in the orthodox manner; that is, the realization gains and losses have not been included as a part of the supplementary charges or credits. The cost of goods sold is an interesting element in this statement. By reference to the preceding chapter, it is noted that the cost of goods sold was $162,200. This figure does not appear in the realization and liquidation statement. The beginning inventory and the purchases for the period are included on the debit side and the ending inventory is included on the credit side. The cost of merchandise sold is the difference between these two quantities, and by its omission from the statement it is made a part of the final net gain. The difference here is $164,200. In the income statement on page 740, the purchase discount of $2,000 was deducted from the cost of goods sold to arrive at the cost of $162,200.

The charges for depreciation and bad debt expense are also excluded from the statement itself. Again the net gain is reduced by the amount of these two elements because the asset contra accounts are deducted from the cost of the asset, thereby reducing the carrying value of fixed assets and receivables in the section of the statement entitled "assets not realized."

The purchases and sales of merchandise have been handled as supplementary charges and credits, respectively. The purchases might have been considered assets acquired and the sales might have been treated as assets realized. Perhaps if we think of sales being portrayed as assets realized, this will help to make the treatment of the cost of sales more understandable. The inventory was sold for $260,000 although its gross cost was only $164,200; thus, there was a realization gain on this asset of $95,800. This gain is reduced, however, before the net gain is derived, by expenses of operations, asset expirations and write-offs, and realization losses on other assets.

In the illustration, purchase and sales discounts were treated as supplementary credits and charges, respectively. These items might have been handled by reducing the accounts payable liquidated by $2,000 and the accounts receivable realized

TYLER TRADING COMPANY, IN RECEIVERSHIP
J. Thompson, Receiver
Statement of Realization and Liquidation
for the year ended January 31, 1967

Debits

Assets to be realized:		
Notes receivable	$ 90,000	
Less: Discounted note	10,000	$ 80,000
Accrued interest receivable		3,000
Accounts receivable	$138,000	
Less: Allowance for bad debts	7,500	130,500
Inventory		174,200
Subscription receivable: Common stock		20,500
U.S. government bonds		25,000
Buildings	$121,400	
Less: Allowance for depreciation	56,540	64,860
Prepaid insurance		1,400
		$ 499,460
Assets acquired:		
Accounts receivable		262,525
Securities (discovered)		4,700
Accrued interest receivable		300
Supplementary charges:		
Merchandise purchases		110,000
Selling and general expense		46,000
Interest expense		10,200
Tax expense		3,700
Receiver's expense		8,000
Sales discount		12,600
Liabilities liquidated:		
Accounts payable—old		260,000
Notes payable		65,200
Accrued interest		11,000
Accounts payable—new		124,000
Receiver's certificates		40,000
Liabilities not liquidated:		
Notes payable		62,300
Accrued interest payable		4,900
Accrued taxes payable		3,700
Accounts payable—old		36,000
Accounts payable—new		32,000
Mortgage payable		60,000
Receiver's certificates		80,000
Net gain		10,710
Total		$1,747,295

Credits

Liabilities to be liquidated:		
Notes payable		$ 127,500
Accrued interest payable		11,000
Accounts payable		296,000
Mortgage payable		60,000
		$ 494,500
Liabilities incurred:		
Accounts payable		156,000
Receiver's certificates		120,000
Accrued taxes payable		3,700
Accrued interest payable		4,900
Supplementary credits:		
Sales		260,000
Interest revenue		2,200
Discount on payables		7,000
Assets realized:		
Notes receivable		70,910
Accounts receivable—old		106,500
Accrued interest receivable		3,000
Subscriptions receivable: common stock		19,500
Securities		4,700
Accounts receivable—new		225,000
Assets not realized:		
Notes receivable		1,000
Accrued interest receivable		300
Accounts receivable—old	$ 28,000	
Accounts receivable—new	37,525	
	$ 65,525	
Less: Allowance for bad debts	4,800	60,725
Inventory		120,000
U.S. government bonds		25,000
Buildings	$121,400	
Less: Allowance for depreciation	60,140	61,260
Prepaid insurance		1,100
Total		$1,747,295

TYLER TRADING COMPANY, IN RECEIVERSHIP
J. Thompson, Receiver
Cash Account Summary
for the year ended January 31, 1967

Balance—Jan. 31, 1966	48,000	Payment of defaulted note	2,525
Collection of accounts receivable —old	104,500	Payment of accounts payable—old	255,000
Collection of notes receivable	70,910	Payment of notes payable	65,200
Collection of interest	4,900	Payment of interest	16,300
Collection of common stock subscriptions	19,500	Payment of accounts payable—new	122,000
Sale of securities	4,700	Payment of receiver's certificates	40,000
Sale of receiver's certificates	120,000	Payment of receiver's expenses	8,000
Collection of accounts receivable —new	214,400	Balance—Jan. 31, 1967	77,885
	586,910		586,910

TYLER TRADING COMPANY, IN RECEIVERSHIP
J. Thompson, Receiver
Capital Account Summary
for the year ended January 31, 1967

Deficit	47,040	Capital stock	100,000
		Discovered securities	4,700
Balance	68,370	Realization and operating gain	10,710
	115,410		115,410

by $10,600. Either procedure is entirely acceptable. For purposes of explanation, the disclosure of the discounts seems desirable here.

The discovery of the securities was treated as an acquired asset. The credit part of the entry was entered in the owners' capital account. This is consistent with the concept that the discovery of assets is in fact a correction of the beginning balances. The credit might have been reported as a "supplementary credit." The problem with such disclosure is that it implies that the discovery was the result of the receiver's activities, when in fact the asset existed in the name of the bankrupt for the entire period.

The discount on the liability was indicated as a "supplementary credit" without setting up a new liability as being incurred because the reduction and the payment occurred simultaneously.

The discounted note was not paid in full at maturity; however, the contingent liability and the contingent receivable were offset. In turn, a liability was incurred to pay $2,525, the defaulted amount plus the bank charge. When the $2,525 was paid a claim arose against the maker for this amount, giving Tyler Trading Company an acquired asset in the form of a receivable. Instead of recording the liability as an "incurred liability" and then setting up the receivable as an "acquired asset,'' the procedure was shortened by setting up the acquired asset simultaneously with the payment. The same entry was made in the receiver's books in the preceding chapter.

Appraisal of the realization and liquidation statement

The use of the supplementary charge and supplementary credit categories varies widely among accountants, with the most popular method seeming to be that which shows the least detail. Valid arguments exist for the opposite point of view in connection with this particular statement, however. The statement is usually prepared for a court comprised of nonaccountants; therefore, explicitness would seem to be a virtue. As a matter of fact, a beginning and ending balance sheet, accompanied by a resumé of the cash transactions and the owners' equity, together with a statement of realization gains and losses, would seem to constitute a more adequate statement of the receiver's activity than the traditional realization and liquidation statement does. The problem of reading the realization and liquidation statement derives mainly from the fact that it is organized in a manner which is unfamiliar to the reader. Financial reporting for many solvent companies covers the same data as reported for companies in receivership. The reporting problem differs significantly only for the company which is undergoing liquidation. Modifications and reorientation of the traditional income statement, as suggested earlier for The Specialty Shops Company (page 764), may offer the most useful reporting techniques for many companies in process of liquidation.

Reorganization of bankrupt corporations

Chapter X of the National Bankruptcy Act was added in 1938 by an act known as the Chandler Act which dealt primarily with the relief to be afforded debtors. This particular amendment governs corporate reorganizations when there is a proposal to realign the capital structure. In general this means that reorganizations involving secured debt obligations and owners' equity are governed by this provision of the law. [Secs. 501–502]

Since the Chandler Act was enacted as a provision to accelerate the bankruptcy proceedings and to reduce the cost of such proceedings normally handled as an equity receivership, many people expected it to replace the equity receivership procedure for corporations. Although these expectations were not fully realized, the corporate reorganization remedy has tended to replace the equity receivership in the case of corporate bankrupts.

Legal procedures

The action which precedes filing a bankruptcy petition under Chapter X and that which precedes a filing under the equity receivership are quite similar. The petition to effect a reorganization plan may be filed with the court by the corporation or by any of the equity interests or their legal representatives. Filing of the reorganization petition is not considered an act of bankruptcy; therefore, the court may approve the petition even though a bankruptcy proceeding is currently pending against the corporation. [Secs. 526–530]

The provisions for an equity receivership proceeding and for a corporate reorganization proceeding are so similar that the act provides that "the court shall have and may exercise all the powers . . . which a court of the United States would have if it had appointed a receiver in equity of the property of the debtor on the ground of insolvency or inability to meet its debts as they mature." This means that one of the first acts of the court will be to appoint one or more receivers or trustees to take over the affairs of the corporation or approve the management to remain in control. [Sec. 515]

The duties of the trustee are to investigate the current condition of the debtor and the desirability of continuing the operation of the business as well as any other matter which is pertinent to the formulation of a reorganization plan. He then reports his findings on these matters to the judge, with special attention to any facts pertaining to fraud or mismanagement. The trustee also submits a brief report of his findings, in the manner prescribed by the judge, to the creditors, stockholders, indenture trustees, the SEC, and such other persons as the judge may designate. He then notifies the equity interests that within a stated time period they may submit suggestions for the formulation of a reorganization plan, or proposals in the form of plans. [Secs. 75 and 586]

Provisions of a reorganization plan

Subchapter X of Chapter X sets out clearly and specifically what the plan for reorganization must include and indicates what other things may be included. In summary, the plan must include provisions relating to (1) the rights of the creditors and stockholders, (2) the payment of costs and expenses of administration, (3) the claims to be paid in full, (4) the creditors and stockholders not affected by the plan, (5) the protection of any class of affected creditors who do not accept the plan by the two-thirds majority as measured by the amount of the claim, (6) the protection of any class of affected stockholders who do not accept the plan by majority vote of the shares outstanding, (7) the execution of the plan, (8) the selection of directors or voting trustees and successors upon consummation of the plan, and (9) the equitable distribution of voting power among the classes of securities, the maintenance of fair terms, rights, and privileges of the several classes of securities, and the filing of periodic financial reports. [Sec. 616]

The plan may also include provisions relating to (1) the property of the debtor, (2) the performance under executory contracts, (3) the retirement of indebtedness created or extended for more than five years, (4) the settlement of claims belonging to the debtor, and (5) any other matters which are not inconsistent with the provisions of this section of the law. [Sec. 616]

Approval of the plan. After the reorganization plan has been completed and filed with the court, a hearing will be held. After this hearing, where all interested parties are invited to state their objections to the plan, and after the SEC has made its report or made known its intention not to make such a report, the judge will enter an order approving the plan which in his opinion complies with the provisions of the act and which is fair, equitable, and feasible. At the same time he will fix a time within which the creditors and stockholders affected thereby may accept the plan. [Sec. 574]

The judge will set a time for a second hearing for consideration of the confirmation of the plan and of such objections as may be made to the confirmation. The plan must be accepted in writing by (1) creditors holding two-thirds in amount of the claims filed and allowed of each class and (2) stockholders holding the majority of stock of each class, if the debtor is solvent. If the plan is in compliance with the provisions of Chapter X of the National Bankruptcy Act and if the plan is fair, equitable, and feasible and if the proposal and acceptance of the plan are in good faith and have not been made or procured by means or premises forbidden by the law, then the judge will confirm the plan as being acceptable to the court. [Secs. 579 and 621]

Effect of confirmation and final decree. Once confirmed by the court, the plan becomes binding on the debtor and on all creditors and stockholders, whether or not they are affected by the plan or have accepted it. The debtor and any corporation organized for the purpose of carrying out the plan must comply with the provisions and the orders of the court and must take all action necessary to carry out the plan.

A reorganization plan is considered to be substantially consummated upon:

1. Transfer, sale, or other disposition of substantially all of the property dealt with in the plan in accordance with its provisions

2. Assumption by the debtor of operation of the business and management of substantially all of the property dealt with by the plan

3. Commencement of the distribution to creditors and stockholders of cash and securities specified in the plan [Sec. 629]

When the plan has been substantially consummated, the judge having jurisdiction over the proceeding will enter a final decree:

1. Discharging the debtor from all its debts and liabilities and terminating all rights and interests of stockholders of the debtor, except as provided in the plan

2. Discharging the trustee, if any

3. Making such provisions by way of injunction or otherwise as may be equitable

4. Closing the estate [Sec. 628]

Accounting problems in reorganization

The accounting aspects of a reorganization proceeding are of three types: (1) general advice on asset valuation and earnings prediction, (2) record keeping during the period while the proceeding is taking place, and (3) effectuation of the plan in the accounts.

In the first of these problem areas, the accountant's contribution is based on his extensive knowledge of the business and his general knowledge of the competitive situation. The accountant is cast in the role of a business adviser or consultant. For this reason there are no specific procedures, forms, or statements to be discussed. A typical problem facing the accountant in such a situation is the following:

Example. Adams Corporation has filed a petition for corporate reorganization asking that its equity be recapitalized in order to relieve it of a tremendous drain on cash. The accountant is asked his opinion of the proposed plan of reorganization. Will the plan provide adequate relief to allow Adams to become an effective, viable competitor in the field?

To answer the question, the accountant would want to make some cash flow projections. What are cash inflows likely to be, what are the requirements of the new capital structure? Can cash outflows be reduced enough to enable the company to finance its replacements and necessary growth to remain competitive? These are not easy questions under the most favorable circumstances, but they are considerably more difficult in a situation where the subject is facing bankruptcy.

The second of these accounting problems has already been discussed under the topic of receivership accounts. The problem here is limited to assumption of control by the receiver and to the record keeping for the operations and activities during the period the receiver or trustee is in control. The accounts and records the accountant must maintain are those which are necessary to permit him to make complete and accurate periodic reports on the trustee's activities. The problems he faces are not substantially different from those he would face in accounting for any operating activity.

The third accounting problem has to do with the implementation of the reorganization plan. This may entail the disposal of assets, the carrying out of a composition agreement, the adjustment of asset values, and the exchanges or adjustments which are made in the various equities. While it is true that the reorganization plan is generally very specific in its various provisions, the accountant must possess considerable skill to incorporate the plan as a part of the accounts of the corporation. There are many different reorganization plans; in fact, each one is likely to be unique. The accountant must keep in mind that he is not writing the reorganization plan. No matter what he thinks of a plan, his job is merely to transform it from a plan into transactions in the records of the corporation.

Many reorganization plans deal with revaluation of assets as well as with the exchange of securities and extension of repayment dates. This means that the changes in asset values reflect accumulated differences in book value and market value. The accountant is concerned with a proper determination of enterprise income, which means that he attempts to reflect all changes in asset values in net income over time. In the case of a reorganization, the AICPA permits these changes to be written off against paid-in capital to the extent that they exceed retained earnings. The Institute states:

> Assets should be carried forward as of the date of readjustment at fair and not unduly conservative amounts, determined with due regard for the accounting to be employed by the company thereafter. If the fair value of any asset is not readily determinable a conservative estimate may be made, but in that case the amount should be described as an estimate and any material difference arising through realization or otherwise and not attributable to events occurring or circumstances arising after that date should not be carried to income or earned surplus.

The bulletin continues by stating:

> When the amounts to be written off in a readjustment have been determined, they should be charged first against earned surplus to the full extent of such surplus; any balance may then be charged against capital surplus. A company which has subsidiaries should apply this rule in such a way that no consolidated

earned surplus survives a readjustment in which any part of losses has been charged to capital surplus.[1]

Upon completion of the reorganization, the accounts are kept in accordance with accepted accounting procedures. Any retained earnings remaining after the reorganization should be separated from earnings retained subsequent to the reorganization. The AICPA has taken the position that a new earned surplus account should be established and dated to show that it runs from the effective date of the readjustment. In the opinion of the Institute, the dating of retained earnings is rarely of significance after a period of ten years.[2] Any other capital accounts arising from the reorganization are treated as contributed capital. Charges against these accounts are limited to those which might be made against the contributed capital accounts of any corporation.

Although each plan is different, the technique used in implementing a particular plan can be illustrated with the following example:

Illustration. The Halvorson Corporation is a manufacturer of cotton goods. The company had been operating since 1949 with a plant and machines which it acquired in a used state after 25 years of use. In 1963 the management decided that the only way to reverse the profit trend, more properly called the loss trend, was to modernize the plant. In order to finance the modernization, the management borrowed $5.5 million from an insurance company. The loan required annual repayments on the debt of $700,000 each year beginning December 31, 1965, plus interest on the unpaid balance at 6%. The company also sold $1.5 million, 6¾% subordinated bonds, due January 1, 1983, to local businessmen. All of this was accomplished by the overwhelming confidence of the owners that this modernization plan would produce profits. In 1966 the management found that, although they had reversed the loss trend and in fact had earned $175,000 after taxes in 1965, new profit opportunities lay ahead with greater automation of the plant. Increased profits were practically assured, but there was no cash for expansion. Upon a second reading of the terms of the insurance loan agreement, they found that no additional funds could be borrowed because of the restrictive provisions of the loan agreement. The officers of the corporation met with representatives of the various equity interests during 1966. By December 15 all parties had agreed to and the court had confirmed the following plan of reorganization. The plan was to be made effective on February 1, 1967.

The condensed balance sheet for Halvorson Corporation as of January 31, 1967, the end of the fiscal year, is presented on page 774.

The provisions of the confirmed plan of reorganization were as follows:

1. Revalue inventory at current cost prices to a total of $9 million, write land and plant assets up to $7.5 million, and write off the intangibles.

2. Pay current payables in full as due. Current creditors have agreed to a temporary extension of time as and if necessary because of cash shortages.

3. Reduce the credit restrictions of the insurance company note, reduce the interest rate to 5%, and defer annual repayments of principle for three years,

[1] AICPA, *Accounting Research and Terminology Bulletins—Final Edition* (New York: 1961), chap. 7a, p. 46.

[2] *Ibid.,* Bulletin No. 46.

HALVORSON CORPORATION *Balance Sheet* *as of January 31, 1967*	
Assets	
Cash	*$ 450,000*
Receivables	*1,750,000*
Inventories	*3,400,000*
Land and plant assets (net)	*6,000,000*
Patents and other intangibles	*300,000*
Total assets	*$11,900,000*
Equities	
Current payables	*$ 600,000*
6% note payable	*4,100,000*
6¾% subordinated debentures	*1,500,000*
6% cumulative preferred stock, $100 par value (dividends in arrears since Jan. 31, 1957)	*2,000,000*
Common stock (par value $10, 500,000 shares issued, 1 million authorized)	*5,000,000*
Paid-in capital	*2,500,000*
Accumulated deficit	*(3,800,000)*
Total equities	*$11,900,000*

extending the maturing date accordingly. Issue 200,000 shares of common stock to the insurance company as consideration for extension of repayment date and reduction of interest charge.

4. Exchange each 6¾% subordinated debenture for 5½% subordinated debenture and ten $50 par value, 5%, noncumulative preferred shares, which are preferred in liquidation only to the common stock. Dividends on the new preferred are to be paid only if net income after interest, taxes, and cumulative preferred dividends exceeds $100,000 per year and if net working capital exceeds $10 million.

5. Issue 1.2 shares of the new noncumulative preferred to the holder of each old 6% cumulative preferred share, in full settlement of all dividend arrearages through 1966.

The entries necessary to effect this plan are as follows:

1. Revaluation of assets:

Inventory	*5,600,000*	
Land and Plant Assets	*1,500,000*	
Patents and Other Intangibles		*300,000*
Reorganization Gain or Loss		*6,800,000*

This entry gives effect to the new values of assets as directed in the reorganization plan and creates a temporary account, Reorganization Gain or Loss, to be used primarily as a clearing account. Upon completion of the reorganization, this account will be closed as a net adjustment to the stock equity in the last entry of the reorganization.

2. *Current payables:*

No entry necessary since there is no change.

3. *6% note payable:*

6% Note Payable	*4,100,000*	
Reorganization Gain or Loss	*2,400,000*	
5% Note Payable		*4,100,000*
Common Stock, Par Value $10		*2,000,000*
Paid-in Capital		*400,000*

This entry records the exchange of the 6% note, payable to the insurance company, for the 5% note and reflects the issuance of 200,000 shares of common stock, with a current market price of $12 per share, in exchange for the reduction in interest rate and the deferral for three years of the annual repayment of the loan.

4. *6¾% subordinated debentures:*

6¾% Subordinated Debentures	*1,500,000*	
Reorganization Gain or Loss	*750,000*	
5½% Subordinated Debentures		*1,500,000*
5% Preferred Stock, $50 Par Value		*750,000*

This entry records (1) the exchange of the 6¾% debentures for the 5½% debentures and (2) the issue of 15,000 shares of a new 5% noncumulative preferred stock in exchange for the reduction in interest rates.

5. *6% cumulative preferred stock:*

Reorganization Gain or Loss	*1,200,000*	
5% Preferred Stock, $50 Par Value		*1,200,000*

This entry reflects the settlement of all dividend arrearages on the 6% preferred.

6. *Transfer of accumulated operating deficit:*

Reorganization Gain or Loss	*3,800,000*	
Accumulated Deficit		*3,800,000*

This entry eliminates the accumulated operating deficit by writing it off against the reorganization gain or loss created by revaluation of the inventory, land, and plant assets. In effect a new entity exists and accumulated profits or losses will be indicative of success or failure from this day forward. Profits or losses of prior periods are made a part of permanent capital.

7. Close-out of reorganization gain or loss to paid-in capital:

Paid-in Capital	*1,350,000*	
Reorganization Gain or Loss		*1,350,000*

This entry concludes the reorganization procedure by transferring the balance in the Reorganization Gain or Loss account to the Paid-in Capital account. The reorganization plan has now been reflected in the accounts.

The balance sheet of the reorganized Halvorson Corporation can now be prepared and compared with the balance sheet as of the same date but before reorganization.

HALVORSON CORPORATION
Balance Sheet
as of January 31, 1967

Assets

	After reorganization	*Before reorganization*
Cash	*$ 450,000*	*$ 450,000*
Receivables	*1,750,000*	*1,750,000*
Inventory	*9,000,000*	*3,400,000*
Land and plant assets (net)	*7,500,000*	*6,000,000*
Patents and other intangibles	*-0-*	*300,000*
Total assets	*$18,700,000*	*$11,900,000*

Equities

	After reorganization	*Before reorganization*
Current payables	*$ 600,000*	*$ 600,000*
6% note payable	*-0-*	*4,100,000*
5% note payable	*4,100,000*	*-0-*
6¾% subordinated debentures	*-0-*	*1,500,000*
5½% subordinated debentures	*1,500,000*	*-0-*
6% cumulative preferred stock, $100 par value (before reorganization dividends in arrears since Jan. 31, 1957)	*2,000,000*	*2,000,000*
5% preferred stock, $50 par value	*1,950,000*	*-0-*
Common stock (par value $10, 200,000 shares issued after reorganization, 500,000 shares before, 1 million authorized)	*7,000,000*	*5,000,000*
Paid-in capital	*1,550,000*	*2,500,000*
Accumulated deficit	*-0-*	*(3,800,000)*
Total equities	*$18,700,000*	*$11,900,000*

This reorganization has been planned and carried out in the belief that it will make Halvorson Corporation a more viable enterprise. Obviously there is no way to be sure that this will occur. If the corporation is unable to find additional capital or if the officers do find additional capital and it cannot be used as profitably as they think it can, then liquidation may come soon. On the other hand, if things go as planned, then Halvorson could became a strong competitor in its field.

The many complicated tax problems associated with such a reorganization plan have deliberately been omitted; although tax problems complicate the preparation of a fair and equitable plan they have little effect on the accountant's work in carrying out the plan.

Arrangements

Chapter XI of the National Bankruptcy Act provides debtors with another form of relief. This is known as the *arrangement*. Arrangement within the terms of the law refers to any plan of a debtor for the settlement, satisfaction, or extension of the time of payment of his unsecured debts. The debtor may work out an informal plan similar to that which might be set out in a legal arrangement. Such a plan would not have legal sanction, however, and, indeed, it would constitute an act of bankruptcy. In a sense an arrangement is a reorganization. The distinction between an arrangement and a reorganization is that an arrangement deals primarily with the rights of unsecured creditors, whereas a reorganization may deal with the rights of all classes of equity, including the stockholders. [Secs. 706–708]

Provisions of arrangement

The act provides for the modification of the rights of the unsecured creditors in the following way: "An arrangement within the meaning of this chapter shall include provisions modifying or altering the rights of unsecured creditors generally or of some class of them, upon any items or for any consideration." [Sec. 756]

An arrangement within the meaning of Chapter XI may include permissive provisions for

1. Treatment of unsecured debts on a parity one with the other

2. Rejection of an executory contract

3. Specific undertakings of the debtor during any period of extension provided for by the arrangement

4. Termination of any period of extension provided by the arrangement

5. Continuation of the debtor's business with or without supervision or control by a receiver only or by a committee of creditors or otherwise

6. Payment of debts incurred after the filing of the petition, and during the pendency of the arrangement, in priority over the debts affected by such arrangement

7. Retention of jurisdiction by the court until provisions of the arrangement have been performed

8. Any other appropriate provisions not inconsistent with Chapter XI [Sec. 757]

Acceptance of proposed arrangement. After a proposed arrangement has been prepared, the court will call a meeting of the debtor and creditors for the purpose of receiving proofs of claim, of examining the debtor, of receiving other testimony relevant to the proceeding, and of receiving the written acceptances of the creditors of the proposed arrangement. If the arrangement is accepted by all creditors, the court will confirm the arrangement. If it is accepted by a majority in number of the creditors, the court will confirm the arrangement upon application for confirmation. As in most other actions under the bankruptcy act, the court will appoint a trustee or receiver or leave the debtor in control, if deemed competent, to assure that the arrangement is carried out in accordance with the court order. [Secs. 761–762]

Effect of confirmation. The confirmation by the court of an arrangement binds all parties, including the debtor and his creditors. Once an arrangement has been confirmed, it can be modified or altered under certain circumstances. Specifically, the law provides that upon confirmation of an arrangement:

1. The arrangement and its provisions shall be binding upon the debtor, upon any person issuing securities or acquiring property under the arrangement and upon all creditors of the debtor, whether or not they are affected by the arrangement or have filed their claims, and whether or not their claims have been scheduled or allowed, and are allowable.

2. The money deposited for priority debts and for the costs and expenses shall be disbursed to the persons entitled thereto.

3. The consideration deposited, if any, shall be distributed, and the rights provided by the arrangement shall inure to the creditors affected by the arrangement whose claims (a) have been filed prior to the date of confirmation . . . and are allowed or (b) whether or not filed have been scheduled by the debtor and are not contingent, unliquidated, or disputed.

4. Except as otherwise provided in sections 769 and 770 of this title, the case shall be dismissed. [Sec. 767]

Accounting problems of an arrangement

The accountant is faced with problems similar to those encountered under Chapter X of the National Bankruptcy Act. The arrangement plan generally does not involve the extensive revaluation of assets, and the secured debts and ownership equities are not involved in the plan at all. The accountant's function related to recording the arrangement on the books of account is restricted, therefore, to changes in unsecured debt terms. The first function, the projection of future prospects and the valuation of assets, is the more important aspect of the accountant's work.

Questions

1. What information is provided on the realization and liquidation statement?
2. In what ways is the realization and liquidation statement similar to or dissimilar from the typical ledger account?
3. Why is little or no information provided about gains and losses resulting from the receiver's activities on the realization and liquidation statement?
4. What items are included in the supplementary charges and supplementary credits category on the realization and liquidation statement?

5. How would each of the following transactions be reported on the realization and liquidation statement? Where there are alternatives, indicate what they are and how they differ from the way you reported the transaction.
   a. Sale of merchandise on account for $10,000 which cost $8,000.
   b. Depreciation of plant assets, for the period, $3,000.
   c. Payment of accounts payable—new of $6,000 less a discount of 3%.

6. As used in the National Bankruptcy Act, what does the term *reorganization* mean?

7. Why is there insistence by the AICPA that retained earnings shall not be carried forward following a reorganization, in which any part of the loss has been charged to retained earnings, unless a new retained earnings account is established and dated?

8. What does the term *arrangement* mean as used in the National Bankruptcy Act? How is it different from a reorganization.

9. Using the realization and liquidation statement below, explain the source of the net loss.

Statement of Realization and Liquidation

Assets to be realized:		*Liabilities to be liquidated:*	
Accounts receivable	$ 6,000	*Accounts payable*	$18,000
Merchandise	12,000	*Notes payable*	4,800
Plant assets (net)	20,000	*Accrued interest*	200
	$38,000		$23,000
Supplementary charges:		*Liabilities assumed:*	
Liquidation expenses	2,500	*Accrued interest*	100
Interest expense	100	*Assets realized:*	
Liabilities liquidated:		*Accounts receivable*	3,000
Accounts payable	5,000	*Merchandise*	9,000
Liabilities not liquidated:		*Assets not realized:*	
Accounts payable	12,000	*Accounts receivable*	2,000
Notes payable	4,800	*Merchandise*	5,000
Accrued interest	300	*Plant assets (net)*	18,000
		Net loss	2,600
Total	$62,700	*Total*	$62,700

10. What is a composition agreement with creditors? How would such an agreement be reflected on the realization and liquidation statement?

Short cases for analysis

22-1 You have just heard Madison Harrell, CPA, explain that the realization and liquidation account with its supporting statements or schedules should be prepared by a process of journalizing in the statements.

Instructions

Explain what the offsetting debit and credit entries would be with respect to the following:

a. Assets, liabilities, and capital at the beginning of the period
b. The discovery of additional assets
c. The sale of merchandise
d. The collection of accounts receivable at a loss
e. The collection of interest on notes
f. The payment of receiver's expenses
g. The incurrence of liabilities by the receiver
h. The destruction of assets by fire and the subsequent collection of insurance for 120% of the book value of the assets destroyed

22-2 In making an audit of Jackson Company as of December 31, you find the following items had been charged or credited to retained earnings during the six months immediately following a Chapter X reorganization, which was finalized and made effective July 1:

(1) Debit of $13,246 arising from an income tax assessment applicable to prior years.
(2) Credit of $30,387 resulting from gain on sale of equipment which was no longer used in the business. This equipment had been written down by a $16,000 increase in the allowance for depreciation at the time of the reorganization.
(3) Debit of $9,627 resulting from the loss on fixed assets destroyed in a fire on November 2.
(4) Debit of $13,500, representing dividends declared on common and preferred stock.
(5) Credit of $52,565, the net income for the year.

Instructions

For each of these items, state whether you believe it to be correctly charged or credited to retained earnings. Give the reasons for your conclusion. If, in your opinion, the item was not handled properly, give the necessary correcting entry.

AICPA adapted

22-3 Mr. Jones, controller of Winedot Corporation, advises you that a friend of his has suggested that the statement of affairs should be prepared for business firms instead of the traditional balance sheet. He is also concerned about a statement he saw recently for Radot Corporation which was headed "Statement of Realization and Liquidation." Jones wonders if this statement is a new form of income statement and, if so, then why has he not been informed about recent trends?

Instructions

Write a report to Jones in which you explain by contrast the form, use, and underlying assumptions of the typical balance sheet, statement of affairs, statement of realization and liquidation, and income statement.

AICPA adapted

22-4 The XYZ Corporation was unable to meet its obligations under maturing debt and lease obligations on March 1. The company, therefore, filed a petition for an arrangement with the courts. The following plan was about to be accepted by all parties when you were hired by the creditor group:

(1) The noteholders agreed to exchange 10-year, 6% subordinated debentures for notes they now hold which require quarterly repayments of $200,000. They also agreed to accept 500 shares of $10 par value common stock with market value of $18.75 in lieu of the interest for two months which was unpaid on March 1 and in consideration of the extension of the maturity date.

(2) The debenture holders agreed to exchange their 5% debentures maturing next year for the new 6%, 10-year debentures and 700 shares of $10 par value common stock with market value of $18.75 in lieu of unpaid interest since January 1.

(3) The trade creditors agreed to exchange one-half of their open accounts for 90-day, 5% notes.

(4) The lease, which had 10 years to run, provided for monthly payments of $20,000. The lessor agreed to reduce the monthly rental to $10,000 and to accept 20,000 shares of $10 par value common stock and 400 10-year, 6% subordinated debentures in lieu of the reduced rental.

The balance sheet of XYZ Corporation at February 28 and the income statement for the first two months of the year are presented below:

Balance Sheet
February 28

Cash	*$ 100,000*
Receivables	*1,500,000*
Inventories	*5,000,000*
Equipment	*1,250,000*
Accumulated depreciation	*(600,000)*
Total assets	*$7,250,000*
Accounts payable	*$ 750,000*
Accrued interest payable	*19,167*
Notes payable—5%	*800,000*
Bonds payable—5%	*1,500,000*
Capital stock—par value $10	*3,000,000*
Retained earnings	*1,180,833*
Total liabilities & equity	*$7,250,000*

Income Statement
for the two months ended February 28

Sales		*$3,150,000*
Less:		
Cost of goods sold	*$2,750,000*	
Rent expense	*40,000*	
Depreciation	*20,833*	
Selling and administrative expense	*110,000*	
Interest	*19,167*	
Taxes	*94,300*	*3,034,300*
Net income		*$ 115,700*

Instructions

a. Prepare the journal entries necessary to reflect the changes which would be brought about by acceptance of the arrangement by the creditors.

b. Assuming that a reasonable approximation of cash flow can be made by adding depreciation to the reported net income figure and assuming that operations remain at this level (which is one-sixth of the expected annual level): Does the arrangement allow the firm to meet its obligations as they mature? Base your opinion on a projection of the data provided. (Round all calculations to the nearest dollar.)

c. Would you recommend any restrictions on the future activity of the management?

22-5 Your advice is sought by the board of directors of Razor Corp. in connection with a proposed plan of reorganization. The following is provided by the board for your consideration:

The Razor Corp. is a manufacturer of machine tools. Its business has shown wide fluctuations in recent years and there have been corresponding variations in profits. For a number of years prior to 1966 there had not been any significant earnings and most years had resulted in losses; however, for the year 1966 there was a net income of $942,100. As of December 31, 1966, the following statement of stockholders' equity was prepared:

$3 cumulative preferred stock, $50 par value—outstanding 96,200 shares (dividends in arrears since Sept. 30, 1950)		*$4,810,000*
Common stock, no-par—outstanding 120,000 shares at assigned value of		*3,365,473*
Accumulated deficit, Jan. 1, 1966	*($1,174,280)**	
Net income for 1966	*942,100*	*(232,180)*
Total		*$7,943,293*

**( ) denotes negative figure.*

A plan of capital adjustment had been worked out during 1966, which was ratified by the stockholders and made effective as of January 1, 1967. This plan provided that the $3 preferred was to be reduced from $50 par value to $40 par value; that it continue to be preferred for $3 per share dividends on a cumulative basis and that it be preferred in liquidation at $50 per share and redeemable at the option of the company at $55 per share. In settlement of dividends in arrears, the company paid $360,750 cash and issued 216,450 shares of B stock having a par value of $10 per share. The B shares are nonvoting and are not entitled to dividends. They are redeemable at $20 per share and are entitled to $20 per share after preferred but before common in liquidation. The agreement under which they are issued provides that a cash redemption fund shall be set up equal to 50% of the yearly net profits in excess of dividend requirements on preferred stock. The fund is to be used to purchase and retire B stock. "Tenders" are to be accepted from stockholders, those shares offered at the lowest prices being redeemed first. If no tenders are received within three months after January 1 of each year, the shares to be retired will be selected by lot. The provisions of issue also state that as long as any B stock is outstanding, no dividends may be paid on common stock. The assigned value of the common was also reduced to $600,000.

The surplus created by this restatement of stock was treated in accordance with accepted accounting practice. All stockholders accepted the exchange offer.

The operations for the year 1967 resulted in a net profit, after taxes, of $1,631,316. Dividends for the full year were paid on the preferred stock. Assume a tax rate of 22% on the first $25,000 of income and of 48% on all income in excess of $25,000.

It now appears that operations are going to be profitable for an indefinite period and the board of directors desires to work out a plan whereby common stock can be put on a dividend basis. Preferred is currently selling for $52 per share and B stock for $9.50 per share.

Based on these values, a plan is under consideration by the board of directors, which it is hoped will enable them to place common on a dividend basis if good earnings continue. This plan calls for authorizing a 5% debenture issue which will be offered to the preferred stockholders in exchange for their stock at the rate of $100 of debentures and two shares of common for each two shares of preferred. It is anticipated that the common will be put on a $1 annual dividend basis after the capital adjustments proposed. Holders of B stock are to be offered one share of new 6% preferred which is to be issued having $100 par value, and five shares of common for each 10 shares of B stock, all before use of the retirement fund. The common stock is to have a stated value of $5 per share.

Instructions

a. Prepare a statement in good form of the stockholders' equity for the Razor Corp. as of December 31, 1967.

b. Prepare a statement in good form of long-term debt and stockholders' equity for the Razor Corp. as of January 1, 1968, assuming that the proposed reorganization plan was approved and made effective as of that date.

c. Prepare a statement showing the earnings per share of common stock in 1967 if the proposed plan could have been in effect as of January 1, 1967.

d. Make your recommendations to the board of directors and give the reasons for your decision.

AICPA adapted

Problems

22-6 The stockholders of Mason Equipment Company resolved at their meeting of June 13, 1966, to liquidate as of August 31, 1966. The May 31, 1966 financial statement on which the stockholders predicated their decision to liquidate appears on page 784.

According to the stockholders' resolution of June 13, the liquidation is to be effected by the directors (who, being principal stockholders, serve without compensation).

Balance Sheet
as of May 31, 1966

Assets

Cash		*$ 36,750*
Accounts receivable		*33,500*
Merchandise inventory		*120,250*
Total current assets		*$190,500*
Furniture, fixtures, trucks (net)		*20,500*
Land and building (net)		*30,000*
Total assets		*$241,000*

Liabilities & Equities

Accounts payable, including taxes		*$ 15,600*
Interest accrued on mortgage		*250*
Accrued payroll		*450*
Total current liabilities		*$ 16,300*
6% mortgage, due Jan. 1, 1968		*10,000*
Capital stock, 4,200 shares, par value $50		*210,000*
Retained earnings—balance at Jan. 1, 1966	*$24,050*	
Less: Loss for five months to May 31, 1966	*19,350*	
Balance		*4,700*
Total liabilities & equity		*$241,000*

The $15,000 cash bid of a local real estate operator for the equity in the land and building is to be accepted immediately, the purchaser to assume the outstanding mortgage of $10,000 and to pay all expenses of title search, closing, etc. Title is to pass as of June 30, 1966; Mason Equipment Company is to pay mortgage interest accrued to that date. Insurance and taxes prepaid prior to June 30, 1966, are to be absorbed by the vendor.

All merchandise on hand is to be offered for sale at 80% of regular sales prices, such special sale to be conducted from June 17 to June 26 (both dates inclusive). These sales are to be on a strictly cash basis and to be final—no returns permitted.

An auction is to be conducted on June 29 on the company's premises, to include all merchandise not disposed of during the previous 10-day sale. All furniture, fixtures, trucks, and other equipment are also to be auctioned at this time. All sales made at such auction are to be strictly cash and final.

Any merchandise still remaining unsold after the auction is to be advertised daily in newspapers of neighboring communities and disposed of at best prices obtainable.

All employees, except the manager-bookkeeper, are to be given immediate notice of their release, at the close of business on June 30, and to be paid up to July 31. The manager-bookkeeper is to be given immediate notice of his release August 31, 1966, on which date he will be paid his salary for the four months ending December 31.

A liquidating dividend (final) is to be paid on September 2, 1966, to all stockholders of record as of August 31, 1966.

Sales of merchandise to regular customers on credit for the period from June 1 to 16, inclusive, amounted to $9,500 and were merged with the liquidation sales. All merchandise unsold after the auction was finally disposed of in August.

Depreciation subsequent to May 31, 1966, may be ignored.

Following is a summary of the cash transactions for the three months ended August 31, 1966:

Cash Transactions

June	*Dr*	*Cr*
Cash sales—regular	*$ 5,850*	
Accounts receivable collections	*23,500*	
Cash sales (special 20% discount)	*47,350*	
Cash received from auction sales:		
Merchandise	*31,500*	
Furniture, fixtures, and trucks	*8,250*	
Auctioneer's commission and expenses		*$ 2,850*
Interest on mortgage paid to June 30		*300*
Proceeds from sale of land and building	*15,000*	
Officers and office salaries (including separation payments and $450 accrued payroll)		*5,550*
Accounts payable		*15,600*
July		
Accounts receivable collections	*1,250*	
Post-auction sales:		
Merchandise	*3,500*	
Furniture, fixtures, and trucks	*2,300*	
Salary of manager-bookkeeper for July		*400*
August		
Accounts receivable collections (final)	*3,700*	
Collection agency fees		*375*
Salary of manager-bookkeeper (including separation payment)		*2,000*
Legal fees and expenses re liquidation		*675*
	$142,200	*$27,750*

Instructions

On the basis of the foregoing data, prepare:

a. Necessary journal entries to summarize the activity from June 1 through August 31. (You may ignore closing entries.)

b. A statement of loss on realization and expenses of liquidation.

c. A statement showing the amount of cash to be distributed as a liquidating dividend to each of the following stockholders:

	Shares
A	*1,600*
B	*1,200*
C	*900*
D	*360*
E	*140*
Total	*4,200*

AICPA adapted

22-7 The Jackson Company was unable to meet its obligations. As a result, Harry Caudle was appointed receiver on April 5, 1966. The following trial balance was taken from the books as of that date:

Cash	*$ 1,528*
Accounts receivable	*11,856*
Merchandise	*33,072*
Prepaid expenses	*1,408*
Fixtures	*24,684*
Total debits	*$72,548*
Accounts payable	*$31,974*
Notes payable	*7,000*
Accrued wages, taxes, etc.	*2,550*
Accrued rent	*1,200*
Accumulated depreciation	*7,606*
Capital stock	*20,000*
Earned surplus	*2,218*
Total credits	*$72,548*

In the period from April 5 to June 30, 1966, the receiver's actions resulted in:

(1) An audit of the accounts receivable disclosed that there were an additional $846 of accounts receivable which had not been brought on the books.

(2) Merchandise costing $16,620 was sold for cash.

(3) A portion of the fixtures, which cost $10,752 and had accumulated depreciation credits of $1,884, was sold.

(4) Accounts receivable totaling $3,764 were collected. Other accounts amounting to $1,482 were determined to be worthless.

(5) Claims were approved and paid for $1,806 of the wages and taxes which were accrued at April 5. Wage claims for $250 which were unrecorded on April 5 have also been approved and paid. Other claims have not yet been paid.

(6) Expenses for wages and supplies used in liquidating the business to June 30 amounted to $2,490. Fees for the receiver need not be considered.

(7) Rent under leases has continued to accrue in the amount of $1,800. Interest of $140 has accrued on notes payable.

(8) *Cash receipts:*

Collection of accounts	*$ 3,764*
Sales of merchandise	*18,216*
Sale of fixtures	*2,000*

Cash disbursements:

Accrued wages and taxes	*$ 2,056*
Expenses of the receivership	*2,490*

Instructions

Prepare a statement of realization and liquidation and the related gain and loss account for the period ended June 30, 1966.

AICPA adapted

22-8 Using data presented for the John Burton Company in Problem 21-7, prepare:

a. A realization and liquidation statement.

b. A statement of gains and losses from receiver's activities.

c. A capital account summary following the distribution of any remaining cash to the owners. Indicate how the cash was divided among the owners.

22-9 The Wilford Manufacturing Company was put under the control of a court-appointed receiver on June 15. The receiver has proceeded with an orderly liquidation of the company and you have been appointed by the court as the accountant to assist the receiver in the preparation of his interim report to the court.

Instructions

Using the data in Problem 21-8,

a. Prepare a report showing the realization of assets, liquidation of liabilities, and operations during the six-month period of the receivership.

b. Also prepare a statement of unsecured creditors' claims and the available assets on December 15.

22-10 The Jason Corporation had $105,000 of dividends in arrears on its preferred stock as of March 31, 1966. While retained earnings were adequate to permit the payment of accumulated dividends, the company's management did not wish to weaken its working capital position. They also realized that a portion of the fixed assets were no longer used or useful in their operation. Therefore, they proposed the following reorganization, which was approved by stockholders, to be effective as of April 1, 1966:

(1) The preferred stock was to be exchanged for $300,000 of 5% debenture bonds. Dividends in arrears were to be settled by the issuance of $120,000 of $10 par value, 5%, noncumulative preferred stock.
(2) Common stock was to be assigned a value of $50 per share.
(3) Goodwill was to be written off.
(4) Property, plant, and equipment were to be written down, based on appraisal and estimates of useful value, by a total of $103,200 consisting of $85,400 increase in allowance for depreciation and $17,800 decrease in certain assets.
(5) Other currents assets were to be written down by $10,460 to reduce certain items to expected realizable values.

The condensed balance sheet as of March 31, 1966, is presented on page 788.

Instructions

a. Prepare the journal entries to give effect to the reorganization as of April 1, 1966. Give complete explanations with each entry and comment on any possible options in recording the reorganization.

b. Prepare a balance sheet as of April 30, 1966, assuming that net income for April was $10,320 after provision for taxes. The operations resulted in $5,290 increase in cash, $10,660 increase in other current assets, $2,010 increase in current liabilities, and $3,620 increase in allowance for depreciation.

JASON CORPORATION
Balance Sheet
as of March 31, 1966

Assets

Cash		*$ 34,690*
Other current assets		*252,890*
Property, plant, and equipment	*$1,458,731*	
Accumulated depreciation	*512,481*	*946,250*
Goodwill		*50,000*
Total assets		*$1,283,830*

Liabilities & Capital

Current liabilities	*$ 136,860*
7% cumulative preferred stock, $100 par ($105,000 dividends in arrears)	*300,000*
Common stock, no-par, 9,000 shares outstanding	*648,430*
Premium on preferred stock	*22,470*
Retained earnings	*176,070*
Total liabilities & capital	*$1,283,830*

AICPA adapted

22-11 Goodman Hardware is facing insolvency as a result of an unexpected decline in sales volume after a large buildup in inventory and a move to larger facilities. The company has been negotiating with its general creditors for an informal agreement of some way to settle its obligations.

The most recent plan for the informal arrangement is for the trade creditors to accept 86 cents for each dollar of claim, with one-fourth of this to be paid within 15 days and the remainder to be paid in three equal installments on the first of May, June, and July. The owner of the facility is to reduce the monthly rental by 50% and take 2% of net sales in lieu of this reduction. The bank loan is fully secured by the inventory, and the accrued wages have priority.

The balance sheet for March 15 and the income statement for 2½ months are shown below:

GOODMAN HARDWARE
Balance Sheet
March 15

Assets

Cash	*$ 24,500.00*
Receivables	*104,200.00*
Inventory	*370,200.00*
Furniture and fixtures (net)	*82,500.00*
Total assets	*$581,400.00*

Liabilities

Accounts payable	*$203,600.00*
Note payable (secured by inventory)	*275,000.00*
Accrued rent	*5,000.00*
Accrued wages	*4,000.00*
Accrued income taxes	*4,500.00*
Accrued interest	*3,437.50*
Capital stock	*75,000.00*
Retained earnings	*10,862.50*
Total liabilities	*$581,400.00*

GOODMAN HARDWARE
Income Statement
for the 2½ months ended March 15

Sales		*$600,000.00*
Less:		
Cost of goods sold	*$522,400.00*	
Depreciation	*800.00*	
Rent expense	*25,000.00*	
Selling and administrative expense	*32,500.00*	
Interest expense	*3,437.50*	
Income taxes	*4,500.00*	
Net income		*$ 11,362.50*

You are hired as the accountant by the creditors to ascertain whether they should accept this proposal or push for liquidation at this time. In the course of your investigation, you ascertain that reasonable liquidation values for the assets are receivables, $78,150; inventory, $342,000; and, furniture and fixtures, $40,000. Liabilities for rent, wages, and taxes have priority. The estimated cost of liquidating the firm is estimated to be $25,000. The applicable income tax rates are 22% on income of $25,000 or less and 48% on all income in excess of $25,000 on an annual basis.

Instructions

Prepare a report for the trade creditors which will indicate clearly their alternative courses of action.

22-12 Hawthorne Shops is on the verge of insolvency. Accordingly, a receiver in equity, R. Robinson, is appointed by the court to take legal possession of the company's assets at February 1. The following January 31 the business was returned to the owners by the receiver with the blessings of the court.

A post-closing trial balance of the company's general ledger on February 1 follows:

HAWTHORNE SHOPS
Post-closing Trial Balance
February 1

Cash	$ 96,000	
Notes receivable	180,000	
Notes receivable discounted		$ 20,000
Accrued interest on notes receivable	6,000	
Accounts receivable	276,000	
Estimated uncollectibles		15,000
Inventory	348,400	
Subscribers to capital stock	41,000	
U.S. government bonds	50,000	
Buildings	242,800	
Accumulated depreciation—building		113,080
Prepaid insurance	2,800	
Deficit	94,080	
Notes payable		255,000
Accrued interest on notes payable		19,600
Accounts payable		592,000
Mortgage payable on buildings		120,000
Accrued interest on mortgage payable		2,400
Common stock		200,000
Totals	$1,337,080	$1,337,080

The transactions during the year of receivership are summarized below:

Cash collections:	
Notes receivable—old (gross $158,000, less written off $16,180)	$ 141,820
Interest on notes receivable, including accrual of $6,000	8,800
Accounts receivable—old (gross $220,000, less discount $4,000 and uncollectible accounts written off $7,000)	209,000
Subscribers to capital stock ($2,000 uncollectible)	39,000
Securities considered worthless Feb. 1 and not included in post-closing trial balance	9,400
Receiver's certificates issued, interest at 4½%	240,000
Accounts receivable—new (gross $450,000, less discounts $21,200)	428,800
Interest on U.S. government bonds	1,000
	$1,077,820

Cash payments:	
Notes receivable discounted, not paid by makers (remaining $15,000 paid by makers at maturity)	$ 5,000
Notes payable—old	130,400
Accounts payable—old (retired at a discount of 10%)	90,000
Accounts payable—old (retired at face amount)	420,000
Accounts payable—new (gross $248,000, less discount $4,000)	244,000
Interest on notes payable, including accrual of $19,600	22,000
Interest on mortgage payable, including accrual of $2,400	5,200

Receiver's certificates	*80,000*
Interest on receiver's certificates	*11,620*
Receiver's fees	*16,000*
	$1,024,220

Other transactions:	
Sales of merchandise (before discounts)	*$ 520,000*
Purchase of merchandise (before discounts)	*220,000*
Selling expenses	*66,000*
General expenses	*26,000*
Adjustments at Jan. 31:	
Merchandise inventory	*$ 240,000*
Depreciation of buildings	*7,200*
Accrued taxes	*7,400*
Accrued interest on notes receivable	*600*
Provision for doubtful accounts—new account receivable	*1,600*
Insurance expired	*600*
Interest on old notes payable	*5,600*
Interest on old mortgage payable	*2,400*

Instructions

a. Prepare a statement of realization and liquidation summarizing the receiver's transactions by setting forth his accountability at the beginning of the receivership, the operations during receivership, and the accountability at the consumation of receivership.

b. Prepare a balance sheet for Hawthorne Shops as of January 31.

AICPA adapted

FIDUCIARY ACCOUNTING

PART SEVEN

23 ESTATE ADMINISTRATION

This chapter and the following one deal with the problems of accounting for the estate of a deceased and for the activities of a trust. In these chapters we shall be emphasizing fiduciary relationships rather than the proprietary relationships typical of most accounting problems. Our starting point is therefore to study the responsibilities and activities of the administrator in order to understand the problems he faces. As in corporate accounting, we need to understand the function of the enterprise and the need for information so that we can set up effective accounting procedures. These two chapters constitute a generalized survey of the applicable laws and present the usual accounting techniques and reports. Many states have specific requirements which may be slightly different from the ones discussed here.

Fiduciary

A fiduciary relationship exists when a person is entrusted with the care, management, and disposition of the property of others and is accountable for his activities in connection with this property. The relationship is usually created by a will, by a trust indenture, or by court appointment. Receivers and trustees in bankruptcy, executors and administrators of estates, and trustees of assets placed in trusts are all persons acting in a fiduciary capacity.

Because of these relationships the purpose and function of fiduciary accounting are quite different from the purpose and function of enterprise accounting. Sprague, in discussing the nature of the difference and the reason for its existence, points out that in fiduciary accounting:

> This idea of proprietorship is nearly or entirely absent, and its place is taken by responsibility or accountability. It always arises from delegated authority, the affairs being placed under the control of some person as representative of the actual owner whose object in keeping accounts is to prove that he has faithfully administered them. . . . The essence of fiduciary accounting is the ascertaining to what extent the person holding these delegated powers has fulfilled his duties and to what extent he is still accountable. He is *charged* with all property coming under his control, and he is *discharged* by any lawful disposal of it for the good of the estate.[1]

Administration of the estate

The origin of the decedent's estate is the death of a person who owns property, either personal or real or both. If the deceased leaves a will indicating the manner in which he, the testator, wishes his property distributed, then the executor named in the will is responsible for carrying out the provisions of the will and/or the applicable laws. If the executor named in the will is unable to serve or if none is named, the fiduciary function may be performed by an administrator appointed by the court.

If the decedent died without leaving a valid will, his estate will be distributed among his heirs in accordance with the statutes of descent and distribution of the state having jurisdiction over the property. A person who dies without a valid will is said to have died *intestate*.

All matters relating to a deceased's estate are handled through the jurisdiction of a county court known as the probate, surrogate's, or orphan's court. The active administration of the estate lies with the executor or administrator; however, the court must issue letters testamentary to an executor or letters of administration to an administrator before he is authorized to proceed with the distribution of the property. Before issuing the letters testamentary, the court will conduct a hearing with appropriate witnesses. If the court is satisfied that the will is a valid instrument and that it was executed without fraud when the decedent was of age, competent, and free from undue influence, then the court will admit the will to probate and issue the letters testamentary.

Duties of the fiduciary

The first duty of the executor or administrator is to prepare an inventory of the estate property and to take charge of all personal property of the decedent except for that exempted under the prevailing state statute, such as household furnishings, family items, domestic animals, the family automobile, and a specified small sum of money. Title to real property usually passes directly to the heirs or devisees and therefore does not come under the control of the fiduciary. However, the court may, under some circumstances, order the real property to be sold as a means of paying valid debts, or the state law may require that the real property be administered by the fiduciary. The fiduciary is required to exercise due diligence in the discovery of all assets and to take the necessary legal steps to obtain possession of them. Any records kept by the decedent are usually very helpful in the discovery

[1] Charles E. Sprague, *Philosophy of Accounts,* 5th ed., The Ronald Press Company (New York: 1922), pp. 148–149.

of assets and any books kept by the decedent must be closed by the executor. The fiduciary is also responsible for the collection of rents, interest, or other items of income owed to or belonging to the decedent, and for the payment of funeral and administrative expenses, legal debts of the decedent, taxes on the estate, and other expenses related to the affairs of the estate. After the payment of debts and expenses, he must distribute the remaining properties to the designated beneficiaries. Finally, an accounting of his administration must be made to the court and other interested parties.

Inventory of assets. In most states the law requires an inventory to be taken by the fiduciary as the basis for his accountability. The inventory includes cash on hand and on deposit, furniture, fixtures and personal articles, claims against others, contract rights which do not involve personal services of the decedent, unpaid fees, commissions and salaries, life insurance policies payable to the estate, interest in partnerships, dividends declared or income accrued before the decedent's death, leases, and all other personal property owned by the decedent. Also included in the inventory are claims canceled by will, articles exempted for the family, and items of no apparent value. The inventory does not include moneys or goods held by the decedent for others. Liabilities are not a part of this listing; if the decedent had pledged some of his assets as collateral for debts owed, the pledged assets are listed without deducting the liabilities they secure.

The items in the inventory are valued by competent appraisers at a value which purports to be market value at the time of death. The details of this list comprise the beginnings of the fiduciary's accounts. These items should be posted to ledgers as a first step in the bookkeeping procedure by entering in ledger accounts the amounts established by the inventory. The credit side of the entry is to an accountability account, Estate Principal.

Custody of funds. The fiduciary is responsible for converting personal property in the estate into cash as rapidly as possible. Perishable goods, speculative investments, and other burdensome property should be sold at the earliest possible date to derive as much as possible of its full value at the date of death. Income-bearing investments which give evidence of being well protected from loss may be held as a matter of increasing the value of the estate. All accounts due should be collected at the earliest possible date; the fiduciary is expected to take vigorous action to accomplish such collection. Items of a personal nature are usually distributed to the heirs at appraised value.

All funds should be kept physically separate from those of the fiduciary. A separate bank account is opened for this purpose, and all disbursements are made by check. Although the fiduciary is not responsible for investing the funds of the estate to earn a return, where the funds can be deposited in an insured, interest-bearing savings account they should be so placed. Adequate risk insurance should be carried to protect the assets in the event of loss from disaster of any kind. In general if the fiduciary is to avoid liability for losses of estate property, he must care for the assets of the estate as diligently as a reasonable man would care for similar assets of his own.

The fiduciary is seldom justified in continuing the operation of a business. If a partnership interest is involved, he should be guided by the partnership agreement or the provisions of the will; in the absence of either, he should ascertain that the surviving partners are liquidating the business.

Payment of debts. In most states debts for funeral expenses, last illness, and allowances for support of the family take precedence over all other debts. These obligations with statutory priority may be paid by the fiduciary as soon as the inventory is complete. Except for these claims, the expenses of administration of the estate have precedence over other debts. The fiduciary is not required to make payment on the other debts until he has ascertained the total liabilities of the decedent. If payments are made before all claims against the estate are determined and if assets prove insufficient to pay all claims, the fiduciary can be held personally liable for the unpaid debts. Assessments against real estate and mortgages assumed when acquiring real estate usually go with the property; however, mortgages entered into by the decedent are liabilities of the estate.

To facilitate prompt discovery of all liabilities, the fiduciary will usually advertise to notify creditors to present their claims. All claims should be reviewed to ascertain that they are legal and proper. Charitable subscriptions are frequently invalid claims because no consideration was given for the subscription.

State law generally specifies the order of priority for payment of various types of debt in the event that the assets are not sufficient to pay all claims. Generally certain types of claims are given first preference; then state and Federal government taxes must be paid; next are court awards against the decedent; and finally unsecured claims.

Taxes on the estate. The income tax on the decedent's income for the period between his last tax return and the date of his death is paid from the estate assets. The income earned on the assets of the estate is subject to Federal income tax at the regular individual rate.

State inheritance taxes are levied on the right of an individual to receive a bequest. When the fiduciary pays state inheritance taxes, he acquires a receivable which he may collect from the various beneficiaries or deduct from the distribution which would otherwise be payable to each beneficiary. State inheritance taxes are usually based on the relationship of the beneficiary to the decedent. The closer the relationship between the beneficiary and the decedent, the lower the rates of tax and the larger the exemptions.

The Federal estate tax is a tax on the right of the decedent to give his property to others upon his death. This tax is based on the gross estate, which for Federal estate tax purposes includes all property of all kinds except real property located outside the United States. The values to be used in establishing the gross value of the estate are those determined by appraisal at (1) the date of the decedent's death, or (2) a date one year after the decedent's death, or (3) in the case of property disposed of at an earlier date, the value at the date of disposition. Deductions from the gross estate are allowed for funeral and administrative expenses, claims against the estate, bequests to public, charitable, and religious organizations, and a marital deduction for certain types of properties that pass to the spouse. A $60,000 exemption is allowed in addition to the above deductions in arriving at the taxable value of the estate. Federal estate tax rates follow a graduated scale based on the taxable value of the estate in a manner similar to the personal income tax. A credit is allowed against the Federal estate tax for payment of state inheritance taxes, subject to a limit stated as a percentage of the taxable estate.

Life insurance benefits payable directly to designated beneficiaries are subject to the state inheritance tax as a part of the beneficiaries' right to receive but may be excluded from the gross estate for Federal estate tax purposes.

Distribution of estate properties. Upon payment of all claims against the estate, the fiduciary begins to distribute the estate property in his possession in accordance with the provisions of the will or applicable state laws.

When there is no will, the inheritance laws of the state stipulate how the property is to be distributed to the heirs or next of kin of the deceased. These laws usually relate the distribution of the estate property to blood and marriage relationships. In some states there are different laws governing the distribution of real and personal property. The laws pertaining to distribution of real property are referred to as the *laws of descent* and those pertaining to distribution of personal property are referred to as the *laws of distribution.*

When there is a will, the property is distributed according to the provisions of the will. The disposition of personal property is referred to as a *legacy* with the person receiving such distribution being called the *legatee.* The disposition of the real property is referred to as a *devise* and the person receiving the real property is known as the *devisee.*

There are several classes of legacies. These various types have different claims against the assets or different rights in the event that the estate assets are not adequate to meet all debts and legacies. A *general* legacy is one payable out of the general personal property. As a result this legacy can be satisfied by distributing any personal property with appraised value equal to the amount of the legacy. A *specific* legacy is one payable only by distributing a particular asset. Any income earned by the asset after the testator's death is the property of the legatee. A specific legacy fails, however, if the asset specified is not in the estate at the testator's death. A *demonstrative* legacy is a gift of money or other property payable out of a specified fund or out of a particular group of assets. If the particular assets are not sufficient to satisfy the legacy, it becomes a general legacy. A *residuary* legacy is one which is paid out of the residuary assets after all others have been satisfied. It is usually specified as a percentage of the residuary estate.

All types of legacies lapse if the legatee dies before the testator; the assets revert to the residuary portion of the estate. An exception to this general rule may be made when the deceased legatee is a child or close relative of the testator and the legatee is survived by children. In such situations the children of the legatee usually receive the legacy.

As mentioned earlier, certain deductions may be made from the legacy. The most frequent is the state inheritance tax. A legatee may also deduct a debt, owed by him to the deceased, from his legacy if the debt does not exceed the distribution he would otherwise receive.

Devises of real property may also be divided into classes. There are *general devises, specific devises,* and *residuary devises* which relate to real property in the same way as these classes of legacies relate to personal property.

If an estate has insufficient assets to meet the debts and other prior claims, the legacies and devises will have to be reduced. The following general rules serve as a guideline; however, the individual state laws may prescribe a different order.

1. A specific legacy takes priority over a general legacy. General legacies may be wiped out completely before the specific legacy is reduced at all.

2. A legacy for the support of the decedent's wife and family where other support is not available will frequently receive precedence over legacies to more distant relatives and others.

3. The personal assets are used to pay debts before any real estate is mortgaged or sold; therefore, all legacies may be wiped out and none of the devisees of real estate will be affected.

4. Except for the above preferences, all legacies are usually reduced proportionately in the event of a deficiency in the estate.

State laws frequently provide for deferral of the distribution of estate assets, at the discretion of the fiduciary, for periods of six months to a year. If the property is not distributed at this time, a payment representing interest on the legacy may be required. In some cases when a payment is made to a legatee before the general distribution, the legatee is required to pay interest to the estate for the period of the advance.

Intermediate and final accounting. Reports are made by the fiduciary to the proper court as required by statute or by the court, or at his convenience if no requirements are made. The fiduciary will file intermediate reports at varying times depending upon the size and complexity of the estate. He will file a final report when he has converted to cash those assets which need to be converted because of their nature or the needs of the estate, and when he has determined and settled all the debts and expenses of the estate. The term *final* does not mean that this is the last report the fiduciary will file; it merely means a final reporting with respect to certain items, particularly claims against the estate.

If the court accepts the final report, it will allow the expenses and fee of the fiduciary and issue a decree which disposes of the remainder of the estate. If a will was left by the deceased, the decree will merely indicate amounts to be distributed to the unpaid general and residuary legacies. If a will was not left, then the decree will indicate the amounts to be received by the heirs in accordance with the statutes covering descent and distribution. When the fiduciary makes this final distribution, the court, upon notification, will declare the estate closed with the settlements made to be final and binding on all parties.

Fiduciary's accounts

The accounts which the fiduciary keeps are not prescribed by law; therefore, they should be designed to provide in sufficient detail the information required of the fiduciary by the courts and other interested parties. This means that the accounts must provide a record of the events involving the estate properties and the actions of the fiduciary with respect to these properties.

The fiduciary is accounting for his responsibility over the assets charged to him. He, therefore, does not recognize any liabilities or equity on his books of account. His accounting equation is assets = accountability, rather than assets = liabilities + equity. He is accountable for all assets in the inventory of the deceased and any assets subsequently discovered or coming into his control as a result of gains on the assets he is holding. He is responsible for paying the debts of the estate and any debts he incurs on behalf of the estate. The payment of these liabilities reduces his accountability. Similarly, he must receive all income that rightfully belongs to the estate from investments comprising the principal or investments made by him on behalf of the estate. These receipts increase his accountability.

The fiduciary, therefore, needs records which will indicate the assets comprising the estate and their source, that is, estate inventory, assets discovered, income, or gain in value. For the small uninvolved estate, a system of asset and accountability accounts may be adequate. In larger estates, the complexity of the activity demands the use of nominal accounts to explain the causes of change in accountability. These nominal accounts are used to record the payment of debts, the collection of receivables, the gain or loss in principal assets, and the distribution of the estate to the legatees. The nominal accounts are closed to the accountability account at the end of each accounting period.

In estate accounting the length of the accounting period is not fixed except as there is need to file annual income tax returns on the income earned by the estate. For purposes of the court, the accounting period is the period elapsed since the last report; therefore, the period is usually established according to the need for intermediate and final reports.

The essential difference between accounting for estates and accounting for the usual business operation is that in estate accounting a clear distinction must be made between the principal of the estate and its income. This distinction rests on the legal interpretation of the meaning of the terms *principal* and *income*. The principal of an estate is represented by a group of assets which can be isolated from other assets deemed to be undistributed income. In other words, the principal of an estate is not the monetary value of the assets; rather it is the assets themselves.

Receipts and disbursements of the estate must be separated as to principal or income. Such a division is essential for tax purposes even though not required by will. Receipts of principal are items which were the property of the decedent which had not been converted into cash, such as interest, rent, appreciation of assets, profits of a business earned prior to death, and dividends which were declared prior to date of death. Disbursements of principal include debts owed at date of death, including funeral expenses and debts arising from last illness, losses on realization of assets, taxes assessed prior to date of death, insurance premiums to avoid loss of principal, losses due to casualty or theft, expenses of administration, carrying charges on unproductive real estate, improvements in real estate, natural wear and tear on property, and estate and inheritance taxes.

All other receipts are generally considered income to the estate. Specifically, they include receipts from accruals arising after the death of the decedent and any profits from a business, including dividends declared after the death of the decedent. Disbursements chargeable against income are generally limited to those related to the collection of income, taxes on income, and those related to keeping income-producing property in as good condition as when the decedent died.

Some differences exist in the treatment of any bond discount or premium which may exist on bond investments. The majority view is that bonds should be inventoried at market price and that no amortization of premium or accumulation of discount should be recorded. Instead, the gain or loss resulting from sale or maturity is an adjustment of principal. This opinion is based on the fact that principal is not impaired if it contains the actual assets left by the decedent or the proceeds of these assets. With respect to bonds purchased by the fiduciary as an investment, a premium is frequently amortized but a discount is seldom accumulated. In several states the applicable statutes provide that neither discount nor premium should be amortized, regardless of the date of purchase.

The accounting entries to record the data discussed above are described in the following paragraphs.

Memorandum entries. Memorandum entries, narrative statements written in the general journal, can be very useful and informative in tracing the history of an organization or activity. The fiduciary may employ this technique rather liberally in setting up his accounts. Elements of information recorded by memorandum entries include the dates of various events such as the death, reading of the will, date of letters testamentary, names of appraisers, any court actions, and any other events without monetary significance which appear important to the administration of the estate.

Opening accounts. The inventory of the assets of the decedent is compiled immediately following his death and valued by appraisers appointed by the court. This inventory forms the basis for the opening entry by the fiduciary. The entry will include a debit to Cash and to other individual assets; or, as an alternative, noncash assets may be debited to a control account and supported by a subsidiary ledger. The credit is to an accountability account, Estate Principal.

Assets discovered subsequent to inventory. Assets discovered after the inventory has been completed are recorded by debiting asset accounts and crediting Estate Principal or a separate accountability account, Assets Discovered. The recorded value of these assets should be the value at the date of the decedent's death.

Realization of assets. Any assets of the estate which are not distributable in their original form to beneficiaries must be converted into cash. If the realization proceeds are more or less than the appraised value of the asset, the accountability of the fiduciary is changed. The difference between the proceeds realized, debit Cash, and the appraised value, credit specific asset, is usually entered in a nominal account, such as Realization Gain or Loss, to be closed to the accountability account at the end of the period.

Payment of expenses or receipt of income. When expenses of the estate are paid, assets are decreased, with a corresponding effect on the fiduciary's accountability. When income is received, assets are increased and accountability rises. Nominal accounts are used to record expenses and income with the offsetting debit or credit to Cash.

Payment of debts or collection of claims. The fiduciary usually does not record the liabilities existing at the date of the decedent's death; consequently, when he pays a liability he reduces his accountability. The debit is usually made to a nominal account, Debts Paid, and Cash is credited.

The collection of claims owed the decedent at the date of his death does not change the fiduciary's accountability because the claim is included in the inventory of assets and is merely being converted into another asset, cash. The conversion is recorded by a debit to Cash and a credit to the receivable being collected.

Payment of expense or collection of income for a legatee. Occasionally the fiduciary will pay expenses for a legatee, such as state inheritance taxes or some payment that is required because of the property that is willed to a legatee. Similarly he may collect money for the legatee, such as interest accrued or dividends declared after the death of the testator. In such cases an account will be opened to indicate an amount due from or due to the particular legatee. If the account represents a due from or receivable to the estate, then it is considered an asset of the estate at the time an accounting is made to the courts. In the distribution of assets, the receivable from the legatee will be deducted from the legacy to which he is otherwise entitled.

If the income is collected for the legatee by the fiduciary, the assets of the estate and the accountability of the executor are increased. The credit to the legacy account would indicate a specific accountability to the legatee for the income received.

Operation of a going business. Although the fiduciary is seldom expected to operate a business owned by the decedent, in some cases the court may order that operation of the business be continued, especially if it is a sole proprietorship not requiring the personal services of the decedent. The records of the business are maintained separately from those of the remainder of the estate and a controlling account is included among the estate assets for the investment in the business at appraised values.

When the fiduciary takes charge of the estate, the books of the business are closed and a complete inventory is taken of the assets. The liabilities then existing are transferred to the list of debts to be paid by the fiduciary. The company's books are then reopened with the assets valued at the appraised amount. Subsequent depreciation and write-off of these assets will be based on these revised values, and a new basis of accountability is established at the date of the decedent's death.

All revenues, expenses, and new liabilities are recorded on the books of the business in the normal manner. When the fiduciary is required to file a report with the court, the books of the business are closed and the gain or loss for the period is determined in the usual fashion. The fiduciary then adjusts the investment account and his accountability account to reflect the results of operating the business during the preceding period. In accounting for this change in the investment, the accountant must be certain to classify the change according to the terms of the will as to estate principal, estate income, or income to a specific legatee.

Distribution of estate assets to legatees. When the specific legacies are distributed, the assets of the estate and the accountability of the executor are both reduced. Distributions may be recorded by debits to a general distribution account entitled Legacies Distributed, but if specific legacies are numerous a better procedure is to use a separate account for each legatee.

Entries after the final accounting. The final accounting of the fiduciary includes a plan for distribution of the remaining assets, a statement of the expenses connected with the accounting, and a statement of the commission due the fiduciary. If the accounting is approved, the court will issue a decree putting its proposals into effect. The expenses are then paid and the distributions to the legatees are made. Finally the nominal accounts for expenses, income, and distribution to legatees are closed.

At all times after the nominal accounts have been closed, the accountability account should equal the total value of the assets under the fiduciary's control. After the final distribution to the legatees, the estate's books are closed and the fiduciary is relieved of his responsibility by the court. Since all accounts have been closed, the fiduciary needs only to inform the court that he has complied with its final order of distributing the assets.

Reports of the fiduciary

The form of the fiduciary's report to court depends upon the requirements of the judge; however, the general form and content are well established. The report is usually divided into two parts. In the first part, the fiduciary *charges* himself with the assets of the estate for which he is responsible, including the estate principal, any discovered assets, and realized gains. He *credits* himself with all property disbursed and with realized losses. The balance must equal the cash and appraised value of the other property on hand. In effect the statement is one of cash receipts and disbursements, although the beginning balance is at least partially composed of property.

In the second part of the statement, the fiduciary *charges* himself with the cash receipts or income derived from the estate assets. He *credits* himself with the cash disbursements or expenses related to the income and with the cash disbursements made to legatees out of income. The balance of the income portion represents the assets derived as income for which the fiduciary is responsible. The combined balance of the principal and income sections represents the assets for which the executor is accountable. These assets are to be ultimately distributed to the legatees subject to the deduction of the fiduciary's commission, legal fees, the expense of the accounting, and other expenses which will be incurred in the administration of the estate. The charge and discharge statement is usually supported in detail by schedules for each line appearing on the face of the statement, although when the detail is not voluminous it may be included on the face of the statement.

The following form is illustrative of a fiduciary's statement:

ESTATE OF D. SMITH
John Doe, Executor or Administrator

Summary of Activity
March 6, 1967, to September 30, 1967

As to Principal:
- The Executor charges himself as follows:
  - Estate corpus (the inventory of the deceased assets at appraised values as originally charged)
  - Discovered assets (assets discovered subsequent to the inventory belonging to deceased at date of death)
  - Gain on realization of principal assets (the excess of sale or distribution value over carrying or appraised value of assets)
- The Executor credits himself as follows:
  - Funeral, last illness, and administrative expenses paid
  - Federal estate and state inheritance taxes paid
  - Debts of the estate paid
  - Distributions to legatees
  - Loss on realization of principal assets
- Balance of principal assets

As to Income:
- The Executor charges himself as follows:
  - Income received on estate assets
- The Executor credits himself as follows:
  - Administrative and other expenses paid chargeable to income
  - Distribution of income assets to legatees
- Balance of income assets

Balance of principal and income assets for which Executor is accountable

Illustration

The accounting and bookkeeping required by the executor of the estate of James Clayton is illustrated in the remaining pages of this chapter. Clayton died on September 23, 1966. His will, dated February 15, 1962, provides that his eldest son, James Clayton, Jr., act as executor of the estate. The will further provides that all just debts and expenses be paid and that his property be disposed of as follows:

Personal residence	devised to Martha Clayton, wife
Rental property as follows:	
210 Marion St. 684 Edgefield Ave. 709 Dogwood Lane	devised to Martha Clayton, wife
644 Main St.	devised to James Clayton, Jr., son
650 Main St.	devised to Colin Clayton, son
400 shares of Queen City Co.	bequeathed to Mary Clayton, daughter
800 shares of Southern Coach	bequeathed to Sally Clayton, daughter
Cash	a bequest of $10,000 to James Clayton, Jr., in lieu of any other executor's commission
All property in residence	bequeathed to Martha Clayton, wife

Remainder of the estate to be divided one-half to Martha Clayton, wife; the other one-half to be divided equally among the four children: James, Jr., Colin, Mary, and Sally Clayton.

The will further provided that $600 per month be paid to Martha Clayton out of income of the estate during the administration period.

All estate and inheritance taxes are to be paid out of the residue of the estate.

The following inventory of the decedent's property, excluding exempt property set aside for the widow, is stated at fair market value as of the date of death. Values were set by a board of three appraisers appointed by the court. No recognition was given to accrued interest on bond investments or to any other accruals.

Personal residence property	*$ 20,000*
Decedent's personal automobile	*3,400*
Cascade Life Insurance Co.—life insurance policy on life of James Clayton, beneficiary Martha Clayton	*150,000*
Upstate Life Insurance Co.—life insurance policy on life of James Clayton, beneficiary estate	*40,000*
1,000 shares of Adams Co. common stock	*47,500*
1,500 shares of King County Bank common stock	*82,600*
1,200 shares of Madison, Inc., common stock	*71,800*
1,000 shares of Queen City Co. common stock	*80,000*
1,600 shares of Southern Coach common stock	*64,000*
First National Bank checking account	*85,640*
$20,000 King County sewer bonds, 3¾%, 1986, interest payable Feb. 1 and Aug. 1	*20,600*
$70,000 U.S. Treasury bonds, 3%, 1992, interest payable Apr. 1 and Oct. 1	*71,400*

James Clayton, Jr., opened an estate banking account on October 10, 1966, after the will was probated on October 8, to which he transferred the balance of the checking account. Other cash transactions were as follows:

Cash Receipts

Interest:		
U.S. Treasury bonds, 3%, 1992		
Oct. 1, 1966		*$ 1,050*
Apr. 1, 1967		*1,050*
Oct. 1, 1967		*1,050*
King County sewer bonds, 3¾%, 1986		
Feb. 1, 1967		*375*
Dividends:		
Adams Co. @ 50¢ per share per quarter and Madison, Inc., @ 75¢ per share per quarter		
Dec. 15, 1966		*1,400*
Mar. 15, 1967		*1,400*
June 15, 1967		*1,400*
Sept. 15, 1967		*1,400*
King County Bank		
Oct. 1, 1966, declared Sept. 3, 1966, payable to holders of record Sept. 20, 1966		*750*
Apr. 1, 1967		*750*
Oct. 1, 1967		*1,125*
Queen City Co. @ 40¢ per share per quarter and Southern Coach @ 25¢ per share per quarter		
Nov. 15, 1966		*440*
Feb. 15, 1967		*440*
May 15, 1967		*440*
Aug. 15, 1967		*440*
Oct. 15, 1966	*Net proceeds of Oct. 15, 1966, sale of decedent's personal automobile*	*3,550*
	Proceeds of Upstate life insurance policy collected Oct. 15, 1966	*40,000*
Feb. 1, 1967	*Net proceeds of Feb. 1, 1967, sale of $20,000 King County sewer bonds, 3¾%, 1986*	*19,700*
Oct. 1, 1967	*Net proceeds of Oct. 1, 1967, sale of $70,000 U.S. Treasury bonds, 3%, 1992*	*72,100*

Cash Disbursements

Oct. 15, 1966	*Funeral expenses to Jones Funeral Home*	*$ 1,850*
Dec. 20, 1966	*Decedent's debts*	*18,782*
Apr. 15, 1967	*Income taxes (state and Federal of Clayton for 1966)*	*25,000*
Sept. 30, 1967	*Federal estate and state inheritance taxes*	*86,000*
Oct. 31, 1967	*Fiduciary income taxes (Federal and state) for fiscal years ended Oct. 31, 1966 ($0), and 1967 ($2,300)*	*2,300*
Each month	*Monthly payments to Martha Clayton, Oct., 1966, to Oct., 1967*	*7,800*

All specific legacies were delivered by November 1, 1966. Attorneys' and accountants' fees and executor's expenses, for which approval was requested in

JAMES CLAYTON ESTATE
James Clayton, Jr., Executor
General Journal

Date	Accounts and explanations	Dr	Cr
1966			
Oct. 8	Will of James Clayton was admitted to probate and letters testamentary were issued to James Clayton, Jr.		
Oct. 10	Personal Residence Property	20,000	
	Life Insurance, Upstate	40,000	
	Personal Automobile	3,400	
	Adams Co.—1,000 common shares	47,500	
	King County Bank—1,500 common shares	82,600	
	Madison, Inc.—1,200 common shares	71,800	
	Queen City Co.—1,000 common shares	80,000	
	Southern Coach—1,600 common shares	64,000	
	First National Bank—checking account	85,640	
	King County Sewer Bonds—3¾%, 1986	20,600	
	U.S. Treasury Bonds—3%, 1992	71,400	
	Accrued Interest on King County Bonds	112	
	Accrued Interest on U.S. Treasury Bonds	1,009	
	Dividends Receivable—King County Bank	750	
	Estate Principal		588,811
	To record the assets of the estate of James Clayton as of Sept., 1966, for which James Clayton, Jr., is accountable. All exempt property set aside for the widow is excluded from this inventory. (Accrued interest rounded to nearest dollar.)		
Oct. 15	Legacy—Mary Clayton	32,000	
	Legacy—Sally Clayton	32,000	
	Queen City Co.—400 common shares		32,000
	Southern Coach—800 common shares		32,000
	To record distribution of common stock to legatees as provided in will probated Oct. 8, 1966.		
Nov. 1	Legacy—Martha Clayton	20,000	
	Personal Residence Property		20,000
	To record distribution of household property to legatee as provided in will probated Oct. 8, 1966.		
1967			
Oct. 20	Dividend Receivable	440	
	Income		440
	To record declaration of regular quarterly dividend by Queen City Co. and Southern Coach payable to stockholders of record Oct. 20, 1967.		
	Note: Although the cash basis accounting is followed almost exclusively in estate accounting, accruals are frequently necessary at the time of the final accounting to effect a proper distribution of the assets.		

JAMES CLAYTON ESTATE
James Clayton, Jr., Executor
Cash Disbursements Journal

Date	Payee	Check no.	Cash in bank Cr	Debts paid Dr	Martha Clayton Dr	Miscellaneous debits	
						Account	Amount
1966							
Oct. 15	Jones Funeral Home	1001	1,850			Funeral Expense	1,850
Oct. 15	Martha Clayton	1002	600		600		
Nov. 1	Martha Clayton	1003	600		600		
Dec. 1	Martha Clayton	1004	600		600		
Dec. 20	Various	Various	18,782	18,782			
1967							
Jan. 1	Martha Clayton	1012	600		600		
Feb. 1	Martha Clayton	1013	600		600		
Mar. 1	Martha Clayton	1014	600		600		
Apr. 1	Martha Clayton	1015	600		600		
Apr. 15	Various	Various	25,000			Personal Tax Expense	25,000
May 1 to Sept. 1	Martha Clayton	Various	3,000		3,000		
Sept. 30	Various	Various	86,000			Estate & Inheritance Tax	86,000
Oct. 1	Martha Clayton	1030	600		600		
Oct. 31	Various	Various	2,300			Fiduciary Income Tax	2,300
			141,732	18,782	7,800		115,150

JAMES CLAYTON ESTATE
James Clayton, Jr., Executor
Cash Receipts Journal

Date	Explanation	Cash in bank Dr	Loss on realization Dr	Gain on realization Cr	Income Cr	Miscellaneous credits	
						Account	Amount
1966							
Oct. 10	Deposit	85,640				First National Bank	85,640
Oct. 15	Sale of auto	3,550		150		Personal Auto	3,400
Oct. 15	Life insurance	40,000				Life Ins.—Upstate	40,000
Oct. 15	Dividend—bank	750				Dividend Received—Bank	750
Oct. 15	Interest	1,050			41	Interest Received—Treas.	1,009
Nov. 15	Dividend	440			440		
Dec. 15	Dividend	1,400			1,400		
1967							
Feb. 1	Interest	375			263	Interest Received—King	112
Feb. 1	Sale—bond	19,700	900			King Co. Bond	20,600
Feb. 15	Dividend	440			440		
Mar. 15	Dividend	1,400			1,400		
Apr. 1	Interest	1,050			1,050		
Apr. 1	Dividend	750			750		
May 15	Dividend	440			440		
June 15	Dividend	1,400			1,400		
Aug. 15	Dividend	440			440		
Sept. 15	Dividend	1,400			1,400		
Oct. 1	Dividend	1,125			1,125		
Oct. 1	Interest	1,050			1,050		
Oct. 1	Sale of bond	72,100		700		U.S. Treas. Bonds	71,400
		234,500	900	850	11,639		222,911

the final accounting of October 31, 1967, totaled $37,660. Regular quarterly dividends declared by Queen City Co. (40 cents per share) and Southern Coach Co. (25 cents per share) to stockholders of record October 20, 1967, payable November 15, 1967, were received by the executor on November 17, 1967, and were immediately delivered to legatees.

The executor's general journal and his cash receipts and disbursements journals are reproduced to show the accounting entries, with all amounts rounded to the nearest dollar. The posting of the journals to the ledger accounts is not illustrated, but the executor's final accounting statement is shown with all detailed schedules. To gain facility with the problems of estate accounting, the student might find it useful to work through these transactions in T accounts to prove the balances in the final charge and discharge statement.

Trial balance. A trial balance prepared from the books of the executor has the same purpose and form as for any business. The asset and nominal account balances are the end of the period balances; however, the accountability account, like the equity accounts, shows the beginning of the period balance. This is true because the nominal accounts represent adjustments to this account and they have not been closed as yet.

JAMES CLAYTON ESTATE
James Clayton, Jr., Executor
Trial Balance
October 31, 1967

	Debit	Credit
Cash	$ 92,768	
Adams Co.—1,000 shares common	47,500	
King County Bank—1,500 shares common	82,600	
Madison, Inc.—1,200 shares common	71,800	
Queen City Co.—600 shares common	48,000	
Southern Coach—800 shares common	32,000	
Dividend receivable	440	
Estate principal		$588,811
Funeral expenses	1,850	
Personal income tax—1966	25,000	
Estate and inheritance taxes	86,000	
Fiduciary income tax	2,300	
Debts paid	18,782	
Martha Clayton—support	7,800	
Loss on realization	900	
Gain on realization		850
Income		12,079
Legacy—Mary Clayton	32,000	
Legacy—Sally Clayton	32,000	
Legacy—Martha Clayton	20,000	
Total	$601,740	$601,740

Charge and discharge statement. The charge and discharge statement, together with the supporting exhibits and schedules, shows the beginning asset balances, the changes during the period, and the ending balance. It is in effect a recapitulation of the accountability account, just as a realization and liquidation statement is a recapitulation of the receiver's account. The assets included in principal as shown at the beginning of the statement are those for which the executor is responsible at the beginning of the period. These asset values are not the same as those found in the trial balance at the end of the period. The figure "balance as to principal" at the end of the period does correspond with the asset balances on the trial balance except that it does not include assets considered to be income. In the illustration the "balance as to income and principal" is the same as the assets shown on the trial balance and can be verified by reference to Schedules E and H.

JAMES CLAYTON ESTATE — *Exhibit I*
James Clayton, Jr., Executor
Charge and Discharge Statement
for the period October 8, 1966, to October 31, 1967

As to Principal I Charge Myself with:		
Assets per inventory (Schedule A)	$588,811	
Gain on realization (Schedule B)	850	
Total charges		$589,661
As to Principal I Credit Myself with:		
Funeral expenses	$ 1,850	
Estate, inheritance, and income taxes (Schedule C)	111,000	
Debts paid	18,782	
Loss on realization (Schedule D)	900	
Legacies delivered	84,000	
Total credits		216,532
Balance as to principal (Schedule E)		$373,129
As to Income I Charge Myself with:		
Dividends received (Schedule F)	$ 9,675	
Interest received (Schedule G)	2,404	
Total charges		$ 12,079
As to Income I Credit Myself with:		
Fiduciary income tax expense	$ 2,300	
Support expense—Martha Clayton	7,800	
Total credits		10,100
Balance as to income (Schedule H)		$ 1,979
Balance as to income and principal		$375,108

JAMES CLAYTON ESTATE — **Schedule A**

James Clayton, Jr., Executor

Inventory of Principal Assets

(exclusive of exempt property set aside for widow)

September 23, 1966

First National Bank—checking account	$ 85,640
Personal residence property	20,000
Personal automobile	3,400
Upstate Life Insurance Co.—beneficiary, estate	40,000
Adams Co. common stock—1,000 shares	47,500
King County Bank common stock—1,500 shares	82,600
Madison, Inc., common stock—1,200 shares	71,800
Queen City Co. common stock—1,000 shares	80,000
Southern Coach common stock—1,600 shares	64,000
King County sewer bonds, 3¾%, 1986	20,600
U.S. Treasury bonds, 3%, 1992	71,400
Dividend receivable—King County Bank	750
Interest receivable—U.S. Treasury bonds	1,009*
Interest receivable—King County sewer bonds	112*
	$588,811

* Calculation of Accrued Interest as of Sept. 23, 1966:
U.S. Treasury bonds, 3% interest payable Apr. 1 and Oct. 1:
$173/180 \times .015 \times \$70{,}000 = \$1{,}009$ (rounded to nearest dollar)
King County sewer bonds, 3¾% interest payable Feb. 1 and Aug. 1:
$54/180 \times .01875 \times \$20{,}000 = \$112$ (rounded to nearest dollar)

JAMES CLAYTON ESTATE — **Schedule B**

James Clayton, Jr., Executor

Gain on Realization

October 8, 1966, to October 31, 1967

Cash proceeds from sale of auto	$ 3,550	
Appraised value per inventory	3,400	
Realization gain		$150
Cash proceeds from sale of U.S. Treasury bonds	$72,100	
Market value per inventory	71,400	
Realization gain		700
Total realization gain—Exhibit I		$850

JAMES CLAYTON ESTATE — **Schedule C**

James Clayton, Jr., Executor

Estate, Inheritance, and Income Taxes

October 8, 1966, to October 31, 1967

Federal estate and state inheritance taxes	$ 86,000
Income tax of James Clayton—1966	25,000
Total taxes—Exhibit I	$111,000

JAMES CLAYTON ESTATE — **Schedule D**
James Clayton, Jr., Executor
Loss on Realization
October 8, 1966, to October 31, 1967

Market value of King County bonds per inventory	$20,600
Cash proceeds from sale	19,700
Realization loss—Exhibit I	$ 900

JAMES CLAYTON ESTATE — **Schedule E**
James Clayton, Jr., Executor
Principal Assets
October 31, 1967

Cash	$ 91,229
Adams Co. common stock, 1,000 shares	47,500
King County Bank common stock, 1,500 shares	82,600
Madison, Inc., common stock, 1,200 shares	71,800
Queen City Co. common stock, 600 shares	48,000
Southern Coach common stock, 800 shares	32,000
Total principal assets—Exhibit I	$373,129

JAMES CLAYTON ESTATE — **Schedule F**
James Clayton, Jr., Executor
Dividend Income
October 8, 1966, to October 31, 1967

Adams Co. common stock	$2,000
Madison, Inc., common stock	3,600
King County Bank common stock	1,875
Queen City Co. common stock	1,200
Southern Coach common stock	1,000
Total dividend income—Exhibit I	$9,675

JAMES CLAYTON ESTATE — **Schedule G**
James Clayton, Jr., Executor
Interest Income
October 8, 1966, to October 31, 1967

U.S. Treasury bonds, 3% (rounded to nearest dollar)	$2,141
King County sewer bonds, 3¾% (rounded to nearest dollar)	263
Total interest income—Exhibit I	$2,404

JAMES CLAYTON ESTATE — **Schedule H**
James Clayton, Jr., Executor
Inventory of Income Assets
October 31, 1967

Cash	$1,539
Dividends receivable	440
Total income assets—Exhibit I	$1,979

JAMES CLAYTON ESTATE — *Exhibit II*
James Clayton, Jr., Executor
Proposed Final Distribution of Assets
October 31, 1967

Balance of estate assets		*$375,108*
Less: Attorneys' and accountants' fees and executor's expenses	*$ 37,660*	
Executor's commission as provided by the will	*10,000*	*47,660*
Remainder of the estate		*$327,448*
Distribution of residuary to legatees:		
Martha Clayton—½ of residual	*$163,724*	
James Clayton, Jr.—⅛ of residual	*40,931*	
Colin Clayton—⅛ of residual	*40,931*	
Mary Clayton—⅛ of residual	*40,931*	
Sally Clayton—⅛ of residual	*40,931*	
Total distribution		*327,448*
Undistributed portion of the assets		*$ -0-*
To Martha Clayton:		
Cash	*$ 22,554*	
Adams Co. common stock, 500 shares	*23,750*	
King County Bank common stock, 750 shares	*41,300*	
Madison, Inc., common stock, 600 shares	*35,900*	
Queen City Co. common stock, 300 shares	*24,000*	
Southern Coach common stock, 400 shares	*16,000*	
Dividend receivable	*220*	
Total		*$163,724*
To James Clayton, Jr., and Colin Clayton:		
Cash	*$ 5,666*	
Adams Co. common stock, 125 shares	*5,938*	
King County Bank common stock, 187 shares	*10,297*	
Madison, Inc., common stock, 150 shares	*8,975*	
Queen City Co. common stock, 75 shares	*6,000*	
Southern Coach common stock, 100 shares	*4,000*	
Dividend receivable	*55*	
Distribution to each	*$ 40,931*	
Total		*81,862*
To Mary Clayton and Sally Clayton:		
Cash	*$ 5,611*	
Adams Co. common stock, 125 shares	*5,937*	
King County Bank common stock, 188 shares	*10,353*	
Madison, Inc., common stock, 150 shares	*8,975*	
Queen City common stock, 75 shares	*6,000*	
Southern Coach common stock, 100 shares	*4,000*	
Dividend receivable	*55*	
Distribution to each	*$ 40,931*	
Total		*81,862*
Total distributed (all figures rounded to nearest dollar)		*$327,448*

Closing entries. After the fiduciary has made his final accounting and the court has approved the fees, the administrative expenses, and the plan for final distribution of the assets, the payment of expenses and distribution of assets must be completed. The entries to record final activity are made here in the general journal.

The following entries will record the payment of approved bills and the distribution of assets to the legatees.

Attorneys', Accountants', and Administrative Expenses	*37,660*	
Executor's Commission	*10,000*	
Cash		*47,660*
To record payment of estate expenses as approved by the court.		
Legacy—Martha Clayton	*163,724*	
Cash		*22,554*
Adams Co. Common Stock		*23,750*
King County Bank Common Stock		*41,300*
Madison, Inc., Common Stock		*35,900*
Queen City Co. Common Stock		*24,000*
Southern Coach Common Stock		*16,000*
Dividends Receivable		*220*
To record distribution of residuary legacy to Martha Clayton, wife of the deceased.		
Legacy—James Clayton, Jr.	*40,931*	
Legacy—Colin Clayton	*40,931*	
Legacy—Mary Clayton	*40,931*	
Legacy—Sally Clayton	*40,931*	
Cash		*22,554*
Adams Co. Common Stock		*23,750*
King County Bank Common Stock		*41,300*
Madison, Inc., Common Stock		*35,900*
Queen City Co. Common Stock		*24,000*
Southern Coach Common Stock		*16,000*
Dividends Receivable		*220*
To record distribution of residuary legacy, 1/8 to each legatee, James, Colin, Mary, and Sally Clayton, children of the deceased.		

Once the final distribution of assets is completed, the executor can then proceed to close out the nominal accounts to his accountability account. If the bookkeeping has been handled properly, the assets will all be distributed and the accountability account will indicate a zero balance.

Estate Principal	*588,811*	
Gain on Realization	*850*	
Income	*12,079*	
Funeral Expenses		*1,850*
Personal Income Tax		*25,000*
Estate and Inheritance Tax		*86,000*
Fiduciary Income Tax		*2,300*
Debts Paid		*18,782*
Martha Clayton—Support		*7,800*
Loss on Realization		*900*
Legacy—Martha Clayton		*183,724*
Legacy—Mary Clayton		*72,931*
Legacy—Sally Clayton		*72,931*
Legacy—James Clayton, Jr.		*40,931*
Legacy—Colin Clayton		*40,931*
Attorneys', Accountants', and Administrative Expenses		*37,660*
Executor's Commission		*10,000*
To close the executor's accounts.		

Questions

1. What conditions constitute a fiduciary relationship? How are these conditions related to the problems of the estate?
2. What are the duties of a fiduciary, acting as executor or administrator of an estate?
3. What are the general guidelines for the payment of debts and distribution of estate assets if the claims against the assets exceed the value of the assets?
4. Distinguish between the inheritance tax and the estate tax.
5. Define the following terms as they are used in the context of estate affairs:
   a. general legacy
   b. specific devise
   c. demonstrative legacy
   d. residuary legacy
6. The accounting equation which is most often discussed is stated as follows: Assets = liabilities + owners' equity. The equation used in connection with fiduciary accounts is assets = accountability. Why is there a difference and what is the meaning of the difference?
7. What is the generalized rule for the separation of items of principal and income?
8. John Caldwell was named executor of an estate with the following assets:

Cash	$ 1,200
Bonds (market value)	10,000
Stock (market value)	5,600
Total	$16,800

Subsequent to assuming his position as executor of the estate, a savings account with a balance of $18,400 was discovered. Caldwell sold the stock for $5,300. Record these data in journal entry form and close the nominal accounts.

9. Helen Mays was executrix of her father's estate, during which time the following events occurred:

(1) Last illness and funeral expenses of $1,950 were paid.
(2) Interest was received on bonds held in the amount of $800; one-half of the interest was accrued at the date of the decedent's death.
(3) The courts authorized the payment of claims against the estate of $12,800.
(4) Notes receivable amounting to $8,000 with interest of $250, one-fifth accrued at the date of death, were collected.
(5) Inheritance taxes were paid out of estate assets for Helen, $2,000; Mrs. Mays, $20,000; John, William, and Thomas, $1,500 each.

Record these transactions in journal entry form.

10. John Mason, executor of his father's estate, must record the following data relating to a business his father was operating at the time of his death:

(1) Debts of the business amounting to $25,500 were paid.
(2) Cash sales for the period following death totaled $250,000.
(3) Merchandise was purchased at a cost of $160,000.
(4) Salaries and wages of $80,000 were paid.
(5) Net income for the period was $20,200.

Make any necessary entries in the executor's accounts.

11. J. Adams, executor of the P. Adams estate, gives you the following summary of his activity for the period:

Estate principal—appraised value	*$95,000*
Funeral and last illness expenses paid	*2,950*
Interest income	*450*
Expenses of executor in collecting income	*60*
Loss on realization of assets	*2,400*
Discovered assets	*4,320*
Distributions to legatees	*10,000*
Income tax on estate income	*15*
Federal estate tax paid	*5,000*

Prepare a charge and discharge statement for the estate of P. Adams.

Short cases for analysis

23-1 In analyzing the accounts of J. Cleveland, executor of the estate of a decedent who died January 17, 1967, you review the will and other documents which reveal that the decedent's son had been specifically bequeathed the decedent's only rental property and bonds of the Pacific Corporation ($100,000 maturity value, 3%, due February 28, 1981); the decedent's daughter was the beneficiary of a life insurance policy (face amount $150,000) on which the decedent had paid the premiums; and his widow had been left the remainder of the estate in trust, with full powers of appointment.

Your examination reveals the following transactions occurring from the time of the decedent's death to March 1, 1967.

(1) *Jan. 20* $3,450 was collected in connection with the redemption of $3,000 par value of Edison Corporation 3% bonds due Jan. 15.

(2) *Jan. 20* $1,000 was collected from Patterson Corporation as a cash dividend of $1 per share on common stock declared Dec. 1, 1966, payable Jan. 15, 1967, to stockholders of record Jan. 2, 1967.

(3) *Jan. 20* $3,250.50 was paid to Smith and Co., brokers, for the purchase of three $1,000 of Atlantic Coast Line 5% bonds due June 30, 1978.

(4) *Jan. 21* 30 shares of common stock were received from Danials Corp., constituting receipt of an ordinary 3% stock dividend declared Dec. 14, 1966, payable Jan. 20, 1967, to holders of record Jan. 15, 1967.

(5) *Feb. 1* $400 quarterly interest was paid on a promissory note due Jan. 31, 1968.

(6) *Feb. 1* Dr. Mathews, the decedent's physician, was paid $1,000 for professional services rendered during the deceased's final illness.

(7) *Feb. 1* $1,600 was collected from Taylor Corporation, as a cash dividend of $.50 per share on common stock declared Jan. 18, 1967, payable Jan. 30, 1967, to holders of record Jan. 27, 1967.

(8) *Feb. 1* $400 rental income for February was received and deposited in the bank.

(9) *Feb. 10* $500 was paid for real estate taxes covering the period from Feb. 1 to July 31, 1967.

(10) *Mar. 1* $1,572 was paid to the District Director of Internal Revenue as the remaining income tax owed by the decedent on his 1966 income.

Instructions

Indicate whether each transaction should be:

a. Allocated between corpus (principal) and income

b. Allocated between corpus (principal) and beneficiaries

c. Attributed solely to income

d. Attributed solely to corpus (principal)

e. Attributed solely to beneficiaries (or devisees)

Give reasons supporting your conclusions as to how each transaction should be handled.

AICPA adapted

23-2 The estate of Gordon Childs included the following items at the date of his death November 16:

(1) A. B. Co. bonds, 4½%, due Dec. 31, 1973; par value $50,000; appraised value as of Nov. 16, $56,000; interest payable Jan. 1 and July 1.

(2) M. Y. Co. common stock, 1,000 shares, dividend of $3 declared Nov. 1, payable Dec. 1 to stockholders of record Nov. 15.
(3) M. Y. Co. 6% cumulative preferred stock, 1,000 shares. (Dividends are paid semiannually on Mar. 5 and Sept. 15 and there are no dividends in arrears.)

Instructions

a. The executor of the estate asks that you advise him as to which items constitute income and which principal of the estate.

b. Suppose that there were dividends in arrears on the preferred stock; would your answer to (a) be any different? If so, in what way? Explain.

AICPA adapted

23-3 The following accounts appear in the trial balance of George Taylor, executor of the estate of his father:

(1) Expenses of last illness
(2) Funeral expense
(3) Expenses of probating will
(4) General expenses of executor
(5) Loss on sale of investment
(6) Legal fees for defending claims against the estate
(7) Legal fees for collection of rents
(8) Executor's commissions
(9) Repairs to office buildings
(10) Estate and inheritance taxes
(11) Fire insurance premium
(12) Special assessments adding permanent value to real estate
(13) Monthly allowance to beneficiaries
(14) Expenses incident to a change in executor

Instructions

Indicate how the balance in each of the above accounts should be classified on the charge and discharge statement.

AICPA adapted

Problems

23-4 Harold Jackson, executor of the estate of T. A. Wells, has entered into the following transactions since inventorying the assets of the estate:

(1) Sold for cash 3,000 shares of the common stock of Cascade Corporation at $24 per share. The shares had been entered in the inventory at $26.50 per share.
(2) Received a check for semiannual interest on Electric Company 5% bonds with a maturity value of $10,000 carried in the inventory at $10,600. One-half

of the interest was accrued at the date of the decedent's death and was included in the inventory of assets.

(3) Paid bills relating to last illness and funeral expenses of $2,475.

(4) Received a check for $2,000 representing a cash dividend of $2 per share on the common stock of Pacific Northwest Co., declared subsequent to date of death. These shares were not included in the inventory. Upon investigation they were found in a safe deposit box at a local bank. The shares have a current market price of $14 per share. Also found in this safe deposit box was a savings account deposit book indicating a balance $10,000 on deposit at First National Bank. Upon checking with the bank, it was learned that the account still existed and had accumulated $1,650 interest at the date of the decedent's death.

(5) Paid $8,760 to various creditors whom the decedent owed at the date of his death.

(6) Collected $5,300 from J. Smith, who borrowed $5,000 from the decedent a year ago. Of the $300 interest collected, $200 was accrued at the date of the decedent's death. The note and accrued interest were included in the inventory of assets by the executor.

(7) Paid state inheritance taxes of $5,000 for the legacies out of estate assets chargeable against the legacies as follows:

Wife, Mary	$2,000
Son, Don	1,000
Son, Ralph	1,000
Daughter, Ruth	1,000

(8) Distributed a specific legacy of personal property valued at $4,600 to Ruth.

Instructions

Make journal entries to record these transactions involving the estate of T. A. Wells.

23-5 The following trial balance was taken from the books of J. E. Jackson, executor of the estate of George Olive, who died March 31. The assets are to be turned over to A. B. Jones on October 31.

Trial Balance
October 31

Estate corpus		*$164,120*
Assets not inventoried		*900*
Parks common stock	*$ 20,000*	
State bonds	*50,000*	
Lowell Co. bonds	*10,000*	
Accrued interest receivable	*900*	
Dividends receivable	*1,000*	
Loss on asset realization	*600*	
Gain on asset realization		*1,600*

Funeral and administrative expense	*1,070*	
Debts of decedent	*6,720*	
Legacy—Mary Olive	*56,000*	
Legacy—J. E. Jackson	*2,000*	
Income		*3,550*
Expense chargeable to income	*220*	
Distribution of income cash	*1,000*	
Principal cash	*20,230*	
Income cash	*430*	
Totals	*$170,170*	*$170,170*

Instructions

a. Prepare the executor's charge and discharge statement. (Supporting schedules are not required.)

b. Prepare journal entries to close the executor's books at October 31.

23-6 The following inventory of personal property was prepared by G. Hillman, executor of the estate of Mrs. A. H. Money:

Cash	*$ 520*
Savings deposits	*6,430*
200 common shares of Southwest, Inc.	*8,700*
400 common shares of Madison Co.	*19,400*
Household furnishings	*6,000*
Automobile	*2,600*
Total	*$43,650*

Mrs. Money's will provided for the following legacies:

To her son, Andrew, the household furnishings, automobile, and $20,000
To her sister, Mary, $10,000
The First Baptist Church, $5,000
To University College, the residuary of the estate

During the period of the administration of the estate, the following transactions occurred:

(1) Last illness and funeral expenses of $3,670 were paid.
(2) Dividends of $1 per share of Southwest, Inc., common stock and of $1.20 per share on Madison Co. common stock were received. Both were declared after Mrs. Money's death.
(3) Debts incurred by Mrs. Money were paid in the amount of $4,950.
(4) Accumulated interest of $125 was added to the savings account.
(5) The specific legacy to the son, Andrew, was distributed.
(6) A bill for the executor's services and expenses in the amount of $1,575 was presented to the estate.
(7) The common stock of Southwest, Inc., was sold for $41 per share; the brokerage fee totaled $250. The common shares of Madison were sold for $43 per share; the brokerage fee was $420.

Instructions

a. Prepare a charge and discharge statement to be presented to the court as a final accounting.

b. Prepare a schedule indicating the proposed distribution of assets to the legatees.

23-7 A. H. Peck, named executor of the John Harris estate, filed the following inventory of assets with the court:

Cash in checking account	$ 4,860
Household furnishings	2,900
Automobile	1,800
Life insurance policy payable to estate	10,000
Savings account	8,640
U.S. government bonds, Series E (maturity value $10,000)	9,220
100 shares of Alpine, Inc., common stock	6,750
Total	$44,170

During the course of the administration of the estate, the following transactions were completed:

(1) Paid last illness and funeral expenses of $1,600.
(2) Received cash dividend of $1.20 per share on the common stock of Alpine, Inc., declared subsequent to date of death.
(3) Sold household furnishings for $2,750 and automobile for $1,900.
(4) Received $10,000 cash in settlement of life insurance policy.
(5) Distributed U.S. government bonds to Albert Harris, in accordance with specific bequest.
(6) Distributed $7,500 out of the funds on deposit in the savings account to Mary Baker, sister of the deceased.
(7) Received interest on savings deposits of $145, which was added to the balance in the savings account.
(8) Paid debts owed to various creditors a total of $4,080.
(9) Distributed $10,000 to Community Hospital in accordance with terms of the will.
(10) Made application to the court and received approval for the payment of executor's fees and expenses of $1,750 and for permission to distribute the residuary assets to John Harris, Jr.

Instructions

a. Make the journal entries required to record the affairs of the John Harris estate.

b. Prepare a charge and discharge statement summarizing the executor's activities.

c. Make any entries necessary to close the accounts of the estate.

23-8 Alex Dunn, Jr., died on January 15, 1967. His records disclose the following estate:

Cash in bank	*$ 3,750*
6% note receivable, including $50 accrued interest	*5,050*
Stock	*50,000*
Dividends declared on stocks	*600*
6% mortgage receivable, including $100 accrued interest	*20,100*
Real estate—apartment house	*35,000*
Household effects	*8,250*
Dividend receivable from Alex Dunn, Sr., trust fund	*250,000*
Total	*$372,750*

On July 1, 1953, the late Alex Dunn, Sr., created a trust fund with his son, Alex Dunn, Jr., as life tenant and his grandson as remainderman. The assets in the fund consist solely of the outstanding capital stock of Dunn, Inc., namely, 2,000 shares of $100 par value stock. At the creation of the trust, the book as well as the market value of the Dunn, Inc., shares was $400,000; at December 31, 1966, market value was $500,000. On January 2, 1967, Dunn, Inc., declared a cash dividend equal to 125% of par value payable February 2, 1967, to shareholders of record January 12, 1967.

The executor's transactions from January 15 to 31, 1967, were as follows:

Cash receipts:

Jan. 20	*Dividends*	*$ 1,500.00*
25	*6% note receivable*	*5,000.00*
	Interest accrued on note	*58.33*
	Stock sold, inventoried at $22,500	*20,000.00*
	6% mortgage sold	*20,100.00*
	Interest accrued on mortgage	*133.33*
28	*Sale of assets not inventoried*	*250.00*
29	*Real estate sold*	*30,000.00*
		$77,041.66

Cash disbursements:

Jan. 20	*Funeral expenses*	*$ 750.00*
23	*Decedent's debts*	*8,000.00*
25	*Decedent's bequests*	*10,000.00*
31	*Advanced to widow*	*500.00*
		$19,250.00

Instructions

Prepare a charge and discharge statement for the executor, covering the period from January 15 to January 31, 1967.

AICPA adapted

23-9 Henry White, a partner in the investment banking firm of Black and White, died on December 31, 1966.

The assets and liabilities of the firm, at that date, were as follows. The partners had agreed to share all profits and losses on the basis of their capital balances at the beginning of each year.

Cash in bank	$ 11,526.90	
Life insurance proceeds receivable	44,700.02	
Marketable securities	978,663.77	
Notes and accounts receivable	23,268.63	
Bonds of Kiln Lumber Co., bankrupt, at 25% of par	56,250.00	
75% interest in log, lumber, machinery, and logging equipment	22,604,25	
Notes payable		$ 500,000.00
Accrued interest		1,500.00
Liability as guarantors of note of Kiln Lumber Co., bankrupt		38,170.31
Accounts payable		14,357.33
Agreement to repurchase $10,000 bonds of Kiln Lumber Co. at 97½		9,750.00
Capital—James Black, 40%		229,294.37
Capital—Henry White, 60%		343,941.56
Totals	$1,137,013.57	$1,137,013.57

James Black, surviving partner, was appointed trustee to continue the business for a limited period of time.

The transactions of the business to September 30, 1967, were as follows:

(1) The amount due from the life insurance company was collected.

(2) $712,554.07 was realized on securities which cost $619,483.

(3) $3,725 was expended in exercising rights, the original and newly acquired shares being among those unsold at Sept. 30.

(4) Notes and accounts receivable realized $17,429.30, but of the balance outstanding at Sept. 30 only $1,000 was considered collectible.

(5) Foreclosure proceedings were instituted on the bonds of the Kiln Lumber Co. In the final settlement, $4,603.97 was realized in cash and the firm acquired a 75% interest in 10,000 acres of timberlands.

(6) The interest in logs, lumber machinery, and logging equipment realized $2,725.09.

(7) A claim receivable for damages, which was pending Dec. 31, 1966, but not entered on the books, was settled for $3,000.

(8) Notes payable with interest, amounting to $27,500, were paid.

(9) The liability as guaranters of the note of the Kiln Lumber Co. was discharged by payment of $36,149.73.

(10) The accounts payable, together with an additional item of $1,275 owing at Dec. 31 but not discovered until later, were duly paid.

(11) The sum of $200,000 was withdrawn in the proportion of the partner's investments at Dec. 31, 1966.

(12) Expenses of operations incurred, exclusive of interest, totaled $7,328.30, of which $432.15 were unpaid Sept. 30, 1967. Revenue from operations amounted to $14,732.03, of which $2,500 had not been received Sept. 30, 1967.

Instructions

Prepare the journal entries required in the accounts of the estate of Henry White to record the effect of the operation of the business for nine months.

AICPA adapted

23-10 Samuel Gifford died on July 18, 1965. The executor, having paid all debts, bequests, and expenses and expecting no more transactions after June 30, 1966, desired to ask the court for his discharge and for an order to turn the remaining assets of the estate over to the trustee named in the will.

An inventory had been filed with the courts on August 15, 1965, consisting of the following items:

Cash in First National Bank	*$ 4,533.12*
Cash in closed bank	*2,050.50*
Real estate, valued by court appraiser at	*38,750.00*
Home furnishings	*6,824.00*
Stock, at market:	
AB Company preferred	*22,865.00*
AB Company common	*3,738.20*
Parkhurst Transit Co. common, at nominal value	*100.00*
U.S. savings bonds, dated Apr. 1, 1965, due Apr. 1, 1975, in the amount of $50,000	*37,500.00*
Accrued interest at 2.9%	*326.25*
Total	*$116,687.07*

In the latter part of September, 1965, a discovery was made of another checking account in the Second National Bank with a balance in the amount of $2,500 and of $125.50 cash in the office safe. Insurance was collected in the amount of $58,000, also a dividend of $1,250 on the AB Company preferred, which had been declared on June 1, 1965, payable to stockholders of record July 10.

On June 15, 1966, the executor sold one-half of the AB Company preferred stock for $13,500 and the Parkhurst Transit Company common for $200. Other receipts during the executor's administration consisted of rents, $4,526; dividends, including those declared before the testator's death, $4,025; collection on deposit in closed bank, $465. All receipts were deposited by the executor in the First National Bank.

Property taxes, accrued at date of death, were $1,575.20 and household debts on that date amounted to $2,111. The executor paid $20,000 bequests and $1,000 executor's fee as specified in the will; also $18,262.50 estate tax, $3,336.95 property taxes, including those accrued at date of death, $750 funeral expenses, $88.50 court costs, as well as the household debts. The widow received allowances to the aggregate sum of $4,800 as directed by the court.

The accrued interest on U.S. savings bonds, $326.25, and the annual rate of 2.9% applied to purchase price are assumed to be correct. Interest is accumulated on these bonds to maturity date.

Instructions

From the foregoing information, prepare:

a. The executor's charge and discharge statement at June 30, 1966.

b. Inventory of principal and income assets at June 30, 1966.

AICPA adapted

23-11 Richard Wills died in an accident on May 31, 1966. His will, dated February 28, 1964, provided that all just debts and expenses be paid and that his property be disposed of as follows:

Personal residence—devised to Bertha Wills, widow.

United States Treasury bonds and Puritan Co. stock—to be placed in trust. All income to go to Bertha Wills during her lifetime, with the right of appointment upon her death.

Seneca Co. mortgage notes—bequeathed to Elsie Wills Johnson, daughter.

Cash—a bequest of $10,000 to David Wills, son.

Remainder of estate—to be divided equally between the two children, Elsie Wills Johnson and David Wills.

The will further provided that during the administration period Bertha Wills was to be paid $300 a month out of estate income. Estate and inheritance taxes are to be borne by the residue. David Wills was named as executor and trustee.

An inventory of the decedent's property was prepared. The preliminary inventory, before the computations of any appropriate income accrual on inventory items, follows:

Personal residence property	*$ 45,000*
Jewelry—diamond ring	*9,600*
York Life Insurance Co.—term life insurance policy on life of Richard Wills. Beneficiary—Bertha Wills, widow	*120,000*
Granite Trust Co.—3% savings bank account, Richard Wills, in trust for Philip Johnson (grandchild), interest credited Jan. 1 and July 1; balance May 31, 1966	*400*
Fidelity National Bank—checking account; balance May 31, 1966	*143,000*
$100,000 U.S. Treasury bonds, 3%, 1999, interest payable Mar. 1 and Sept. 1	*100,000*
$9,700 Seneca Co. first mortgage notes, 6%, 1975, interest payable May 31 and Nov. 30	*9,900*
800 shares Puritan Co. common stock	*64,000*
700 shares Meta Mfg. Co. common stock	*70,000*

The executor opened an estate bank account to which he transferred the decedent's checking account balance. Other deposits, through July 1, 1967, were as follows:

Interest collected on bonds:	
$100,000 U.S. Treasury	
Sept. 1, 1966	*$ 1,500*
Mar. 1, 1967	*1,500*
Dividends received on stock:	
800 shares Puritan Co. stock:	
June 15, 1966, declared May 7, 1966, payable to holders of record May 27, 1966	*800*
Sept. 15, 1966	*800*
Dec. 15, 1966	*1,200*
Mar. 15, 1967	*800*
June 15, 1967	*800*
Net proceeds of June 19, 1966, sale of Meta Mfg. Co. 700 shares of common stock	*68,810*

Payments were made from the estate's checking account through July 1, 1967, for the following:

Funeral expenses	*$ 2,000*
Assessments for additional 1964 Federal and state income tax ($1,700) plus interest ($110) to May 31	*1,810*
1966 income taxes of Richard Wills for the period Jan. 1, 1966, through May 31, 1966, in excess of amounts paid by the decedent on declarations of estimated tax	*9,100*
Federal and state fiduciary income taxes, fiscal years ending June 30, 1966 ($75), and June 30, 1967 ($1,400)	*1,475*
Federal and state estate taxes	*58,000*
Monthly payments to Bertha Wills: 13 payments	*3,900*
Attorney's and accountant's fees	*25,000*

The executor waived his commission. However, he desired to receive his father's diamond ring in lieu of the $10,000 specific legacy. All parties agreed to this in writing, and the court's approval was secured. All other specific legacies were delivered by July 15, 1966.

Instructions

Prepare a charge and discharge statement as to principal and income, with supporting schedules, to accompany the attorney's formal court accounting on behalf of the executor of the Estate of Richard Wills for the period from May 31, 1966, through July 1, 1967.

AICPA adapted

23-12 Ben East died July 7, 1966. His will appointed two executors to administer his estate and provided for the payment of funeral and other necessary expenses and of general bequests, namely, $10,000 to Cemetery on the Mount; $15,000 to PMW, a sister; and to each executor, $5,000 in lieu of fees.

The testator at date of death was possessed of the following:

Cash	*$ 52,000*
Accounts receivable	*18,000*
Non-interest-bearing notes receivable	*10,000*
First mortgage bonds 6%, interest Jan. 1 and July 1, principal amount $8,000, appraised	*6,500*
U.S. bonds, 3% interest Jan. 15 and July 15, par value $100,000, appraised	*101,500*
5,000 shares Shell Mining Co., no par value, cost $50,000, appraised	*-0-*
1,000 shares Atlas Amusement Corp., par value $100,000, appraised	*102,000*
Semiprecious stones	*5,280*
Clothing	*1,375*
Furniture	*7,500*

A summary of cash transactions from July 7, 1966, to September 30, 1967, is presented as follows:

Cash receipts:	
Accounts receivable collected (remainder uncollectible)	*$15,000*
Proceeds—sale of $70,000 U.S. savings bonds on Jan. 15, 1967, at $102 without interest	*71,400*
Dividends:	
$2.50 per share of Atlas Amusement Corp., declared payable to stockholders of record on July 5, 1966, and paid July 25, 1966	*2,500*
$2.50 per share of Atlas Amusement Corp., declared payable to stockholders of record Jan. 5, 1967, and paid Jan. 25, 1967	*2,500*
Proceeds—5,000 shares of Shell Mining Co. at 10 cents per share	*500*
Refund of 1966 overpayment of U.S. income tax (declaration tax paid $5,725, actual tax payable $5,350)	*375*
Proceeds—sale of furniture	*5,150*
Other transactions—6% short-term notes collected at maturity; interest on all investments collected.	
Cash disbursements:	
Funeral expenses, etc.	*$ 1,750*
Administration expenses (corpus, $5,250; income, $1,250)	*6,500*
Legal and accounting services incident to probating will	*3,750*
Debts of testator	*14,450*
U.S. Treasury Dept.—tax deficiency, 1963, and interest thereon, $72	*522*
Paya Co., 4½% bonds—$20,000 acquired Aug. 15, 1966, at $101 and accrued interest (interest dates Mar. 15 and Sept. 15)	*20,575*

Short-term notes—$5,000, 6% purchased on Jan. 16, 1967, at 100½, interest Jan. 15 and July 15, maturing in six months from date of purchase.

Other transactions—general bequests paid in full, PMW taking semiprecious stones at appraised value to apply against bequest of $15,000.

Other transactions—clothing given to charity.

Instructions

Prepare, as of September 30, 1967, a summary statement of principal and income (charge and discharge statement) of the Estate of Ben East, Deceased.

AICPA adapted

24 TRUST ACCOUNTING

A trust is created by the segregation of assets to be used for the benefit of some designated person or organization. A trust relationship exists whenever one person holds property for the benefit of some other person. The person responsible for the assets comprising the trust is referred to as the *trustee;* in general he holds legal title to the property in the trust for the benefit of the beneficiary. Beneficiaries, in turn, are usually designated by the party who has placed the property in trust, called variously the grantor, donor, creator, or trustor. The named beneficiaries possess equitable or beneficial title to the trust property.

Trusts may, and frequently do, provide for two types of beneficiaries: (1) the *income beneficiary* who is entitled to receive the income from the trust for a stated period of time or until the occurrence of some event such as death or the attainment of a specific age; (2) the *principal beneficiary* or the remainderman who is entitled to receive the property of the trust at the termination of the income beneficiary's interest as indicated in the trust agreement. One person may be both income and principal beneficiary; on the other hand, there may be several income and principal beneficiaries. A trust is highly individualistic and can take almost any form subject to the limitations imposed by the laws of the several states.

A private trust may not suspend indefinitely the power of anyone to transfer the trust property. The common-law rule limits the duration of a private trust to 21 years following the death of a specified beneficiary living at the time the trust is created. A private trust must, therefore, provide for a remainderman if the income beneficiary is to receive the income for his lifetime, or the income beneficiary must be given the prerogative of disposing of the trust property in his last will and testament. A public or charitable trust, on the other hand, may be established for an indefinite period of time. In most states, however, the accumulation of income in the trust is restricted; for example, a trust created for the benefit of a minor may accumulate income only until the minor reaches the age of majority. Even the income of a charitable trust may not be accumulated for an unreasonable period.

The title to trust property is held by the trustee because a trust is seldom revocable. The trustee has sole authority over the assets of the irrevocable trust, restricted only by certain rights of the beneficiary which will be discussed later. The grantor, of course, may reserve the right to revoke a trust at any time during his lifetime. If the grantor chooses to reserve this right to himself, the tax situation regarding the trust is quite different from the one which governs an irrevocable trust. The only other way that a trust can be revoked is by the unanimous consent of the beneficiaries.

Types of trusts

Several types of trusts need to be distinguished. A person may set aside a portion of his assets during his lifetime and create a trust to benefit specific individuals or organizations. A trust created in this manner is called a *living trust* or a trust *inter vivos*. The same person might also choose to create a trust upon his death for the benefit of named persons or organizations. A trust created by will is referred to as a *testamentary trust*. The living trust and the testamentary trust are both *express trusts*. This means that the trustee, beneficiary, subject matter, and method of administration are expressly stated in a will or other instrument. An *implied trust* is a trust which is created when the language of an instrument does not expressly provide for the creation of a trust but it indicates the need for or desirability of a trust under certain circumstances. On certain occasions, especially when a minor is involved, the court will order a trust relationship created to prevent fraud or misuse of the assets.

Because the legal and accounting principles applied to them frequently vary, it is necessary to distinguish between a private and a public or charitable trust. A private trust is established for the benefit of one or more particular individuals. A public or charitable trust is usually established to benefit institutions or organizations in specific ways as indicated in the trust agreement.

Duties of the trustee

The powers of the trustee derive from two sources: (1) the instrument creating the trust and (2) the general laws pertaining to trust relationships. The instrument may either expand or contract the general laws of trusteeship, except that it may not relieve the trustee of gross negligence or misconduct in the execution of his functions. The powers of the trustee may be either (1) imperative and mandatory or (2) permissive and discretionary. The general powers of the trustee permit him to take and retain title to property, to sell and reinvest, to pay necessary expenses in the maintenance of the trust property, to sue and defend suits related to trust property, to enter into contracts, and to pay out trust assets to those entitled to receive them.

The duties of the trustee are usually quite similar to those assigned the executor of an estate. He is expected to manage, protect, and conserve the trust property as any prudent man would care for his own property. If the trustee has abilities which are greater than those of the average man, he is expected to use these abilities in the administration of the trust. He is required to keep the trust properties separate from his own and to keep principal and income separate, at least for accounting purposes. Unlike the estate executor, he is responsible for keeping the principal funds invested in acceptable income-producing investments. The trustee is responsible for the distribution of the income funds to the designated beneficiaries at reasonable intervals and for impartiality in the distribution of these assets among the beneficiaries. He must provide the beneficiaries with complete and accurate information concerning the trust and he must make available to the beneficiaries all records of the trust as well as the trust assets themselves.

Investment of the trust assets is restricted to "legal" investments unless specific directions are included in the trust instrument. Legal investments include: (1) bonds of the United States government, the state where the trust is being administered, and the municipalities of that state; (2) first mortgages on improved real estate; and (3) in some states, preferred and common stocks of large well-known corporations. If the trust includes property which does not meet the standards of "legal" investments and the trust instrument does not make explicit directions for holding this property, the trustee is required to dispose of these assets within a reasonable time. The trustee, like the executor, is required to make periodic reports; upon final distribution of the trust properties, he may be required to make a final accounting before he can be officially discharged from his responsibilities as a trustee.

If the will creating the trust names the same individual executor of the estate and trustee of the trust, then this individual may act in a dual capacity for a period of time. In doing this he must maintain two sets of records and administer the estate in accordance with the powers and duties governing estate administration. His function as trustee must also be carried out in accordance with the directions and laws pertaining to trust administration. The estate books will show the transfer of properties to the trust and the trust records will indicate their receipt. Real property which is devised to the trust will go directly to the trust in the same manner that other real property is transferred and will not pass through the estate books. If the trust is created out of the residuary of the estate, the trust will not be opened until the estate is closed and the residuary is determined.

Rights of the beneficiary

The beneficiary has an equitable title in the property of the trust and accordingly has certain rights. He can bring suit in a court of equity to enforce his rights or to prevent misuse of trust property by the trustee. The beneficiary has the right to inspect the trust property and to have an accounting ordered if there is reason to doubt that the trustee is acting in good faith. The beneficiary may also have an injunction issued to restrain the trustee from proceeding with any unauthorized act. If the beneficiary is of age, he may ratify actions of the trustee which would otherwise be in violation of the duties or responsibilities of the trustee.

Principal and income distinguished

The problem of distinguishing between trust principal and income is one of the most difficult faced by the accountant. In some cases the intent of the grantor is expressed or implied; however, in the absence of any clear expression of intent, the general legal rules apply. The importance of this problem arises from the fact that there may be two beneficiaries: (1) the life tenant who is entitled to the income from the trust principal and who is responsible for the expenses of earning this income to the limit of gross income, and (2) the remainderman who is entitled to receive the trust principal at some point in time or upon the occurrence of some event such as the death of the life tenant.

The trust principal includes the property which originally constitutes the trust plus any property which is subsequently added by the grantor; the trust income is the accumulation of funds derived from the investment of the trust principal. Increases or decreases in the assets which constitute the trust principal are considered as a part of the principal and not as income. Income determined for trust purposes is not necessarily the same as income determined for general accounting or tax purposes; it is the income determined in accordance with specific laws, which may on occasion require the interpretation of a court. The items which frequently require designation as principal or income can be classified into three categories: (1) items involving accrual of income or expense at the time the trust is created, (2) items involving classification after the trust is created, and (3) items involving subsequent impairment or improvement of trust assets.

Accruals. Trust accounting generally conforms to the cash basis of accounting; however, there are at least two dates when accrual concepts are used. These dates are: (1) the date the trust is created and (2) the date the tenancy is terminated and the corpus held for the remainderman. At these two dates it becomes important to determine what is income and what is principal if the two beneficiaries are to receive equitable treatment.

The general rule of accrual is that income and expense accruing to the trust at the time the trust assets are delivered to the trustee belong to or are claims against the trust corpus. All income accruing after this date and before the date that the trust assets are deliverable to the remainderman is the income of the income beneficiary. Similarly, expenses incurred in the earning of income between these dates are expenses to be paid from income assets. The date of collection or payment in these two cases is unimportant in the division between principal and income. The various states have laws which relate to specific items of revenue and expense, and where applicable these must be followed.

The general rule of accrual will be given with respect to the following items; in each case there may be a conflict with an existing state law. These general rules are presented merely as guides to discussions and problem solutions; they should not be regarded as definitive in all cases.

1. *Interest.* Interest accrued on receivables and investments at the date the trust is established is considered part of the trust corpus. Exceptions are interest on (*a*) savings accounts when the interest is paid only if the deposit remains until the end of the interest period, and (*b*) coupon bonds when the payment is contingent upon the owner presenting the coupon, in which case the date of receipt is controlling. Similar rules apply to the accrual of interest expense.

2. *Rent.* The accrual of rent prior to the beginning of the trust is considered by many states as a portion of a trust corpus. Any rent accruing between the date of the establishment of the trust and the termination of the tenancy belongs to the income beneficiary. Rent expense is handled similarly.

3. *Dividends.* Ordinary cash dividends are not divisible. If the dividend is de-

clared and the date of record has passed before the trust is created, the dividend is a part of the corpus. Otherwise it is considered income of the trust. A stock dividend is treated in the same manner in many states; however, in those states which follow the Massachusetts rule, the stock dividend is considered a part of the corpus regardless of the date of declaration. The Massachusetts rule also dictates that all cash dividends, no matter how large, if declared during the period of the tenancy, are income to the trust.

The Pennsylvania rule states that extraordinarily large dividends in whatever form should be distributed between principal and income. The amount given to the corpus should be sufficient to keep intact the value of the shares as they were on the date the trust was established; the remainder of the dividend is then considered income. In essence the Pennsylvania rule adheres to the philosophy that the earnings of a corporation belong to the person who was entitled to the income on the date the income was recognized. Under the Pennsylvania rule, the criterion for determining whether or not an extraordinarily large dividend has been declared is the change in book value of the stock. If as a result of the dividend the book value of the stock is reduced below its book value at the date the stock was made a part of the trust, then that part of the dividend required to restore the original book value would be considered principal and the remainder would be income.

4. *Property taxes.* Taxes which have been levied on trust property prior to the beginning of the trust are charges against the principal. Any taxes assessed on the basis of trust property held for the benefit of the income beneficiary are chargeable against income. Special assessments made during the administration of the trust are usually paid by the remainderman, although in some cases where the assessment is for improvements which benefit the life tenant, a part or all of the assessment may be charged against income. When the assessment is paid from the corpus, interest on the funds advanced may be charged against income.

5. *Profits.* Income earned by a partnership or proprietorship does not accrue. The income which is earned prior to the creation of the trust is considered a part of the principal of the trust. In many cases a partnership is dissolved upon the death of a partner, and there may be no income earned after the trust is established. In the event that the business continues by specific direction of the grantor or provision of the partnership agreement, any income earned after the trust is created is income of the trust.

6. *Executory contracts.* Any profit earned on the completion of an executory contract by the trustee is an addition to the principal of the trust.

7. *Livestock and crops.* Any livestock born during the tenancy under the trust is considered income, except to the extent that the herd must be maintained as directed by the grantor, in which case the increase must be divided between principal and income in a manner which honors this intention. If the principal includes land, any crops harvested during the tenancy are considered income of the trust.

8. *Premium returns.* Any return of premium or dividend on insurance policies which was paid prior to the creation of the trust is a part of the principal. This is considered realization of assets.

9. *Royalties.* Royalties or other income from the operation of mines or other natural resource deposits which were made operative before the trust was created or which were developed in cooperation with the remainderman are income to the trust.

Classification of receipts and disbursements. Many receipts and disbursements do not involve accrual or apportionment on a time basis; these items generally involve classification as to principal or income. The classification of these items follows the general rule that increases or decreases in assets composing the trust corpus are items of principal and similar changes in the assets composing undistributed income are income items. The classification of a number of important kinds of receipts and disbursements is enumerated below:

Classified as principal

1. Proceeds of borrowing when principal assets are pledged as security, although there is no increase in the remainderman's equity.

2. Losses due to casualty or theft of principal assets.

3. Proceeds from insurance received for casualty losses when the assets are held for the use of the trust in general.

4. Carrying charges on unproductive real estate.

5. Expenses of administration, except those directly related to the administration of income.

6. Any expenditures which improve the property and any expenditures on acquired property necessary to its installation and operation, except those made voluntarily by the income beneficiary.

7. Payment of claims against trust assets existing upon creation of the trust.

8. The value of the assets in existence at the date the inventory was taken but which were not included in the inventory.

Classified as income

1. Expenses incurred earning and collecting income.

2. Income taxes, except those on gains derived from the sale of principal assets.

3. Taxes assessed or levied on assets held by the trust for the life tenant.

4. All expenses in connection with owning and using property necessary to maintain its condition at the date received by the trust, except for natural decreases such as depreciation and depletion.

5. Amortization, depletion, or depreciation of a wasting asset unless the grantor has indicated that the life tenant is to receive the full income of the trust.

6. Losses due to casualty and theft of income assets.

7. Casualty insurance premiums unless they provide some special protection to the remainderman, in which case they will be apportioned between principal and income.

Impairment or improvement of trust assets. In general, any impairment of the trust property is charged to the trust corpus unless the impairment arises out of the use of the property for the production of income. Here as in practically all other trust matters, the wishes of the grantor and the laws of the state are governing in specific instances. One area in particular where the desire of the grantor is important is in policies of depreciation and depletion. If the grantor wants full income without deduction for the decline in value of the assets to go to the income beneficiary, then these items are charged to principal. If he wants to preserve the trust assets for the remainderman, then charges for depreciation and depletion are charged to income. In the absence of any expressed intent, the general rule given above under classification of receipts and disbursements will be in effect.

Extraordinary repairs and permanent improvements to trust property are generally charged against the trust property; however, ordinary repairs made in the course of using the property and improvements made primarily for the benefit of the life tenant are chargeable against income.

All losses and gains resulting from the realization of assets composing the trust corpus are generally considered to be applicable to the principal. Accordingly, if bonds are inventoried at a premium, the premium is not amortized and the income beneficiary does not have to absorb the amortization of the premium as a reduction of income. Instead the loss is charged against the principal when the bonds are sold. Similarly, when bonds are inventoried at a discount, the income beneficiary is not given the benefit of the increased income resulting from the accumulation of the discount.

When the trustee buys bonds as an investment of trust funds, a slightly different situation may exist. In some states the premium on a bond purchased by the trustee is amortized and charged against the income from the trust; however, the discount is seldom accumulated. Such a position may be criticized as inconsistent. The Principal and Income Act provides that neither premium nor discount will be amortized. This act states that the inventory value of assets, purchased after the trust is created, is cost. Any gain or loss resulting from holding such assets to maturity or from realization by sale shall inure to the trust principal. When and if amortization of premium or accumulation of discount is required, either the straight-line method or the effective yield method is acceptable.

If corporate stocks are held as a part of the trust principal, the right to acquire additional shares at a price below market may be available to the trust as an existing stockholder. If the trustee elects to sell these rights rather than to exercise them, the proceeds are considered a part of the principal. By electing to sell the rights, the trustee has reduced the percentage ownership in the corporation, thereby reducing the asset value of the shares held. A portion of the ownership has been realized. Any gain or loss on the sale is considered a part of the trust corpus. The same concept is involved in accounting for any equity investment when the cost of the original shares is prorated between the old shares and the rights.

Private trusts

Accounting for the private trust

The trust, like the estate, has a unique accounting orientation because it involves responsibility reporting almost exclusively, rather than the traditional proprietorship accounting associated with business firms. Since the trust typically exists over a rather long period of time, the concept of the accounting period is more important in trust accounting than in estate accounting. The trustee will usually be expected to file complete reports of his activity with the trust beneficiaries at least once a year. Upon the request of the beneficiaries, he may file reports more often; however, these are generally thought of as interim reports.

The trust is operated for the benefit of the income beneficiary and the distributions which may be made to him are limited to the cash in the income account. Since the main purpose of trust accounting is to provide a record of the trustee's activities for the beneficiaries, the cash basis of accounting is quite satisfactory and is generally used. Accruals need to be recognized at two times only: (1) at the creation of the trust and (2) at the time when the income beneficiary's rights cease and the principal is distributed to the remainderman. At these two times the trustee must record the accrued receivables and payables in order to achieve an equitable distribution of the assets under his control.

From a legal viewpoint, the trust corpus consists of a specific group of assets which can be physically separated from the income assets. This concept is quite different from saying that the trust corpus is a given dollar amount of assets and that the income is the increase in the total dollar amount of the trust. The prevalence of the legal theory can be observed in the rules stated earlier concerning the distinction between income and principal. The accounting records must be organized and maintained in a way which will provide information about specific assets as well as dollar aggregates. Information is needed about specific assets in order to distinguish between gains and losses arising from the realization of corpus and income assets.

Recording principal and income. The bookkeeping system for the trust will vary according to the complexity of the operation. The trustee needs records to support his actions, to make reports, and as a basis for filing the tax return. The cash basis is perfectly acceptable; however, a double-entry system should be used. A system of multicolumn journals and control and subsidiary ledger accounts is frequently found to be the most efficient system for keeping detailed records.

The income of a private trust is subject to Federal income taxes; however, the portion of the income currently distributable to the income beneficiaries is taxable to them, with the undistributable portion of the income taxed to the trust. For this reason the tax on trust income is frequently referred to as a tax on undistributed earnings of the trust. In the field of taxation, the trust is characterized as a *conduit* through which income passes to the beneficiary. Each item of income distributable to the beneficiary has the identical tax status to the recipient that it would have had to the trust; for example, capital gains and losses and tax-exempt income are identified as such when they are distributed.

Trustee's reports. The form of the trustee's report will vary widely depending upon court jurisdiction, frequency of the report, and specific provisions of the trust instrument. The assets should be carried by the trustee at original inventory value or cost so long as they compose a portion of the trust assets. Assets whose value has declined to zero should be carried in the trustee's accounts and should be kept even though their value is written off as a loss. Needless to say, the report should indicate clearly the distinction between property which is trust principal and property which is the undistributed income of the trust.

In essence the report is an analysis of the trust principal and income accounts supported, where necessary for complete disclosure, by supplementary schedules. Since the responsibilities of the trustee and estate executor are quite similar, the trustee's report frequently resembles the executor's charge and discharge statement.

Illustration of accounting procedures. Henry James, executor of his father's estate, has filed a final accounting of his actions as executor with the probate court. The court has approved his statement and the payment of the attorney, the accountant, and the executor's commission. The plan of distribution of the residuary assets, which is in accord with his father's will, is also approved by the court.

The will provides for the creation of a trust with the residuary of the estate comprising the principal. Mrs. Jane James is designated as the life tenant to receive the income of the trust for the remainder of her lifetime. Henry James and William James are named as remaindermen to share equally the trust principal at their mother's death. Henry James is named as the trustee of the trust. The inventory of the estate residuary as filed with the court is reproduced below:

WILLIAM JAMES ESTATE
Inventory of Principal Assets
May 15, 1966

Cash	$ 69,650
3½% U.S. Treasury bonds, due Feb. 15, 1986, interest payable Feb. 15 and Aug. 15, par $100,000	100,750
6% Wilson Manufacturing Co. bonds, due Apr. 1, 1972, interest payable Apr. 1 and Oct. 1, par $100,000	98,500
Prairie View Mining Co. common stock, 5,000 shares	162,500
Jasper Trading Co. common stock, 6,800 shares	151,300
Total	$582,700

WILLIAM JAMES ESTATE
Inventory of Income Assets
May 15, 1966

Cash	$14,345
Accrued interest receivable	1,625
Dividends receivable (declared but not received)	2,040
Total	$18,010

The executor must pay from the estate assets the attorney's fee of $22,375, the accountant's fee of $8,500, and the executor's commission of $18,625. The remaining assets, principal and income, will become the trust principal at May 20, 1966.

The entries (on page 838) to record the payment of the unpaid obligations, the transfer of estate assets to the trust, and the closing of the estate are recorded in the accounts kept by the executor.

After the opening of the trust books on May 20, the following transactions were entered into by the trustee on account of the trust:

1966

June 10	Received dividend of $2,040 from Jasper Trading Co. declared payable to stockholders of record May 8, 1966.
July 15	Sold Wilson Manufacturing Co. bonds for $99,000 plus interest of $1,750. The brokerage commission deducted from the sale was $150.
Aug. 15	Received semiannual interest on U.S. Treasury bonds.
Sept. 15	Mailed a check for $1,500 to Mrs. Jane James.
Oct. 1	Purchased 2,000 shares of Meadow Brook, Inc., common stock at $30 per share plus commission of $548; also purchased 1,500 shares of

Attorney's Fees	*22,375*	
Accountant's Fee	*8,500*	
Executor's Commission	*18,625*	
Cash		*49,500*
To record payment of unpaid obligations of the estate.		
Estate Principal	*551,210*	
Cash		*34,495*
3½% U.S. Treasury Bonds		*100,750*
6% Wilson Manufacturing Co. Bonds		*98,500*
Prairie View Mining Co. Common Stock		*162,500*
Jasper Trading Co. Common Stock		*151,300*
Accrued Interest Receivable		*1,625*
Dividends Receivable		*2,040*
To record transfer of residuary assets of the estate to trust in accordance with provisions of the will.		
Estate Principal	*49,500*	
Attorney's Fees		*22,375*
Accountant's Fee		*8,500*
Executor's Commission		*18,625*
To close estate of William James by order of the probate court.		

Standard Products common stock at $46 per share plus commission of $594 through Hutzler Securities, broker.

Nov. 1 Received cash dividend on Prairie View common stock at the rate of $1.25 per share.

Dec. 10 Received cash dividend on common stock of Jasper Trading Co. at the rate of $.40 per share.

1967

Jan. 1 Mailed a check to Mrs. Jane James for $7,000.

Feb. 15 Received semiannual interest of $1,750 on U.S. Treasury bonds.

Mar. 20 Received cash dividend on common stock of Meadow Brook, Inc., of $.45 per share and Standard Products of $.60 per share.

May 1 Received cash dividend on Prairie View common stock at the rate of $1.25 per share plus a 2% stock dividend. (The applicable statute states that stock dividends are to be treated as income and should be transferred to the income beneficiary immediately.)

May 15 Purchased 100 shares of common stock of Jenkins, Inc., through Hutzler Securities at $26.50 per share net, with income cash, to hold as an income-producing investment for the benefit of the life tenant.

May 31 Mailed check to Mrs. Jane James for $5,500; also paid trustee's expenses and commission of $1,500 to be charged 60% to principal and 40% to income.

The above transactions are recorded in the multicolumn journals and general journal as shown on pages 839 and 840.

Cash Receipts Journal

Date	Explanation	Cash in bank Dr	Principal: Investments control Cr	Principal: Realization gain Cr	Principal: Realization loss Dr	Principal: Miscellaneous credits: Amount	Ref	Account	Income: Dividend Cr	Income: Interest Cr	Income: Miscellaneous credits: Amount	Ref	Account
1966													
May 20	Record cash included in principal	34,495				34,495		Trust Principal					
June 10	Rec'd dividend, Jasper	2,040	2,040										
July 15	Sold Wilson bonds	100,600	99,250	350						1,000			
Aug. 15	Rec'd interest, U.S. Treasury bonds	1,750	875							875			
Nov. 1	Rec'd dividend, Prairie View	6,250							6,250				
Dec. 10	Rec'd dividend, Jasper Co.	2,720							2,720				
1967													
Feb. 15	Rec'd interest, U.S. Treas. bonds	1,750								1,750			
Mar. 20	Rec'd dividend, Meadow Brook	900							900				
	Rec'd dividend, Standard Products	900							900				
May 1	Rec'd dividend, Prairie View	6,250							6,250				
		157,655	102,165	350	-0-	34,495			17,020	3,625	-0-		

WILLIAM JAMES TRUST
Cash Disbursements Journal

Date	Payee	Check no.	Cash in bank Cr	Principal: Investments control Dr	Principal: Miscellaneous debits: Amount	Ref	Account	Income: Expenses Dr	Income: Distributed to beneficiary Dr	Income: Investments Dr	Income: Miscellaneous debits: Amount	Ref	Account
1966													
Sept. 15	Mrs. Jane James	1001	1,500						1,500				
Oct. 1	Hutzler Securities	1002	130,142	130,142									
1967													
Jan. 1	Mrs. Jane James	1003	7,000						7,000				
May 15	Hutzler Securities	1004	2,650							2,650			
May 31	Mrs. Jane James	1005	5,500						5,500				
31	Henry James, trustee	1006	1,500		900		Trustee's Expenses	600					
			148,292	130,142	900			600	14,000	2,650	-0-		

WILLIAM JAMES TRUST
General Journal

1966			
May 20	*Investment Control*	*516,715*	
	Trust Principal		*516,715*
	To establish the William James Trust for the benefit of Mrs. Jane James during her life and for Henry and William James at her death with the residuary assets of the estate as follows:		
	U.S. Treasury bonds, 3½% . . . $100,750		
	Wilson Manufacturing Co. bonds 98,500		
	Prairie View Mining Co. common stock . . . 162,500		
	Jasper Trading Co. common stock 151,300		
	Accrued interest receivable . . . 1,625		
	Dividends receivable . . . 2,040		
	Total . . . $516,715		
1967			
May 1	*Memorandum entry to record the receipt of 100 shares of Prairie View stock as a 2% stock dividend. These shares were reregistered in the name of Mrs. Jane James and distributed to her in accordance with the state law governing trusts.*		

These journal forms are merely suggestive of a type which might be used in accounting for the affairs of the trust. Of course, all these transactions could be recorded in a simple two-column general journal; however, where the trust is an active one, the multicolumn journal is a useful device for recording daily transactions.

The James trust has adopted the fiscal year June 1–May 31 as its accounting period, with the first period extending from the date the trust was established, May 20, 1966, to May 31, 1967. The closing entries for the first period are illustrated below in a traditional two-column journal:

Realization Gain	*350*	
Trust Principal	*550*	
Trustee's Expenses		*900*
To close gains and expenses to trust principal.		
Dividend Income	*17,020*	
Interest Income	*3,625*	
Trustee's Expenses		*600*
Distribution to Income Beneficiary		*14,000*
Trust Income		*6,045*
To close income, expenses, and distribution accounts to trust income.		

The trustee's report as illustrated is designed to stress the stewardship aspect of a trust. The trustee's accountability for principal and income is shown separately, each with the related changes in the accountability during the year. The trustee may employ a control account and subsidiary ledger arrangement in the ledger; however, the main assets composing the principal and income of the trust should be indicated on the statement or in accompanying schedules. In the present illustration a portion of the income retained in the trust is held in the form of cash; since only one cash account is maintained in this illustration, the two elements of cash must be added to obtain the cash balance reflected by the cash receipts and disbursements journals.

WILLIAM JAMES TRUST
Henry James, Trustee
Statement of Trust Principal
for the period May 20, 1966, to May 31, 1967

Trust principal—May 20, 1966:		
Cash	$ 34,495	
U.S. Treasury bonds, 3½%	100,750	
Wilson Manufacturing Co. bonds, 6%	98,500	
Prairie View Mining Co. common stock	162,500	
Jasper Trading Co. common stock	151,300	
Accrued interest receivable	1,625	
Dividends receivable	2,040	$551,210
Increases:		
Realization gain		350
		$551,560
Decreases:		
Trustee's expenses		900
Trust principal—May 31, 1967 (Schedule A)		$550,660

Schedule A

Inventory of Trust Principal
May 31, 1967

Cash	$ 5,968
U.S. Treasury bonds, 3½%	100,750
Prairie View Mining Co. common stock	162,500
Jasper Trading Co. common stock	151,300
Meadow Brook common stock	60,548
Standard Products common stock	69,594
Total	$550,660

Charitable trusts and foundations

Charitable trusts and foundations are, in a general way, governed by the same legal principles and requirements as the private trust. There are, however, some differences, the most important being that no specific beneficiaries need to be

WILLIAM JAMES TRUST
Henry James, Trustee
Statement of Trust Income

Revenue received for benefit of life tenant:		
Dividends	$17,020	
Interest	3,625	$20,645
Expenses chargeable to trust income:		
Trustee expense		600
		$20,045
Income distribution:		
Cash distributed to Mrs. Jane James	$14,000	
100 shares of common stock of Prairie View common stock received as stock dividend on trust principal	-0-	14,000
Undistributed trust income at May 31, 1967 (Schedule B)		$ 6,045

Schedule B

Inventory of Trust Income
May 31, 1967

Cash	$ 3,395
Jenkins, Inc., common stock	2,650
Total	$ 6,045

named. A particular segment of the general public may be the recipient of the income from the trust through various organizations such as schools, hospitals, and churches which receive trust support. In addition, charitable trusts may be established for an indefinite period of time. Since there is no direct beneficiary in many cases and since the life of the trust may be indefinite, the Attorney General is customarily given the responsibility for protecting the public's interest in these trusts.

The charitable trust usually operates under a board of trustees rather than a single trustee as is generally found in a private trust. The board is frequently self-perpetuating, with new members being elected by the existing members. The board makes decisions regarding the use of the assets within the limitations imposed upon them by the trust instrument or the applicable laws. Should it become impossible or impractical for the specific provisions of the trust instrument to be carried out, action may be taken by the courts to approve the use of the assets for purposes similar to those provided for originally.

Accounting problems of charitable trusts

In general the accounting procedures are the same for charitable trusts as for private trusts. Annual reports are required by the Internal Revenue Service, and many foundations attempt to obtain widespread circulation of their annual reports in order to solicit funds or applications for grants and to provide information to the public about their activities.

Many of the differences which exist in accounting for charitable trusts arise out of the unlimited life of the trust. In private trusts bond discounts and premiums are seldom amortized; in a charitable trust, because of the time interval which may transpire between acquisition and maturity or sale, bond premiums and discounts are frequently amortized. Amortization tends to avoid large adjustments in the investment account which might otherwise be necessary. Depreciation of income-producing properties is also provided for in order to assure the continued existence of the trust. Without adequate provision for depreciation, a trust which has a sizable investment in depreciable property would ultimately liquidate itself. However, foundations often charge to expense their acquisitions of furniture and fixtures for use in administering the trust. Cash flow is regarded as more important than income measurement; however, in charitable trusts as well as private ones, a separation of principal and income assets is essential.

A charitable trust or foundation may commit itself to pay a given sum of money to a particular beneficiary over a period of years. Because of these forward commitments, additional information is needed from the accounts. The trustees need to know what their commitments are at any point in time so that they can determine the availability of funds for distribution. Unlike the trustee of a private trust, the trustees of public trusts need an accounting system which shows appropriations and unpaid balances on specific grants.

The accounting system used by these organizations is frequently referred to as *fund accounting*. In essence this means that the system must report the funds available for a particular purpose and the commitments which have been made for the use of these funds. Because of the time interval between the date of approval for expenditures and the date the liability is actually created, a temporary account known as an appropriation account is used to indicate the commitment of funds. When the obligation to pay arises, the appropriation is converted to a liability and ultimately the payment is made. This procedure is illustrated as follows:

1. When the trustees decide how much money will be paid in total to various beneficiaries they make a general appropriation. The appropriation is usually from income; however, in some situations the principal may be appropriated. The appropriation of income in the amount of $250,000 is illustrated as follows:

Appropriations of Income	*250,000*	
Authorized Appropriations		*250,000*
To record the authorization of appropriations of $250,000 from income for the year 1967.		

2. When a grant is made by the awards committee, the foundation or trust is obligated to pay and a liability is created. Payment may be made immediately as a lump sum or it may be spread over several months. Since payment is not always made simultaneously with the grant, the accounting system must provide for the reflection of these liabilities or claims against the assets of the trust. Assume that a grant of $50,000 is made to City University to be paid in equal quarterly payments. The entry to record the award is:

Authorized Appropriations	*50,000*	
Unpaid Grants		*50,000*
To record the award of a grant to City University of $50,000 to support an inquiry into the nature of accounting principles, to be paid in equal quarterly installments.		

3. At the designated dates the checks will be written and mailed to the beneficiary. The payment of the first quarterly installment to City University is illustrated below:

Unpaid Grants	*12,500*	
Cash in Bank		*12,500*
To record the payment of the first installment to City University under grant out of income.		

Any appropriation from principal would be handled in the same manner after it is approved by the trustees. The only difference in the journal entries would be the original debit to record the appropriation; it would be made to Appropriations of Principal rather than to Appropriations of Income.

Special-purpose funds

Occasionally a public trust or foundation is given assets for a particular type of endeavor specified by the grantor. The use of either income or principal or both may be required by the terms of the donation. The assets are deposited with the trust for purposes of administration only, and the trustees are required to establish a separate set of records for these special-purpose funds in order to make appropriate reports to the donor. In most cases the assets may be commingled with other trust assets, but separate records should be maintained. Special funds are also sometimes created out of trust principal by action of the trustees.

The entries to create a special-purpose fund when additional assets are donated to the trust and when the assets are merely separated from the trust principal or income are similar. In the first case securities with a market value of $100,000 are donated to the trust for the purpose of supporting research in accounting. The trustees are to screen applications carefully, but awards may be made out of income or principal. The entry to create the special fund is as follows:

Investments	*100,000*	
Accounting Research Fund		*100,000*
To record the receipt of securities with a market value of $100,000 to be used together with any income for the support of accounting research.		

To illustrate the case of a special fund created out of the trust principal, assume that assets with a book value of $100,000 are to be set aside for a special purpose. The entry will be:

Transfers from Trust Principal	*100,000*	
Accounting Research Fund		*100,000*
To record the establishment of an accounting research fund from the general trust assets.		

Grants made from a special-purpose fund will usually state whether payment is to be made from income or principal. The normal appropriation entry may not be used in special-purpose funds because there is no implied or express intention to maintain the fund. The entry to record a grant of $10,000 to John Doe is thus recorded as follows:

Accounting Research Fund	*10,000*	
Unpaid Grant		*10,000*
To record the grant of $10,000 to John Doe to support his research into the problem of trust accounting.		

Administrative expenses may be charged against the fund granted for reseach activity. Entries to record such expenses vary, depending upon the manner in which the accounts of the special fund are kept. If the accounts are a part of the general records of the trust rather than a self-balancing set of accounts, the entry to record administrative expenses of $600, chargeable to the special fund, would be as follows:

Accounting Research Fund	*600*	
Administrative Expenses		*600*
To record the assignment of a portion of the administrative expenses to the accounting research fund. Expenses represent the cost of reviewing applications for grants for the period from January to April.		

The original charge for administrative expenses was made against trust income; the above entry is made merely to charge the accounting research fund and to relieve the income of the main trust.

Lapsed appropriations and grants

In some cases a particular grant will not be distributed in full because the recipient becomes unable to use it. Similarly, an appropriation may not be fully utilized because the acceptable applications are not equal to the appropriation. In either case the original entry authorizing the appropriation or the grant should be reversed to remove it from the records. The funds will thereby be available for other grants in the present year or in future years if the trustees elect to increase the appropriation by the amount of the unutilized portion. In any event the assets of the trust are not decreased by the amount which was originally appropriated or granted.

Financial statements

The statement of operations for a charitable trust is similar to the statement of income prepared for the ordinary business. The revenue category on the trust statement will usually include gifts to the trust, if the gifts are to be used to cover operating expenses or to provide additional grants. Gifts of a nature designed to increase the principal of the trust would not be so classified; they would be credited to the trust principal and would be reflected as an increase in this category on the balance sheet. The operating statement of the trust may take many forms and may be called by a variety of titles. It may report only revenue and expenses or it may also include a summary of unappropriated income. In most cases the statement is accompanied by a series of schedules reporting details which are not included on the face of the statement except in summary form. Schedules are generally included for the details of grants and appropriations as a matter of course, with others being included when the circumstances seem to warrant their preparation. One form of an operating statement for a trust is illustrated below:

THE ABLE FOUNDATION
Statement of Revenue, Expenses, and Appropriations
for the year 1967

Revenue:		
Dividends	$56,700	
Interest	32,450	
Gifts	15,000	
Miscellaneous	1,750	
Total		$105,900
Expenses:		
Salaries and employee benefits	$19,600	
Travel	5,200	
Legal and accounting	7,500	
Depreciation	600	
Rent	3,600	
Telephone and telegraph	2,500	
Janitorial services	1,200	
Miscellaneous	800	
Total		41,000
Excess of revenue over expenses		$ 64,900
Unappropriated income, beginning of year		18,300
Transfers from principal and special-purpose funds		40,000
Lapses of prior year's appropriations available		5,000
Total funds available for appropriations		$128,200
Authorized appropriations		125,000
Unappropriated income, end of year		$ 3,200

In the balance sheet of a charitable trust, the assets are usually carried at cost or fair value at date of receipt. However, since the assets often consist of securities for which daily market quotations are available, it is customary to indicate the current market value parenthetically, by footnote, or by a schedule accompanying the balance sheet. The liabilities usually consist of unpaid grants. To provide information on the types of organizations being supported by the foundation, a schedule of unpaid grants may be included.

The trust principal and the unappropriated income are treated as the capital or equity of the foundation. The balance of authorized appropriations will also be included in the equity section of the balance sheet. This portion of the equity represents the assets which have been officially committed but which have not been formally awarded to any recipient at the date the statement is prepared. These assets, in other words, are not free and available for any use except that specified in the appropriation.

The report of the trust or foundation may also include any other statements or information which the trustees think will be useful or helpful to the reader of the statement. Additional information will of course vary widely from one trust to another, depending upon the use the trustees wish to make of the statements.

Questions

1. What are the principal duties of the trustee?
2. What are the rights of a beneficiary of a trust?
3. What is the rule involving accrual of income or expense as it relates to the division between principal and income?
4. What is the difference between the Massachusetts rule and the Pennsylvania rule regarding the classification of dividends as principal or income?
5. Indicate whether each of the following receipts and disbursements should be classified as principal or income:
   - **a.** Losses due to casualty or theft of principal asset
   - **b.** Taxes levied on assets held for life tenant
   - **c.** Payment of claims existing at date trust is created
   - **d.** Expenses of maintaining condition of property held by the trust
   - **e.** Expenses of general administration of the trust
   - **f.** Carrying charges on unproductive real estate
   - **g.** Casualty insurance premiums
   - **h.** Expenses incurred in earning and collecting income
   - **i.** Proceeds from casualty insurance to insure against loss of trust assets
6. If the trust corpus includes as an investment bonds which were acquired at a value above or below maturity value, how should the adjustment to maturity value be treated?
7. ABC Trust holds 1,000 shares of XYZ company carried in the accounts at a cost of $50,000. XYZ company issues rights to its stockholders to acquire one share of stock at $40 for each 10 shares held. The rights are selling for $2 and the stock exrights for $58. The trustee sells the rights. How should this transaction be accounted for?

8. The Baxter Trust is created from the remainder of the C. W. Baxter estate. The assets held by the estate and all unpaid obligations are itemized as follows:

Cash	*$ 92,400*
U.S. Treasury bonds	*100,250*
Corporation bonds	*60,600*
Common stock	*192,400*
Interest accrued receivable	*3,600*
Dividends declared on which day of record has passed	*10,500*
Total	*$459,750*

The executor's fee of $12,000, the attorney's fee of $16,000, and the accountant's fee of $7,500 are to be paid by the estate. The remainder of the assets are to be deposited with the trustee of the Baxter Trust. Record the creation of the trust, assuming these assets constitute the first and only contribution to the trust.

9. The following trial balance was prepared from the accounts of the Richards Trust:

RICHARDS TRUST
Trial Balance

Principal cash	*$ 25,000*	
Income cash	*4,000*	
Investment control	*620,000*	
Dividend income		*$ 12,250*
Interest income		*15,100*
Trustee's expenses	*4,200*	
Distribution to income beneficiary	*25,000*	
Realization gain		*5,400*
Realization loss	*300*	
Trust principal		*642,000*
Trust income		*3,750*
Total	*$678,500*	*$678,500*

Prepare the closing entries, assuming the trustee's expenses are divided equally between principal and income.

10. The Accountants Research Trust was established by a major donation of common stock. The purpose of the trust is to support accounting research. The following selected events occurred during the first year:

(1) The trustees appropriated $50,000 out of income to be awarded to support worthy research projects.
(2) Two grants of $10,000 each were made.
(3) Payments of $5,000 were made under each of the grants.

Record these events in journal entry form.

Short cases for analysis

24-1 The McCannon Trust was created from the residuary assets of the estate of John McCannon. Included among the residuary assets were 5% bonds of Adams Supply Co. due July 1, 1970, with par value of $100,000. The market value of the bonds on October 1, 1967, the date that these bonds were delivered to the trust, was 102½ plus accrued interest. Interest is payable on these bonds on July 1 and January 1.

Instructions

a. Make all entries required to account for this bondholding during the period it is held by the trust. (Assume that it is held to maturity.)

b. Explain your reasons for accounting for the bondholding as you have.

c. Would your answer have been any different if the trustee had purchased these bonds for the trust with cash held by the trust?

d. What do you understand to be the major distinction between income earned on trust assets for the benefit of the income beneficiary and gains realized on trust assets for the benefit of the remainderman?

24-2 The Mason Trust acquired 5,000 shares of the common stock of Electric Power Company on January 2, 1955, at a cost of $50 per share. On January 2, 1967, Electric Power Company declared a 50% stock dividend payable to stockholders of record January 10, 1967. The common stock equity of the balance sheets of Electric Power Company indicated the following facts:

	Dec. 31, 1954	*Dec. 31, 1966*
Common stock, par value $10, authorized 2,000,000 shares; issued and outstanding, 1954, 800,000 shares; 1966, 950,000 shares	*$ 8,000,000*	*$ 9,500,000*
Capital paid-in in excess of par value	*16,000,000*	*22,400,000*
Retained earnings	*14,000,000*	*27,200,000*
	$38,000,000	*$59,100,000*

Instructions

a. Allocate the stock dividend between principal and income in accordance with the Pennsylvania rule.

b. What difference would there be, if any, if the Massachusetts rule were followed?

c. What central issue is at stake in the rulings of these two states?

d. What might be a more equitable rule to follow in accounting for the division between principal and income when common stock is held by a trust? What problems might be encountered?

24-3 Thomas transferred his transistor manufacturing business and 1,000 shares of Zeno Company common stock to Central Trust Company to be held in trust for the benefit of his son, Peter, for life, with the remainder to go to Peter's son, James. The Central Trust Company insured the transistor business with the Mutual Insurance Company by buying two policies. One policy was a standard fire insurance policy covering the building, equipment, etc. The other policy was secured for the purpose of covering loss of income during periods when the business was inoperable as a result of tornado, earthquake, or fire. The buildings and equipment were subsequently destroyed by fire and the Mutual Insurance Company paid claims under both policies to the Central Trust Company.

Shortly after the 1,000 common shares of Zeno Company had been transferred to Central Trust Company, Zeno declared a dividend of 10 common shares of Maddox Corporation for each 100 shares of Zeno Company common stock held. The Maddox Corporation common stock had been purchased as an investment by Zeno Company.

During the same year Zeno Company directors declared that the common stock would be split on a basis of two new shares for each old share. After the distribution of the new shares, Central Trust Company decided to sell 1,000 shares of Zeno Company common stock.

Instructions

a. How should the Central Trust Company handle the events which have been described above as to distribution between the life beneficiary and the remainderman?

b. State your reasons for making the distribution in the manner in which you did.

AICPA adapted

24-4 In accounting for a testamentary trust, there is a problem of separating the items that should be charged against principal from the items that should be charged against income. You are to state whether each of the following items would be charged to principal or to income, assuming that the most general rule is to be followed. Give explanations for each of your answers.

(1) Federal estate taxes paid
(2) Interest paid on mortgage on real estate
(3) Depreciation of real estate
(4) Legal fees for collection of rent
(5) Special assessment tax levied on real estate for street improvements
(6) Amortization of premium on bonds which had been purchased by the testator
(7) Loss on sale of trust investments
(8) Taxes on vacant city lots

AICPA adapted

24-5 Ash Bryce, a resident of Boston, Massachusetts, died September 1, 1967, and by his will established a trust providing that the income, after costs of administration, be paid to his widow Bertha for and during her life. During the first year of the trust, the trustee received the following:

1. *Dividends:*

Cash dividends declared Aug. 5, 1967, payable to stock of record Aug. 30	*$ 8,000*
Cash dividends declared at various times from Sept. 1, 1967, to July 31, 1968	*20,000*
Stock dividends declared on Dec. 1. The market value of the stock at date of declaration was $10, the book value was $8. The book value of the stock at Sept. 1, 1967, was $7.50.	

2. *Interest:*

Semiannual interest on municipal bonds paid on Dec. 1	*5,000*
Semiannual interest on municipal bonds paid on June 1	*5,000*
Semiannual interest on corporate bonds paid on Feb. 28 and Aug. 31 for the two periods	*20,000*

3. *Sale of securities:*
   Securities with an inventory value of $20,000 were sold for $27,600.

The trustee's expenses and fees paid in accordance with the provisions of the trust indenture totaled $1,650.

Instructions

a. Prepare a schedule of income for the year to which Bertha Bryce is entitled in accordance with the terms of the trust agreement.

b. For those items not considered income, explain why they are excluded.

AICPA adapted

Problems

24-6 J. A. Alexander established a testamentary trust. The will provided that the trust would be composed of the residuary of his estate. On March 1, 1967, the court gave its permission for the estate to be closed and the assets to be delivered to the trustee. The residuary assets of the estate were as follows:

5% bonds (market value)	*$ 40,000*
Common stock (market value)	*65,400*
Real estate (market value)	*120,000*
Cash in bank	*34,000*
Total	*$259,400*

Activities of the trustee during the first year were:

(1) Received interest on bonds (par value, $50,000) on Aug. 30, 1967.

(2) Made repairs to real estate, necessary in order to maintain the property, totaling $5,000.

(3) Sold bonds (par value, $20,000) on Nov. 30 for $16,800 plus accrued interest.
(4) Received dividend on stock, $2,000.
(5) Received rent from rental property for the year in the amount of $14,400.
(6) Distributed income to the life tenant in the amount of $12,000.
(7) Received interest on remaining bonds on Feb. 29, 1968.
(8) Paid trustee's expenses and commission of $2,000 chargeable 60% to principal and 40% to income.

Instructions

Prepare statements of trust principal and income for the period March 1, 1967, through February 29, 1968.

24-7 Mason Schaffer, Jr., executor of his father's estate, has filed a final accounting of his actions as executor with the court. The court has approved his statement and the payment of the attorney's fees, $14,500; the accountant's fees, $5,525; and the executor's commission, $12,100. The will provides that the residuary of the estate should be used to establish a trust with Mrs. Mary Schaffer as life tenant, to receive the income of the trust for the remainder of her lifetime. Mason Schaffer and Alexander Schaffer are named as remaindermen to share equally the trust principal at their mother's death. Mason Schaffer is named as trustee and is to be paid $2,000 per year, chargeable against income, for his services. The inventory of the estate residuary as filed with the court is presented below:

MASON SCHAFFER, SR., ESTATE
Inventory of Principal Assets
February 1, 1967

Cash	*$ 45,275*
3% of U.S. Treasury bonds, due Nov. 1, 1987, interest payable Nov. 1 and May 1, par $65,000	*65,500*
6% Raeford Manufacturing Co. bonds, due Apr. 1, 1982, interest payable Apr. 1 and Oct. 1, par $65,000	*64,025*
Mountain Mining Co. common stock, 3,250 shares	*105,625*
Crafton Trading Co. common stock, 4,450 shares	*98,350*
Total	*$378,775*

MASON SCHAFFER, SR., ESTATE
Inventory of Income Assets
February 1, 1967

Cash	*$ 9,325*
Accrued interest receivable	*1,788*
Dividends receivable	*1,325*
Total	*$ 12,438*

The following transactions occurred during the first year of the trust:

Feb. 10 Received dividend of $1,325 from Crafton Trading Co. declared payable to stockholders of record January 20.

Mar. 1 Sold Raeford Manufacturing Co. bonds for $64,350 plus accrued interest. Brokerage commission of $100 was deducted from the proceeds of the sale.

May 1 Received semiannual interest on U.S. Treasury bonds.

June 15 Mailed a check for $975 to Mrs. Mary Schaffer.

July 1 Purchased 1,300 shares of Talbot Supply Co. common stock at $20 per share plus commission of $356; also purchased 975 shares of General Products common stock at $30 per share plus commission of $386.

July 1 Received cash dividend on Mountain Mining Co. at rate of $.82 per share.

Oct. 10 Received cash dividend on common stock of Crafton Trading Co. at rate of $.26 per share.

Nov. 1 Mailed a check to Mrs. Mary Schaffer for $4,550.

Nov. 1 Received semiannual interest on U.S. Treasury bonds.

Dec. 20 Received cash dividend on common stock of Talbot Supply Co. of $.30 per share and General Products of $.40 per share.

Jan. 2 Received cash dividend on Mountain Mining Co. common stock at the rate of $.82 per share plus a 2% stock dividend. (The applicable statute requires that stock dividends be treated as income and be transferred to the income beneficiary.)

Jan. 15 Purchased 100 shares of common stock of Darkins, Inc., at $17.25 per share net, with income cash, to hold as an income-producing investment for the benefit of the life tenant.

Jan. 31 Mailed check to Mrs. Mary Schaffer for $3,575; also paid trustee's commission of $2,000.

Instructions

a. Record the entries to close the estate.

b. Set up the trust accounts and record the above transactions in general journal form.

24-8 A. J. Adamson created a charitable trust January 1, 1967, by executing an indenture providing for the income from his trust to be used to support research in the social sciences and by depositing the following securities with Alex Johns as trustee:

	Current market quote
1,000 shares of Adamson, Inc., common stock	56¼
1,500 shares of Motors, Inc., common stock	82½
500 5% first mortgage bonds of Amalgamated Utilities, $1,000 par value, interest payable Dec. 1 and June 1, maturing June 1, 1975	101½

The following events occurred during the first year of the trust's existence:

(1) The trustee authorized appropriations of income in the amount of $25,000.
(2) Interest received on the bonds totaled $25,000.

(3) Dividends of $3 per share were received on Adamson, Inc., stock and of $1.50 per share were received on Motors, Inc., stock.
(4) Motors, Inc., offered the common stockholders the right to buy one new share of common stock for each 20 shares they held at the time for $40 per share. The market price of the common stock at the date the shares sold ex rights was $92.50 and of the right $2.50. The trustee elected to sell the rights later at a price of $2.75 per right.
(5) Grants were made for research in the amount of $21,500.
(6) Trustee's expenses associated with investigating the various proposals totaled $1,750.
(7) Payments to researches under the terms of the grant were made in the amount of $18,500. All unpaid balances were authorized to be carried over into the next year, with one exception where the unpaid portion totaled $45 and the research had been completed.
(8) The trustee's fees, in accordance with the indenture, were paid in the amount of $1,500.

Instructions

a. Prepare journal entries to record the creation of the trust and all transactions occurring during the course of the year.

b. Prepare financial statements as of December 31, 1967.

24-9 The endowment trust fund of Prep School has been accumulated over the years by an original grant by the founder of $1 million and subsequent contributions by alumni. The following trial balance was prepared from the accounts of the endowment at the beginning of the current year.

Cash	*$ 85,000*	
Accrued interest receivable	*8,000*	
Investments	*1,760,000*	
Trust, principal		*$1,810,000*
Trust, income		*43,000*
Totals	*$1,853,000*	*$1,853,000*

The trust indenture provides that the income from the trust is to be used solely for the support of the operations of the school. The following transactions occurred during the fiscal year:

(1) The trustees appropriated $100,000 for operating expenses of the school.
(2) Endowment investments having a book value of $250,000 were sold for $275,000, including accrued interest of $1,500.
(3) Investments were purchased by the endowment fund trustees at a cost of $310,000 plus accrued interest of $2,000.
(4) Interest earned on endowment investments during the year totaled $72,300. Accrued interest receivable at the end of the year amounted to $9,600.

(5) Cash in the amount of $82,500 was transferred from the endowment bank account to the general fund account of the school.
(6) $10,000 was received as a bequest from an alumnus to be added to the endowment principal.
(7) The trustees authorized and paid a grant of $40,000 from the principal of the endowment fund to the school for purposes of planning a new library building.

Instructions

a. Prepare all journal entries necessary to account for the endowment for the year. (Assume that unused appropriations are canceled at the end of the year.)

b. Prepare financial statements for the endowment trust for the year.

24-10 John Gibbon died January 1, 1962, and left his property in trust to his daughter, Ethel. The income was to be paid to her as long as she lived and at her death the trust principal was to go to his nephew, William Gibbon. He appointed John Doe trustee at a fixed fee of $5,000 per annum. All expenses of settling the estate were paid and accounted for by the executor before the trustee took over.

Ethel died on September 30, 1965, and left all her property in trust to her cousin, Joseph Hart. John Doe was appointed executor and trustee of her estate and he agreed not to make any additional charges for these services. All income was to be paid to Joseph Hart. The estate, which consisted solely of Ethel's unexpended income from the John Gibbon trust, was immediately invested in 4% certificates of deposit.

The property received under the will of John Gibbon on January 1, 1962, was:
10,000 shares of the K. O. Corporation, valued at $100 each.
$300,000 bonds of K. O. Corporation, valued at par, paying interest on June 30 and Dec. 31 at 6% per annum.

In the five years ended December 31, 1966, the trustee received the following dividends on the stock:
Feb. 1, 1962, 1963, and 1964, $40,000 per year
Feb. 1, 1965, and 1966, $60,000 per year
He made the following payments:
Expenses: $100 per month
Trustee's fees: $5,000 per annum
To beneficiaries:

Ethel Gibbon:	
1962	$27,250
1963	35,000
1964	25,000
1965	37,000
William Gibbon:	
1965	$17,000
1966	46,000
Joseph Hart:	
1966	$3,000

The surplus cash was left on deposit in the bank and drew no interest.

Instructions

Prepare the trustee's accounts including the beneficiaries' interest, covering the five-year period ended December 31, 1966, when the remainder of the John Gibbon trust is turned over to William Gibbon.

AICPA adapted

24-11 John Jones set up an irrevocable trust for the benefit of his eldest daughter, Joan Jones, to run until 1971, when she would be thirty years old and could receive the principal of the trust. If she should die before attaining the age of thirty, the trust principal would go to her younger sister, Ethel Jones. The income of the trust could be withdrawn by the beneficiary at any time.

By terms of the trust agreement, John Jones was to be trustee during his life and was to receive a fee of $1,000 a year, chargeable to income, in lieu of commissions.

Any investments made for the trust were to be subject to the approval of the trustee only and not to be bound by any legal rulings regarding trust investments.

There was paid into the trust by gift from John Jones on January 1, 1957, the sum of $100,000 which was to be invested by the trustee.

On December 31, 1966, Joan died and bequeathed her entire estate, composed entirely of the undistributed income of the trust created by her father, to her brother, Paul Jones, to be held in trust for him. He was to receive the income and had the right of appointment of principal. John Jones was made trustee and was to receive an annual fee of $1,000 instead of commission.

The trial balance of John Jones, trustee, at December 31, 1966, was as follows:

Debits	
Cash—principal	*$ 7,000*
Cash—income	*9,550*
$300,000 par bonds 4% RR & I, due 1991, at cost, investment of principal	*275,000*
Stocks—2,000 shares of North Cascade, Inc., $10 par value common at cost, investment of undistributed income funds	*150,000*
Oil Venture Syndicate—investment of undistributed income funds	*12,500*
Accrued interest on bonds	*950*
Payment to beneficiary during 1966	*2,500*
Expenses applicable to income for the year	*1,850*
Expenses applicable to principal paid during the year	*1,250*
Trustee's fee for the year	*1,000*
Total	*$461,600*

Credits	
Principal of trust—Jan. 1, 1966	*$275,000*
Undistributed income balance, Jan. 1, 1966	*138,500*
Interest on bonds	*12,800*

Dividends	*14,000*
Profits on sale of principal investment bonds	*9,200*
Profits on sale of stocks held as income investment	*9,600*
Due to trustee for fees	*2,500*
Total	*$461,600*

Analysis of undistributed income at Jan. 1, 1966:	
Interest received	*$ 80,000*
Dividends received	*89,000*
Profits on stocks sold	*30,000*
Total revenue	*$199,000*
Expenses charged to income	*$ 16,500*
Fees to trustee	*9,000*
Payments to beneficiary	*35,000*
Total expenses	*$ 60,500*
Balance, Jan. 1, 1966	*$138,500*

Analysis of principal at Jan. 1, 1966:	
Jan. 1, 1957	*$100,000*
Increase in principal through sale of investments	*190,000*
Total	*$290,000*
Payment of expenses applicable to principal	*15,000*
Balance, Jan. 1, 1966	*$275,000*

During the three years ended December 31, 1969, the following transactions took place:

On December 31, 1967, the Oil Venture Syndicate was liquidated by receiving:

(1) 1,000 shares no-par value stock of Oklahoma Oil Producers, Incorporated, of which the market value at December 31, 1967, was $10 a share.

(2) $6,250 in cash.

(3) $12,500 par value 5% Stanton Oils of California bonds, due in 1992, of which the market value at December 31, 1967, was 80% of par value.

During the year 1968 the trustee sold $150,000 par value of the 4% RR & I bonds at a net profit of $25,000 and invested the cash in U.S. government 3¾% bonds at 100 net.

During 1968 the trustee invested $10,000 of undistributed income funds of the Paul Jones trust in Standard Oils common stock at $40 per share, receiving 250 shares; the expenses of the purchase amounted to $50.

On January 25, 1969, the trustee sold $12,500 par value bonds of Stanton Oils of California for $12,500 net and invested the proceeds in Tulsa City 4% bonds at 100 net.

During the three years ended December 31, 1969, there was collected:

Interest on RR & I bonds	*$26,321.25*
Interest on Stanton Oils of California bonds	*625.00*
Interest on U.S. government bonds	*10,053.75*
Interest on Tulsa City bonds	*500.00*
Dividends on stocks	*40,000.00*

During the same three years there was disbursed:

Payments to Ethel Jones as beneficiary	*$ 6,000.00*
Payments to Paul Jones as beneficiary	*10,000.00*
Expenses chargeable to income of the principal trust	*4,000.00*
Expenses paid chargeable to income of undistributed income trust	*3,500.00*
Fees paid trustee	*3,000.00*
The account payable to trustee at Dec. 31, 1966, was liquidated in addition.	

No accounting of the trustee's actions has been filed during this three-year period.

Instructions

Prepare statements summarizing the trustee's actions during the three-year period.

AICPA adapted

PART EIGHT

GOVERNMENTAL ACCOUNTING

25 FUND ACCOUNTING: GOVERNMENTS AND INSTITUTIONS

The focus of much of the discussion in this and the preceding volumes of this series has been on accounting for the activities of an enterprise, the objective of the accounting being to measure and report performance and financial condition of the enterprise. The focus of the discussion in this and the following chapter is on accounting for a specific group of resources. The accounting entity is the fund rather than the enterprise. The emphasis in accounting for funds is one of accountability rather than ownership. Stewardship over resources is the focal point rather than measurement of operating results.

Since we will be using the fund as the focal point of the accounting procedures to be developed here, a definition of the term is in order. It has been defined as "a sum of money or other resources segregated for the purpose of carrying on specific activities or attaining certain objectives in accordance with special regulations, restrictions, or limitations and constituting an independent fiscal and accounting entity."[1] We can readily see the difference between this definition and that which accountants generally state when talking about funds. In financial accounting the term *fund* most often refers to a sum of money or other assets which have been earmarked for a particular purpose. There is seldom any implication that a separate accounting system will be set up. It is important, therefore, that for purposes of this chapter we understand that a fund represents not only a sum of resources but also an accounting entity.

If we look at the fund as the accounting entity, then what should the accounting system be designed to show? Essentially the accounting system must reveal what resources were or became available and what disposition was made of them during

[1] *Municipal Accounting and Auditing,* National Committee on Governmental Accounting (Chicago: 1951), pp. 3–4.

the period. The requirements of the system support the concept of accountability. In general, the emphasis on stewardship, as opposed to performance, means that fund accounting is used most widely in areas where the primary need for an accounting system is to establish control over resources. Resources flowing in must be accounted for and all disbursements must be checked against the authority to use the resources. Fund accounting quite naturally then fits the needs of many nonprofit organizations, such as government, hospitals, schools, libraries, and churches.

The primary reason for the adoption of fund accounting by these organizations can be found in legal restrictions which have been placed on the use of assets available to them. Since the objective of these organizations is to provide a service to a segment of the population at a minimal charge, at a charge unrelated to value, or at no charge at all, the administrator is responsible for seeing that the funds are administered in accordance with the prevailing law. The number of separate funds employed by an organization will vary widely, depending on the legal requirements and the administrative practices which are applicable. Funds are usually classified on a functional basis, which means that they are classified as to the source of receipts or as to the use to be made of the assets. Such a classification generally complies with the legal requirements established by state statute, municipal charter requirements, and ordinances; it is in accordance with good accounting practice and provides valuable financial statistics. Adhering to this general philosophy, the National Committee on Governmental Accounting[2] has recommended the following classification of funds and has suggested the general purpose of each fund as follows:

The general fund is used to account for all revenues and the activities financed by them, which are not accounted for in some special fund.

Special revenue funds are established to account for taxes and other revenues (except special assessments) set aside for a particular purpose. Usually a separate revenue fund is set up for each purpose for which revenues are dedicated; for example, if a special tax levy is made for schools, a special revenue fund is set up to account for the schools' finances and activities.

Working capital funds are used to account for services provided to other departments for which a charge is made, usually to cover only the cost. These are *revolving* funds.

Special assessment funds are established to account for special assessments levied to finance improvements or services deemed to benefit the properties against which the assessments are levied.

Bond funds are used to account for the proceeds of general bond issues.

Sinking funds are set up to account for the accumulation of resources for retiring term bonds at their maturity.

Trust and agency funds are established to account for cash or other assets held by the municipality as a trustee or agent, respectively. The two classes of funds are so similar that for accounting purposes they are grouped together.

Utility or other enterprise funds are established to account for the financing of services rendered primarily to the general public for compensation, such as those of water works, electric plants, docks, wharves, and airports.

[2] *Ibid.*, p. 5.

General fixed asset accounts are set up to account for all fixed assets held by the municipality which are not part of a revolving or trust fund.

General bonded debt accounts are established as a self-balancing system to account for all unmatured bond contracts which are not payable from a special assessment fund or utility fund and, therefore, are not carried as a liability to these funds.

These funds relate particularly to governmental activity, and the remaining discussion will be centered around this activity; however, the principles of fund accounting can be applied whenever the focus is upon the use made of a specific group of resources. Terminology may vary, but the principles of fund accounting are the same whether the activity to be accounted for relates to a government, hospital, school, or library.

Budgeting

The budget of any business activity, whether it is profit-oriented or not, is a plan of financial activity. The budget is no different for the governmental activity. As a matter of fact, it is often more important as a guiding factor to the nonprofit activity than it is to the profit-seeking activity. This is true because in many cases, especially in those funds governed by public officials, the authority for spending any money for any purpose depends upon legislative approval. In such situations the budget is essential. It usually specifies (1) the time period covered by the budget; (2) the organizational units which are to spend the money and the amount each unit may spend; and (3) the object for which the money can be spent, such as salaries, supplies, equipment, etc., and the amount designated for each.

Before the expenditure budget can be adopted by the legislative body, a revenue budget must be prepared to ascertain that the expenditure appropriations are within the limits of the organization's resources. The revenue budget is obviously a forecast of expected events, not all of which are under the control of the legislative body making the appropriation; however, the long-term success of the organization for which the budget is being prepared is dependent upon the ability of this body to forecast the revenue accurately. In most cases this means that the revenue will be forecast by source: for example, taxes, licenses, fines, penalties, etc. In each case there is a problem of estimating the total revenue to which the unit is entitled and the extent of the uncollectibles from each source.

Unlike profit-seeking enterprises, governmental units usually make the budget a part of the formal accounts. The reason for this is probably found in the authority represented by the budget. In a firm the budget is prepared and administered by the management. In a governmental unit the budget is also prepared by management and submitted to a legislative body for approval. The authority to spend funds is granted by the legislative body and the administration of the program is then carried out by the management, usually without any authority over the amount of the appropriation. The entry generally used to formalize the budget is:

Estimated Revenues	*785,000*	
Appropriations		*725,000*
Unappropriated Surplus		*60,000*

There are accountants who argue that the recording of the budget should have no effect on the surplus accounts of the fund. They maintain that any change in surplus should be the result of the excess (or deficiency) of revenues over expenditures. The advocates of this position create another account, frequently referred to as Budgetary Surplus. In situations where this latter procedure is followed the entry to record the budget is as follows:

Estimated Revenues	*785,000*	
Appropriations		*725,000*
Budgetary Surplus		*60,000*

The advantages of this alternative procedure are that:

1. A single account indicates the status of the current year's budget. A debit balance indicates that authorized appropriations exceed estimated revenues for the current year and a credit balance indicates that estimated revenues exceed appropriations.

2. The separation of the budgetary and operating data facilitates the preparation of financial statements and the comparison of budget and results.

Of course, at the end of the period the budgetary accounts are reversed and the actual revenues and expenditures are closed to unappropriated surplus.

Lapsing and continuing appropriations. Since an appropriation is usually made for one year, there may be times when an appropriation will not have been used fully by the end of the budget period. In many cases commitments will have been made to spend a portion of this unexpended balance. There may also exist a portion of the appropriation which has not been committed for any purpose. In such circumstances, the budget procedure is to increase the appropriation for the following year by the amount of the committed and unexpended funds, thereby granting the administrator the privilege to spend more money in the second period than he would have had if he had been able to complete his plans for the first period. Any funds which have not been so committed at the end of the first period usually revert to the general pool of resources to be budgeted for the second period. Of course there are occasions when a budget period will extend beyond one year; this is particularly true when the budget is to cover the construction of some facility which will remain under construction for several periods.

As a result of this emphasis on a strict budget, most governmental units will follow a system of encumbering the appropriation whenever they have committed themselves to the expenditure of funds. Such a system is desirable to obtain information about the funds which are uncommitted at any time during the year as well as about the amount of funds committed at the end of the year which have not been expended.

Another device which is commonly used in fund accounting is the *allotment*. Frequently the administrator of a fund will allot his total budget into components, such as quarterly allotments or allotment by specific activity. This procedure is instituted primarily as a control device of the administrator so that he may ascertain that the money which is appropriated is used in the manner which seems best in view of his directive for administering the unit. There is no question here of matching expenditures with revenues or, for that matter, of deciding which purpose deserves more financial support than the other, both of which are problems of the legislative body in appropriating money for an entire unit. The administrator acts as one man charged with a specific responsibility and he does not have to convince others that any given allotment is better than some other which they might propose. The allotment scheme is a highly useful device; however, it is not necessary to the functioning of the fund accounting system.

If it is found desirable to formalize the allotment of funds, then the journal entry to record the appropriation would probably be changed as follows:

Estimated Revenues	*785,000*	
Unallotted Appropriations		*725,000*
Unappropriated Surplus or Budgetary Surplus		*60,000*

When the appropriation is allotted, the following entry would be made:

Unallotted Appropriations	*125,000*	
Allotments		*125,000*

Annual financial report and the budget. The annual financial report is very helpful in the preparation of the budget in many instances and it is also helpful in reviewing the past year's activity as compared with the planned activity. In many ways this relationship of the budget and the financial report places the budget bureau and the legislative body on the horns of a dilemma. In the first place, most budgets have their beginnings in the history of past activity. This naturally means that the preparation of the budget begins with a review of what has happened in past years. How much money was appropriated for a particular purpose and how much was spent? This usually forms a basis for opinion as to how much should be appropriated for the next period. If all the money was spent and the administrator was clamoring for more, then perhaps the budget for this activity should be enlarged. On the other hand, if the money which was appropriated last period was not needed, then there may be evidence that this particular activity does not need any increase; instead its appropriation may be decreased. Such reliance on past data, while in many ways desirable, does in many cases lead to waste on the part of the administrator. He may feel it a disgrace to have his budget cut; his reputation as an administrator tends to change as the size of his budget changes. We might add as an aside that although we often criticize government officials for this type of behavior, there is no reason to believe that it does not extend into the realm of the corporate world also. Wherever success is measured by the size of the budget one controls and where budgets are based on past activity, this situation is likely to occur. This is not to say that the budget director should ignore the past when seeking guidance, but he needs a special sort of clairvoyance to determine what activities are most important to the government or the enterprise as a whole and what the cost of carrying on these activities is likely to be. In the absence of this type of information, the budget and financial statements of past years are likely to continue to be the basis for estimating future requirements.

Cash or accrual basis of accounting

In fund accounting there must be some consideration of the basis of accounting. Should the accounts be kept on the accrual or the cash basis? The accrual basis requires that revenues be recognized as the revenue is earned, not necessarily when cash is received, and that expenses be recognized when incurred, not necessarily when cash is paid. In fund accounting, especially when related to governmental units, there may be some question of when revenue is earned. In the case of taxes, the revenue is considered to be earned at the time that the bills are sent to the taxpayer or at the time when the tax is considered due, whether paid or not. In the case of licenses and fines, there may be very little time lapse between the date the revenue is earned, that is, the date that application for the license is made or that the illegal act causing the fine to be levied took place, and the date that the cash is collected. As a result the municipality may record these items on the cash basis even though they are purportedly on the accrual basis of accounting. There is also some conflict in the full accrual treatment for expenses. In the case of accrued items such as interest on borrowed money, the accrual may not be recorded at the end of the period because the appropriation for the current year did not make provision for this expenditure in the current period. In such cases the accrual must be omitted and recorded in the following period or omitted until the payment is actually made. This latter procedure seems to be the one that has gained the most favor among municipal accountants. It is frequently referred to as the *modified accrual basis of accounting.*

The cash basis of accounting requires that no revenues or expenses be recognized until the cash is actually received or disbursed. This method has its limitations because it does not allow, in all cases, the matching of services provided during a period with the cost of providing those services. The argument has been advanced that the accrual basis of accounting is not necessary in fund accounting. There is no need to worry about matching revenues and expenses because in many cases the fund has no revenues. The source of its resources is an appropriation from the general fund. This may be true, but there does seem to be a need to recognize the cost of providing a service in the period when that service is provided. In addition, in order to reconcile the appropriation with the actual costs incurred, it seems essential to recognize the cost when it is incurred rather than when cash is expended, especially since the payment may not be made until a later period. As a result of these arguments, the advocates of the cash basis of accounting have proposed a modified cash basis, which approximates the modified accrual basis. The major difference in the two methods is that under the modified cash basis the revenue is not recognized until the cash is received. Expenses are recognized at the time when the costs are incurred rather than at the time payment is made. The major objection to such a scheme is that there seems to be no real reason for not recording the revenue when it is considered to be earned and there are times when the matching of revenues and expenditures may be desirable in utility or working capital funds. Moreover, the recognition of revenue when it is billed or earned provides an additional control over the revenue and assures that all reasonable effort will be exerted to collect it. At least the fact that it was never collected will not be easily forgotten. In addition the recording of revenue when it is billed or earned provides for a more complete accounting record. For these reasons the accrual method seems to be preferable except where there is some legal restriction which would prevent its use.

When the cash or modified cash basis of accounting is followed, it is necessary for purposes of control and financial reporting to use some system of memorandum or self-balancing accounts to record the fact that a receivable or payable exists. One procedure which might be used to obtain this information is suggested here. The entries illustrated below reflect receivables; however, a similar system for payables can easily be designed. This illustration is designed to show the self-balancing nature of the accounts.

Taxes Receivable	*200,000*	
Uncollected Taxes		*200,000*
To record the billing of taxes for the fiscal year 1966.		
Cash	*80,000*	
Revenues		*80,000*
To record the collection of a portion of the tax levy for the fiscal year 1966.		
Uncollected Taxes	*80,000*	
Taxes Receivable		*80,000*
To reflect the taxes collected to date in the receivable accounts.		

If a balance sheet were prepared at this time, the accounts receivable would probably be shown as follows:

Taxes receivable	*$120,000*
Less: Uncollected taxes	*120,000*

There are other methods for controlling taxes receivable which do not require formal journal entries and ledger accounts, but the system described above is simple and inexpensive to maintain, and for a fund that is subject to public scrutiny it provides complete information about the activity for the period.

Encumbrances and the basis of accounting. The encumbrance is the earmarking of an appropriation to indicate that the funds are committed. Under any system of accounting, the encumbrance does not result in the recognition of an expense or expenditure. Since the purpose of the encumbrance is to earmark appropriations which have been committed, it is desirable to use the system regardless of the basis of accounting adopted for the fund. As a matter of fact, the encumbrance system may be more desirable when the cash basis of accounting is used. This is frequently the only way of determining the obligations which remain to be met from a particular appropriation. The expense is recognized in accordance with the system of accounting adopted. If the accrual basis is adopted, then the expense is recognized when the liability is recognized. On the other hand, if the cash basis is adopted, the expense is not recognized until the cash is expended. The entries required to account for encumbrances and the subsequent recognition of the expense and payment of the liability for each basis of accounting are illustrated as follows:

Accrual basis accounting:		
Encumbrances	*75,000*	
Reserve for Encumbrances		*75,000*
To record the encumbrances of appropriations for project X.		
Appropriation Expenditures	*20,000*	
Accounts Payable		*20,000*
To record the acquisition of materials to be used on project X.		
Reserve for Encumbrances	*20,000*	
Encumbrances		*20,000*
To relieve the encumbrances for the materials received to date on project X.		
Accounts Payable	*20,000*	
Cash		*20,000*
To record the payment of accounts.		
Cash basis accounting:		
Encumbrances	*75,000*	
Reserve for Encumbrances		*75,000*
To record the encumbrance of appropriations for project X.		
Appropriation Expenditures	*20,000*	
Cash		*20,000*
To record the purchase of materials for use on project X.		
Reserve for Encumbrances	*20,000*	
Encumbrances		*20,000*
To relieve the encumbrances for the materials received to date on project X.		

Special problems

There are several features of fund accounting which are not found in traditional financial accounting. Several of these features are necessary because of the control which is exercised over the unit by the governing body, and some of them are peculiar to fund accounting without regard to the element of control.

Appropriations are required when a fund is under the strict surveillance of a governing board or legislative body. Appropriations are the authority given by the controlling group for the administrator of a fund to commit the resources of the organization in carrying out his activities. The appropriation is based on the formal budget which is prepared estimating the revenues and authorizing the expenditure of cash. The journal entry necessary to record the appropriation was illustrated earlier on page 863.

After the budget is adopted, the tax bills for the year are mailed and the receivables and the associated revenues are recognized. Before cash is expended, the control group will frequently require that an encumbrance system be adopted to assure proper budgetary controls. The *encumbrance* is the commitment of moneys to a particular use. In general, this means that an order has been placed. The system is employed to prevent the administrator from committing more cash than he has authority to commit. The control aspect of the system may be overstressed, however, as the administrator usually has to add the encumbered amount and the expended amount together to determine the total spent and/or committed. This total must then be subtracted from the appropriated amount to determine whether or not there are uncommitted appropriations available. Of course, we must recognize that the information is available for him to use, whereas it might not be under a traditional accounting system. After all, a control system is worthless if it is not used for the purpose for which it is designed. The journal entry to record an encumbrance was presented earlier.

Since the prime concern in fund accounting is to account for the resources and the claims against those resources, frequently there is less emphasis on the revenue and expense accounts. In many cases a control account will be used in the general ledger to account for all expenditures, with a subsidiary ledger to allow for the classification of these expenditures. The account so used is frequently referred to as *appropriation expenditures.* Any debit to an expense account is made to this control account and the expenditure is then classified by type in the subsidiary ledger. There is little concern with measuring income; therefore, both revenue and expense control accounts are closed to unappropriated surplus. The entries required to close a typical fund are as follows:

Revenues	*266,000*	
Unappropriated Surplus	*9,000*	
Estimated Revenues		*275,000*
To close actual and estimated revenues.		
Appropriations	*262,000*	
Encumbrances		*28,000*
Appropriation Expenditures		*230,000*
Unappropriated Surplus		*4,000*
To close appropriations, encumbrances, and appropriation expenditures.		

In this illustration, it is assumed that the appropriation for the current year will be left open to the extent of outstanding encumbrances. The reserve for encumbrances is transferred to a new account, indicating that it is applicable to the appropriation of a prior year. The new account is closed when the expenditures are made in settlement of the encumbrance. Any difference between the actual cost and the amount encumbered is an adjustment of unappropriated surplus. The entries to record this procedure follow:

Reserve for Encumbrances	*28,000*	
Reserve for Encumbrances of Prior Years		*28,000*
To transfer the reserve for encumbrances to a new account identifying it as applicable to a prior year's budget.		
Expenditures Chargeable against Reserve for Encumbrances of Prior Years	*27,500*	
Accounts Payable		*27,500*
To record the receipt of goods ordered under appropriation of prior year.		
Reserve for Encumbrances of Prior Years	*28,000*	
Expenditures Chargeable against Reserve for Encumbrances of Prior Years		*27,500*
Unappropriated Surplus		*500*
To close the expenditures chargeable against encumbrances and appropriations of prior years.		

Interfund receivables and payables. Since each fund is a separate entity, there will be occasions when one fund will borrow money from another fund or sell something to another fund on credit. In these cases the receivable or payable must be recognized as any other asset or liability. There is a general rule against offsetting assets and liabilities in fund accounting as there is in financial accounting; therefore, when a fund has a receivable from another fund and at the same time owes that fund money, the payable should not be offset against the receivable.

Use of the term revenue. In fund accounting, the term *revenue* is used to refer to increases in or additions to assets without a corresponding increase in a liability or reduction in an expenditure. In addition, the cancellation of liabilities without a corresponding decrease in assets or increase in another liability is also termed revenue. With such a definition, situations arise where revenue may accrue to a fund but not to the organization as a whole, or in fact there may be revenue to one fund and an expenditure to another. Consider the sale of bonds by a governmental unit: The proceeds of the sale are entered in the bond fund; however, the bond fund is not responsible for the payment of the bonds at maturity; therefore, the proceeds are considered to be revenue to the bond fund. Some other fund will recognize the payable and the expenditure when the bonds are paid. A similar situation occurs when the general fund makes a deposit to the sinking fund for the retirement of the bonds. The cash deposit is considered an expenditure of the general fund and a revenue to the sinking fund.

Illustration of fund accounting

The process of recording routine transactions in fund accounting is highly repetitive. The purpose of the following illustrative transactions is, therefore, not to present a complete recording of all the financial events which are likely to transpire during the accounting period, but rather to illustrate the various types of transactions which one is likely to encounter in accounting for the various funds of a municipal government. In recording these transactions, we shall adhere to the terminology suggested by the National Committee on Governmental Accounting. There are many places where the terminology might be improved by making it more descriptive; nevertheless, there is some advantage to conforming to accepted terminology. We are concerned here, primarily, with the general ledger accounts and only secondarily with the subsidiary ledger. As in commercial accounting, the desired information dictates the detail which must be found in the ledger system. Let it suffice to say that the system with a minimum of detail is not always the most desirable system.

General fund

The purpose of the general fund, as stated earlier, is to account for all revenues and activities which are not accounted for by one of several special funds. This is not meant to imply that the general fund handles only miscellaneous transactions. As a matter of fact, the general fund is the central and most important fund of municipal governments. The general fund receives a large portion of all revenues which support most of the municipality's current operations.

Budget. The first step in accounting for the general fund is to record the adoption of the budget, as illustrated earlier.

Estimated Revenues	*960,000*	
Appropriations		*948,000*
Unappropriated Surplus		*12,000*
To record the adoption of the annual budget.		

Revenue. A record of the tax levy is provided as a matter of record and as a matter of compliance with the accrual basis of accounting. In many cases an allowance for uncollectible taxes is created simultaneously with the recognition of the receivable. The purpose of such a procedure is to obtain a realistic appraisal of tax receipts. The recognition of uncollectibles might be deferred until the end of the budget period except for the fact that appropriations are limited by the estimate of revenues.

Taxes Receivable—Current	*745,000*	
Estimated Uncollectible Taxes—Current		*7,000*
Tax Revenues		*738,000*
To record the tax levy of $1.50 per $100 evaluation of real and personal property.		

As the cash is received from the taxpayers, the receivables are reduced and the receipts of cash are recorded.

Cash	*670,000*	
Taxes Receivable—Current		*670,000*
To record collection of taxes before the penalty date.		

Other transactions relating to the collection and write-off of receivables and the collection of fines, licenses, and fees are illustrated below:

Taxes Receivable—Delinquent	*75,000*	
Estimated Uncollectible Taxes—Current	*7,000*	
Taxes Receivable—Current		*75,000*
Estimated Uncollectible Taxes—Delinquent		*7,000*
To record delinquent taxes.		
Interest and Penalties Receivable on Taxes	*3,750*	
Estimated Uncollectible Interest and Penalties		*350*
Interest and Penalty Revenue		*3,400*
To record estimated interest and penalties due on delinquent taxes.		
Cash	*72,450*	
Taxes Receivable—Delinquent		*69,000*
Interest and Penalties Receivable on Taxes		*3,450*
To record collection of delinquent taxes with applicable interest and penalities.		
Cash	*92,000*	
Fines, Fees, and License Revenue		*92,000*
To record collection of fines, fees, and licenses.		
Estimated Uncollectible Taxes—Delinquent	*1,000*	
Estimated Uncollectible Interest and Penalties	*50*	
Tax Revenue		*1,000*
Interest and Penalty Revenue		*50*
To adjust estimated uncollectible taxes and interest and penalties to 100% allowance for delinquent taxes.		

Encumbrances and expenditures. In cases where budgetary control is facilitated by the use of an encumbrance system, each time an order is placed the appropriation should be encumbered to assure that the appropriation is not exceeded during the interval between the time when the order is placed and the time when the goods are received. At the time the order is placed the following entry is made:

Encumbrances	*18,500*	
Reserve for Encumbrances		*18,500*
To record encumbrance for purchase orders issued.		

When the materials and services are received and the liability therefore is established, the encumbrance is removed by reversing the above entry and the liability is recognized as indicated on the next page:

Appropriation Expenditures	*8,700*	
Accounts Payable		*8,700*
To record the receipt of materials and supplies and the actual liability for orders in the encumbered amount of $8,500.		
Reserve for Encumbrances	*8,500*	
Encumbrances		*8,500*
To cancel encumbrances for orders received.		

In the event that expenditures are made to acquire goods or services which are not consumed during the period in which the expenditure is made, the asset should be recognized at the end of the period. This is usually accomplished by debiting an asset account, such as Inventory of Materials and Supplies, and crediting an equity account, such as Reserve for Inventory. The additional equity account is created so that the Unappropriated Surplus account may continue to represent the resources presently available to the municipality for appropriation during the next period. Assume that materials and supplies costing $2,000 are on hand at the end of the accounting period. These materials are a part of those acquired during the present period at a total cost of $8,700. The entry to recognize the asset is illustrated here:

Inventory of Materials and Supplies	*2,000*	
Reserve for Inventory		*2,000*
To record inventory of materials and supplies on hand at the end of the period.		

In the subsequent period when the asset is consumed, the above entry will be reversed.

In cases where purchase orders have not been filled at the end of the year, the appropriation for that year is charged for the encumbered amount. In the following period when the goods are received and the liability is established, the expenditure will be recorded in a special account to be offset against the reserve for encumbrances of prior years. To illustrate, assume that one purchase order for $25,500 has not been filled at the end of the period. During the following year the order is filled and the invoice is for $25,500. The transfer of the reserve for encumbrances and the transaction are recorded as shown at the top of page 874.

In the event that the expenditure is not equal to the encumbrance, the difference is an adjustment of unappropriated surplus. The encumbrance system is designed as a control device, as indicated earlier; however, it is not the only system which may be used for this purpose. Many municipalities have eliminated the encumbrance system and in its place they have substituted an unfilled order file, which provides similar information and avoids some of the routine bookkeeping.

Expenditures which are budgeted specifically, such as payroll, bond interest, bond retirement, and other similar items, are seldom encumbered, since nothing

Reserve for Encumbrances	*25,500*	
Reserve for Encumbrances of Prior Year		*25,500*
To transfer reserve for encumbrance to new account.		
Expenditures Chargeable against Reserve for Encumbrances of Prior Year	*25,500*	
Accounts Payable		*25,500*
To record expenditure resulting from encumbrance of prior period.		
Reserve for Encumbrances of Prior Year	*25,500*	
Expenditures Chargeable against Reserve for Encumbrances of Prior Year		*25,500*
To close the reserve for encumbrances remaining from a prior year to an expenditure applicable to prior year's appropriation.		

is gained by the encumbrance procedure. When the definite sum payable is known at budget time, the budget is specific; when the sum is merely estimated and no greater knowledge of the amount owed is gained until the liability is definite, there is no need to perform the extra work of encumbering and reversing the entry. When items of cost are specifically budgeted, the following entries are made at the time the expenditure is made:

Appropriation Expenditures	*23,400*	
Withholding Taxes Payable		*3,600*
Social Security Taxes Payable		*800*
Cash		*19,000*
To record payroll for month of June, the last month of the budget year.		
Appropriation Expenditures	*12,000*	
Bond Interest Payable		*12,000*
To record interest liability on 3% general obligation bonds.		

When cash is transferred from the general fund to other funds, it may be transferred as a loan or as a grant. In either case the transfer should be authorized by the legislative body charged with establishing the annual budget for all funds. The entries required to record both types of transfer are illustrated as follows:

Due from Special Assessment Fund	*20,000*	
Cash		*20,000*
To record temporary loan to special assessment fund to be repaid without interest when assessments are collected.		
Appropriation Expenditures	*50,000*	
Due to Sinking Fund		*50,000*
To record liability for annual deposit to sinking fund for bond retirement.		

Closing entries. At the end of the budget period, both the budgetary and operating accounts must be closed. There are two procedures which are used to close these accounts:

1. The budget entries made at the beginning of the period are reversed and the revenue and expenditure accounts are closed to unappropriated surplus.

2. The estimated revenue is offset against the actual revenue, with the balance being treated as an adjustment to unappropriated surplus. Similarly, the appropriations are offset against the appropriation expenditures, with the difference being closed to the unappropriated surplus.

The first procedure seems preferable because it allows a comparison of actual receipts with actual outlays, with the resultant being an adjustment to surplus. The second procedure accomplishes the same thing but the emphasis is on a comparison of budgeted receipts and actual receipts and budgeted expenditures and actual expenditures rather than a comparison of actual events. The accountant should use that closing procedure which emphasizes the information which in his opinion is more important. Both procedures are illustrated below:

		Debit	Credit
(1)	*Appropriations*	*948,000*	
	Unappropriated Surplus	*12,000*	
	Estimated Revenues		*960,000*
	To close budget accounts.		
	Revenues	*978,400*	
	Appropriation Expenditures		*930,600*
	Encumbrances		*16,800*
	Unappropriated Surplus		*31,000*
	To close revenue, expenditure, and encumbrance accounts.		
(2)	*Appropriations*	*948,000*	
	Appropriation Expenditures		*930,600*
	Unappropriated Surplus		*600*
	Encumbrances		*16,800*
	To close expenditures and appropriations.		
	Revenues	*978,400*	
	Estimated Revenues		*960,000*
	Unappropriated Surplus		*18,400*
	To close revenues and estimated revenues.		

In each case there is an increase in unappropriated surplus of $31,000 for the year. Under procedure (1) the $12,000 budget surplus is removed by reversing the budget entry and an actual surplus of $31,000 is recorded. In procedure (2) the $12,000 budget surplus was recorded at the beginning of the year, actual revenues exceeded estimated revenues by $18,400, and actual expenditures were less than budgeted expenditures by $600, for a total increase in surplus of $31,000.

Questions

1. Contrast the meaning of the term *fund* as used in this chapter and the meaning generally implied by accountants.
2. What is the essence of a fund accounting system?
3. Why is the fund accounting system, as opposed to the enterprise accounting system, frequently adopted by many nonprofit organizations?
4. Compare and contrast the purpose of the following sets of funds:
   a. Special revenue and special assessment funds
   b. Bond fund and general bonded debt accounts
   c. Working capital and utility funds
5. Why are the budgets of governmental units made a part of the formal accounting system?
6. Record the following budget of the general fund in journal entry form:

Estimated revenues:	
Property tax	*$240,500*
Fines and penalties	*4,000*
Surplus from water fund	*20,000*
Total	*$264,500*
Appropriations	*$272,000*

7. What does the term *to encumber* mean? Why is the encumbrance system used in fund accounting?
8. The city of A uses the modified accrual system of accounting and the encumbrance system for all purchases which require a purchase order. The following information is available for a given order:
   Materials were ordered at an estimated cost of $25,000. When they were delivered, the invoice was for $24,750 and freight charges were $175. Make all entries necessary to record this transaction.
9. The City of B had an encumbrance on its books at the end of the year of $12,000. The appropriations for the year were left open to the extent of amounts encumbered at year-end. Early in the new year, the goods on order at the end of the preceding year were delivered. The invoice was in the amount of $12,600. Make all journal entries required at the end of the year and when the goods are received.
10. What does the term *revenue* mean in fund accounting?
11. The following partial list of accounts and their balances have been taken from the ledger of the general fund of Metro:

Appropriations	*$275,000*
Tax revenue	*262,500*
Fines and penalties revenue	*18,600*
Appropriation expenditures	*262,400*

Encumbrances	*10,000*
Estimated revenue	*280,000*
Reserve for encumbrances	*10,000*

Make the closing entries for the end of the year.

Short cases for analysis

25-1 Mr. Barston has come to you as the city's CPA and asked that you explain the differences between fund accounting and enterprise accounting. He points out that he finds that both fund accounting and enterprise accounting are stewardship systems. One of the objectives of both systems is to report on the assets received by the entity and the disposition made of them. Both systems must provide information about cash flows in order for management to plan activities.

Instructions

Explain to Mr. Barston why the accounting systems for the two entities differ so markedly.

25-2 Appropriation expenditures from the general fund of Union City totaled $855,000 for the current year. $40,000 of this total was for the purchase of a fire truck for the city and $10,000 was for purchase of supplies, of which $6,000 are still on hand at the end of the year.

Instructions

Make any adjusting entries which you deem necessary. Explain why you do or do not make entries to adjust the expenditure account for the purchase of the fire truck and the supplies.

25-3 The city of Woodville has lost certain of its records of the past year's activity. You are asked to review the comparative trial balances and unappropriated surplus ledger account for the current year and answer certain questions.

CITY OF WOODVILLE
General Fund
Comparative Trial Balances

	Current year	*Prior year*
Cash	*$ 91,000*	*$60,000*
Taxes receivable—current	*45,000*	*30,000*
Allowance for bad debts	*(12,000)*	*(10,000)*
Taxes receivable—delinquent	*15,000*	*12,000*
Allowance for bad debts	*(8,500)*	*(8,000)*
Total assets	*$130,500*	*$84,000*

Accounts payable	*$ 22,000*	*$18,000*
Reserve for encumbrances	*40,000*	*25,000*
Unappropriated surplus	*68,500*	*41,000*
Total liabilities & surplus	*$130,500*	*$84,000*

Unappropriated Surplus

Beginning balance	*$41,000*
Add: Excess of estimated revenue over appropriations	*5,000*
Excess of revenue over estimated revenue	*12,500*
Excess of appropriations over appropriation expenditures of $287,500 and encumbrances	*12,500*
Excess of reserve for encumbrances of prior years over actual bill	*2,500*
	$73,500
Less: Increase in allowance for bad debts applicable to receivables of prior years	*5,000*
Ending balance	*$68,500*

Instructions

a. Determine the following quantities for the current year:
(1) Appropriations
(2) Total cash disbursed
(3) Total revenue
(4) Total cash collected
(5) Total receivables of prior years written off

b. Are the general fund accounts kept on the cash basis or modified accrual basis? Explain.

c. What entry was made to record the budget?

25-4 The trial balance of Central City's General Fund for the current year is presented below:

CENTRAL CITY
General Fund
Trial Balance

Cash	*$ 22,400*	
Taxes receivable—delinquent	*138,000*	
Allowance for uncollectibles		*$ 22,000*
Interest and penalties receivable	*1,100*	
Allowance for uncollectibles		*100*
Accounts receivable	*42,000*	
Allowance for uncollectibles		*2,000*
Estimated revenues	*862,000*	
Vouchers payable		*59,800*
Due to working capital fund		*60,000*

Taxes collected in advance		2,000
Appropriations		852,000
Reserve for encumbrances		40,000
Unappropriated surplus		10,000
Revenues		857,400
Encumbranoes	40,000	
Appropriation expenditures	799,800	
Total	*$1,905,300*	*$1,905,300*

Instructions

a. Prepare closing entries.

b. What can you say about the operations of Central City's General Fund for the current year?

Problems

25-5 The City of Pineville made the following budget estimates and entered into the following transactions during the year.

(1) Revenues were estimated as follows:

Property taxes	*$150,000*
City auto licenses	11,000
Business licenses	25,000
Fines	16,000

(2) General fund appropriations totaled $200,000.

(3) Property taxes totaling $152,000 were levied, with $5,000 estimated uncollectible.

(4) Purchase orders were issued for goods and services totaling $28,500.

(5) Goods and services represented by purchase orders of $20,000 were received at a cost of $21,500.

(6) Cash receipts totaled $188,200 from the following sources:

Property taxes	*$137,000*
City auto licenses	11,700
Business licenses	21,000
Fines and penalties	18,500

(7) Cash disbursements were made as follows:

Accounts payable (see 5)	*$21,500*
Wages and salaries	86,400
Encumbrances of prior period	12,500
(Reserve for encumbrances was carried at $13,400 on the books.)	

Rent on buildings and equipment	*42,300*
Deposit to sinking fund	*30,000*
Services from water works	*5,000*
Services from working capital fund	*3,500*
Interest on general bonded indebtedness	*22,750*

Instructions

Record the above budget and transactions in general journal entry form.

25-6 The trial balance of the general fund of the County of Y on July 1, 1966, is presented below:

Trial Balance
July 1, 1966

Cash	*$ 25,000*	
Taxes receivable—delinquent	*50,000*	
Allowance for uncollectibles—delinquent		*$ 7,500*
Interest and penalties receivable	*1,250*	
Allowance for uncollectibles—interest and penalties		*187*
Accounts receivable	*25,000*	
Allowances for uncollectibles—accounts receivable		*2,500*
Vouchers payable		*40,000*
Reserve encumbrances of prior period		*25,000*
Unappropriated surplus		*26,063*
Totals	*$101,250*	*$101,250*

The following transactions occurred during the fiscal year 1967:

(1) Revenues were estimated at $250,000; appropriations of $270,000 were made.
(2) Orders placed during the prior period in the amount of $25,000 were received at an actual invoice price of $23,250.
(3) An order was placed for materials estimated to cost $50,000.
(4) Property taxes of $250,000 were levied and it was estimated that 5% will be uncollectible.
(5) Collections were made as follows:

Current taxes	*$200,000*
Delinquent taxes	*25,000*
Interest and penalties receivable	*750*
Accounts receivable	*12,500*

(6) Payments were made as follows:

Vouchers payable	*$63,750*
Payrolls	*50,000*

(7) Materials ordered were received at an actual cost of $52,500.
(8) Taxes amounting to $50,000 have become delinquent.
(9) Delinquent taxes amounting to $5,000 and interest and penalties of $50 were written off as uncollectible.
(10) Delinquent taxes amounting to $500, which were written off in a prior period, were collected with interest and penalties of $82.
(11) An order was placed for an automobile for the sheriff at a cost of $2,500.
(12) An order was placed for materials at an estimated cost of $50,000.
(13) Payrolls of $62,500 were paid.
(14) The automobile ordered for the sheriff was received and a check in the amount of $2,500 was issued in payment.
(15) Bonds payable in the amount of $25,000 matured. The payment of this obligation was included in the current year's appropriation.
(16) The matured bonds were paid.
(17) Interest on general bonded debt amounting to $12,500 was paid.
(18) Interest of $600 accrued on delinquent taxes; 5% of the amount accrued was added to the allowance for uncollectible interest and taxes.

Instructions

a. Record all activities of the general fund for the fiscal year 1967, including the budget in journal entry form.

b. Prepare a pre-closing trial balance.

c. Make the closing entries in journal form.

25-7 The accounts of the general fund of Madisonville as of January 1, 1966, were as follows:

Cash	*$1,000*
Taxes receivable—delinquent	*8,000*
Accounts payable	*7,000*
Reserve for encumbrances	*1,500*
Unappropriated surplus	*500*

The following transactions for the current year are to be considered:

(1) The budget which was adopted for 1966 provided for taxes of $275,000, special assessments of $100,000, fees of $15,000, and license revenues of $10,000. Appropriations were $290,000 for general fund operations, and $100,000 for the purpose of establishing a working capital fund.
(2) All taxes and special assessments became receivable.
(3) Cash receipts for the general fund included:

Taxes from 1966	*$260,000*
Special assessments	*100,000*
Fees	*16,000*
Licenses	*9,500*
Taxes receivable—delinquent plus interest of $500. Tax liens were obtained on the remainder of the delinquent taxes	*5,500*

(4) Contracts amounting to $75,000 were let by the general fund.
(5) Services rendered by the working capital fund to the general fund totaled $40,000.
(6) The following cash disbursements were made by the general fund:

Working capital fund	*$100,000*
Accounts payable of the preceding year	*7,000*
Outstanding orders at beginning of year all received and paid for	*2,000*
Expenses of fund incurred during year	*145,000*
Stores purchased for central storeroom established during year	*5,000*
Contracts let during year	*30,000*
Permanent advance to newly created petty cash fund	*1,000*
Services performed by working capital fund	*35,000*
Salaries paid during year	*30,000*

(7) All unpaid taxes became delinquent.
(8) Stores inventory in general fund amounted to $2,000 on December 31, 1966.

Instructions

Prepare a working paper showing the transactions, closing entries, and balance sheet for the general fund for 1966.

AICPA adapted

25-8 The following information pertains to the operations of the General Fund of the X County. Functions of this county government include operating the county jail and caring for the county courts.

Funds to finance the operations are provided from a levy of county tax against the various towns of the county, from the state distribution of unincorporated business taxes, from board of jail prisoners assessed against the towns and against the state, and from interest on savings accounts.

The balances in the accounts of the fund on January 1, 1966, were as follows:

Cash in savings accounts	*$ 60,650*
Cash in checking accounts	*41,380*
Cash on hand (undeposited prisoners' board receipts)	*320*
Inventory of jail supplies	*3,070*
Due from towns and state for board of prisoners	*3,550*
General Fund surplus	*108,970*

The budget for the year 1966, as adopted by the county commissioners, provided for the following items of revenue and expenditure:

(1) Town and county taxes	*$20,000*
(2) Jail operating costs	*55,500*
(3) Court operating costs	*7,500*

(4) *Unincorporated business tax*	*18,000*
(5) *Board of prisoners (revenue)*	*5,000*
(6) *Commissioners' salaries and expenses*	*8,000*
(7) *Interest on savings*	*1,000*
(8) *Miscellaneous expenses*	*1,000*

General Fund surplus was appropriated in sufficient amount to balance the budget. At December 31, 1966, the jail supply inventory amounted to $5,120, cash of $380 was on hand, and $1,325 of prisoners' board bills were unpaid by towns and state. The following items represent all the transactions which occurred during the year, with all current bills vouchered and paid by December 31, 1966.

Item (1) was transacted exactly as budgeted.

Item (2) cash expenditures amounted to	$55,230
Item (3) amounted to	7,110
Item (4) amounted to	18,070
Item (5) billings amounted to	4,550
Item (6) amounted to	6,670
Item (7) amounted to	1,050
Item (8) amounted to	2,310

During the year, $25,000 was transferred from the savings accounts to the checking accounts.

Instructions

From the above information, prepare a work sheet providing columns to show:

a. Trial balance as of January 1, 1966

b. The transactions for the year

c. Variances between budgeted and actual revenues and expenditures for the year

d. Balance sheet of the General Fund, December 31, 1966

AICPA adapted

25-9 The data at the top of page 884 were taken from accounts of the Town of Ridgedale after the books had been closed for the fiscal year ending June 30, 1967.

The following additional data are available:

(1) The budget for the year provided for estimated revenues of $1,000,000 and appropriations of $965,000.

(2) Expenditures totaling $895,000, in addition to those chargeable against Reserve for Encumbrances, were made.

(3) The actual expenditure chargeable against Reserve for Encumbrances of Prior Years was $37,000.

(4) Only the annual tax levy is accrued by debiting a receivable.

	Balances, June 30, 1966	1967 changes		Balances, June 30, 1967
		Debits	Credits	
Cash	$180,000	$ 955,000	$ 880,000	$255,000
Taxes receivable	20,000	809,000	781,000	48,000
	$200,000			$303,000
Allowances for uncollectible taxes	$ 4,000	6,000	9,000	$ 7,000
Vouchers payable	44,000	880,000	889,000	53,000
Due to Working Capital Fund	2,000	7,000	10,000	5,000
Due to Sinking Fund	10,000	60,000	100,000	50,000
Reserve for encumbrances	40,000	40,000	47,000	47,000
Unappropriated surplus	100,000	20,000	61,000	141,000
	$200,000	$2,777,000	$2,777,000	$303,000

Instructions

Prepare a work sheet to compare estimated revenues with actual revenues, and encumbrances and expenditures with appropriations and other authorizations. The work sheet should have the following column headings:

Balance sheet, June 30, 1966
1967 transactions (debit & credit)
Estimated revenues
Actual revenues
Encumbrances and expenditures
Appropriations and other authorizations
Balance sheet, June 30, 1967

AICPA adapted

25-10 The Sleepy Haven Township's adjusted trial balance for the General Fund as at the close of its fiscal year ending June 30, 1967, is shown below.

SLEEPY HAVEN TOWNSHIP
General Fund Trial Balance
June 30, 1967

Cash	$ 1,100	
Taxes receivable—current (Note 1)	8,200	
Allowance for uncollectible taxes—current		$ 150
Taxes receivable—delinquent	2,500	
Allowance for uncollectible taxes—delinquent		1,650
Miscellaneous accounts receivable	4,000	
Allowance for uncollectible accounts		400
Due from Working Capital Fund	5,000	

Appropriation expenditures (Note 2)	*75,500*	
Encumbrances	*3,700*	
Revenues (Note 3)		*6,000*
Due to Utility Fund		*1,000*
Vouchers payable		*2,000*
Reserve for encumbrances—prior year		*4,400*
Reserve for encumbrances		*3,700*
Surplus receipts (Note 4)		*700*
Appropriations		*72,000*
Unappropriated surplus		*8,000*
Totals	*$100,000*	*$100,000*

Note 1 The current tax roll and miscellaneous accounts receivable, recorded on the accrual basis as sources of revenue, amounted to $50,000 and $20,000, respectively. These items have been recorded on the books subject to a 2% provision for uncollectible accounts.

Note 2 Includes $4,250 paid during the fiscal year in settlement of all purchase orders outstanding at the beginning of the fiscal year.

Note 3 Represents the difference between the budgeted (estimated) revenue of $70,000 and the actual revenue realized during the fiscal year.

Note 4 Represents the proceeds from sale of equipment damaged by fire.

Instructions

a. Prepare in columnar form an Analysis of Changes in Unappropriated Surplus for the year ending June 30, 1967, with column headings: Estimated, Actual, and Excess or Deficiency of Actual Compared with Estimated.

b. Prepare a formal balance sheet at June 30, 1967.

AICPA adapted

25-11 The Crescent City Council has employed you to examine the General Fund. The following information is made available to you directly or as the result of your examination:

(1) The account balances of the General Fund at the end of the fiscal year are as follows:

Debits

Cash	*$ 600,000*
Taxes receivable—current	*500,000*
Appropriation expenditures	*9,300,000*
	$10,400,000

Credits

Revenues received	*$ 9,900,000*
Deferred tax collections	*500,000*
	$10,400,000

(2) At the beginning of the year the council formally approved the budget for the fiscal year, which is presented with the cash receipts and disbursements information in (3) below.

(3) Cash receipts and disbursements, together with budget information, is presented below.

	Estimated revenues	Actual receipts
Taxes:		
Current year	*$ 9,700,000*	*$9,500,000*
Collected in advance	*-0-*	*20,000*
Licenses and permits	*200,000*	*250,000*
Fines and forfeits	*70,000*	*78,000*
Rentals from use of properties	*30,000*	*32,000*
Miscellaneous:		
Refunds and rebates of current service charges by other agencies:		
Utility Fund	*-0-*	*6,000*
Working Capital Fund	*-0-*	*4,000*
Unused (excess) cash from Bond Fund	*-0-*	*10,000*
Total	*$10,000,000*	*$9,900,000*

	Planned expenditures	Actual disbursements
*Departmental expenses**	*$ 7,100,000*	*$6,894,000*
Contribution to Retirement Pension Fund	*150,000*	*140,000*
Creation of a petty cash fund	*-0-*	*5,000*
City's share of cost of special assessments	*150,000*	*150,000*
Establishment of Working Capital Fund	*50,000*	*50,000*
Equipment—general office	*420,000*	*421,000*
Land for building site	*500,000*	*500,000*
Sinking Fund contribution	*1,000,000*	*1,000,000*
Matured serial general obligation bonds	*100,000*	*100,000*
Interest on bonds:		
Sinking Fund bonds	*20,000*	*20,000*
Serial bonds	*10,000*	*10,000*
Temporary loan to Working Capital Fund	*-0-*	*10,000*
	$ 9,500,000	*$9,300,000*
** Include the following:*		
Billed by Utility Fund	*$ 70,000*	*$ 80,000*
Billed by Working Capital Fund	*-0-*	*$ 39,000*

(4) City taxes receivable, per tax roll, amounted to $10,000,000.

(5) All unpaid city taxes become delinquent at the end of the year in which levied.

(6) Unrecorded amounts at the close of the fiscal year consisted of

Accrued salaries	*$60,000*	
Invoices for materials and supplies received	*19,000*	*$79,000*
Orders placed by the city but not filled		*30,000*

(7) Services billed by the Working Capital Fund, not recorded on the books of the General Fund, amounted to $1,000.

(8) The General Fund stores inventory amounted to $35,000 at the end of the period and is to be recorded. The city's charter provides that expenditures are based on purchases.

(9) The city's charter specifies that purchase orders unfilled at the end of the year do not lapse.

Instructions

Prepare a work sheet for the General Fund with columns for Balances per Books, Corrections and Adjustments, and Corrected Balances. Key the corrections and adjustments to the related transaction numbers. Formal general journal entries are not required.

AICPA adapted

26 FUND ACCOUNTING: GOVERNMENTS AND INSTITUTIONS (CONCLUDED)

Special revenue funds

Special revenue funds are established to account for revenues obtained for specific purposes, for example, for the support of particular activities such as libraries, parks, zoos, and schools. This support may be in the form of a tax levy with a designated purpose or in the form of contributions from individuals or from the general fund. Frequently these special revenues are handled through the general fund and are merely earmarked by the appropriation budget for use in a special manner. In any event the journal entries to record identical transactions are the same for special revenue and the general fund.

Working capital or revolving funds

Working capital funds are established to finance service activities of the government such as garage, central purchasing, and stores departments. These activities are provided centrally for all the departments of the government in order to gain economies of centralization.

The working capital fund is a revolving fund in that costs are incurred in the production of a product or service and revenues are derived from the sale of that product or service to other units of the government. This means that the fund operates in a manner similar to a commercial-type enterprise and the accounting problems are similar. The fund is financed in many ways; however, the most common is by an appropriation from the general fund. The cash so received is used to buy the goods and services needed to provide the desired services. Each unit is charged for the services received from the working capital fund. The charge for these services is usually based on cost of providing the service. The fund, therefore, operates on a revolving cash cycle with only the original capital being received from outside sources.

At first glance one is likely to conclude that this is one way to bring an element of control into government. The administrator is charged with selling a product or service; therefore, he must hold costs in line. The fallacy of such thinking lies in the fact that the various buying departments seldom have any choice in the selection of the supplier. In other words, they must buy the service from the working capital fund if it can be provided. This means that the working capital fund does not have to compete in the open market; therefore, any inefficiencies which occur are absorbed by increasing the price to the other departments.

The entries to record the transactions of the working capital fund are quite similar to those which would be made to record the transactions of any commercial activity. The entry to establish the fund follows:

Cash	*200,000*	
Contribution from General Fund		*200,000*
To record the establishment of a working capital fund to operate the central garage.		

Subsequently the cash will be used to acquire assets. A summary entry of acquisitions is illustrated below:

Inventory of Materials and Supplies	*74,000*	
Land	*15,000*	
Building	*45,000*	
Equipment	*20,000*	
Cash		*90,000*
Vouchers Payable		*64,000*
To record the acquisition of assets to be used in the operation of the central garage.		

The operations of the working capital fund are summarized for the period as follows:

Administrative Salaries	*8,000*	
Wages of Workmen	*24,000*	
Shop Supplies	*4,000*	
Heat, Light, and Power	*1,800*	
Office Salaries	*4,800*	
Vouchers Payable		*42,600*
To record costs of operating the central garage for the period.		

Cost of Materials and Supplies Used	*46,000*	
Inventory of Materials and Supplies		*46,000*
To record cost of materials and supplies used during the period.		
Depreciation—Building	*1,000*	
Depreciation—Equipment	*2,000*	
Accumulated Depreciation—Building		*1,000*
Accumulated Depreciation—Equipment		*2,000*
To record depreciation of facilities.		
Due from Other Funds	*94,600*	
Charges to Departments		*94,600*
To record billings to other departments based on services provided.		
Cash	*82,000*	
Due from Other Funds		*82,000*
To record receipt of cash in payment of bills rendered.		
Vouchers Payable	*95,000*	
Cash		*95,000*
To record payment of vouchers.		

Operating costs and revenue accounts for the period must be closed at the end of each period for the working capital fund as for other funds and commercial businesses. Although the administrator is not responsible for making a profit, he is responsible for covering his costs. For this reason there is an attempt to match revenues and costs associated with the production of those revenues. The closing entries for the central garage are illustrated below:

Charges to Departments	*94,600*	
Cost of Materials and Supplies Used		*46,000*
Depreciation—Building		*1,000*
Depreciation—Equipment		*2,000*
Administrative Salaries		*8,000*
Wages of Workmen		*24,000*
Shop Supplies		*4,000*
Heat, Light, and Power		*1,800*
Office Salaries		*4,800*
Excess of Charges to Department over Costs		*3,000*
To close revenue and expense accounts.		
Excess of Charges to Departments over Costs	*3,000*	
Unappropriated Surplus		*3,000*
To close the excess of charges over cost to unappropriated surplus.		

The budget is not made a part of the formal accounts of the working capital fund. The working capital fund is not dependent on an annual appropriation for its continued operation, and for this reason the appropriation-type budget is not applicable to this fund. An operating budget is more desirable for the revolving funds. The activity of working capital funds depends upon the demands placed upon them by other departments and this demand is a function of the appropriation in the using department. Once the original grant is made to the working capital fund, no further resources of the government are required unless the fund is expanded. Instead, the resources revolve. The problems of planning and budgeting, therefore, are quite similar to those faced by commercial enterprises.

Special assessment fund

The special assessment fund is created to account for the receipt and disbursement of special assessments levied against the owners of specific properties which benefit from improvements or increased services financed with funds from the assessment. The function of the accounting is, therefore, to record and control the receipts and record the expenditures as they are made. In many cases the original cash will be raised by the sale of bonds which will be retired from the assessments paid over a period of years by the landowners. Where this is the case, the landowners are assessed not only for the cost of the improvement but for the cost of servicing the debt as well.

In the great majority of cases, the special assessment is approved by vote of the property owners affected so that a maximum cost for the improvement is authorized. In these cases a legal budget must be prepared which reflects the total assessment and the appropriation to carry out the improvement. The entry to record the authorization is as follows:

Improvement Authorized	*900,000*	
Appropriations		*900,000*
To record authorization of special project 29.		

We shall assume that special project 29 is the extension of water mains to a part of the city. The general fund will pay one-fourth of the total cost and the property owners will pay the remainder, with 20% due immediately and the balance to be paid in 10 equal installments on July 1 of each year, with interest at 4% per year on the unpaid balance as of July 1 of the previous year. Bonds are to be sold to enable the project to be completed at the earliest date. The entries to record these data are indicated below:

Special Assessments Receivable—Current	*135,000*	
Special Assessments Receivable—Deferred	*540,000*	
Due from General Fund	*225,000*	
Improvements Authorized		*900,000*
To record levy of special assessment and the amount due from the general fund as the city's proportionate share of the cost.		

Cash for Construction	*360,000*	
Special Assessments Receivable—Current		*135,000*
Due from General Fund		*225,000*
To record collection of the first installment and the amount due from the general fund.		
Unissued Bonds	*540,000*	
Bonds Eligible to Be Sold		*540,000*
To record authorization to sell bonds.		
Cash for Construction	*540,000*	
Bonds Payable, 4%		*540,000*
To record sale of bonds at par value.		
Bonds Eligible to Be Sold	*540,000*	
Unissued Bonds		*540,000*
To reverse the authorization entry: bonds have been issued.		

The entries to record the actual construction activity are the same in this fund as they are to record expenditures in any fund where there is a legal appropriation. The encumbrance system would probably be used. At the end of the fiscal period, the appropriation expenditures would be closed to appropriations or, if not closed, deducted from appropriations in the statements. Until the project is completed, there is generally no charge or credit to unappropriated surplus because until such time as all costs have been incurred, there is no way of knowing whether the cost of construction will be greater or less than the appropriation. In addition, at the end of each fiscal period an entry is made in the general fixed asset accounts to debit Work in Progress for the total cost incurred in the project during the year and to credit Investment in General Fixed Assets—from Property Owners' Share of Assessment Improvement Cost, for the proportion of the cost provided by the assessment, and Investment in General Fixed Assets—from Municipality's Share of Assessment Improvement Cost, for the proportion of the cost provided by the municipality's contribution.

In addition to the construction transactions, there are financial transactions to be recorded. The entries for the first year are illustrated below, assuming that all assessments are paid when due and interest on bonds is payable annually.

Interest Receivable	*21,600*	
Interest Revenue		*21,600*
To record interest on unpaid assessments.		
Interest Expense	*21,600*	
Interest Payable		*21,600*
To record interest expense on bonds payable.		

Special Assessments Receivable—Current	*54,000*	
Special Assessments Receivable—Deferred		*54,000*
To record the deferred assessments which are now current receivables.		
Cash for Bond Payments	*54,000*	
Cash for Interest Payment	*21,600*	
Interest Receivable		*21,600*
Special Assessments Receivable—Current		*54,000*
To record collection of cash for bond and interest payment.		
Bonds Payable	*54,000*	
Interest Payable	*21,600*	
Cash for Bond Payments		*54,000*
Cash for Interest Payments		*21,600*
To record payment of bonds and interest.		
Interest Revenue	*21,600*	
Interest Expense		*21,600*
To close expense and revenue account.		

Actual costs of a special assessment project will seldom be equal to the appropriation. Where there is a difference, the question arises as to the disposition to be made of any surplus and the source of cash to settle any deficit. Each case is slightly different and the applicable legal provisions govern each individual situation. If the appropriation has been exceeded by $5,000, there will be a liability for this amount and a debit balance in unappropriated surplus. If the liability is to the general fund and the municipality has voted to underwrite excesses of this kind, the final entry will be:

Due to General Fund	*5,000*	
Unappropriated Surplus		*5,000*
To write off the liability owed to the general fund in accordance with directive 4189.		

Of course if the liability is owed to an outside party, the cash will have to be made available from some other source.

If there was $8,000 cash remaining at the end of the project, the cash would probably be returned to the property owners or the general fund of the municipality. The entry would be as follows:

Unappropriated Surplus	*8,000*	
Cash		*8,000*
To record the return of excess cash to the general fund in accordance with public order 596.		

Bond funds

Bond funds are used to account for the receipt and disbursement of the proceeds of all bonds issued by a municipality except for special assessment and utility or other enterprise bonds. A separate self-balancing fund is usually set up to account for each bond issue. Before a bond issue may be sold, it must be authorized; in essence, this is the budget entry which is usually recorded as follows:

Bonds Authorized—Unissued	*1,000,000*	
Appropriations		*1,000,000*
To record authorization to issue 4%, 20-year bonds for construction of new municipal building.		

Subsequently, when bonds are sold, the following entry is recorded in the bond fund:

Cash	*1,005,000*	
Bonds Authorized—Unissued		*1,000,000*
Premium on Bonds		*5,000*
To record sale of bonds at a premium.		

Simultaneously an entry should be made in the general bonded debt accounts to record the liability which exists. This entry will be discussed later; however, it is presented here to illustrate the interfund relationship.

Amount to Be Provided for Payment of Principal	*1,000,000*	
Bonds Payable		*1,000,000*
To record liability associated with bonds payable.		

Any premium or discount resulting from the sale of a bond is considered to be an adjustment of the interest charge. The extra cash represented by the premium is, therefore, usually transferred to the fund responsible for the payment of interest, usually the general fund. The entry is illustrated as follows:

Premium on Bonds	*5,000*	
Cash		*5,000*
To record transfer of premiums collected on bonds payable to general fund for payment of interest.		

Similarly, a discount would require the deposit of additional cash in the bond fund by the fund responsible for paying the interest. Accordingly, the entry would be:

Cash	*8,000*	
Discount on Bonds		*8,000*
To record transfer of cash equal to discount on bonds to the bond fund.		

If there were legal restrictions against the general fund making up the discount, then the appropriation would have to be reduced by the amount of the discount.

The usual encumbrance system is followed for recording commitments in the bond fund, with a subsequent set of entries to reverse the encumbrance and record the expenditure.

If the bonds are sold for the purpose of acquiring or constructing long-lived assets, then at the end of each accounting period an entry is made in the general fixed asset accounts to record any cost incurred. Generally the entry would be as follows:

Construction in Progress	*675,000*	
Investment in Fixed Assets—from General Bonds		*675,000*
To record cost of construction financed during the year with funds derived from the sale of bonds.		

In the year in which the construction or acquisition is completed, the construction in progress account is closed to the particular asset accounts involved, also in the general fixed asset accounts, as follows:

Building	*993,000*	
Construction in Progress		*675,000*
Investment in Fixed Assets—from General Bonds		*318,000*
To record cost of completed construction financed by sale of bonds.		

The usual closing entry may be made each period for the bond fund except that no surplus or deficit is realized until the project for which the bonds were sold has been completed.

During interim periods, the closing entry is merely:

Appropriations	*675,000*	
Expenditures		*675,000*
To close construction expenditures for the year.		

In some cases the expenditures account may remain open until the project is complete. In financial statements the expenditures are deducted from appropriations to indicate the unexpended appropriation. When the surplus or deficit is finally known as a result of the construction being completed, it is recognized in the closing entry as follows:

Appropriations	325,000	
Expenditures		318,000
Unappropriated Surplus		7,000
To close construction expenditures for the year and to recognize the excess of appropriations over expenditures.		

The cash balance represented by this surplus balance would probably be transferred to the general fund or to the fund charged with the retirement of the bonds, probably the sinking fund. The transfer would be recorded as follows:

Bond Fund

Unappropriated Surplus	7,000	
Cash		7,000
To record transfer of cash remaining upon completion of construction to the sinking fund.		

Sinking Fund

Cash	7,000	
Deposit from Bond Fund		7,000
To record deposit of cash remaining in bond fund upon completion of construction.		

Thus the bond fund would be closed since its function has been fulfilled.

Sinking funds

The sinking fund is created to retire bonds when the contract requires the periodic deposit of moneys in a separate fund for the purpose of retiring the bond at maturity. This fund is not normally concerned with the payment of periodic interest on these obligations. Frequently a municipality will levy a special tax to allow for the orderly retirement of the bonds. In most cases the general fund is responsible for accounting for the levy and collection of the special tax and for the contribution to the sinking fund. The accounts of the sinking fund are ordinarily restricted to receipt of the contribution from the general fund, the investment of the funds, the collection of income from the investments, and the final retirement of matured bonds. Occasionally the special tax levy and the collection of the tax will be accounted for in the accounts of the sinking fund. When such is the case, the journal entries to record these activities are the same as those that would appear in the general fund or a special revenue fund.

The annual contribution to be made by the general fund to the sinking fund is determined on the basis of some assumed level of earnings to be derived from the investment of the funds deposited in the sinking fund. The annual contribution may be modified as the earnings exceed or fall below the expected level. The technique of estimating annual contributions to the sinking fund is discussed in Chapter 18.

The journal entries which are required to account for the activities of the sinking fund are illustrated below. The first entry each year is to record the planned contribution and earnings on the invested funds.

Required Contributions	*48,700*	
Required Earnings	*1,300*	
Reserve for Retirement of Sinking Fund Bonds		*50,000*
To record required contribution and earnings for the year based on present value calculations.		

The required earnings, of course, represents the expected earnings on the total cash invested; therefore, this portion of the entry increases as the investment grows.

The actual transactions of the period are then recorded as follows:

Cash	*48,700*	
Contribution Revenues		*48,700*
To record receipt of contribution from the general fund.		
Investment	*40,000*	
Unamortized Premiums	*1,200*	
Accrued Interest on Investments	*400*	
Cash		*41,600*
To record purchase of investment securities at premium plus accrued interest.		
Cash	*1,570*	
Interest Earnings		*1,170*
Accrued Interest on Investments		*400*
To record receipt of interest on investment.		
Interest Receivable on Investment	*400*	
Interest Earnings		*400*
To record accrual of interest on investments at end of year.		
Interest Earnings	*120*	
Unamortized Premiums		*120*
To record amortization of premium on investments.		
Contribution Revenues	*48,700*	
Required Contributions		*48,700*
To close required and actual contributions.		
Interest Earnings	*1,450*	
Required Interest Earnings		*1,300*
Unappropriated Surplus		*150*
To close required and actual interest earnings.		

Similar entries would be made each year as the sinking fund continues to grow. At maturity, bonds must be recorded as a liability of the sinking fund and the general bonded debt accounts must be relieved of the liability. The entry necessary to record the liability in the accounts of the sinking fund depends on whether an appropriation is required or not. Logic would indicate that since the fund has been established by appropriation for a particular purpose, no further appropriation is necessary. If this is the situation, the entry to bring the matured bonds into the accounts would be:

Reserve for Retirement of Sinking Fund Bonds....	*1,000,000*	
Matured Bonds Payable................		*1,000,000*
To record matured bonds as a liability of the sinking fund.		

If an appropriation is required under the laws of the municipality, it would be recorded as follows:

Reserve for Retirement of Sinking Fund Bonds....	*1,000,000*	
Appropriations........................		*1,000,000*
To record appropriation for retirement of bonds payable.		
Appropriations...........................	*1,000,000*	
Matured Bonds Payable................		*1,000,000*
To record matured bonds as a liability of the sinking fund.		

The matured bonds may now be paid or the accumulated cash may be transferred to a fiscal agent who is responsible for retiring the bonds. If the cash is transferred to a fiscal agent, the matured bonds payable is canceled when the agent reports that he has acquired the bonds. The following entries are made:

Cash in Hands of Fiscal Agent................	*1,000,000*	
Cash................................		*1,000,000*
To record transfer of cash to fiscal agent.		
Matured Bonds Payable.....................	*1,000,000*	
Cash in Hands of Fiscal Agent..........		*1,000,000*
To record retirement of bonds by fiscal agent.		

Trust and agency funds

Trust and agency funds are established to account for cash deposits or other property received and held by the municipality as trustee or custodian. The two types of funds are substantially identical and from an accounting standpoint are considered as one class. In common usage the term *trust fund* describes a custodial fund that will exist over relatively long periods of time where there are investment decisions to be made. The *agency fund* designation is used when the term of the custodial function is shorter and investment operations are limited. Trust funds are frequently classified as public or private and as expendable or nonexpendable. A public trust fund is one whose principal and income are used for the benefit of the public. An expendable trust fund is one whose principal and income may be expended. A nonexpendable one requires that the principal be kept intact.

Governmental trust funds, like those established by individuals, are usually governed by trust indentures, which are very specific as to the nature and purpose of the fund. The operations of the fund include receipt of money by donation, grant, or income from investments; the making of investments; and the spending of resources in accordance with the terms of the indenture or other regulatory provisions.

The problems of accounting for a trust fund are simple ones. If the fund is set up as a means of holding cash for some specific purpose, then the entry to record the receipt of cash is to debit cash and to credit the fund balance. Similarly, withdrawals are handled as reductions of the fund balance and cash. In cases where the cash is invested and there are expenditures of various types, it is frequently desirable to set up accounts to reflect revenues earned and expenditures incurred. At the end of the period, these revenue and expenditure accounts are closed to the fund balance. The operation of such a trust fund is in essence the same as that of a sinking fund.

Where the trust fund is established to pay off some commitment at some future date, a reserve account should be used to indicate the estimated liability owed at any particular time. Where such a fund is in operation, the unappropriated surplus or deficit is an indication of the adequacy of the assets to meet the estimated requirements of the fund. Such a fund is commonly employed in the case of an employees' pension plan. The required contributions are determined on the basis of the provisions of the particular plan. Accordingly, the required contributions are recorded each period and at the end of the period the actual contribution is compared with the required contribution to determine the adjustment to the surplus account. The reserve account established when the required contribution is recorded is the estimated claim against the assets of the fund. Again the procedures illustrated for the sinking fund apply; for example, the entry to record the required contribution for a period when the employer and employees share equally the payment to the fund is as follows:

Required Contribution—Employer	*7,500*	
Required Contribution—Employees	*7,500*	
Required Earnings	*2,400*	
Reserve for Retirements		*17,400*
To record required annual contribution and earnings on investments.		

The general fixed asset accounts

The self-balancing set of accounts referred to as the general fixed asset accounts are quite different from the funds which have been illustrated. This set of accounts is primarily for the purpose of accounting for and controlling the assets which are the property of the municipality. These accounts do not constitute an operating fund in any sense of the word. The fixed assets which are included in this set of accounts are those which are considered the general property of the organization. Fixed assets acquired by the utility and other enterprise, working capital, and trust and agency funds are not general fixed assets but are the fixed assets of these specific funds. The general fixed assets are carried at their cost of acquisition or construction or, in the case of gifts, at fair market value at date of acquisition. The source of the funds used to acquire general fixed assets is the credit side of the journal entry and most acquisitions are financed from bonds funds, special assessments, appropriations from the general fund, or gifts and grants. Several instances involving acquisition of fixed assets have been illustrated in the preceding discussion. The entry to record the acquisition of assets in the general fixed asset accounts is illustrated below:

Land	*500,000*	
Building	*450,000*	
Equipment	*1,000,000*	
Construction in Progress	*600,000*	
Investment in General Fixed Assets:		
from Bonds		*750,000*
from Federal Grants		*500,000*
from Property Owners' Share of Assessment Improvement Cost		*600,000*
from Current Revenues		*300,000*
from Municipality's Share of Assessment Improvement Cost		*400,000*
To record acquisition of fixed assets.		
Building	*1,250,000*	
Construction in Progress		*600,000*
Investment in General Fixed Assets from Bonds		*650,000*
To record completion of construction in progress.		

The retirement, sale, or disposal of general fixed assets must be recorded in the self-balancing accounts by reversing the entry made to record the acquisition of the asset. Any cash derived from the sale or disposal of the asset would generally be recorded in the general fund. Illustrative entries for the sale of obsolete equipment for $20,000 are presented on page 901.

There is some reason to question the need for or the desirability of recording the source of the cash used to acquire individual assets. As Professor Lorig[1] suggests, the information is seldom if ever used. In his opinion, a perpetual record

[1] A. M. Lorig, "Suggested Improvements in Governmental Accounting," *Accounting Review*, October, 1963, pp. 759–760.

General Fixed Asset Accounts

Investment in General Fixed Assets:		
from Bonds	*250,000*	
from Current Revenues	*50,000*	
from Federal Grant	*300,000*	
Equipment		*600,000*
To record the sale of equipment.		

General Fund

Cash	*20,000*	
Revenue from Sale of Equipment		*20,000*
To record cash received from the sale of obsolete equipment which is carried as a part of the general fixed assets.		

of the asset cost with a counterbalancing account, Investment in Fixed Assets, is all that is needed. If information as to the source of capital is desired, this can be provided on a perpetual inventory record of all fixed assets.

The question of whether or not depreciation of fixed assets should be recorded in the accounts is one that never ceases to cause debate among accountants. The argument is invariably made that if depreciation calculations are justified at all, they are justified in governmental as well as commercial accounting. Such a position overlooks the fact that the purpose of accounting may be different under different circumstances and consequently the desirability of recording depreciation may vary. In all circumstances we agree that depreciation represents the expiration of the usefulness of the asset to the owner. Surely the usefulness of assets held by municipalities decreases as the services provided by the assets are consumed. Then why do we not record depreciation? The answer lies in the purpose for which the accounting records are kept. Except for municipal utilities or other self-supporting activities, the municipality is not concerned with the measurement of profit or loss for the period. Instead the concern is with comparison between the budgeted and the actual expenditures and revenues.

Unless cash is to be set aside for the purpose of replacing certain assets, depreciation cannot be included in a budget which appropriates the cash to be spent during the coming period. If the depreciation is not a part of the budget but is then included as an expense of the period, there will be little value in comparing the budgeted and actual results of operations. The reports of the municipality may even give the impression that the appropriation has been overexpended unless detailed and elaborate explanations are made. In essence we can say then that, for annual report purposes, the calculation of depreciation provides no useful information and may lead to erroneous conclusions. Fund accounting is concerned with showing the sources of cash and the uses of the cash and not with the measurement of cost expirations and resulting revenues.

There are occasions when depreciation calculations are important in fund accounting, however. When the accountant provides information about the total cost of providing a service, depreciation must be included as a part of this total cost. Decisions relating to future action must be made with a full knowledge of all the facts, and the cost of facilities required is one of the important facts. In summary, we can conclude that plant assets do lose their usefulness, whether owned by government or private business, but whether or not depreciation should be included in the financial statements is determined by the purpose for which these statements are prepared. Some government agencies regularly include depreciation on general fixed assets in their operating statements prepared for internal use and exclude it from the annual financial statements.

General bonded debt and interest accounts

The general bonded debt and interest group of self-balancing accounts is used to preserve the identity of the other funds of the municipality. The unmatured bonds and interest to be paid from general revenues are recorded here because no assets presently on hand in the general fund or other funds will be used to pay these liabilities (except for sinking fund assets specifically held for this purpose). This same condition generally prevails in commercial accounting also. The difference in these two situations is that in commercial accounting the enterprise is the accounting entity, whereas in fund accounting the fund is the accounting entity. The life of a fund is frequently continuing, however, for the purposes of accounting and reporting its life is considered to coincide with the budget period, which is usually one or two years. For this reason debts owed in future years are not considered claims against the assets of specific funds, but rather claims against the ability of the organization to obtain the cash for payment of the debt. On the other hand, the commercial enterprise is viewed in long-term perspective, even though annual statements are prepared. For this reason the bonds are considered an obligation of the enterprise, in spite of the fact that the liability may not be paid for many years.

The entries to be recorded in the general bonded debt accounts are usually restricted to recognition of liabilities owed in future periods. No proceeds from the sale of bonds are ever recorded in this group of accounts. In most cases the proceeds will be handled through separate bond funds, as illustrated earlier. The entries to be recorded here are:

Amount to Be Provided for Payment of Principal	*1,000,000*	
Bonds Payable		*1,000,000*
To record liability arising upon sale of 4%, 20-year bonds.		
Amount to Be Provided for Payment of Interest	*800,000*	
Interest Payable in Future Years		*800,000*
To record liability for interest to be paid during the term of the bond contract; $40,000 of the interest will be paid during the current year from the general fund.		

As the liability matures, it will be eliminated from the general bonded debt accounts and entered in the accounts of the fund where the appropriation for payment has been made. Each year, for example, the following entry would be made to reduce the interest liability:

Interest Payable in Future Years	*40,000*	
Amount to Be Provided for Payment of Interest		*40,000*
To reduce the future liability for the interest which is due and payable by the general fund during the current year.		

Where a sinking fund has been established for the retirement of an issue of bonds payable, we frequently find it desirable to indicate in the self-balancing accounts the amount of cash so accumulated. The purpose of such information is to inform interested parties of the balance which must still be provided for bond retirement. This information is usually recorded as follows:

Amount in Sinking Fund	*50,150*	
Amount to Be Provided for Payment of Principal		*50,150*
To record the amount which has been provided for payment of principal by deposit and earnings during the year.		

Of course the amount in the sinking fund will grow yearly. At the maturity date, the bond liability must be transferred to that fund which is responsible for its retirement, in the present case the sinking fund. The following entry would be required in the general bonded debt accounts:

Bond Payable	*1,000,000*	
Amount in Sinking Fund		*985,788*
Amount to Be Provided for Payment of Principal		*14,212*
To record transfer of bond payable to sinking fund for final payment.		

The above entry assumes that earnings of the sinking fund have not been adequate in recent years. The deficit must be made up from the resources of some fund. The entries to be recorded in the sinking fund have been illustrated earlier.

There is some question as to the desirability of including the total interest to be paid on general bonds in the general bonded debt accounts. What purpose does this entry serve? As we have discovered earlier in our study of bonds payable, the liability owed by the debtor at any one time may be viewed as the present value of a series of semiannual interest payments plus the present value of a sum due at the end of a stated period of years. There seems to be no good and logical reason, therefore, for introducing the liability for interest to be paid over the life of the bond into the accounts of the municipality. The reason often cited is one of permitting the planning of future cash requirements. This objective can certainly be accomplished without making a formal journal entry in the accounts. The objection to this procedure is simply that it is inconsistent with current commercial accounting practice and it seems to have no logic or support in fund accounting.

Utility or other enterprise funds

Utility or other enterprise funds are established to account for the activities of self-supporting enterprises which operate as an arm of the government. These enterprises usually provide some service to the people of the community and the charge for the service is related to customer's usage. Such funds could be established to account for water, electricity, and gas services and for the operation of airports, docks, hospitals, and public housing. Operations of the government which may be supported by outside revenues which are not derived by sale of service to consumers, such as libraries, parks, and zoos, are not accounted for as utilities and other enterprises. The operations discussed under this heading are those which resemble commercial businesses. These government enterprises are operating to make a profit or at a very minimum to be self-supporting; therefore, the accounts should be kept in such a way as to allow the administrator to determine whether or not this goal is achieved.

The budget prepared for a utility or other enterprise is much like a budget prepared for any commercial operation. The level of revenues and expenditures is primarily a function of the demand by the consumers for the service rather than a function of a legislative decision as to how much of the available resources can be expended for the purpose.

In accounting for the utility or other enterprise, we must remember that the accounting procedures employed are exactly the same as those used in commercial accounts. Revenue is recognized when the service is provided to the customer. Costs are incurred when the liability arises; these costs must then be allocated to periods as expired costs or expenses as the usefulness of the asset expires. Plant assets are, therefore, depreciated and inventoriable costs of all kinds are included in the financial statements as assets.

In essence the difference between the utility funds and the other funds discussed here is that the utility is selling a service to the customer at a stated price per unit, whereas the other funds are controlling a given quantity of assets or providing services to the public without any correlation between the service received by the individual and the support provided by individuals in the form of taxes.

Financial statements

When one considers preparation of financial reports for an accounting entity, his objective is to organize the report in a manner which reveals the maximum information to the prospective user. In fund accounting this objective is the same. The central questions here are: Who is the user? and What information will be useful to him? There are at least four parties who are concerned with the reports of the municipal government: (1) the legislative body, (2) the chief executive, (3) the bondholders, and (4) the citizens of the community. What information do these parties want about the operation of the government? The legislative body and chief executive want to know how the fund actually operated relative to the budget and what assets it has on hand at the end of the year as well as what commitments it has made against these assets. The report will be used to ascertain whether the administrator stayed within his authority and as a basis for preparing future budgets. The bondholder is concerned with the status of his claim against the entity. This means that he wants to know that the terms of the bond contract are being observed and that the administrators are acting in a responsible manner which will assure regular interest payments and orderly retirement of the debt at maturity. The citizens want to know what their tax money is being used for. This means that they want to know how much was collected and from what sources. They want to know what this money was spent for in terms of services provided, for example, the cost of fire protection, garbage collection, etc. The question is: Does he want or need to know the total cost of the service for the period or does he merely want to know the total cash outlay for these services for the period? At the present time financial statements of municipal funds are limited to a report of cash flows and a statement of assets on hand and liabilities owed at year-end.

As we can readily see, there is some doubt as to what constitutes a useful report of the activities of a nonprofit organization. At least a part of the doubt arises because we do not know what information is useful. Nevertheless, some report must be prepared at least annually. Should this report be a unified report for the organization as a whole or a separate report for each fund? Because of the diversity of interest in the affairs of the government and because of the accountant's orientation to report the affairs of each entity separately, individual reports are usually prepared for each fund. In many cases combined balance sheets are also prepared. The emphasis on the balance sheet is probably related to the strong feeling of stewardship which generally pervades nonprofit organizations.

The statements normally prepared for the various funds are (1) the balance sheet; (2) a comparative statement of expenditures, encumbrances, and appropriations; (3) a comparative statement of budgeted and actual revenues; and (4) a reconciliation of unappropriated surplus. Not all of these statements are prepared for every fund because in many cases the information is not needed or the transactions which would be reflected on the statement did not occur in the fund for the year of the report. A balance sheet is prepared for each fund where there are assets in the fund at the end of the year and supporting schedules are prepared in those cases where additional explanatory information is desired. The self-supporting activities of the municipality usually prepare a commercial type of income statement to indicate the success or failure of the operation for the year.

The balance sheet is prepared in the traditional form with the assets arrayed beginning with cash, the most liquid, to inventories, generally considered to be the least liquid of the assets held. The balance sheets of the general funds seldom reflect any fixed or plant assets. The statements of the special-purpose funds will include fixed assets when they are held by the fund. The liabilities, reserves, and surplus appear on the right side of the balance sheet. There are no capital accounts, of course. The liabilities are usually presented first in the order of liquidation date followed by any reserves, such as reserve for encumbrances, and finally the unappropriated surplus balance is presented as the balancing figure. The principles followed for the preparation of any balance sheet are followed in the case of funds, the main difference being that certain accounts do not appear because they are not kept by the fund. Most fund balance sheets are concerned with cash, claims to cash, and obligations to pay cash. A typical balance sheet for the general fund would appear as follows:

CITY OF GREENSTICKS
General Fund
Balance Sheet
at the close of the fiscal period ended June 30, 1966

Assets

Cash		*$145,500*
Temporary investments		*36,400*
Accrued interest on investments		*100*
Accounts receivable	*$ 40,600*	
Less: Estimated uncollectible accounts	*8,000*	*32,600*
Taxes receivable—delinquent	*$ 98,600*	
Less: Estimated uncollectible taxes	*25,600*	*73,000*
Interest and penalties receivable on taxes	*$ 11,200*	
Less: Estimated uncollectible interest and penalties	*3,200*	*8,000*
Tax liens receivable	*$120,200*	
Less: Estimated uncollectible tax liens	*33,400*	*86,800*
Due from other funds		*32,000*
Inventory of supplies		*11,400*
Total assets		*$425,800*

Liabilities, Reserves, & Surplus

Vouchers payable	*$ 69,800*
Judgments payable	*20,000*
Matured bonds payable	*25,000*
Matured interest payable	*15,000*
Contracts payable	*151,915*
Due to other funds	*20,000*
Taxes collected in advance	*30,000*
Total liabilities	*$331,715*
Reserve for encumbrances—current year	*28,000*
Unappropriated surplus	*66,085*
Total liabilities, reserves, & surplus	*$425,800*

The comparative statement of expenditures, encumbrances, and appropriations is designed to portray a comparison of actual expenditures with appropriations for the period. It is divided into functions with a breakdown of the expenses by function. The statement provides the reader with a quick visual comparison of the beginning of the period with the expenditures of the period and the encumbrances at the end of the period; finally, any unencumbered balance is shown by deducting the expenditures and commitments from the funds appropriated. The statement is illustrated for the general fund on page 907.

The comparative statement of budgeted and actual revenue is prepared to indicate a comparison of planned and estimated activity. The final column reports the excess or deficiency of actual revenue over estimated revenue by source. This statement for the general fund appears on page 908.

CITY OF GREENSTICKS
General Fund
Comparative Statement of Expenditures, Encumbrances, and Appropriations for the fiscal period ended June 30, 1966

	Appropriations	Reserve for encumbrances outstanding at beginning of year	Total	Expenditures	Unexpended balance	Encumbrances outstanding at close of year	Unencumbered balance
General government:							
Legislative:							
Personal services	$ 30,000	$ -0-	$ 30,000	$ 29,500	$ 500	$ 200	$ 300
Other expenses	10,000	-0-	10,000	10,000	-0-	-0-	-0-
Total	$ 40,000	$ -0-	$ 40,000	$ 39,500	$ 500	$ 200	$ 300
Executive:							
Personal services	$ 10,000	$ -0-	$ 10,000	$ 10,000	$ -0-	$ -0-	$ -0-
Other expenses	3,000	150	3,150	2,950	200	50	150
Total	$ 13,000	$ 150	$ 13,150	$ 12,950	$ 200	$ 50	$ 150
Total general government	$ 130,000	$ 800	$ 130,800	$ 128,600	$ 2,200	$ 1,050	$ 1,150
Public safety	288,700	5,500	294,200	269,695	24,505	6,550	17,955
Highways	84,000	6,000	90,000	87,300	2,700	-0-	2,700
Sanitation and waste removal	47,500	2,500	50,000	44,600	5,400	3,900	1,500
Health and hospitals	62,400	3,000	65,400	61,400	4,000	3,850	150
Public welfare	46,300	500	46,800	44,900	1,900	200	1,700
Schools	473,500	19,250	492,750	481,700	11,050	10,000	1,050
Libraries	35,000	2,000	37,000	34,300	2,700	2,200	500
Recreation	18,500	1,500	20,000	19,700	300	250	50
Pension	6,700	-0-	6,700	6,000	700	-0-	700
Interest on debt	7,805	-0-	7,805	7,805	-0-	-0-	-0-
Grand total	$1,200,405	$41,050	$1,241,455	$1,186,000	$55,455	$28,000	$27,455

CITY OF GREENSTICKS
General Fund
Comparative Statement of Estimated and Actual Revenue
for the fiscal period ended June 30, 1966

	Estimated revenue	Actual revenue	Excess or deficiency* of actual compared with estimated
General property taxes:			
Current year's levy	$ 749,000	$ 738,000	$11,000*
Interest and penalties	3,900	3,950	50
Total	$ 752,900	$ 741,950	$10,950*
Other local taxes:			
Poll tax	$ 1,050	$ 1,175	$ 125
Licenses and permits:			
Auto licenses	$ 36,700	$ 37,000	$ 300
Business licenses	74,300	72,600	1,700*
Peddlers' permits	100	80	20*
Building permits	3,000	2,800	200*
Total	$ 114,100	$ 112,480	$ 1,620*
Fines and penalties:			
Fines	$ 14,700	$ 18,900	$ 4,200
Penalties	7,000	8,280	1,280
Total	$ 21,700	$ 27,180	$ 5,480
Revenue from use of money and property:			
Interest earned	$ 1,750	$ 1,900	$ 150
Rents and concessions	34,500	42,600	8,100
Total	$ 36,250	$ 44,500	$ 8,250
Revenue from other agencies:			
Shared state taxes	$ 88,000	$ 89,200	$ 1,200
Grants from Federal government	68,500	68,500	-0-
State grants-in-aid	41,000	40,000	1,000*
Total	$ 197,500	$ 197,700	$ 200
Charges for current services:			
General government	$ 40,000	$ 42,000	$ 2,000
Public safety	8,000	9,200	1,200
Sanitation and waste removal	10,000	7,400	2,600*
Recreation	4,000	6,800	2,800
Total	$ 62,000	$ 65,400	$ 3,400
Grand total	$1,185,500	$1,190,385	$ 4,885

The fourth statement, frequently prepared as a supporting schedule, is the analysis of changes in unappropriated surplus. This statement reconciles the changes in the fund balance from the beginning to the end of the fiscal period.

At the same time a comparison is usually made between the estimated and the actual changes in order to tie the comparative statement of revenue and expenditures to the balance sheet. The statement follows:

CITY OF GREENSTICKS
General Fund
Analysis of Changes in Unappropriated Surplus
for the fiscal period ended June 30, 1966

	Estimated	*Actual*	*Excess or deficiency* of actual compared with estimated*
Unappropriated surplus (beginning of period)	$ 48,650	$ 48,650	$-0-
Add:			
Reserve for encumbrances of prior years	41,050	41,050	-0-
Revenues	1,185,500	1,190,385	4,885
Total	$1,275,200	$1,280,085	$ 4,885
Less:			
Expenditures	1,241,455	1,186,000	55,455*
Reserve for encumbrances (end of year)		28,000	28,000
Total	$1,241,455	$1,214,000	$27,455*
Unappropriated surplus (end of period)	$ 33,745	$ 66,085	$32,340*

The appropriateness of combined or consolidated statements for a municipality has been discussed for many years. The main question seems to be whether or not any information is provided by the combined statements which is not presented by the individual statements. There are two forms of the combined balance sheet which are in use. One of these is simply the presentation of the various fund balance sheets in sequence. The other is a columnar form which contains a column for each fund and a total column of the aggregate account balances in the various funds. There is some question concerning the significance of the total column. If they do not provide useful information, then why present the aggregate data? The National Committee on Governmental Accounting has indicated that the total column is relatively unimportant and has recommended that no statement of combined revenues and expenditures be prepared. The reason for this seems to be that the revenues and expenditures of the various funds are frequently not comparable in the manner in which they are accumulated. When the funds are combined, unlike sums must be added, which results in a meaningless total. The committee is also opposed to any attempt to prepare consolidated balance sheets because "each fund is an independent entity over which the administrative official, and often even the legislative body, have no unlimited control. The funds are so tied up legally that they cannot be said to represent one economic entity."[2]

[2] *Municipal Accounting and Auditing,* National Committee on Governmental Accounting (Chicago: 1951), p. 141.

Questions

1. The City of Greenville decides to establish a Working Capital Fund to account for the operation of the city's motor pool. It is estimated that the rental charges will amount to $1,200,000 the first year and operating expenses will total $1,175,000. The general fund appropriates $175,000 to be used by the Working Capital Fund to finance its operations. Make any necessary entries on the books of the Working Capital Fund to record these facts.

2. Why is depreciation expense recorded in the working capital fund when it is not recorded by the general fund, when the same assets are held by the various operating departments within the general fund, rather than by the working capital fund?

3. Why do we carry bonds payable in the special assessment fund as a liability instead of carrying it in the general bonded debt accounts?

4. In most funds we close the appropriations and appropriation expenditures accounts at the end of each accounting period. In the case of special assessment funds, these accounts may not be closed routinely at the end of the accounting period. Why?

5. If the appropriation expenditures do not exactly equal the appropriation of a special assessment fund, what disposition is made of the surplus assets or how is the shortage covered?

6. When general obligation bonds are sold by a municipality, the proceeds are accounted for in the bond fund. In what fund is the liability accounted for and why?

7. Premiums or discounts on bonds are usually considered adjustments of the periodic interest charges. How are such matters handled in fund accounting?

8. When a sinking fund is created for the purpose of repaying a general obligation bond, an appropriation is made in the general fund for the deposit of cash in the sinking fund. In addition, the fund grows by investing the money so deposited. What entry is required each year to record the budget of the sinking fund?

9. Make the entries in the general bonded debt accounts and the sinking fund to record the retirement of a bond issue totaling $1.5 million.

10. Distinguish between a trust fund and an agency fund.

11. Why is depreciation seldom recorded in fund accounting except for utilities and other self-supporting activities?

12. Are depreciation calculations ever important in fund accounting in areas other than self-supporting activities?

13. When a sinking fund is established for the purpose of repaying a general obligation bond, what entry is frequently made in the general bonded debt accounts as the sinking fund is accumulated and why?

14. Why are the following entries made in the general bonded debt accounts:

	Dr.	Cr.
(1) Amount to Be Provided for Payment of Interest	yyy	
Interest Payable in Future Years		yyy
(2) Interest Payable in Future Years	xxx	
Amount to Be Provided for Payment of Interest		xxx

15. What financial statements are typically prepared for the various funds?

Problems

26-1 The town council of Youngsville voted to establish a working capital fund as of July 1, 1966. Accordingly an appropriation of $100,000 was made from the general fund to establish the fund. The cash was transferred on July 1.

During the course of the year the working capital fund provided services to various funds, and billings for the first year were:

General fund	*$40,000*
Utility fund	*20,000*
Water fund	*30,000*
	$90,000

At the end of the first year of operation, the general fund and the water fund each owed the working capital fund $5,000.

The following cash disbursements were made by the working capital fund during the year:

Purchase of equipment (estimated useful life 10 years)	*$60,000*
Purchase of materials and supplies of which one-fifth remained at June 30, 1967	*40,000*
Salaries and wages as follows:	
Direct labor	*19,000*
Office salaries	*12,000*
Superintendent's salary	*8,000*
Heat, light, and power	*4,000*
Office expenses	*2,500*

Instructions

Prepare a statement of operations for the year, and a balance sheet at the end of the first year of operations for the working capital fund.

26-2 The City of Riverside issued $600,000 of bonds at par value on January 2, 1966, for the purpose of constructing a bridge. The trial balance of the bond fund on January 1, 1967, is presented on page 912.

Bond Fund
Trial Balance
January 1, 1967

Cash	$375,300	
Vouchers payable		$ 9,300
Judgments payable		34,500
Reserve for encumbrances of prior year		90,000
Appropriations		241,500
Totals	$375,300	$375,300

The trial balance of the sinking fund established for the purpose of providing for retirement of the bonds is presented below as of January 1, 1967:

Sinking Fund
Trial Balance
January 1, 1967

Cash	$ 7,233	
Taxes receivable—delinquent	13,050	
Allowance for uncollectibles—delinquent		$ 4,500
Interest and penalities receivable	405	
Allowance for uncollectibles—interest and penalities		60
Investments	36,000	
Reserve for retirement of sinking fund bonds		51,972
Unappropriated surplus		156
Totals	$56,688	$56,688

The following transactions relating to these funds occurred during the year ending December 31, 1967:

(1) Sinking fund requirements for the year were:

Required contributions	$49,974
Required earnings	4,077

(2) Taxes were levied in the amount of $52,974 and the allowance for uncollectibles was increased $3,000.

(3) Court judgments were paid in full.

(4) Vouchers payable were paid.

(5) The materials ordered last year were received at the estimated price plus $1,500 transportation cost.

(6) Collections of current taxes totaled $31,308.

(7) Payroll of $78,000 was approved for payment and paid.

(8) Uncollected balance of taxes receivable—current became delinquent.

(9) Interest and penalties accrued on delinquent taxes amounted to $495; however, expected uncollectibles total $75 of this amount.

(10) Collections were made:

Delinquent taxes	$21,300
Interest and penalties	360

(11) Structural steel estimated to cost $45,000 was ordered for the bridge.
(12) Vouchers paid amounted to $91,500.
(13) Investments were acquired for $60,000.
(14) Engineering expenses of $23,700 were paid.
(15) Interest collected on investments amounted to $4,200.
(16) The structural steel was received. Actual billed cost was $44,400.
(17) Payrolls amounting to $90,000 were approved and paid.
(18) Delinquent taxes of $225 were written off.
(19) The bridge was completed and all bills paid.

Instructions

a. Prepare journal entries for the bond fund and sinking fund to record the activity for the year.

b. Prepare pre-closing trial balances for each fund.

c. Prepare journal entries to close the accounts at the end of the year; assume that any cash balance in the bond fund is transferred to the sinking fund.

26-3 The City Hall Bond Fund was established on July 1, 1966, to account for the construction of a new City Hall financed by the sale of bonds. The building was to be constructed on a site owned by the city.

The building construction was to be financed by the issuance of 10-year $2 million general obligation bonds bearing interest at 4%. Through prior arrangements, $1 million of these bonds were sold on July 1, 1966. The remaining bonds are to be sold on July 1, 1967.

The only funds in which transactions pertaining to the new City Hall were recorded were the City Hall Bond Fund and the General Fund. The Bond Fund's trial balance follows:

CITY OF LARNACA
City Hall Bond Fund
June 30, 1967

	Debit	*Credit*
Cash	*$ 893,000*	
Appropriation expenditures	*140,500*	
Encumbrances	*715,500*	
Accounts payable		*$ 11,000*
Reserve for encumbrances		*723,000*
Appropriations		*1,015,000*
Totals	*$1,749,000*	*$1,749,000*

An analysis of the Appropriation Expenditures account follows:

	Debit
(1) A progress billing invoice from General Construction Company (with which the city contracted for the construction of the new City Hall for $750,000; other contracts will be let for heating, air conditioning, etc.) showing 10% of the work completed	$ 75,000

(2) A charge from the General Fund for work done in clearing the building site	11,000
(3) Payments to suppliers for building materials and supplies purchased	14,500
(4) Payment of interest on bonds outstanding	40,000
	$140,500

An analysis of the Reserve for Encumbrances account follows:

	Debit (Credit)
(1) To record contract with General Construction Company	$(750,000)
(2) Purchase orders placed for materials and supplies	(55,000)
(3) Receipt of materials and supplies and payment therefor	14,500
(4) Payment of General Construction Company invoice, less 10% retention	67,500
	$(723,000)

An analysis of the Appropriations account follows:

	Debit (Credit)
(1) Face value of bonds sold	$(1,000,000)
(2) Premium realized on sale of bonds	(15,000)
	$(1,015,000)

Instructions

a. Prepare a work sheet for the City Hall Bond Fund at June 30, 1967, showing
(1) Preliminary trial balance
(2) Adjustments (Formal journal entries are not required.)
(3) Adjusted trial balance

b. Prepare the formal adjusting journal entries for the following funds and groups of accounts: (Closing entries are not required.)
(1) General Fixed Assets Fund
(2) General Fund
(3) General Bonded Debt and Interest Fund

AICPA adapted

26-4 The City of Bergen entered into the following transactions during the year 1966:

(1) A bond issue was authorized by vote to provide funds for the construction of a new municipal building which, it was estimated, would cost $500,000. The bonds were to be paid in 10 equal installments from a sinking fund, payments being due March 1 of each year. Any balance of the bond fund is to be transferred directly to the sinking fund.

(2) An advance of $40,000 was received from the General Fund to underwrite a deposit on the land contract of $60,000. The deposit was made.

(3) Bonds of $450,000 were sold for cash at 102. It was decided not to sell all the bonds because the cost of the land was less than was expected.

(4) Contracts amounting to $390,000 were let to Michela and Company, the lowest bidder, for the construction of the municipal building.
(5) The temporary advance from the General Fund was repaid and the balance on the land contract was paid.
(6) Based on the architect's certificate, warrants were issued for $320,000 for the work completed to date.
(7) Warrants paid in cash by the treasurer amounted to $310,000.
(8) As a result of changes in the plans, the contract with Michela and Company was revised to $440,000; the remainder of the bonds were sold at 101.
(9) Before the end of the year, the building had been completed and additional warrants amounting to $115,000 were issued to the contractor in final payment for the work. All warrants were paid by the treasurer.

Instructions

a. Record the information and closing entries in bond fund T accounts. Designate the entries in the T accounts by the numbers which identify the data.

b. Prepare applicable fund balance sheets as of December 31, 1966, considering only the proceeds and expenditures from bond fund transactions.

AICPA adapted

26-5 You were engaged as auditor of the City of Druid as of July 1, 1966. You found the following accounts, among others, in the General Fund for the fiscal year ending June 30, 1966:

Special Cash

Date		*Ref*	*Dr*	*Cr*	*Balance*
Aug. 1, 1965		*CR 58*	*301,000*		*301,000*
Sept. 1, 1965		*CR 60*	*80,000*		*381,000*
Dec. 1, 1965		*CD 41*		*185,000*	*196,000*
Feb. 1, 1966		*CD 45*		*4,500*	*191,500*
June 1, 1966		*CR 64*	*50,500*		*242,000*
June 30, 1966		*CD 65*		*167,000*	*75,000*

Bonds Payable

Date		*Ref*	*Dr*	*Cr*	*Balance*
Aug. 1, 1965		*CR 58*		*300,000*	*300,000*
June 1, 1966		*CR 64*		*50,000*	*350,000*

Construction in Progress—Main Street Sewer

Date		*Ref*	*Dr*	*Cr*	*Balance*
Dec. 1, 1965		*CD 41*	*185,000*		*185,000*
June 30, 1966		*CD 65*	*167,000*		*352,000*

Interest Expense

Date		Ref	Dr	Cr	Balance
Feb. 1, 1966		CD 45	4,500		4,500
June 1, 1966		CR 64		500	4,000

Assessment Income

Date		Ref	Dr	Cr	Balance
Sept. 1, 1965		CR 60		80,000	80,000

Premium on Bonds

Date		Ref	Dr	Cr	Balance
Aug. 1, 1965		CR 58		1,000	1,000

The accounts resulted from the project described below:

The City Council authorized the Main Street Sewer Project and a bond issue of $350,000 to permit deferral of assessment payments. According to the terms of the authorization, the property owners were to be assessed 80% of the estimated cost of construction and the balance was made available by the city during October, 1965. On September 1, 1965, the first of five equal annual assessment installments was collected from the property owners. The deferred assessments were to bear interest at 5⅝% from September 1, 1965.

The project was expected to be completed by October 31, 1966.

Instructions

a. Prepare a Special Assessment Fund work sheet in which you record the transactions of the Main Street Sewer Project as they should have been made by the client. Show the closing entries at June 30, 1966, and show the accounts balances at that date. (Formal journal entries are not required.)

b. Prepare the formal journal entries that should be made in funds other than the Special Assessment Fund to record properly therein the results of transactions of the Main Street Sewer Project.

AICPA adapted

26-6 The Town of Big Springs had not been operating a public library prior to October 1, 1965. On October 1, 1965, James Jones died, having made a valid will which provided for the gift of his residence and various securities to the town for the establishment and operation of a free public library. The gift was accepted by the town. The library funds and operation were placed under the control of trustees. The terms of the gift provided that not in excess of $5,000 of the principal of the fund could be used for the purchase of equipment, building rearrangement, and purchase of such "standard" library reference books as, in the opinion of the trustees, were needed for starting the library. Except for this $5,000, the principal of the fund is to be invested and the income therefrom used to operate the library in accordance with appropriations made by the trustees.

The property received from the estate by the trustees was as follows:

Description	*Face or par value*	*Appraised value*
Residence of James Jones:		
Land		*$ 2,500*
Building (25-year estimated life)		*20,000*
Bonds:		
AB Company	*$34,000*	*32,000*
C & D Company	*10,000*	*11,200*
D & G Company	*20,000*	*20,000*
Stocks:		
M Company, 6% preferred	*12,000*	*12,600*
S Company, 5% preferred	*10,000*	*9,600*
K Company, common (300 shares)	*No par*	*12,900*
GF Company (200 shares)	*4,000*	*14,500*

The following events occurred in connection with the library operations up to June 30, 1966:

(1) 100 shares of GF Company stock were sold on November 17 for $6,875.

(2) Cash payments were made for: (a) alteration of the house, $1,310; (b) general reference books, $725; (c) equipment having an estimated life of 10 years, $2,180. The trustees state that these amounts are to be charged to principal under the applicable provision of the gift.

(3) The library started operation on January 1, 1966. The trustees adopted the following budget for the year ended December 31, 1966:

Estimated income from investments	*$5,000*
Estimated income from fines, etc.	*200*
Appropriation for salaries	*3,600*
Appropriation for subscriptions	*300*
Appropriation for purchase of books	*800*
Appropriation for utilities, supplies, etc.	*400*

(4) The following cash receipts were reported during the six months to June 30, 1966:

Sale of C & D Company bonds, including accrued interest of $80	*$11,550*
Interest and dividends	*3,100*
Fines	*20*
Gift for purchase of books	*200*
Total	*$14,870*

(5) The following cash payments were made during the six months to June 30, 1966:

Purchase of 100 shares of no-par common stock of L & M Company, including commission and tax cost of $42.50	*$ 9,655*
Payment of salaries	*1,500*
Payment of property taxes applicable to the year ended Dec. 31, 1965, based on an assessment as of June 30, 1965	*200*
Purchase of books	*900*
Magazine subscriptions	*230*
Supplies and other expense	*260*
Total	*$12,745*

(6) On June 30, 1966, there were miscellaneous expenses unpaid but accrued, amounting to $90. Also there were outstanding purchase orders for books in the amount of $70.

Instructions

Assuming that the town records budgetary accounts, prepare all statements necessary to show results of operations to June 30, 1966, and the financial position of the library funds, both expendable and nonexpendable, as of June 30, 1966. Where another treatment of an item is possible, explain the other treatment and state the justification of your choice.

AICPA adapted

26-7 The City of Larkspur provides electric energy for its citizens through an operating department. All transactions of the Electric Department are recorded in a self-sustaining fund supported by revenue from the sales of energy. Plant expansion is financed by the issuance of bonds which are repaid out of revenues.

All cash of the Electric Department is held by the City Treasurer. Receipts from customers and others are deposited in the Treasurer's account. Disbursements are made by drawing warrants on the Treasurer.

The following is the post-closing trial balance of the Electric Department as at June 30, 1965:

Cash on deposit with City Treasurer	*$ 2,250,000*	
Due from customers	*2,120,000*	
Other current assets	*130,000*	
Construction in progress	*500,000*	
Land	*5,000,000*	
Electric plant	*50,000,000°*	
Accumulated depreciation—electric plant		*$10,000,000*
Accounts payable and accrued liabilities		*3,270,000*
5% electric revenue bonds		*20,000,000*
Accumulated earnings		*26,730,000*
Totals	*$60,000,000*	*$60,000,000*

° *The plant is being depreciated on the basis of a 50-year composite life.*

The transactions of the Electric Department for the year ended June 30, 1966, are summarized below:

(1) Sales of electric energy—$10,700,000.
(2) Purchases of fuel and operating supplies—$2,950,000.
(3) Construction of miscellaneous system improvements (financed from operations)—$750,000.
(4) Fuel consumed—$2,790,000.
(5) Miscellaneous plant additions and improvements placed in service—$1,000,000.
(6) Wages and salaries paid—$4,280,000.
(7) Sale on December 31, 1965, of 20-year 5% Electric Revenue bonds, with interest payable semiannually—$5,000,000.
(8) Expenditures out of bond proceeds for construction of Larkspur Steam Plant Unit No. 1 and control house—$2,800,000.
(9) Operating materials and supplies consumed—$150,000.
(10) Payments received from customers—$10,500,000.
(11) Expenditures out of bond proceeds for construction of Larkspur Steam Plant Unit No. 2—$2,200,000.
(12) Warrants drawn on City Treasurer in settlement of accounts payable—$3,045,000.
(13) Larkspur Steam Plant placed in service, June 30, 1966.

Instructions

Prepare a work sheet for the Utility Fund, the Electric Department, showing:

a. The balance sheet amounts at June 30, 1965.

b. The transactions for the year. (Journal entries supporting your transactions are not required.)

c. The balance sheet amounts at June 30, 1966.

d. The sources and applications of funds during the year.

AICPA adapted

26-8 The following information pertains to the operation of the water fund of the City of Meridian. Included in the operations of this fund are those of a special replacement fund for the water department, the accounts of which are a part of the accounts of the water fund.

The balances in the accounts of this fund on January 1, 1966, were as follows:

Cash	*$ 6,126*
Accounts receivable	*7,645*
Stores	*13,826*
Investments of replacement fund	*21,700*
Permanent property	*212,604*
Accounts payable	*4,324*
Customers' deposits	*1,500*
Replacement fund reserve	*21,700*

Operating surplus	*21,773*
Bonds payable	*60,000*
Capital surplus	*152,604*

The following items represent the total transactions of the fund for the year ended December 31, 1966:

(1) Services billed	$146,867
(2) Accounts collected	147,842
(3) Uncollectible accounts of prior years written off	1,097
(4) Invoices and payrolls approved for current expense	69,826
(5) Invoices approved for purchase of water department stores	31,424
(6) Stores issued for use in operation	32,615
(7) Supplies secured from general fund stores and used in operation (cash transferred to general fund)	7,197
(8) Vouchers approved for payment of bonds and interest of $3,000	23,000
(9) Depreciation entered as charge against current income and credited to replacement reserve	10,600
(10) Deposits received	400
Deposits refunded	240
(11) Invoices approved for replacements of equipment which cost $6,200	7,800
(12) Invoices approved for additions to plant	12,460
(13) Vouchers approved for purchase of securities necessary fully to invest the replacement fund	compute
(14) Income received on investments	1,102
(15) Warrants drawn for invoices, payrolls, and vouchers approved	147,316

Instructions

From the above information you are to prepare:

a. A balance sheet of the fund as of December 31, 1966.

b. An operating statement of the water department for 1966.

c. An analysis of the operating surplus of the department for 1966.

AICPA adapted

26-9 The following data are presented for the City of Megopolis for the year 1966:

(1) Balance sheet—January 1, 1966:

Assets		*Liabilities*	
Cash	*$ 2,000*	*Allowance for uncollectible taxes—arrears*	*$10,000*
Taxes receivable—arrears	*15,000*	*Accounts payable*	*3,000*
		Unappropriated surplus	*4,000*
Total assets	*$17,000*	*Total liabilities*	*$17,000*

Statement of bonded debt—January 1, 1966:

Assets		*Liabilities*	
Amount to be provided for retirement of bonds	*$285,000*	*4½% serial bonds payable*	*$285,000*

(2) Budget for the year 1966:

Estimated revenues:		*Current appropriations:*	
Taxes receivable—1966 levy	*$225,000*	*General government*	*$68,000*
Court fines	*10,000*	*Police department*	*61,000*
Licenses	*6,000*	*Fire department*	*12,000*
Permits	*10,000*	*Highway department*	*44,000*
Interest and penalties	*8,000*	*Sanitation department*	*39,000*
		Retirement of serial bonds	*15,000*
		Interest on bonds	*17,000*
		Interest on tax notes	*3,000*
	$259,000		*$259,000*

(3) The amount of taxes levied for the year 1966 is $236,250, which includes a 5% allowance for uncollectible accounts.

(4) Receipts and disbursements in 1966:

Receipts:		
Current taxes		*$223,000*
Taxes in arrears		*6,000*
Tax anticipation notes		*90,000*
Other revenues:		
Court fines	*$10,600*	
Licenses	*6,100*	
Permits	*9,800*	
Interest and penalties	*8,400*	*34,900*
		$353,900
Disbursements:		
Sundry appropriations:		
General government	*$67,000*	
Police department	*59,250*	
Fire department	*10,750*	
Highway department	*42,000*	
Sanitation department	*40,000*	
Retirement of serial bonds	*15,000*	
Interest on bonds	*17,000*	
Interest on tax notes	*2,700*	*$253,700*
Tax anticipation notes		*90,000*
Accounts payable		*3,000*
		$346,700

(5) Bills unpaid at December 31, 1966, amounted to $2,600.

(6) The uncollected taxes originating prior to January 1, 1966, should be fully reserved for.

(7) Other transactions in 1966:
   (a) The construction of a new municipal center was authorized at an estimated cost of $100,000.
   (b) 4½% serial bonds in the principal amount of $100,000 were authorized and issued at par.
   (c) Contracts were let for construction of the municipal center, aggregating $95,000.
   (d) $60,000 was paid on these contracts.
   (e) On December 31, 1966, $80,000 of the construction work was completed.

Instructions

Prepare a working paper showing (*a*) the financial transactions of the City of Megopolis for 1966 and (*b*) the balance sheets of the general fund and bond fund and a statement of bonded debt at December 31, 1966.

26-10 The following budget was proposed for 1967 for the Mohawk Valley School District General Fund:

Unappropriated surplus, Jan. 1, 1967	*$128,000*
Revenues:	
Taxes	*112,000*
Investment income	*4,000*
Total	*$244,000*
Expenditures:	
Operating	*$120,000*
County Treasurer's fees	*1,120*
Bond interest	*50,000*
Unappropriated surplus, Dec. 31, 1967	*72,880*
Total	*$244,000*

A general obligation bond issue of the School District was proposed in 1966, proceeds to be used for a new school. There are no other outstanding bond issues. Information about the bond issue follows:

Face	*$1,000,000*
Interest rate	*5%*
Bonds dated	*Jan. 1, 1967*
Coupons mature	*Jan. 1 and July 1, beginning July 1, 1967*

Bonds mature serially at $100,000 per year starting Jan. 1, 1969.

The School District uses a separate bank account for each fund.

The General Fund trial balance at December 31, 1966 follows:

	Debit	*Credit*
Cash	*$ 28,000*	
Temporary investments—U.S. 4% bonds, interest payable May 1 and Nov. 1	*100,000*	
Unappropriated surplus		*$128,000*
Totals	*$128,000*	*$128,000*

The County Treasurer will collect the taxes and charge a standard fee of 1% on all collections. The transactions for 1967 were as follows:

Jan. 1 The proposed budget was adopted; the general obligation bond issue was authorized; and the taxes were levied.
Feb. 28 Tax receipts from County Treasurer, $49,500, were deposited.
Apr. 1 Bond issue was sold at 101 plus accrued interest. It was directed that the premium be used for payment of interest.
Apr. 2 The School District disbursed $47,000 for the new school site.
Apr. 3 A contract for $950,000 for the new school was approved.
May 1 Interest was received on temporary investments.
July 1 Interest was paid on bonds.
Aug. 31 Tax receipts from County Treasurer, $59,400, were deposited.
Nov. 1 Payment on new school construction contract, $200,000, was made.
Dec. 31 Operating expenses paid during year were $115,000.

Instructions

Prepare the formal journal entries to record the foregoing 1967 transaction in the following funds or groups of accounts:

General Fund
Bond Fund
General Fixed Assets
General Bonded Debt and Interest

AICPA adapted

26-11 You have been engaged by the Town of Nihill to examine its June 30, 1967, balance sheet. You are the first CPA to be engaged by the town and find that acceptable methods of municipal accounting have not been employed. The Town Clerk stated that the books had been closed and presented the following balance sheet:

TOWN OF NIHILL
Balance Sheet
June 30, 1967

Assets	
Cash	*$ 36,200*
Taxes receivable	*21,900*
Accounts receivable	*9,000*
Investments	*84,200*
Prepaid expenses	*21,000*
Fixed assets	*245,400*
Total assets	*$417,700*
Liabilities	
Accounts payable	*$ 6,500*
Bonds payable	*200,000*
Unappropriated surplus	*211,200*
Total liabilities	*$417,700*

The Town of Nihill was formed as a separate political unit on July 1, 1965. The town was formerly a real estate development within the Township of Hamton. Your audit disclosed the following information:

(1) On July 1, 1965, the town received a bequest of $50,000 in cash and a house with a fair market value of $40,000. The house was recorded on the books as an investment at its fair market value at July 1, 1966. The bequest arose under the terms of a will which provided that the house would be used as a public library and the $50,000 would be established as a nonexpendable trust fund whose income would be used to buy library books. Securities costing $49,200 were purchased in July by the town for the trust fund, and in the following June, securities with a cost of $5,000 were sold for $6,800. The trust fund had dividend and interest income of $2,100 during the year, of which $1,900 was expended. In addition the town expended from general funds $9,000 for conversion of the house to library purposes and $19,000 for books; these last amounts were charged to expenditures. The town has no other investments. The decision was made to account for the library operations in a separate fund.

(2) Taxes levied for the year amounted to $84,300, of which $62,400 was collected and $800 has been identified as requiring abatement. It is anticipated that $1,400 of the 1966–1967 levy will prove uncollectible.

(3) The water company that had been formed by the developer to service the real estate development was purchased by the town on July 1, 1966. The seller accepted 3% general obligation bonds in settlement. Details of the sales contract follow:

Plant and equipment		*$108,000*
Assets and liabilities assumed:		
Prepaid expenses (inventories)	*$19,000*	
Accounts receivable	*8,000*	
Total	*$27,000*	
Accounts payable	*5,000*	*22,000*
Sales price		*$130,000*

Cash arising from the operation of the water plant, except for a $1,000 working fund, is used for the general purposes of the town. At June 30, 1967, the following accounts pertain solely to the operation of the water plant: Accounts Receivable, Prepaid Expenses, and Accounts Payable.

(4) A $300,000 issue of 3% general obligation bonds was authorized on July 1, 1966. In addition to the settlement for the purchase of the water company, bonds in the amount of $70,000 were sold at 100 on that date, and $65,400 of the proceeds had been used up to June 30, 1967, to obtain other equipment for the town. Interest is payable on June 30 and December 31. Commencing June 30, 1968, bonds in the amount of $10,000 are to be retired each June 30.

(5) A shipment of supplies for the water plant was received in June, 1967, and included in Prepaid Expenses but the invoice for $700 was recorded in July. An order was placed in June with a printer for stationery to be used by the town's governing body. The stationery was delivered in July and cost $500.

Instructions

Prepare a balance sheet work sheet to adjust the Town Clerk's account accumulations as of June 30, 1967, and distribute them to the appropriate funds or groups of accounts. The work sheet should be in the format of the Town Clerk's balance sheet and have the following column headings:

Balance per books
Adjustments—Debits
Adjustments—Credits
General fund
Library endowment principal fund
Library fund
General fixed assets
Water utility fund
Bond fund
General bonded debt and interest

AICPA adapted

COMPOUND INTEREST TABLES

Table 1. Present value of \$1 due in n periods at i interest per period

Table 2. Present value of an annuity of \$1 per period for n periods at i interest per period

Table 3. Amount of \$1 due in n periods at i interest per period

Table 4. Amount of an annuity of \$1 per period for n periods at i interest per period

Table 1. Present Value of $1 Due in n Periods: $p_{\overline{n}|i} = \frac{1}{(1 + i)^n}$

	Rate of interest, %						
n	.5	1.0	1.5	2.0	2.5	3.0	4.0
1	.9950	.9901	.9852	.9804	.9756	.9709	.9615
2	.9901	.9803	.9707	.9612	.9518	.9426	.9246
3	.9851	.9706	.9563	.9423	.9286	.9151	.8890
4	.9802	.9610	.9422	.9238	.9060	.8885	.8548
5	.9754	.9515	.9283	.9057	.8839	.8626	.8219
6	.9705	.9420	.9145	.8880	.8623	.8375	.7903
7	.9657	.9327	.9010	.8706	.8413	.8131	.7599
8	.9609	.9235	.8877	.8535	.8207	.7894	.7307
9	.9561	.9143	.8746	.8368	.8007	.7664	.7026
10	.9513	.9053	.8617	.8203	.7812	.7441	.6756
11	.9466	.8963	.8489	.8043	.7621	.7224	.6496
12	.9419	.8874	.8364	.7885	.7436	.7014	.6246
13	.9372	.8787	.8240	.7730	.7254	.6810	.6006
14	.9326	.8700	.8118	.7579	.7077	.6611	.5775
15	.9279	.8613	.7999	.7430	.6905	.6419	.5553
16	.9233	.8528	.7880	.7284	.6736	.6232	.5339
17	.9187	.8444	.7764	.7142	.6572	.6050	.5134
18	.9141	.8360	.7649	.7002	.6412	.5874	.4936
19	.9096	.8277	.7536	.6864	.6255	.5703	.4746
20	.9051	.8195	.7425	.6730	.6103	.5537	.4564
21	.9006	.8114	.7315	.6598	.5954	.5375	.4388
22	.8961	.8034	.7207	.6468	.5809	.5219	.4220
23	.8916	.7954	.7100	.6342	.5667	.5067	.4057
24	.8872	.7876	.6995	.6217	.5529	.4919	.3901
25	.8828	.7798	.6892	.6095	.5394	.4776	.3751
26	.8784	.7720	.6790	.5976	.5262	.4637	.3607
27	.8740	.7644	.6690	.5859	.5134	.4502	.3468
28	.8697	.7568	.6591	.5744	.5009	.4371	.3335
29	.8653	.7493	.6494	.5631	.4887	.4243	.3207
30	.8610	.7419	.6398	.5521	.4767	.4120	.3083
35	.8398	.7059	.5939	.5000	.4214	.3554	.2534
40	.8191	.6717	.5513	.4529	.3724	.3066	.2083
45	.7990	.6391	.5117	.4102	.3292	.2644	.1712
50	.7793	.6080	.4750	.3715	.2909	.2281	.1407

Rate of interest, %						
5.0	6.0	8.0	10.0	15.0	20.0	25.0
.9524	.9434	.9259	.9091	.8696	.8333	.8000
.9070	.8900	.8573	.8264	.7561	.6944	.6400
.8638	.8396	.7938	.7513	.6575	.5787	.5120
.8227	.7921	.7350	.6830	.5718	.4823	.4096
.7835	.7473	.6806	.6209	.4972	.4019	.3277
.7462	.7050	.6302	.5645	.4323	.3349	.2621
.7107	.6651	.5835	.5132	.3759	.2791	.2097
.6768	.6274	.5403	.4665	.3269	.2326	.1678
.6446	.5919	.5002	.4241	.2843	.1938	.1342
.6139	.5584	.4632	.3855	.2472	.1615	.1074
.5847	.5268	.4289	.3505	.2149	.1346	.0859
.5568	.4970	.3971	.3186	.1869	.1122	.0687
.5303	.4688	.3677	.2897	.1625	.0935	.0550
.5051	.4423	.3405	.2633	.1413	.0779	.0440
.4810	.4173	.3152	.2394	.1229	.0649	.0352
.4581	.3936	.2919	.2176	.1069	.0541	.0281
.4363	.3714	.2703	.1978	.0929	.0451	.0225
.4155	.3503	.2502	.1799	.0808	.0376	.0180
.3957	.3305	.2317	.1635	.0703	.0313	.0144
.3769	.3118	.2145	.1486	.0611	.0261	.0115
.3589	.2942	.1987	.1351	.0531	.0217	.0092
.3418	.2775	.1839	.1228	.0462	.0181	.0074
.3256	.2618	.1703	.1117	.0402	.0151	.0059
.3101	.2470	.1577	.1015	.0349	.0126	.0047
.2953	.2330	.1460	.0923	.0304	.0105	.0038
.2812	.2198	.1352	.0839	.0264	.0087	.0030
.2678	.2074	.1252	.0763	.0230	.0073	.0024
.2551	.1956	.1159	.0693	.0200	.0061	.0019
.2429	.1846	.1073	.0630	.0174	.0051	.0015
.2314	.1741	.0994	.0573	.0151	.0042	.0012
.1813	.1301	.0676	.0356	.0075	.0017	.0004
.1420	.0972	.0460	.0221	.0037	.0007	.0001
.1113	.0727	.0313	.0137	.0019	.0003	0.0000
.0872	.0543	.0213	.0085	.0009	.0001	0.0000

Table 2. Present Value of an Annuity of \$1 per Period: $P_{\overline{n}|i} = \dfrac{1 - \dfrac{1}{(1+i)^n}}{i}$

	Rate of interest, %						
n	.5	1.0	1.5	2.0	2.5	3.0	4.0
1	.9950	.9901	.9852	.9804	.9756	.9709	.9615
2	1.9851	1.9704	1.9559	1.9416	1.9274	1.9135	1.8861
3	2.9702	2.9410	2.9122	2.8839	2.8560	2.8286	2.7751
4	3.9505	3.9020	3.8544	3.8077	3.7620	3.7171	3.6299
5	4.9259	4.8534	4.7826	4.7135	4.6458	4.5797	4.4518
6	5.8964	5.7955	5.6972	5.6014	5.5081	5.4172	5.2421
7	6.8621	6.7282	6.5982	6.4720	6.3494	6.2303	6.0021
8	7.8230	7.6517	7.4859	7.3255	7.1701	7.0197	6.7327
9	8.7791	8.5660	8.3605	8.1622	7.9709	7.7861	7.4353
10	9.7304	9.4713	9.2222	8.9826	8.7521	8.5302	8.1109
11	10.6770	10.3676	10.0711	9.7868	9.5142	9.2526	8.7605
12	11.6189	11.2551	10.9075	10.5753	10.2578	9.9540	9.3851
13	12.5562	12.1337	11.7315	11.3484	10.9832	10.6350	9.9856
14	13.4887	13.0037	12.5434	12.1062	11.6909	11.2961	10.5631
15	14.4166	13.8651	13.3432	12.8493	12.3814	11.9379	11.1184
16	15.3399	14.7179	14.1313	13.5777	13.0550	12.5611	11.6523
17	16.2586	15.5623	14.9076	14.2919	13.7122	13.1661	12.1657
18	17.1728	16.3983	15.6726	14.9920	14.3534	13.7535	12.6593
19	18.0824	17.2260	16.4262	15.6785	14.9789	14.3238	13.1339
20	18.9874	18.0456	17.1686	16.3514	15.5892	14.8775	13.5903
21	19.8880	18.8570	17.9001	17.0112	16.1845	15.4150	14.0292
22	20.7841	19.6604	18.6208	17.6580	16.7654	15.9369	14.4511
23	21.6757	20.4558	19.3309	18.2922	17.3321	16.4436	14.8568
24	22.5629	21.2434	20.0304	18.9139	17.8850	16.9355	15.2470
25	23.4456	22.0232	20.7196	19.5235	18.4244	17.4131	15.6221
26	24.3240	22.7952	21.3986	20.1210	18.9506	17.8768	15.9828
27	25.1980	23.5596	22.0676	20.7069	19.4640	18.3270	16.3296
28	26.0677	24.3164	22.7267	21.2813	19.9649	18.7641	16.6631
29	26.9330	25.0658	23.3761	21.8444	20.4535	19.1885	16.9837
30	27.7941	25.8077	24.0158	22.3965	20.9303	19.6004	17.2920
35	32.0354	29.4086	27.0756	24.9986	23.1452	21.4872	18.6646
40	36.1722	32.8347	29.9158	27.3555	25.1028	23.1148	19.7928
45	40.2072	36.0945	32.5523	29.4902	26.8330	24.5187	20.7200
50	44.1428	39.1961	34.9997	31.4236	28.3623	25.7298	21.4822

Rate of interest, %						
5.0	6.0	8.0	10.0	15.0	20.0	25.0
.9524	.9434	.9259	.9091	.8696	.8333	.8000
1.8594	1.8334	1.7833	1.7355	1.6257	1.5278	1.4400
2.7232	2.6730	2.5771	2.4869	2.2832	2.1065	1.9520
3.5460	3.4651	3.3121	3.1699	2.8550	2.5887	2.3616
4.3295	4.2124	3.9927	3.7908	3.3522	2.9906	2.6893
5.0757	4.9173	4.6229	4.3553	3.7845	3.3255	2.9514
5.7864	5.5824	5.2064	4.8684	4.1604	3.6046	3.1611
6.4632	6.2098	5.7466	5.3349	4.4873	3.8372	3.3289
7.1078	6.8017	6.2469	5.7590	4.7716	4.0310	3.4631
7.7217	7.3601	6.7101	6.1446	5.0188	4.1925	3.5705
8.3064	7.8869	7.1390	6.4951	5.2337	4.3271	3.6564
8.8633	8.3838	7.5361	6.8137	5.4206	4.4392	3.7251
9.3936	8.8527	7.9038	7.1034	5.5831	4.5327	3.7801
9.8986	9.2950	8.2442	7.3667	5.7245	4.6106	3.8241
10.3797	9.7122	8.5595	7.6061	5.8474	4.6755	3.8593
10.8378	10.1059	8.8514	7.8237	5.9542	4.7296	3.8874
11.2741	10.4773	9.1216	8.0216	6.0472	4.7746	3.9099
11.6896	10.8276	9.3719	8.2014	6.1280	4.8122	3.9279
12.0853	11.1581	9.6036	8.3649	6.1982	4.8435	3.9424
12.4622	11.4699	9.8181	8.5136	6.2593	4.8696	3.9539
12.8212	11.7641	10.0168	8.6487	6.3125	4.8913	3.9631
13.1630	12.0416	10.2007	8.7715	6.3587	4.9094	3.9705
13.4886	12.3034	10.3711	8.8832	6.3988	4.9245	3.9764
13.7986	12.5504	10.5288	8.9847	6.4338	4.9371	3.9811
14.0939	12.7834	10.6748	9.0770	6.4641	4.9476	3.9849
14.3752	13.0032	10.8100	9.1609	6.4906	4.9563	3.9879
14.6430	13.2105	10.9352	9.2372	6.5135	4.9636	3.9903
14.8981	13.4062	11.0511	9.3066	6.5335	4.9697	3.9923
15.1411	13.5907	11.1584	9.3696	6.5509	4.9747	3.9938
15.3725	13.7648	11.2578	9.4269	6.5660	4.9789	3.9950
16.3742	14.4982	11.6546	9.6442	6.6166	4.9915	3.9984
17.1591	15.0463	11.9246	9.7791	6.6418	4.9966	3.9995
17.7741	15.4558	12.1084	9.8628	6.6543	4.9986	3.9998
18.2559	15.7619	12.2335	9.9148	6.6605	4.9995	3.9999

Table 3. Amount of \$1 Due in n Periods: $a_{\overline{n}|i} = (1 + i)^n$

n	Rate of interest, % .5	1.0	1.5	2.0	2.5
1	1.0050	1.0100	1.0150	1.0200	1.0250
2	1.0100	1.0201	1.0302	1.0404	1.0506
3	1.0151	1.0303	1.0457	1.0612	1.0769
4	1.0202	1.0406	1.0614	1.0824	1.1038
5	1.0253	1.0510	1.0773	1.1041	1.1314
6	1.0304	1.0615	1.0934	1.1262	1.1597
7	1.0355	1.0721	1.1098	1.1487	1.1887
8	1.0407	1.0829	1.1265	1.1717	1.2184
9	1.0459	1.0937	1.1434	1.1951	1.2489
10	1.0511	1.1046	1.1605	1.2190	1.2801
11	1.0564	1.1157	1.1779	1.2434	1.3121
12	1.0617	1.1268	1.1956	1.2682	1.3449
13	1.0670	1.1381	1.2136	1.2936	1.3785
14	1.0723	1.1495	1.2318	1.3195	1.4130
15	1.0777	1.1610	1.2502	1.3459	1.4483
16	1.0831	1.1726	1.2690	1.3728	1.4845
17	1.0885	1.1843	1.2880	1.4002	1.5216
18	1.0939	1.1961	1.3073	1.4282	1.5597
19	1.0994	1.2081	1.3270	1.4568	1.5987
20	1.1049	1.2202	1.3469	1.4859	1.6386
21	1.1104	1.2324	1.3671	1.5157	1.6796
22	1.1160	1.2447	1.3876	1.5460	1.7216
23	1.1216	1.2572	1.4084	1.5769	1.7646
24	1.1272	1.2697	1.4295	1.6084	1.8087
25	1.1328	1.2824	1.4509	1.6406	1.8539
26	1.1385	1.2953	1.4727	1.6734	1.9003
27	1.1442	1.3082	1.4948	1.7069	1.9478
28	1.1499	1.3213	1.5172	1.7410	1.9965
29	1.1556	1.3345	1.5400	1.7758	2.0464
30	1.1614	1.3478	1.5631	1.8114	2.0976
35	1.1907	1.4166	1.6839	1.9999	2.3732
40	1.2208	1.4889	1.8140	2.2080	2.6851
45	1.2516	1.5648	1.9542	2.4379	3.0379
50	1.2832	1.6446	2.1052	2.6916	3.4371

Rate of interest, %

3.0	4.0	5.0	6.0	8.0	10.0
1.0300	1.0400	1.0500	1.0600	1.0800	1.1000
1.0609	1.0816	1.1025	1.1236	1.1664	1.2100
1.0927	1.1249	1.1576	1.1910	1.2597	1.3310
1.1255	1.1699	1.2155	1.2625	1.3605	1.4641
1.1593	1.2167	1.2763	1.3382	1.4693	1.6105
1.1941	1.2653	1.3401	1.4185	1.5869	1.7716
1.2299	1.3159	1.4071	1.5036	1.7138	1.9487
1.2668	1.3686	1.4775	1.5938	1.8509	2.1436
1.3048	1.4233	1.5513	1.6895	1.9990	2.3579
1.3439	1.4802	1.6289	1.7908	2.1589	2.5937
1.3842	1.5395	1.7103	1.8983	2.3316	2.8531
1.4258	1.6010	1.7959	2.0122	2.5182	3.1384
1.4685	1.6651	1.8856	2.1329	2.7196	3.4523
1.5126	1.7317	1.9799	2.2609	2.9372	3.7975
1.5580	1.8009	2.0789	2.3966	3.1722	4.1772
1.6047	1.8730	2.1829	2.5404	3.4259	4.5950
1.6528	1.9479	2.2920	2.6928	3.7000	5.0545
1.7024	2.0258	2.4066	2.8543	3.9960	5.5599
1.7535	2.1068	2.5270	3.0256	4.3157	6.1159
1.8061	2.1911	2.6533	3.2071	4.6610	6.7275
1.8603	2.2788	2.7860	3.3996	5.0338	7.4002
1.9161	2.3699	2.9253	3.6035	5.4365	8.1403
1.9736	2.4647	3.0715	3.8197	5.8715	8.9543
2.0328	2.5633	3.2251	4.0489	6.3412	9.8497
2.0938	2.6658	3.3864	4.2919	6.8485	10.8347
2.1566	2.7725	3.5557	4.5494	7.3964	11.9182
2.2213	2.8834	3.7335	4.8223	7.9881	13.1100
2.2879	2.9987	3.9201	5.1117	8.6271	14.4210
2.3566	3.1187	4.1161	5.4184	9.3173	15.8631
2.4273	3.2434	4.3219	5.7435	10.0627	17.4494
2.8139	3.9461	5.5160	7.6861	14.7853	28.1024
3.2620	4.8010	7.0400	10.2857	21.7245	45.2593
3.7816	5.8412	8.9850	13.7646	31.9204	72.8905
4.3839	7.1067	11.4674	18.4202	46.9016	117.3909

Table 4. Amount of an Annuity of $1 per Period: $A_{\overline{n}|i} = \dfrac{(1 + i)^n - 1}{i}$

n	.5	1.0	1.5	2.0	2.5
			Rate of interest, %		
1	1.0000	1.0000	1.0000	1.0000	1.0000
2	2.0050	2.0100	2.0150	2.0200	2.0250
3	3.0150	3.0301	3.0452	3.0604	3.0756
4	4.0301	4.0604	4.0909	4.1216	4.1525
5	5.0503	5.1010	5.1523	5.2040	5.2563
6	6.0755	6.1520	6.2296	6.3081	6.3877
7	7.1059	7.2135	7.3230	7.4343	7.5474
8	8.1414	8.2857	8.4328	8.5830	8.7361
9	9.1821	9.3685	9.5593	9.7546	9.9545
10	10.2280	10.4622	10.7027	10.9497	11.2034
11	11.2792	11.5668	11.8633	12.1687	12.4835
12	12.3356	12.6825	13.0412	13.4121	13.7956
13	13.3972	13.8093	14.2368	14.6803	15.1404
14	14.4642	14.9474	15.4504	15.9739	16.5190
15	15.5365	16.0969	16.6821	17.2934	17.9319
16	16.6142	17.2579	17.9324	18.6393	19.3802
17	17.6973	18.4304	19.2014	20.0121	20.8647
18	18.7858	19.6147	20.4894	21.4123	22.3863
19	19.8797	20.8109	21.7967	22.8406	23.9460
20	20.9791	22.0190	23.1237	24.2974	25.5447
21	22.0840	23.2392	24.4705	25.7833	27.1833
22	23.1944	24.4716	25.8376	27.2990	28.8629
23	24.3104	25.7163	27.2251	28.8450	30.5844
24	25.4320	26.9735	28.6335	30.4219	32.3490
25	26.5591	28.2432	30.0630	32.0303	34.1578
26	27.6919	29.5256	31.5140	33.6709	36.0117
27	28.8304	30.8209	32.9867	35.3443	37.9120
28	29.9745	32.1291	34.4815	37.0512	39.8598
29	31.1244	33.4504	35.9987	38.7922	41.8563
30	32.2800	34.7849	37.5387	40.5681	43.9027
35	38.1454	41.6603	45.5921	49.9945	54.9282
40	44.1588	48.8864	54.2679	60.4020	67.4026
45	50.3242	56.4811	63.6142	71.8927	81.5161
50	56.6452	64.4632	73.6828	84.5794	97.4843

Rate of interest, %					
3.0	4.0	5.0	6.0	8.0	10.0
1.0000	1.0000	1.0000	1.0000	1.0000	1.0000
2.0300	2.0400	2.0500	2.0600	2.0800	2.1000
3.0909	3.1216	3.1525	3.1836	3.2464	3.3100
4.1836	4.2465	4.3101	4.3746	4.5061	4.6410
5.3091	5.4163	5.5256	5.6371	5.8666	6.1051
6.4684	6.6330	6.8019	6.9753	7.3359	7.7156
7.6625	7.8983	8.1420	8.3938	8.9228	9.4872
8.8923	9.2142	9.5491	9.8975	10.6366	11.4359
10.1591	10.5828	11.0266	11.4913	12.4876	13.5795
11.4639	12.0061	12.5779	13.1808	14.4866	15.9374
12.8078	13.4864	14.2068	14.9716	16.6455	18.5312
14.1920	15.0258	15.9171	16.8699	18.9771	21.3843
15.6178	16.6268	17.7130	18.8821	21.4953	24.5227
17.0863	18.2919	19.5986	21.0151	24.2149	27.9750
18.5989	20.0236	21.5786	23.2760	27.1521	31.7725
20.1569	21.8245	23.6575	25.6725	30.3243	35.9497
21.7616	23.6975	25.8404	28.2129	33.7502	40.5447
23.4144	25.6454	28.1324	30.9057	37.4502	45.5992
25.1169	27.6712	30.5390	33.7600	41.4463	51.1591
26.8704	29.7781	33.0660	36.7856	45.7620	57.2750
28.6765	31.9692	35.7193	39.9927	50.4229	64.0025
30.5368	34.2480	38.5052	43.3923	55.4568	71.4027
32.4529	36.6179	41.4305	46.9958	60.8933	79.5430
34.4265	39.0826	44.5020	50.8156	66.7648	88.4973
36.4593	41.6459	47.7271	54.8645	73.1059	98.3471
38.5530	44.3117	51.1135	59.1564	79.9544	109.1818
40.7096	47.0842	54.6691	63.7058	87.3508	121.0999
42.9309	49.9676	58.4026	68.5281	95.3388	134.2099
45.2189	52.9663	62.3227	73.6398	103.9659	148.6309
47.5754	56.0849	66.4388	79.0582	113.2832	164.4940
60.4621	73.6522	90.3203	111.4348	172.3168	271.0244
75.4013	95.0255	120.7998	154.7620	259.0565	442.5926
92.7199	121.0294	159.7002	212.7435	386.5056	718.9048
112.7969	152.6671	209.3480	290.3359	573.7702	1163.9085

INDEX

Accounting Principles Board, 636
Accounting Research Bulletins (AICPA), bargain-purchase assumption, 254
  consolidated statements, 475
  control of subsidiary, 394
  equity method, 298
  foreign exchange rates, 456
  intercompany profits, 323
  pooling of interest, 357
  retained earnings, 773
  translation of foreign accounts, 463, 465, 466, 470
  treasury stock, 439
  unrealized gains, 460
Accounting Research Studies (AICPA), consolidated statements (No. 7) 243
  leases (No. 5), 637
  price-level changes (No. 6), 497, 501
  purchase versus pooling (No. 5), 356
  replacement cost (No. 3), 539
Accounting system, for branch, 202–203
  for sales agency, 201–202
Affiliated companies (*see* Consolidations)
American Accounting Association, intercompany profits, 323
  price-level changes, 499
  treasury stock, 439
American Institute of Certified Public Accountants (AICPA), 297
  (*See also* Accounting Principles Board; *Accounting Research Bulletins; Accounting Research Studies*)

Annuity, 581–603
  amounts of, 582–589
  deferred, 596–597
  due, 585–588
  finding interest rate, 600–602
  open-end, 588–590
  ordinary, 582–585
  present value of, 590–598
  types of, 582
  value over time, 598
Anton, Hector R., 644*n.*
Appropriation expenditures, 869
Arrangement, 777–778
Assignment of assets, 691–692

Bankrupt, reorganization of a, 769–773
Bankruptcy, involuntary, 693–694
  proceedings, 693–696
  voluntary, 693–694
  (*See also* Realization; Receivership)
Beneficiary, income, 829
  principal, 829
  rights of, 831
Bierman, Harold, 659*n.*
Bonds, call provision on, 628–629
  serial type, 633
Bonus, to new partner upon admission to partnership, 48–49, 51–52
  to old partners upon admission of partner, 44–48, 50
  upon retirement of partner, 55–56

Branches, accounting for, 202–203
billings above cost, 210–214
establishment of, 200
financial statements of, 204–205
start-up expenses, 224
transactions between, 222–224
Budgeting, governments, 863–865

Call provision, 628–629
Capital, cost of, 663–668
Capital budgeting, 653
Changing price levels, recognition of, 556–561
replacement cost and, 552–555
stable monetary unit assumption and, 501
Charge and discharge statement, 804
Charitable trust, 841–844
Composition agreements, 691, 765–766
Compound discount, 580
Compound interest, 574
formulas, 576–581
Consolidated balance sheet, equity method, 283–285
Consolidated financial statements, 285–287, 298–299
Consolidated net income, equity method, 282–283
Consolidated statements, cost basis, 275–281
cost and equity methods compared, 274–275, 297–298
equity basis, 281–285
legal status of, 242
why prepared, 243–244
Consolidated working papers, balance sheet, 279–281
income statement, 276–277
Consolidations, after acquisition, 287–296
at acquisition—partially owned subsidiary, 255–262
balance sheet at date of acquisition, 262–264
changes in ownership of subsidiary, 388–405
changes in parent's interest, 388–396
excess of book value over cost, 253–255
excess of cost over book value, 250–253
growth in subsidiaries since acquisition, 425–434
intercompany bond holdings, 345–356
intercompany profits, 317–328
in beginning inventories, 325
determination of, 324
in inventories, 317–321
in inventories at date of acquisition, 325
Consolidations, intercompany profits, losses on inventories, 324–325
procedures to remove, 323–324
on sale of depreciable assets, 340–345
sale of land, 318
why eliminate, 321–323
working papers, 326–328
intercompany transactions, 312–317
discounting notes, 312–314
dividends, 316–317
receivables and payables, 312
revenues and expenses, 314–315
mutual holdings, 434–444
one year after acquisition, 275–287
pooling of interest concept, 356–362
pooling of interest versus purchase concept, 357–361
purchase concept, 356
sale or purchase of shares by parent, 396–400
stock dividend by subsidiary, 386–388
subsidiary dividends in excess of earnings since acquisition, 388
subsidiary holding company, 420–425
subsidiary preferred and common stock, 380–386
terminology of, 241–242
wholly owned subsidiary, 244–245
why affiliate, 242
Corporation, choice between partnership and, 4–5
Creditor committees, 691
Creditors, preferred, 694
with priority, 694
secured, 694
unsecured, 694–795

Deferred gross profit, on real estate sale, 164–168
Deficiency account, 699
Depreciation, annuity method of, 639–641
and the interest factor, 638–644
sinking-fund method of, 641–643
Devise, 799
Devisee, 799
Direct valuation, 613
Direct valuation and bond issues, 620–633
Dividend, to unsecured creditors, 695

Effective interest versus straight-line average, 627–628
Encumbrances, 867–869
Equity receivership, 692–693
Estate, accounting for an, 800
administration, 796
assets discovered, 802

Estate, custody of funds, 797
  debt payment, 798
  distribution of the, 799
  inventory of assets, 797
  legacy, 799
  payments from, 802–803
  realization of assets, 802
  taxes on the, 798
Exchange restrictions, 470–471
Express trusts, 830

Fiduciary, accounts of, 800–803
  charge and discharge statement, 804
  duties of, 796–800
  summary of activity of, 804
  (*See also* Estate)
Financial report, governments, 865, 904–909
Financial statements, charitable trust, 846–847
Foreign exchange rates, 456–457
Foreign operations, 455–480
  balance sheet accounts, 463–466
  devaluation, 467–470
  by domestic company, 457–461
  exchange rates, 456–457
  exchange restrictions, 470–471
  foreign investments, 462–463
  foreign subsidiary, 475–480
  home office and branch, 471–475
  income statement accounts, 466–467
  inventory on consignment, 461–462
Foundations (*see* Trust)
Fund, 861
  bond, 862, 894–896
  general, 862, 871–875
  sinking, 862, 896–898
  special assessment, 862, 891–893
  special revenue, 862, 888
  trust and agency, 862, 898–899
  utility, 862, 904
  working capital, 862, 888–891

General Fund, 871–875
Goodwill, to new partner, 49–52
  when new partner purchases interest, 42–43
  to old partner, 45–48, 50
  upon partner's retirement, 54–55
Gordon, M. J., 665*n.*
Governments, accounting for, 866–870
  appropriation expenditures, 869
  appropriations, 864–865
  asset accounts, 900–902
  bonded debt and interest, 902–903
  budgeting, 863–865
Governments, encumbrances, 867–869
  financial reports, 865, 904–909
  fund(s), 862, 871–875, 888–904
    general, 871–875
    revenue, 870
Gross Profit, departmental rates of, 179–180
  recognition of, 168–169

Hepworth, Samuel R., 457*n.*
Holding gains and losses, 532–533, 539–542
Home office and branch, beginning inventory priced above cost, 214–219
  combined statements, 205
  foreign operations, 471–475
  perpetual inventories, 219–220
  reciprocal accounts, 203
  reconciliation of reciprocal accounts, 220–222
  working papers, 205–210

Implied trust, 830
Income, measurement of, 536–538
  prior periods' adjustment of, 22–23
  receiver, 727
  statements, partnerships, 21
  trust, 831–835
Income beneficiary, 829
Income tax, factors, on bond refunding, 670–673
    on leases, 669–670
  and investment decisions, 663–668
Incorporation of partnership, 57–58
Indices of general price change, 496–497
Inflation, 506–510
Inheritance (*see* Estate)
Insolvency, 689–690
  of partners, 81, 85–87
  of partnership, 83–87
Insolvent business, judicial procedures, 692
  nonjudicial procedures, 690
Insolvent debtors, 690–696
Installment contracts receivable, aging of, 175–176
Installment method of accounting, 164–165
  for income tax purposes, 177–179
Installment sales, buyer's viewpoint, 189
  expenses of, 183–184
  interest on, 185–188
  of merchandise, 169–175
  with periodic inventory, 179
  of real estate, 165–168
  recognition of profit on, 163–164
  repossessions, 181–183

Installment sales, special characteristics of, 161–162
statement presentation, 184–185
trade-ins, 180–181
Institutions (*see* Governments)
Interest, compound, 574, 576–581
effective versus straight-line, 627–628
simple, 574–575
Interest factor on leased property, 638–643
Intestate, 796
Investment decisions and income taxes, 663–668
Investment proposals, 668–676
bond refunding, 670–673
lease or buy, 668–670
property replacement, 673–676
Involuntary bankrupt, 693–694

Kane, John E., 498*n.*

Laws of descent, 799
Laws of distribution, 799
Leasehold, 634
Leases, depreciation and interest factor on, 638–643
income tax factors on, 669–670
long-term, 633–638
periodic payments, 635–638
Legacy, 799
Legatee, 799
Liabilities of bankrupt, 697–698
Liquidation, 74–75
Littleton, A. C., 536*n.*
Living trust, 830
Loans, partnerships, 9
Long-term leases, 633–638
Long-term liabilities, and the changing price level, 509–510
Lorie, James H., 653*n.*
Lorig, A. M., 900*n.*

Marshal, 694
Marshaling of assets, 85
May, George O., 501*n.*
Measures of price changes, 496–500
Monetary accounts, 506
Monetary units, 501
Moonitz, Maurice, 257*n.*, 298*n.*, 323*n.*
Myers, John H., 638*n.*

National Committee on Governmental Accounting, 861, 909
Net present value (*see* Present value)

Opportunity costs, 667–668

Partnership, asset valuation, 47–48
choice between corporation and, 4–5
Partnerships, admission of partner, 38–53
by investment, 44–52
by purchase of interest, 39–43
an appraisal, 3
beginning agreement, 6–7
bonus to new partner, 48–49, 51–52
changes in partners, 37–38
characteristics of, 4
death of partner, 56–57
dissolution of, 37–38
income statement, 21
incorporation of, 57–58
internal reports for management, 23–24
limited partner, 4
liquidation, distribution of assets, 75–79
distribution of gain or loss, 75, 76–87
installments, 101
partner with debit balance after loss, 79–83
partnership insolvent but partners solvent, 83–85
partnership and partners insolvent, 85–87
settlement with partners, 76
owners' equity, 7–8
partners' drawings, 19
partners' loans, 9
prior periods' adjustment of income, 22–23
profit sharing plans, 10–21
refusal to admit partner, 43–44
retirement of partner, 53–57
statement of liquidation, 76
statement of partners' capitals, 21–22
valuation of partners' investments, 9
Paton, William A., 507*n.*, 533*n.*
Paxon, Lloyd, 507*n.*
Periodic inventory, installment sales with use of, 179
Pooling of interest concept, 356–362
Preferred creditors, 694
Preferred stock, subsidiary, 380–386
Present value, 613–620
of annuity, 590–598
of deferred annuity, 596–597
of a future amount, 578–580
index, 660
method of valuation, 654–655
at various interest rates, 602–603
versus yield method, 663
Price indices, 495–500
Price level changes, 495–517
Price levels and replacement cost, 552–555

Principal beneficiary, 829
Principal of trust, 831–835
Private trust, 835–836
Profit, recognition of at time of sale, 163–164
Purchase concept, consolidations, 356–362

Realization, 536–538
Realization and liquidation statement, 756–758
  accounting for the, 763–766
  appraisal of the, 769
Receiver, 694
Receivership, accounting for, 723–727
  in equity, 722–723
  statements, 727
  working papers, 735–737
  (*See also* Realization and liquidation statement)
Reciprocal accounts, 203
Referee, 694
Remainderman, 829
Rents, 581
Reorganization, accounting for a, 771–773
  of a bankrupt, 769–773
  plan, 770–771
Replacement cost, 533
  advantages and disadvantages of, 538–539
  and changing price levels, 552–555
Reports of fiduciary, 803–804
Revenue, governmental, 870
Right of offset, 76

Sales agency, 200–201
  accounting for, 201–202
Savage, L. J., 653***n.***
Secured creditors, 694
Securities and Exchange Commission, consolidated statements, 242
Serial Bonds, 633
Shapiro, E., 665***n.***
Shipments to branch, 204
Simple interest, 574
  formulas, 574–575
Smidt, S., 659***n.***
Solomons, Ezra, 666
Special-purpose trust fund, 844–845
Sprague, Charles E., 796***n.***
Sprouse, Robert T., 533***n.***
Stable monetary unit, 501
Statement of affairs, 697–705
  for going concern, 705
Statement of liquidation, partnerships, 76
Stock dividends, by subsidiary, 386–388
Subsidiary, as a holding company, 420–425
  preferred stock, 380–386
Summary of activity of fiduciary, 804
Survey of Consolidated Financial Statement Practices (AICPA), 297

Taxes (***see*** Income tax)
Testamentary trust, 830
Testator, 796
Treasury stock, subsidiary transactions in, 404–405
Trust, accruals for, 832–834
  beneficiaries of, 829
  charitable, 841–844
    financial statements, 846–847
    lapsed appropriations, 845
  private, 835–836
  receipts and disbursements, 834
  special-purpose funds in, 844–845
  types of, 830
Trust income, 831–835
Trust principal, 831–835
Trustee, 694, 829
  duties of, 830–831

Unstable monetary unit, assumption of, 510–512

Valuation, 612
  compound interest applications of, 612
  investment proposal, 653–663
  long-term leases, 633–638
  present value method of, 654–655
  yield method of, 653–654
Values compared over time, 598–599
Voluntary bankrupt, 693–694

Wyatt, Arthur R., 356***n.***, 357***n.***

Yield, finding unknown rate of, 600–603
Yield method of valuation, 653–654